INTRODUCTION TO Desktop Publishing

With Digital Graphics

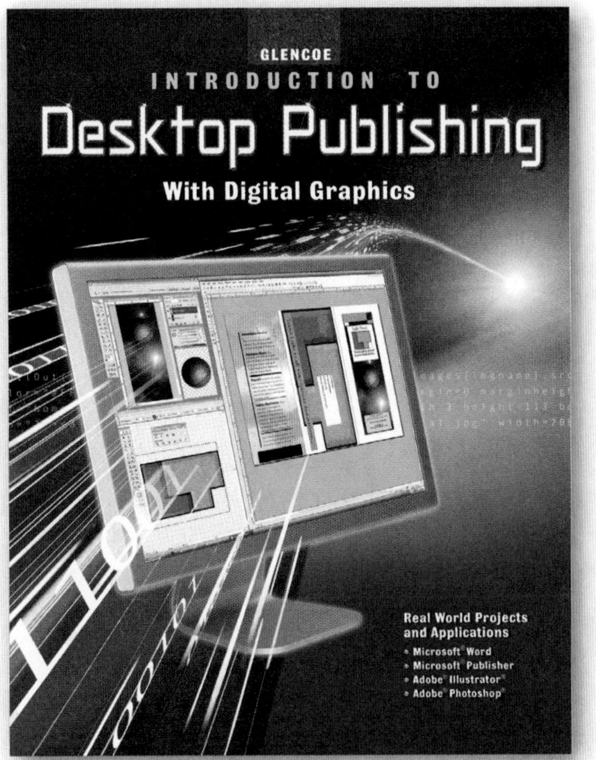

Kevin Niemeyer

Klein Independent School District

Houston, TX

McGraw Hill Glencoe

New York, New York   Columbus, Ohio   Chicago, Illinois   Woodland Hills, California

Glencoe

The McGraw·Hill Companies

Between the time that Web site information is gathered and published, it is not unusual for some sites to have changed URLs or closed. URLs will be updated in reprints or on the Online Resource Center when possible.

Printed in the United States of America.

Send all inquiries to:
Glencoe/McGraw-Hill
21600 Oxnard Street, Suite 500
Woodland Hills, CA 91367

ISBN: 978-0-07-872913-3 (Student Edition)
MHID: 0-07-872913-0 (Student Edition)
ISBN: 978-0-07-876045-7 (Teacher Resource Manual)
MHID: 0-07-876045-3 (Teacher Resource Manual)

3 4 5 6 7 8 9 027/043 12 11 10 09 08

About the Author

Kevin Niemeyer is a teacher for the Klein Independent School District (KISD) in Houston, Texas. He provides instruction in English, Technology Applications, and Desktop Publishing. Kevin is part of a teaching team for KISD's professional development courses. He conducts teacher training in computer education courses such as Microsoft Publisher, Excel, PowerPoint, and Adobe Photoshop. He also develops extensive Web-based teaching materials for his students. Kevin holds a BA in English with a teaching certificate for English and History from Sam Houston State University in Huntsville, Texas. He has over ten years of experience in the field of education, including teaching English as a Second Language in the United States and English as a Foreign Language overseas. Kevin was a contributing writer for two Glencoe textbooks, *Computer Concepts in Action* and *Introduction to Multimedia,* prior to authoring this book.

Kevin lives in Houston, Texas, with his wife, Karen, and his three sons: Jacob, Daniel, and Benjamin. When not teaching or writing, Kevin showcases his desktop publishing talents locally as a freelance designer, and he has designed numerous flyers, posters, books, and business packages for various companies.

Advisory Review Board

Erik Amerikaner
Westlake High School
Westlake Village, California

Douglas M. Bergman
Porter-Gaud School
Charleston, South Carolina

Linda Mallinson
Mid Florida Technical Center
Orlando, Florida

Pam McCarthy
North Canton City Schools
North Canton, Ohio

Academic Reviewers

Jane Brammer
Lake Region High School
Eagle Lake, Florida

Leah Goldman
White Knoll Middle School
W. Columbia, South Carolina

Audrey Marshall
Auburn High School
Auburn, Alabama

Elizabeth Nilsen
Cape Elizabeth High School
Cape Elizabeth, Maine

Linda Robinson
Winter Haven High School
Winter Haven, Florida

Ann Rosborough
Decatur Middle School
Indianapolis, Indiana

Stacy Sherman
Atlantic Technical Center
Coconut Creek, Florida

Polly White
Wawasee High School
Syracuse, Indiana

Rick White
Santa Susana High School
Simi Valley, California

Diane Williamson
Raleigh Egypt Middle School
Memphis, Tennessee

Technical Reviewers

Jason Converse
North Canton City Schools
North Canton, OH

Kimberly Nidy
North Canton City Schools
North Canton, OH

SCREEN CAPTURE CREDITS

Microsoft product screen shots reprinted with permission from Microsoft Corporation.

Adobe product screen shots reprinted with permission from Adobe Systems Incorporated.

Microsoft Word 2003, copyright © 1983–2003 Microsoft Corporation, **3, 5, 6, 7, 8, 9, 10, 11, 12, 13, 14, 15, 16, 17, 18, 19, 20, 21, 22, 23, 24, 25, 26, 27, 28, 29, 30, 31, 32, 33, 34, 35, 36, 38, 39, 40, 41, 42, 43, 44, 45, 46, 47, 48, 50, 51, 54, 58, 60, 61, 62, 63, 64, 65, 66, 67, 68, 69, 70, 71, 72, 73, 74, 75, 76, 77, 78, 79, 80, 81, 82, 83, 84, 85, 86, 87, 88, 90, 91, 92, 93, 94, 95, 98, 331, 375, 385, 393, 411, 446, 466;** © 1995–2006, The Weather Channel Interactive, Inc. **99**; Microsoft Publisher 2003, copyright © 1991–2003 Microsoft Corporation, **104, 106, 107, 108, 109, 110, 111, 112, 113, 114, 115, 116, 117, 118, 119, 120, 121, 122, 123, 124, 125, 126, 127, 128, 129, 131, 132, 133, 134, 135, 137, 138, 139, 140, 141, 142, 143, 144, 152, 155, 156, 158, 159, 160, 164, 165, 166, 168, 169, 170, 171, 174, 175, 176, 177, 178, 180, 181, 182, 183, 184, 187, 188, 193, 259, 260, 267, 268, 275, 280, 281, 382, 383, 384, 386, 394, 397, 399, 401, 402, 409, 412, 414, 415, 416, 419, 420, 421, 424, 425, 427, 429, 436;** Adobe Photoshop, copyright © 1990–2005, Adobe Systems Incorporated. All rights reserved, **201, 202, 203, 204, 205, 206, 207, 208, 209, 210, 211, 212, 213, 214, 215, 216, 217, 218, 219, 220, 221, 222, 223, 224, 225, 226, 227, 228, 230, 231, 232, 233, 234, 235, 236, 237, 238, 242, 244, 245, 254, 255, 256, 257, 258, 261, 262, 263, 264, 265, 269, 270, 271, 283, 284, 424;** © 2000–2006 The McGraw-Hill Companies, Inc. All rights reserved, **251;** 2001–2006 Corbis Corporation. All rights reserved, **252**; © Microsoft Windows XP, copyright © 2001 Microsoft Corporation, **292, 459, 462, 465, 466, 467, 468, 469, 470, 471, 472, 473, 474, 475;** Adobe Illustrator, copyright © 1987–2005, Adobe Systems Incorporated. All rights reserved, **293, 294, 295, 296, 297, 298, 299, 300, 301, 302, 303, 304, 305, 306, 307, 308, 309, 310, 311, 312, 313, 314, 315, 316, 317, 318, 319, 321, 322, 323, 325, 326, 327, 328, 336, 337, 338, 339, 340, 341, 342, 343, 344, 346, 347, 348, 349, 350, 351, 352, 353, 354, 355, 356, 360, 361, 362, 363, 364, 365, 367, 368, 369, 370, 391, 392, 408, 412, 497, 505, 506;** Excel 2003 copyright © 1983–2003 Microsoft Corporation, **381, 387, 388, 389, 390, 393, 398, 474;** U.S. Department of Education, **407;** © 2006 Apple Computer, Inc. All rights reserved, **410**; royalty-free/PhotoDisc/Getty Images, **417, 421, 428;** National Aeronautics and Space Administration (NASA), **418, 420, 422, 422, 424, 427, 430, 431, 434, 435, 438, 441;** copyright © 2006 Jeff Bateman, **421;** © 1996–2006 Travelocity.com LP. All rights reserved, **426;** PowerPoint 2003 copyright © 1983–2003 Microsoft Corporation, **431, 433, 434, 435, 439, 440, 441;** © 1995–2006 Symantec Corporation, **461;** U.S. Department of the Interior, National Park Service, **483, 484;** © 2006 Google, **484**; Microsoft Outlook 2003, copyright © 1983–2003 Microsoft Corporation, **487, 488, 489, 490;** © 2004, Microsoft Corporation, **488, 489, 502;** Washington State Department of Printing, **501, 507, 508, 509, 510, 512.**

Table of Contents

PHOTO CREDITS

Courtesy of Adesso Inc. **450**(tc); Vincent Besnault/Getty Images **448**(tr); Bettmann/CORBIS **477**; Matthew Borkoski/Index Stock **vii**, **290**; Andreas Buck/Peter Arnold, Inc. **xiii**, **442**; Mark Burnett **453**(bl), **454**(tcl); Cooperphoto/CORBIS **453**(br); Dex Images/CORBIS **448**(b); Digital Art/CORBIS **127**(b), **127**(t); Lonnie Duka/Index Stock **329**; Nicholas Eveleigh/SuperStock **129**; Hunter Freeman photo2002/ courtesy Apple Computer, Inc. **449**(cr); Tony Freeman/PhotoEdit **455**(tl); courtesy of Tim Fuller Photography **xi**, **52**, **286, 403**; Getty Images **100**; Aaron Haupt **449**(br); Hewlett Packard **454**(t); courtesy of International Business Machine Corp. **448**(c), **450**(c), **451**(tcl), **451**(tl), **478**(b); Intel Corp.©2002 **452**; courtesy of Iomega Corp. **453**(bc); Lars Klove/Gettty Images **451**(tcr); Andrew Kolb/Masterfile **vi**, **196**; Gregg Manuso/International Stock **371**; MTPA Stock/Masterfile **96**; Mug Shots/CORBIS **448**(cl); Michael Newman/PhotoEdit **viii**, **376**, **450**(tr), **455**(bl), **455**(br); Nikon USA **450**(br); Richard T. Nowitz/Phototake Inc./Alamy Images **479** (l); David Raymer/CORBIS **191**; Mark Richards/PhotoEdit **450**(bcr), **485**; Charles E. Rotkin/CORBIS **478**(t); royalty-free/BananaStock/Alamy Images **480**; royalty-free/CORBIS **449**(cl), **449**(t), **450**(cl), **450**(cr), **451**(tr), **454**(tcr), **479**(c), **479**(r); royalty-free/Getty Images **xiv**, **145**, **455**(cl); royalty-free/ Masterfile **448**(tl); royalty-free/Photodisc/Getty Images **xv**; royalty-free/SuperStock **v**, **101**; royalty-free/Veer **iv**, **1**; Seagate **453**(tl), **453**(tr); Joe Skipper/Reuters/CORBIS **247**; Phillip and Karen Smith/SuperStock **448**(cr); courtesy of Sony **451**(b), **454**(b); Sutherland Photodesign **455**(tr); Stephen Swintek/Getty Images **449**(bl); SW Productions/Brand X Pictures/PictureQuest **xxi**; David Young-Wolff/ PhotoEdit **462**; Vaughn Youtz/CORBIS **450**(bcl).

Photo of the 1999 Lamborghini Diablo VT contributed by Luigi Ballatori, **212–214, 216–219**; photos of castle and Stonehenge contributed by Douglas S. Jantz, **79, 84, 86; 221–223**; photo of downtown Houston contributed by Karen Niemeyer, **262-265, 267-268**; photo of Lamborghini profile contributed by Kevin Niemeyer, **212-214, 216-219**; photo of Texas sky contributed by Kevin Niemeyer, **221**; photo of Freeport Beach ocean horizon contributed by Kevin Niemeyer, **225-228**; photo of baby contributed by Kevin Niemeyer, **230-233**; photo of Morning Glory contributed by Kevin Niemeyer, **230-233**; photo of Texas Bluebonnets contributed by Jerry Upton, **254, 257**.

Table of Contents

U

V

W

X

Z

Q

R

S

Table of Contents

T

Table of Contents

P

Skill Development

Spotlight On Skills

Chapter 1 Projects

1-1	Format Fonts	
	Change Font Size	
1-2	Apply Formatting Attributes	
1-3	Use Font Families	
1-4	Cut and Paste	
	Align Text	
	Insert a Drop Cap	
	Add a Page Border	
	Check Spelling	
1-5	Find and Replace Text	
	Insert a Text Box	
	Add a Fill Color	
	Insert a Graphic	
	Move and Resize an Object	
1-6	Change Page Orientation	
	Format a Page Border	
	Insert a Watermark	
	Add WordArt	
	Apply Kerning	
1-7	Adjust Leading	
	Add a Bulleted List	
	Kern Text	
	Insert Page Numbers	
1-8	Create a Numbered List	
	Insert Symbols	
1-9	Create a Table	
	Sort Data	
	Add Footnotes	
	Resize Columns	
	Format a Table	
	Center Vertically	
1-10	Use a Template	
1-11	Determine Message, Audience, and Content	
	Design Flyer Layout	

Chapter 2 Projects

2-1	Draw Circles	
	Apply Color Fill Options	
	Draw and Format Lines	
2-2	Apply Different Font Styles	
	Add a Page Border	
	Edit and Resize Clip Art	
	Group Drawing Elements	
	Wrap Text	
	Add a Header	
2-3	Create Shapes	
	Group Drawing Objects	
	Resize Clip Art	
	Duplicate Clip Art	
2-4	Format WordArt	
	Combine Text and Graphics	
	Add Callouts	
	Add a Background Color	
2-5	Lay Out a Quad-fold Document	
	Use the Zoom Tool	
	Rotate Images	
	Print Four Pages on a Sheet	
2-6	Create a Masthead	
	Format Columns	
	Create Styles	
2-7	Crop and Size a Photograph	
	Add a Caption	
2-8	Create Tabs with Leaders	
	Format Columns	
	Apply Format Painter	
2-9	Design a Front Panel	
	Add a Texture Background	

Chapter 3 Projects

3-1	Use Templates and Wizards	
	Rotate a Shape	
	Add Clip Art/Pictures	
	Add/Change Color	
3-2	Modify a Template	
	Apply Layout Guides	
	Change Brightness and Contrast	
	Add a Background Image	
3-3	Insert and Format WordArt	
	Create and Format a Bulleted List	
	Flip an Image	
	Insert a Design Gallery Object	
	Create Tear-Offs	
3-4	Create a Custom-sized Document	
	Crop an Image	
	Create a Coupon	
	Insert and Resize Dingbats	
3-5	Lay Out a Two-page Brochure	
	Apply Ruler Guides	
	Link Text Boxes	
	Add Pull-quotes	
3-6	Lay Out Web pages	
	Create a Master Page	
	Publish a File as a Web Page	
3-7	Insert Hyperlinks	
3-8	Lay Out Text and Graphics	
	Create a Master Page	
3-9	Apply Styles to Text	
	Create and Apply a Second Master Page	

N

O

Skill Development

Chapter 4 Projects

4-1 Create Repetition
Adjust White Space
4-2 Add a Contrasting Color
Insert an Attention Getter
4-3 Apply the Golden Ratio
Group Related Content
4-4 Apply PARC to a List
Create New Styles
Apply Style Sheets
4-5 Import a Style Sheet
Apply CMYK Custom Colors
Align Objects
4-6 Link Text Boxes
Re-align Orphan Text
4-7 Resize a Web Page
Resize a Design Gallery Object
4-8 Lay Out a Booklet
Position and Resize Graphics
Apply Style Sheets
Link Text Boxes
4-9 Insert a Calendar Template

Chapter 5 Projects

5-1 Apply the Zoom
Select with the Polygonal Lasso
Copy and Move an Object
Select with the Magic Wand
Flip an Object
Select with Marquee Tools
Scale an Object
5-2 Select with the Magnetic Lasso
Separate Background Images
Resize and Rotate Objects
Crop an Image
5-3 Use the Navigator Palette
Add to Selection
Subtract from Selection
Add a Layer
5-4 Change Color
Create New Layers
Reorder Layers
Add a New Background
Adjust Contrast
Insert a New Image
Erase Parts of an Image
5-5 Resize a Document
Add a Layer Mask
Set an RGB Color
Add Text
Align Objects
5-6 Straighten a Photo
Remove Red Eye
Apply the Clone Stamp
Adjust Color Levels
5-7 Add a Layer for a Selection
Add a Shadow
Apply a Filter
Flatten an Image
Create a Vignette Effect
5-8 Change the Workspace Color
Apply Filters
Apply the Magic Eraser
Add a Gradient Fill
5-9 Take a Digital Photograph
Upload a Photo from a Camera
Remove a Background
Insert a Picture into an Image
Apply Blending Modes
5-10 Group Layers
Insert Magazine Cover Objects
Add Text

Chapter 6 Projects

6-1 Insert a Custom Shape
Add Filters
Apply a Type Mask
Add Styles
Save in a New Format
6-2 Insert a Photoshop File
Lay Out a Postcard
Print Multiple Copies on a Sheet
6-3 Saturate Colors
Add Layer Masks
Apply Gradients
Add a Layer Style
6-4 Set Print Specifications
Assemble Printed Pages
6-5 Blend Layers
Apply the Clone Tool
Apply the Smudge Tool
6-6 Apply PARC Principles
6-7 Lay Out Text Elements
Design the First Page
Design the Final Page
6-8 Create a Texture
Insert Page Numbers
Insert a Textured Background

M

Skill Development

Chapter 7 Projects

- **7-1** Create Geometric Shapes
  - Apply the Selection Tool
  - Add Fill Color
  - Drag Objects
  - Apply the Direct Selection Tool
- **7-2** Display Grids and Guides
  - Apply the Zoom Tool
  - Align Objects
  - Format a Line
  - Add Text
  - Rotate an Object
- **7-3** Duplicate an Image
  - Work with the Color Palette
  - Work with the Swatches Palette
- **7-4** Work with the Gradient Palette
  - Create Colors with the Color Picker
- **7-5** Use the Transparency Palette
  - Compare Opacity Levels
- **7-6** Apply Blending Options
- **7-7** Distort an Image
  - Add a Drop Shadow
  - Warp Text
- **7-8** Add Shape to Area
  - Apply Text Outlines
- **7-9** Create a Text Path
  - Add a Gradient
  - Apply Envelope Distort

Chapter 8 Projects

- **8-1** Apply Pathfinder Palette Tools
  - Create Custom Colors
  - Work with the Layers Palette
  - Draw with the Pen Tool
- **8-2** Apply the Pathfinder Palette
  - Add Word Clip Art
  - Apply Text Outlines
  - Apply Expand Appearance
  - Customize Print Output
- **8-3** Lay Out a Tent Card
  - Insert an Illustrator File
  - Format Text Boxes
  - Apply a Master Page
  - Add Border Art
  - Create a Custom Color
- **8-4** Copy and Paste Clip Art
  - Apply Live Trace
- **8-5** Apply Text Outlines
  - Apply Pathfinder Divide
  - Apply 3D Effects
- **8-6** Set Poster Layout
  - Apply Gradient Transparency
  - Set Print Specifications
- **8-7** Apply 3D Effects
- **8-8** Create a Logo
- **8-9** Add Clip Art to Logo
  - Apply Text Outlines
  - Add Symbols

Chapter 9 Projects

- **9-1** Create a Flowchart
  - Add Connectors
- **9-2** Modify a Calendar Template
- **9-3** Create a Spreadsheet
  - Apply the Sum Function
  - Enter Formulas
  - Copy Formulas
- **9-4** Brainstorm Ideas
  - Create a Design
- **9-5** Lay Out a Business Card
  - Insert a Logo
- **9-6** Lay Out a Letterhead
  - Insert a Logo
- **9-7** Lay Out a Business Envelope
  - Add a Return Address

Chapter 10 Projects

- **10-1** Transfer Style Sheets in Microsoft Word
  - Transfer Style Sheets in Microsoft Publisher
  - Transfer Style Sheets in Adobe Illustrator
- **10-2** Design the Front Panel
  - Create the Address Panel
  - Add Styles to the Back Panel
- **10-3** Add Text and Graphics
  - Apply a Style Sheet
- **10-4** Lay out a booklet
  - Apply a Master Page
  - Create a Cover Image
  - Add a Table of Contents
  - Import Style Sheets
  - Cite Sources
- **10-5** Create an Image in Photoshop
  - Format a Web Page in Publisher
  - Add Pages to a Publication
- **10-6** Ignore the Master Page
  - Create Hyperlinks
- **10-7** Import an Outline
  - Set up a Slide Master
  - Add a Title Master
  - Apply the Master Slides
- **10-8** Add Text to Slides
  - Take Screen Captures of Documents
- **10-9** Add Custom Animation
  - Adjust Timing

H

I

J

K

L

Academic Integration

Language Arts

Math

G

Academic Integration

Science

Social Studies

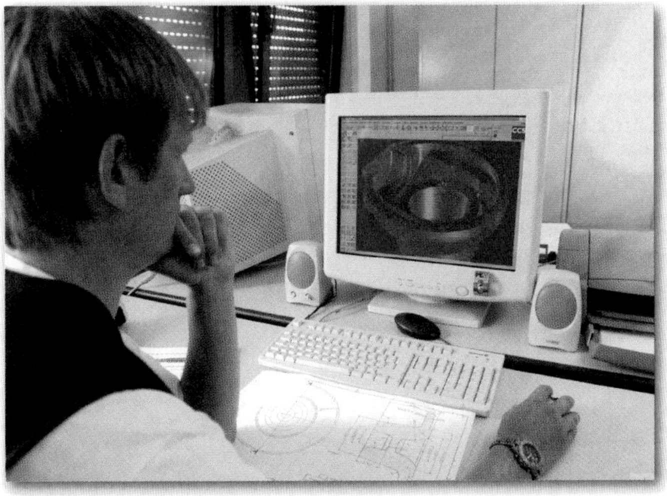

E

F

Why Study Desktop Publishing?

Desktop publishing is one of the most important skills and trades in society today. By understanding how to use various types of desktop publishing and graphics software, you will learn how to create effective and interesting documents and publications.

Introduction to Desktop Publishing with Digital Graphics is intended to provide you with project-based instruction that will give you the skills needed for planning and creating desktop-published documents. This textbook was written and designed to help you achieve each of the following goals:

Become a 21st Century Citizen

- Understand how to use technology wisely and safely.
- Understand how computers and the Internet work.
- Evaluate the accuracy and usefulness of information on the Web.
- Find and share information quickly, safely, and ethically.

Become an Effective Desktop Publisher

- Demonstrate your understanding of fundamental desktop publishing principles.
- Become a skilled and creative user of desktop publishing technology such as Microsoft Word, Microsoft Publisher, Adobe Photoshop, and Adobe Illustrator.
- Create your own unique and engaging desktop publishing documents for your audience.
- Become an expert at evaluating desktop-published documents.
- Offer constructive feedback to improve your own and others' published documents.

Develop Learning and Study Skills for All Subjects

- Improve reading comprehension with both guided and independent reading strategies.
- Develop critical thinking skills.
- Build teamwork skills.
- Integrate technology skills across the curriculum.

D

How Can I Develop My Reading Skills?

When you read this textbook, you will be learning about technology and how it is used in the world around you. This textbook is a good example of non-fiction writing—it describes real-world ideas and facts. It is also an example of technical writing because it gives you specific step-by-step instructions for how to complete different tasks.

Below and on the next page are some reading strategies that will help you become an active textbook reader. Choose the strategies that work best for you. If you have trouble as you read your textbook, look back at these strategies for help. If you do not understand the material or need additional help, ask your teacher or a parent.

Before You Read

SET A PURPOSE

- Why am I reading the textbook?
- How might I be able to use what I learn in my own life?

PREVIEW

- Read the chapter title to find out what the topic will be.
- Read the subtitles to see what you will learn about the topic.
- Skim the photos, charts, graphs, or maps.
- Look for vocabulary words that are boldfaced. How are they defined?

DRAW FROM YOUR OWN BACKGROUND

- What do I already know about the topic?
- How is the new information different from what I already know?

C

As You Read

QUESTION

- What is the main idea?
- How well do the details support the main idea?
- How do the photos, charts, graphs, and maps support the main idea?

CONNECT

- Think about people, places, and events in your own life. Are there any similarities with those in your textbook?

PREDICT

- Can you predict events or outcomes by using clues and information that you already know?

VISUALIZE

- Can you imagine the settings, actions, and people that are described?
- Can you create graphic organizers to help me see relationships found in the information?

IF YOU DON'T KNOW WHAT A WORD MEANS...

- think about the setting, or context, in which the word is used.
- check if prefixes such as *un-*, *non-*, or *pre-* can help you break down the word.
- look up the word's definition in a dictionary or glossary.

READING DOs

Do...

- ✓ establish a purpose for reading.
- ✓ think about how your own experiences relate to the topic.
- ✓ try different reading strategies.

READING DON'Ts

Don't...

- ⃠ ignore how the textbook is organized.
- ⃠ allow yourself to be easily distracted.
- ⃠ hurry to finish the material.

After You Read

SUMMARIZE

- What have I learned from this text?
- How can I apply what I have learned?

ASSESS

- What was the main idea?
- Did the text clearly support the main idea?
- Can I use this new information in other school subjects or at home?

Take the Desktop Publishing Challenge!

Many features in this text—such as colorful headings, illustrations with captions, tables and charts—have been carefully constructed to help you read, understand, and remember key ideas and concepts. Taking advantage of these features can help you improve your reading and study skills.

Get Started

The scavenger hunt on these pages highlights features that will help you get the most out of your textbook. Collect points as you complete each step.

1. **How many projects are in Chapter 1?** [*6 points. Hint: The Table of Contents gives you at-a-glance information about the major divisions and topics in the book.*]

2. **How many times does the Glencoe Online URL www.glencoe.com appear in Chapter 1?** [*8 points*]

3. **What is the purpose of the Sidebar feature on page 10? Why is it important?** [*6 points*]

4. **What are the skills you expect to learn in Chapter 1, Project 1-4?** [*6 points*]

5. **What study tip do you learn in the Before You Read activity on page 103?** [*6 points*]

6. **What is the purpose of the Eye on Ethics feature on page 36? What is the feature teaching you?** [*7 points*]

7. **What three key terms are defined in Project 3-2?** [*3 points.* Hint: Key terms stand out from the rest of the text because they are printed in bold and highlighted.]

transparency The level at which an object can be seen through, in order to see another object behind it. (p. 215)

transparent A quality which lets you see through an object, making the objects underneath visible. (p. 315)

typeface A design for a set of characters (letters, numbers, and punctuation marks). (p. 7)

typography The study of type and its characteristics. (p. 7)

U

ungroup To break a larger object or image into its smaller pieces, each with its own set of handles. (p. 64)

V

vector graphic An image that is created by using mathematical reference points. Vector graphics can be resized without losing clarity. (pp. 56, 293)

vignette An image that has a border that fades into the background. (p. 229)

W

warp To bend or distort. (p. 321)

watermark An image that is barely visible and often cannot be seen until the paper it is on is held up to the light. (p. 25)

Web page One file or document within a Web site. (p. 423)

Web site A collection of files or documents located on the World Wide Web. A Web site can be one file or many. (p. 423)

white space Empty space that sets off the text or graphics on a page. (pp. 25, 151)

widow The last line of a paragraph (or text group) carried forward to the top of the next page or column. (p. 177)

WMF (Windows MetaFile) A vector file format not generally considered suitable for high-quality printing. (p. 294)

WordArt Decorative text that comes in many interesting shapes and colors. (p. 25)

wrap To flow text around an image or object. (p. 21)

WYSIWYG (pronounced *wizzy-wig*) An acronym that means "What You See Is What You Get." What you see on the monitor screen is the same as what you see on the printed page. (p. 3)

8 What are the five design process elements listed in the Design Process table in each Chapter? [6 points]

9 What topic is covered in the Instant Message on page 227? [6 points]

10 How can the Go Online Preview feature help you learn more about the documents you will create? [4 points]

11 What kind of illustration will you create in Independent Practice 2 at the end of Chapter 7? [4 points]

12 How many steps will it take you to complete Project 1-3? [4 points]

13 How can you tell when you need to use a Data File in a project? [5 points]

14 Why is it important to read the You Will Learn To before you read the Workshop Foundations and Toolbox? [5 points]

15 Which feature helps you check your work at the completion of a project? [4 points]

16 On what page of each project will you find Spotlight on Skills, Key Terms, and Academic Focus? [5 points]

17 How can you tell what the academic focus of an Independent Practice project is? [4 points]

18 Which Appendix can help you edit and correct a fellow student's document? [4 points]

19 What information can you find about careers from the In the Workplace feature? [3 points]

20 What type of activities can you find when you read the Go Online Activities feature? [4 points]

service bureau A company or organization that provides desktop publishing services, such as scanning and high-resolution printing. (p. 334)

signature The number of pages that are created when a sheet of paper is folded. Books are made up of one or more signatures. (p. 511)

single lens reflex A single lens reflex (SLR) camera allows the photographer to look through the camera's viewfinder and actually see the exact image that will be captured by the camera lens. (p. 240)

sizing handle A small circle or square that is visible on the sides or corners of an object. (p. 21)

SLR See *Single Lens Reflex.*

snap A feature that pulls objects to align with the nearest guide, ruler position, or object. (p. 110)

sort To arrange data in a table or spreadsheet according to particular values or criteria. You can sort from highest to lowest, alphabetically, etc. (p. 41)

spectrum The entire range of color from white to black.(p. 311)

splash page The page where users enter a Web site. (p. 426)

spot color A color not created by combining cyan, magenta, yellow, and black. These colors are premixed and can be special ordered when printing at a professional print shop. (p. 158)

spread Pages that face each other, like in an open book. (p. 104)

spreadsheet A grid or table that arranges numbers or text so that it is easy to manage and manipulate information. (p. 387)

style sheet Formatting rules that allow you to easily format specific text consistently. (pp. 79, 167)

synchronization A process that allows you to create or edit one object while all the related objects automatically display the same information (such as tear-offs). (p. 115)

T

table A grid of rows and columns that organizes information so that it is easy to find and compare. (p. 41)

tagline A slogan. (p. 393)

teamwork Working as a group in a way that encourages close cooperation between group members. (p. 378)

tear-off A tab that can easily be torn off a flyer or advertisement and contains contact information such as an address or phone number. (p. 115)

template A pre-formatted, fill-in-the-blank document. (pp. 46, 106)

text box A frame that contains text and can be placed anywhere in a document. (p. 21)

three-dimensional (3D) The illusion that a drawn object displays depth, width, and height. (p. 359)

3D modeling The process of using a computer to virtually create an object in three dimensions (3D). (p. 359)

thumbnail sketches Simple drawings that give a sense of the layout and basic elements of your design. (p. 49)

TIFF, also TIF (Tagged Integrated File Format) A lossless raster file format that preserves image detail. Since file sizes tend to be quite large, this file format works best for high-quality printing. New versions of this format preserve transparent information. (pp. 200, 259)

tile printing A method of printing an image that is larger than what the printer could normally print by separating the image onto different pages that are later assembled into the complete image. (p. 354)

timeline A visual representation, often a chart, that shows when each stage of a project will be completed. (p. 379)

tracking An adjustment of the horizontal spacing between a series of characters. (p. 361)

transition An animation or other device that occurs between slides in a presentation. (p. 439)

What Is Your Desktop Publishing Skill Rating?

POINTS	SKILL RATING
90 to 100	You really know how to let your textbook work for you!
70 to 89	Researching and organizing are skills you possess!
Less than 70	Consider working with your teacher or classmates to learn how to use your book more effectively—you will gain skills you can use your whole life.

1. 10
2. Eight times
3. To teach keyboard shortcuts. It is important because not only do shortcuts save time, but they also help you familiarize yourself with the keyboard and its many functions.
4. Read the Spotlight on Skills information at the beginning of the project.
5. Adjust your reading speed to match the difficulty of the text. Re-read the text, if necessary.
6. The Eye on Ethics feature discusses the importance of legal symbols in order to protect one's work, names, or logos.
7. Layout guides (layout grids), gutter, and snap
8. Purpose, audience, content, layout, and publication
9. Interpret a histogram.
10. Go Online Activities Preview directs you to PowerPoint presentations and rubrics at the Glencoe Online Learning Center.
11. An illustration of breakfast food
12. Eight steps
13. An icon that looks like a CD appears at the beginning of the Step-by-Step.
14. The You Will Learn To section helps you focus on what you need to be learning in that particular section.
15. Review and Revise
16. The first page of every project
17. Note the icon and description preceding the project. There are projects in math, language arts, science, or social studies.
18. Appendix C
19. In the Workplace describes careers using desktop publishing skills. The feature also gives information about the future outlook, training, salary ranges, and skills and talents required for the career.
20. Enrichment activities that allow you to learn more about desktop publishing

process color A color created by mixing colors—such as cyan, magenta, yellow, and black—in specific proportions. (p. 497)

project manager The person leading or supervising a team. (p. 378)

promotion A special offer used to persuade people to buy products or services. (p. 423)

proportional Size relationships between different objects or parts of the same object. In a proportional font, letters take up a space that relates to their size. (p. 8)

proximity How close together elements are on a page. (p. 151)

publication A document containing text and graphics that is distributed in print or online. (p. 3)

public domain Materials that are so old that they no longer have a copyright, or materials that are published by the government or are declared free to the public. (p. 251)

pull handles Used to make circles or squares larger or smaller. (p. 61)

Q

quad-fold A document that is folded in half twice, so that there are four (quad) folds. (p. 75)

R

radial A circular effect. (p. 311)

raster graphic (Also called *bitmap graphic.*) A graphic made up of tiny colored squares (pixels) that work together to form an image. Raster images do not look as smooth and crisp as vector graphics when they are enlarged because the software tries to adjust the size of the pixels. (pp. 56, 198)

ratio The relationship between objects based on size or quantity. (p. 162)

repetition The consistent use of important design elements that are echoed, or repeated, in some way throughout the design. (p. 152)

resize To reduce or increase the size of a picture so that the page looks balanced and visually appealing. (p. 84)

resolution The clarity of an image, expressed in number of *pixels per inch* (ppi) or *dots per inch* (dpi). (p. 180, 198)

retouch To fix or edit an image. (p. 224)

RGB (Red, Green, Blue) The primary colors of light. When mixed in different proportions, these three colors can create a large range of colors that can be displayed on a monitor. (p. 306)

royalty A fee that is paid in order to use copyrighted material. (p. 251)

Rule of Six A presentation principle of using no more than six words per line and no more than six lines per slide, or six short bullet points, in a PowerPoint presentation. (p. 431)

S

sans serif Sans (pronounced *san* or *sanz*) means "without" in French; so a sans serif font does not have the extra strokes. (p. 7) See *serif.*

saturation The intensity of a color. (p. 215)

scalable The ability of a graphic to be resized without losing image quality. (pp. 7, 71, 198, 293)

scale Size of an object. (p. 68)

search engine A program that finds Web sites or other information by searching for key words. (p. 426)

serif (rhymes with *sheriff*) A stroke on a letterform. Serif fonts have a small cross stroke at the top or bottom of most letters. (p. 7)

What Hardware and Software Do I Need?

Specific directions and illustrations are given for the Microsoft Windows XP platform. Projects and figures in *Introduction to Desktop Publishing with Digital Graphics* were created using Microsoft Word 2003, Microsoft Publisher 2003, Adobe Photoshop CS2, and Adobe Illustrator CS2. However, teachers can easily tailor activities to previous versions of Windows and the above-mentioned software applications. (Note to Macintosh users: Material in this textbook can be modified and used in the Mac platform. Mac User icons have been provided in step-by-steps where the steps may be somewhat different from Microsoft Windows.)

Equipment Needs

	Hardware	Software
Required	• Computer • Color monitor • (Make sure your equipment meets or exceeds the minimum system requirements of your software.) • Mouse • Keyboard	• Internet browser (such as Microsoft Internet Explorer or Mozilla Firefox) • Microsoft Windows XP, 2000, or 98 • Microsoft Word • Microsoft Publisher • Adobe Photoshop • Adobe Illustrator
Recommended	• Flash, CD, or DVD drive • Printer • Scanner • Digital camera	• Microsoft Excel • Microsoft PowerPoint

Using Student Data Files

To complete some activities and projects in this book, Student Data Files are required.

- When you see the Student Data File icon, locate needed files before beginning the activity.
- Student Data Files are available on the book's Online Learning Center at www.glencoe.com. All files are also provided on the Teacher Resource DVD. Your teacher will tell you where to find these files.
- Some projects require you to continue working on a file you created in an earlier project. If you are absent and cannot complete the previous project, your teacher may choose to provide you with the Solution File for the missed project (Solution Files are only available on the Teacher Resource DVD or on the Online Learning Center, Teacher Center).

Student Data File

monotype A type of font where all characters take up the same amount of space. Sometimes called fixed pitch fonts. (p. 8)

montage Similar to a collage, except that the separate images combine to create a new image. (p. 229)

morph To gradually blend two images together in such a manner that the first image appears to be transforming into the other image. (p. 317)

N

nameplate See *masthead.* (p. 79)

native format A format created specifically for a single software program. (pp. 258, 346)

negative space Another term for white space, or the space without text or graphics. (p. 155)

O

object Any individual shape, image, or text that can be moved, edited, or manipulated. (p. 297)

opacity How dark an object is, making it more difficult to see through. (p. 215)

opaque An object's *opacity*, a quality which makes an object too dark to see through. (pp. 215, 315)

optical zoom A lens in a camera that magnifies the subject without losing image quality. (p. 240)

orphan A first line of a paragraph (or other text group) that is left at the bottom of a page or column. (p. 177)

P

palette A set of tools, located in a separate floating toolbar, that relates to a particular action, such as adding color or working with layers. (pp. 201, 295)

Pantone A color system used by professional print shops that matches computer data with specialized inks. See *spot color.* (p. 391)

parallel Describes lines that stay an equal distance from each other and never intersect. (p. 61)

path The line that is created when an object is drawn or traced. (p.297)

PDF (Portable Document Format) A format developed by Adobe that creates an image of a document that can be viewed on any computer. (p. 436)

perpendicular Describes lines that intersect at a right angle (90 degrees). (p. 61)

pixel Short for *picture-element,* the smallest unit of color in an image, or on a computer monitor. (pp. 56, 198)

pixelated Describes when individual pixels are visible in an image. (pp. 199, 349)

pixels per inch (ppi) The measurement used in order to keep track of an image's resolution. (p. 253)

plagiarism The practice of using someone else's material without crediting the source. It is like stealing, and can result in stiff penalties. (p. 273)

PNG (Portable Network Graphics) A lossless raster file format that preserves image detail. File sizes can vary, and this format preserves transparent information. (pp. 200, 259)

point A font and spacing measurement that is $^1/_{72}$ of an inch. (p. 8)

polygon A multisided geometric figure. (p. 203)

portrait orientation A page layout where the short edge of the paper is along the top. (p. 26)

PostScript A computer language that translates a raster file into a format that can be printed on a high-resolution printer. (p. 506)

Print Layout View A viewing option that allows you to see how the text and graphics in a document will print on the page. (p. 5)

Technology Standards

Most educators today believe that in order to live, learn, and work successfully in an increasingly complex society, students must be able to use technology effectively.

What Are Standards?

Standards give educators a benchmark that lets them and their students know what skills every student should master in a particular subject area. Students who know what standards they are expected to meet before they begin a course are better prepared to succeed and meet expectations. The technology standards described below and on the next pages are designed to help students understand and apply the skills needed to be technologically literate in today's society.

ISTE and NETS

The International Society for Technology in Education (ISTE) has developed National Educational Technology Standards for students (NETS-S). The ISTE standards identify skills that students can practice and master in school, but the skills are also used outside of school, at home and at work. The activities in this book are designed to meet ISTE standards. For more information about ISTE and the NETS, please visit www.iste.org.

K

kern To adjust the horizontal spacing between two characters. (p. 26)

L

landscape orientation A page layout where the long edge of the paper is along the top. (p. 26)

layering The process used to precisely position and align different graphic objects and effects within one design; also called stacking. (p. 336)

layout guides A series of evenly spaced lines that form the basic framework under a design and allow objects to be precisely aligned and sized. (p. 110)

layout software A software application used to combine text and graphics together on a page. (pp. 3, 103)

leader A line or series of dots connecting information. Leaders can be inserted before tab stops, or they can be attached to a text box to point to a specific part of an image. (p. 71)

leading The spacing between lines of text. Many modern word processors call this line spacing. (pp. 30, 89)

letterform The shape of a letter. (p. 13)

letterhead The heading at the top of stationery, usually containing a name and address and sometimes a company logo. (p. 396)

link To connect. When text boxes are linked, text from one box can automatically flow into another box no matter where the boxes are located. (pp. 125, 177)

logo A combination of text and graphics used to identify a business or product. (p. 71)

lossless Refers to raster file formats that do not compress file sizes. (p. 200)

lossy Refers to raster file formats that compress file sizes by removing or simplifying data. (p. 200)

M

magnify To enlarge your view of an image so that you can see close details. (p. 301)

mailing list A large list of people who are intended to receive a copy of a letter or publication in a mass mailing. (p. 400)

mail merge A process for producing mass mailings with personalized addresses on form letters, envelopes, and labels. (p. 400)

main publication The document in a mail merge (such as a form letter or envelope) that does not change text, punctuation, spacing, or graphics when it is merged with the data source. (p. 400)

map An illustration that is wrapped around the outside of an object, as wallpaper is attached to a wall. (p. 366)

marketing A process that a company uses to promote and distribute its products or services. (p. 410)

marquee A dotted outline around sections you have selected. (pp. 203, 297)

mask A feature that hides areas of an image so that the data cannot be edited. (pp. 220, 342)

master page A special layer that allows design elements in a document to be repeated automatically on any number of pages. This layer is usually behind all other layers. (pp. 104, 130)

masthead A title of a newsletter, newspaper, or other periodical that stands out from the rest of the text by using style, color, or size to grab the reader's attention. (p. 79)

medium The delivery method of publications, such as print, CDs or DVDs, television and radio broadcasts, and Internet publishing. (p. 334)

megapixel A unit that contains over one million pixels. (p. 240)

milestone A critical point in a project. (p. 381)

National Educational Technology Standards for Students (NETS•S)

The NETS are divided into six broad categories that are listed below. Activities in the book are specificially designed to meet the standards within each category.

1. Basic operations and concepts

- Students demonstrate a sound understanding of the nature and operation of technology systems.
- Students are proficient in the use of technology.

2. Social, ethical, and human issues

- Students understand the ethical, cultural, and societal issues related to technology.
- Students practice responsible use of technology systems, information, and software.
- Students develop positive attitudes toward technology uses that support lifelong learning, collaboration, personal pursuits, and productivity.

3. Technology productivity tools

- Students use technology tools to enhance learning, increase productivity, and promote creativity.
- Students use productivity tools to collaborate in constructing technology-enhanced models, prepare publications, and produce other creative works.

4. Technology communications tools

- Students use telecommunications to collaborate, publish, and interact with peers, experts, and other audiences.
- Students use a variety of media and formats to communicate information and ideas effectively to multiple audiences.

5. Technology research tools

- Students use technology to locate, evaluate, and collect information from a variety of sources.
- Students use technology tools to process data and report results.
- Students evaluate and select new information resources and technological innovations based on the appropriateness of specific tasks.

6. Technology problem-solving and decision-making tools

- Students use technology resources for solving problems and making informed decisions.
- Students employ technology in the development of strategies for solving problems in the real world.

footer Information that appears at the bottom of every page. (p. 16)

frame A holder for an object, such as text or a picture, in a publication. (p. 104)

freeware A software program that is downloadable at no charge. (p. 354)

G

GIF (Graphic Interchange Format) A lossy raster file format that reduces the number of colors in an image. This file format works best for Internet Web pages and preserves transparent data. (pp. 200, 259)

gradient A gradual change from one color to another. (p. 311)

gradient stop The beginning or end colors used in a gradient. (p. 311)

grayscale A color system that ranges from white to black with shades of gray in between. (pp. 261, 306)

gridlines Lines and borders that separate rows and columns. (p. 41)

grids The framework upon which you place objects for alignment and sizing. (p. 301)

group To combine separate simple objects into a single, more complex image. (p. 64)

gutter The space between columns of text or between the publication's binding and the first column in a page spread. (p. 110)

H

header Information that appears at the top of every page. (p.16)

hexadecimal value A six-digit code that defines one color. (p. 499)

highlight An effect showing the light reflected off a surface. (p. 229)

histogram A graph that shows the number of pixels for each color and tone in an image. (p. 225)

hot spot A hyperlink location on a Web page. (p. 133)

HSB (Hue, Saturation, Brightness) A method of describing color to a computer. (p. 306)

HTML (HyperText Markup Language) A computer language used for creating Web sites. (p. 130)

hue Color (p. 215)

hyperlink A clickable area in a document, often represented as colored text or a graphic, that takes you to information within the same document or to another location. (p. 133)

I

icon A picture button in a software application. Used as a shortcut to a menu item. (p. 5)

imagesetter A high-resolution printer used for high-quality, professional print jobs. (p. 501)

import To bring in a file or product. (pp. 172, 409)

indirect channel of distribution When a company uses a middleman to give out marketing materials or products to customers. (p. 413)

interface All of the onscreen elements—such as graphics, menus, and tools—that allow you to communicate with the computer. (p. 5)

J

JPEG, also JPG (Joint Photographic Experts Group) A raster file format commonly used for photographs and images. This efficient format is often used on the Internet, for low to medium resolution needs, or for pictures that do not require transparency. (p. 254)

National Educational Technology Standards for Students: Performance Indicators for Technology-Literate Students

In this text, all students should have opportunities to demonstrate the following performance indicators for technological literacy. Each performance indicator refers to the standards category or categories (listed on previous page) to which the performance is linked.

1. Identify capabilities and limitations of contemporary and emerging technology resources and assess the potential of these systems and services to address personal, lifelong learning, and workplace needs. (2)
2. Make informed choices among technology systems, resources and services. (1, 2)
3. Analyze advantages and disadvantages of widespread use and reliance on technology in the workplace and in society as a whole. (2)
4. Demonstrate and advocate for legal and ethical behaviors among peers, family, and community regarding the use of technology and information. (2)
5. Use technology tools and resources for managing and communicating personal/professional information (e.g., finances, schedules, addresses, purchases, correspondence). (3, 4)
6. Evaluate technology-based options, including distance and distributed education, for lifelong learning. (5)
7. Routinely and efficiently use online information resources to meet needs for collaboration, research, publications, communications, and productivity. (4, 5, 6)
8. Select and apply technology tools for research, information analysis, problem-solving, and decision-making in content learning. (4, 5)
9. Investigate and apply expert systems, intelligent agents, and simulations in real-world situations. (3, 5, 6)
10. Collaborate with peers, experts, and others to contribute to content-related knowledge base by using technology to compile, synthesize, produce, and disseminate information, models, and other creative works. (4, 5, 6)

copyright The legal rights of a writer, musician, artist, or creator of a work to protect his or her property from unauthorized use. A copyrighted work cannot be used without permission of the creator or holder of the copyright, and a fee might have to be paid for its use. (p. 4)

crop To trim an image. (p. 84)

D

data source A database of names, addresses, and other useful information, used in a mail merge. (p. 400)

deadline A time goal. (p. 385)

default The automatic or built-in setting for a feature in a computer program. (p. 58)

design process A step-by-step system used to create effective designs and documents. (p. 49)

desktop publishing (DTP) The use of a computer to combine text and graphics together on a page. (p. 3)

dingbats A variety of graphic icons and symbols included in the Wingdings and Webdings fonts. (pp. 36, 120)

direct channel of distribution When a company gives out marketing materials and products directly to customers. (p. 413)

dithering When a visiting computer substitutes colors on Web pages that use colors not included in the standard 216 colors. (p. 180)

drop cap A large, decorative letter used as the first letter of a paragraph. (p. 16)

duplex printing To print on both sides of the paper before going on to the next copy. (pp. 93, 140)

E

economy of scale Achieving a lower cost per item by producing large volumes of the item. (p. 416)

embedded font Fonts that are saved as part of the document itself. This allows a print shop to use the exact font that was intended. (p. 504)

EMF (Enhanced MetaFile) A vector file format not generally considered suitable for high-quality printing. (p. 294)

EPS (Encapsulated PostScript) A vector file format used to print high-quality images on professional printers. (p. 294)

export To send out a product or file to be used in another location. (pp. 172, 409)

extrude To give an object visual depth. (p. 351)

F

fair use An exception to copyright law that allows copyrighted products to be used for certain educational purposes without requiring permission or royalty payments. (p. 251)

fastening points Points that anchor a line and start a new line segment. (p. 207)

file name extension The letters displayed after a file name that describe the file format. (For example, Word documents end with .doc.) (pp. 200, 293)

filter A tool that can create effects like distortions, textures, blurs, and more. (p. 234)

flatten A command that merges all layers of an image into one layer to reduce the file size and make the image more difficult to change when sent to a client. (p. 229)

flowchart A chart showing the parts of a larger procedure, illustrated by using a set of standard symbols. (p. 379)

focal point An area to which your eye is drawn. (p. 153)

font A specific typeface combined with variations such as size, style, and spacing. (p. 7)

font attributes Characteristics or qualities of text, such as underline, bold, italics, superscript, and subscript. (p. 10)

UNIT 1

Design with Microsoft Word

Contents

A

advertising Using or paying a magazine, television station, Web site, or other medium to promote a company's products or services. (p. 410)

align To arrange items so that they line up. (p. 16)

alignment The horizontal and vertical placement of objects. (p. 152)

anchor point The spot where you begin or end a line segment. (pp. 203, 297)

animation An effect where elements on the screen appear to move. (p. 439)

audience The person or group of people whom a publication is meant to influence or entertain. (p. 2)

B

bevel Refers to the angled edges of an object. (p. 351)

Bézier curve (pronounced *bay-zee-yeah*) A precise method of drawing curves that uses anchor points on a path and control points that describe the direction of the path. (p. 337)

bi-fold Folded in half, therefore creating two pages with one fold in the middle, like a book. (p. 89)

binding The method used to hold the pages of a document together. Binding can be anything from a single staple to complex stitching and gluing. (p. 509)

bitmap graphic See *raster graphic.* (p. 56)

blending modes Tools that control the way the pixels on one layer blend with the pixels in underlying layers. (p. 215)

booklet A publication with multiple pages printed front and back that is smaller or shorter than a book. (p. 418)

border A line or a design that outlines a specific section or a page in a document. (p. 16)

brand Words, symbols, designs, or even sounds that identify a product or service and that customers immediately associate with a particular product or service. (p. 410)

bullet A character such as a dot or diamond, often placed before items in a list. (p. 31)

byline The credit line showing the name of an article's writer, usually added below an article's title. (p. 79)

C

callout A type of text box that calls attention to parts of an image. (p. 71)

channel of distribution The path by which a product moves from producer to consumer. (p. 413)

client The person or group of people who commission a publication. (p. 334)

clipboard A temporary storage area that a computer program uses when you cut or copy material. (p. 15)

clone To copy a range of pixels and paste the pixels into another location. (pp. 224, 269)

CMYK (Cyan, Magenta, Yellow, Black) Many printers use these four colors as primary colors for ink. (p. 306)

collage A collection of assembled images. (p. 211)

connector A line that stays attached to a shape regardless of where the shape is moved. (p. 382)

consistency Repetition of the same elements or principles in designs. (p. 407)

contrast Design elements that look different from surrounding features to create visual interest or specific focal points. (pp. 13, 153)

control point A drawing point defining the angle of a path to its next anchor point. (p. 337)

Chapter 1 Introducing Desktop Publishing

Skills You Will Learn

Think about the publications you use or see every day. There are magazines and newspapers, flyers and brochures, textbooks you read in school, and books you read for fun. Even though these publications have certain elements in common, they each follow a specific design and layout.

Publishing and Design

In this book, you will learn the desktop publishing skills you need to create a variety of documents. More importantly, you will be introduced to the principles that guide layout and design. Without an effective design, your publication will not reach the people you want to reach or get the results for which it was created.

The table below describes the questions you should ask yourself before designing any type of document.

DESIGN PROCESS: Overview

Elements	Issues
Purpose	What is this publication meant to do? Is the intent of the publication to educate, inform, entertain, or advertise? What information, product, or service is it describing or selling?
Audience	Who do you want to read your publication? What do they like, and what appeals to them? How does your message meet their needs?
Content	What content and graphics do you need to effectively achieve your purpose and get the response you want from your audience? Should you use mostly written information, or is it better to use lots of illustrations?
Layout	How do you make your content visually appealing and easy to read for your audience? How can you capture the audience's attention? What size text should you have, and how should it be organized? Where should the graphics go? How do you guide the reader to important information?
Publication	Is factual information accurate? Has it been proofread and edited? Should it be printed, published as a Web page, or both? If it is printed, is it on a single page, two-sided pages, or in multiple pages? If it is a Web page, do you need hyperlinks or interactivity?

APPENDIX C

Proofreaders' Marks	Draft	Final Copy
Omit space	data base	database
∨ or ∧ Insert	if he's going (insert: ', not ,)	if he's not going,
Capitalize	Maple street	Maple Street
Delete	a ~~final~~ draft	a draft
# Insert space	allready to	all ready to
when / ~~if~~ Change word	and ~~if~~ you (when)	and when you
Use lowercase letter	our President	our president
¶ Paragraph	¶ Most of the	Most of the
• • • Don't delete	a ~~true~~ story	a true story
Spell out	the only (1)	the only one
Transpose	they all see	they see all
ss Single-space	ss first line second line	first line second line
ds Double-space	ds first line second line	first line second line
Move right	Please send	Please send
Move left	May I	May I
Bold	Column Heading	**Column Heading**
ital Italic	ital Time magazine	*Time* magazine
u/l Underline	u/l Time magazine	Time magazine readers
Move as shown	readers will see	will see

WORK SHOP

Foundations

You Will Learn To

- Identify elements of desktop publishing
- Apply design process skills

Key Terms

publication
layout software
WYSIWYG
desktop publishing

Before You Read

Key Terms Journal As you read, you will come across important desktop publishing words, or *key terms.* To help you understand these words and recall their meanings, draw four columns on a piece of paper. Label them: *Key Term, What is it?, What else is it like?, Examples.* Whenever you read a key term, write it down, and fill in the other three columns.

Desktop Publishing

In 1985, a quiet revolution began in the publishing industry with the introduction of desktop publishing. Until then, books, brochures, newspapers, magazines, and other publications were created by teams of professionals, using very specialized equipment. Desktop publishing software made it possible for anybody with a computer to create a professional-looking **publication,** or printed work.

What Is Desktop Publishing?

Desktop publishing was started by Paul Brainerd, an executive in a publishing company. He saw the possibilities of a new type of software, called **layout software,** that combined text and graphics together on a page. Layout software uses a principle known as **WYSIWYG** (pronounced *wizzy-wig*), an acronym that means "What You See Is What You Get." With a team of specialists, Brainerd created PageMaker, the first desktop publishing application.

Desktop publishing, or DTP, is the use of a computer to combine text and graphics together on a page. This alone, however, is not enough to make a publication look good or achieve the purpose for which it was created. To be truly effective, desktop publishing requires planning and design.

Desktop publishing has become an important part of doing business. Organizations use it for advertising, newsletters, and other documents. However, when businesses send publications that are poorly designed, they give customers a bad impression. Instead of promoting professionalism and high-quality service and products, the business looks careless.

► Notice the misspellings in this flyer and how hard it is to read. What is your impression of the company that created it?

Eight-page, right-angle fold This fold is used to create eight-page signatures and documents with a large image or chart on one side and text on the other.

Common dimensions		
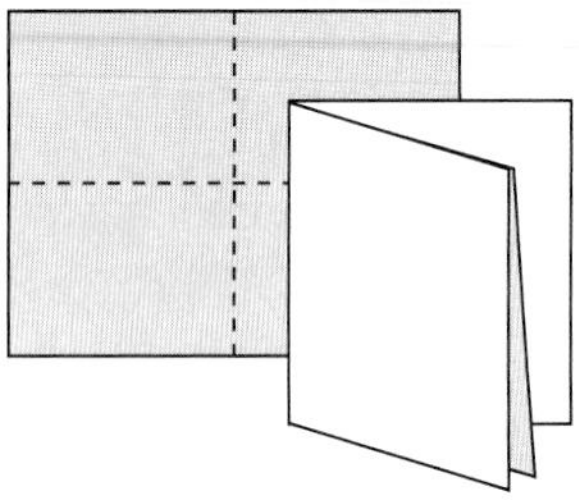	*Flat size*	*Finished size*
	22″ × 34″	11″ × 17″ tabloid
	17″ × 22″	8½″ × 11″
	11″ × 17″	5½″ × 8½″

Twelve-page fold This fold is used mostly for 12-page newsletters and book signatures.

Common dimensions		
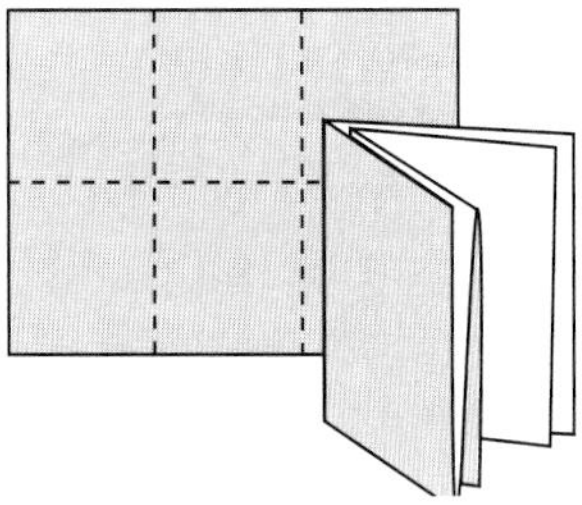	*Flat size*	*Finished size*
	17″ × 33″	8½″ × 11″
	11″ × 25½″	5½″ × 8½″

Sixteen-page fold This fold is used mostly to make 16-page newsletters and book signatures.

Common dimensions		
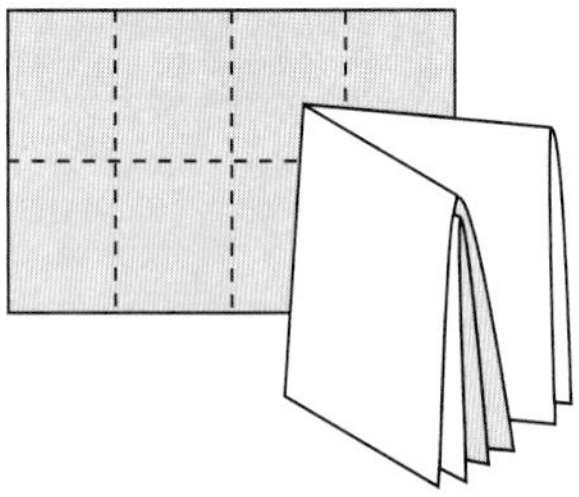	*Flat size*	*Finished size*
	34″ × 22″	8½″ × 11″
	22″ × 17″	5½″ × 8½″

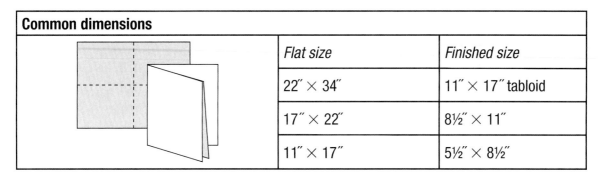

The information above, and more information about printing, can be found in the Washington State Department of Printing *Guide to Services* (www.prt.wa.gov).

Before you begin a project, determine what signature the printer will use to produce your book. Knowing how the printer will use paper can help you better manage printing costs. When creating long publications, try to match the page count to the signature count. If designing a project of less than a full signature, consider using the leftover paper for letterhead or even notepads.

How Does the Design Process Work?

In Chapters 1–3 of this book, you will be guided through the design elements you will need for a project. You will see how design principles apply to every publication that you create. As you become more skilled in using desktop publishing tools, you will learn broader principles of design so that you can apply design and layout guidelines on your own.

It is fun and easy to learn about design. Think about the designs used in magazines and why you prefer one magazine design over another. Good designs are the ones that catch your eye and your attention. The chart below offers some tips for developing your design skills.

Design Basics

- **Look for examples of good design.** Keep copies of brochures, newsletters, flyers, or other publications that you think are well designed.
- **Determine the purpose of a publication's message.** Consider the audience, the message you want to convey, the budget, and how the material will be distributed. These factors will determine the graphics you will need and the best software to use.
- **Sketch a few ideas on paper.** On paper, you can quickly experiment with different design ideas. Sketching your ideas helps you think creatively and saves time at the computer.
- **Use your sketches to create your ideas on the computer.** If budget and timeframe permit, you can submit several ideas to a client or team.
- **Seek input from others.** Is the document readable? Is it visually appealing? Is the message clear? Are the fonts appropriate?
- **Keep your design simple.** Remove any unnecessary elements and make sure nothing distracts from the intended message.

After you have finished your document, proofread it, then edit and revise it. Remember, though, that good design is never finished, but recognize when you have done all that you can.

Reading Check

1. **Define** What is desktop publishing?
2. **Describe** What are three ways you can develop design skills?

Eye On Ethics

Copyright Laws A copyright protects someone who creates something such as a book, song, or art. The work cannot be copied or used without permission.

Copying music, information, or images from the Internet may be illegal. Even if material is not registered with the United States Copyright Office, all artistic works are considered copyrighted *as soon as the author saves the material.* Using it without permission is a breach of copyright law that can result in criminal prosecution.

Identify What kind of material can be copyrighted?

Special Folds

Most multipage documents are created by folding a large sheet of paper to create two or more smaller pages. The following chart shows layouts for some of the most common standard folds. The folded group of pages is called a "signature." A long book may contain many signatures. You can often see the signatures in a book by looking at the top or side of the book.

Single-parallel fold This type of fold is used for invitations, brochures, and four-page book signatures.

Common dimensions

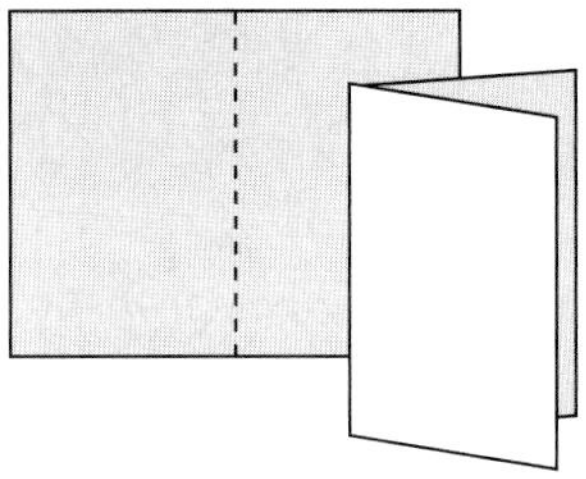

Flat size	*Finished size*
22″ × 17″	11″ × 17″ tabloid
17″ × 11″	8½″ × 11″
11″ × 8½″	5½″ × 8½″
5½″ × 8½″	5½″ × 4¼″

Letter fold The letter fold or c-fold is most commonly used for brochures and mailing inserts.

Common dimensions

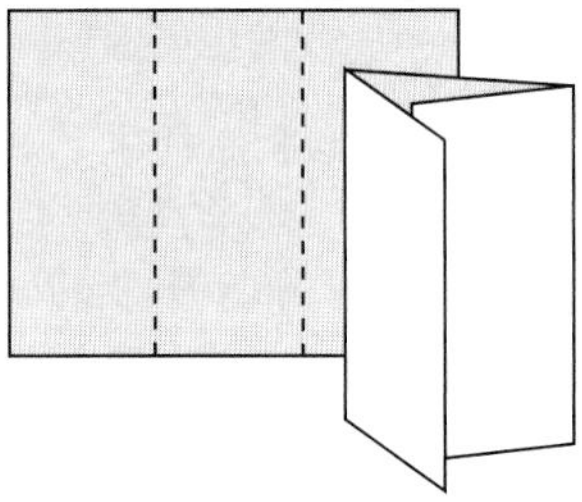

Flat size	*Finished size*
17″ × 11″	5⅝″ × 11″
14″ × 8½″	4⅝″ × 8½″
11″ × 8½″	3⅝″ × 8½″

Double-parallel fold The double-parallel fold is often used for brochures printed on legal-size paper.

Common dimensions

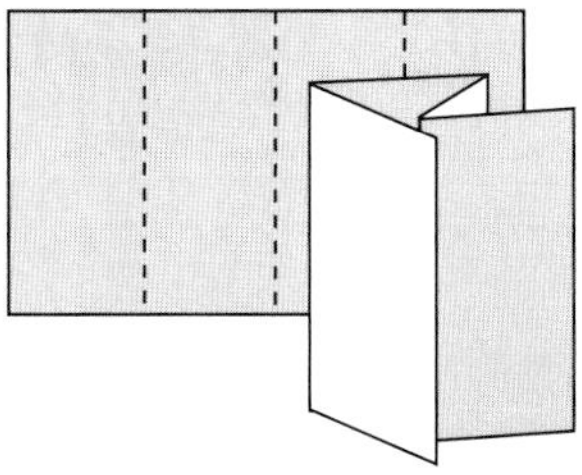

Flat size	*Finished size*
34″ × 11″	8½″ × 11″
17″ × 11″	4¼″ × 11″
14″ × 8½″	3½″ × 8½″

Introducing Word

You Will Learn To

- Identify Word's toolbars
- Identify Word's menu bar
- Find the scroll bars and ruler

Key Terms

interface

Print Layout View

icons

Sidebar

GUI In 1985, computers with a graphical user interface (GUI) were introduced. A GUI (pronounced *gooey*) interface allows users to interact with the computer through graphic elements such as icons, menus, and windows. Before GUIs, commands were entered as text only. GUIs made computers easy to use and popular for everyday users. Most commercial software today uses a GUI.

Define What is a graphical user interface?

Microsoft® Word is the most popular software application for personal computers. Word includes many tools that can be used to create desktop publishing documents such as simple newsletters, flyers, resumes, stationery, and even cards.

What Is a User Interface?

In order to work effectively in any program, you have to know the elements of the user interface. The **interface** is all of the onscreen elements (such as graphics, menus, and tools) that allow you to communicate with the computer. Study the figure below, and memorize Word's features and the special terminology used for desktop publishing. With your teacher's permission, open Microsoft Word and locate the tools shown here. **Print Layout View** allows you to see how text and graphics will print on the page.

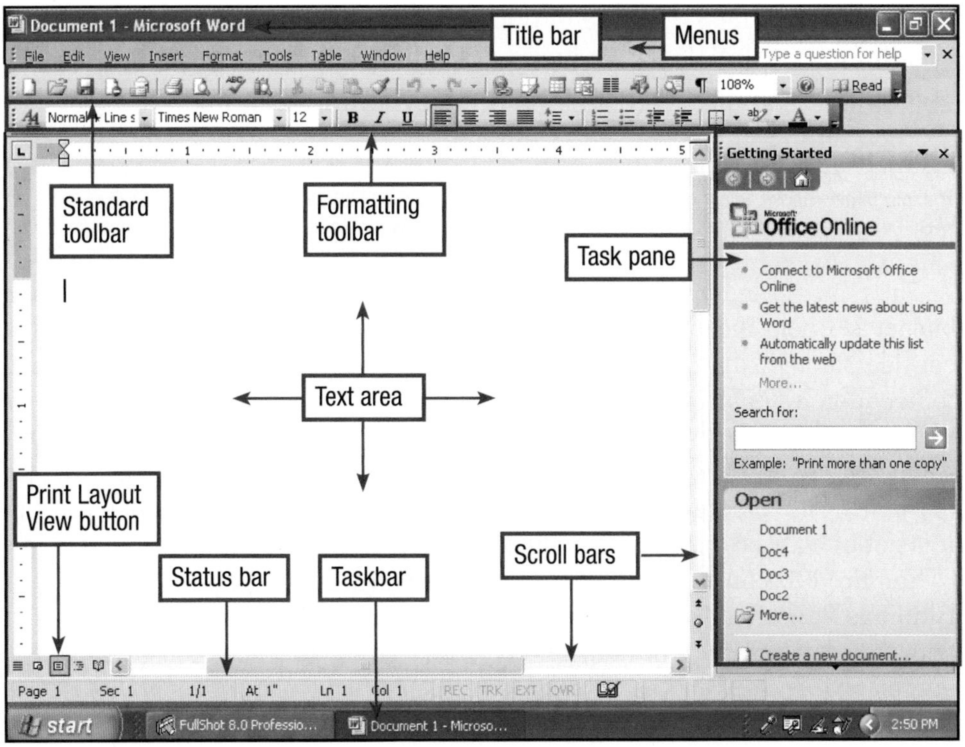

▲ Your screen may not look exactly like this image, but it should have the same elements.

Thermal Binding Thermal-bound books are created by applying a strip of colored cloth tape with heat-activated adhesive to the spine of the book. This type of binding is very economical and available in a variety of colors.	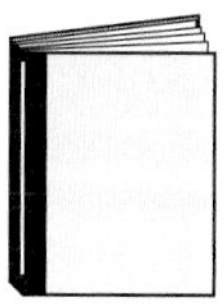
Comb Binding This type of binding involves punching rectangular holes down the spine edge of a book and inserting a plastic comb. Combs are available in a variety of colors. Combs also may be imprinted with the title of the book.	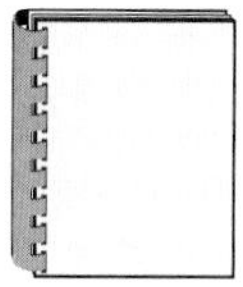
Spiral Binding A spiral bound book uses one continuous plastic or wire spiral inserted into round holes punched along the edge of the spine. Spiral binding is slightly more expensive than comb binding, but is much more durable. This binding style is recommended for instruction manuals or workbooks that must lie flat when open.	
Wire-o Binding Wire-o binding is similar to spiral binding, except it uses a series of double wire loops instead of a continuous spiral. Besides being extremely durable, wire-o binding lets you lay the book completely flat or even fold the pages completely around to the back.	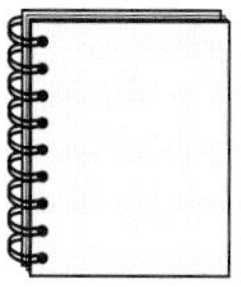

The information above, and more information about printing, can be found in the Washington State Department of Printing *Guide to Services* (www.prt.wa.gov).

The type of binding you use depends on how you plan to use the publication and what your budget is. Books that need to lie flat, like an instruction manual, might be spiral bound. You might consider, though, that it is easy to tear pages out of a spiral book, which might make it impractical for a children's publication.

Hardcover books use a method of binding called *case binding*. In case binding, the pages are stitched together, then hard covers are added by using end sheets and a strip of cloth attached to the spine. Case binding is used for textbooks and the commercial books you find in bookstores. It is not often used in business publications, which is why it is not discussed in the chart above.

You need to consider the type of binding you will use before you lay out your documents. Bindings will affect the margins of a publication. A book that does not lay flat, such as one with side stitching, will need larger center margins than a book that is stapled at the fold. Spiral bindings and comb bindings need margins that allow for the holes in the pages.

WORKSHOP Toolbox

Title Bar

The title bar is the bar that runs across the top of the screen. It displays the name of the document. When you open a new document, the name is always *Document 1* (or another number), but when you save the document, the name on the title bar changes to reflect the new document name.

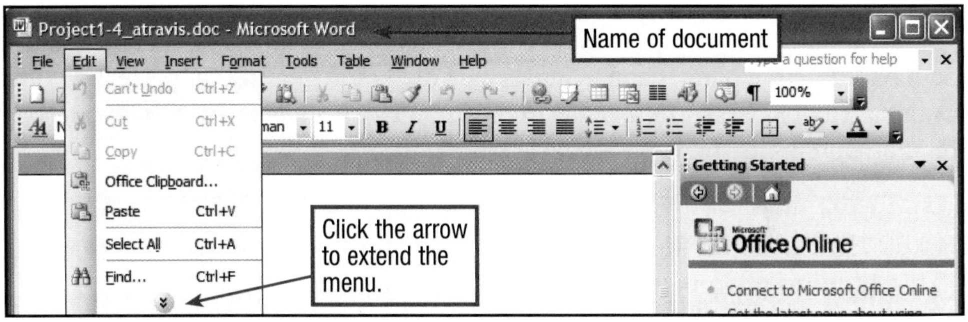

▲ The menu bar has the same commands found in the toolbars.

Menu Bar

The menu bar has general menu categories (such as Edit, View, Format, etc.) from which you can carry out any command in Word. The other bars, called toolbars, display clickable **icons**, or picture buttons, which are shortcuts to the menu items. Unlike the toolbars, the menu bar must always be displayed. Closing the menu bar will close the program.

When a menu option is clicked, a drop-down menu is displayed. Usually the menu only shows the commands that are used most often. To see all the options on the menu, simply click the double arrow at the bottom of the menu, or just wait a few seconds.

Standard and Formatting Toolbars

The Standard toolbar displays icons for many common commands such as Save, Print, Copy, etc. The Formatting toolbar contains commands that control the appearance of the text. You will learn more about the commands in the Standard and Formatting toolbars later in this chapter.

Reading Check

1. **Define** What is a user interface?
2. **Compare and Contrast** How is the menu bar similar to a toolbar, and how is it different?

Sidebar

Moving Toolbars
Toolbars can be moved. Click the toolbar's gripper (the four dots on the toolbar). You can drag the toolbars to the top, bottom, or either side of the screen, or they can be undocked and float in the workspace itself.

When toolbars are closed, they disappear. Open or close them by clicking **View>Toolbars**, then choose a toolbar.

Identify Which menu lets you open or close a toolbar?

Choose a Binding

After you have printed a multipage document, you may need to fasten, or bind, the pages together. Document binding can be as simple as stapling one corner of the pages. You might staple a simple document, like a report, that has few pages and is printed on one side.

Evaluate Binding Options

Larger publications require more complex bindings. Magazines and booklets are often stapled on the fold. Large reports and manuals may use spiral bindings or perfect bindings. Books, such as this textbook, are sewn together and then glued. Print shops generally offer a wide variety of binding options as shown in the table below.

Bindings	
Stapling Stapling is one of the simplest types of binding. The document is stapled in the upper left corner, which can be done automatically on a photocopy machine.	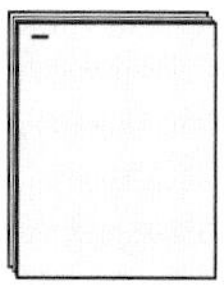
Side Stitching In this type of binding, the booklet is stapled two or more times about ¼ inch from the edge of the sheet of paper. Depending on the dimensions and thickness of the book, this type of binding will be done by machine at the same time the book is collated, or by hand after the job is collated. Side stitched books cannot be opened completely flat and require larger inside margins.	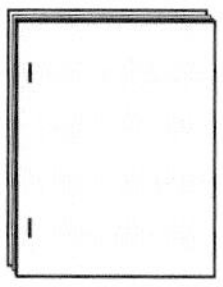
Saddle Stitching Saddle stitching uses wire to "staple" books through the fold. The flat edge of the staple is outside the document, as in most magazines. This method can be used to bind a book with up to 120 pages plus a heavy cover. It is a fast, cost-effective way to bind small- to medium-sized books.	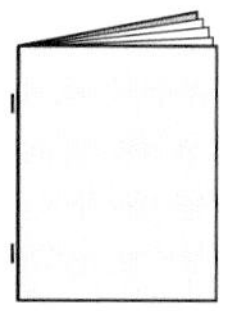
Perfect Binding Perfect binding is often the most cost-effective way of binding books over ⅛ inch thick. Perfect-bound books use a heavyweight, wrap-around cover glued down the spine, like telephone books. If the book is over ¼ inch thick, you may also have the title printed on the spine.	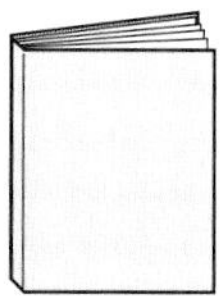

Project 1-1

Format with Fonts

Spotlight on Skills

- Format fonts
- Change font size

Key Terms

- typography
- typeface
- font
- serif
- sans serif
- scalable
- points

Academic Focus

Social Studies
Format the American National Anthem

Go Online PREVIEW
www.glencoe.com

Before You Begin
Go to **Chapter 1**, and choose **PowerPoint Presentations** to preview the documents you will be creating. Also, use the individual project **Rubrics** to help create and evaluate your work.

Type conveys the message, creates visual interest, and sets the tone. Its proper use is essential. One clear distinction between an expert design and an unprofessional one is how the graphic designer uses type. The study of type and its characteristics is called **typography**.

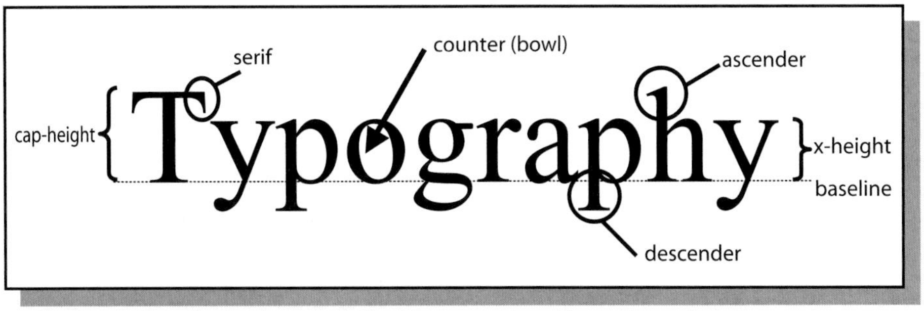

▲ Fonts are described using specialized terms such as those shown here.

Fonts and Typeface

A **typeface** is a design for a set of characters (letters, numbers, and punctuation marks). Typeface is not the same as font. A **font** is a specific typeface combined with variations such as size, style, and spacing.

Categorizing Fonts

Professionals categorize fonts in order to better describe them, to explain their usage, and to show how different fonts relate to one another.

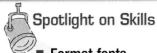

▲ Serif fonts are usually easier to read than sans serif fonts when there is a lot of text.

Serif One of the most important features used to describe a font is the presence or absence of a **serif** (rhymes with *sheriff*), or stroke. Serif fonts have a small cross-stroke at the top or bottom of most letters. (Also see the chart on page 13.)

Sans serif *Sans* (pronounced san or sanz) means "without" in French, so a **sans serif** font does not have the extra cross-strokes. These fonts are easier to read when there is not a lot of text. They are not as easy to read as serif fonts, so they are usually used for titles, headings, or short blocks of text.

Fill Out Forms Completely

When you submit a document to a professional printer, you will most likely need to fill out a form explaining all your requirements. The following is a sample form from the Washington State Department of Printing. Each number represents required information that you must provide so that the document is printed to your specifications.

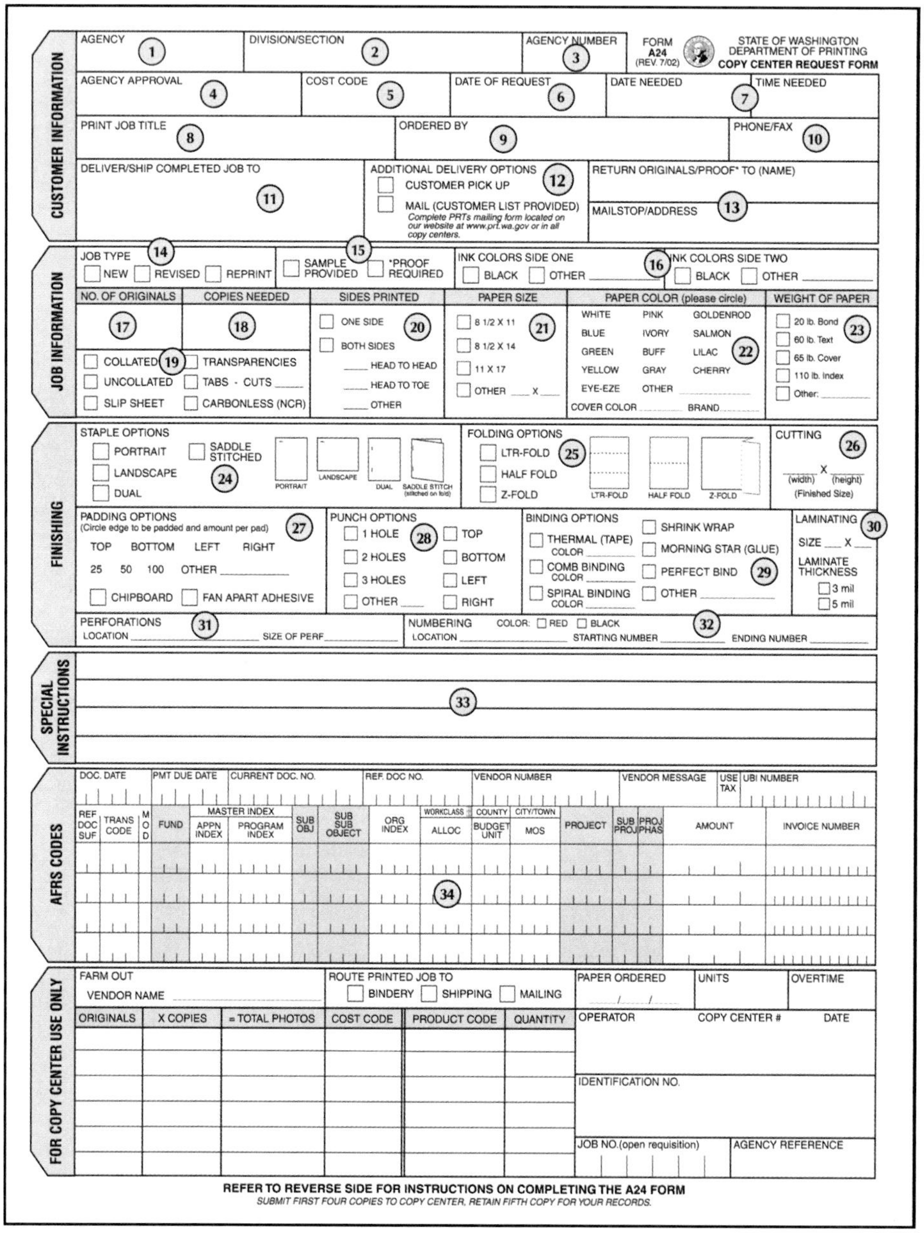

STATE OF WASHINGTON
DEPARTMENT OF PRINTING
COPY CENTER REQUEST FORM
FORM A24 (REV. 7/02)

CUSTOMER INFORMATION
AGENCY (1) | DIVISION/SECTION (2) | AGENCY NUMBER (3)
AGENCY APPROVAL (4) | COST CODE (5) | DATE OF REQUEST (6) | DATE NEEDED (7) | TIME NEEDED
PRINT JOB TITLE (8) | ORDERED BY (9) | PHONE/FAX (10)
DELIVER/SHIP COMPLETED JOB TO (11)
ADDITIONAL DELIVERY OPTIONS (12): ☐ CUSTOMER PICK UP ☐ MAIL (CUSTOMER LIST PROVIDED) Complete PRTs mailing form located on our website at www.prt.wa.gov or in all copy centers.
RETURN ORIGINALS/PROOF* TO (NAME)
MAILSTOP/ADDRESS (13)

JOB INFORMATION
JOB TYPE (14): ☐ NEW ☐ REVISED ☐ REPRINT
(15) ☐ SAMPLE PROVIDED ☐ *PROOF REQUIRED
INK COLORS SIDE ONE: ☐ BLACK ☐ OTHER ____
(16) INK COLORS SIDE TWO: ☐ BLACK ☐ OTHER ____
NO. OF ORIGINALS (17) | COPIES NEEDED (18) | SIDES PRINTED (20) | PAPER SIZE (21) | PAPER COLOR (please circle) (22) | WEIGHT OF PAPER (23)
(19) ☐ COLLATED ☐ TRANSPARENCIES ☐ UNCOLLATED ☐ TABS - CUTS ____ ☐ SLIP SHEET ☐ CARBONLESS (NCR)
SIDES PRINTED: ☐ ONE SIDE ☐ BOTH SIDES ____ HEAD TO HEAD ____ HEAD TO TOE ____ OTHER
PAPER SIZE: ☐ 8 1/2 X 11 ☐ 8 1/2 X 14 ☐ 11 X 17 ☐ OTHER ___ X ___
PAPER COLOR: WHITE PINK GOLDENROD BLUE IVORY SALMON GREEN BUFF LILAC YELLOW GRAY CHERRY EYE-EZE OTHER ____ COVER COLOR ____ BRAND ____
WEIGHT OF PAPER: ☐ 20 lb. Bond ☐ 60 lb. Text ☐ 65 lb. Cover ☐ 110 lb. Index ☐ Other: ____

FINISHING
STAPLE OPTIONS (24): ☐ PORTRAIT ☐ LANDSCAPE ☐ DUAL ☐ SADDLE STITCHED — PORTRAIT LANDSCAPE DUAL SADDLE STITCH (stitched on fold)
FOLDING OPTIONS (25): ☐ LTR-FOLD ☐ HALF FOLD ☐ Z-FOLD — LTR-FOLD HALF FOLD Z-FOLD
CUTTING (26): ___ X ___ (width) (height) (Finished Size)
PADDING OPTIONS (27) (Circle edge to be padded and amount per pad): TOP BOTTOM LEFT RIGHT 25 50 100 OTHER ____ ☐ CHIPBOARD ☐ FAN APART ADHESIVE
PUNCH OPTIONS (28): ☐ 1 HOLE ☐ 2 HOLES ☐ 3 HOLES ☐ OTHER ___ ☐ TOP ☐ BOTTOM ☐ LEFT ☐ RIGHT
BINDING OPTIONS (29): ☐ THERMAL (TAPE) COLOR ____ ☐ COMB BINDING COLOR ____ ☐ SPIRAL BINDING COLOR ____ ☐ SHRINK WRAP ☐ MORNING STAR (GLUE) ☐ PERFECT BIND ☐ OTHER ____
LAMINATING (30): SIZE ___ X ___ LAMINATE THICKNESS ☐ 3 mil ☐ 5 mil
PERFORATIONS (31): LOCATION ____ SIZE OF PERF ____
NUMBERING (32): COLOR: ☐ RED ☐ BLACK LOCATION ____ STARTING NUMBER ____ ENDING NUMBER ____

SPECIAL INSTRUCTIONS (33)

AFRS CODES (34)
DOC. DATE | PMT DUE DATE | CURRENT DOC. NO. | REF. DOC NO. | VENDOR NUMBER | VENDOR MESSAGE | USE TAX | UBI NUMBER
REF DOC SUF | TRANS CODE | M O D | FUND | MASTER INDEX: APPN INDEX, PROGRAM INDEX | SUB OBJ | SUB SUB OBJECT | ORG INDEX | WORKCLASS ALLOC | COUNTY BUDGET UNIT | CITY/TOWN MOS | PROJECT | SUB PROJ | PROJ PHAS | AMOUNT | INVOICE NUMBER

FOR COPY CENTER USE ONLY
FARM OUT VENDOR NAME ____ | ROUTE PRINTED JOB TO ☐ BINDERY ☐ SHIPPING ☐ MAILING | PAPER ORDERED | UNITS | OVERTIME
ORIGINALS | X COPIES | = TOTAL PHOTOS | COST CODE | PRODUCT CODE | QUANTITY | OPERATOR | COPY CENTER # | DATE
IDENTIFICATION NO.
JOB NO.(open requisition) | AGENCY REFERENCE

REFER TO REVERSE SIDE FOR INSTRUCTIONS ON COMPLETING THE A24 FORM
SUBMIT FIRST FOUR COPIES TO COPY CENTER, RETAIN FIFTH COPY FOR YOUR RECORDS.

The information above, and more information about printing, can be found in the Washington State Department of Printing *Guide to Services* (www.prt.wa.gov).

Font Size

Technology has made it very easy to display a font in any size, without any distortion of the typeface. Fonts that can be resized this way are called **scalable** fonts. The computer stores the shape of each character (the typeface) but not the size, which allows it to be reproduced in any proportion.

Measuring Fonts Font size is measured in **points**. A point is about $1/72$ of an inch. Body text is usually between 9 to 12 points in size, depending on the relative size of the font's x-height. The x-height is the height of a lowercase x in a font. (See the illustration on page 7.)

Compare Font x-Heights

This is Times New Roman 12 point	This is Arial 11 point
This is Times New Roman 13 point	This is Arial 12 point

▲ If you want Arial text to be the same height as Times New Roman, the Arial font must be one point less than the Times New Roman.

You can see that the x-height for Times New Roman is smaller than Arial. Although the fonts are measured by the same point standard, the sizes are different because the points measure the entire body of the letters.

Monotype Fonts All characters in monotype fonts take up the same amount of space. (Sometimes these are called *fixed pitch* fonts.) For example, an *i* uses the same amount of space as an *m*, even though they are different sizes. These fonts are generally not used for large bodies of text because they can create awkward spacing.

Proportional Fonts In a proportional font, letters take up a space that is proportional to their size. Since an *i* is not as wide as an *m*, it uses approximately 33% of the space of the *m*. Most fonts work this way.

Monotype font (Courier)

The quick brown fox jumped over the lazy dog.

The quick brown fox jumped over the lazy dog.

Proportional font (Palatino)

▲ The monotype font (top) takes up more space than the proportional font (bottom).

▶ **In this project,** you will compare the use of serif and sans serif fonts when you format the lyrics of the national anthem.

Sidebar

TrueType and PostScript Fonts TrueType and PostScript fonts use two types of instructions, one for displaying clearly on a monitor (which is low resolution) and the other for printing on high resolution printers such as imagesetters.

TrueType fonts are becoming the more popular technology for both everyday and professional use because it provides more control over how the fonts are displayed.

Draw Conclusions Why would a font be displayed differently on a monitor and a printed document?

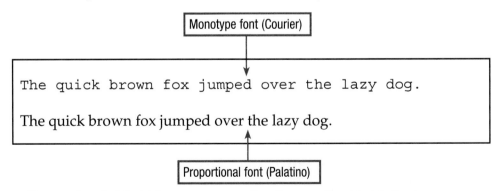

Deliver Your Document

It used to be difficult to get a design to a publisher. Jobs had to be saved on multiple disks and compressed to fit as much data as possible. Today, if the service bureau you intend to use is local, you can put your work on a CD-R, DVD-R, or a large volume, portable flash-drive to give to the service bureau. Since Macintosh computers can now read PC formats, the service bureau should have no trouble reading your files.

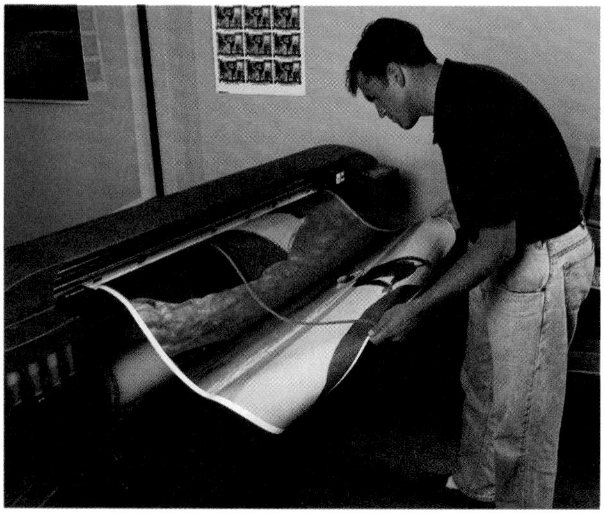

◀ The service bureau provides you with printing services that are beyond your desktop printing options.

e-Mail

For smaller files, you may choose to e-mail your file to the service bureau. This option does not work for large files since many e-mail servers will not accept files over a certain size. It could also take a very long time for the printer to download it.

Web Sites

Many copy shops also have Web sites that allow you to upload files and complete order forms. You should still talk to a representative, and you may need to get a password that allows you to access this part of their Web site. If your connection speed is slow, however, uploading files may take some time.

FTP (File Transfer Protocol) Sites

The World Wide Web is only one part of the Internet. Another area is for FTP (File Transfer Protocol) interchanges. Many companies have an FTP site that allows for faster file transfer from one location to another. Like a Web site, an FTP site needs to be hosted on a server computer and access is strictly limited to protect the site against malicious users. You will often need a login name and password to gain access to a company's FTP site.

Student Data File

Step-by-Step

1. In Microsoft Word, click **File>Open**, and browse to **Data File 1-1**. Save the file according to your teacher's instructions.

Format Fonts

2. Select the title. On the **Formatting** toolbar, click the **Font** drop-down menu (Figure 1.1). Select a sans serif font such as **Arial**.

Change Font Size

3. With the title still selected, click the **Font Size** drop-down menu [12 ▾] (Figure 1.1). Click **18**. Deselect title.

4. Select the author's name and date. Format and **center** in a serif font such as **Palatino**. Then change the font size to **10 pt.**

5. Select all the verses of the anthem. Choose a serif font such as **Palatino**. Increase the font size to **12 pt** (Figure 1.2).

6. Click **Print Layout View** [▤] to see how your document will look when printed. Save and close the file.

7. Open the data file again, and save it with a new name. Format the national anthem with font and font sizes of your choice.

▼ **Figure 1.1** A sans serif font is usually used for titles.

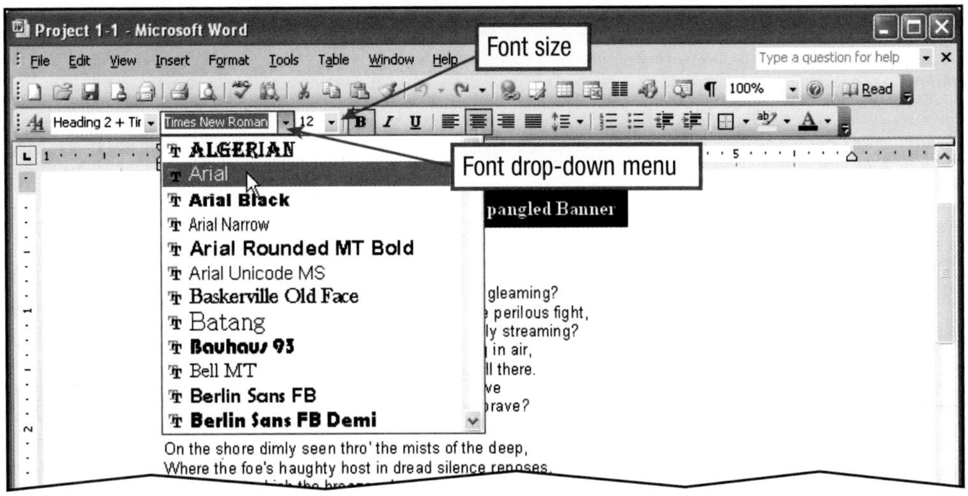

▼ **Figure 1.2** Your final document should look similar to this.

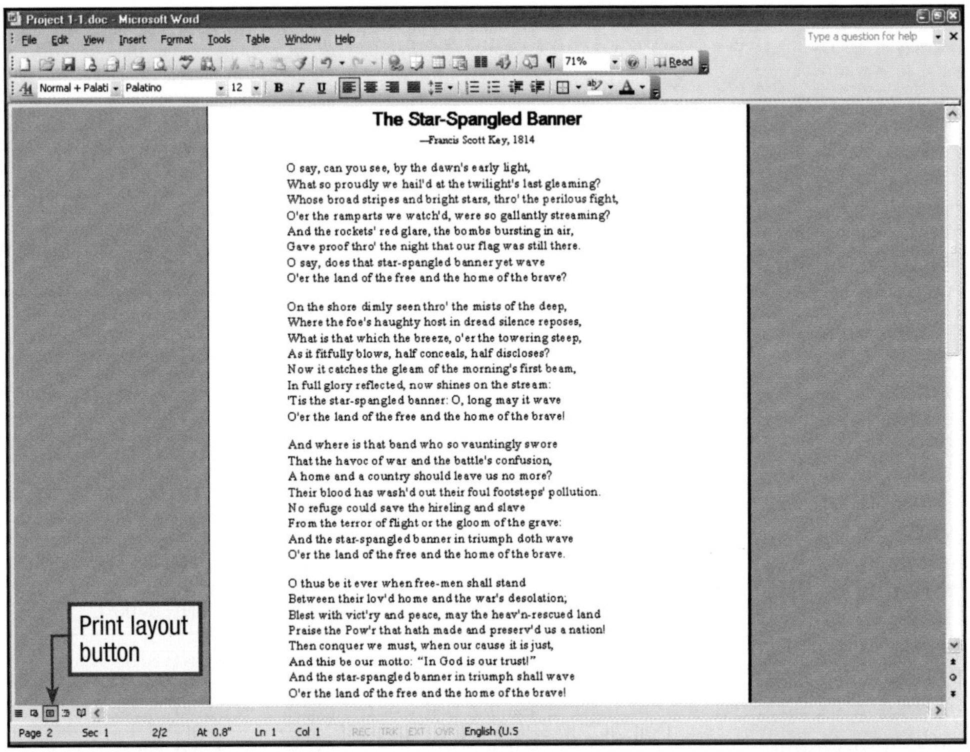

Instant Message

Selecting Text or Graphics When you are told to *select* an item, you are either clicking on it or dragging your mouse pointer over it to highlight it. When an item is selected, you can perform specific commands on it, such as editing, moving, or formatting it.

Use PostScript® Files

PostScript is a computer language, developed by Adobe, that is used by professional-grade printers. It creates high-resolution images, even from raster files, that can be printed on imagesetters or other PostScript printers. Until recently, professional print shops would only accept PostScript files for publication.

Most layout software will allow you to save your document as a PostScript-type file, such as EPS format. Word processors, however, do not usually have this ability. PostScript documents are used for printing only, and cannot be viewed. Like a PDF, the font descriptions are saved with the file.

Add Spot Colors

There are times when you want to use colors that cannot be created accurately by mixing the CMYK colors. While most colors can be created using these four "process colors," there are other colors (florescent colors, extremely saturated colors, and metallic colors are some examples) that cannot be created through this process. Adding spot colors to the printer's instructions will increase the cost (ink, setup costs, and cleaning costs), but they can also help to make a design stand out from the rest.

Prepare a Mock-up

For important print jobs, prepare an example (a mock-up or "go-by") to give to the print shop. This makes it easier for them to compare their results with your expectations and make adjustments accordingly.

You can also require that the print shop create proofs for you to inspect before printing the publication. A proof lets you check that the color is correct and that the text and graphics have not been moved or changed. If your budget is low, however, you might find the proof process to be expensive, time consuming, and impractical if the print shop is far away.

You can also instruct the printer to create cut-outs in the design, such as windows in the cover, or special sized paper with tabs or cut corners. The cost is generally given per cut.

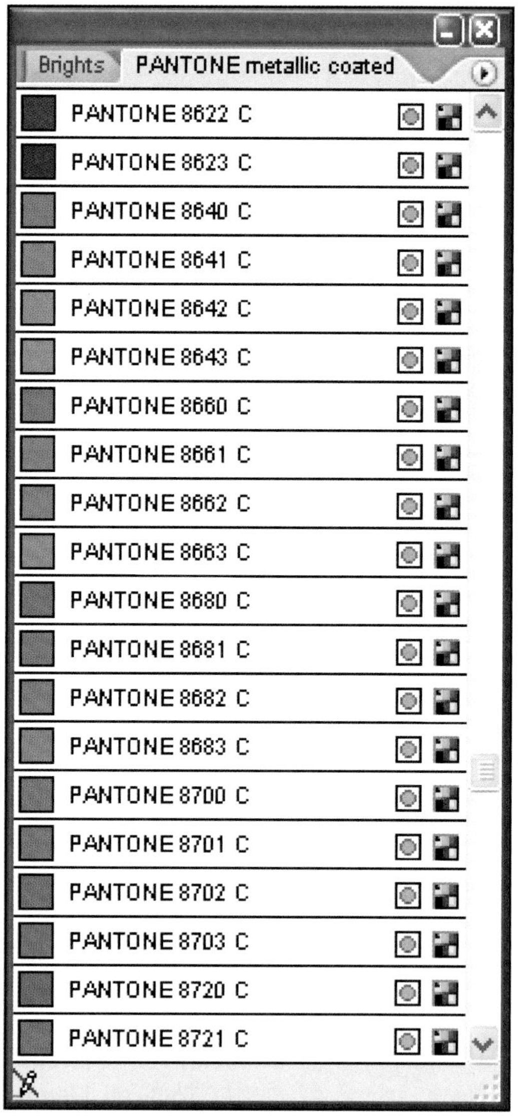

▲ You can find spot colors in Illustrator's Swatch library. Spot colors are indicated by a round spot.

Project 1-2 Design with Font Attributes

Spotlight on Skills

- Apply formatting attributes

Key Term

- font attributes

Academic Focus

Science
Format chemical formulas

Most word processing applications allow users to change **font attributes** to text. These are characteristics or qualities such as <u>underline</u>, **bold**, *italics*, $^{\text{superscript,}}$ and $_{\text{subscript}}$.

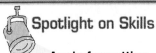

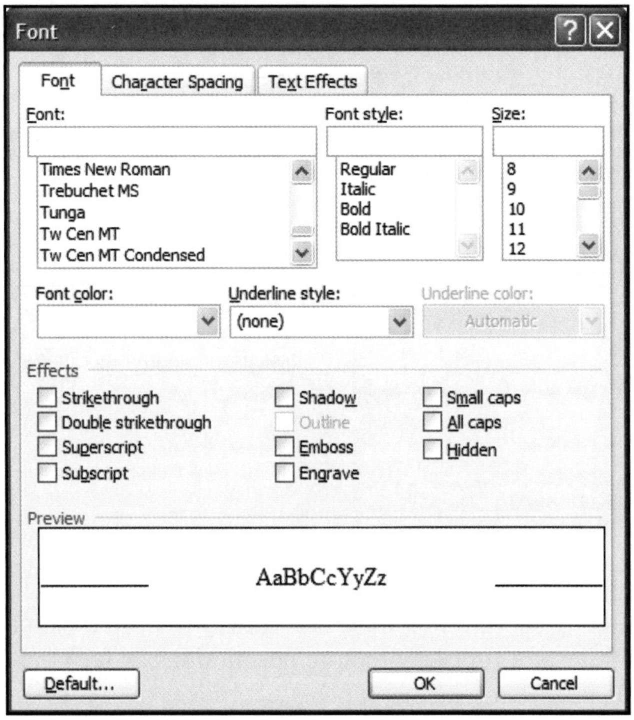

◄ You can find many different font attributes in the Font dialog box, which is accessed through the Format menu.

<u>Underlining</u> is not used much in professional documents. It can distract from nearby text and reduces readability (how easy it is to read and understand text). Underlining, however, is still used to format Web site addresses.

Bolding text adds extra weight to a character and increases its contrast with those things around it, making it more noticeable. Do not overuse bold, or it will lose its impact.

Italics are often used to call out special content such as titles, headings, non-English or unfamiliar words, and even dialogue.

Use ^{Superscript} to make text smaller and place it above the baseline, and use $_{\text{Subscript}}$ to move text below the baseline. Superscript is commonly used for numbers like 1st and 2nd and also for footnote citations. Subscript is commonly used in chemical formulas such as Fe_2O_3.

ALL CAPS can be created by pressing the [CAPS LOCK] key on the keyboard. It is a font attribute that should usually not be used with a lot of text. It reduces readability because words written in all caps look like a rectangular block and individual letters are not easily distinguished.

Sidebar

Keyboard Shortcuts Listed below are some text styles that are used so often that they are not only included in Word's Formatting toolbar, but they also have their own keyboard shortcut.

<u>Underline</u>	CTRL + U
Bold	CTRL + B
Italics	CTRL + I
^{Superscript}	CTRL SHIFT +
$_{\text{Subscript}}$	CTRL +

Identify What is the keyboard shortcut for bolding?

► **In this project,** you will format a report using font attributes. You will learn about Poland's famous tourist attraction, the Wieliczka Salt Mine.

Preflight the Files

Your next step is to get the files ready for the printer, or preflight the files. Publisher has a feature called Pack and Go that will prepare color separations, copy the fonts used in the publication, and create a form that includes settings information that the print shop will need to determine your printing needs.

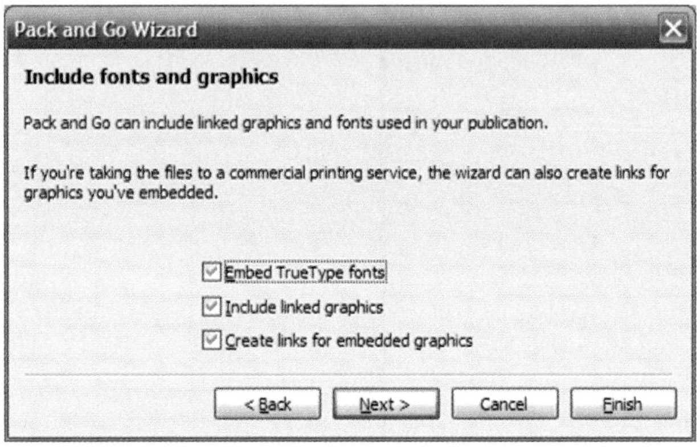

◄ The Pack and Go feature in Publisher lets you embed fonts and prepare a publication for transfer to another computer or a commercial printer.

Pack and Go will even save your printing specifications in a compressed folder so it is easier to send the large files to the copy shop. Since fonts are copyright protected material, however, providing the service with copies of a font may require permissions or fees.

Use Adobe Portable Document Format (PDF)

PDF format is becoming the preferred method for sending complex documents. It also solves the problem of fonts and copyright issues. Files saved in a PDF format are saved as images of the file. They can be opened on any computer using the Acrobat Reader, software that Adobe will download for free. The reader, however, cannot be used to edit PDF documents, which can only be edited using Adobe Acrobat software.

Creating PDF files is usually easy. Some applications such as Illustrator let you save work as a PDF. Others require special software. The software lets you change the printer setting to your PDF maker or choose File>Create PDF. Instead of printing, the computer will print to a file—a PDF that you can save and share.

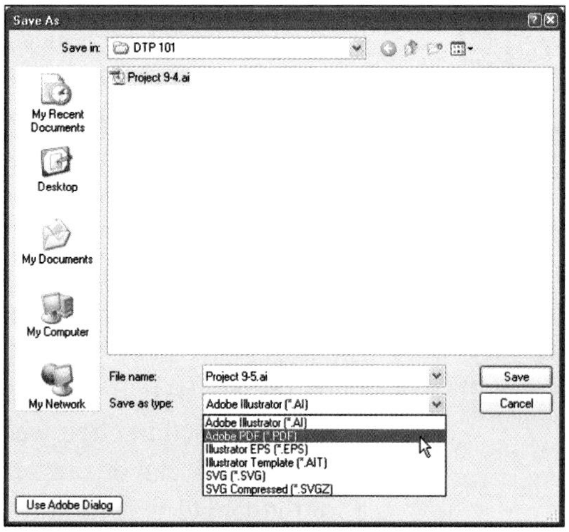

▲ Adobe Illustrator lets you save files as PDFs without needing additional software.

Student Data File

Step-by-Step

1 In Word, click **File>Open**, and browse to **Data File 1-2**. Save the file according to your teacher's instructions.

Apply Formatting Attributes

2 Select the essay title. On the **Formatting** toolbar, click the **Font** drop-down menu [Times New Roman ▾] Select a sans serif font such as **Arial 16 pt**.

3 With the title still selected, click **Bold** [B] on the **Formatting** toolbar.

4 If necessary, select the title. Then click **Format>Font>Font color**. Click **Blue**.

5 Under **Effects**, click **All caps**. Then click **OK** (Figure 1.3).

6 Select the number **2** in the formula for magnesium chloride. Then click **Format>Font**.

7 Under **Effects**, click **Subscript**. Then click **OK**.

8 Repeat Steps 6 and 7 for the numbers in the formulas for magnesium sulphate, calcium sulphate, and magnesium bromide. See **Figure 1.4**.

▼ **Figure 1.3** Enhance a document by using font attributes.

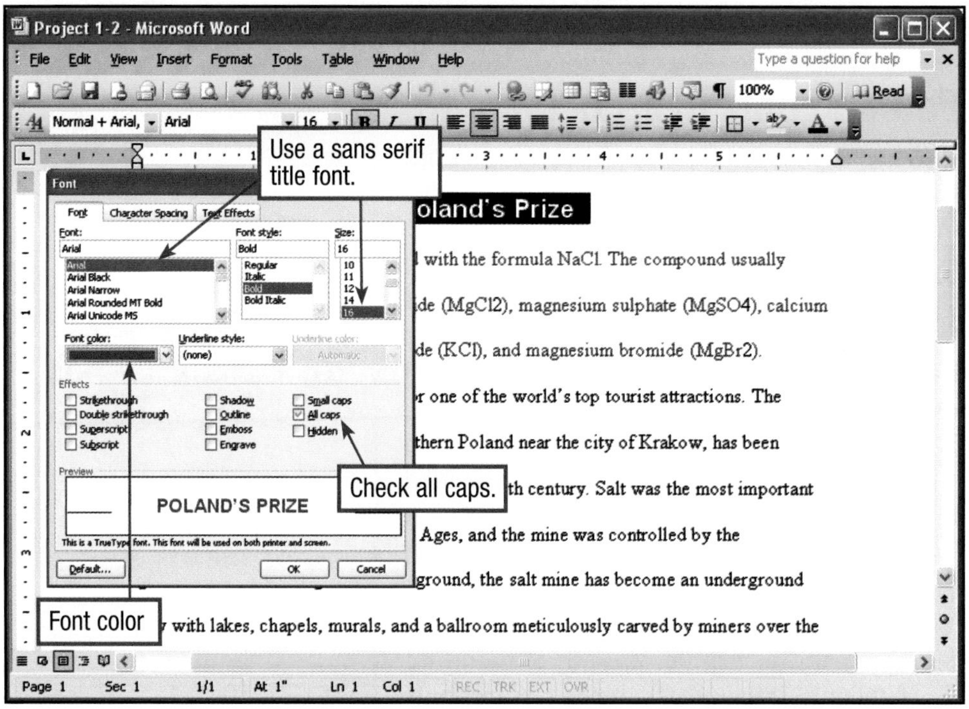

▼ **Figure 1.4** Change font attributes to make a document more technically accurate.

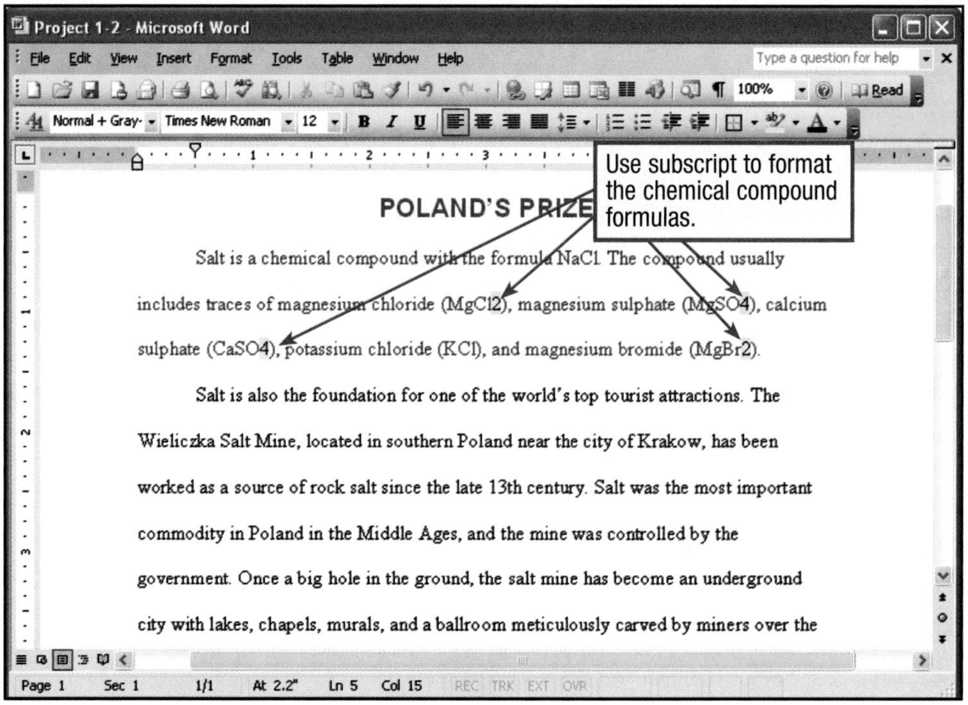

Embed Fonts in a Document

When saving your work to be used by a print shop, you may choose to embed your fonts. This means that all the fonts you used to create the document are saved with the file. That way you can be sure the print shop will use the correct fonts in your document. For example, if you use Bodoni MT Condensed, the printer service will use the exact same Bodoni font.

You can usually embed fonts as an option when you save a document. Since embedded font information is saved in the document itself, the fonts travel with the document. Embedding also avoids copyright issues related to distributing fonts.

There can be problems with embedding fonts, though. Documents with embedded fonts cannot be edited by someone who does not have all the same fonts. Also, embedding fonts in a publication will greatly increase the file size.

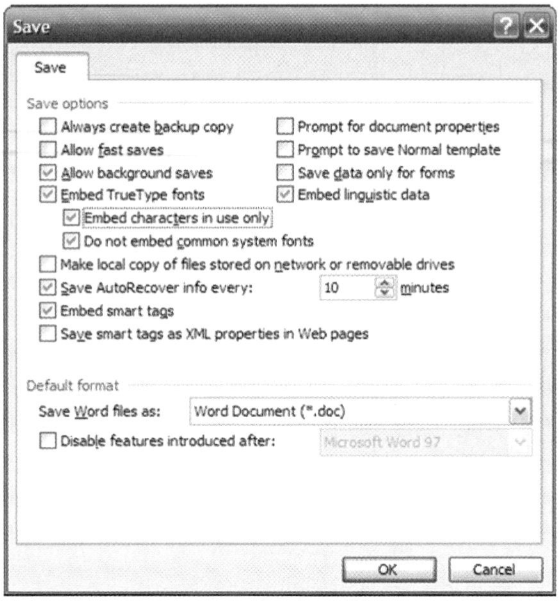

▲ In Word, click **File>Save As>Tools>Save Options** to embed fonts in your document. Most Windows and MacIntosh applications include font embed technology.

Create Text Outlines in Adobe Applications

Some software applications (Illustrator and InDesign, for example) have the ability to create text outlines, which are images of the text itself. Using this method, the print shop does not have to have the specific fonts in order to accurately reproduce your document. Like embedded fonts, text outlines cannot easily be edited, and computer work time to make changes is usually expensive.

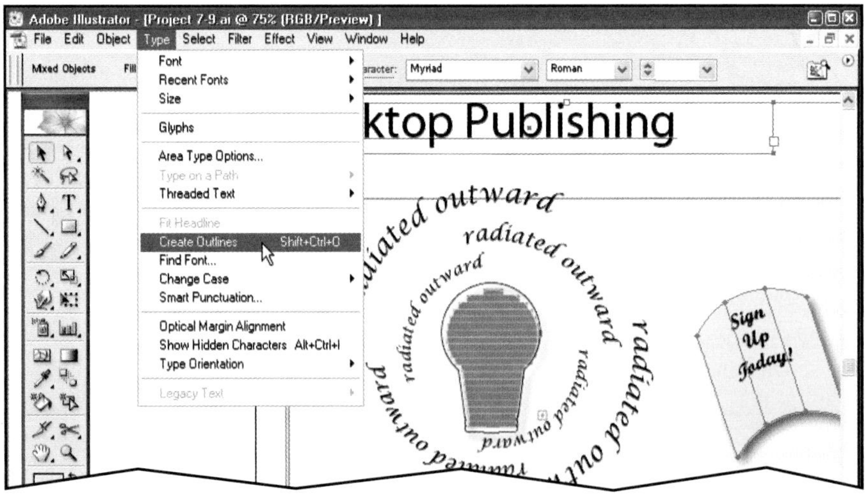

◄ Text outlines can ensure that documents will be printed as designed, though they may not be edited easily after the text has been converted.

9. This essay about salt needs a footnote reference. Click at the end of the first paragraph. Key the number **1,** then select it.

10. Click **Format>Font**. Under **Effects**, click **Superscript**. Click **OK**.

11. Repeat Steps 9 and 10 to add a superscript number **1** before the word *Salt* (Figure 1.5).

12. You are ready to use font attributes to create the title page. Place your insertion point at the beginning of the document (Figure 1.6).

13. Press CTRL + ENTER to insert a hard page break. Press ↑ key on the keyboard to move to the top of the new page.

14. Click **Center** on the **Formatting** toolbar.

15. Key a title page similar to the one shown in Figure 1.6. Use the figure as a guide. Choose font attributes for the text. Include the title, your name, your teacher's name, your class name, and the date.

16. Click **File>Page Setup> Layout Tab**. Under **Page**, **Vertical** alignment, choose **Center**. Click **OK**.

17. Follow your teacher's instructions for saving and printing your work.

Figure 1.5 Use superscript numbers for footnote references.

Use superscript to format the footnote number.

POLAND'S PRIZE

Salt is a chemical compound with the formula NaCl. The compound usually includes traces of magnesium chloride ($MgCl_2$), magnesium sulphate ($MgSO_4$), calcium sulphate ($CaSO_4$), potassium chloride (KCl), and magnesium bromide ($MgBr_2$).[1]

The salt mine is on the United Nations Educational Scientific and Cultural Organization's (UNESCO) list of World Class Landmarks of Cultural and Natural Heritage, where it was listed among the top twelve attractions in the world.

[1]"Salt (compound)," *Microsoft® Encarta® Online Encyclopedia* 2005 http://encarta.msn.com © 1997-2005 Microsoft Corporation. All Rights Reserved.

Add the footnote number to the reference.

Figure 1.6 Font attributes add interest on a title page.

↓ Press ENTER 3 times

POLAND'S PRIZE

↓ Press ENTER 13 times

Prepared by

↓ Press ENTER 2 times

Eva Luczyk

↓ Press ENTER 13 times

Prepared for

↓ Press ENTER 2 times

Mrs. Westphal
Science, Period 1

↓ Press ENTER 2 times

February 25, 20--

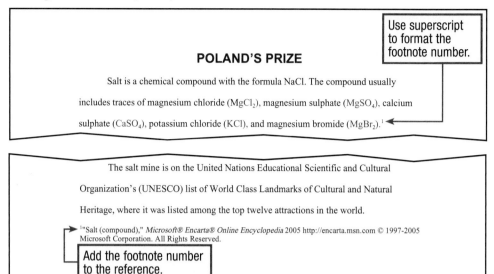

Prepare for Publication

Because of the variety of publishing processes, be sure and talk to your service bureau before even beginning work on a design. Some print shops prefer to receive the file in certain file formats such as TIFF, or Publisher, Photoshop, Illustrator, or InDesign native formats. They may even require that the document be saved as a high-definition PDF, or a PostScript file.

Some print shops will not take file formats from a PC platform, preferring a Macintosh platform. These requirements may change the way that you work. Find out before you begin a project. Discovering that you used the wrong software when you think you are finished can cause you a lot of stress and may make you miss an important deadline! Also keep in mind that if a service bureau does not support the type of file you need to create with your software, you can find another one. There are many service bureaus, and one can probably provide the services you need.

Use Your Software's Help Feature

Depending upon your software, you may wish to search your software's Help files for information about color separations or preparing for commercial printing. Not all software applications can create color separations and they will have different tools for commercial printing requirements.

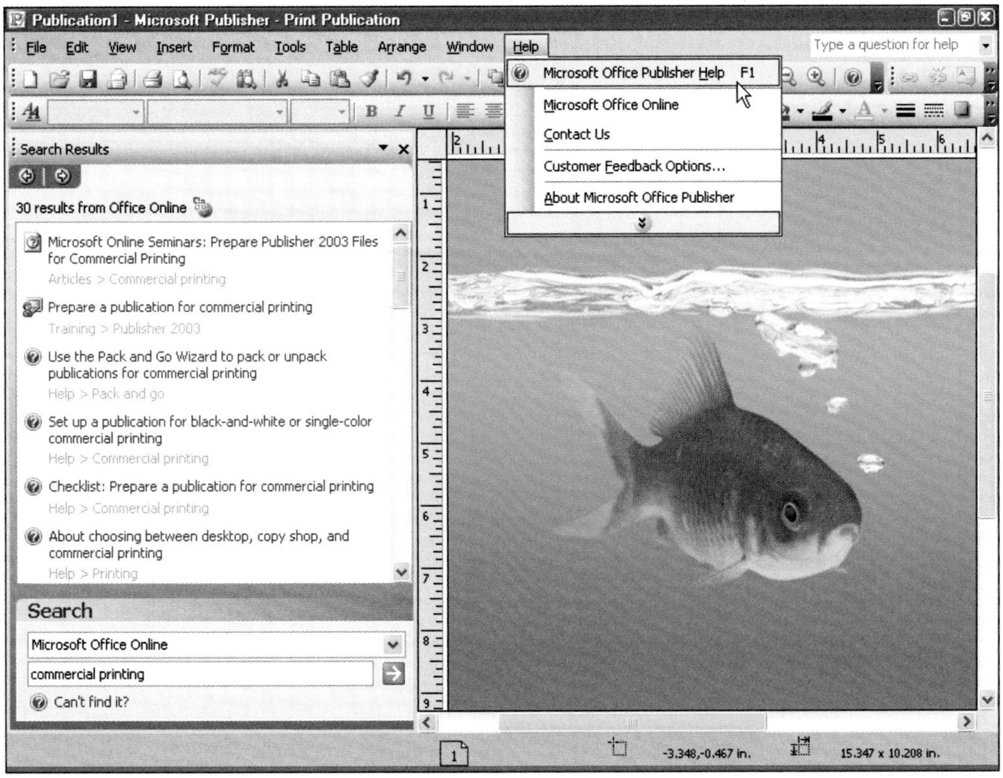

▲ Use software Help files to find important information on file preparation.

Project 1-3

Design with Font Families

Spotlight on Skills

- Use font families

Key Terms

- letterform
- contrast

Academic Focus

Language Arts
Interpret words visually

The chart below shows different font families and how the fonts in each family have a related typeface. Families are further organized by characteristics such as whether they have a serif or whether they are script (like handwriting), decorative, or graphics fonts like dingbats. Relationships within the font families are further characterized by the **letterform**, or the shape of a letter.

FONT FAMILIES	
Serif Families	**Sans Serif Families**
Oldstyle	**Sans Serif**
Book Antiqua	Arial
Centaur	**Impact**
Garamond	Verdana
Palatino Linotype	**Script**
Times	Comic Sans
Slab Serif	*Freestyle Script*
GOUDY STOUT	Old English
Playbill	**Decorative**
Rockwell Extra Bold	Jokerman
Wide Latin	OCR A
Modern	**STENCIL**
Bernard MT Condensed	**Dingbats**
Bodoni MT Black	▯✔✕⌜⌜▲▲⌜ (Marlette)
Century Schoolbook	Σψμβολ (Symbol)
Modern No. 20	▶■🚲♥ⓘ●■? (Webdings)

▲ Use this chart to determine which kinds of fonts go well together.

When designing a page, you must choose fonts from different families in order to provide good contrast and visual interest. **Contrast** is a difference that sets off an element from the others in your document.

For example, if you were designing a brochure, you might use:

- An oldstyle serif font, such as Palatino Linotype, for the text paragraphs to make them more readable
- A sans serif font, like Verdana, for headers to contrast with the paragraphs
- A slab serif font like Wide Latin for the title on the front panel

Never use more than three fonts in the whole document. It is always best to keep your design simple and focused on your message.

▶ **In this project,** you will create a guide to identify fonts in serif and sans serif families. You can use this guide in later projects to help you choose appropriate fonts for your designs.

Sidebar

Fonts and Readability When desktop publishing design principles are followed closely, the publication is engaging. It is easy to read and understand. The focus is clear to anyone reading the publication. Do not combine sans serif fonts with all caps and tight spacing. This keeps people from reading content carefully. Use fonts, spacing, and font attributes that encourage your audience to read your entire message so the message is clearly understood.

Interpret Why is it important to design readable publications?

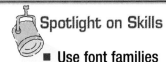

Offset Press

An offset press is a printing press, and it is the most common choice for commercial printing. Ink is spread on printing plates that have the image of the document on them. When a sheet of paper is passed over the plate, the image of the document is transferred to the paper.

In professional printing, each document file is separated into individual colors, with one plate for each color ink. Inks might include CMYK colors, as well as a spot color or a glossy varnish. An offset press may have 6–12 units, each containing one color and one printing plate. The document is passed from unit to unit until the entire design is printed.

◀ When a file is separated into colors, each page will print at least four times, once for each color: 1) Yellow, 2) Cyan, 3) Magenta, and 4) Black. A page will print more times if there are spot colors or other inks or finishes.

Offset printers can print on paper, vinyl, fabric, or even ceramic and plastic. The more colors that are used, the higher the printing costs will be. Documents that use more colors than the number of units on the printer may have to be passed through a second time for additional setup and cleaning fees. Since the price per document decreases with higher quantities, offset press work is best for large print runs or for specialty print jobs.

Screen Printing

Screen printing is most commonly used to print T-shirt designs, though this process can be used to print on almost any surface. In this type of printing, the ink is passed through a wire mesh that serves as a printing plate to apply the ink to the surface. Screen printing generally does not reproduce photographs or areas with small details well.

Thermography

In this printing process, the printer combines a special powder with the ink and then passes the document under heat. This causes the ink to swell, creating a raised, embossed feeling. Thermography printing is commonly used on business cards and can be done at most print shops.

Step-by-Step

1. In Word, open **Data File 1-3**. Save the file according to your teacher's instructions.

Use Font Families

2. Under the **Serif Families Oldstyle**, key an example of the font family in the blank cell. Select a serif font such as **Times**.

3. Under the **Serif Families Slab Serif**, key an example of the font family in the blank cell. Refer to the Font Families table on page 13, if you need help.

4. Key an example of a font for each font family in the remaining blank cells.

5. Select the word *heavy* for word list. From the Font Families table, choose a font such as **Goudy Stout** that reflects the mood of the word *heavy*.

6. Select the word *airy*. Pick a font style such as **OCR A** that reflects its mood.

7. Continue formatting each word with an appropriate font.

8. Follow your teacher's instructions for saving and printing your work.

▼ Figure 1.7 Use the table on page 13 to add font examples in the blank cells for each font family. Serif fonts go in the left column and sans serif in the right.

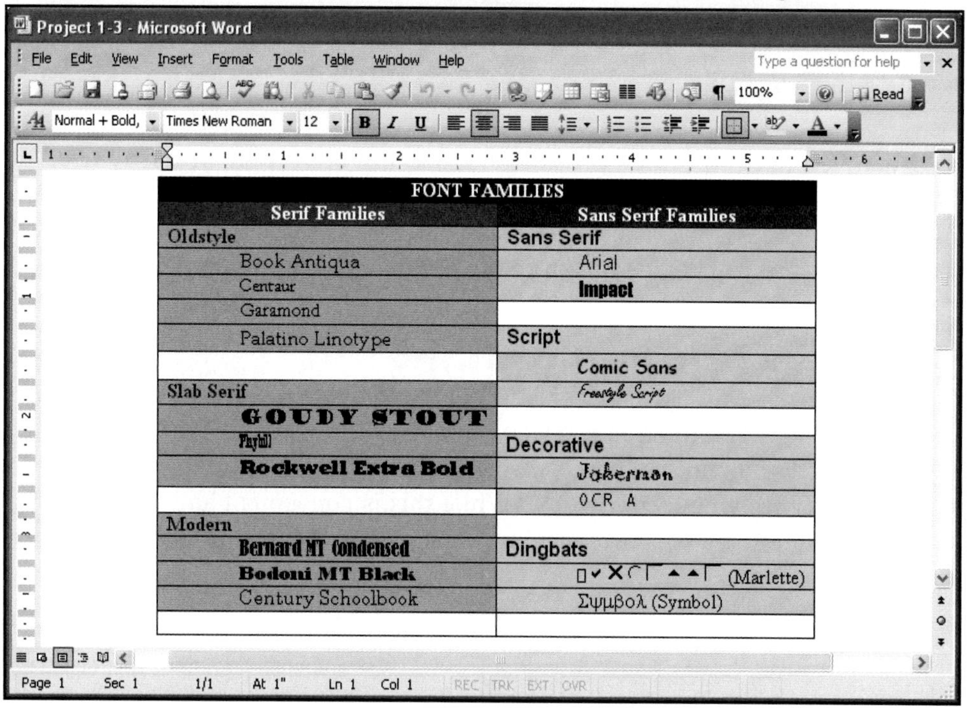

FONT FAMILIES	
Serif Families	Sans Serif Families
Oldstyle	Sans Serif
Book Antiqua	Arial
Centaur	Impact
Garamond	
Palatino Linotype	Script
	Comic Sans
Slab Serif	Freestyle Script
GOUDY STOUT	
Playbill	Decorative
Rockwell Extra Bold	Jokerman
	OCR A
Modern	
Bernard MT Condensed	Dingbats
Bodoni MT Black	(Marlette)
Century Schoolbook	Συμβολ (Symbol)

▼ Figure 1.8 Carefully selecting a font can help convey your intended message or mood.

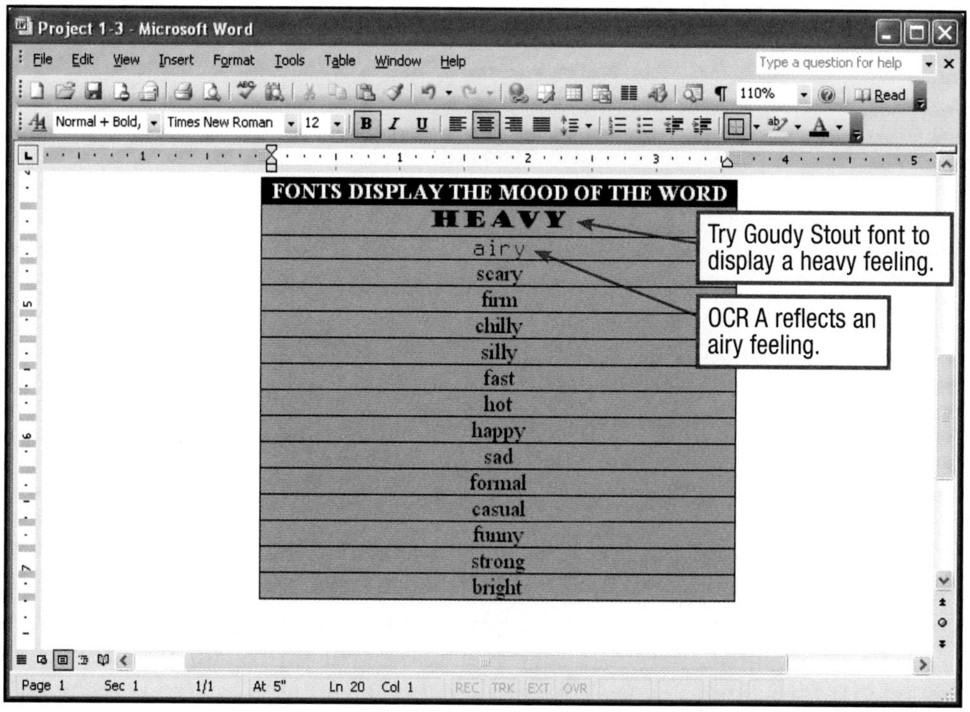

FONTS DISPLAY THE MOOD OF THE WORD
HEAVY
airy
scary
firm
chilly
silly
fast
hot
happy
sad
formal
casual
funny
strong
bright

Professional Printing and Binding

When you need to print a professional-looking document, you may need to go to a service bureau that handles both the printing and the binding. Besides a professional look, however, you must also consider price. The more copies you make of your publication, the less it will cost you per copy. Before you decide on a printing method, always compare costs.

Evaluate Printing Options

When printing to a desktop printer, you may have noticed that the cost of printing stays steady, regardless of the number of copies to be printed. Ink and paper costs remain constant, no matter how many copies you need to make. While this is convenient and highly appropriate for only a few copies, it quickly becomes inappropriate when you must print many copies.

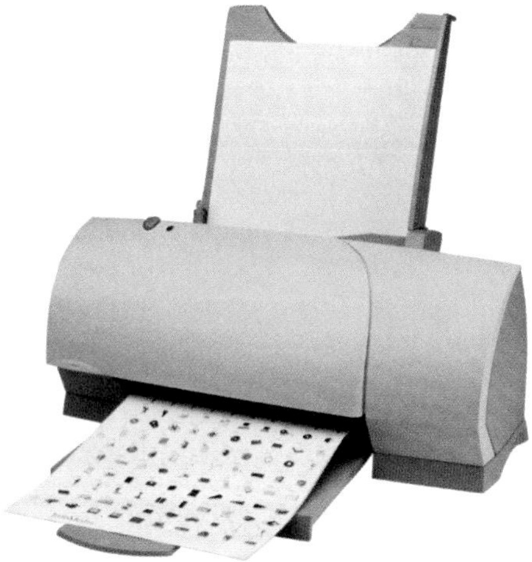

◄ For small print runs, your desktop printer is probably the most cost-effective choice. For larger quantities, however, you should check other printing options.

Photocopier

You may decide to take a trip to your local print shop and use a photocopier. Copy machines are not very sensitive devices and often cannot print pictures, gradients, or subtle colors very well. They are fine if the run is less than 500 copies and high quality is not necessary. Costs may decrease depending on the number of copies.

Imagesetter

An imagesetter is a professional-level printing device, much like a computer printer. It is capable of printing high-quality graphics and subtle shading. The high cost of an imagesetter ($30,000–$100,000) makes this printer too expensive for most small businesses and individuals.

Most professional printers, or service bureaus, will have an imagesetter and charge customers about $10 for a single page. While the cost of printing one page is somewhat high, the cost decreases as the number of copies increases above five hundred.

Project 1-4 Format with Word Tools

Spotlight on Skills

- Cut and paste
- Align text
- Insert a drop cap
- Add a page border
- Check spelling

Key Terms

- clipboard
- align
- drop cap
- border
- header
- footer

Academic Focus

Social Studies
Format the Gettysburg Address

> **Sidebar**
>
> **Keyboard Shortcuts** Here are some useful shortcuts:
>
> Cut CTRL + X
> Copy CTRL + C
> Paste CTRL + V
> Decrease Font Size CTRL + SHIFT + <
> Increase Font Size CTRL + SHIFT + >
> Spell Check F7
>
> **Explain** Why is it sometimes easier to use keyboard shortcuts than toolbar buttons?

Most of the commands that you will use can be carried out by clicking an icon on Word's Standard and Formatting toolbars. If you cannot find the command you want on a toolbar, you can access it through one of the options on the menu bar.

Formatting Tools

Cut, Copy, & Paste Use the cut or copy commands to move or copy text or graphics in a document. Use **Cut** to remove material. Use **Copy** to duplicate material without removing it. You can then **Paste** the cut or copied items anywhere in your document.

When you cut or copy material, the information is saved in a temporary storage area called the **clipboard**. The material can be pasted in the same document or even into a different document or other applications, such as PowerPoint. The clipboard saves an item until it is deleted or replaced or the program is turned off.

You can display the copied items by clicking **Edit>Clipboard**. When the clipboard is not visible, however, you can only save one item on the clipboard at a time. When a new item is copied or cut, it replaces the old item.

Spell Check It is essential that you always check your spelling before you submit a document. Word can be set to automatically check spelling as you write. To check an individual word or the whole document at once, you can click **Tools>Spelling and Grammar** on the Menu bar, or click the **Spelling and Grammar** button on the Standard toolbar.

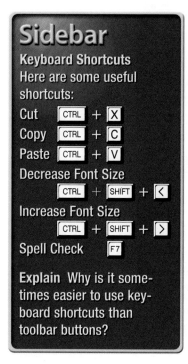

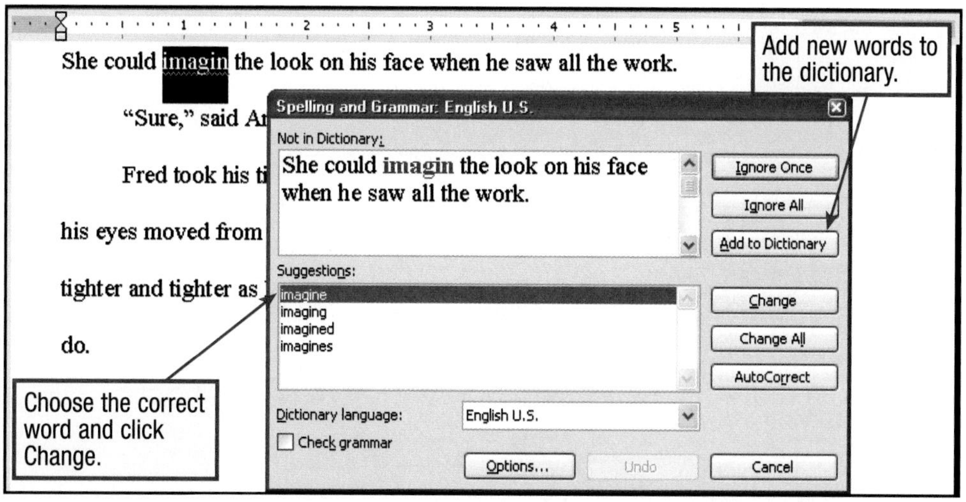

▲ You can add new words to the dictionary. Check with your teacher before adding any words to Word's dictionary.

Word's default setting checks for spellings that are not in Word's dictionary. When it finds a word that it does not recognize, a red squiggly line is displayed beneath the word. Right-click the word to see suggested spellings.

The Web-Safe Color Palette

Colors in the chart are notated in both their hexadecimal values for use in Web design programs and their RGB (red, green, blue) values for use in graphics programs.

- The first number/letter combination shown represents the color's hexadecimal value. You can use hexadecimal values to select colors in Adobe Illustrator's or Photoshop's color palettes or color pickers.
- The second set of numbers shown represents the color's RGB value. Each of these numbers correlates to an intensity value of red, green, and blue as displayed on a monitor. For example, an orange color would have the RGB color designation of: red 255, green 102, and blue 51.

FFFFFF R=255 G=255 B=255	FFFFCC R=255 G=255 B=204	FFFF99 R=255 G=255 B=153	FFFF66 R=255 G=255 B=102	FFFF33 R=255 G=255 B=51	FFFF00 R=255 G=255 B=0	66FFFF R=102 G=255 B=255	66FFCC R=102 G=255 B=204	66FF99 R=102 G=255 B=153	66FF66 R=102 G=255 B=102	66FF33 R=102 G=255 B=51	66FF00 R=102 G=255 B=0
FFCCFF R=255 G=204 B=255	FFCCCC R=255 G=204 B=204	FFCC99 R=255 G=204 B=153	FFCC66 R=255 G=204 B=102	FFCC33 R=255 G=204 B=51	FFCC00 R=255 G=204 B=0	66CCFF R=102 G=204 B=255	66CCCC R=102 G=204 B=204	66CC99 R=102 G=204 B=153	66CC66 R=102 G=204 B=102	66CC33 R=102 G=204 B=51	66FF00 R=102 G=204 B=0
FF99FF R=255 G=153 B=255	FF99CC R=255 G=153 B=204	FF9999 R=255 G=153 B=153	FF9966 R=255 G=153 B=102	FF9933 R=255 G=153 B=51	FF9900 R=255 G=153 B=0	6699FF R=102 G=153 B=255	6699CC R=102 G=153 B=204	669999 R=102 G=153 B=153	669966 R=102 G=153 B=102	669933 R=102 G=153 B=51	669900 R=102 G=153 B=0
FF66FF R=255 G=102 B=255	FF66CC R=255 G=102 B=204	FF6699 R=255 G=102 B=153	FF6666 R=255 G=102 B=102	FF6633 R=255 G=102 B=51	FF6600 R=255 G=102 B=0	6666FF R=102 G=102 B=255	6666CC R=102 G=102 B=204	666699 R=102 G=102 B=153	666666 R=102 G=102 B=102	666633 R=102 G=102 B=51	666600 R=102 G=102 B=0
FF33FF R=255 G=51 B=255	FF33CC R=255 G=51 B=204	FF3399 R=255 G=51 B=153	FF3366 R=255 G=51 B=102	FF3333 R=255 G=51 B=51	FF3300 R=255 G=51 B=0	6633FF R=102 G=51 B=255	6633CC R=102 G=51 B=204	663399 R=102 G=51 B=153	663366 R=102 G=51 B=102	663333 R=102 G=51 B=51	663300 R=102 G=51 B=0
FF00FF R=255 G=0 B=255	FF00CC R=255 G=0 B=204	FF0099 R=255 G=0 B=153	FF0066 R=255 G=0 B=102	FF0033 R=255 G=0 B=51	FF0000 R=255 G=0 B=0	6600FF R=102 G=0 B=255	6600CC R=102 G=0 B=204	660099 R=102 G=0 B=153	660066 R=102 G=0 B=102	660033 R=102 G=0 B=51	660000 R=102 G=0 B=0
CCFFFF R=204 G=255 B=255	CCFFCC R=204 G=255 B=204	CCFF99 R=204 G=255 B=153	CCFF66 R=204 G=255 B=102	CCFF33 R=204 G=255 B=51	CCFF00 R=204 G=255 B=0	33FFFF R=51 G=255 B=255	33FFCC R=51 G=255 B=204	33FF99 R=51 G=255 B=153	33FF66 R=51 G=255 B=102	33FF33 R=51 G=255 B=51	33FF00 R=51 G=255 B=0
CCCCFF R=204 G=204 B=255	CCCCCC R=204 G=204 B=204	CCCC99 R=204 G=204 B=153	CCCC66 R=204 G=204 B=102	CCCC33 R=204 G=204 B=51	CCCC00 R=204 G=204 B=0	33CCFF R=51 G=204 B=255	33CCCC R=51 G=204 B=204	33CC99 R=51 G=204 B=153	33CC66 R=51 G=204 B=102	33CC33 R=51 G=204 B=51	33CC00 R=51 G=204 B=0
CC99FF R=204 G=153 B=255	CC99CC R=204 G=153 B=204	CC9999 R=204 G=153 B=153	CC9966 R=204 G=153 B=102	CC9933 R=204 G=153 B=51	CC9900 R=204 G=153 B=0	3399FF R=51 G=153 B=255	3399CC R=51 G=153 B=204	339999 R=51 G=153 B=153	339966 R=51 G=153 B=102	339933 R=51 G=153 B=51	339900 R=51 G=153 B=0
CC66FF R=204 G=102 B=255	CC66CC R=204 G=102 B=204	CC6699 R=204 G=102 B=153	CC6666 R=204 G=102 B=102	CC6633 R=204 G=102 B=51	CC6600 R=204 G=102 B=0	3366FF R=51 G=102 B=255	3366CC R=51 G=102 B=204	336699 R=51 G=102 B=153	336666 R=51 G=102 B=102	336633 R=51 G=102 B=51	336600 R=51 G=102 B=0
CC33FF R=204 G=51 B=255	CC33CC R=204 G=51 B=204	CC3399 R=204 G=51 B=153	CC3366 R=204 G=51 B=102	CC3333 R=204 G=51 B=51	CC3300 R=204 G=51 B=0	3333FF R=51 G=51 B=255	3333CC R=51 G=51 B=204	333399 R=51 G=51 B=153	333366 R=51 G=51 B=102	333333 R=51 G=51 B=51	333300 R=51 G=51 B=0
CC00FF R=204 G=0 B=255	CC00CC R=204 G=0 B=204	CC0099 R=204 G=0 B=153	CC0066 R=204 G=0 B=102	CC0033 R=204 G=0 B=51	CC0000 R=204 G=0 B=0	3300FF R=51 G=0 B=255	3300CC R=51 G=0 B=204	330099 R=51 G=0 B=153	330066 R=51 G=0 B=102	330033 R=51 G=0 B=51	330000 R=51 G=0 B=0
99FFFF R=153 G=255 B=255	99FFCC R=153 G=255 B=204	99FF99 R=153 G=255 B=153	99FF66 R=153 G=255 B=102	99FF33 R=153 G=255 B=51	99FF00 R=153 G=255 B=0	00FFFF R=0 G=255 B=255	00FFCC R=0 G=255 B=204	00FF99 R=0 G=255 B=153	00FF66 R=0 G=255 B=102	00FF33 R=0 G=255 B=51	00FF00 R=0 G=255 B=0
99CCFF R=153 G=204 B=255	99CCCC R=153 G=204 B=204	99CC99 R=153 G=204 B=153	99CC66 R=153 G=204 B=102	99CC33 R=153 G=204 B=51	99CC00 R=153 G=204 B=0	00CCFF R=0 G=204 B=255	00CCCC R=0 G=204 B=204	00CC99 R=0 G=204 B=153	00CC66 R=0 G=204 B=102	00CC33 R=0 G=204 B=51	00CC00 R=0 G=204 B=0
9999FF R=153 G=153 B=255	9999CC R=153 G=153 B=204	999999 R=153 G=153 B=153	999966 R=153 G=153 B=102	999933 R=153 G=153 B=51	999900 R=153 G=153 B=0	0099FF R=0 G=153 B=255	0099CC R=0 G=153 B=204	009999 R=0 G=153 B=153	009966 R=0 G=153 B=102	009933 R=0 G=153 B=51	009900 R=0 G=153 B=0
9966FF R=153 G=102 B=255	9966CC R=153 G=102 B=204	996699 R=153 G=102 B=153	996666 R=153 G=102 B=102	996633 R=153 G=102 B=51	996600 R=153 G=102 B=0	0066FF R=0 G=102 B=255	0066CC R=0 G=102 B=204	006699 R=0 G=102 B=153	006666 R=0 G=102 B=102	006633 R=0 G=102 B=51	006600 R=0 G=102 B=0
9933FF R=153 G=51 B=255	9933CC R=153 G=51 B=204	993399 R=153 G=51 B=153	993366 R=153 G=51 B=102	993333 R=153 G=51 B=51	993300 R=153 G=51 B=0	0033FF R=0 G=51 B=255	0033CC R=0 G=51 B=204	003399 R=0 G=51 B=153	003366 R=0 G=51 B=102	003333 R=0 G=51 B=51	003300 R=0 G=51 B=0
9900FF R=153 G=0 B=255	9900CC R=153 G=0 B=204	990099 R=153 G=0 B=153	990066 R=153 G=0 B=102	990033 R=153 G=0 B=51	990000 R=153 G=0 B=0	0000FF R=0 G=0 B=255	0000CC R=0 G=0 B=204	000099 R=0 G=0 B=153	000066 R=0 G=0 B=102	000033 R=0 G=0 B=51	000000 R=0 G=0 B=0

Additional Formatting Tools

Align Text When you **align** text, you are arranging items so that they line up. The Formatting toolbar has four buttons to align text in different positions from left to right. You can also change the vertical text alignment between the top and bottom margin through the **File>Page Setup** box.

Text Alignment Options

Alignment	Button	Description
Align left		Text lines up along the left margin.
Center		Text is centered between margins.
Align right		Text lines up along the right margin.
Justify		Text spreads from left to right margins.

Format for Visual Interest Change fonts, point sizes, and font styles by using either the buttons on the Formatting toolbar or by clicking **Format>Font**. You can also use the Format menu to enhance a document with decorative elements such as a drop cap or a page border. A **drop cap** is a large decorative letter used as the first letter of a paragraph. A **border** is a line or a design that outlines a specific section or a page in a document.

Add Headers and Footers

A **header** is information that appears at the top of every page. A **footer** is information that appears at the bottom of every page. Click **View>Header and Footer** to open the Header and Footer toolbar.

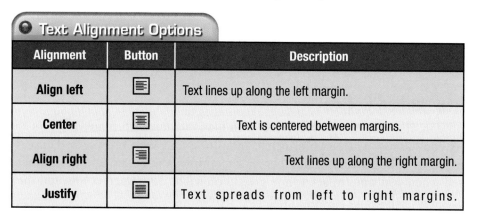

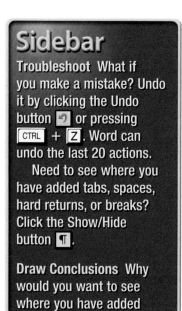

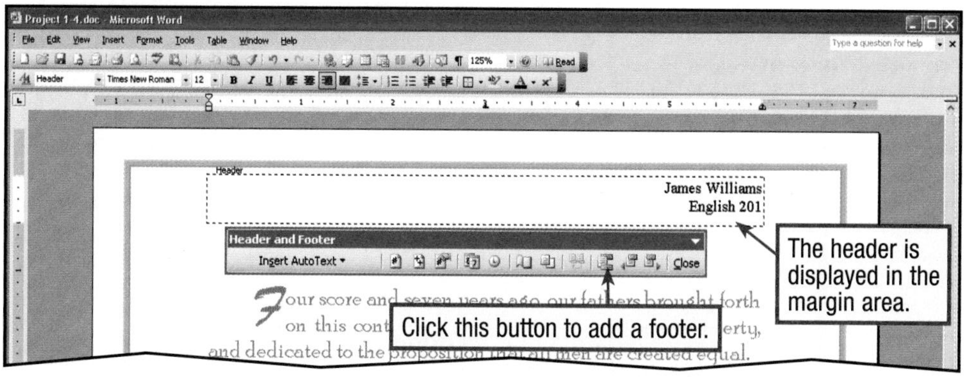

▲ The text in a header or footer appears on every page of your document.

▶ **In this project,** you will use Word tools to format the Gettysburg Address as a visually interesting and easily readable document.

Sidebar

Troubleshoot What if you make a mistake? Undo it by clicking the Undo button or pressing CTRL + Z. Word can undo the last 20 actions.

Need to see where you have added tabs, spaces, hard returns, or breaks? Click the Show/Hide button ¶.

Draw Conclusions Why would you want to see where you have added extra spaces?

APPENDIX A

Web-Safe Color Reference Guide

Not every monitor displays color in the same way. To avoid complications, you should select colors from the 216-color Web-safe color palette when formatting text, choosing backgrounds, and creating basic graphics for your site. Using this limited color palette (shown on the next page) helps ensure that colors will display properly no matter what computer system, monitor settings, or Web browser people use to view your pages.

The 16 Named Colors

You can also use the World Wide Web Consortium's 16 named colors to maintain color consistency across various platforms, monitors, and Web browsers. These 16 colors can be specified by a hexadecimal number. For example, the hexadecimal number 00FF00 can be entered when you want to set a lime green color. The 16 named colors and their corresponding hexadecimal values are shown in the table below.

16 Named Colors

Color Name	Hexadecimal Value	Example
Aqua	#00FFFF	
Black	#000000	
Blue	#0000FF	
Fuchsia	#FF00FF	
Gray	#808080	
Green	#008000	
Lime	#00FF00	
Maroon	#800000	
Navy	#000080	
Olive	#808000	
Purple	#800080	
Red	#FF0000	
Silver	#C0C0C0	
Teal	#008080	
White	#FFFFFF	
Yellow	#FFFF00	

Student Data File

Step-by-Step

1. In Word, click open **Data File 1-4**. Save the file according to your teacher's instructions.

Cut and Paste

2. The document is out of order! Select the second paragraph by clicking anywhere in it three times (Figure 1.9).

3. On the **Standard** toolbar, click **Cut** [icon] to remove the paragraph from the document. This places it on the clipboard.

4. Place your insertion point before the first letter of the first paragraph. Click **Paste** [icon]. The paragraph you cut in Step 3 should now be the first paragraph. If necessary, press the ENTER key to separate the first and second paragraphs.

5. On the **menu** bar, click **Edit>Select All**, or press CTRL + A to select the entire document. On the **Formatting** toolbar, change the font to **Poor Richard** or a similar old-fashioned font (Figure 1.10).

6. Increase the typeface to a more readable size like **16 pt**.

▼ **Figure 1.9** When you cut text, it can be pasted anywhere.

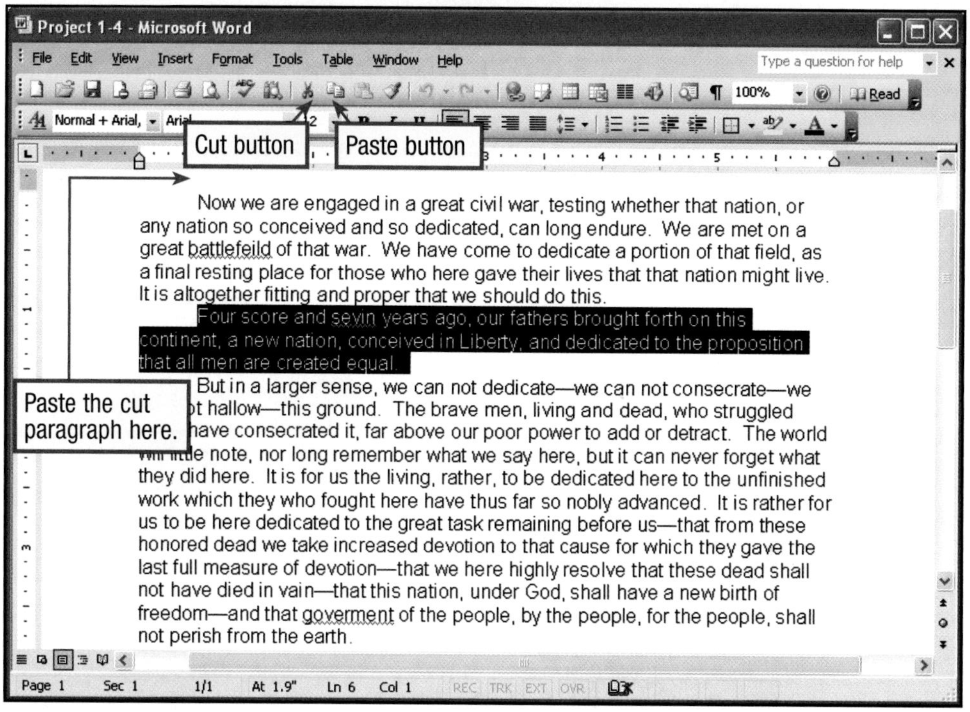

▼ **Figure 1.10** The Formatting toolbar has many tools for changing fonts.

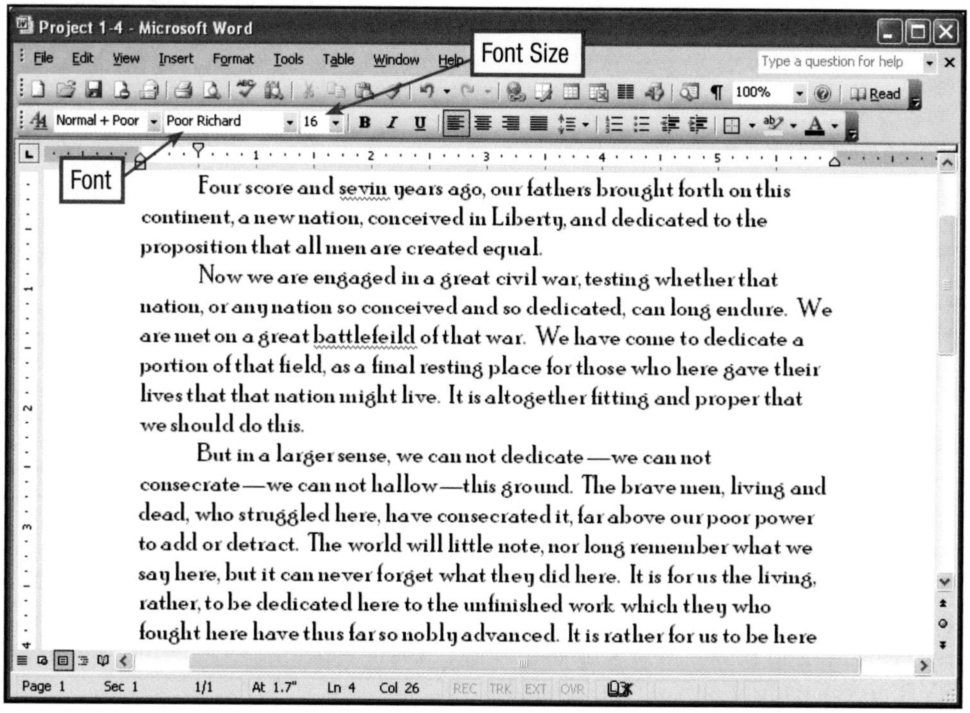

Printer Colors Versus Monitor Colors

Even with monitor calibration, you can still expect some colors to change when they are printed. The monitor and the printer operate under two completely different color theories. The computer monitor uses light (an *addition* color model), while the printer uses paint (a *subtraction* color model).

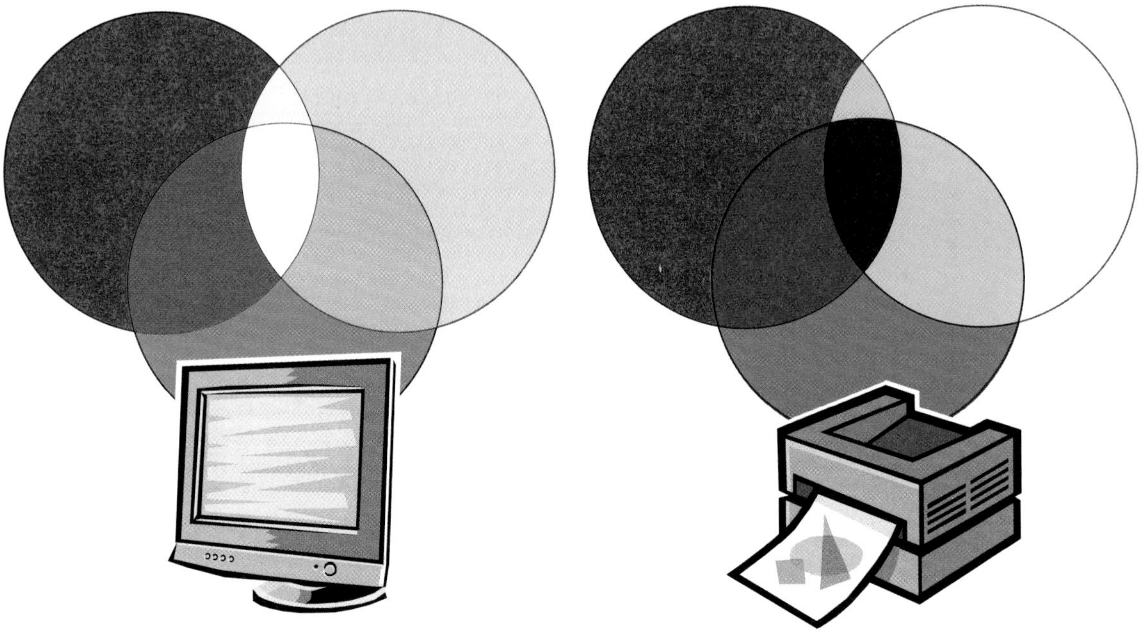

Your computer monitor and your printer use two completely different principles for creating colors. As a result, colors on the monitor may look different when they are printed.

When a color is created by addition, it means that two or more wave lengths can combined to create a new color. The primary colors of light—red, green, and blue (RGB)—are used to create all the colors you see on a computer monitor. The RGB color scheme uses 256 shades of red, green, and blue, which can be combined to display 16,777,216 colors.

When a color is created by subtraction, combining colors causes some wave lengths to be absorbed so that they are removed from a color. You only see the color that is left. The ink used in printing absorbs some colors and reflects others. For example, blue text might be created when two colored inks are combined, causing all the red and yellow wave lengths to be absorbed, and the green and blue wave lengths to reflect.

Printers can use two color processes to create a huge range of colors. The CMYK scheme uses the colors cyan (a shade of blue), magenta (a shade of red), yellow, and black. RYB printers use red, yellow, and blue. CMYK is used more often, especially with high-quality printers because RYB colors cannot create a pure black.

Align Text

7 Click **Justify** [Justify icon]. Click once to deselect the text.

8 Click in front of the first word in the speech. Key The Gettysburg Address.

9 Press [ENTER] two times. Then select the title, and change the **Font Size** to **24 pt**.

10 With the title still selected, click **Center** [Center icon] on the **Formatting** toolbar.

11 On the **Standard** toolbar, click **Show/Hide** [¶] (Figure 1.11). There should be only one space after a period. Find and remove the seven double spaces in the document.

12 Click after the last word in the document, and press [ENTER] two times. Then press **Align right** [Align right icon], or press [CTRL] + [R].

13 On the **Formatting** toolbar, change the **Font** to **Brush Script**, change the **Font Size** to **28 pt**. Click **Bold** [B], or press [CTRL] + [B]. Then key Abraham Lincoln.

Insert a Drop Cap

14 Select the **F** in the first word of the first paragraph. Click **Format>Drop Cap**.

15 In the **Drop Cap** box, click the **Dropped** option, change the **Font** to **Brush Script**, and choose a **2-line drop**. Click **OK** (Figure 1.12).

Figure 1.11 Use the Show/Hide tool to view your spacing, indents, and hard returns.

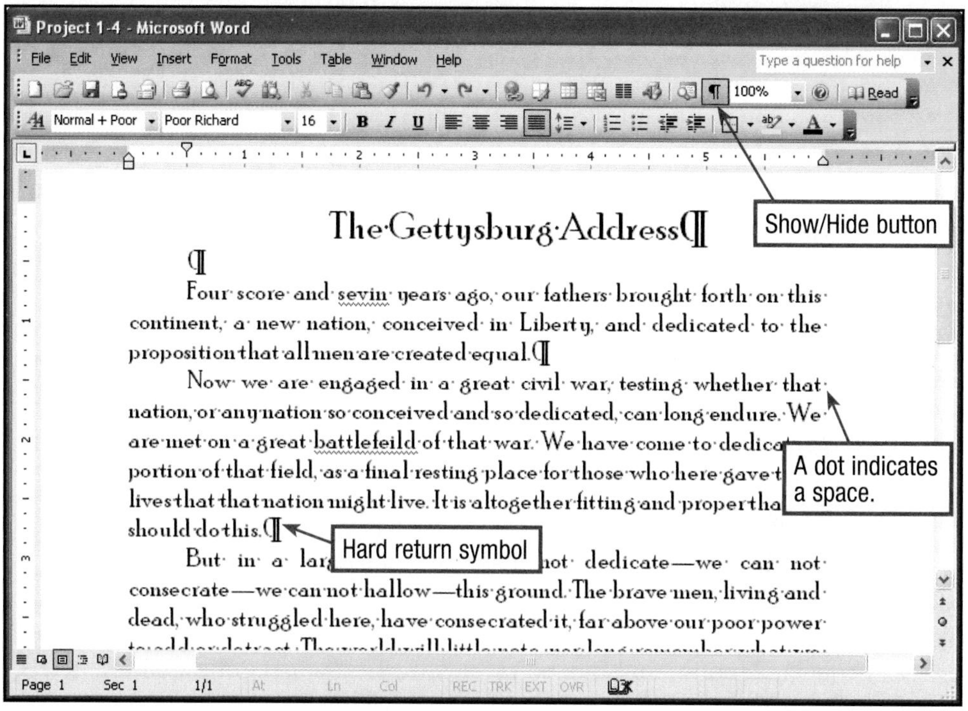

Figure 1.12 Drop caps can make a text document visually interesting.

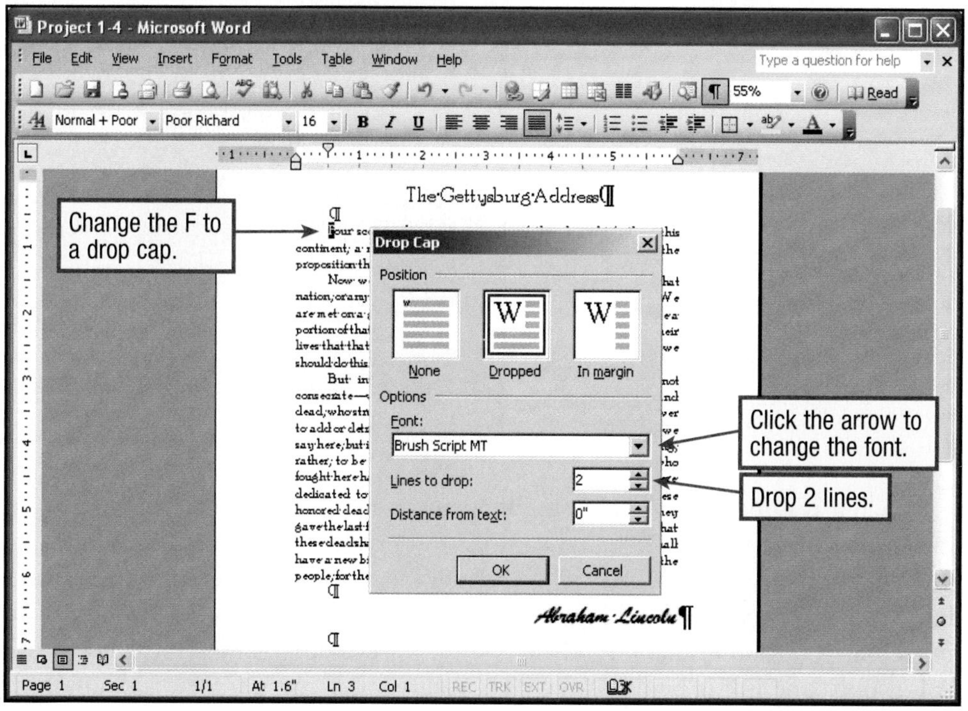

Adjust Color to Light

When viewed in different kinds of lighting, colors also appear to change. This is called *metamerism*. Sunlight (at noon) is the standard by which colors are measured. Colors viewed under a fluorescent light will appear a bit more blue, and colors viewed under a light bulb are not as vibrant and warm as in sunlight.

Colors also change from your computer monitor to your printer. Sometimes, you can calibrate your monitor to help colors look like they will on the actual printed page. With Photoshop, Adobe also packages a program called Adobe Gamma (located in your Control Panel) that will help you calibrate your monitor. Technically, however, the monitor's colors will also change based on the surrounding light source. To help counteract this problem, professionals will also purchase devices which sense the surrounding light and recalibrate the monitor accordingly.

Choose Exact Colors

Since there are so many different shades of each color, it is not very helpful to simply describe a color as "red." If you did, you might find the "red" you used looks different on each page of your document. Tell a group member to use "red," and you will discover that nobody in your group is using the same color! Instead, be more specific by using the CMYK, RGB, or hexadecimal values to describe colors (see page 500 of this Appendix).

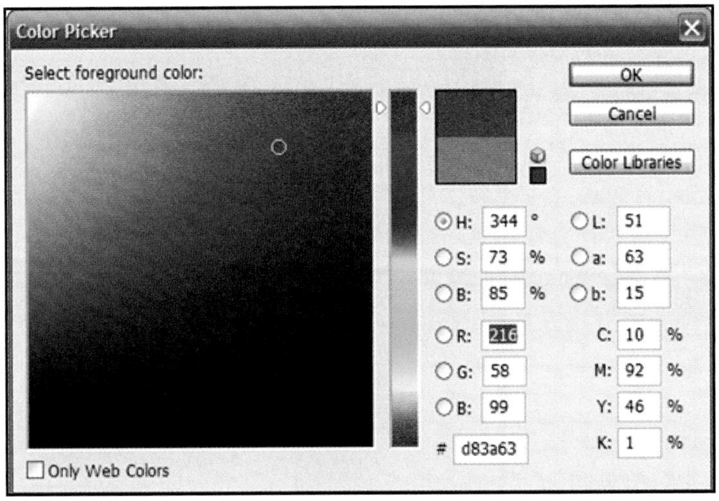

► With 16.7 million colors at your disposal, you need to use specific numbers to describe a color.

When it is important to make sure that colors are always exactly the same (like for a company logo), use a color model such as Pantone to describe to the print shop the specific colors you need. Pantone is a type of *spot color*, which means that each color has its own special shade of ink, unlike a *process color*. Process colors are created by mixing a few colors of ink—like cyan, magenta, yellow, and black (CMYK)—in different proportions. So when a printer uses a spot color, only one ink is being use, which ensures that you get the exact color your job requires. Since this type of service can be expensive, it should be used sparingly.

Add a Page Border

16 Click anywhere in the document to deselect the drop cap. On the **menu** bar, click **Format>Borders and Shading**, then click the **Page Border** tab.

17 Choose **Box** setting and the style and size settings shown in Figure 1.13. Click **OK**.

18 On the **menu** bar, click **View>Header and Footer**. Your insertion point should be in the **Header** box. Click **Align Right** [icon]. Key your name, press ENTER, and key the date.

19 On the **Header and Footer** toolbar, click **Switch Between Header and Footer** [icon]. Key November 19, 1863.

20 Select the text in the footer. Click **Center** [icon] and **Italic** *I*.

21 On the Header and Footer toolbar, click **Close**.

Check Spelling

22 On the **Standard** toolbar, click **Spelling and Grammar** [icon]. Correct any mistakes.

23 Your document should look similar to Figure 1.14.

24 Follow your teacher's instructions for saving and printing your work.

▼ **Figure 1.13** Choose a page border that does not distract from the text.

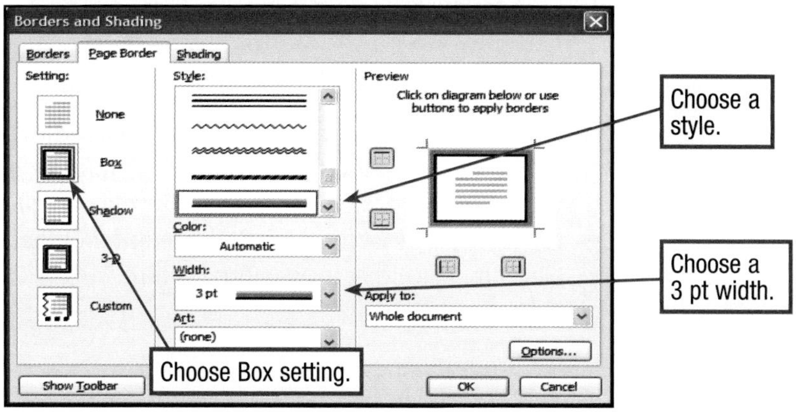

▼ **Figure 1.14** Your final document should look similar to this example.

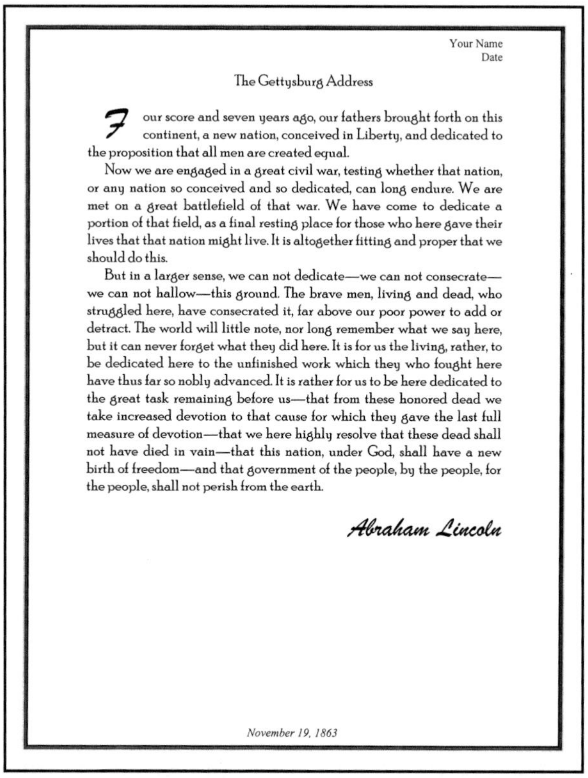

Your Name
Date

The Gettysburg Address

Four score and seven years ago, our fathers brought forth on this continent, a new nation, conceived in Liberty, and dedicated to the proposition that all men are created equal.

Now we are engaged in a great civil war, testing whether that nation, or any nation so conceived and so dedicated, can long endure. We are met on a great battlefield of that war. We have come to dedicate a portion of that field, as a final resting place for those who here gave their lives that that nation might live. It is altogether fitting and proper that we should do this.

But in a larger sense, we can not dedicate—we can not consecrate—we can not hallow—this ground. The brave men, living and dead, who struggled here, have consecrated it, far above our poor power to add or detract. The world will little note, nor long remember what we say here, but it can never forget what they did here. It is for us the living, rather, to be dedicated here to the unfinished work which they who fought here have thus far so nobly advanced. It is rather for us to be here dedicated to the great task remaining before us—that from these honored dead we take increased devotion to that cause for which they gave the last full measure of devotion—that we here highly resolve that these dead shall not have died in vain—that this nation, under God, shall have a new birth of freedom—and that government of the people, by the people, for the people, shall not perish from the earth.

Abraham Lincoln

November 19, 1863

REVIEW AND REVISE

Check your work Use Figure 1.14 as a guide and check that:

- ☑ Text alignment is justified.
- ☑ There is a drop cap, page border, header, and footer.
- ☑ There are no spelling errors or typos.

Complementary A complementary color scheme uses colors that are opposite each other on the color wheel. This can create a high energy design that can be visually difficult to process. Use tints or tones of these colors for maximum impact. Be careful of color associations! Red-green combinations suggest the Christmas holiday in Western culture.

Split-complementary Split-complementary color schemes use one harmonious and one complementary color. This means that two of the colors used are next to each other on the color wheel, and one color is opposite. This scheme is typically used to create contrast, but can also be used in an elegant design.

Use these color schemes when planning your next design. Experiment on an image in Photoshop. Try to create duotones (two colors, usually black and another color) to reduce the number of colors in an image, or create a monochromatic or complementary design. See what your experimentation can help you create!

How Do I Create Consistent Colors?

Colors do not stay consistent. Since the perception of color is based on interpreting wavelengths of light, a color looks different when the colors around it change. This is referred to as *color context*. Sometimes, when the right color combinations are evident, the colors will even seem to shimmer and blink.

Color properties change based on color context. The blue circle is the same color in all three boxes, but appears darker when placed against darker backgrounds. Also, the lighter color appears to be in front of the darker color.

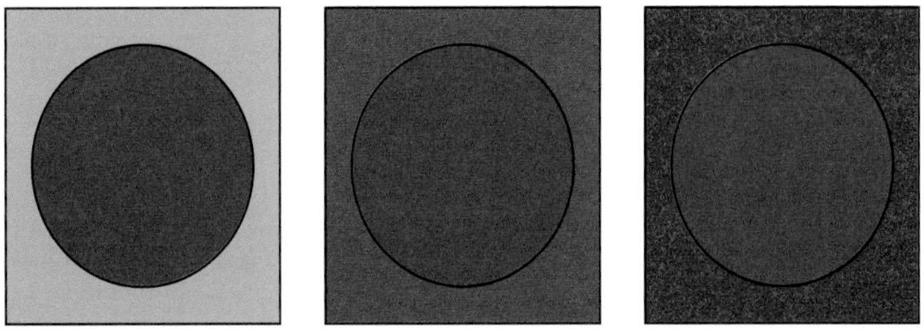

Project 1-5

Insert and Wrap Clip Art

Spotlight on Skills

- Find and replace text
- Insert a text box
- Add a fill color
- Insert a graphic
- Move and resize an object

Key Terms

- wrap
- sizing handle
- text box

Academic Focus

Language Arts
Illustrate an Aesop's Fable and find synonyms

Illustrate a Story

Desktop publishing is used to create documents that combine text and graphics. Graphics can include pictures like clip art and photos, as well as icons, borders, and even tables and charts.

When you place an image into a document, you must consider a number of factors, such as:

- Does the image enhance the message of the text?
- Is the image attractive or visually interesting?
- Where should the image be placed in the document?
- How large should the image be?

The wrong image or the wrong placement can make a document uninteresting, confusing, or unprofessional.

Insert an Image

You can insert a picture into a Word document in a number of ways. You can use **Insert>Picture** to find a specific clip art or photo file. You can also copy and paste an image into a document from another document or from an electronic source such as a Web site or CD-ROM.

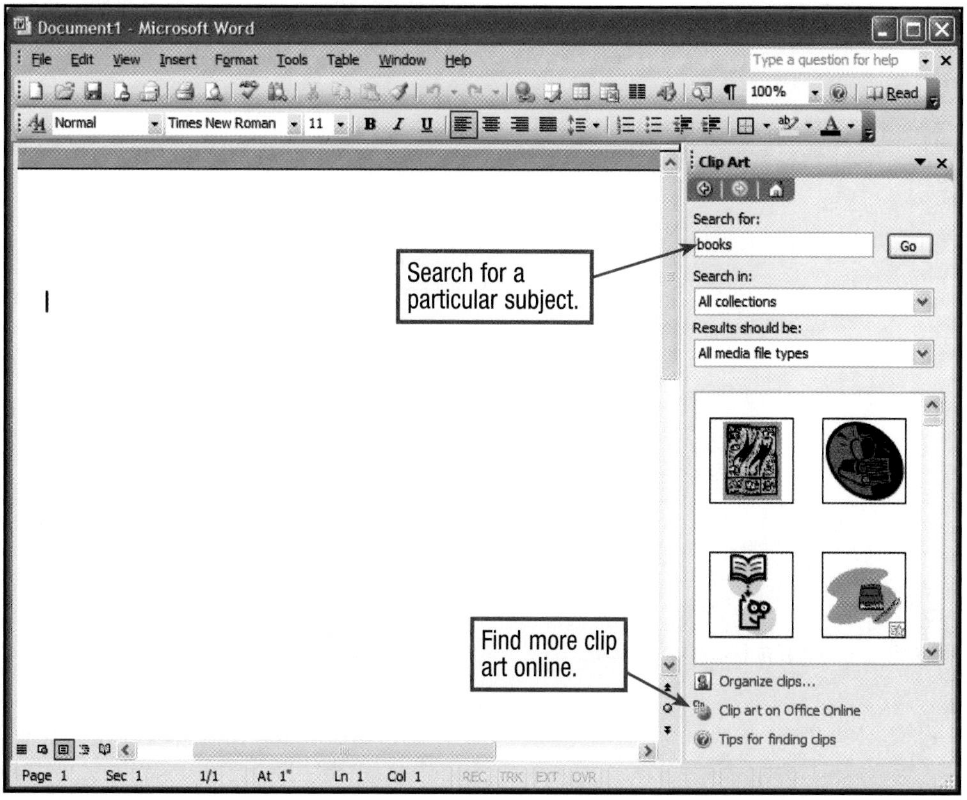

► Word has an assortment of clip art from which you can choose. Double-click an image to insert it.

How Do I Combine Colors Effectively?

In 1666, Sir Isaac Newton first invented the color wheel that we are so familiar with today. Using this color wheel, we can create a framework for the colors you can safely and effectively use together.

The color wheel shows the relationship between different colors. The highlights on each color are color tints, and the shadows are color shades.

The following diagrams show the four most common color schemes. Whites, blacks, grays, and browns are neutral and can be used in most color schemes.

Monochromatic A monochromatic color scheme uses shades and tints of only one color. To create contrast, different tints (lighter shades) and tones (darker shades) are used.

Harmonious Harmonious colors are side by side on the color wheel. This color scheme is used most often in advertisements and sends an elegant message.

Wrap Text When you **wrap** text, you flow text around a graphic. The text on this page is wrapped around the two figures. Depending on the layout you want for the text, you can wrap text above, below, to the side, or all around a picture. You can choose a style by opening the Format Picture box and choosing the **Layout** tab.

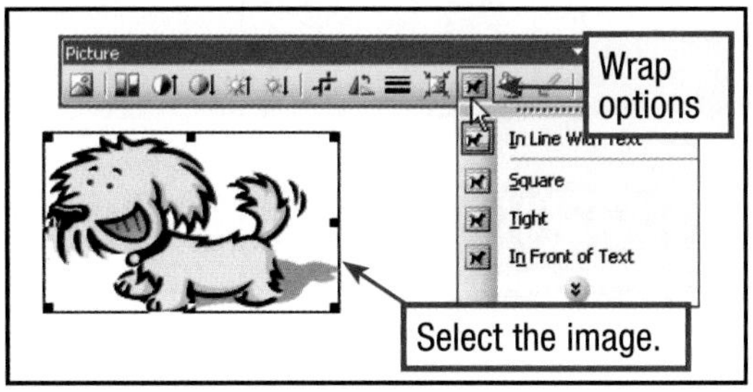

▲ Display the Picture toolbar by clicking the image.

You can also choose a wrapping style by using the **Picture toolbar**. Click the image to display the toolbar. You can then click the **Text Wrapping** button. If the toolbar is not displayed, right-click the image and choose **Show Picture Toolbar**.

When you insert the image into the document, your insertion point should already be in the spot where you want the figure to be placed. Once it is inserted, you may have to resize it and wrap text around it.

Resize an Image When you place a picture into a document, it will probably disrupt the layout of the text, but it can be easily fixed by changing the size of the image.

You can resize an image by selecting it and then dragging a **sizing handle**, a small circle or square that is visible on the sides or corners of an object (see the figure). You can also double-click on the object, or click **Format>Picture** to display the **Format Picture** box. You can key specific dimensions in the **Size** tab of the Format Picture box.

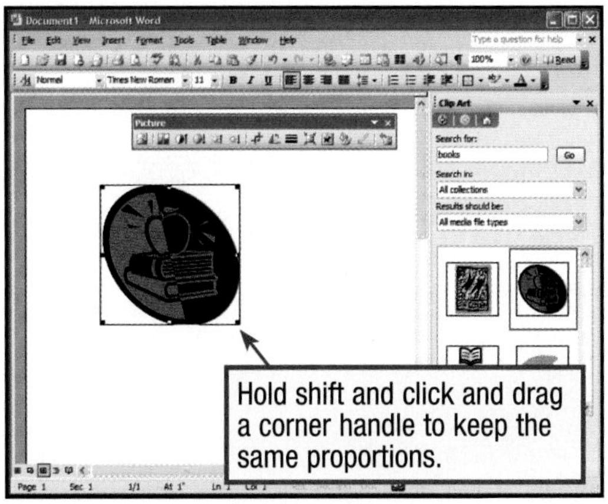

▲ You must click on the image to select it in order to display the sizing handles.

Insert a Text Box A **text box** is a graphic element that holds text and graphics. When you put text or graphics into the box, you can set the text box off from other content and move it around. Like an image, it can be resized and text can be wrapped around it. Text boxes can be filled with different colors and have a border. You can also change the direction of the text, as you will see in the following project.

Sidebar

Search for Synonyms When searching for a word in the Thesaurus, it is usually best to use single nouns (*flower*, not *flowers*), and verbs in first person present tense (*go*, not *goes* or *went*). If you do search for a word that derives from another word, the thesaurus will offer a suggestion for your search. For example, if you keyed *goes*, it would give you the related word *go*.

Draw Conclusions Why is it important to know how to use a thesaurus to create desktop published documents?

▶ **In this project,** you will illustrate an Aesop's Fable by adding clip art. You will also use the Thesaurus and Find/Replace tools to revise your story. Consider the audience. This story is meant for a younger age group, which means you should use a larger font, a shorter line length, and brighter colors.

Color Choice and Design

Not only do designs in color get more attention than those without, but color itself can be a powerful tool to help deliver the message to the reader. People tend to relate colors to certain feelings, though these associations are mostly based upon culture. The following associations are based on Western culture.

COLOR ASSOCIATIONS			
Color	*Warm/Cool*	*Positive Response*	*Negative Response*
Red	Warm	Authority, passion, courage	Fire, anger, danger
Orange	Warm	Cheerful, energetic, creative	Shock, unpleasantness
Yellow	Warm	Energetic, fun, golden	Cautiousness, fearfulness
Green	Cool	Safety, luckiness, nature	Guilt, greed
Blue	Cool	Calmness, faithfulness, justice, loyalty	Sadness, loneliness
Violet	Cool	Royalty, intelligence, wisdom	Apprehension, loneliness

As you can see from the chart, warm colors tend to be associated with excitement and strong, expressive emotions like anger or cheerfulness. Cool colors call less attention to themselves and can be overpowered by warm colors like red or yellow. Neutral colors like black, white, grey, and brown can be used to make other colors stand out or to tone them down. Neutral colors can be cool or warm, and they also have associations. For example, black and grey are considered sophisticated or formal. Browns might be used to express earthiness.

Like all elements of design, choose colors that are likely to enhance your message, rather than distract from it. Make sure you also know which colors are most likely to appeal to your intended audience and how the audience will interpret those colors.

Student Data File

Step-by-Step

1. Open **Data File 1-5a**, and save it according to your teacher's instructions.

2. On the **menu** bar, click **File>Page Setup**. In the **Margins** tab, change the **Left margin** to **2.5**. Then click **OK**.

3. On the **menu** bar, click **Edit>Select All** (or press CTRL + A) to select all the text. Change the font to **Times New Roman**, and change the **Font Size** to **20**.

4. Select the third sentence. On the **Standard** toolbar, click **Cut** (Figure 1.15). Press ENTER once, should you need to separate paragraphs 1 and 2.

5. Place your insertion point at the end of the fable, then press ENTER twice. Click **Paste** to move the sentence there.

Find and Replace Text

6. On the **menu** bar, click **Edit>Replace** (or press CTRL + H). In the **Find what** box, key skunk. In the **Replace with** box, key bear. (Figure 1.16)

7. Click **Replace all**, then click **OK** when the confirmation box pops up. Close the **Find and Replace** box.

Figure 1.15 Use the Cut and Paste buttons to move text.

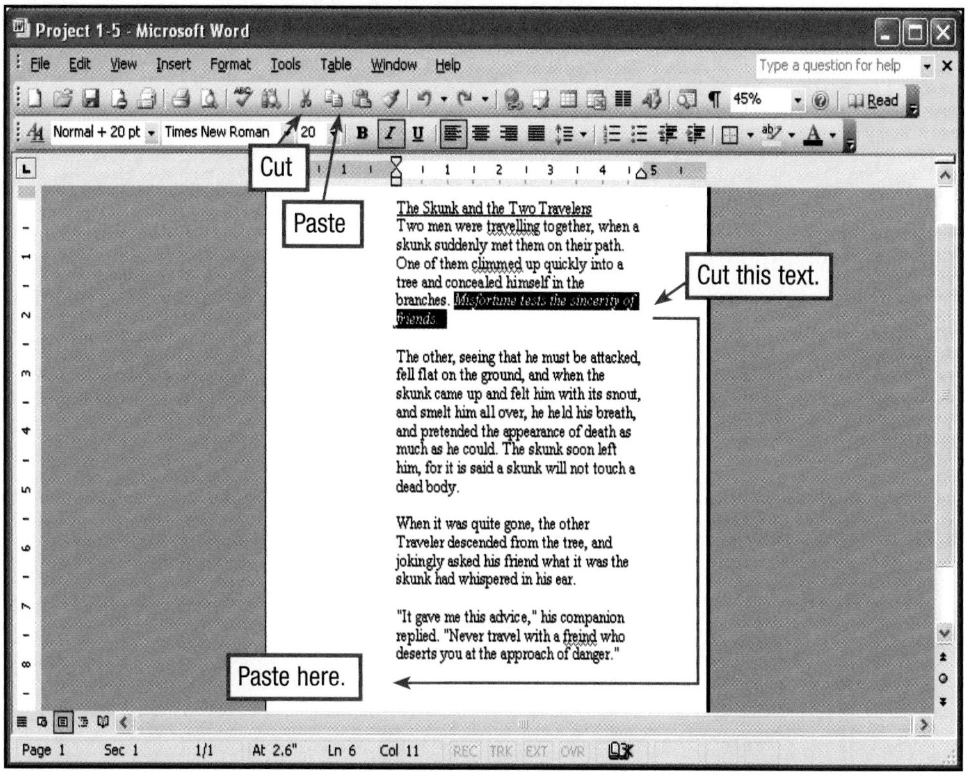

Figure 1.16 You can choose to replace all the words at once, or you can replace them one at a time.

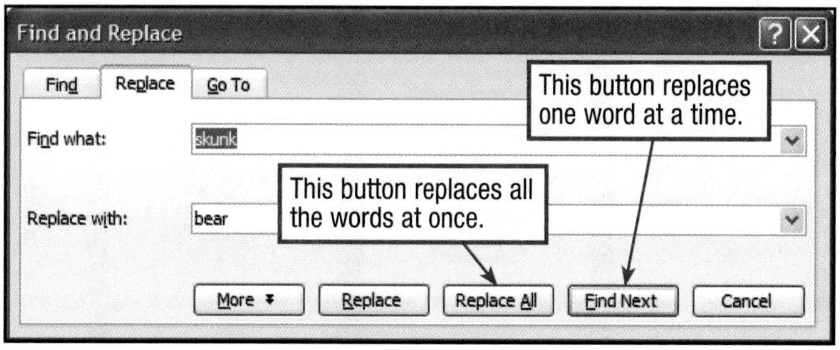

Instant Message

Find and Replace The Find and Replace feature allows you to quickly replace words, symbols, and even formatting everywhere in documents at once. You can also search for and replace or remove character formatting such as bold or italics, paragraph marks, page breaks, and tabs. Use the Find feature on its own if you are just looking for specific text that does not need to be replaced.

What Is Color Blindness?

People do not all see colors the same way. Light and wavelength signals can be distorted because eyes may be somewhat misshapen (most of them are), and cones can miss their signal. In fact, approximately 10 percent of all males are "color-blind," though less than 1 percent of all females have this difficulty. Color blindness does not mean that people see in black and white. Most people who are color-blind have difficulties seeing the difference between reds and purples, reds and greens, or blues and greens.

Many people are not aware that they are color-blind until they take a test like the one below. A color-blind person would have trouble seeing the figures and lines in circles 6, 7, 13, 14, and 15. People who are not color-blind would not see the numbers in circles 8 and 9 or the line in circle 12.

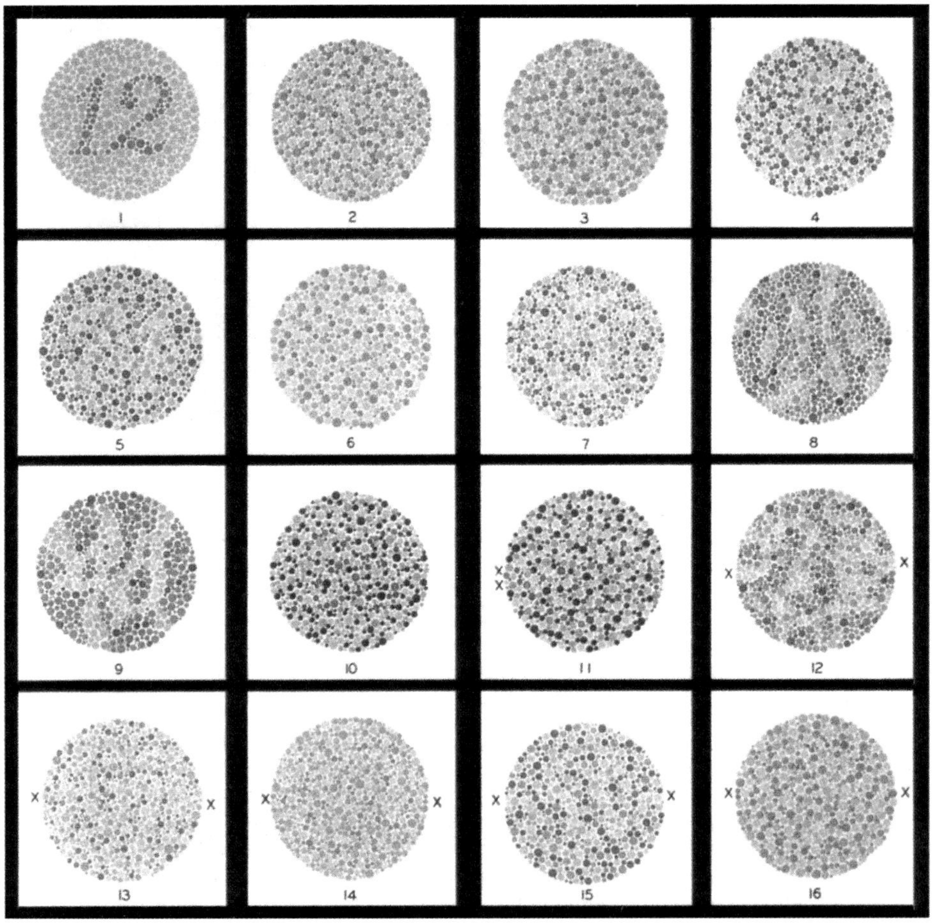

▲ The Ishihara test is one method of assessing color blindness.

The fact that a portion of an audience is color-blind may require a change of the colors used in a design. If 10 percent of an audience cannot easily read a design due to the color choices, then those colors should have been chosen more carefully.

8. Select the word *pretended* in the second paragraph. On the **menu** bar, click **Tools>Language>Thesaurus**. The task pane opens.

9. Move your mouse over the synonym *fake*. Then click the arrow next to it, and choose **Insert**. (**Note:** Make sure you change the new word to the past tense.)

10. Close the task pane. Place your insertion point at the beginning of the document, and check your spelling.

Insert a Text Box

11. Select the title, and click **Underline** [U] to remove the underline. Then click **Insert>Text Box** to put the title into a text box.

12. With the text box selected, click **Format>Text Direction**. In the **Text Direction** box, choose the orientation to the left. Click **OK**.

13. Move your mouse pointer over the edge of the text box until the pointer becomes a 4-headed arrow. Drag the text box to the left side of the document.

14. Click and drag a corner sizing handle to enlarge the box. It should run the full length of the page and be about 1½ inches wide (Figure 1.18).

▼ **Figure 1.17** Remember to change the inserted word to the correct tense so it matches the grammar in the sentence.

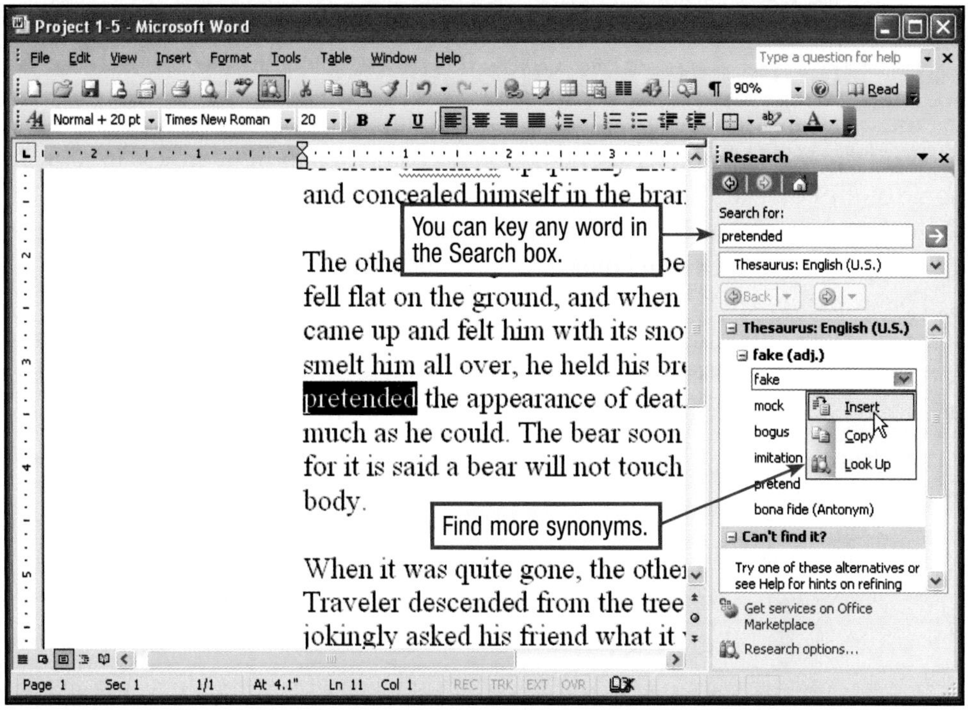

▼ **Figure 1.18** Check the size of the text box with the horizontal ruler.

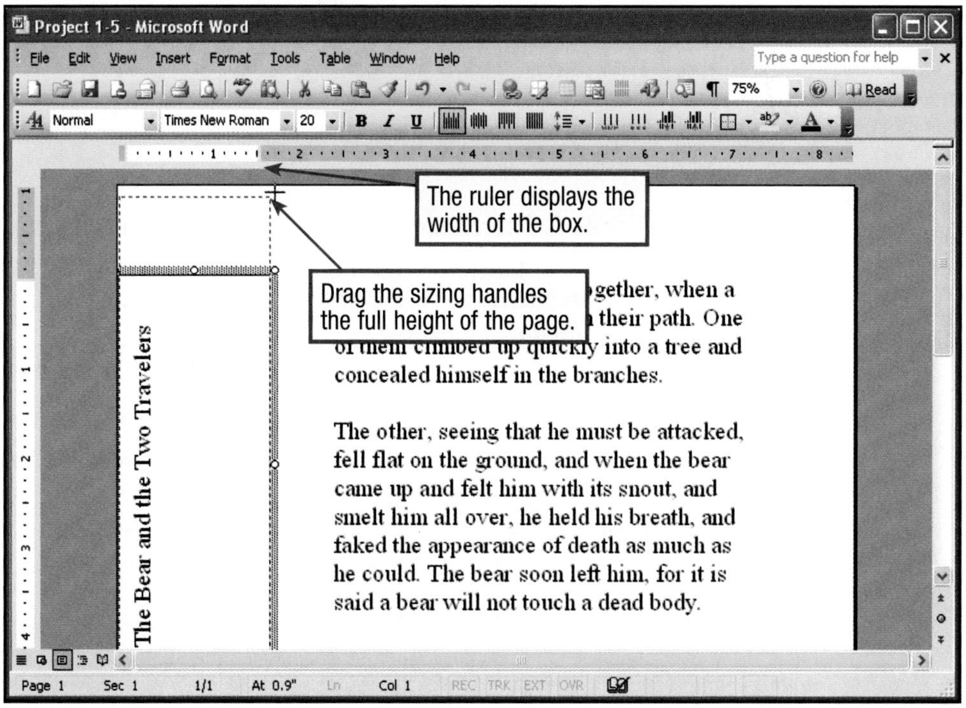

How Do Our Eyes Perceive Color?

You can see colors because of the way the light travels from an object to our eyes. Our minds then interpret the signals as being a certain color. When light strikes an object, such as a ball, some of the color wave lengths are reflected and some are absorbed. The reflected light waves are the colors that we see directly. The absorbed color wave lengths cannot be seen and they cannot combine with the reflected colors.

For example, when you see a yellow lemon, you perceive it to be yellow for two possible reasons. The lemon might be reflecting back only a yellow wave length, or it might be reflecting a few different wave lengths that combine to create the color yellow. The lemon might also be absorbing other wave lengths, such as blue, that would interfere with the color yellow.

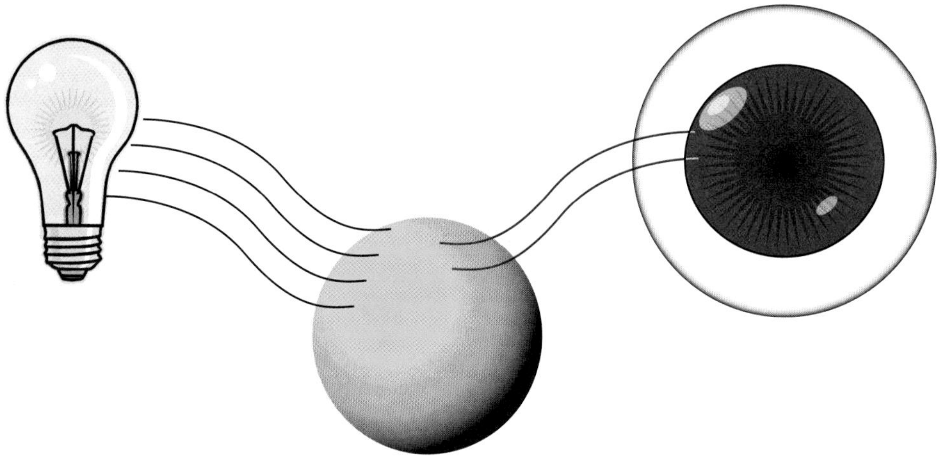

▲ Our eyes interpret the reflected light wave frequencies as colors. In this case, the lemon is perceived as yellow.

Our eyes can detect millions of different colors, though we do not all interpret any particular color in the exact same way. When light enters through the pupil, receptors in the back of the eyes, called *cones,* detect the wave length present and send a signal to the brain. The brain then reassembles and interprets the image.

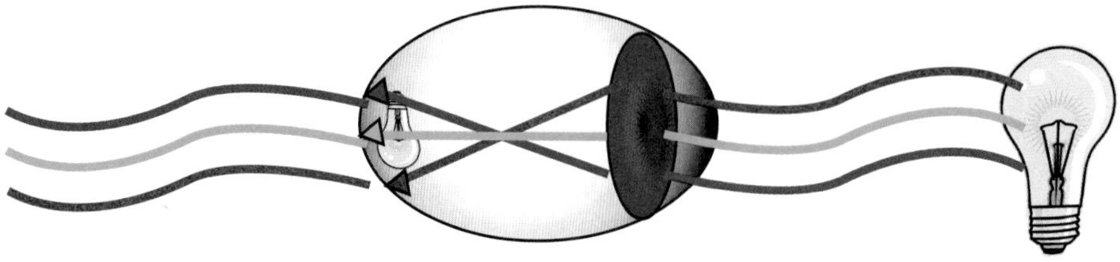

▲ The light waves reflected from an object enter the pupil and are reversed onto the back of the eye. Cone receptors sensitive to light frequencies then send signals for the brain to interpret.

15 Select the title. Center it, and change the format to **Arial Rounded MT Bold, 36 pt** (Figure 1.19).

16 Click **Format>Font**. In the **Font** tab, under **Effects**, click the **Shadow** box. Click **OK**.

Add a Fill Color

17 Select the text box, then click **Format>Text Box**. Choose the **Colors and Lines** tab. Under **Fill**, click the **Color** drop-down menu. Choose a **gold** color. Click **OK**.

Insert a Graphic

18 Place your insertion point in the space below the second paragraph. Click **Insert>Picture>From File**. Scroll to **Data File 1-5b**, and double-click to insert it into your document.

19 Select the picture, then click **Format>Picture**. In the **Layout** tab, choose **Square**, and then click **OK**.

Move and Resize an Object

20 Move and resize the clip art so that your document looks similar to Figure 1.19. (Use the same techniques you used to resize the text box in Steps 13–14.)

21 Follow your teacher's instructions for saving and printing your work.

▼ **Figure 1.19** Your final document should look similar to this.

The Bear and the Two Travelers

Two men were traveling together, when a bear suddenly met them on their path. One of them climbed up quickly into a tree and concealed himself in the branches.

The other, seeing that he must be attacked, fell flat on the ground, and when the bear came up and felt him with its snout, and smelt him all over, he held his breath, and faked the appearance of death as much as he could. The bear soon left him, for it is said a bear will not touch a dead body.

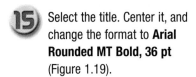

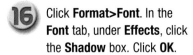

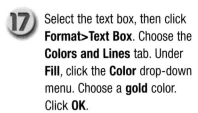

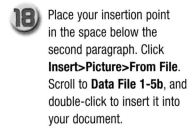

When it was quite gone, the other Traveler descended from the tree, and jokingly asked his friend what it was the bear had whispered in his ear.

"It gave me this advice," his companion replied. "Never travel with a friend who deserts you at the approach of danger."

Misfortune tests the sincerity of friends.

REVIEW AND REVISE

Check your work Use Figure 1.19 as a guide and check that:

- ☑ Fonts are consistent and readable.
- ☑ The title is in a colored text box, and the text direction is correct.
- ☑ All references to *skunk* have been replaced with *bear.*
- ☑ The image is laid out attractively, and text wraps around it.
- ☑ There are no spelling errors or typos.

Color Theory and Design

When Henry Ford first created the Model T automobile, he famously declared that customers could have any color they wanted…*so long as it was black!*

In the past, it was impractical to produce and manufacture goods, such as cars or newspapers, with different color choices. Today, however, the price of color printing has become more affordable, and the lower printing costs have made color documents the standard choice.

Light and Color

Scientific studies, as well as years of practical experiences, have shown that color documents receive more attention than black and white. When a person views colors, the mind and eye work together so that the colors convey meaning and influence attitudes. For example, green might be considered calming and associated with nature. Red might be exciting or associated with danger. Clearly, the use of color is an important aspect of a designer's job. Not only do color documents attract the eye, but color itself can help to communicate the message.

What Is Color?

Rainbows and prisms all display the amazing qualities of a single beam of light. The light from the sun or a light bulb appears to be white or colorless. When raw white light (from a sunbeam or a direct beam from a light bulb) strikes a prism, the light wave is bent, revealing a spectrum of different colors. Each color is actually a different wave length of light. Rainbows display their multicolored spectrum when the water droplets in a light rain bend the rays of the sun.

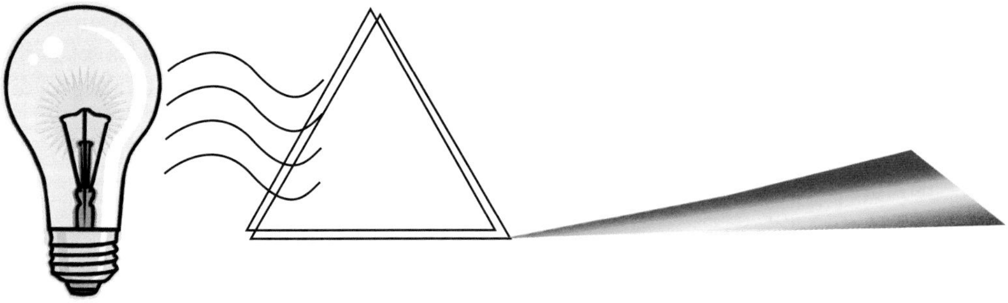

▲ When raw white light passes through a prism, you can see that it is composed of different wave lengths, which we perceive as color.

Some wave lengths, such as blue, do not take much bending, or refraction, to be produced. In fact, our sky appears to be blue during the day because the sun's angle to the earth is slight. Some colors require much sharper refraction. At sunset, the sky works like a prism, bending the sun's light and revealing colors that require much sharper refraction such as reds and oranges.

Colors separated by a prism display a precise color spectrum that is always in the same order: red, orange, yellow, green, blue, indigo, and violet. You can remember the colors by using the mnemonic (memory device) ROY G BV (pronounced *roy gee biv*).

Project 1-6 Create a Certificate

Spotlight on Skills

- Change page orientation
- Format a page border
- Insert a watermark
- Add WordArt
- Apply kerning

Key Terms

- white space
- watermark
- WordArt
- kern
- portrait orientation
- landscape orientation

Academic Focus

Math
Evaluate spatial consistency

Certificates are documents that give special recognition to a person or team. They usually do not contain much text, but the text that is there must be eye-catching and impressive. The information should be clearly laid out, with a lot of **white space**, or empty space, to set off the text. Below are some features you can use when you create a certificate.

Add a Watermark

A **watermark** is an image that is barely visible and often cannot be seen until the paper it is on is held up to the light. If you hold up a $5.00 bill, you can tell it is authentic if you see a watermark of Abraham Lincoln's face. This type of watermark is actually placed into the paper when the paper is manufactured.

Watermarks are often created by placing very light images behind text. This type of watermark is not used to prove authenticity, but to add visual interest to a document, or to identify a type of document, such as a Customer Copy.

Watermarks are only visible in Print Layout View or when the document is printed. Create watermarks by clicking the **Format** menu and choosing the **Background** option.

PERSONAL FINANCIAL STATEMENT

Lydia Kwan

Assets		**Amount in Dollars**
Cash - checking accounts	$	1,500
Cash - savings accounts		4,750
Certificates of deposit		-
Securities - stocks / bonds / mutual funds		-
Life insurance *(cash surrender value)*		-
Personal property *(autos, jewelry, etc.)*		25,000
Retirement Funds *(eg. IRAs, 401k)*		-
Real estate *(market value)*		-
Other assets *(specify)*		-
Total Assets	**$**	**31,250**
Liabilities		**Amount in Dollars**
Current Debt *(Credit cards, Accounts)*	$	275
Notes payable *(describe below)*		-
Taxes payable		-
Real estate mortgages *(describe)*		-
Other liabilities *(specify)*		-
Total Liabilities	**$**	**275**
Net Worth	**$**	**30,975**

▲ A watermark can be a picture or text.

Insert WordArt

You can create text that stands out by using WordArt. **WordArt** is decorative text that comes in many interesting shapes and colors. It can have effects such as shadows added to it, and it can be rotated, stretched, or made 3-dimensional.

WordArt can make a document more distinctive, or it can add color, playfulness, or dramatic effect. It is a useful tool for creating titles, certificates, newsletter mastheads, and greeting cards for personal use.

▲ WordArt combines text with art qualities.

PART 5 Assessment

Key Term Review

Answer the following questions on a separate piece of paper.

1. The Microsoft Office software that sends and receives e-mail is _______________. (p. 487)
2. _______________ is a system for sending messages and files electronically from one computer to another. (p. 487)
3. A(n) _______________ is a list of e-mail addresses.(p. 488)
4. A(n) _______________ is an online discussion of a particular issue. (p. 488)
5. _______________ is like having a telephone conversation using text. (p. 488)
6. The _______________ feature in Microsoft Office can answer questions you might have about how to do something in Outlook. (p. 489)

Concept Review

Answer the following questions on a separate piece of paper.

7. What are two ways messages can be entered into an e-mail? (p. 487)
8. Name two things Outlook can do in addition to sending and receiving e-mail. (p. 487)
9. What are three types of online communication? (p. 488)
10. Explain how instant messaging is similar to having a telephone conversation. (p. 488)
11. What is a newsgroup? (p. 488)
12. Where can you access Help in Outlook? (p. 489)
13. What is the function of the Help feature? (p. 489)
14. Which of the following is *not* true about Outlook? (p. 487)
    a. You can view your schedule by the year.
    b. You can view your schedule by the month.
    c. You can view your schedule by the week.
    d. You can view your schedule by the day.
15. To use Help in Outlook (p. 489)
    a. Open the Help menu and choose Outlook Tools.
    b. Open the Help menu and choose Outlook Help.
    c. Open the Outlook menu and choose Help.
    d. Open the Outlook menu and choose Go Online.

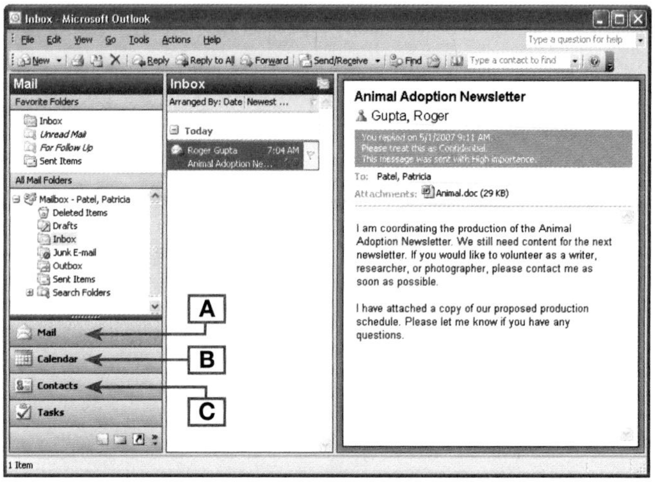

16. Match the labeled buttons on the Outlook screen with the following tasks:
    a. Check incoming messages (p. 487)
    b. View a list of stored e-mail addresses (p. 487)
    c. Switch to Day view (p. 487)
17. In the Outlook screen above, how many messages are in the Inbox? (p. 487)
18. In the Outlook screen above, whose Outlook mailbox is shown? (p. 487)

Critical Thinking

Complete the following exercises to reinforce your understanding of the lesson.

19. **Explain** Write a paragraph in which you explain how you think e-mail has changed the way people do business and communicate.
20. **Use** Use the Outlook calendar to create a weekly schedule for yourself. Include the times that your classes meet as well as time for extracurricular activities and time for homework.

ISTE Standards

The following ISTE standards are covered in Part 5. Refer to pages xxii to xxiii for a description of the standards listed here.

NETS•S	Performance Indicator
4, 5	5, 7

Sidebar

Ligatures If some letter combinations are brought close together, they interfere with each other's readability, such as the letters *f* and *i*. Ligatures are characters that combine two or more letters into a single character. The first recorded ligature is the ampersand (&). It is a combination of *e* and *t*, and *et* is the Latin for *and*.

Explain Why are some letters combined to form ligatures?

Kern Between Characters

When you work with titles or any text using a large font, you might notice that the spacing between letters looks very uneven. To fix this, you can **kern**, or adjust the space between characters.

Kerning is generally not needed for body text, since the space between letters is too small to be noticeable, but titles and headlines can look better when the spacing between letters is adjusted. Often, kerning is applied to specific letter pairs like Ve, To, Aw, and LT, which appear to have extra space around the letter combination. Sometimes graphic designers will kern to achieve an interesting effect. Basically, kerning is a purely visual art where the space surrounding the letters is adjusted to appear consistent.

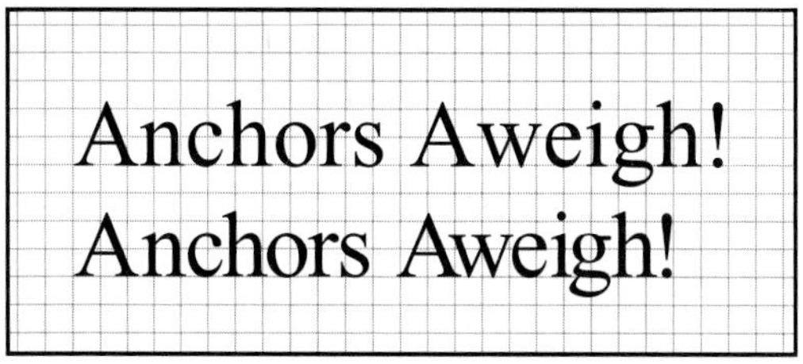

▲ The Aw pair looks better when the letters are kerned, as shown in the bottom example.

In Word, it can be hard to adjust the amount of space between characters. In later chapters you will see how specialized desktop publishing programs like Adobe Illustrator can make kerning easier.

► Portrait Orientation

▲ Landscape Orientation

Change Page Orientation

Page orientation is the direction of the page or printed document. In a **portrait orientation**, the short edge of the paper is along the top. In a **landscape orientation**, the long edge of the paper is along the top.

Different kinds of documents generally use different orientations. For example, certificates and brochures are usually printed in landscape orientation. Letters and newsletters are in portrait orientation. Flyers can be laid out in either orientation.

► **In this project,** you will create a certificate that will include a watermark and WordArt. The certificate appears to be a rather simple document, but it requires consistent and careful spacing between characters and in the layout of the text on the page.

Using Help and Other Productivity Tools

Key Terms

Help menu

Outlook, like the other applications in Microsoft Office, has many features, so it can sometimes be difficult to remember how to do something. The **Help menu** feature offers instructions and tips about many topics.

To use Help, open the Help menu and choose Outlook Help. Enter a keyword or keywords to search for the topic you want.

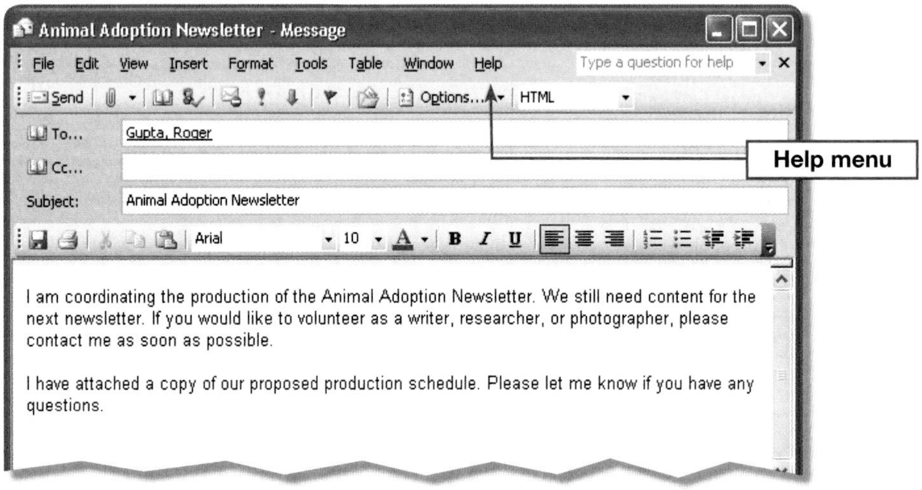

The Microsoft Office Web site provides help and other useful information.

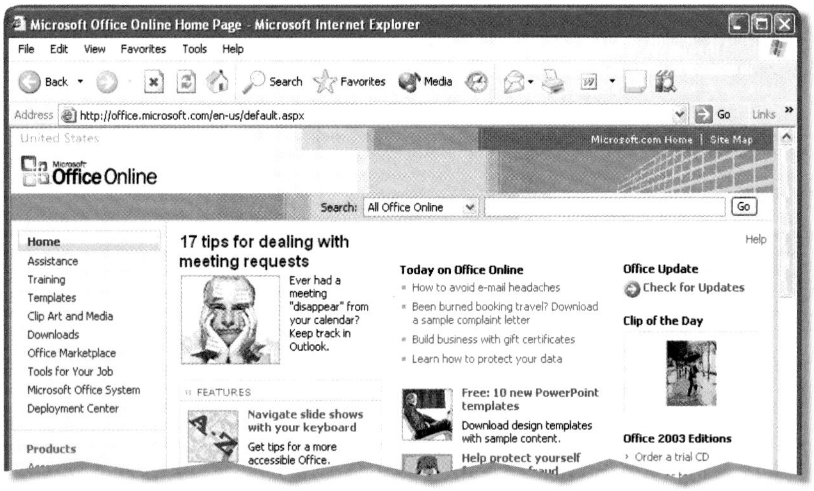

TECH CHECK

1. **Demonstrate** Use Online Help to retrieve information about sending e-mail.
2. **Demonstrate** Use the Microsoft Office Online Web site to retrieve online tools.

Student Data File

Step-by-Step

1. Open a **New** Word document, and save it according to your teacher's instructions.

Change Page Orientation

2. On the **menu** bar, click **File>Page Setup**. Click the **Margins** tab, and choose **Landscape**. Click **OK**.

Format a Page Border

3. On the **menu** bar, click **Format>Borders and Shading**. Then choose the **Page Border** tab. Click the box setting.

4. Click the **Art** drop-down menu. Choose a border like the one shown in Figure 1.20. Under the **Color** option, choose **Aqua**. Click **OK**.

Insert a Watermark

5. On the **menu** bar, click **Format>Background**. In the drop-down menu, choose **Printed Watermark**.

6. In the **Printed Watermark** box, choose **Picture Watermark**, and click the **Select Picture** button.

7. Scroll to **Data File 1-6 Watermark**. Select the file, and then click **Insert**. Click **OK**. Your document should look like Figure 1.21.

▼ **Figure 1.20** Note that the ruler changes when you change page orientation.

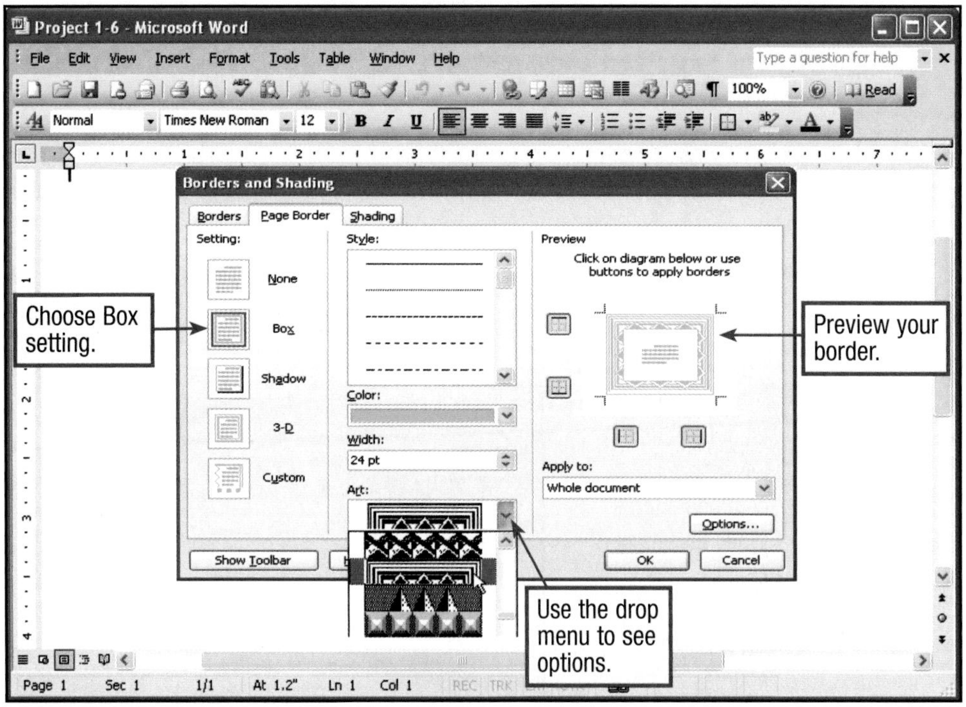
Project 1-6 - Microsoft Word
Borders and Shading
Choose Box setting.
Preview your border.
Use the drop menu to see options.

▼ **Figure 1.21** The watermark stays behind any text you add.

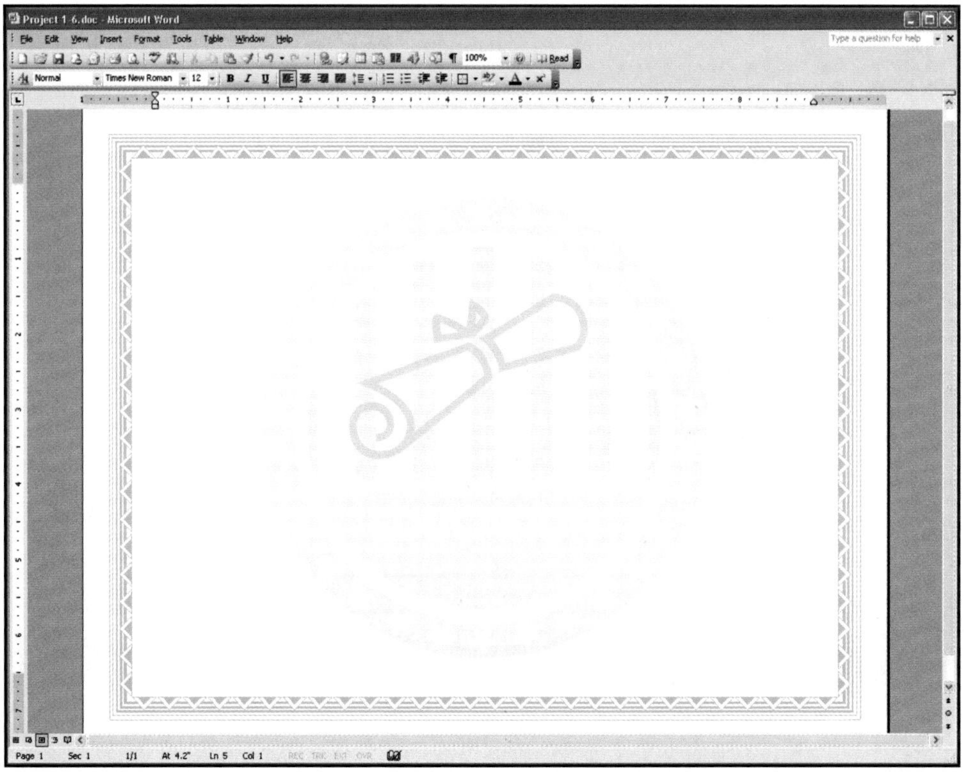

Online Communication

Key Terms
Distribution list
Instant messaging
Newsgroup

You can share information with whole groups at one time using online communication. A **newsgroup** is an online discussion group where people can discuss specific topics.

A **distribution list** identifies people who share a common interest. When an e-mail is sent to a distribution list, every e-mail address on the list receives the e-mail.

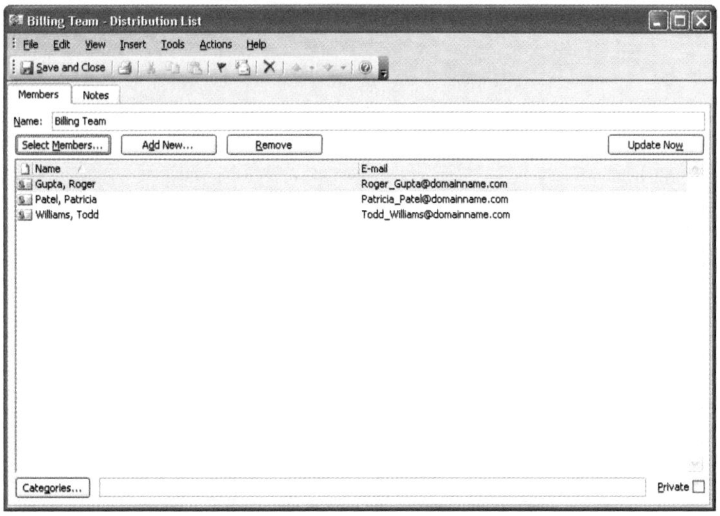

Instant messaging is like having a telephone conversation with text. As soon as you key a message, everyone in the conversation will receive it. They can then respond with their own messages.

TECH CHECK

1. **Use** Send your teacher an e-mail explaining instant messaging.
2. **Explain** How are distribution lists and newsgroups different?

8. On the **Format** toolbar, click **Center** .

Add WordArt

9. On the **menu** bar, click **Insert>Picture>WordArt**.

10. In the **WordArt Gallery**, choose the style shown in Figure 1.22. Then click **OK**.

11. In the **Edit WordArt Text** box, choose **Lucida Calligraphy**, or a similar font, **54 pt**. Then in the text box, key Certificate of Completion. Click **OK**.

▼ **Figure 1.22** WordArt provides many options for creating visually interesting text.

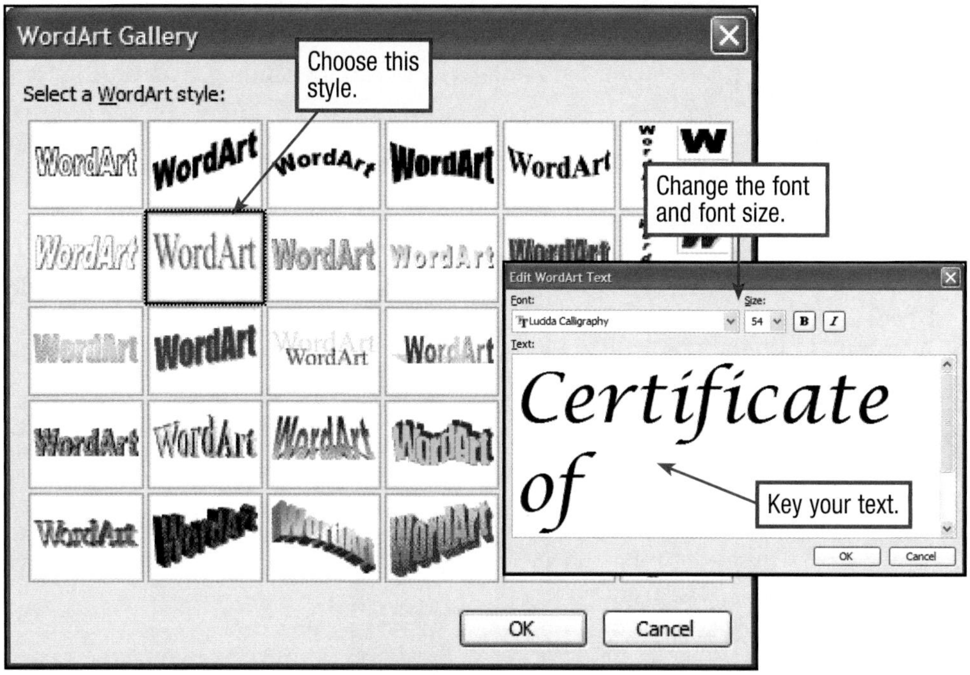

12. Click on your WordArt to show the **WordArt** toolbar. Click **Format WordArt** . Under the **Colors and Lines** tab, change the **Fill Color** to **red**.

13. Your WordArt should look like Figure 1.23. Place your insertion point below the WordArt. Press ENTER twice.

14. Change the **font** to a script typeface such as **Script MT Bold**. Change the **font size** to **48 pt**. Key your name (Figure 1.23).

▼ **Figure 1.23** Placing extra spaces below the WordArt makes it easier to add text to the document.

Microsoft Outlook

Key Terms

- **E-mail**
- **Outlook**

E-mail is a system for sending electronic messages from one computer to another. The messages can be text entered on the keyboard or they can be from files stored on a computer. Microsoft **Outlook** is a program that sends and receives e-mail.

In addition to sending and receiving e-mail, Outlook saves contact information, such as phone numbers and e-mail addresses. Outlook also has a calendar for scheduling.

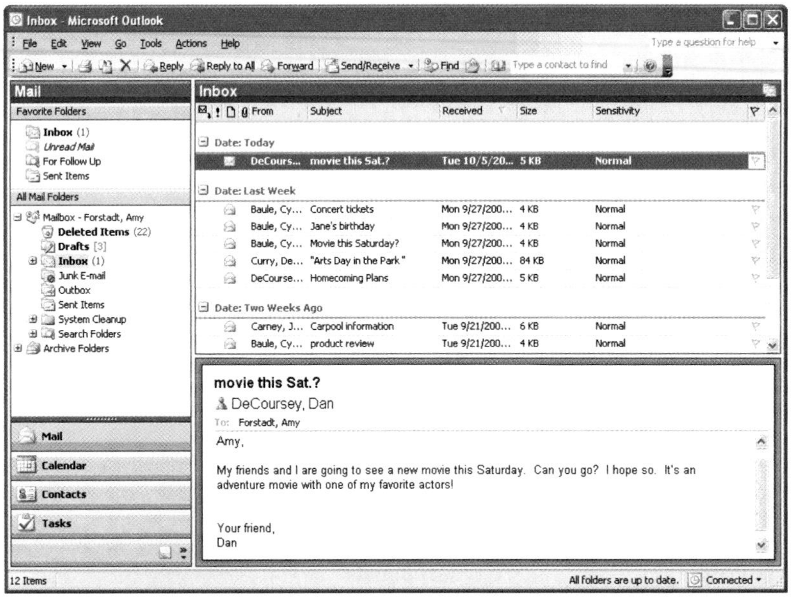

The Outlook calendar is a useful time-management tool. You can view your schedule by the month, by the week, or by the day. The Day view, shown here, allows you to schedule your time by the hour.

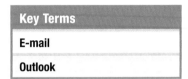

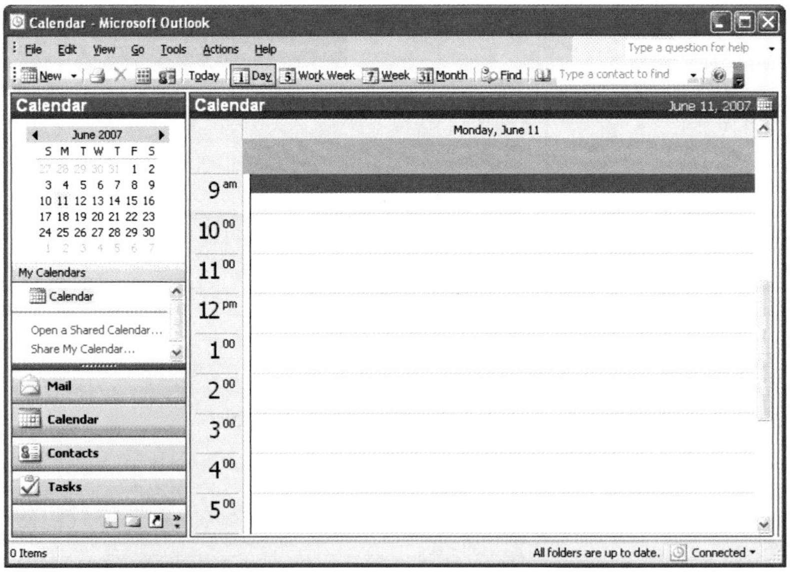

TECH CHECK

1. **Define** Define e-mail.
2. **Reproduce** Name three functions for which Outlook is useful.

15 Change the **font** to **Lucida Sans**, **28**, and then press ENTER two times. Key has completed.

16 Press ENTER twice, and change the **font size** to **36**. Key Desktop Publishing Design. Press ENTER once, and change the **font size** to **20**. Key Word Processing.

17 Click **File>Page Setup**. In the **Layout** tab under **Page**, change the **Vertical alignment** to **Center**.

Apply Kerning

18 To see how kerning affects your text, select the line *has completed*, and click **Format>Font**. Choose the **Character Spacing** tab.

19 Next to **Spacing**, click the drop-down menu arrow, and choose **Condensed** by **2 pt**. Click **OK** (Figure 1.24).

20 Select your name. Repeat steps 18 and 19 to change the **character spacing** so it is **Expanded** by **2 pt**.

21 Kern any other text that you think needs it. Follow your teacher's instructions for saving and printing your work. Your document should look similar to Figure 1.25.

▼ **Figure 1.24** Condense (reduce) or expand (increase) the space between letters.

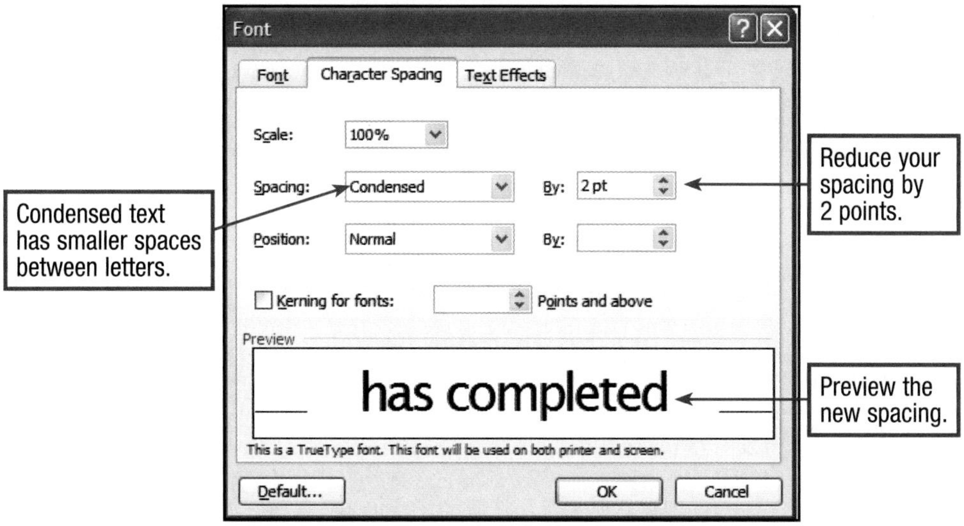

▼ **Figure 1.25** Your finished document should look like this.

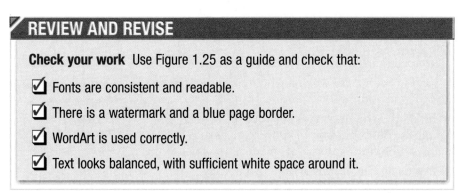

REVIEW AND REVISE

Check your work Use Figure 1.25 as a guide and check that:

☑ Fonts are consistent and readable.

☑ There is a watermark and a blue page border.

☑ WordArt is used correctly.

☑ Text looks balanced, with sufficient white space around it.

PART 4 Assessment

Key Term Review

Answer the following questions on a separate piece of paper.

1. A(n) ____________ is the software that sends and retrieves information on the Internet. (p. 483)
2. Web pages that contain information in many forms, like sound and movies, are called ____________ pages. (p. 483)
3. A(n) ____________ searches the Internet for keywords or phrases that a user enters. (p. 484)
4. ____________ states that the number of transistors in a computer circuit will double every couple of years. (p. 478)
5. A(n) ________________________ connects homes and businesses to the Internet. (p. 483)
6. Dialup, DSL, and cable are three types of ____________ that connect a computer to the Internet. (p. 483)
7. A(n) ____________ is an item on a Web page that links to another Web page. (p. 483)
8. A refrigerator that could order more eggs for you is an example of a ____________. (p. 485)
9. A(n) ____________ might have technology that automatically adjusts lights and temperature, opens doors for residents, and include motion sensors to track movement. (p. 485)

Concept Review

Answer the following questions on a separate piece of paper.

10. What was the first fully functional computer? (p. 477)
11. Describe the ENIAC, first American computer. (p. 477)
12. What was one major outcome of the increase in the number of transistors in a computer? (p. 478)
13. Explain how computers have both increased and decreased the demand for jobs. (p. 479)
14. Give one example of when it would be appropriate to key your address in a Web site. (p. 480)
15. Why should you never give out your social security number, your birth date, or your mother's maiden name without the consent of an adult? (p. 480)
16. When using e-mail, why should you not say something about someone that you would not want them to hear? (p. 481)
17. Why should you never send "spam" or junk e-mail? (p. 481)
18. What is a "flame"? (p. 481)
19. How does a search engine find information on the Internet? (p. 484)
20. How might a smart house help an elderly or disabled person? (p. 485)

Critical Thinking

Complete the following exercises to reinforce your understanding of the lesson.

21. **Defend** Is the Internet a positive or negative influence on society? Write a short three-paragraph essay in which you argue that the Internet is either a positive or negative influence on society.
22. **Compile** With a classmate, create a list of ten Web sites that would be useful for school research. All the Web sites should contain information on a variety of topics, and all of the sites should contain reliable and accurate information.
23. **Develop** Create a diagram similar to the one below. Fill in the diagram with five events in the history of computers. (p. 477)

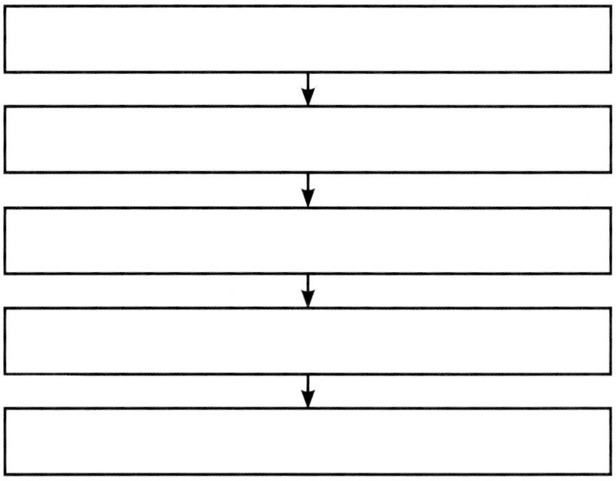

ISTE Standards

The following ISTE standards are covered in Part 4. Refer to pages xxii to xxiii for a description of the standards listed here.

NETS•S	Performance Indicator
2	1, 3, 4

Project 1-7

Create a Business Flyer

Spotlight on Skills

- Adjust leading
- Add a bulleted list
- Kern text
- Insert page numbers

Key Terms

- leading
- bullet

Academic Focus

Math
Calculate line spacing

Effective business documents should make it easy to find and interpret information. Lay out information clearly by using proper line spacing and, when appropriate, present your important points as lists.

Determine Line Spacing

Back in the days of movable-type printing presses, printers would separate lines of text by putting lead strips between them. The process of spacing lines of text came to be known as **leading** (rhymes with *wedding*). Today, many modern word processors call this process *line spacing*.

Although leading refers to the space between lines, it is actually measured from the baseline of a line of text to the baseline of the text below it. Generally, leading is 120–150 percent of the font size, though that can vary depending upon the type of font. Many programs will automatically choose leading for particular fonts, though they also allow you to set your own spacing.

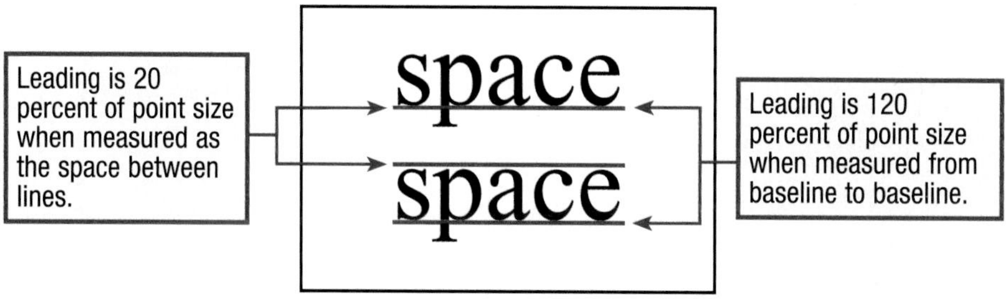
Leading is 20 percent of point size when measured as the space between lines.
space
space
Leading is 120 percent of point size when measured from baseline to baseline.

▲ Leading is sometimes measured as the space between lines, and sometimes it is measured as the distance between baselines.

With a 120 percent leading, if your font size is 10 points, the measurement between baselines is 12 points (10 pt font × 1.20 = 12 pt leading). You can also say that the actual space between lines is 20 percent of the font size. In other words, a 10 point font would have a 2 point space between lines (10 pt font + 2 pt space = 12 pt leading).

If the leading is too tight, readers will find the material too dense and too hard to read without a comfortable amount of white space between the lines. If line spacing is set way too close, even the letters themselves may not have enough room to be displayed.

If the leading is too wide, readers will find that the material is too slow to read, taking too much time to track and find the next line after reading the previous one. In fact, it becomes difficult to follow the train of thought.

▲ Poor leading makes a document hard to read.

Sidebar

Percent Leading The following kinds of text may require more than 120 percent leading:

- Larger or higher fonts
- Very small type
- Sans serif type
- Bold type
- Long lines of text
- Audience needs

Draw Conclusions Why might small fonts need more than 120 percent leading?

Emerging Technology

Key Terms
Smart appliance
Smart house

Computer technology is constantly changing. Today, many workers carry a laptop PC, a cell phone, and a PDA. Single, small devices able to do the work of all three are gaining in popularity. With improvements in wireless technology, workers are able to work in many different places—the kitchen table, a park bench, or a lounge chair by the pool.

Smart appliances with computers that are connected to the Internet are also becoming a reality. Refrigerators could warn you when the milk is about to spoil, order more eggs for you, or schedule a repair visit. Microwaves could have an Internet browser to search the Web for recipes. Such inventions could lead to **smart houses** with networks that control Internet-enabled appliances. Technology already exists to automatically monitor and adjust lights, temperature, and TV or stereo volume. Smart houses might be able to open doors automatically for an elderly or disabled resident. A smart house might include motion sensors to track movement—if they detect no motion for a certain amount of time, the house could call for help in case the person has fallen or lost consciousness.

TECH CHECK

1. **Define** What is a smart appliance?
2. **Predict** Name three features that a smart house might have.
3. **Create** Draw a diagram of your own smart appliance. Label all of its features.

Create Lists

Putting information into lists can help readers immediately see the most important points. The two kinds of lists you will usually find in documents are bulleted lists and numbered lists.

Bulleted Lists present information in no particular order. For example, if you listed the contents of your backpack, the order would not matter. In front of each item on the list is a **bullet**, which is a character such as a dot or diamond.

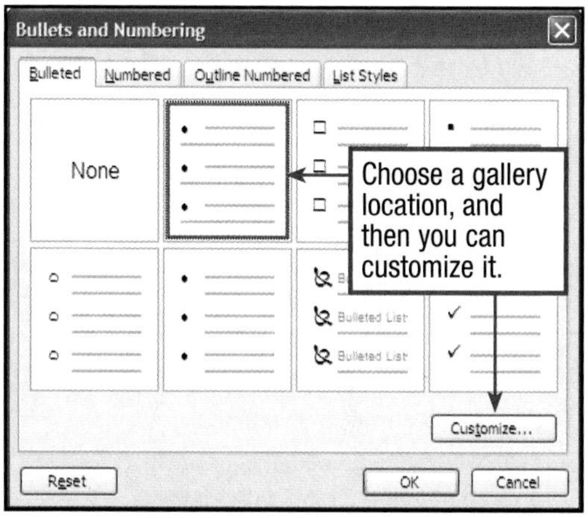

▲ You can customize the bullets or numbers you use in a list.

Numbered Lists present information in a specific order, such as steps or ranking. For example, if you listed your classes, you might want to format them as a numbered list by period.

When you add bullets (or numbers) to a document, Microsoft Word automatically changes the horizontal ruler to align the bullets and text. If the text and bullets in your list do not align the way you like, you can adjust them by clicking **Format>Bullets and Numbering**. From this dialog box, you can change settings and bullet or number styles.

You can also adjust spacing and alignment by using the horizontal ruler. The ruler displays and lets you adjust indents, tabs, and margins in any part of a document. Generally, the space between text and a bullet or number is about 0.2 inches. The text usually is aligned to the right of the bullet or number, as shown below.

Sidebar

Apply Parallel Structure When you create a list, you should always try to have all the items in it follow the same grammatical structure. For example, in the document you create in this project (see Figure 1.32), each list item completes the sentence that starts the paragraph. Therefore, each item uses wording that sounds correct when added to the sentence. In this case, the items all start with a verb. Since they complete a sentence, they all end with a period.

Compose Use parallel structure to write a new item for the bulleted list in Figure 1.32 (on page 35).

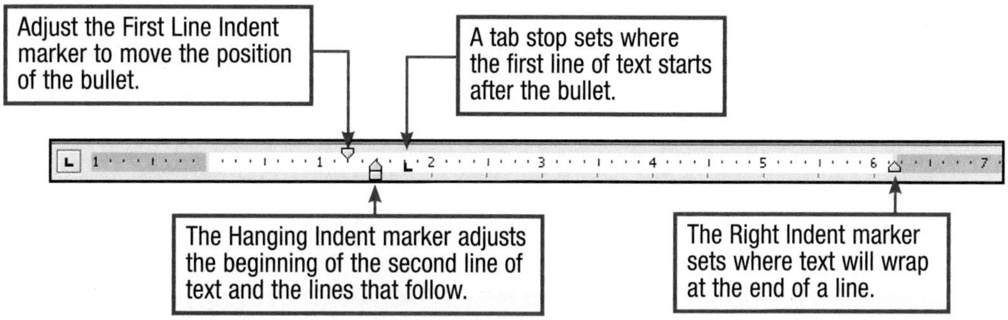

Adjust the First Line Indent marker to move the position of the bullet.
A tab stop sets where the first line of text starts after the bullet.
The Hanging Indent marker adjusts the beginning of the second line of text and the lines that follow.
The Right Indent marker sets where text will wrap at the end of a line.

▲ Use the ruler to adjust indents and text alignment.

▶ **In this project,** you will create one page of an annual report for an imaginary company, HypothetiCo. Annual reports analyze a company's performance for shareholders, managers, and investors to see. Your report will include graphics and a bulleted list.

Navigating the Internet Continued

The Internet contains so much information that it is often hard to find what you are looking for. **Search engines** search the Internet for keywords that you provide.

In addition to the search engine in Internet Explorer, there are several very good search engines such as Google, on the Internet. Regardless of which search engine you use, it is important for you to be able to search effectively.

Click here to use the search engine Internet Explorer

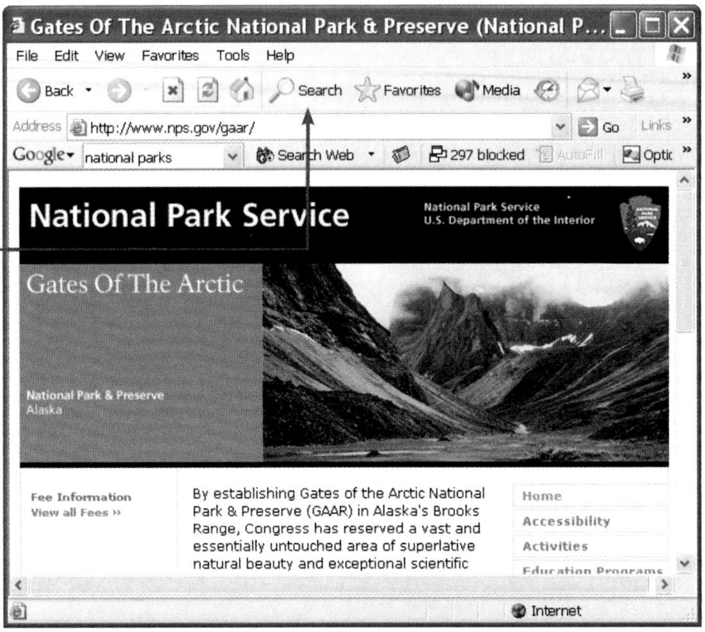

The first step towards searching effectively is choosing appropriate keywords. When you are searching for something that is not easily summed up in one word, you can enter two or more words.

Many search engines also have an advanced search that allows you to indicate exactly what you want the engine to search for and what you want it to ignore.

Different types of searches

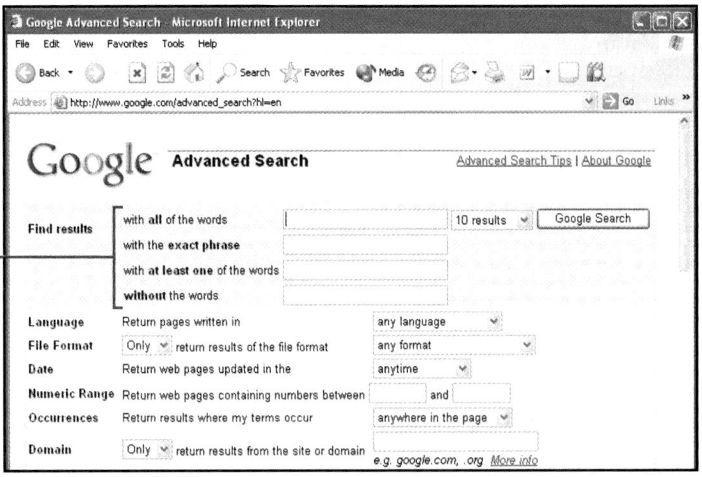

TECH CHECK

1. **Define** What is a browser?
2. **Explain** Why are bookmarks useful?
3. **Predict** Describe a situation in which it would be best to use an advanced search.

Student Data File

Step-by-Step

1. Open **Data File 1-7a**, and save it according to your teacher's instructions.

2. Change the title's font size to **24 pt** and **center** it.

3. Select the body text and **justify** the alignment.

Adjust Leading

4. Click **Format>Paragraph** and choose the **Indent and Spacing** tab.

5. Change the **After** setting to **6**. Click the arrow below **Line Spacing** to change it to **At least** and choose **15 pt**. Your document should look similar to Figure 1.26.

6. Reformat the information in the second paragraph into a list, as shown in Figure 1.27. Press ENTER between each item in the list.

▼ **Figure 1.26** Before and After spacing is applied when you insert a hard return (press the Enter key) between lines.

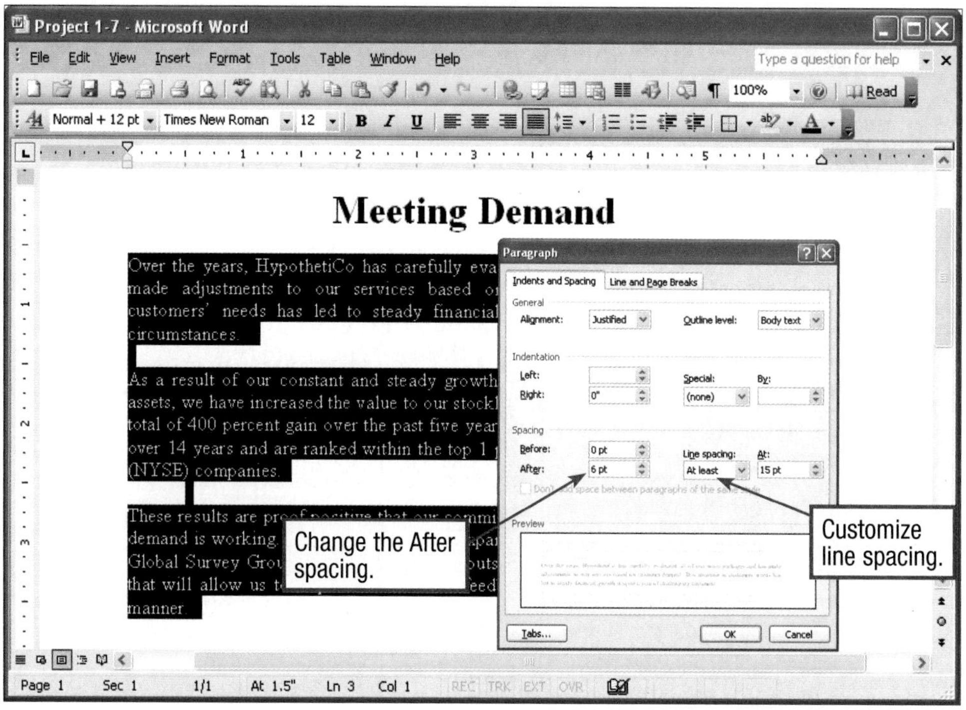

▼ **Figure 1.27** There should be a hard return between each item in the list.

Meeting Demand

Over the years, HypothetiCo has carefully evaluated all of our travel packages and has made adjustments to our services based on customer demand. This attention to customers' needs has led to steady financial growth despite a year of challenging circumstances.

As a result of our constant and steady growth and our policy of reinvesting in capital assets, we have:

Increased the value to our stockholders by 150 percent last year.

Gained a total of 400 percent gain over the past five years.

Paid a consistent dividend for over 14 years.

Been ranked within the top 1 percent of all New York Stock Exchange (NYSE) companies.

These results are proof positive that our commitment to quality and to meeting customer demand is working. This year, we plan to expand this business model by partnering with Global Survey Group (GSG). GSG has an outstanding record for providing quality data that will allow us to respond to customer feedback in a more timely and cost-effective manner.

Using the Internet

Key Terms

- Browser
- Hyperlink
- ISP (Internet Service Provider)
- Modem
- Multimedia page
- Search engine

Computers are connected to the Internet in different ways. Homes and businesses pay an **ISP, or Internet Service Provider,** to connect to the Internet. A **modem** allows a computer to be connected to the Internet. Dialup modems and DSL modems use phone lines to connect to the Internet. A cable modem uses cable TV wires to connect. A **browser** is the software that sends and retrieves information on the Internet. Study the figure below to learn about some important browser functions.

A **hyperlink** is an item on a Web page that links to another Web page. When you click a hyperlink, the browser will display the page the hyperlink connects to.

The Favorites menu allows you to bookmark Web pages. A bookmark sends the browser automatically to a page that you specify. Web pages that contain information in many forms, like sound and movies, are called **multimedia pages**.

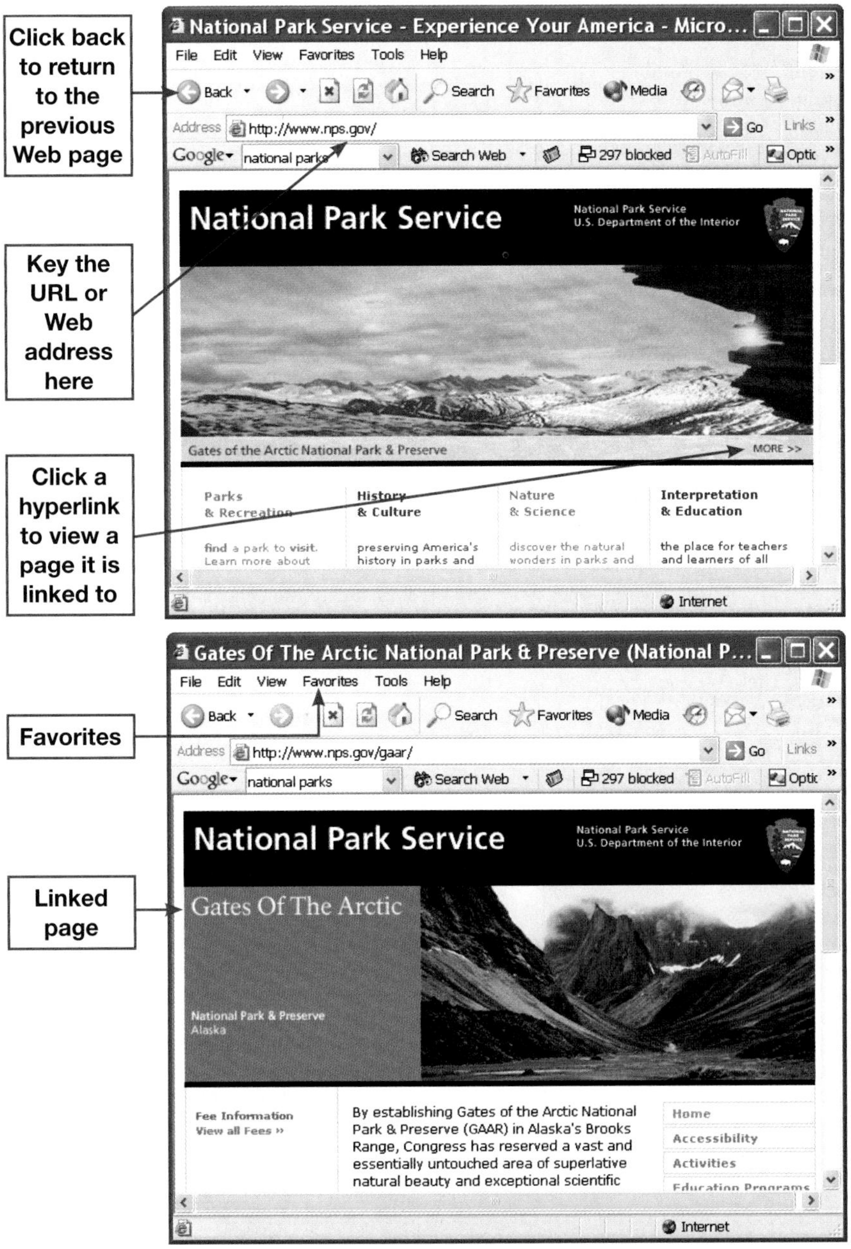

Add a Bulleted List

7 **Select** the list, then click **Format>Bullets and Numbering**. Click any option except None. Then choose the **Customize** button.

8 In the Customize Bulleted List box, set the **Bullet position** to **0.25**. Change both **Text position** settings to **0.5**.

9 In the **Customize Bulleted List** box, click the **Character** button to open the **Symbol** box.

10 Change the font to **Wingdings**, then scroll to find a bullet similar to the one in Figure 1.28. Click the symbol, and then click **OK** to insert the bullets.

Kern Text

11 The title needs to be kerned. Select the **M** in *Meeting*. Click **Format>Font**. Then choose the **Character Spacing** tab. Change **Spacing** to **Condensed** by **1 pt**.

12 Kern the **D** in *Demand*. Continue adjusting the spacing until all letters appear to be equally separated. (**Note:** Spacing will vary depending on the font.) (Figure 1.29)

▼ **Figure 1.28** Customize your list's bullets and indents.

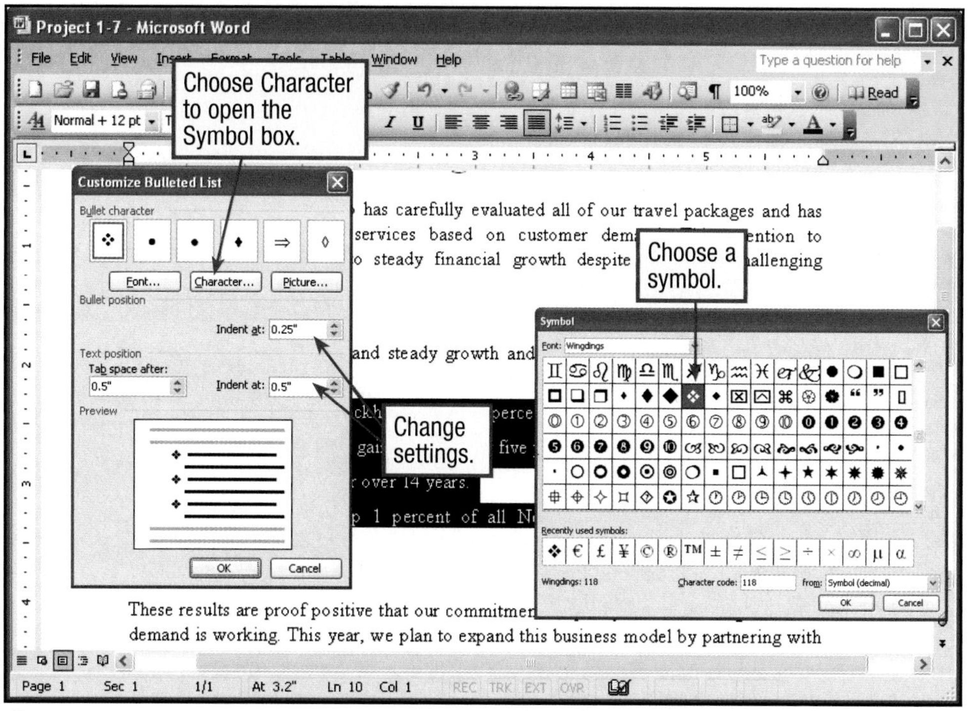

▼ **Figure 1.29** It may take a few tries to adjust spacing between characters.

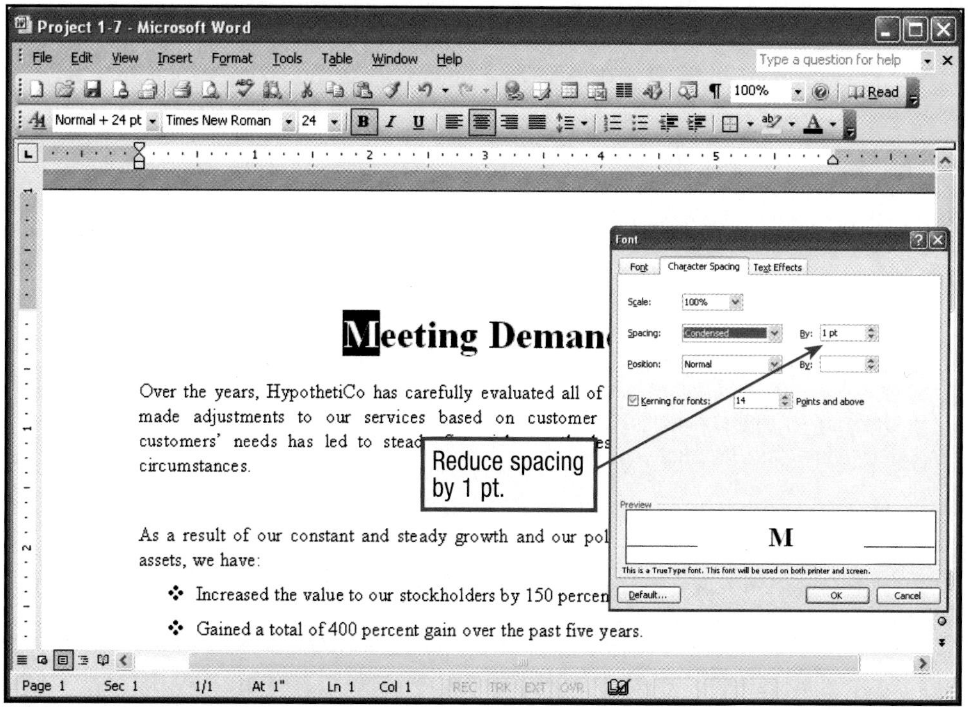

Ethics and Technology

Computers can be used to do wonderful things, but they can also be misused. Knowing some simple ethical guidelines will ensure that you are always doing the right thing.

USING THE INTERNET RESPONSIBLY

- ✓ Because your school may have a fast Internet connection, you may be tempted to use these connections to download large files. Check with your teacher first, as there may be policies forbidding this.
- ✓ Remember that the school computer is there to help you get your work done. If you instead use the computer to play games, check your personal e-mail, or look at offensive material on the Internet, you are inappropriately using the resource that is being provided for you.
- ✓ If you engage in inappropriate activity on a school computer, you could be suspended from school, or perhaps even prosecuted.
- ✓ Do not do anything on a computer that you would not do if your teacher or parents were standing behind you, watching.
- ✓ E-mail systems leave a "digital paper trail." This means that what you type into an e-mail can be found by a system administrator. Be sure not to abuse company or school e-mail systems—it may come back to haunt you!
- ✓ You would not steal office supplies from your office or school, so make sure you do not take home computer-related resources like CD-ROMs or floppy disks.
- ✓ If you download any files or applications, be sure to check with your system administrator before using them. Downloaded files are a chief source of viruses, which cause millions of dollars in damages to computer networks every year.
- ✓ Avoid plagiarism, or copying someone else's work. It is acceptable to quote online sources in your work, but you must make sure you identify those sources and give them proper credit.
- ✓ Follow copyright laws. If you want to use part of an online work that has been copyrighted, contact the Webmaster of the site or the author of the article to request permission.
- ✓ It is not legal to download copyrighted music and videos and share them for free. Only use legal file sharing sites, which usually charge a small fee.
- ✓ If you need graphic images for a document you are creating, look for sources of license-free images that you do not have to pay to use. The owner of the image should be able to provide proof of ownership of the image and grant or deny permission to use it. If you cannot get this type of documentation in writing, do not use the image.
- ✓ Evaluate the information listed in a Web site. Sites that include bibliographical information tend to be more reliable.
- ✓ Do not engage in cyberbullying. Cyberbullying involves using the Internet or other digital communication devices to send or post information that is harmful or cruel. It might include harassment, put-downs, or making private information about an individual public. Be sure to report any instances of cyberbullying.
- ✓ Do not interfere with or tamper with anyone else's computer files.
- ✓ Always show consideration and respect for others in the way you use your computer.

TECH CHECK

1. **Explain** What is a "digital paper trail"?
2. **Predict** When is it acceptable to quote from someone else's work?
3. **Analyze** Why do you think music companies are trying to stop illegal downloading of music files?

13 Click in front of the word *Meeting*, and press ENTER to create a blank line above the title. Move the cursor back up to the blank line.

14 Click **Insert>Picture>From File**, and browse to **Data File 1-7b**. Double-click the file to insert the HypothetiCo logo (Figure 1.30).

15 Place your insertion point between paragraphs 1 and 2. Then click **Insert>Picture>From File** to insert **Data File 1-7c**.

16 Center the logo and graph by selecting the image and clicking **Center** (Figure 1.31).

Figure 1.30 A logo is a combination of text and graphics.

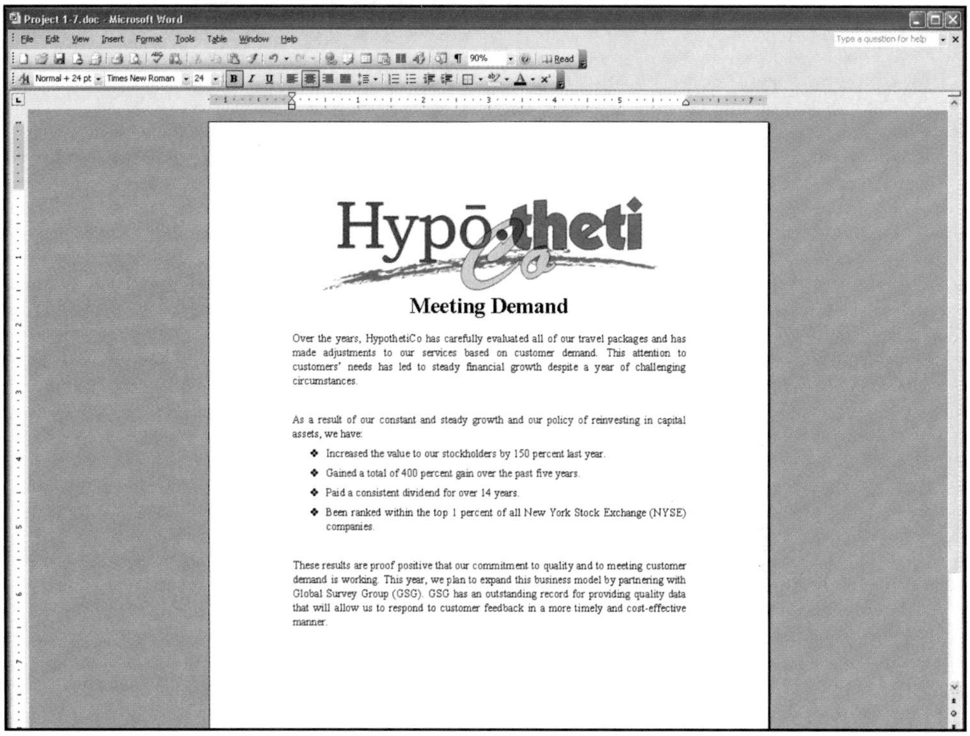

17 Place your insertion point at the end of the document. Click **Insert>Picture>From File** to insert **Data File 1-7d**, the sidebar image. (**Note:** Do not worry if your page layout shifts. Just continue to the next step.)

18 Select the sidebar picture, and then click **Format>Picture**. In the **Layout** tab, change the layout to **Square**.

19 Click and drag the green rotate handle at the top of the picture. (Figure 1.31) Rotate the picture so that the star is at the top.

Figure 1.31 Graphs and charts convey information visually.

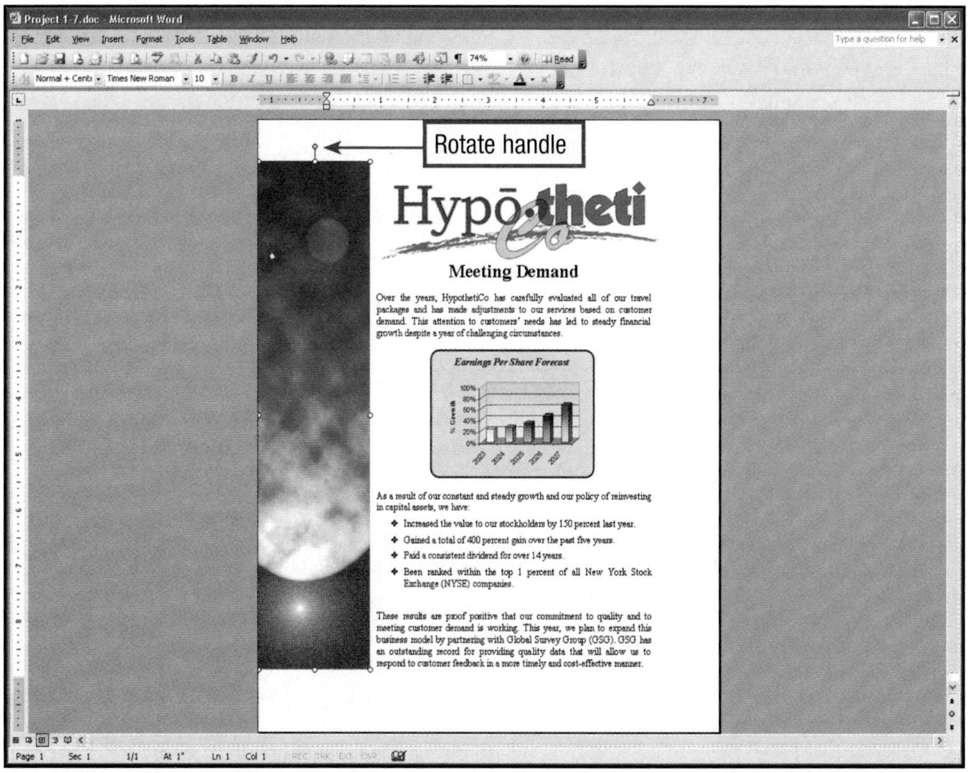

Netiquette

New rules of etiquette have evolved for the communication media provided by the Internet: e-mail, chat rooms, and newsgroups. Nicknamed "netiquette," these basic guidelines are important to keep in mind whenever you are communicating with someone online.

NETIQUETTE GUIDELINES

E-MAIL

- ✓ Do not send large attachments, unless the recipient is expecting them.
- ✓ When forwarding e-mails, trim off unnecessary information like old headers and quotes—these can build up quickly!
- ✓ Do not say anything about someone that you would not want them to hear. Even after you click Delete, the e-mail is not really gone. E-mail records stay in the system for a long time.
- ✓ Never send or forward chain letters. Even if they seem like a good idea, they are often fraudulent.
- ✓ Do not "spam." Spam, or junk e-mail, is a billion-dollar problem, clogging e-mail systems and wasting time. Do not add to the problem.
- ✓ Do not SHOUT. Make sure your Caps Lock key is off.

CHAT ROOMS

- ✓ Choose chat rooms wisely. Some chat rooms have questionable people, so do some research first.
- ✓ Behave in a chat room as though you were communicating face-to-face. Remember that words can be misinterpreted, and things like sarcasm and body language may not come across online.
- ✓ Do not threaten, harass, or abuse any participants in a chat room.
- ✓ Take turns with the conversation. Just like in a real conversation, allow people to finish their thoughts, and do not interrupt.
- ✓ Be aware of "lurkers," people who are reading the conversation but not taking part.

NEWSGROUPS

- ✓ Stay on topic. Most newsgroups are very specific, and readers do not appreciate posts (contributed information) that do not fit the topic.
- ✓ Do not "flame." A flame is an aggressive or insulting letter. People in newsgroups often get passionate or excited in these conversations, which makes it easy to flame. Never key something that you would not want to say out loud.
- ✓ Know your facts. There is no fact-checking process in newsgroups. Just because someone makes a statement does not mean it is true. Remember this when quoting or replying to someone.
- ✓ Behave online as you normally would—honestly, ethically, and wisely.

TECH CHECK

1. **Predict** What information will you need to give if you order something online?
2. **Summarize** What are some general "netiquette" rules?
3. **Discuss** Write a paragraph that discusses the benefits and dangers of the Internet.

20 Click and drag the picture to the left side of the page, as shown in Figure 1.32.

21 Position and resize the sidebar graphic so that it looks like Figure 1.32.

Insert Page Numbers

22 Click **Insert>Page Numbers**.

23 Under **Position**, choose **Bottom of Page**. For **Alignment**, choose **Right**. Click **OK**. (**Note:** If you added more pages to this document, each page would be numbered sequentially.)

24 Your document should look similar to Figure 1.32. Save and print your work according to your teacher's instructions.

▼ **Figure 1.32** The final document.

HypōtheticCo

Meeting Demand

Over the years, HypotheticCo has carefully evaluated all of our travel packages and has made adjustments to our services based on customer demand. This attention to customers' needs has led to steady financial growth despite a year of challenging circumstances.

As a result of our constant and steady growth and our policy of reinvesting in capital assets, we have:

- ❖ Increased the value to our stockholders by 150 percent last year.
- ❖ Gained a total of 400 percent over the past five years.
- ❖ Paid a consistent dividend for over 14 years.
- ❖ Been ranked within the top 1 percent of all New York Stock Exchange (NYSE) companies.

These results are proof positive that our commitment to quality and to meeting customer demand is working. This year, we plan to expand this business model by partnering with Global Survey Group (GSG). GSG has an outstanding record for providing quality data that will allow us to respond to customer feedback in a more timely and cost-effective manner.

1

REVIEW AND REVISE

Check your work Use Figure 1.32 as a guide and check that:

- ☑ Line spacing makes text readable and attractive.
- ☑ Content in the bulleted list is written and aligned correctly.
- ☑ Graphics are effectively laid out.
- ☑ A page number is inserted in the lower right corner.

Staying Safe Online

The Internet can be a wonderful place. There is much to learn, explore, and discover. But it can also be a dangerous place. Many Web sites seek information from their users. Although some of these Web sites are legitimate, there are many questionable sites that are looking for data as well. Before you key any information into an online form or chat room, you need to evaluate that Web site. Take the following precautions to stay safe online.

Know to whom you are giving the information. Check the URL in your browser. Does it match the domain you visited? Or were you redirected to another site without your knowledge?

Why are you giving the information? For example, if you are ordering something online, you will need to give your address in order for the product to be shipped. There should always be a good reason for all the information you provide.

Never give out your social security number, your birth date, or your mother's maiden name without adult consent. This information is often used to secure credit reports, and giving this information to a dishonest source can ruin your credit.

Never give personal information of any sort to someone you meet in a chat room. Always remain anonymous.

If you are still unsure whether it is safe to give the information, check with a parent or another trusted adult.

Project 1-8

Design with Symbols

Spotlight on Skills

- Create a numbered list
- Insert symbols

Key Term

- dingbats

Academic Focus

Math
Use math symbols and fractions

Recipes require certain elements that you will find useful in other documents too. Since they almost always follow a step-by-step process, you generally need to format a recipe as a numbered list. Recipes also use special characters such as fractions for measurements and symbols such as degree (°) signs.

Add Symbols and Special Characters

Many symbols, such as the dollar sign ($), asterisk (*), and percent (%), can be accessed through the keyboard. However, there are many other symbols that you cannot find on your keyboard, such as the ¢ sign. Also, if you were to key a fraction, you could key 7/8, but not ⅞.

You can find these symbols through the Insert menu. Click **Insert>Symbol** to open the Symbol box, as shown in the figure.

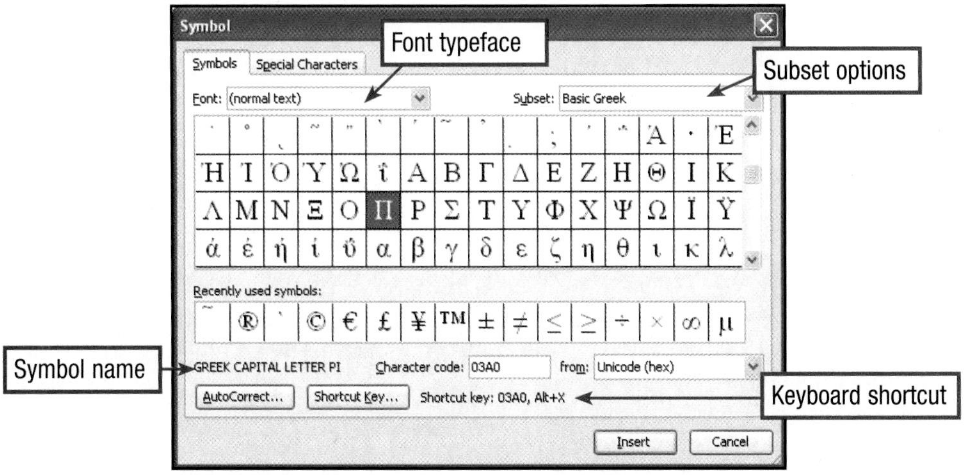

▲ You can use the Subset option to find specific types of characters.

You will find many of the same symbols in different fonts, though some fonts support some symbols that other fonts do not. The Wingdings and Webdings fonts also include a variety of graphic icons and symbols, called **dingbats**.

Symbols are grouped into categories, and you can use the Subset option to help locate them. For example, there are categories for mathematical operators, currency symbols, and punctuation marks. Click on one of these subsets to look for specific types of characters.

If you use a character a lot, you might prefer to learn its shortcut on the keyboard. When you click a symbol in the Symbol box, a shortcut is displayed, usually with a number sequence. Hold the ALT key, and then key the numbers on the keypad. (Make sure Num Lock NUM LOCK is on when you use the keypad.)

Eye On Ethics

Legal Symbols Companies and individuals protect their work, names, or logos by adding symbols such as © (copyright), ® (registered trademark), or ™ (trademark). When you see these symbols, it means you cannot use the material without permission from the owner.

You can use keystrokes to create these symbols in Word.

©	Ctrl+Alt+C
®	Ctrl+Alt+R
™	Ctrl+Alt+T

Identify What do the copyright, registered, and trademark symbols signify?

Impact of Computers on Society Continued

Computers have changed the world. They have changed everything from shopping, to movies, to the kinds of jobs that are available.

Overall, computers have made it easier for businesses to exchange information. E-mail and access to information, such as stock market data, has increased the speed of business. Computers have made surveillance (monitoring and watching people) easier than ever. Privacy and security issues are being debated in courtrooms every day. Data is being collected on millions of people and sold to virtually all types of businesses. People who work together today do not have to do so at the same time. Many services and information are available 24 hours per day. Technologists believe that we have only begun to imagine the impact of computers on our society.

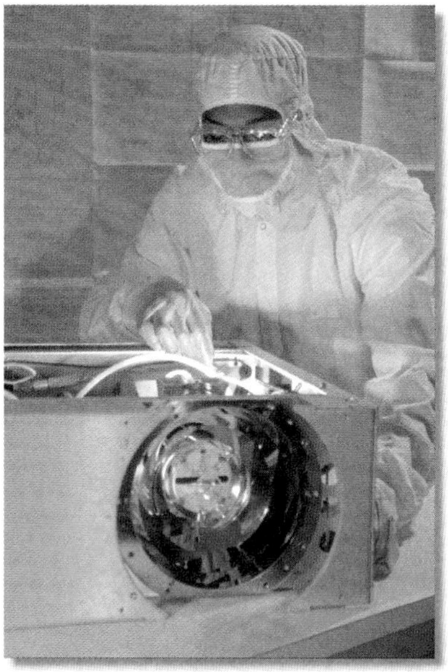

There are dozens of jobs that help people keep computers running smoothly. People are also needed to create software for computers.

In addition to creating new jobs, computers have decreased the demand for other jobs. Computers have reduced the number of bank tellers, telephone operators, mail sorters, and loan interviewers.

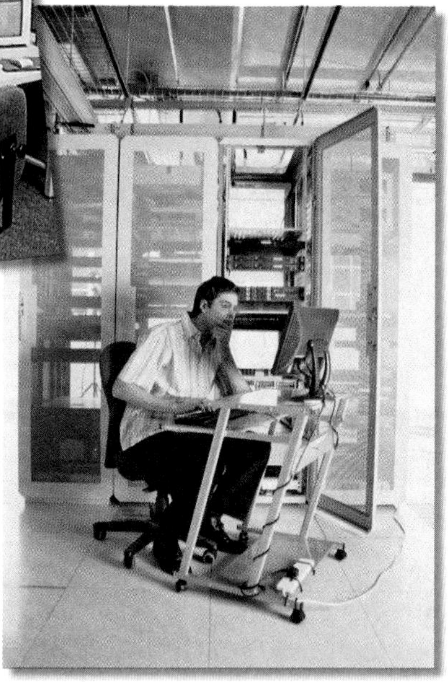

TECH CHECK

1. **Reproduce** What is Moore's Law?
2. **Summarize** Write a paragraph that summarizes the invention and development of computers.
3. **Discuss** Write a paragraph that discusses the positive and negative impacts that computers have had on society.

Sidebar

Format Automatically Word can automatically format certain keystrokes as symbols. Click **Tools>AutoCorrect Options**. AutoCorrect allows you to automatically apply formatting styles, such as changing hyphens to dashes. Click the **AutoCorrect** tab to find what keystrokes to use to insert symbols such as ☺ or →. Make sure the *Replace text as you type* box is checked, and try some keystrokes for yourself.

Explain What does the AutoCorrect tool allow you to do?

Options for Dashes and Fractions

Insert Dashes Many people do not realize that there are actually three kinds of dashes. You can learn about these in the table below. En and Em dashes can both be found by clicking the **Insert>Symbol>Special Characters** tab.

Create Dashes

Type of Dash	Use	Keyboard Shortcut
Hyphen (-)	To hyphenate words like e-mail or break a word into syllables.	Hyphen key is on the top row of the keyboard
En Dash (–)	To show a range: The recipe serves 2–4 people.	Hold ALT and key 0150 on the numeric keypad. Or, use CTRL + − (minus sign on numeric keypad)
Em Dash (—)	To indicate a sudden break in thought or to add emphasis to a sentence: Tea cakes—despite the name—taste best with milk.	Hold ALT and key 0150 on the numeric keypad. Or, use ALT CTRL + − (minus sign on numeric keypad)

Format Fractions While Microsoft Word recognizes many fractions and will instantly convert numbers like 1/2 to ½, there are instances where Word will not recognize a particular fraction. You can turn on or off automatic formatting of fractions in the **AutoFormat** dialog box. Some of these fractions can be found through **Insert>Symbol**, in the Number Forms subset category.

▼ You can find some fractions in the Symbols options.

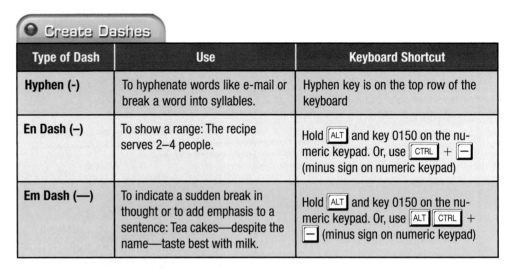

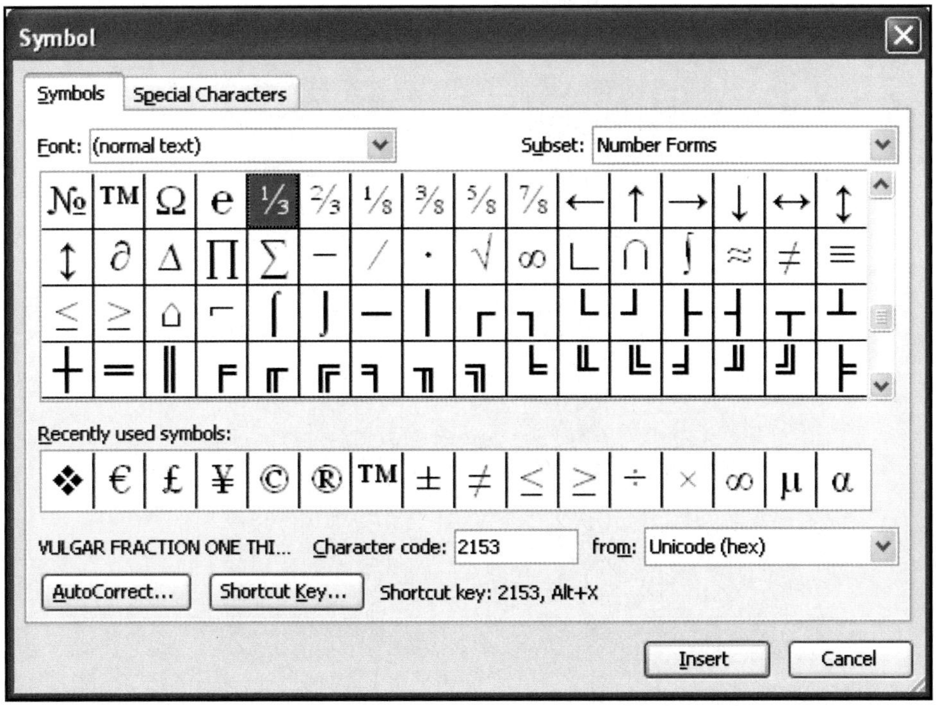

You can also format fractions by using the following steps:

- Key the fraction, like 1/7.
- Select the top number (numerator), click **Format>Font**, and choose **Superscript**. This moves the number above the baseline, like $^{1}/7$.
- Select the bottom number (denominator), click **Format>Font**, then choose **Subscript**. Your fraction is now complete and should look like $^{1}/_{7}$.

Impact of Computers on Society Continued

Moore's Law

Computers were mostly used by large businesses and by the government until the mid-1970s when personal computers were first built. However, in 1965 Gordon Moore made a prediction that became known as **Moore's Law**. Moore predicted that the number of transistors in computer circuits would double every couple of years. As it turns out, his prediction has been fairly accurate.

The increase in the number of transistors made it possible for computers to become much smaller than the ENIAC and the Harvard mark I. Compared to the room-filling ENIAC, today's laptops are about the size of a coffee table book. And they are far more powerful. An average laptop today is about 300,000 times faster than the ENIAC.

Circuit board used in the 1960s.

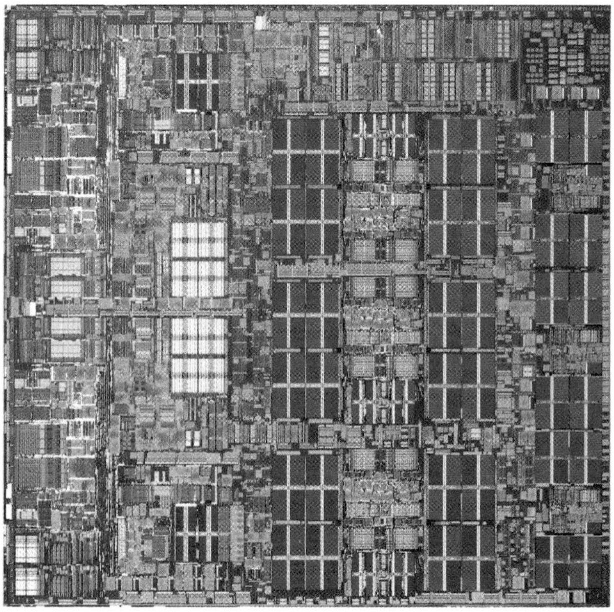

Recent circuit board.

Student Data File

Step-by-Step

1. Open **Data File 1-8a**, and save it according to your teacher's instructions.

2. Format the text as shown in Figure 1.33.

Create a Numbered List

3. Select the text under *Directions*, then click **Numbering** on the **Formatting** toolbar to automatically number the items in the list.

4. Key the following step after Step 6: Let cool for 2 minutes before removing from cookie sheet. (The list should automatically renumber.)

Insert Symbols

5. Replace text with the highlighted symbols shown in Figure 1.33.

6. Select the step-by-step instructions. Click **Format>Paragraph**. Set both the **Before** and **After** spacing to **6 pt**. (**Note:** Do not use double spacing!)

7. Format the title *Tea Cakes* in a **sans serif** font similar to the one in Figure 1.33.

▼ **Figure 1.33** Use the information called out in this example to format the recipe.

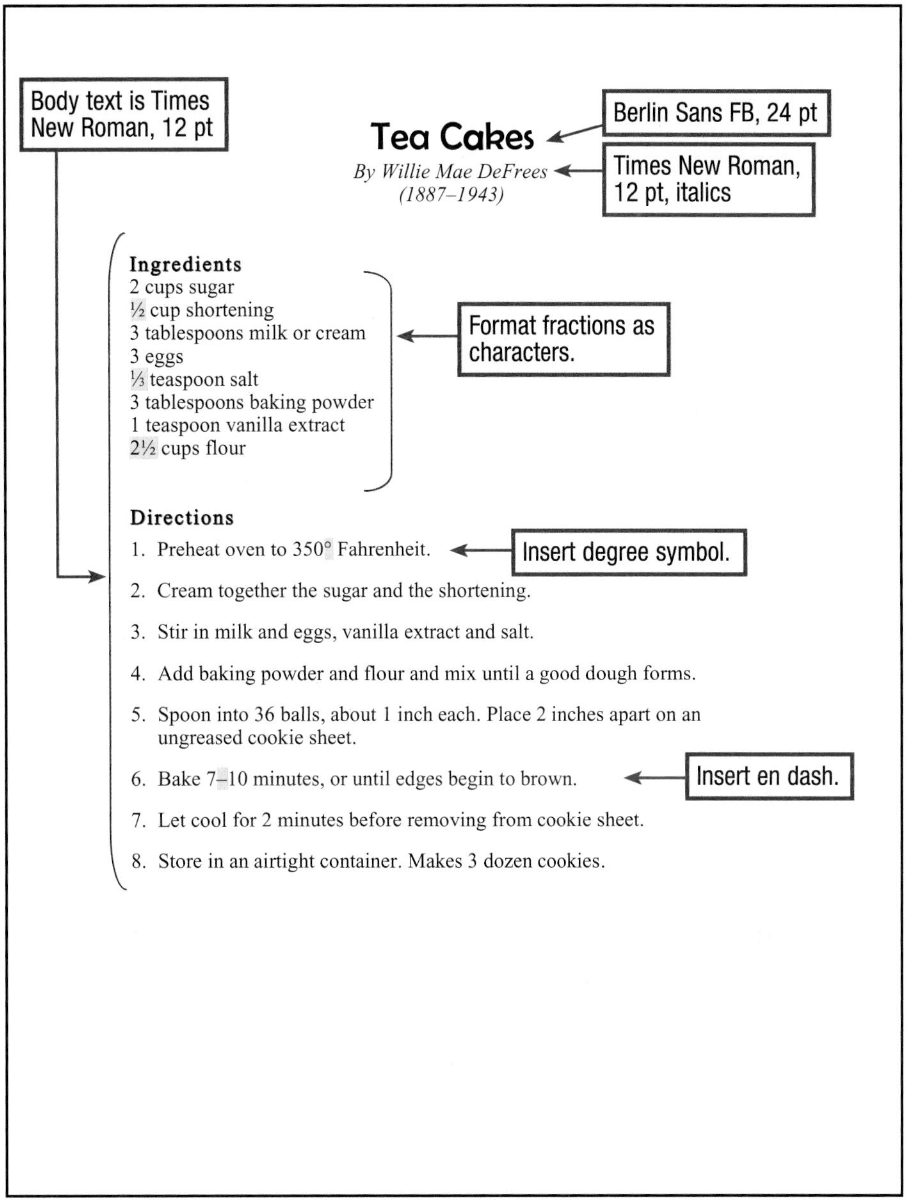

Body text is Times New Roman, 12 pt

Tea Cakes ← Berlin Sans FB, 24 pt

By Willie Mae DeFrees ← Times New Roman, 12 pt, italics
(1887–1943)

Ingredients
2 cups sugar
½ cup shortening
3 tablespoons milk or cream
3 eggs
⅓ teaspoon salt
3 tablespoons baking powder
1 teaspoon vanilla extract
2½ cups flour

← Format fractions as characters.

Directions

1. Preheat oven to 350° Fahrenheit. ← Insert degree symbol.
2. Cream together the sugar and the shortening.
3. Stir in milk and eggs, vanilla extract and salt.
4. Add baking powder and flour and mix until a good dough forms.
5. Spoon into 36 balls, about 1 inch each. Place 2 inches apart on an ungreased cookie sheet.
6. Bake 7–10 minutes, or until edges begin to brown. ← Insert en dash.
7. Let cool for 2 minutes before removing from cookie sheet.
8. Store in an airtight container. Makes 3 dozen cookies.

Instant Message

Adjust Automatic Numbering Word's automatic numbering feature sometimes needs fine-tuning. Use the ruler to adjust number settings if the text is not aligned properly or the spacing between numbers and text is off. You can also change the settings or number style by clicking the **Format>Bullets and Numbering>Numbered** tab. Choose different numbering options such as Roman numerals or letters, or you can start your list with a number higher than one.

Impact of Computers on Society

Key Terms

Moore's law

Some of the first computers were built during WWII. They were built to perform the many calculations necessary to break codes.

The first American computer, which was built during WWII, was called the ENIAC. The ENIAC filled a 30 by 50 foot room and had 18,000 vacuum tubes and 6,000 switches. At 5,000 calculations per second, the ENIAC was much faster than any computer before it. However, it had to be rewired for each new calculation.

In **1944**, Howard Aiken introduced the first fully functional computer: the Harvard Mark I.

The Harvard Mark I was 55 feet long and 8 feet high. It was slower than the ENIAC, but it did not have to be rewired for new calculations.

The first "personal computer" was the Altair 880. It became available for commercial purchase in **1975** and cost about $400. The Altair 880 came in a kit that the user had to assemble.

The Apple II came out in **1977**. It came fully assembled with a built-in keyboard. However, users had to plug the computer into their own television sets to use the monitor.

In **1989** the World Wide Web was created at a physics laboratory in Geneva, Switzerland. It was originally intended for use by scientific researchers.

A personal digital assistant called the Pilot was released in **1996**. It was extremely popular because of its capabilities and ease of use.

2005 saw more advances in wireless networking. The ability to access the Internet by wireless connections with handheld computers was a main focus in business and school environments.

8 Select the text under *Ingredients*, and click the ruler at the 1-inch mark. A tab mark will appear (Figure 1.34).

9 Click **Increase Indent** until the text aligns with that point on the ruler.

10 Repeat Steps 8–9 for the text under *Directions.*

11 Place your insertion point at the end of the document, and click **Insert>Picture>WordArt**. Choose the first style in the Gallery, and click **OK** (Figure 1.34).

12 In the **Edit WordArt** box with **Lucida Sans 14 pt**, key Do not overwork the dough! ENTER It will be tough! Click **OK**.

13 Select the WordArt, and click **Format>WordArt**. Choose the **Colors and Lines** tab. Change both the **Fill** color and the **Line** color to **blue**.

14 While still in the **Format WordArt** box, click the **Layout** tab. Choose **In front of text**, and then click **OK**.

15 **Rotate** and **move** the WordArt into the position shown in Figure 1.35.

▼ Figure 1.34 WordArt can be placed anywhere in the document.

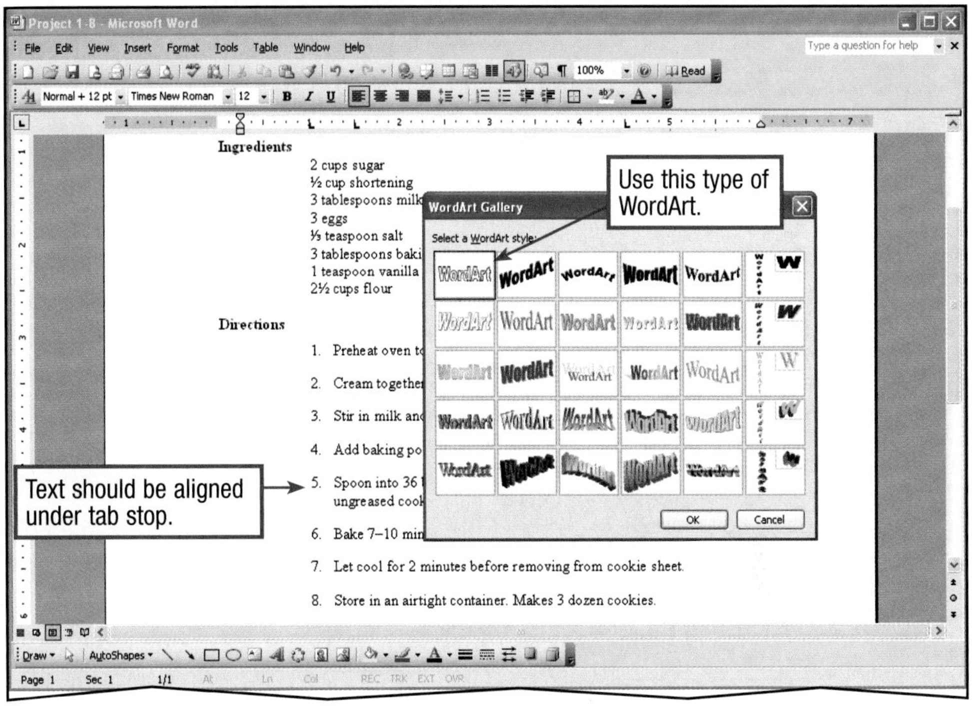

Use this type of WordArt.
Text should be aligned under tab stop.

▼ Figure 1.35 Format WordArt by using the WordArt toolbar or **Format>WordArt**.

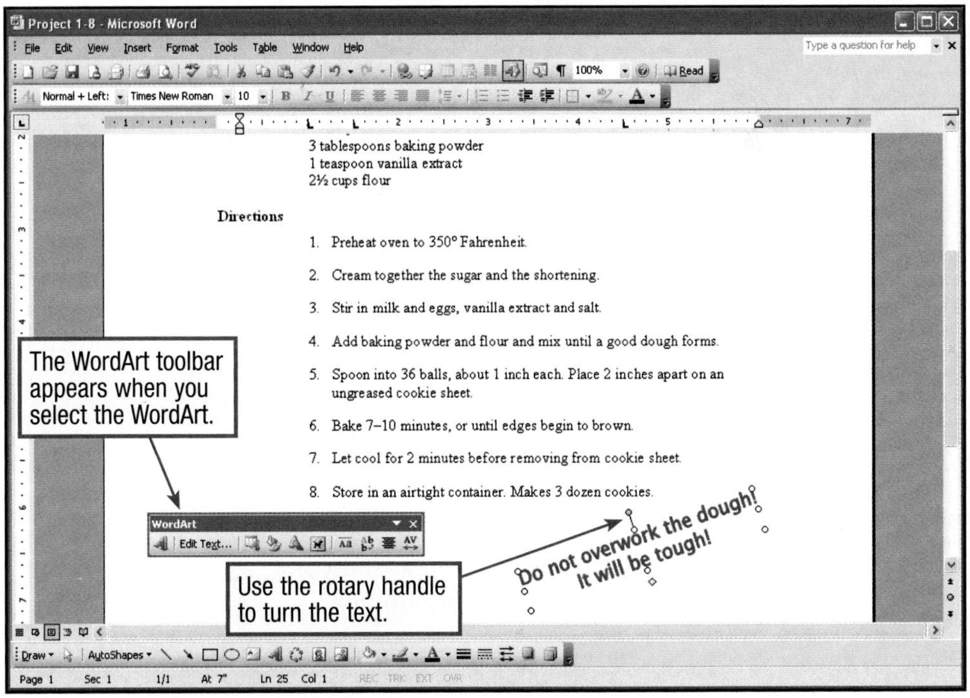

Use the rotary handle to turn the text.

PART 3 Assessment

Key Term Review

Answer the following questions on a separate piece of paper.

1. A(n) ______________ is a container for files and folders. (p. 468)

2. The ______________ is the visual representation of a file system on a computer. (p. 465)

3. A directory that contains other directories is called a ______________. (p. 468)

4. The ______________ is used to delete items permanently. (p. 465)

5. A(n) ______________ is a list of options. The ______________ opens files and applications. A(n) ______________ can be opened by right-clicking the mouse. (p. 465)

6. Graphic representations of files or applications are called ______________. (p. 465)

7. A(n) ______________ is the box that moves inside the scroll bar. (p. 466)

8. ______________ is a program that shows the entire file system on a computer. (p. 468)

9. A(n) ______________ is an icon that will automatically open a particular program, folder, or file, no matter where the shortcut is in the file system. (p. 473)

10. A window that appears inside an application and has buttons and menus to carry out various commands is called a ______________. (p. 474)

11. The ______________ contains tools that allow a user to change the way Windows appears and functions. (p. 474)

12. To ______________ a window means to make it larger or smaller. (p. 466)

13. The ______________ shows what file and applications are open. (p. 465)

14. The ______________ deletes files or applications from the computer. (p. 465)

15. A(n) ______________ is a box that shows what is inside a file or folder. (p. 466)

Concept Review

Answer the following questions on a separate piece of paper.

16. Explain the difference between maximizing a window and minimizing a window. (p. 466)

17. How would you move a window? (p. 466)

18. Describe how to delete a file or folder. (p. 467)

19. Explain what the desktop is in a graphical user interface. (p. 465)

20. Explain where the monitor should be located to help avoid soreness while working at the computer. (p. 464)

21. Write detailed directions explaining to a friend how to use Search to find a particular file or folder. (p. 469)

22. Explain the similarities and differences between folders and subfolders. (p. 470)

23. What steps would you take to copy a folder? (p. 471)

Critical Thinking

Complete the following exercises to reinforce your understanding of the lesson.

24. Design Design a file system to store information, such as homework, related to school. Sketch the file system with the highest directory at the top of the page. Use lines to show which folders are in each directory. Be sure to label each folder.

25. Explain Write a paragraph in which you explain the different parts of a Windows desktop to someone who has never seen it before. Mention at least three parts of the desktop and explain the function of each part.

ISTE Standards

The following ISTE standards are covered in Part 3. Refer to pages xxii to xxiii for a description of the standards listed here.

NETS•S	Performance Indicator
1, 3	2, 5

16 Select the title, and click **Format>Borders and Shading**. Choose the **Shading** tab.

17 Choose **blue** for the color, and under **Apply to**, choose **paragraph**. Click **OK**. The text will automatically change to white (Figure 1.36).

18 With your insertion point still in the blue box, click **Insert>Picture>From File**, then insert **Data File 1-8b**.

19 Select the clip art, and click **Format>Picture**. Then choose the **Layout** tab. Click **In front of text**, and move the image to the top of the page (Figure 1.36).

20 Resize the clip art to fit by dragging the handles or by changing the settings in the **Size** tab of the **Format Picture** box.

21 Move your insertion point to the bottom of your document, and insert **Data File 1-8c**.

22 Repeat steps 19–20 to move and resize the image. Your final document should look similar to Figure 1.36.

23 Follow your teacher's instructions for saving and printing your work.

▼ **Figure 1.36** Your recipe should look similar to the illustration.

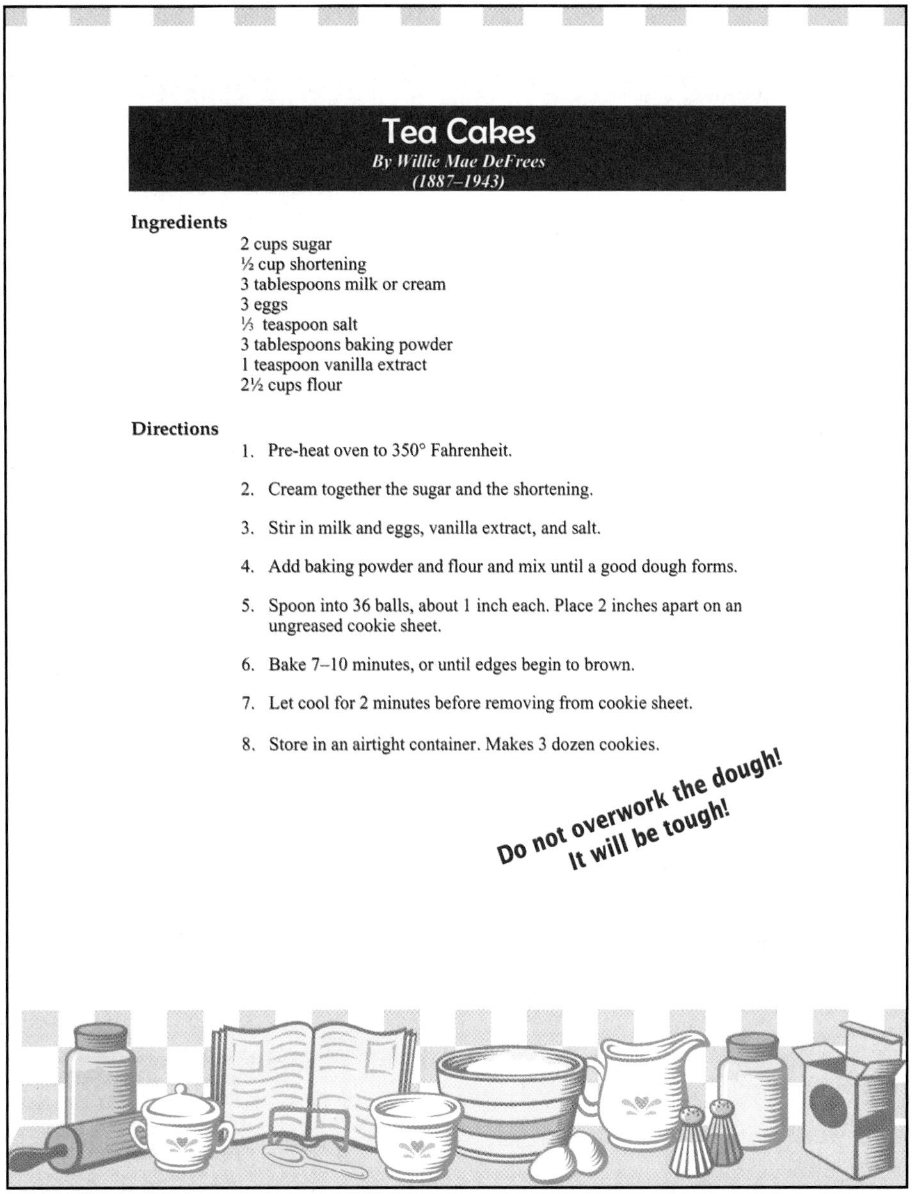

Tea Cakes

By Willie Mae DeFrees
(1887–1943)

Ingredients

2 cups sugar
½ cup shortening
3 tablespoons milk or cream
3 eggs
⅓ teaspoon salt
3 tablespoons baking powder
1 teaspoon vanilla extract
2½ cups flour

Directions

1. Pre-heat oven to 350° Fahrenheit.
2. Cream together the sugar and the shortening.
3. Stir in milk and eggs, vanilla extract, and salt.
4. Add baking powder and flour and mix until a good dough forms.
5. Spoon into 36 balls, about 1 inch each. Place 2 inches apart on an ungreased cookie sheet.
6. Bake 7–10 minutes, or until edges begin to brown.
7. Let cool for 2 minutes before removing from cookie sheet.
8. Store in an airtight container. Makes 3 dozen cookies.

Do not overwork the dough!
It will be tough!

REVIEW AND REVISE

Check your work Use Figure 1.36 as a guide and check that:

- ☑ The text is accurate, laid out attractively, and easy to read.
- ☑ Symbols and fractions have been added correctly.
- ☑ The numbered list presents information in the correct order.
- ☑ Graphics relate to content and are sized and placed effectively.

Processing: Shutting Down Windows

Follow these steps to shut down, or turn off, Windows once you have finished using the computer.

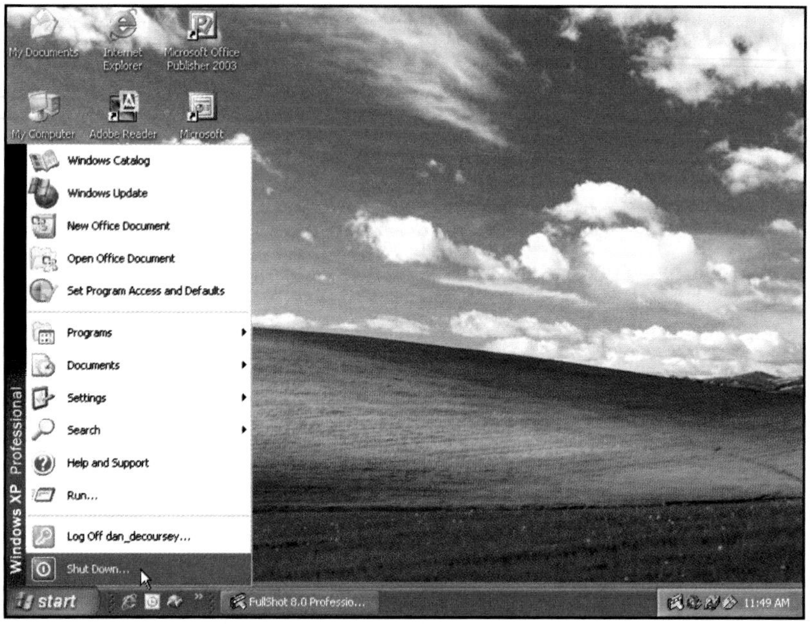

1. Close all files and programs.
2. Click **Start**.
3. Choose **Shut Down**...

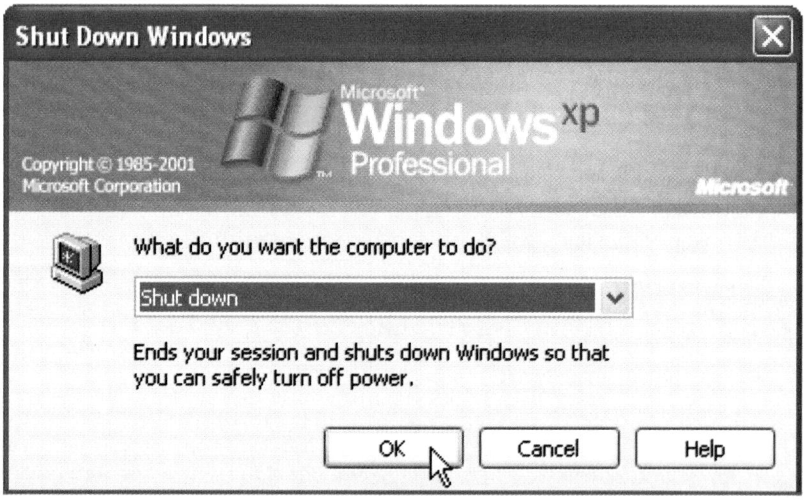

4. When the Shut Down Windows dialog box appears, click the drop-down arrow and choose **Shut down** if necessary.
5. Click **OK.**

TECH CHECK

1. Demonstrate Use the Control Panel to do the following:

a) Change screen displays.

b) Change mouse settings.

c) Change the date and time.

2. Demonstrate Use the Printers and Faxes option in the Control Panel to perform the following tasks:

a) Change the default printer.

b) Change printer properties.

3. Recall What are two places in a Microsoft application that commands can be found?

Project 1-9

Create a Table

Spotlight on Skills

- Create a table
- Sort data
- Add footnotes
- Resize columns
- Format a table
- Center vertically

Key Terms

- table
- gridlines
- sort

Academic Focus

Social Studies
Compare state populations

A **table** is a grid of rows and columns that organizes information so that it is easy to find and understand. As you work more in desktop publishing, you will find that tables make it easier to:

- Format and sort information
- Move formatted information on the page
- Create stable Web pages

Block Schedule for Monday		
Time	**Class**	**Teacher**
8:00 – 9:50	English	Loh
10:00 – 11:50	Math	Aldrich
12:00 – 12:30	Lunch	
12:30 – 2:20	Spanish	Garcia

Merged cells
Row
Column
Cell

▲ Tables make it easy to quickly find information.

As you can see in the figure above, **columns** list information vertically, from top to bottom. **Rows** list information horizontally, from left to right. A **cell** is where a column and row cross.

Create Tables

Microsoft Word has a number of ways to create tables. You can use the **Table** menu on the menu bar, or click the **Insert Table** button or the **Tables and Borders** button on the Standard toolbar.

Tables can have any number of rows and columns, which can be separated by **gridlines**, or borders. When gridlines are hidden, the table format can be used to create a column layout on a page. The information in a table can be formatted easily, and the table itself can have different types of borders or be filled with color. You even have a choice of attractive table formats to choose from under **Table>Autoformats**.

Tables in Word allow you to perform simple calculations and automatically **sort**, or arrange information. You can arrange your data in ascending or descending order. Ascending data is arranged alphabetically from A–Z, or from lowest to highest number. Descending order is from Z–A, or from highest to lowest number.

▶ **In this project,** you will create and format a table to compare the populations and other facts about certain U.S. states. You will also use superscript numerals to footnote and cite the sources of your information.

Processing: Working with Windows

Key Terms

- Control panel
- Dialog box
- Task pane
- Toolbar

In Windows, the Start menu launches applications. To launch an application, click the Start button and then choose Programs. Click the application you want to launch.

After launching a Microsoft application, notice the following parts of the screen.

The **Control Panel** contains tools that allow a user to change the way Windows appears and functions. Visit the Student Online Learning Center to learn about using the control panel to change monitor, mouse, and printer settings.

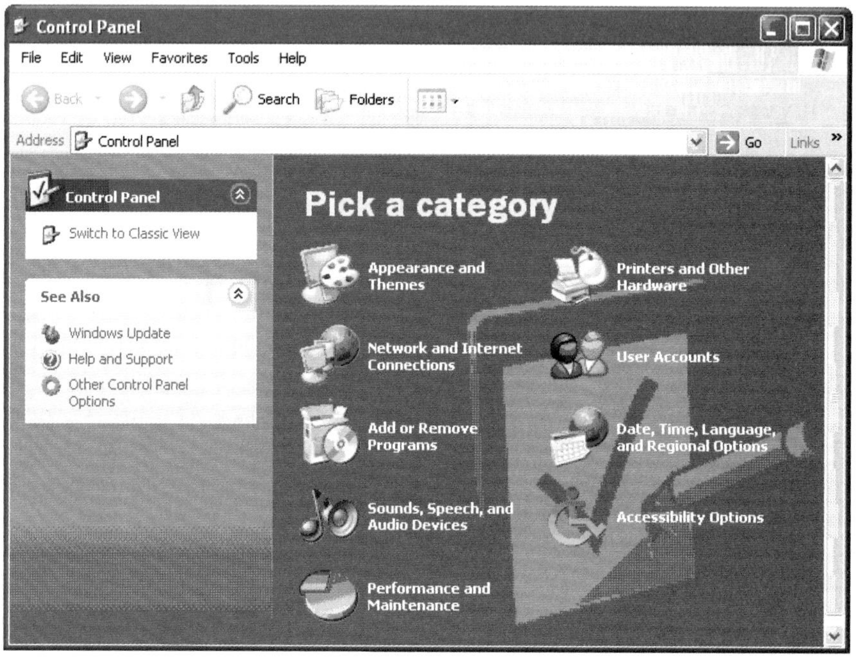

The **task pane** helps complete basic tasks.

The **toolbars** provide a quick way to give the application commands. The menus also contain commands. A **dialog box** is a window that appears inside an application and has buttons and menus to carry out various commands.

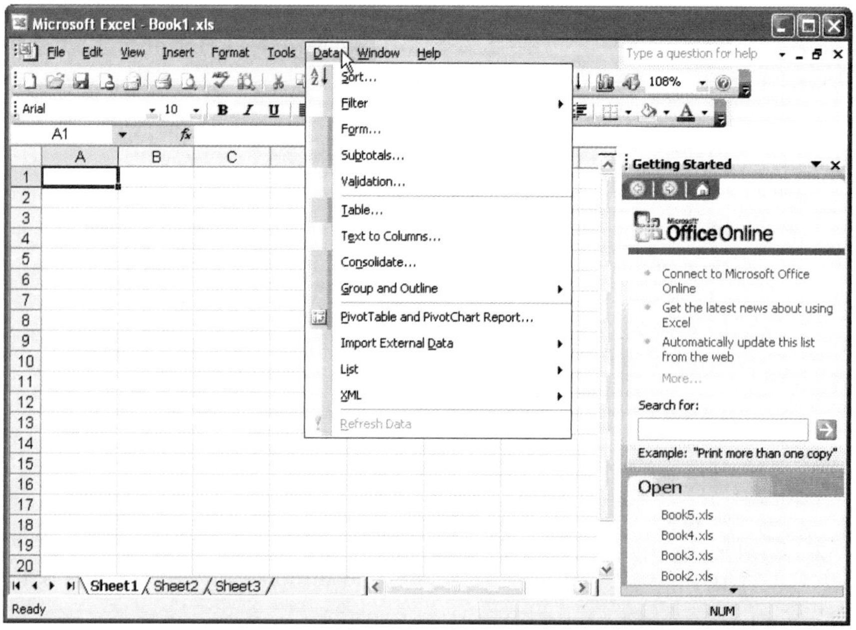

Step-by-Step

1 Open a new Word document, and save it according to your teacher's instructions.

Create a Table

2 On the **menu** bar, click **Table>Insert>Table**. In the Insert Table box, under **Table Size**, choose **5 columns** and **7 rows**. Click **OK**.

3 Select the entire first row. Click **Table>Merge Cells.** This makes the first row into one large cell.

4 Key the data as shown in Figure 1.37. Press the TAB key to move between cells. (**Note:** If the data in a cell does not align properly, click in the cell and check the ruler. Make sure the Right Indent slider is set at the right edge of the column.)

5 Select the number data in all rows of columns 2–5. Click **Align Right**.

6 Insert a new row by placing your insertion point in the bottom row, then clicking **Table>Insert>Row Above**. Key the following information in the five columns:

New Jersey
8,700,000
1,134
$27,006
82.1%
(Figure 1.38)

▼ **Figure 1.37** Key the data in this table. Do not worry if your table layout looks wider than this figure.

Merged cells, Arial, 16 pt, bold, centered

Times New Roman, 14 pt bold, centered

Times New Roman, 12 pt

State Quick Facts				
	Population	**Persons Per Square Mile**	**Per Capita Income**	**High School Graduates**
U.S.A.	293,700,000	80	$21,587	80.4%
California	35,900,000	217	$22,711	76.8%
Florida	17,400,000	296	$21,557	79.9%
Illinois	12,700,000	223	$23,104	81.4%
Texas	22,500,000	80	$19,617	75.7%

▼ **Figure 1.38** Numbers in a table should be right-aligned.

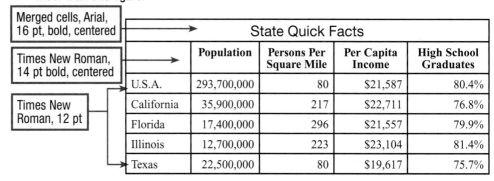

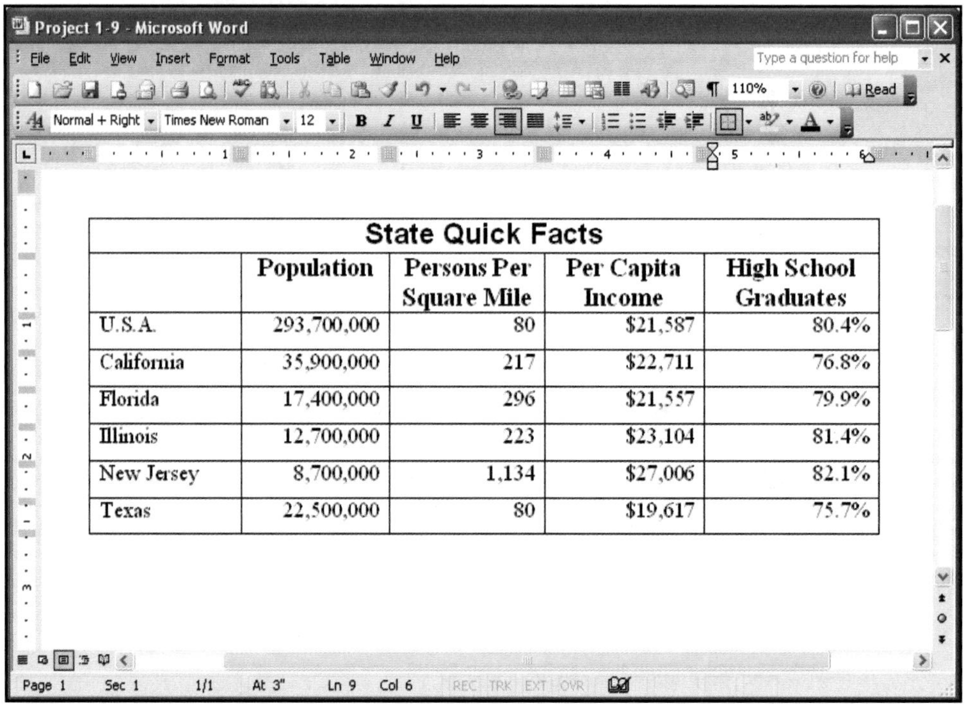

State Quick Facts				
	Population	**Persons Per Square Mile**	**Per Capita Income**	**High School Graduates**
U.S.A.	293,700,000	80	$21,587	80.4%
California	35,900,000	217	$22,711	76.8%
Florida	17,400,000	296	$21,557	79.9%
Illinois	12,700,000	223	$23,104	81.4%
New Jersey	8,700,000	1,134	$27,006	82.1%
Texas	22,500,000	80	$19,617	75.7%

Instant Message

Create Tabs in Tables When you press TAB in a table, your insertion point moves to the next cell. However, you can create a tab stop in a cell. Place your insertion point in the cell. Insert a tab stop as you normally would, by clicking on the ruler or using the **Insert** menu. To move your insertion point to the tab stop, press the CTRL key, and then press TAB.

Getting Set: Using Shortcuts

A **shortcut** is an icon that will automatically open a particular program, folder, or file, no matter where the shortcut is in the file system. For resources that people use often, shortcuts save the time of clicking through multiple folders to get to the program.

Follow these instructions to create a shortcut.

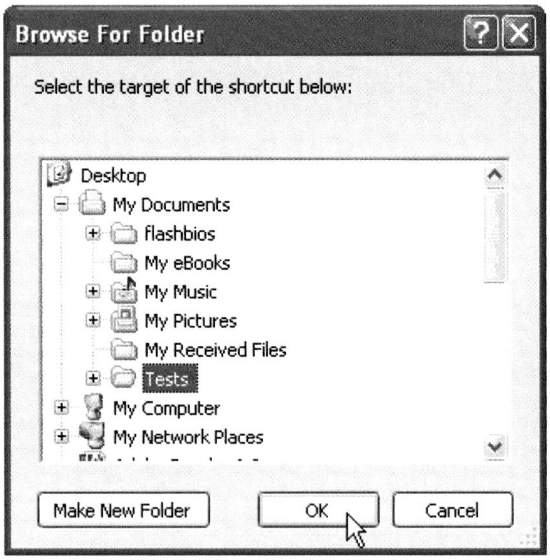

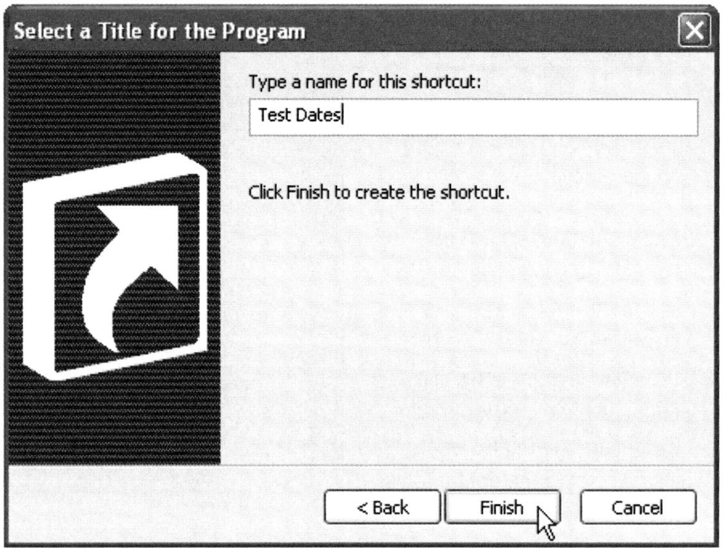

1. Right-click the place where you want to put the shortcut. Choose **New>Shortcut.**
2. In the Create Shortcut box, click **Browse.**
3. Select the location of the program or folder to which you want the shortcut to lead. Click **OK.**
4. In the Create Shortcut box, click **Next.**
5. Key a name for the shortcut in the line at the top of the box. Click **Finish.**

TECH CHECK

1. **Analyze** Explain the difference between a file that is text and a file that is a program.
2. **Describe** Describe the relationship between a parent directory and a subdirectory.
3. **Demonstrate** Use the search function in Windows to search for files and folders.
4. **Demonstrate** Complete the following actions:
   a) Create, name, and rename a folder.
   b) Format a floppy disk.
   c) Copy a folder to another directory and to a diskette.
5. **Demonstrate** Create a new shortcut.

Sort Data

7 Select all data columns in Rows 4–8 (California to Texas). Click **Table>Sort** to display the Sort options.

8 Under **Sort by**, choose **Column 2**. Next to **Type**, choose **Number**. Click the **Descending** option, then **OK**. Your table is now organized by population.

Add Footnotes

9 Place your insertion point after *State Quick Facts.* Click **Format>Fonts**. Under *Effects*, check the **Superscript** box. Click **OK**.

10 Key a superscript 1. Your title should look like Figure 1.40.

11 Repeat steps 9 and 10 to add superscript numbers to each header as shown in Figure 1.40.

12 Place your insertion point below the table. Add the footnotes shown in Figure 1.40. Use a **10 pt, serif font**.

Resize Columns

13 Click in one of the columns to display the table settings on the ruler.

14 On the ruler, click and drag the square sliders between the columns to make the columns wider.

Figure 1.39 Select all the columns before you perform a sort.

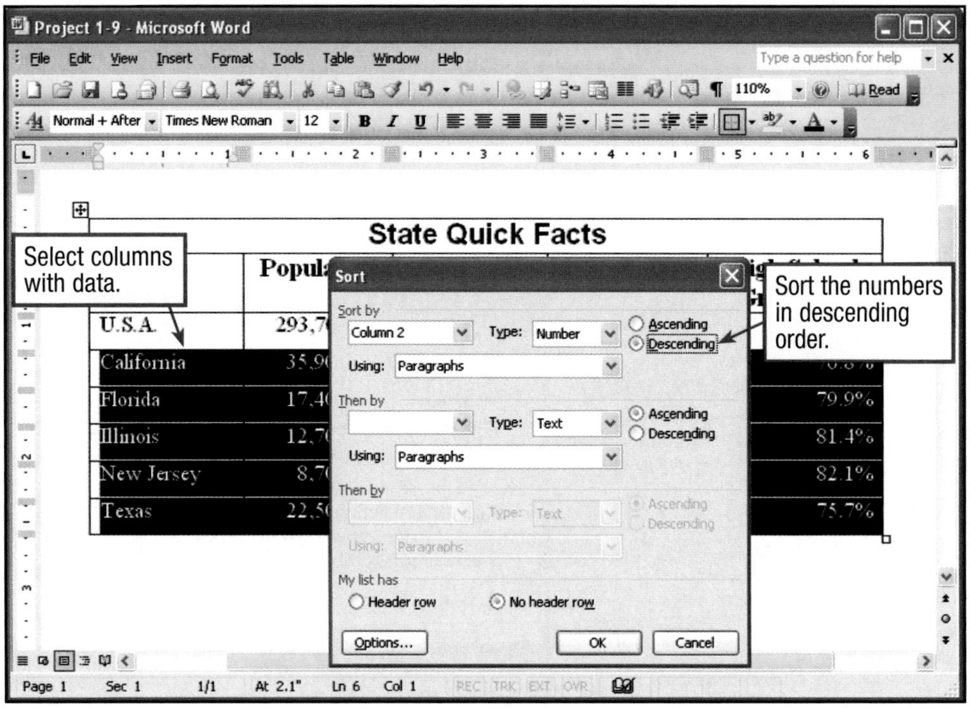

Figure 1.40 Your table is now sorted by population instead of alphabetically by state.

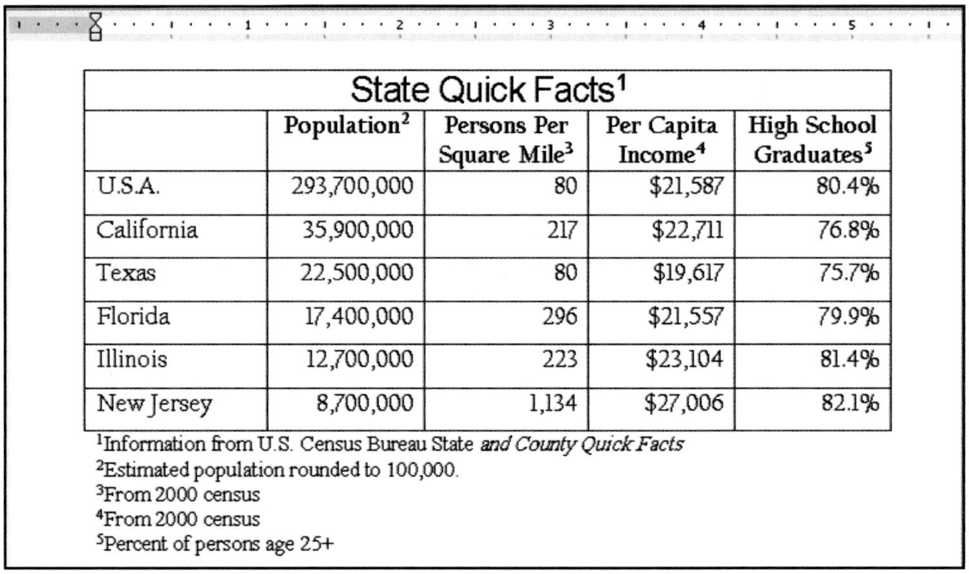

State Quick Facts[1]				
	Population[2]	Persons Per Square Mile[3]	Per Capita Income[4]	High School Graduates[5]
U.S.A.	293,700,000	80	$21,587	80.4%
California	35,900,000	217	$22,711	76.8%
Texas	22,500,000	80	$19,617	75.7%
Florida	17,400,000	296	$21,557	79.9%
Illinois	12,700,000	223	$23,104	81.4%
New Jersey	8,700,000	1,134	$27,006	82.1%

[1]Information from U.S. Census Bureau State *and County Quick Facts*
[2]Estimated population rounded to 100,000.
[3]From 2000 census
[4]From 2000 census
[5]Percent of persons age 25+

Getting Set: Using Floppy Disks

Before you can use a blank floppy disk, you must **format** the disk. When a disk is formatted, the computer first checks to make sure the disk works. Then the computer creates addresses for the information on the disk.

To format a disk, first place the disk in the floppy drive. Then open the **My Computer** directory. Click the **3½ Floppy (A:)** drive. Choose **File>Format**.

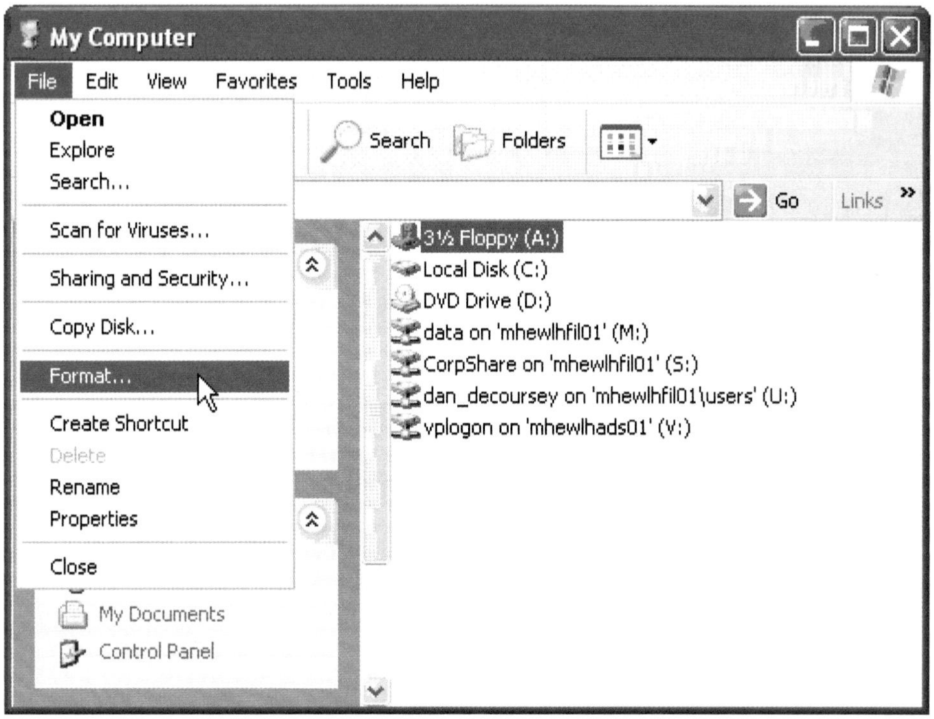

To copy a file to a floppy disk, drag the file to the My Computer window and drop the file on the icon for the 3½ Floppy (A:) drive.

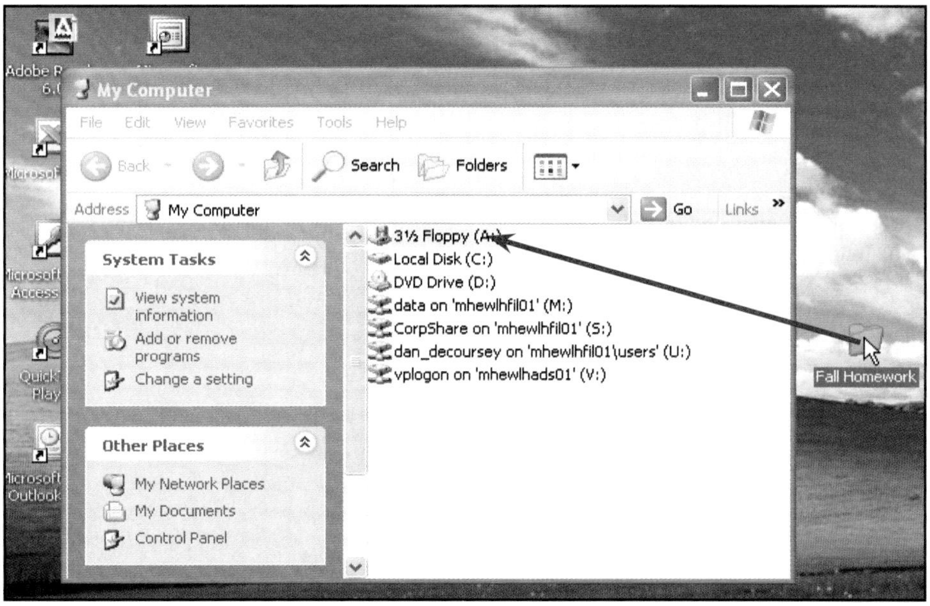

Format a Table

15 Select the text below the table, then click the **Increase Indent** button on the **Formatting** toolbar.

16 Highlight Rows 3–8. Click **Format>Paragraph**, and change the spacing **After** to **6 pt**.

17 Select the first row. Click **Format>Borders and Shading**, then change the **shading** color to **dark red**. Click **OK**.

18 If the text in Row 1 does not automatically turn white, select the row. Click the **Font Color** drop-down menu, and change the text color to **white**.

19 Select the third row. Open the **Borders and Shading** box, and change the **shading** color to **10% gray** (Figure 1.41).

20 Select the entire table. Click **Tables and Borders** on the **Standard** toolbar.

21 In the **Tables and Borders** box, click the **Border** drop-down menu. Click the **No Border** option (Figure 1.42). All borders should be removed.

▼ **Figure 1.41** Use a color fill to call attention to specific information.

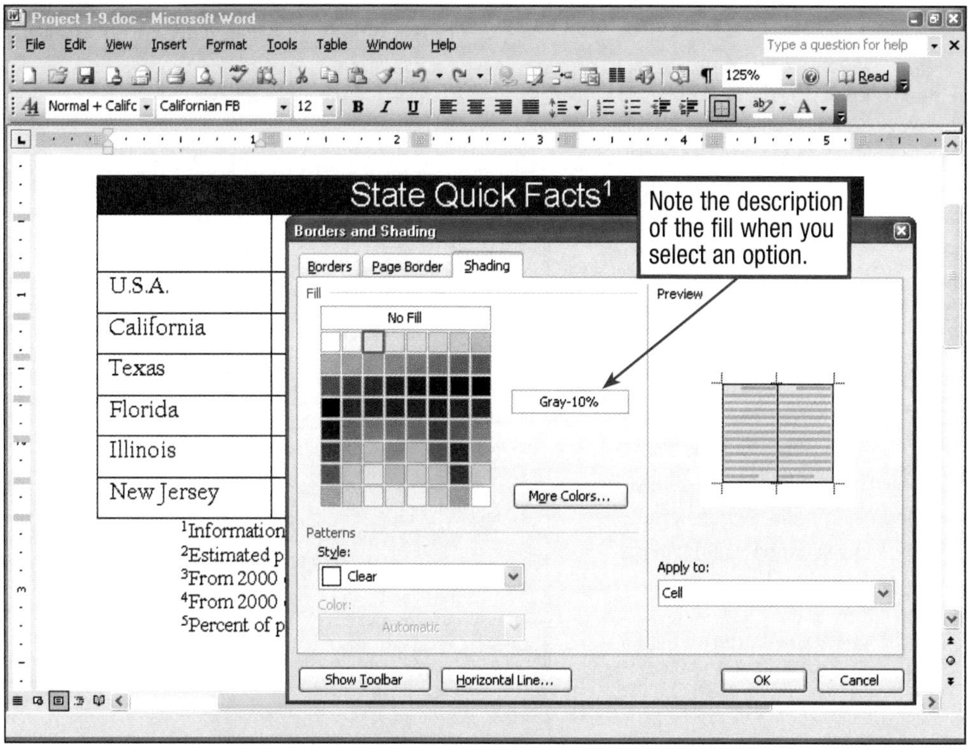

▼ **Figure 1.42** You can add or remove borders from any part of the table.

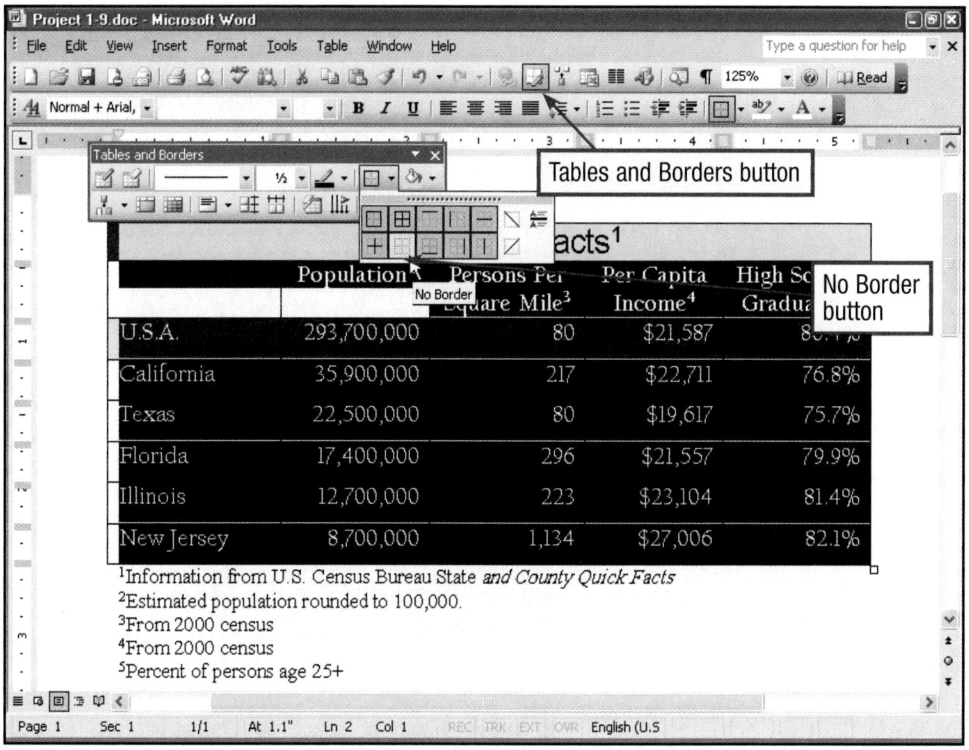

Getting Set: Working with Files and Folders Continued

To copy the Social Studies folder, right-click the folder and choose **Copy**. Then right-click the empty space in the window and choose **Paste**.

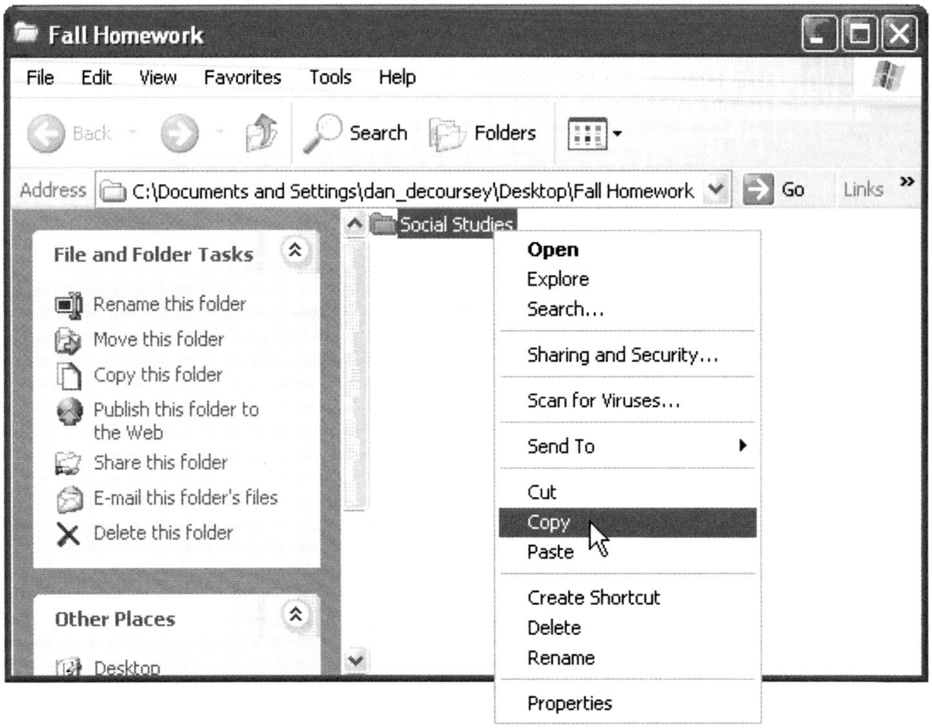

To delete the copy of Social Studies, right-click the copy and choose **Delete**. Then click **Yes** in the Confirm Folder Delete box.

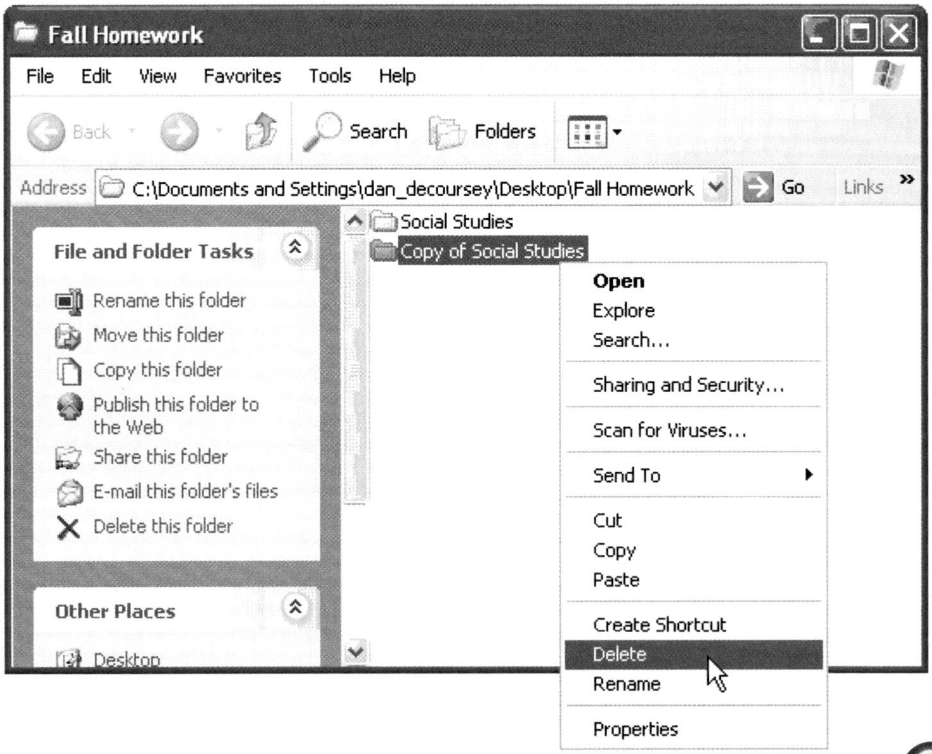

22. In the **Tables and Borders** box, click the **Line Weight** drop-down menu ½, and choose **2¼ pt**.

23. With the table still selected, click the **Outside Border** option. Close the **Tables and Borders** box

24. Select the table, and click **Table>Table Properties>Table** tab. Choose **Center** alignment. Click **OK**.

Center Vertically

25. Click **File>Page Setup>Layout** tab. Under *Page*, change the **Vertical alignment** to **Center**.

26. Click **Table>Hide Gridlines**. Right-align **Row 2**.

27. Your table should look like Figure 1.43. Follow your teacher's instructions for saving and printing your work.

▼ **Figure 1.43** **The table is centered vertically and horizontally.**

State Quick Facts[1]				
	Population[2]	Persons Per Square Mile[3]	Per Capita Income[4]	High School Graduates[5]
U.S.A.	293,700,000	80	$21,587	80.4%
California	35,900,000	217	$22,711	76.8%
Texas	22,500,000	80	$19,617	75.7%
Florida	17,400,000	296	$21,557	79.9%
Illinois	12,700,000	223	$23,104	81.4%
New Jersey	8,700,000	1,134	$27,006	82.1%

[1]Information from U.S. Census Bureau State and County Quick Facts
[2]Estimated population rounded to 100,000.
[3]From 2000 census
[4]From 2000 census
[5]Percent of persons age 25+

REVIEW AND REVISE

Check your work Use Figure 1.43 as a guide and check that:

- ☑ The table colors and borders match Figure 1.43.
- ☑ Text is complete and accurate.
- ☑ The table is sorted from highest to lowest city population.
- ☑ There are citations below the table.
- ☑ The table is centered.

Getting Set: Working with Files and Folders Continued

To create a folder, right-click the desktop. Then choose **New> Folder**. When the new folder appears, key Homework and press ENTER on your keyboard. Right-click the **Homework** folder and choose **Rename**. Key Fall Homework. Press ENTER.

To create a subfolder, open the folder in which you want to create the new folder. On the left side of the window, click **Make a new folder**. Finally, key Social Studies and press ENTER.

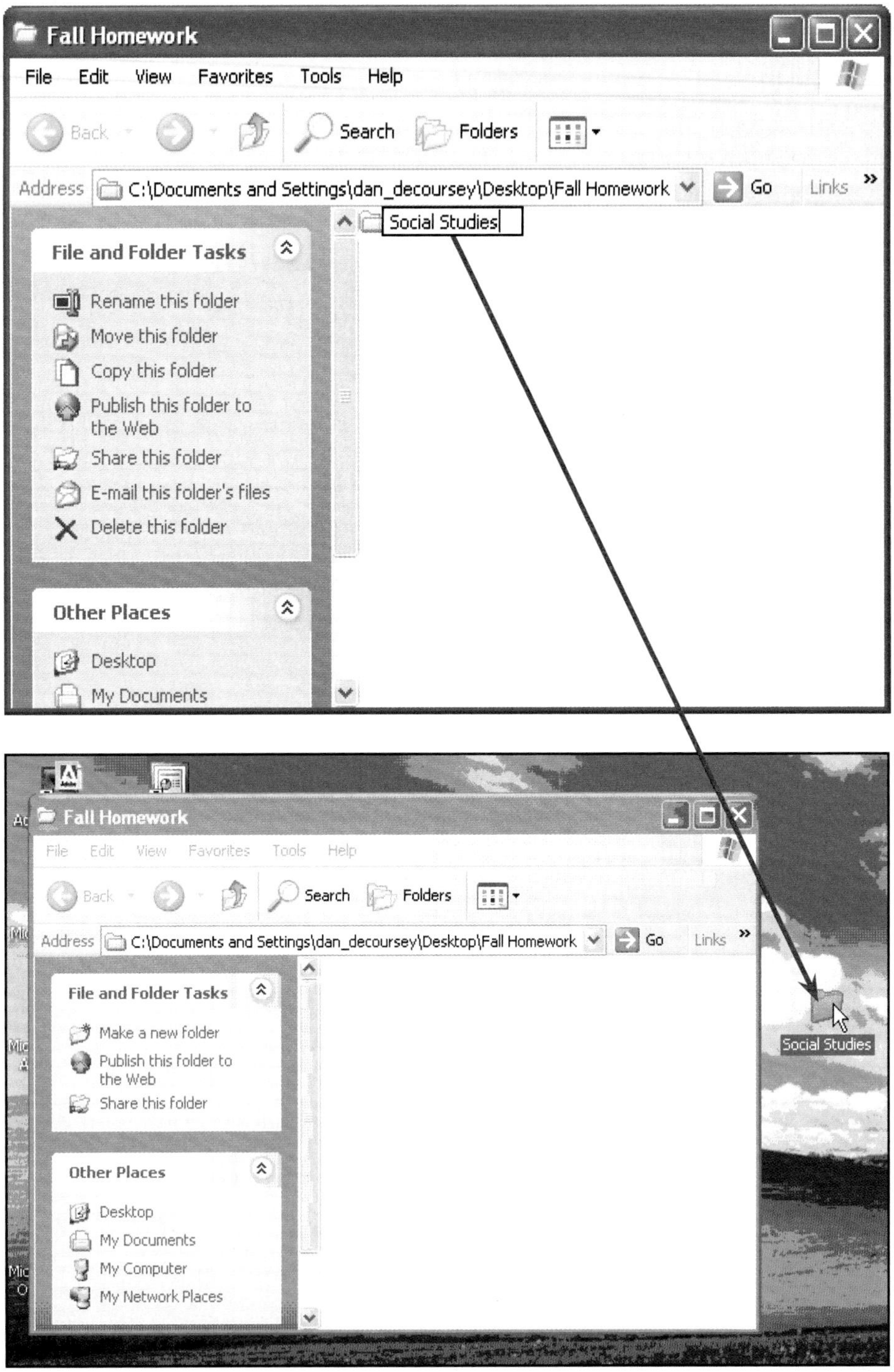

To move a folder, grab the folder and drop it in its new location. Drag **Social Studies** to the desktop. Then drag it back into the **Fall Homework** folder.

Project 1-10

Create a Résumé with a Template

Spotlight on Skills

- Use a template

Key Term

- template

Academic Focus

Social Studies
Create Ben Franklin's résumé

If you do not have a résumé already, you will probably need to have one in the next few years. A résumé lists your education, employment history, and skills. It is one of the most important documents that you will create. If an employer is impressed by your résumé, then you will be invited to a face-to-face interview. A good résumé can help you get hired.

Create with Templates and Wizards

Writing an effective résumé takes careful consideration, and there are books and online sources that can help you find the best way to present your background.

Employers frequently scan the résumés they receive, so it is important to have a résumé that is clearly presented. A résumé might also be searched for key phrases and job skills that match the requirements of the position. A well-organized, attractive résumé has a better chance of being noticed.

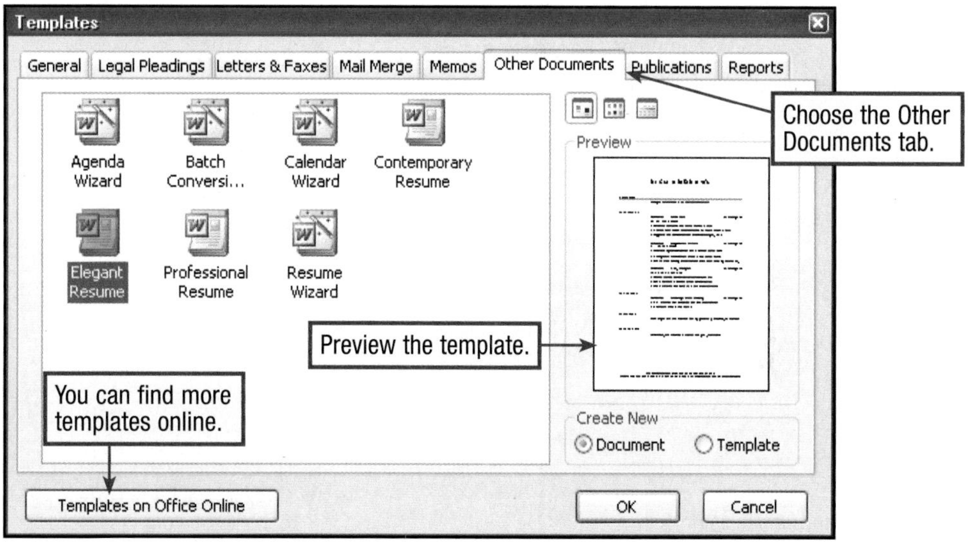

▲ Word offers templates and wizards for creating different résumé styles and many other types of documents.

Documents like résumés lay out information in a way that it is easy to find and read. You can create your own layout, but it is often easier to use a template. A **template** is a pre-formatted, fill-in-the-blank document. Microsoft Word has a variety of templates that you can use for many types of documents. You can find a selection of résumés in Word itself or online. Word also has wizards, which are step-by-step questions that create templates tailored to your specific needs.

► **In this project,** you will use a template to create a résumé for 20-year-old Benjamin Franklin.

Getting Set: Working with Files and Folders Continued

With so many places to look, finding folders and files can be difficult. Use the Search window to find files and folders when you do not know where they are.

To search for a folder, you can choose **Start>Search>For Files or Folders**. To search all of the files and folders on the computer, click **All Files and Folders** on the left side of the Search window.

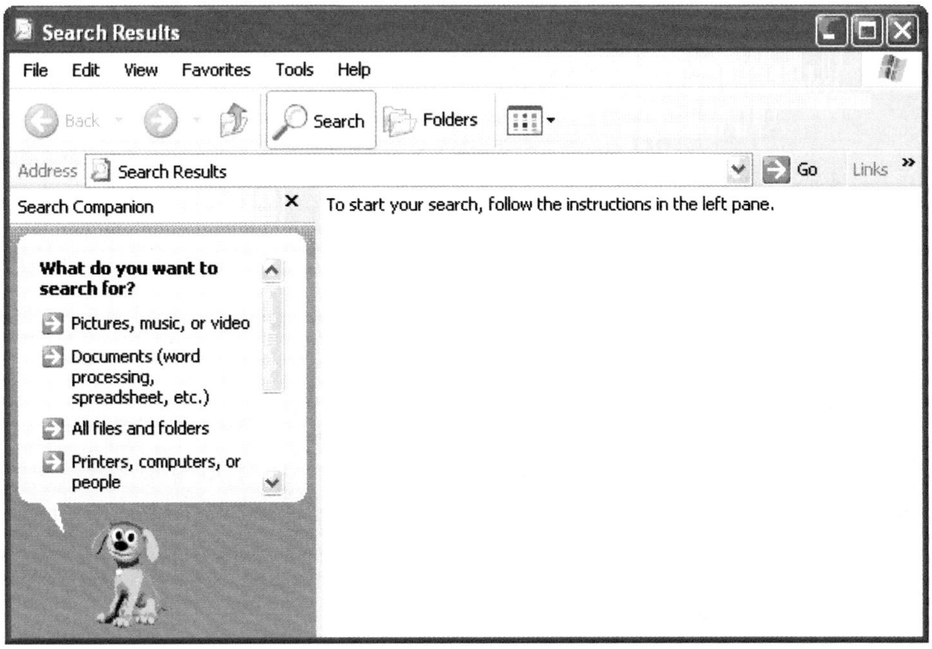

To search for files or folders that contain the word *computer*, key computer below **All or part of the file name**. Then click **Search**. If you are not sure if the name of a file is *Computer, Computers*, or *Computing*, use an asterisk for the part you are not sure about. For example, enter Comput* in **All or part of the file name**. This tells the computer to show all files that start with *Comput*.

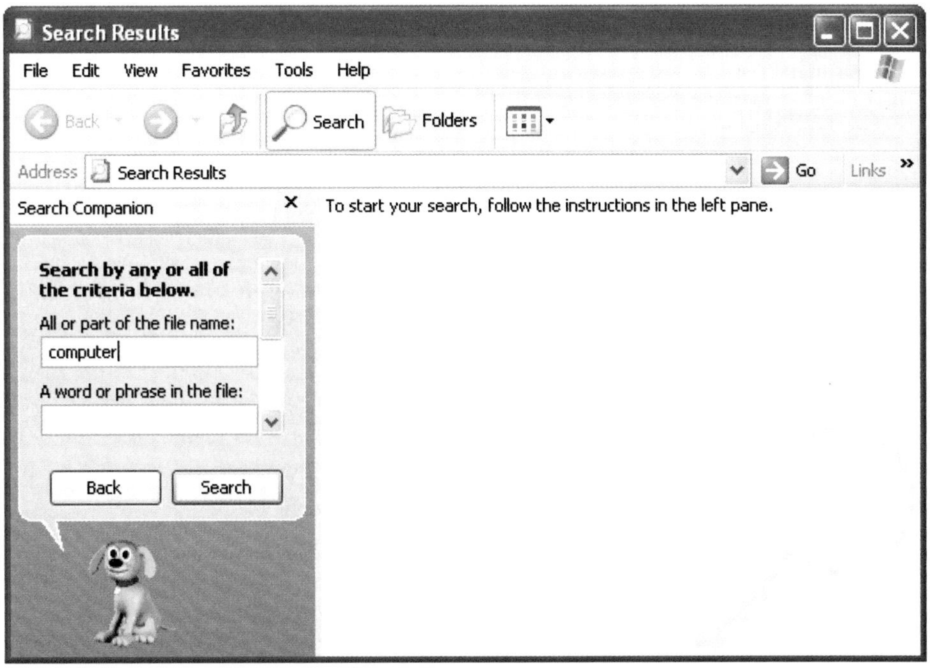

Student Data File

Step-by-Step

1. Open a blank Word document. Click **File>New** to display the New Document task pane.

Use a Template

2. In the task pane, choose **On My Computer** to display Word's template options.

3. In the Templates box, click the **Other Documents** tab, and choose **Professional Resume**.

4. Click the word **Objective**. Then click **Table>Show Gridlines**.

5. Select the last row of the table that reads *Tips.* Click **Table>Delete>Row** to remove the row.

6. Open **Data File 1-10**. Replace the information in the template by **either** of the following methods:
   - Copy and paste the material from the data file into the résumé template.
   - Key the information into the template.

7. Run a spell-check. Your final résumé should look like Figure 1.45. Follow your teacher's instructions for saving and printing your document.

Figure 1.44 The table gridlines will not be visible when you print.

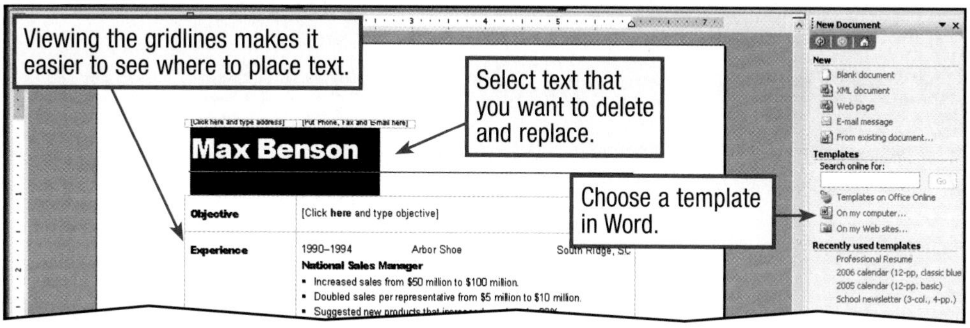

Figure 1.45 Replace the placeholder text in the template with your content.

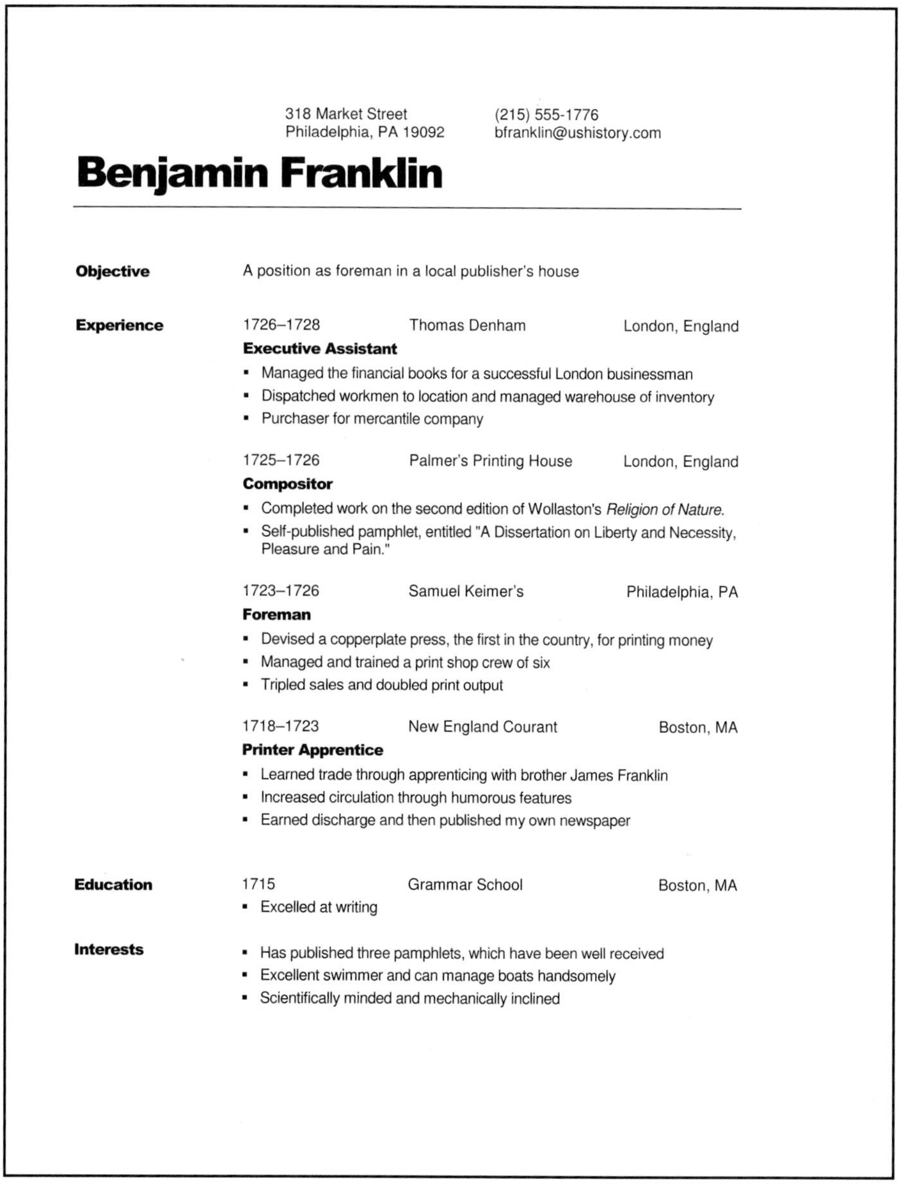

318 Market Street
Philadelphia, PA 19092

(215) 555-1776
bfranklin@ushistory.com

Benjamin Franklin

Objective A position as foreman in a local publisher's house

Experience

1726–1728 Thomas Denham London, England
Executive Assistant
- Managed the financial books for a successful London businessman
- Dispatched workmen to location and managed warehouse of inventory
- Purchaser for mercantile company

1725–1726 Palmer's Printing House London, England
Compositor
- Completed work on the second edition of Wollaston's *Religion of Nature.*
- Self-published pamphlet, entitled "A Dissertation on Liberty and Necessity, Pleasure and Pain."

1723–1726 Samuel Keimer's Philadelphia, PA
Foreman
- Devised a copperplate press, the first in the country, for printing money
- Managed and trained a print shop crew of six
- Tripled sales and doubled print output

1718–1723 New England Courant Boston, MA
Printer Apprentice
- Learned trade through apprenticing with brother James Franklin
- Increased circulation through humorous features
- Earned discharge and then published my own newspaper

Education 1715 Grammar School Boston, MA
- Excelled at writing

Interests
- Has published three pamphlets, which have been well received
- Excellent swimmer and can manage boats handsomely
- Scientifically minded and mechanically inclined

Getting Set: Working with Files and Folders

Key Terms
Directory
Format
Parent directory
Shortcut
Subdirectory
Windows Explorer

Windows Explorer is a program that shows the entire file system on a computer. To open Windows Explorer, choose **Start>Programs>Accessories>Windows Explorer**.

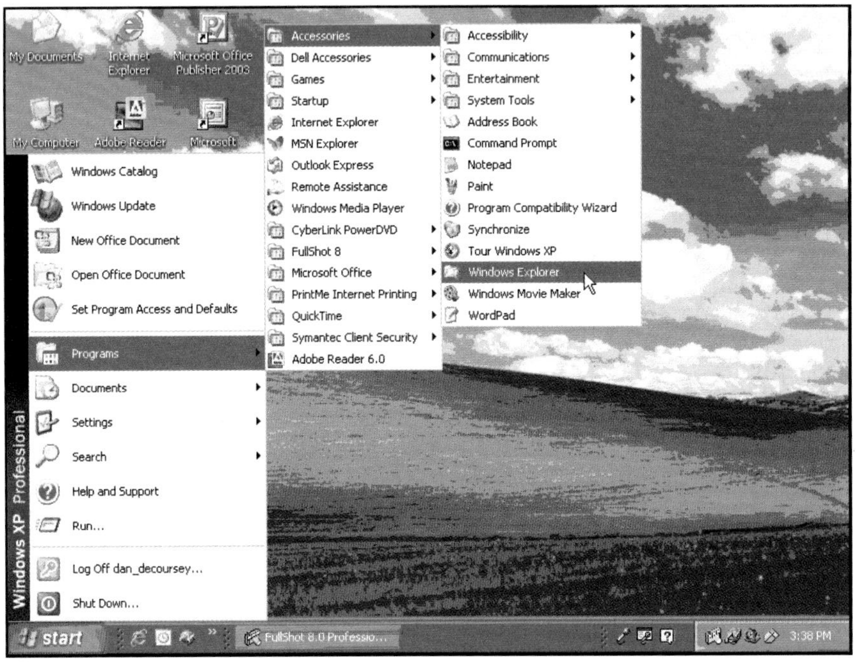

At the top left of the Desktop window, click the Desktop icon. All of the files and folders on the desktop will be displayed on the right side of the window.

One of the **directories**, or containers for files and folders, on the desktop is called My Documents. To view the files of this directory, click the My Documents icon on the left. Files can be data, text, programs, and more. To find out more about a file, right-click the file and choose Properties.

A directory can hold other directories. A directory that holds other directories is called a **parent directory**. A directory that is located in another directory is called a **subdirectory**. For instance, My Computer is a parent directory for 3½ Floppy (A:), and 3½ Floppy (A:) is a subdirectory of My Computer.

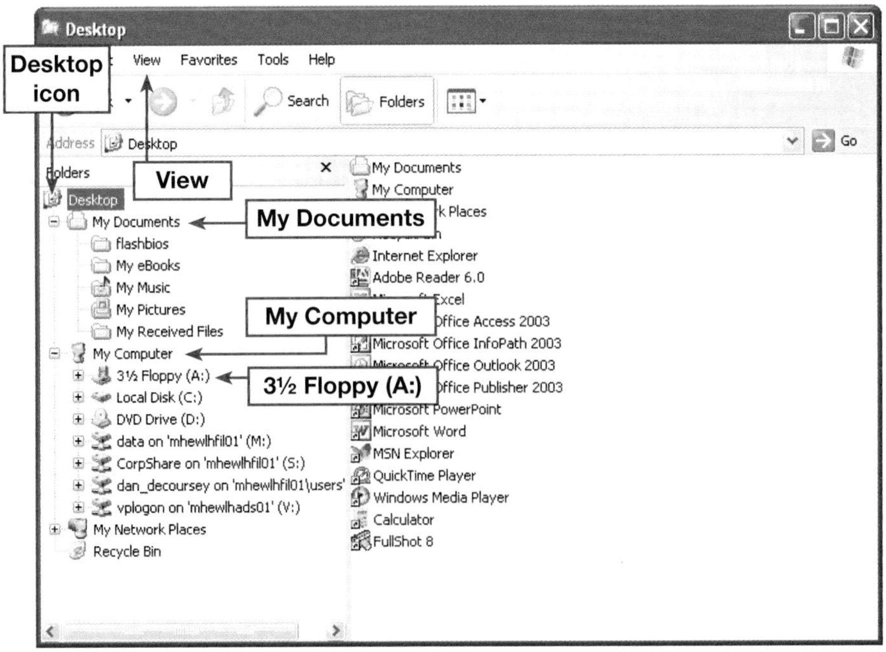

Skills Studio

Reinforce Your Skills

- **Project 1-11**
  Create thumbnail sketches
  Apply planned elements
  Format text for readability and attractive presentation
  Insert clip art
  Format flyer layout

Go Online ACTIVITIES
www.glencoe.com

Challenge Yourself Go to **Chapter 1**, and choose **Enrichment Activities** for more practice with the skills you have learned.

Lay Out One-Page Flyers

The following project will take you through the steps you need to create a well-designed flyer:

◆ **Project 1-11** Create a flyer

Grab Attention

Flyers are inexpensive ways of advertising. They are generally produced by the thousands and are printed on a single side, usually in one color. They might be posted on walls, telephone poles, or bulletin boards. They are often handed out or placed on counters for people to take.

Since flyers tend to be mass produced, they need to stand out from the crowd of other flyers. While studies show that color documents are read more often than ones without color, a full-color process on flyers is often too expensive an option.

Alternatives to using full color include using colored paper when printing, using an ink color other than black, or using only one spot color somewhere in the document. Each of these solutions increases the cost of printing, but it can make the difference between an effective flyer and one that is ignored because it looks like all the rest.

Getting Ready Continued

You can **restore** a window that was minimized to make it visible again. To restore a window, click the title of the window in the task bar.

To close a window, click the Close Window button.

To delete a file or folder, drag the item to the Recycle Bin and drop it on top. This places the item in the Recycle Bin, but does not delete the item. To delete the item, right click the Recycle Bin. Locate and click Empty Recycle Bin to permanently delete all of the items in your Recycle Bin.

Icons on the desktop can be arranged and rearranged to fit your needs. You can click and drag icons to various places on the desktop. You can also right click the mouse and choose Arrange Icons By. A submenu will open that allows you to arrange the icons by Name, Size, Type, or Modified. Icons can be arranged using Auto Arrange or they can be placed in a grid by choosing Align to Grid. You can also choose to hide the icons by deselecting Show Desktop Icons.

TECH CHECK

1. **Recall** List three parts of the Windows desktop.
2. **Reproduce** Make a sketch of a window. On the sketch, label the following items: Maximize button, Minimize button, Scroll bar, and Title bar.

Skills Studio

Project 1-11 Create a Flyer

Skills You Will Apply

- Determine message, audience, and content
- Design flyer layout

Key Terms

- design process
- thumbnail sketch

Academic Focus

Social Studies
Initiate a time capsule

The **design process** is a step-by-step system used to create effective designs and documents. While the design process will be explained in more detail in Chapter 4, the main point is *planning*. Effective planning will help you create better projects in a shorter time. Planning usually involves the following steps:

Planning Your Design

1. **Message** Decide what message needs to be on the flyer. What is the most important information you want readers to see?
2. **Audience** Determine the audience for your flyer. To whom do you want to deliver this information?
3. **Content** Consider the text and images that will appeal to your specific audience. Is the audience young and trendy, or do you want to attract more traditional people?
4. **Budget** Estimate costs for creating your design. How much time will it take? How many copies will be made? What will printing expenses be?

Sidebar

Printing Problems You should always ask a client how the flyer will be published. If a copy machine will be used, be aware that copy machines usually do not handle shades of gray, watermarks, or photographs very well. Avoid these elements when designing a flyer that will be printed on a copy machine.

Evaluate Why must you know how a document will be printed?

Create Thumbnails

After understanding the requirements of a project, the next step is creating thumbnail sketches of your ideas. Imagine what the finished design will look like, and sketch your ideas on paper. A **thumbnail sketch** is a simple drawing that gives a sense of the layout and basic elements of your design. Sketches are not detailed illustrations of the final document and do not really require good drawing skills. They will, however, let you try out different designs without taking up too much time.

Do not start designing on the computer! This can limit your design to what you think the computer is capable of doing. By designing on paper, you will be less worried about what the computer can do, and instead try to get the computer to match your vision.

▶ **In this project,** you will create a flyer advertising a school-wide time capsule project. A time capsule is a container that holds objects that represent the culture from a particular time. The time capsule will be uncovered in 10 years for future history classes to analyze and learn about your time. Students are being asked to contribute items that they think describe current social, cultural, and technological trends.

Getting Ready Continued

Double-clicking on a folder opens it. The contents of the folder are displayed in a **window,** which is simply a box that shows what is inside a folder or file. A different window can be opened for each file or folder you want to use. You can have many windows open at one time, but you can only work in one window, the active window, at a time.

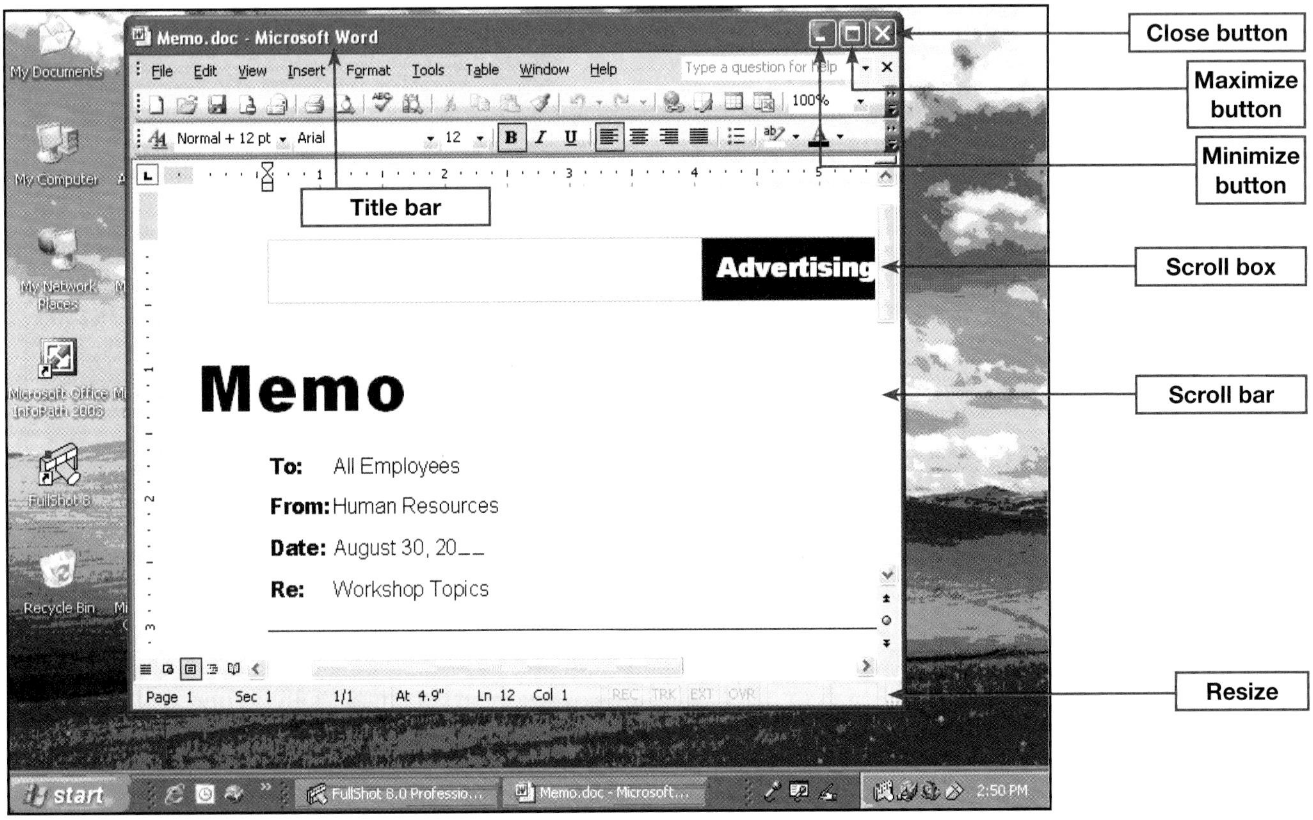

To move a window, place your pointer on the Title bar. Press and hold the left mouse button and then move the pointer to where you want the window to be. Holding down the mouse button and moving the mouse is called dragging.

Often, the entire contents of a window are not visible. To view the rest of the window, grab the scroll bar and drag it downward. The box that moves inside the scroll bar is called the **scroll box.**

To **resize** a window, or to make it larger or smaller, place the pointer over one of the corners of the window. When the small black arrows appear, drag the corner outward to make the window larger. Drag the corner inward to make the window smaller.

To **maximize** a window, or to make it fill up the screen, click the maximize button in the upper right corner of the window. To return the window to its original size, click the button again.

You can **minimize** a window to take the window off the desktop without closing it. To minimize a window, click the minimize button in the upper right corner of the window.

Student Data File

Step-by-Step

1. Use the project description to create a thumbnail sketch based on the message, audience, and content.

2. Open a new Word document, and save it according to your teacher's instructions.

3. Create a flyer using your thumbnail sketch, or follow the instructions below to create a flyer based on Figure 1.49 on page 51.

4. Change the page orientation to **landscape**. Then **center** and **key** the text: Student Council Time Capsule and Deadline. Use a large, bold font.

5. Create a text box below the word *Deadline.* Use **Format>Text Box** to add a **black fill** color.

6. Insert **WordArt** in the text box. Key June 1 as the WordArt text. Use a tech-like font such as **Sydnie**, **72 pt**.

7. Use the sizing handles to resize the text box so that it looks similar to Figure 1.47.

▼ **Figure 1.46** Thumbnail sketches can use simple shapes and labels to express design concepts.

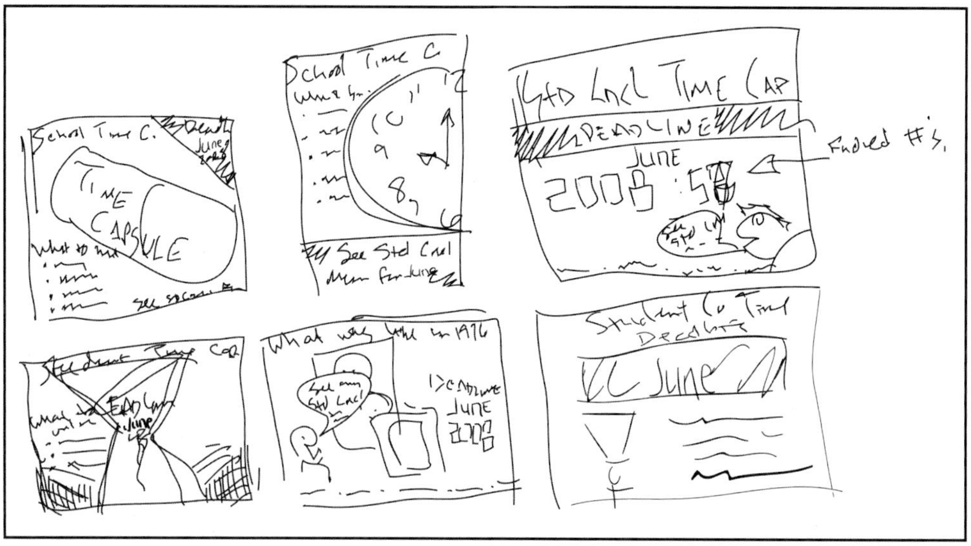

▼ **Figure 1.47** Your flyer should be in landscape orientation.

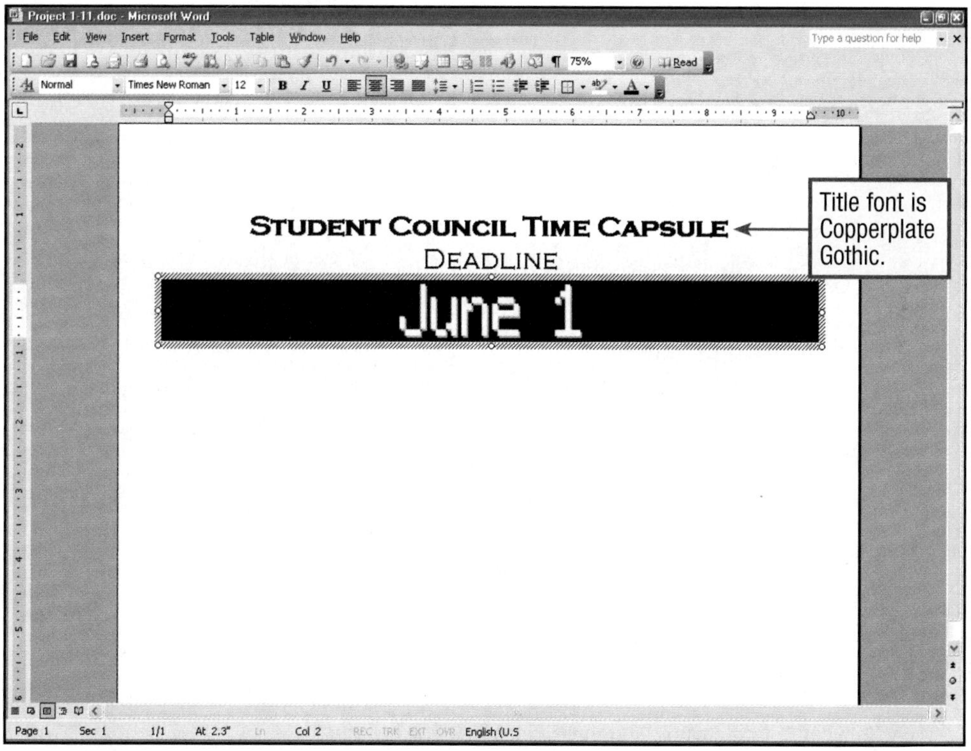

Getting Ready Continued

Once the computer is on, you will see the **desktop.** In a graphical user interface (GUI), the desktop is the visual representation of the file system on a computer. All of the files and applications on a computer can be accessed through the desktop.

A GUI allows you to issue commands to the computer by using visual objects instead of typing commands. A mouse or other pointing device is used to access the icons and menues in a GUI.

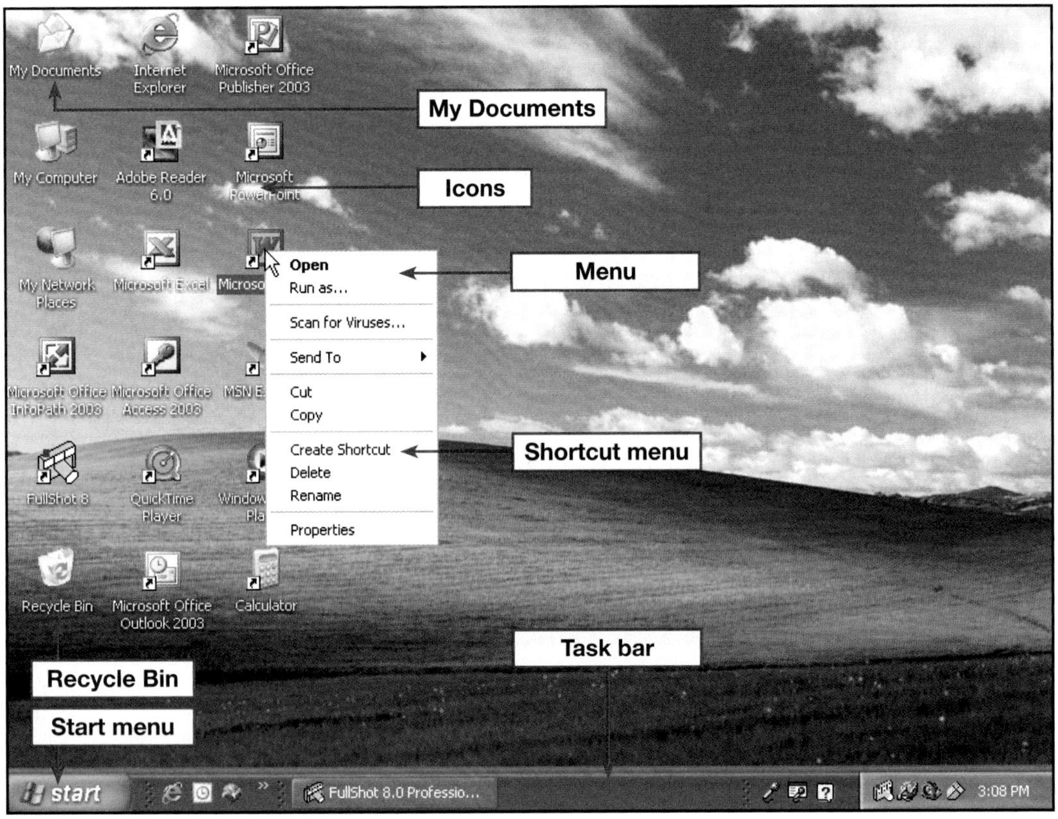

Icons are graphic representations of files or applications.

The **Start Menu** opens files and applications. It gives you access to all the resources and programs on your computer. A **menu** is a list of options.

The **Task bar** shows what files and applications are open. It allows you to launch and manage programs.

The **Recycle Bin** deletes files or applications from the computer.

Right-click once on the mouse to open a **shortcut menu.**

Double-click on the My Documents icon to open a list of your documents.

8) **Center** the **WordArt**.

9) Insert a text box on the bottom right side of your page. Size it to be **3.25″ height**, **5.0″ width**. Remove the border.

10) Key the text in Figure 1.48. Use a red sans serif font such as **Arial 20 pt**, **centered**, for the red text and a larger font size for the black text. Use ALT + **0149** for the bullet symbol.

11) Place your insertion point under the black text box. Then click **Insert>Picture>From File** to insert **Data File 1-11**.

12) Use **Format>Picture** to change the clip art layout to **In Front of Text**. Then reposition and resize the clip art so that it looks similar to Figure 1.49.

13) Add a page border.

14) Follow your teacher's instructions for saving and printing your work. Although the document is created in color, it should print well in black and white.

▼ **Figure 1.48** You can add other items that you think belong in a time capsule.

Current Events Clippings • Scrapbooks • CDs and Books • Food Menus • Popular Toys • Concert Programs • Maps • Popular Magazines • Lists of Favorite Things • Photos • School Projects • Favorite Web Site Printouts

SEE ANY STUDENT COUNCIL MEMBER FOR MORE DETAILS

▼ **Figure 1.49** The final document has changed slightly from the thumbnail but retains the basic concepts.

STUDENT COUNCIL TIME CAPSULE

DEADLINE

June 1

Current Events Clippings • Scrapbooks • CDs and Books • Food Menus • Popular Toys • Concert Programs • Maps • Popular Magazines • Lists of Favorite Things • Photos • School Projects • Favorite Web Site Printouts

SEE ANY STUDENT COUNCIL MEMBER FOR MORE DETAILS

PART 3 Ready, Set, Process

Getting Ready

Key Terms
Desktop
Icon
Maximize
Menu
Minimize
Recycle bin
Resize
Restore
Scroll box
Shortcut menu
Start menu
Task bar
Window

While computers do not usually require a lot of care and upkeeping, there are many things you can do to help keep your computer functioning properly.

- **Do not eat or drink near the computer.** Food and drinks can ruin the computer. Crumbs from food can get stuck between the keys on the keyboard. Some foods can make the keyboard, mouse, or other computer parts sticky. A spilled drink can cause an electrical shortage.
- **Keep your computer work area free of clutter.** This will help you work more efficiently while at the computer.
- **Insert disks and CDs gently into the disk drive and CD drive.** Never force a disk or CD into the drive.
- **Check that there are no disks or CDs in any of the drives** before turning on the computer.

Now, locate the power button POWER on the front of your computer. Press the button to start up the computer. Follow your teacher's instructions to logon once the computer has powered on.

Many hours of typing at a computer can make your wrists, arms, and back tired and sore. Here are a few tips that can help you avoid fatigue and soreness.

1. Sit with your hips as far back in your chair as they will go. Your back should rest against the back of the chair. The chair should support your upper and lower back.
2. Place the keyboard close enough to your body that you don't have to stretch to reach it. Your abdomen should be approximately one hand's span from the keyboard.
3. If you can, adjust the height of your chair so that your knees are even with your hips.
4. Center the keyboard on your body.
5. Place the monitor directly in front of you and slightly below your line of sight. The monitor should be between 20 and 24 inches from your eyes.

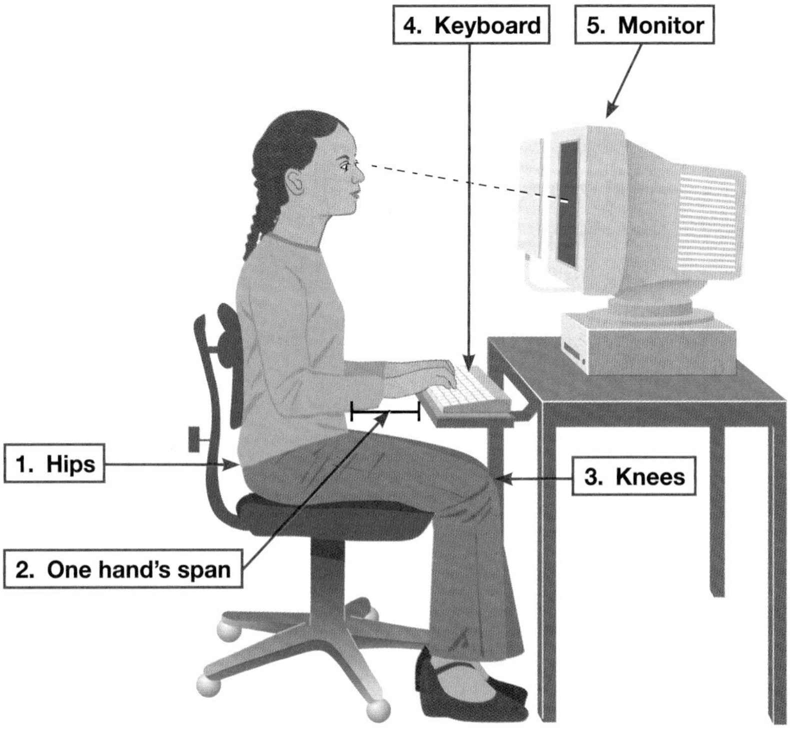

In The Workplace

Administrative Assistants

At one time, administrative assistants mostly keyed documents and answered phones. The computer changed these roles. Many of today's administrative assistants are responsible for a wide range of tasks, including desktop publishing. Businesses often create newsletters or other documents that are designed and produced by administrative assistants.

On the Job

In many businesses, an administrative assistant position is an entry-level job that is a stepping stone to other positions in the company. Although administrative assistants often work for one particular person, they may also work for a specific department or group of people. Communication skills are very important. Administrative assistants are often the middlemen between their supervisors and other departments or outside customers and contractors. They need to have good writing skills, including good grammar and spelling. If they create a document that looks unprofessional or contains mistakes, that will reflect on their company or employer.

Administrative assistants may not need to use specialized desktop publishing programs such as Microsoft Publisher or Adobe InDesign. However, they should know how to use the desktop publishing tools in Word. They need to know how to format and lay out attractive newsletters that can be printed or published on a Web site. They may also be responsible for documents such as financial reports, flyers, and even advertisements or catalogs.

Besides desktop publishing and word processing, administrative assistants might manage databases and file systems, create spreadsheets, or do bookkeeping and billing. People in this position might act as receptionists, office managers, or executive assistants.

Future Outlook

Many people now use computers to do many of the tasks that administrative assistants did. However, this career will continue to be in demand for people who have the technology and communication skills that are becoming increasingly important for all businesses.

For more information about this career, look for job descriptions on Web sites such as **monster.com** and **CareerBuilder.com**.

Training

Many high schools and community colleges offer the vocational and technology skills that are needed to be an administrative assistant. Companies may also offer training for jobs that require skills specific to their needs.

Salary Range

Depending on experience and required duties, the salary that administrative assistants may earn is between $22,000 to $50,000.

Skills and Talents

Administrative Assistants need to have:

- Knowledge of various software programs
- Good communication skills
- Good writing skills
- Good problem-solving skills
- Good communication skills.
- The ability to work independently and meet deadlines

Career *Activity*

Why is it important for administrative assistants to have desktop publishing skills?

PART 2 Assessment

Key Term Review

Answer the following questions on a separate piece of paper.

1. A(n) ______________________ is the program responsible for running a computer. (p. 459)

2. A(n) ______________________ uses images on a monitor to make an operating system easier to use. (p. 459)

3. ______________________ tell the computer what to do and allow the computer user to control the computer. (p. 459)

4. A program that runs "on top" of an operating system is called a(n) ______________________. (p. 460)

5. An application that uses values organized into rows and columns is a(n) ______________________. (p. 460)

6. A(n) ______________________ is an organized way to store information so that it is easy for the computer to search the information. (p. 460)

7. A(n) ______________________ is more efficient than a typewriter because you can correct mistakes on the screen before you print a document. (p. 460)

8. A ______________________ is an unwanted program that can copy itself. (p. 461)

9. ______________________ data is data that has been put into a code. (p. 461)

10. A program that performs a specific task within an operating system is called a ______________________. (p. 461)

11. The hierarchical file system is one example of a ______________________. (p. 462)

12. A(n) ______________________ protects computers against unwanted connections. (p. 461)

Concept Review

Answer the following questions on a separate piece of paper.

13. Explain the relationship between commands and a computer's operating system. (p. 459)

14. List two differences between word processor applications and spreadsheet applications. (p. 460)

15. List three things for which you could use a database. (p. 460)

16. Will an operating system work without an application? (p. 460)

17. Will an application work without an operating system? (p. 460)

18. Explain the importance of firewalls. (p. 461)

Critical Thinking

Complete the following exercises to reinforce your understanding of the lesson.

19. Predict Think of three types of businesses that you think use application software to help make business easier. Write down the type of business and then describe how an application could help that type of business.

20. Collect Think of three school-related activities, such as keeping track of your homework, which you think might be easier with the help of a computer and a software application. Go online and try to locate an application that meets your needs. Try using search terms that combine the words "application" or "software" with the activity (sample search term: homework software).

21. Compare Many people who run their own small office or home office use sophisticated application suites that allow them to create documents, spreadsheets, databases, and presentations. These suites help small business owners solve many of their own problems without the use of accountants, marketers, or designers and without a large financial investment. Research and compare the capabilities of three applications suites. Determine which suite you would prefer to use and explain why.

ISTE Standards

The following ISTE standards are covered in Part 2. Refer to pages xxii to xxiii for a description of the standards listed here.

NETS•S	Performance Indicator
3	5

Chapter 1 Assessment

Reading Check

1. **Define** Define what a *sans serif* font is and name at least three examples.
2. **Explain** Why is it easy to change the size of a scalable font?
3. **Identify** What part of the Word screen should you check to make sure you are in the correct document?
4. **Describe** What are four different ways you can align text on a page?
5. **Evaluate** Why should you use fonts from different font families when creating publications?

Critical Thinking

6. **Compare and Contrast** How would you use an oldstyle font in a document, and how would you use a slab serif font?
7. **Analyze** Why is underlining not used much?
8. **Describe** What kind of spelling mistakes might not be caught by the Spelling and Grammar tool?
9. **Explain** How would you correct your document if you found that you had used two spaces instead of one after every period?
10. **Evaluate** What are three advantages of using a table format?

1 Independent Practice

MATH **Create a Daily Schedule** Break down your school day into categories that can be presented as a table.

a. Plan Draw out a table with your daily schedule.
- The table is four columns. Use the following categories for your column headers: Period, Class, Time, Teacher. (For block schedules, use Day/Time for the third category.)
- Determine how many rows you need. This will vary depending on the number of school periods and after-school activities you have.

b. Create Use Word's table tools to create a table.
- Use your handwritten table as a model for creating your table in Word.
- Merge the cells in the first row, and then add a centered heading.
- Use **Table>Insert** to add a new column labeled *Room*.
- Fill in the table with your classes and the other information.
- Use **Borders and Shading** or **Table AutoFormat** to add color shading and interesting borders to your table.
- Adjust column and text spacing as needed.
- Use **AutoFit to Contents**.

c. Publish Check your schedule to make sure you have not made any errors. Follow your teacher's instructions for saving and printing your work.

Go Online **RUBRICS**
www.glencoe.com

Independent Practice
Go to **Chapter 1**, and choose **Rubrics**. Use the rubrics to help create and evaluate your projects.

Utility Programs Continued

Utility programs accomplish a number of tasks aside from maintaining the security of a computer.

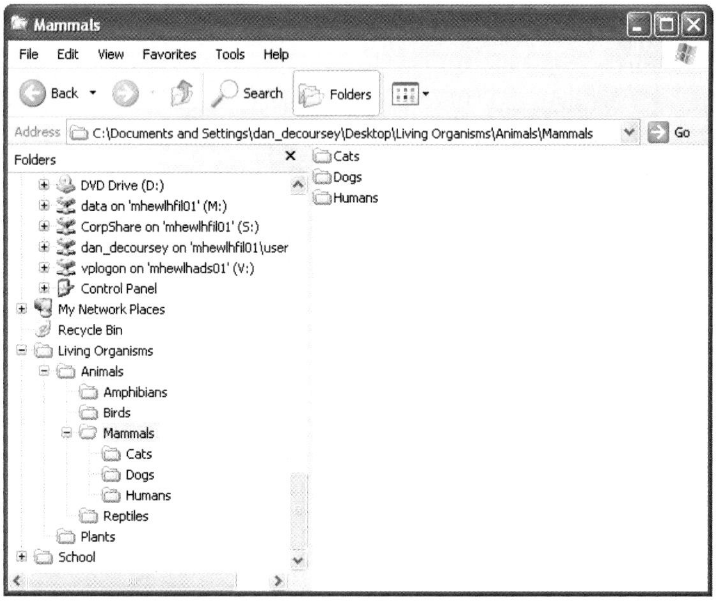

A **file management** utility organizes files and information so that they are easy to locate. The most common file system is called a hierarchical file system. In a hierarchical file system, information is organized by categories, starting with broad categories that get more and more specific as files are opened.

Some utility programs, such as Windows Media Player, allow a user to listen to music or watch movies on his or her computer.

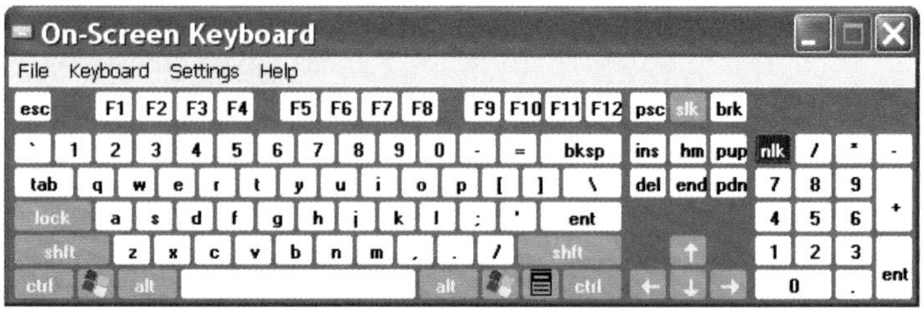

Windows has a group of utilities that make computers easier for people with visual or mobility impairments to use. For instance, a person who cannot type can use the virtual keyboard to click the letters.

TECH CHECK

1. **Discuss** What are the benefits of antivirus programs?
2. **Construct** Create a hierarchical file system for your favorite pastime. The first item should be the broadest category to which your pastime belongs. Each new item should be more specific than the previous item, ending with your pastime.

Chapter 1 Assessment

2 Independent Practice ★★

LANGUAGE ARTS **Illustrate a Poem** Find a short poem and create a visual interpretation of the poem.

a. Plan Choose a poem that has strong visual imagery or themes that can be presented graphically.

b. Create Key the poem, using margins, spacing, and fonts that allow the poem and graphics to fit on one page.

- Use attractive fonts for the title and text that suit the mood of the poem.
- Insert a drop cap at the beginning of the poem.
- Add a page border.
- Insert clip art to illustrate the poem.

c. Evaluate Follow your teacher's instructions for saving and printing your work. Exchange poems with a classmate. Use a rubric to evaluate each other's work for accuracy and how well the visuals enhance the poem.

Go Online ACTIVITIES
www.glencoe.com

Enrichment Go to **Chapter 1**, and choose **Enrichment Activities.** Find more desktop publishing projects using Microsoft Word.

3 Independent Practice ★★★

SCIENCE **Create a Pet Flyer** Imagine that you have been asked to help your local pet shop sell a pet—only the pet is not an everyday dog, cat, rabbit, or goldfish. Find an interesting animal, and create a For Sale flyer that makes the chosen pet seem like the best pet in the world.

For Sale
World's Cutest Fruit Bat
Here's a unique pet that will:
➤ Keep you company at night.
➤ Hang around during the day.
➤ Pollinate your flowers.
➤ Disperse seeds throughout your neighborhood.
➤ Definitely not drive you batty!

a. Plan Do research to find an animal, and learn about its characteristics.

- Determine who your audience is and the content you want to include in your flyer.
- Create a thumbnail sketch showing the layout and content. Include a bulleted list and at least one image of the animal.

b. Create Use your thumbnail sketch to create a flyer in Word. Include:

- The design elements in your thumbnail
- WordArt
- At least one text box

c. Evaluate Follow your teacher's instructions for saving and printing your work. Exchange flyers with a classmate, and use a rubric to evaluate each other's work for accuracy, visual appeal, and content.

Utility Programs

Key Terms

- Encryption
- File management
- Firewall
- Utility program
- Virus

A **utility program** is a program that performs a specific task within an operating system. Utility programs perform a variety of tasks.

Computer Security

Computer security is very important because there are more threats to computers than ever before.

One of the most common threats is called a **virus.** A virus is an unwanted program running on a computer. A virus makes copies of itself and, in some cases, sends copies to other computers. Viruses can use up a computer's memory or harm the data stored on the computer. Another threat is unwanted connections to or from the Internet. These connections can be from viruses or from other users who are attempting to gain control of another computer illegally. A **firewall** is a utility that protects computers against unwanted connections.

Some people have information stored on their computer that they do not want everyone to see. For instance, a company that has created a new invention might want to keep the plans secret until they can patent the invention. People can protect their information by using **encryption,** or putting data into a code.

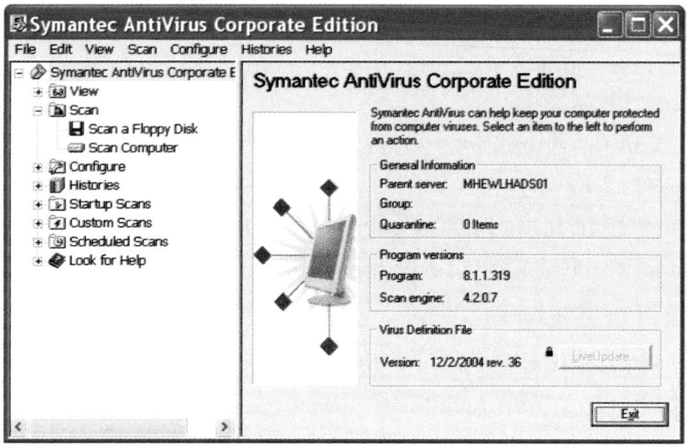

An antivirus program detects and eliminates viruses before they can harm a computer. Good antivirus programs obtain new information about viruses from the Internet.

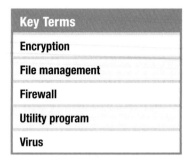

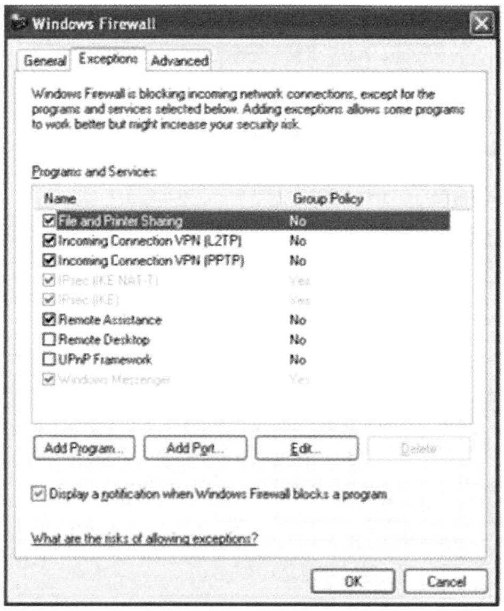

A firewall examines each piece of data that comes into a computer or leaves a computer. If the firewall detects a threat, it will block the data.

<a href="mailto:%65%6E%68%61%6E%63%65%72%40%68%63%70%64%2E%63%6F%6D">janedoe@aol.com</a>

In order to view an encryption, a user must know the key. The key is a string of numbers without which the information will not make sense.

Chapter 2 Vector Graphics in Word

Skills You Will Learn

In this chapter, you will learn more about clip art and vector graphics and use Word's Drawing toolbar to create and manipulate images. You will then use these skills to create flyers, cards, and brochures.

Design an Effective Flyer or Brochure

A flyer is generally a one-page information sheet, while brochures are usually printed on two sides of a page and folded. Both flyers and brochures have a limited amount of space to present information. They must also catch the reader's attention so they are not immediately set aside or thrown out.

In both cases, the design must have a specific purpose and be aimed at a particular audience. Before creating either type of publication, you need to determine the most important information to be presented and the images that best convey that content. You must then lay out the text and images in an attractive way that lets readers understand the information at a glance. Finally, you must edit and proofread the document before publishing it in a format that is most likely to reach your audience. Keep the budget in mind as you consider these design issues.

Below is a table showing the elements you should consider when designing a flyer or brochure.

DESIGN PROCESS: Flyers and Brochures

Elements	Issues
Purpose	To provide information about a product, business, or event in a visual, easy-to-read format that can be widely distributed.
Audience	Varies. (A brochure for a restaurant that targets college students would look different from a restaurant brochure aimed at families or upscale customers.)
Content	Gather or create content and design elements such as graphics, logos, headings, lists, text boxes, tear-off elements (for example, coupons or contact information).
Layout	Flyers are usually a single page. Brochures are usually a two-sided page with multiple folds.
Publication	Publish as print or Web documents. Printed documents can be color or black and white. Brochures may require duplex printing. The number of copies needed will vary.

Application Software

Key Terms

- Application
- Database
- Presentation
- Spreadsheet
- Word processor

Today, people use computers for everything from writing a letter to calculating a budget. But it is not a computer's operating system that does these things. The operating system only runs the computer. **Applications** are the programs designed for a particular type of task, like writing a letter or calculating a budget. Applications, however, will not work without an operating system.

Many types of applications serve different purposes. Four of the most common application types are **word processors, spreadsheets, presentations,** and **databases.** The table below explains each of these types. Other common applications include Internet browsers, used for viewing Internet content; e-mail programs, used for sending and receiving mail electronically; and graphics programs, used to create images on the computer.

Four Common Applications

Application Type	What does it do?	Example
Word Processor	A word processor produces text documents. You key words into the computer using a keyboard just as if you were using a typewriter. However, a word processor is more efficient because you can correct mistakes on the screen before you print a document.	**Microsoft Word** **WordPerfect** **Wordpro** **AppleWorks Word Processing** **Microsoft Works Word Processing**
Spreadsheet	A spreadsheet is a table organized into rows and columns. You enter numbers in the table. The spreadsheet can do calculations with the numbers in the table.	**Microsoft Excel** **Lotus 1-2-3** **AppleWorks Spreadsheet** **Microsoft Works Spreadsheet**
Presentation	A presentation is composed of slides that contain information and graphics. A presentation program helps you make a presentation look organized and eye-catching.	**Microsoft PowerPoint** **Apple Keynote** **AppleWorks Presentation**
Database	A database is an organized way to store information so that it is easy for the computer to search the information. For instance, you might use a database to store your friends' names, phone numbers, and addresses so that you can easily look up a number or address using a friend's name.	**Microsoft Access** **FileMaker** **AppleWorks Database** **Microsoft Works Database**

TECH CHECK

1. **Distinguish** How are operating systems and applications different?
2. **Discuss** List three things you could use a word processor for.

WORKSHOP Foundations

Understanding Graphics

A well-written document that is largely ignored by its audience is virtually useless. Like spices in cooking, desktop publishing adds flavor to text documents and varies the texture and color to create a visually attractive message with a clear focus.

Without graphics, desktop publishing is merely word processing. In addition to providing visual appeal, graphics such as maps, charts, graphs, and illustrations make complex information easy to understand. Skillfully created illustrations can defy the limitations of time, space, and imagination to communicate effectively.

What Are Vector and Raster Graphics?

There are two kinds of graphics: vector graphics and raster graphics. The difference between these images is in the way that computers store the information which affects the way they can be used.

▲ A vector graphic can be resized without loss of definition. It looks crisp and smooth, whether it is small or large.

▲ The same image in raster graphic format shows the pixels when the image is enlarged to the same size as the vector graphic.

A **vector graphic** is usually a drawing, such as clip art, and is made up of lines and curves. A **raster (or bitmap) graphic** is a complex picture, made up of **pixels**, or small squares of color in a grid. *Bitmap* and *raster* are interchangeable terms. Raster graphics are created with software such as Adobe® Photoshop® or Corel® Paint Shop. Raster images do not look as smooth and crisp as vector graphics when they are resized because the software tries to adjust the pixels. However, raster graphics can also look as realistic as a photograph. Chapters 5 and 6 will discuss raster graphics in more detail.

You Will Learn To

- Identify vector and raster graphics
- Compare vector and raster graphics

Key Terms

vector graphic
raster graphic
bitmap graphic
pixels

Before You Read

Survey Before You Read Before starting the chapter, do a quick survey of the content by reading the colored headings. Think about what you already know about the topic. Look for the bolded terms. Jot down words you do not recognize so you can find the meaning as you read. Study the pictures, charts, and illustrations. Do they help you predict what information will appear in the chapter? Finally, read the end-of-chapter questions. This will help you pay attention to important concepts in the reading.

Operating System Software

Key Terms
Command
Graphical User Interface (GUI)
Operating system

A computer's **operating system** is a program that runs the computer. It recognizes input from input devices, sends output to output devices, and saves data and information on the hard disk. A computer user controls the operating system with **commands.** A command tells the computer to perform a particular task. Users of operating systems such as Linux and DOS need to type in commands to tell the computer what to do. More popular operating systems such as Windows and Macintosh use a **graphical user interface (GUI).** A GUI uses images on a monitor to make an operating system easier to use. Instead of learning command words, a GUI user can choose from a list of options.

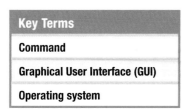

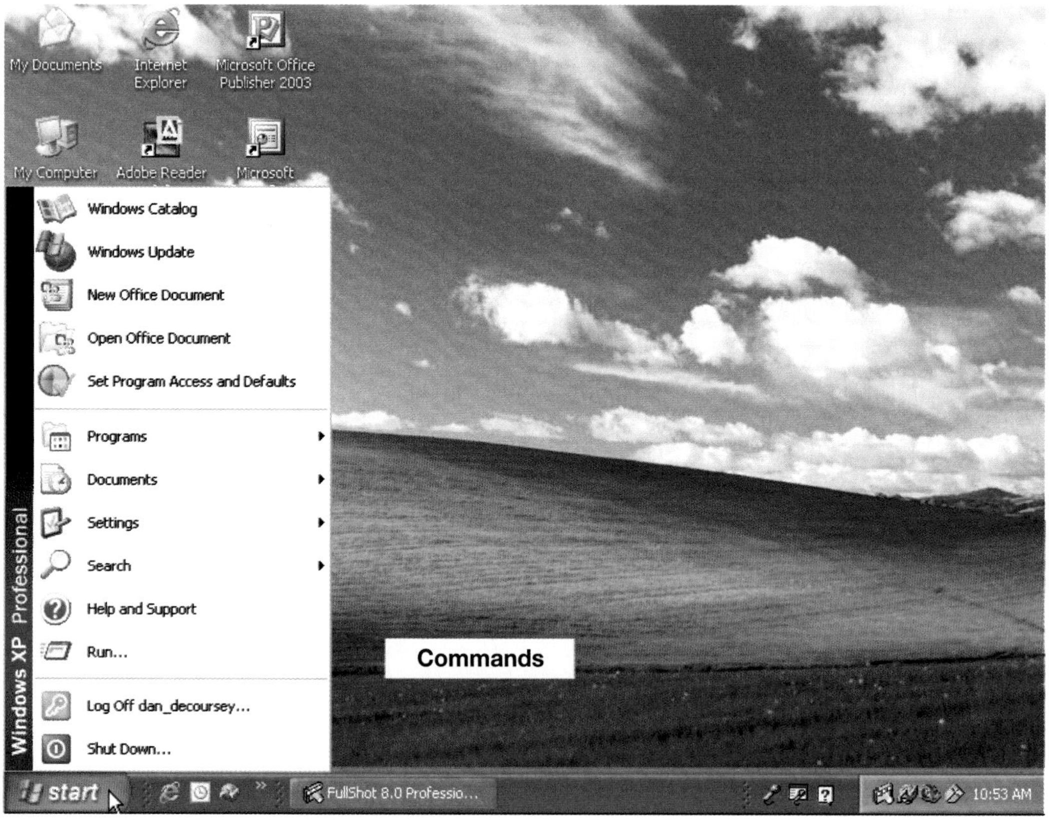

Windows is an operating system that employs a graphical user interface that uses images and a list of options instead of keyed commands.

TECH CHECK

1. **Explain** Why are commands important?
2. **Predict** Why do you think operating systems with GUIs are more popular than those that use word commands?

How Are Vector Graphics Created?

Computers create vector graphics by using math formulas. For example, if you draw a circle, the computer does not "remember" exactly what the circle looks like. Instead, it remembers the center point and area of the circle so that it may *redraw* the object again.

Adobe® Illustrator® is popular software that is used to create vector images. Every time you create an image, the program saves instructions on how the graphic should be drawn. When you zoom in or move the object, the computer *redraws* the entire image without losing any quality. Eventually, all images must be converted to raster images by a computer so they can be sent to a monitor or printer, where they are displayed as pixels.

Sidebar

What Is a Pixel? The word *pixel* is a combination of the words *picture element.* Pixels are tiny squares that are used to create an image. You can find pixels in a graphic, and you can find pixels in your computer monitor, too. So *pixel* can refer to information or to hardware. The higher the number of pixels in an image (the greater the resolution or individual points of color), the more detail the image can contain.

Identify What is the word *pixel* short for?

Which Type of Image Should I Use?

Vector and raster images serve different purposes, as shown in the table below. It is important to know if an image will be resized.

Vector vs. Raster Graphics

Type of Graphic	Purpose	Types of Image	File Size	Stored As	Resizeability
Vector	Allows you to create and manipulate shapes with precision for display on a computer	Line drawings, maps, cartoons, diagrams	Small	Math formulas	Excellent
Raster	Allows you to create and manipulate drawings that are easily edited	Realistic images or photos	Large	Pixels	Poor

▲ Determine the purpose of the graphics in a publication before choosing the type of graphics to use.

In this chapter, you will explore some of the drawing tools available in Microsoft Word for creating vector graphics.

Reading Check

1. **Compare and Contrast** How do raster and vector graphics differ? How are they the same?
2. **Draw Conclusions** What kind of graphic is clip art?

PART 1 Assessment

Key Term Review

Answer the following questions on a separate piece of paper.

1. ______________________ refers to the practical application of an art or skill. (p. 448)

2. A computer designed to remain in one location is a(n) ______________________. (p. 449)

3. A computer designed to be carried from place to place is a(n) ______________________. (p. 449)

4 ______________________ are powerful computers that can do many things at once. (p. 449)

5. Keyboards and printers are examples of ______________________. (p. 450)

6. An input device that has buttons to push and a control stick is called a(n) ______________________. (p. 450)

7. You must connect peripheral devices to the computer through a(n) ______________________. (p. 450)

8. A(n) ______________________ displays visual information similar to a television set. (p. 451)

9. The brain of a computer is called the ______________________. (p. 452)

10. All circuit boards in a computer connect to the ______________________, or main circuit board. (p. 452)

11. Three types of optical storage disks are __________, __________ and __________. (p. 454)

12. A group of computers that are connected to each other is called a(n) ______________________. (p. 456)

13. A(n) ______________________ allows network resources to run smoothly by managing the flow of information on a network. (p. 456)

14. A connected group of computers that are close to each other is called a(n) ______________________. (p. 456)

15. The actual arrangement of computers in a network is called a(n) ______________________. (p. 457)

Concept Review

Answer the following questions on a separate piece of paper.

16. Information goes into a computer through ______________________ and comes out through ______________________. (pp. 450–451)

17. Most of the calculations done in a computer take place in the ______________________. (p. 452)

18. Tapes or disks that are used to store information for a long time are called ______________________. (p. 453)

19. A mainframe is the best type of computer for ______________________ users. (p. 449)

20. A group of connected computers that are far apart is called a ______________________. (p. 456)

Critical Thinking

Complete the following exercises to reinforce your understanding of the lesson.

21. Organize Create a diagram that shows how a basic microcomputer system handles information. The diagram should show the flow of information, where information is stored, and where it is processed. Locate and label the following items:

- at least three input devices
- at least three output devices
- memory
- storage devices
- processing locations

22. Compile Create a table that you can use to evaluate or compare microcomputer systems.

- On the left side of your paper, create a column that contains at least seven categories (such as "Amount of Memory" and "Cost") that you can use to evaluate a computer system.
- Find an online computer store or look at an advertising flyer.
- Look up two different computer systems and fill in the categories you have created.
- Compare your results. Which system seems the better bargain?

ISTE Standards

The following ISTE standards are covered in Part 1. Refer to pages xxii to xxiii for a description of the standards listed here.

NETS•S	Performance Indicator
3	5

WORK SHOP

Toolbox

You Will Learn To

- Display the Drawing toolbar
- Identify drawing tools

Key Term

default

Word's Drawing Toolbar

The Drawing toolbar contains buttons that you can use for creating line drawings and shapes, inserting images, and manipulating graphics.

How Do I Display the Drawing Toolbar?

In Microsoft Word, choose **View>Toolbars>Drawing** to display the Drawing toolbar. Word usually displays the toolbar at the bottom of the window, which is the automatic, or **default**, setting. However, if it has been moved in the past, the toolbar may appear anywhere on your screen. Your toolbar should look like the image below.

What Drawing Tools Are in Word?

Word is considered a word processing program, but it contains tools that allow it to function as desktop publishing software. Whether you are drawing a simple shape around text or changing the features of complex clip art, Word provides useful options that can give your document visual appeal.

Use the Drawing toolbar to create straight or freeform lines, add arrows and shapes, and change colors or styles.

AutoShapes [AutoShapes] provides an assortment of drawing options, as well as common shapes that save time when drawing, including stars, arrows, and banners (see the illustration below).

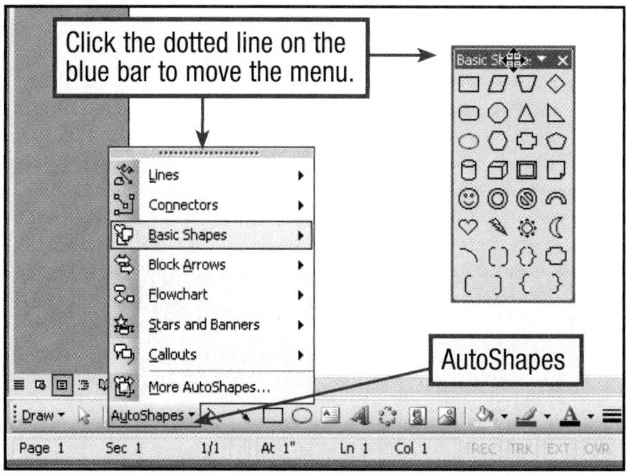

Word provides you with many tools to create your publications. Practice using these tools so you understand how to use each tool effectively. Knowing which tools to use will help you complete the projects in this chapter.

► Click the dotted line at the top of most drawing menus to drag the menu into the workspace. This is helpful when creating drawings.

Networks Continued

Connecting computers properly so that they can communicate is challenging. Devices called **network hardware** and software called **network operating systems (NOS)** help computers share information.

A **network topology** is the actual arrangement of computers in a network. Three network topologies are shown below.

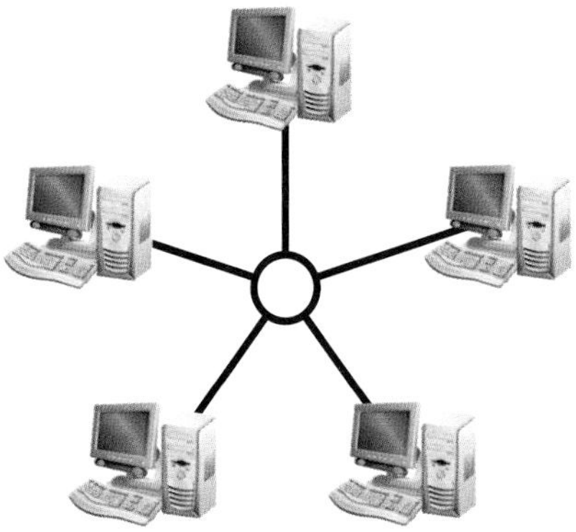

Star

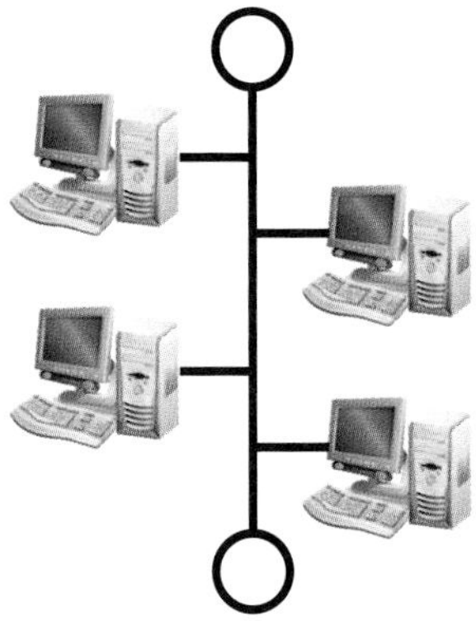

Bus

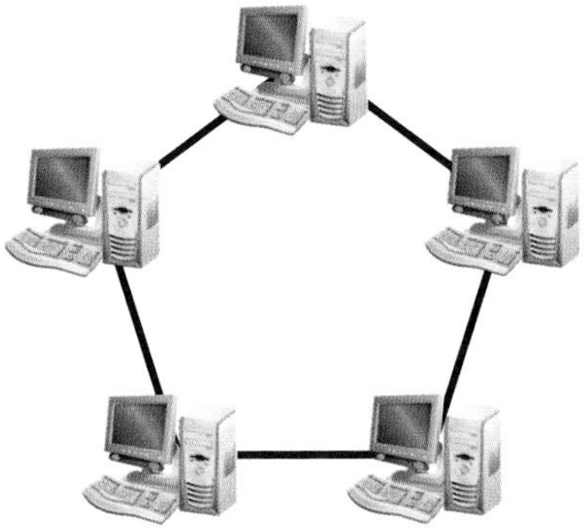

Ring

Networks can also have combinations of these topologies, such as a star-bus network or a star-ring network.

TECH CHECK

1. **Differentiate** What is the difference between a LAN and a WAN? Describe one use for a LAN and one for a WAN.
2. **Construct** Draw a diagram of a star-ring network.

WORKSHOP Toolbox

Eye On Ethics

What Is a Copyright? The first copyright laws were introduced in England in 1709. The term literally comes from the *right* of an individual to prevent his or her work from being *copied* without permission. Before then, anyone with the means could print and sell books without paying the author a cent!

Draw Conclusions How were writers protected before copyright laws?

Drawing Tools in Microsoft Word

Button	Function	Button	Function
Draw ▾ **Draw**	Opens options, such as grouping and rotating objects, and wrapping text around objects.	**Insert Clip Art**	Inserts pre-drawn art from the program or the Internet.
Select Objects	Selects an object (shape, picture, WordArt) or parts of an object.	**Insert Picture**	Inserts a digital picture into the document.
Line Color	Adds color to the outside line around a drawing object.	**Fill Color**	Adds a color, texture, pattern, or even a picture to an enclosed figure.
Line	Creates straight lines.	**Font Color**	Changes the text color, just like the button on the Formatting toolbar.
Rectangle	Creates squares or rectangles of any size.	**Line Style**	Changes properties like line thickness or number of lines.
Oval	Creates ovals and circles.	**Dash Style**	Makes the lines in a selected figure dashed, dotted, or both.
Text Box	Creates a rectangle in which you can place graphics or text.	**Arrow Style**	Gives options to set different arrow heads, end points, or pointer direction.
Insert WordArt	Creates text with graphic effects.	**Shadow Style**	Adds a drop shadow behind objects.
Insert Diagram or Chart	Creates organization charts, such as flowcharts.	**3-D Style**	Adds three-dimensional effects to drawing objects.

Networks

Key Terms
Ethernet cable
LAN
Network
Network hardware
Network interface card (NIC)
Network operating system (NOS)
Network topology
Router
Server
WAN

A **network** is a group of computers that are connected to each other. There are two basic types of networks.

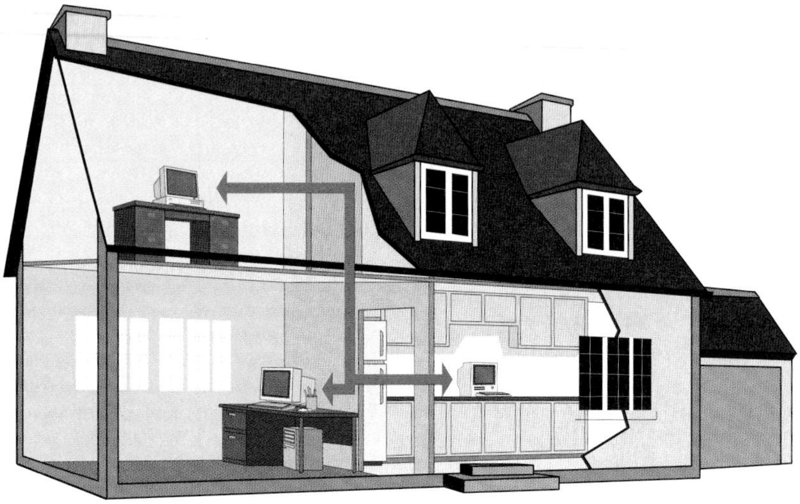

A **LAN,** or **L**ocal **A**rea **N**etwork, is a connected group of computers that are close to each other. For example, a connected group of computers in a home or in an office is a LAN.

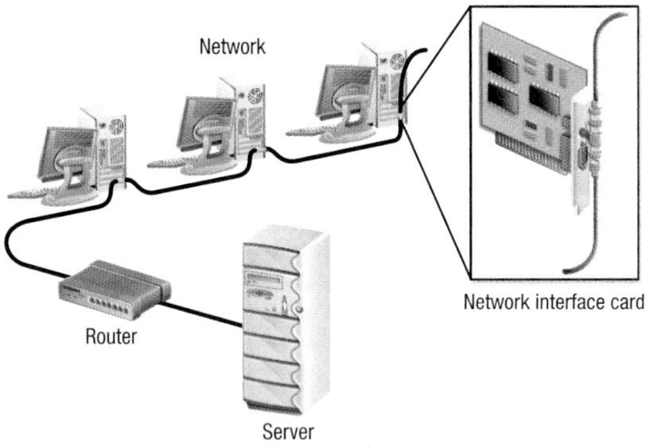

All computers on a network need a **network interface card (NIC)** so that the computers can communicate over the network. One way to connect computers is by **Ethernet cable.** A **router** connects multiple computers to each other as well as to a WAN (like the Internet). A **server** manages the flow of information on a network. This allows network resources, like files and printers, to run smoothly.

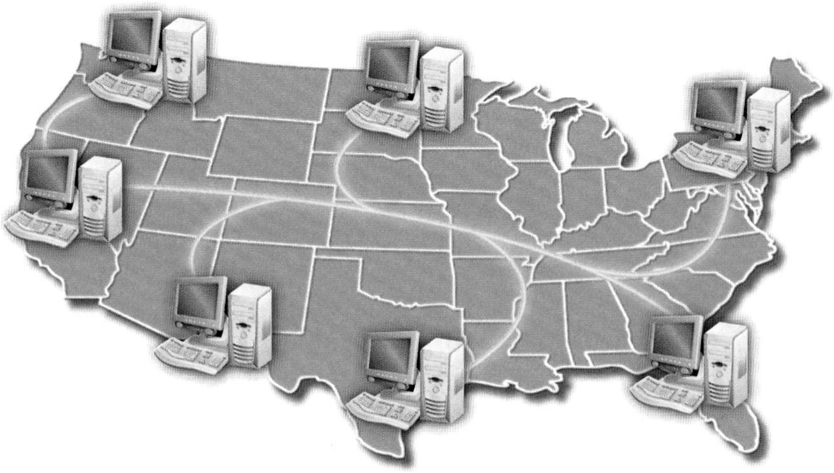

A **WAN,** or **W**ide **A**rea **N**etwork, is a connected group of computers that are not close to each other. For example, the Internet is a WAN. A WAN provides users with access to large amounts of information.

WORKSHOP Toolbox

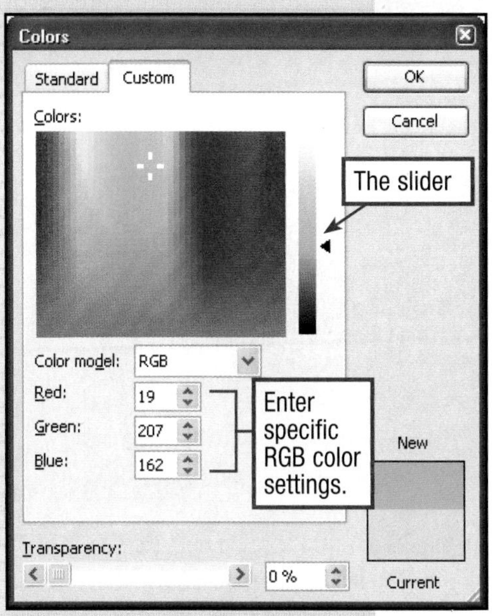

▲ The computer uses a mixture of red, green, and blue (RGB) to display colors on the monitor. You can use the slider to adjust color, or key specific settings to get an exact color.

Using Colors in Word

When you open a menu from the fill or line color buttons (or effects like textures), you will not see the names of the colors displayed. If you want to find a specific color by name, slowly move your mouse over the squares. The color name should pop up.

If you want to create a color that is not one of the default colors, you can click *More Colors*. The Colors dialog box (shown at the left) lets you set a wide range of colors.

Shadow Settings and 3-D Effects

The **Shadow Style** button and the **3-D Style** button are useful tools to give your publications depth. However, do not overuse the tools in a publication, or your audience may be distracted from the focus of your message.

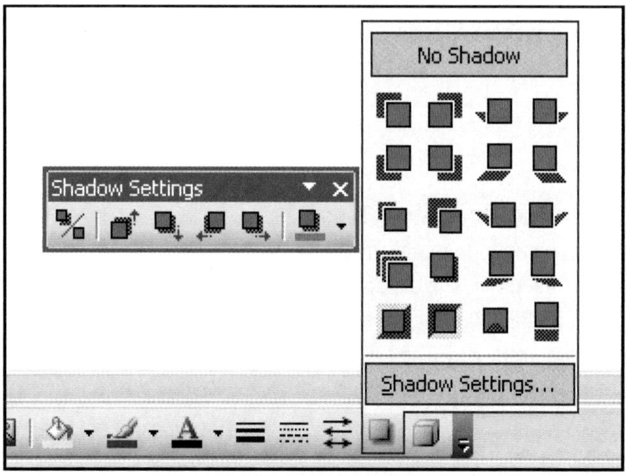

▲ In the Shadow menu, choose **Shadow Settings** to adjust the look, direction, color, and length of your shadow.

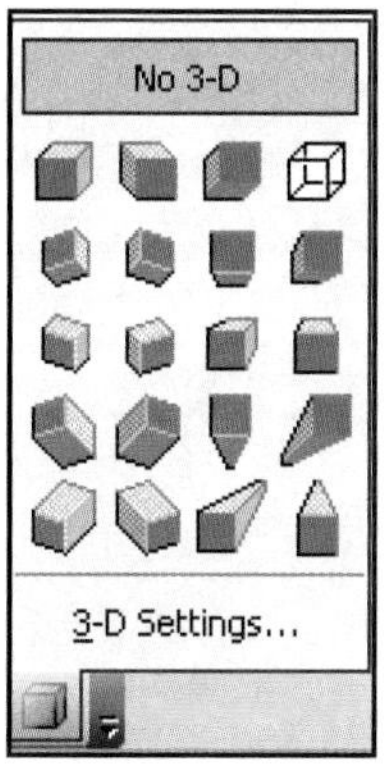

▲ The 3-D style menu effects created by this button cannot be used in combination with other buttons.

Reading Check

1. **Evaluate** Which Drawing toolbar button do you think you will use most often and why?
2. **Draw Conclusions** Why is it important to familiarize yourself with the many drawing tools?

Storage Devices Continued

If you have problems using a storage device, try the basic troubleshooting procedures below.

For Floppy Disks:

Make sure the write-protect tab is in the locked position. Look at the bottom right and bottom left corners of the disk. If there is a hole in both corners, turn the disk over. Then move the tab in the bottom right corner to cover the hole.

Make sure there is not a disk in the drive already.

Make sure the disk is right side up and the metal side is facing the drive. The disk being inserted in this photo is not facing the correct way. The bottom disk is facing the correct way.

Put a different floppy disk into the drive. If neither floppy works, the disk drive may be broken.

For Optical Disks:

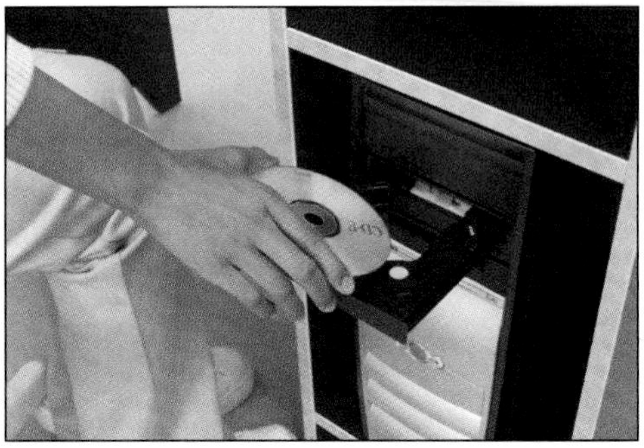

Make sure the CD or DVD is seated right side up in the disk tray. The shiny side should be on the bottom. Make sure there is not more than one CD or DVD in the tray.

If a CD will not work, as a last resort, wipe it with a very soft cloth. Wipe the shiny side gently from the center of the disk outward. Ask your teacher or a parent before attempting this.

TECH CHECK

1. **Evaluate** If you wanted to save a copy of a short story you wrote, could you use a floppy disk? Why or why not?
2. **Identify** What are the storage capacities of floppy disks, ZIP disks, and hard drives?
3. **Describe** Describe three things you can do if your CD-ROM is not working.

Project 2-1

Drawing Basics

Spotlight on Skills

- Draw circles
- Apply color fill options
- Draw and format lines

Key Terms

- perpendicular
- parallel
- pull handles

Academic Focus

Math
Create geometric shapes

Go Online PREVIEW
www.glencoe.com

Before You Begin Go to **Chapter 2**, and choose **PowerPoint Presentations** to preview the documents you will be creating. Also, use the individual project **Rubrics** to help create and evaluate your work.

The Drawing toolbar contains the shapes and tools you need to create and modify your own simple drawings.

Helpful Keyboard Keys

Your keyboard can make it easier to use the tools on the Drawing toolbar more precisely.

▲ You can create sophisticated images by adding gradient fill patterns to simple shapes like rectangles.

Shift Key By holding down the SHIFT key, you can:

- Make perfect squares or circles when using the Rectangle or Oval drawing tools.
- Create lines that are **perpendicular** (lines that join at a right angle), **parallel** (lines that never intersect), or at a 45-degree angle when using the Line drawing tool.
- Select multiple items.

Control (Ctrl) Key Holding down the CTRL key allows you to:

- *Nudge* or move drawing objects a tiny amount. Select the object, and then use the arrow keys on the keyboard.
- Create a copy of the object. Click it, and then drag the object with the mouse.

Mac users should press the ALT key instead of the CTRL Key.

Alt Key You also have more control in placing and sizing objects when you press the ALT key while dragging the object with the mouse.

Customize AutoShapes Most AutoShapes can be customized. You can use **pull handles** (either squares or circles) to make them larger or smaller and the green circles to rotate them.

If your AutoShape has a yellow diamond (some shapes have more than one), you can click and drag the diamond to change the appearance of the shape. You can make happy faces look sad or change an arc into a ring.

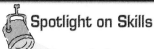

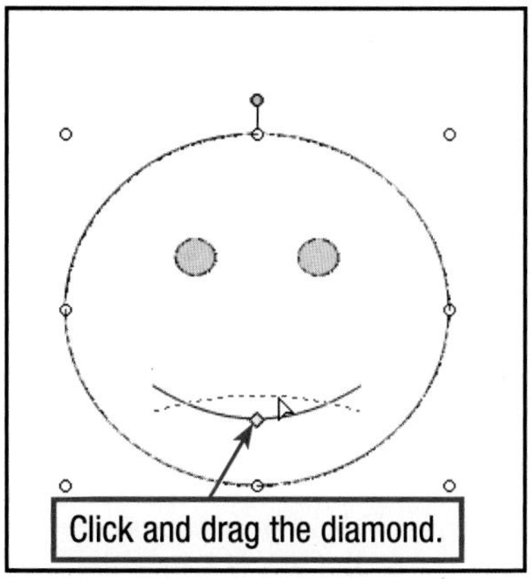

▲ The yellow diamond that appears on many AutoShapes allows the user to customize the shape's appearance.

► **In this project,** you will create a drawing of a pizza using a number of simple shapes. Then you will divide the pizza into equal slices using Word's drawing tools.

Storage Devices Continued

All of the storage devices you have read about so far use electric charges to store information. **Optical disks,** another type of storage device, use lasers to read and write information. Four types of optical disks are explained below.

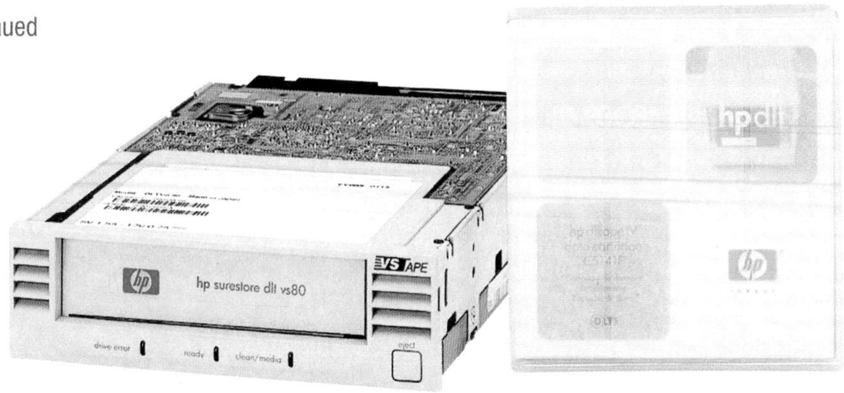

Information can only be put on CD-ROM and CD-R disk once. A **CD-RW** is an optical disk that can record information many times. CD-RW disks are useful for making copies of important information for backup.

A **CD-R,** which stands for **C**ompact **D**isk-**R**ecordable, is a CD-ROM disk that does not yet contain any information. A CD-R drive writes information onto the CD-R disk. A CD-R can hold about the same amount of information that the CD-ROM can hold.

A **CD-ROM** is an optical disk that can hold up to 1 gigabyte of information. One gigabyte of information is equal to 700 floppy disks or 300,000 pages of text. CD-ROM drives are very common in PCs because the CD-ROM is a cheap way to store lots of information.

A **flash drive** is a portable storage device that plugs directly into a computer's USB port. Some are as small as a pen or keychain and hold 256MB to 4GB of information or more.

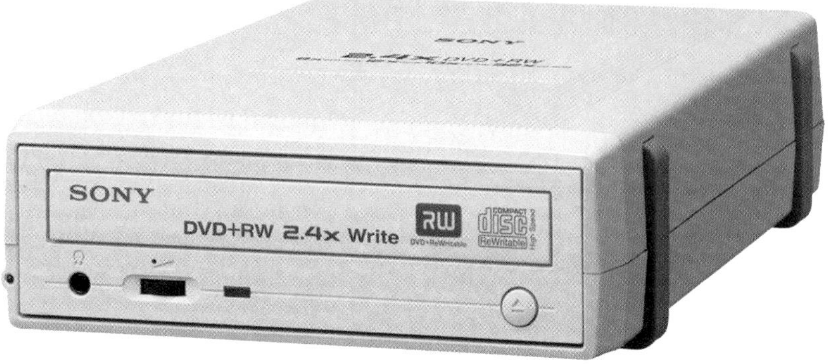

Like the CD-ROM, a **DVD-ROM** is an optical disk. However, the DVD-ROM can hold up to 17 gigabytes of information. It would take 17 CD-ROMs to hold the information in one DVD-ROM. DVD-ROM disks are commonly used to store movies.

Step-by-Step

1. Open a new Word document. Save it according to your teacher's instructions.

Draw Circles

2. If the **Drawing** toolbar is not displayed, on the **menu** toolbar, click **View>Toolbars>Drawing**.

3. On the **Drawing** toolbar, click the **Oval** button, then click anywhere on the page.

4. Hold the SHIFT key while dragging the mouse to create a circle. Make the circle about 5 inches in diameter.

Apply Color Fill Options

5. If your circle does not display sizing handles, click the circle to select it. On the **Drawing** toolbar, click **Fill Color**, then choose **Tan**.

6. Create a smaller circle, and place it inside the first one. Press the arrow keys to nudge it into place (Figure 2.1). Mac users should press the ALT and arrow keys.

7. On the **Drawing** toolbar, click the **Fill Color** button, and choose **Fill Effects**.

8. Under the **Pattern** tab, choose **Large Confetti** (Figure 2.2). Click **OK**.

9. Change the foreground to **Gold** and the background to **Red**. Then click **OK**.

Figure 2.1 Use the Oval button and Shift key to draw perfect circles.

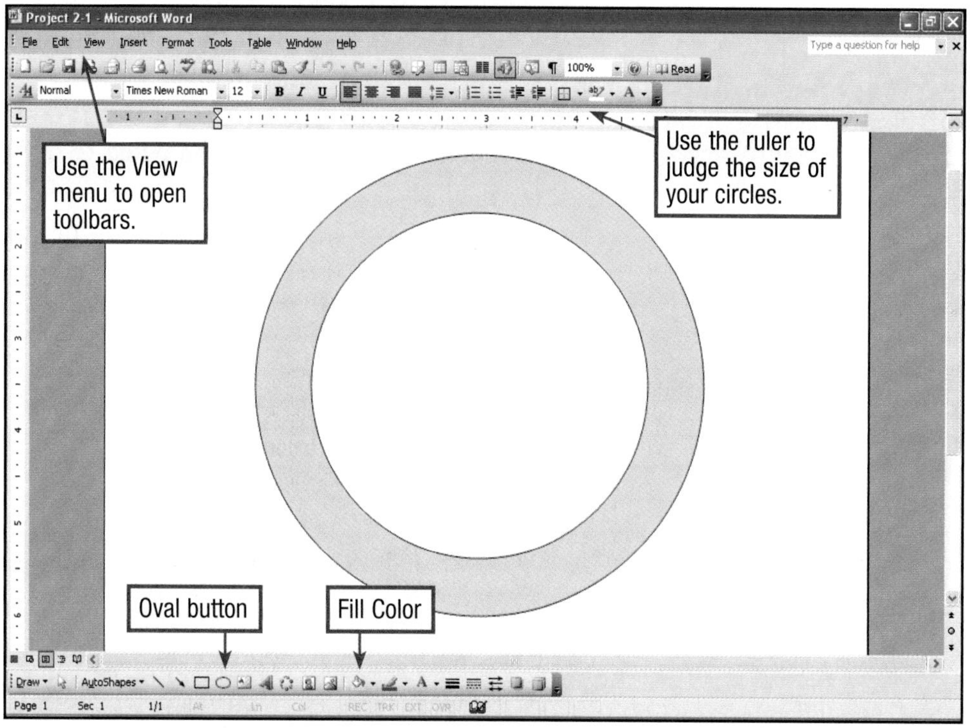

Figure 2.2. Use a pattern to give texture to a color.

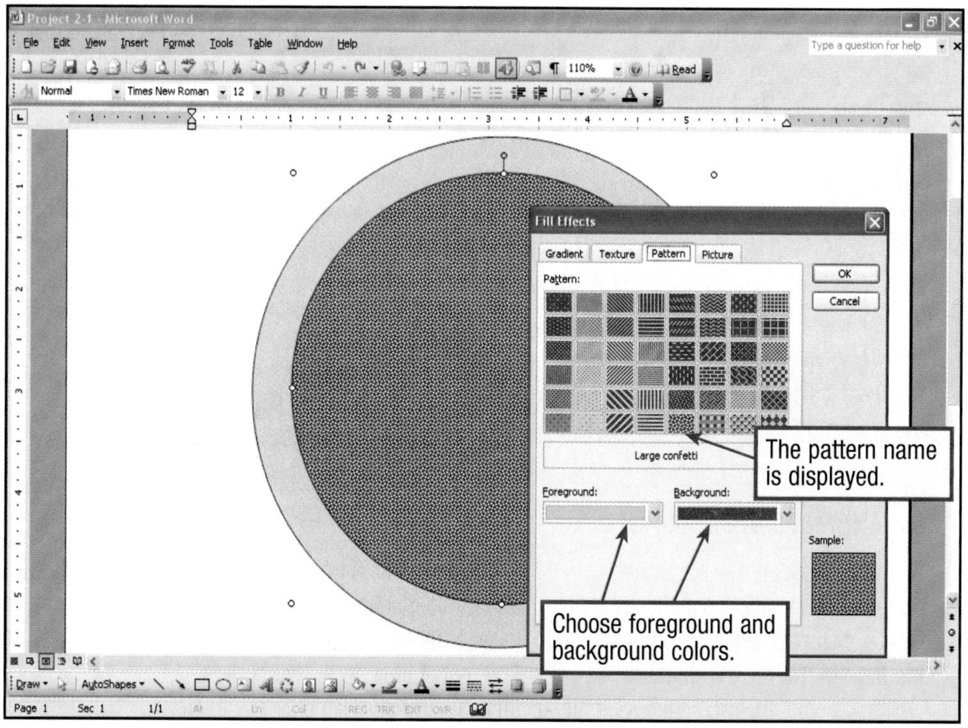

Storage Devices

Key Terms
CD-R
CD-ROM
CD-RW
DVD-ROM
Flash drive
Flash memory
Floppy disk
Hard drive
Optical disk
ZIP disk

As you have already learned, computers change data into useful information. Computers are also useful for storing information. In this section, you will learn about some of the devices that are used to store information.

A **hard drive,** also called a hard disk, is the most widely used secondary storage device. A hard drive can be internal or external. Hard drives today can usually hold 10 to 100 gigabytes (GB) of data. One GB equals one million kilobytes (KB). A five-page research paper uses about 40 KB.

A **floppy disk** contains a small portable disk inside a plastic cover. Floppy disks can hold up to 1.4 megabytes (MB) of information, which is about enough space to store the words in a small book.

A **ZIP disk,** like a floppy disk, has a portable disk inside a plastic case. A ZIP disk can hold 100 to 750 megabytes (MB). Two hundred fifty megabytes is roughly equal to five volumes of an encyclopedia!

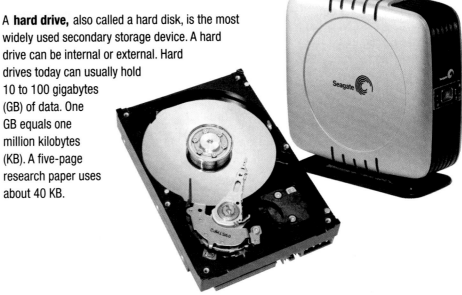

Flash memory is used in digital cameras, some MP3 players, portable storage drives, and other devices. It uses chips to hold information.

10 Create a small circle on top of the previous two to create a pepperoni (Figure 2.3).

11 On the **Drawing** toolbar, click the **Fill Color** button. Then choose **Fill Effects**, and select the **Gradient** tab.

12 Click **One Color**, and change **Color 1** to **Red**. Choose the **Horizontal** shading style (Figure 2.3). Click **OK**.

13 Hold the CTRL key, click on the pepperoni. A small + sign will appear. Drag away from the pepperoni to create a copy of the pepperonis.

Mac users press ALT instead of CTRL.

14 Continue selecting, dragging, and distributing pepperoni all around the pizza (Figure 2.4).

Draw and Format Lines

15 On the **Drawing** toolbar, double-click **Line** so it stays selected.

16 Click and drag 4 lines to create 8 equal "slices" on the pizza. See Figure 2.4. (**Note**: Press ALT to make line placement more precise.)

17 Hold the SHIFT key, and select each of the lines.

18 On the **Drawing** toolbar, change the **Line Color** to **Gray-50 percent**. Your finished drawing should look similar to Figure 2.4.

▼ **Figure 2.3** A gradient fill blends color together and helps create realistic shading.

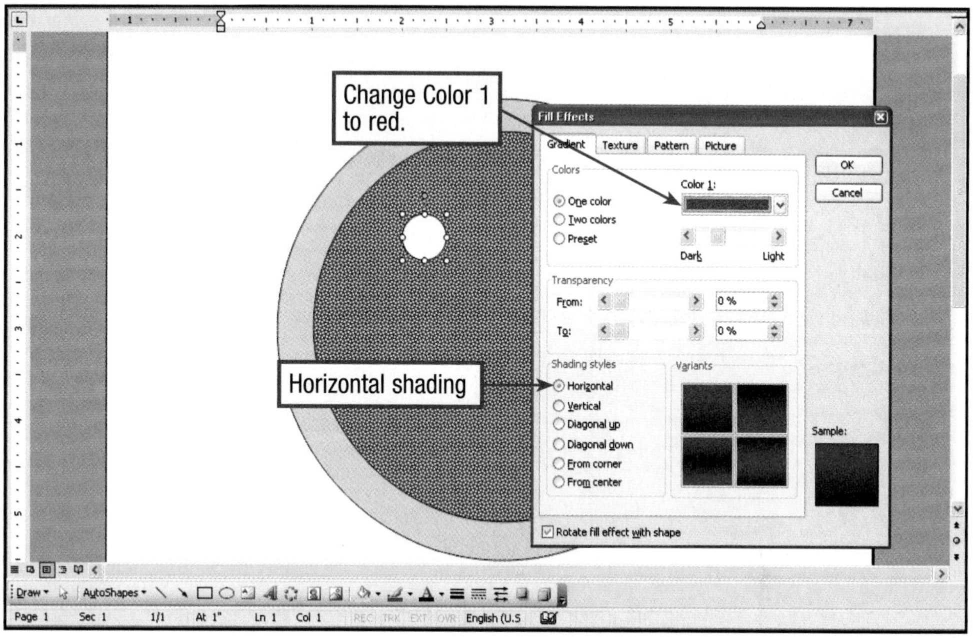

▼ **Figure 2.4** Your final pepperoni pizza should look similar to this.

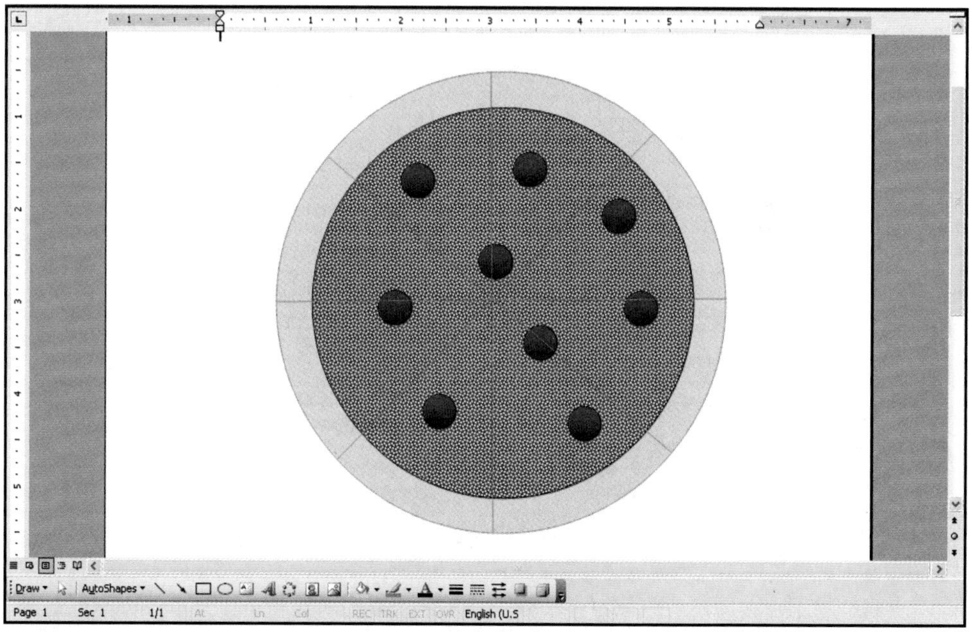

Instant Message

Remove the Drawing Canvas The default setting of Word will create a drawing canvas when you first click on a drawing tool. If you do not want to create an image in the drawing canvas, press DELETE on your keyboard.

Processing Components

Key Terms
CPU
Memory
Microprocessor
Motherboard
RAM
ROM
Process

A computer uses hardware to **process** data into useful information. The part of the computer that processes information has many parts that work together. The **microprocessor** is the brain of a computer. A computer makes almost all of its calculations in the microprocessor. Not all microprocessors are the same. Some can perform more calculations per second than others. Today's handheld PDAs process data many times faster than the early mainframe computers.

Computers use **memory** to hold information and perform tasks.

- Random access memory **(RAM)** holds information temporarily, when you are working in a particular file. It is erased when you turn off the computer
- Read-only memory **(ROM)** is permanent information on your computer that cannot be changed. It holds your computer's built-in instructions and works when you turn on or shut down your computer.

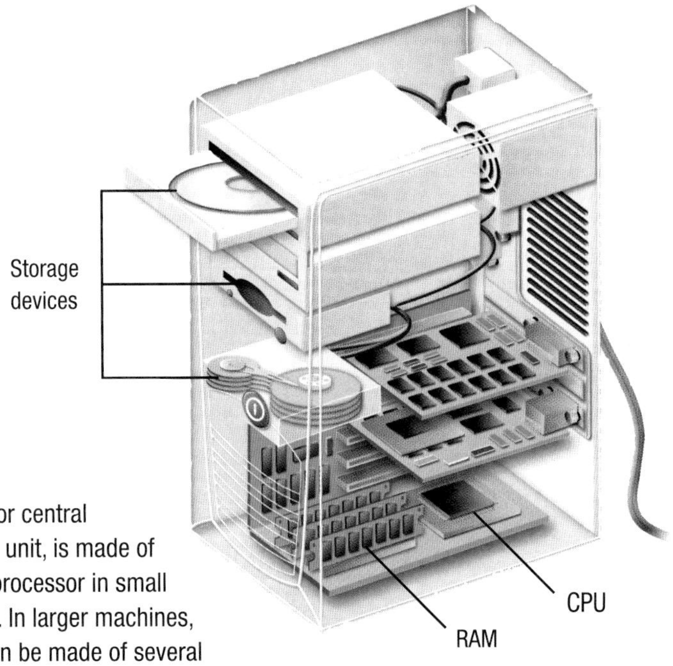

The **CPU,** or central processing unit, is made of one microprocessor in small computers. In larger machines, the CPU can be made of several microprocessors working together.

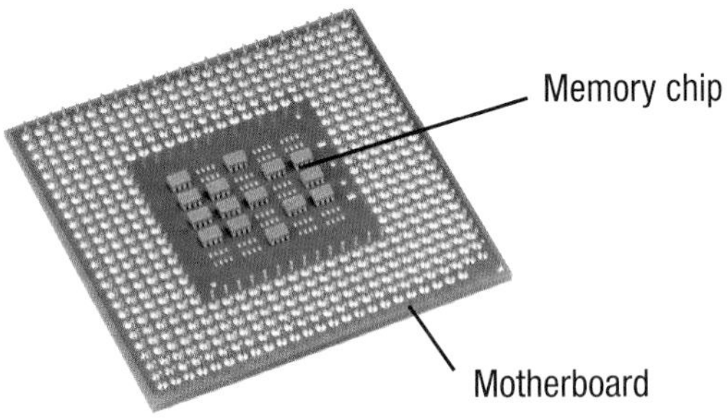

The **motherboard** is the main circuit board in a computer. All of the other circuit boards connect to the motherboard. In many computers, the microprocessor and memory can be found on the motherboard.

TECH CHECK

1. **Describe** List three processing components in a computer and explain what each does.
2. **Evaluate** What does the CPU have to do with the speed of a computer?
3. **Compare** What is the difference between RAM and ROM?

Project 2-2

Group Drawing Objects

Spotlight on Skills

- Apply different font styles
- Add a page border
- Edit and resize clip art
- Group drawing elements
- Wrap text
- Add a header

Key Terms

- group
- ungroup

Academic Focus

Language Arts
Communicate your message clearly

The graphics you created in Project 2-1 were vector images. In vector images, complex drawings are made of simple lines and shapes. The dog to the right was created in Microsoft Word by combining circles, trapezoids, lines, an arc, and a rectangle. A shadow was added to some of the shapes. All these tools are on the Drawing toolbar.

▲ You can create this picture using the Drawing toolbar.

Group and Ungroup

When you combine separate simple objects into a single, more complex image, you **group** the objects. Grouping keeps all the pieces of the image together so that you can easily move and resize the image.

In the dog image, the eyes can be grouped so that the two circles can be moved or resized together. Notice that each eye is made up of a white and black circle. Grouping these objects helps make the image easier to manage.

Objects that have been grouped together can also be separated by using the **ungroup** command. When you ungroup, you break a drawing into smaller pieces, each with its own set of handles, as shown in the clip art of the bus. The group and ungroup commands can be found in the Draw [Draw ▾] menu on the Drawing toolbar.

◀ When you ungroup a clip art image, you can see the handles of each individual element making up the image.

▶ **In this project,** you will create a flyer that advertises guitar lessons. You will then edit the image and lay out the text to make your message visually interesting.

Output Devices

Key Terms

- Monitor
- Output device
- Printer
- Speaker

You have learned that input devices put information *into* a computer. **Output devices** carry information *out* of a computer. First, the computer changes the information into a useable format. Then, the output devices present the information to the computer user.

You use a **printer** to transfer images from a monitor to paper. For instance, when you key an essay on a computer, you can then print it out to turn in for class. You can also use a printer to print pictures.

A **monitor,** which is also called a computer screen, displays information visually, just like a television set. An LCD (liquid crystal display) monitor is much thinner than a CRT (cathode ray tube) monitor.

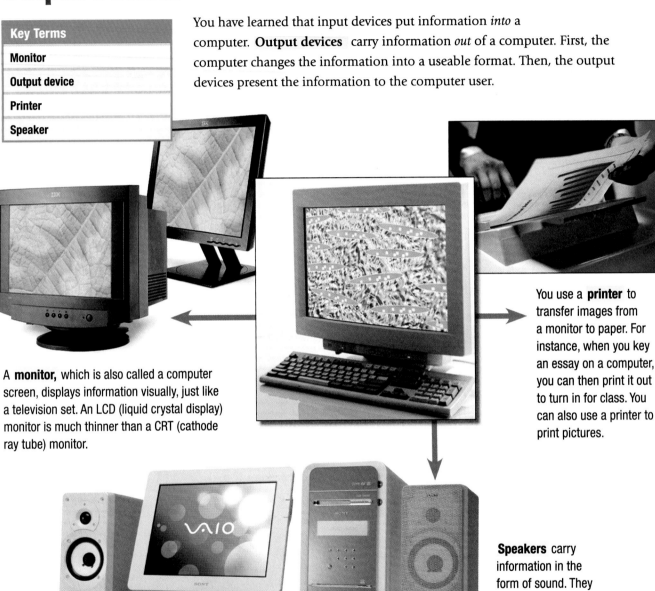

Speakers carry information in the form of sound. They can output music, speech, and noises.

TECH CHECK

Illustrate Information flows out of a computer through output devices. Create a diagram that shows information flowing from a computer to three different output devices. Write a brief explanation next to each output device that explains what sort of information the device outputs.

Student Data File

Step-by-Step

1. Open a **New** Word document. Create the flyer in Figure 2.5 following Steps 2–7. Save your file according to your teacher's instructions.

2. Key the flyer heading Learn to Play Guitar!

3. Under the heading, insert **Data File 2-2**, clip art of a guitar. Size the clip art to fit.

Apply Different Font Styles

4. Under the clip art, key Guitar Lessons for All Ages.

5. Double space, and then key the paragraph as shown.

6. Press ENTER three times. Key Call 555-281-1234 now to reserve your spot!

Add a Page Border

7. On the **menu** bar, click **Format>Borders and Shading**. In the **Page Borders** tab, choose from the Setting, Style, Color, and Art options to add a page border. Click **OK**.

▼ **Figure 2.5** Use the suggested fonts, or similar ones, to create this flyer.

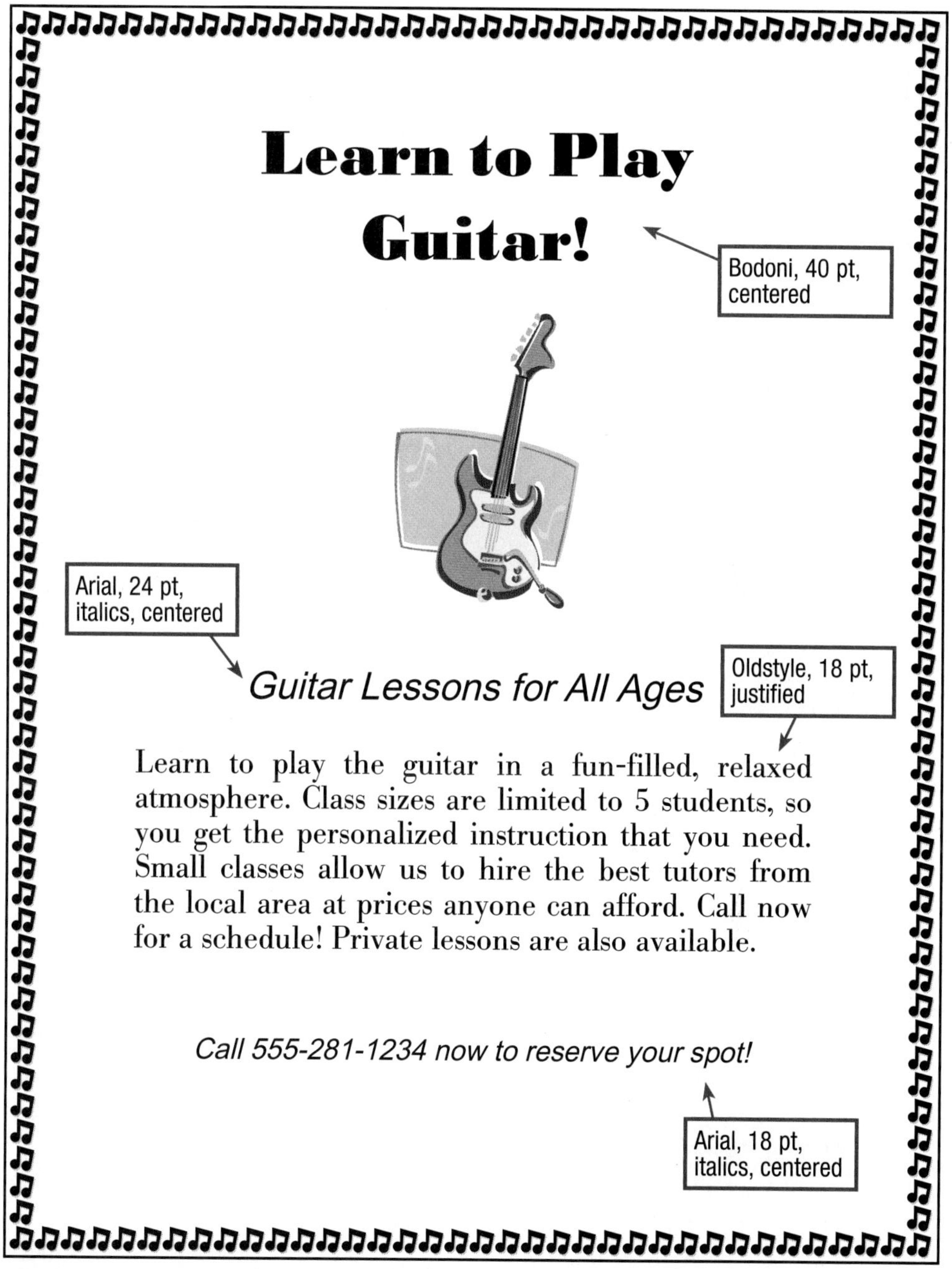
Learn to Play Guitar!
Bodoni, 40 pt, centered
Arial, 24 pt, italics, centered
Guitar Lessons for All Ages
Oldstyle, 18 pt, justified
Learn to play the guitar in a fun-filled, relaxed atmosphere. Class sizes are limited to 5 students, so you get the personalized instruction that you need. Small classes allow us to hire the best tutors from the local area at prices anyone can afford. Call now for a schedule! Private lessons are also available.
Call 555-281-1234 now to reserve your spot!
Arial, 18 pt, italics, centered

Instant Message

Selecting Objects To select more than one object for grouping you can:

- Press CTRL and click each element you want to add to the group.
- Use the **Select Objects** button, and drag a box around the group. Then click **Draw>Group** on the Drawing toolbar.

Input Devices

Key Terms

- Input device
- Joystick
- Keyboard
- Microphone
- Mouse
- Peripheral
- Port
- Scanner

Anything connected to your computer is considered a **peripheral.** In order for a computer to work, it must first have data. You can use peripherals called **input devices** to put information into a computer.

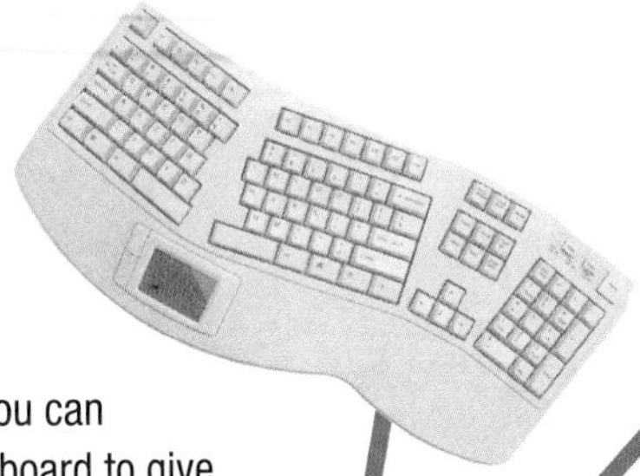

A **keyboard** is used to enter information in the form of words, numbers, and punctuation. You can also use a keyboard to give commands to some programs.

A **scanner** collects information in the form of pictures and sends the information to the computer.

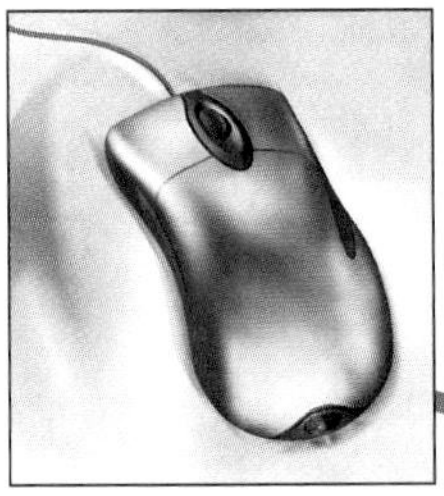

A **mouse** is used to control objects seen on a computer screen. A mouse can be used as an alternate to the keyboard for inputting instructions.

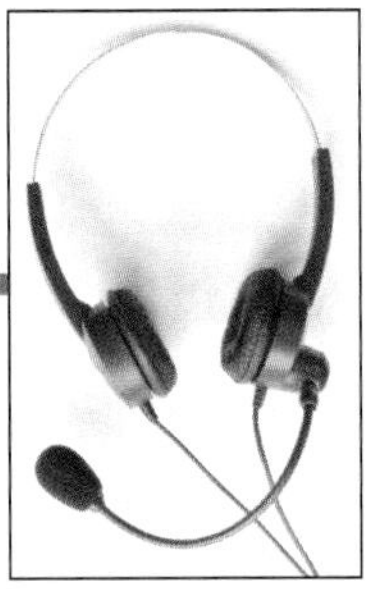

A **microphone** can be used to input audio such as music or voice commands into a computer.

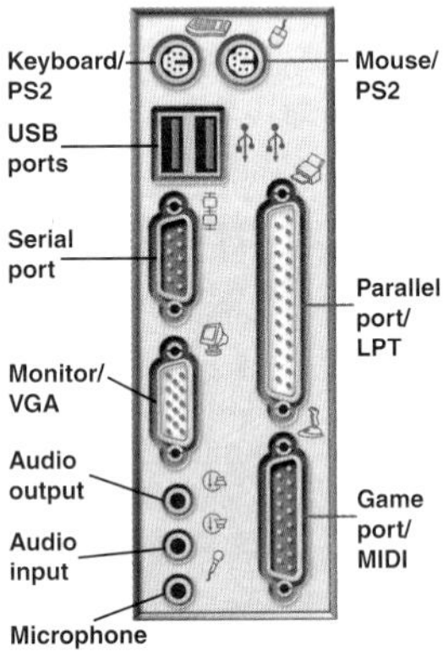

A **port** allows users to connect external input devices to the computer system.

A **joystick** is an input device used for playing games. The buttons send instructions to the computer.

A digital camera captures photographs as digital files that can be uploaded directly to a computer. A digital camcorder is used to create original video files.

TECH CHECK

1. **Differentiate** What type of information would you enter into a computer using a keyboard?
2. **Identify** In this topic, you learned about keyboards, mice, and scanners. Name three other devices that can be used as input devices.

Edit and Resize Clip Art

8 Select the clip art, and then **right-click**. Choose **Edit Picture**. Your clip art will separate into individual objects (Figure 2.6).
Mac users press CTRL, and click the mouse instead of right-clicking.

9 Hold SHIFT and click each of the elements that make up the background of the clip art.

10 Press DELETE. The selected elements should disappear. Repeat the process, if necessary.

11 Hold the CTRL key, and click on each of the salmon-colored guitar pieces.

12 Click **Fill Color**, and choose a color for the selected elements.

Group Drawing Elements

13 On the **Drawing** toolbar, click **Select Objects**. Then click above and to the left of your clip art. Drag a selection box around all the ungrouped elements.

14 Click **Draw** Draw ▾. Choose **Group**.

15 Click and drag the clip art away from the drawing canvas. (If some of the clip art remains behind, click **Undo**. Then group again.)

16 Select and delete the drawing canvas (Figure 2.7).

▼ **Figure 2.6** When editing a vector image, Word separates the drawing into its parts.

Learn to Play Guitar!
Remove the background.
Guitar Lessons for All Ages

▼ **Figure 2.7** The Drawing Canvas and the clip art are separate elements and can be edited separately.

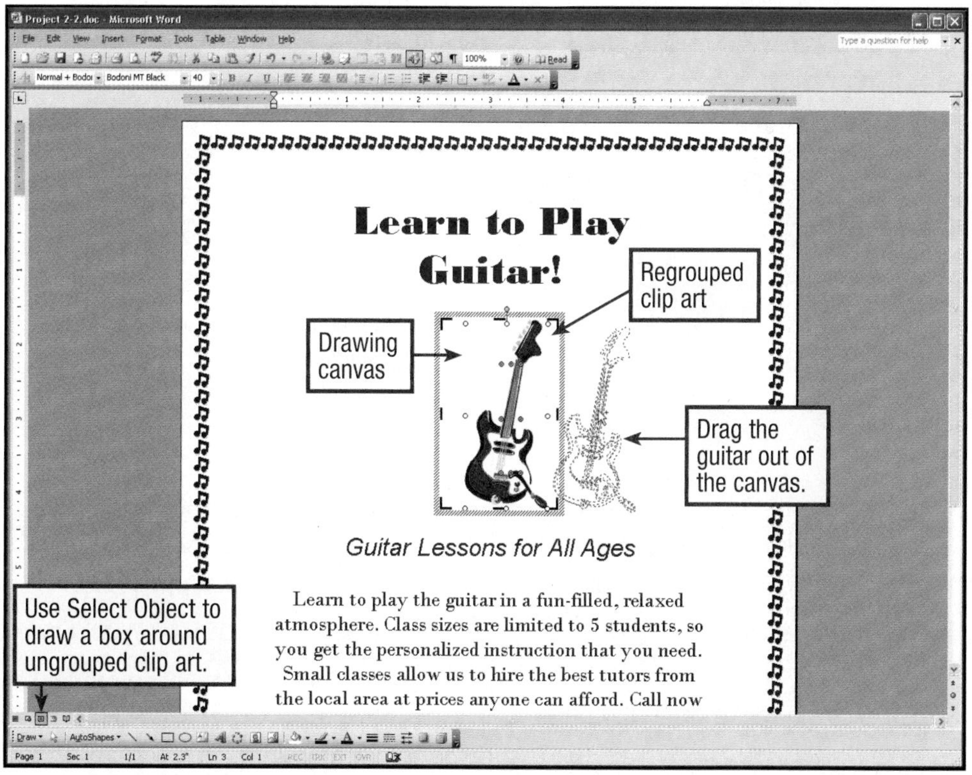
Project 2-2.doc - Microsoft Word
Learn to Play Guitar!
Regrouped clip art
Drawing canvas
Drag the guitar out of the canvas.
Guitar Lessons for All Ages
Use Select Object to draw a box around ungrouped clip art.
Learn to play the guitar in a fun-filled, relaxed atmosphere. Class sizes are limited to 5 students, so you get the personalized instruction that you need. Small classes allow us to hire the best tutors from the local area at prices anyone can afford. Call now

Types of Computers and Computer Systems

Key Terms
Desktop
Laptop
Macintosh
Mainframe
Personal computer (PC)
Personal digital assistant (PDA)

In today's world, computers are everywhere. They come in different shapes and sizes and they serve vastly different purposes.

A **desktop** computer is designed to remain in one location. The **personal computer (PC)** and the **Macintosh** support one user at a time. A company called Apple makes Macintosh computers. Several different companies make PCs.

Windows PC

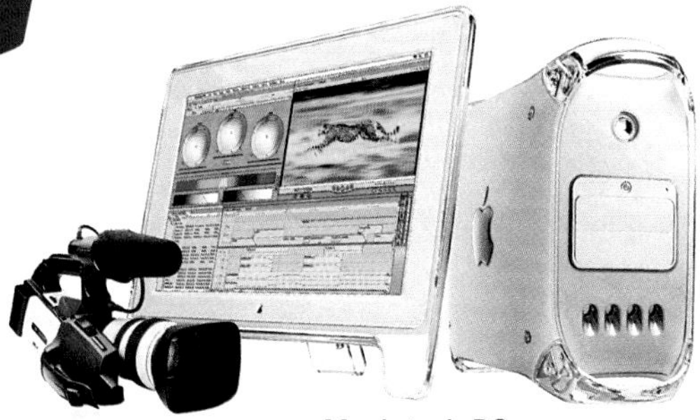

Macintosh PC

A **laptop** computer is designed to be carried from place to place.

Mainframes are very powerful computers that can do many things at once. While only one person at a time can use a PC or Macintosh, hundreds of people can use a mainframe at once.

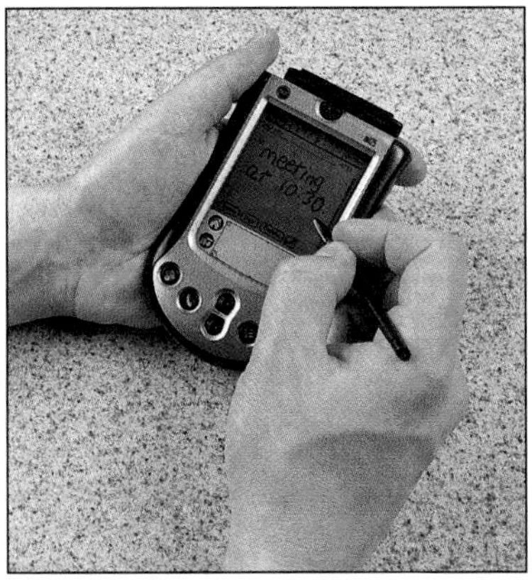

A **personal digital assistant (PDA)** is a computer that is small enough to hold in one's hand.

TECH CHECK

1. **Describe** What is the difference between a laptop and a desktop?
2. **Evaluate** Give three reasons why a person might prefer a laptop to a desktop computer.
3. **Explain** How are PCs and a mainframe different? Which type of computer might be used by a large company? Why?

Wrap Text

17 Select the guitar. On the **menu** bar, click **Format>Object**. In the **Layout** tab, choose **Tight**. Click **OK**.

18 Click and drag a corner handle on the clip art to increase the size of the guitar until it stretches the length of the page (Figure 2.8).

19 Select all the text in the body of the document, and click **Align Left** ☰. Resize the text, if necessary, and position the clip art so the text does not overlap it.

Add a Header

20 Click **View** on the **menu** bar. Choose **Header and Footer**. Click inside the **Header** text box at the top of your page. Key your name and the date at top of your page.

21 On the **Formatting** toolbar, click **Align Right** ☰. Click **Close** on the Header and Footer toolbar.

22 Your finished document should look similar to Figure 2.8. Save your flyer according to your teacher's instructions.

▼ **Figure 2.8** Your finished flyer should include your name and the date in a header.

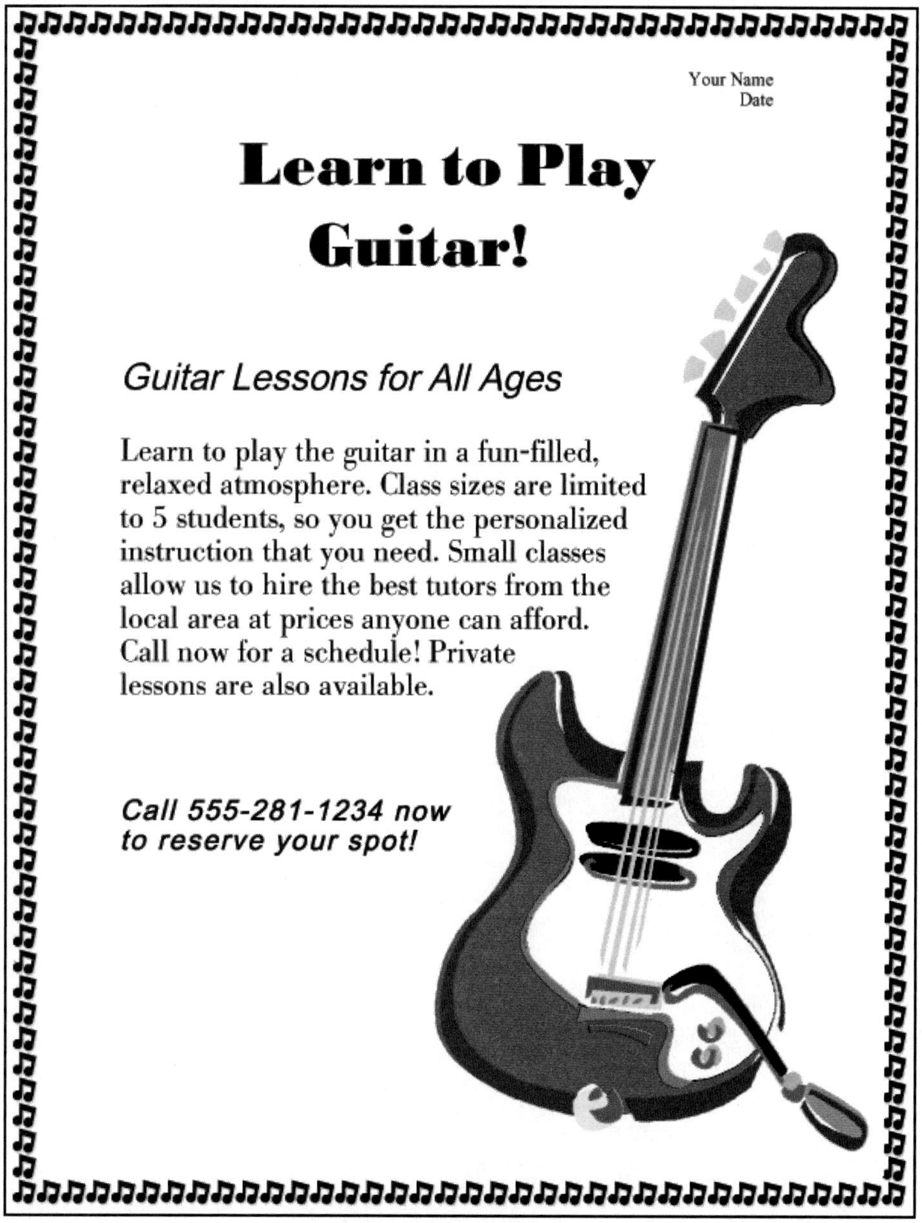
Your Name
Date
Learn to Play Guitar!
Guitar Lessons for All Ages
Learn to play the guitar in a fun-filled, relaxed atmosphere. Class sizes are limited to 5 students, so you get the personalized instruction that you need. Small classes allow us to hire the best tutors from the local area at prices anyone can afford. Call now for a schedule! Private lessons are also available.
Call 555-281-1234 now to reserve your spot!

REVIEW AND REVISE

Check your work Use Figure 2.8 as a guide and check that:

- ☑ The fonts and image are attractive, accurate, and easy to read.
- ☑ The guitar's color is changed and background elements removed.
- ☑ Text is left-aligned and not wrapped too tightly around the graphic.
- ☑ There is a header and a page border.

How Have Computers Changed the World?

Key Terms
Computer
Technology

A **computer** is an electronic device that processes data and converts it into information that people can use. Chances are you cannot imagine a world without computers!

Common conveniences such as fast food restaurants and ATMs use computers to provide quick, easy service to customers.

Some computer-created games are so realistic that it seems as if you can see, hear, and sometimes even feel the action around you!

Doctors and medical technicians depend on heart monitors, full-body scanners, and other computer-based devices.

E-mail and cell phones make it easy to contact friends and family—even if they live on the other side of the world!

The term **technology** refers to the practical application of an art or skill. Nearly every part of the globe has been touched by technology.

TECH CHECK

1. **Identify** What aspects of your life do not involve computers?
2. **Make Predictions** What would life be like without computers? How would your life change if computers suddenly disappeared from the world?
3. **Interview** Talk to someone who is older than you, such as a parent or a grandparent. Did they use computers when they were young? How was their life different from the way you live now?

Project 2-3 Layer Drawing Objects

Spotlight on Skills

- Create shapes
- Group drawing objects
- Resize clip art
- Duplicate clip art

Key Terms

- layers
- scale

Academic Focus

Math
Work with shapes and ratios

The individual parts of a graphic are stacked on top of each other so that the image is actually made up of **layers**, or different levels. Each element is on its own separate layer, similar to the floors of a multistory building. The text layer is the first floor, with each new drawing object built upon the previous layer.

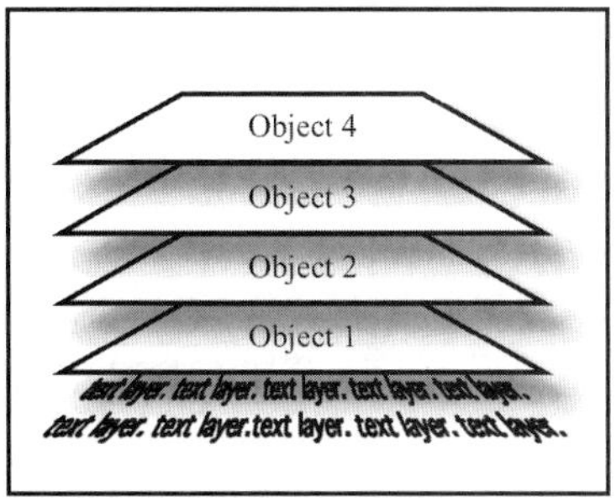

▲ Objects build upon each other.

Graphic layers can be reordered and rearranged (*unlike* a building). When you break clip art into its individual pieces, some of the elements will be in the front layers. Others will be behind. You can send an object to the front or back of an image that has layers.

The image you create in this project will use layering to make it look like a slice of pizza has been removed. Drawing objects like stationery watermarks can be placed behind a text layer. Objects can be placed so far into the background that they appear on every page. The Header and Footer area is usually behind *all* other layers. When you work with Photoshop and Illustrator, you will see how layers work to create a complex image.

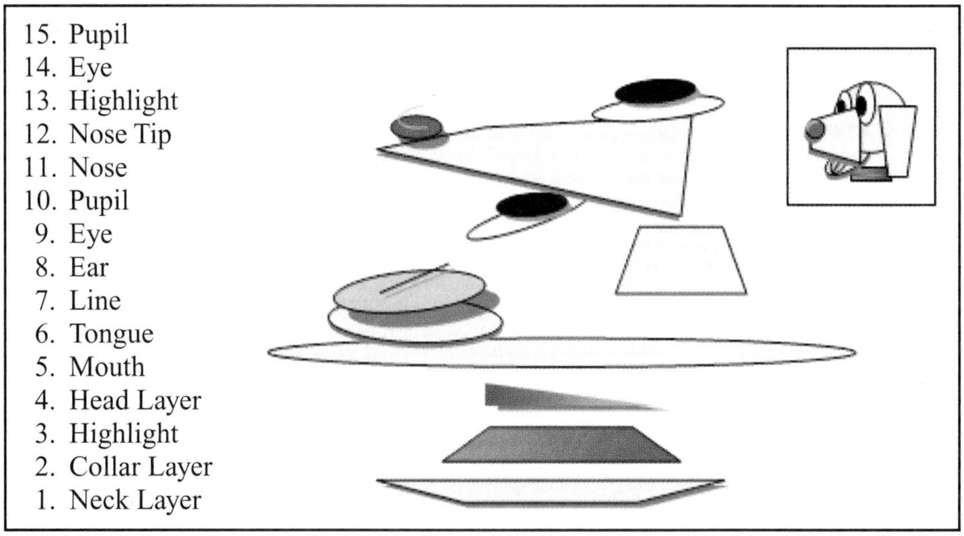

► A simple drawing of a dog requires fifteen layers. Looking from the top, however, the drawing appears to have no depth.

► **In this project,** you will be using the pizza image you created in Project 2-1 to create a flyer to advertise a pizza parlor. The flyer's page orientation will be landscape. You will also copy and paste clip art to create a page border. You will need to reduce the **scale**, or size, of the clip art. To do this without changing the way it looks, you will *lock the aspect ratio* so that the width and height of the image will keep the same proportion no matter how much you reduce the size of the image.

Technology *Handbook*

Computers are everywhere—in businesses, schools, and homes, in ATMs, drive-up windows, and cars. Learning about how computers work can help make your life a little easier. The information in this *Technology Handbook* will help you better understand how to make computers work for you!

Contents

Student Data File

Step-by-Step

1. Open the **Pizza Art** file that you created in Project 2-1, and save it as a new file. (Or use **Data File 2-3a**.)

2. On the **menu** bar, click **File>Page Setup**, and change the **Page Orientation** to **Landscape**. Click **OK**.

Create Shapes

3. On the **Drawing** toolbar, click **AutoShapes** >**Basic Shapes**. Choose the **Isosceles Triangle**.

4. Click and drag a triangle to position over one of the pizza "slices" (Figure 2.9). **Note**: It will not be a perfect fit, and the fill color should be white.

5. With the triangle still selected, click **Line Color** . Then choose **No Line**.

Group Drawing Objects

6. Hold the CTRL key, and select both the pizza and the triangle. Click **Draw>Group** to group both objects together.

7. Click **Insert Clip Art** . Search for a picture of a **chef**, or use **Data File 2-3b**. Double-click the image to insert it in your document (Figure 2.10).

▼ **Figure 2.9** Word does not have a way to remove a section of an image like this. Use shapes to create a mask that covers sections you want to "remove."

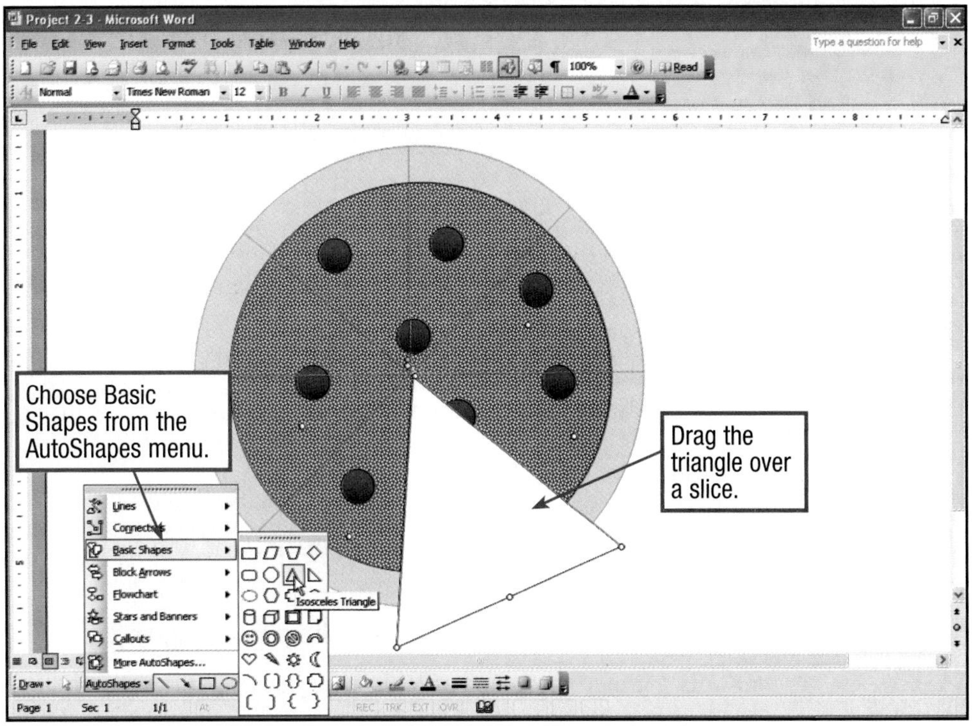

▼ **Figure 2.10** The Clip Art task pane opens when you click Insert ClipArt.

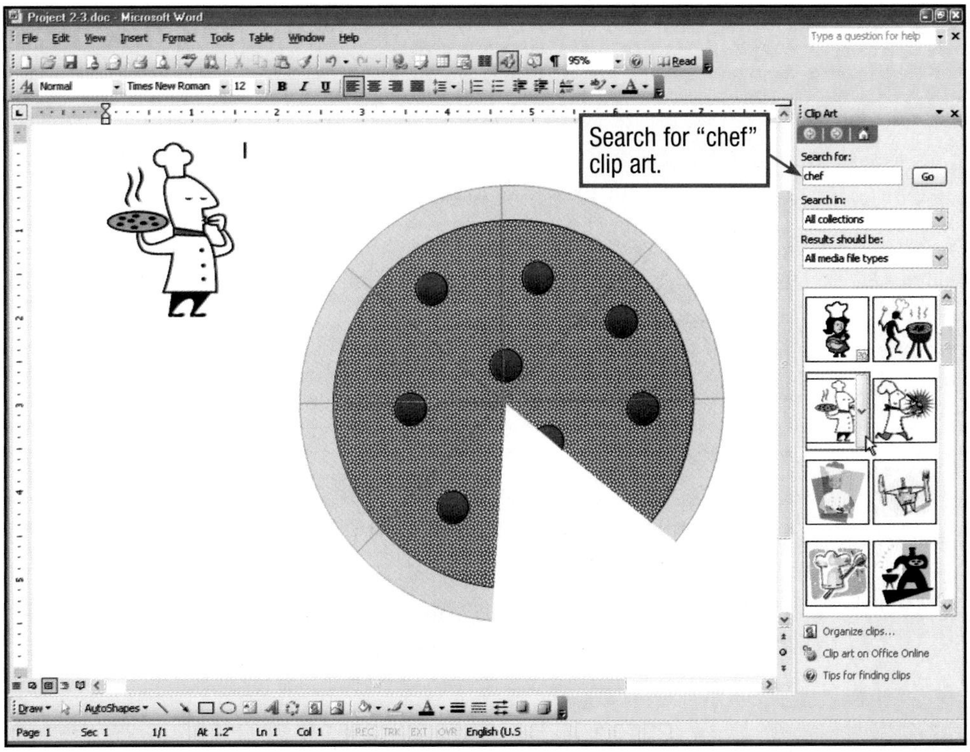

UNIT 5

Projects Across the Curriculum

Project 3 Market a Political Campaign ★★

SOCIAL STUDIES You and a partner are creating the campaign materials for the city councilman (or woman) from your district. You will create the designs for the councilman's campaign buttons and a banner.

Plan

1. Determine the images you want for your button and banner. Include a photograph of the candidate. Use the Internet to find examples of political images.
2. Come up with a campaign slogan.

Create

3. Create a logo or other graphic elements that will be repeated on both the buttons and the banner.
4. Your buttons should include a photograph, text, and graphics.
5. Your banner should be at least 8 inches by 40 inches. Include a photograph, your candidate's slogan, and at least two other images created in Illustrator or edited in Photoshop.

Project 4 Create a Healthy Lifestyle Campaign ★★★

SCIENCE Imagine that you are part of a team promoting a healthy teen lifestyle. As a group, create a positive message to students by creating a newsletter and Web site to promote health ideas.

Plan

1. Brainstorm ideas on the content you want in your publication. Assign tasks to each team member.
2. Research content, such as nutrition, exercise, smoking, drinking, and dating. Your team may decide to interview health teachers.

Create

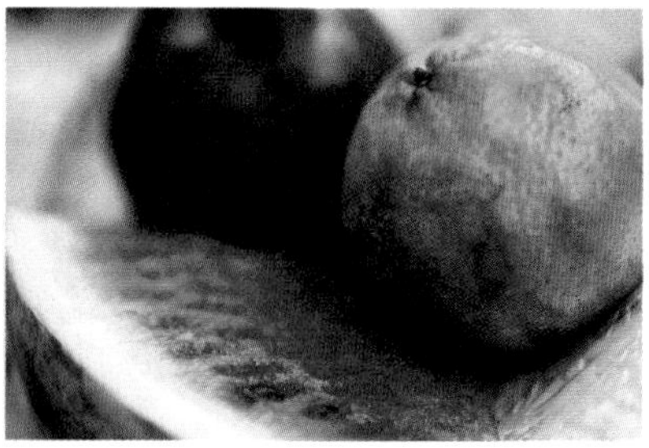

3. Lay out a four-page newsletter. Include at least two paragraphs, a masthead, table of contents, and repeating design elements.
4. Use the content from your newsletter to create a Web site with at least a splash page and four other pages. Link the pages.

Resize Clip Art

8. Select the clip art. Click **Format> Picture**.

9. In the **Format Picture** box, choose the **Size** tab. Under **Scale**, check the **Lock aspect ratio** box. Change the **Height** and **Width** to **25 percent** of the original size.

10. In the **Format Picture** box, choose the **Layout** tab. Then choose **Square**. Click **OK**.

Duplicate Clip Art

11. Position the clip art in the corner of the page, select it, and press CTRL + D to duplicate the image.

12. Position the new duplicate below the original copy. To nudge the graphic, hold CTRL and press the arrow keys. **Mac** users press ALT instead of CTRL.

13. Press CTRL + D again. This time, the copy should be in the same relative position. Repeat until you have completed one side.

14. **Group** the side you have finished. Repeat the steps to add clip art to all. (Figure 2.11).

15. Resize and reposition your borders to fill the space equally on all sides.

16. Your document should look similar to Figure 2.12. **Save** your document to continue in Project 2-4.

▼ **Figure 2.11** Repeating simple clip art allows you to create your own borders.

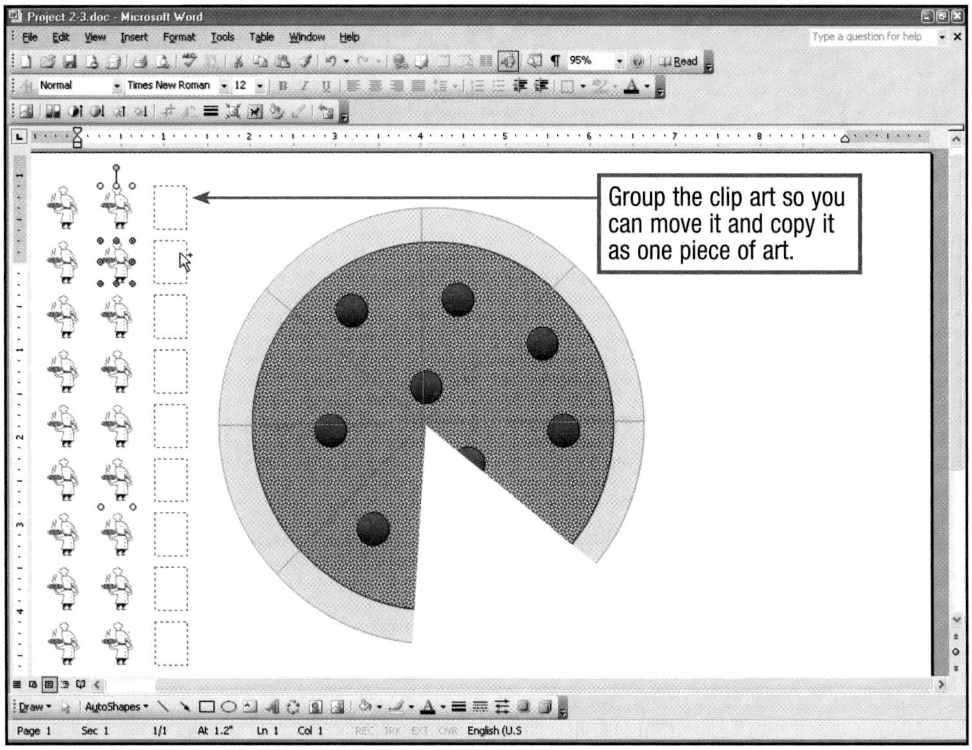
Project 2-3.doc - Microsoft Word
Group the clip art so you can move it and copy it as one piece of art.

▼ **Figure 2.12** Your document should look similar to this one.

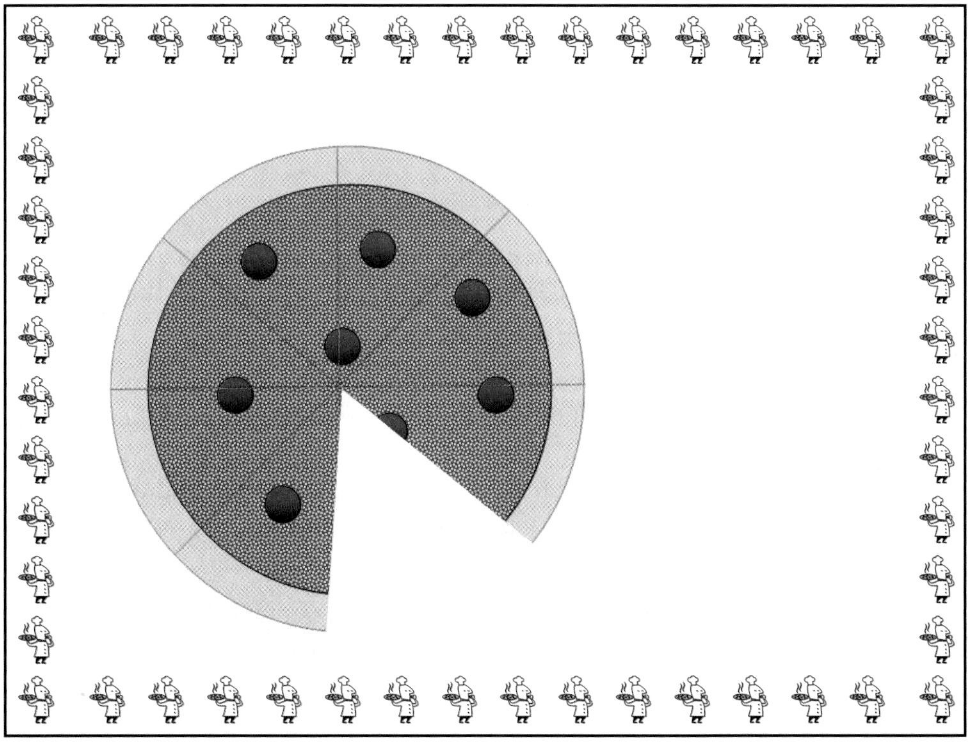

UNIT 5

Projects Across the Curriculum

The skills you learned in this unit will help you in your other classes, too. Use your desktop publishing skills to complete the following projects. Follow your teacher's instructions for saving or printing your work.

Project 1 Create a Marketing Brochure ★

LANGUAGE ARTS Follow your teacher's instructions to form a team that is creating a marketing brochure for a local store or restaurant. The business wants you to create a logo for them, which will be used in a promotional brochure.

Go Online RUBRICS
www.glencoe.com

Unit: Projects Go to **Unit 5,** and choose **Rubrics**. Use the projects to help create and evaluate your work.

Plan

1. Determine the content you need to include, the audience you want to attract, and the graphics you want to use.

2. Assign tasks to the members of your team and create a timeline.

Create

3. Create at least three thumbnails of logos and then create the logo in Illustrator.

4. In Publisher, lay out a tri-fold brochure. Repeat font styles and design features throughout the brochure. Insert at least two photographs and add a promotional coupon.

Project 2 Create a Math Study Guide ★★

MATH You want to help younger students who have difficulty with math. You have decided to create a visually appealing math study guide.

Plan

1. Meet with elementary teachers to find what content would be most helpful. Decide what grade level you will create the guide for.

2. Determine the math concepts you will cover and the text and images you will need to illustrate them.

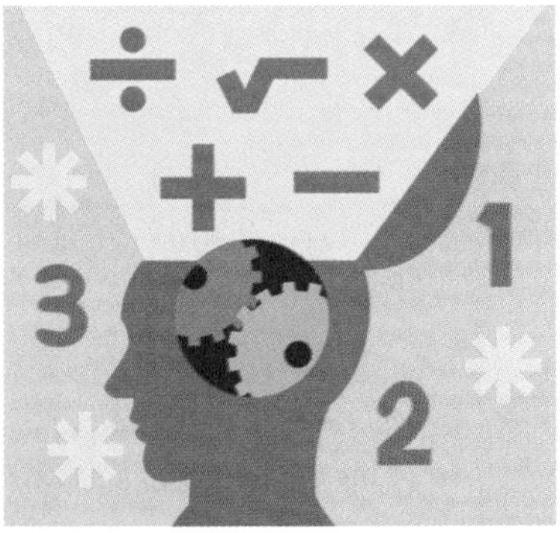

Create

3. Lay out an eight-page study guide booklet in Publisher. Create a master page to repeat design elements.

4. Create or modify digital images using Adobe Photoshop or Illustrator.

Project 2-4

Create a Logo and Add Callouts

Spotlight on Skills

- Format WordArt
- Combine text and graphics
- Add callouts
- Add a background color

Key Terms

- logo
- scalable
- callout
- leader

Academic Focus

Language Arts
Communicate with clear visual messages

Sidebar

Logo Design
Organizations want people to instantly recognize their logos, whether it is an apple on an MP3 player or a red cross on an ambulance. A good logo has that power. Original logo design can be costly when designed by a graphic artist.

Analyze Describe two logos that you think are effective. Explain why.

A **logo** is a combination of text and graphics used to identify a business or product. An effective logo is very important to an organization because it must convey the company's message and must be instantly recognizable to customers.

Logos are almost always vector graphics. By using vector graphics, the same logo can be used whether the design is on a business card or a billboard. Vector graphics are **scalable**, retaining smooth and crisp images at any size. Vector graphics are typically created using illustration software, such as Adobe Illustrator (see Chapter 7), but simple ones can be created in Word.

Combine Text and Graphics in Logos

While logos tend to incorporate graphics, many logos simply use one or more fonts. Even in logos, you should apply the typeface rules you learned in Chapter 1:

- Use only typefaces from separate families.
- Do not use more than two fonts.
- Use fonts with dramatically different characteristics.

Also, be aware of the higher production costs when you use many colors in your logo. If your budget is limited, you need to limit the number of colors in the logo.

Logos often have some sort of graphic element to go along with the font. Perhaps an image can be substituted for a letter, as in the CapCo logo. Sometimes the graphic element goes alongside the word, as in the Midnight Writer logo.

▶ **In this project,** you will create a logo for the pizza flyer you started in Project 2-3. You will also add callouts and a text box to the flyer. A **callout** is a type of text box that acts as a label for a graphic. A **leader** (a line or series of dots connecting information) points from the text box to a specific part of an image.

2 Independent Practice ★★

TEAM PROJECT Market a Movie Follow your teacher's instructions to organize a team that will create an exciting marketing campaign for the latest blockbuster movie. Your team plans to create a poster and a Web site to promote the movie.

a. Plan What kind of movie is it and who is its target audience?

- Use a real movie or decide on a title for your own movie. Come up with a slogan for the movie, and find images to use.
- Brainstorm the content you will include on your poster and Web site. The poster design can be used for a splash page, and there will be at least four other pages.
- Assign tasks to each group member and create a timeline.

b. Create Use Publisher to create the poster and the Web pages.

- Use Illustrator to create an interesting logo or title design for the movie.
- Create a master page for the Web pages so you can repeat design elements in each page. Add different images to illustrate content on each page.
- Add hyperlinks to the pages.

c. Publish Preview your Web pages and revise if necessary.

3 Independent Practice ★★★

TEAM PROJECT Promote a Fund Raiser One of your school's student organizations needs to raise money. Follow your teacher's instructions for forming a team. You and your team plan to create a booklet and PowerPoint presentation that the organization can use to get donations.

a. Plan Talk to a teacher or student in charge of a club, team, or theater production who needs to raise money.

- Determine the information they need to include in marketing materials.
- Decide on a budget and use that to determine how many pages the booklet will have, how it will be printed, and the number of copies you will need.

b. Create Use Publisher to create your booklet.

- Use a master page to repeat design elements, and include at least three photographs. Add Photoshop filter effects to the cover.
- Use Illustrator to create an interesting logo or title effect that you can use in the booklet and the presentation.
- Repeat the content and design element used in the booklet in your presentation.

Go Online ACTIVITIES
www.glencoe.com

Enrichment Go to **Chapter 10**, and choose **Enrichment Activities.** Find more integrated desktop publishing projects.

Step-by-Step

1. In your pizza flyer, center your pizza. Then place the insertion point at the top of the page.

2. On the **Drawing** toolbar, click **Insert WordArt**. Choose the first style, and key the text The Missing Slice.

Format WordArt

3. On the **WordArt** toolbar, click **Format WordArt**. In the **Colors and Lines** tab, choose **Brown** fill.

4. In the **Layout** tab choose **Behind text** for the Wrapping style, and choose **Center** for Horizontal Alignment. Click **OK**.

Combine Text and Graphics

5. Create a small triangle. With the triangle still selected, click **Line Color**. Then choose **No Line**.

6. Repeat the **Fill Effects** pattern and colors for the logo pizza slice to match the pizza.

7. Position the triangle by the first letter of the **WordArt** logo as in Figure 2.14. Right-click, and choose **Order>Send to Back**.

8. Select both the logo pizza slice and the WordArt, and choose **Draw>Group**.

▼ **Figure 2.13** Use the Layout tab to place your WordArt where you want it.

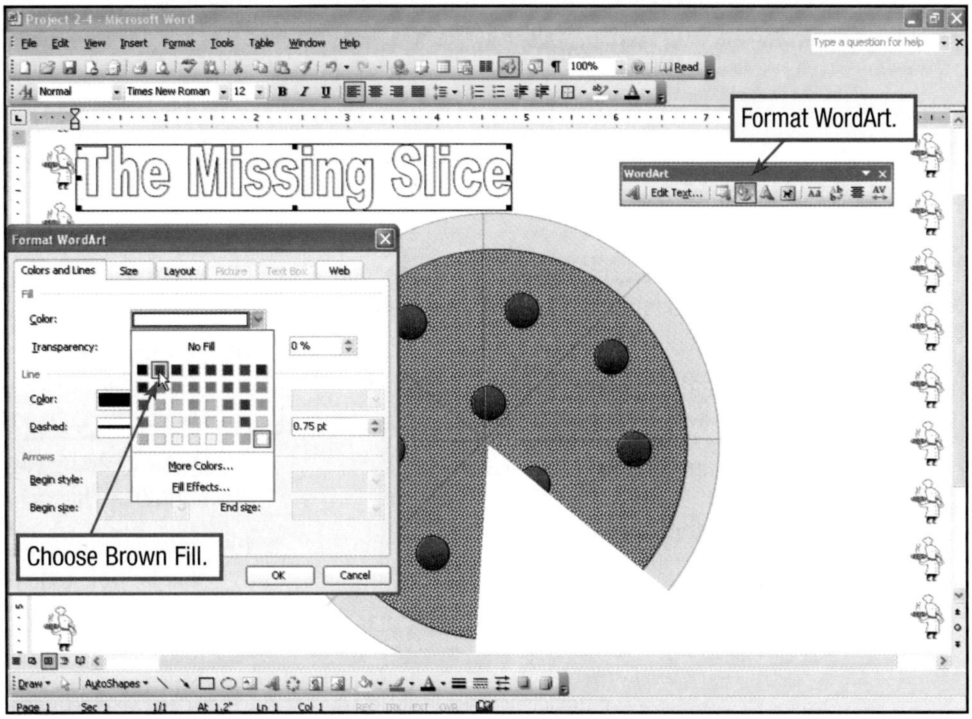

▼ **Figure 2.14** Use the group option to keep the logo's line and WordArt together as a single object.

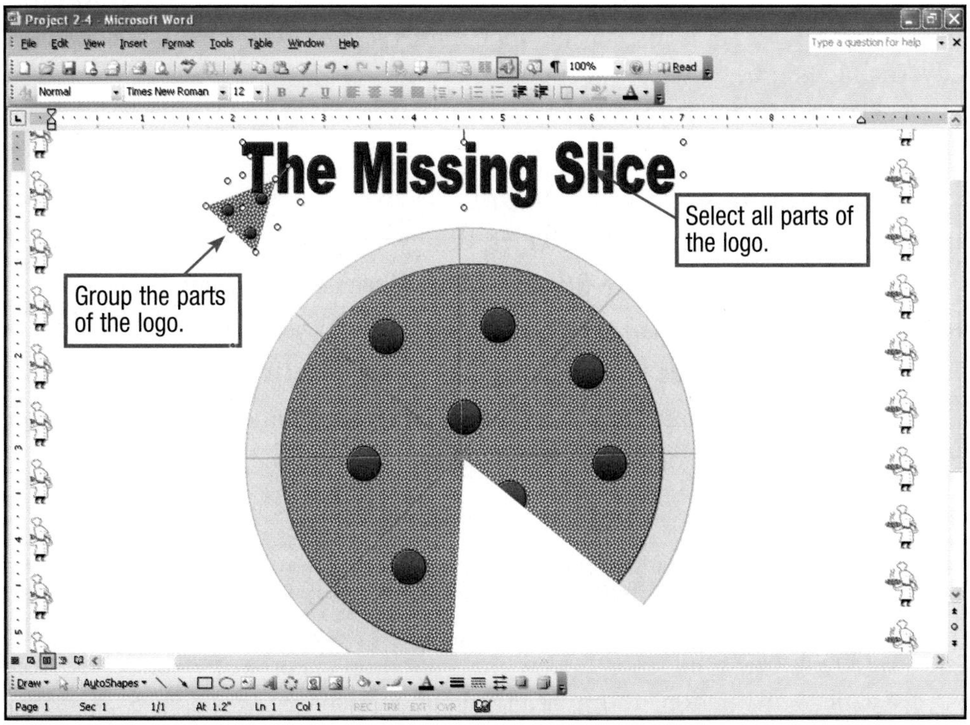

Chapter 10 Assessment

Reading Check

1. **Identify** List three essential components of a typical business package.
2. **Explain** Of the four PARC principles, how is repetition the most responsible for helping a publication achieve a professional appearance?
3. **Differentiate** What does it mean to import a style sheet? To export a style sheet?
4. **Describe** What are three types of design elements that can be added to style sheets to help ensure consistency in your publications?
5. **Evaluate** How does branding promote a company?

Critical Thinking

6. **Draw Conclusions** Why is it so important to use style sheets, especially when you are part of a design team?
7. **Analyze** What types of challenges do designers face when incorporating repetition into publications?
8. **Compare and Contrast** How does the process of transferring style sheets in Microsoft Word and Microsoft Publisher differ?
9. **Make Connections** What design elements are most often used in each component of a business package?
10. **Make Predictions** What are some ways companies can control costs in planning marketing publications?

1 Independent Practice

TEAM PROJECT **Promote a Rock Band** Imagine that you have been asked to market a new garage band. The band has a loyal following and is on the verge of becoming a big success. Follow your teacher's instructions for forming a team. Your team is responsible for creating a logo for the band and a poster advertising their next concert at a local teen club.

a. Plan Brainstorm what kind of band this is. What kind of music do they play and who is their audience?
- Create a name for the band and write the text to promote their concert.
- As a group, brainstorm the images, design elements, and colors you will use.
- Assign tasks and create a timeline for each part of the project.

b. Design Create thumbnail sketches of the logos and posters.
- Design at least three logos and decide on one. Use Illustrator to create it.
- Create or find images to include on the poster. Use Photoshop to edit photos.

c. Create Use Illustrator to design the logo.
- Use Publisher to create a poster that is at least 16 inches wide and 20 inches high.
- Insert the logo and other images in the poster. Use Photoshop to add effects to the images.
- Add text. Use Photoshop to add glow and drop shadow effects. Follow your teacher's instructions for printing the publications.

Go Online RUBRICS
www.glencoe.com

Independent Practice
Go to **Chapter 10**, and choose **Rubrics**. Use the rubrics to help create and evaluate your projects.

Add Callouts

9. On the **Drawing** toolbar, click the **AutoShapes** button, and then choose **Callouts**.

10. Choose callout style **Line Callout 2** or one that is similar to those shown in Figures 2.15 and 2.16.

11. **Click and drag** a callout box to a pepperoni. Click on the line leader to display yellow diamonds. Then drag the diamond until the leader points to the pepperoni.

▼ **Figure 2.15** Use the diamonds to move the leaders so they point to the right spot.

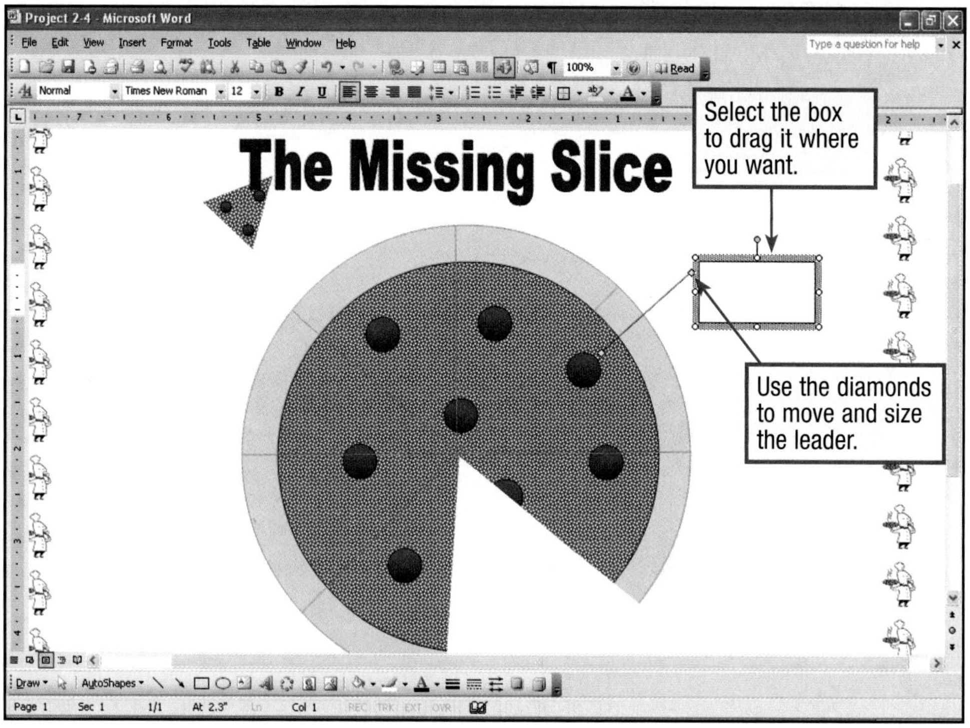

12. **Click and drag** a callout box to each of the features shown in Figure 2.16.

13. To add text, click inside a box. Key the descriptions from Figure 2.16. Use a **12 pt sans serif** font.

14. Add the description to each callout, making sure to use the same font size and style in each.

15. **Center** the text in each box. Your flyer should look similar to Figure 2.16.

▼ **Figure 2.16** Text boxes, like callouts, allow you to place text anywhere on the page.

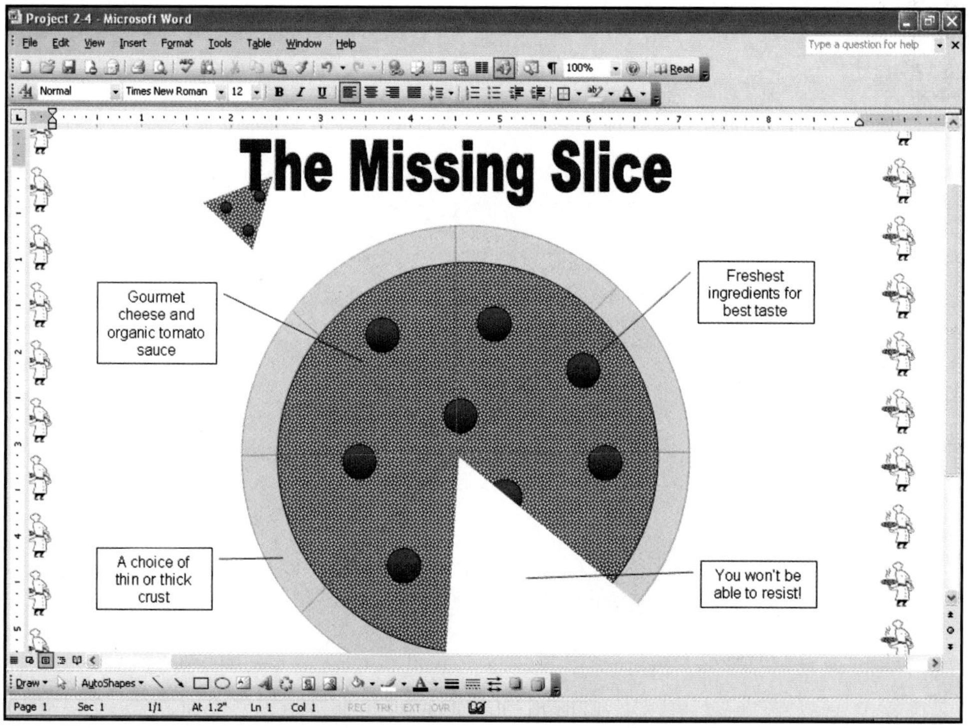

In The Workplace

Web Designer

Web designers (also referred to as Web developers) create Web sites. They organize, develop, and design the many elements that make up a site. Designers determine the style, colors, graphics, fonts, and other visual elements, determine the layout and content of each page, and develop the navigation tools used to move from page to page. Web designers diagnose and fix technical problems. Although Webmasters generally maintain the site once it is built, Web designers are sometimes responsible for adding new elements and keeping sites updated.

On the Job

Web designers often coordinate the work of specialists such as illustrators, photographers, copywriters, animators, computer programmers, Web security specialists, and multimedia experts. They might use HTML, XML, JavaScript, and other programming languages for creating Web pages or Web development applications such as Dreamweaver®.

Designers ensure that the e-commerce interface is easy to use. Since more and more people log on through high-speed Internet connections, Web designers incorporate features that take advantage of the increased bandwidth. They may use Macromedia Flash® to add animation to sites or embed movie clips using QuickTime® or RealPlayer®.

Web designers work for Web development companies, advertising agencies, multimedia design firms, and companies who hire Web designers to develop and maintain their sites "in-house." Some Web designers are freelancers who develop sites for various companies.

Future Outlook

There is strong demand for skilled Web designers. For more information about these careers, consult the following Web sites:

- **Webmaster Organization (webmaster.org)** provides resources for Web designers.
- **World Organization of Webmasters (WOW) (joinwow.org)** provides certification and educational resources to Web professionals.

Training

Web design requires advanced training and experience with computers. Certification programs and degrees are offered by community colleges, vocational schools, technical colleges, online programs, and universities.

Salary Range

The salary for Web designers ranges from $36,000 to $95,000 per year depending upon experience, skill, responsibility, and location.

Skills and Talents

Web designers need to have:

- Good computer skills.
- Knowledge of Internet, design, and multimedia programs.
- Good communication skills.
- The ability to work in teams or independently to meet deadlines.

Career Activity

Why is it important for Web designers to have graphic design skills?

16 Select all the callouts and the pizza graphic, and choose **Draw>Group**.

17 Click **Text Box** . Drag a text box below the pizza, all the way across the bottom of the document.

18 In the text box, key Call 552-555-1234 now to place your order! in a **serif** font, **24 pt**, **centered**, and **bold**.

19 Select the new text box. Then click **Fill Color** , and choose **No Fill**. Click **Line Color** , and choose **No Line**.

Add a Background Color

20 To add a background to your flyer, draw a rectangle that completely covers the document.

21 Select the rectangle, and click **Fill Color** . Then choose a color.

22 Select the rectangle, and choose **Draw>Order>Send to Back**. The pizza is displayed in front of the background color.

23 Change the color of the missing triangle to match the background color.

24 Your flyer should look similar to Figure 2.17. Follow your teacher's instructions for saving and printing your work.

▼ **Figure 2.17** To save ink, you can create a colored background by printing on colored paper.

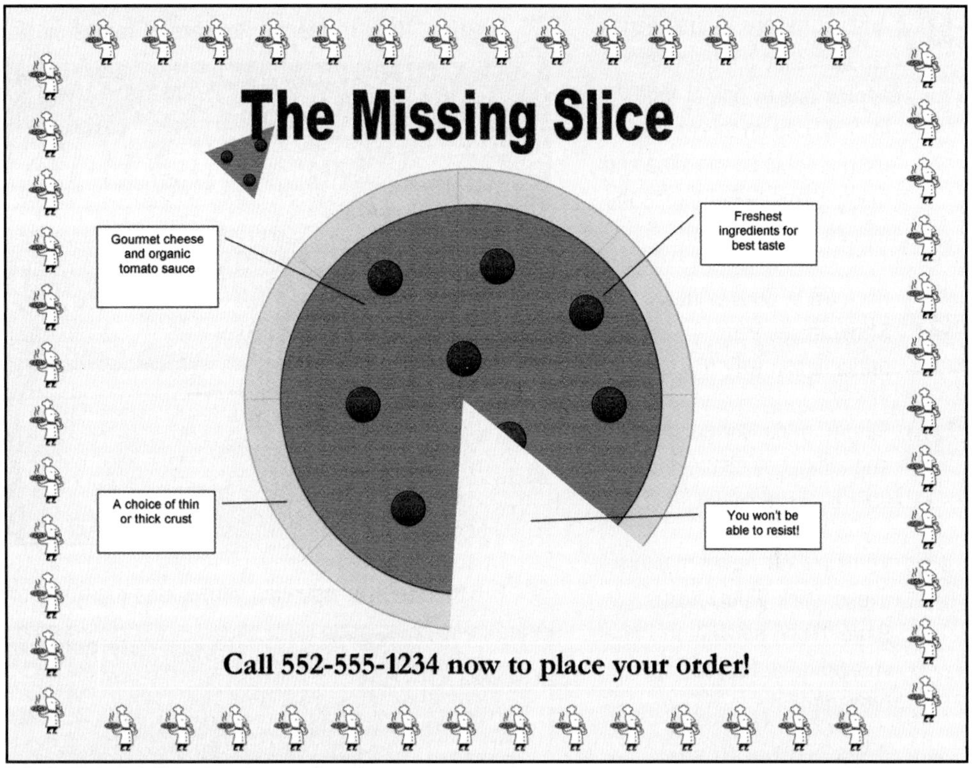

REVIEW AND REVISE

Check your work Use Figure 2.17 as a guide and check that:

- ☑ There are no spelling or grammar errors.
- ☑ The fonts are used consistently—consistent sizing, typeface, and style in the callouts.
- ☑ The callouts are readable and pointing to the correct location.
- ☑ The logo is complete and accurate.
- ☑ The graphics used in the border are consistently spaced.
- ☑ The line and the triangle used for the missing slice effectively hide the graphics behind.
- ☑ The text box at the bottom has no fill color and no line color.
- ☑ The background color covers the entire flyer.

8. Add animations to the images on each slide so that they appear one by one or fade in slowly. To do this, select each graphic on the slide and follow Steps 3–6. Change the effects as appropriate.

9. Click **Slide Show>View Show** to see your presentation with transitions.

10. Return to the **Normal** view and make any changes to your slides. Save your work.

11. Add **speaker notes** to your slides. Click **View>Notes Page** to add notes that you can print for your presentation.

12. Practice giving your presentation. Click **Slide Show>Rehearse Timings**. Time yourself as you move through the slides manually by clicking your mouse (Figure 10.39).

13. If you want the slides to advance automatically, click **Slide Show>Slide Transitions**.

14. In the Slide Transition task pane, under **Advance Slide**, check **Automatically** and set it to a speed that matches your timing requirements in Step 12 (Figure 10.40).

15. With your teacher's permission, print your notes and present your PowerPoint slide show to the class.

▼ **Figure 10.39** Use the Rehearse Timings clock to time your presentation.

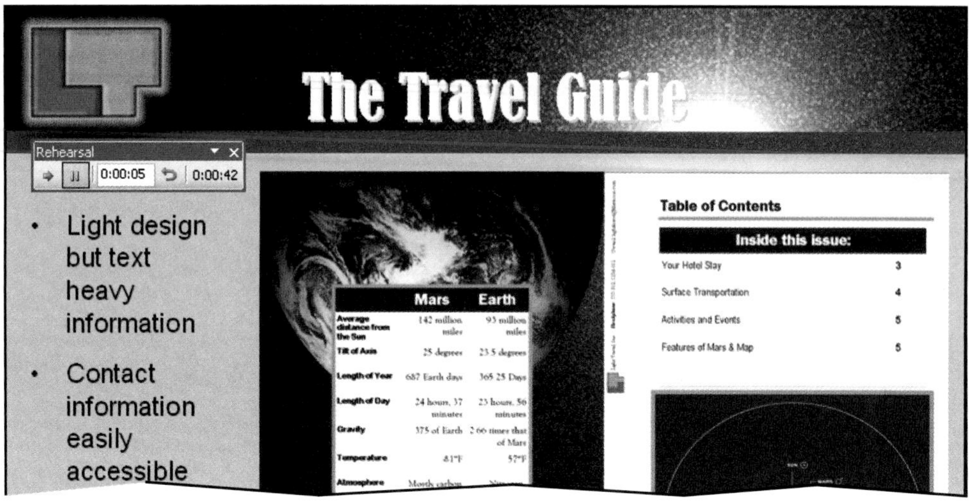

▼ **Figure 10.40** Advance your slides manually or use an automatic setting.

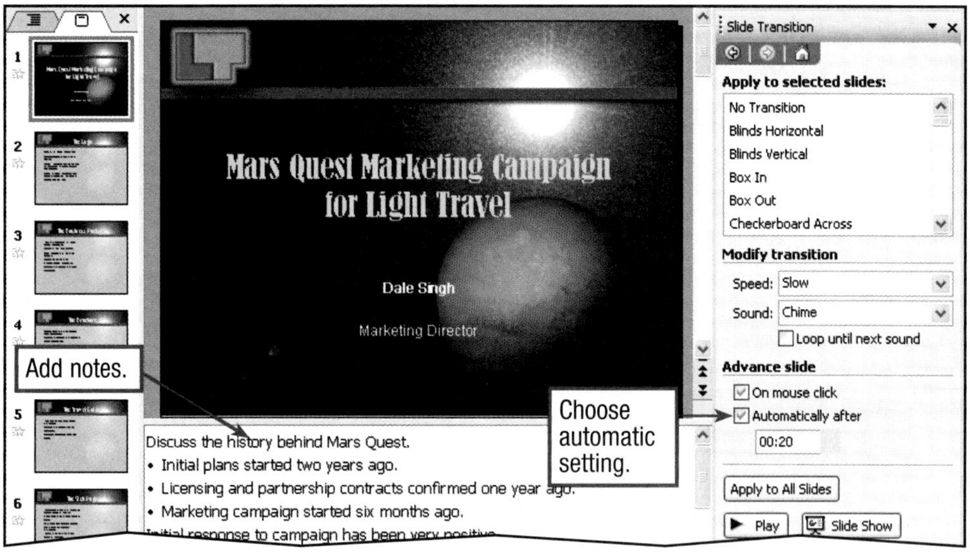

REVIEW AND REVISE

Check your work View your slides and check that:

- ☑ The master slide design elements are applied to each slide effectively.
- ☑ Images illustrate the text and are placed effectively.
- ☑ Text is readable with no spelling or grammar errors.
- ☑ Animations have been added to the presentation.

Project 2-5 Create Quad-fold Documents

Spotlight on Skills

- Lay out a quad-fold document
- Use the zoom tool
- Rotate images
- Print four pages on a sheet

Key Term

- quad-fold

Academic Focus

Math
Evaluate spatial relationships

A **quad-fold** document is one that is folded in half twice, so that there are four (quad) folds. Cards are often folded twice. Before creating a quad-fold card, it is a good idea to use a model to help visualize the layout. Follow the steps below.

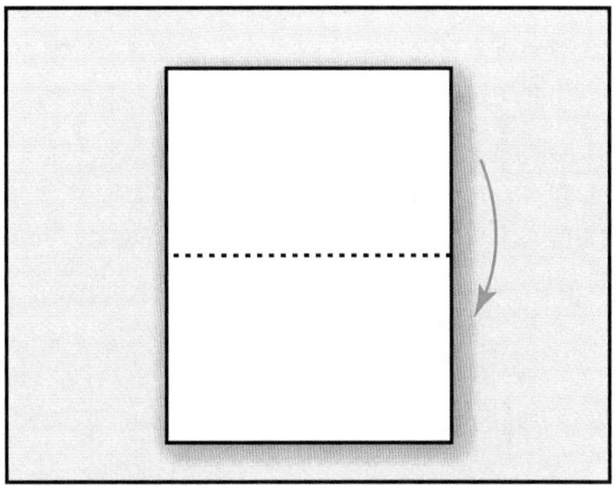

▲ 1. Hold a sheet of paper in portrait position, and fold it in half from top to bottom.

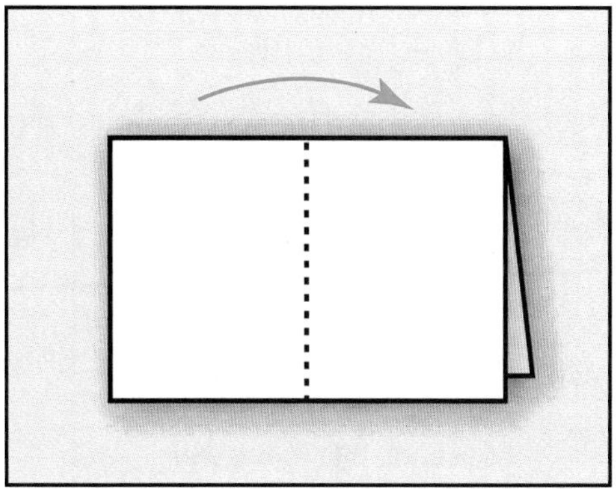

▲ 2. Then fold it in half again (from side to side) so that it looks like a greeting card.

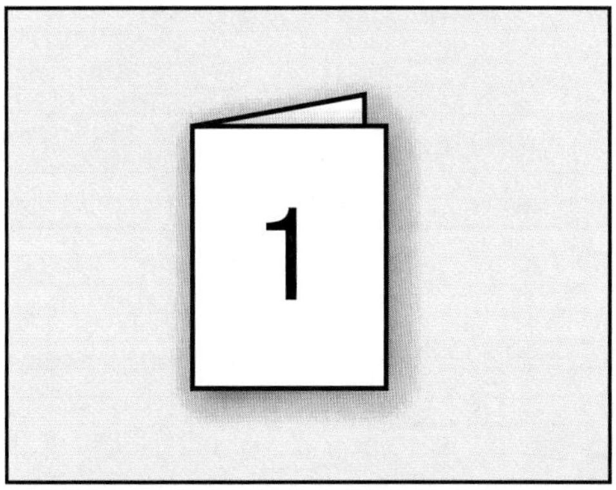

▲ 3. Hold the card so the folds are at the top and left. Then number each page of the card 1, 2, 3, and 4, as shown in the illustration.

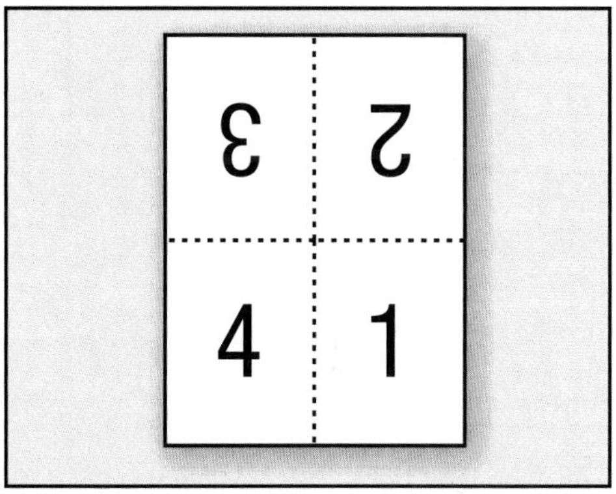

▲ 4. Open the paper. It should look like the figure shown.

Notice that all four panels are on the same side of the page and two of the panels are upside-down. (Which two, depends on how you folded the paper.) The panels are probably in a different order from what you expected.

Page layout software, such as Microsoft® Publisher, Adobe® InDesign®, and QuarkXpress®, can make creating a quad-fold layout much easier.

► **In this project,** you will lay out and create a quad-fold party invitation. You will use WordArt to create text that can be rotated. Regular text cannot be turned upside down. If your printer allows, you can use the Print Zoom option to print all four pages on one sheet.

Step-by-Step

1. Open the PowerPoint presentation that you started in **Project 10-8**. Save it according to your teacher's instructions.

2. Click **View>Master>Slide Master.** Select the bottom text box in the first Slide Master.

Add Custom Animation

3. Click **Slide Show>Custom Animation**.

4. In the **Custom Animation** task pane, click the **Add Effect** button. Choose **Entrance>Blinds**.

5. Change **Start** to **After Previous**. In the drop-down menu shown in Figure 10.37, click **Effect Options**.

Adjust Timing

6. In the **Effect Options** dialog box, click the **Timings** tab and change the **Delay** to **1 second**. Click **OK** (Figure 10.39).

7. Choose **View>Normal** to return to editing your presentation. All the slides that are assigned to this slide master have now been changed.

Figure 10.37 Add your own custom animations.

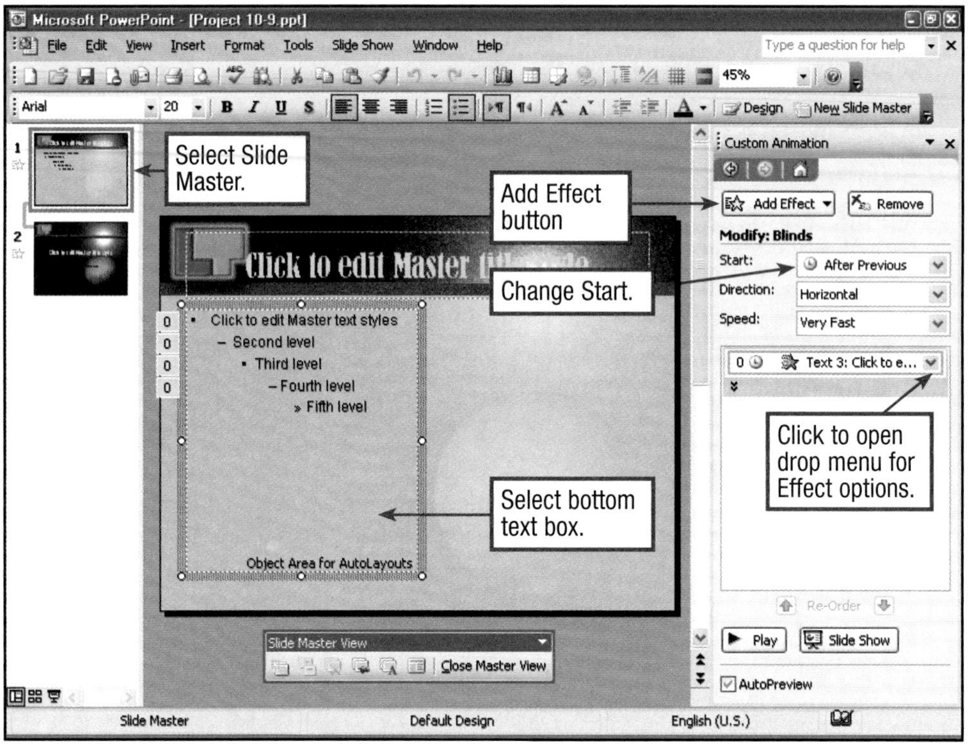

Figure 10.38 View your presentation as a slide show to see the transitions.

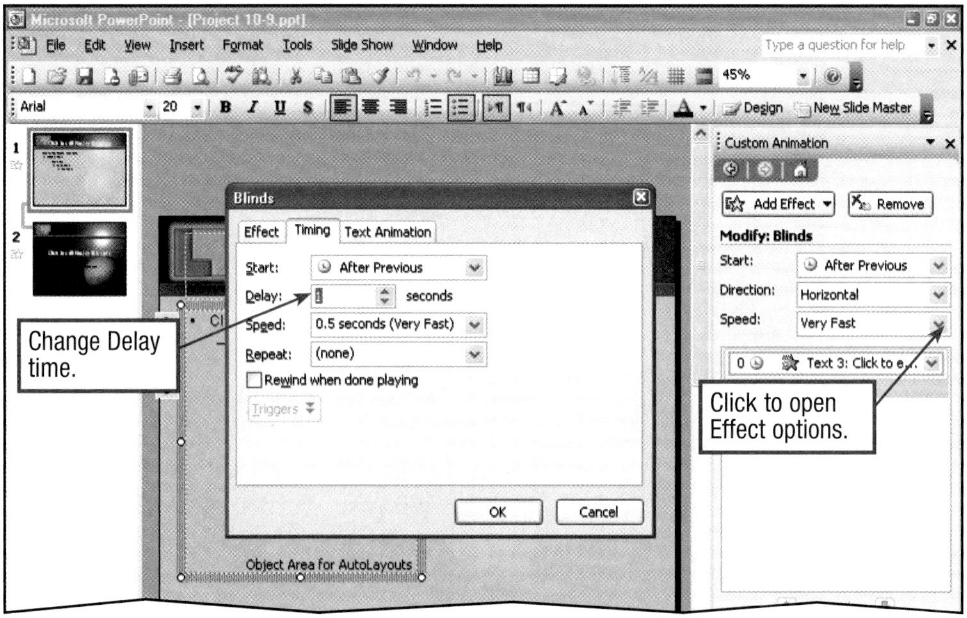

Student Data File

Step-by-Step

1. Open a new Word document, and save it according to your teacher's instructions.

Lay Out a Quad-fold Document

2. On the **menu** bar, click **Insert>Break>Page Break** to create a second page. Click **OK**. Insert two more page breaks so that you have four pages.

3. Click **File>Print Preview**. Click **Multiple Page** [icon], and choose the **2×2** layout (Figure 2.18).

Use the Zoom Tool

4. **Close** the Print Preview screen. On the **Standard** toolbar, reduce the **Zoom** [100%] until your pages are in a 2×2 layout (Figure 2.19).

5. Place your insertion point in **page 4** (bottom right) on your screen. This is **panel 1** of the card. (Review the diagram on page 75 for your layout.)

6. Use **80 pt WordArt** or a playful font, such as **Curlz MT**, to key You have been invited....

7. Center the text horizontally and vertically. (**Hint:** Use **File>Page Setup** to center vertically.) See Figure 2.19.

Figure 2.18 Print Preview lets you can see how the four panels of the card look.

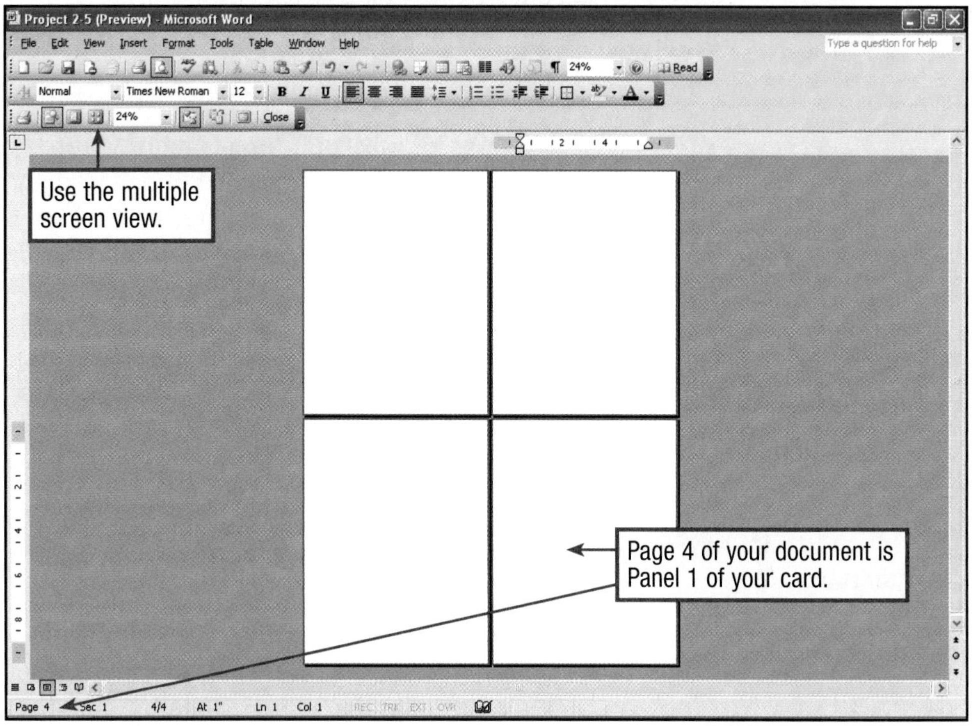
Project 2-5 (Preview) - Microsoft Word
Use the multiple screen view.
Page 4 of your document is Panel 1 of your card.

Figure 2.19 The first panel of the card is Page 4 of your document in this layout.

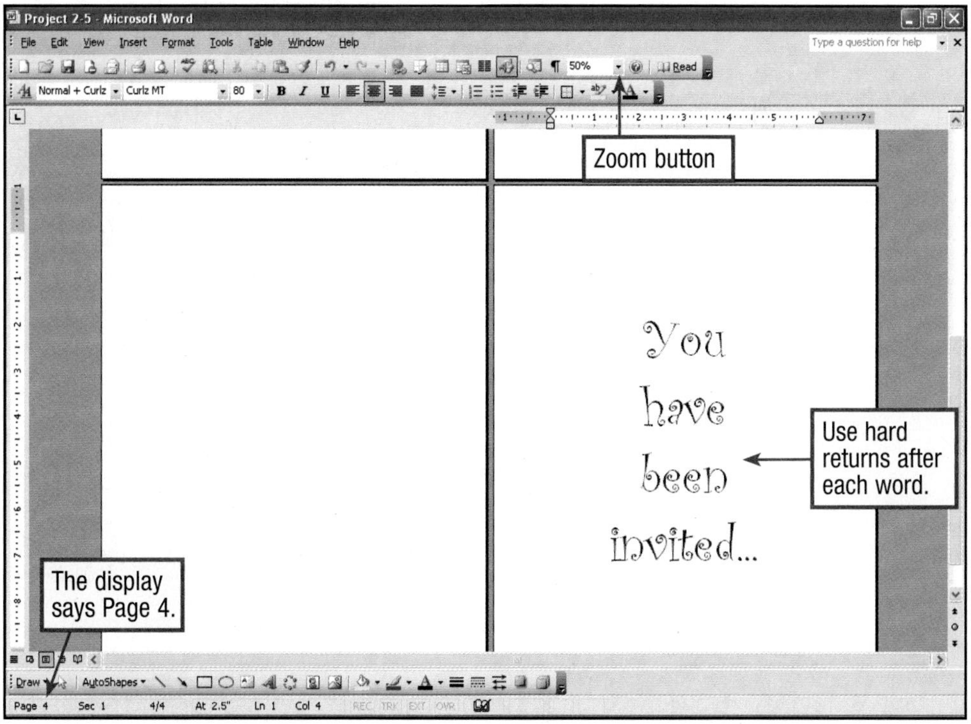
Project 2-5 - Microsoft Word
Zoom button
You have been invited...
Use hard returns after each word.
The display says Page 4.

Project 10-9 Add Effects to a Presentation

Skills You Will Apply

- Add custom animation
- Adjust timing

Key Terms

- animation
- transition

Academic Focus

Language Arts
Present information to an audience

Before PowerPoint, presentations were typically given as photographic slide shows. Photographs had to be taken and processed into a 35mm slide. The slides were then placed one by one into the slide projector by hand. Not only was this a time-consuming and expensive process, but slides were presented without the benefit of animations or other special effects.

Animate Your Presentation

Most of the features you need to create an impressive PowerPoint presentation are under the Slide Show menu. Here, you will find the preset and custom animation options. An **animation** is an effect where elements on the screen move. The preset animations are somewhat limited and overused. Once you become more familiar with PowerPoint, you can create your own effects through the Custom Animation task pane.

A **transition** is an animation that occurs between slides. Transitions add a nice touch to the presentation. You can choose from dozens of transitions: wipe left, dissolve, checkerboard, fade through black, and more. You can access these from the Slide Show task pane or by clicking **Slide Show>Slide Transitions**. You can also add sounds to the transitions and set the slides to automatically advance without having to press a key.

► Use the Slide Show task pane to apply preset effects.

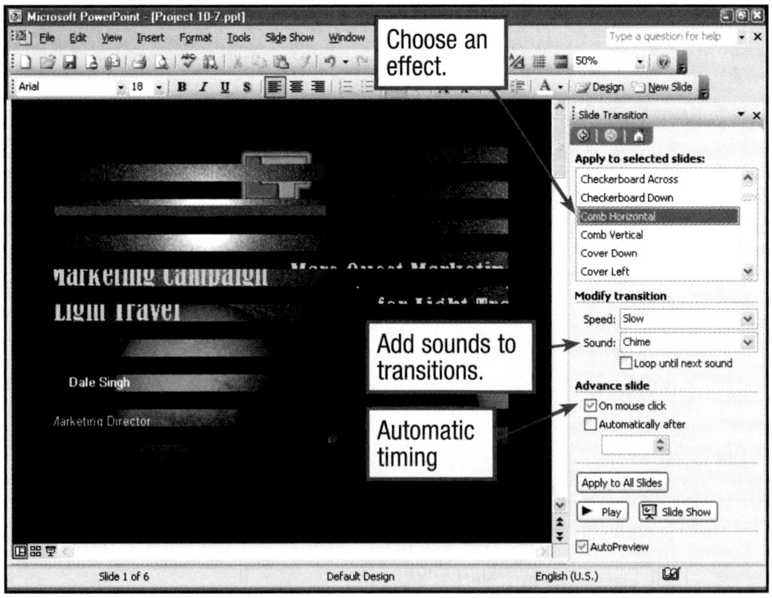

► **In this project,** you will finish the PowerPoint presentation you worked on in Project 10-8. You will add animation and other effects to the slides.

8. On **page 2** (the top right panel), insert a **WordArt** message in a different style: The party is at my house and starts at 7! (Figure 2.20).

Rotate Images

9. Select the WordArt. On the **Drawing** toolbar, choose **Draw>Rotate or Flip**. Then rotate the text until the WordArt is upside down (Figure 2.20).

▼ **Figure 2.20** Use the Rotate option to position your text.

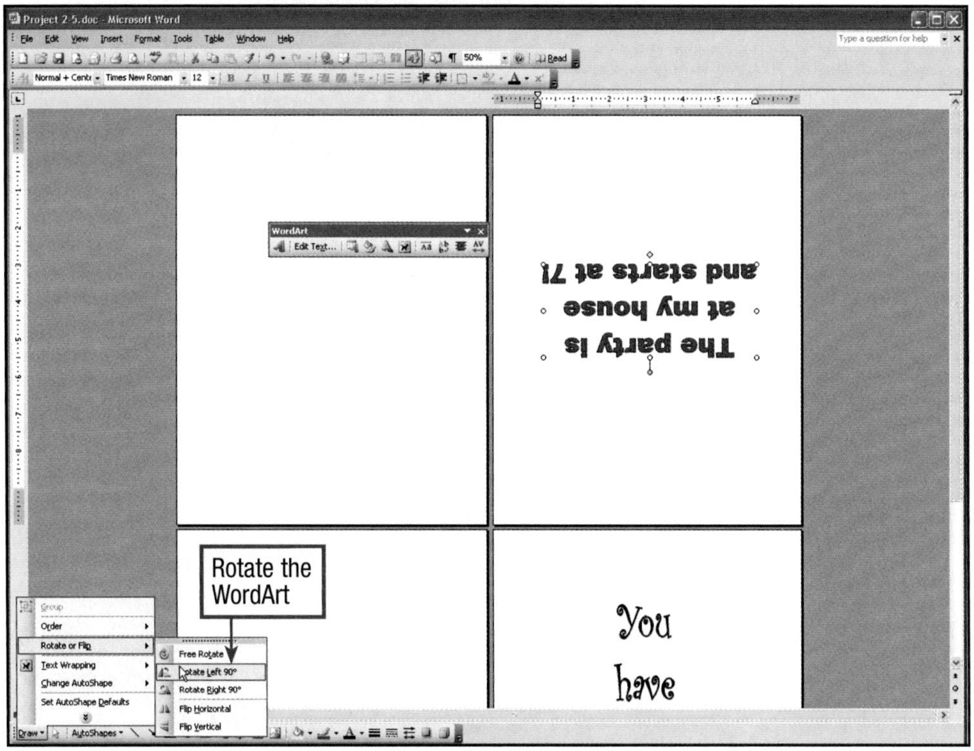

10. Place your insertion point in **page 1** (top left) on your screen. This is **panel 3** of the card. (**Hint**: Check the status bar to view the page number.)

11. Use **WordArt** to create a message that says: …to a party!

12. Select the WordArt. On the **WordArt** toolbar, click **Format WordArt** , and choose the **Size** tab.

13. Click the **Rotation** arrow until the text is positioned similarly to Figure 2.21.

▼ **Figure 2.21** Pages 1 and 2 are the inside of the card.

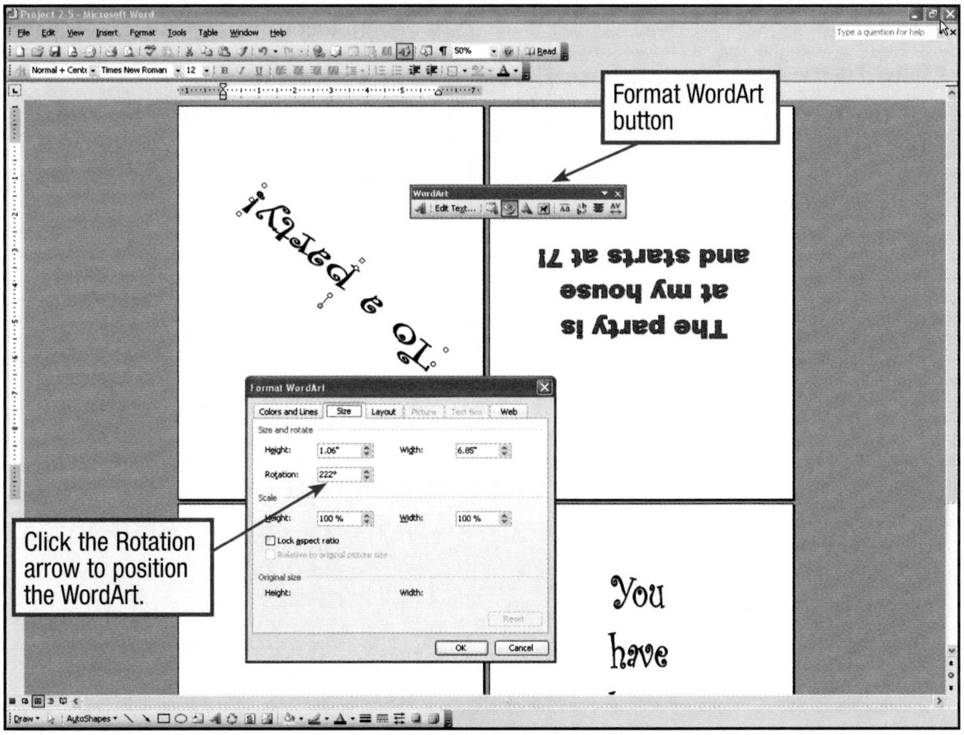

7. If your version of Publisher does not allow you to save in a graphic format, open the file and position the document on your screen so that you can capture the best image.

8. Press PRINT SCREEN. You will not see anything yet. Open the slide where you want to insert the image. Click **Edit>Paste** to display the screen capture.

9. To capture your Web pages, you will probably have to use **Print Screen**.

10. Use the **Picture** toolbar to crop and edit the screen capture as needed.

11. Use Photoshop to further edit your images. You can make them look like an open book, or combine them into one figure.

12. Insert images saved as files by clicking **Insert>Picture>From File**. Then position and size the image to fit on the slide.

13. View your slides as they will look in the presentation by clicking **Slide Show>View Show**.

14. Follow your teacher's instructions for saving the file. You will continue working on the presentation in Project 10-9.

▼ **Figure 10.35** A large product like a booklet might require more than one slide.

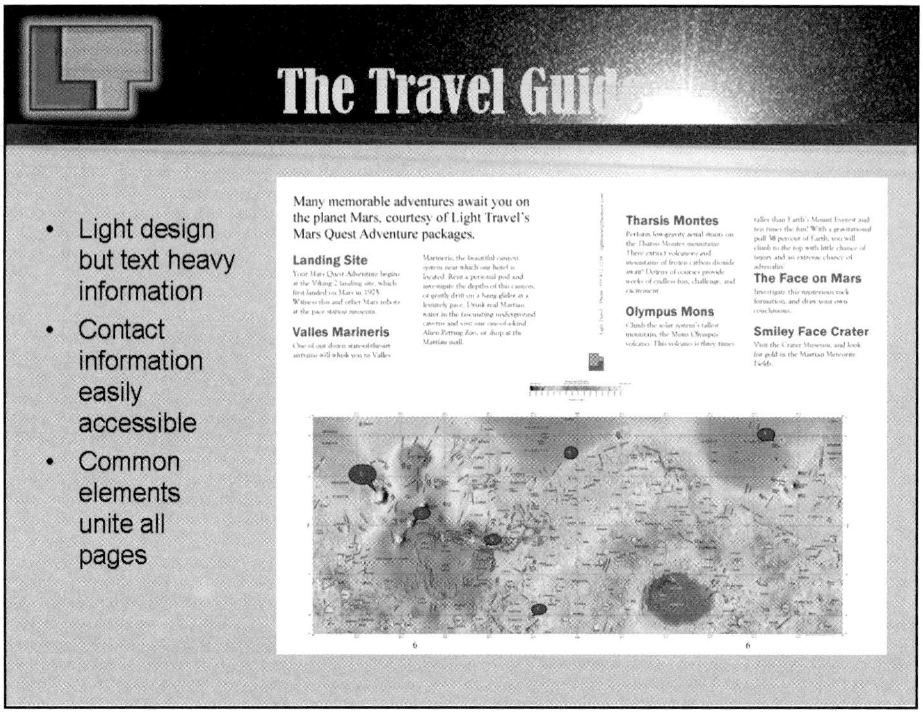

▼ **Figure 10.36** Use Photoshop to combine pages.

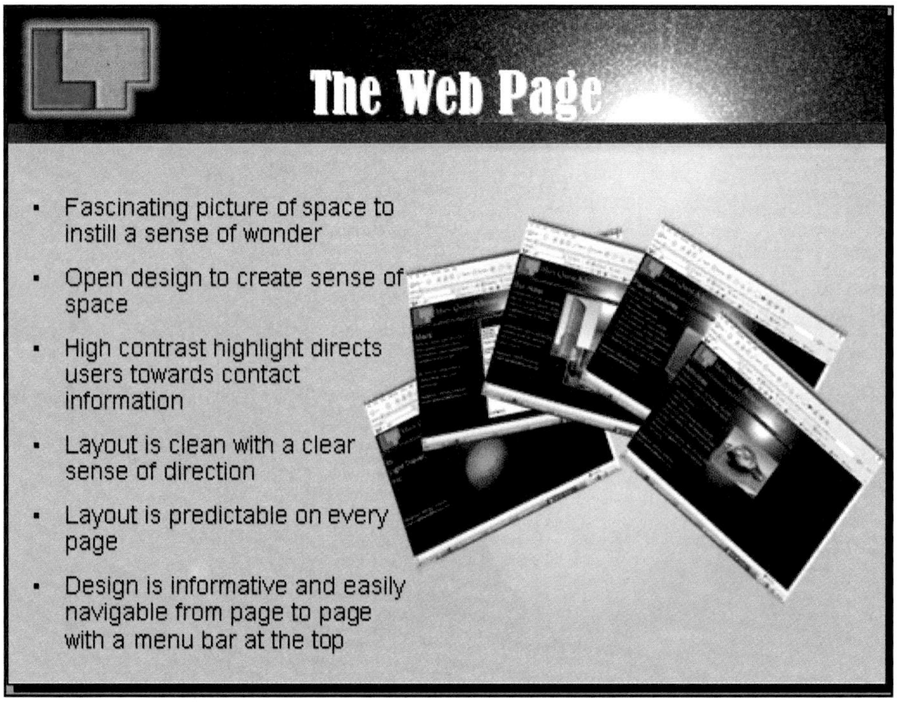

14. Place your insertion point in **page 3** (bottom left) on your screen. This is **panel 4** of the card.

15. Use WordArt, text boxes, or key directly onto the page. Key Designed By and add your name (Figure 2.22).

16. Under your name, add a © symbol and the date. (Hint: You can use the keyboard to create the copyright symbol. Press CTRL + ALT + C.)

17. Use the clip art in **Data File 2-5** (or choose your own clip art) to add graphics that will enhance your message.

18. Your unfolded card should look similar to Figure 2.22. **Save** your work. Then, with your teacher's permission, you are ready to print the card.

Print Four Pages on a Sheet

19. Click **File>Print**. In the Print box under **Zoom**, choose **4 pages** in the **Pages per sheet** window. Click **OK**.

20. All four pages should be printed on one sheet of paper. Fold your card and see how well it works!

▼ **Figure 2.22** Use borders, shading, and clip art to make your finished card visually interesting.

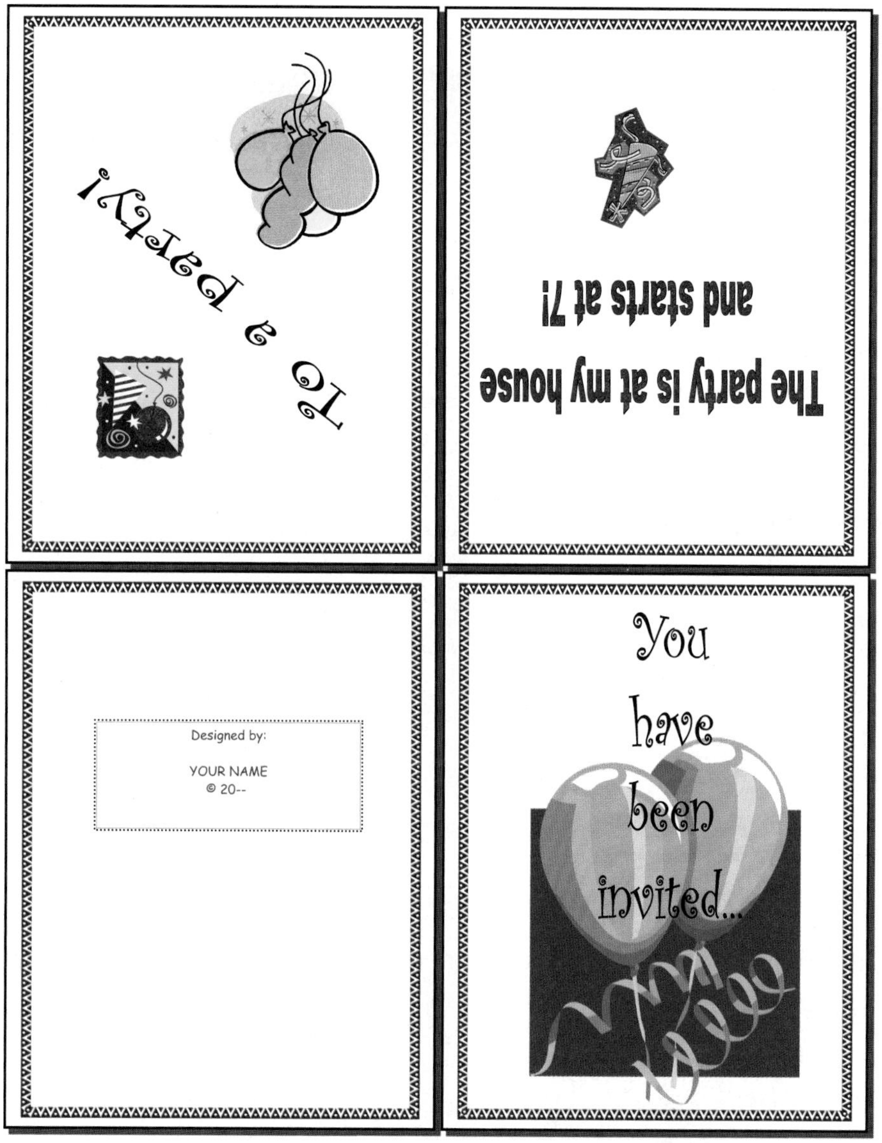

REVIEW AND REVISE

Check your work Use Figure 2.22 as a guide and check that:

- ☑ Text is printed and positioned correctly on each panel.
- ☑ The graphics are effective.
- ☑ There is enough white space so elements are not too crowded.
- ☑ There are no spelling or grammar errors.

Student Data File

Step-by-Step

1. Open the PowerPoint Presentation you started in Project 10-7. Save it according to your teacher's instructions.

2. Click **View>Normal** to design your presentation and display the slide thumbnails.

Add Text to Slides

3. If you want to add more slides, click the **New Slide** button New Slide on the tool bar.

4. For each slide, edit the items from the original outline you imported. If you want to write your own content, add 3–6 bulleted items on each slide.

Take Screen Captures of Documents

5. Use any method described in the **Spotlight on Skills** or in the steps below to create your images. You can also use **Data Files 10-8a** to **10-8d**.

6. For capturing the stationery, brochure, and booklet, use Publisher's **Save As** command and save the file in a graphic format such as **JPEG**, **GIF**, or **TIFF**.

▼ **Figure 10.34** Remember the Rule of Six when adding text to a slide.

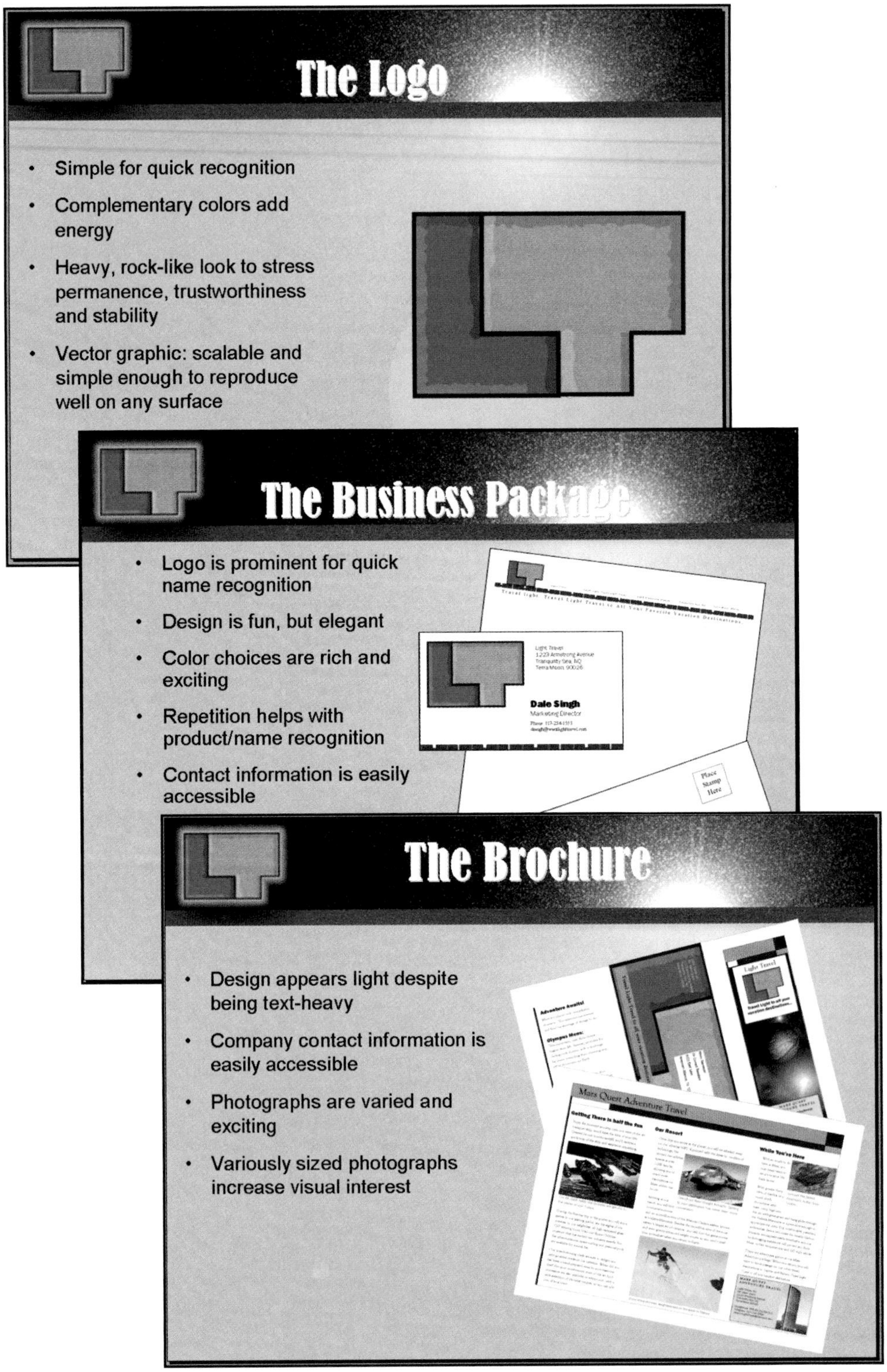

The Logo
• Simple for quick recognition
• Complementary colors add energy
• Heavy, rock-like look to stress permanence, trustworthiness and stability
• Vector graphic: scalable and simple enough to reproduce well on any surface
The Business Package
• Logo is prominent for quick name recognition
• Design is fun, but elegant
• Color choices are rich and exciting
• Repetition helps with product/name recognition
• Contact information is easily accessible
Dale Singh
Place Stamp Here
The Brochure
• Design appears light despite being text-heavy
• Company contact information is easily accessible
• Photographs are varied and exciting
• Variously sized photographs increase visual interest
Mars Quest Adventure Travel

Project 2-6 Create a Newsletter

Spotlight on Skills

- Create a masthead
- Format columns
- Create styles

Key Terms

- masthead
- byline
- style sheet

Academic Focus

Language Arts
Create a newsletter based on the legend of King Arthur

Desktop publishing has made it possible for personal newsletters to look very professional and include sophisticated text and graphics. Newsletters often contain a lot of text and information, which means they have to be both visually interesting and easy to read. Below are some of the elements that you should consider in order to create an effective newsletter.

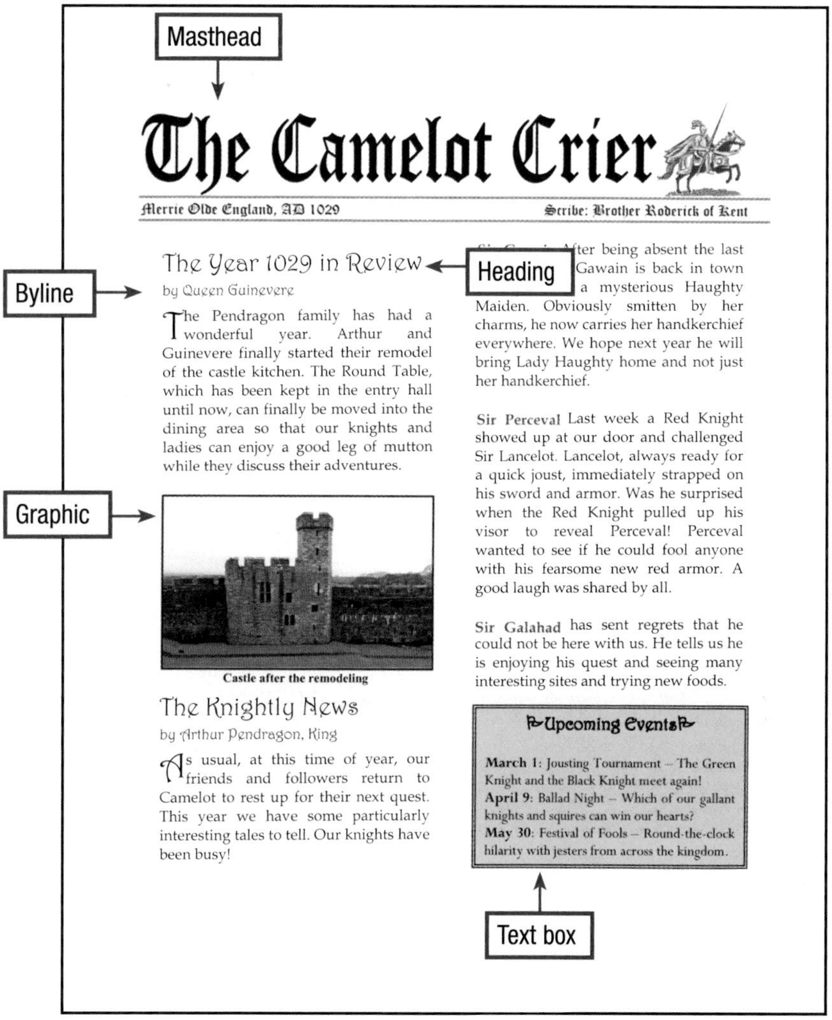

The Camelot Crier

Merrie Olde England, AD 1029 — Scribe: Brother Roderick of Kent

The Year 1029 in Review

by Queen Guinevere

The Pendragon family has had a wonderful year. Arthur and Guinevere finally started their remodel of the castle kitchen. The Round Table, which has been kept in the entry hall until now, can finally be moved into the dining area so that our knights and ladies can enjoy a good leg of mutton while they discuss their adventures.

Castle after the remodeling

The Knightly News

by Arthur Pendragon, King

As usual, at this time of year, our friends and followers return to Camelot to rest up for their next quest. This year we have some particularly interesting tales to tell. Our knights have been busy!

...fter being absent the last ... Gawain is back in town ... a mysterious Haughty Maiden. Obviously smitten by her charms, he now carries her handkerchief everywhere. We hope next year he will bring Lady Haughty home and not just her handkerchief.

Sir Perceval Last week a Red Knight showed up at our door and challenged Sir Lancelot. Lancelot, always ready for a quick joust, immediately strapped on his sword and armor. Was he surprised when the Red Knight pulled up his visor to reveal Perceval! Perceval wanted to see if he could fool anyone with his fearsome new red armor. A good laugh was shared by all.

Sir Galahad has sent regrets that he could not be here with us. He tells us he is enjoying his quest and seeing many interesting sites and trying new foods.

Upcoming Events

March 1: Jousting Tournament – The Green Knight and the Black Knight meet again!
April 9: Ballad Night – Which of our gallant knights and squires can win our hearts?
May 30: Festival of Fools – Round-the-clock hilarity with jesters from across the kingdom.

- A **masthead** (also called a nameplate) is the title of a newspaper or newsletter. It uses style, color, or size to grab the reader's attention.
- A **byline** tells who wrote the article.
- A column format gives readers shorter lines to scan.
- Graphics or photographs add color and visual interest.
- Text boxes call out specific information.
- Headings and body text use consistent formatting.

Project 10-8

Create Images for a Presentation

Skills You Will Apply

- Add text to slides
- Take screen captures of documents

Key Terms

- PDF
- screen capture

Academic Focus

Language Arts
Enhance a presentation

In this presentation, you are showing your colleagues all the elements of your marketing campaign. To create images of your business package, brochure, or any of the products you created, you can use the methods described for the following applications.

Publisher Publisher 2003 lets you save pages as a picture. This lets you send documents to people who may not otherwise be able to open an electronic copy. For example, if their computer did not have the fonts that you want to use in a design, a picture would let them view them. Click **File>Save As** and change the file type to a GIF, JPG, BMP, TIFF, PNG, or WMF. Each page has to be saved separately, so this option is impractical for long documents. In older versions of Publisher, you can use the Print Screen method discussed below.

Illustrator A **PDF** is a Portable Document Format, which is a type of file format developed by Adobe. It is like a picture of the document. This format is becoming the standard format for exchanging documents, no matter what kind of computer or software you use.

Other Methods A **screen capture** is a picture of an image that is displayed on your monitor's screen. Even without screen capture software, a picture of the entire screen can be taken with the Prt Scrn (Print Screen) button on your keyboard. When you press this button, it copies the whole screen. You must then paste the image into any program that accepts images: Word, Photoshop, PowerPoint, or Publisher. The image resolution is usually not good enough for professional publishing on an Imagesetter, but it is usually fine for desktop publishing.

You can also scan images into your computer using a scanner and then saving them in a suitable graphic format. Microsoft Office 2003 comes with a Document Image Writer. Save the file in Document Imaging Format (mdi). Then a preview window will open, and the page can be saved as a TIFF.

▼ In Publisher you can save your file as graphic images.

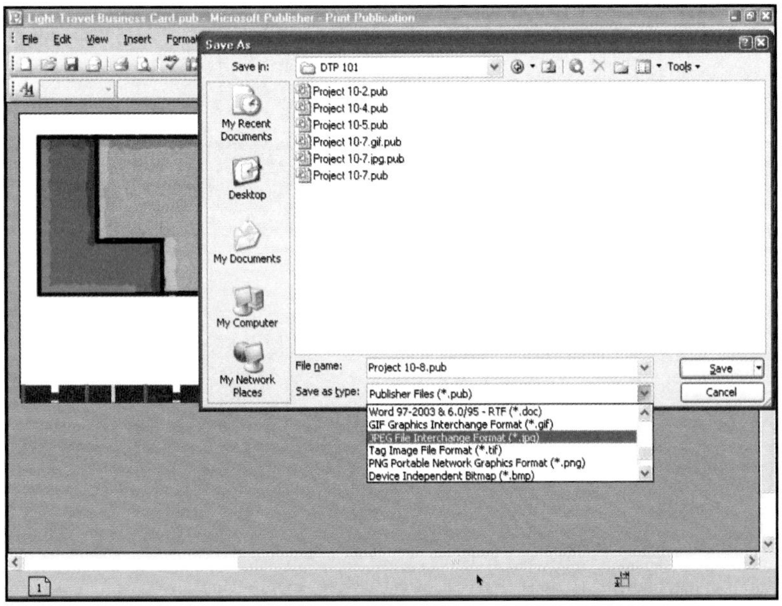

► **In this project,** your team will add images of your marketing materials to the slides that you started in Project 10-7.

Create Styles

Desktop publishing applications allow you to create your own **style sheet**, or formatting rules. These allow you to easily format specific types of text consistently. For example, you can create a style named *Main Heading* with text that is bold, 24 pt, Arial. To apply that style to a main heading in your document, you merely have to click on the style you have created. Word has a style list on the formatting toolbar.

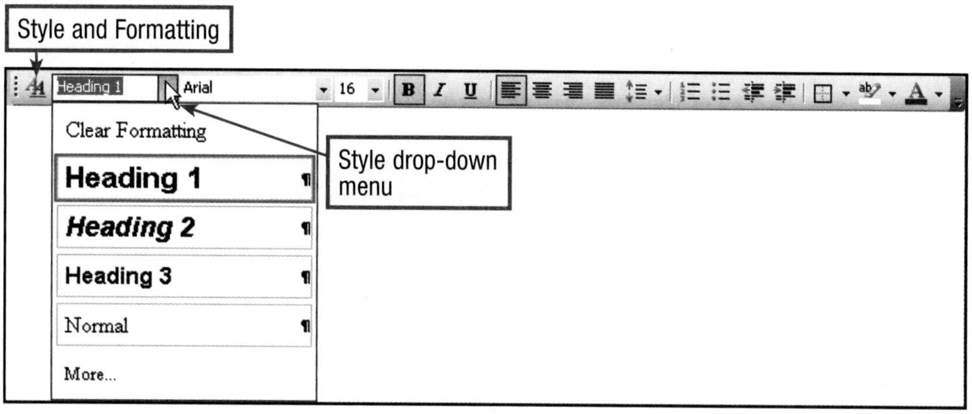

▲ You can create your own styles or use ones that are included in Word.

► **In this project,** you will begin formatting a personal-style newsletter, describing the deeds of King Arthur and his court. You will create a masthead and columns, and apply styles to text. You will continue the newsletter in Project 2-7.

Student Data File

Step-by-Step

1. Open a new document. Save it according to your teacher's instructions.

2. Click **File>Page Setup.** Under the **Margins** tab, change the **Left** and **Right margins** to **0.75**.

Create a Masthead

3. Click **Insert WordArt** , and choose the first style. Change the font to **Old English Text**, **54 pt**. Key The Camelot Crier. Click **OK**.

▼ **Figure 2.23** You can change the font in WordArt.

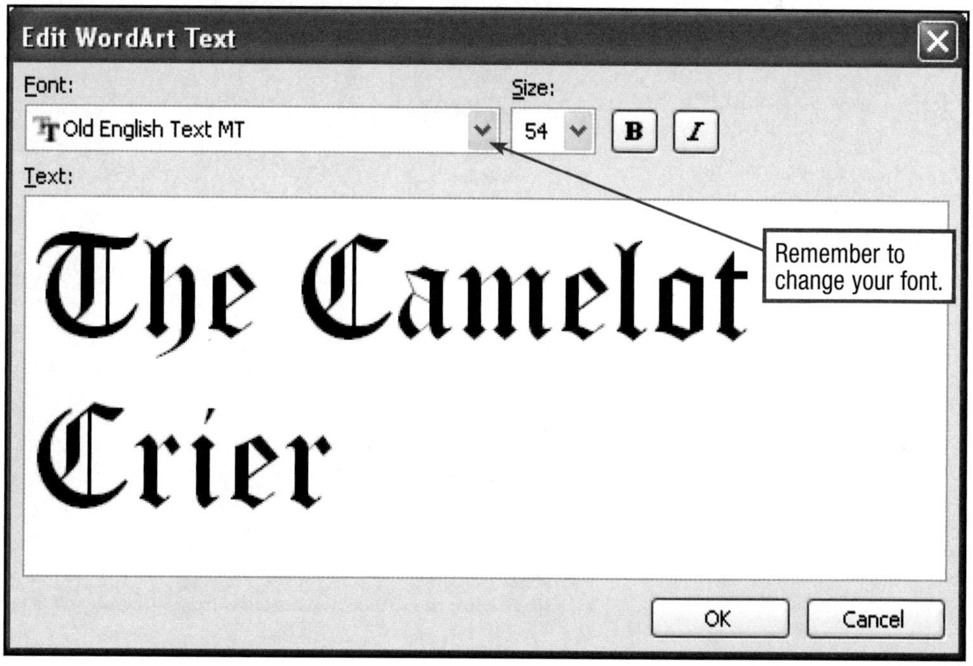

Apply the Master Slides

16 Click **View>Normal** to return to the presentation. Your slides should have the background images from the master slides.

17 If **Slide 1** is not displayed on the workspace, click the thumbnail in the slide view on the left (Figure 10.32).

18 Right-click **Slide 1** and choose **Slide Layout**. In the **Slide Layout** task pane, choose the **Title Slide** layout (Figure 10.33).

19 Key the following title in the top text box: Mars Quest Marketing Campaign for Light Travel.

20 In the bottom text box, format and key your own name, followed by the title Marketing Director.

21 Follow your teacher's instructions for saving the file. You will continue in Project 10-8.

▼ **Figure 10.32** All your slides should have a consistent look.

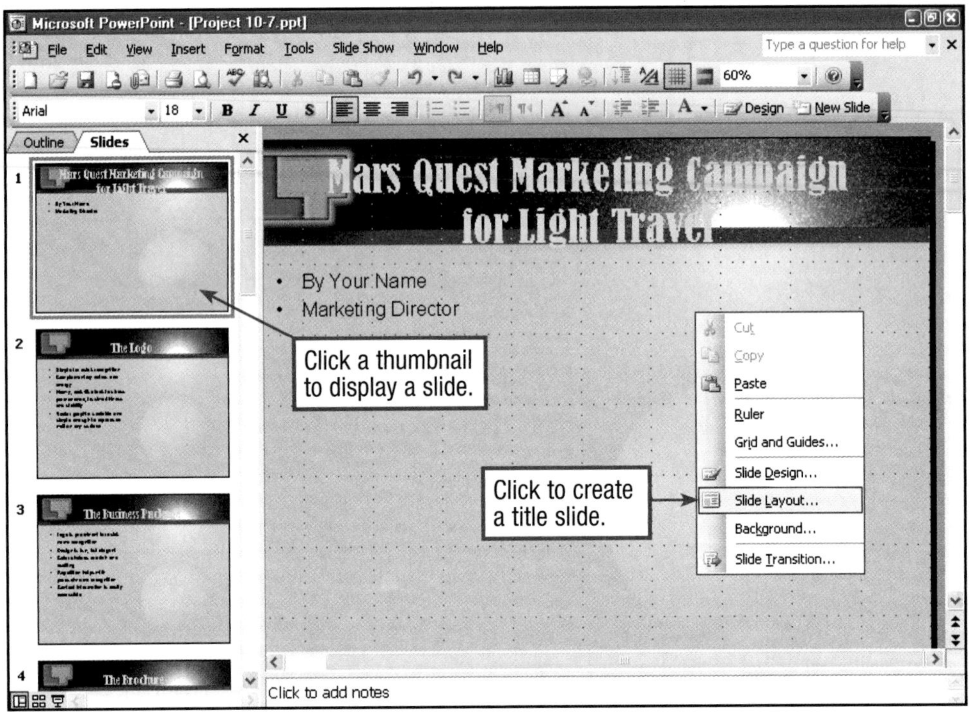

▼ **Figure 10.33** Your title slide will look different from the content slides.

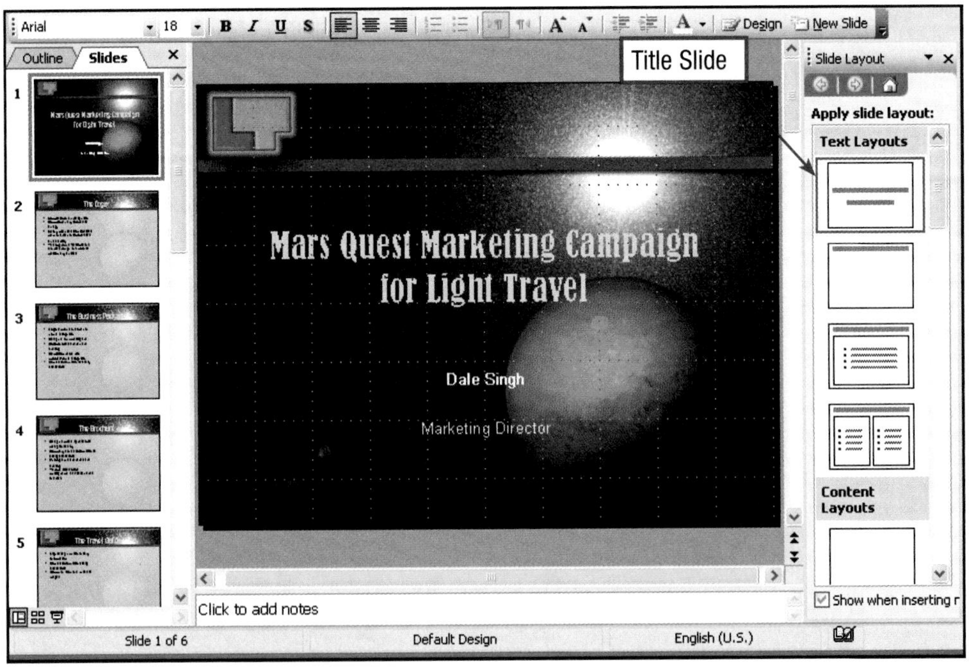

4. Click the WordArt to open the **WordArt** toolbar, and click **Format WordArt** .

5. Choose the **Colors and Lines** tab, and change the **Fill Color** to **Black**. Click **OK** (Figure 2.24).

6. Press ENTER twice to create two spaces under the WordArt. Then move the insertion point up one space so it is under the WordArt.

7. In **12 pt Old English Text** (or a similar font) key Merrie Olde England, AD 1029.

8. Tab to the 4½ inch mark on the ruler and key Scribe: Brother Roderick of Kent.

9. Select the text from Steps 7 and 8. Click **Format>Borders and Shading**. Choose:
   - **Apply to** paragraph
   - **Custom** setting
   - **Double line** style
   - **Borders** on the **top** and **bottom** of the box

10. Be sure to unselect the side borders in the **Preview**. Click **OK** (Figure 2.25).

▼ **Figure 2.24** You can change colors, size, and direction of WordArt text.

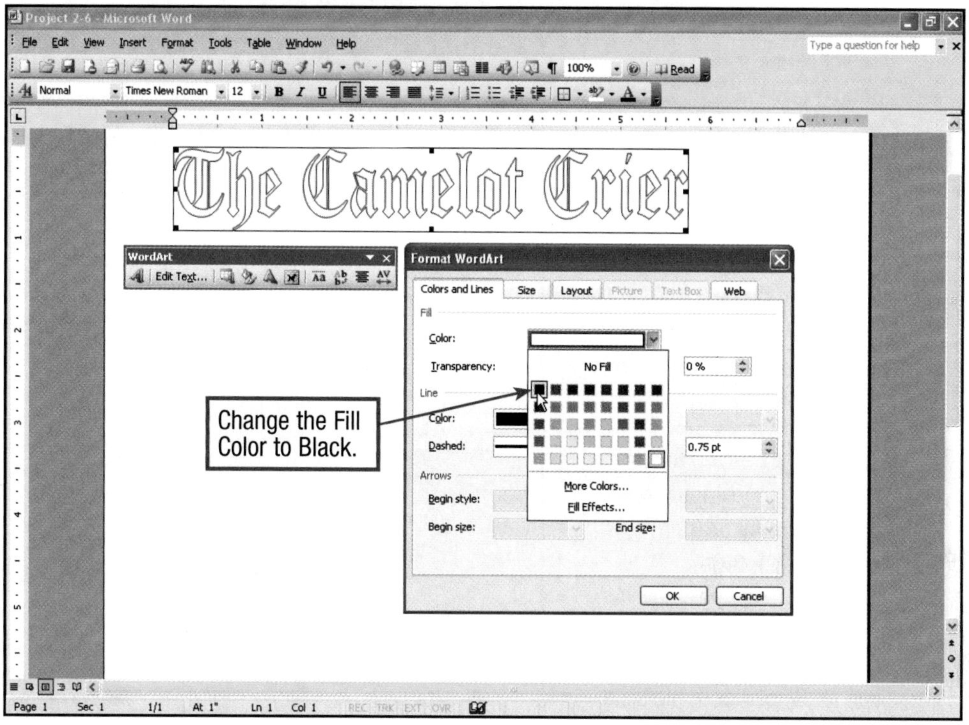

▼ **Figure 2.25** Leave a space below the box you create.

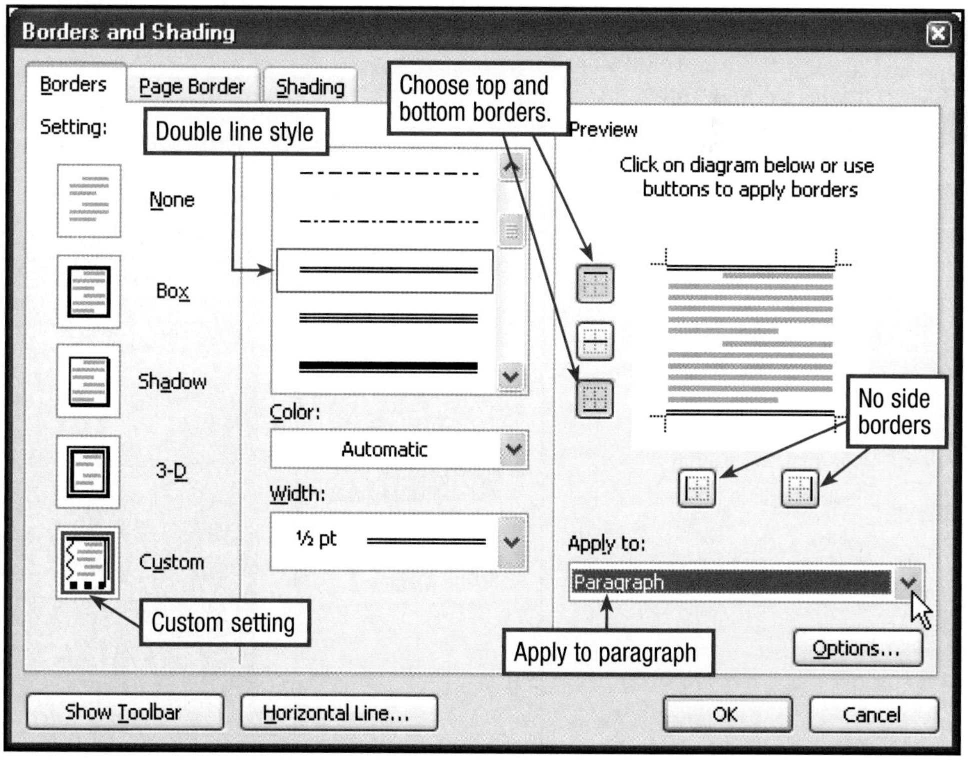

7. Select all the text in the bottom text box **Edit Master Text Styles**.

8. Change the font to **20 pt**.

9. Click **Format>Line Spacing** and set the **After paragraph spacing** to **0.25 lines**. Click **OK**.

10. Press CTRL + G to open the **Grid and Guides** box. Check **Display grid on screen**. Click **OK**.

11. Reduce the text box size so it extends to the vertical grid line at the center of the slide. It should fill only the left side of the slide (Figure 10.30).

▼ Figure 10.30 Use grid guides to help you align objects consistently.

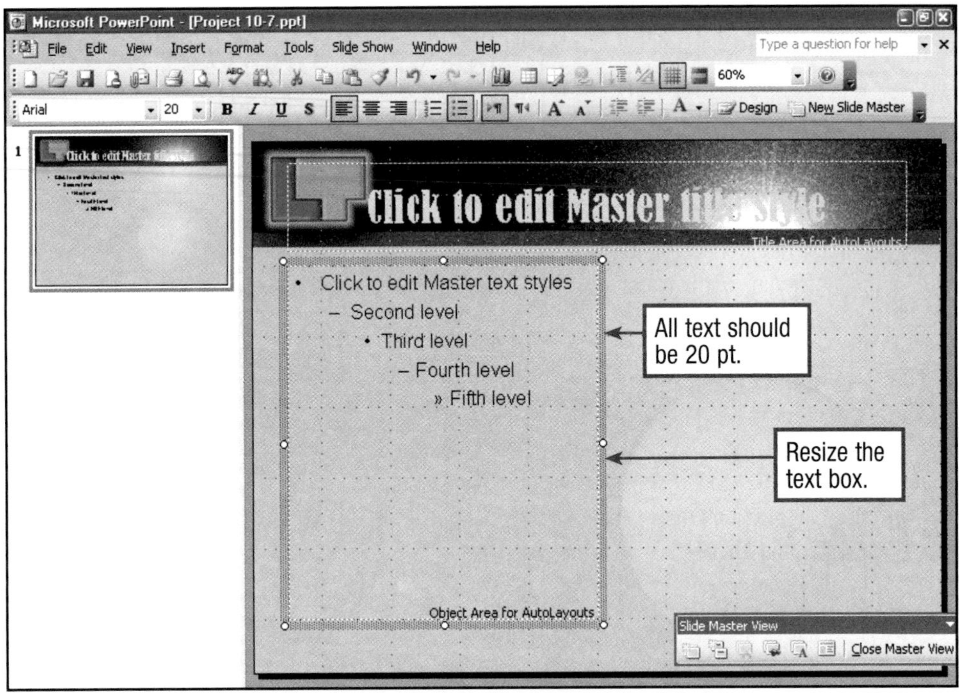

Add a Title Master

12. Click **Insert>New Title Master**.

13. In the Title Master slide, select the top **Master title style** text box. Insert **Data File 10-7c**.

14. Resize the picture to fill the slide, then **Send to Back**.

15. Change the title text to the same font you used for the title in the Slide Master.

▼ Figure 10.31 The Title Master will apply a different design to your title slide.

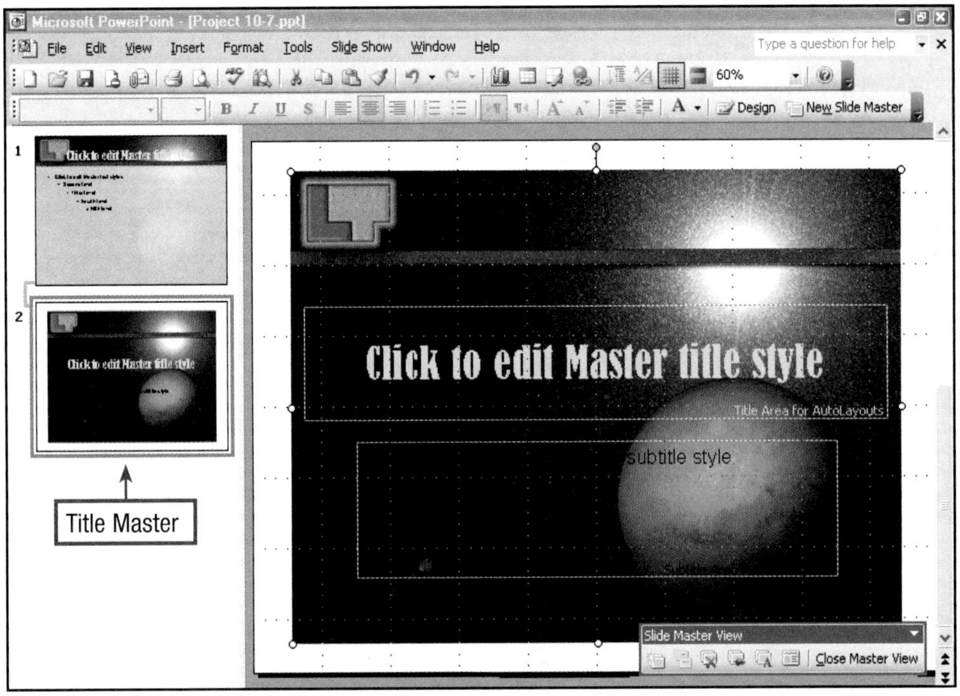

11. If necessary, delete blank line spaces above the borderline. Place your insertion point next to the WordArt. Insert the clip art **Data File 2-6a**, or choose your own clip art.

12. Drag the clip art to the right of the WordArt. Adjust the size so it looks similar to Figure 2.26. (**Note**: If the clip art does not have round handles, change the **Text Wrap** setting to **Square** so you can move the image.)

13. Place your insertion point below the borderlines you created. Click **Insert>Break**. Under Section break types, click **Continuous**.

14. Open **Page Setup** again, and change the **Left** and **Right margins** to **1.0**. Under Preview, apply to **This section**.

Format Columns

15. Insert **Data File 2-6b**. Format the text as two columns by clicking **Format>Columns** and choosing **Two** under **Presets**.

16. Select the first bold heading *The Year 1029 in Review.* Change the font to **Harrington 20 pt, not bold** (or a similar font).

17. With the heading selected, click **Format>Paragraph**. Set the **Spacing before** to **6 pt** and the **Spacing after** to **3 pt**.

Figure 2.26 A section break lets you use different margins on one page.

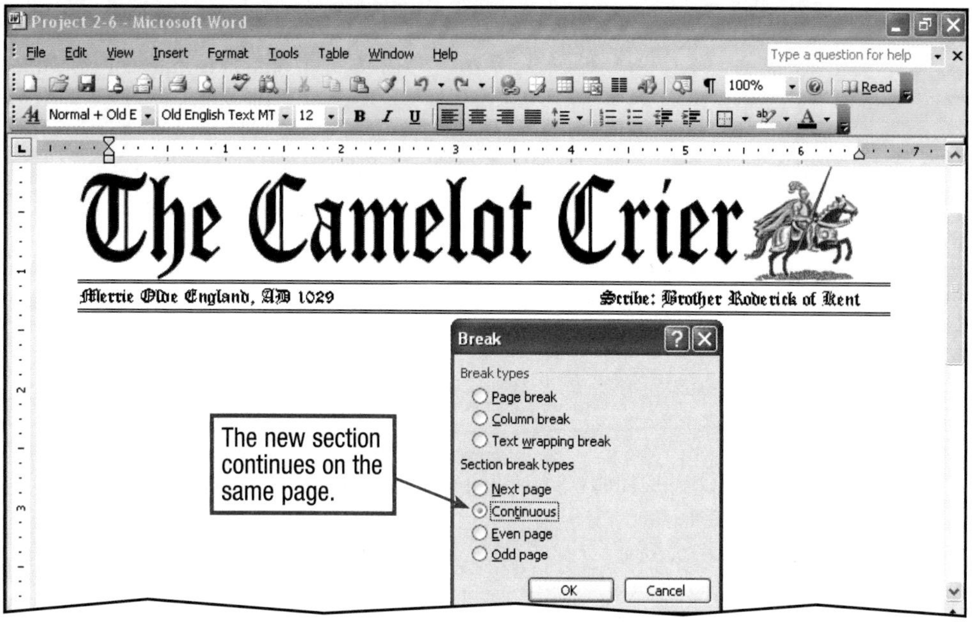

Figure 2.27 Narrow columns make it easier to read text.

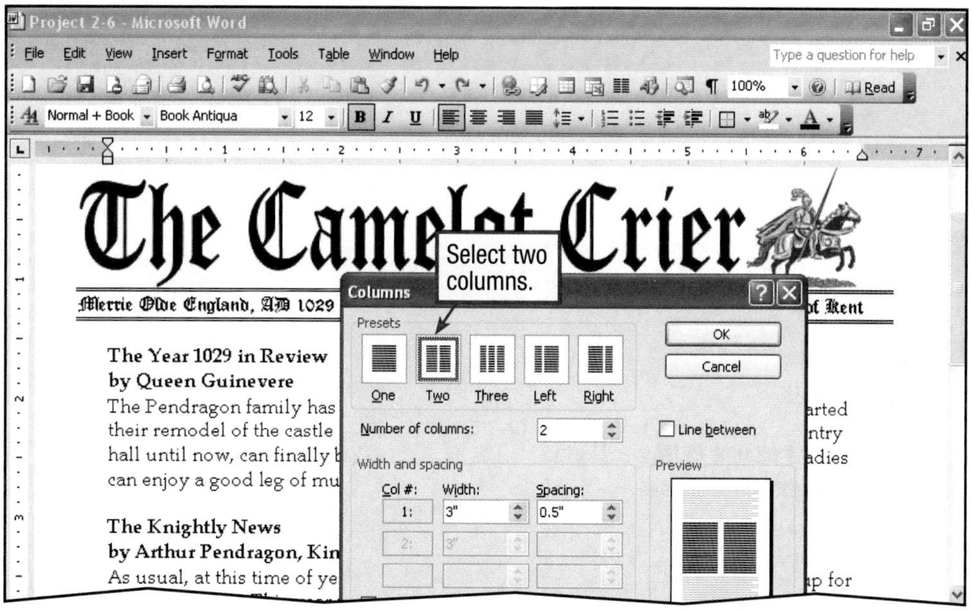

Instant Message

View Formatting Click **Show/Hide** ¶ on the Standard toolbar to see where you have added section or page breaks, hard returns, and tabs. Often this is the first step you should take when text on the screen is not where you want it to be.

Student Data File

Step-by-Step

1 Open Microsoft PowerPoint.

Import an Outline

2 Click **File>Open**. Change **Files of type** to **All Outlines** and open **Data File 10-7a**. Save according to your teacher's instructions (Figure 10.28).

Set Up a Slide Master

3 Click **View>Master>Slide Master**. This is the master slide. Any changes made here will apply to all slides that apply to this master.

4 Select the **Master title style** text box on the top and click **Insert>Picture>From File**. Insert **Data File 10-7b** (Figure 10.29).

5 Resize the picture to fill the slide. **Right-click** on the Picture. On the menu, click **Order>Send to Back**.

6 Change the title text to a light colored, modern font to create contrast with the background.

Figure 10.28 The outline is automatically imported into slide format.

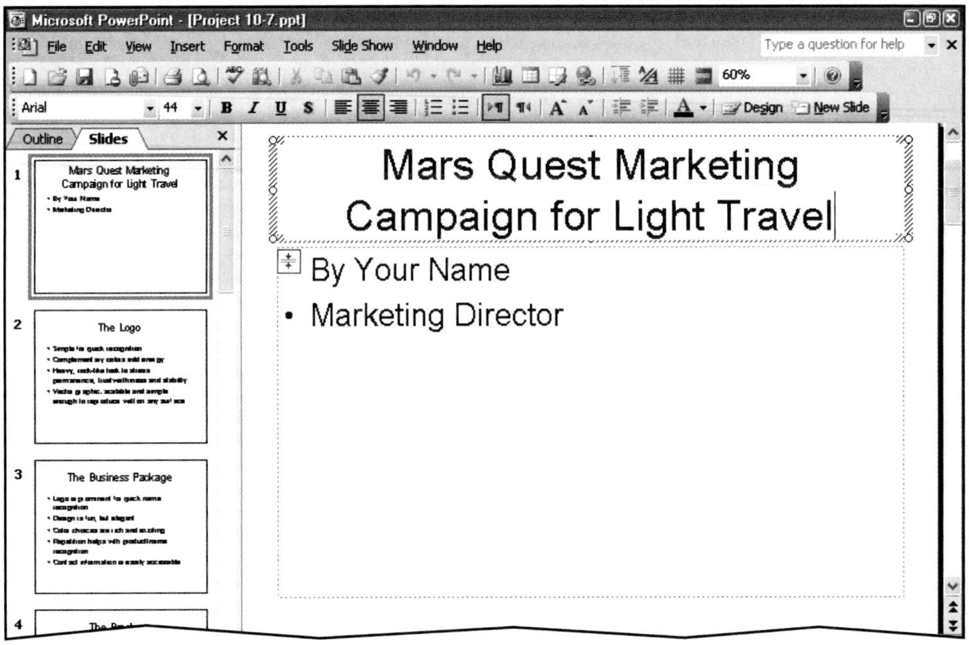

Figure 10.29 A master slide allows you to repeat its design on any slides.

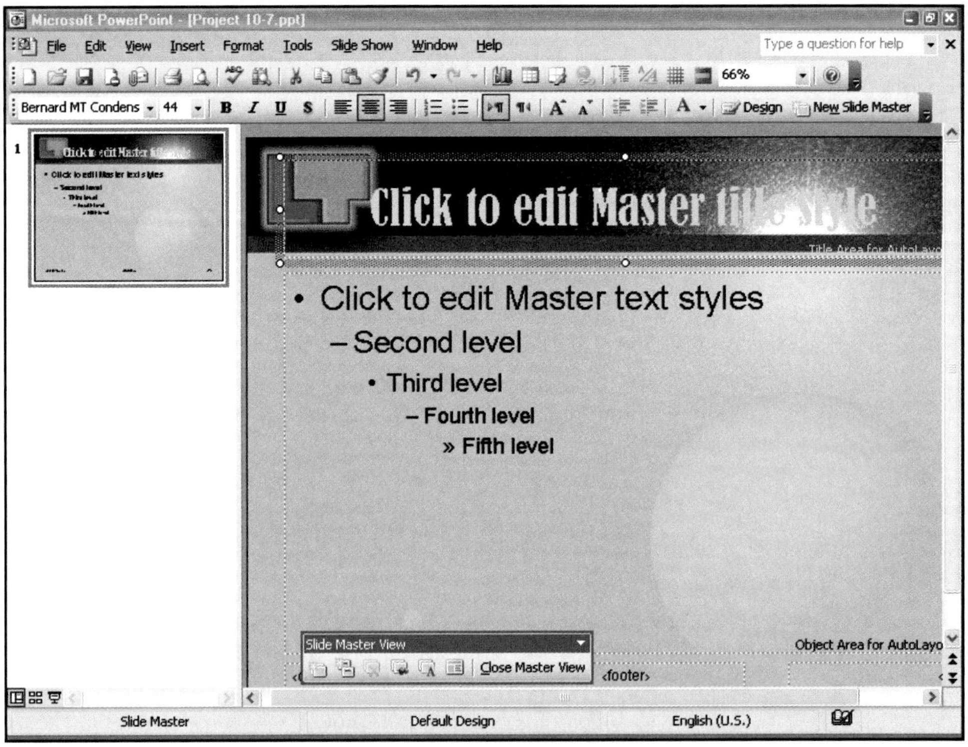

Create Styles

18 With the heading still selected, click **Styles and Formatting** [icon]. Then, in the task pane, click **New Style** [New Style...].

19 In the **New Style** box, next to **Name,** key Newsletter heading.

20 In each of the three boxes below Name, choose the settings shown in Figure 2.28. Click **OK** to save your new style.

21 Select the second heading *The Knightly News.* On the **Formatting** toolbar, click the **Style** window drop-down menu. Scroll down to the **Newsletter heading** style you just created. Click to apply the style.

22 Select the byline *by Queen Guinevere.* Follow Steps 15–19 to create a new style.
- Use the font **Harrington, 12 pt, not bold**.
- Add spacing **0 pt Before** and **6 pt After**.
- Name it Newsletter byline.

23 Apply the new style to the second byline *by Arthur Pendragon, King.*

24 Your newsletter should look similar to Figure 2.29. Save your newsletter for Project 2-7.

Figure 2.28 Style sheets make it easy to apply styles consistently.

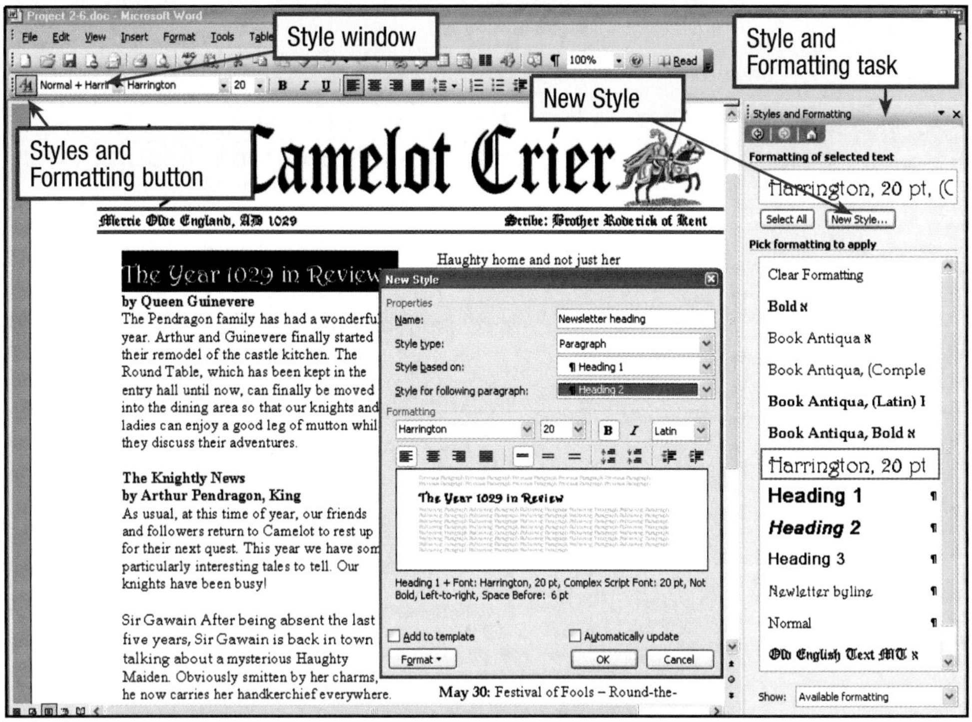

Figure 2.29 Headings should stand out from the rest of the text.

The Camelot Crier

Merrie Olde England, AD 1029 | Scribe: Brother Roderick of Kent

The Year 1029 in Review

by Queen Guinevere

The Pendragon family has had a wonderful year. Arthur and Guinevere finally started their remodel of the castle kitchen. The Round Table, which has been kept in the entry hall until now, can finally be moved into the dining area so that our knights and ladies can enjoy a good leg of mutton while they discuss their adventures.

The Knightly News

by Arthur Pendragon, King

As usual, at this time of year, our friends and followers return to Camelot to rest up for their next quest. This year we have some particularly interesting

bring Lady Haughty home and not just her handkerchief.

Sir Perceval Last week a Red Knight showed up at our door and challenged Sir Lancelot. Lancelot, always ready for a quick joust, immediately strapped on his sword and armor. Was he surprised when the Red Knight pulled up his visor to reveal Perceval! Perceval wanted to see if he could fool anyone with his fearsome new red armor. A good laugh was shared by all.

Sir Galahad has sent regrets that he could not be here with us. He tells us he is enjoying his quest and seeing many interesting sites and trying new foods.

Upcoming Events

March 1: Jousting Tournament – The

Plan Your Presentation

When designing a PowerPoint presentation, keep in mind that the audience may view the presentation in a variety of ways:

Computer screen PowerPoint presentations can be presented on a single computer or multiple computers. Only a few people at a time can view a presentation on a computer monitor.

- Design as you would for a Web page, except that all the text should be visible on the page without scrolling.
- Titles should use a serif font and body text should be sans serif.

Projector screen A special projector enlarges your presentation on a screen, like a slideshow. This is the best way to make a presentation to a large audience. Design elements need to be visible from a distance.

- Follow the **Rule of Six**: Use no more than six words per line, and no more than six short bullet points per slide.
- Letters should be 1 inch (72 pixels) high for every ten feet away from the screen that the audience is sitting.
- Choose high-contrast colors and use uncluttered backgrounds.

Printed handouts You may want to print out your presentation so the audience can take notes and keep a hard copy of the information. Choose colors that are also clear and attractive when printed in black and white.

- You have options for how many slides can be printed on a page. Three is usually best.
- You can print your speaker notes for the audience to take home, or just print the slide images.

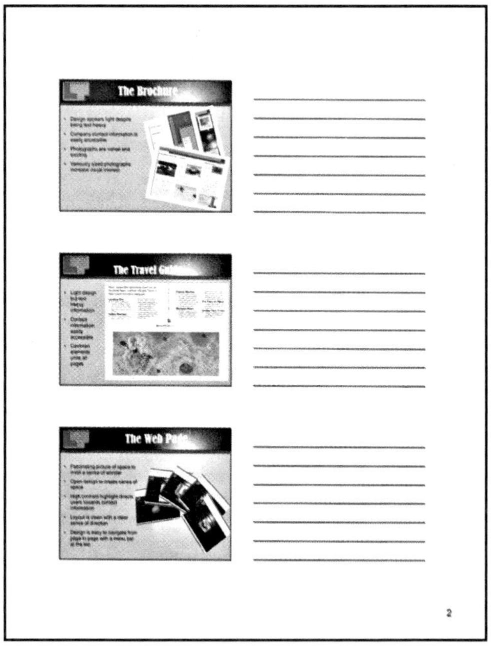

▲ You can print 3 slides to a page with room for the audience to write down notes.

▶ **In this project,** your team will begin creating a PowerPoint presentation that describes your Mars Quest marketing campaign to your associates. Your team will continue to develop the presentation in the next two projects.

Project 2-7 Crop and Resize a Photograph

Spotlight on Skills

- Crop and resize a photograph
- Add a caption

Key Terms

- resize
- crop

Academic Focus

Math
Modify proportions of a photograph

For a more eye-catching newsletter, add appropriate graphics and text boxes. Both elements can help break up the text and make the document more interesting for the reader. Text boxes also call out specific information to which you might want to draw a reader's attention.

When you insert a photograph into the first column, your text will automatically flow into the second column. You may have to **resize** the photograph. When you resize, you reduce or increase the size of the picture so that the page looks balanced and visually appealing.

You can also **crop**, or trim, an image. This allows you to display the parts of the picture that are most important. It is also useful for changing the proportions of a photo. For example, if you have a photo that is in portrait layout, you can crop the top and/or bottom, to change the shape to a landscape layout. This can be useful if you do not have much space and need to fit the photo to specific dimensions. Cropping also improves the composition of a photo, making designs more interesting and attractive.

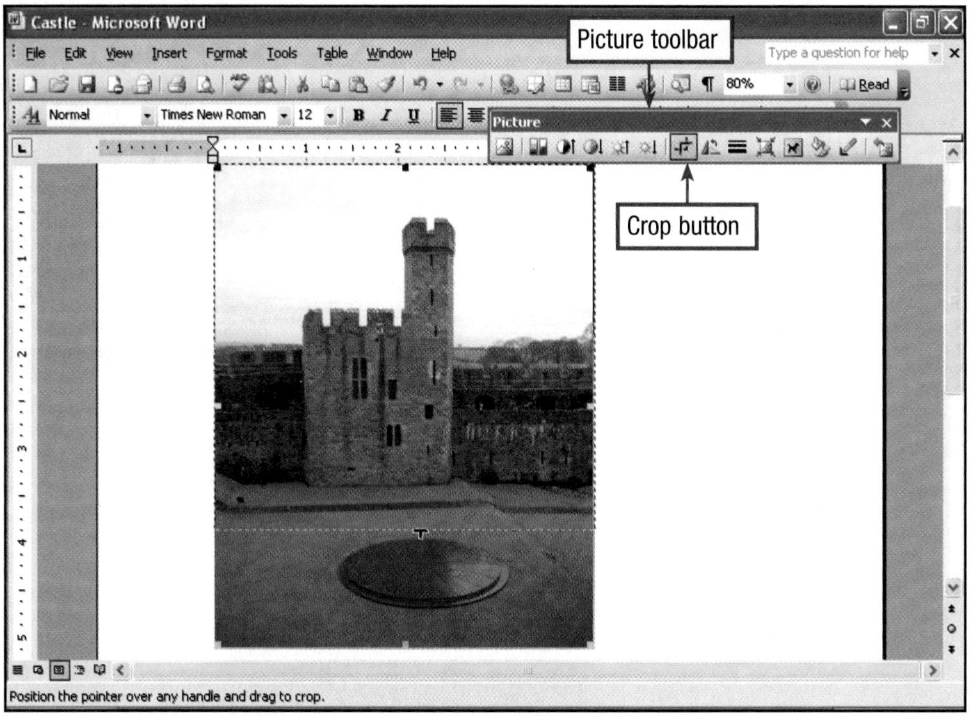

▲ Cropping displays more of the castle and less of the sky and grass.

▶ **In this project,** you will continue to format your Camelot newsletter and add a text box and a photograph. You will crop and resize the photo to fit the dimensions of the newsletter so that the columns will align properly. Drop caps and a caption will also add interest to the page.

Skills Studio

Project 10-7

Create a PowerPoint Presentation

Skills You Will Apply

- Import an outline
- Set up a Slide Master
- Add a Title Master
- Apply the master slides

Key Term

- Rule of Six

Academic Focus

Language Arts
Create an oral presentation

Using PowerPoint, you can easily create a professional-looking presentation that will capture your audience's attention. PowerPoint's user interface is similar to that of Word and Publisher. It provides different options for creating and viewing your slides.

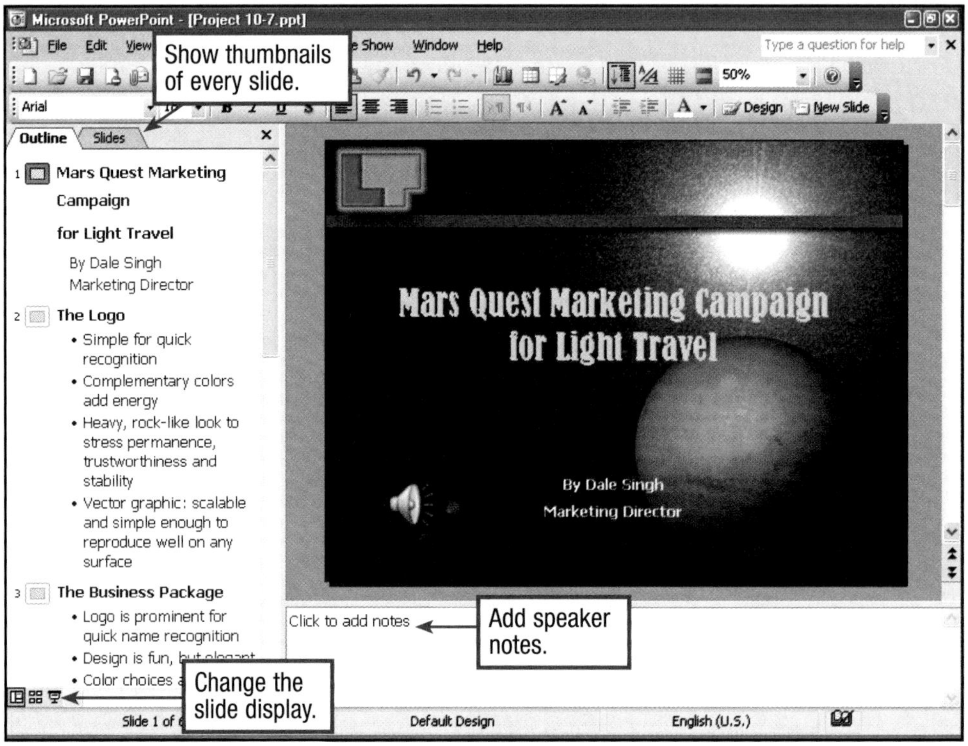
Microsoft PowerPoint - [Project 10-7.ppt]
Show thumbnails of every slide.
Outline
Slides
Mars Quest Marketing Campaign
for Light Travel
By Dale Singh
Marketing Director
The Logo
Simple for quick recognition
Complementary colors add energy
Heavy, rock-like look to stress permanence, trustworthiness and stability
Vector graphic: scalable and simple enough to reproduce well on any surface
The Business Package
Logo is prominent for quick name recognition
Mars Quest Marketing Campaign for Light Travel
By Dale Singh
Marketing Director
Click to add notes
Add speaker notes.
Change the slide display.
Default Design
English (U.S.)

Outline View Choosing this option on the task pane is the fastest way to input content into a presentation. Formatting and graphics are not displayed in this view, just the text.

Slide View This task pane shows small thumbnails of each slide in the presentation, making it easy to see the layout of the presentation at a glance. You can see an example on page 430. Clicking a thumbnail displays the slide on the workspace.

Speaker Notes You have the option to add notes to each slide. These notes are not displayed on the screen during a presentation. They can be printed, though, so that the presenter can remember what information to say during the presentation. They can also be used as a handout for the audience or co-presenters.

Step-by-Step

1. In your Camelot newsletter, select the first **T** in the first article. Then click **Format>Drop Cap**.
2. In the **Drop Cap** box, choose **Dropped**, and change the font to **Harrington**. Then change **Lines to drop** to **2.** Click **OK**.
3. Repeat Steps 1 and 2 to create a dropped **A** at the start of the second article (Figure 2.30).
4. In the second article, select **Sir Gawain** at the beginning of the second paragraph. Change the font to **dark red**.
5. Apply the same formatting to **Sir Perceval** and **Sir Galahad** in the next two paragraphs (Figure 2.31).
6. Select all the text, and click **Justify** ▤.

▼ **Figure 2.30** Drop caps can give a document an old-fashioned look.

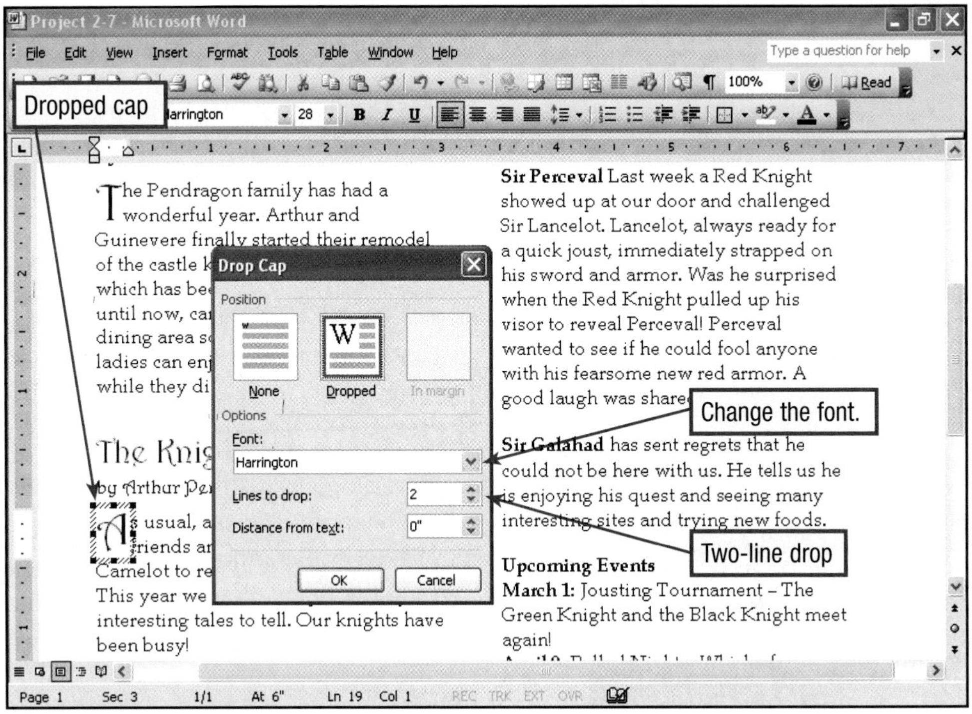

▼ **Figure 2.31** If you have gaps between words in justified text, add text or use a hyphen to break a word between lines.

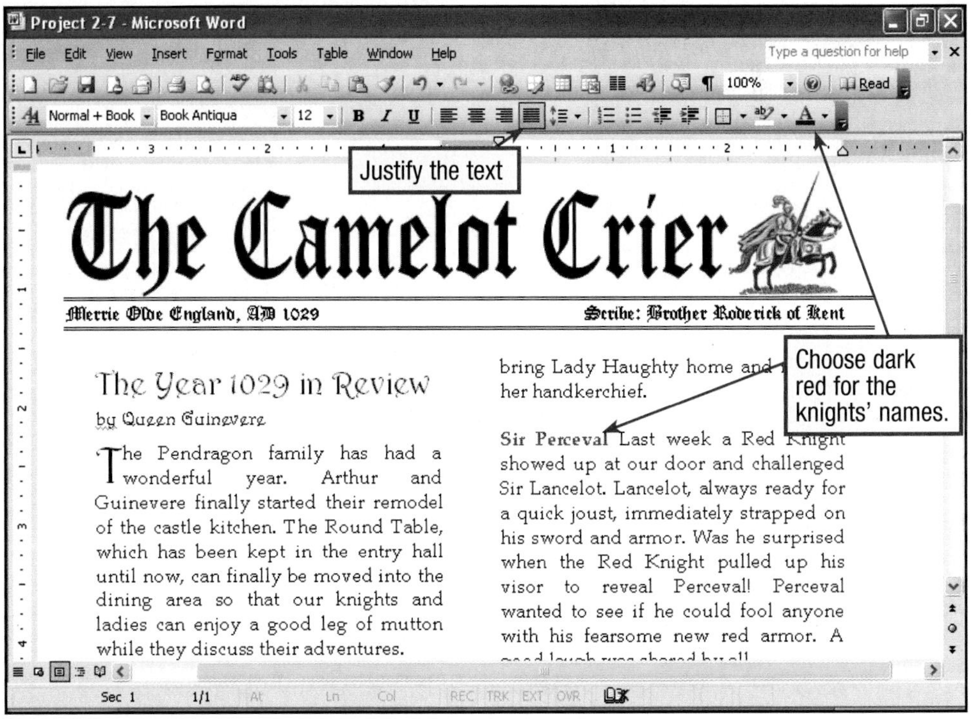

Skills Studio

Reinforce Your Skills

- **Project 10-7**
  - Identify Powerpoint features
  - Plan a presentation
  - Import an outline
  - Apply master slides
- **Project 10-8**
  - Add text to slides
  - Take screen captures
  - Insert images into slides
- **Project 10-9**
  - Add custom animation
  - Adjust timing
  - Preview and rehearse a presentation

Go Online ACTIVITIES
www.glencoe.com

Challenge Yourself Go to **Chapter 10**, and choose **Enrichment Activities** for more practice with the skills you have learned.

Design PowerPoint Presentations

The following three projects will take you through the steps you need to create a PowerPoint presentation:

- **Project 10-7** Create a PowerPoint presentation
- **Project 10-8** Create images for a presentation
- **Project 10-9** Add effects to a presentation

Present Your Product

PowerPoint is a software application that is used to create business and educational presentations and custom slide shows. Presentations can have simple animations, hyperlinks to other slides or files, music, and sound effects. PowerPoint has many tools for creating presentations that will inform and instruct your audience while keeping their interest.

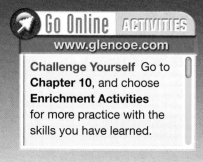

A good presentation will use PowerPoint's features to visually communicate information without overdoing the special effects. Too many sounds and animations can distract from the message and end up being annoying, rather than entertaining.

7. Select the *Upcoming Events* text. Click **Text Box** to add a text box around the text.

8. Format the text using the following or similar fonts (Figure 2.32):
   - **Harrington 14 pt**, **center aligned**, for the title
   - **Perpetua 12 pt** for the body text

9. Use the **Wingding** font to insert a banner symbol on both sides of the title (Figure 2.32). Add a blank line.

10. Add a gold fill to the text box and a black border with a line style similar to Figure 2.32.

Crop and Resize a Photograph

11. Place your insertion point at the end of the first article, and press ENTER to add a space. Then insert **Data File 2-7**.

12. On the **Picture** toolbar, click **Crop** . Your mouse pointer will display the crop symbol.

13. Click the picture handle closest to the section you want to crop. Drag the handle inward until you have removed that section (Figure 2.33).

14. When you finish cropping, drag the photo's pull handles and size the photo to fit the space.

▼ Figure 2.32 **Add a text box to set off important information.**

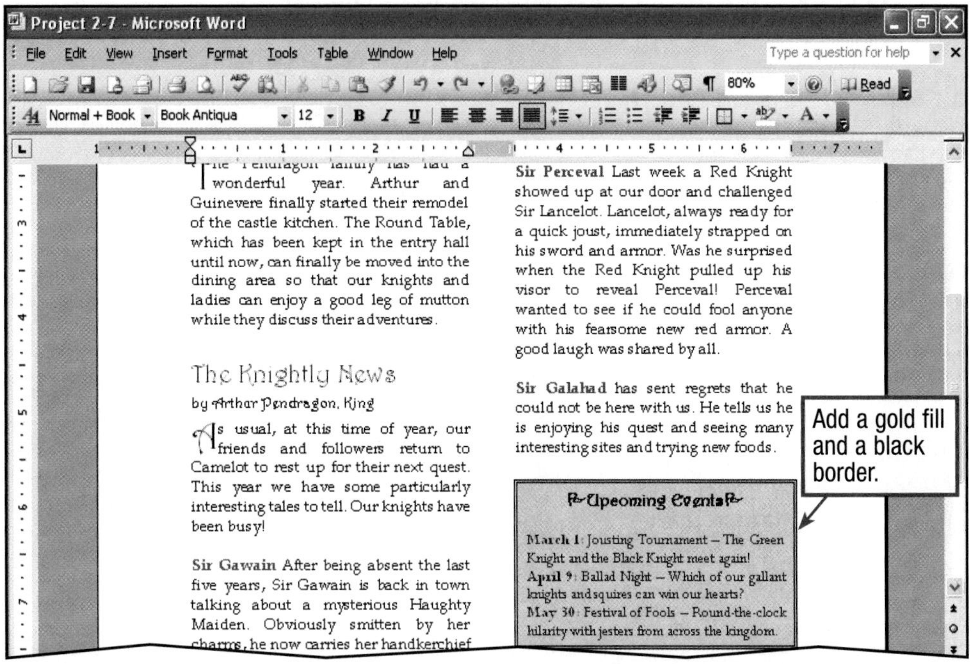

▼ Figure 2.33 **Click a picture handle to use the cropping tool.**

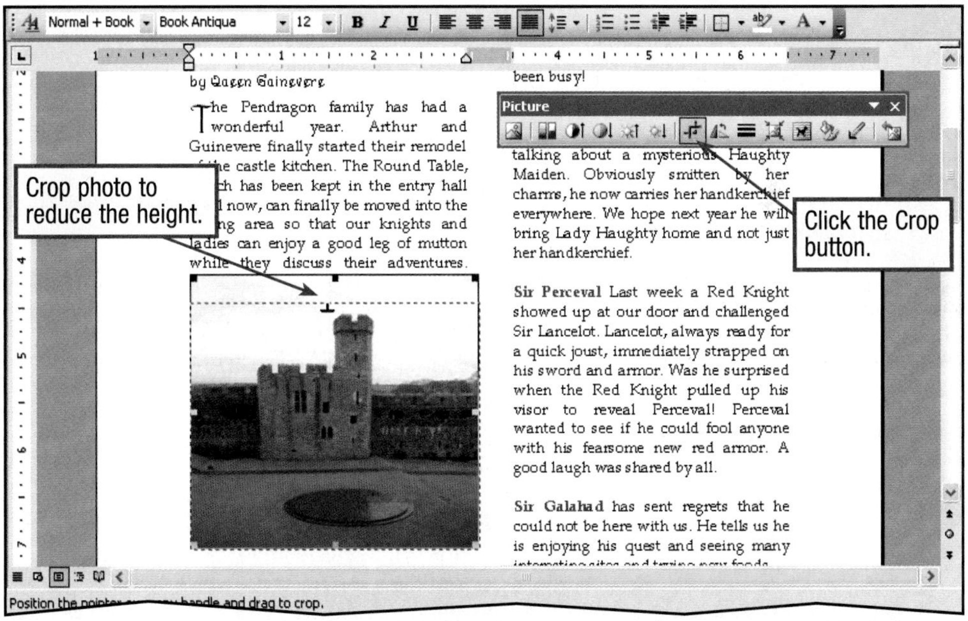

Instant Message

Display the Picture Toolbar If the Picture toolbar is not displayed, right-click the photo, and choose **Show Picture toolbar**. You can also display the toolbar by clicking **View>Toolbars>Picture**.

13 Repeat the steps to create **Page 5**, as shown in Figure 10.26.

Create Hyperlinks

14 Click **View>Toolbars>Web Tools** to display the **Web Tools** toolbar.

15 Go to **Page 2**. On the **Web Tools** toolbar, click **Hot Spot**. Drag a hot spot over the page title in the navigation bar.

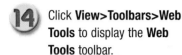

16 In the **Insert Hyperlink** dialog box, click **Place in This Document**, then choose **Page 2** (Figure 10.27).

17 Click **Change Title**, and rename the page to **Mars**.

18 Click **OK** to close all the dialog boxes, then click **Arrange>Send to Master Page**.

19 Repeat **Steps 15–18** to add **hyperlinks** to all the pages.

20 On the **Web Tools** toolbar, click **Web Page Preview**. Test your hyperlinks, and check to make sure your layout does not change.

21 Proofread your work. Follow your teacher's instructions for saving the Web pages.

▼ **Figure 10.26** Make sure items on a bulleted list are aligned.

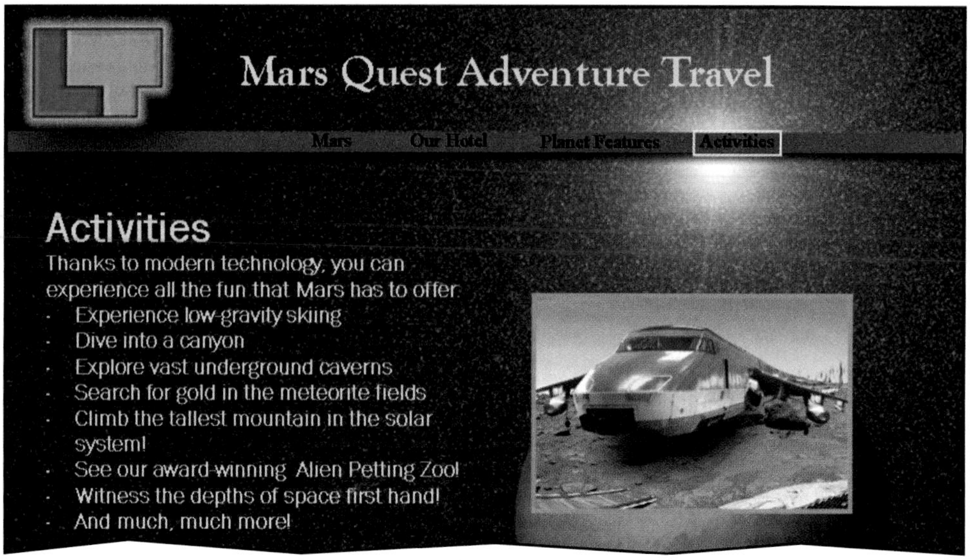

▼ **Figure 10.27** Add a hyperlink to each page.

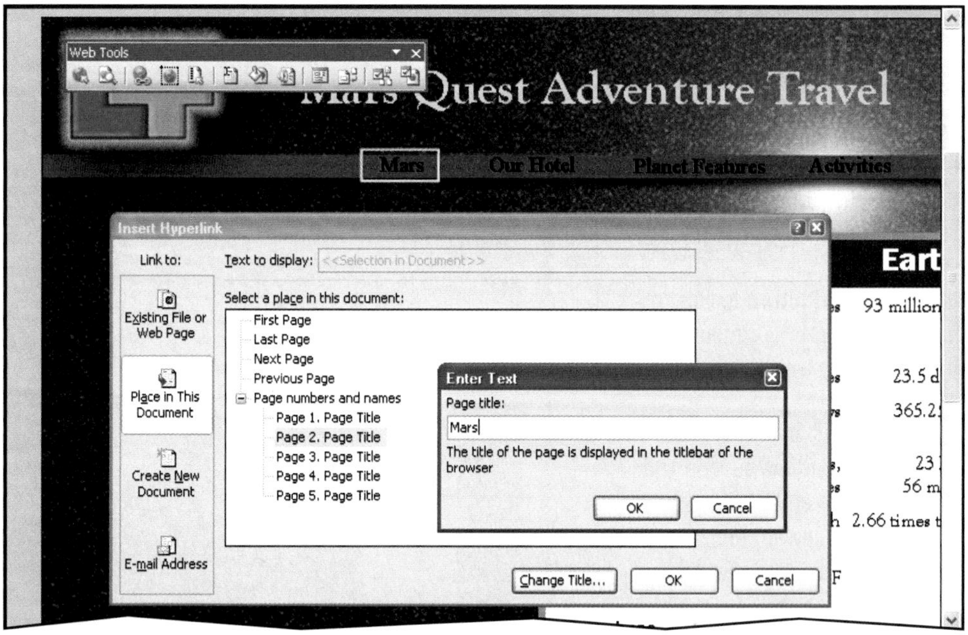

REVIEW AND REVISE

Check your work Use Figures 10.22–10.26 as guides and check that:

☑ The master page design elements are applied to each Web page.

☑ In Web page preview, the layout is effective and the hyperlinks work.

☑ Text is readable with no spelling or grammar errors.

15 Select the picture, and choose **Format>Picture>Picture** tab. Adjust the sliders for **Brightness** and **Contrast**. Click **OK**. Repeat until the image looks best.

Add a Caption

16 Right-click the photo, and choose **Caption** from the drop menu.

Mac users click **Insert>Reference>Caption**.

17 In the **Caption** box, check **Exclude Label**. Then add a short descriptive caption for the photo. Click **OK**.

18 Select the photo, and click **center align**. Center the caption.

19 Click **Format>Borders and Shading** to add a **1½ pt line** around the photo.

20 Resize your photograph and text box to balance the columns, if necessary. Your newsletter should look similar to Figure 2.34.

21 Follow your teacher's instructions for saving and printing your newsletter.

▼ **Figure 2.34** Size the photo and text box so that the two columns are aligned.

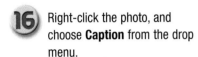

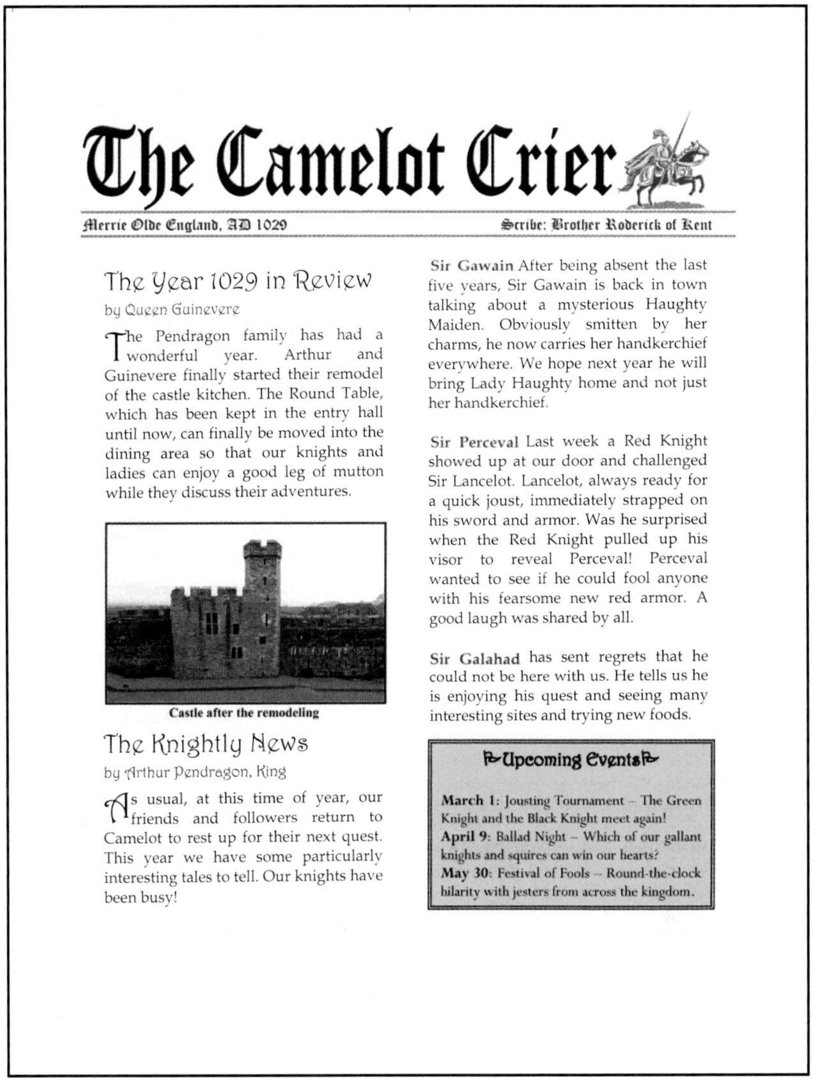

The Camelot Crier

Merrie Olde England, AD 1029 — Scribe: Brother Roderick of Kent

The Year 1029 in Review

by Queen Guinevere

The Pendragon family has had a wonderful year. Arthur and Guinevere finally started their remodel of the castle kitchen. The Round Table, which has been kept in the entry hall until now, can finally be moved into the dining area so that our knights and ladies can enjoy a good leg of mutton while they discuss their adventures.

Castle after the remodeling

The Knightly News

by Arthur Pendragon, King

As usual, at this time of year, our friends and followers return to Camelot to rest up for their next quest. This year we have some particularly interesting tales to tell. Our knights have been busy!

Sir Gawain After being absent the last five years, Sir Gawain is back in town talking about a mysterious Haughty Maiden. Obviously smitten by her charms, he now carries her handkerchief everywhere. We hope next year he will bring Lady Haughty home and not just her handkerchief.

Sir Perceval Last week a Red Knight showed up at our door and challenged Sir Lancelot. Lancelot, always ready for a quick joust, immediately strapped on his sword and armor. Was he surprised when the Red Knight pulled up his visor to reveal Perceval! Perceval wanted to see if he could fool anyone with his fearsome new red armor. A good laugh was shared by all.

Sir Galahad has sent regrets that he could not be here with us. He tells us he is enjoying his quest and seeing many interesting sites and trying new foods.

Upcoming Events

March 1: Jousting Tournament – The Green Knight and the Black Knight meet again!
April 9: Ballad Night – Which of our gallant knights and squires can win our hearts?
May 30: Festival of Fools – Round-the-clock hilarity with jesters from across the kingdom.

REVIEW AND REVISE

Check your work Use Figure 2.34 as a guide and check that:

- ☑ The masthead is sized effectively and contains a graphic.
- ☑ Two sets of double lines separate the masthead from the articles.
- ☑ Text is formatted in two columns that are aligned at top and bottom.
- ☑ Text styles are applied consistently to headings and body text.
- ☑ The photo is cropped effectively and sized properly.
- ☑ The text box uses a different font and has a colored background.

8. On **Page 3**, add the text shown in Figure 10.24 or create your own descriptions of the hotel.

9. Insert pictures that you used in the brochure and booklet, or create new images. Add **border lines** around the images.

10. Use **grid guides** to align the objects on the page. Repeat design elements from the first page and master page.

11. Add a **yellow line** around the **page title** on the **navigation bar**.

▼ **Figure 10.24** Reuse images from other publications to keep costs down.

12. Repeat the steps to create **Page 4**, as shown in Figure 10.25. Make sure you add a **line** around the **page title** on the **navigation** bar. Add a **border** to the picture.

▼ **Figure 10.25** Repeat styles, alignment, and design elements from previous pages.

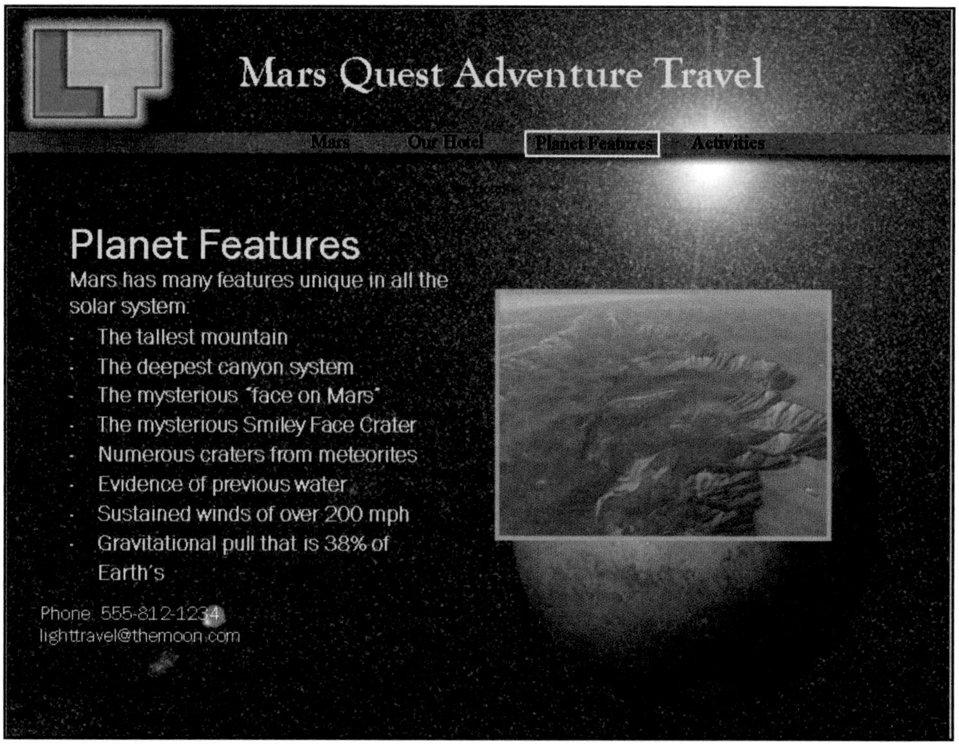

Skills Studio

Create a Bi-fold Brochure

The following two projects will take you through the steps you need to create a bi-fold brochure:

- **Project 2-8** Design a brochure
- **Project 2-9** Design the front panel

Reinforce Your Skills

- **Project 2-8**
  - Create tabs with leaders
  - Format columns
  - Apply Format Painter
  - Format line spacing
- **Project 2-9**
  - Format brochure layout
  - Design a front panel
  - Print on two sides

Design Balanced Brochures

One of the most challenging publications to design is a brochure. Brochures must relay a lot of information in a small amount of space. To do this effectively, brochures must be visually interesting, or the reader will not read the document.

Brochures are typically folded in half (bi-fold) or in thirds (tri-fold), and are printed on the front and back of a page. Folding affects the layout of a document, as you will see in following projects.

Brochures must provide information in a way that is easy to read and understand at a glance. Usually the outside of the brochure will display graphics and titles, with a few important specifics. The inside of the brochure contains most of the text content.

Winter Jazz Concert
Taft Auditorium
Saturday, December 10
7:00 p.m.

Winter Jazz Concert
Taft Auditorium
Saturday, December 10
7:00 p.m.
.....By Richard Rodgers
.....By Artie Shaw
.....By Scott Joplin
.....By Glenn Miller
.....By Stevie Wonder

This is a program, but brochures are also used for marketing products, destinations, or businesses. When done well, they attract readers' attention by balancing text with graphics.

Go Online ACTIVITIES
www.glencoe.com

Challenge Yourself Go to **Chapter 2**, and choose **Enrichment Activities** for more practice with the skills you have learned.

Step-by-Step

1. In Publisher, open the Web pages that you started in Project 10-5. Save the document according to your teacher's instructions.

2. Use the **page sorter** at the bottom of the screen to move between pages.

3. On **Page 1**, your splash page, add the name of your company (Figure 10.22).

4. On **Page 2**, add a text box and add the text shown in Figure 10.23 or create your own descriptions.

Ignore the Master Page

5. To align objects on your Web page, use grid guides. You may have to have to click **View>Ignore Master Page** to see the lines.

6. Insert the table that you created for your booklet in **Project 10-4.** Resize it as necessary.

7. On the navigation bar, create a text box around the page title. Add a thick yellow line to let readers know what page they are on (Figure 10.23).

▼ **Figure 10.22** The splash page is the first page customers see.

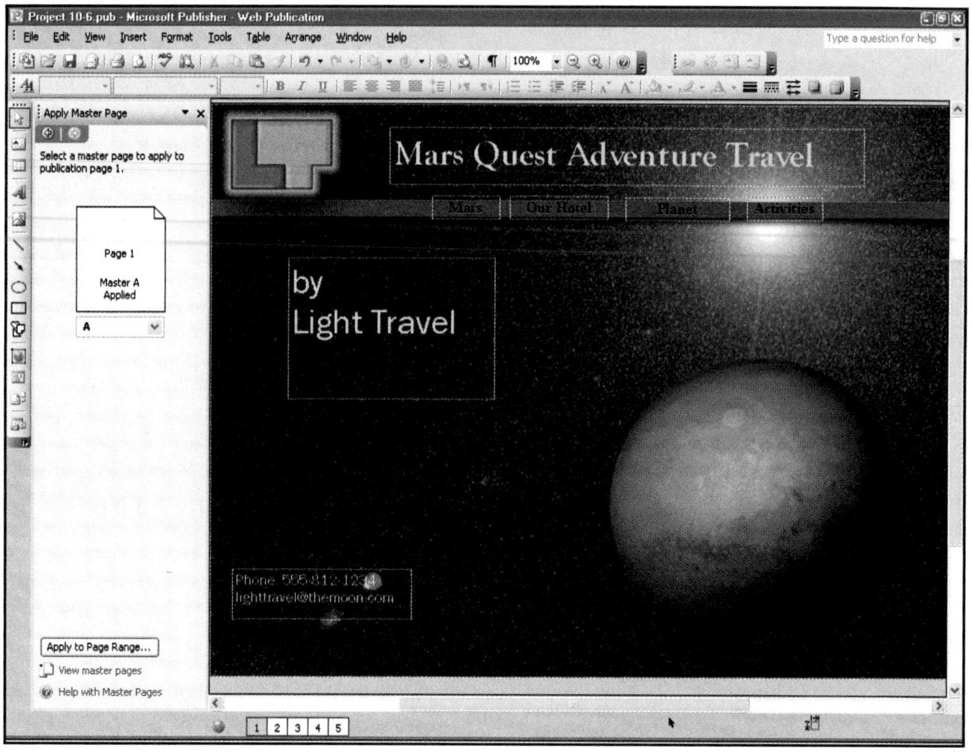

▼ **Figure 10.23** Highlight the page title on the navigation bar so users know what page they are on.

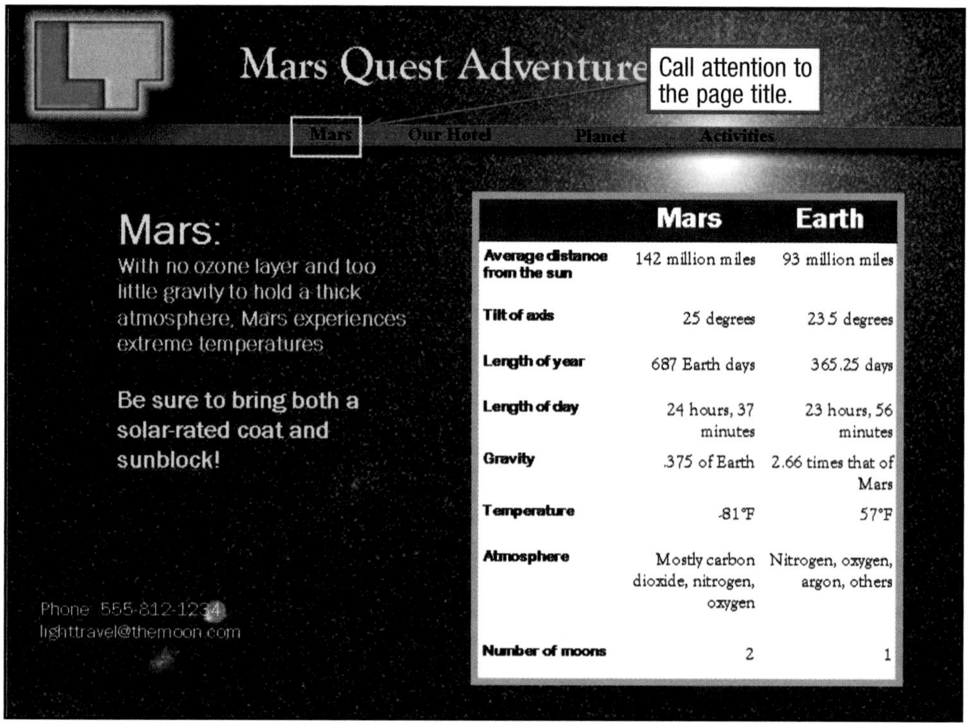

Skills Studio

Project 2-8

Design a Brochure

Skills You Will Apply

- Add tabs with leaders
- Format columns
- Apply Format Painter

Key Terms

- bi-fold
- leading

Academic Focus

Math
Use a ruler for layout

Sidebar

Templates Microsoft Word provides a brochure template to help create tri-fold brochures. A **template** is a document that is already formatted and can be used as a pattern. To find the brochure template or other types of templates, choose **File>New**, choose **Templates On My Computer**. Click the **Publications** tab.

Evaluate Why would a template be useful?

A **bi-fold** brochure is folded in half and therefore has two pages with one fold in the middle, like a book. The first panel is usually like the cover of the book. The inside of the brochure is formatted as two columns, so it reads like two separate pages.

The text in a brochure should be formatted so that it is easy to read and find specific information. Use the design guidelines summarized in the checklist below.

Design Guidelines

- Similar content should be grouped together. Use spacing to separate groups of information.
- Levels of importance are clearly displayed by aligning main headers at the left margin and indenting supporting information so that it stands apart.
- Different types of information are set off by different fonts. For example, headers often have a larger font than supporting information.
- Consistent formatting helps readers immediately identify certain information. For example, in the jazz concert brochure you will create, leaders, or small dots, always set off the names of composers.
- Graphic elements, such as clip art and borders, can be repeated on exterior and interior pages to tie the design together.

Paragraph spacing (also known as **leading**, pronounced "led-ding") lets you adjust the space between paragraphs, items in a bulleted or numbered list, or lines that end with a hard return. You can format paragraph spacing through the Format menu or by right-clicking selected text.

Create Consistency with Format Painter

You can easily copy formatting to new text by using the **Format Painter**. This button is located on the **Standard** toolbar. The **Format Painter** can copy format options such as font styles, color, size, tab stops, and spacing. Copying format is an easy way to maintain consistency within a document.

▶ **In this project,** you will use Word's ruler to format the inside pages of a jazz concert program, applying a two-column layout and uniform tabs with leaders. You will make the brochure more readable by changing the spacing and text formatting.

Project 10-6

Add Hyperlinks

Spotlight on Skills

- Ignore the master page
- Create hyperlinks

Key Term

- splash page

Academic Focus

Science
Organize information about Mars

In Project 10-2, you read about channels of distribution for getting marketing materials from a company to its customers. Web sites are excellent channels of distribution.

Benefits of Web Sites

Although there are costs for creating and maintaining a Web site, there are no printing or mailing costs. Unlike print materials, it is easy to change and update information whenever necessary. Best of all, a Web presence makes it possible for companies to reach a much wider group of customers from across the world. Often, customers will seek out the company rather than the company having to find the customer.

Web sites can also contain a much larger range of information than print materials, yet still make it easy to find specific details. For example, your company, Light Travel, might have pages describing each of its tours. Under each tour, there can be Web pages describing hotels, activities, and costs. Other pages may allow customers to immediately book a tour or contact a travel agent. These services are a great way to attract customers and lower business costs.

The Internet provides other marketing options to companies besides creating their own Web sites. Discount sites like Expedia® and Travelocity® will list travel-related businesses that offer tours, hotels, and transportation. Search engines such as Yahoo®, Google®, and MSN® can also be an effective way to lead customers to your site.

▶ Web sites like Travelocity, Expedia, and many more are good distribution channels for companies in the travel industry.

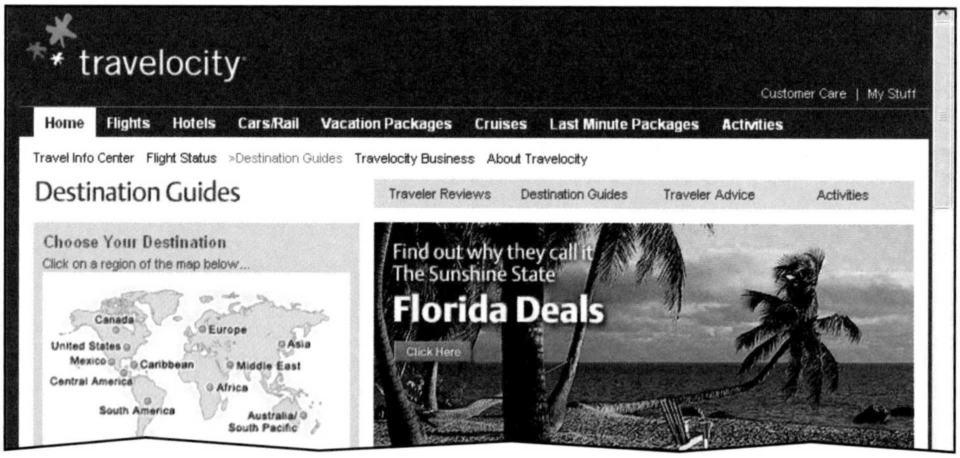

▶ **In this project,** you will create pages for your Mars Quest Web site, including a **splash page**, the page where users enter the site. A splash page sets up the overall mood and tone of the site. You will also add hyperlinks so that users can easily navigate from page to page.

Student Data File

Step-by-Step

1. Open **Data File 2-8**, and save it according to your teacher's instructions.

2. Change to **Landscape** orientation.

3. Select all of the text by clicking CTRL + A.
Mac users click ⌘ + A.

Add Tabs with Leaders

4. Click **Format>Tabs**. In the **Tabs** box, key 2.75 in the **Tab stop position.**

5. Under **Leader**, click the small dots leaders (**Option #2**), then click **Set** and **OK** (Figure 2.35).

6. At the first song, place the insertion point in front of the **By**. Then press TAB to align the text at **2.75** inches.

7. Repeat Step 6 until all songs are formatted the same.

8. Select all of the text in the document. Set a new **Tab stop position** at **0.72**.

9. Click in front of ***Soloists***. Press TAB. Repeat to indent all soloists' groups (Figure 2.36).

▼ **Figure 2.35** Default tabs are 0.5 inches.

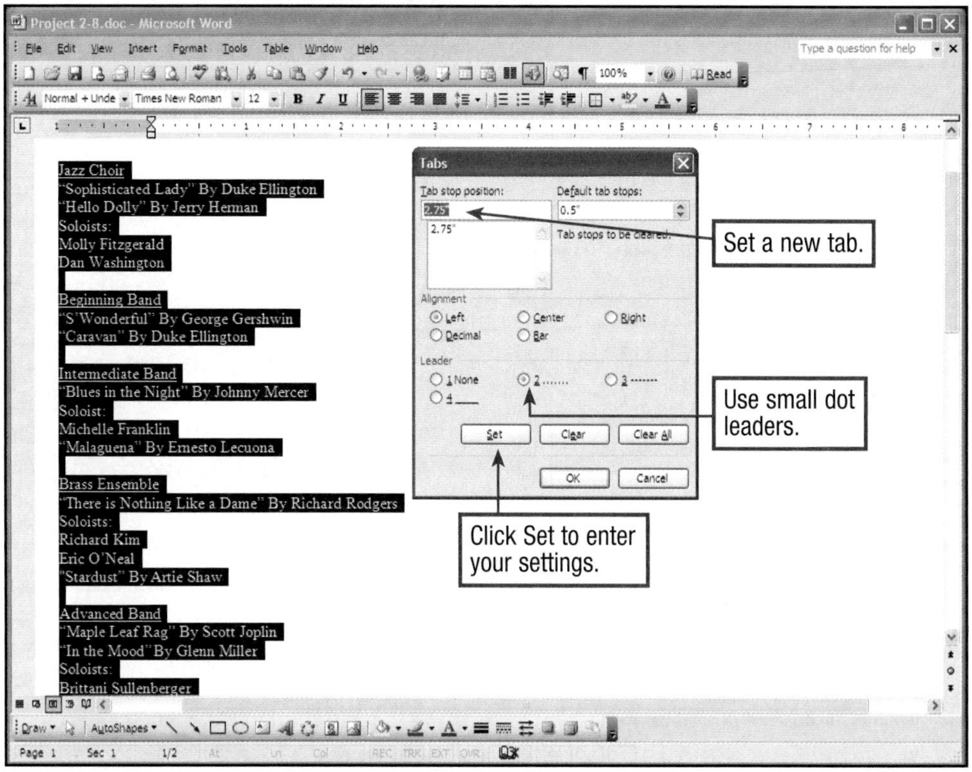

▼ **Figure 2.36** Use indents to group related information.

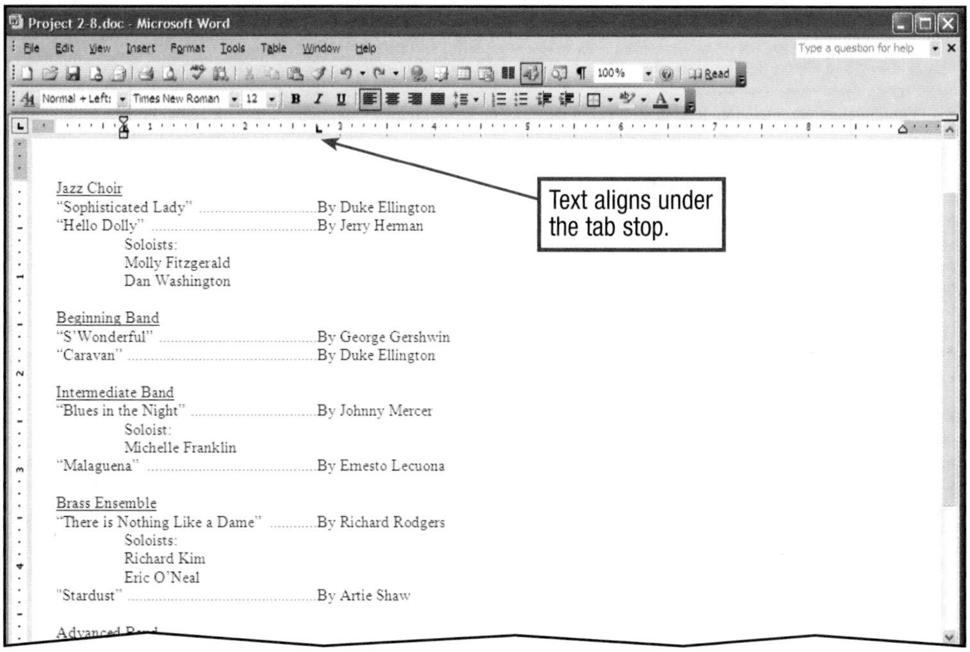

8 Click **View>Master Page** to open the **Edit Master Page** task pane.

9 Insert the Photoshop image into the Publisher Master page.

10 Select the picture. Click **Format>Picture**. Change the size to **600 pixels high** by **800 pixels wide**. Reposition the picture as needed.

11 Add a title for your Web site next to the logo (Figure 10.20).

12 On the **navigation bar**, add **four** text boxes. In each text box, add a title for the other four pages in the Web site.

13 Create another text box near the bottom of the screen. Key in the company's contact information (Figure 10.20).

Add Pages to a Publication

14 Press CTRL + M to return to the publication page (Figure 10.21).

15 Click **Insert>Page>Blank** to create a new page. Repeat until you have **five** pages total.

16 Follow your teacher's instructions for saving your Web pages. You will continue your Web site in Project 10-6.

▼ Figure 10.20 Use a master page to have a consistent design on every page.

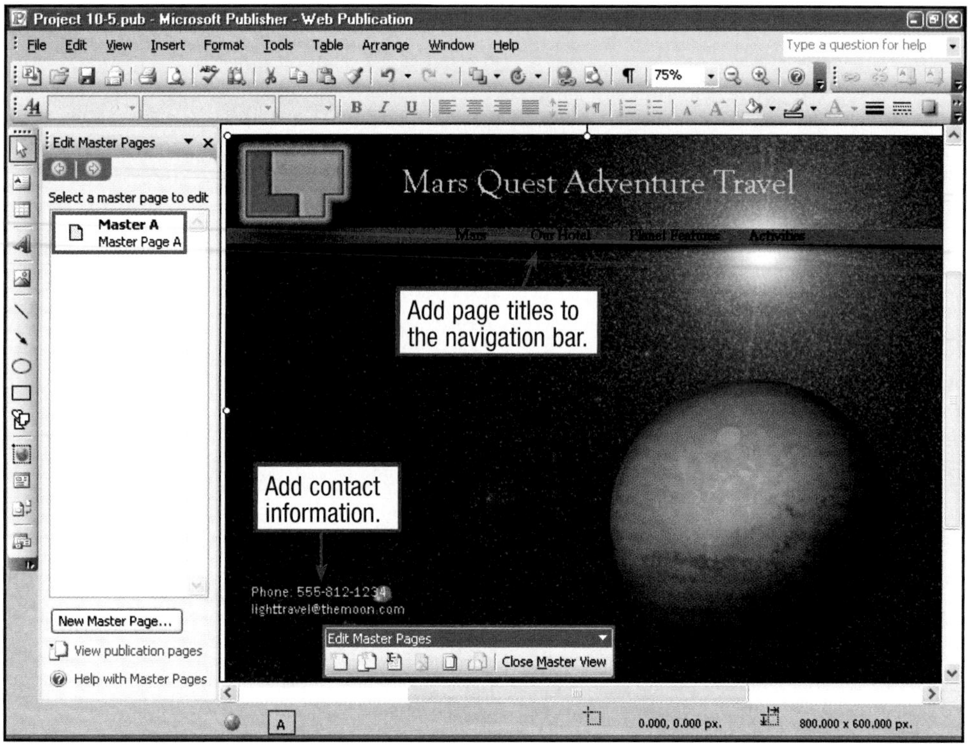

▼ Figure 10.21 Return to publication pages in order to add new pages.

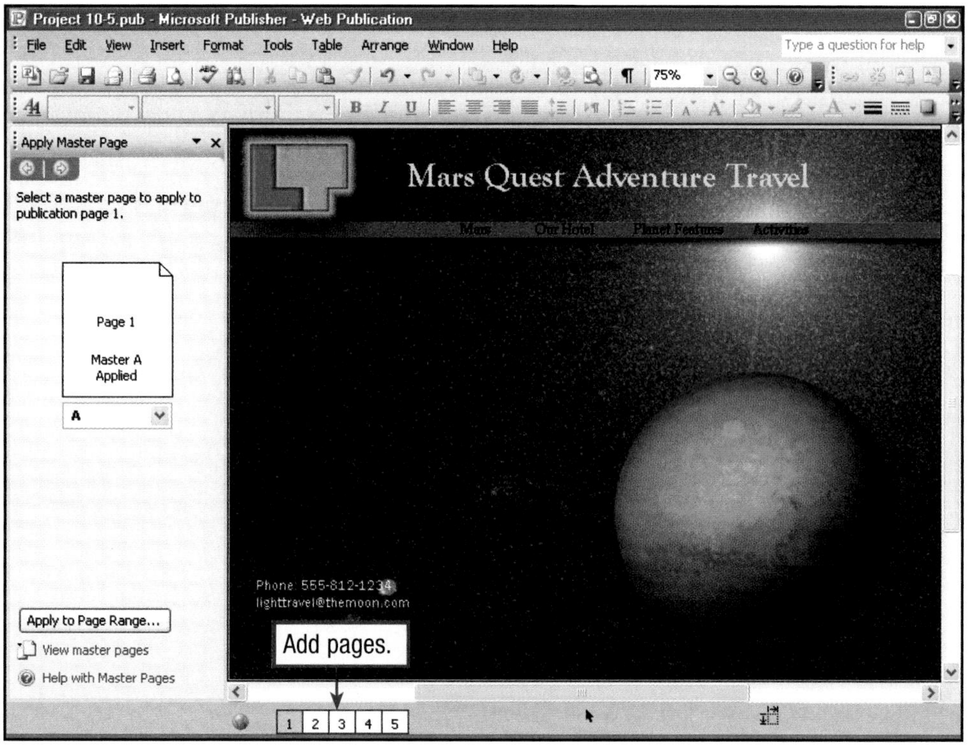

Format Columns

10 Select all of the text in the document. On the **Formatting** toolbar, click **Columns**, and choose **2 Columns**.

11 In your brochure, select the first group name *Jazz Choir*, and format with **Harrington, 24 pt, bold**. Click **Underline** to remove the underline.

12 With the section head still selected, change the **Spacing Before** to **28** (Figure 2.37).

13 With the section head still selected, click in the **Styles** window on the **Formatting** toolbar. Key Section Head. Press ENTER.

Apply Format Painter

14 With the section head still selected, double-click **Format Painter**. The mouse pointer should change to a paintbrush (Figure 2.38).

15 Select each jazz group name with the paintbrush to format the text like *Jazz Choir*. Press ESC to turn off the Format Painter.

16 Select the first song name and the composer. Format the text with a sans serif font, such as **Franklin Gothic Book**, **12 pt**.

Figure 2.37 Use spacing so your text does not look too crowded or far apart.

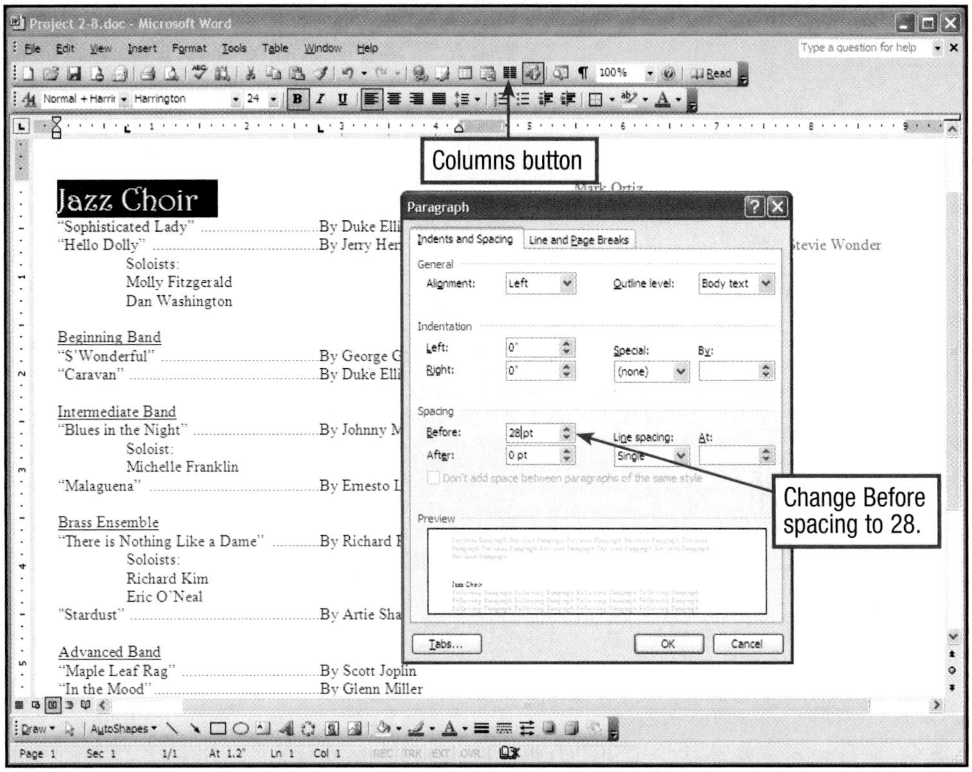

Figure 2.38 Format Painter copies formatting options from one item to another.

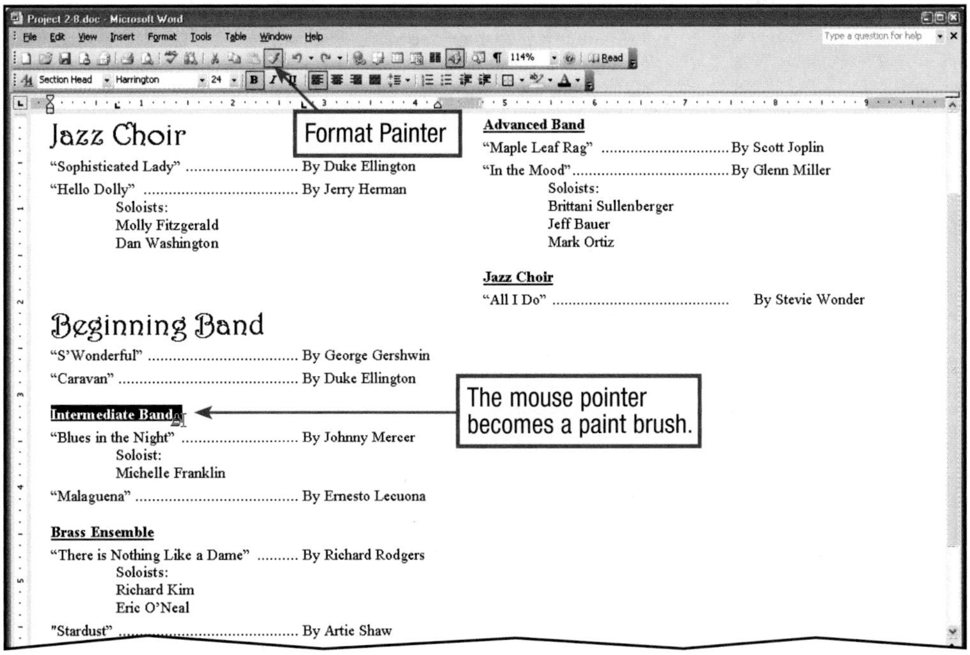

Student Data File

Step-by-Step

Create an Image in Photoshop

1. In Photoshop, follow Steps 2–5 to create an image similar to the one shown in Figure 10.18. Or you can open **Data File 10-5a** in Photoshop, and skip to Step 6.

2. Create a background layer with a star, then add another layer and insert a photograph of Mars (**Data File 10-5b**). Add light and shadow effects.

3. Add a layer with the logo you created in Project 9-4. Add a glow and drop shadow.

4. Create a new layer. Insert a narrow rectangle, below the logo, that extends the width of the page. This is the navigation bar (Figure 10.18).

5. Add a fill and drop shadow to the navigation bar. Save the image.

Format a Web Page in Publisher

6. In Microsoft Publisher, open a new document. In the **New Publication** task pane, click **Blank Web Page**.

7. Click **File>Page Setup**. Under the **Layout** tab, choose **Custom** and key 800 for **width** and 600 for **height** (Figure 10.19).

▼ **Figure 10.18** Use drop shadows and glow effects to make objects stand out.

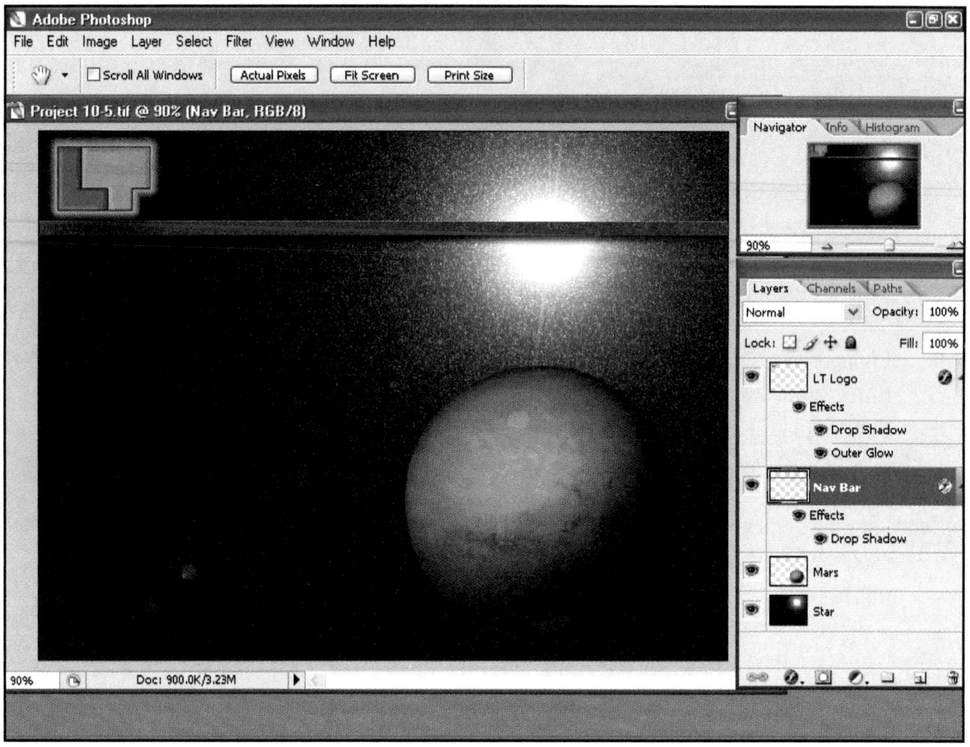

▼ **Figure 10.19** Choose a page size that will display correctly on most monitors.

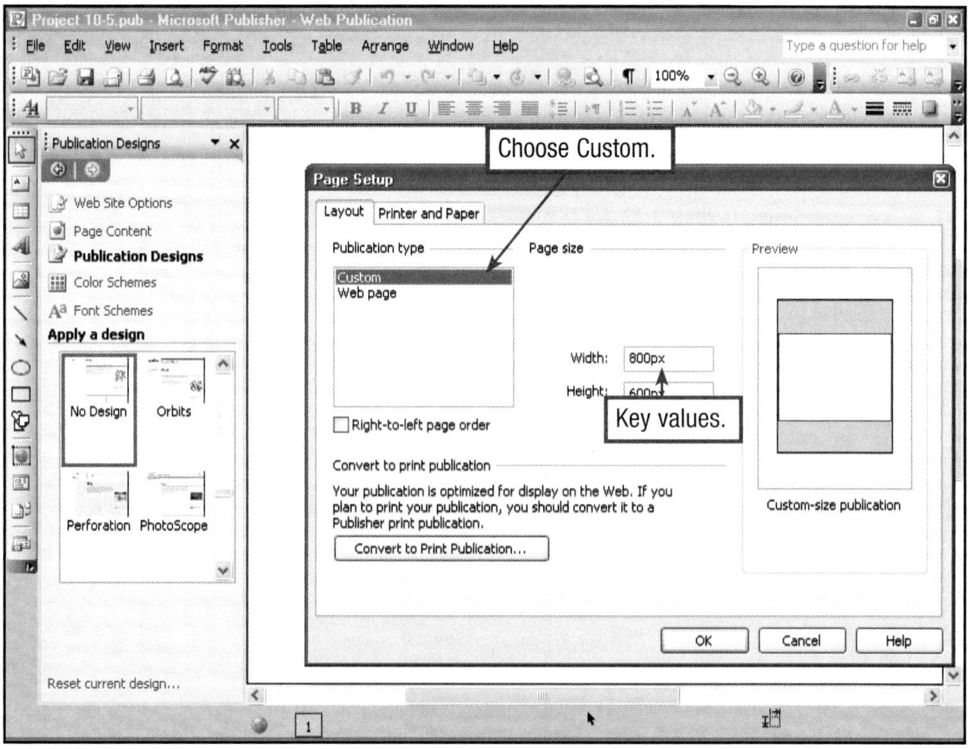

17 With the text still selected, click **Format>Paragraph**, and then change the **Spacing Before** to **4**.

18 Use this example to define a style, and name it *Song.* Use the **Format Painter** to apply the new formatting to each song and its composer.

19 Select each group of soloists, and format the text with **Harrington 12 pt**.

20 If your brochure does not have equal columns, place your insertion point in front of the text *Brass Ensemble.* Click **Insert>Break>Column Break**.

21 Adjust column alignment and spacing, if necessary. Your document should look similar to Figure 2.40.

22 Follow your teacher's instructions for saving your work. You will use this file in Project 2-9.

▼ **Figure 2.39** You can use the Format Painter to define a style.

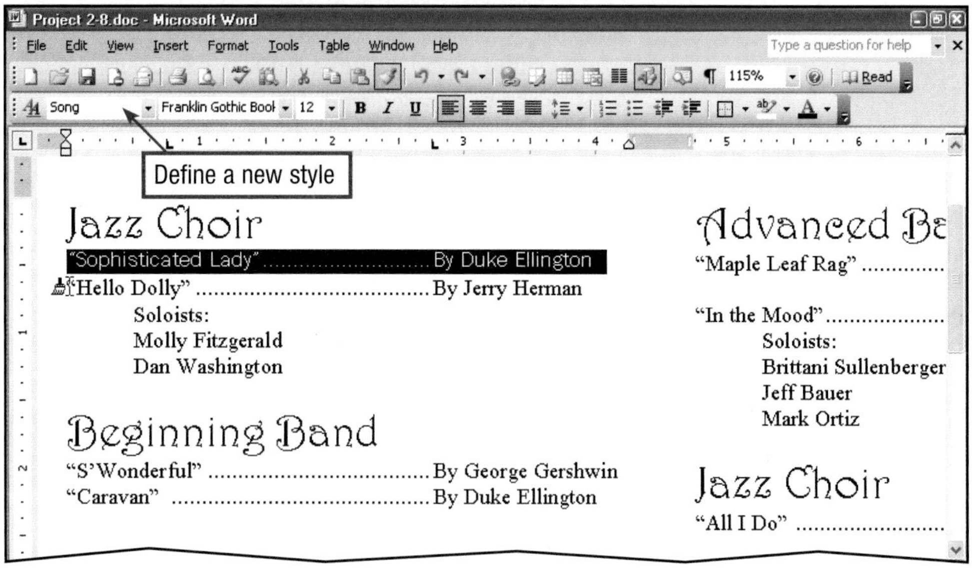

▼ **Figure 2.40** Formatting is consistent for each type of information, and the spacing makes the page look less crowded.

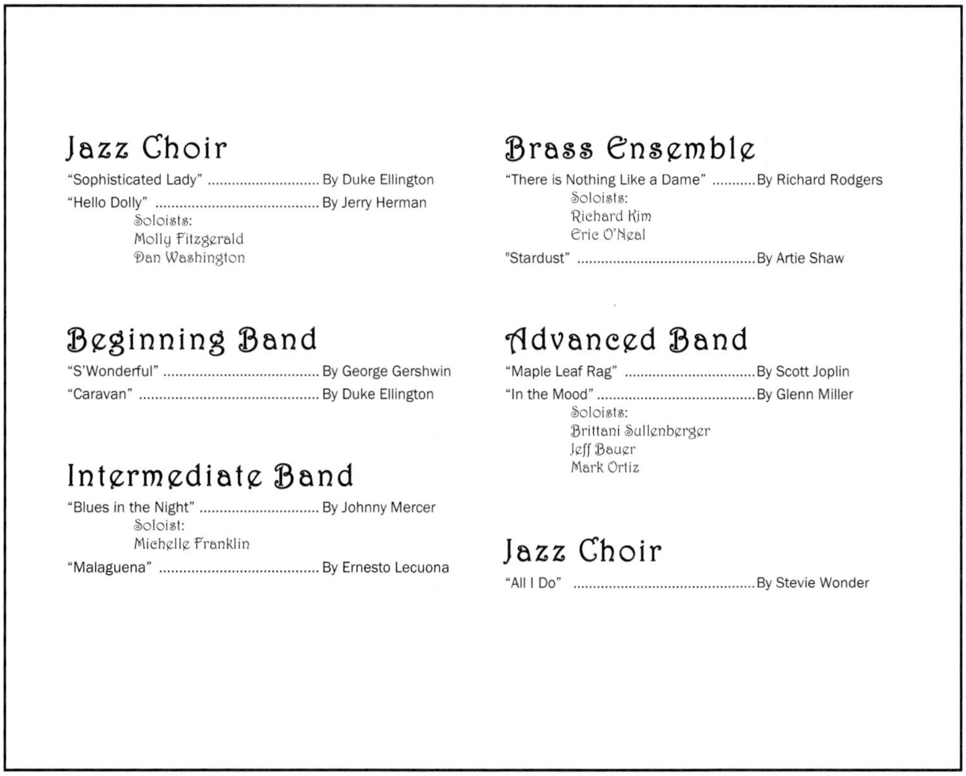

Jazz Choir

"Sophisticated Lady" .... By Duke Ellington
"Hello Dolly" .... By Jerry Herman
Soloists:
Molly Fitzgerald
Dan Washington

Beginning Band

"S'Wonderful" .... By George Gershwin
"Caravan" .... By Duke Ellington

Intermediate Band

"Blues in the Night" .... By Johnny Mercer
Soloist:
Michelle Franklin
"Malaguena" .... By Ernesto Lecuona

Brass Ensemble

"There is Nothing Like a Dame" .... By Richard Rodgers
Soloists:
Richard Kim
Eric O'Neal
"Stardust" .... By Artie Shaw

Advanced Band

"Maple Leaf Rag" .... By Scott Joplin
"In the Mood" .... By Glenn Miller
Soloists:
Brittani Sullenberger
Jeff Bauer
Mark Ortiz

Jazz Choir

"All I Do" .... By Stevie Wonder

Project 10-5

Design Web Pages

Spotlight on Skills

- Create an image in Photoshop
- Format a Web page in Publisher
- Add pages to a publication

Key Terms

- Web site
- promotion
- Web page

Academic Focus

Science
Create a Mars Web site

A **Web site** is a group of interlinked files about a single topic on the Internet. Web sites have become a standard element of modern business communication. Businesses use Web sites to highlight special services, display an online catalog, post employee news, or advertise a **promotion**, which is a special offer used to persuade people to buy products. In comparison to traditional advertisements, Web sites are an extremely affordable way to get a message out.

Software programs such as Adobe Dreamweaver® and Microsoft® FrontPage® are typically used to create Web sites, but you can use Publisher as well, even though it has limited tools. Regardless of the software you use, creating an effective Web site comes down to good design principles. The PARC principles still apply: group related items, align everything, create repetitive elements from page to page, and be sure that contrast is obvious.

Web Design Versus Print Design

Although similar, there are a few key differences between print page design and Web design. A **Web page** is one file within a Web site. There must be consistency between pages in a Web site, though there is no need to worry about continuing text between pages. A Web page can generally hold as much text as you want, though readers may have to scroll to read long pages. Keep in mind, however, that it is harder to read text on a monitor. When possible, keep text short on a Web page and use clear fonts and white space.

The most important difference between Web and print pages is that Web pages are viewed on a variety of computers, at a variety of screen resolutions, over which you have little or no control. Therefore, whether using text, graphics, multimedia, or hyperlinks, you must choose your design elements to be effective no matter how they are displayed.

Create Effective Web Pages

Method	Reason
Use a common page size like 800 × 600.	A Web page created at too high a resolution may not display properly on all monitors, especially older monitors that do not have those settings.
Use common colors.	A base set of 216 colors is the same for all Web browsers. The computer will dither (substitute) other colors outside this range.
Use simple fonts.	Fonts not installed on the user's computer will look different from your design.

▶ **In this project,** your team will begin to design Web pages for your Mars Quest business. Your team will create a master page with an image and design elements that will be applied to all the pages on the Web site. You will finish your Web pages in Project 10-6.

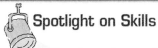

Project 2-9 Lay Out a Front Panel

Skills You Will Apply

- Design a front panel
- Add a texture background

Key Term

- duplex printing

Academic Focus

Math
Use a ruler for layout

In the figure below, you can see that when the outside of a brochure is folded in half like a book, the right panel becomes the first page of the brochure. The left panel is the last page of the brochure.

You must keep this layout in mind when you create the content for the exterior of the brochure. As you look at the figure, notice that the right outside panel is the front of the brochure. The front of the brochure is used to attract the reader's attention. Important information such as the name of the event, location, and time appears here. An attention-grabbing graphic is usually included. Borders are often added for visual appeal. The attractiveness of the front panel often determines whether or not readers open the brochure.

In this project, you create the front page by inserting a text box in the right panel. You could also format the page as two columns to create the two sides of a bi-fold document.

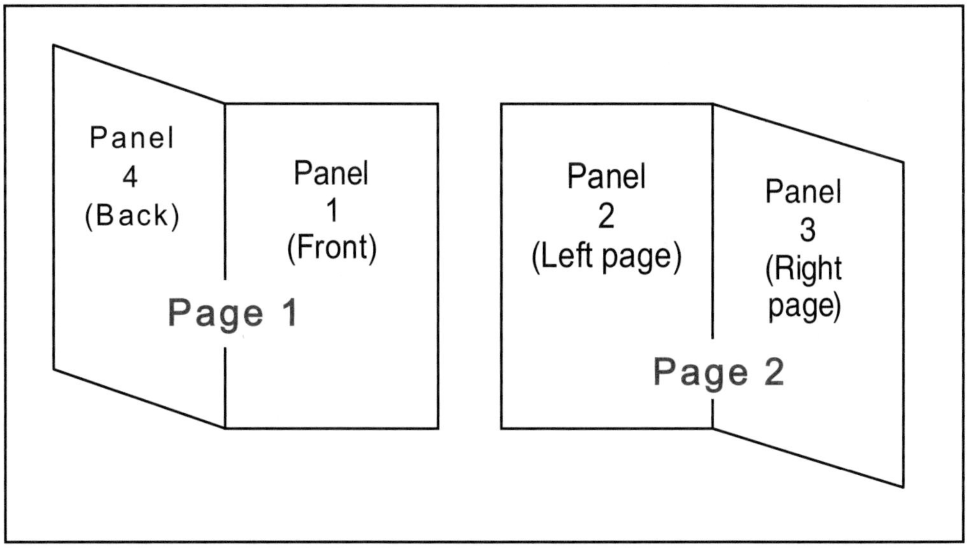

Brochures are printed on two sides. To do this, you can use a printer that has **duplex printing**, which prints on both sides of the paper before printing the next copy. If a duplex printer is unavailable, print on one side, then flip the paper over to print on the other side. Make sure, though, that the paper is inserted into the printer so that the back prints in the same direction as the front of the brochure.

▶ **In this project,** you will complete the brochure that you started in Project 2-8 by laying out the front panel for your brochure. You will also add graphic elements to the exterior and interior of the brochure that unify the design.

21. On **Pages 6–7**, describe the planet's sites and activities. You can use the text from **Data File 10-4a**.

22. Add a map that spans both pages (**Data File 10-4i**) and add callouts that show where each site is located (Figure 10.17).

23. Apply the master page and style sheets to Pages 6 and 7.

24. On **Page 8**, the back cover, insert the same image you used on the front cover, but modify it so that it is not identical (Figure 10.17).

25. Add the company logo and contact information, and repeat previous format styles.

Cite Sources

26. Add a text box, and properly cite all of your research and picture sources.

27. Review your document to check for errors in spelling and grammar. Also, check that it follows PARC principles.

28. Follow your teacher's instructions for saving, printing, and assembling your booklet.

▼ **Figure 10.17** **Add callouts to the map and repeat the cover design on the back.**

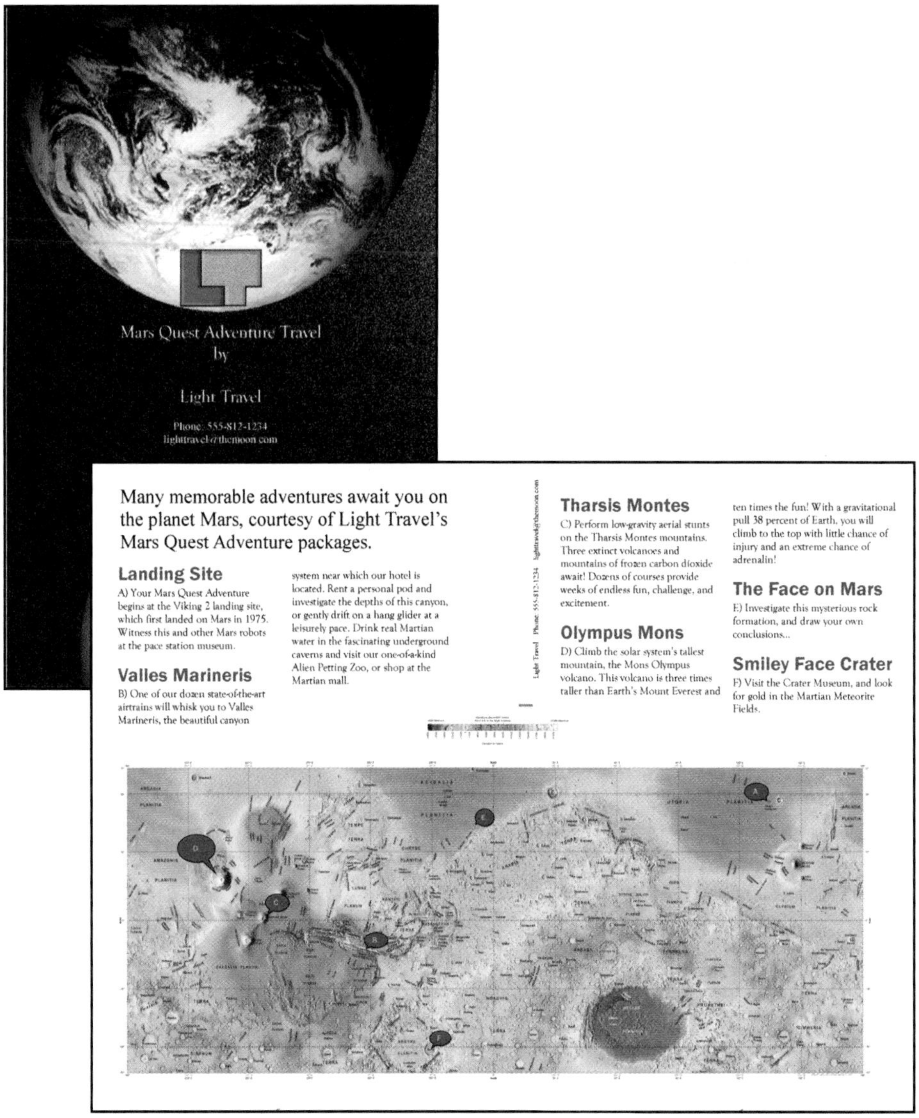

REVIEW AND REVISE

Check your work Use Figures 10.14–10.17 as guides and check that:

- ☑ The pages in the booklet are in the correct order when it is assembled.
- ☑ Design elements have been applied consistently using style sheets and a master page.
- ☑ Images illustrate the content and are sized and placed effectively.
- ☑ Text is accurate and grammatical, and sources are cited correctly.

Student Data File

Step-by-Step

1. Place your insertion point at the beginning of the jazz program.

2. On the **menu** bar, choose **Insert>Break>Page Break**. This creates a new page before the jazz program schedule.

Design a Front Panel

3. Create a text box that is **6.75" high** and **4.0" wide**. Use the ruler as a guide to center the box in the right column (Figure 2.41).

4. Key and center the following text on the new page:
   Winter Jazz Concert ENTER
   Taft Auditorium ENTER
   Saturday, December 10 ENTER
   7:00 p.m.

5. Select the first line. Then format it with a **dark red** decorative font such as **Harrington 48 pt.**

6. Format the remaining lines with a **dark green** font such as **Lucida Calligraphy**. Use **24 pt** for *Taft Auditorium* and **16 pt** for the date and time (Figure 2.42).

Figure 2.41 The ruler shows the two sides of the page. The right side is the front panel of the brochure.

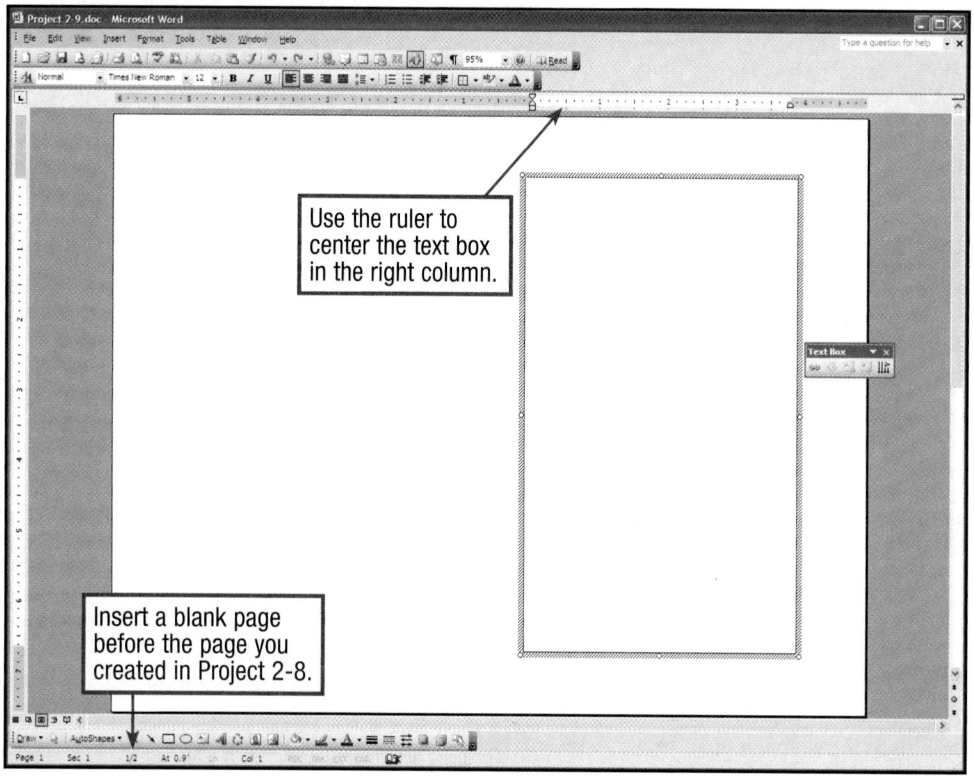
Project 2-9.doc - Microsoft Word
Use the ruler to center the text box in the right column.
Insert a blank page before the page you created in Project 2-8.

Figure 2.42 Use a combination of the same fonts for the front of the program.

Project 2-9.doc - Microsoft Word
Winter Jazz Concert
Taft Auditorium
Saturday, December 10
7:00 p.m.

14 On **Page 4**, describe the hotel accommodations, or insert that text from **Data File 10-4a** (Figure 10.16).

Import Style Sheets

15 **Import style sheets** from the brochure you created in **Projects 10-2** and **10-3.** Apply the styles or create new styles (Figure 10.15).

16 Find photos of hotels or hotel rooms and use Photoshop to make them appear to be on Mars. If you prefer, you can use **Data Files 10-4d** to **10-4f.**

17 Add text boxes to insert captions for each picture and to display the hotel prices. Apply the master page.

18 On **Page 5**, describe the transportation for traveling to Mars and on the planet's surface. You can use the content from **Data File 10-4a**.

19 Add repetitive design elements by applying style sheets to the text and the master page.

20 Create or find images of vehicles, or insert **Data Files 10-4g** and **10-4h**. Add captions (Figure 10.16).

▼ **Figure 10.15** Import style sheets to create a specific look in all your documents.

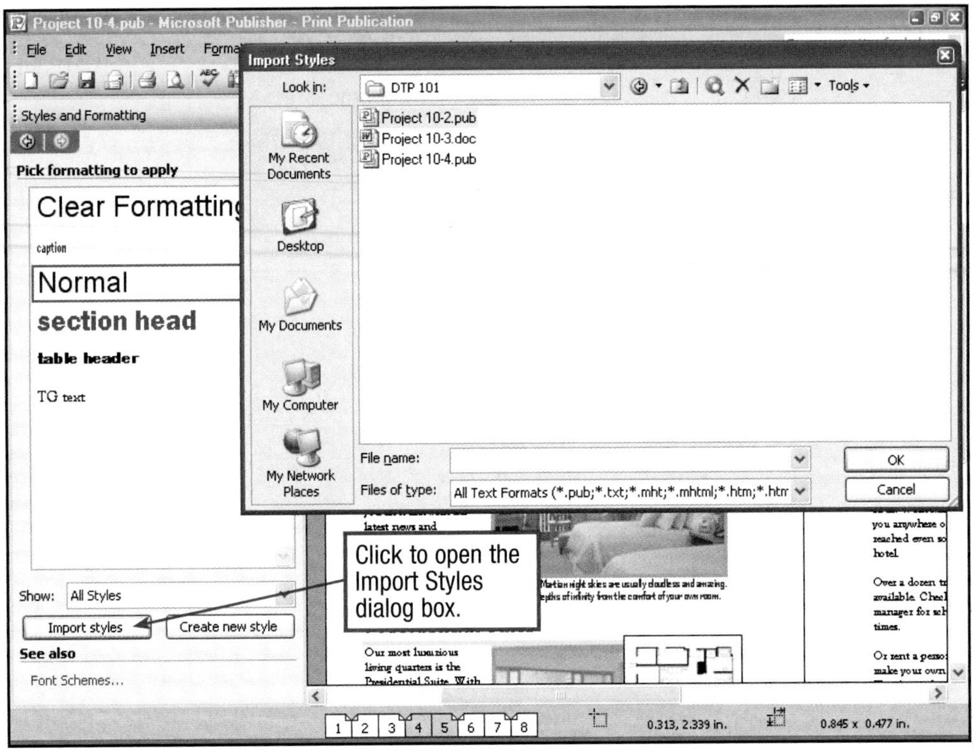

▼ **Figure 10.16** Pictures should be sized and aligned properly.

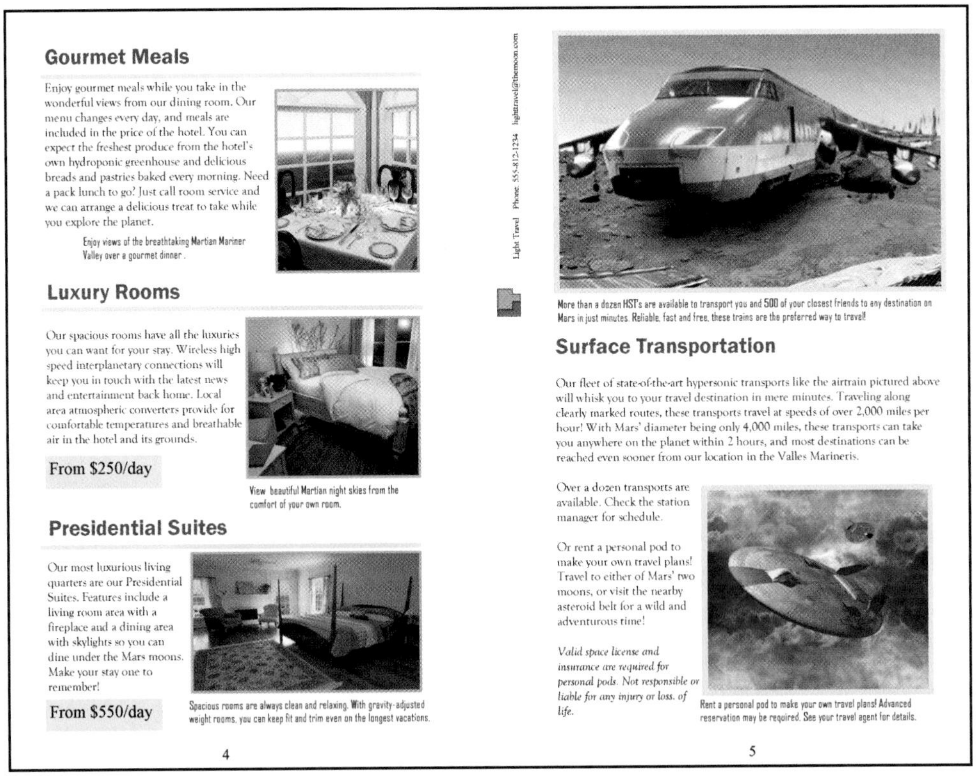

7 Select the title text, and then click **Format>Font**. Change the **Style** to **Emboss**.

Add a Texture Background

8 Add a fill to the text box. Click **Format>Text Box> Colors and Lines** tab. In the **Fill Color** menu, choose **Fill Effects>Texture>Parchment**.

9 Add a **plum colored** border line to the text box, with a similar style to the one shown in Figure 2.43.

10 Insert a space before ***Taft Auditorium***. Insert the clip art from **Data File 2-9**.

11 Adjust the space between text and images so your page looks similar to Figure 2.43.

12 Return to the interior of your brochure. Insert a smaller copy of the clip art on the front panel.

13 Add a border that matches the one on the exterior. (**Hint:** Draw a rectangle around the text and use the **Order** command to **Send it to the Back**.)

14 Your brochure should look similar to Figure 2.43. Follow your teacher's instructions for saving and printing your work. If possible, use duplex printing.

▼ **Figure 2.43** Design elements should repeat on the interior and exterior.

Jazz Choir
"Sophisticated Lady" .... By Duke Ellington
"Hello Dolly" .... By Jerry Herman
Soloists:
Molly Fitzgerald
Dan Washington
Beginning Band
"S'Wonderful" .... By George Gershwin
"Caravan" .... By Duke Ellington
Intermediate Band
"Blues in the Night" .... By Johnny Mercer
Soloist:
Michelle Franklin
"Malaguena" .... By Ernesto Lecuona
Brass Ensemble
"There is Nothing Like a Dame" .... By Richard Rodgers
Soloists:
Richard Kim
Eric O'Neal
"Stardust" .... By Artie Shaw
Advanced Band
"Maple Leaf Rag" .... By Scott Joplin
"In the Mood" .... By Glenn Miller
Soloists:
Brittani Sullenberger
Jeff Bauer
Mark Ortiz
Jazz Choir
"All I Do" .... By Stevie Wonder
Winter Jazz Concert
Taft Auditorium
Saturday, December 10
7:00 p.m.

REVIEW AND REVISE

Check your work Use Figure 2.43 a guide and check that:

- ☑ Fonts have consistent sizing, typeface, and style.
- ☑ Text is correct and positioned correctly on each panel.
- ☑ Graphics and borders are repeated and used effectively.
- ☑ Elements are not too crowded or distant.

Create a Cover Image

7 On **Page 1**, the cover, create an image in Photoshop or Illustrator. It can be a separate picture or a background, as shown in Figure 10.13. You can use the image in **Data File 10-4b**.

8 Add your logo to the front cover, as well as text about Mars Quest and your company's contact information.

9 On **Page 2**, repeat the same image you created for the cover, or add new images.

10 Design a table comparing the characteristics of Earth and Mars. Use the chart in **Data File 10-4a**, or find your own data (Figure 10.14).

11 Apply the design elements from the master page, and add any new elements that repeat the design.

Add a Table of Contents

12 On **Page 3**, create a Table of Contents. Use the text you added to determine the items and page numbers you will list (Figure 10.14).

13 Add an image to the page. You can create one yourself, find one to insert, or use **Data File 10-4c**. Apply the master page.

▼ **Figure 10.13** Add design elements that connect the cover to the interior pages.

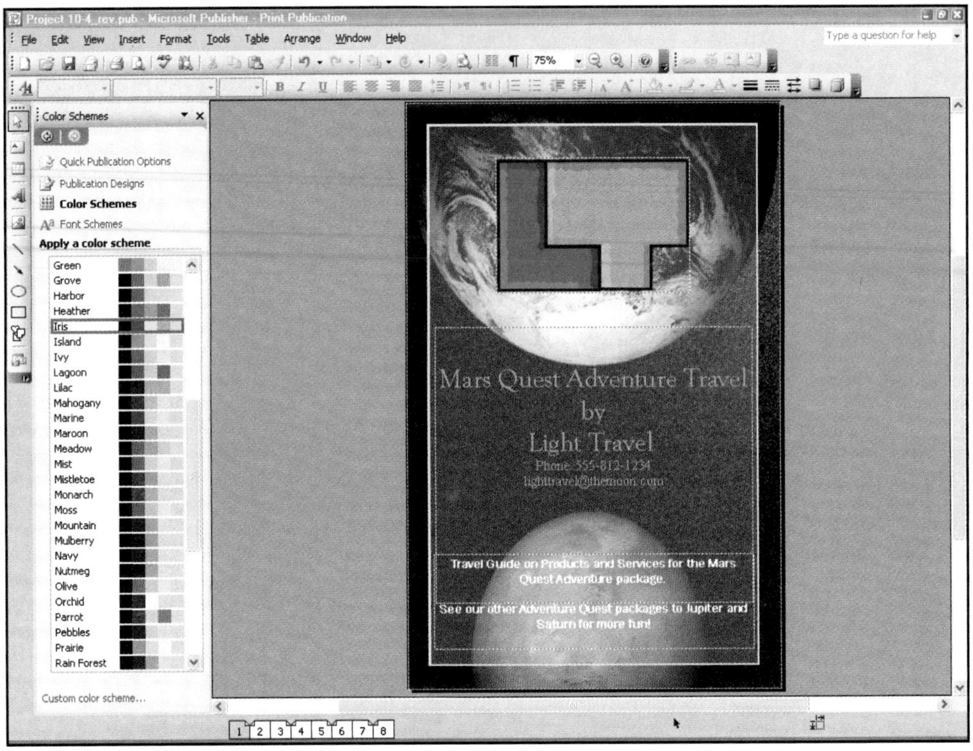

▼ **Figure 10.14** Make sure the page numbers are aligned in the Table of Contents.

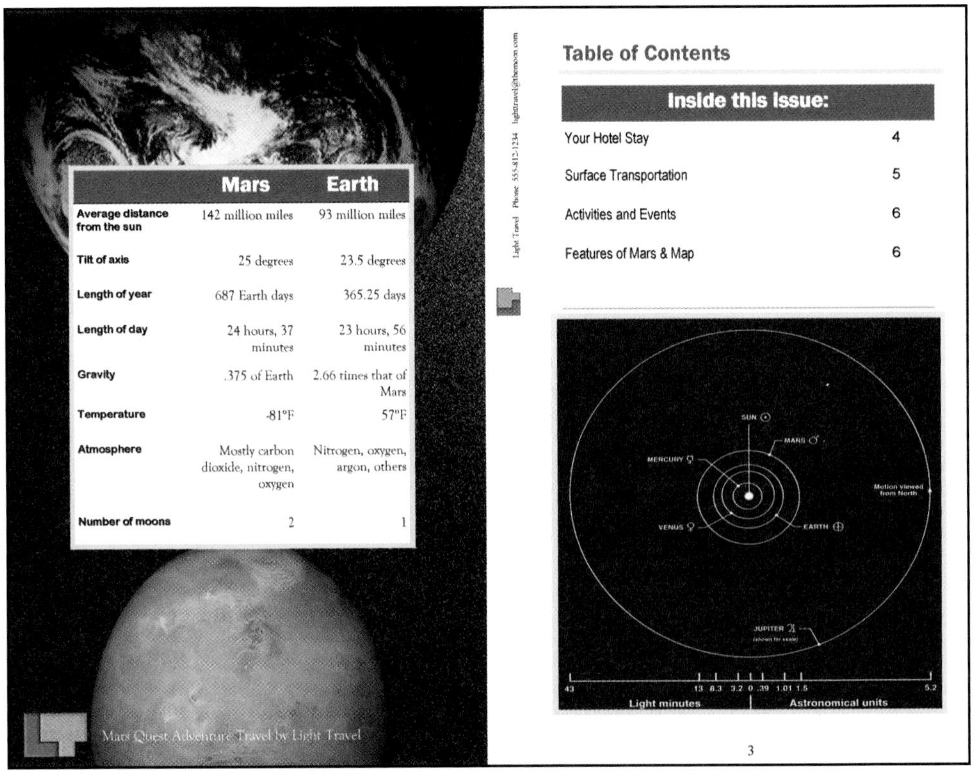

In The Workplace

Writers and Editors

Writers and editors communicate with the written word. Writers and authors may develop fiction or non-fiction material for books, magazines, Web sites, radio, television, films, advertisements, technical journals, and other outlets. Some editors plan content, review proposals, and supervise writers, while other editors do original writing or review, correct, and rewrite the work of others.

On the Job

Writers and editors usually work on a computer and use desktop publishing tools every day. They should be knowledgeable about graphic design, page layout, and multimedia technology. Writers and editors should be able to blend text, graphics, and sound together. Microsoft Word and other word processing programs are commonly used for writing and tracking changes in a manuscript. Some writers may create their own desktop-published materials using Microsoft Publisher or Adobe InDesign. Many writers publish their work directly on the Internet and are familiar with Web tools such as Dreamweaver.

Nonfiction writers have strong research skills and may work for newspapers, magazines, or write books. Creative writers may write fiction, poetry plays, or scripts. Technical writers communicate complex information using clear, understandable, and accurate language, and produce manuals, instructions, proposals, and other materials. Copy writers create advertising material for print and broadcast media.

Magazines, newspapers, and book publishers employ editors to oversee all aspects of a publication. Copy editors check content, accuracy, grammar, and style.

Future Outlook

Employment for writers and editors is extremely competitive, because many people are attracted to this occupation. There is strong demand for technical and specialized writers and those with Web expertise. For more inf ormation about these careers, consult the following Web sites:

- **Society for Technical Communication (stc.org)**
- **American Copy Editors Society (copydesk.org)**

Training

A college degree is usually essential for a position as a writer or editor, especially degrees in English, communications, and journalism. Technical writing generally requires a degree in a specialized field.

Salary Range

The annual salary for writers and authors ranges from $23,000 to $91,000, depending upon experience, responsibility, location, and talent.

Skills and Talents

Writers and editors need to have:

Good writing skills.

Knowledge of word processing and desktop publishing software programs.

Excellent communication skills.

The ability to work independently and meet deadlines.

Good researching skills.

Career Activity

Why is it important for writers and editors to have desktop publishing skills?

Student Data File

Step-by-Step

1. In Microsoft Publisher, open a new blank document. Save it according to your teacher's instructions.

Lay Out a Booklet

2. Click **File>Page Setup**, and choose **Booklet** as the Publication Type. The page should be in **landscape**, and the size should be **5.5 inches wide** and **8.5 inches tall**.

3. Click **Insert>Pages**, and add **7 more pages** for a total of 8. Click **View>Two-Page Spread**.

4. Add **grid guides** to help with layout and alignment. Use the figures in this project to help you determine the layout guides you will need.

Apply a Master Page

5. Click **View>Master Page**. Create a master page that includes design elements that will repeat through the booklet. Include page numbers, the logo, and contact information (Figure 10.12).

6. In your publication, you can use the text from **Data File 10-4a**, or research and write your own text. Refer to the figures and steps in this project for suggestions.

▼ **Figure 10.11** Create the layout before you add the content.

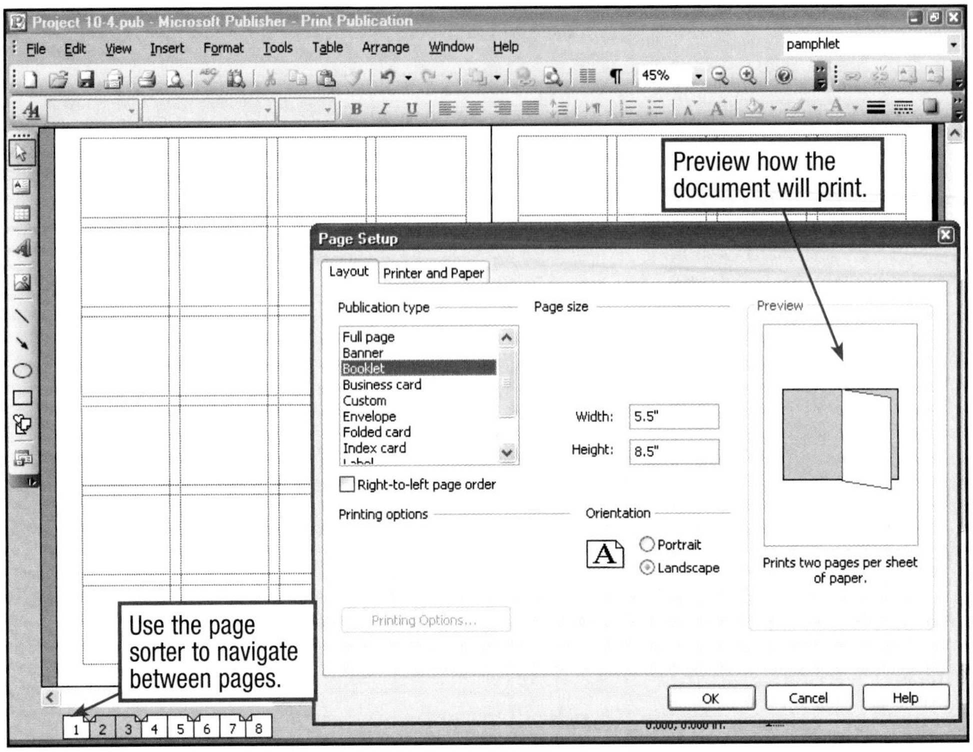

▼ **Figure 10.12** The master page makes it easy to repeat design elements.

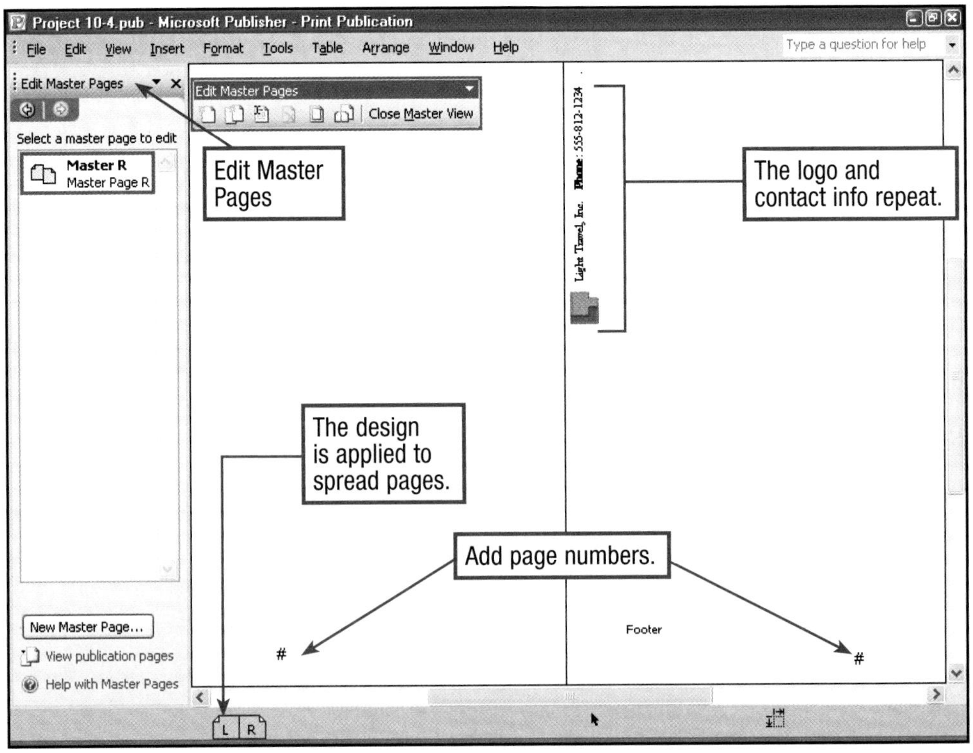

Chapter 2 Assessment

Reading Check

1. **Define** What are vector images and raster images?
2. **Identify** Which keyboard button would you press to make a perfect circle with the Oval drawing tool?
3. **Identify** Which panel would be the front cover of a bi-fold brochure?
4. **Explain** How can you make several drawing objects behave as a single object?
5. **Contrast** What is the difference between resizing and cropping a picture?

Critical Thinking

6. **Evaluate** What happens to clip art when you use the Edit Picture command?
7. **Explain** In Word, how do you rotate text to any angle and even turn text upside down?
8. **Describe** What steps would you take to create a picture of a doughnut using the Drawing toolbar?
9. **Evaluate** Describe a brand logo that you think is effective and explain why.
10. **Analyze** What are the advantages of using a vector image rather than a raster image?

1 Independent Practice

TEAM PROJECT **Create a Logo** With a partner, design a logo for a small business that you can start. Decide what product or service the business offers and what to name your business.

a. Plan Brainstorm what text and images will convey the message you want to get across to customers.

b. Design By hand, sketch a logo that:
- Uses text for the name of your business.
- Includes a graphic, either as part of the text or as a separate image next to the text.

c. Create Use the Microsoft drawing tools to create your logo.
- Use WordArt for the text.
- Use at least two colors.
- Insert AutoShapes or clip art for the image.
- Group the separate objects to create one object.

d. Present Follow your teacher's instructions to determine which of the following methods you should use to evaluate your logo's effectiveness:
- Print the logo with a brief summary describing your company and the products/services it offers.
- Introduce and describe the logo to your class, and see if your classmates can determine what your business does.

Go Online RUBRICS
www.glencoe.com

Independent Practice
Go to **Chapter 2**, and choose **Rubrics**. Use the rubrics to help create and evaluate your projects.

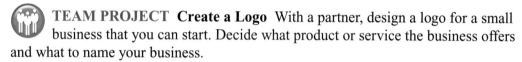

Project 10-4 Design a Booklet

Spotlight on Skills

- Lay out a booklet
- Apply a master page
- Create a cover image
- Add a table of contents
- Import style sheets
- Cite sources

Key Term

- booklet

Academic Focus

Language Arts
Create content for a booklet

Some types of publications are difficult to create without the use of layout software. In the last project, you saw how Publisher made it easy to lay out a brochure with a complex tri-fold design. A booklet is another example of a publication for which layout software is very useful.

A **booklet** is a publication with multiple pages printed front and back. Page layout in a booklet can be complicated. In an eight-page booklet, for example, pages 8 and 1 are two panels printed on the same page. Pages 2 and 7 are printed on the back of pages 8 and 1. Pages 3 and 6 are printed on the back of pages 4 and 5. Fortunately, layout software handles this complexity and allows the designer to simply concentrate on the design.

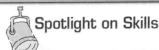

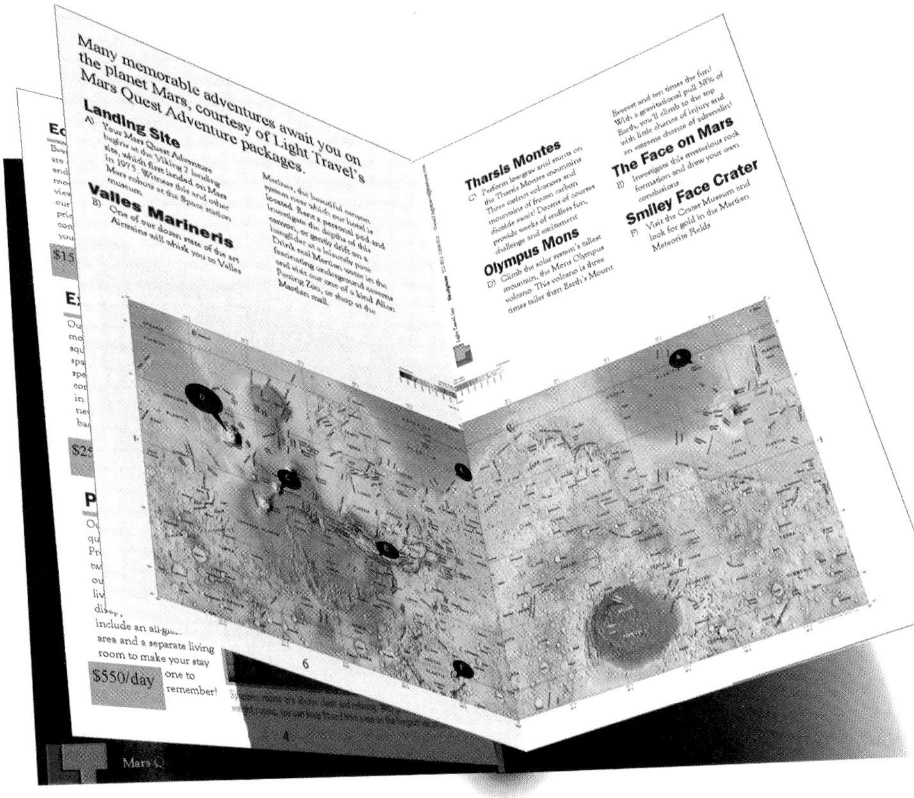

▶ Booklets have complex pagination that can be handled easily with layout software such as Microsoft Publisher.

Marketing booklets are large enough to describe one or more products in detail. Although similar in layout to a newsletter, they are not published as frequently and are often printed in full color on glossy paper. Like brochures, they are usually printed professionally in large quantities to benefit from economy of scale.

▶ **In this project,** you will begin an eight-page Mars Quest Travel Guide that provides important information for your customers.

Chapter 2 Assessment

2 Independent Practice ★★

LANGUAGE ARTS **Create a Flyer** Imagine that you are opening an ice cream shop. You offer 25 flavors, fabulous ice cream creations, and an old-fashioned soda fountain. Create a flyer to advertise your new shop.

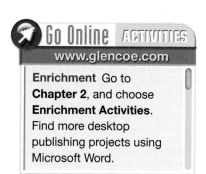

a. Plan Write the text that you will need in your flyer to attract customers. Include the hours and location.

b. Design Decide what graphics and fonts you want to use. By hand, sketch the layout of your flyer.

c. Create Combine your text and graphics into a one-page flyer. Include:
- A header or logo created using WordArt with the name of the shop.
- At least two different fonts, font sizes, and font formats.
- At least one clip art image.
- A page border.

d. Evaluate Follow your teacher's instructions for printing your flyer. Exchange flyers with a classmate. Go to the **Chapter 2 Rubrics** at the Online Learning Center. Use the project rubric to evaluate each other's work for accuracy, visual appeal, and content.

3 Independent Practice ★★★

SOCIAL STUDIES **Create a Brochure with a Map** Imagine that your school is giving a tour to prospective students. You have volunteered to create a bi-fold brochure that gives a brief description of the school, a tour schedule, and a simple map showing where the tour begins.

a. Design Determine the elements you need to create your brochure and where they will be placed. For the interior of the brochure:
- Write the text that describes the school and the tour schedule.
- Create a simple map with Word's drawing tools.

b. Create Lay out your text and graphics.
- Use two columns for the interior of the brochure.
- The exterior of the brochure should include the name of the school, the date of the tour, clip art, and a border.

c. Publish Before printing, have a classmate evaluate your work using a rubric from the Online Learning Center. Follow your teacher's instructions for printing your brochure as a two-sided document.

Go Online ACTIVITIES
www.glencoe.com

Enrichment Go to **Chapter 2**, and choose **Enrichment Activities.** Find more desktop publishing projects using Microsoft Word.

Apply a Style Sheet

4. Format the text using the style sheet that you created for the headers and body text in the back panel.

5. Locate photos or art that you can use to illustrate your text. If you do not have time, use **Data Files 10-3b to 10-3f**.

6. Use Photoshop to alter photos as needed. (For example, Mars' atmosphere is sandy colored in daylight, and sunsets are a spectacular blue.)

7. Lay out the images so that they align using the grid guides.

8. Use text boxes to add captions below each of the pictures.

9. Add design elements that repeat between pages to visually tie the pages together. This can include decorative bars and color schemes.

10. Your final design should look similar to Figure 10.10. Follow your teacher's instructions for saving and printing your work.

▼ **Figure 10.10** The final brochure should repeat design elements on the exterior and the interior.

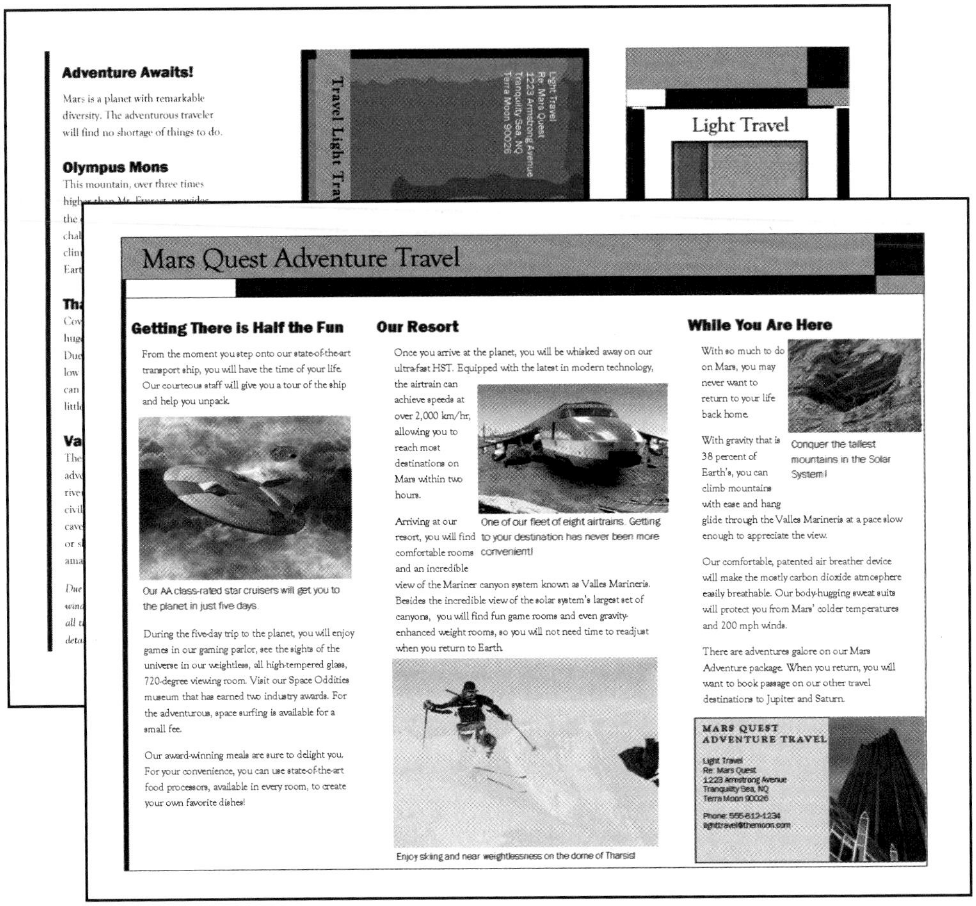

REVIEW AND REVISE

Check your work Use Figures 10.8 and 10.10 as guides and check that:

- ☑ The panels of the brochure are placed in the correct positions on the exterior and the interior.
- ☑ The front panel has an illustration designed in Photoshop.
- ☑ The logo and company slogan are repeated on the brochure's front panel and address panel.
- ☑ The address panel has a return address and a box for the addressee.
- ☑ Headers and body text have consistent formatting.
- ☑ Design elements are repeated on the exterior and interior.
- ☑ The design follows PARC principles.
- ☑ Text is readable and has been proofread and edited.

UNIT 1 Projects Across the Curriculum

The skills you learned in this unit will help you in your other classes, too. Use your desktop publishing skills to complete the following projects. Follow your teacher's instructions for saving or printing your work.

Project 1 Draw a Castle ★

MATH Use Word's drawing tools to draw a castle.

Go Online RUBRICS
www.glencoe.com
Unit: Projects Go to **Unit 1**, and choose **Rubrics**. Use the projects to help create and evaluate your work.

Plan

1. Draw a simple castle before you begin. Use different shapes, such as rectangles, trapezoids, circles, triangles, and so on, to create towers, doors, windows, moats, and whatever you would like to design your castle.

Create

2. Use the following tools to create your castle:
   - **a.** Autoshapes to create the basic outlines of your castle
   - **b.** Line Style and Line Color to emphasize specific elements
   - **c.** Fill Color to add color and textures to the different structures

Project 2 Create a Visual Report ★★

SCIENCE Create a one-page flyer that uses graphics to illustrate a science-related topic that interests you. It can be on a subject you are studying in your science class, the environment, weather, volcanoes, magnets, or space.

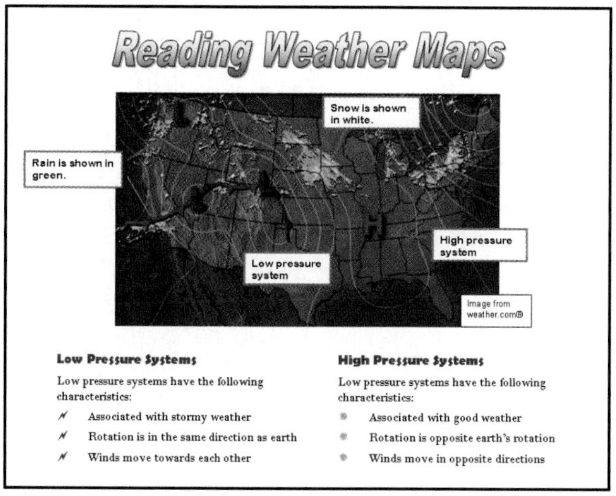

Plan

1. Before you begin, determine the images and content you will need and the size and layout of the text and images.

Create

2. Create a title with WordArt.
3. Separate text into smaller sections or lists with headers.
4. Add one or two images with callouts and/or captions

Project 10-3 Create the Brochure Interior

Spotlight on Skills

- Add text and graphics
- Apply a style sheet

Key Term

- economy of scale

Academic Focus

Science
Describe conditions on Mars

Student Data File

When you create your brochure, ask yourself what kind of customer would be attracted to your product. Who would want to take a vacation on Mars? Most likely your customers would be looking for adventure, no matter how much it costs. With that in mind, your text and images should convey the excitement and uniqueness of such a trip. Remember that you have to get your message across in a relatively small document.

You should also try to keep the information in the brochure fairly general so that it does not quickly become out of date. Brochures are usually printed in large batches and are used for years and seldom changed. This publishing practice creates economy of scale. **Economy of scale** means that producing large volumes of an item results in a lower cost per item. When companies print many copies of a brochure, they can usually afford high quality, full color designs on glossy paper. The cost per brochure may amount to only pennies, depending upon the number of copies printed.

▶ **In this project,** you will complete the brochure that you started in Project 10-2. You will use consistent design elements when you add images and text to the interior.

Step-by-Step

1. Open the brochure you started in Project 10-2. Save it according to your teacher's instructions.

2. Create three text frames, one on each panel on **Page 2**.

Add Text and Graphics

3. Insert the text from **Data File 10-3a**. Or research and key your own text about activities that visitors can do on Mars. Consider the atmosphere, temperature, gravity, and other features (Figure 10.9).

▼ **Figure 10.9** You may have to cut and edit your text after you add the images.

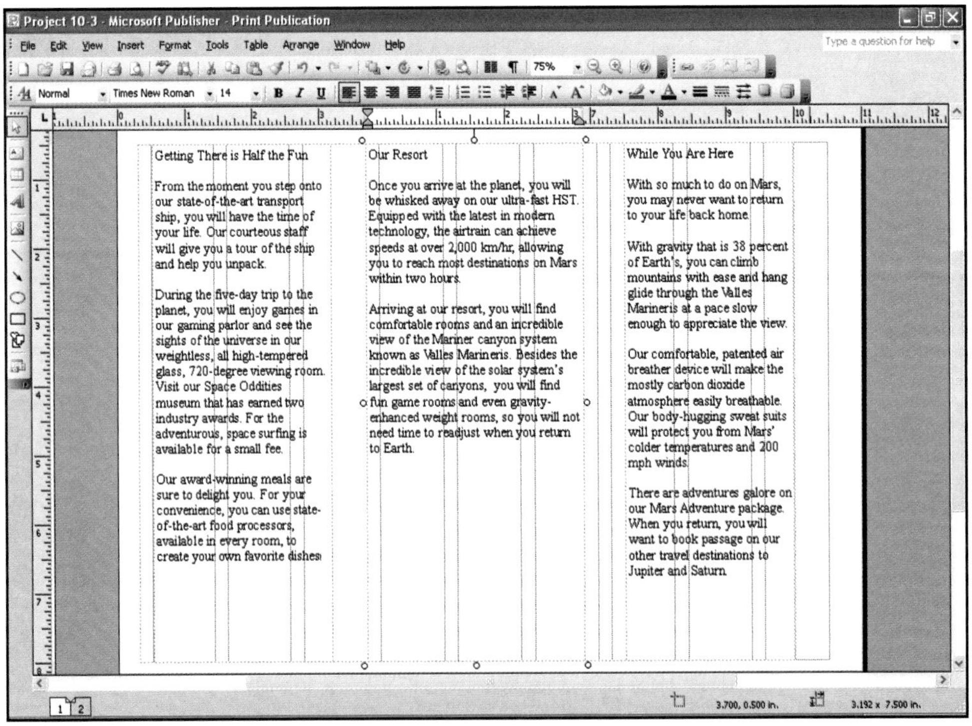

Projects Across the Curriculum

Project 3 Create a Greeting Card ★★

LANGUAGE ARTS Create a quad-fold greeting card for a special occasion, a holiday, or a thank you. Your card should contain colorful images and deliver an appropriate message.

Plan

1. Write a short poem or short message for the occasion.
2. Decide on images or designs to make the card attractive and eye-catching.

Create

3. Use WordArt or an interesting font to add text to the first panel of your card.
4. Insert the message you wrote in Step 1 on the third panel.
5. Add clip art or other design elements to the card.
6. Add a "Created by" credit on the last panel of the card.

Project 4 Create a Travel Brochure ★★★

SOCIAL STUDIES Create a two-column brochure about a popular travel destination. The brochure should provide helpful information to families who want to visit the area.

Plan

1. Determine a place that you would like to feature in the brochure. It can be a national park or recreation area, a famous town, or a resort.
2. Use the Internet to find images and information for your content.

Create

3. Your brochure should include:
   a. A title created with WordArt.
   b. At least two articles that you have written.
   c. At least three graphics. (clip art, photos, charts, etc.).

Publish

4. Proofread and edit your brochure. Follow your teacher's instructions for printing.

9 Create a gray text box at the bottom of the panel. Key the company contact information in the box.

10 Add a design at the top of the panel similar to the one shown in Figure 10.7.

Create the Address Panel

11 In the middle panel, insert your logo. Resize and crop it as needed.

12 Use text boxes to add the return address and company slogan. Create a placeholder for the mailing address (Figure 10.7).

Add Styles to the Back Panel

13 On the back panel of your brochure (the left side of the page), add a text box. Research information about Mars and key it in the text box, or insert **Data File 10-2**.

14 Use style sheets to keep headers, body text, and leading consistent.

15 Set **body text** in an **Oldstyle** font. Use **140 percent leading** for the **body text**, with a **9 pt space after** each paragraph.

16 Section headers should use a **colored, heavy sans serif font** and have a **6–9 pt space before** them (Figure 10.8).

17 Follow your teacher's instructions for saving your file. You will continue the brochure in Project 10-3.

▼ **Figure 10.7** Your logo and slogan on the address panel make your mailed brochure instantly recognizable.

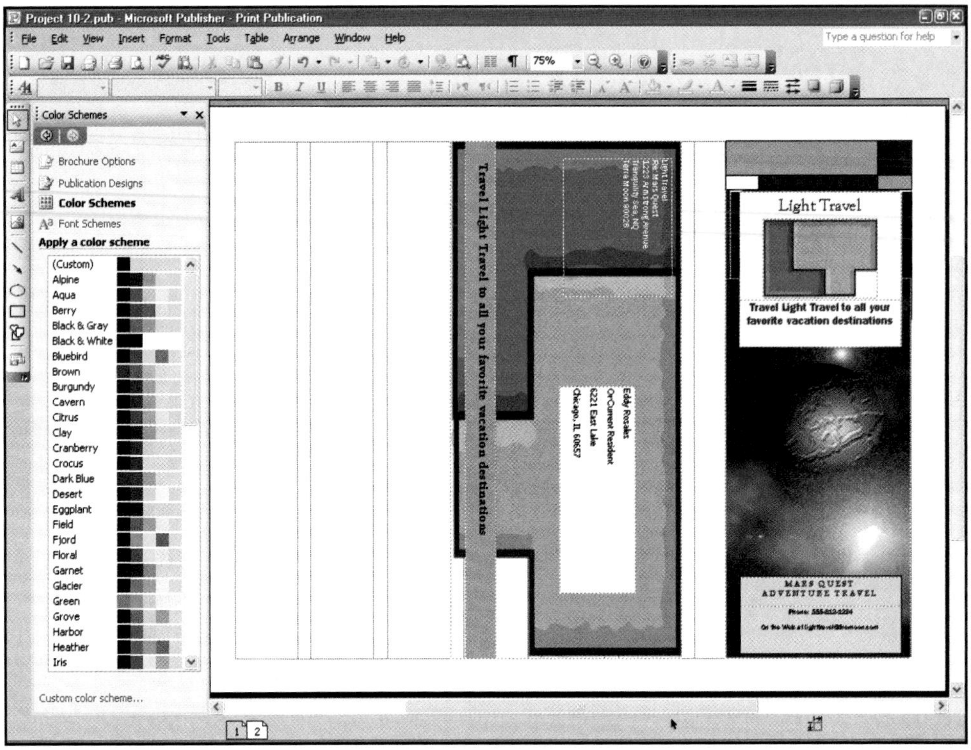

▼ **Figure 10.8** Make sure your final document follows PARC principles.

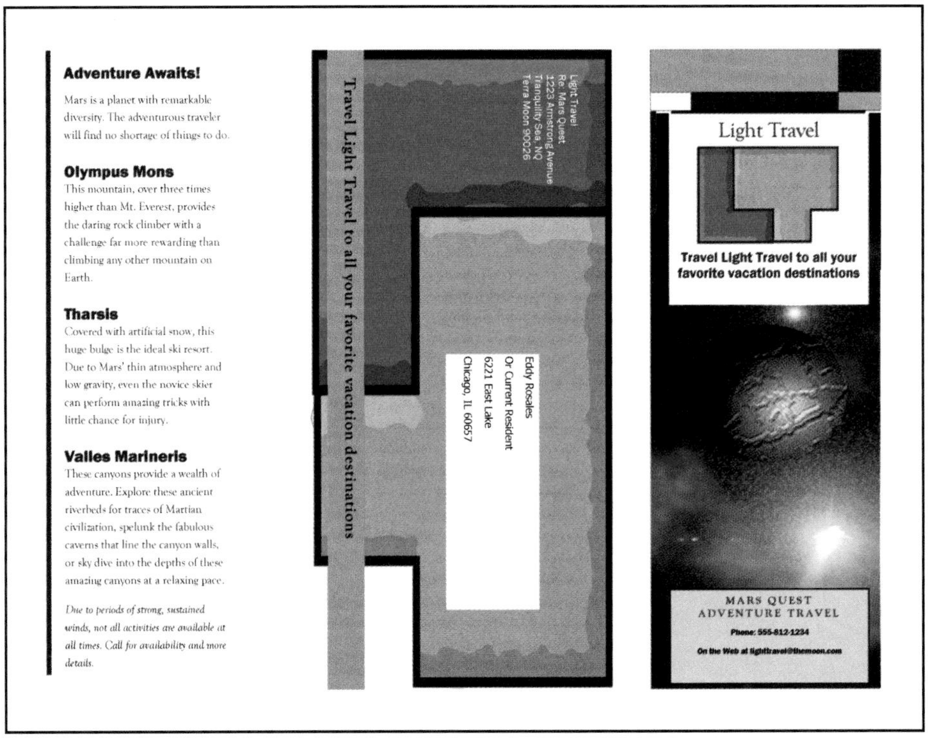

UNIT 2

Design with Microsoft Publisher

Contents

Step-by-Step

1. Open a new document in Microsoft Publisher. Save the file according to your teacher's instructions.
2. Click **Insert>Page**, and add one more page to your design. The first page will be the outside of the brochure, and the second page will be the inside.
3. Change to **Landscape** orientation.
4. Set **0.5 inch margins.** Add a **9 column** layout grid with a **0.2 inch gutter** (Figure 10.5).

Design the Front Panel

5. For the front panel of your brochure, use Photoshop to create a space illustration, similar to the one you created in Project 5-8.
6. Size the illustration so it fits effectively on the right hand panel of the page (Figure 10.6).
7. Create a white rectangle at the top of the panel and insert the logo you created in Project 9-4.
8. Add a text box to the rectangle with the company slogan: Travel Light Travel to all your favorite vacation destinations.

Figure 10.5 The outside of your tri-fold brochure should lay out from right to left.

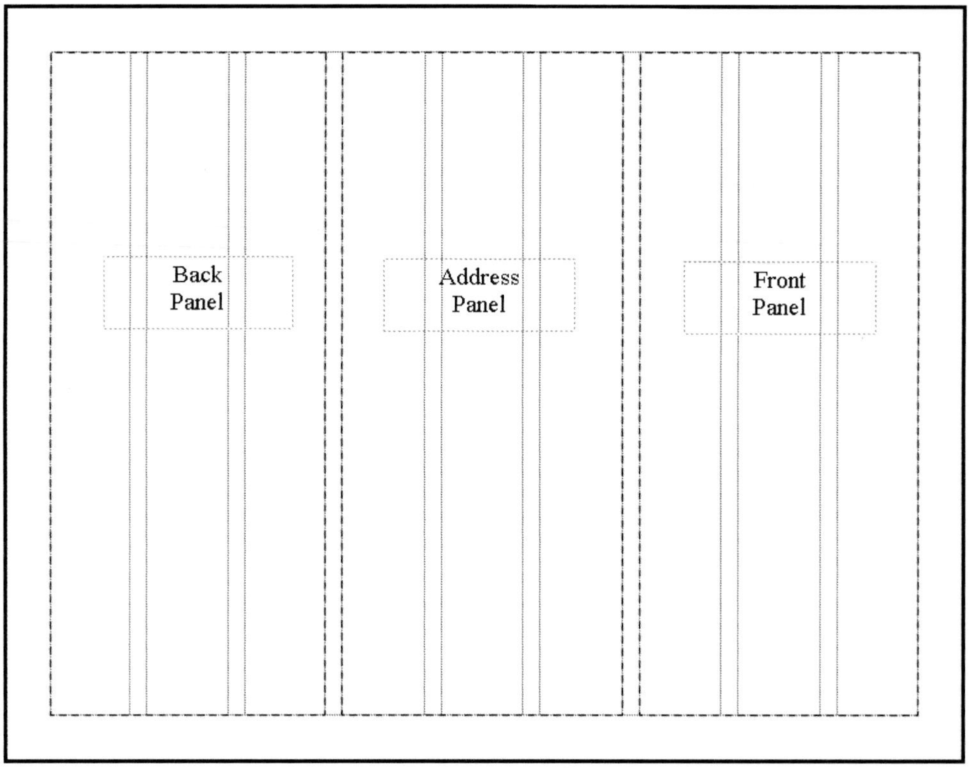

Figure 10.6 Use a color scheme that complements the logo.

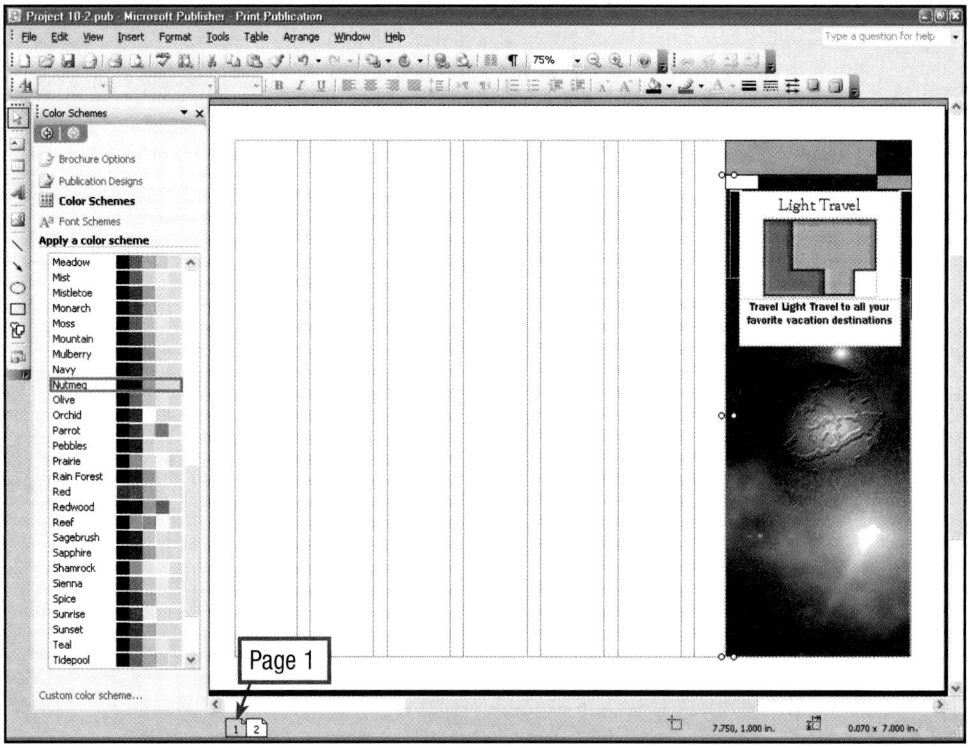

Chapter 3 Introducing Microsoft Publisher

Skills You Will Learn

In this chapter, you will see how much easier it is to use layout software, rather than a word processor, for desktop publishing. Microsoft® Publisher has the tools you need to place design elements exactly where you want on a page. It also provides layouts for numerous kinds of documents, including newsletters, brochures, calendars, business forms, and even Web pages.

Design Effective Advertisements

In Unit 1, you learned about logos, which are visual designs that immediately identify an organization. Logos tell people a lot about an organization: what it produces or what services it offers, whether it is conservative or modern, or whether it is traditional or innovative.

The same is true of an advertisement. Businesses want people to immediately recognize them and their message when they see a print ad, flyer, brochure, or Web site. No matter how exciting or visually interesting an advertisement is, it is not doing its job if the audience does not know its purpose or who is behind it.

DESIGN PROCESS: Advertisements

Elements	Issues
Purpose	To provide information that persuades people to do business with a company or organization.
Audience	Varies, depending on the product or service that the company is offering. Could be customers or business partners. Customers can be any age or demographic.
Content	Design elements might include headings, text boxes, charts, bulleted lists, and graphics. A company logo, contact information, and product information are typically included.
Layout	Sized to use as a magazine, phone book, or Internet ad; postcard; multifold brochure; single-page flyer; or Web page.
Publication	Published as print and Web documents. Printed documents can be color or black and white, single sided or duplex printed. Many copies can be printed and distributed individually, or one copy can be submitted.

Project 10-2 Create a Brochure

Spotlight on Skills

- Design the front panel
- Create the address panel
- Add styles to the back panel

Key Terms

- channel of distribution
- direct channel
- indirect channel

Academic Focus

Science
Create images and text relating to Mars

Even though marketing materials are often given away free to customers or business partners, it can cost a lot of money to develop them. Teams like yours must determine what information needs to be explained and how best to present it.

A business will often develop a variety of marketing materials including brochures and pamphlets, newsletters, a Web site, CD-ROMs, and even items like mouse pads or key chains. Print publications such as brochures might highlight individual products or services, while a larger booklet would summarize all the company's products or services.

► The brochure should include the company logo and a design that is similar to the company's other marketing materials.

After the materials are created, they reach customers through a **channel of distribution**, the path from producer to consumer. A **direct channel** means that the company gives out the material directly to the consumer. An **indirect channel** will use a "middle man," like a travel agency, to distribute the publications. Companies often use both methods.

► **In this project,** you will begin a brochure for your Mars Quest travel business. It will have a tri-fold layout and a full-color design. The brochure will describe the tours your company offers, transportation, special activities, and contact information. You can research and create your own images and content, or use the Data Files that are provided.

WORKSHOP Foundations

Layout Software

You Will Learn To

- Define layout software
- Compare layout and word processing software

Key Term

layout software

Before You Read

Adjust Reading Speed When you are learning new concepts, it helps to adjust your reading speed to match the difficulty of the text. Slow down your reading speed when you have difficulty understanding a concept. Look over illustrations. If needed, re-read the text to make sure you have absorbed the material. It may take longer to read the assignment, but you will understand and remember more.

Microsoft Publisher is **layout software**, a desktop publishing application that allows you to place images and text exactly where and how you want them on the page.

How Is Publisher Different from Word?

Microsoft Publisher is designed to handle lots of text and pictures with complex layouts and printing needs. In Publisher, pictures stay where they are placed, and pages always print the way they look onscreen. Professional graphic designers most often use layout software like Adobe® InDesign® or QuarkXpress®.

These programs also make it easier to send files to a professional print shop. Publisher's *Pack and Go* feature stores fonts in a special file with the document. When files are sent to a print shop, the fonts and specific instructions are available for the prepress technician.

Desktop Publishing with Publisher and Word

Publisher	Word
Remains stable when dealing with long, complex documents with lots of graphics.	May be unstable. Graphics often move on the page, and text boxes can get lost.
Minimizes lay out and print issues on complex documents.	Requires special planning for laying out multifold or multipage documents.
Includes alignment features that help place objects exactly where you want on the page.	Provides basic alignment features, but it is difficult to place objects precisely on the page.
Ensures portability because the fonts and the document travel together from one computer to another.	Problems can occur when documents are sent to another computer. Fonts can shift if not installed on the second computer.

Reading Check

1. **Draw Conclusions** Which software would you use to create a five-page research paper with three graphics? Explain your choice.
2. **Compare** Why is layout easier to do in Publisher than in Word?

Transfer Style Sheets in Microsoft Publisher

8 Open a new, blank Publisher document. Click **Format>Styles and Formatting** to open the Styles and Formatting task pane.

9 Click the **Import Styles** button. In the **Import Styles** dialog box, browse to the menu file you created in **Project 3-9**. Click **OK**.

10 All the styles from Project 3-9 will be imported. Delete or modify styles as needed using the **Styles and Formatting** task pane.

Transfer Style Sheets in Adobe Illustrator

11 Open a new Illustrator document. Click **Window>Type>Paragraph Styles**.

12 On the **Paragraph Styles** palette, click the **Options** button (Figure 10.4).

13 Choose **Load Paragraph Styles**, and browse to an Illustrator file. **Note:** Since no styles were defined in Illustrator projects, choose any one.

14 All the styles in the chosen document will be imported. Delete or modify styles as needed using the **Paragraph Styles** palette.

▼ **Figure 10.3** Import Styles adds the styles from the document you choose.

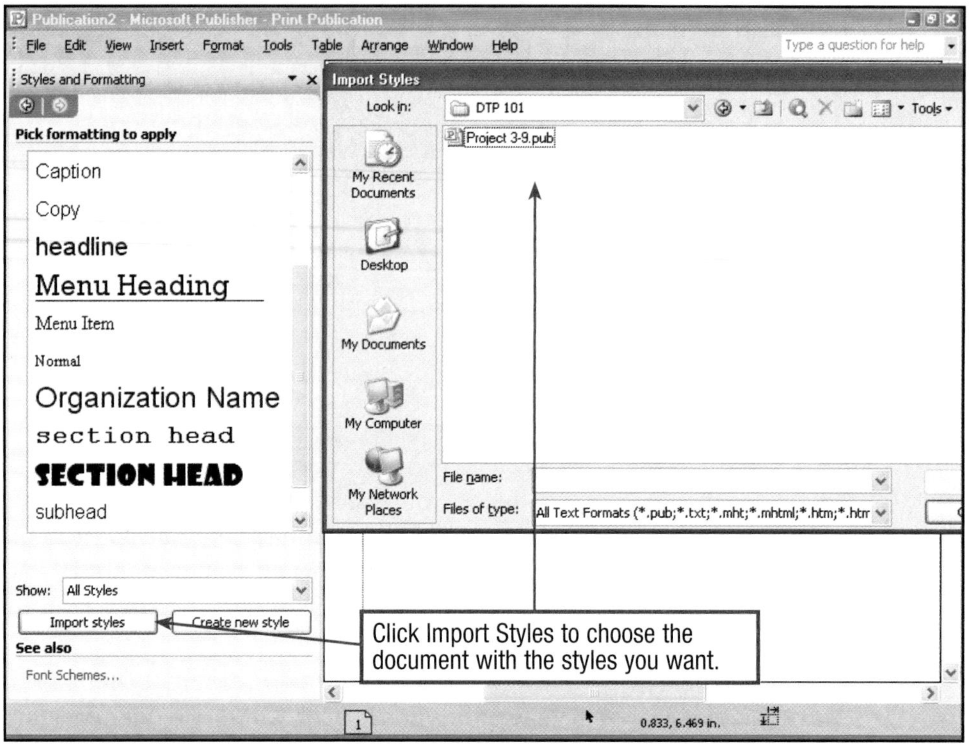

▼ **Figure 10.4** You can use the Paragraph Styles palette to import and export styles in Adobe Illustrator and Adobe InDesign, a professional layout program.

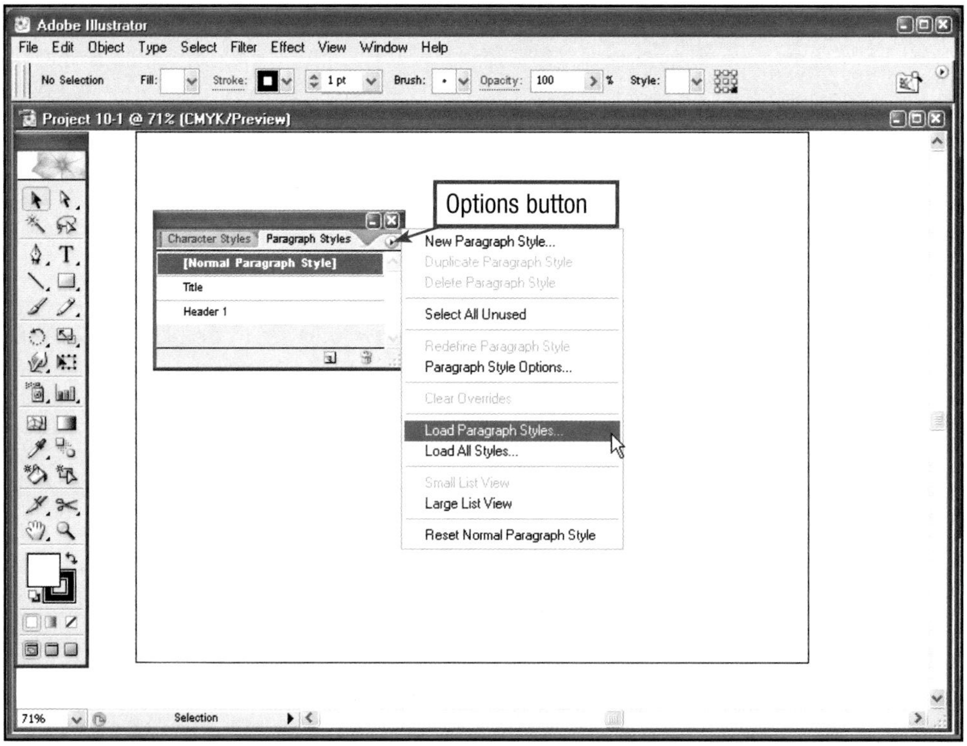

WORKSHOP

Toolbox

The Publisher Interface

You Will Learn To

- Identify Publisher's interface and features
- Compare Word's and Publisher's interface

Key Terms

frame
spread
master page

Publisher's interface is similar to Word's, but there are several additional features. These page layout features help you place design objects exactly where you want on the page.

Object Toolbar The Object toolbar displays buttons for frames, some drawing tools, and Design Gallery Objects. A **frame** is a type of border that holds an object in a publication. In Microsoft Word, text and graphics can be added either directly onto the page or inside of a frame such as a text box or drawing canvas. In Publisher, *everything* is in its own frame—text, tables, clip art, and pictures.

Scratch Area Objects placed in the scratch area are displayed so they will be accessible, no matter which page you are working on.

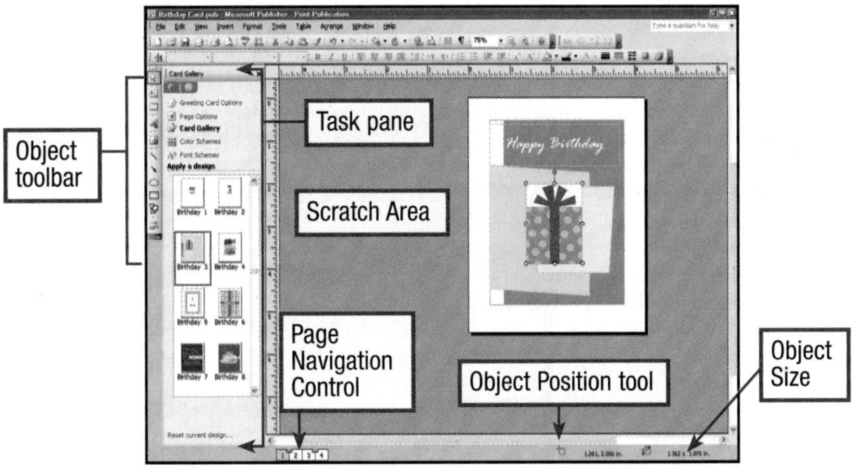

Page Navigation Control Click a page icon to move between pages, or drag the icon to move a page. You can also see which pages are in a **spread** (pages that face each other, like in a book), or whether you are working on a **master page**, a tool that allows design elements to repeat automatically on any number of pages.

Object Position Use this tool to see exactly where the top left corner of an object is positioned on the page.

Object Size Keep an eye on the horizontal and vertical measurements of an object. It is very important where physical space is carefully budgeted.

Step-by-Step

Transfer Style Sheets in Microsoft Word

1. Open a new Word document. Save it according to your teacher's instructions.

2. Click **Tools>Templates and Add-Ins**. In the **Templates** window, click the **Organizer** button.

3. In the **Organizer** dialog box, choose the **Styles** tab. Click the left **Close File** button. The button changes to Open File. Click **Open File** (Figure 10.1).

4. In the **Open** dialog box, change **Files of type** to **All Files**. Then browse to the Camelot newsletter file you created in **Project 2-7**. Click **Open**.

5. In the **Organizer** dialog box, click the **Close File** button on the right.

6. Repeat Steps 3–4 to open the file you are working in now in the right-hand box.

7. In the left box, select two styles to copy, then click the **Copy** button to copy the style to the current document or the default template (Normal.dot).

▼ **Figure 10.1** You can add a style to the global template or to a specific document.

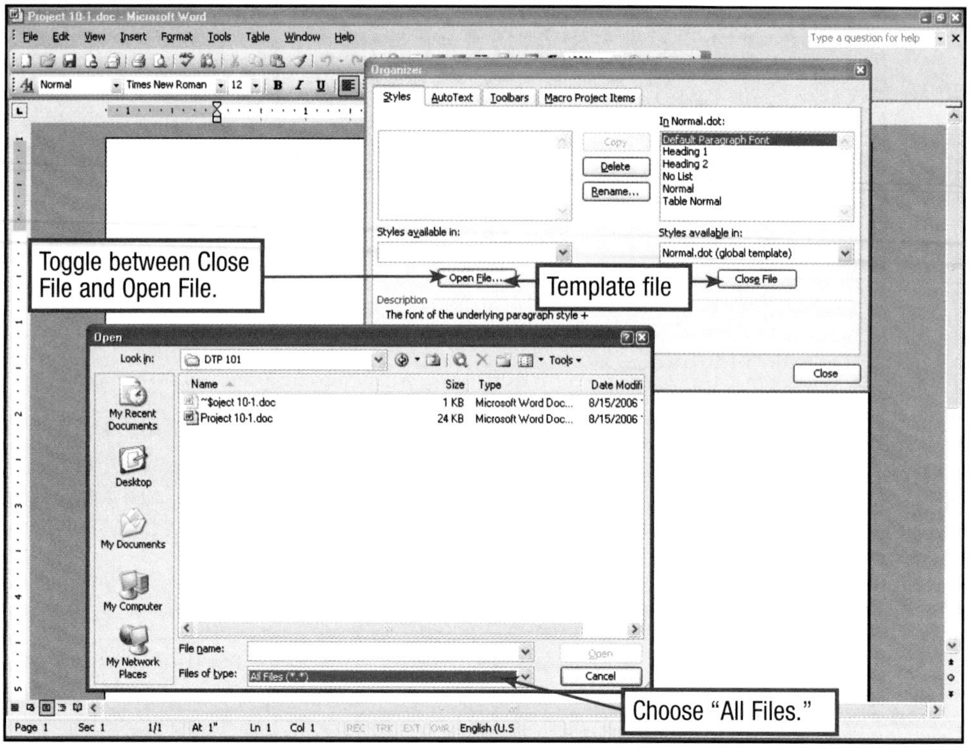

Toggle between Close File and Open File.

Choose "All Files."

▼ **Figure 10.2** Copy styles from the left box to the right, or the other way.

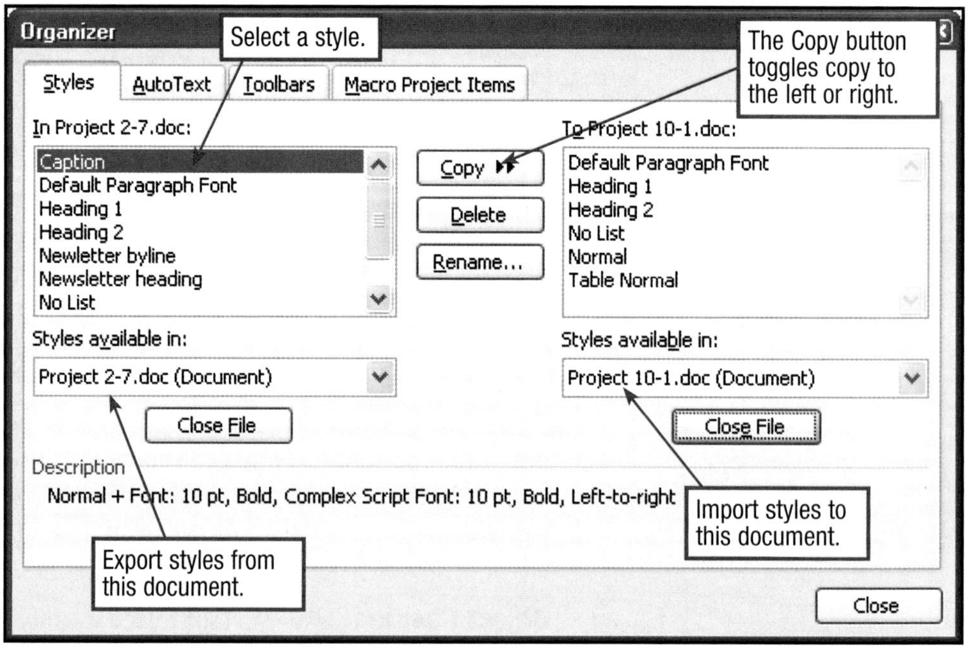

Select a style.
The Copy button toggles copy to the left or right.
Export styles from this document.
Import styles to this document.

Compare the Word and Publisher Interface

The menus, toolbars, and task panes of both programs share many of the same features and icons. Most of the commands that you use in Word, including mouse and keyboard commands, are the same in Publisher.

Compare Publisher and Word Interfaces

Feature	What is the same as Word?	What is unique to Publisher?
Title bar	Shows the document's last saved name	Works the same way
Menu bar	Allows access to most common commands	Includes an Arrange menu
Standard toolbar	Displays buttons for common commands such as open, save, print, cut, copy, etc.	Includes new buttons like *Zoom In* and *Zoom Out*. Buttons for tables and spreadsheets have moved to the Object toolbar
Formatting toolbar	Includes basic tools for formatting text	Only accessible when a text box is selected. Includes buttons for formatting text boxes
Task pane	Lets you switch between tasks and manage features like clip art and style sheets	Displays design options. Can act as a wizard, taking you through steps
Workspace	Shows the page layout, orientation, and paper size	Also displays layout lines such as ruler and layout guides
Rulers	Can be used to set tab stops	Can be moved and re-centered to measure distances and can be used to create ruler guides for layout
Scrollbars	Move the document on the screen	Can only scroll the page you are viewing, not move from page to page

Reading Check

1. **Explain** What is the scratch area around the workspace used for?
2. **Identify** How do you move from page to page in Publisher?

Eye On Ethics

Legal Use of Images Images that you find on the Internet are often copyrighted even though it may not say so on the site. If you use an image for a school report, it usually is considered **fair use**, which means you can use material without permission. However, if you use the image in a business publication, you may be breaking copyright laws. Always check with the Web site administrator if you are not sure.

Define What is fair use?

Project 10-1 Import and Export Style Sheets

Spotlight on Skills

- Transfer style sheets in Microsoft Word
- Transfer style sheets in Microsoft Publisher
- Transfer style sheets in Adobe Illustrator

Key Terms

- marketing
- advertising
- brand

Academic Focus

Social Studies
Discuss marketing practices

Go Online PREVIEW
www.glencoe.com

Before You Begin Go to **Chapter 10**, and choose **PowerPoint Presentations** to preview the documents you will be creating. Also, use the individual project **Rubrics** to help create and evaluate your work.

In Chapter 9, you formed a marketing team for Light Travel, a company that sells adventure travel packages to Mars. You and your team are putting together a set of marketing materials that promotes your latest venture: the Mars Quest vacation package. The travel arrangements include transportation and luxury accommodations. However, since Mars is still a relatively new holiday destination, you are going to have come up with a very convincing marketing campaign.

Advertising is only one part of marketing. **Marketing** is a process that a company uses to develop, promote, and distribute its products. **Advertising** is when a company pays a magazine, television station, Web site, or other medium to promote its products or services. In order to market effectively, companies must take into account their customers' wants and needs. They must then create a message and identity that meets those standards.

One way to create a strong identity, or a **brand,** is by using words, symbols, designs, or even sounds that customers immediately associate with a particular product or service. Think of Macintosh's apple logo or the Microsoft flying window logo. You can easily identify a product from either of those companies.

▲ You can recognize the Macintosh apple logo no matter where you see it.

Marketing materials must promote brand recognition, which means that they must use consistent design elements from one type of document to the next. You have already created a logo and a business package, and you will be repeating those designs in a brochure, booklet, Web page, and even a PowerPoint presentation.

▶ **In this project,** you will learn how to import and export style sheets into different documents, using different software applications. This is an easy way to add repetition and consistency between your marketing products. If you use a style often, you can even add it to the default template.

Project 3-1

Spotlight on Skills

- Use templates and wizards
- Rotate a shape
- Add clip art/pictures
- Add/change color

Key Term

- template

Academic Focus

Social Studies
Identify important dates

Go Online PREVIEW
www.glencoe.com

Before You Begin Go to **Chapter 3**, and choose **PowerPoint Presentations** to preview the documents you will be creating. Also, use the individual project **Rubrics** to help create and evaluate your work.

Create a Calendar with a Template

In Unit 1 you created a résumé with a **template**, or a guide that contains the formatting, layout, and design elements for publications. In Publisher, when you start a new publication from the New Document task pane, a copy of the template file opens so that the original template cannot be altered by mistake.

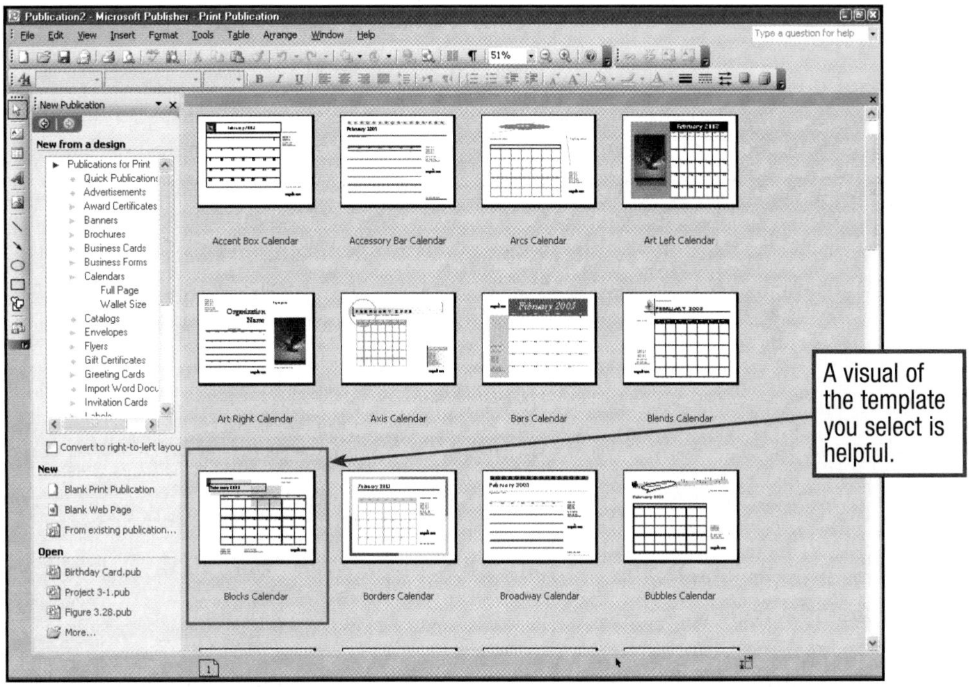

▲ Publisher offers many varieties of templates for each type of document.

Templates are a fast way to create a document. All you need to do is replace the placeholder text and graphics with your own. However, templates may also be customized, and you can create your own templates. You should use a template when:

- You do not have enough time to develop an idea from scratch.
- You need to keep a consistent design from one document to another, like in a monthly newsletter.

In Publisher, if the templates are not visible:

- Make sure that the task pane is open by choosing **View>Task Pane**.
- Use the task pane drop-down menu, and select **Publication Designs**.
- To change the type of publications, click the drop-down menu, and choose **New Publications>Publications for Print**.

▶ **In this project,** you will create a calendar from a template. Then you will modify the template, adding clip art and text boxes.

Workshop Toolbox

Transfer Style Sheets

You Will Learn To

- Maintain consistency between documents

Key Terms

import
export

As you have seen in earlier chapters, style sheets help keep formatting consistent. Style sheets are particularly helpful when working with teams. They help keep your designs consistent from job to job, designer to designer, and document to document.

Most software applications allow you to transfer style sheets to other documents or other computers. You can **import**, or bring in, a style sheet to use in a document you are working on. Or you can **export**, or send out, a style sheet to use in another document. You cannot, however, transfer style sheets to other software applications. For example, if you create a document in Illustrator, you cannot transfer your style sheet to a document in Microsoft Word.

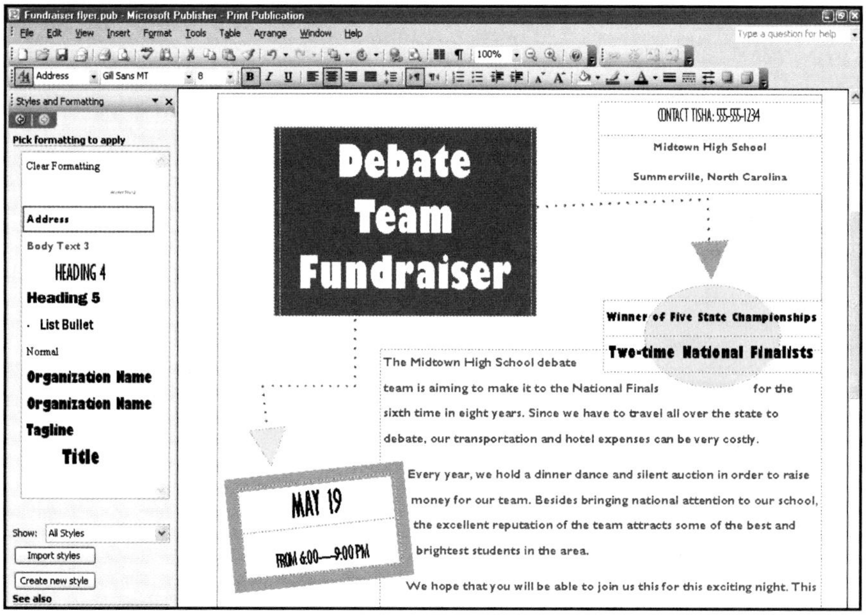

▲ You can import or export style sheets to give the same look to different documents.

Eye On Ethics

Case Study A friend has created a graphic novel using characters and settings from Star Wars®. She published her novel online at a fan fiction site and received rave reviews. Now someone has offered to publish the novel, but before she can decide, a "cease and desist" order is issued by the court. If she continues, she can be sued.

Evaluate Do you think your friend published her work on a fan fiction site without violating copyright laws? Why would the courts prevent her from printing her book?

Reading Check

1. **Explain** Describe three advantages of using style sheets.
2. **Draw Conclusions** When you are working on a group project, why would it be helpful for group members to all use the same software applications?

Student Data File

Step-by-Step

Use Templates and Wizards

1. Open Microsoft Publisher, and click **Publications for Print**. Choose **Calendars**, and then select **Travel Calendar**. Save the file.

2. In the task pane, click the **Change Date Range** button. Change the start date and end date to **November 2008**.

3. Click **Color Schemes**. Choose **Grove** color scheme (Figure 3.1). Click **Back** [Back button icon].

Rotate a Shape

4. Select the month name. Hold SHIFT as you use the green rotate handle. Move the text box to the left side of the calendar and resize it.

5. Right-click the center picture. From the pop-up menu, choose **Delete Object**. Delete the frame. Then delete the right picture and its frame.

Add Clip Art/Pictures

6. Double-click the left picture to open the Clip Art window.

7. Use **Data File 3-1**, or search through the clip art for *autumn*, and insert the picture. Resize and reposition it to look like Figure 3.2.

Figure 3.1 Use the options in the task pane to modify your template.

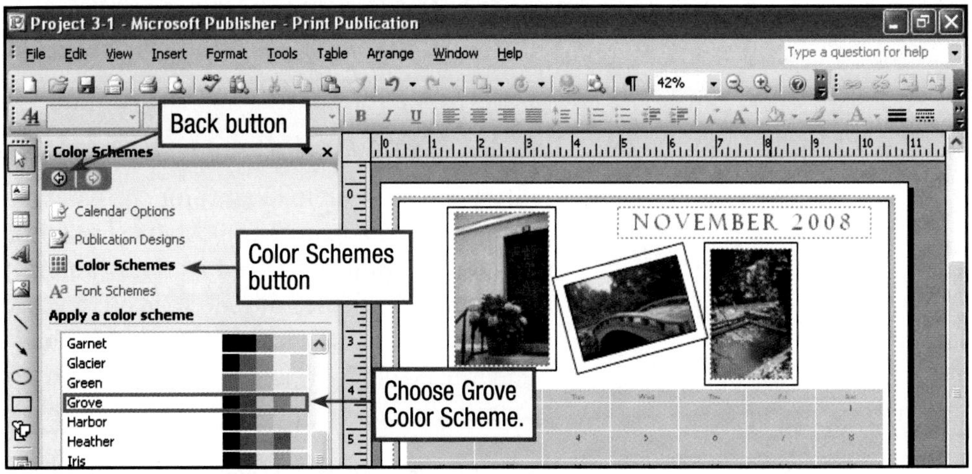

Figure 3.2 Hold the Shift key when you rotate an object for more control.

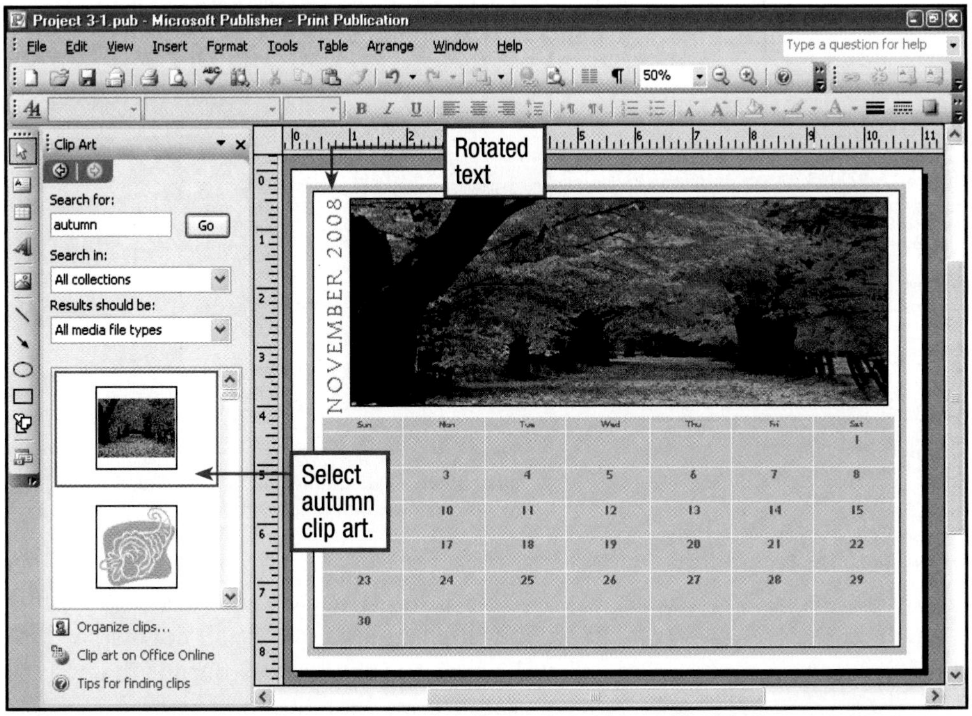

Instant Message

Template Tips When using templates, be aware that some templates, such as the advertisements, are **NOT** a full-page design! Always check the rulers when working with a new template. Some templates, such as certificates, require special paper that may already have a design printed upon it. This paper can be purchased through catalogs or office supply stores.

WORKSHOP Foundations

How Do I Keep Colors Consistent?

It can be difficult to keep color consistent in a design, especially when you are working with many people and using different software applications. Your team may decide to use red as the primary color in your design, but there are at least 256 shades of red! To avoid confusion when communicating with your team, use CMYK or RGB color values. **Pantone** is another common standardized color system. It offers custom-colored inks used in professional printing. (To review the use of color, see Appendix A.)

▼ RGB values for Ruby Red

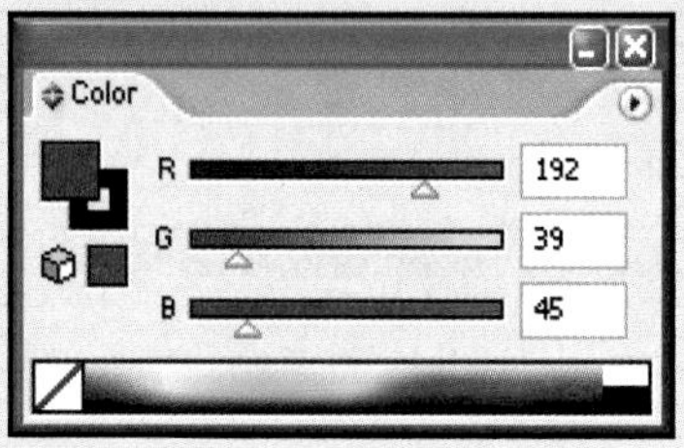

▼ CMYK values for Ruby Red

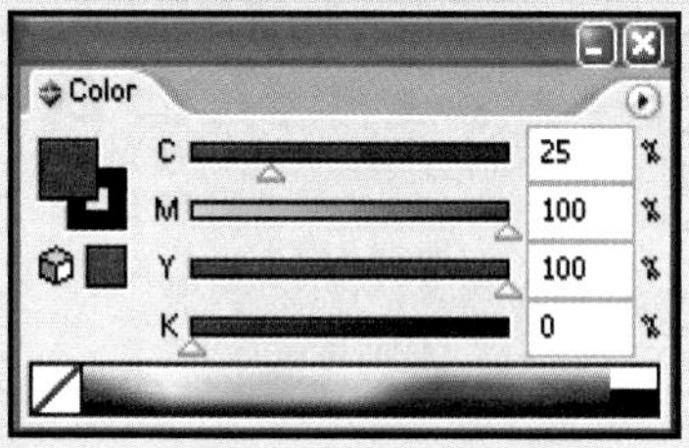

▲ There are hundreds of shades of red, so you must use specific color values if you want all team members to use the same shade.

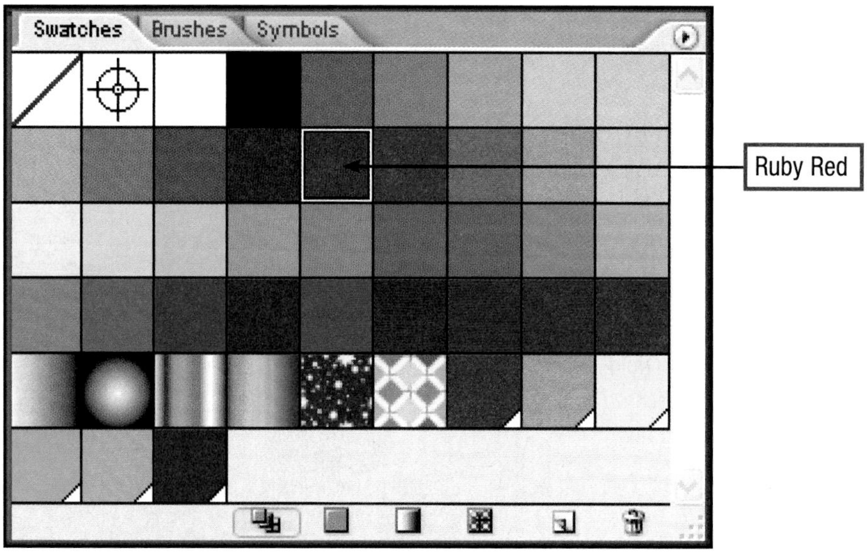

▲ Each swatch has a different color value, which varies according to the color system being used.

Also, do not trust your monitor when evaluating colors for a print publication. Your monitor will not display the colors the same as your printer will, and it is the printer output that your audience will see. Whenever possible, print your colors to make sure they are the shade that you want.

Reading Check

1. **Compare and Contrast** Make a chart comparing ten color swatches in Illustrator. Identify each color's name, RGB, and CMYK settings. Print and compare the chart to your computer monitor. Describe how they are different.
2. **Describe** How can repetition be incorporated into a brochure design?

8. Click after the date on the first Tuesday of the month. **(Note**: Press [Zoom In icon] to **Zoom In** closer and **Zoom Out** [Zoom Out icon] to return to the original view.) Or, press F9.

9. Press ENTER to add a space. Use a **14 pt** font to key Election Day. (Figure 3.3)

10. Use the same font and same font size on November 11th to key Veterans Day.

11. Select the dates for the fourth Wednesday, Thursday, and Friday.

Add/Change Color

12. On the **Formatting** toolbar, click **Fill Color** [icon]. Then change the color to **Accent 4** (RGB 204, 204, 204), the 5th color over.

13. On the **Object** toolbar, click **Text Box** [icon]. Drag a text box below the dates of the three gray days.

14. In the text box, use the same font as Step 9, but at **22 pts**. Key No school!.

15. Select the text. On the Formatting toolbar, click **Center** [icon] to center the text within the box (Figure 3.4).

▼ **Figure 3.3** Run the mouse pointer over the colors to display the names.

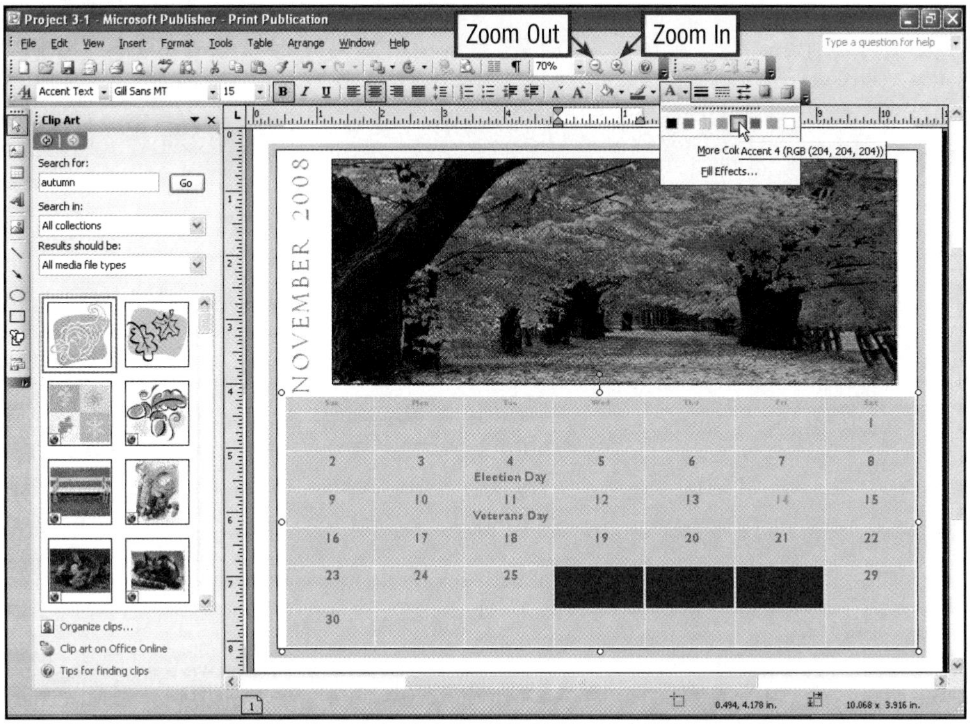

▼ **Figure 3.4** Center the text in the text box. Do not center it on the page.

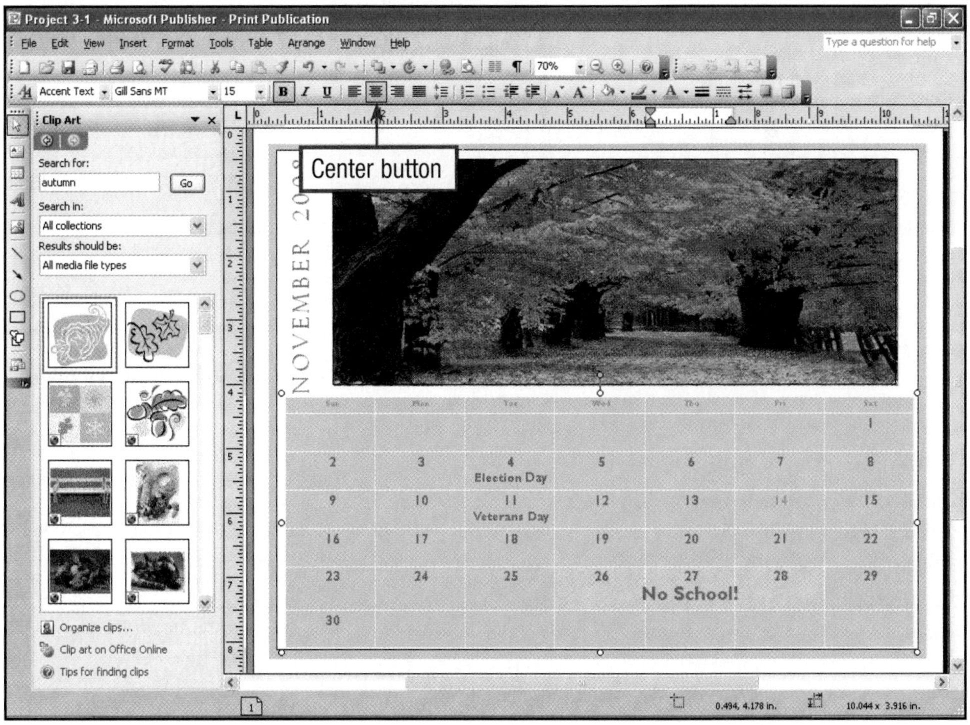

WORKSHOP Foundations

You Will Learn To

- Recognize consistent design elements
- Evaluate effective use of color

Key Term

Pantone

Before You Read

How Can You Improve? If you do well on a test, you know your study strategies were successful. If you do poorly, think about how to improve your studying for the next test. What methods worked? Which did not? How can you improve your understanding of the material? Discuss study techniques with classmates, and find the ones that help you learn best.

Maintain Consistency

In Chapter 4, you learned about the four main design principles: Proximity, Alignment, Repetition, and Contrast (PARC). Of these four principles, note that repetition is a primary design focus in marketing materials. Repeating design elements and consistent use of type and graphic styles across publications, both in print and on Web sites, helps tie publications together visually. This creates a professional identity for your organization that clients will easily recognize.

▲ This Web page reinforces PARC principles through the use of consistent colors, font styles, and box shapes.

Repetition needs to be developed throughout a design, whether the design is for a 12-page booklet or a two-page brochure. What are some things you should repeat throughout a design? Certainly, dominant design elements should be repeated, such as a company's logo, certain colors, clip art, or graphic elements like lines or shapes. But other, more subtle elements, such as the font scheme, the leading, or page margins should be repeated as well. The challenge to the designer is to create a design that is suitably consistent and harmonious but not monotonous and dull.

16 Select the first row of the calendar that contains the days of the week. Fill the cells with **black**, and change the text color to **white**.

17 To check for common printing problems, on the **menu** bar, click **Tools>Design Checker**.

18 Review the problems listed in the task pane. Click the arrow next to each one, and choose **Go To This Item**.

19 Determine whether the problem needs to be fixed. Choose **Explain** to find out more about potential troubles. A Help window will open to discuss the topic.

20 On the **menu** bar, click **View>Boundaries and Guides** or **File>Print Preview** to see what the design will look like so you can make changes before printing.

21 Your final calendar should look similar to Figure 3.5. Follow your teacher's instructions for saving and printing your work.

Figure 3.5 You easily created a customized publication with a template.

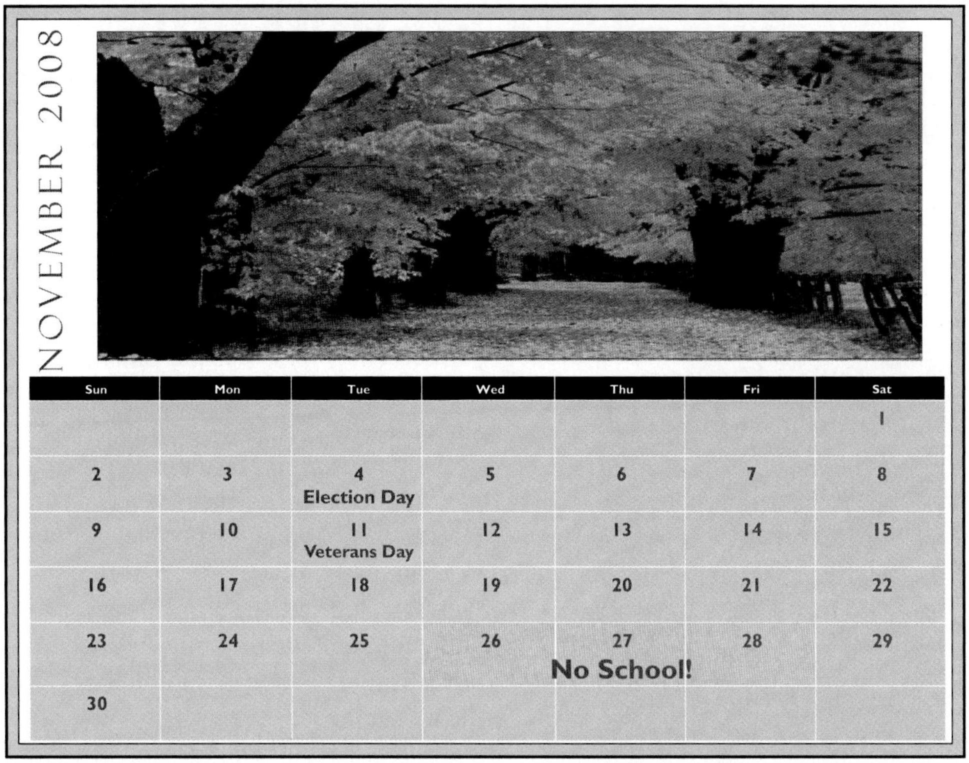

NOVEMBER 2008
Sun
Mon
Tue
Wed
Thu
Fri
Sat
1
2
3
4
Election Day
5
6
7
8
9
10
11
Veterans Day
12
13
14
15
16
17
18
19
20
21
22
23
24
25
26
27
No School!
28
29
30

Instant Message

Troubleshoot Templates Do not worry if the text you see when you open a template is different than that in the figures. Publisher has tools that save information that has been added to a template. These tools allow the information to be automaticallly inserted into any new template that is created.

REVIEW AND REVISE

Check your work Use Figure 3.5 as a guide and check that:

- ☑ The month and year are rotated and aligned with the left edge of the calendar.
- ☑ The image extends across the top of the page.
- ☑ The color scheme is correct.
- ☑ Election Day and Veterans Day have been correctly marked.
- ☑ The correct three days have been shaded and marked "No School."
- ☑ The first row is filled, and the text color has been changed.

Chapter 10 Creating Marketing Materials

Skills You Will Learn

Workshop Foundations
Maintain Consistency

Workshop Toolbox
Transfer Style Sheets

Project 10-1
Import and Export Style Sheets

Project 10-2
Create a Brochure

Project 10-3
Create the Brochure Interior

Project 10-4
Design a Booklet

Project 10-5
Design Web Pages

Project 10-6
Add Hyperlinks

Skills Studio

Design PowerPoint Presentations

Project 10-7
Create a PowerPoint Presentation

Project 10-8
Create Images for a Presentation

Project 10-9
Add Effects to a Presentation

In this chapter, your team will continue its work marketing the Mars Quest interplanetary travel agency. The team will create a brochure, a booklet, a Web page, and a PowerPoint presentation.

Advertise Your Product

Advertisements can be placed in magazines and newspapers, and on Web pages, baseball stadium walls, city buses, and movie theater screens. Some large companies may spend months and thousands of dollars creating their advertising campaigns. However, with a clever idea and the right software, you can create a professional-looking, low-budget ad in a matter of hours.

Businesses place advertisements based on their target audience. Gender, age, and income level all play a part in determining the audience's personality and motivation. The audience helps define the advertising strategy, including the type of publication or medium where the ad is placed.

Advertisers use a formula called the CPM (Cost per Page per Thousand) to help compare the value of advertising rates in various media. A full-page, full-color advertisement in a national magazine with a high CPM, can cost more than $200,000 for a year. A magazine with a low CPM would cost less.

Cost, however, is only one part of the puzzle. An advertiser also needs to consider which media outlets are popular with its audience. It would not make sense to advertise a product in a magazine that the target audience would never read, regardless of the cost.

Design Process: Marketing Materials

Elements	Issues
Purpose	To position products and services so they are attractive to customers.
Audience	Varies, depending on the product or service being offered.
Content	Some marketing materials may use a lot of text; others may use mainly pictures. Most fall somewhere in between.
Layout	Should be easy to read, with an attention-grabbing design that clearly identifies the company and its message.
Publication	May be published as separate pamphlets or brochures or placed in other print media or online. Marketing materials may range from black and white to full color, and be any size.

Project 3-2

Design a Business Card

Spotlight on Skills

- Modify a template
- Apply layout guides
- Change brightness and contrast
- Add a background image

Key Terms

- layout guides
- gutter
- snap

Academic Focus

Math
Create a grid

Layout guides, also called layout grids, are lines that form a framework under a document, helping to create a consistent design. Three different types of layout guides are offered in Publisher: margin guides, grid guides, and baseline guides. Blue dotted lines indicate the layout choices that you make, such as the margin settings. The lines appear on the screen, but they do not print.

Apply Layout Guides

Layout guides divide the workspace into evenly spaced rows and columns. These gridlines help determine how wide an object should be and where to place it effectively. Objects that are laid out without regard to the grid may stand out in a way that distracts from your document's design and message.

In the figure to the right, evenly spaced gridlines help determine the placement of articles, graphics, tables, and headlines. The space between columns is called a **gutter**. Even though every article has a different layout, the entire design itself seems consistent thanks to the underlying grid structure.

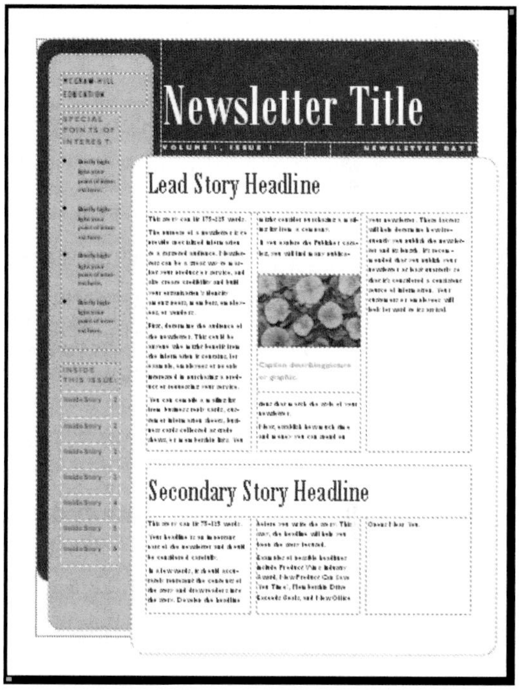

▲ The layout guides in this template keep the newsletter design consistent.

You determine the number of columns and rows you need for your grid. If you have too many columns or rows, it will be difficult to create an orderly layout. If you use too few, your objects will be too far apart. The more you use layout guides, the easier it will be to set them up for the most effective design.

To make it easy to align objects along a gridline, Publisher has a **snap** command on the **Arrange** menu, which pulls, or snaps, objects to the nearest guide line, ruler, or even another object.

► **In this project,** you will use a template and layout guides to create a business card. Business cards are usually a standard size (2 inches high by 3½ inches wide). They are meant to fit easily into wallets and card files. Like a logo, the look of a business card says a lot about an organization, its product, and its message.

2 Independent Practice ★★

TEAM PROJECT **Plan a Children's Book** Imagine that you and your team have just signed a contract to publish a new children's book. Follow your teacher's instructions to organize a team.

a. **Plan** Brainstorm ideas for a book.
   - Locate examples of children's books and decide upon the design.
   - Decide which software will be needed and the budget for the project.
   - Break the overall project into smaller tasks and assign team members to each task.
   - Establish a timeline for the completion of each part of the project.

b. **Create** Sketch thumbnails showing the design for each page.
   - Create one page of the book.
   - Create a title page with the name and logo of your company at the bottom.

c. **Evaluate** Exchange plans with another group, and use a rubric to evaluate each other's work for accuracy, visual appeal, and content. Follow your teacher's instructions for printing your publications.

3 Independent Practice ★★★

TEAM PROJECT **Plan a Fund-Raising Campaign** Your school has asked students to volunteer to raise money for a local non-profit organization. Follow your teacher's instructions to organize a team that will create materials to promote this school-wide community service activity.

a. **Plan**
   - Determine which organization you would like to support and the materials you will need to create.
   - Determine the budget and a timeline for the campaign.
   - Break the project into smaller tasks. Assign team members to each task.

b. **Create** Draw thumbnail sketches of the promotional materials.
   - If the organization does not have a logo, create one for them and design letterhead stationery.
   - Request permission to use photos from the organization or create your own.
   - Create at least one of your promotional documents in Publisher.

c. **Evaluate** Exchange your work with another group, and evaluate each other's work for accuracy, visual appeal, and content. Follow your teacher's instructions for printing your publications.

Go Online ACTIVITIES
www.glencoe.com

Enrichment Go to **Chapter 9**, and choose **Enrichment Activities** to find more desktop publishing projects.

Step-by-Step

Modify a Template

1. In the task pane, click **Publications for Print**. Choose **Business Cards**. Save the file according to your teacher's instructions.

2. Scroll down and choose the **Brocade Business Card**.

3. Replace the placeholder text in the template with your own information (Figure 3.6). Use your own name and your school's address.

4. Move the phone, fax, and e-mail information into the address text box.

5. A **Text in Overflow Indicator** should appear below the address box (Figure 3.7). This means that the content does not fit in the text box frame.

6. Select the empty text box, and click **Edit>Delete Object**.

7. Click and drag down the bottom middle handle of the address text box until all the text in the frame is displayed.

8. Repeat Step 6 to delete the Organization Name text box and the text box with the floral graphic on the right (Figure 3.7).

Figure 3.6 Replace the placeholder text in the template.

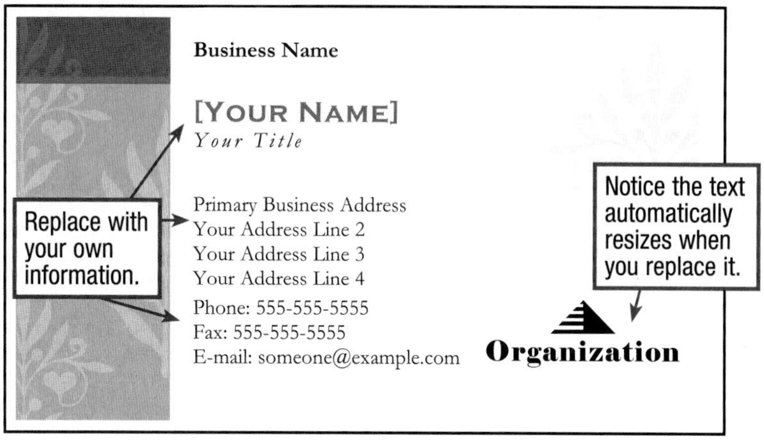

Figure 3.7 You can combine information so that there are fewer text boxes.

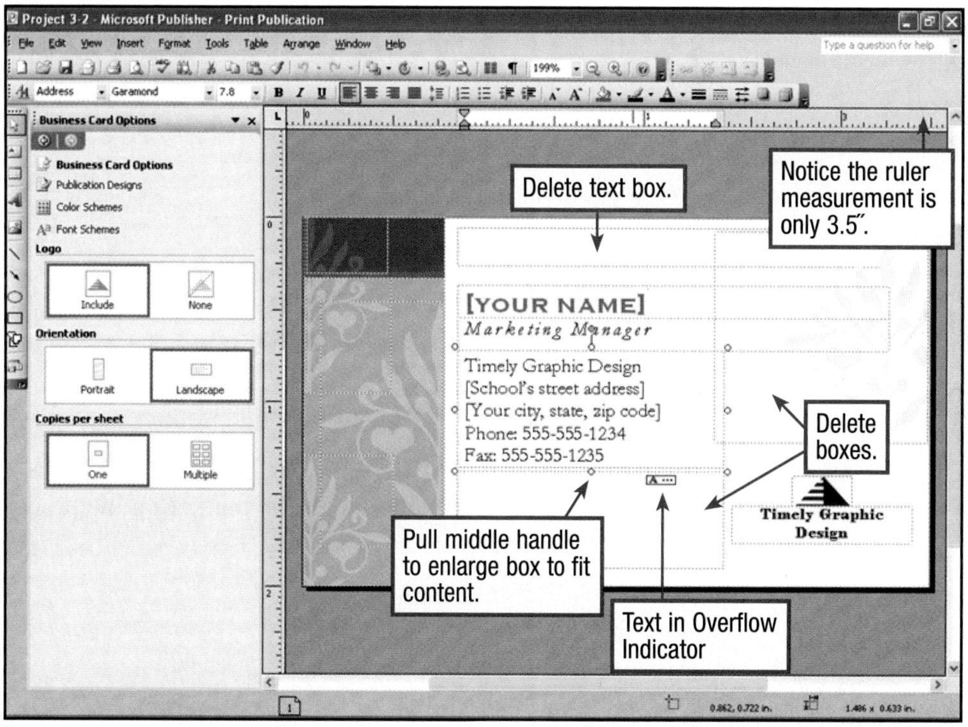

Instant Message

Check the Ruler Notice that the business card you are working on fills the screen. Check the measurement on the ruler. Your card is only 3½ inches wide and 2 inches high. Use the **Zoom Out** button to reduce the image to the card's actual size.

Chapter 9 Assessment

Reading Check	Critical Thinking
1. Define What is a timeline?	**6. Explain** Why is it important to establish project milestones?
2. Identify Name three different ways to avoid conflicts between team members.	**7. Compare and Contrast** What is the difference between a Win-Win conflict resolution strategy and an I-Win conflict resolution strategy?
3. Describe How can conflicts among team members be resolved?	**8. Describe** How can you help a team member who is falling behind schedule?
4. Explain Why is it important to use a flow chart to assign tasks to team members?	**9. Summarize** Describe three kinds of software that a project manager might need to use.
5. Summarize What are the responsibilities of a project manager?	**10. Analyze** What problems might arise if team members do not work well together?

1 Independent Practice

TEAM PROJECT **Create a New Product** Follow your teacher's instructions to form a group. You will be creating a company that is creating a brand new product. It might be a new video game, jackets with built-in MP3 players, or whatever you can dream of. You need to create the business package for the company and begin planning the marketing campaign for the product.

a. Plan Brainstorm ideas for a product and the name of your company.
- Describe the audience and the appropriate tone of the marketing materials that would appeal to your audience.
- Break the project into smaller tasks.
- Assign responsibility for each aspect of the project.
- Create a timeline.

b. Design Draw thumbnail sketches of a company logo and letterhead.
- Ask your teacher to evaluate your sketches.
- Revise your best sketches, as needed.

c. Create Create a business package that reflects your company's vision.
- Use Illustrator to create your logo.
- Use Publisher to create a business card and letterhead stationery.

d. Evaluate Exchange your work with another group, and evaluate each other's work for accuracy, visual appeal, and content. Follow your teacher's instructions for printing your publications.

Go Online RUBRICS
www.glencoe.com

Independent Practice
Go to **Chapter 9**, and choose **Rubrics**. Use the rubrics to help create and evaluate your projects.

Apply Layout Guides

9. Click **Arrange>Layout Guides**. In the **Grid Guides** tab, change **Columns** to **5** with **0 spacing**. Change **Rows** to **4** with **0 spacing**. Click **OK** (Figure 3.8).

10. Click **Arrange>Snap**. Make sure the **To Guides** option is checked, and then close the menu.

11. Hold SHIFT to select both the **Name** text box and the **Title** text box. A **Group Objects** icon should appear.

12. Click the **Group Objects** icon to group the text boxes as one object. (**Note**: If the **Group Objects** icon is not displayed, click **Arrange>Group**.)

13. Drag the **Name** and **Title** text boxes to the left and below the gridline, as shown in Figure 3.9. Resize the text box, if necessary.

14. Drag the **Address** text box down to the lower gridline and resize, if necessary. Format *Timely Graphic Design* in bold.

15. Drag the logo (the pyramid icon and organization name) to the top left corner, and resize it to fit. (**Hint:** Resize the height of the text box also). See Figure 3.9.

16. If the logo disappears behind the design, click the right side of the organization logo. Then click **Arrange>Order>Send to Front**.

▼ **Figure 3.8** Use layout guides to break the workspace into even spaces.

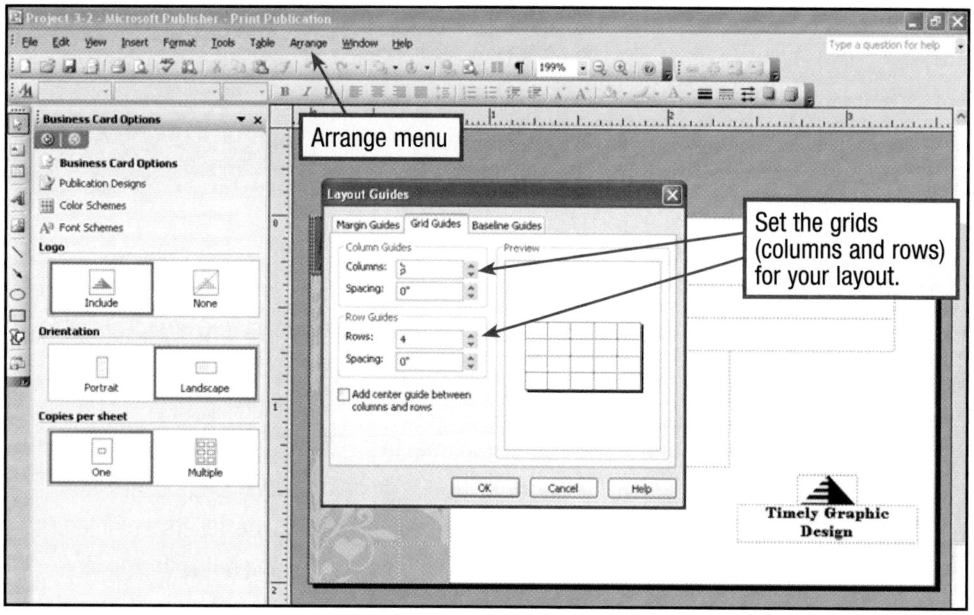

▼ **Figure 3.9** The layout guides make it easy to resize and align objects.

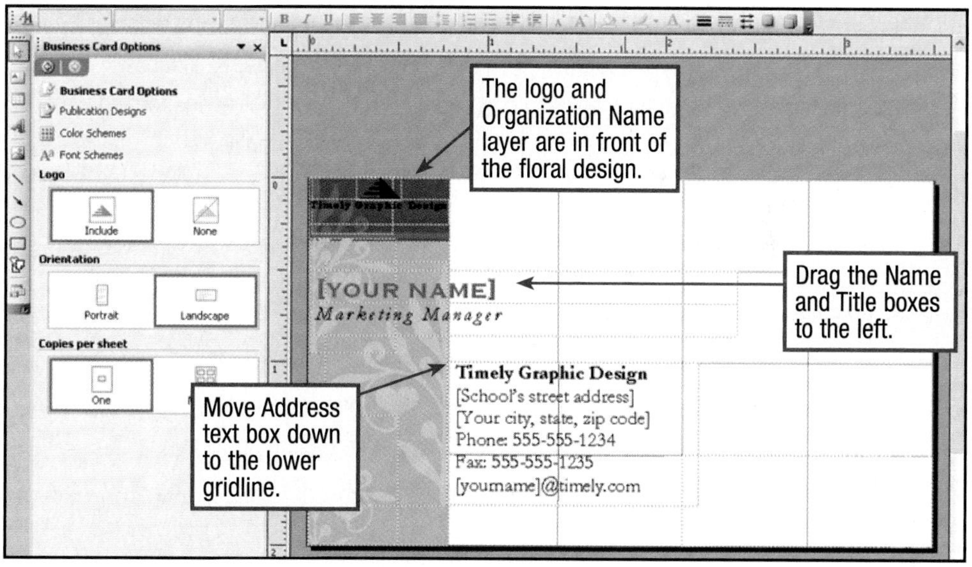

Instant Message

Size Text to Fit If the *Text in Overflow Indicator* is displayed, you can resize the text box to fit the text. However, if you have limited space, you might prefer to resize the text to fit the box. For example, the logo's organization name should shrink if there is not enough room for the text in the text box. To automatically resize text, click **Format>AutoFit Text>Best Fit**.

In The Workplace

Team Project Managers

Project managers supervise a team and are responsible for making sure that a project is created on time, within its budget, and that all the project elements are consistent with the clients' wishes. A marketing team might include graphic designers, layout artists, copywriters, photographers, Web designers, commercial directors, and other production and marketing staff.

On the Job

A project manager organizes workflow, makes sure each milestone is met, tracks expenses, and meets regularly with clients. Project managers in marketing and advertising work for advertising agencies, graphic design firms, publishing companies, broadcast stations, Internet companies, and in-house marketing departments. They are involved in creating print advertising, television commercials, billboards, Web sites, and other media.

Project managers may specialize in one industry, advertising medium, or market niche. In large companies, workers have specific roles. In smaller firms, jobs may be more fluid; the owner of an agency may also be its creative director and copywriter, or an art director might both manage projects and generate creative solutions.

Managers communicate with their teams using software such as Word and Outlook. Directors of design or publishing teams may work with design software like Photoshop and Illustrator, layout applications such as InDesign, and Web design applications like Dreamweaver. Project managers often use software like Microsoft Project or Excel to track scheduling and budgets.

Future Outlook

Companies are often in need of qualified project managers, but they often promote people to the position from within the company. For more information about this career, consult the following Web site:

- **Future Business Leaders of America (FBLA)** promotes leadership qualities and provides good training for future managers **(www.fbla.org).**

Training

A college degree or certificate in advertising, marketing, graphic design, or a related field can be earned at community colleges, universities, art schools, and specialized design programs. Business courses may also be helpful. Team leaders often are promoted from other positions after working in a company for several years.

Salary Range

Earnings for art directors and project managers range from $35,000 to $123,000 per year.

Skills and Talents

Team Project Managers must have:

Excellent communication skills.

Creativity and flexibility.

Knowledge of relevant software.

Knowledge of marketing, advertising, and public relations concepts.

Strategic thinking skills.

The ability to meet deadlines.

Career Activity

How do project managers ensure that a company's image is consistent?

17 Select the pyramid icon. Then right-click. From the drop-down menu, choose **Change Picture>From File**. Insert **Data File 3-2a**, a clock.

Change Brightness and Contrast

18 Select the clock. Click **Format>Picture>Picture** tab. Adjust the **Brightness** to **82%** and the **Contrast** to **95%**. Click **OK**.

19 To enlarge the clock without resizing the name, you must ungroup the logo. Select the logo, and click **Arrange>Ungroup**. When asked if you are sure you want to ungroup, click **Yes**.

20 Hold SHIFT and resize the clock to fit in the area (Figure 3.10). (**Note:** The image may look like it has a white background.)

Add a Background Image

21 Click outside the card. Click **Insert>Picture>From File** to insert **Data File 3-2b**. The clock image will cover your card.

22 With the clock picture selected, click **Arrange>Order>Send to Back**. Your card should appear over the picture (Figure 3.11).

▼ **Figure 3.10** Brightness and contrast can make your picture stand out.

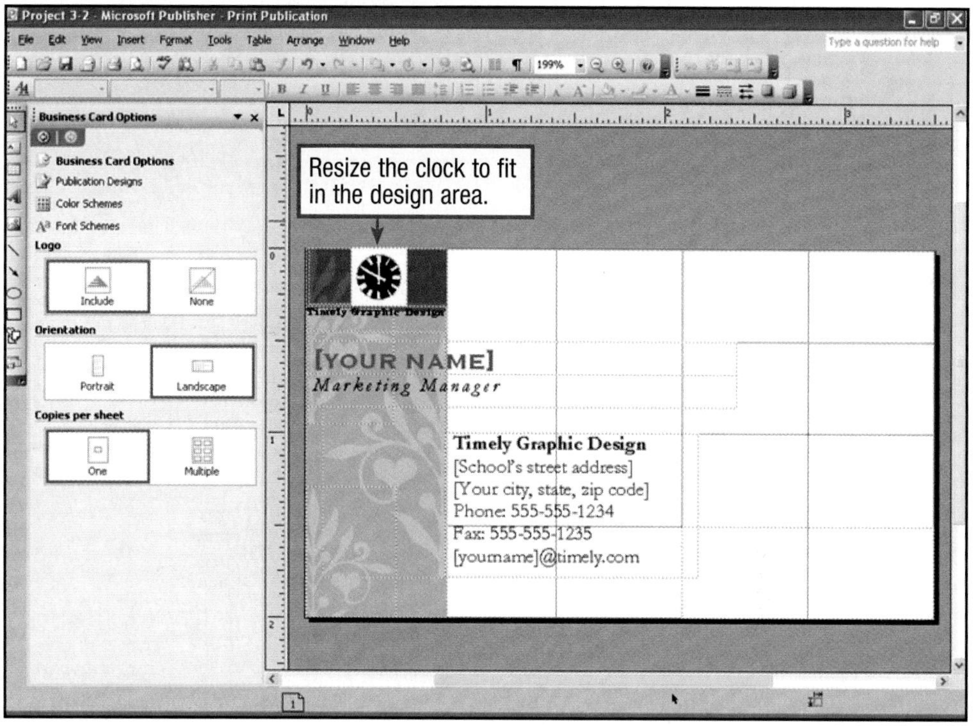

▼ **Figure 3.11** Bringing an object to the front or back rearranges the layers of text and graphics in a document.

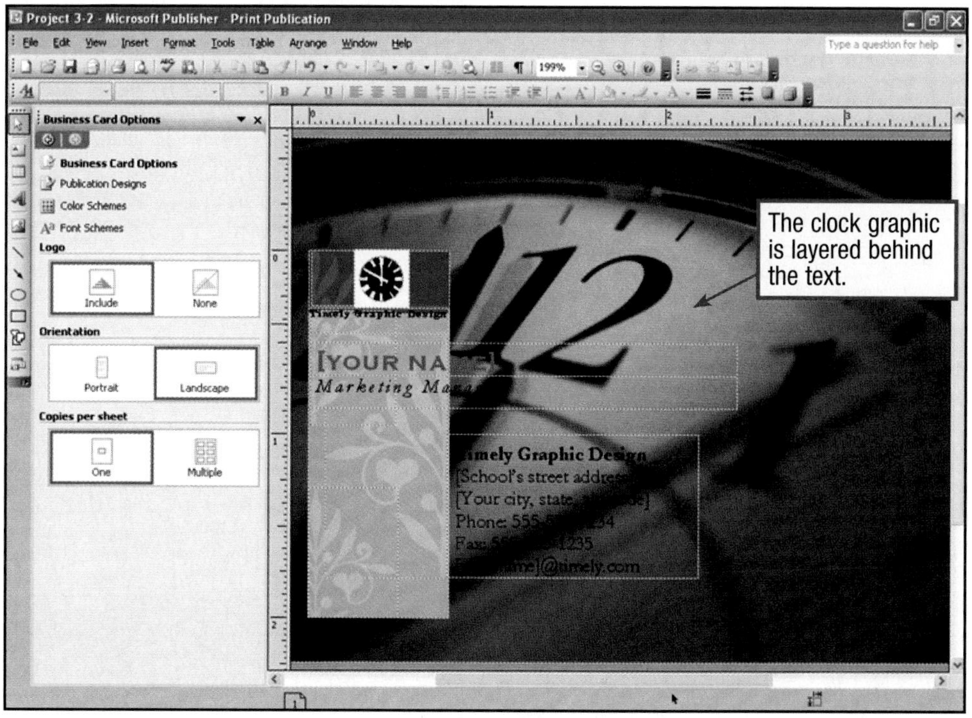

Merge the Data and Envelopes

6. In the Mail and Catalog Merge task pane, check that **Use an existing list** is marked under **Select data** source. Under Step 2 of 5, click **Next: Create your publication**.

7. Click the **Address block** link in the task pane. Choose the address name format that includes the title, complete first name, and complete last name (Figure 9.24). Click **Ok.**

8. On your envelope, the words *AddressBlock* appear with chevrons to indicate a merged field. Resize the address text box, if necessary.

9. At the bottom of the task pane, click **Next: Preview your publication**. Use the << and >> to view each addressed publication.

10. Click **Next: Complete the merge**. Then on the **Menu** bar, choose **File>Print Preview**. Close the dialog box.

11. Follow your teacher's instructions for saving and printing your publication.

▼ **Figure 9.24** The Address block link allows you to customize the address format. The preview box reflects your choices.

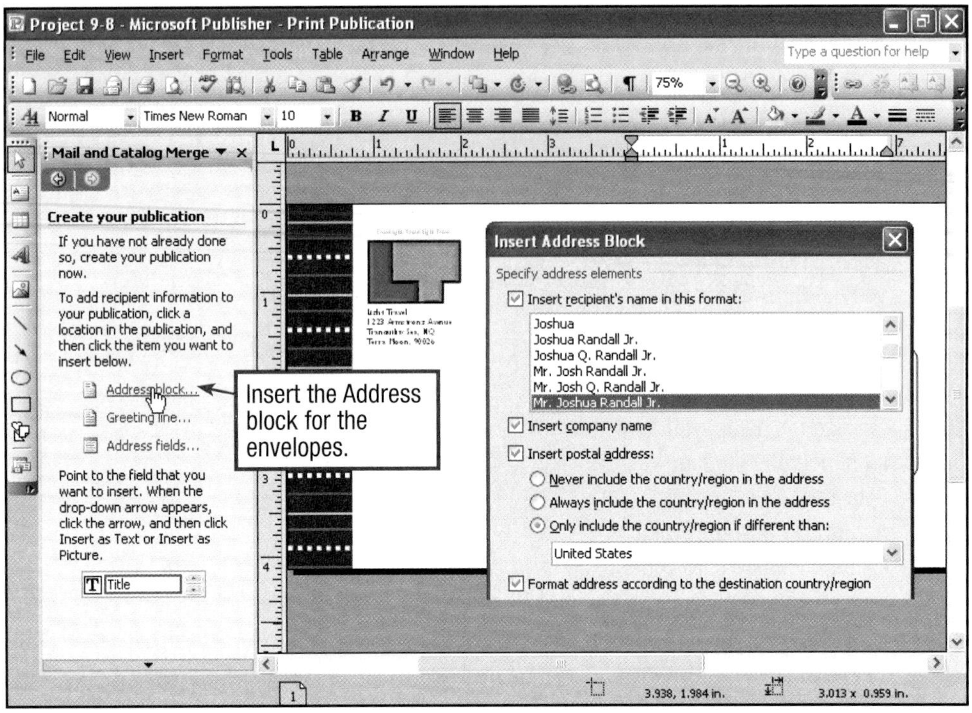

▼ **Figure 9.25** Use the previous publication and next publication arrows to view all the records in the merged publication.

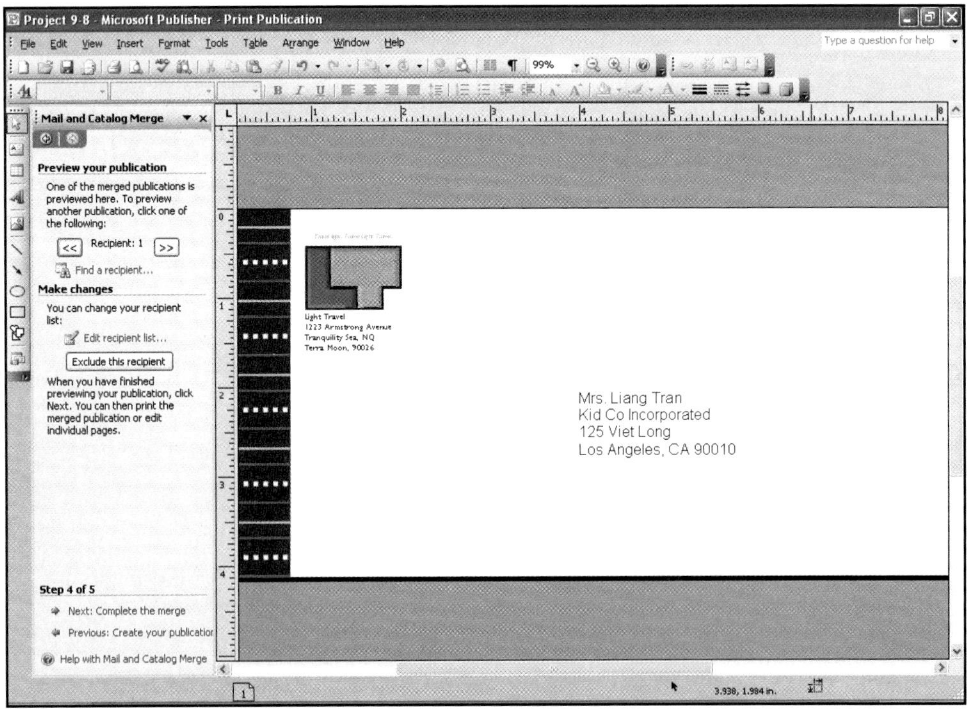

23 Click **Zoom Out** to see the edge of the clock picture. Resize the image to the approximate size of the card.

24 Crop excess parts of the picture. On the **Picture** toolbar, click **Crop**. Then click on the right corner picture handle, and drag inward (Figure 3.12).

25 On the **Picture** toolbar, click **Format Picture**.

26 In the **Picture** tab, under **Image Control**, choose **Washout** from the **Color** drop-down list. Click **OK**.

27 Follow your teacher's instructions for saving and printing your work.

Sidebar

Troubleshoot It is easy to fix common problems:

- If text moves, it might be trying to wrap around objects. Click **Arrange>Order>Bring to Front.**
- If text keeps resizing automatically, remove the Best Fit option by selecting the text, and clicking **Format>AutoFit Text>Do Not AutoFit.**
- If text is not breaking the way you want, click **Tools>Options>Edit tab** to turn off Automatic Hyphenation.

Explain What does AutoFit do?

Figure 3.12 The mouse pointer becomes a cropping tool when placed over a handle.

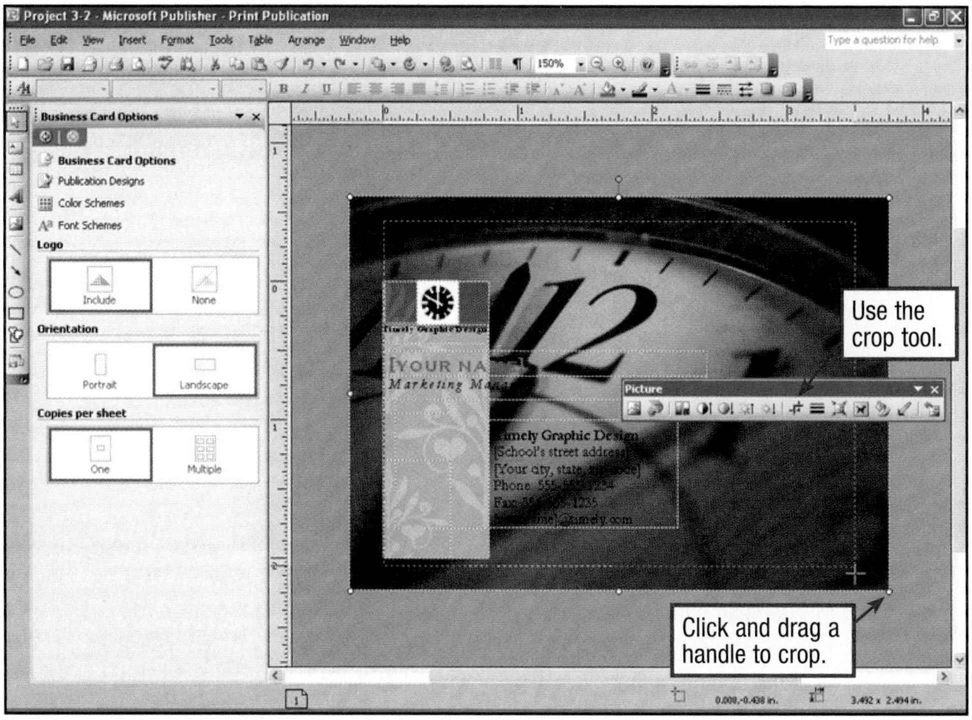

Figure 3.13 The final business card (approximate size).

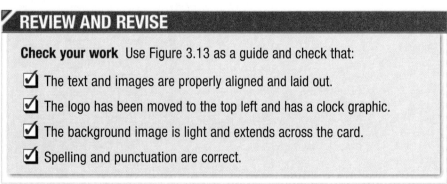

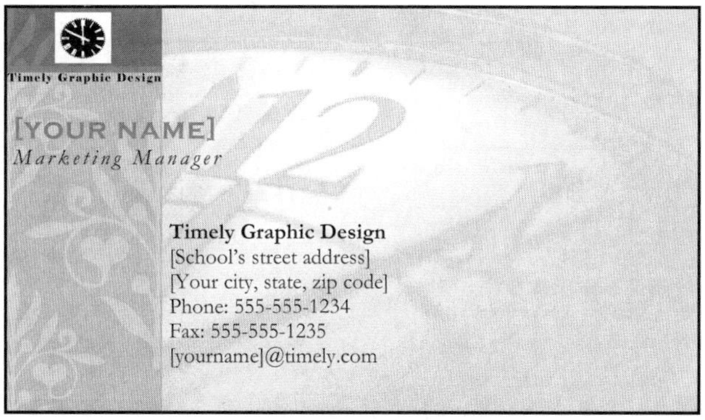

REVIEW AND REVISE

Check your work Use Figure 3.13 as a guide and check that:

- ☑ The text and images are properly aligned and laid out.
- ☑ The logo has been moved to the top left and has a clock graphic.
- ☑ The background image is light and extends across the card.
- ☑ Spelling and punctuation are correct.

Student Data File

Step-by-Step

1. In Publisher, open your envelope project created in **Project 9-7.** Save according to your teacher's instructions.

2. On the Menu bar, click **Tools>Mail and Catalog Merge>Mail and Catalog Merge Wizard (Figure 9.22).**

3. In the **Mail and Catalog Merge** task pane, click the **Mail Merge** radio button. Then click **Next: Select data source** at the bottom of the task pane.

Import a Data Source File

4. Click **Browse** under **Use an existing list**, and open **Data File 9-8**, an Access database file.

5. The **Mail Merge Recipients** dialog box is displayed (Figure 9.23). Click **OK**.

▼ **Figure 9.22** Use Publisher's Mail and Catalog Merge Wizard to generate individualized publications for mass mailings.

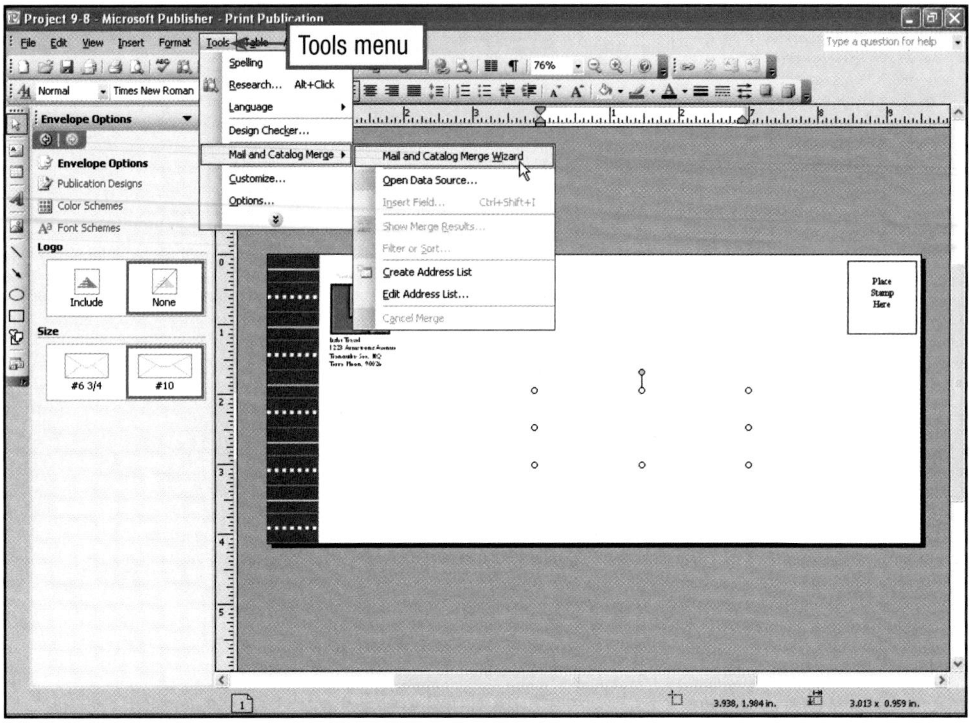

▼ **Figure 9.23** The data source is a list of names, companies, and addresses to use for a mass mailing.

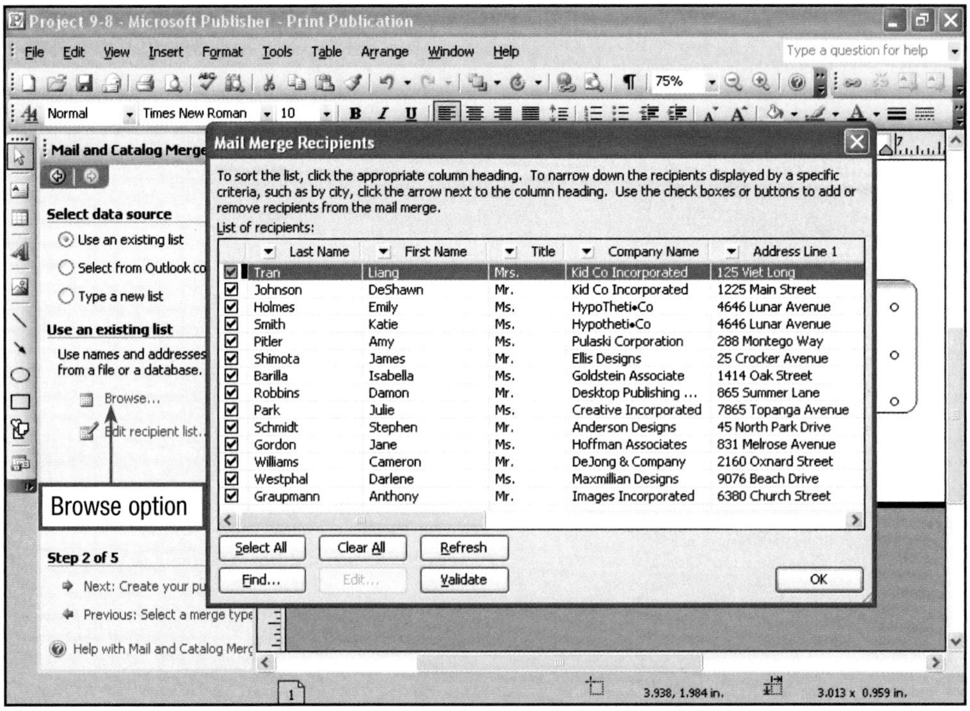

Lay Out a Business Envelope

1. In Publisher, choose **Publications from Print** and choose **Envelope**.
2. In the **Envelope Options** task pane, choose size **#10.** Delete all the objects on the template.
3. Click **Arrange>Layout** Guides. Change the **Margin Guides** to: **Top: .25″**, **Left: .5″**, **Right: .5″**, **Bottom: .625″**.
4. Add grid guides of **2 columns** with a **0 inch gutter** and **3 rows** with a **.2 inch gutter**. (Figure 9.20).
5. In the left margin, insert the same **Design Gallery** object used in your letterhead.

Add a Return Address

6. Insert the company logo that you created in Project 9-4 in the return address area.
7. Use a text box to key the company tagline.
8. Use text boxes to add the return address information and the name and address of the recipient.
9. In the postage area, create a 1 inch square text box. Key and center the following: Place Stamp Here.
10. Follow your teacher's instructions for saving and printing the envelope.

▼ **Figure 9.20** Use Publisher's grid guides to design your business envelope.

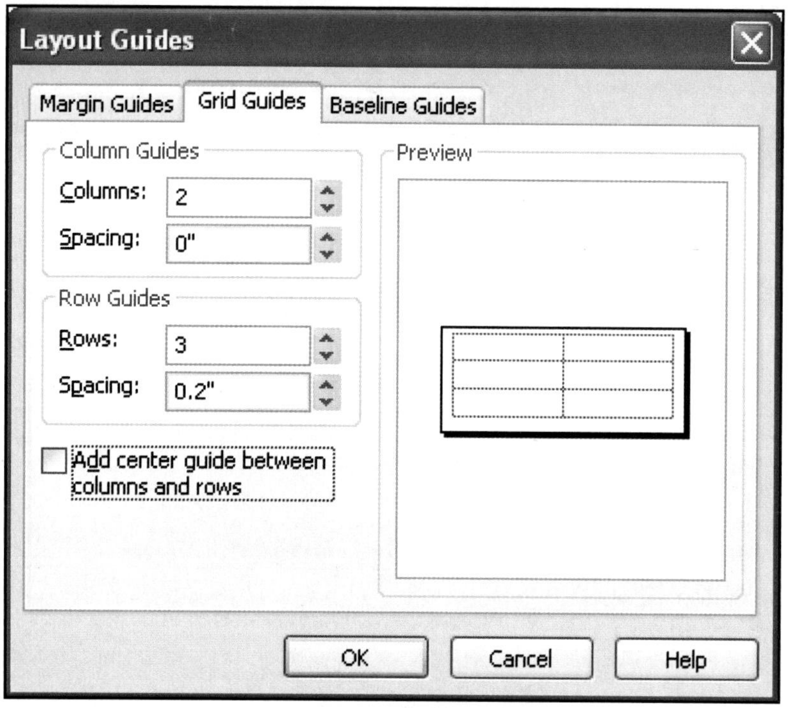

▼ **Figure 9.21** Contact information and similar design elements are repeated.

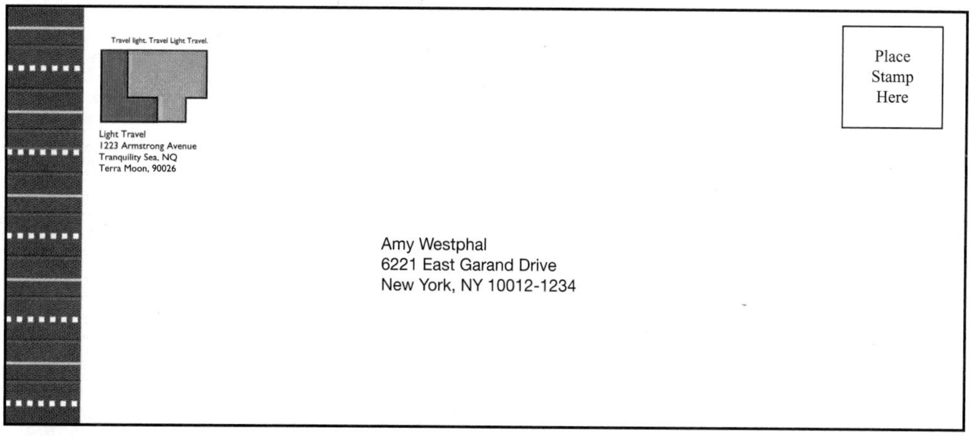

REVIEW AND REVISE

Check your work Use Figure 9.21 as a guide and check that:

- ☑ The envelope follows the United States Postal Service guidelines.
- ☑ The envelope includes the name, street address, and city, state, and ZIP code on separate lines.
- ☑ A text box is added to indicate where the stamp will go.

Student Data File

Step-by-Step

1. In the **New Publication** task pane, click **Blank Publications**, **Full Page**. Save according to your teacher's instructions.

2. Choose **Arrange>Layout Guides>Margin Guides**. Set the **Left**, **Right**, and **Bottom margins** at **0.5″**.

3. Click the **Grid Guides** tab, and set **4 columns** and **10 rows** with **0″ spacing**.

Insert and Format WordArt

4. On the **Object** toolbar, click **Insert WordArt** [icon]. Choose the style shown in Figure 3.14.

5. In the **Edit WordArt Text** box, change the font to **Berlin Sans FB 36 pt** and key Baby-Sitter.

6. On the **WordArt** toolbar, choose **Format WordArt**. (If the toolbar is not displayed, click **View>Toolbars>WordArt**.) In the **Format WordArt** box, choose the **Color and Lines** tab. Change the **Fill Color** to **Fill Effects**.

7. In the **Gradient** tab under **Colors**, click **Preset**. Under **Preset colors**, choose **Ocean**. (Figure 3.15).

▼ **Figure 3.14** Layout guides help when you create a document without a template.

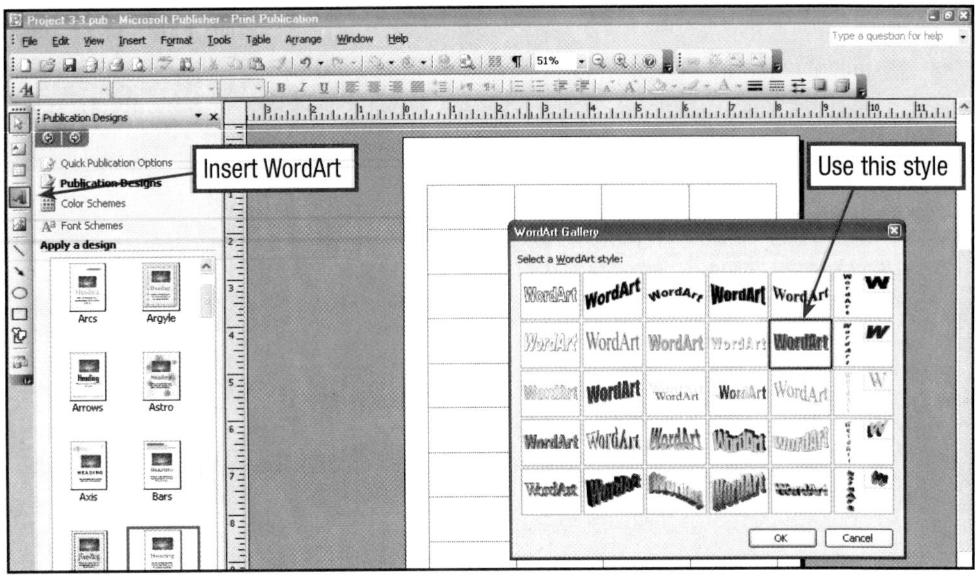

▼ **Figure 3.15** WordArt tools in Publisher are very similar to those in Word.

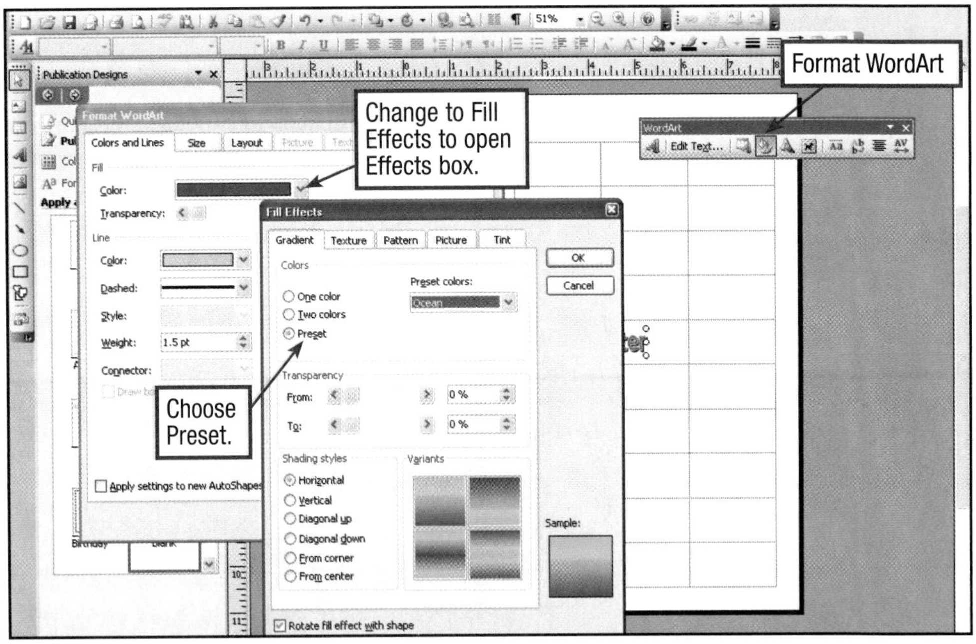

Instant Message

Turn Off Hyphenation If you do not want words to be broken between two lines, remember that you can turn off the automatic hyphenation feature. Select the text within the text box by pressing CTRL + A, then click **Tools >Language>Hyphenation**. Remove the check from the automatic hyphenation. This feature does not work on WordArt text.

Project 9-8

Perform a Mail Merge

Spotlight on Skills

- Import a data source file
- Merge the data and envelopes

Key Terms

- mailing list
- mail merge
- data source
- main publication
- import

Academic Focus

Science
Apply a database

Now that you have created a business package, you are ready to send a customized mass mailing to all the potential customers that might be interested in a vacation on Mars. You have collected the names and addresses of people on a **mailing list**, which is a list of intended recipients. A mailing list can have fewer than fifty names or be as large as several thousand names. Publisher's Mail Merge tools make it easy and quick to create individualized letters, envelopes, or personalized mailing labels.

A **mail merge** is a process that creates personalized letters and envelopes in a mass mailing. Rather than having a general greeting, a form letter can be addressed to the individual receiving it. Companies can automatically generate personally addressed communications to customers, business associates, or any large group.

With Publisher, you can add customer mailing addresses and other information onto the publication itself, or you create mailing labels and then place the labels on the publication. The mail merge process requires a **data source**, or a database of names, addresses, and other useful information, and a **main publication** with unchanging text, punctuation, spacing, and graphics. The first step in preparing a mass mailing is to create the data source.

The data source can be created within Publisher, or data can come from another application. You can **import**, or bring in data from other applications such as an Excel spreadsheet, an Access database, a Word table, or even a Contacts list from Outlook. The information in the data source is variable, changing as records are edited, added, or deleted. The table below shows data formats that can be imported to Publisher.

Although it may take a while to create a database, once it is done it is easy to add names or make changes. You can also send mailings to the whole group, or create smaller sub-groups for sending different types of communications.

Data Formats

Software Application	File Extension
Microsoft Access	.mdb
Microsoft Excel	.xls
Microsoft Outlook	.pst
Microsoft Word tables or merge data documents	.doc

► **In this project,** you will use Access database table as the data source to perform a mail merge. The mail merge will generate individualized envelopes to mail a publication or other communication.

Project 3-3 Add Tear-Offs to a Flyer

Spotlight on Skills

- Insert and format WordArt
- Create and format a bulleted list
- Flip an image
- Insert a Design Gallery object
- Create tear-offs

Key Terms

- tear-off
- synchronization

Academic Focus

Language Arts
Use parallel structure in a list

Design Gallery Objects

One of Publisher's most helpful features is the **Design Gallery Object** tool. The Design Gallery contains objects like formatted advertisements, sidebars, logos, calendars, and nameplates. These pieces can be used to build a newsletter, brochure, or flyer. Each Design Gallery object works like a miniature template with its fill-in-the-blank text boxes.

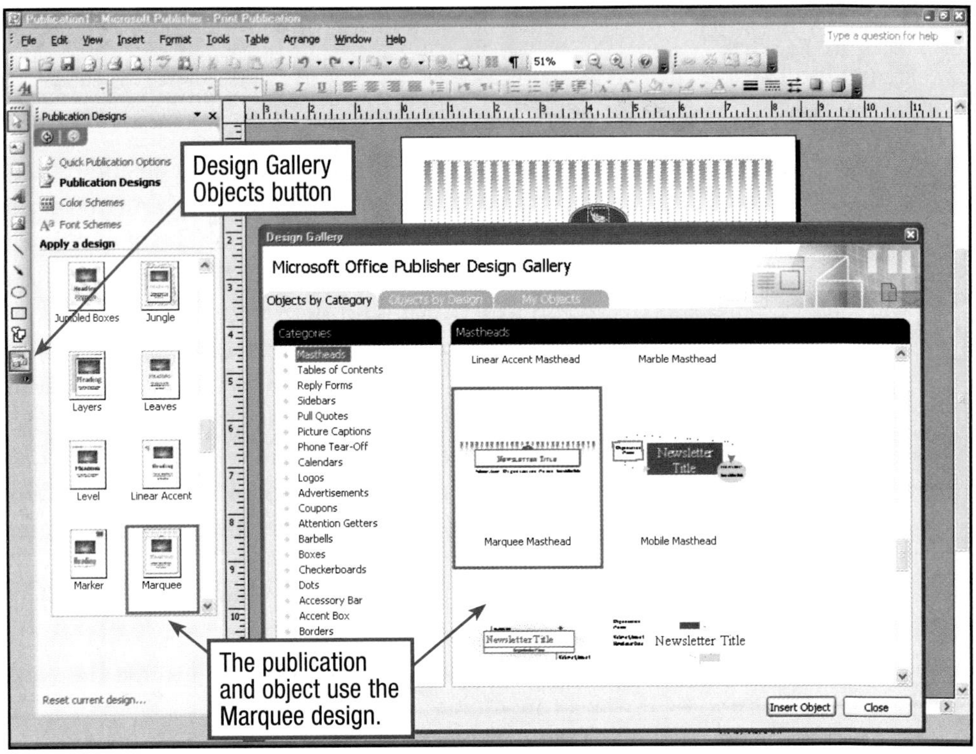

▲ Design Gallery objects can match the design of the publication.

Tear-offs If you ever need to advertise a business or want to sell a product or service, you might find it useful to include a Design Gallery object called a tear-off. A **tear-off** is a tab that can easily be torn off a flyer or advertisement and contains contact information such as an address or phone number.

Tear-offs can be edited easily using Publisher's **synchronization** tool. When you edit a synchronized object, all the related objects automatically change to display the same information. With tear-offs, you only have to enter the contact information in one tab, and it will be copied automatically.

▶ **In this project,** you will create a flyer advertising babysitting services. The flyer will include tear-offs at the bottom.

8. Resize the WordArt across all four columns of the document, stretching it from margin to margin. Move it to the second row.

9. On the **Object** toolbar, click **Text Box** [icon]. Create a text box that stretches across **columns 2–3** in the **first row**, above the WordArt.

10. In this new text box, click **Center** [icon]. In a **serif font**, key Need to go shopping?. Press [ENTER]. Key Want to go to a movie? (Figure 3.16).

11. Select all of the text in the text box. On the Formatting toolbar, click **Increase Font Size** [icon] until the text fills the box.

Create and Format a Bulleted List

12. Create a text box that spans **rows 3–7** and **columns 3–4**. Use the same font as Step 11 to key the list in Figure 3.17 without bullets. Increase the font size to fit the text box.

13. Select the list. Click **Format>Bullets and Numbering**, and choose a bullet character. Click the **Character** button.

14. Change the font to **Wingdings**. Choose a graphic to use as a bullet, and then click **OK**.

15. Change the size of the bullet to match the font size. Click **OK** (Figure 3.17).

▼ **Figure 3.16** Objects fit into the gridlines like puzzle pieces.

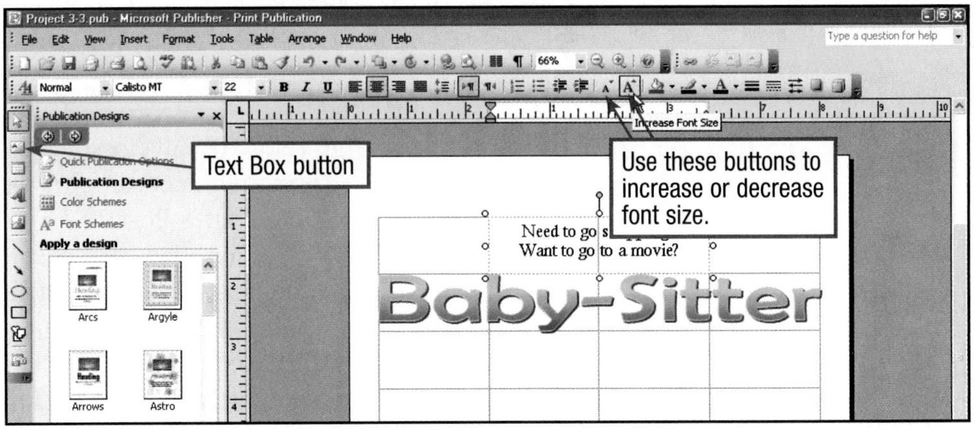
Text Box button
Use these buttons to increase or decrease font size.
Increase Font Size
Need to go shopping?
Want to go to a movie?
Baby-Sitter

▼ **Figure 3.17** Key the list in the text box you create in Step 12.

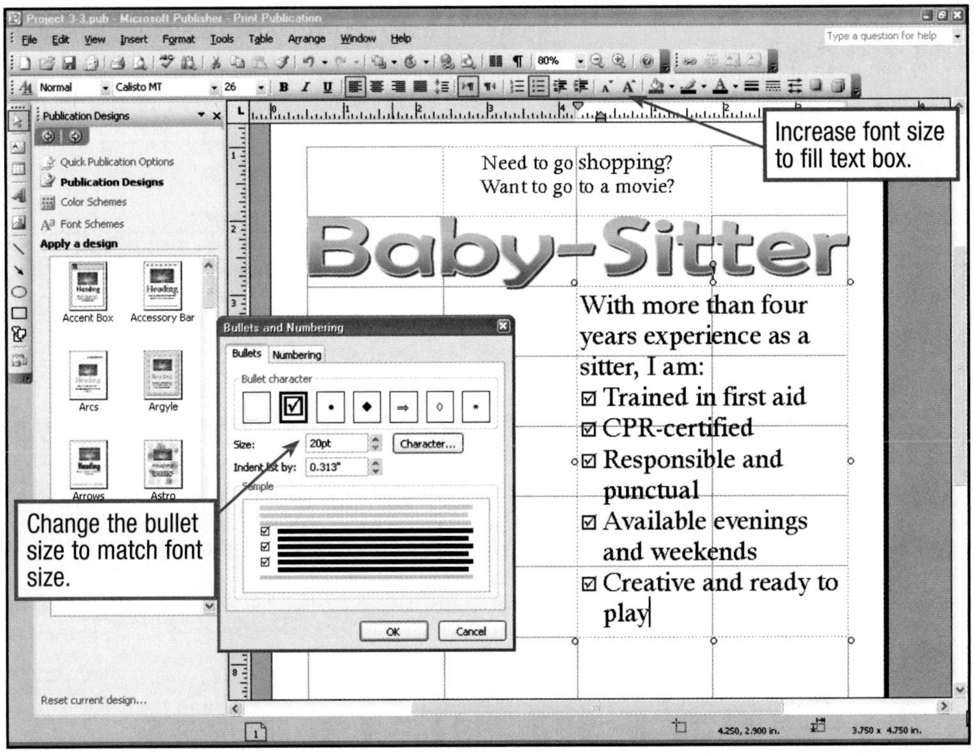
Increase font size to fill text box.
Need to go shopping?
Want to go to a movie?
Baby-Sitter
With more than four years experience as a sitter, I am:
Trained in first aid
CPR-certified
Responsible and punctual
Available evenings and weekends
Creative and ready to play
Bullets and Numbering
Change the bullet size to match font size.

Instant Message

Use Parallel Wording When you create a bulleted list, make sure the items in the list use a parallel structure. For example, in the list above, each bulleted item is a descriptive phrase that sounds correct when added after *I am*. An additional phrase such as *References available upon request* would not be part of the list because it uses a different structure from the other items.

Skills Studio

Project 9-7 Design Business Envelopes

Skills You Will Apply

- Lay out a business envelope
- Add a return address

Academic Focus

Math
Lay out on a grid

A standard large (No. 10) envelope is 9½ inches by 4½ inches. The envelope should be formatted according to the guidelines for business mail developed by the United States Postal Service **(www.usps.com).**

The Postal Service recommends that envelopes be formatted in all capital letters without punctuation marks. Automated mail processing machines read the addresses on envelopes from the bottom up. The equipment will first look for a city, state, and ZIP Code. If you do not know the ZIP code, you can find the information on the United States Postal Service Web site.

Next, the machines look for the delivery address. The delivery address should be on a separate line from the city, state, and ZIP code. Any information that is below the delivery address line such as a logo, a slogan, or an attention line) can confuse the machines and misdirect your mail.

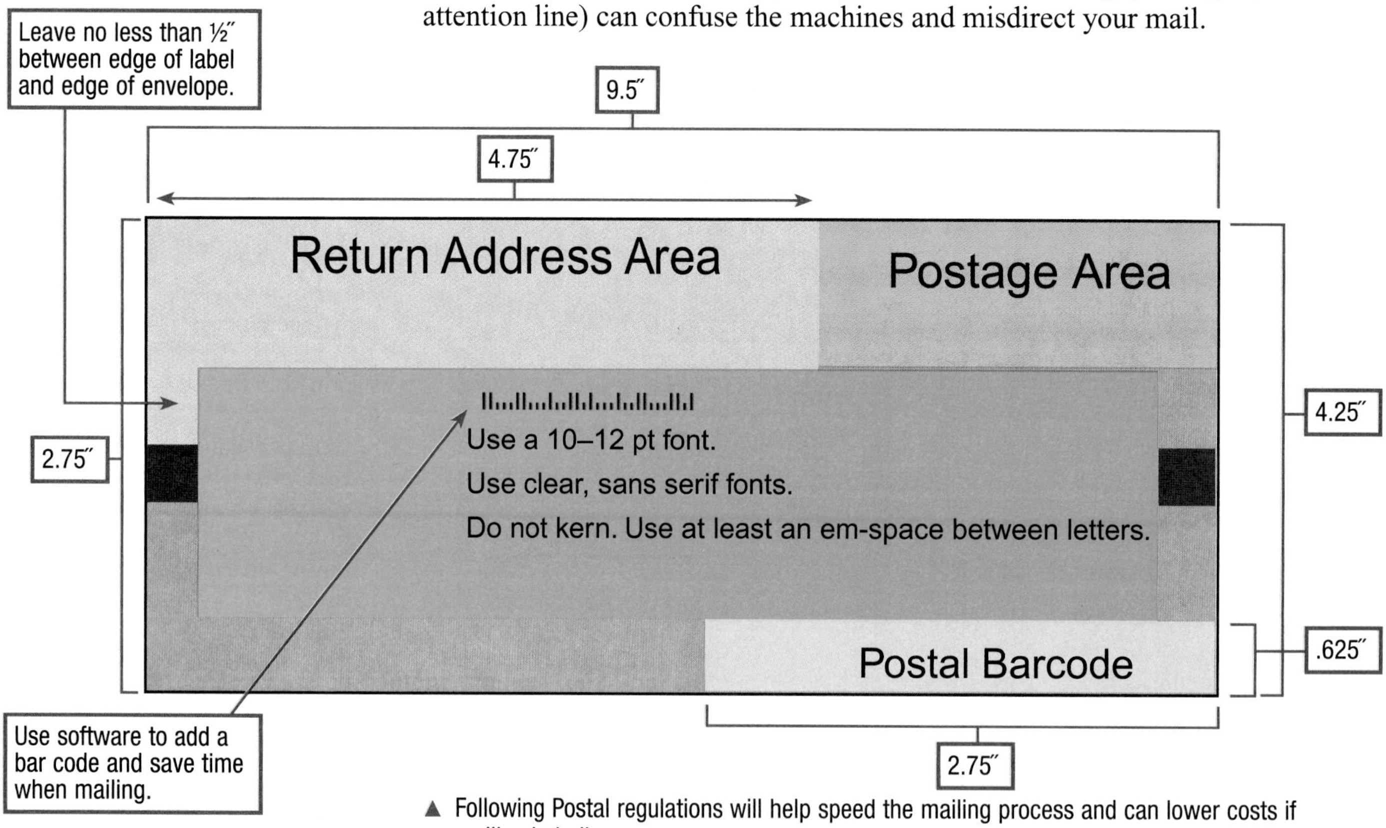

Leave no less than ½″ between edge of label and edge of envelope.
9.5″
4.75″
Return Address Area
Postage Area
Use a 10–12 pt font.
Use clear, sans serif fonts.
Do not kern. Use at least an em-space between letters.
2.75″
4.25″
Postal Barcode
.625″
Use software to add a bar code and save time when mailing.
2.75″

▲ Following Postal regulations will help speed the mailing process and can lower costs if mailing in bulk.

▶ **In this project,** you will complete your business package. The business envelope will include the logo and design elements used on your business card and business letterhead. You will use the layout grid to help you set up usable space for the envelope.

16 Click outside the text box. Insert the clip art from **Data File 3-3**. Resize the picture so that it fills **columns 1–2**, **rows 3–7** (Figure 3.18).

Flip an Image

17 Your clip art should face the text to direct attention to the information. Flip the picture by selecting it and clicking **Arrange>Rotate or Flip>Flip Horizontal**.

18 Create another text box at **row 8**, spanning **columns 2–3**. Use a **sans serif font**, **center**, and key Contact Laura Gilbert [ENTER] 555-555-1234 (Figure 3.19).

19 Select the text box. Click **Format>AutoFit Text>Best Fit** to enlarge the text to fit the frame (Figure 3.19).

Insert a Design Gallery Object

20 On the Object toolbar, click **Design Gallery Object** [icon]. Choose **Phone Tear-Off**, and click the Phone Tear-Off object.

21 Click **Insert Object**. Drag the tear-off object to the bottom row.

▼ **Figure 3.18** Flip your picture so it faces towards important information.

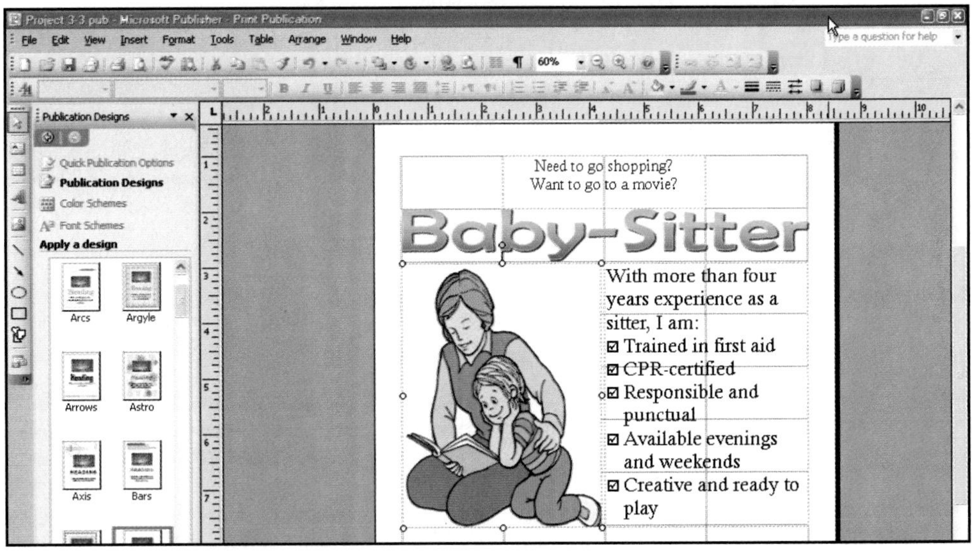

▼ **Figure 3.19** Place the tear-offs at the bottom of the page.

Instant Message

Change Your View Zoom out to view an overall layout.

- Press [CTRL] and roll the wheel on your mouse, or
- Press the [F9] key, or
- Click **Zoom Out** [icon] on the **Standard** toolbar.

Step-by-Step

Lay Out a Letterhead

1. In Microsoft Publisher, create a new, blank document.
2. Click **Arrange>Layout Guides**. Set all margins to **0.25 inches.**
3. Add the same **Design Gallery** object you used for the business card (a marquee or accessory bar).

Insert a Logo

4. Insert the company logo in a prominent position at the top of the page.
5. Use text boxes to add the company name, address, and contact information.
6. Use a text box to key the company tagline Travel Light. Travel Light Travel to All Your Favorite Vacation Destinations..
7. Add a dominant design element such as a bold line to help separate the logo and text from the rest of the page.
8. Size the letterhead so it does not take up too much space. Most of the space needs to remain empty for the letter content.
9. Follow your teacher's instructions for saving and printing your work.

▼ **Figure 9.18** Use margins to guide you as you place text and objects at the top of the page.

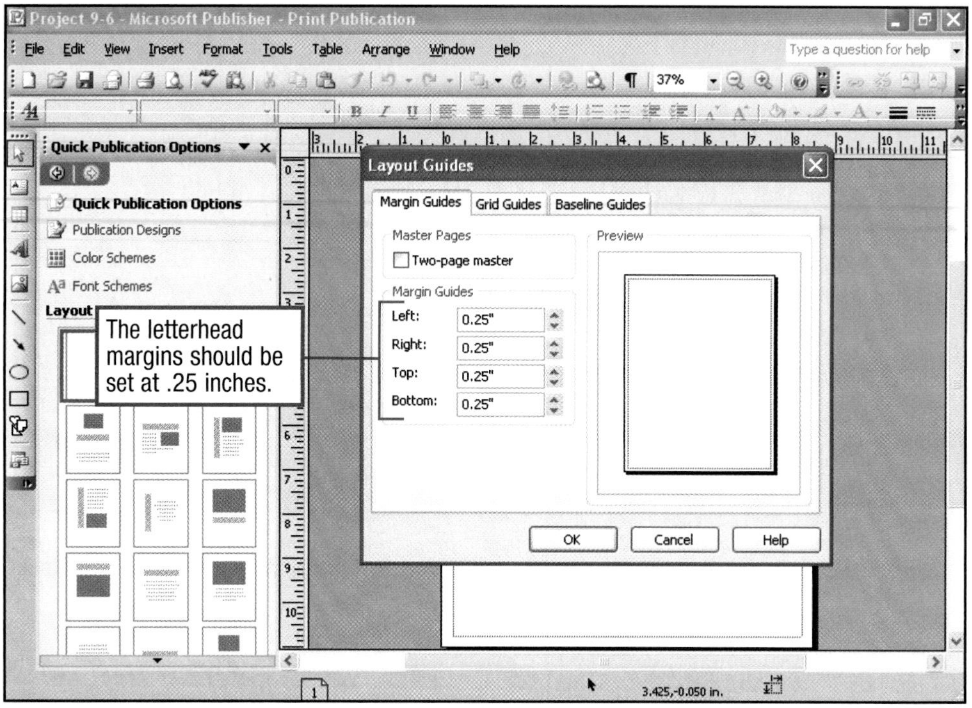

▼ **Figure 9.19** Contact information and similar design elements help the reader to easily identify the company.

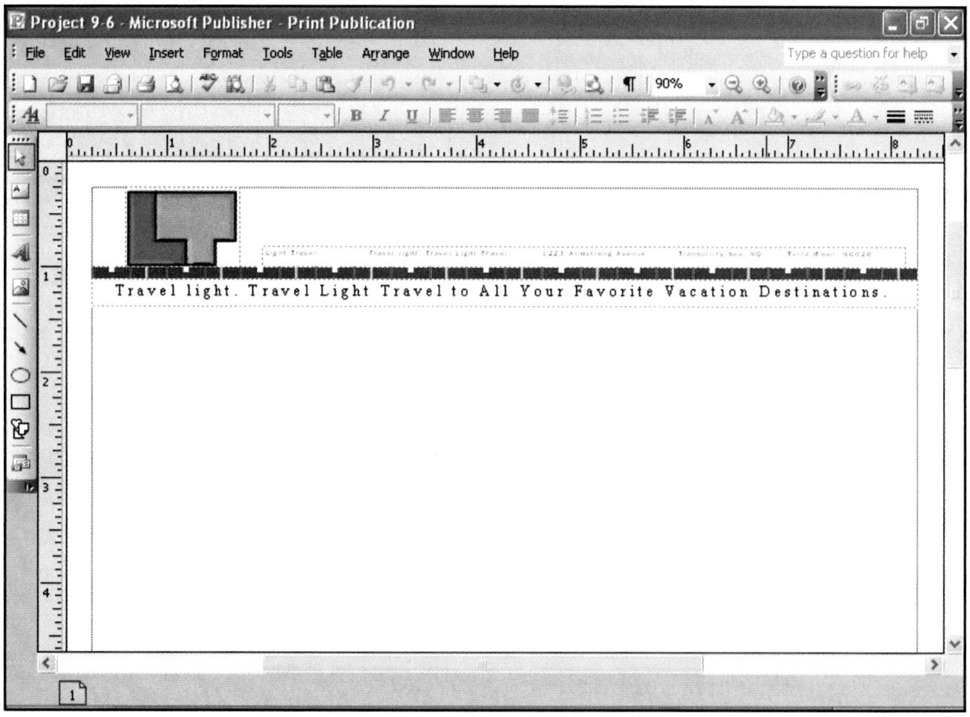

Create Tear-Offs

22 **Copy** the information from the text box you created in **Step 18**. Then select the text in a tear-off and **paste** (Figure 3.20).

23 Select the text, and resize the text with the **AutoFit** tool.

24 Click outside the tear-off frame. All the tear-offs will display the same information!

25 Pull the **middle right handle** of the tear-off frame to stretch the tear-offs across the bottom of the flyer. More tear-offs will be added.

26 Click **View>Boundaries and Guides** to hide the boundaries. Hold ALT, and use the arrow keys to nudge objects up or down to adjust white space.

27 Evaluate your design. Follow your teacher's instructions for saving and printing your flyer.

▼ **Figure 3.20** The final product. Use this image to help you proof your design.

Need to go shopping?
Want to go to a movie?

Baby-Sitter

With more than four years experience as a sitter, I am:

☑ Trained in first aid
☑ CPR-certified
☑ Responsible and punctual
☑ Available evenings and weekends
☑ Creative and ready to play

Contact Laura Gilbert
555-555-1234

Contact Laura Gilbert 555-555-1234
Contact Laura Gilbert 555-555-1234
Contact Laura Gilbert 555-555-1234
Contact Laura Gilbert 555-555-1234
Contact Laura Gilbert 555-555-1234
Contact Laura Gilbert 555-555-1234
Contact Laura Gilbert 555-555-1234
Contact Laura Gilbert 555-555-1234
Contact Laura Gilbert 555-555-1234
Contact Laura Gilbert 555-555-1234

REVIEW AND REVISE

Check your work Use Figure 3.20 as a guide and check that:

☑ The text and images are properly aligned and laid out.

☑ Text is sized properly to the text box.

☑ WordArt is Ocean colored and extends the width of the page.

☑ The bullets in the list are Wingdings font.

☑ The image has been flipped to face the bulleted list.

☑ Tear-offs contain the correct contact information and extend across the width of the page.

☑ Spelling and punctuation are correct.

Project 9-6 — Design Business Letterhead

Company letterhead is used to indicate to the reader that a message is official. A **letterhead** is the heading at the top of stationery which usually contains a name and address. Businesses often include a logo and company colors in the letterhead. While contact information can be designed to be on the top, bottom, or one of the sides, it should never interfere with the ability to write and print a letter.

Skills You Will Apply

- Lay out a letterhead
- Insert a logo

Key Term

- letterhead

Academic Focus

Language Arts
Add descriptive text

Include company name, logo, and contact information.

A dominant design element should be repeated throughout the business package.

The company tagline (slogan) is often included on the business stationery.

Some companies include graphics, contact information, or company product listings at the bottom of the letterhead.

Light Travel *Travel light. Travel Light Travel.* 1223 Armstrong Avenue Tranquility Sea, NQ Terra Moon, 73620

Travel light. Travel Light Travel to All Your Favorite Vacation Destinations.

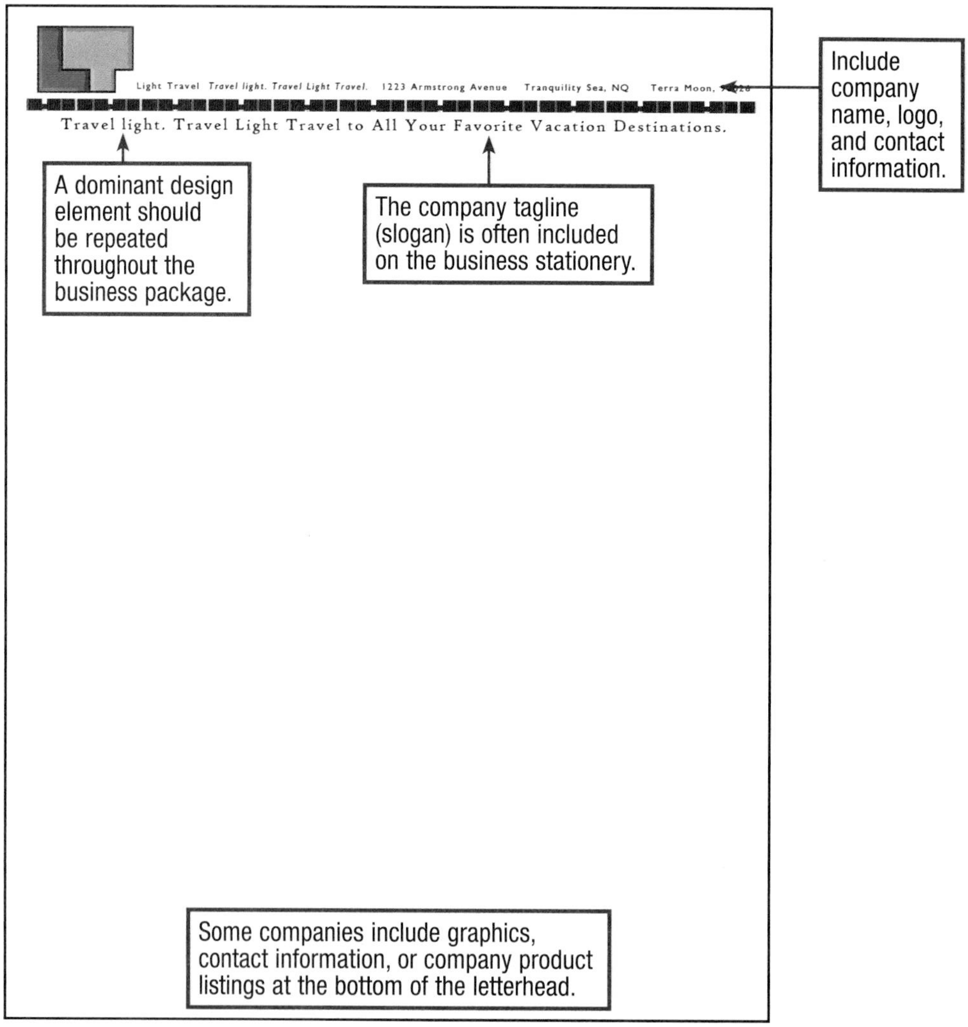

► Most of the space on a business letterhead is needed for the content of the letter.

► **In this project,** you will create the business letterhead for Light Travel, again using the logo you created in Project 9-4. You will incorporate some of the design elements that you used on your business card. Although you have been given an example, you can use the directions to create your own letterhead design.

Project 3-4 Create a Coupon Mailer

Spotlight on Skills

- Create a custom-size document
- Crop an image
- Create a coupon
- Insert and resize dingbats

Key Term

- dingbat

Academic Focus

Language Arts
Create an advertisement

In Project 3-3, you added tear-offs to a flyer by using a Design Gallery object. The Design Gallery is an easy way to create tear-offs because they would require a lot of formatting if made from scratch. Coupons are also Design Gallery objects. Unlike tear-offs, however, coupons are relatively easy to create from scratch.

▲ Coupons can be printed or posted online.

Coupons are often used by merchants and businesses to attract customers and to track the effectiveness of advertising. They can be included as part of a larger flyer, or the entire coupon can be a separate document. Many companies now include coupons on their Web sites for special online promotions.

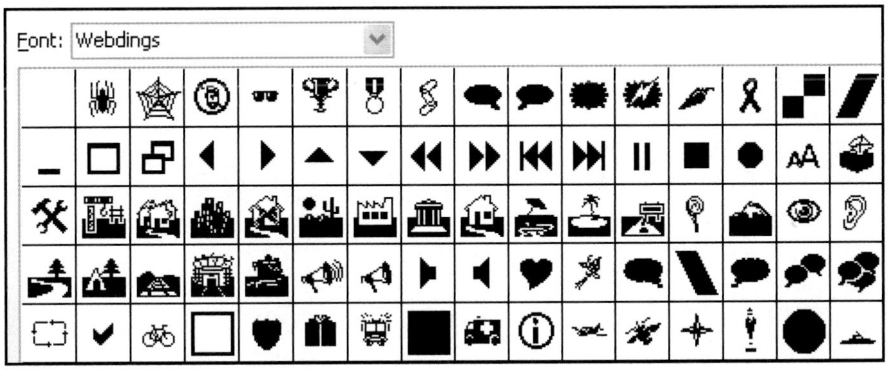

▲ Dingbats can draw readers' attention in a publication.

Notice the scissors on the dotted line in the coupon; this type of font is called a dingbat. A **dingbat** is a font represented by a symbol or picture. To find dingbats, you can choose to insert a symbol and then select a font such as Webdings.

▶ **In this project,** you will create an advertisement flyer that contains a clip-out coupon.

Sidebar

Dingbat Fonts Dingbat fonts are similar to clip art. These small graphics are stored on your computer like any other font, but they are not used for reading. You can find them in your font list with names like Marlette, Bookshelf Symbol, Webdings, and Wingdings. Some may not even be readable in your font window. Scroll through Publisher's font menu to see what is available.

Draw Conclusions When might you want to use a dingbat font?

Skills Studio

Reinforce Your Skills

- **Project 9-6**
  - Lay out a letterhead
  - Insert a logo
- **Project 9-7**
  - Lay out a business envelope
  - Add a return address
- **Project 9-8**
  - Import a data source file
  - Merge the data and envelopes

Go Online ACTIVITIES

www.glencoe.com

Challenge Yourself Go to **Chapter 9**, and choose **Enrichment Activities** for more practice with the skills you have learned.

Design Business Stationery

The following three projects will take you through the steps you need to create business stationery.

- **Project 9-6** Design business letterhead
- **Project 9-7** Design business envelopes
- **Project 9-8** Perform a mail merge

Correspond with Class

Just as you choose personal stationery that expresses a sense of your personality, companies create letterhead stationery that represents the way they want to be perceived by customers. A firm that wants to emphasize traditional values would have stationery that looks very different from that of a company that designs trendy clothes.

With the popularity of online businesses, letterhead stationery may not seem as important as it once was. Yet even Internet-based businesses must use regular mail at times. Companies may follow up with a customer to check customer satisfaction, send promotional material, or resolve problems. Business contacts with suppliers, contractors, and partners often require letters.

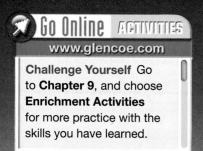

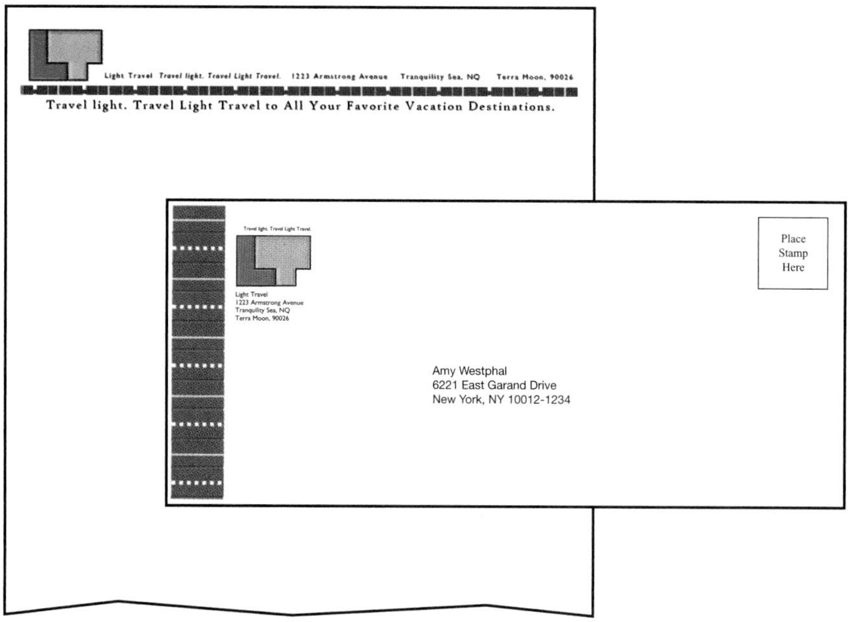

The same design that is created for a letterhead can be used on envelopes, on postcards, and even on the address portion of marketing brochures or newsletters. Once a company creates a recognizable branding, it should use it on all forms of communication.

Student Data File

Step-by-Step

1. Open Microsoft Publisher, and choose **Blank Publications>Full Page**.

Create a Custom-Size Document

2. Click **File>Page Setup>Layout** tab. Under **Publication type**, choose **Custom**. Change the **Width** to **8.25″** and the **Height** to **3.5″**.

3. Click **Change Copies per Sheet**, and then choose **Print one copy per sheet**. Click **OK** until you return to the workspace (Figure 3.21).

4. Click **Arrange>Layout Guides>Margin Guides** tab. Change the margin to **0.25″** for all sides. Click **OK**.

5. Click **Arrange>Layout Guides>Grid Guides** tab. Set **2 columns** with **0.1″ spacing**. Set **4 rows** with **0″ spacing**.

6. On the **Object** toolbar, click **Picture Frame**, and choose **Picture from File**. Drag a frame over the left column.

Crop an Image

7. Insert **Data File 3-4.** Resize the picture, and crop if necessary to fit the space (Figure 3.22).

Figure 3.21 This custom size normally prints three copies per page.

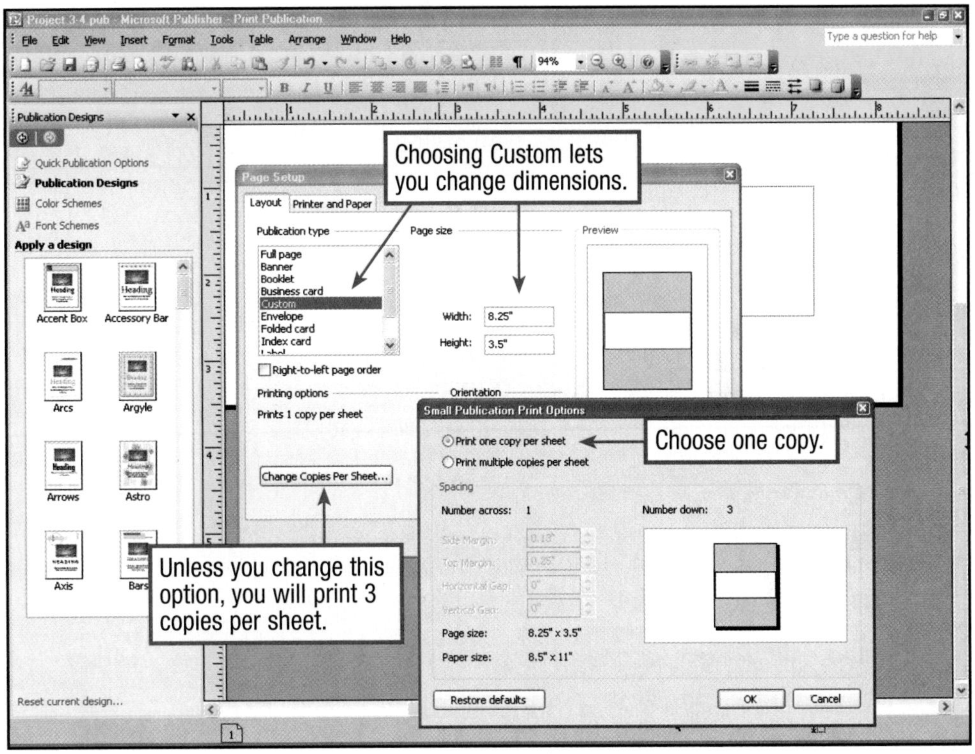

Choosing Custom lets you change dimensions.
Choose one copy.
Unless you change this option, you will print 3 copies per sheet.

Figure 3.22 Resize and crop the photo so the image fits the grid.

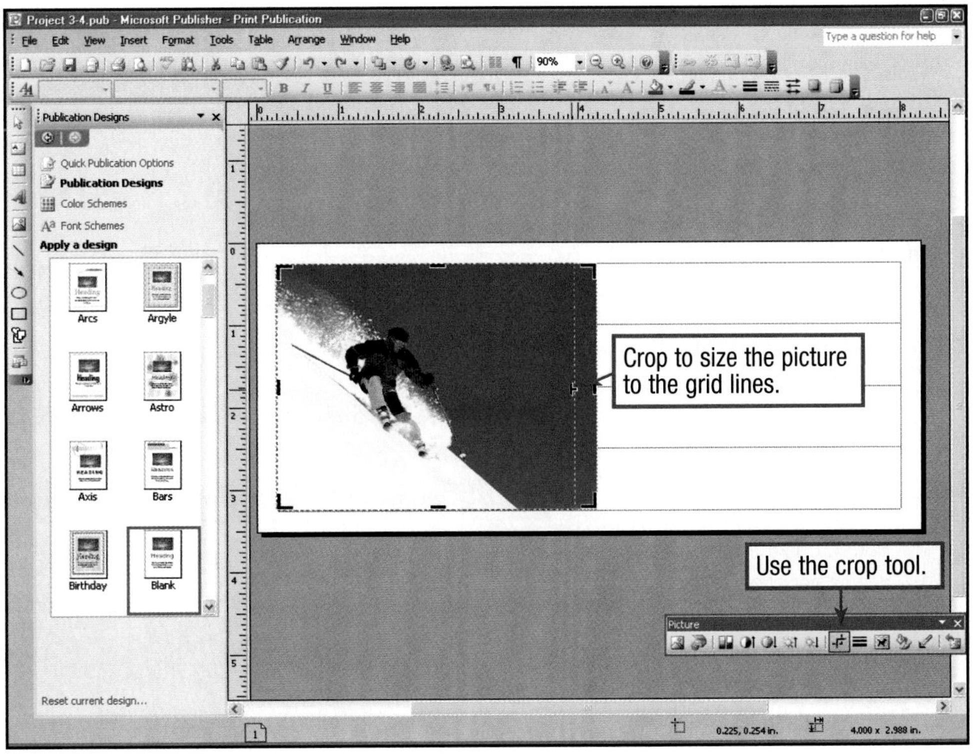

Crop to size the picture to the grid lines.
Use the crop tool.

Step-by-Step

Lay Out a Business Card

1. In Microsoft Publisher, choose **Blank Publications** and choose any business card.

2. Delete the objects in the template, and create a business card of your own design. The position title on the card should read *Director of Marketing*.

3. Include all company information, including company address and all personal contact information.

4. Use the figure to help you create a business card. A six-column layout grid will help with the placement of the objects (Figure 9.16).

Insert a Logo

5. Insert the company logo you created in Project 9-4.

6. Use the **Design Gallery Objects** to add a marquee or accessory bar at the bottom of the card.

7. Use text boxes to add company contact information and personal information.

8. Choose **File>Page Setup**, and choose **Change Copies per Sheet**. Change the number of copies per sheet to 1.

9. Follow your teacher's instructions for saving and printing the business card.

▼ Figure 9.16 Business cards should be readable and reflect the company's corporate culture.

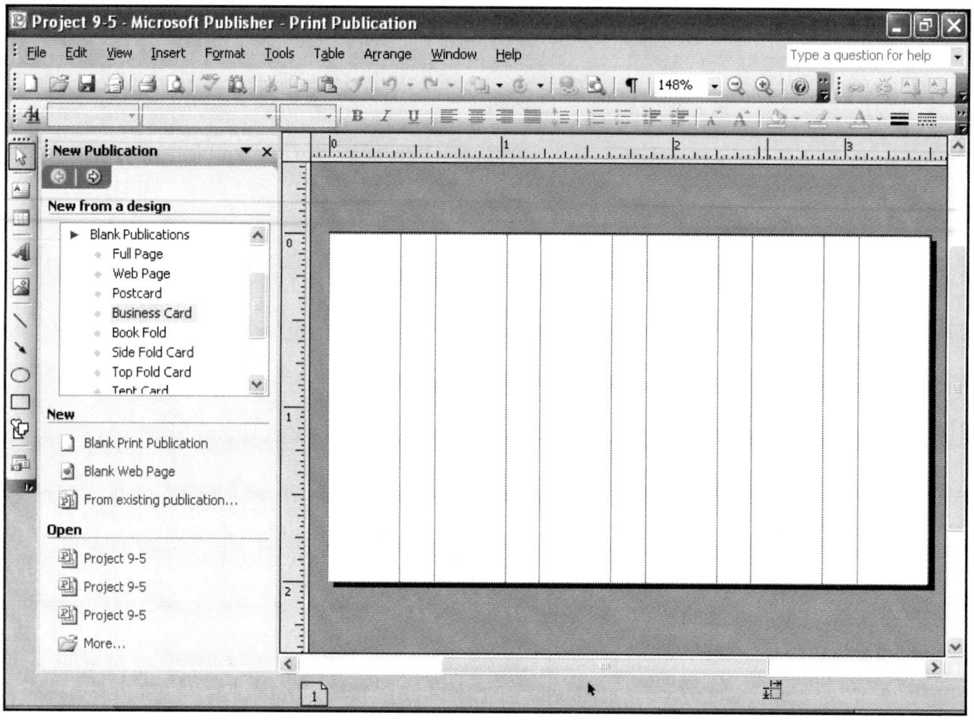

▼ Figure 9.17 A simple but eye-catching logo is easily remembered.

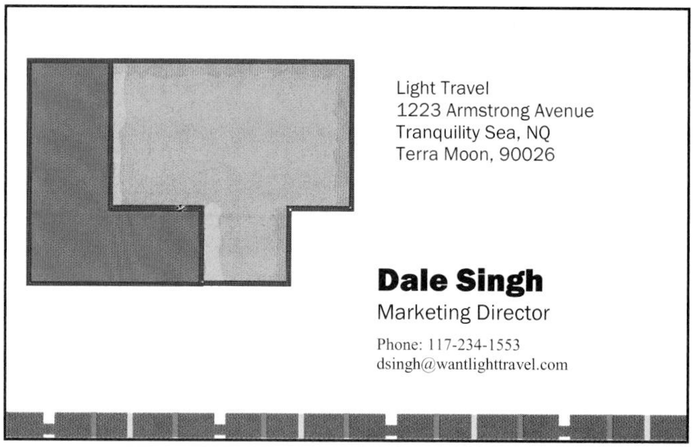

REVIEW AND REVISE

Check your work Use Figure 9.17 as a guide and check that:

- ☑ The company logo is clearly visible.
- ☑ Contact information is correct, complete, and readable.
- ☑ There is sufficient white space and the design follows PARC principles.

8. Create a text box that spans both columns across the top row.

9. In the text box, **center** text and use a **serif 20 pt** font to key Check out our Ski Shoppe sale ENTER to Buy One, Get One Free! See Figure 3.23.

10. Hold ALT and drag the left side of the text box to the right until the text straddles the center line, as shown in Figure 3.23.

11. Select the text that covers the picture, and change the font color to **White**.

Create a Coupon

12. Create another text box in the right-hand column of the second row.

13. Use the fonts in Figure 3.24 to key and center Come down now! ENTER Bring this ad and buy one item in our Ski Shoppe and get a second one free!

14. Press SHIFT + ENTER to create a soft return after *Shoppe*. Adjust text size so it fits the box as shown in Figure 3.24.

Figure 3.23 Adjust the color of the text to increase contrast and help readability.

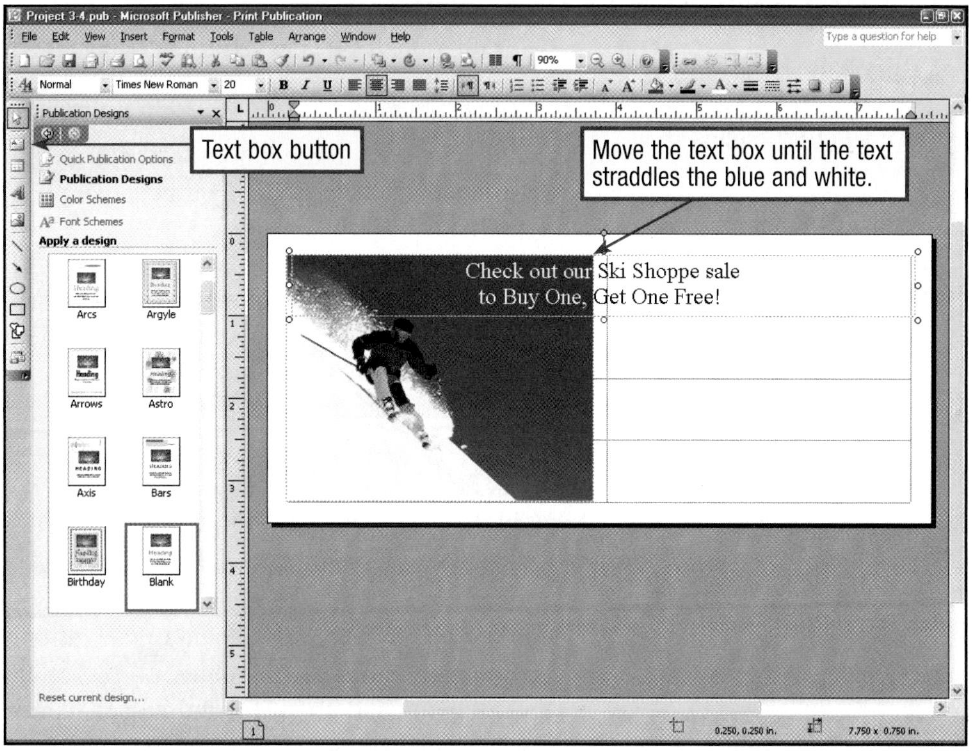

Figure 3.24 A forced soft return lets you break a line where you want.

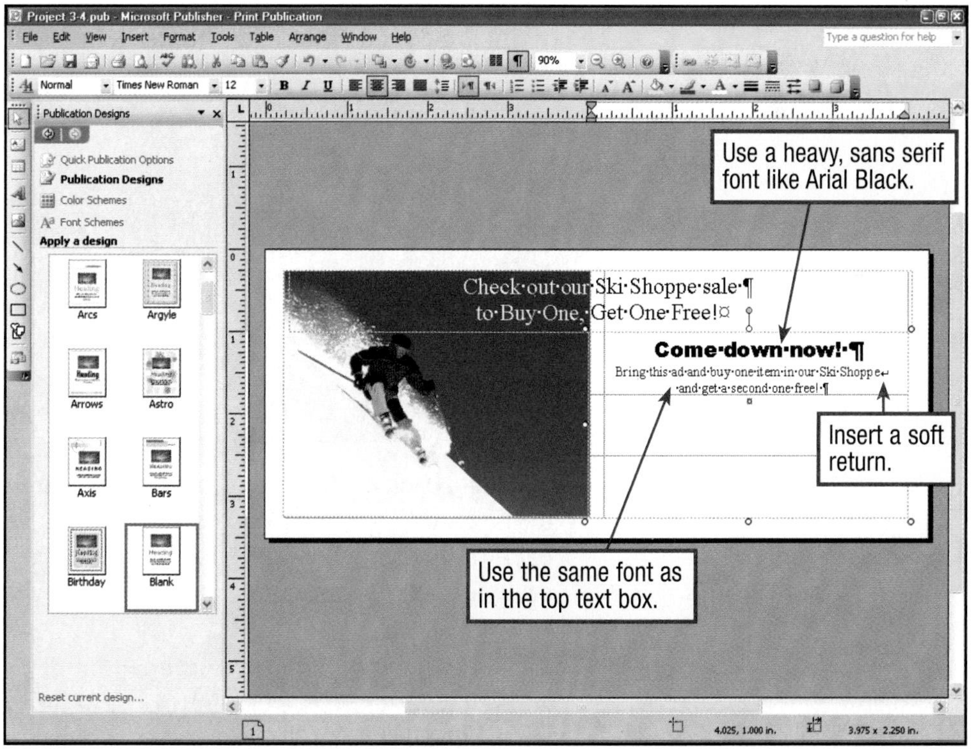

Project 9-5

Spotlight on Skills

- Lay out a business card
- Insert a logo

Key Term

tagline

Academic Focus

Language Arts

Add descriptive text

Design a Business Card

Professionals like lawyers and officers of large corporations carry business cards that usually have a simple, traditional design. They display the name of the person, his or her title, and the company. They almost always use one or two color inks and are embossed on high quality, heavy paper. This kind of card is meant to be exchanged between people who intend to make contact again.

Smaller businesses, however, use business cards to attract attention. A sales representative may be competing with half a dozen other sales people to get your business. After a personal meeting, the business card that is left behind will reinforce any impressions that were made. It must include an image and information that stand out from the rest.

Business Card Layout

Business cards should be clear and easy to read and should reflect the company's corporate culture. Business cards that are too busy, or are a non-standard size, will probably be thrown away and reflect poorly upon the company's professionalism and organization.

Business cards must include all the relevant contact information about the company and about the individual representing the company. Company information includes the name, logo, **tagline** or slogan, and company address. Individual information includes the person's name, official company position, phone number(s), fax number, and e-mail address.

Designs should be kept simple, yet they should send an impressive message about your organization. Although landscape orientation is more often used, portrait design is becoming more popular. Avoid any unnecessary text because most business cards are only 3.5 inches by 2 inches. You should allow for adequate white space.

Sometimes it is necessary to use both the front and back of a business card. Create designs that use both the front and back of the card when necessary information would crowd the front of the card. For example, some companies list products and services on the back of a card, when there is not enough room on the front of the card to provide such information.

▶ **In this project,** you will create a design for a business card for the Director of Marketing. In your designs, you will use the logo you created in Project 9-4.

15. Create a text box in the third row. Use **Arial Black** font to key Sports World.

16. Change the font to **red**, and **center** it. **Enlarge** the text to the size of the box (Figure 3.25).

Insert and Resize Dingbats

17. Select the "o" in *World*, and then click **Insert>Symbol**. Change the font to **Webdings**. Choose an image of a **globe** (near the bottom of the box). Click **Insert**.

18. Make the globe **bold** and **black**. **Resize** it to match the other letters. (**Hint**: Use the **Decrease/Increase Font Size** buttons to resize the dingbat.)

19. Create a text box in the bottom right row. In a small serif font such as 10 pt, key Valid until February 26. Free item must be the same price or less than purchased item. Excludes merchandise over $100.00. One offer per family. © 20-- Sports World. All rights reserved. (Figure 3.26).

20. Select the text in the text box, and click **Format>Horizontal Rules**. In the dialog box, set the thickness at **1 pt** for the **Rule before paragraph** and **Rule after paragraph**. Click **OK**.

Figure 3.25 The Webdings font includes many useful images.

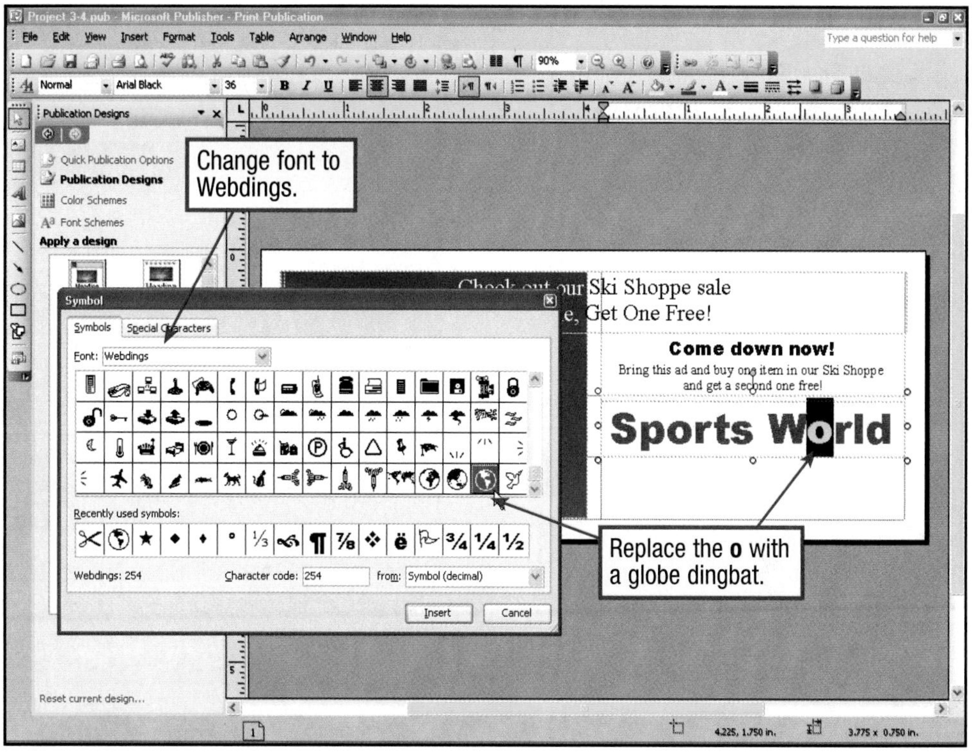

Figure 3.26 It is easy to format border lines in Publisher.

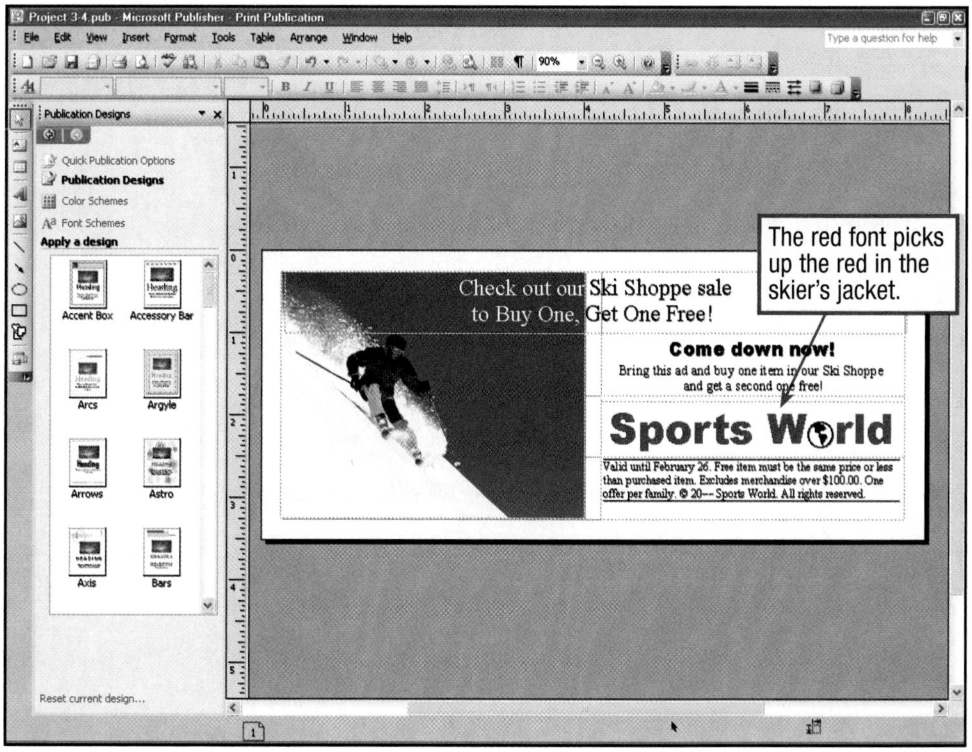

Step-by-Step

1. With your group, brainstorm the words, images, and colors you might want to use.

2. By hand, sketch three different sample logo designs.

3. Use Adobe Illustrator to create your logo. If you would like to create the design that is shown in Figure 9.14, use the following steps.

4. To create the L and T shapes, use the **Rectangle** drawing tool. Open the **Pathfinder** palette to **Add to shape** or **Subtract from shape**, as needed.

5. Fill the **T** with the color **0066cc**. Fill the **L** with the color **FF9933**. Use the **Stroke** palette to create a thick stroke around the letters.

6. Create the highlights and shadow with the **Paintbrush** tool using white and black lines.

7. Use **the Transparency** palette blending modes and **Opacity** settings to adjust the highlights and shadows.

8. Follow your teacher's instructions for saving and printing your work.

9. If possible, print out the design and again review it with your group. Make any final modifications.

▼ Figure 9.14 Use a thick stroke to hide imperfections and create contrast.

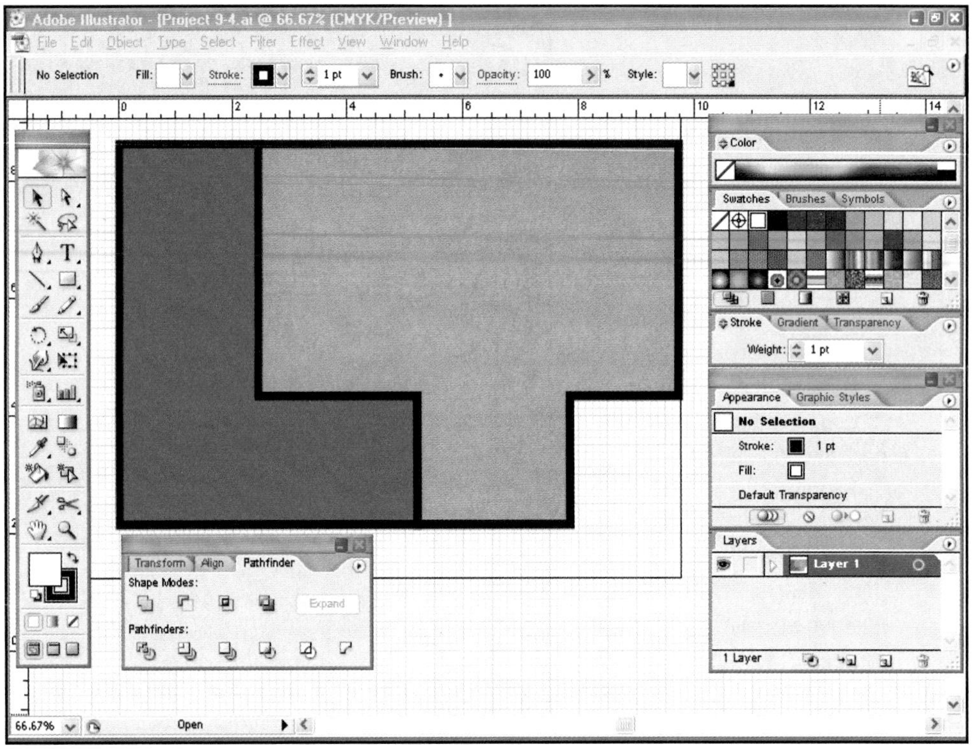

▼ Figure 9.15 Use blending modes and filters to add highlights, shadows, and textures.

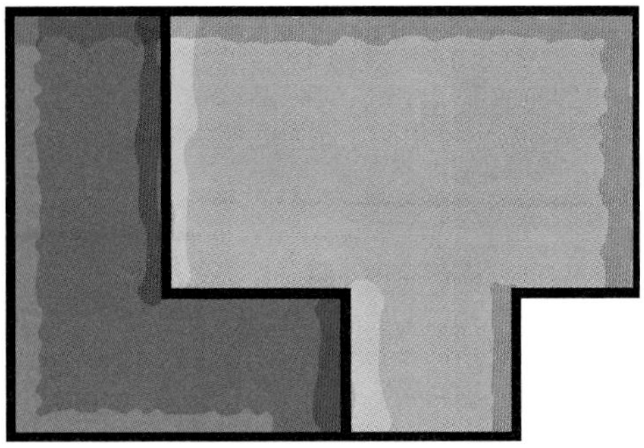

REVIEW AND REVISE

Check your work Use Figure 9.15 as a guide and check that:

- ☑ The graphic is a vector image.
- ☑ Edges are clean of any distortions caused by rectangle blends.
- ☑ The stroke is heavy and dark.
- ☑ Colors are accurate.

21 On the **Object** toolbar, click **Rectangle**, and drag a rectangle around the coupon text (Figure 3.28).

22 Select the rectangle. On the **Formatting** toolbar, click the **Line/Border Style** button and change the line's weight to **2¼ points**.

23 Click **Dash Style**, and choose the **Dash** line.

24 Create a small text box above the coupon. Click **Insert>Symbol**, change the font to **Wingdings**, and choose a **scissors** dingbat.

25 Notice that the text to the left of the scissors has shifted. Select the scissors text box, and click **Format>Text Box>Layout** tab. Choose **None** for the **Wrapping Style**.

26 Select the scissors dingbat, and resize it as shown in Figure 3.28. Move the text box as shown in the figure.

27 Proofread your work. Follow your teacher's instructions for saving and printing.

▼ **Figure 3.27** The scissors dingbat is found in the Wingdings font.

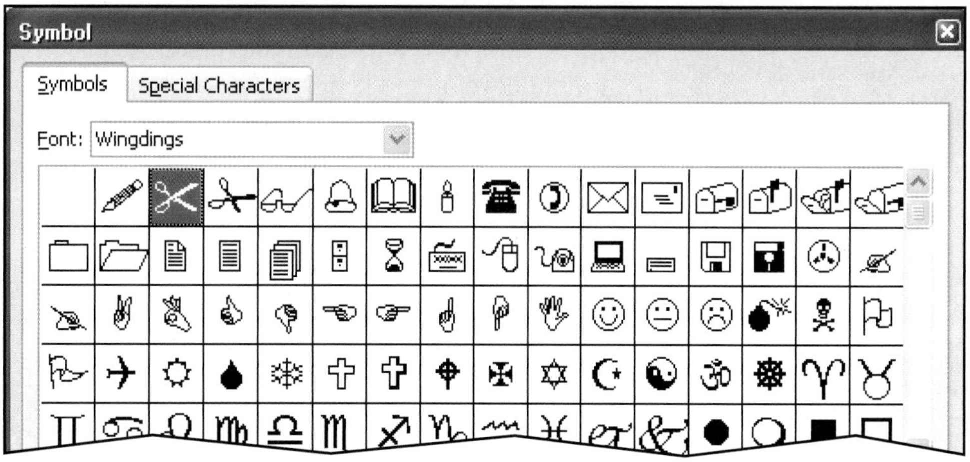

▼ **Figure 3.28** Use the final flyer to evaluate your work.

REVIEW AND REVISE

Check your work Use Figure 3.28 as a guide and check that:

- ☑ The text and images are properly aligned and laid out.
- ☑ Photo is cropped and sized effectively.
- ☑ Text is sized properly to the text box and easy to read.
- ☑ Dingbats are inserted in *World* and above the coupon and are sized and placed effectively.
- ☑ The coupon has a heavy, dashed line around it.
- ☑ Spelling and punctuation are correct.

Project 9-4

Design a Logo

Spotlight on Skills

- Brainstorm ideas
- Create a design

Key Term

- Pantone

Academic Focus

Language Arts
Create a visual message

You have organized your team, created a timeline, and established a budget to develop marketing materials for the Mars Quest division of Light Travel. You are now ready to develop a logo, which you will need for all your marketing materials.

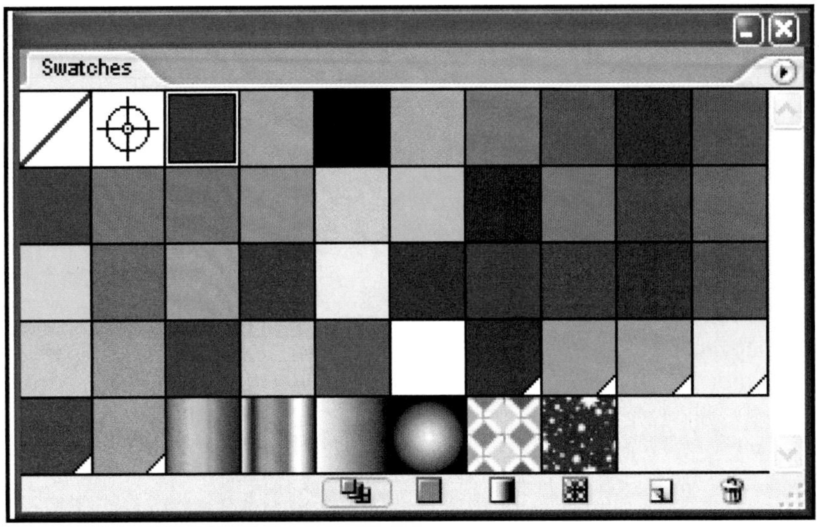

▲ To avoid printing problems, use standard colors like color swatches for your logo.

Logo Guidelines

Review the logos you have created in previous projects. When creating a logo, remember to:

- Keep the design simple. Text-only treatments often use contrasting font families and most logos with graphics use only basic shapes.
- Create them as scalable vector images. These types of graphics will look as clean on a business card as they do when on a billboard. This means logos must be created in a drawing program such as Illustrator.
- Use colors that can be reproduced reliably regardless of the printer. Choose color swatches or custom colors, like **Pantone**, which is a color system used by professional printers. See Appendix A: Color Theory for more information.
- Do your research. Companies pay a lot of money to create logos, and they expect them to be unique. Logos that are too similar to another company's logo can result in product confusion and may even end up in a lawsuit.

▶ **In this project,** you and your group will use Adobe Illustrator to create a logo for your company. You can create the logo used to illustrate this project, but try to come up with a design of your own.

Sidebar

Brainstorming To come up with as many ideas as possible, brainstorm with your group. Assign one team member the job of writing down everything. Set a time limit. Then encourage everyone to call out ideas. Do not criticize or evaluate anything during the session. Instead, focus on coming up with as many ideas as you can—even if they seem impractical. It is amazing how many great products resulted from "crazy" ideas!

Explain Why should a time limit be set on a brainstorming session?

Project 3-5

Spotlight on Skills

- Lay out a two-page brochure
- Apply ruler guides
- Link text boxes
- Add pull-quotes

Key Term

- link

Academic Focus

Science
Consider technology of the future

Design a Bi-Fold Brochure

Brochures can be created in all shapes and sizes. For example, a small square bi-fold brochure can be used as the liner for CD and DVD packaging. In Word, you created a bi-fold brochure that required some complicated formatting. You will see that in Publisher, it is much easier to create a consistent design and layout in a two-sided, multifold brochure. With the options in Publisher's brochure templates, you can create exactly the shape and size brochure that you need.

Work with Multipage Documents

Publisher has a number of tools to help you maintain the same layout and alignment in every page of your document. The program also makes it easy to create and edit content that is laid out on more than one page.

Layout Guides You have seen how layout guides can help create a consistent space within a one-page document. Layout guides are especially helpful in creating consistent design in multipage documents. One set of layout guides can be applied over a large number of pages.

Ruler Guides Unlike layout guides, ruler guides are temporary settings, used when alignment needs to be checked and set on a specific page. Although they may be set so they are visible on every page, ruler guides are generally used on individual pages. There is no limit to the number of ruler guides that one may set on a page.

Connect Text Boxes Toolbar In multipage documents, such as newsletters, an article might begin on one page and then continue on a different page. Publisher lets you **link**, or connect, text boxes so that text from one box can automatically flow into another box no matter where the boxes are located.

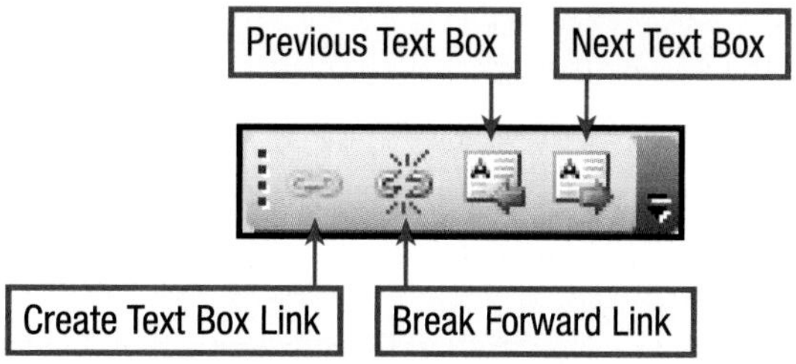

▶ **In this project,** you will create a bi-fold brochure that describes *The Home of the Future*. Remember that the first page of the brochure will be laid out so that the brochure cover is on the right, and the final panel is on the left.

To help visualize the bi-fold brochure, you can fold a piece of paper and use sketches or labels to determine where the design elements will be placed.

14 In *rows 12–22* (columns A–C), key the text shown in Figure 9.12.

15 Select cell **C18** and click the **Sum** button to add cells **C13–C16**.

16 In cell **C19**, calculate the ink costs per sheet by **dividing** the **Total (C18)** by the **number of sheets** that can be printed by one cartridge (20,000). Key =C18/20000. (**Hint:** Click cell C18 instead of keying it.)

17 In cell **F20**, calculate the total ink costs for your project by **multiplying** the **Ink costs per sheet (C19)** by the **Total sheets of paper (C10)** needed. Key =C19*C10. (**Hint:** Click the cells and use the asterisk sign.)

18 Select cell **F22**, and click the **Sum** button. Then hold SHIFT and click cell **F10** to include it in the formula. Press ENTER for your total costs.

19 Select **Row 10**. Fill it with a **light blue** fill. Repeat for **Row 20** and **Row 22**.

20 Format currency by selecting all columns with currency figures and clicking $ on the **Formatting** toolbar.

21 Follow your teacher's instructions for saving and printing your spreadsheet.

Figure 9.12 Make sure you enter the text in the correct cells.

	A	B	C	D
11				
12	**Ink Cartridges**	**Quantity**	**Costs per unit**	
13	Cyan	1	$170	
14	Magenta	1	$170	
15	Yellow	1	$170	
16	Black	1	$170	
17				
18	**Total cartridge costs**			
19	**Ink costs per sheet**			
20	**Total ink costs**			
21				
22	**Total project costs**			
23				

Use bold.

Figure 9.13 Use the final spreadsheet to see what your costs are.

	A	B	C	D	E	F	G
1	**Mars Marketing Project**						
2							
3	**Product**	**Quantity**	**Total sheets of paper**	**Type of paper**	**Paper cost per sales unit**	**Total paper cost**	**Paper cost per unit**
4	Business cards	600	60	Card stock, 10 cds/sheet	$13/200 cards	$ 39.00	$ 0.07
5	Stationery	500	500	20 lb weight	$17/500 sheets	$ 17.00	$ 0.03
6	Envelopes	500	500	#10 size	$27/250 envelopes	$ 52.00	$ 0.10
7	2-page, 4-color brochure	500	1000	color laser, 28 lb	$10/500 sheets	$ 20.00	$ 0.04
8	4-page, 4-color pamphlet	500	2000	Same	Same	$ 40.00	$ 0.08
9							
10	**Total paper costs**		**4060**			**$ 168.00**	
11							
12	**Ink Cartridges**	**Quantity**	**Cost per unit**				
13	Cyan	1	$ 170.00				
14	Magenta	1	$ 170.00				
15	Yellow	1	$ 170.00				
16	Black	1	$ 170.00				
17							
18	**Total cartridge costs**		**$ 680.00**				
19	**Ink costs per sheet**		**$ 0.03**				
20	**Total ink costs**					**$ 138.04**	
21							
22	**Total project costs**					**$ 306.04**	
23							
24							

REVIEW AND REVISE

Check your work Use Figure 9.13 as a guide and check that:

- ☑ Text and data have been entered accurately and in the correct cells.
- ☑ Calculations based on formulas are correct.
- ☑ Total costs are calculated for paper, ink, and the whole project.
- ☑ Rows 10, 20, and 22 are light blue and currency data is formatted.

Step-by-Step

1. Open a new full page **Blank Print Publication**, and save it according to your teacher's instructions.

Lay Out a Two-Page Brochure

2. Click **File>Page Setup>Layout** tab, and choose **Landscape** orientation.

3. Click **Arrange>Layout Guides**. In the **Margins** tab, set **0.5 inches** for all sides. In the **Grid Guides** tab, create **6 columns**, with a **0.2 inches gutter** (Spacing). Click **OK**.

Apply Ruler Guides

4. Drag a ruler guide to the 1" mark on the vertical ruler. Use the guide to align a text box in **columns 4–6** that is **1.125 inches** high (Figure 3.29).

5. Use **bold, Felix Titling** (or another title font) to key: Your (**24 pt**) Future Home **(36 pt)** as shown.

6. **Center** the text and change the font color to **gold**. Select the text box, and change the **Fill** color to **Black** (Figure 3.30).

Figure 3.29 Drag the horizontal ruler to create a ruler guide.

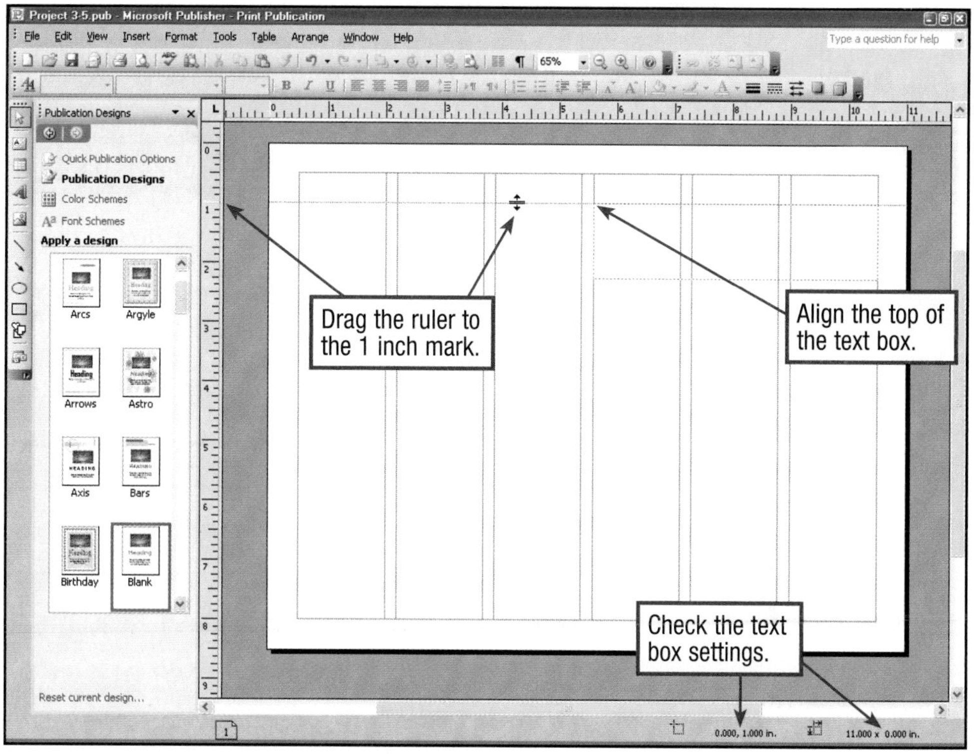

Figure 3.30 The front panel of the brochure is on the right.

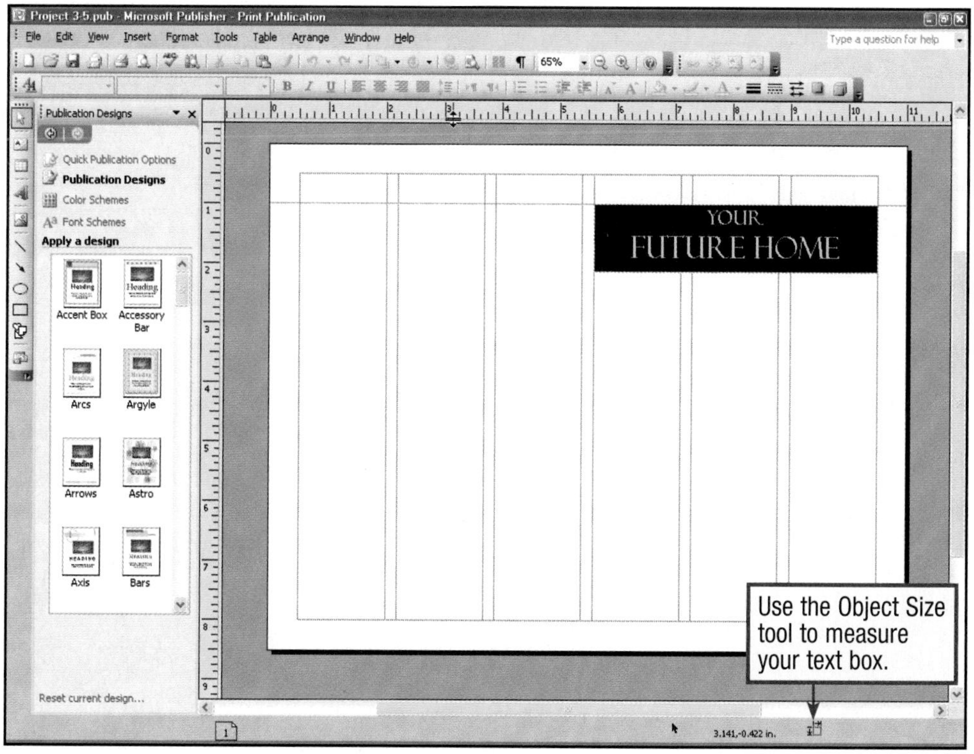

9 Select cell **F10**, and repeat Steps 6 and 7 to get the total paper costs for all the products.

10 In cell **G3**, key Paper cost per unit. This amount is how much you pay for paper to produce one business card, one brochure, one pamphlet, and so on.

Enter Formulas

11 To find paper cost per unit, you must **divide** the **Total Paper Cost** by the **Quantity** of the product. To create the formula in cell G4 (Figure 9.10):

- Click in cell **G4**.
- Press [=].
- Click cell **F4**.
- Press [/]. (This is the division sign.)
- Click cell **B4**.
- Press [ENTER].

Copy Formulas

12 To copy the formula in the other cells, click cell **G4**, then click **Edit>Copy**. Click in cell **G5** and click **Edit>Paste**. Excel automatically recalculates the formula using the data in cells F5 and C5.

13 Repeat Step 11 to copy the formula in cells **G6**, **G7**, **G8** (Figure 9.11).

▼ **Figure 9.10** The formula is displayed in the formula bar and in the cell where it is entered.

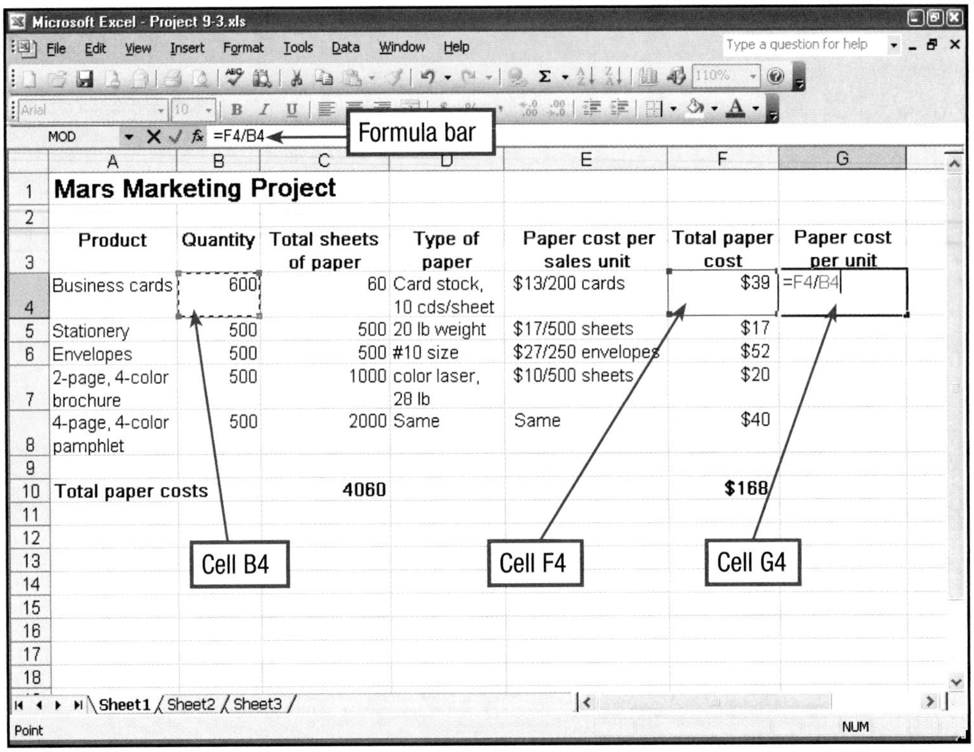

▼ **Figure 9.11** The formula changes when it is pasted in the new cell. It now uses data from that row for the calculation.

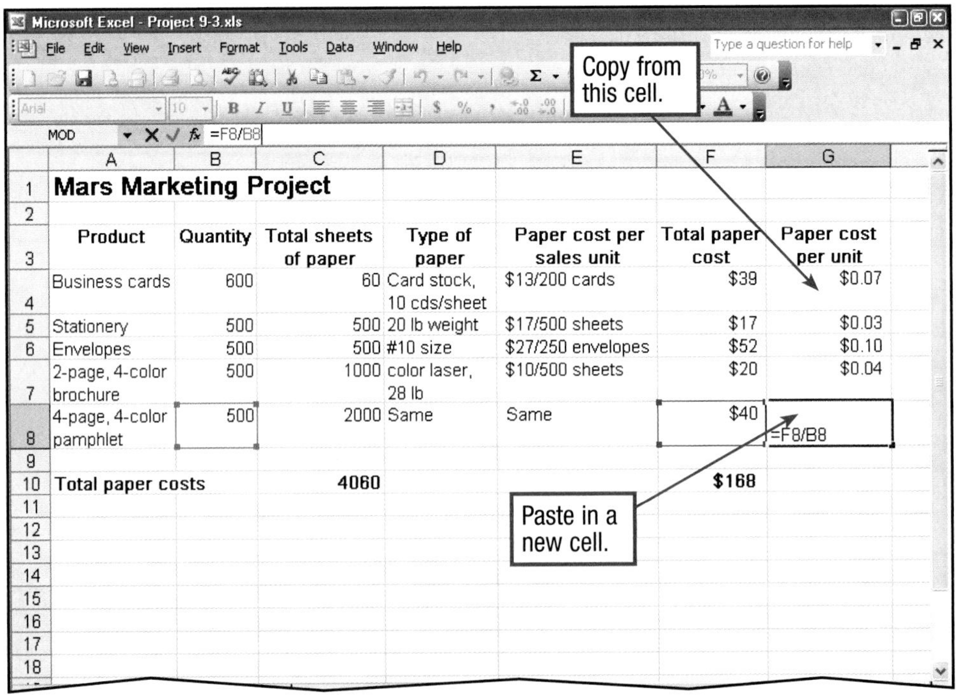

Kern Text

7. Select *Future Home*. Click **Format>Character Spacing**. Under **Kerning**, change the drop menu to **Expand**, and change **By this amount** to **7.5 pt**. Click **OK**.

8. Insert the image from **Data File 3-5a**. **Resize** and **crop** it to fit **columns 4-6**. (**Hint**: Use the **Zoom Out** tool.)

9. Select the photo. Then click **Arrange>Order>Send to back** to move it behind the nameplate (Figure 3.31).

10. Select the photo frame. Click **Line/Border Style** , and choose a **3 pt** line.

11. Use the top margin guide to align a **1 inch** text box across **columns 1–3**. Add a **black fill** (Figure 3.31).

12. In the box, **center** align and use **bold**, **gold Felix Titling**, **32 pt** to key Coming Home.

13. Repeat Step 7 to **kern** the text (Figure 3.31).

14. Create a text box that fills the space below the box you created in Step 11. Add a **gold fill** and a black **3 pt line** as a border.

15. Click **Insert>Text File** to insert **Data File 3-5b** in the text box. Adjust text or objects for the most effective layout (Figure 3.32).

▼ **Figure 3.31** Use the Align or Distribute menu to arrange the objects.

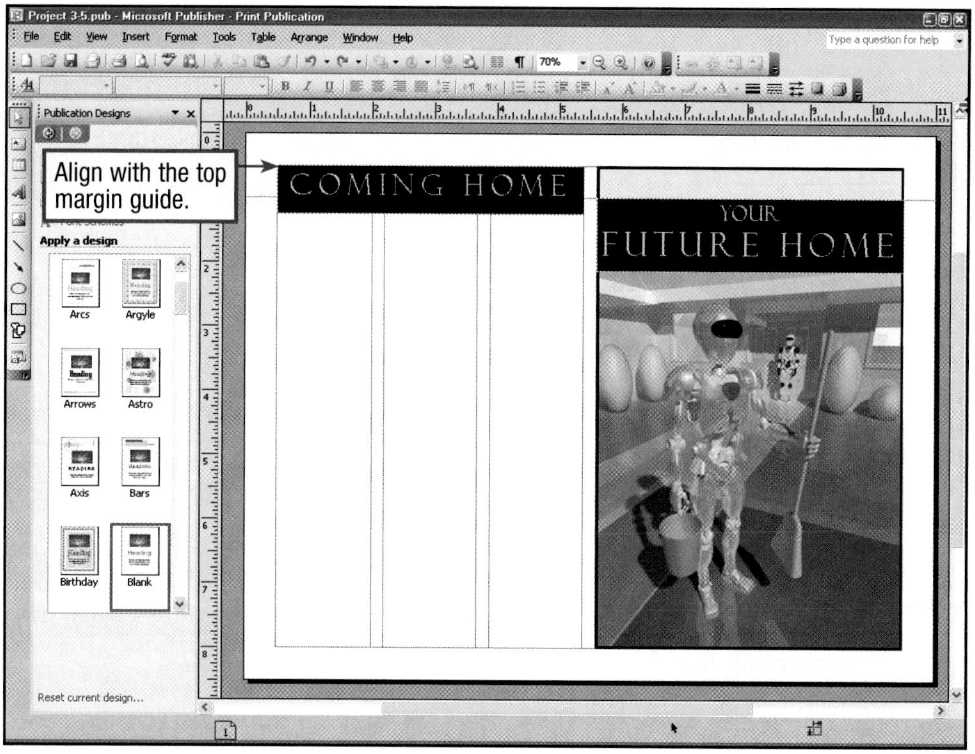

▼ **Figure 3.32** The exterior of your brochure should have repeating design elements.

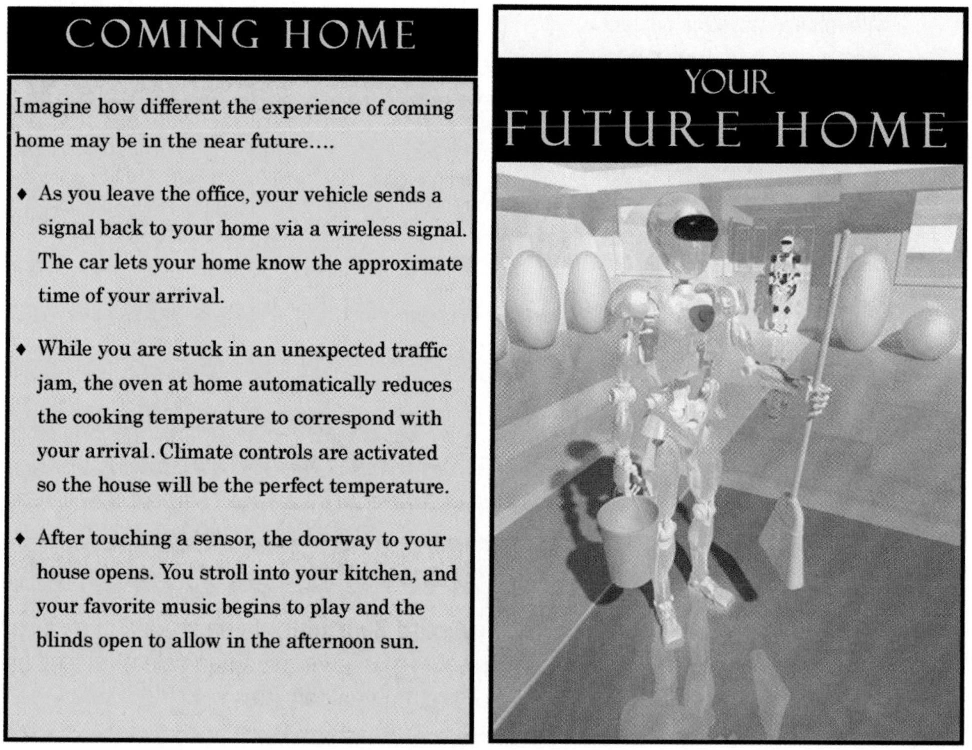

Step-by-Step

1 Open Microsoft Excel. Save the file according to your teacher's instructions.

Create a Spreadsheet

2 Key the information shown in Figure 9.8, using the steps below. Press TAB or ENTER after each entry. Use your mouse or the keyboard arrows to move between cells.

3 In Row 1, key Mars Marketing Project in **14 pt**, **bold**.

4 In **Row 3**, key the headers in **bold**. To wrap text in a cell, click **Format>Cells**. In the **Alignment** tab, click the **Wrap Text** box.

5 To widen a column, move your mouse to the top row with letters. Move the pointer over the line that divides the columns until you see a two-headed arrow ✥. Click and drag the line to the desired width (Figure 9.8).

6 Finish keying the information in Figure 9.8 in each of the columns.

Apply the Sum Function

7 Click cell **C10** to select it. Then click **Sum** Σ. Your screen should look similar to Figure 9.9.

8 Press ENTER to add the total number of sheets for all the products.

▼ **Figure 9.8** Key the information in the correct columns.

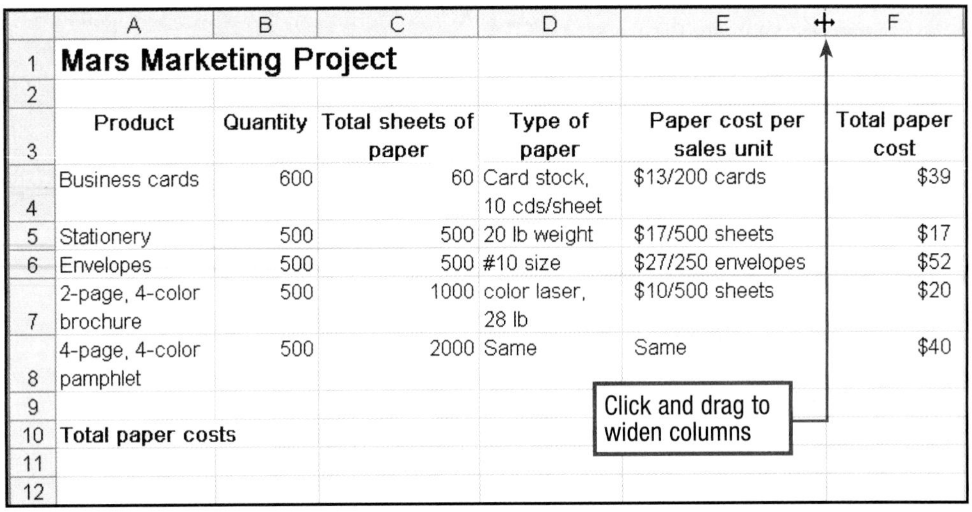

	A	B	C	D	E	F
1	**Mars Marketing Project**					
2						
3	**Product**	**Quantity**	**Total sheets of paper**	**Type of paper**	**Paper cost per sales unit**	**Total paper cost**
4	Business cards	600	60	Card stock, 10 cds/sheet	$13/200 cards	$39
5	Stationery	500	500	20 lb weight	$17/500 sheets	$17
6	Envelopes	500	500	#10 size	$27/250 envelopes	$52
7	2-page, 4-color brochure	500	1000	color laser, 28 lb	$10/500 sheets	$20
8	4-page, 4-color pamphlet	500	2000	Same	Same	$40
9						
10	**Total paper costs**					
11						
12						

▼ **Figure 9.9** Excel automatically selects all the numbers in the column above the cell with the Sum function.

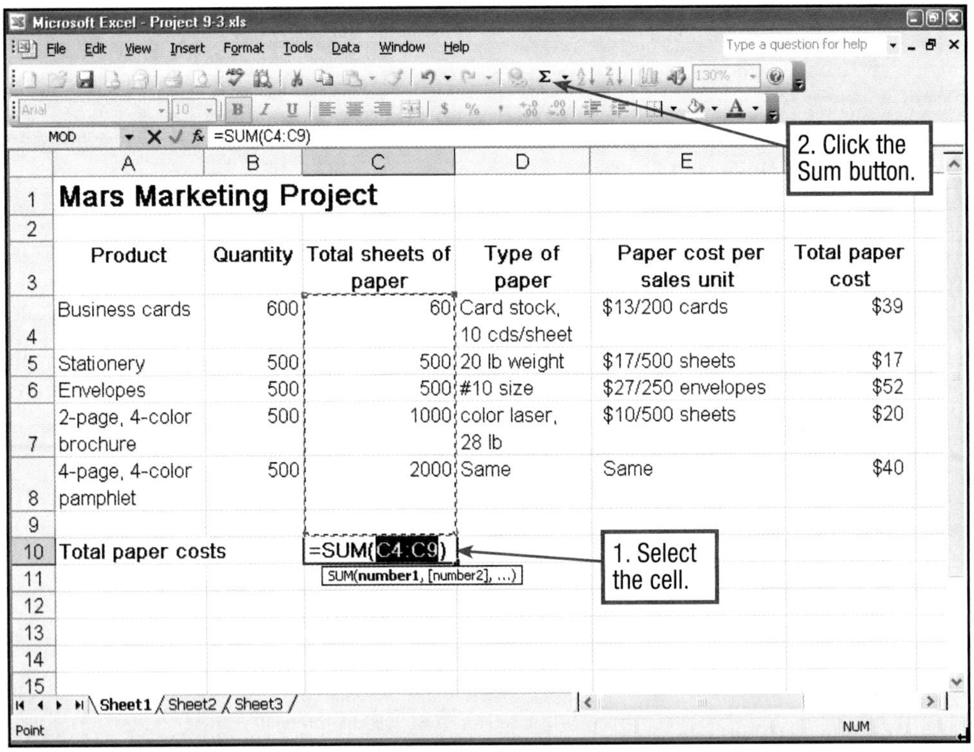

	A	B	C	D	E
1	**Mars Marketing Project**				
2					
3	**Product**	**Quantity**	**Total sheets of paper**	**Type of paper**	**Paper cost per sales unit**
4	Business cards	600	60	Card stock, 10 cds/sheet	$13/200 cards
5	Stationery	500	500	20 lb weight	$17/500 sheets
6	Envelopes	500	500	#10 size	$27/250 envelopes
7	2-page, 4-color brochure	500	1000	color laser, 28 lb	$10/500 sheets
8	4-page, 4-color pamphlet	500	2000	Same	Same
9					
10	**Total paper costs**		=SUM(C4:C9)		

Instant Message

Keyboard Shortcuts To enter data in a cell and select the cell to the right, press TAB. To enter data and select the cell below, press ENTER. To add a hard return in a cell, press ALT + ENTER.

16 Click **Insert>Page**. Set **1 page**. Choose **After current page** and **Insert blank pages**. Click **OK**.

17 On the new page, create a text box that spans **columns 1–2**. Insert **Data File 3-5c**. (**Note**: If the computer asks if you wish to use autoflow, click **No**.)

18 The text box is too small, so the **Text in Overflow** [A ···] indicator is displayed. Create a second text box that spans **columns 4–5** (Figure 3.33).

Link Text Boxes

19 Select the first text box. On the Connect Text Boxes toolbar, click **Create Text Box Link**.

20 Move your mouse pointer to the second text box. The pointer becomes a pouring cup. Click the empty text box. (Press ESC to turn off the **Connect Text Box** feature.)

21 Click the bottom middle handle of the first column and drag up (to reduce the height) until *Recreation* moves to the top of the second column.

Figure 3.33 You can "pour" the excess text between linked text boxes.

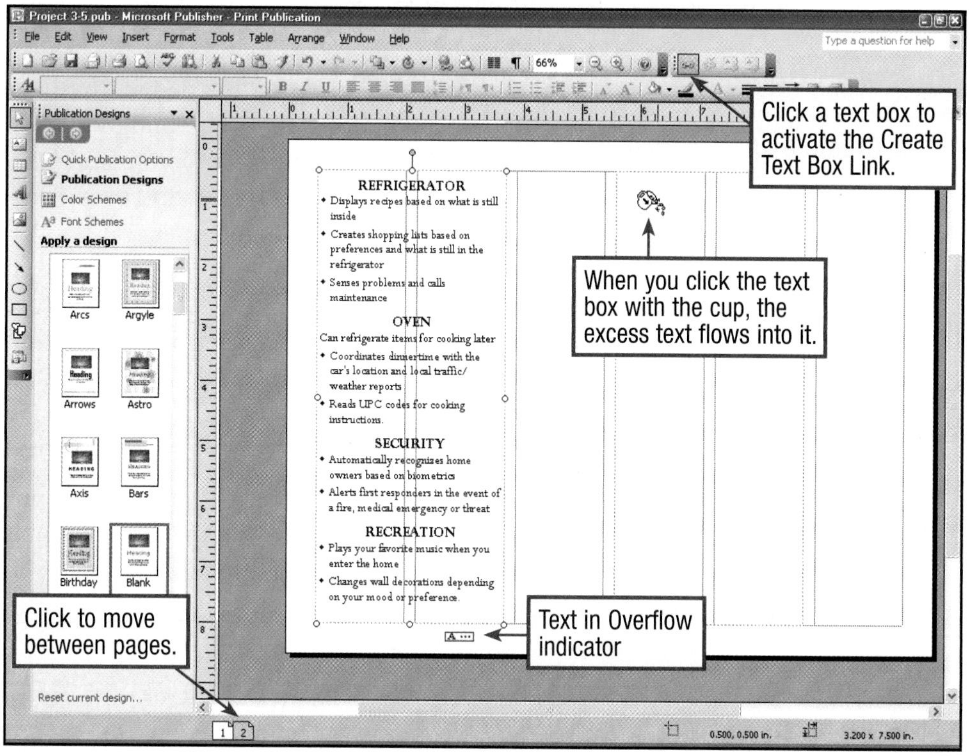

Project 3-5.pub - Microsoft Publisher - Print Publication
Click a text box to activate the Create Text Box Link.
When you click the text box with the cup, the excess text flows into it.
Click to move between pages.
Text in Overflow indicator

Figure 3.34 The excess text automatically flows to the second box.

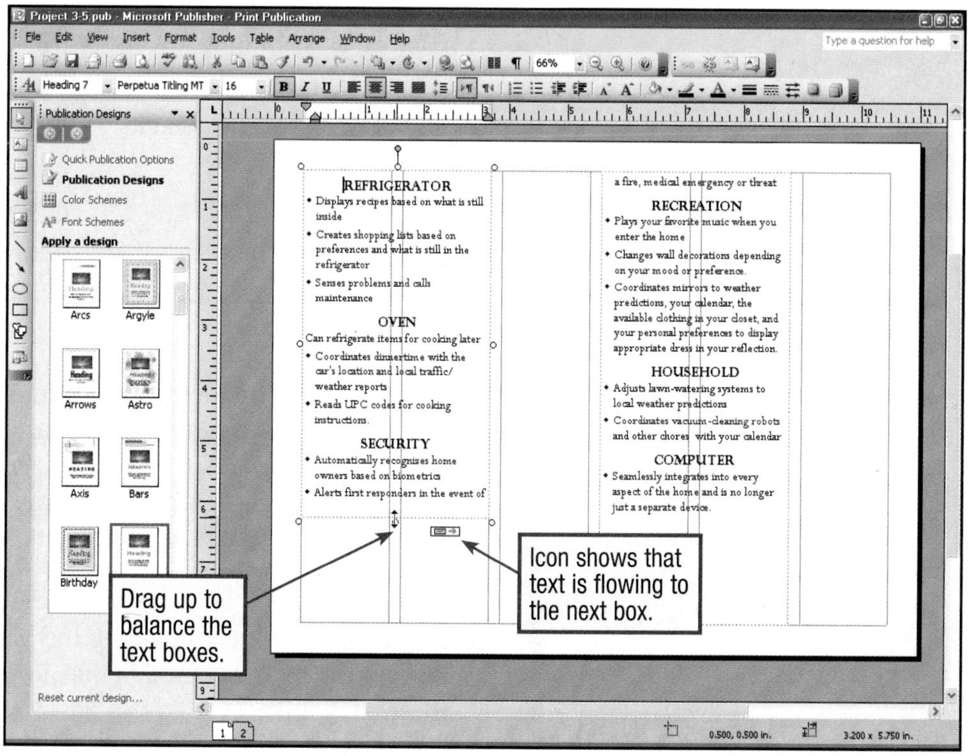

Project 3-5.pub - Microsoft Publisher - Print Publication
Drag up to balance the text boxes.
Icon shows that text is flowing to the next box.

Project 9-3

Spotlight on Skills

- Create a spreadsheet
- Apply the Sum function
- Enter formulas
- Copy formulas

Key Term

- spreadsheet

Academic Focus

Math
Apply math formulas

Create a Budget

Before anyone starts working on the project—or even brainstorming about it—your team must know the budget for the project and understand how that affects the final product. The budget determines what can and should be included in the design, from colors and font choices to document size and layout, types of graphics used, and even file types.

Will the budget allow the materials to be professionally printed? If so, perhaps you can then use special inks and high quality pictures, or special types of paper. Does the budget limit the project to being printed in black and white, or with only one spot color? Knowing these things before you begin can save time that might otherwise be wasted on effects you cannot use.

Crunch Numbers with Spreadsheets

Microsoft Excel is one of the most popular programs used for creating spreadsheets. A **spreadsheet** is a grid or table that arranges numbers or text so that it is easy to manage and manipulate information.

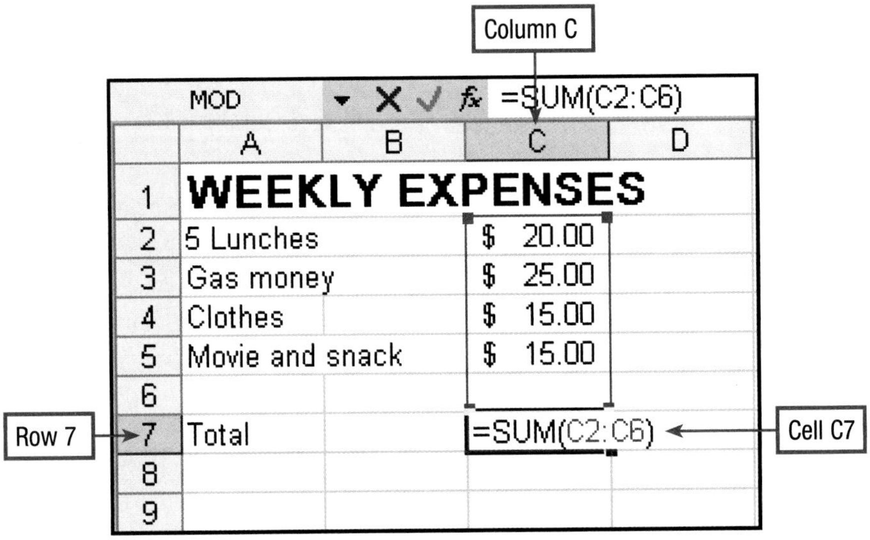

▲ All the numbers in Column C will be added up in Cell C7.

Excel lets you enter mathematical formulas so that numbers can be automatically calculated. For example, in this project you will be adding up numbers to see your total costs. By entering a SUM formula at the bottom of a column, you can automatically total all the numbers in the column. If you need to change a number, a new total will automatically be calculated.

▶ **In this project,** you will consider the printing cost of publishing a set of marketing materials including the business package, brochure, and pamphlet. The amounts used in this project do not cover all the costs of publication. Unlike a real-world business, you will not have to consider costs such as salaries and equipment.

22 Insert the picture in **Data File 3-5d** at the bottom of **column 3**. Resize, if necessary.

Add Pull-Quotes

23 On the **Object** toolbar, click **Design Gallery Object** . In the **Pull-Quote** category, choose **Kid Stuff**. Insert it above the image.

24 Change the font in the pull quote to **black**, **16 pt**. Key Robots will be able to help you with homework or cleaning the dishes. They might even be good companions.

25 Insert **Data File 3-5e** at the top of **column 6**. Copy the first pull-quote, and paste it below the image.

26 Replace the text in the pull quote Computer chips will let your appliances automatically perform tasks and even service themselves.

27 Select the picture and pull-quote in column 3, and click **Arrange>Group**. Add a **black border line**. Repeat with column 6 (Figure 3.35).

28 Follow your teacher's instructions for saving and printing your work. If possible, use duplex printing to print both sides on a single sheet of paper.

▼ **Figure 3.35** Use this figure to proof your brochure.

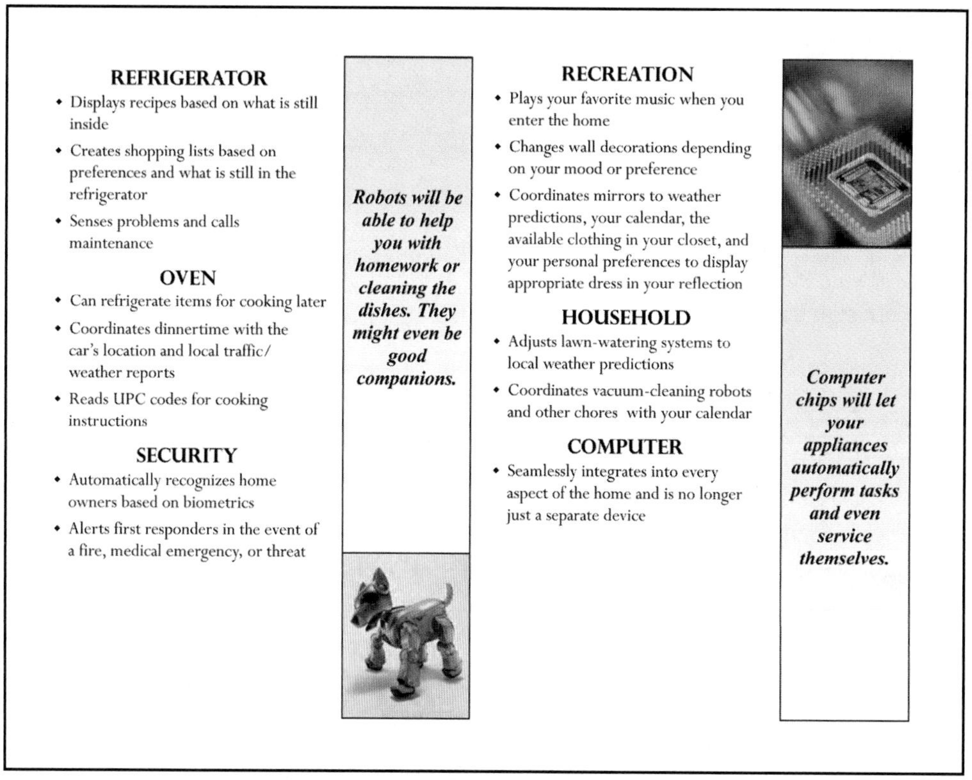

REFRIGERATOR
- Displays recipes based on what is still inside
- Creates shopping lists based on preferences and what is still in the refrigerator
- Senses problems and calls maintenance

OVEN
- Can refrigerate items for cooking later
- Coordinates dinnertime with the car's location and local traffic/weather reports
- Reads UPC codes for cooking instructions

SECURITY
- Automatically recognizes home owners based on biometrics
- Alerts first responders in the event of a fire, medical emergency, or threat

Robots will be able to help you with homework or cleaning the dishes. They might even be good companions.

RECREATION
- Plays your favorite music when you enter the home
- Changes wall decorations depending on your mood or preference
- Coordinates mirrors to weather predictions, your calendar, the available clothing in your closet, and your personal preferences to display appropriate dress in your reflection

HOUSEHOLD
- Adjusts lawn-watering systems to local weather predictions
- Coordinates vacuum-cleaning robots and other chores with your calendar

COMPUTER
- Seamlessly integrates into every aspect of the home and is no longer just a separate device

Computer chips will let your appliances automatically perform tasks and even service themselves.

Instant Message

Printing in Black and White Some font colors (such as gold) used with dark backgrounds may not print well on a black and white printer. If you are printing this brochure in black and white rather than color, use white text instead of gold on the black background.

REVIEW AND REVISE

Check your work Use Figure 3.32 and 3.35 as guides and check that:

- ☑ The text and images are properly aligned and laid out.
- ☑ Exterior has title page on the right and text to the left.
- ☑ Interior text flows between text boxes and is balanced.
- ☑ Pull-quotes and graphics are used effectively.
- ☑ Design uses repetition on all panels of the brochure.
- ☑ Spelling and punctuation are correct.

Step-by-Step

1. In Publisher, open a **blank new publication** in **landscape** orientation. Save it according to your teacher's instructions.
2. On the **Object** toolbar, click **Design Gallery Objects** , and insert a calendar.

Modify a Calendar Template

3. If you need to change the calendar date, select the calendar and click **Wizard** . On the task pane, click the **Change Date Range** button and set the correct date.
4. In the calendar, determine which dates you need. Select rows you do not need and click **Table>Delete>Rows**. Repeat to delete unnecessary columns (Figure 9.6).
5. Select the calendar, and click **Arrange>Ungroup**.
6. Select the section of the calendar with the dates and enlarge it to fill the workspace (Figure 9.7).
7. With your group, determine how long each part of your project will take. Use Figure 9.7 as a model and create colored text boxes spanning the dates of each task.
8. Follow your teacher's instructions for saving and printing your timeline.

Figure 9.6 Keep only the dates that you need for your timeline.

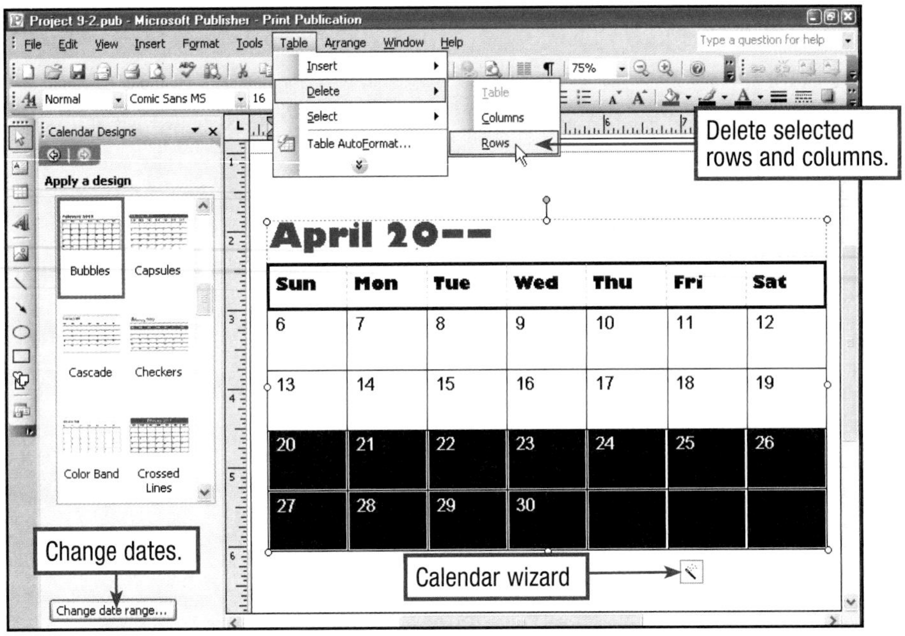

Figure 9.7 You can add the names of team members next to each task.

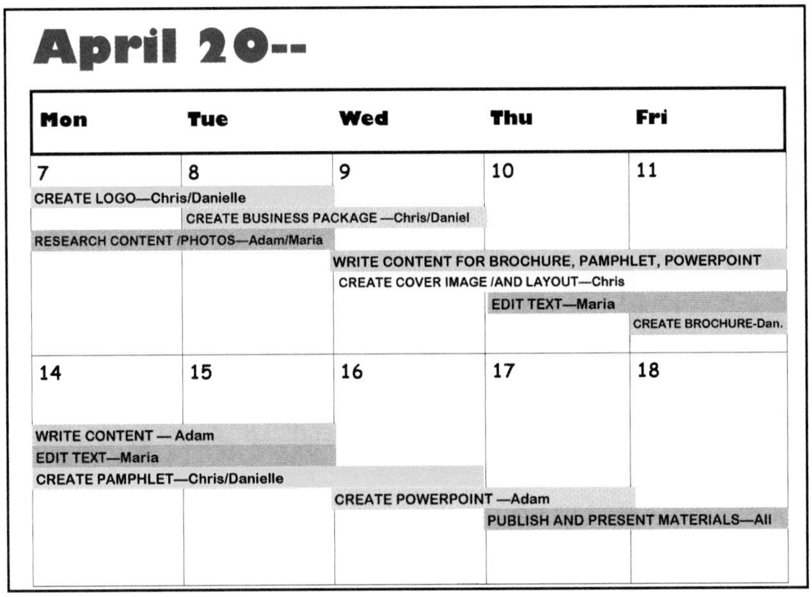

REVIEW AND REVISE

Check your work Use Figure 9.7 as a guide and check that:

- ☑ The calendar only shows the timeframe for the projects.
- ☑ Tasks are logically scheduled, using different colors.

Project 3-6

Create Web Pages Using a Master Page

Spotlight on Skills

- Lay out Web pages
- Create a master page
- Publish a file as a Web page

Key Terms

- HTML (Hypertext Markup Language)
- master page

Academic Focus

Math
Evaluate spatial relationships

The Web is becoming increasingly more important for publishing, and Web pages are common for organizations and individuals.

Compare Web Page Software

Web pages are created using a programming language called **HTML**, an acronym for *Hypertext Markup Language*. Software applications, such as Adobe Dreamweaver® and Microsoft® FrontPage, allow you to create Web pages without knowing HTML. These applications are powerful and versatile tools for creating Web pages, but they can be difficult to master. Microsoft Publisher is easier to use to create simple Web pages.

Repeat Design with a Master Page

You might have noticed that many Web sites have design elements that repeat from page to page. These can be created with a **master page**, a tool that allows design elements to repeat automatically on any number of pages.

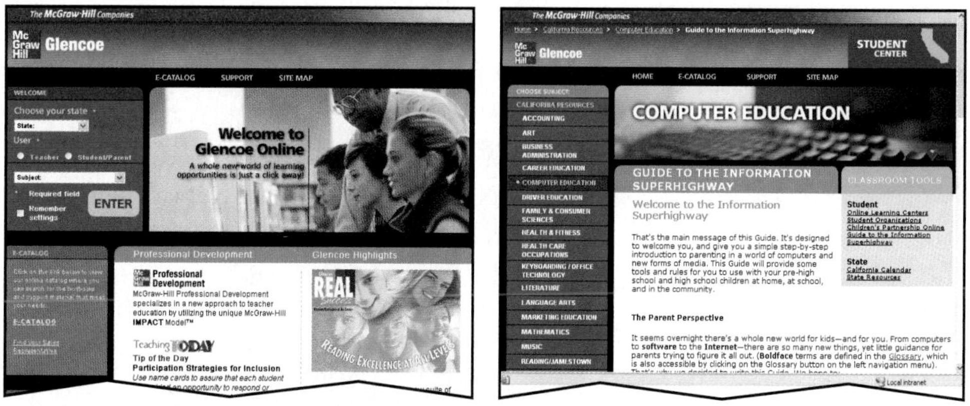

▲ A master page makes it easy to have consistent design on each page of a Web site. What objects are the same on these two pages?

Master pages allow designers to easily set page-to-page consistency, and edit pages quickly when elements on the master page are changed. They also conserve file size because graphic elements are really only counted once, even though they may appear on every page.

▶ **In this project,** you will begin to create pages for a school's Web site, using a master page to create consistent design. In Project 3-7, you will add interactivity to the Web site.

Sidebar

Start a Web Site You can create your own Web sites and domain name (the URL address of your Web page) for extremely affordable rates. Companies such as GeoCities.com offer free Web hosting, provided they are allowed to advertise on the site.

Draw Conclusions What might you expect to see on a Web page posted on a free Web hosting site?

Project 9-2 Create a Timeline

Spotlight on Skills

- Modify a calendar template

Key Term

- deadline

Academic Focus

Science
Break a process into steps

Frequently at the beginning of a project— especially a large one—a team may worry that the project cannot be completed in the given time. Or, the deadline may seem so far away that the team feels there is no need to hurry. As a result, they may wait to start tasks and then panic when the deadline approaches. How can you manage your project so that your team can work calmly and efficiently and complete the project on time?

Set Deadlines

Break a project into its component parts and set a time goal, or **deadline**, for each of those parts. Setting a deadline means making a decision based on how long each part should take to complete and when the project must be turned in. Each member of the group should be responsible for estimating a realistic amount of time that it will take to complete his or her part of the project. The project manager makes sure that group members' tasks are scheduled so that everyone stays busy and the project can move forward without any delays.

Of course, you can only do what you have time to do. Keep this in mind when planning. Not enough time to create something from scratch? Use clip art or stock photos. Simply missing a deadline should never be an option. Modify your design to fit within the timeframe that you are given.

Schedule Meetings

Good groups will check on each member's progress. You may want to meet daily, every couple of days, or even weekly. Schedule meetings so that everyone is up to date, but not so often that the meetings take away from the time you need to complete the project.

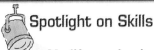

If you find out that a team member is falling behind schedule, try to come up with a solution to help him. Perhaps another team member can help out and make the task go more quickly. Perhaps the task needs to be modified to fit the time given. In any case, keeping track of each team member's progress can help you solve problems along the way—not at the last minute—and enable you to deliver the project on time.

► **In this project,** your group will use Microsoft Publisher to create a timeline. The timeline will show deadlines for each part of the Mars project, which must be completed in two weeks. It will also show which team member is responsible for finishing specific tasks on time.

Student Data File

Step-by-Step

Lay Out Web Pages

1. In the New Publications task pane, click **Blank Publications>Web Page**. Save according to your teacher's instructions.

2. Click **File>Page Setup**. Click **Custom** and set: **Width: 760 px**, **Height: 480 px**. Click **OK**.

Create a Master Page

3. Click **View>Master Page**.

4. Set the **Grid Guides** to **Columns: 4**, with **0 spacing**, **Rows: 10**, with **0 spacing**.

5. In **columns 2–3**, **rows 1–2**, create a text box. Insert **WordArt** with your school name. Use an **Arial**, **40 pt** font.

6. Click **Format>WordArt> Colors and Lines>Fill Effects**. Change the fill to a preset color like **Horizon**.

7. In **column 4**, add separate text boxes to **row 1** and **row 2**. Use **Arial Black**, **10 pt** to key your school's address and phone number.

8. In **column 1**, **rows 1–4**, insert **Data File 3-6a**, or a mascot from clip art of your choice (Figure 3.37).

Figure 3.36 New toolbars automatically display when you create a Web page.

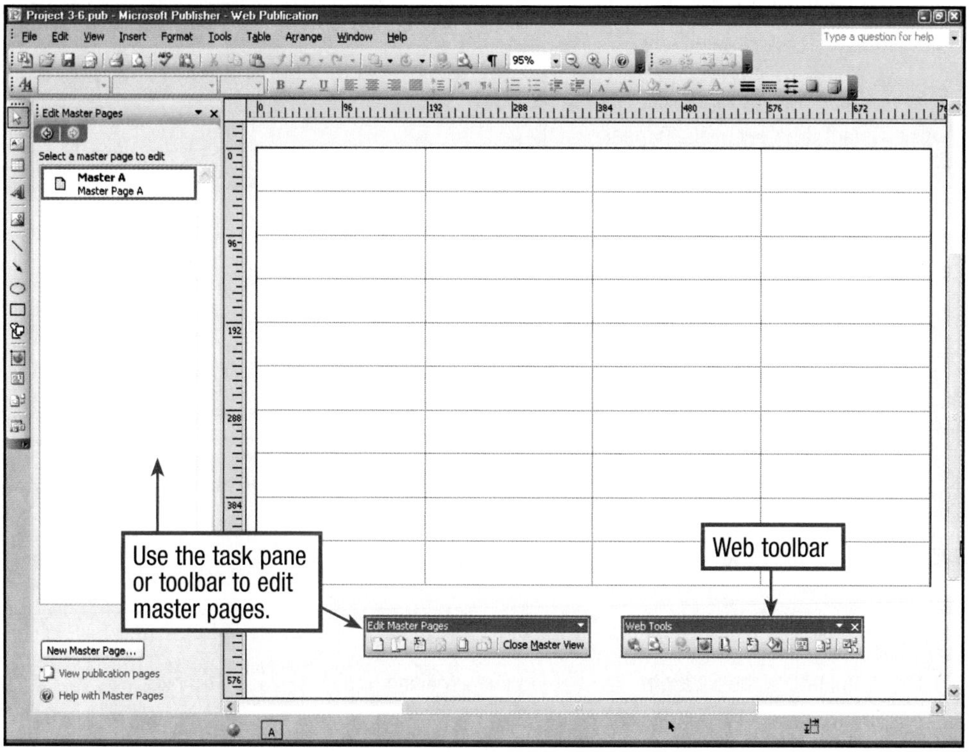

Use the task pane or toolbar to edit master pages.
Web toolbar

Figure 3.37 Master page objects will be displayed on all pages of the document.

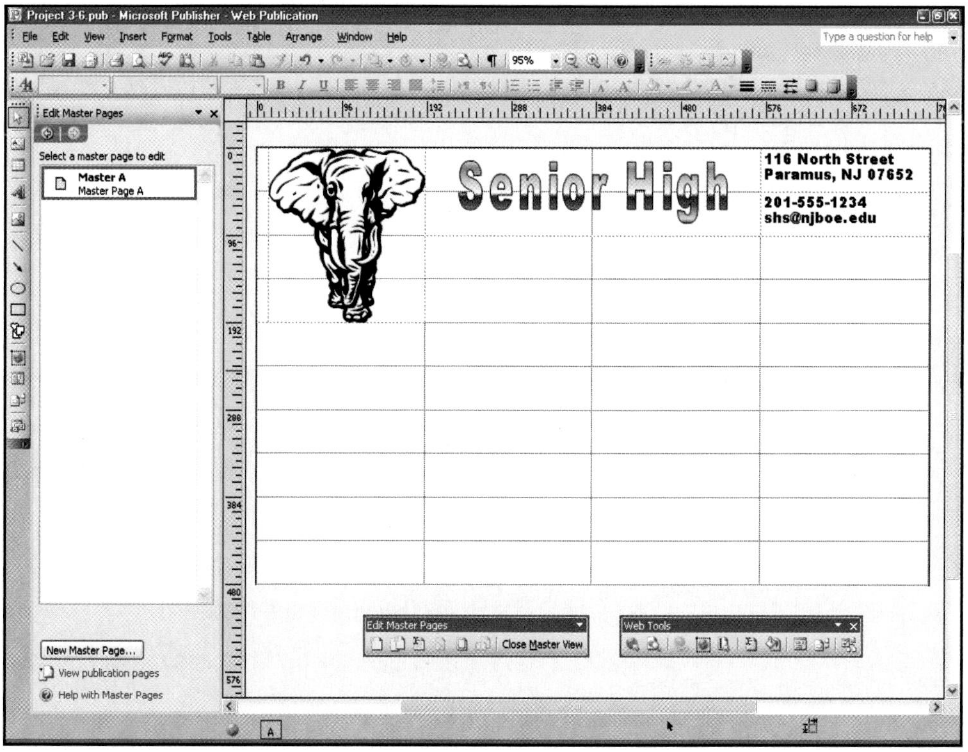

13 Create a new row of ovals beneath the last row. Add text with more detail about each task.

14 Select the new ovals. Repeat **Step 10** to align, and group the new row. Then **Align Center** with the rest of the diagram.

15 Add connectors between the two rows of ovals (Figure 9.4).

16 Below the last row, create more ovals, one for each member of your group. Key in each person's name.

17 In the **Connectors** toolbar, double-click the **Straight Arrow** connector so the button stays active.

18 Click to draw arrows from each group member to the tasks they will be doing. Position the member ovals so it is easier to see the arrows (Figure 9.5).

19 Fill the flowchart boxes with colors that group related jobs and team members.

20 Follow your teacher's instructions for saving and printing your work.

▼ **Figure 9.4** Break the large tasks into smaller parts.

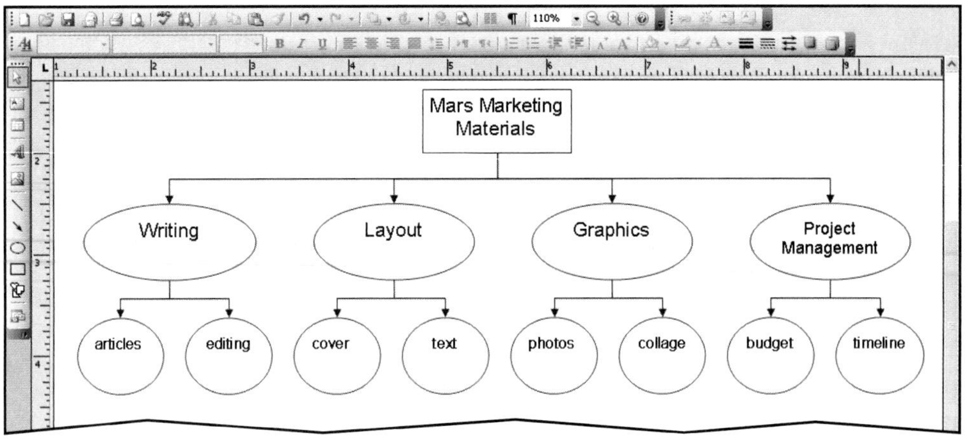

▼ **Figure 9.5** Color the boxes so it is easy to see who is responsible for each task.

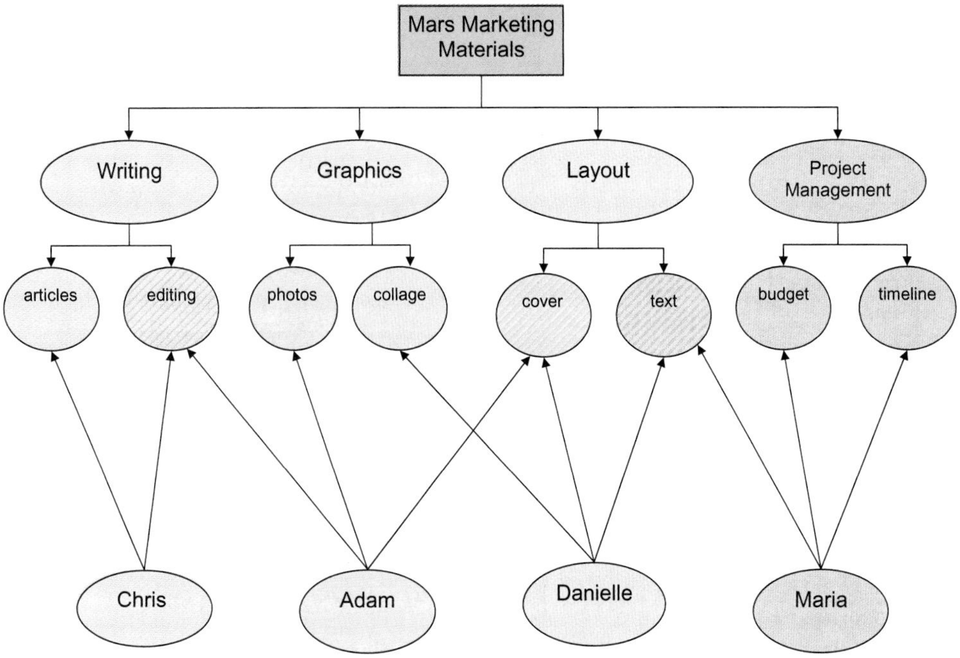

REVIEW AND REVISE

Check your work Use Figure 9.5 as a guide and check that:

- ☑ The boxes in the flowchart are aligned.
- ☑ Connectors are attached to the correct boxes.
- ☑ Text is correct and readable.
- ☑ Boxes are filled with colors that group related tasks.

9. Draw a rectangle across the entire width of rows 1–2. Use **black** fill. Then click **Arrange>Order>Send to Back** to display the clip art and WordArt.

10. Select the hidden text in column 4, and change it to **white**. Add contrast to the WordArt by changing the line color to white.

11. In column 1, insert individual text boxes in **rows 5–9**. Key the text shown in Figure 3.38.

12. Add a **1½ pt line** border and a **light fill** color to the text boxes in **rows 6–9**.

Publish a File as a Web Page

13. Press CTRL + M to move back to the publication page. (**Note**: You can use the same command to return to the master page.)

14. Insert **Data File 3-6b** in **columns 2–4**, **rows 3–8**. You may need to crop the picture to fit the space.

15. Create a text box below the picture. In a **centered**, sans serif font like **Verdana**, **12 pt**, key OUR MISSION To equip young women and men with the skills, knowledge, and character they need to succeed (Figure 3.39).

16. Follow your teacher's instructions for saving your document. You will continue to work on it in Project 3-7.

Figure 3.38 Make text a light color to contrast with the dark background.

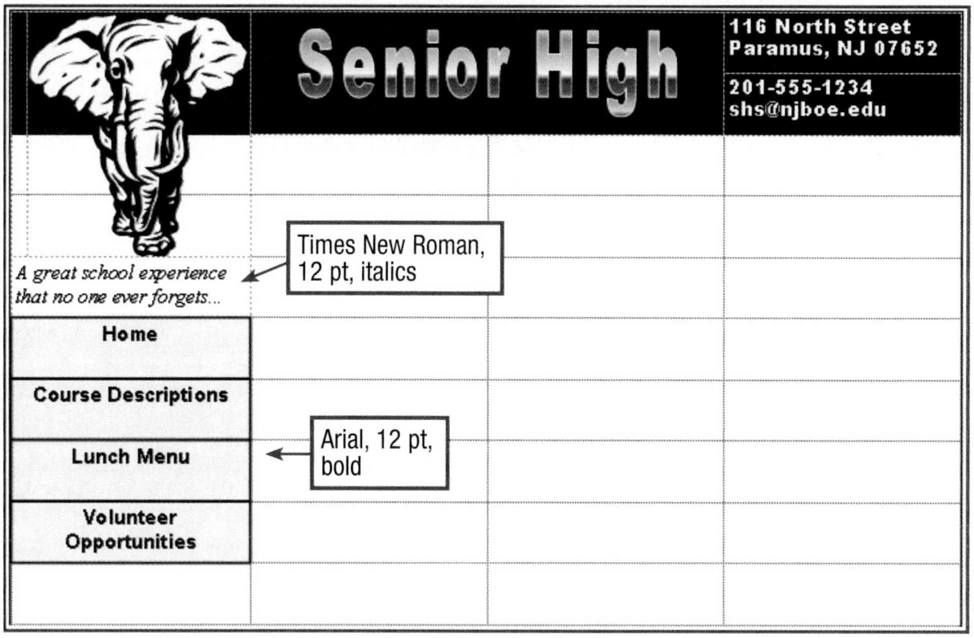

Figure 3.39 You must leave the master page to create each page of the Web site.

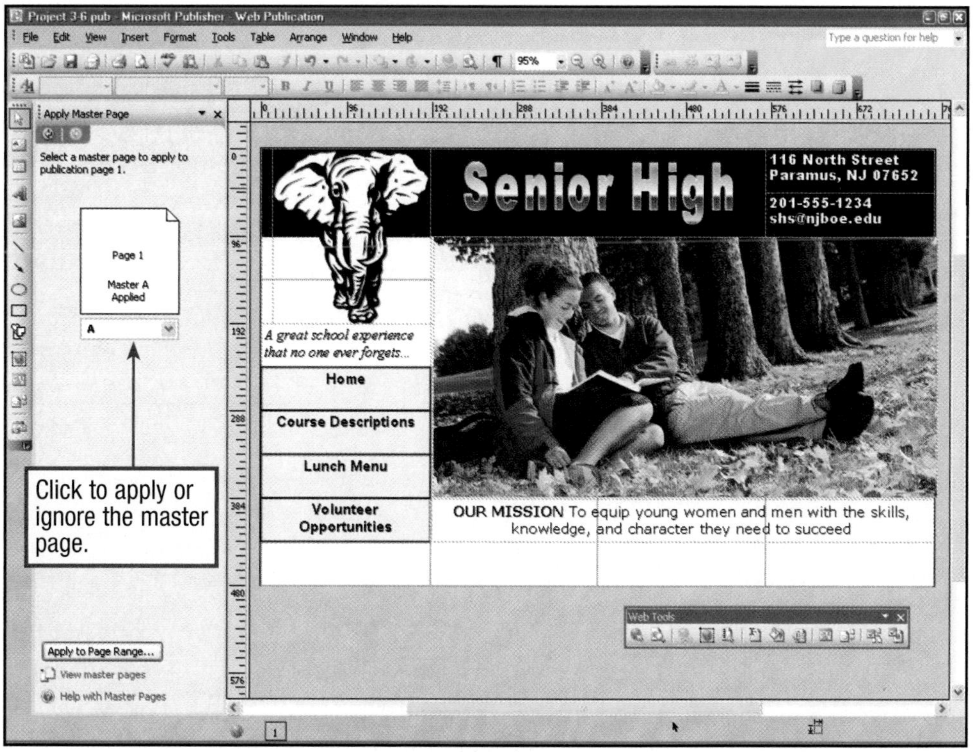

Create a Flowchart

5. On the **Flowchart** toolbar, click and drag the **Process** rectangle box into the workspace.

6. Right-click on the rectangle, and choose **Add Text**. Key Mars Marketing Materials. Resize the box. Center and format the font (Figure 9.2).

7. On the **Flowchart** toolbar, click the **Connector** oval and create an oval. Select the oval, then hold CTRL to drag out three copies across the page.

8. Add text to each oval: Writing, Layout, Graphics, Project Management.

9. Press SHIFT to select all four new ovals. Click **Arrange>Align** or **Distribute**. Choose **Distribute Horizontally**, then in the same menu, click **Align Middle**. Group the ovals together (Figure 9.2).

10. Select the oval group and the rectangle. Click **Arrange>Align or Distribute>Align Center**.

Add Connectors

11. In the **Connector** toolbar, click the **Elbow Arrow** connector. Click the bottom blue handle on the rectangle, then click the top blue handle on the first oval to connect them.

12. Repeat **Step 11** until all the ovals are connected to the rectangle (Figure 9.3).

Figure 9.2 Align the boxes on your chart.

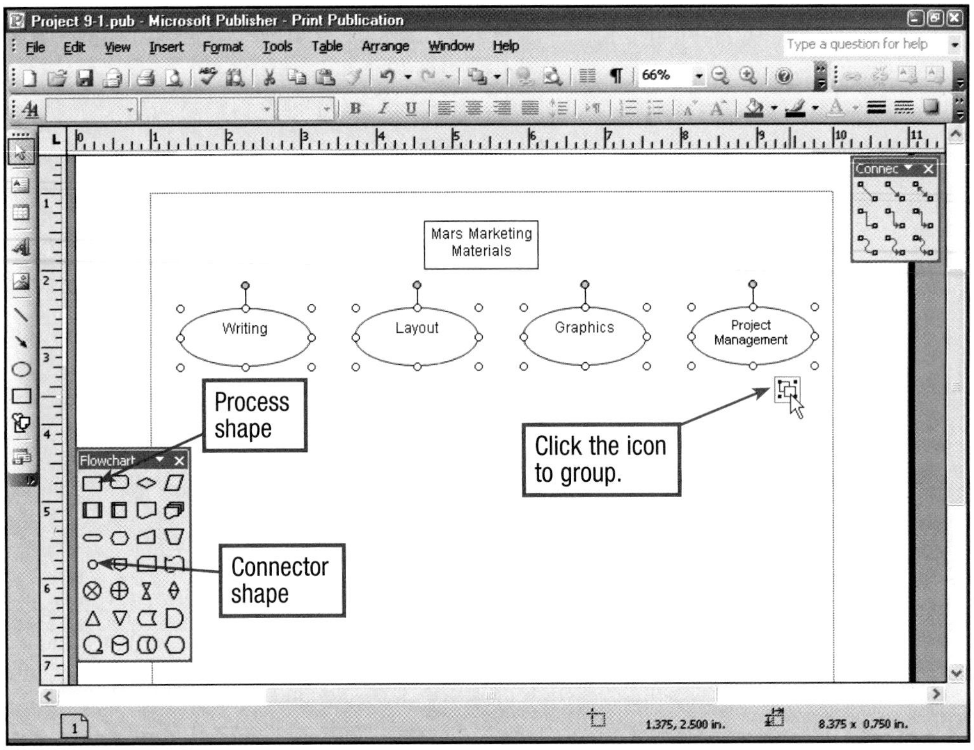

Figure 9.3 Connectors automatically attach to handles on the flowchart boxes.

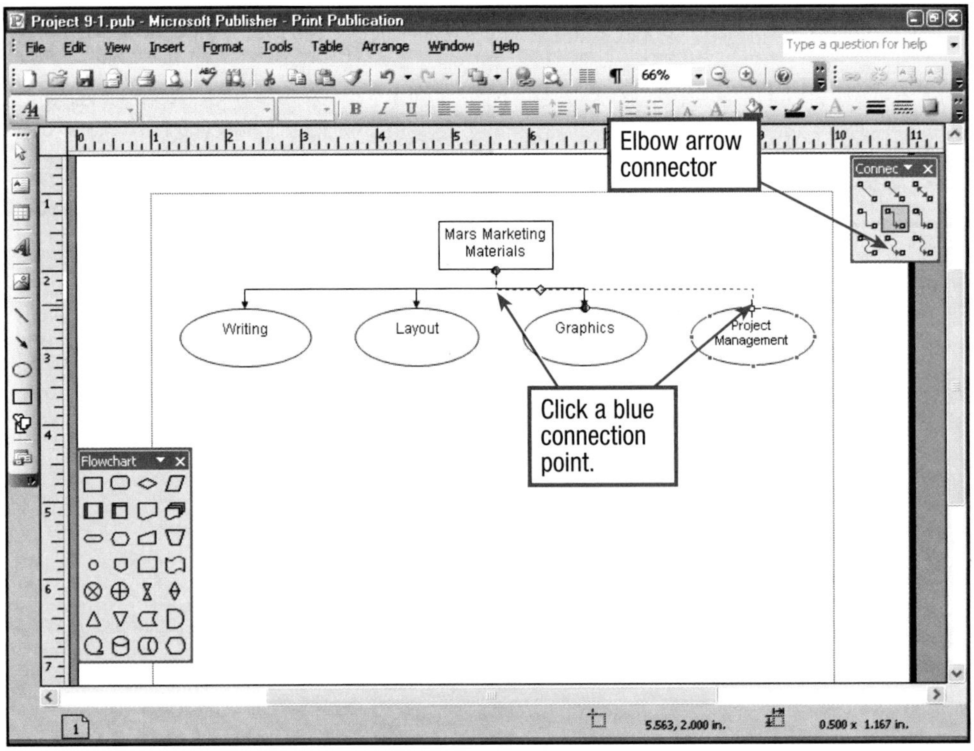

Project 3-7

Add Hyperlinks to Web Pages

Spotlight on Skills

- Insert hyperlinks
- Publish a file as a Web page

Key Terms

- hyperlink
- hot spot

Academic Focus

Language Arts
Organize related content

Student Data File

Hyperlinks create interactivity on a document, slide presentation, or Web site. Microsoft Word®, Publisher®, PowerPoint®, and Excel® all have similar tools for adding hyperlinks.

Hyperlinks

A **hyperlink** is a reference, often represented as colored text or a graphic, that allows you to move to different parts of a page or from one online page to another. Most text links are underlined and are a different color from the rest of the text. This location can be to a Web site anywhere on the Internet. You can even link to another document in a different program.

To create a hyperlink, you must first set a link location (which Publisher calls a **hot spot**) and then set a location to which the link points. When the hyperlink is activated, the computer locates the file and automatically opens the program that can read the file.

▶ **In this project,** you will add pages to the Web publication you started in Project 3-6. You will also create hyperlinks between the pages.

▼ **Figure 3.40** Check the Page Navigation icons on the status bar to see what page you are on.

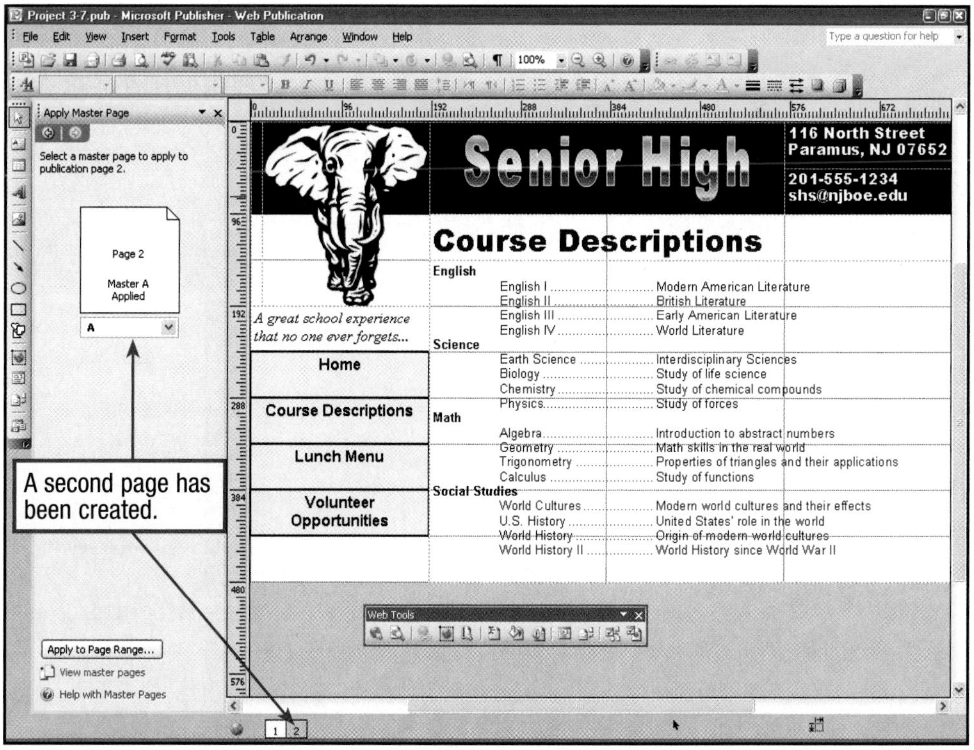

Step-by-Step

1. Open the Web page you started in Project 3-6.
2. Click **Insert>Page>Blank**. Click **OK**. (**Note**: If you need to add layout guides to new pages, create the same grid as in Project 3-6.)
3. Create a text box in **columns 2–4**, **row 3**. In **Arial Black**, **24 pt**, key Course Descriptions.
4. Create a second text box that spans **columns 2–4**, **rows 4–10**. Click **Insert>Text File** and insert **Data File 3-7a**.

Project 9-1 Assign Team Roles

Spotlight on Skills

- Create a flowchart
- Add connectors

Key Term

- connector

Academic Focus

Science
Break a process into steps

Go Online PREVIEW
www.glencoe.com

Before You Begin Go to **Chapter 9**, and choose **PowerPoint Presentations** to preview the documents you will be creating. Also, use the individual project **Rubrics** to help create and evaluate your work.

Imagine that it is the year 2125 and interplanetary travel for vacations is as common as airplane travel is today. You work in the marketing department of Light Travel, a company that sells adventure travel packages to Mars. Your boss wants you and your team to put together a set of marketing materials that highlight your company's services. If your boss likes the materials, it could mean promotions for all of you.

Your team decides to start by creating a logo and business package. Later on, you will create a brochure, booklet, Web page, and PowerPoint presentation. First you need to determine the role each team member will play, and you also need to create a budget and a timeline for the project.

Create a Flowchart

You will start your project by creating a flowchart to help you outline team member roles and responsibilities. A flowchart is made of simple shapes such as ovals, squares, circles, and rectangles that are joined together by connectors. A **connector** is a line that stays attached to a shape regardless of where the shape is moved.

▶ **In this project,** you will use Microsoft Publisher to create a flowchart that divides the work and assigns responsibilities to group members based on their abilities and interests.

Step-by-Step

1. In Publisher, open a blank publication in **Landscape**.
2. Click **Tools>Options>Edit**, and turn off **Hyphenation**.
3. Click **AutoShapes** . Choose **Flowchart**.
4. Click the dotted gripper on the menu, and drag it onto the workspace. Repeat with the **Connectors** menu.

▼ Figure 9.1 **Create a floating toolbar by dragging the gripper at the top of a menu.**

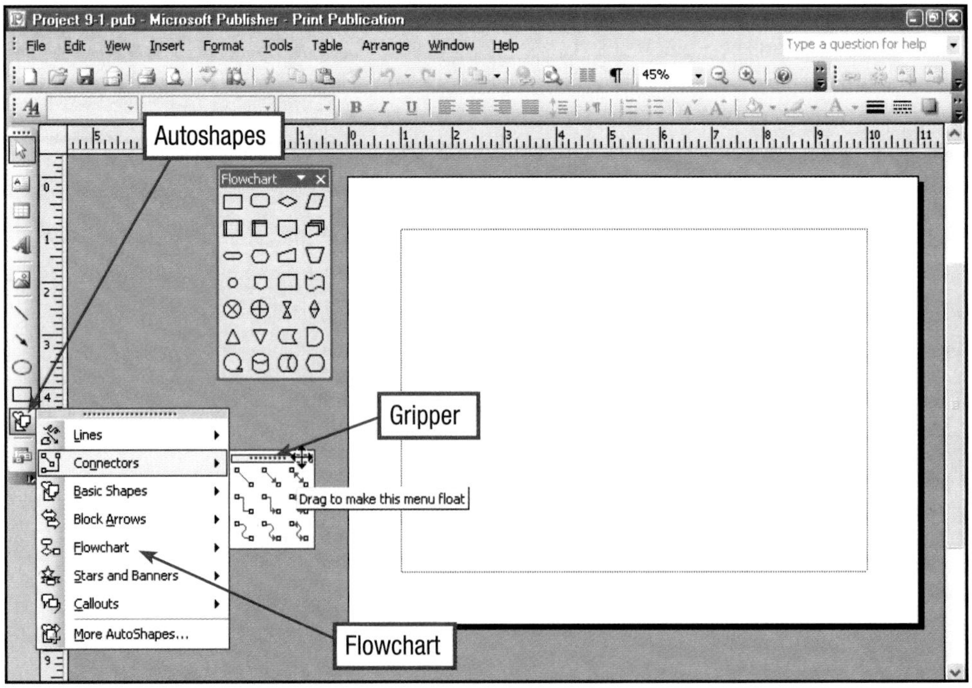

5. Follow Steps 2–3 to insert a new **blank page**, and key the title Lunch Menu in **row 3**.

6. Follow Step 4 to insert **Data File 3-7b** on the new page below the title.

7. Repeat Steps 2–4 to insert a new page titled Volunteer Opportunities. Insert **Data File 3-7c** (Figure 3.41).

8. On the **Page Sorter**, click **Page 1** to return to that page.

Insert Hyperlinks

9. On the **Web Tools** toolbar, click **Hot Spot**. Then click the top left corner of the **Home** box, and drag the hot spot so that it covers the box.

10. In the **Insert Hyperlink** box, click **Place in this Document**. Then choose **Page 1**.

11. Click **Change Title**, and rename Page 1 Senior High Home Page. (Figure 3.42).

12. Click **OK** to close the dialog boxes. Then click **Arrange>Send to Master Page**.

▼ **Figure 3.41** Your document should have 4 pages after Step 7.

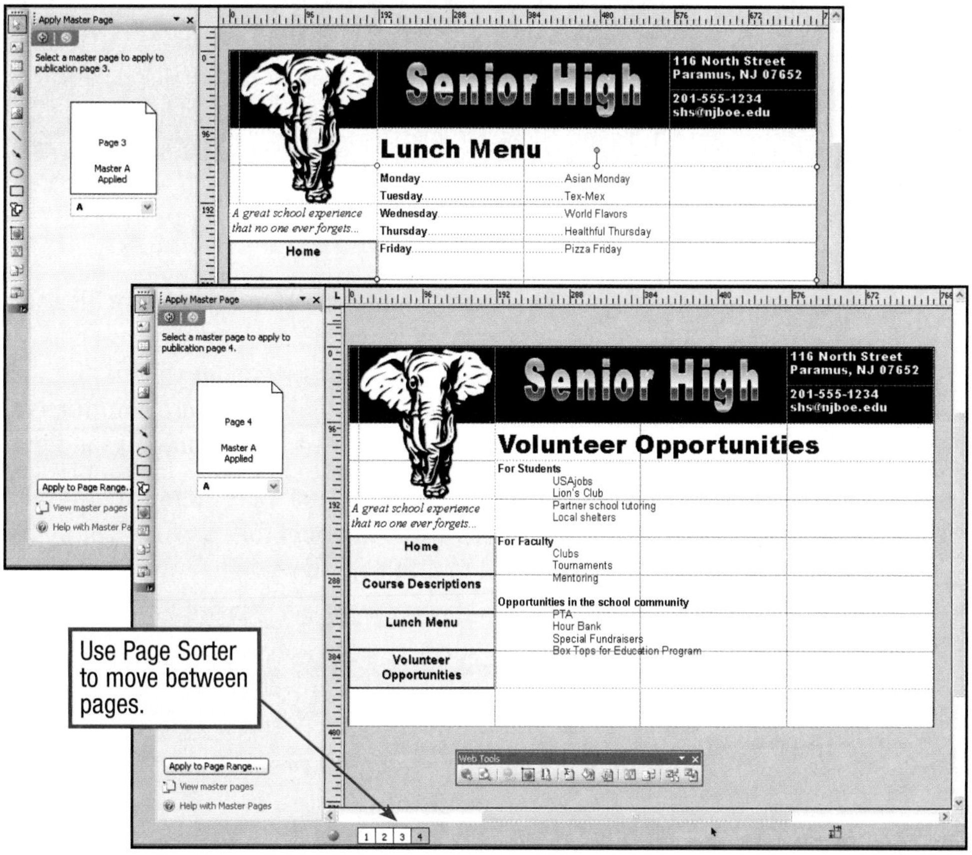

▼ **Figure 3.42** Setting a hot spot creates a link to another page in the document.

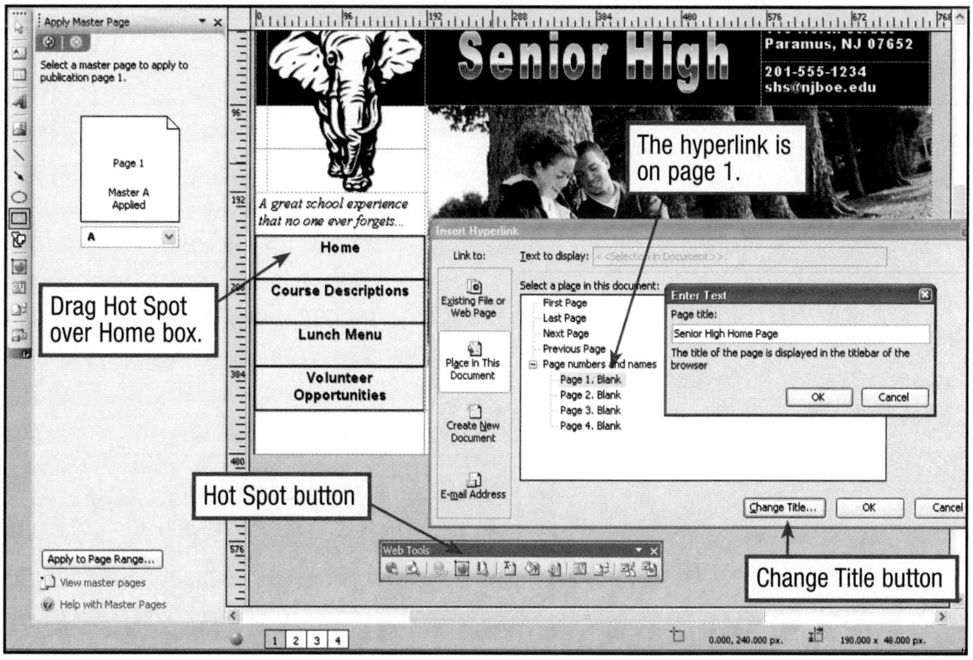

WORKSHOP

Toolbox

Tools for Teams

You Will Learn To

- Identify software for teamwork
- Compare software features

Key Term

milestone

When you are working in a group, clear and ongoing communication is a key strategy for success. Communicating may seem easy if your whole team is working in the same place, but what if all or part of the team work out of their homes? There are many software solutions for helping groups communicate and keep track of deadlines, budgets, and other critical information.

Stay in Touch E-mail programs such as Microsoft Outlook and Outlook Express are great tools for communicating as a team. Instant Messaging is a useful tool that allows you to communicate in real time.

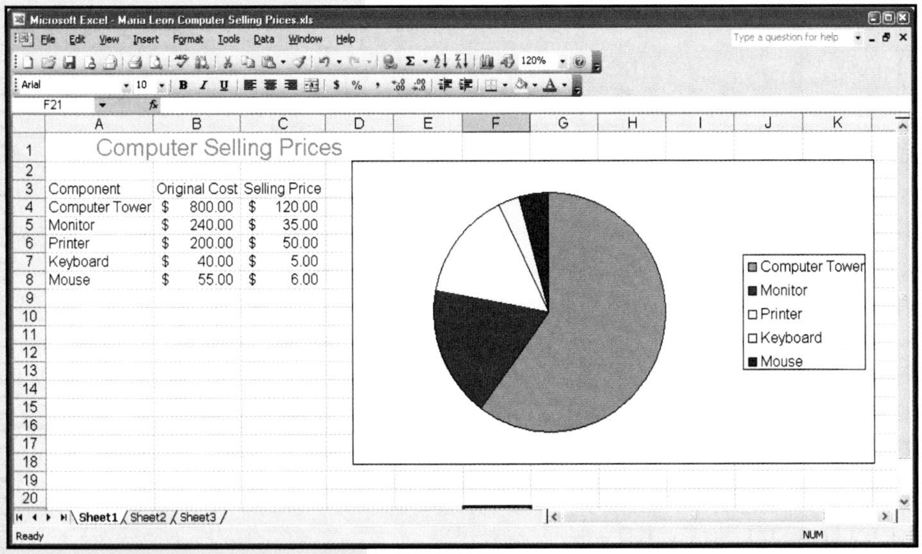

▲ Excel can create charts to compare data.

Track Your Budget Microsoft® Excel is electronic spreadsheet software that is particularly useful for budgeting purposes. With Excel, you can produce professional reports, perform simple financial calculations, and create charts. Excel spreadsheets can be attached to e-mail messages and shared with your team.

Stay on Schedule Project management software such as Microsoft® Project is helpful for many project management tasks, such as setting up and maintaining the project schedule. You can also use Excel to break a larger **milestone**—a critical point in a project—into smaller parts. You can then determine when each component must be finished in order to meet the deadline.

Reading Check

1. **Evaluate** If you wanted to create a chart comparing the costs of each part of a project, which software would you use?
2. **Draw Conclusions** How might a project manager use Microsoft Excel?

13 Repeat Steps 9–12 to create hot spots for the other three boxes in column 1:

- Link each box to the appropriate page.
- Change the page title.
- Send the link to the master page.

14 On Page 1, click **Rectangle**, and drag a rectangle over the **Home** box.

15 On the **Formatting toolbar**, click **Fill Color>More Fill Colors**. Choose green, and adjust the transparency slider to 75 percent.

16 Select the rectangle. On the **Formatting** toolbar, click **Line Color**, and choose **No Line**.

17 **Copy** the rectangle. On **Page 2**, paste the rectangle over the **Course Descriptions** box.

18 On **Page 3**, paste the rectangle over the **Lunch Menu** box. On **Page 4**, paste the rectangle over **Volunteer Opportunities**.

19 Click **Web Page Preview** (or **File>Web Page Preview**) to test your hyperlinks (Figure 3.43).

Publish a File as a Web Page

20 Proofread your work. Follow your teacher's instructions for saving and printing your work.

▼ **Figure 3.43** Your document might look slightly different when it is published as a Web page.

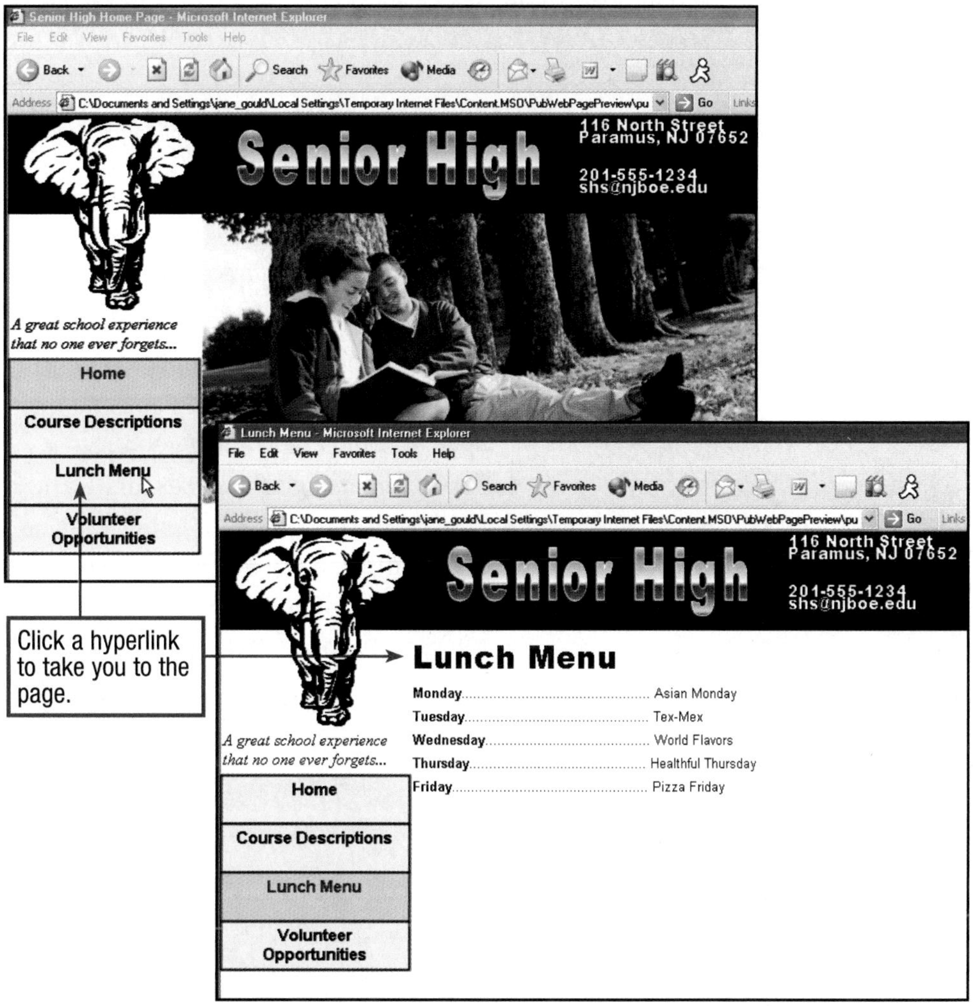

REVIEW AND REVISE

Check your work Use Figure 3.43 as a guide and check that:

- ☑ The text and images are properly aligned and laid out in Publisher and as a Web page.
- ☑ The document has four pages, each with its own content.
- ☑ The master page text and images are on each page of the document.
- ☑ Hyperlinks work correctly and link to the correct pages.
- ☑ Design uses repetition on all pages of the document.
- ☑ Text is easy to read, and spelling and punctuation are correct.

How Do I Resolve Conflicts?

During the course of a project, group members will disagree, but solutions will need to be worked out quickly. Set rules for handling these conflicts in advance. Knowing how to resolve conflicts successfully will help ensure that your team completes its task and achieves its goals. To avoid conflicts:

- Avoid getting personal. Focus on the problem, not the person.
- Provide constructive feedback, not criticism.
- Do not dwell on the past. Focusing on past mistakes does nothing to help with the present problem.
- Try to understand the needs and feelings of your teammates.
- Use nonverbal communication skills to improve relationships. For example, approach team members with a smile.
- Remind group members that you all have a common goal—to achieve a successful outcome.

Conflict Resolution Strategies

Definition	Example
I Win	Unwilling to compromise. "We are going to do a tri-fold brochure for the advertising campaign, not a flyer! And that's final!"
You Win	Yields to the other point of view. "Your idea about the font color choice will work after all."
Win-Win	Solution results from both points of view. "I really want to go to a Chinese restaurant." "I am tired and don't feel like going out to eat." Win-Win: "How about we get Chinese takeout and eat at home?"
Other	The decision is given to another, or a third option is chosen. Identify the times when you can walk away from an issue. "We should forget about this for now and come back to it later in the project."

Reading Check

1. **Describe** What are three strategies that can help teams work effectively?
2. **Evaluate** Which conflict resolution strategies might help resolve a fight between siblings who want to watch different TV shows at the same time?

Skills Studio

Reinforce Your Skills

- **Project 3-8**
  - Apply layout guides
  - Lay out text and graphics
  - Create a master page
- **Project 3-9**
  - Apply styles
  - Create a second master page
  - Print on two sides

Go Online ACTIVITIES
www.glencoe.com

Challenge Yourself Go to **Chapter 3**, and choose **Enrichment Activities** for more practice with the skills you have learned.

Design a Menu

The following two projects will take you through the steps you need to create a bi-fold menu that includes text and graphics.

- **Project 3-8** Design the menu exterior
- **Project 3-9** Design the menu interior

Design an Enticing Menu

A menu often provides the first impression for judging a restaurant and its food. The menu must be laid out clearly so that it is easy to find foods by certain categories and to see the prices. It also must provide interesting descriptions of the dishes, including details that appeal to customers that the restaurant hopes to attract.

Many restaurants include photos in their menus. Photos are a great way to focus the attention of a hungry person on specific items that the restaurant may want to promote.

Menus come in all different shapes, sizes, and layouts. A menu might be one single-sided page or six double-sided pages folded like a book. The design choice depends upon the amount of content, the budget, and the message that the restaurant wants to convey to its customers.

Create a Flowchart When possible, break long processes and large projects into smaller steps and easily attained goals. In the workplace, flowcharts are often used for this purpose. A **flowchart** illustrates procedures by using a set of standard symbols like boxes and arrows. This process makes it easier to concentrate upon the individual tasks that need to be accomplished. In the example on page 378, a simple task is broken into parts, and then each part is assigned to a team member. The relationship between tasks is represented by connector lines and arrows.

Establish a Timeline It also helps to use a **timeline**, a visual representation, often a chart, that shows when each stage of the project will be completed. A timeline can help determine if the group is on target to meet the goal. If part of the project is in danger of not meeting its deadline, then the goals should be re-evaluated. Can the scope of the project be changed? Can others be brought in to assist?

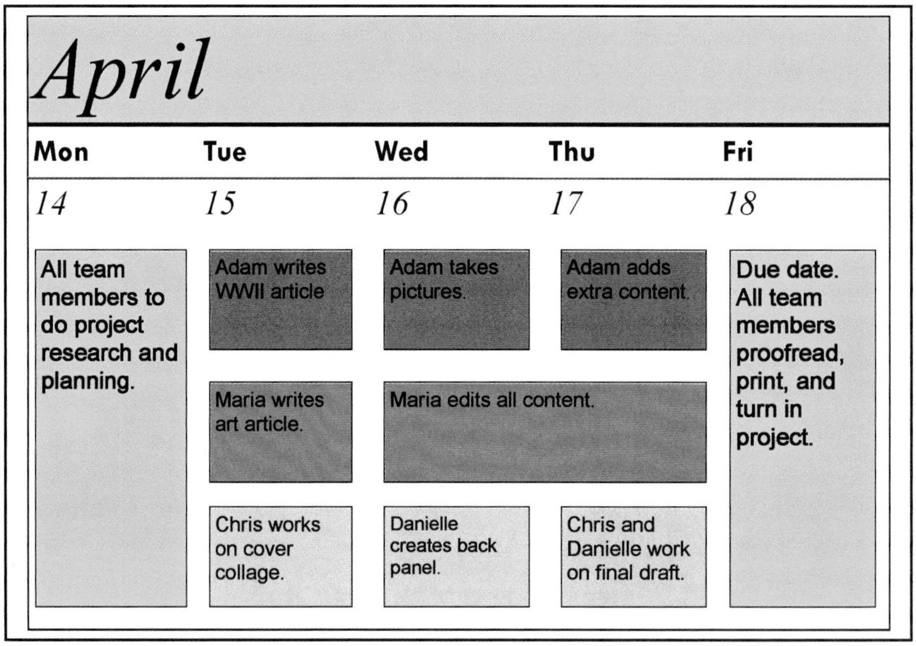
April
Mon
Tue
Wed
Thu
Fri
14
15
16
17
18
All team members to do project research and planning.
Adam writes WWII article
Adam takes pictures.
Adam adds extra content.
Due date. All team members proofread, print, and turn in project.
Maria writes art article.
Maria edits all content.
Chris works on cover collage.
Danielle creates back panel.
Chris and Danielle work on final draft.

▲ All parts of a project can be tracked on a timeline.

Often, conflict will arise when people are working together. The **project manager**, who is the person leading or supervising the team, should always be aware of potential problems. He or she is responsible for making sure that team members work well together in order to complete the project on time.

Eye On Ethics

Case Study Today's technology makes it easy to modify published music, movies, and games. That does not mean it is the right thing to do. What if a friend came up with new lyrics for a popular song that he wanted to publish on a music-swapping Internet site? People who have done this have been sued by the artists who created the original music. There could be stiff fines and legal actions.

Evaluate How would you advise your friend, to be sure that he was using technology ethically?

Skills Studio

Project 3-8 Design the Menu Exterior

Skills You Will Apply

- Apply layout guides
- Lay out text and graphics
- Create a master page

Academic Focus

Math
Evaluate spatial relationships

Student Data File

In Project 3-6, you used a master page to create a consistent design in Web pages. Print books also use repeated design elements. Look at your textbooks (including this book), and notice repetitive elements—headers, footers, borders, and page numbers—that can be created with a master page.

When you create a booklet, or any document with a two-page spread, Publisher automatically assumes you want to create a two-page master with a left and right page design. As you will see in this project, sometimes you may want to use the same page design for both pages in a spread. When you change from a two-page to a single-page master, the left page design is removed, and the right page design is applied to all pages of the document using the master page elements.

▶ **In this project,** you will create the outside of a menu. Unlike the bi-fold brochure you created in Project 3-5, the menu will be laid out like a booklet. Each panel will be created as an individual page. The pages will print so that they are laid out in the correct order when the paper they are on is folded like a booklet.

▼ **Figure 3.44** **The default booklet is four pages.**

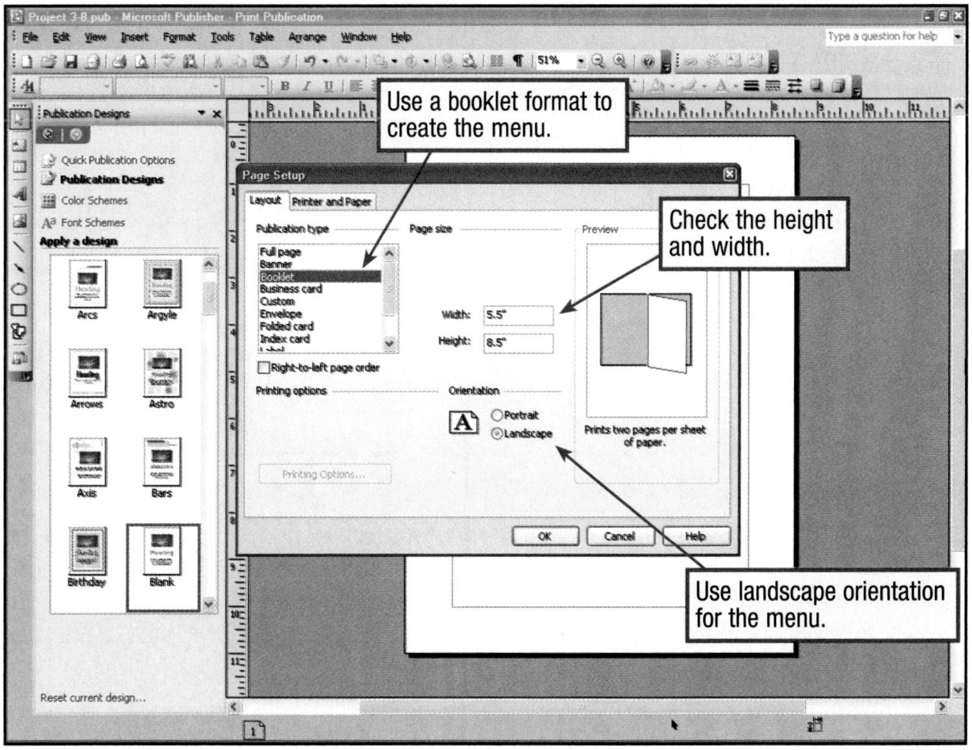

Step-by-Step

1 Open a new full page **Blank Print Publication**, and save the document.

Apply Layout Guides

2 Click **File>Page Setup**, and choose **Booklet**. Set the **Width** at **5.5 inches** and **Height** at **8.5 inches**. Click **OK**. When asked about adding three pages, click **Yes**.

3 Set margin guides. Change the top margin to **1.5 inches** and the rest to **0.5 inch**.

4 Set grid guides. Create **5 columns** and **4 rows**, both with a **0 inch gutter**.

WORK SHOP Foundations

Work with Groups

You Will Learn To

- Work as part of a team
- Resolve conflicts

Key Terms

teamwork
flowchart
timeline
project manager

In the workplace, employees seldom work alone. People work together in groups to get the job done. In stores, for example, managers, salespeople, and stockroom clerks depend upon each other to do their jobs well. Graphic artists have supervisors, co-workers, and clients whose opinions affect the final product. Writers have editors and reviewers whose input influences their work. Working as a group requires cooperation between group members, also known as **teamwork**.

What Makes an Effective Team?

As a student, you have worked in a variety of groups to complete school projects. From this experience, you have probably learned some successful teamwork strategies. For example, you may have noticed that teams work together better when each person clearly knows what he or she needs to do. For this reason, it is important to set clear expectations and use effective communication strategies. Teams also work well when the total workload is divided fairly, with work assigned to group members according to their interests and abilities.

Before You Read

Organize Information If you had to remember the names of everyone in your class on the first day, it would be difficult. However, what if you remembered one row at a time? Grouping information makes it easier to remember. When you read or take notes, think about how topics relate to each other. Then organize the topics by group categories.

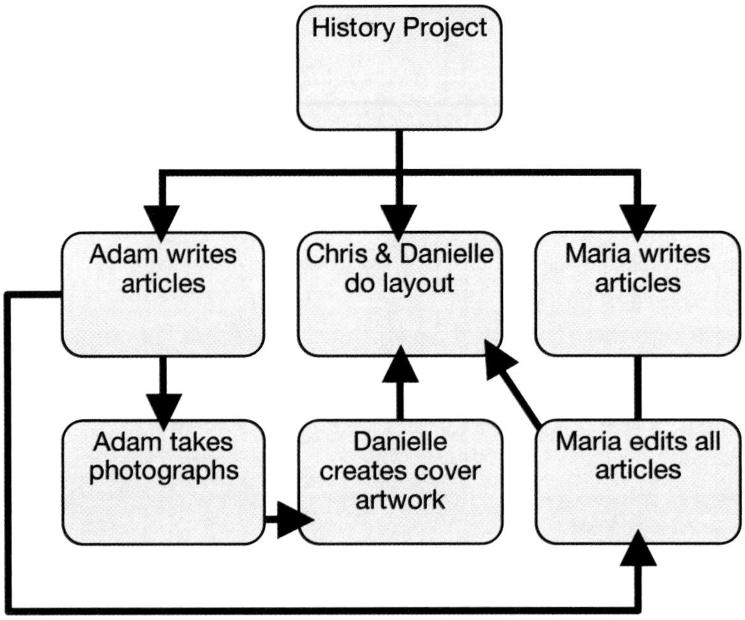

▲ A flowchart shows which group member is assigned to each task.

Lay out Text and Graphics

5 Insert picture **Data File 3-8a** in **row 1**, a logo. Change the **width** to **4 inches**.

6 Select the logo. Click **Arrange>Align** or **Distribute>Relative to Margin Guides**.

7 Select the logo again, and in the **Align** or **Distribute** menu, choose **Align Center**.

8 Create text boxes in **row 2** and **row 4**, between **columns 2–4**.

9 In the top box, use a slab serif font such as **Rockwell**, **18 pt**. **Center** and key
56 Diego Place
Miami, FL 33145
305-555-1234

10 In the bottom box, using **Rockwell**, **11 pt**. **Center** and key:
Monday–Friday 11:00 am–10:30 pm
Saturday 8:00 am–11:30 pm
Sunday closed

11 Select the Monday–Friday line, and click **Format>Horizontal Rules**. Place a **1 pt black** rule **before the paragraph** (Figure 3.45).

12 On **Page 1**, select the logo and **copy** it.

13 On **Page 4**, **paste** the logo at the bottom of the page. Align and center as in Steps 6–7 (Figure 3.46).

▼ **Figure 3.45** Use small caps for AM and PM and an en-dash between times.

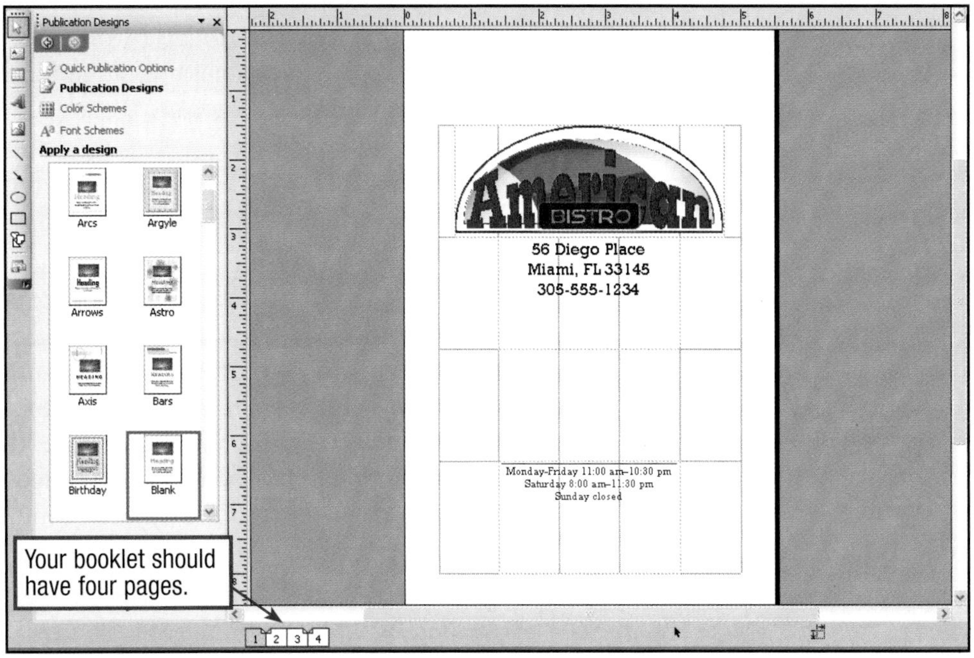

▼ **Figure 3.46** Use the Page Navigation Control buttons to move between pages.

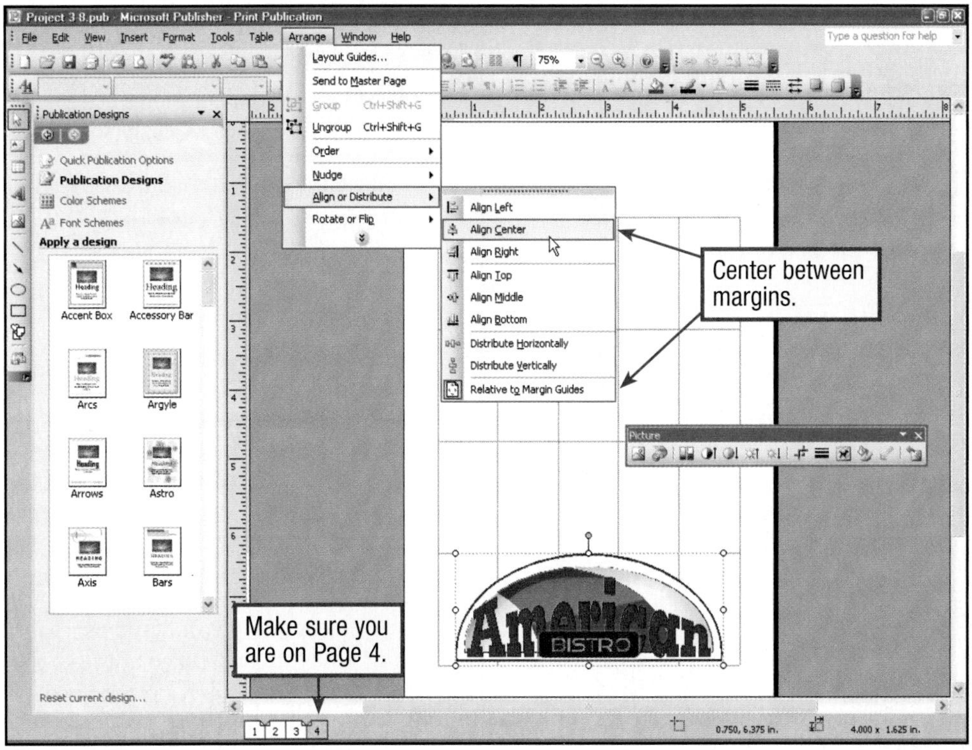

Chapter 9 Focus on Teamwork

Skills You Will Learn

Workshop Foundations
Work with Groups

Workshop Toolbox
Tools for Teams

Project 9-1
Assign Team Roles

Project 9-2
Create a Timeline

Project 9-3
Create a Budget

Project 9-4
Design a Logo

Project 9-5
Design a Business Card

Skills Studio

Design Business Stationery

Project 9-6
Design Business Letterhead

Project 9-7
Design Business Envelopes

Project 9-8
Perform a Mail Merge

In this chapter, you will learn how to work well in groups, which is an important skill in today's workplace. You will use these teamwork skills to create a business package for an interplanetary travel agency you and your classmates are forming.

Create a Business Package

Would you want to go to a college that sent you letters on stationery with orange lettering, balloons in the logo, and fonts like Curlz MT? Would you hire a clown for a children's birthday that had a business card that looked like it came from a college? Business stationery and business cards are often the first impression customers get from a company, and they should convey a message at a glance.

Besides creating a visual message, it is important for companies to create and maintain a consistent image in all of their communications with their customers. One way that companies achieve this is by creating a business package. A business package consists of business cards and company stationery (letterhead and envelopes) that incorporate the company logo and have a consistent overall design (colors, fonts, and borders) to visually tie the elements together.

DESIGN PROCESS: Business Packages

Elements	Issues
Purpose	To provide a consistent, professional looking set of materials for company communication.
Audience	Varies. Business cards are used to leave contact information. Letterhead stationery is used for letters to clients, vendors, or others regarding company business.
Content	Business cards include the employee's name, title, contact information, and the company logo. Letterhead contains the company logo, contact information, and sometimes staff names.
Layout	A letterhead should be placed so that it does not conflict with the formatting of a letter. Business cards should be easy to read with plenty of white space.
Publication	Letterhead and business cards are created on different paper weights. Each company will pick materials that reflect the company image. These materials are typically published by professional printers, though many individuals now publish their own business packages using office color printers.

14 Insert a text box in the row above the logo. In **Rockwell**, **18 pt**. **Center** and key When you need [ENTER] a break from [ENTER] home cooking.

15 Click **Format>Text Box>Text Box**. Under *Vertical Alignment,* choose **Bottom**. The page should look similar to Figure 3.47.

Create a Master Page

16 Click **View>Master Page** (or [CTRL] + [M]).

17 On the **Edit Master Pages** toolbar, click **Change Single/Two Page** [icon]. Click **OK** in the warning dialog box that pops up.

18 Click **Insert>Picture** and choose **Data File 3-8b**. This adds a background to your master page.

19 On the **Edit Master Pages** toolbar, click **Close Master View** to return to the document.

20 See how your pages will print by clicking **File>Print Preview**. The front and back covers should look similar to Figure 3.48. Click **Close** and return to **Normal** view.

21 Follow your teacher's instructions for saving your work. You will continue to work with the menu in Project 3-9.

▼ **Figure 3.47** The master page will automatically apply a background to your pages.

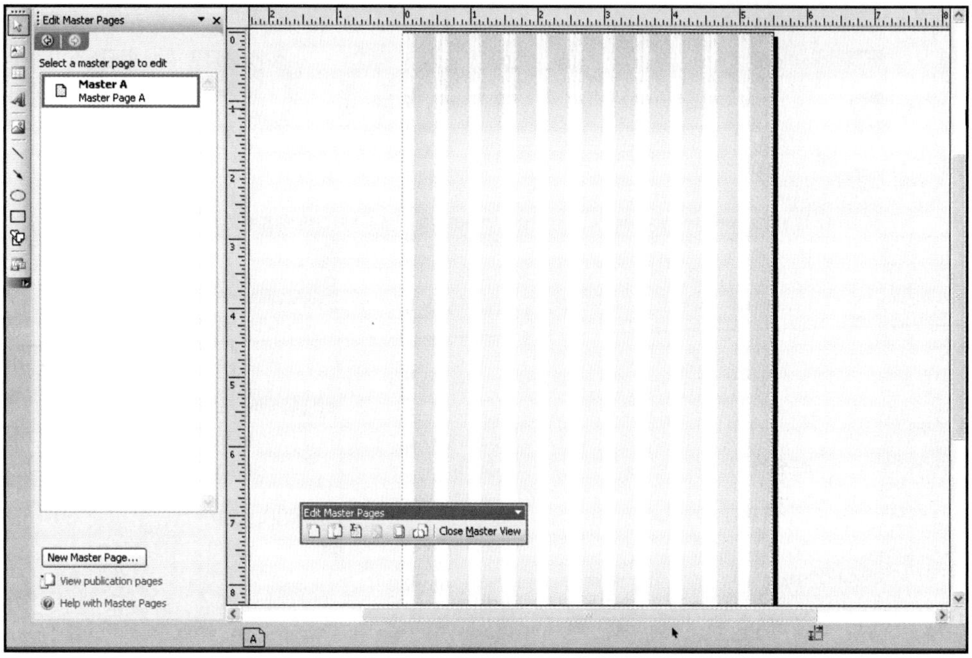

▼ **Figure 3.48** In Print Preview, you can see how the pages will print.

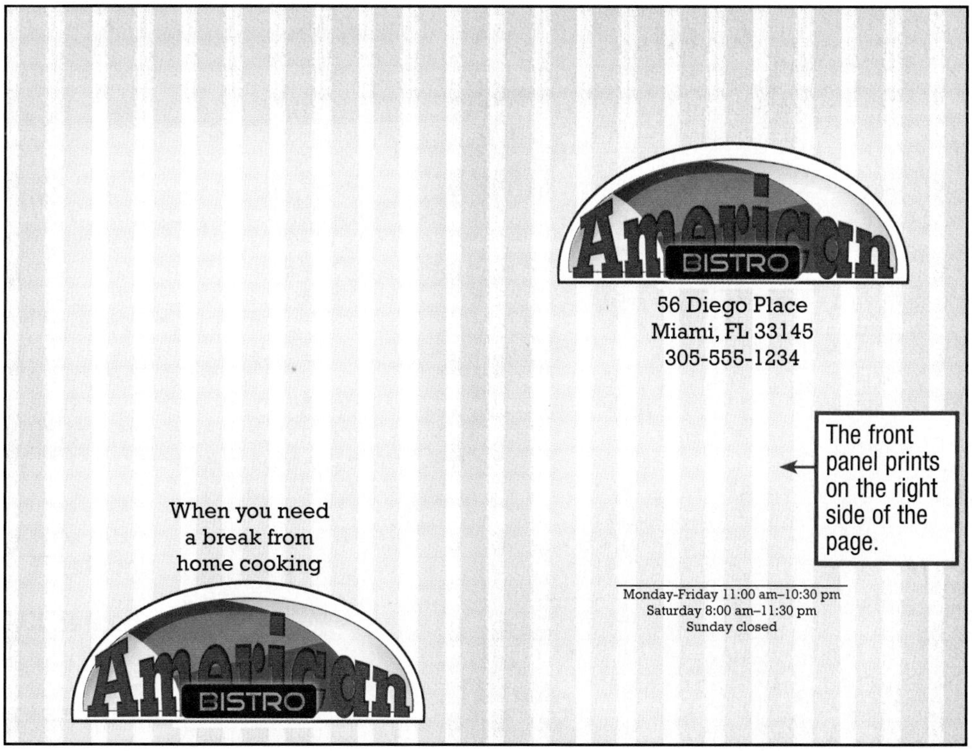

American
BISTRO
56 Diego Place
Miami, FL 33145
305-555-1234
The front panel prints on the right side of the page.
When you need
a break from
home cooking
Monday-Friday 11:00 am–10:30 pm
Saturday 8:00 am–11:30 pm
Sunday closed
American
BISTRO

UNIT

5 Design as a Team

Contents

Project 3-9 Design the Menu Interior

Skills You Will Apply

- Apply styles to text
- Create and apply a second master page

Key Term

- duplex printing

Academic Focus

Math
Evaluate spatial relationships

Sidebar

Align with Tabs
Although text can be set almost anywhere on a page using text boxes, you will find that tabs are still an important part of good design. Tabs should be used to align text (especially in lists). Never use the space bar to align text. It is time consuming, and it can create significant problems when editing a document.

Draw Conclusions How might aligning text with the space bar create problems when you revise a document?

Unlike previous versions of Microsoft Publisher, Publisher 2003 can support multiple masters. This allows you to create separate masters for pages that share some, but not all design elements, of other pages. For example, in this textbook, the Workshop Foundations and the Workshop Toolbox have the same logo and top border, but the border is in a different color.

Apply Styles

Publisher also provides consistency by *applying styles* throughout an entire design. When applied to text, the **Text Styles** tool will keep track of the font typeface, size, color, borders/shading, tab stops, and margin settings. If any of these font characteristics are changed, the change can be quickly applied to *all* items that have been assigned to share the same style—*regardless of how many items that may include*.

The process of applying styles in Microsoft Publisher works exactly the same way as it did in Microsoft Word (see Project 2-6):

1. Apply the required formatting to the text.
2. Select the formatted text, and enter a name in the **New Style** dialog box.
3. Select other text that shares the same style, and click the style name in the **Style** task pane. You can also use the **Format Painter** to apply the style to other text.

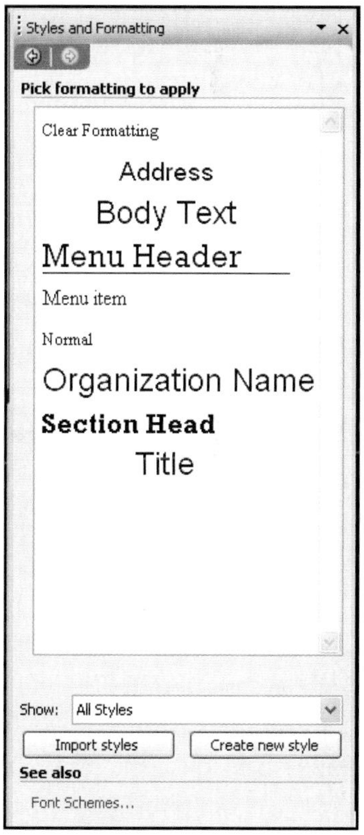

▶ The Styles and Formatting task pane displays the program's default styles as well as styles that you create.

▶ **In this project,** you will create the interior pages of the menu you started in Project 3-8. You will use tabs and leaders, applied styles, and a second master page to give your menu a clear and consistent design. If you print your menu, you will see that Publisher automatically arranges the pages so that the cover and interior print correctly. If possible, use **duplex printing** which allows computers to print both sides of the brochure at the same time.

UNIT 4

Projects Across the Curriculum

Project 3 Create a Board Game Review ★★★

SCIENCE Work together with classmates to create a board game that reviews all of the scientific facts that you have learned this year. Your game should include questions from any of your science classes such as biology, chemistry, and physics.

Plan

1. Determine the type of game and design the game itself: the cards, game board, and box.

Create

2. Use Adobe Illustrator's Symbol Sprayer and Type on a Path features.
3. Use Publisher to create a master page for the cards.

Publish

4. Use Publisher for the layout and for tile printing.
5. Use common objects for game pieces and purchase dice, create a spinner, or use cards to move the pieces forward (or backward) in your game. Have fun!

Project 4 Create a Pottery Design ★★★

SOCIAL STUDIES Use Illustrator to design an original pottery pattern.

▲ Navajo designs tended to be geometric in style.

Plan

1. Research the types of patterns that were used in Native American pottery, Grecian and Roman pottery, or classical Chinese, Japanese, or Korean pottery. Note the colors and types of patterns used by each culture.

Create

2. Use Adobe Illustrator's 3D capabilities to create a historically accurate pottery pattern representation.
3. Write a short description of the pottery and its use (based on shape). Provide background on the culture and the time period that the pottery is from. Explain the significance of the pottery's design for the people who created it, and include examples of other designs that were common among the culture.

Student Data File

Step-by-Step

1. Open the menu you created in Project 3-8. Make sure you are in the publication view, not the master pages.

2. Click on **Page 2**. Notice that **Pages 2–3** are a spread.

3. Open the **Apply Master Pages** task pane. Below the thumbnails, choose **Ignore Master** (Figure 3.49).

4. On **Page 2**, create a text box that spans **columns 3–5, rows 1–4**. Insert **Data File 3-9a** (a text file).

5. On **Page 3**, create a text box that spans **columns 1–3, rows 1–4. Insert Data File 3-9b** (a text file).

Apply Styles to Text

6. Select the first word on **Page 2**, *Drinks*. Change the font to **Rockwell, 24 pt**, and **add a black horizontal rule after the paragraph**. Set paragraph line **spacing** to **12 pt before paragraphs**.

7. Click **Styles and Formatting** [44]. In the task pane, choose **Create new style**, and enter the new style name Menu Heading (Figure 3.50).

▼ **Figure 3.49** You do not need to use the same master for every page of your document.

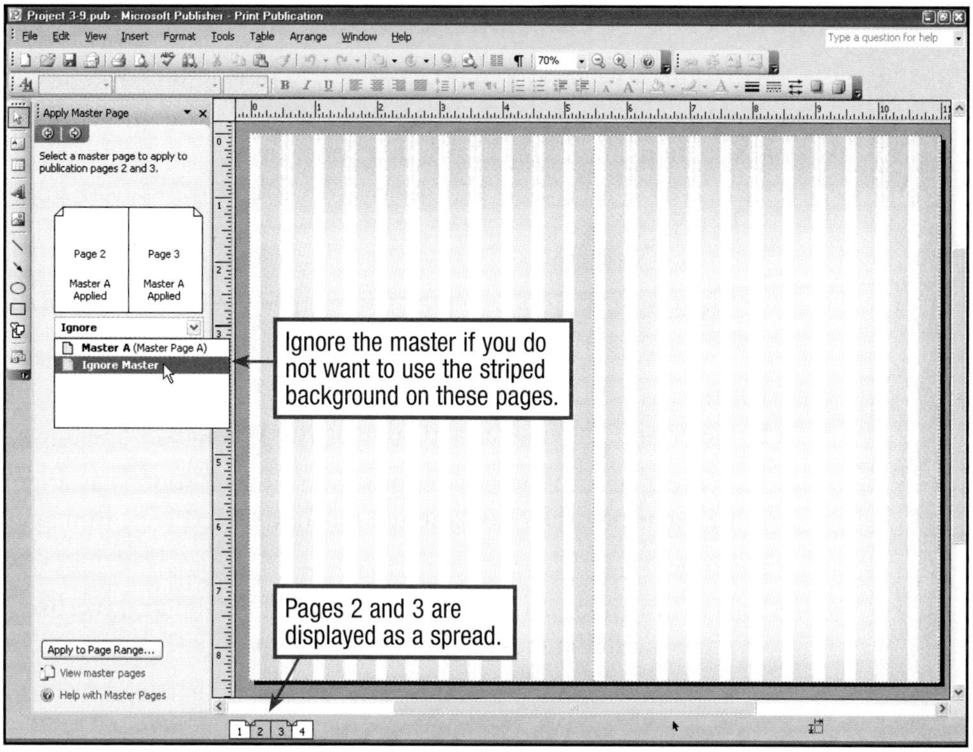

Ignore the master if you do not want to use the striped background on these pages.
Pages 2 and 3 are displayed as a spread.

▼ **Figure 3.50** You can add new text styles to the Styles menu.

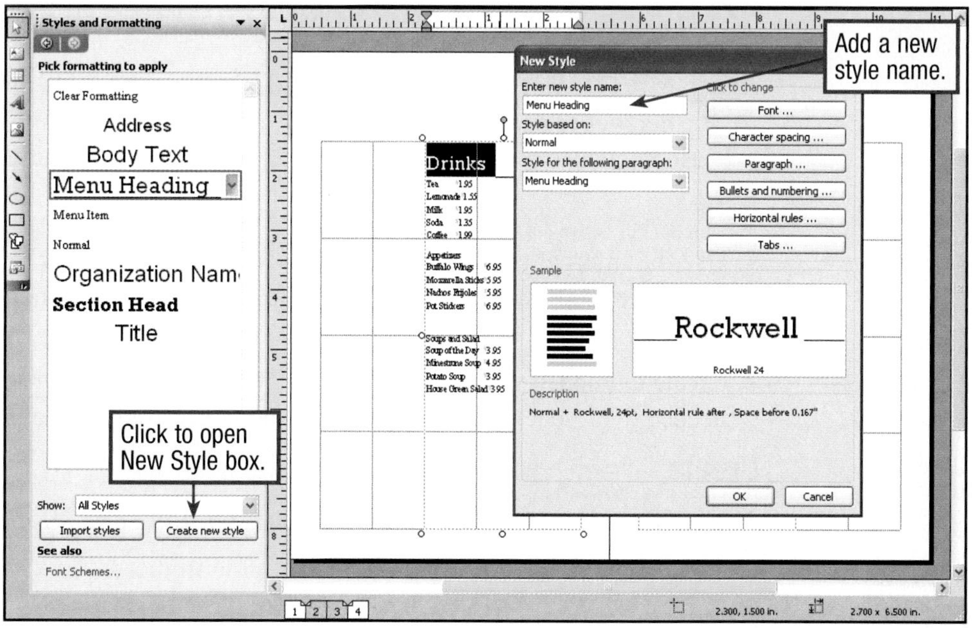

Click to open New Style box.

UNIT 4

Projects Across the Curriculum

The skills you learned in this unit will help you in your other classes, too. Use your desktop publishing skills to complete the following projects. Follow your teacher's instructions for saving or printing your work.

Project 1 Create a Food Product ★

LANGUAGE ARTS Use Publisher and Illustrator to develop an advertisement for your own new food product.

Plan

1. Determine the images and content you will need.

2. Write a description of your product so that it sounds as appetizing as possible. Look online for food advertising strategies.

Create

3. Use Illustrator and Publisher to create a full-color advertisement including the description of your product.

4. Explain why you chose the fonts, colors, effects, and layout. Describe how the graphics appeal to the audience.

Project 2 Create a Graph ★★

MATH You have been asked to design a graph for a magazine comparing the number of sports injuries between male and female high school athletes. Your graph will use images to present the information in a clear, interesting way.

Plan

1. Use the Internet or interview coaches to find statistics for the number of sports-related injuries for high school males and females.

2. Create thumbnail sketches, and determine the design elements needed to present the information in an audience-friendly manner.

> **Go Online RUBRICS**
> www.glencoe.com
> **Unit: Projects** Go to **Unit 4,** and choose **Rubrics**. Use the projects to help create and evaluate your work.

Create

3. Use Illustrator tools to create a visually appealing and informative graph.

4. Try a shattered text title for a connection to injuries.

5. Include source citations in proper format.

8 Select *Drinks*. Double-click **Format Painter** [icon].

9 Use the **Format Painter** to apply the new style to each section head (Figure 3.51). Click [ESC] to turn off **Format Painter**.

10 Select the second line, *Tea...$1.95*. Change the
- Font to **Times New Roman**, **12 pt**.
- Paragraph **line spacing** to **8 after paragraphs**.

11 Click **Format>Tabs**. Clear old tabs. Set a **Right tab** stop at **2.125 inches** with a **Dot leader**. Click **Set** and **OK**.

12 Name the style *Menu Item*, and apply it to the other menu items (Figure 3.51). Check that **Show: All Styles** is selected.

13 Insert the picture files (**Data Files 3-9c**, **3-9d**, **3-9e**, and **3-9f**). Use Figure 3.52 as a guide to determine where to place each photo.

14 Add text boxes above or below each photo. Add a caption describing the pictured dish.

15 Select the first caption. Change the font to **Arial Narrow**, **10 pt**. Add a new style named *Caption*, and apply it to all the captions.

Figure 3.51 To turn off Format Painter, press the Escape key.

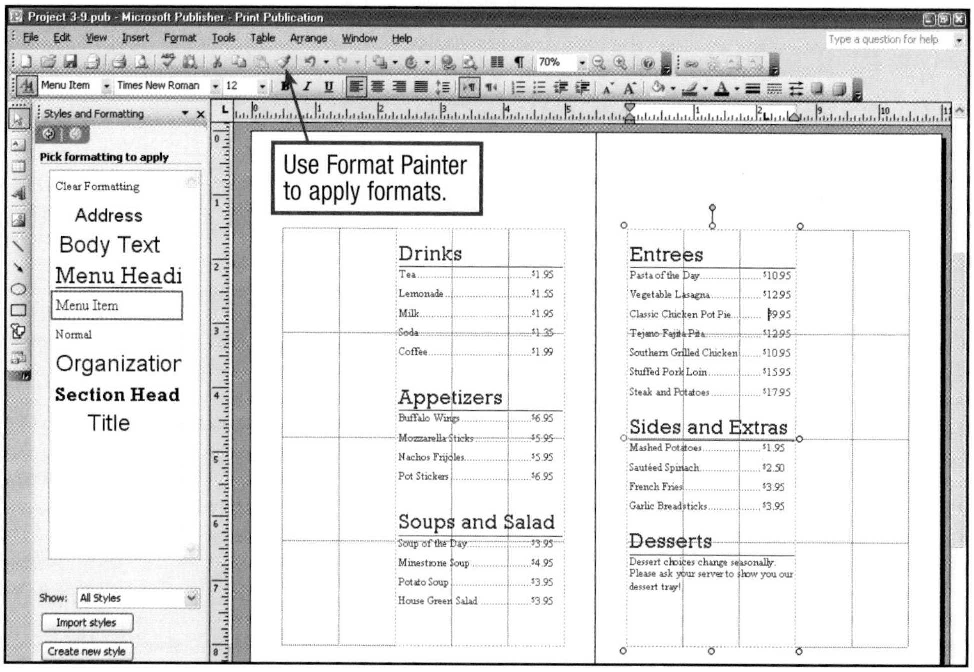

Figure 3.52 Place photos according to the figure.

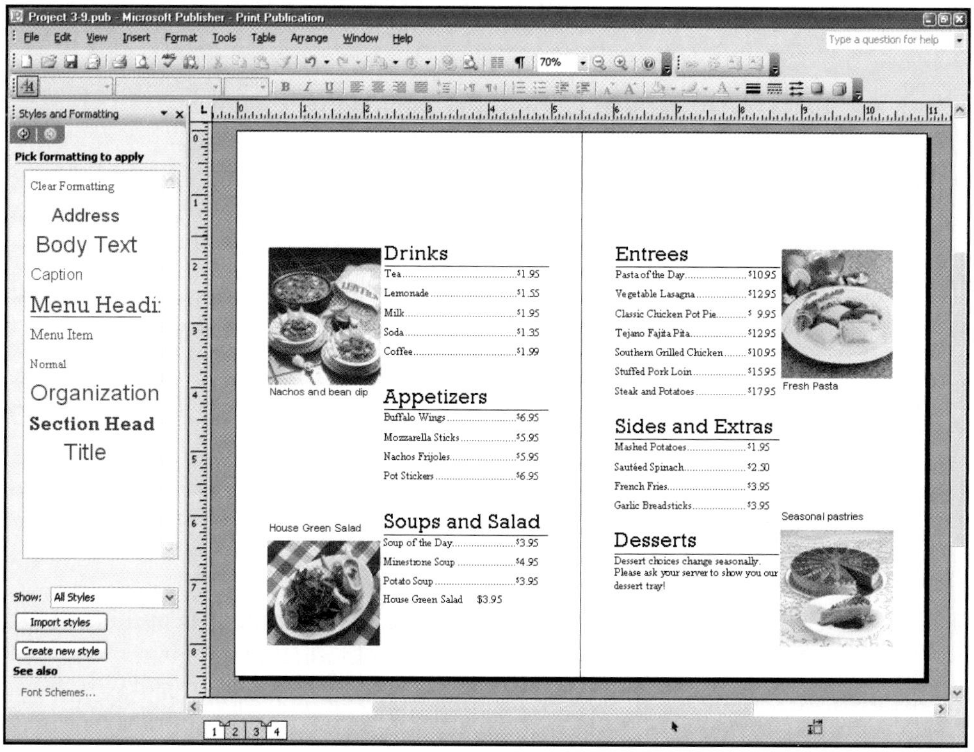

2 Independent Practice ★★

LANGUAGE ARTS Create a Proverb Banner Proverbs are wise sayings that are passed down through the generations, such as "A journey of a thousand miles begins with a single step." Create a banner that illustrates a proverb, its origin, and its meaning.

a. Plan Perform accurate research on your topic. Locate the national origin and author. Use proper format for citing the source.

b. Design Create thumbnail sketches.
- Evaluate the design according to PARC principles and revise as necessary.
- Create a final design sketch.

c. Create Use Illustrator to create special text effects for the proverb.
- Add a background and other design elements.
- Use Publisher for small text and for the layout of individual elements.

d. Publish Use Publisher to tile print your design. Assemble the design by trimming and taping the design together.

Go Online ACTIVITIES
www.glencoe.com

Enrichment Go to **Chapter 8**, and choose **Enrichment Activities.** Find more desktop publishing projects using Adobe Illustrator.

3 Independent Practice ★★★

TEAMWORK Design Cereal Box Packaging Imagine that you are a graphic artist specializing in cereal box packaging. Work with a partner or team of students to brainstorm a theme for a new cereal, and create everything you need to make a compelling product design. The theme should be incorporated throughout the entire design.

a. Plan Flatten a cereal box, and trace a template on construction paper.
- Measure each side carefully, and allow for printable space only.
- Assign responsibilities for each side of the cereal box.
- Determine what design elements belong on each side.

b. Design: Create thumbnail sketches for each side.

c. Create Use Illustrator to create special text effects for the title and drawings. Use Publisher for small text and for the layout of individual elements.

d. Publish Assemble the design by trimming, gluing, and taping the design together. With your teacher's permission, display the design.

Create and Apply a Second Master Page

16 Click **View>Master Page**. On the **Edit Master Page** toolbar, click **New Master Page**.

17 In the **New Master Page** box, key a description: Menu Spread. Click **OK** (Figure 3.53).

18 Change the **top** margin guide to **1.5 inches** and the bottom to **0.5 inches**.

19 Insert the logo file (**Data File 3-8a**), and change the **width** to **2 inches**.

20 Position the logo on the top grid line and **center** relative to the Margin Guides (Figure 3.54).

21 Draw a **1 pt gray line** along the **top** and **bottom** Grid Guides.

22 Click **Insert>Page Number**. Insert a page number in the **bottom center** of the page but **not** on the first page (Figure 3.54).

23 Draw a rectangle over the page. Add a **gradient gold fill**, **horizontal shading** at the **lightest** setting. Change the order to **Send to Back**.

▼ **Figure 3.53** When you use multiple masters, it is helpful to name the master pages.

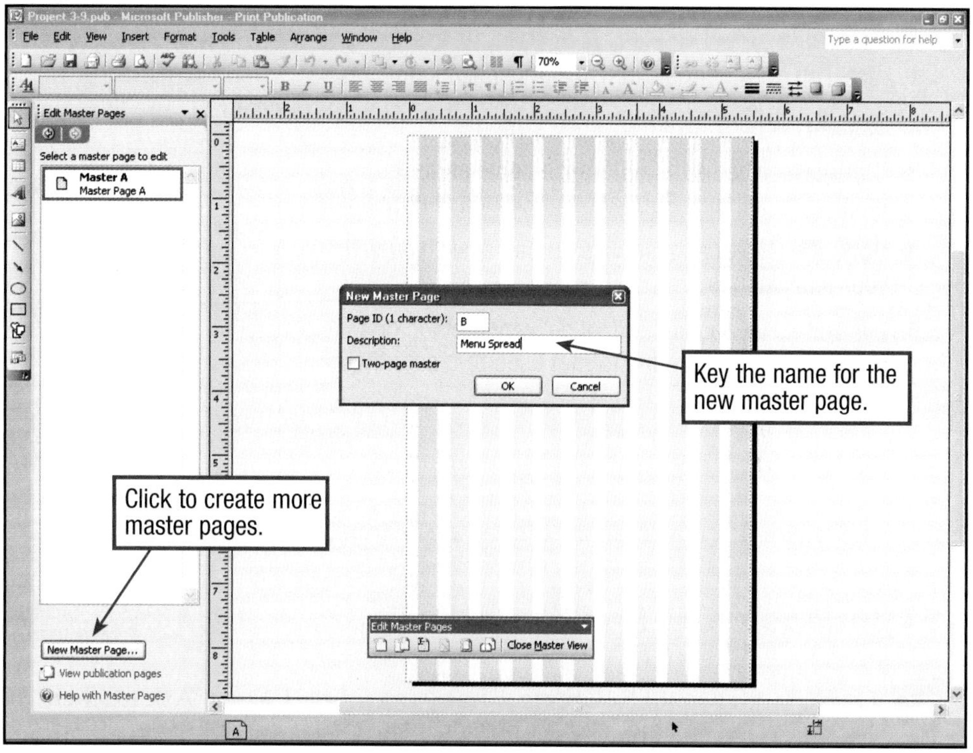

▼ **Figure 3.54** The design elements on this page will be applied to both spread pages.

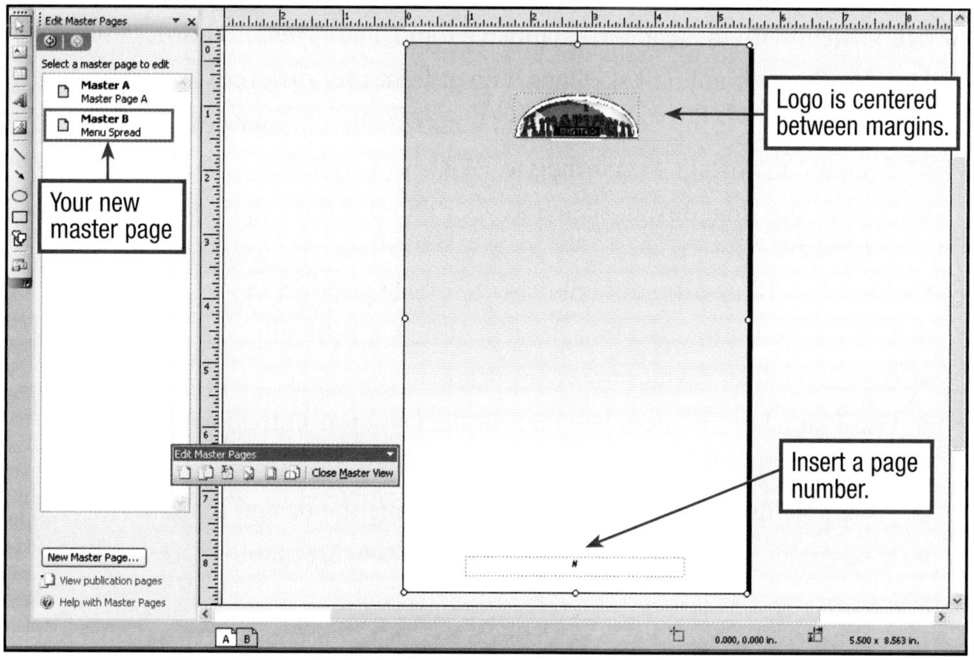

Chapter 8 Assessment

Reading Check

1. **Identify** Name three examples of publication media.
2. **Explain** What is layering?
3. **Compare** What is the difference between the Pathfinder palette's Subtract and Expand commands?
4. **Describe** How can a service bureau assist you with your publications?
5. **Evaluate** How does the final delivery method of a publication affect the file format used to create the publication?

Critical Thinking

6. **Evaluate** Why is it so important to understand a client's design needs before you begin a project?
7. **Analyze** In what situations would it be advantageous to convert a raster graphic into a vector graphic?
8. **Cause and Effect** How do layers help you during the design process?
9. **Make Connections** Give two examples of times when you would use a vector image and two examples of times when you would use a raster image.
10. **Compare** Give three examples of how the Layers palette in Illustrator is similar to the Layers palette in Photoshop.

1 Independent Practice

LANGUAGE ARTS **Create a Language Arts Poster** Ask teachers in your school's language arts department for ideas on creating a teaching poster. They may want a poster on grammar skills, a poster that highlights the achievements of a particular author, or a poster about reading strategies.

a. Plan Meet with the teacher, establish a topic, and research thoroughly.

b. Design Draw thumbnail sketches with at least four different layout ideas.

- Get feedback from classmates and your teacher on your designs.
- Evaluate the designs according to PARC principles.
- Present the final design sketch to your client and get approval. Revise as necessary.

c. Create Use Illustrator and Publisher to create your poster.

- Use Illustrator to create special text effects for the title.
- Create the background for your poster.
- Use Publisher for small text and for the layout of individual elements.

d. Publish Use Publisher to tile print your design.

- Assemble the design by trimming and taping the design together.
- If possible, laminate your design to further ensure stability.

Go Online RUBRICS
www.glencoe.com

Independent Practice
Go to **Chapter 8**, and choose **Rubrics**. Use the rubrics to help create and evaluate your projects.

24 Close the Master View. Go to **Page 2** of the publication. In the Master Page Task Pane, choose **Master B**.

25 Use the **Spelling** tool and **Design Checker** to check your menu.

26 Click **File>Print Preview**.

27 Check both the exterior and interior pages to see how the document will look when it prints. Make any changes, if necessary.

28 Follow your teacher's instructions for saving and printing your work.

Figure 3.55 The interior of your menu should look similar to this.

Sidebar

Dash Shortcuts

Remember to use the proper kind of dash. En-dashes show a change in time, such as 11–12. Use CTRL + − on your keypad to create an en-dash. Use CTRL + ALT + − to create the longer em-dash, which is used for an abrupt break in a sentence—like this.

Identify What is the keyboard shortcut for an en-dash?

REVIEW AND REVISE

Check your work Use Figure 3.55 as a guide and check that:

- ☑ The text and images are properly aligned on all pages.
- ☑ The document has four pages, each with its own content.
- ☑ The interior and exterior pages apply different master page designs.
- ☑ Text on interior pages uses consistent styles for headers, captions, and content.
- ☑ Design uses repetition on all pages of the document.
- ☑ Information is grouped effectively.
- ☑ Images relate to text.
- ☑ Text is easy to read, and spelling and punctuation are correct.

In The Workplace

Brand Identity Designer

Brand identity designers create a visual image, such as a logo or trademark, that expresses an organization's identity. Effective branding creates the customer recognition essential to business survival in an increasingly competitive marketplace. Brand identity designers must be able to combine both marketing and artistic skills.

On the Job

Today, a unique brand identity is an essential marketing tool. Companies reinforce their image by incorporating their brand into all their visual materials, including stationery, product packaging, advertising, and Web pages. The symbols representing Apple and Nike, for example, are so recognizable that including the actual name of the company is unnecessary. For UPS, the color brown is so strongly identified with its corporate signature that consumers easily recognize a UPS delivery truck.

Brand identity designers work for specialized brand identity firms, advertising agencies, and companies with in-house branding departments. To understand the image a company wants to present, they meet with specialists in marketing, sales, communications, packaging, and Web site design. Designers develop their ideas with sketches on paper and with programs such as Photoshop and Illustrator.

Designers must evaluate the distinctiveness of a symbol and its effectiveness when displayed on everything from computer screens and business cards to billboards and airplanes. Many companies update their look frequently, while others, like Coca-Cola, have such a distinctive and widely recognized brand identity that the familiar script is left essentially unchanged.

Future Outlook

Demand for skilled and talented brand identity designers is high. For more information about this career, consult the following Web site:

- **American Institute of Graphic Arts (aiga.org)**, the professional association for graphic design, features resources on brand identity design through the AIGA Center for Brand Experience.

Training

Brand identity designers can study graphic design along with relevant subjects such as advertising, communications, and psychology at community colleges, art schools, universities, and specialized multimedia and design programs.

Salary Range

Salaries for brand identity designers can range from $32,000 to $80,000 per year depending upon experience, skill, industry, and location.

Skills and Talents

Brand identity designers need to have:

- Knowledge of digital illustration and design software
- Knowledge of marketing, advertising, and public relations concepts
- Strategic thinking skills
- Creative flexibility
- Good communication skills
- The ability to meet deadlines

Career Activity

How could an understanding of advertising psychology help a brand identity designer develop effective concepts?

In The Workplace

Graphic Designers

Graphic designers design and create layouts for magazines and newspapers, brochures, advertisements, business marketing materials, Web pages, and other publications. Many graphic designers work in both print and electronic publishing, including film and videogame industries. The skills you are learning in this book are the same skills graphic designers use on the job

On the Job

Graphic designers often work with a variety of software such as illustration software, computer aided design (like CAD) software, two-dimensional (2-D) modeling software, or animation software. Being able to draw by hand is beneficial but not required. Images can be produced with software, downloaded from cameras or scanners, or created with pen tablets, which allow designers to draw or edit by hand.

Often graphic designers are part of a larger team. For example, to create this textbook, the designer worked with writers and editors, who provided the content, and a production coordinator, who used the design to lay out the book. Designers must have good communication skills to create the product that everyone envisions.

According to the U.S. Bureau of Labor Statistics, one-third of all designers work in their own homes as freelancers. Designers who freelance must find new employers when they finish work with one employer, and they also provide their own equipment and their own benefits, such as health care. All designers need a good portfolio (a collection of your best work) when meeting prospective employers.

Future Outlook

Demand for graphic designers is expected to increase as electronic publishing becomes more popular. For more information about this field, go to the following Web sites:

- **American Institute of Graphic Arts (www.aiga.org)** to learn more about the design industry
- **National Association of Schools of Art and Design (nasad.arts.accredit.org)** for information about schools for design education

Training

Training can come from 2–3 year design schools, 4-year colleges, or from apprenticeship programs. Most graphic designers need on the job training for 1–3 years. Student organizations such as Future Business Leaders of America (FBLA) and Business Professionals of America (BPA) also help prepare students for careers in design.

Salary Range

The median average earnings for graphic designers is between $20,000–$60,000, depending on experience, responsibilities, and location.

Skills and Talents

Graphics designers need to have:

- Knowledge of desktop publishing programs such as Illustrator, Photoshop, and InDesign
- A flair for good design
- Active imaginations
- Good problem-solving skills
- Good communication skills
- The ability to work independently and meet deadlines

Career Activity

Why must freelance designers have a portfolio?

15 Click **More Options**. You can adjust the light source on each map. Highlights and intensity add realistic effects. Experiment with the options until you have achieved the result you would like.

16 Save your project as an Illustrator file so that you can make adjustments or changes at another time.

17 Select your can design, and choose **Object>Expand Appearance** to save the artwork.

18 Follow your teacher's instructions for saving and printing your project.

19 Your finished project is ready to be inserted in a Word or Publisher publication, if you want to create an advertisement or packaging.

▼ **Figure 8.46** Lighting options can add visually appealing and more realistic effects to objects.

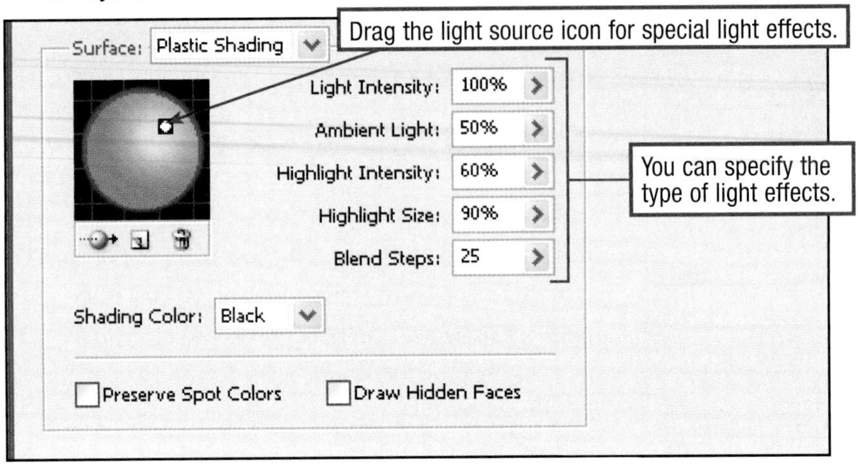

▼ **Figure 8.47** Your final illustration should look three dimensional.

REVIEW AND REVISE

Check your work Use Figure 8.47 as a guide and check that:

- ☑ The fruit drink can is a visually accurate representation.
- ☑ The logo and label are mapped to the object shape.
- ☑ The 3D object shape is rotated so that the logo is readable, and label text is visible.
- ☑ Lighting effects are applied to the can.

Chapter 3 Assessment

Reading Check

1. **Define** What is layout software, and when would you use it?
2. **Identify** Name five interface features that are in Publisher but not Word.
3. **Describe** What are two ways rulers are used in Publisher?
4. **Explain** Give an example of when you would use a master page and explain why.
5. **Define** What are hyperlinks, and when would you use them?

Critical Thinking

6. **Compare** Give three reasons why it is better to use Publisher rather than Word to create a multi-fold brochure.
7. **Explain** Why do you need layout guides to create a document?
8. **Describe** Choose two Design Gallery objects, and describe how you would use them.
9. **Evaluate** Which feature would you use if you started an article on the first page of a newsletter and ended it on the third page?
10. **Analyze** Why might you want to modify a template?

1 Independent Practice

LANGUAGE ARTS **Create a Friendship Coupon** Instead of a card, you might like to give a friend, a family member, or a special teacher a flyer with a coupon to express your appreciation. The coupon can offer a service: *One interior/exterior car detailing to be redeemed by Mom on her birthday*. Or it can just be a way to say thanks: *A hundred thanks to the best coach around!*

As an alternative, you can use tear-offs instead of a coupon: *Tear off a tab whenever you need a hug*.

a. Plan Decide to whom you would like to send a coupon. Write down what you would like to say in the flyer and in the coupon/tear-offs.

b. Design Sketch a flyer that includes a coupon or tear-offs. Determine what kind of graphics and text express your message.

c. Create Use Projects 3-3 or 3-4 as examples.

- Apply layout guides.
- Emphasize important text by using as least one example of WordArt or a background fill behind the text.
- Use 2–3 different fonts or font styles.
- Include at least one image—either clip art or a photograph.

d. Publish Proofread your document, and use the Design Checker. With your teacher's permission, print the document.

Go Online RUBRICS
www.glencoe.com

Independent Practice
Go to **Chapter 3**, and choose **Rubrics**. Use the rubrics to help create and evaluate your projects.

12 In the 3D Resolve Options box, choose **Custom Rotation** in the **Position** drop-down menu. Click on the graphic and rotate it, or key rotation degrees.

13 Click **Window>Appearance** to open the **Appearance** palette. Make additional changes to the object shape.

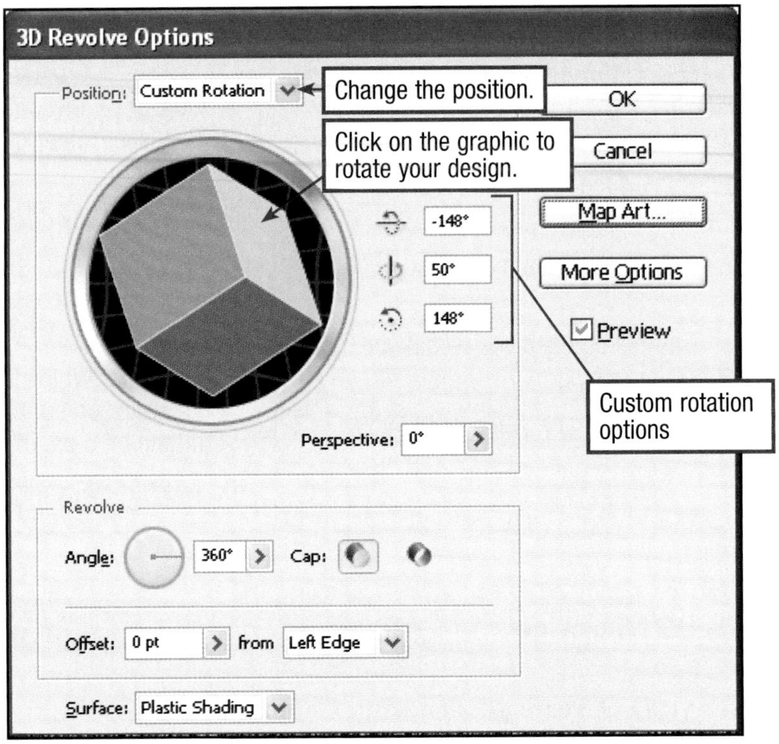

▼ **Figure 8.44** Experiment with different degrees of rotation.

14 Click the **Selection** tool, and then select the fruit drink object. In the **Appearance** palette, double-click the ***f* icon** to open the **3D Revolve Options** dialog box again.

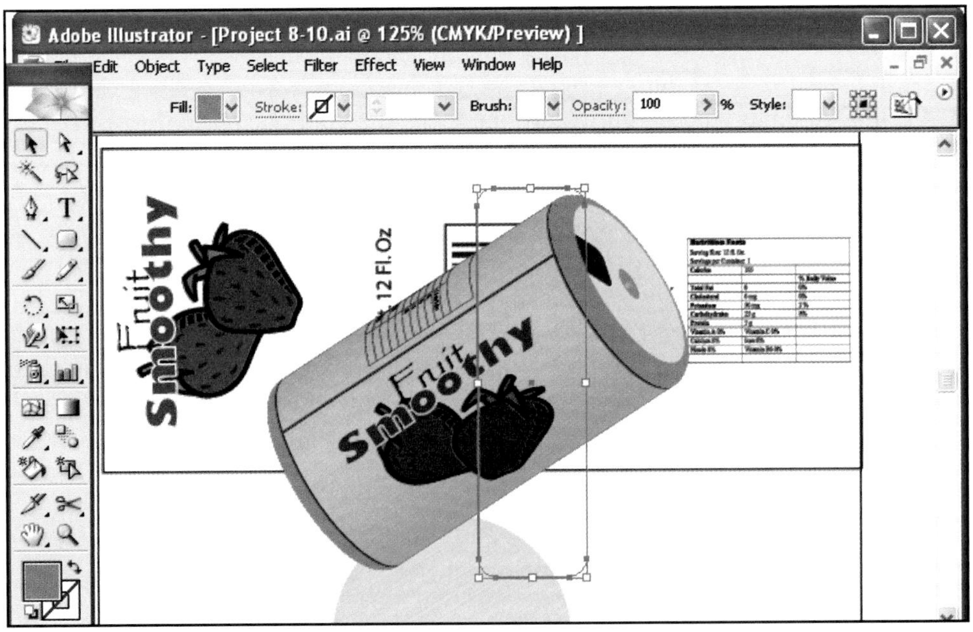

▼ **Figure 8.45** Rotate the object so that you can see the logo, the clip art, and part of the label text.

2 Independent Practice ★★

SCIENCE **Create a Plant Brochure** Imagine that you work for a garden shop or nursery that wants to inform its customers about the plants they buy for their gardens. You have been assigned the task of creating a brochure comparing different varieties of plants and how to care for them.

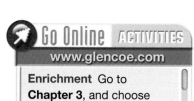

a. Plan Do research using print or online resources or your local nursery.
- Choose a type of plant that has a number of varieties, like tomatoes, roses, or cooking herbs. Choose at least three varieties.
- Write content describing each variety and the type of care it needs.
- Find appropriate images to illustrate the brochure.

b. Design Sketch the layout of the brochure, deciding how many folds you will have and where each panel will appear on the printed page.

c. Create Combine your text and graphics into a two-sided brochure.
- Use linked text boxes to flow text.
- Place an image on the cover and at least three images in the interior.

d. Publish Proofread and follow your teacher's instructions for printing the brochure.

3 Independent Practice ★★★

TEAM PROJECT **Create Community Service Web Pages** There are probably many organizations in your community that can use volunteers. With a partner, compile a list of these groups from classmates or your school. Then choose the five that you would like to present on a Web site.

a. Plan Write the content for each page.
- Find out your school's requirements for community service.
- Gather information about each organization: the name and contact information, its mission, jobs available for volunteers, and volunteer requirements.

b. Create Use a master page to repeat design elements.
- Your home page should describe your school's community service policy, and each organization should have its own page.
- Use hyperlinks and a table of contents to link between pages.

c. Publish Use the Web Page Preview to make sure that hyperlinks work and design elements do not shift. With your teacher's permission, publish your Web pages on your school's Web site.

Go Online ACTIVITIES
www.glencoe.com

Enrichment Go to **Chapter 3**, and choose **Enrichment Activities**. Find more desktop publishing projects using Microsoft Publisher.

6 This Map Art box shows 7 surfaces to map. (**Note**: The number of surfaces on your drawing may vary.) Click the arrows next to **Surface** until you locate the can top surface (Figure 8.42).

7 Click the **Symbol** drop-down arrow to locate the map symbol for the can top (Figure 8.42).

8 Click **Shade Artwork** and **Scale to Fit**.

▼ Figure 8.42 Light gray areas are visible surfaces, and dark gray areas are currently not visible.

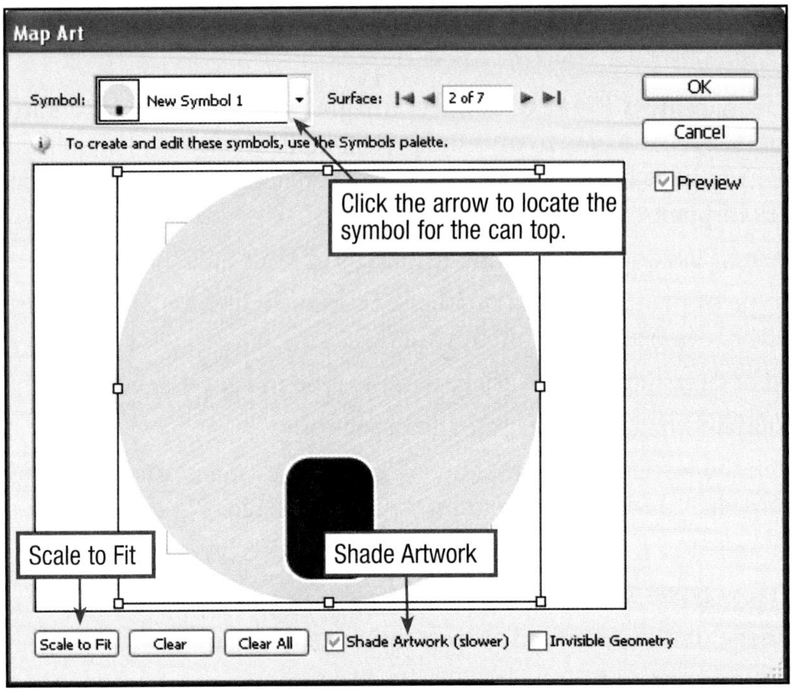

9 In the **Map Art** dialog box, click the arrows next to **Surface** until you locate the can label surface.

10 Click the **Symbol** drop-down arrow to locate the map symbol for the can label (Figure 8.43).

11 Click **Shade Artwork** and **Scale to Fit**. Click **OK** to close the **Map Art** dialog box.

▼ Figure 8.43 The label surface art is displayed.

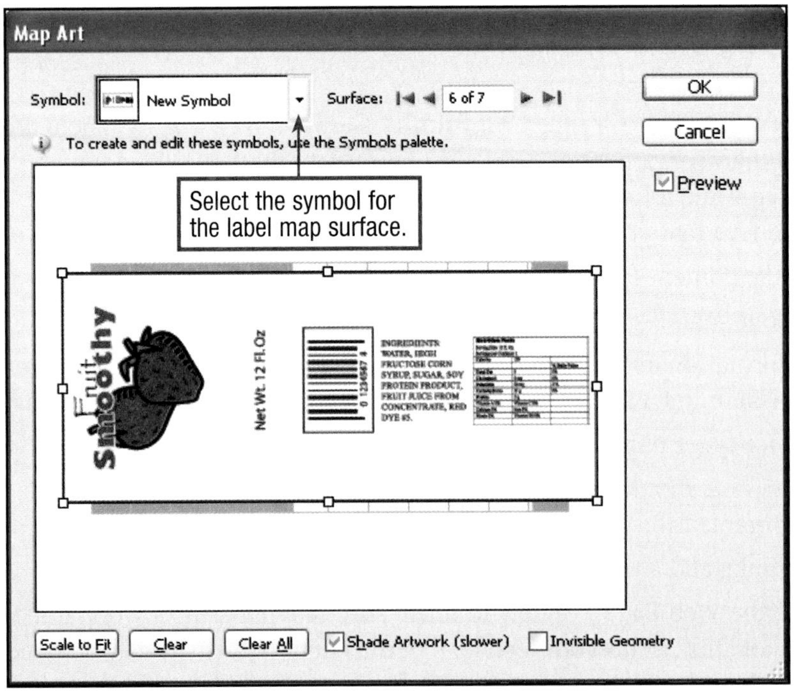

Chapter 4 Focus on Design Makeovers

Skills You Will Learn

- **Workshop Foundations**
  - The Design Process
- **Workshop Toolbox**
  - PARC Design Principles
- **Project 4-1**
  - Evaluate Design in a Flyer
- **Project 4-2**
  - Add Contrast and Focal Points
- **Project 4-3**
  - Apply the Golden Ratio
- **Project 4-4**
  - Apply Styles in a Flyer
- **Project 4-5**
  - Revise a Tri-fold Brochure
- **Project 4-6**
  - Apply PARC to the Brochure Interior
- **Project 4-7**
  - Apply PARC to a Web Page

Skills Studio

Create a Children's Newsletter

Project 4-8
Design for a Young Audience

Project 4-9
Complete Your Newsletter

Have you ever looked at a design and said to yourself, "Wow! I wish I could make something like that!" Chances are that you can.

In this chapter, you will learn how to apply design principles that will help you create visually effective publications. These principles are used in every field of art, from interior decorating to painting and, yes, to desktop publishing.

Publish Interesting Newsletters

Newsletters are like small newspapers. They usually contain many of the same elements, including a masthead, articles with headers, and graphic elements such as photos, charts, and art. Some newsletters might also include tables of contents and advertisements.

Generally businesses and organizations, schools, and even individuals send out newsletters on a regular schedule. Newsletters may be published weekly, monthly, or once or twice a year, but the purpose is always to keep the audience informed about recent or upcoming events.

DESIGN PROCESS: Newsletters

Elements	Issues
Purpose	To provide a variety of information, in the form of articles and graphics.
Audience	Varies. Businesses send newsletters to customers, employees, or investors. Schools publish student and parent newsletters. Families send newsletters to friends or family members.
Content	Articles with graphics such as photos, clip art, or charts. Design content includes mastheads, different headers, and tables of contents.
Layout	Two to three columns on a page with one, two, or more pages. If more than two pages, an even number of pages is generally used in the layout. Articles can continue on a second page.
Publication	Publish as print and/or Web documents. Printed newsletters may be black and white or color, single-sided or duplex printing. They are usually meant to be distributed to a large audience, so they require many copies.

Step-by-Step

1. In Illustrator, open your Project 8-7 file, the fruit drink can. Use **Selection** to select the object shape. On the menu bar, click **Edit>Copy**. Close the Project 8-7 file.

2. Open Project 8-9, the label. Save it according to your teacher's instructions. On the **menu** bar, click **Edit>Paste**. to insert the can in the workspace.

3. In the toolbox, click the **Selection** tool, and then select the fruit drink can object.

4. On the **menu** bar, click **Window>Appearance** to open the **Appearance** palette. Double-click the ***f* icon** to open the **3D Revolve Options** dialog box (Figure 8.40).

Create a Map

5. In the **3D Revolve Options** dialog box, click **Preview**. Then click **Map Art** (Figure 8.41).

Figure 8.40 The object shape is inserted in your fruit drink label file.

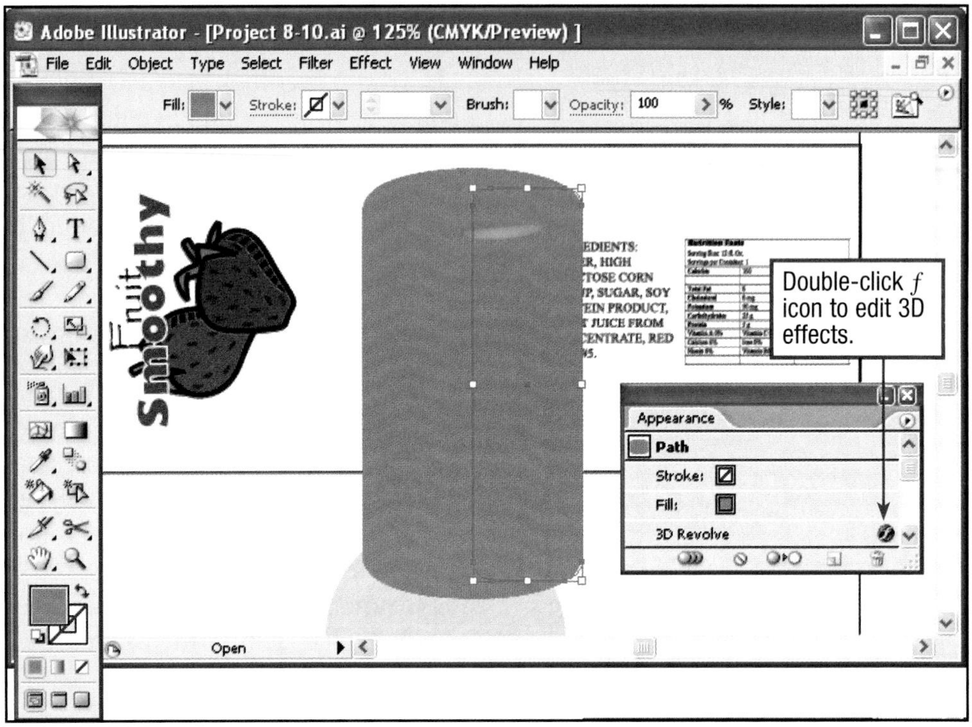

Figure 8.41 The map will wrap around the outside of the object and will rotate with the object for a realistic 3D effect.

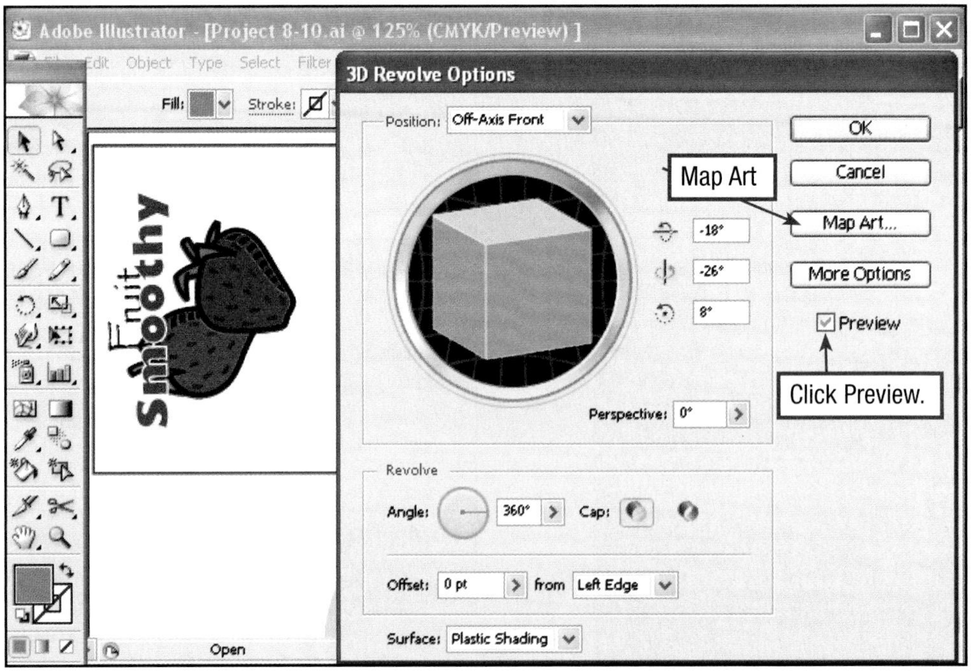

WORKSHOP Foundations

You Will Learn To

- Identify the steps of the design process
- Apply the design process
- Determine client needs in relation to design

Key Terms

design process
client

Before You Read

Use Bookmarks If you do not understand something you read, mark the page with a bookmark or a sticky note if your teacher allows. Jot down a comment or question about the text. Then come back to it later and reread the section. If you are still unsure, ask your teacher for help, or see if the subject can be discussed further in class.

The Design Process

You have already learned and applied some design concepts in the projects you have created. You have experienced for yourself how much thought goes into creating an interesting and effective document. Now you will see how following a specific design process can help you produce professional publications.

Why Is the Design Process Like a Spiral?

Every chapter begins with a table that outlines the design process for a particular type of publication. These tables can help you think of questions you should ask yourself when creating a document.

As you will see, though, the design process is really more of a spiral than a list. The **design process** is a procedure that takes you through steps and actions leading to the best design possible for a client or audience. Like a spiral, the design process sometimes seems to bring you back to the same place, even though you are, in fact, further along than you were.

Throughout the design process, there is a constant need to review your work and determine if you are meeting the needs of the client and the audience. Often it is helpful to ask for another opinion from a colleague, who may give you insight by looking at your design from a fresh perspective. Use the feedback to fine-tune your work until it is the best possible design to meet your client's needs.

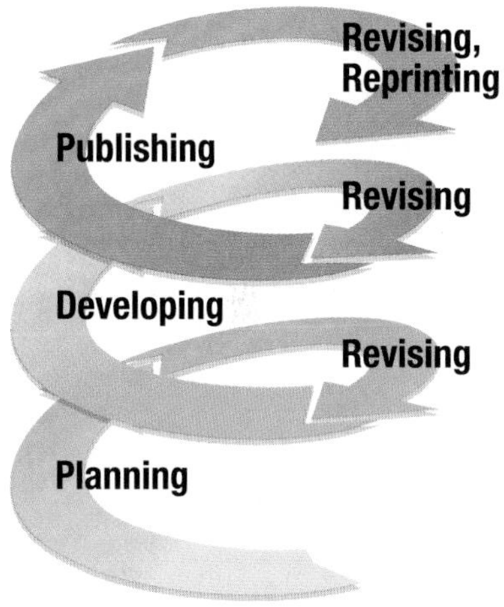

▲ Every stage of the design process requires review and revisions.

How Do I Apply the Design Process?

At each stage of design, whether it is the planning, the development, or the publishing stage, peer response and revision are needed to help target the audience and to include as many creative ideas as possible.

Plan Your design is driven by a **client**, the person or group of people for whom you are designing a publication. The client can be an outside customer who hires you. When a publication is for your own business, the client is the

Skills Studio

Project 8-10

Add Symbols to a Label

Skills You Will Apply

- Create a map
- Affix a map

Key Term

- map

Academic Focus

Language Arts
Create descriptive text

Product design is big business. More and more, advertisers are using research and hard work to create good product designs to help sell products. Imagine looking for a bag of tortilla chips at the grocery store. What tells you if a chip is worth buying? We may look for a familiar brand name or at the price, but next time you are at the store, look to see what other signals are being sent to you. These are probably the signals that influence your decision more than your original intention.

Imagine comparing three different bags of tortilla chips, all similarly priced. The one in a fancy, shiny package with expensive graphics may tell you that it is professionally packaged and is probably a high-quality product. Perhaps another one uses poor graphics and a dull package. This one would probably seem to be a low-quality product, perhaps even one that is unclean. A third package may include traditional Mexican images, quaint graphics, and paper packaging. This one may seem more authentic.

► By building a virtual model using Adobe Illustrator, we can inexpensively test product designs.

Because building real models is expensive and time consuming, graphic designers will often turn first to 3D modeling programs. These programs allow for designs to be created virtually, using the computer. A **map** is an illustration that is wrapped around the outside of an object, as wallpaper is attached to a wall. Maps rotate with the object and can be used to add a touch of realism. Only after designs have been created and approved will designers then build actual models of the product and test the design.

While not a substitute for a dedicated 3D modeling program, Adobe Illustrator does have some capability to create simple product designs. In this final phase, we will be creating a three-dimensional object in cyberspace!

► **In this project,** you will create a map that adds the label to your fruit drink can.

audience that you are trying to attract, or managers who are overseeing the project. Although the client and the intended audience are usually different people, it is critical that the needs of both groups are met with the same design. Use the planning stage to gather information that helps you visualize the final product.

- Get exact information from the client about the purpose, audience, and tone of the material. Determine how the publication will be printed, what the budget is, and when it is due.
- Ask the right questions to help you frame the job, avoid redesigns, and increase customer satisfaction.
- Start a project by drawing quick thumbnail sketches to brainstorm a lot of different ideas. Create more detailed sketches based on your best two or three designs. Do not try to create your ideas on the computer. That will take too much time.
- Do not show your client all your ideas. Show only your best work. Agree on a final sketch with the client before using the computer.

Develop When you create the final design on the computer, you should try to follow the approved plan, but you will still have to make some adjustments.

- Make modifications to match the art or content.
- Simplify the design to make the message clear and cohesive.
- Revise based on feedback from peers or the client. Evaluate each suggestion carefully.

Publish If possible, test print or publish your design. Mistakes are often much easier to see on paper than on screen.

- Try the design in the medium in which it will be published. If it is to be published on the Web, try it out on different computer systems and different Web browsers, such as Internet Explorer.
- If the design is to be published on a copy machine, print it out on the copy machine to make sure that it will print clearly.
- Again, make necessary adjustments based on feedback from peers or the client. Review at every stage of the design process helps achieve the project goals.

Reading Check

1. **Explain** Why is the design process more of a spiral than a list?
2. **Cause and Effect** Why is it important to get a client to commit to a budget?

Sidebar

Prepare Before you begin to work on a specific project, you should already have begun the design process.

- Look for examples of good design in books, magazines, and the Internet. Think about what makes the design effective.
- Keep a file of good designs. Do not copy them, but use them for inspiration.
- Learn from negative examples. When you see a bad design, figure out why it does not work.
- Collect books or magazines that discuss or provide examples of good design.

Analyze Find a magazine ad. Explain why the design features work or do not work well.

Add Symbols

10. All objects should be selected. On the menu bar, click **Windows>Symbols** to open the **Symbols** palette.

11. Drag the label into the **Symbols** palette so that it is added as a symbol. The label appears as an icon in the palette (Figure 8.38).

▼ **Figure 8.38** Move the label to the Symbol palette, adding it to the palette as a new symbol.

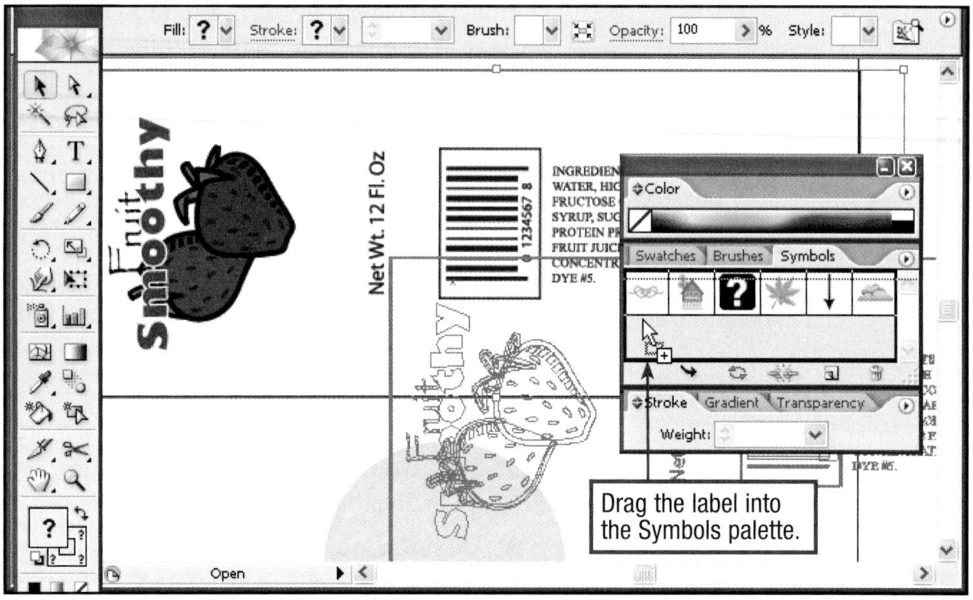

▼ **Figure 8.39** The fruit drink can label should be similar to this illustration.

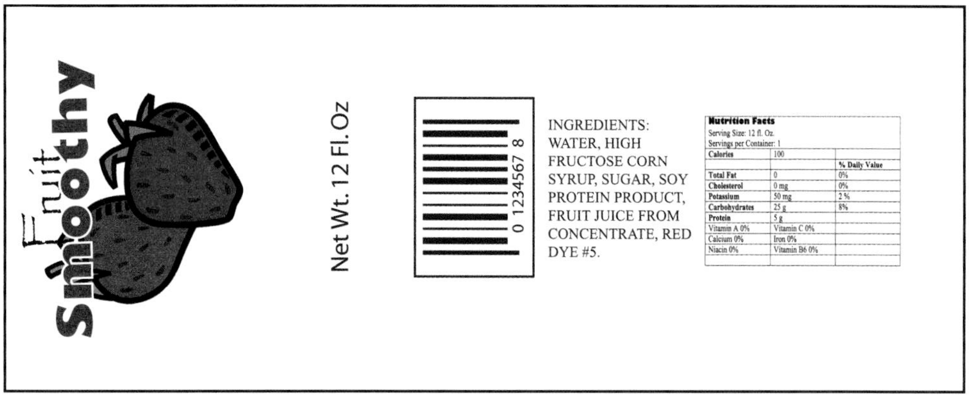

12. Click the **Selection** tool. Select the illustration of the fruit drink can top. Then drag the can top to the **Symbols** palette. The can top appears as an icon in the Symbols palette.

13. Your label should look similar to Figure 8.39.

14. Save the project according to your teacher's instructions. You will use the file in Project 8.10 to complete your product design.

REVIEW AND REVISE

Check your work Use Figure 8.39 as a guide and check that:

- ☑ Visually interesting clip art is added to the logo.
- ☑ The logo is rotated.
- ☑ All objects are vertically aligned.
- ☑ Both the label and the can top are added to the Symbols palette.

WORK SHOP

Toolbox

You Will Learn To

- Identify PARC design principles

Key Terms

proximity
white space
alignment
repetition
contrast
focal point

PARC Design Principles

Although a great design requires creativity and instinct, you can always make sure that your design is attractive and easy to read by applying the PARC principles. PARC stands for

Proximity

Alignment

Repetition

Contrast

You should always check your design using these four concepts.

What Is Proximity?

Proximity is how elements are grouped together on a page. Grouping content into small, related chunks of information makes it easier to understand and digest. Another word for this concept is *grouping*. **White space** is the area on the page without text or graphics and is often used to separate groups. When designing, there are two rules of proximity you should follow:

- Content that logically belongs together physically should be together.
- Content that does not belong together should be clearly separated.

Create Proximity

Grouping Method	Apply Grouping Techniques
Physically adjust the spacing to avoid crowding.	Create white space between items. This gives the reader a chance to absorb what has been read.
Separate groups with lines (horizontal or vertical.)	Lines can separate items to improve readability or enhance a design, but they might also lead the reader's eyes right off the page! Lines may break up the white space in a document.
Enclose with boxes.	Boxes can help content stand out, but too many boxes can make a document fragmented and difficult to read. Too many boxes tend to trap the eye and reduce white space.
Use similar fonts and font sizes.	Titles, headlines, captions, and copy should have a font scheme that visually helps the reader group items together.
Add color.	Colored fonts or fills make information seem as if it is related.

Add Clip Art to Logo

4. Open Microsoft Word Clip Art Gallery to find **strawberry clip art**, or use **Data File 8-9b**.

5. On the **menu** bar, click **Edit>Paste** to insert your clip art into the label design (Figure 8.36).

6. Resize and rotate the clip art as needed, and click **Object>Arrange> Send Backward**.

▼ Figure 8.36 Resize the clip art to complement the logo.

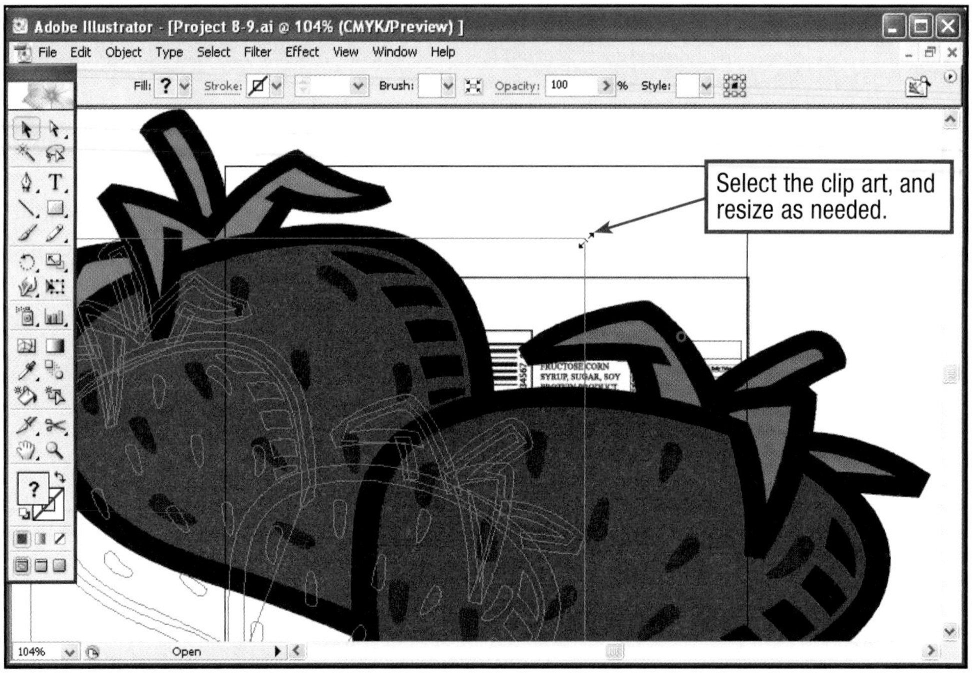

7. Use the **Selection** tool to select all objects. On the **menu** bar, click **Window>Align.** Then on the Align palette, choose **Vertical Align Center** (Figure 8.37).

8. Select all objects. On the **menu** bar, click **Object>Group**.

▼ Figure 8.37 Use the Align palette to align all the objects.

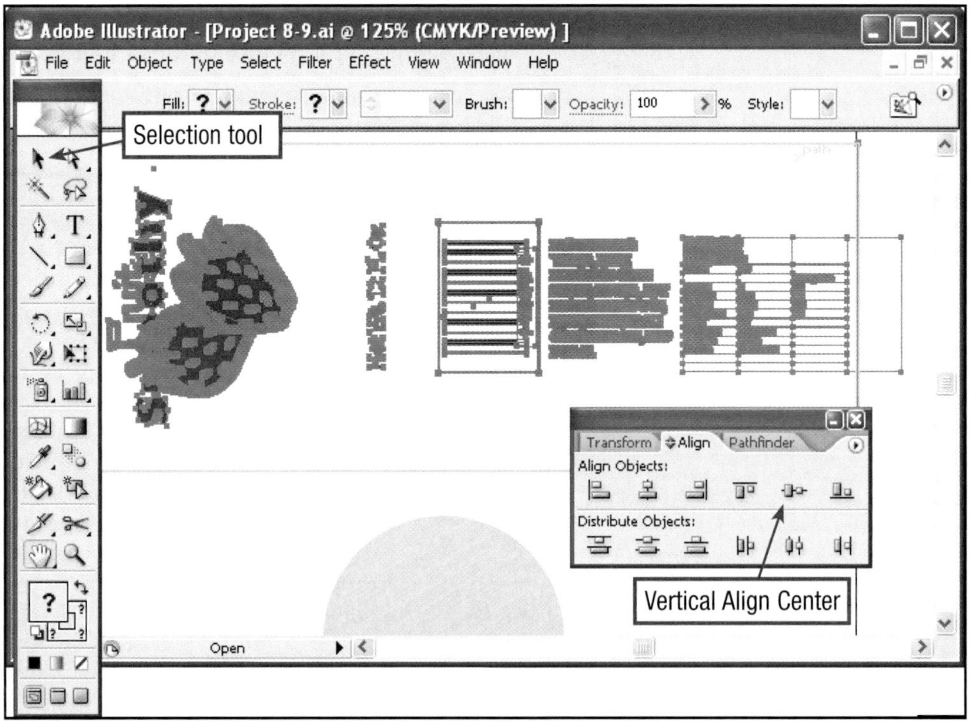

Why Is Alignment Important?

Alignment, or the horizontal and vertical placement of objects, helps readers immediately see what information belongs together. For example, in Chapter 3, you used tabs, margin guides, layout guides, and ruler guides to align objects.

How Is Repetition Used?

You have repeated fonts and design elements within projects to make them consistent. **Repetition** means that important design elements are echoed, or repeated, in some way throughout the design. Repetition creates harmony within a design, though overuse can make a design boring and monotonous.

To make repetition work, you need to have a central, or dominant, design element. How do you find the dominant design element?

- Step back from a design and see if anything naturally catches your eye.
- Look for a shape or color in clip art or a logo to repeat. A special title treatment or page border can be picked up and repeated.
- If you cannot find a dominant design element, add one to the design. Add rules (lines) or drawing objects such as rectangles and circles.

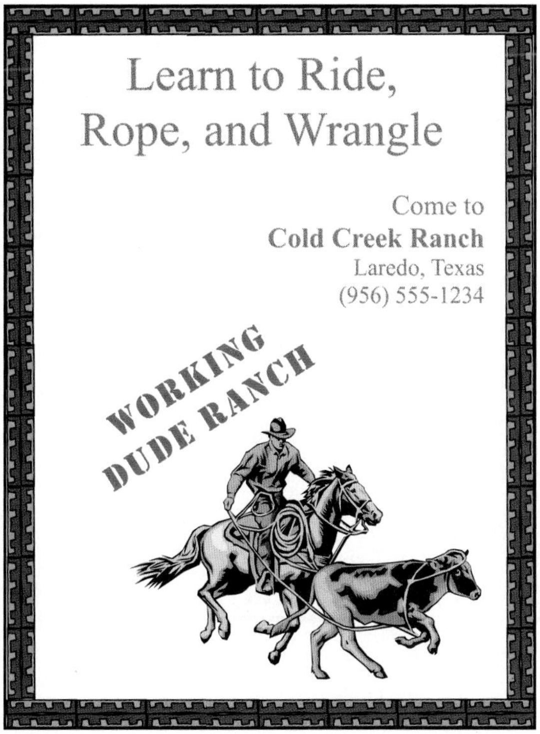

◄ Break up the alignment to draw attention to one feature. Use repetition to draw features together.

Eye On Ethics

Free Graphics There are many places on the Web where you can find free images. You may still have to credit the source of the image, but you will not have to pay a fee or royalty (payment for each use). You can use key words like *free images* to search for sources on a search engine like Google or Yahoo. Make sure you check the terms of use or policies of the Web site to ensure that you are using the images legally. There may be restrictions on how you use the image. You may have to pay if your published work is for profit.

Explain Why should you always check the terms and conditions for using a free image?

Skills Studio

Project 8-9 Design a Product Label

Skills You Will Apply

- Add clip art to logo
- Add symbols

Academic Focus

Language Arts
Create descriptive text

Student Data File

Step-by-Step

1. In Illustrator, open **Data File 8-9a**. This data file includes text for the label and an illustration for the top of your can. Save the file according to your teacher's instructions.

2. Click **File>Open**, and browse to the logo that you created in Project 8-8. Copy and paste the logo into your file. Click **OK** in the PDF dialog box.

3. Use the **Selection** tool, and hold SHIFT as you rotate the logo **90 degrees**. Position the logo to the left of the label text in the blank area (Figure 8.35).

Think about all the labels that you are exposed to on a daily basis. Labeling and packaging influence what products and services we buy every day. A well-designed label is easy to read and inviting so that you want to know more about the product.

These labels are created by graphic artists. An artist has sharp observation skills. Rather than just seeing computers, dogs, or cars, the artist sees a collection of squares, ovals, and other objects. It is hard to draw a dog, but it is easy to draw circles and ovals that can be positioned and shaded to look like a dog.

As you work to design a label with different objects, think about the simple shapes that can be used to make the objects.

▶ **In this project,** you will create a label for the fruit drink can. The label will include a table listing nutritional information, a graphic illustration, and the logo that you created in Project 8-8.

▼ **Figure 8.35** Rotate the logo for better use of the space on the label design for your smoothy can.

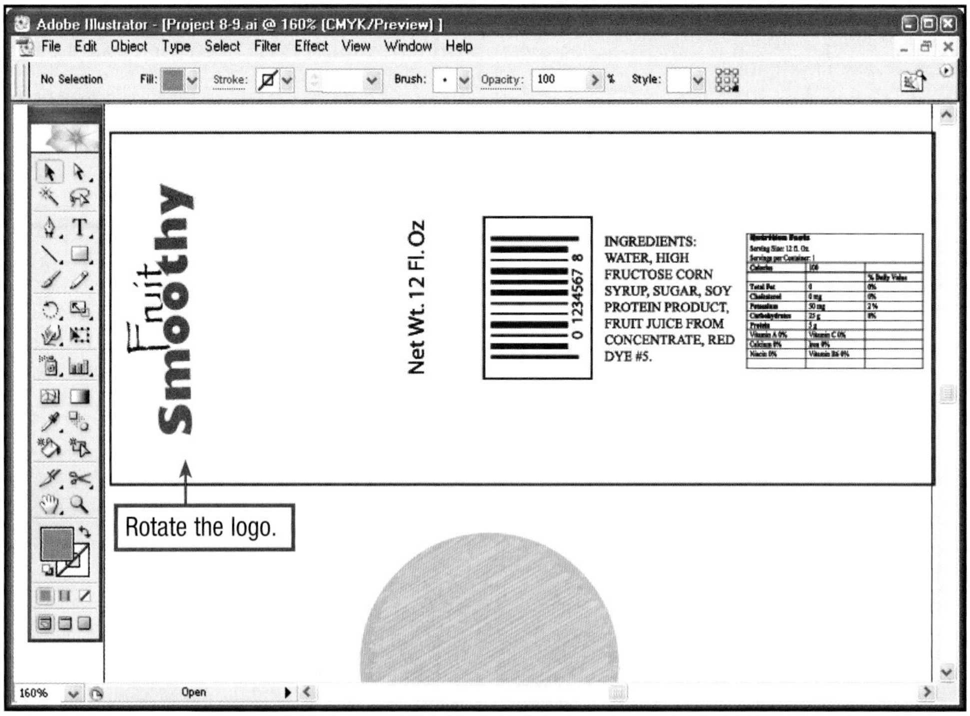

How Do I Add Contrast?

When you add **contrast**, you use design elements that look different from surrounding features to create visual interest or specific focal points. A **focal point** is an area that your eye is drawn to. For example, a document with mostly black serif fonts might use a red sans serif font to call attention to specific content. The focal point is usually the place of highest contrast.

Create Contrast

Design Element	Apply Contrast Techniques
Size/weight	Use heavier or larger text to visually separate titles from body text and to draw the reader's attention. Use smaller text for longer content.
Font	Choose fonts from different families for different functions such as body text, headers, titles, and captions. Use fonts to draw attention to headings and titles.
Alignment	Combine different alignments. Rotate text to different angles. Extend graphics into margins to break up alignment.
Color	Use colors that are different enough to stand out from each other. Reverse text so that light colors are on a dark background. (See Appendix A on Color Theory for more suggestions.)

You can use contrast to create an entry point for the reader. Readers need direction, a visual clue, to show them where to begin looking in a publication. The natural beginning place is one where there is high contrast.

Remember that the PARC principles are not absolute laws. While these principles should be included in every design, they may be ignored if the message is better served without them. For example, your client may specifically request the use of certain colors that do not contrast strongly with one another. Your job as a graphic designer is not merely to showcase your skills, but to ensure that the client's message has been clearly presented.

Eye On Ethics

Public Domain A copyrighted work is in **public domain** if it was published before 1923. Public domain means that the work can be used without permission.

If you wanted to publish a book using authentic Civil War photos, you would not need to get permission. However, if the photographs were from a 1962 *Life* magazine, you would need to get permission. If you are not sure whether you need permission to use an image, always check with the source.

Evaluate Would you need permission to publish a Herman Melville story? Why or why not?

Reading Check

1. **Identify** Describe the four PARC principles that you should always try to apply when creating a publication.
2. **Draw Conclusions** Why should you try not to use too much repetition in a document?

5 Use the **Selection** tool to select the word **Smoothy**. Change the **Fill** color to **red**, then click **Stroke** to add a **white** stroke.

6 Click **Rectangle** to create a rectangle over the letter *S*. Change the **Fill** to **Black.**

7 Click **Object>Arrange>Send to Back** (Figure 8.33).

▼ **Figure 8.33** Create visually appealing logos with color and fonts.

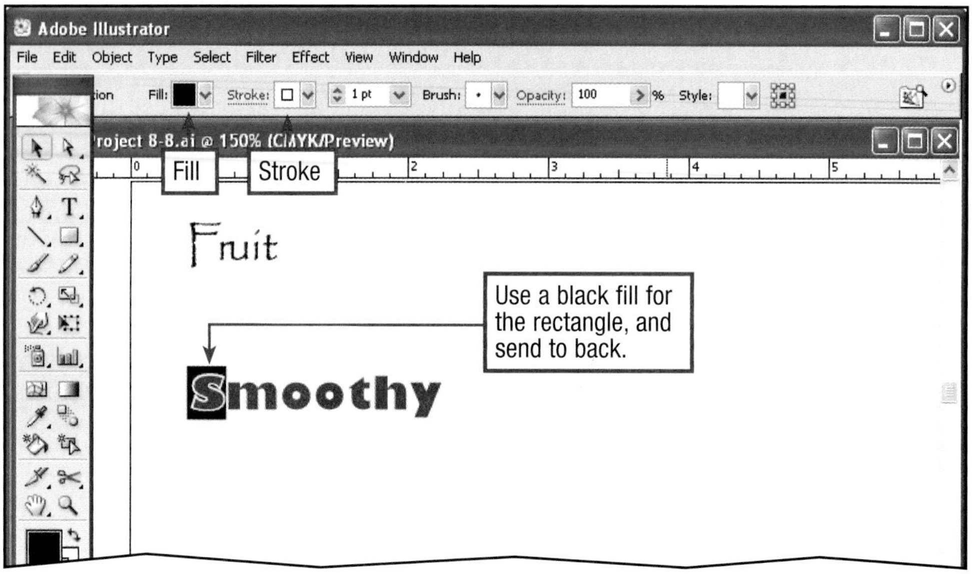

8 Reposition the objects similar to Figure 8.34.

9 Use the **Selection** tool to select all objects. On the **menu** bar, choose **Object>Group**.

10 On the menu bar, choose **Object>Expand** to keep all objects together. Click **OK** in the **Objects Expand** dialog box.

11 Follow your teacher's instructions for saving your work. You will continue your label in Project 8-9.

▼ **Figure 8.34** Expand the two parts of the logo to create one object.

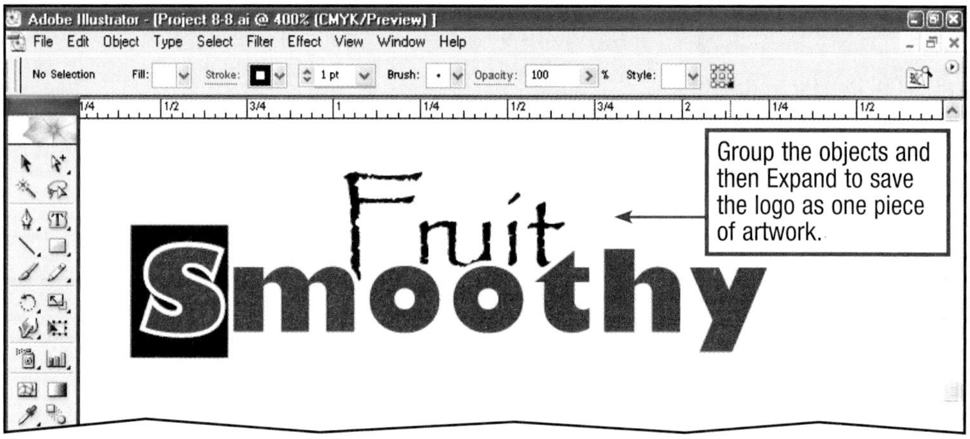

REVIEW AND REVISE

Check your work Use Figure 8.34 as a guide and check that:

- ☑ A red fill with white stroke is used for the word *Smoothy*.
- ☑ Tracking is adjusted for the letters *F* and *r*.
- ☑ Papyrus and Gill Sans Ultra Bold fonts are used.
- ☑ The objects are expanded to remain as one piece of artwork.

Project 4-1 Evaluate Design in a Flyer

Spotlight on Skills

- Create repetition
- Adjust white space

Key Term

- negative space

Academic Focus

Social Studies
Identify international cuisines

Go Online PREVIEW
www.glencoe.com

Before You Begin Go to **Chapter 4**, and choose **PowerPoint Presentations** to preview the documents you will be creating. Also, use the individual project **Rubrics** to help create and evaluate your work.

A flyer can be a successful form of low-cost advertising, if it creates a positive response from its intended audience. A poorly designed flyer, however, can have the opposite effect. This flyer has design problems and incorrect spelling, which reflect negatively on the organizers of the event. Use the table to determine how the design can be improved.

INTERNATIONAL FOOD FAIR

ENJOY EXOTIC DISHES FROM OVER 25 COUNTRIES
PARTICEPATE IN COOKING DEMON-STRATONS
TASTE FOODS FROM AROUND THE WORLD
ALBANIA, BRAZIL, CHINA, FINLAND, FRANCE, GREECE, INDIA, INDONE-SIA, ITALY, JAMAICA, JAPAN, KENYA, KOREA, JAPAN, LEBANON, MEXICO, MOROCO, PERU, RUSSIA, SPAIN, THAI-LAND, AND MORE!
SUNDAY, MAY 14 : 11 AM-2 PM
CLEVELAND HIGH SCHOOL FOOTBALL FIELD
JOIN US FOR A GOURMET FEAST!
BABGANOUJ, PIROJI, DIM SUM, TZAT-ZIKI, TANDOORI, TAMALES, CURRY, CEVICHE, KIM CHEE, FALAFEL, PAD THAI, SASHIMI, COUSCOUS, SHWARMA, BORSCHT, PAELLA, RAITA, SPANIKOPITA, ALL YOUR FA-VORITE FOODS!

Design Blunders

PARC Principle	Design Problems
Proximity	• There is very little grouping: text is evenly distributed across the page, text is all capital letters. • Text is broken awkwardly between lines.
Alignment	• Most text is center-aligned, which is safe, but boring. • White space does not flow through text.
Repetition	• Related serif font is used throughout, which is safe, but boring. • Font style is the only design element used.
Contrast	• Although different font sizes and styles are used, there is very little difference among them. • The first two lines provide the only focal point. • There are no graphics to contrast with the text.

Skills Studio

Project 8-8 Design a Product Logo

Company logos can be found on a variety of products, including business cards, letterhead, company shirts, magazine advertisements, packaging, and even billboards. To ensure a consistent message and increase recognition in product branding, a single logo needs to work in all these situations.

The solution is to create the logo as a vector image. Illustrator is a powerful tool for creating logos. Although Photoshop may be somewhat easier to use, it is simply not the best tool for creating logos. Creating text effects in Photoshop will create results that cannot be resized easily. Spacing between letters as blocks of text, or **tracking**, is easy to do from Illustrator's **Character** palette.

▶ **In this project,** you will design and create a logo for your fruit drink can. Although this logo is created from simple text, you will combine it with graphics in Project 8-9 for the can's label. The text allows you to combine the logo with any image (in this case fruit) that visually represents the specific product. For example, if you had a tropical flavor smoothy, you might add pictures of bananas and mangos to the logo.

Skills You Will Apply

- Create a logo

Key Term

- tracking

Academic Focus

Language Arts
Create descriptive text

Step-by-Step

1. Open a new document in Adobe Illustrator, **4 inches high** and **6 inches wide**. Save the document according to your teacher's instructions.

2. On the menu bar, click **View>Show Rulers**.

3. In the toolbox, click **Type** [T] to key Fruit in **24 pt Papyrus.** Select the *F* and *r*, and then set **Tracking** in the **Character** palette at **-50** to adjust the space between those two letters.

4. Click **Selection** [▶]. Then click the **Type** tool to key Smoothy in **Gill Sans Ultra Bold 24 pt**. Leave space between the two words (Figure 8.32).

▼ **Figure 8.32** Choose complementary, distinctive fonts for the logo.

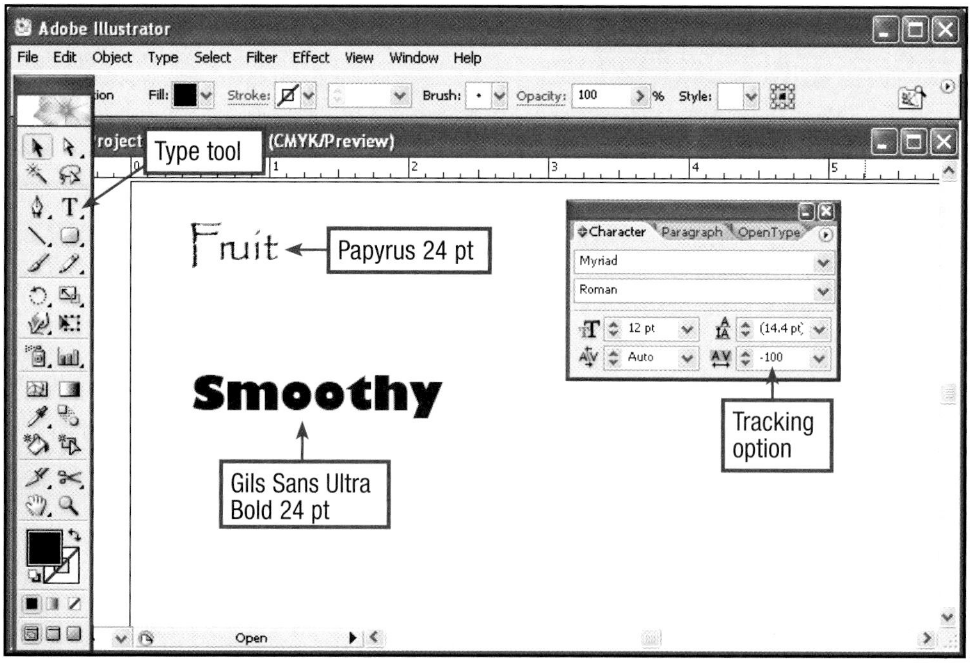

Arrange White Space

Another term for white space is **negative space**. White space should be *active*, able to flow throughout the document, as shown in the figure below on the right. *Passive* white space decreases readability. The shape of the negative space on the page is as important as the text or graphics.

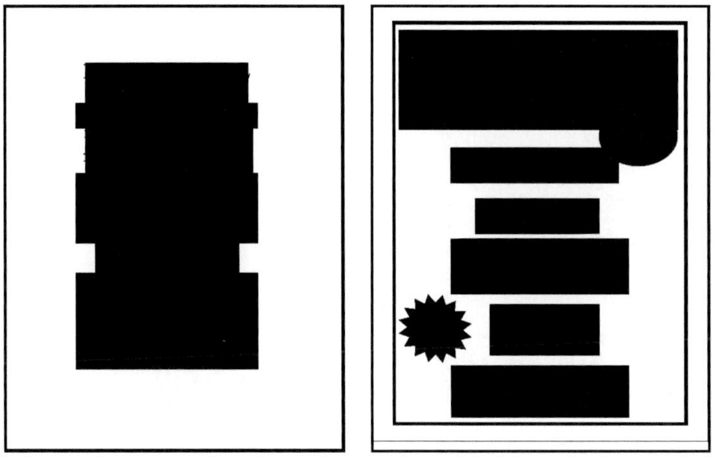

▲ The flyer on the left has passive white space. The white space on the right flows, so the content is easier to read.

▶ **In this project,** you will begin to apply PARC design principles to revise the format in an International Food Fair flyer.

Step-by-Step

1. In Publisher, open **Data File 4-1**. Save it according to your teacher's instructions.

2. Select all the text, then click **Format>Font**. Under **Effects**, turn off All Caps.

3. Run a Spell Check on the text, and correct all mistakes. **(Note:** Ignore spelling on the food names.)

4. Drag the text box into the scratch area (Figure 4.1).

▼ **Figure 4.1** Move text to the scratch area while you work in the workspace.

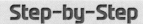

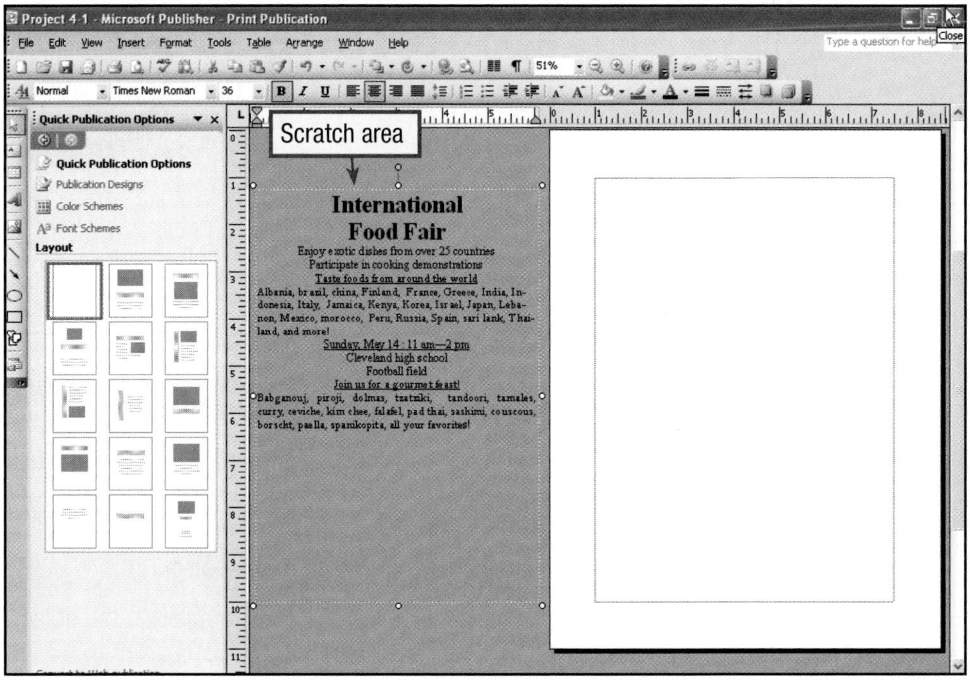

Step-by-Step

1. Open a **New** document in Adobe Illustrator, **8 inches high** and **6 inches wide**. Save it according to your teacher's instructions.

2. In the toolbox, click **Rectangle** ▭, and drag right to open **Rounded Rectangle** ▢.

3. Create a rectangle in the workspace with the following dimensions: **width .85 inch**, **height 3 inches**, **corner radius 10 pt** (Figure 8.30).

4. Click **Fill**, and select a **gray** fill. Or, double-click **Fill** to choose a color in the **Color Picker** dialog box.

Apply 3D Effects

5. Choose **Effect>3D>Revolve**.

6. Adjust the settings in the **3D Revolve Options** dialog box. **Perspective**: **0 inch**, **Revolve Angle 360 degrees**, **Offset 0 pt** from **Left Edge**. Use Figure 8.31 to check your settings. Click the **Preview** check box, and experiment with other settings.

7. Save your work in an Illustrator file format. You will use the object in the final project of the Skills Studio.

▼ **Figure 8.30** Use the Rounded Rectangle tool to create the drink can shape.

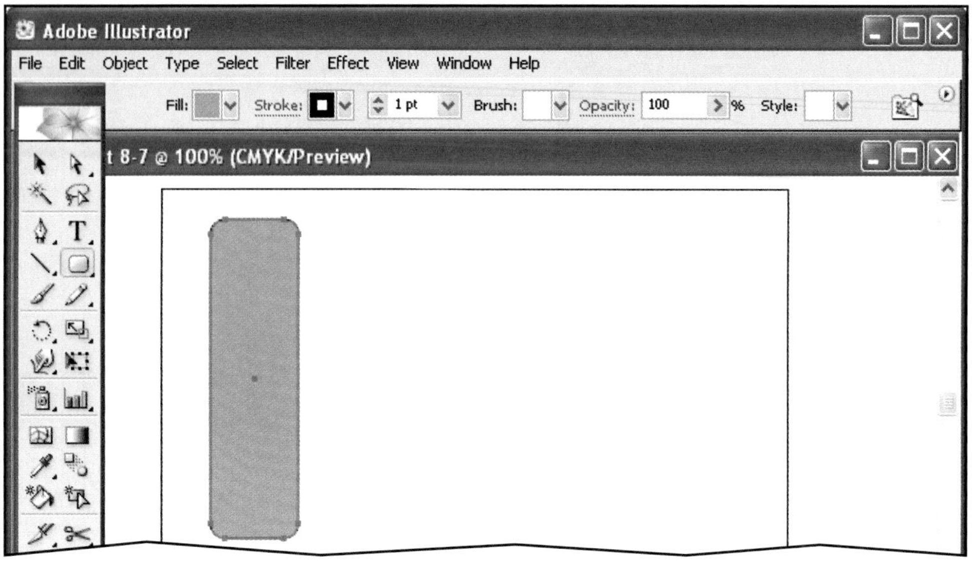

▼ **Figure 8.31** Use 3D Revolve options to make shapes three-dimensional.

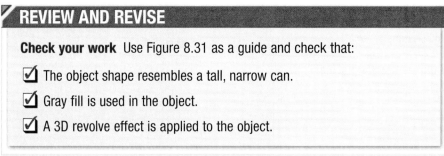

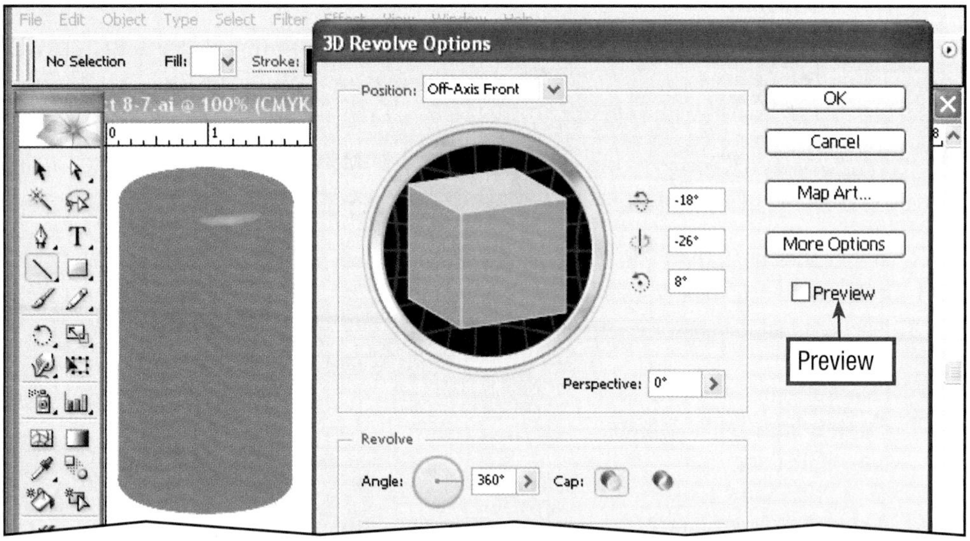

REVIEW AND REVISE

Check your work Use Figure 8.31 as a guide and check that:

- ☑ The object shape resembles a tall, narrow can.
- ☑ Gray fill is used in the object.
- ☑ A 3D revolve effect is applied to the object.

5. Click **Arrange>Layout Guides** to set Grid Guides of **5 columns** with **0 inch gutters**.

6. While in the Layout Guides box, set **0.5 inch margins**.

7. Click **Rectangle** ▭, and drag a rectangle along the margin guides to create a border.

8. Select the new border. On the Formatting toolbar, click **Line/ Border Style** ☰. Choose a **6 pt solid black line**.

Create Repetition

9. On the Object toolbar, click **Insert WordArt** , and choose the style shown in Figure 4.2.

10. In the Edit WordArt box, key International. Use **Impact** typeface.

11. Select the Word Art, and click **Format>Word Art>Size**. Make the **width 7 inches** and **height 1.7 inches**.

12. Select the Word Art. On the **WordArt** toolbar, click **WordArt Shape** , and choose the **Deflate Bottom** style (Figure 4.3).

▼ **Figure 4.2** Use the rectangle tool to create a page border.

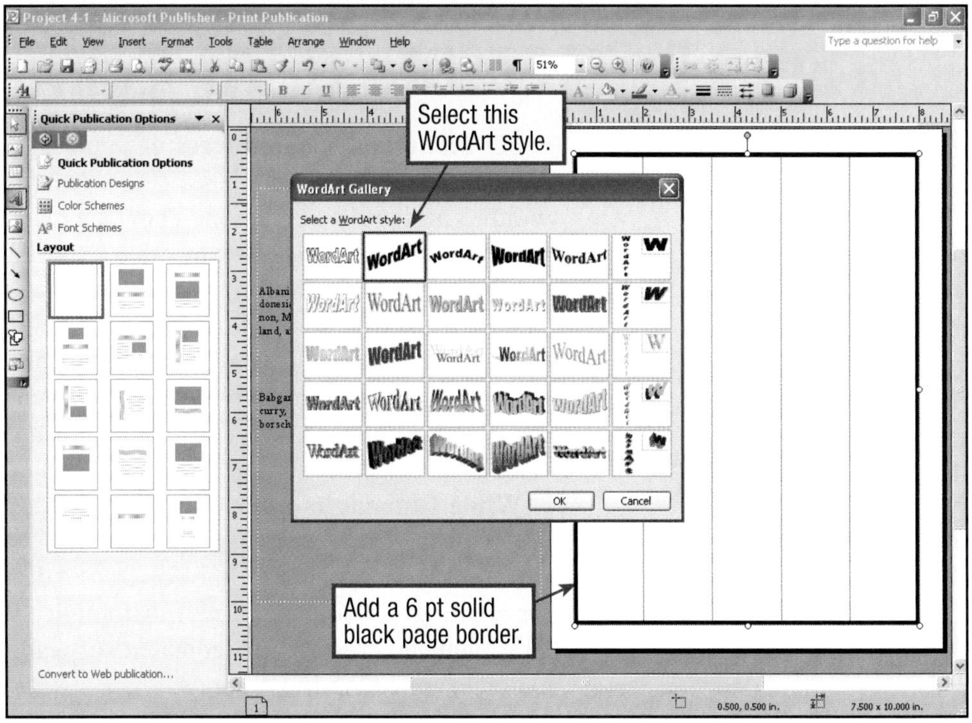

▼ **Figure 4.3** Move your mouse over each shape to display the name.

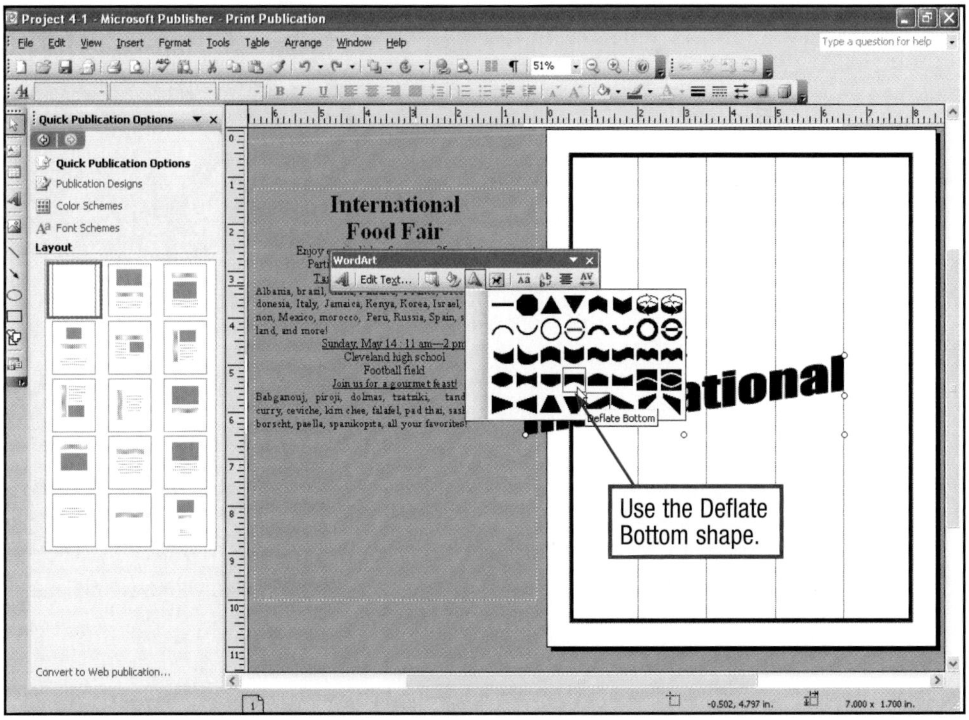

Skills Studio

Project 8-7 Create a 3D Cylinder

Skills You Will Apply

- Apply 3D effects

Key Term

- 3D modeling
- three-dimensional (3D)

Academic Focus

Math
Evaluate three-dimensional objects

3D modeling is the process of using a computer to virtually create an object. The artist first creates a **three-dimensional** object displaying depth, width, and height on screen. Then the artist defines its characteristics—whether it is glass, brick, or any other material or texture. The artist describes the light source's direction, intensity, and color. The computer uses complicated math computations to determine what the object would look like based on this information. It is a complex and time-consuming process. Today's movies require hundreds of the fastest computer systems to achieve realistic 3D effects. The outcome is a fascinating virtual world where the artist's vision can be fully realized.

While filmmakers often create their own proprietary software, other 3D programs are available, such as Caligari/DAZ TrueSpace™ and Bryce™. Anim8or® is available online for free. Adobe Illustrator has modest tools for creating 3D objects as well. Although the results are not as realistic as those you can create with dedicated software, Illustrator's tools can be used to create appealing illustrations.

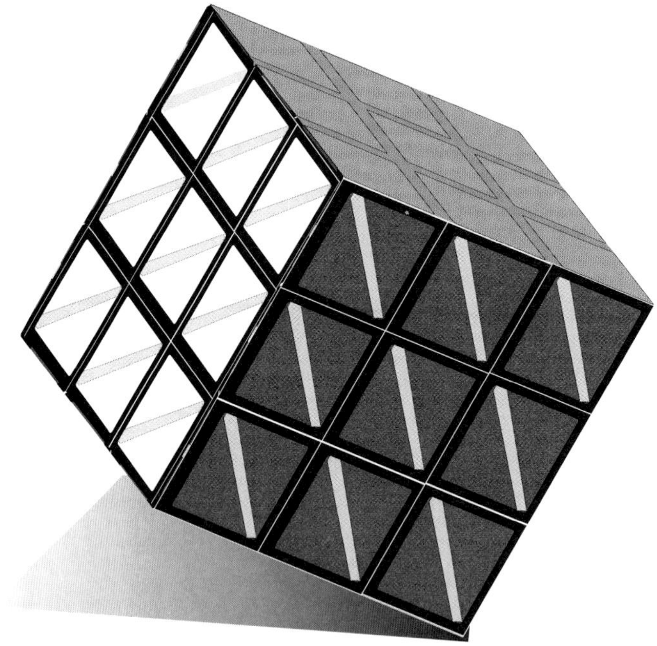

▲ This cube was created with a simple shape and the 3D tools in Illustrator.

► **In this project,** you will create a fruit drink can with Illustrator's Rounded Rectangle tool. The can will have a three-dimensional shape when you apply the 3D revolve effect.

13 Repeat Steps 9–10, but this time key Food Fair.

14 Change the **width** to **3.9 inches** and the **height** to **1.25 inches**. Change the WordArt shape to **Inflate Top**.

Adjust White Space

15 Drag the two WordArt objects to the top of the page as shown in Figure 4.4.

16 Create a **text box** below the WordArt extending over **columns 2–4** to the bottom of the page.

17 Insert the text from the original text box.

18 Delete all underlines. Center and format the text as shown in Figure 4.4.

19 Follow your teacher's instructions for saving your work. You will continue working on this flyer in Project 4-2.

▼ **Figure 4.4** Compare your final document to the original flyer.

REVIEW AND REVISE

Check your work Use Figure 4.4 as a guide, and check that your flyer follows the following design guidelines:

- ☑ There is proximity. Text is grouped logically.
- ☑ There is alignment. This flyer uses conservative center alignment.
- ☑ There is repetition. Fonts come from related families.
- ☑ There is contrast. WordArt provides a focal point.
- ☑ White space flows so that it is easy to read the information.

Skills Studio

Design a 3D Product

The following four projects will take you through the steps you need to create a three dimensional object:

- **Project 8-7** Create a 3D cylinder
- **Project 8-8** Design a product logo
- **Project 8-9** Design a product label
- **Project 8-10** Add symbols to a label

Reinforce Your Skills

Project 8-7
- Apply 3D effects

Project 8-8
- Create a logo

Project 8-9
- Add clip art to a Logo
- Apply text outlines
- Add symbols

Project 8-10
- Create a map
- Affix a map

Go Online ACTIVITIES
www.glencoe.com

Challenge Yourself Go to **Chapter 8**, and choose **Enrichment Activities** for more practice with the skills you have learned.

Product Design

One of the big advances in recent marketing has been a concentrated effort on product design. Although millions of dollars are spent on various forms of advertising, including television, magazine, and radio advertisements, it is the product design that often makes the difference. For example, have you ever gone to the grocery store to buy a bag of chips, but walked out with a different brand because of the way the bag looked? Did the chips look tastier? Did it appear to be a better quality product, with better crunch?

Manufacturers spend years designing a product. Audience preferences and needs are assessed through extensive research. You may have noticed people participating in market surveys while shopping at a store. Manufacturers want to find out what characteristics are most appealing to their target audience. The final product is not ready to go until accountants, marketers, researchers, and graphic designers have determined the best product to fill the greatest market need.

Project 4-2

Add Contrast and Focal Points

Spotlight on Skills

- Add a contrasting color
- Insert an Attention Getter

Key Term

- spot color

Academic Focus

Social Studies
Identify international cuisines

Student Data File

Graphics catch our attention more than most words, and audiences usually understand the meaning of a picture more easily than words. Whenever possible, try to create interest or sell your product or service by using visual elements. They are usually the best entry point for leading readers to other important content.

Designers often use color with graphics. Using one color to contrast with the black ink will help you create a visually attractive and appealing publication. It can also create a focal point that attracts the eye to important information on the page. Printers can use a **spot color**, a specific color ink, to make the contrasting color exactly the shade you want.

Another way to call out important information is with Publisher's *Attention Getter* feature. These design elements may look like star bursts or unusual shapes. They can be found in Publisher's Design Gallery. Attention Getters can be used as focal points. Too many of them, however, can be distracting.

▶ **In this project,** you will continue revising the flyer that you started in Project 4-1, adding color and an attention getter.

Step-by-Step

1. Open the International Food Fair flyer that you revised in Project 4-1. Save it according to your teacher's instructions.
2. Click **Insert>Picture>From File**, and insert **Data File 4-2**.
3. Select the clip art, and click **Format>Picture>Size** tab. Then change the height to **2 inches.** Be sure the **Lock Aspect Ratio** box is checked. Do not close the Format Picture box (Figure 4.5).

▼ **Figure 4.5** Add an image to create visual interest in a document.

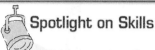

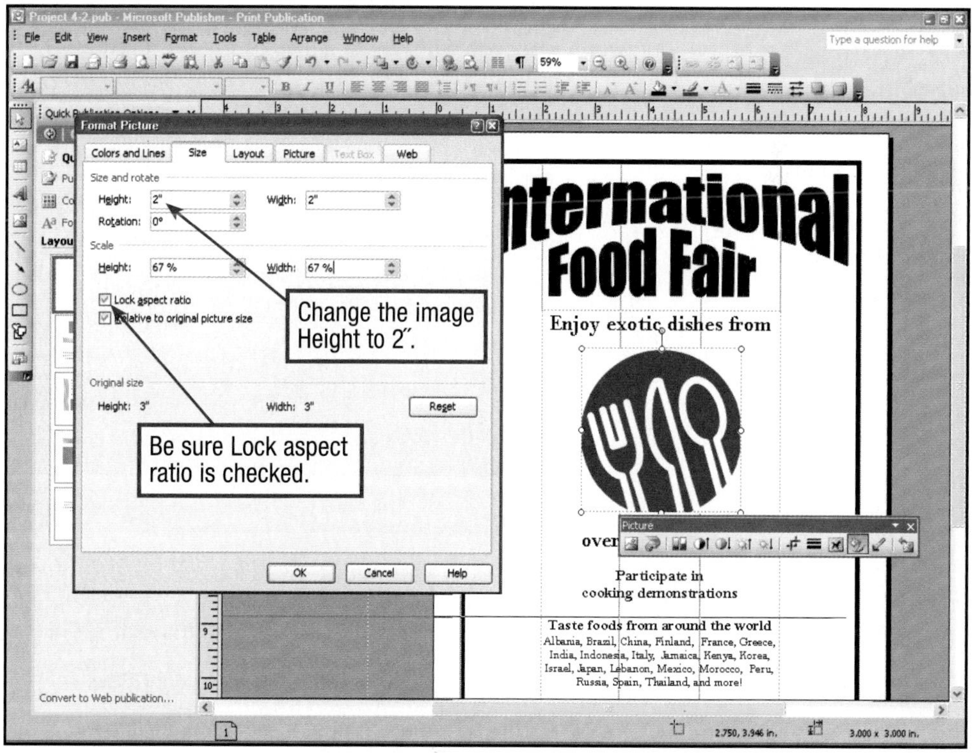

15. In the **Print** dialog box, click the **Advanced Print Settings** button. In the **Page Settings** tab, make sure that **Crop marks** is selected, and click **OK**.

16. Follow your teacher's instructions for printing the poster.

17. On the printed pages, trim the excess, but leave some duplication for overlap.

18. Overlap the pages, aligning the text and images. Tape the backs of the pages together. Your finished poster should look similar to Figure 8.29.

▼ **Figure 8.29** Your finished poster.

REVIEW AND REVISE

Check your work Use Figure 8.29 as a guide and check that:

- ☑ Transparency settings have been applied.
- ☑ The text is readable and accurate.
- ☑ The entire poster design is visible.
- ☑ The four tiled pages are aligned properly.

Add a Contrasting Color

4. In the **Format Picture** box, click the **Picture** tab. Click the **Recolor** button. In the **Color** drop down menu, choose **More Colors**.

5. Click the **Custom** tab, and key 245 in the **red** RGB windows. Set the other colors at **0**. Click **OK** to close all the dialog boxes.

6. Move the clip art into the position shown in Figure 4.6.

7. Right-click the clip art, and click **Order** on the menu. Choose **Send to Back**. The clip art should be behind the WordArt (Figure 4.6).

8. Select the clip art and the two WordArt objects. Click **Group** to group them as one object.

9. Click **Arrange>Align or Distribute>Relative to Margin Guides.** Then click **Arrange>Align or Distribute>Align Center**.

10. Create a final text box along the bottom margin. **Center** and key Profits will be donated to the Red Cross.

11. Change the text to **italic**, **Times New Roman**, **14 pt**. Change the color to the same **red** as in Step 5 (Figure 4.7).

Figure 4.6 Use customized colors to enhance a design.

Figure 4.7 Repetition of a custom color adds unity to the design.

7. Change the font to **36 pt Berlin Sans FB Demi**. Set the **leading** at **86 pt**, with **50 pt** after each paragraph.

8. Insert **Data File 8-6**, a fire background, and then click **Arrange>Order>Send to Back** (Figure 8.27).

9. Create a **white rectangle**, and **send it back** so it is between the text and the background layers.

Apply Gradient Transparency

10. Select the rectangle. Change the border to a **double-line border**. Select the rectangle. On the Formatting toolbar, choose the **Fill Color** and click **Fill Effects**.

11. Click on the **Gradient** tab, choose **One Color** (white), and select the **first Horizontal gradient**. Choose **Transparency** settings: **From 0 percent** and **To 80 percent**.

12. Select all the objects in the design. Choose **Arrange>Align or Distribute>Align Center**. Make other adjustments as needed. See Figure 8.29 on page 357.

13. Save the poster in TIFF format following your teacher's instructions.

Set Print Specifications

14. Click **File>Print**. Click the **Change Overlap** button. Make sure that the **Overlap** is set to **0.25"**. Click **OK** to return to

Figure 8.27 Create visual interest with an appropriate background. Use a gradient to blend the foreground and background.

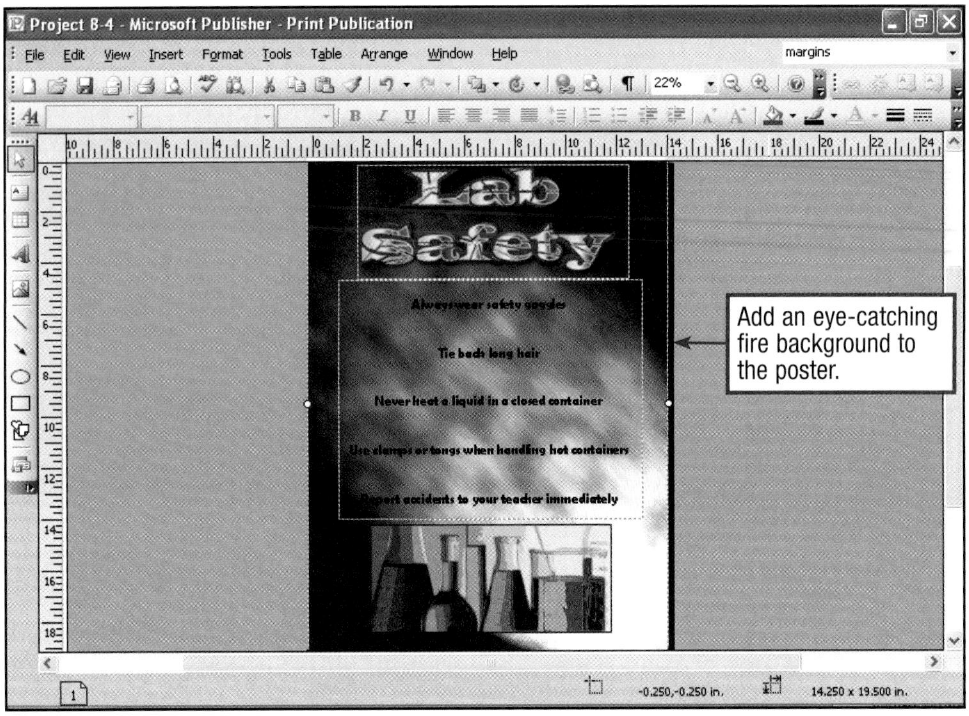

Figure 8.28 To print on one sheet, rather than tile printing, you would need special paper and a printer that handles large formats.

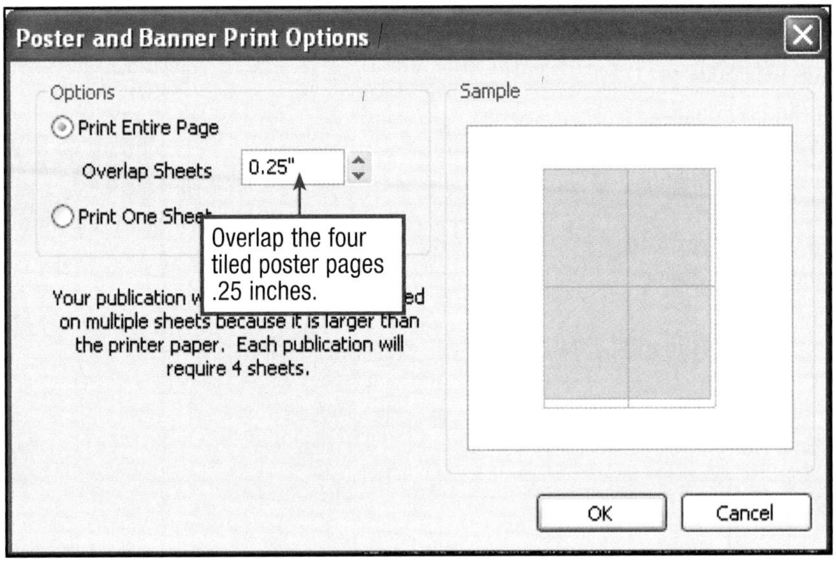

Insert an Attention Getter

12 Click **Design Gallery Objects** . Choose **Attention Getters**.

13 In the **Attention Getters** box, choose the **Shadowed Starburst** style, as shown in Figure 4.8.

14 Resize the Attention Getter, and reposition it as shown in Figure 4.9.

15 Select the Attention Getter, and click **Format>Object>Layout** tab. Change the **Text Wrapping** to **None**.

16 Change the text in the Attention Getter to This weekend! (Make sure **AutoFit Text** is on.)

17 Use the green handle to rotate the Attention Getter to an angle similar to Figure 4.9.

▼ **Figure 4.8** Attention Getters do exactly what their name suggests.

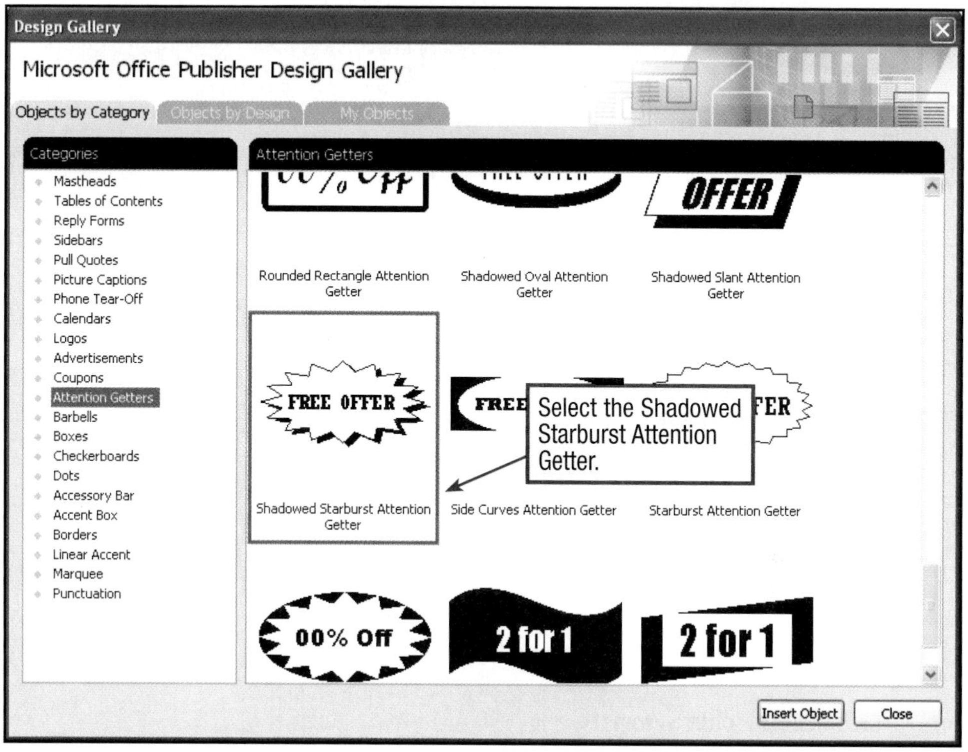

▼ **Figure 4.9** You can modify any part of the Attention Getter.

Student Data File

Step-by-Step

Set Poster Layout

1. Open Microsoft Publisher. In the **New Publications** task pane, click **Poster**.

2. Click **File>Page Setup**. Set the **width** to **14 inches** and the **height** to **19 inches**.

3. Click **Arrange>Layout Guides**, and change all the **margin** settings to **.25 inch**.

4. Click **Insert>Picture>From File**, and browse to the Lab Safety Shattered Text **PNG file** created in Project 8-5. Insert the picture at the top of the workspace (Figure 8.25).

5. Deselect the picture, and then insert the **Live Trace** file you created in Project 8-4 at the bottom of the workspace.

6. Between the text drawing and the clip art, insert a text box. Key and center the following safety guidelines (Figure 8.26):
   - Always wear safety goggles
   - Tie back long hair
   - Never heat a liquid in a closed container
   - Use clamps or tongs when handling hot containers
   - Report accidents to your teacher immediately

Figure 8.25 Eye-catching shattered text will attract attention to the important safety rules in the lab.

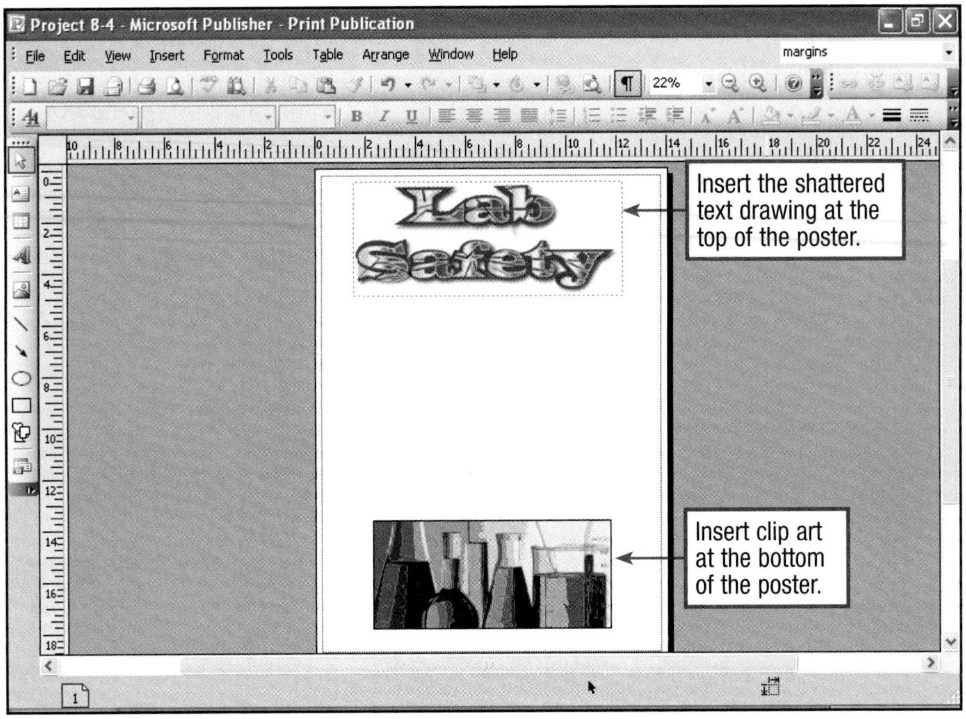

Figure 8.26 Center align text and graphics.

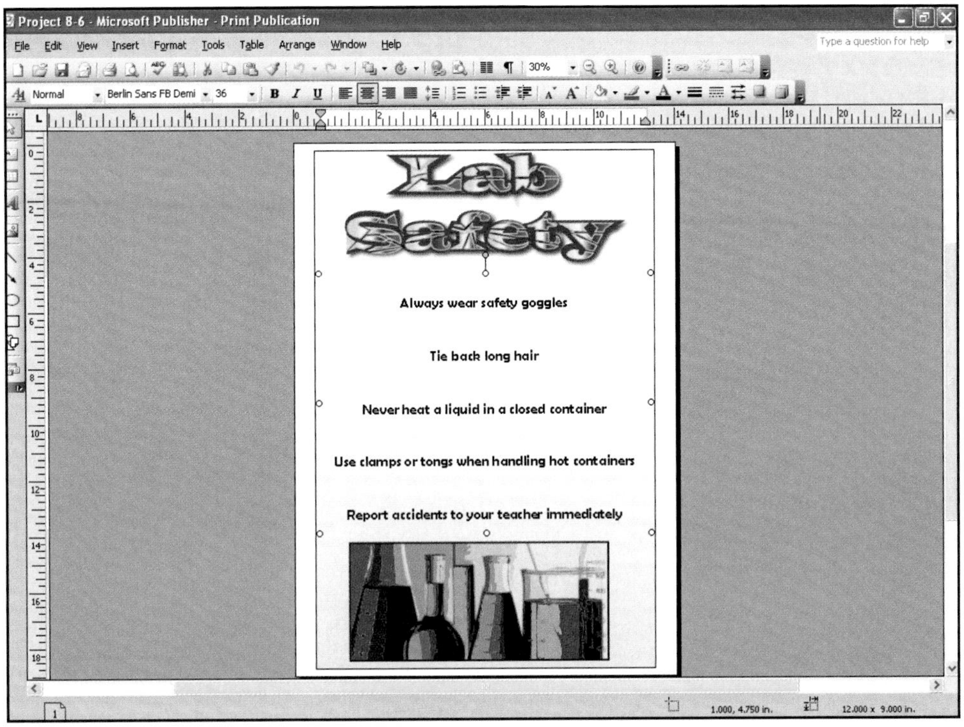

18 Select the Attention Getter. Click **Format>Object>Colors and Lines** tab. Click the **Line color** drop-down menu.

19 Choose **More Colors**. In the **Custom** tab, set the **RGB** values to the same **red** color previously set.

20 If the text box border inside the Attention Getter is red, select the text box only. Click **Line Color**. Choose **No Color**.

21 Select the text in the Attention Getter, and change it to the same **red** previously set.

22 Proofread your work, and use **Design Checker** to make sure there are no design problems.

23 Save and print your work according to your teacher's instructions.

▼ Figure 4.10 The color on the page adds excitement.

REVIEW AND REVISE

Check your work Use Figure 4.10 as a guide and check that:

- ☑ The red spot color is the same throughout the document.
- ☑ The clip art color has been changed to red and is behind the WordArt.
- ☑ The text at the bottom of the page is centered, red, and italic.
- ☑ The Attention Getter is sized and placed according to the figure, with red text and line.

Project 8-6 Lay Out a Poster

Spotlight on Skills

- Set poster layout
- Apply gradient transparency
- Set print specifications

Key Terms

- tile printing
- freeware

Academic Focus

Science
Demonstrate safety awareness in lab

You are learning about the tools and techniques to create drawings using Illustrator. Now you are ready to use those vector-based drawings, both text and illustrations, in real-world design projects. Drawings can be imported into page layout software to create dynamic and appealing products such as posters, book covers, and magazines.

Page layout is the final stage in a project. While it is important to create interesting graphics that support the message, strong page layout software makes the difference between an effective design and one that fails to deliver the message.

Much of the power in page layout software is in its ability to easily move and arrange objects. However, in this project, you will use Publisher layout software for its printing abilities. To print the poster you created in Project 8-5, you will need an oversized printer, or you can tile print.

Tile printing is used when a document is too large to be printed on one sheet of paper. When you tile print, you print parts of the document on different pages. When the pages are joined together and aligned, they form the complete document. Using tile printing options, you can theoretically print a design as big as a house.

Compatible File Formats

In Chapter 6, you learned that Adobe Photoshop and Microsoft Publisher must use compatible file formats so that the programs can work together. File formats also must be compatible when using Adobe Illustrator and Microsoft Publisher.

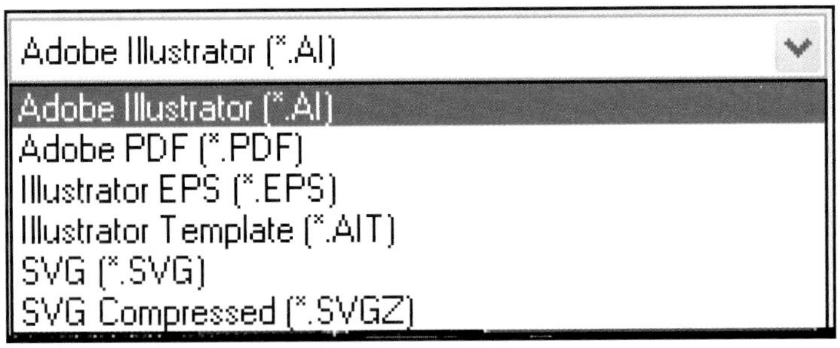

▲ Illustrator lets you save files in many formats recognized by other programs.

Fortunately, most software applications can be made to work together. For example, even though Illustrator creates graphics in its native AI format, it can save the graphics in a format that other programs will recognize, such as PNG.

Adobe Illustrator also lets you save in PDF format which is like a picture of the image. PDF files can usually be opened by any computer and can be used with a variety of software. An important benefit of the PDF format is that files can be retrieved, viewed, and printed with freeware called Adobe Acrobat Reader. As the word implies, **freeware** is software programming that is downloadable at no charge. This software allows you to share documents easily with anyone without additional expense.

▶ **In this project,** you will lay out your poster file in Publisher. You will add safety reminder text and clip art to the poster. Finally, you will tile print the poster, combining four sheets of paper to create the oversized document.

Project 4-3 Apply the Golden Ratio

Spotlight on Skills

- Apply the Golden Ratio
- Group related content

Key Term

- ratio

Academic Focus

Math
Evaluate ratios

► The Greeks used the Golden Ratio to design buildings.

Go Online ACTIVITIES
www.glencoe.com

Golden Ratio Go to **Chapter 4**, and choose **Enrichment Activities** to learn more about the Golden Ratio and page design.

The ancient Greeks noticed a consistent pattern in nature, which they called the Golden Ratio. A **ratio** is the relationship between objects based on size or quantity. The Greeks believed that designs that used proportions based on the Golden Ratio were more pleasing than others.

Calculate the Golden Ratio

The Golden Ratio has the value of 1.618, meaning that the size of the pattern always changes by that amount. It can be used to create many kinds of increasing or decreasing patterns using spirals, rectangles, or other shapes.

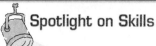

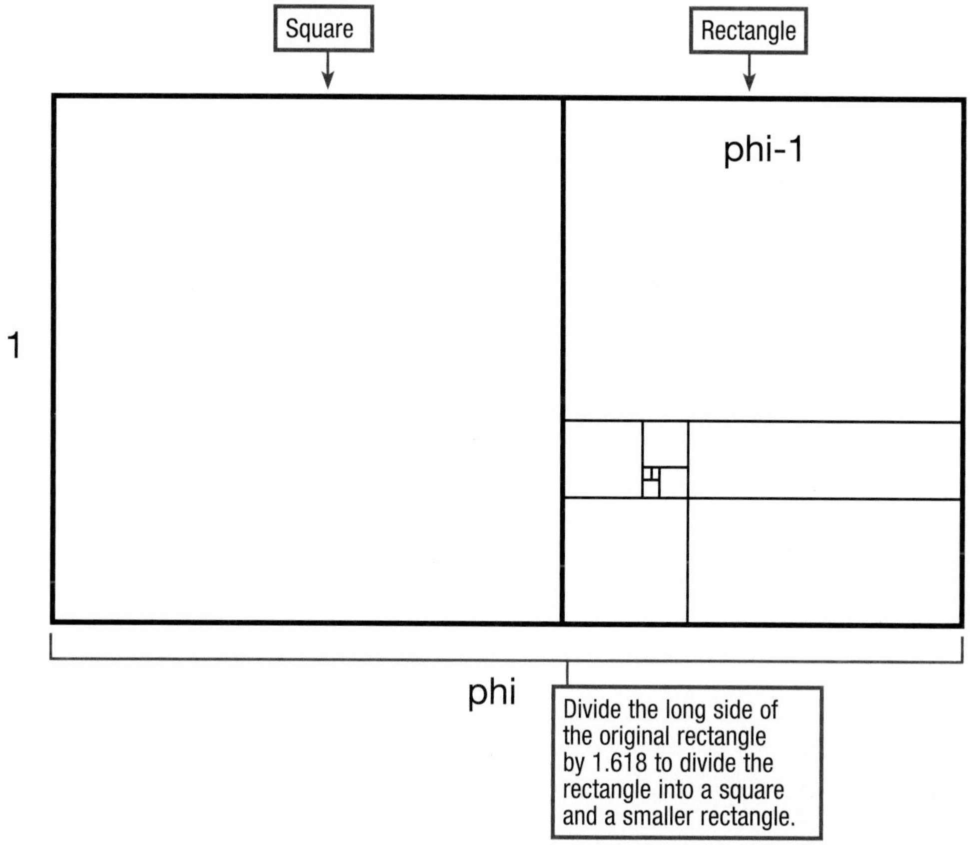

Square
Rectangle
phi-1
1
phi
Divide the long side of the original rectangle by 1.618 to divide the rectangle into a square and a smaller rectangle.

In the example, the long side of the rectangle has a length *phi*, to show that it can be any length. If you divide the long side of the rectangle by 1.618, you find the point where you can divide the rectangle into a square and another rectangle. The new rectangle has the same proportions as the original large rectangle. You can continue the square and rectangle pattern an infinite number of times by dividing the long side of each new, smaller rectangle by 1.618.

8. Select the title, and choose **Object>Ungroup**. **Zoom in**.

9. Use **Selection** [tool icon] to select letter pieces. Use the **arrow** keys to move each letter piece slightly. Rotate letter pieces for additional effect (Figure 8.23).

10. Select shapes. Click **Object>Group**.

Apply 3D Effects

11. With the title selected, click **Effect>3D>Extrude and Bevel**. Change the **Position** to **Front**, the **Extrude Depth** to **20 pt**, the **Bevel** to **Classic**, and the **Height** to **3**.

12. Select the duplicate text in the scratch area. Click **Window>Stroke**, and change the **Weight** thickness to a large size, such as **20 pts**.

13. Click the **Stroke** button. Select a **Stroke** color. Then click **Effect>Stylize>Drop Shadow**. Use the default settings.

14. Drag the text to your illustration, and then click **Object>Arrange>Send to Back** (Figure 8.24).

15. Click **File>Export, Save as type**, and choose **PNG** to save in a vector format that preserves transparency.

16. You will continue your poster in Project 8-6.

▼ Figure 8.23 Create the shattered text effect by separating the letter pieces.

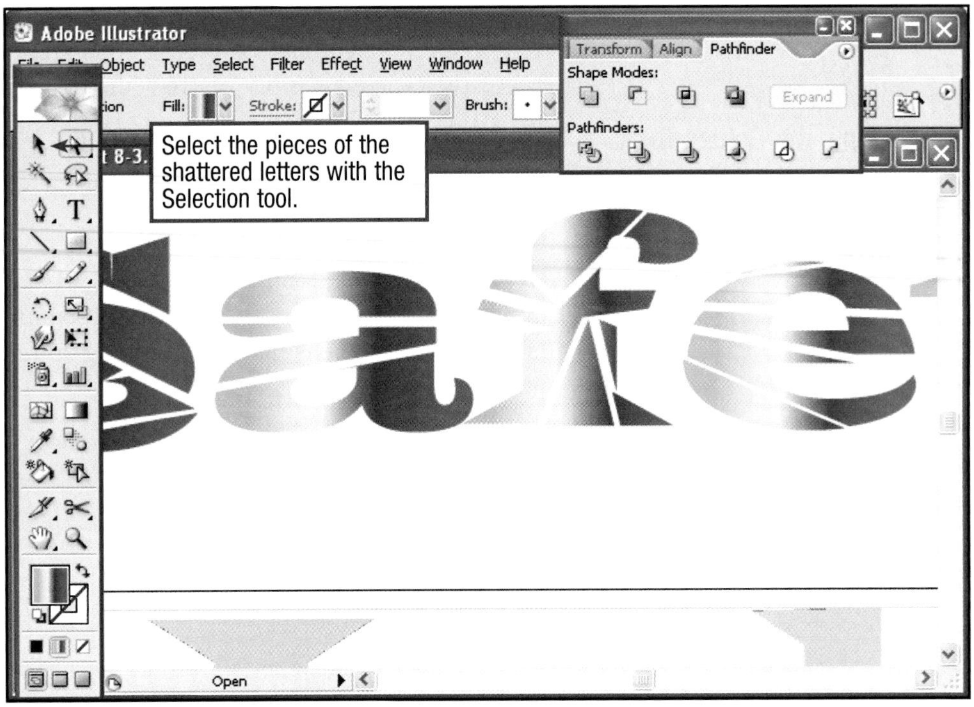

▼ Figure 8.24 Note the dynamic 3D text effect using extrude and bevel tools.

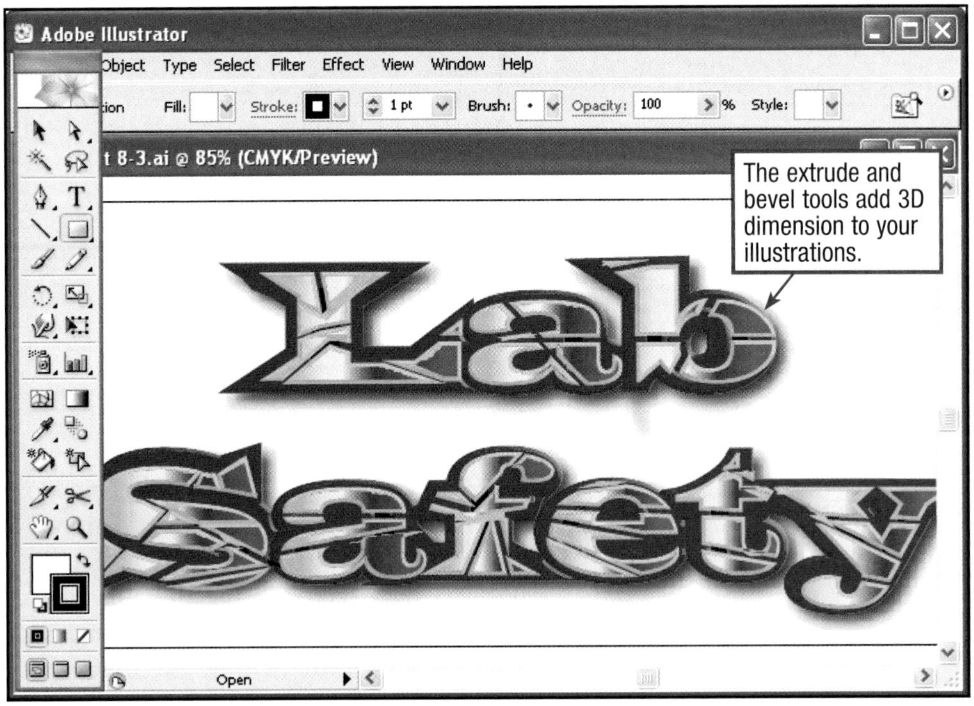

Evaluate an Advertisement

Although this design uses interesting contrast, it is difficult to see how content is grouped, or what information is most important. Use the table below to evaluate the effectiveness of the flyer.

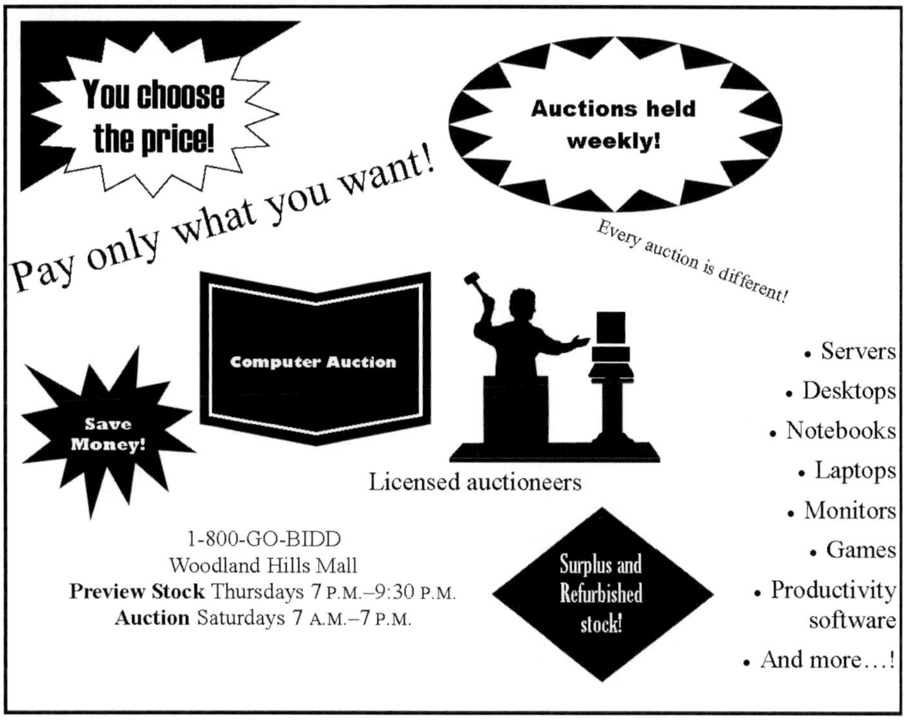

Design Blunders

PARC Principle	Problems
Proximity	• Information is not grouped consistently.
Alignment	• Too many types of alignments send a confused message. • White space is poorly used.
Repetition	• The design uses only two typefaces, which is good, but the reader does not recognize the repetition because there are too many competing elements. • The dominant design element, the reversed rectangle, is echoed by a reversed oval. The repetition does not work because of the random layout.
Contrast	• High contrast points compete, causing the reader's eyes to skip around the page. The reader does not know what to read first.

▶ **In this project,** you will create an advertisement that uses the Golden Ratio to break the space into attractive segments.

Step-by-Step

1. Create a new document **10 inches wide** and **5 inches high** in landscape orientation.

2. Use **Type** [T] to key Lab Safety on two lines in **Wide Latin** font. Use a large font size to fill the workspace. Then click **Window>Type>Paragraph>Align center**.

3. Press [ALT] to make a duplicate copy of the text. Drag it to the scratch area for later use.

Apply Text Outlines

4. Select the text, and click **Type>Create Outlines** to turn the text into an art drawing.

5. Use the **Gradient** palette to add an effect similar to Figure 8.21. **Unselect** the title text object, and then press [D] to set to **default black and white**.

6. Use **Line Segment** [\] to create a series of randomly intersecting lines over the title text. See Figure 8.22.

Apply Pathfinder Divide

7. Select the text and the intersecting lines. Open the **Pathfinder** palette, and click the **Divide** icon. The software makes separate shapes out of the intersecting lines.

▼ Figure 8.21 Use Illustrator to create large title text for flexibility in resizing and adding special effects.

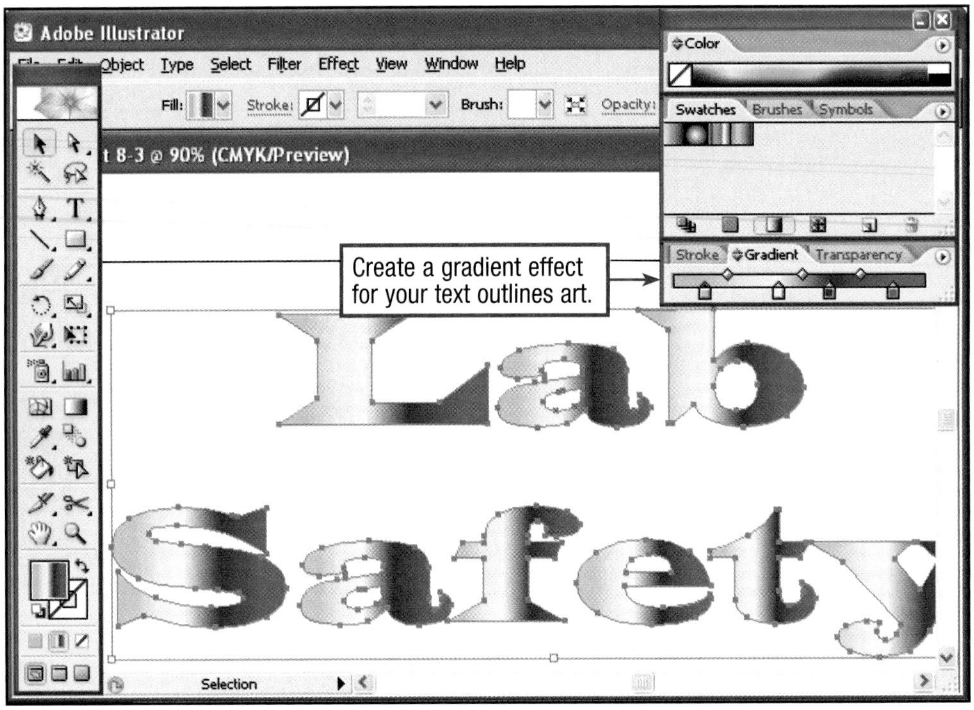

Create a gradient effect
for your text outlines art.

▼ Figure 8.22 Simple lines can be used to create an exciting effect.

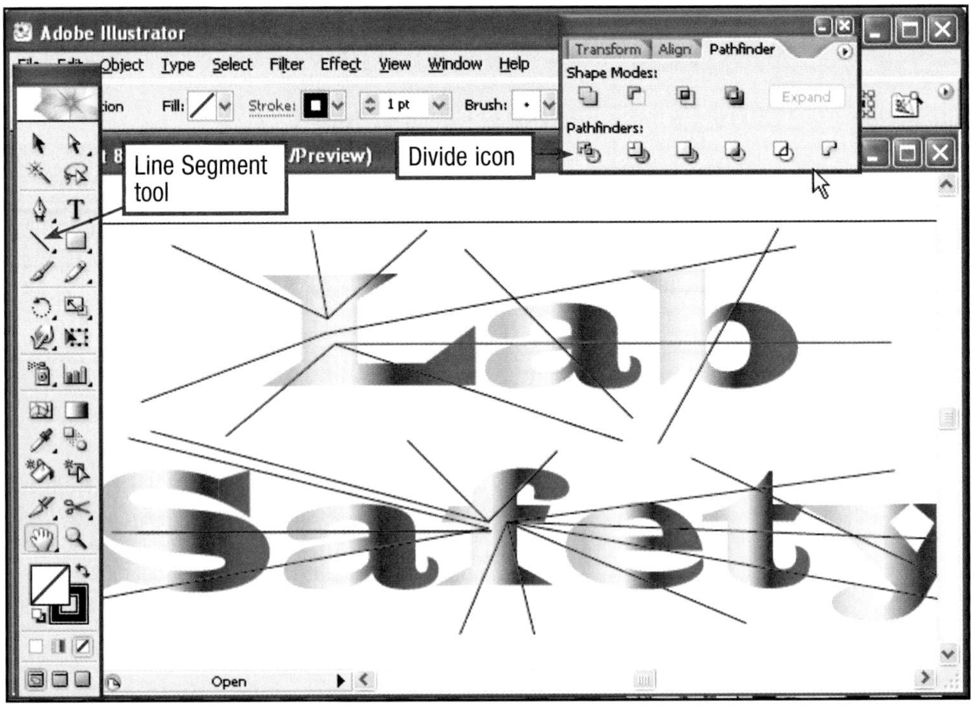

Student Data File

Step-by-Step

1. In Publisher, open **Data File 4-3**. Save it according to your teacher's instructions.

2. Open the **Apply Master Page** task pane. At the bottom of the task pane, click **View Master Pages** (Figure 4.11).

Apply the Golden Ratio

3. In the **Edit Master Page** window, use the **Arrange>Layout Guides** box to set the **right margin** to **3.05 inches**. All other margins should remain **0 inches**.

4. Create a **gray rectangle** that is **3.71 inches high** and **3.05 inches wide**. Place it as shown in Figure 4.12.

5. Create a **black rectangle** that is **2.29 inches high** and **3.05 inches wide**. Place it as shown in Figure 4.12.

6. Draw a rectangle over the white rectangle. Choose **No Fill** and add a **1 pt**, **black** border line.

7. Close the **Master View** to return to your publication.

▼ **Figure 4.11** It is hard to tell where to look in this advertisement.

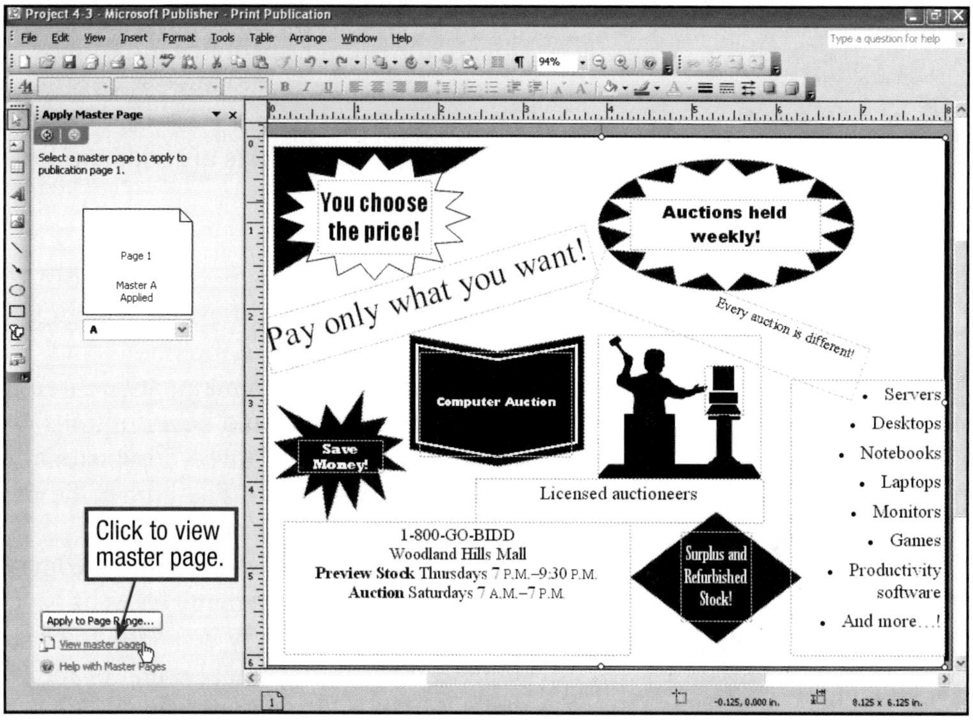

▼ **Figure 4.12** Each rectangle is 1.618 times bigger or smaller than the others.

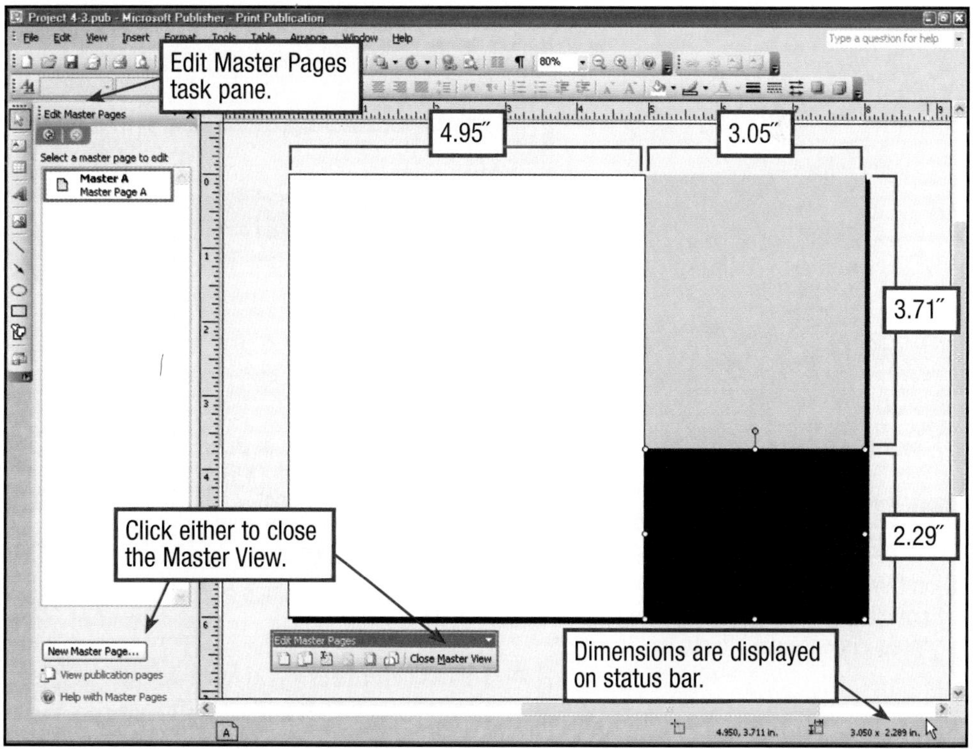

Project 8-5 Create Shattered Text

Spotlight on Skills

- Apply text outlines
- Apply Pathfinder Divide
- Apply three-dimensional (3D) effects

Key Terms

- extrude
- bevel

Academic Focus

Math
Create three dimensional effects

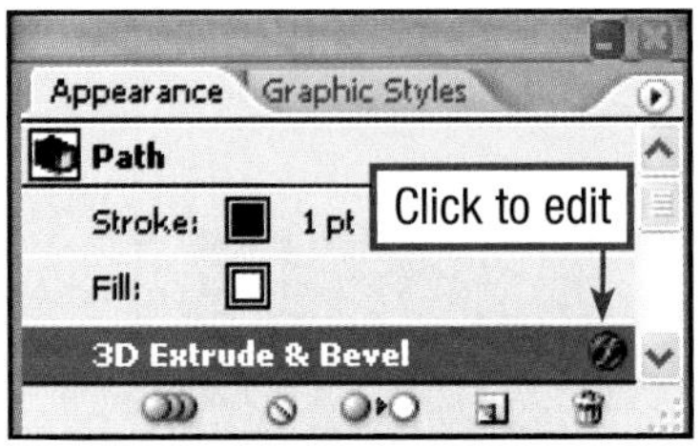

▲ In the Appearance palette, double-click the *f* icon to change three-dimensional effects.

Illustrator is a powerful program that can be used to create title fonts. With large, scalable fonts, impressive effects are fun to create. Because the images are created as vector artwork, they can be enlarged without loss of image quality. Vector files also take up less space.

Helpful Text Tools

Illustrator contains some simple tools to give objects perceived depth and visual interest on the page. You already know how to create three-dimensional text with Adobe Photoshop. With Adobe Illustrator, you can create eye-catching and imaginative three-dimensional objects.

Illustrator's extrude and bevel options are two of the tools that can be used to create realistic three-dimensional effects. To **extrude** an object is to give it visual depth. The higher the point size, the greater the three-dimensional look of the object.

To **bevel** an object is to smooth its edges so that the edges appear to be cut at an angle. There are many types of bevels accessible through the bevel drop-down menu that may be added to objects to give them character.

Once a three-dimensional effect is applied to an object, its appearance must be modified if you wish to change any characteristics of the object. Use the **Appearance** palette to change settings for a 3D object.

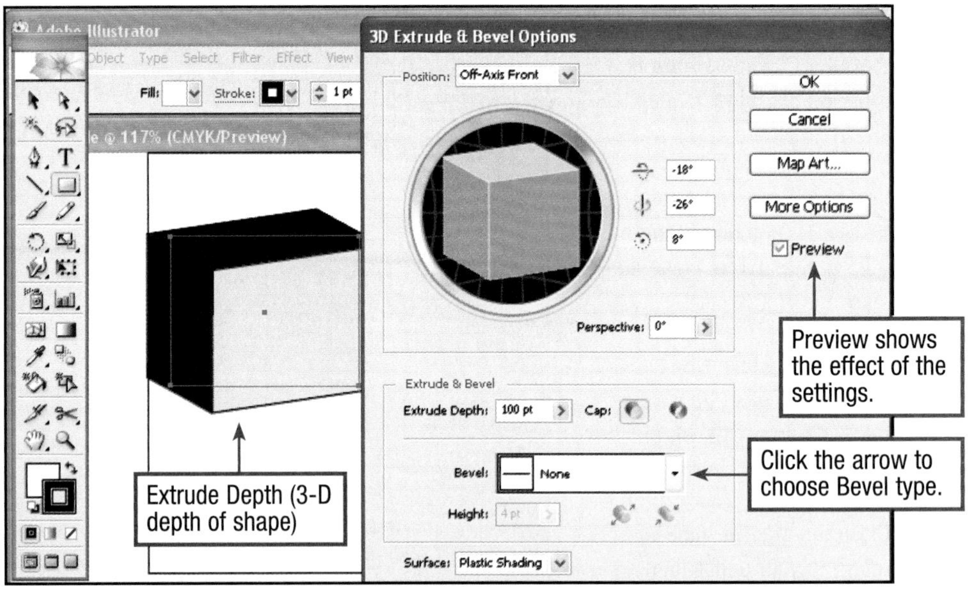

▲ A simple rectangle becomes a rectangular prism when extruded to 100 points.

▶ **In this project,** you will create a science lab safety poster with Illustrator's text tools. You will use the Pathfinder palette to make the text appear shattered, or broken into pieces.

8. Select the design, and drag it into the scratch area. (**Hint:** Set your **Zoom** at 50%.) The master page design is on a separate level.

9. Select the production page, and click **Arrange>Ungroup**. If necessary, click **View>Boundaries and Guides** to display frames. (Figure 4.13).

Group Related Content

10. From the old layout, move the elements to the white area of the new layout. Position and resize objects as shown in Figure 4.14.

11. Select all the newly-moved objects. Click **Arrange>Align or Distribute** and **align center** relative to the margin guides.

12. From the old layout, drag the objects shown in Figure 4.14 to the gray area. Position and resize them as shown in Figure 4.14.

13. Create a new text box in the gray area. Use the font in Figure 4.14 and key Save Money!

14. Move the new box into the position shown in Figure 4.14.

▼ Figure 4.13 The master page keeps the background objects from being disturbed.

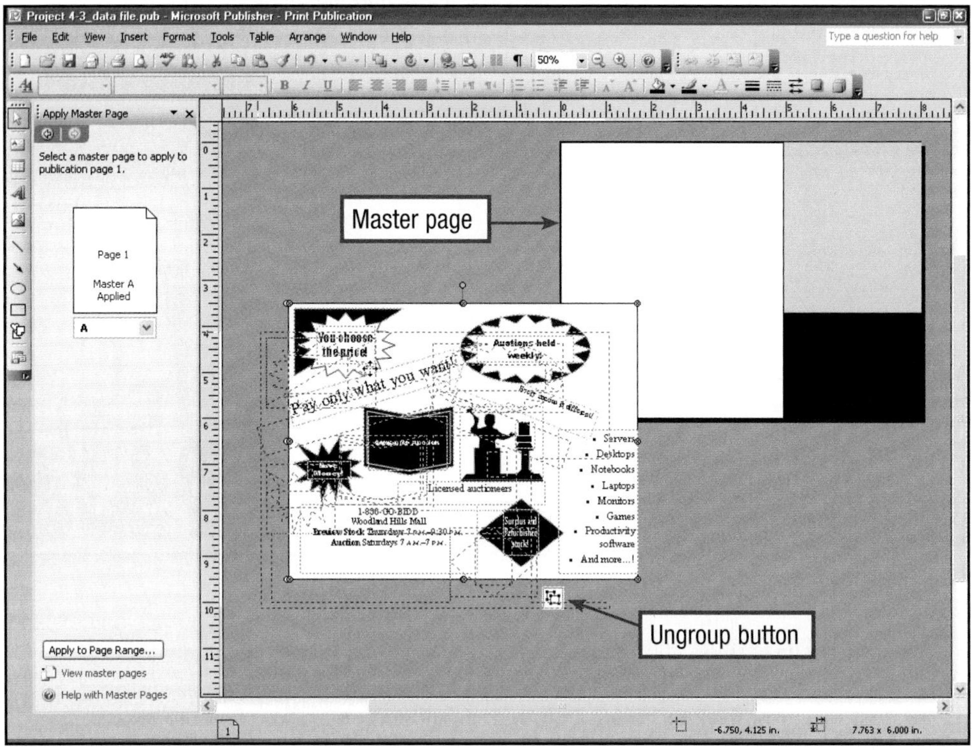

▼ Figure 4.14 Use this figure to arrange your new layout.

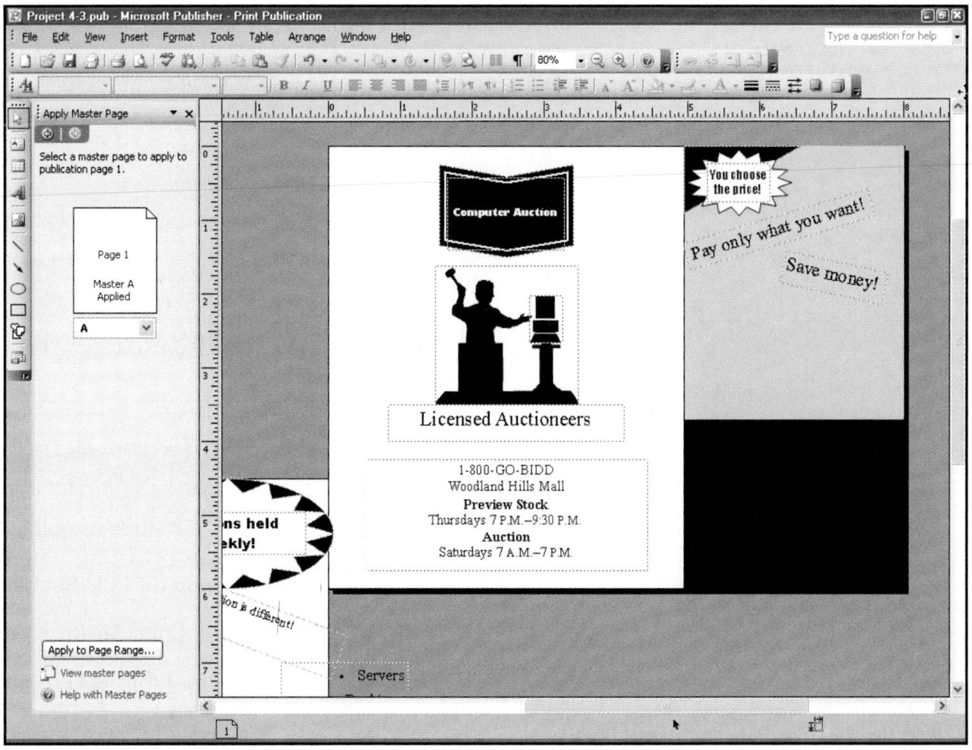

Copy and Paste Clip Art

3. Select the clip art. Click **Edit>Copy**. In your document click **Edit>Paste**.

Apply Live Trace

4. Click **Object>Live Trace>Make**. On the **Object** toolbar, change the **Preset** to **Color 16**.
5. Click **File>Save** to preserve the image if further editing is necessary later.
6. Click **Object>Live Trace>Expand** to make the effect permanent.
7. Choose **File>Export,** and save the file in a file format to use in other programs. Ask your teacher what file format should be used.
8. You will continue your poster in Project 8-5.

▼ **Figure 8.19** Use Illustrator's Live Trace feature to convert a raster graphic into a scalable vector image.

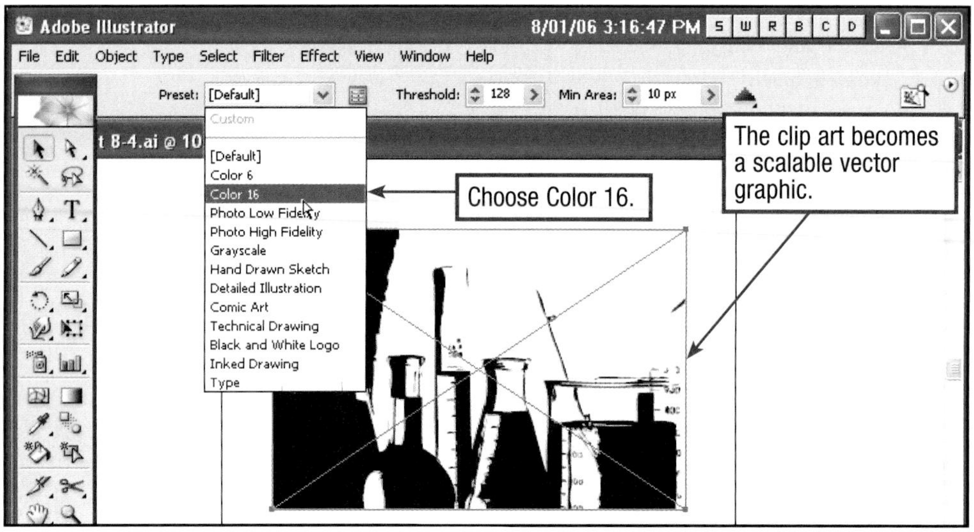

▼ **Figure 8.20** After using Live Trace and expanding the tracing, you can then create scalable clip art from photographs!

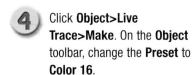

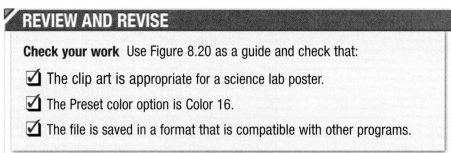

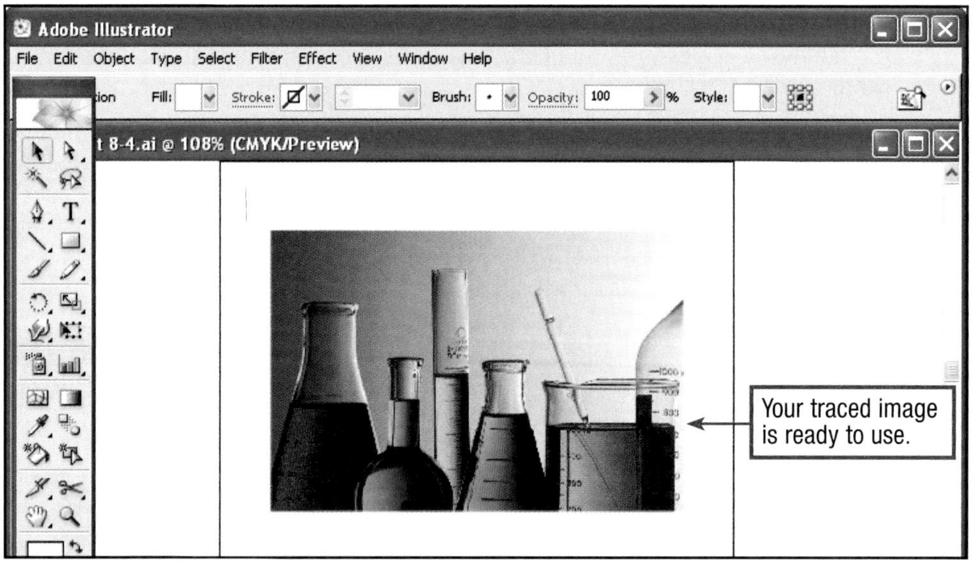

REVIEW AND REVISE

Check your work Use Figure 8.20 as a guide and check that:

- ☑ The clip art is appropriate for a science lab poster.
- ☑ The Preset color option is Color 16.
- ☑ The file is saved in a format that is compatible with other programs.

15. Move the bulleted list into position at the bottom of the gray area. Select all the text, and change the **font size** to **10** and **align left**.

16. Select the text box, and click **Format>Text Box>Text Box**. Click the **Columns** button, and set the columns to **3**.

17. Use the handles to make the text box wider and shorter, until the text is spread evenly in the three columns (Figure 4.15).

18. Move and resize the diamond Attention Getter so that it overlaps the gray and black areas as shown in Figure 4.16.

19. Change the text within the Attention Getter to **black**. Change the fill in the diamond to **white** and the border line to **black**.

20. Create a text box at the bottom of the black area.

21. In a **white serif** font, key Auctions Held Weekly. Every Auction Is Different!

22. Select the text box. **Center** the text. Then click **Format>AutoFit text> Best Fit**.

23. Follow your teacher's instructions for saving and printing your advertisement.

▼ **Figure 4.15** You can format a text box with columns.

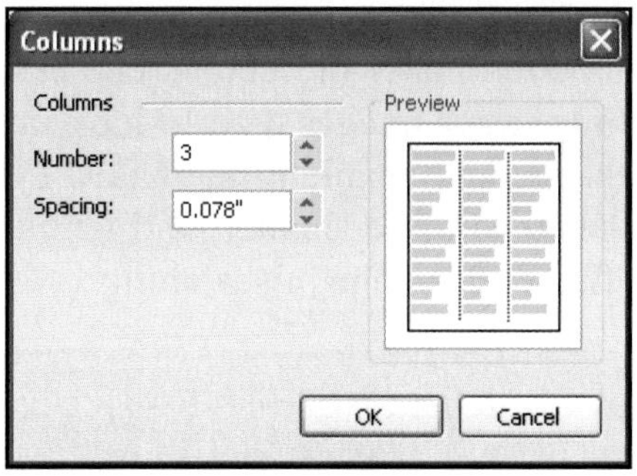

▼ **Figure 4.16** The new layout makes the busy design more appealing and readable.

REVIEW AND REVISE

Check your work Use Figure 4.16 as a guide and check that:

- ☑ Information is grouped so that it is easy to find.
- ☑ Contrast is used effectively to create focal points.
- ☑ Objects in the white area are centered.
- ☑ The bulleted list aligns properly in three columns.
- ☑ The diamond attention getter is white with black text and a black border.

Project 8-4 Apply Live Trace

Spotlight on Skills

- Copy and paste clip art
- Apply Live Trace

Key Term

- pixelated

Academic Focus

Science
Create a lab safety poster

Student Data File

Which is better, raster or vector? The answer lies in the purpose of the graphic. While raster images tend to look more like photographs, the individual pixels become visible to the naked eye, or **pixelated**, when resized. Vector images tend to be smaller, and tend to look like drawings, but they have the definite advantage of scalability.

Raster and Vector Characteristics

Raster	Vector
Photographic quality	Tend to look like drawings
Larger file sizes	Tend to be smaller in size
Resolution dependent	Scalable

It is seldom beneficial to turn a vector graphic into a raster image, but there are times when you may want to convert a raster graphic into a vector one. Until recently, special software such as Adobe Streamline was required to convert raster to vector. With the release of Illustrator CS2, Adobe has incorporated a powerful tracing feature.

▶ **In this project,** you will use Illustrator's Live Trace tool to convert a raster graphic into a scalable vector image. You will use this vector graphic in a science poster that you will create in Project 8-5.

Step-by-Step

1. Open a new document in Illustrator, and save it according to your teacher's instructions.
2. Insert **Data File 8-4**, or open the Microsoft Word **Clip Art Gallery**. Choose clip art that is appropriate for a science lab poster (Figure 8.18).

▼ **Figure 8.18** Choose clip art that relates to the poster message.

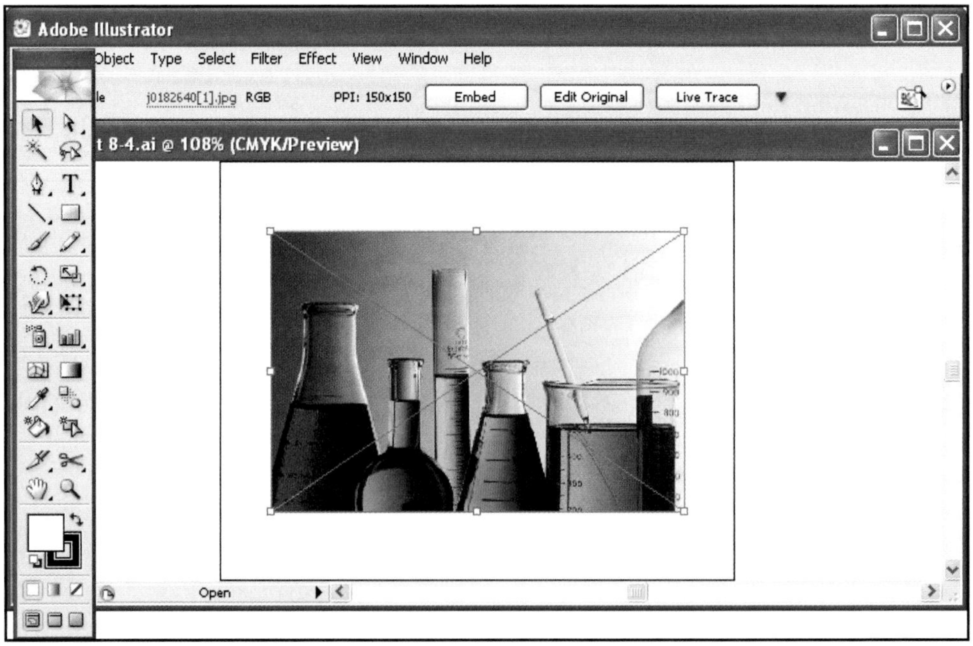

Project 4-4

Apply Styles in a Flyer

Spotlight on Skills

- Apply PARC to a list
- Create new styles
- Apply style sheets

Key Term

- style sheet

Academic Focus

Math
Apply alignment concepts

In previous projects, you created a **style sheet**, a tool that lets you save the name of a style and its font typeface, size, style, color, alignment, tab stops, margins and leading. Style sheets are useful for applying repetition to a document.

In the advertisement above, the message, "Quality you can trust" does not match the impression an audience will get from the poor design. Use the table to evaluate the flyer's effectiveness.

Design Blunders

PARC Principle	Design Problems
Proximity	• The proximity and grouping is weak and inconsistent. • Hyphenation creates awkward word breaks and decreases readability.
Alignment	• Items are misaligned and use conflicting alignments. • Many items line up with nothing else.
Repetition	• Some elements are in all caps, while others use lowercase. • Overuse of a single font is boring.
Contrast	• The reader is not given a focal point. • Other than the large font at the top, there is little use of contrast.

▶ **In this project,** you will use style sheets to make a business flyer more visually interesting and readable.

Apply a Master Page

8 Press CTRL + M to open the **Master Page** to add a custom color border to both pages.

9 On the **Master Page**, use **Rectangle** to draw a rectangle over the entire page.

Add Border Art

10 On the **Formatting** toolbar, click **Line/Border Style** **More Lines**. In the **Colors and Lines** tab, click the **Border Art** button. Choose the **Woodwork** border or a border of your choice (Figure 8.16). Do not close the **Format AutoShape** dialog box.

Create a Custom Color

11 Apply repetition by using the same red sanguine color as on the coat of arms. In the **Format AutoShape** dialog box, under **Line**, choose **More Colors** from the **Color** drop-down menu.

12 In the **Colors** dialog box, click the **Custom** tab. Then choose **CMYK Color model**, and enter the settings for sanguine red: **Cyan 23**, **Magenta 92**, **Yellow 78**, and **Black 14**.

13 Click **OK** until you close all dialog boxes. Click **Close Master Page View**.

14 Your card should look similar to Figure 8.17. Follow your teacher's instructions for printing and saving your work.

▼ Figure 8.16 Use the colors from the coat of arms in the border.

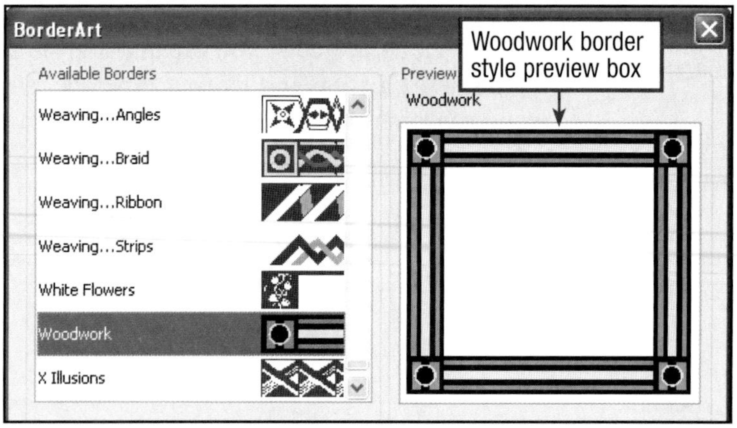

▼ Figure 8.17 Your final document.

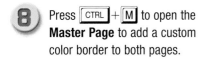

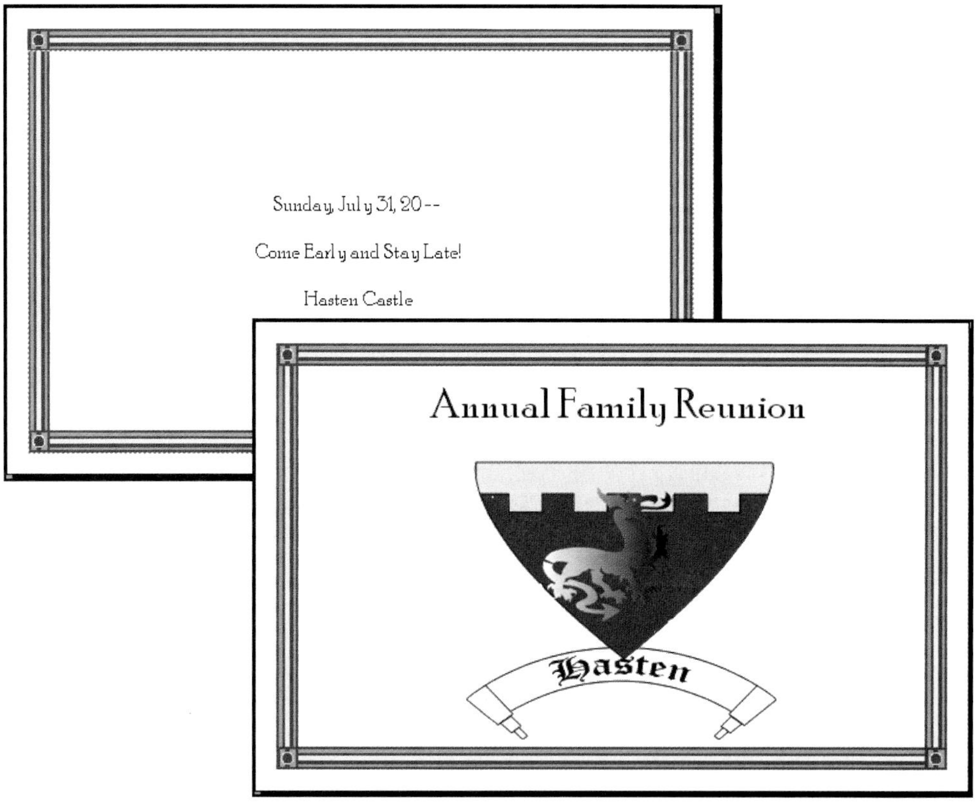

REVIEW AND REVISE

Check your work Use Figure 8.17 as a guide and check that:

- ☑ The coat of arms on Page 1 and text on Page 2 are both centered.
- ☑ Sanguine red color is repeated on the page borders and coat of arms.

Student Data File

1. In Publisher, open **Data File 4-4a**. Save it according to your teacher's instructions.
2. Select all parts of the design, and drag them to the scratch area.
3. Right-click on the clip art, and choose **Delete Object** (Figure 4.17).

▼ **Figure 4.17** Clip art should be selected carefully to send a professional message.

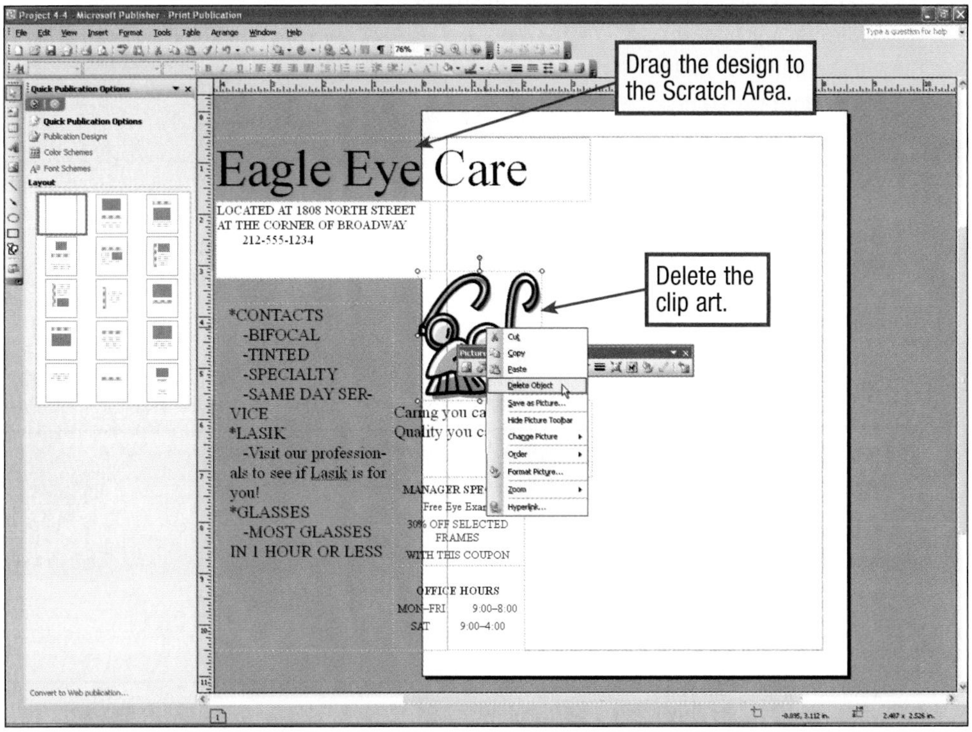

4. Drag the *Eagle Eye Care* text box to the workspace. Resize the text box, and stretch it across the entire top margin (Figure 4.18).
5. Change the font to **Bodoni MT Black**, **48 pt**. Change the **text color** to **white** and the text box **fill** to **black**.
6. Below *Eagle Eye Care*, key the phone number in **24 pt** font.
7. Drag the text box with *Caring you can see...*below the first text box (Figure 4.18).
8. Change the font to **Edwardian Script ITC** (or another elegant script font), at **24 pt**.

▼ **Figure 4.18** Black and white text provides a dynamic and powerful focal point.

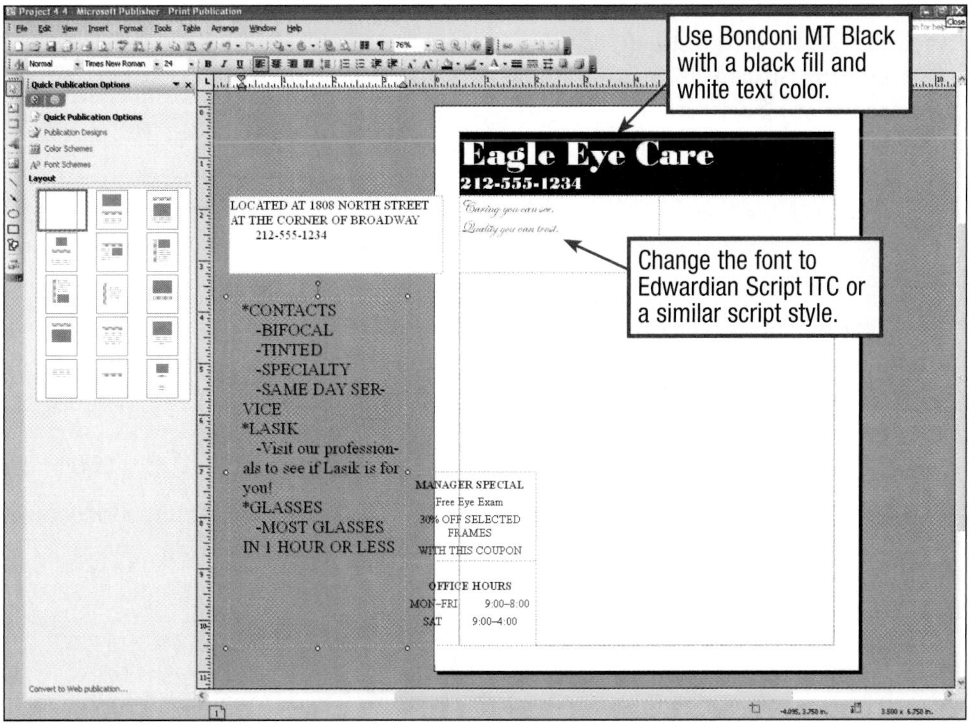

2. Click **Arrange>Layout Guides>Margin Guides**. Confirm margins for **Inside** and **Outside 0.25 inches**, **Top** and **Bottom 0.25 inches**.

3. Click the **Grid Guides** tab, and confirm that the **Grid Guides** are set for **1 column** and **1 row.**

Insert an Illustrator File

4. Click **Insert>Picture> From File**, and select your **Project 8-2** coat of arms (**WMF** file format). **Resize** and **reposition** as shown in Figure 8.14.

5. Add a text box above the coat of arms. Key Annual Family Reunion in **Poor Richard**, **36 pt**, **center aligned** (Figure 8.14).

6. Add a text box on page 2 to key details for the reunion. Use **Poor Richard**, **18 pt center aligned**, to key Sunday, July 31, 2008 [ENTER] Come Early and Stay Late! [ENTER] Hasten Castle.

Format Text Boxes

7. Click **Format>Text Box>Text Box** tab. Under **Vertical alignment**, choose **Middle**. Click **OK** (Figure 8.15).

▼ **Figure 8.14** A drawing created in Illustrator is used for an attention-getting invitation.

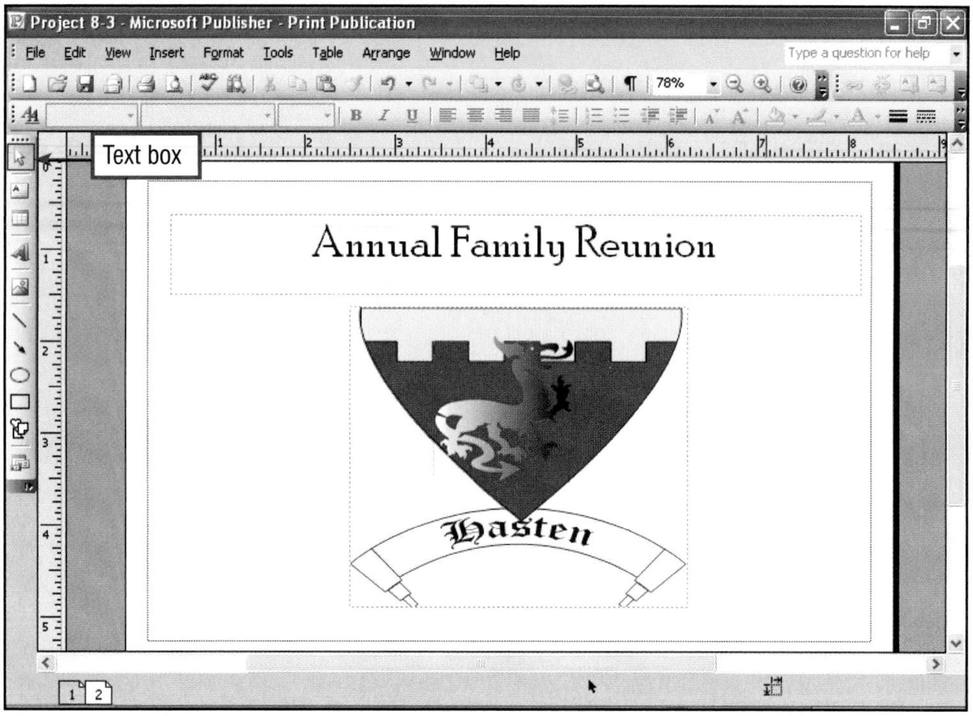

▼ **Figure 8.15** The message is short, but it contains all the information that the audience needs.

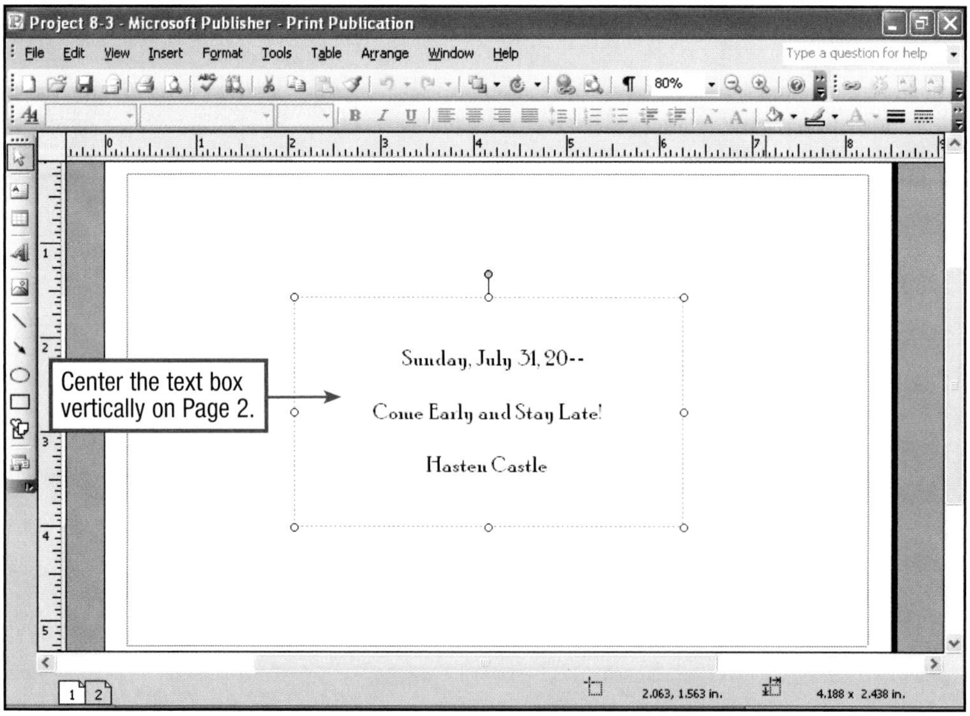

Apply PARC to a List

9. Drag the text box with the bulleted list to align with the left margin of the new design (Figure 4.19).

10. Click **Show/Hide** [¶]. Delete all tabs from the text. Then delete all the asterisks and hyphens.

11. Select all the text. Click **Format>Font**, and turn off **All Caps**.

12. Click **Tools>Language >Hyphenation**. Turn off **Automatically Hyphenate This Story**.

13. In the text box, select the word *Contacts*. Change the font to **Bodoni MT Black**.

14. Click **Format>Paragraphs**. Change the spacing **Before paragraphs** to **12**.

15. On the horizontal ruler, drag the **First Line Indent** slider to the left margin (Figure 4.20).

Create New Styles

16. With *Contacts* still selected, click in the **Styles** window. Key Section Head, then press [ENTER] (Figure 4.20).

Figure 4.19 Use the Special Characters button to reveal tabs and spacing.

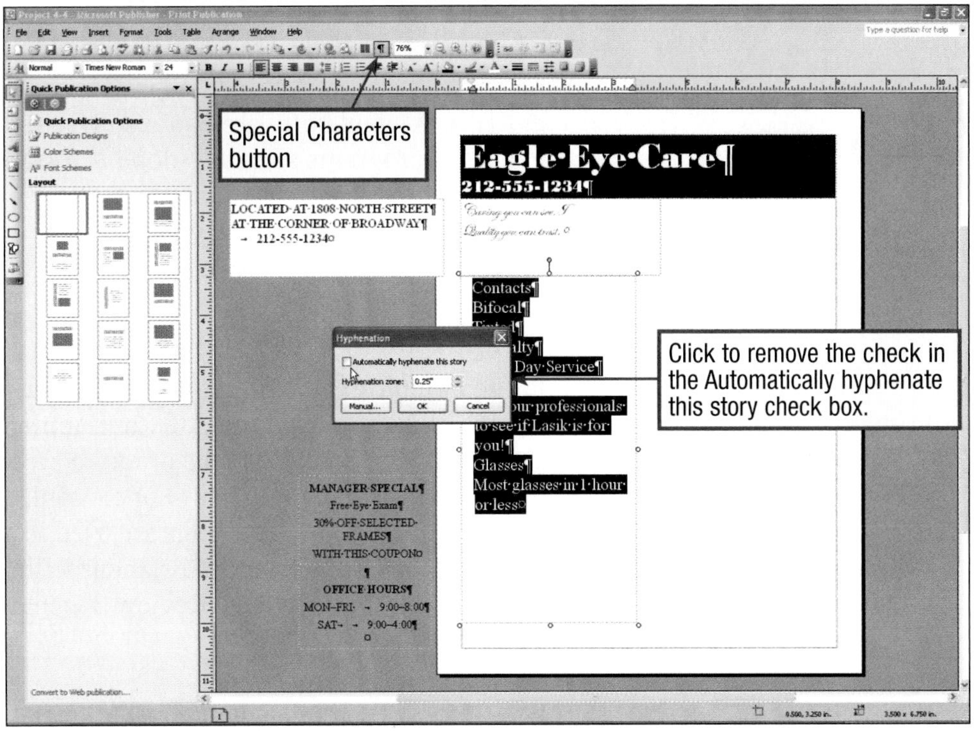

Figure 4.20 Create styles for separate design elements.

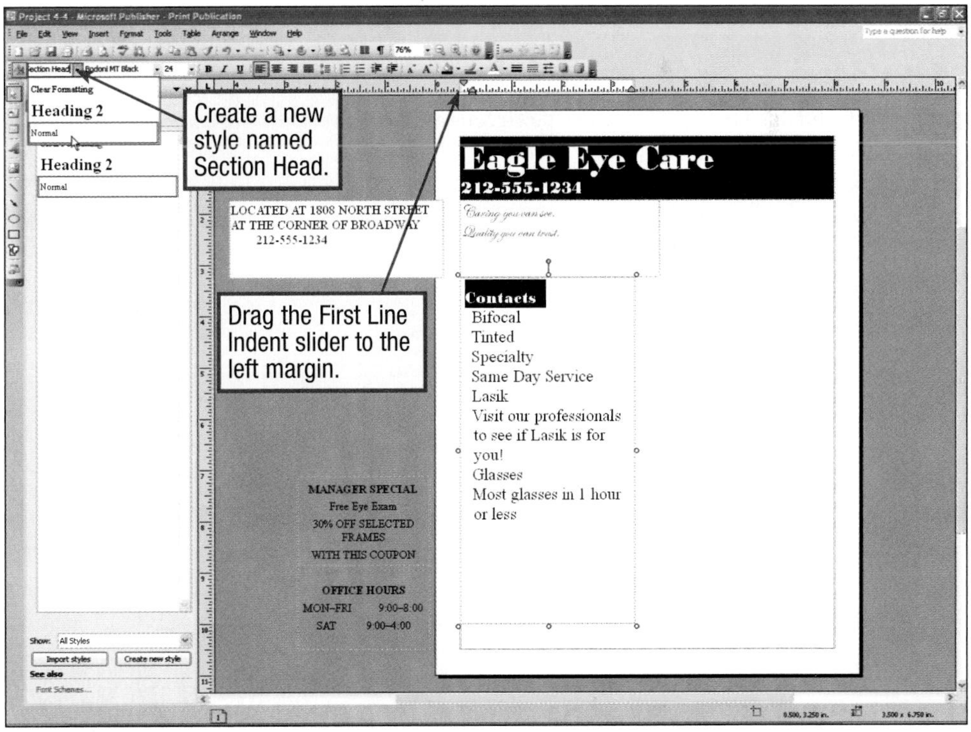

Project 8-3

Create a Tent Card

Spotlight on Skills

- Lay out a tent card
- Insert an Illustrator file
- Format text boxes
- Apply a master page
- Add border art
- Create a custom color

Key Term

- native format

Academic Focus

Language Arts
Add descriptive text

In Unit 3, you used Publisher layout software to create projects that integrated raster images created in Adobe Photoshop with Microsoft Word text files. Layout software can also be used to combine vector drawings created in programs such as Adobe Illustrator with text. Page layout software is ideal for design and production with dynamic tools that encourage creativity. It is the role of layout software to put these different elements together to create a single, consistent product.

Compatible File Formats

The default **native format**—the format created for Illustrator—is AI (Adobe Illustrator). Many software applications have their own native formats. Files created with the program are automatically saved within the program in the native format. For example, Photoshop's native format is PSD. When Illustrator drawings are used in another application, the vector images must be exported to a standard file format so that each program recognizes the file formats. Review the chart on page 259 in Chapter 6 on file compatibility.

▶ **In this project,** you will create a tent card inviting relatives to a family reunion. The coat of arms that you created in Projects 8-1 and 8-2 will be used for the cover of the card.

Step-by-Step

Lay Out a Tent Card

1 In Publisher, click **Blank Publications**, and then choose **Tent Card** design. Respond **Yes** to the question if you want Publisher to automatically insert pages. Save the document according to your teacher's instructions.

▼ **Figure 8.13** A tent card can be used as a reminder of an event or as an invitation.

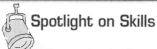

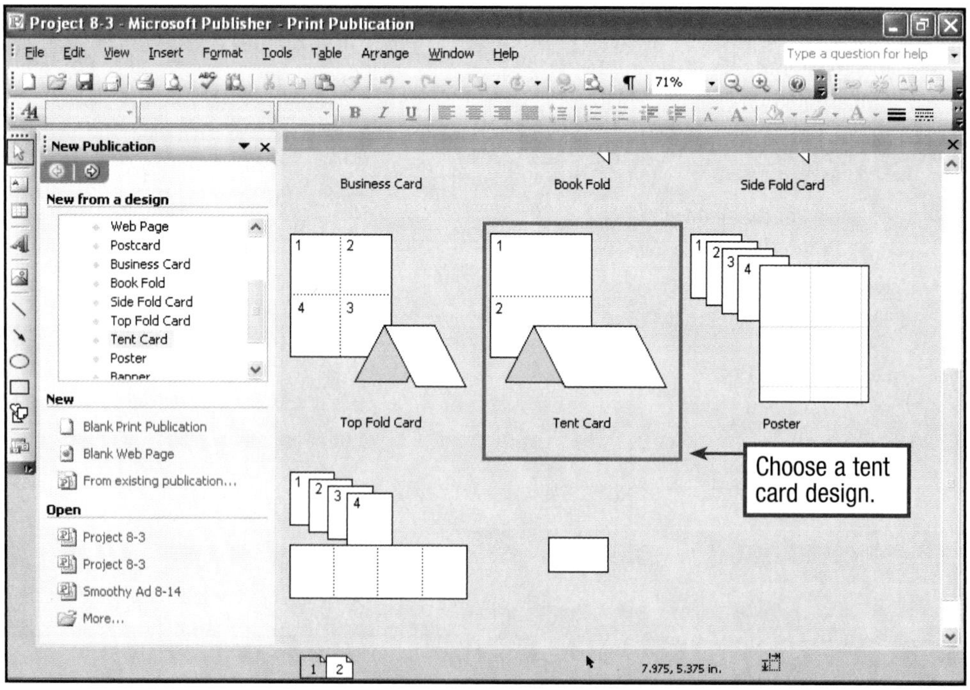

Apply Style Sheets

17 Select the word *Lasik.* Click the **Style** drop-down menu Normal, and click on the new **Section Head** style.

18 Repeat Step 17 to format the word *Glasses* in the new style.

19 Drag the *Manager Special* text box to the new design, as shown in Figure 4.21.

Figure 4.21 Use styles to ensure consistency and save time.

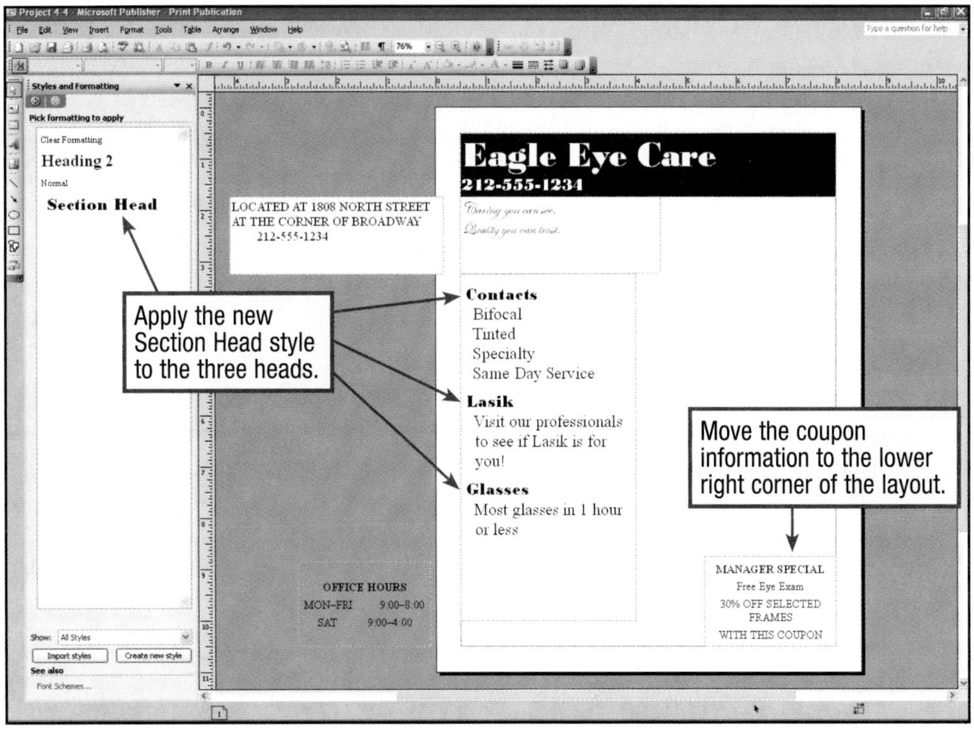

20 Remove **All Caps**, **right align** the text, and use **Format Painter** to apply the script font to the last line.

21 Add a **3 pt dashed line** around the border of the text box (Figure 4.22).

22 Create a small text box at the left of the text box. Click **Insert>Symbol**, and choose the **Wingding** font to insert a dingbat of a scissors.

23 Drag the green rotate handle to rotate the scissors. Resize the scissors to **28 pt** (Figure 4.22).

Figure 4.22 Coupons are often designed within a flyer to attract customers.

Instant Message

Apply Styles There are three ways to apply style sheet formats:

- Select the formatted text, double-click the **Format Painter**, and then select any text to which you want to apply the new style.
- Select the text to which you want to apply the style, then choose the style from the **Style** window on the Formatting toolbar.
- Open the **Style and Formatting** task pane. Select the text to which you want to apply the style, then click the style in the task pane.

Apply Text Outlines

15. Select the text, and then choose **Type>Create Outlines**.

16. Use **Object>Group** to combine the scroll shapes and your family name.

17. Click **Object>Envelope Distort>Make with Warp**. Choose **Arc** style. Move your text and scroll below your coat of arms. Click **Object>Arrange>Send to back**.

18. Select the shield and the scroll group, and open the **Align** palette. Select **Horizontal Align Center**.

Apply Expand Appearance

19. Click **Object>Expand** to make the effects permanent as one piece of artwork.

Customize Print Output

20. Choose **File>Export**, and save your work as a **WMF** to use later.

21. Choose **File>Print**, and choose **Setup**. For placement, choose **Center**.

22. In the **Print** dialog box, under **Marks and Bleed**, check **Trim Marks**. Follow your teacher's instructions before printing.

▼ Figure 8.12 Your family coat of arms should look similar to this illustration.

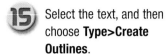

REVIEW AND REVISE

Check your work Use Figure 8.12 as a guide and check that:

☑ The illustration resembles an authentic coat of arms.

☑ The castle group layer is visible.

☑ Dragon clip art has been inserted with a metallic gradient color.

☑ The scroll is an arc shape with your family name.

☑ All objects have been grouped.

☑ The illustration is saved in WMF format.

24 Drag the text box with the office hours to the bottom left corner. **Left align** the text, and use **tabs** to align the hours (Figure 4.23).

25 Cut/paste the address above the office hours, and apply the same font as in *Manager Special*.

26 Insert the picture **Data File 4-4b**. Resize and crop the photo to fit the space shown in Figure 4.23.

27 Click **Arrange>Order>Send to Back**. If necessary, add soft returns (SHIFT ENTER) to the text on the left so it fits.

28 Add a **6 pt border line** to the image.

29 Your flyer should look similar to Figure 4.23. Follow your teacher's instructions for saving and printing your work.

▼ **Figure 4.23** Images of smiling faces produce positive reactions from viewers.

REVIEW AND REVISE

Check your work Use Figure 4.23 as a guide and check that:

- ☑ Information is aligned in a consistent manner.
- ☑ Contrast is used effectively to call out important information.
- ☑ Font styles are applied consistently for effective repetition.
- ☑ The photo is sized and cropped so that the design is not too crowded.
- ☑ A scissors icon is placed on the coupon's cutting line.
- ☑ Hyphenation has been turned off, and no words are split between lines.
- ☑ There are no spelling or grammar mistakes.

Add Word Clip Art

8. Insert **Data File 8.2**, or open Microsoft Word, using the **Clip Art Gallery** to search for a dragon, similar to Figure 8.10.

9. Select the Dragon Clip Art, and choose **Format>Picture**. Click on the **Layout** tab, and be sure that the clip art is set to **In Front of Text**.

10. Select the clip art, and choose **Edit>Copy**.

11. Open your coat of arms, and choose **Edit>Paste**. Then move your dragon emblem into position on the shield (Figure 8.10).

12. Use **Direct Selection** to select the dragon. Change its color to a metallic shade. A gradient with bright highlights will help create this effect.

13. Use **Rectangle** to draw shapes similar to those used in Figure 8.11 to create a scroll. Uncheck **Snap to Guides**.

14. Use **Type** to place your family name on top of the rectangle scroll, and **resize** and **reposition** the text as needed.

▼ Figure 8.10 Clip art from Word may be used, provided it is NOT set to In Line with Text before it is pasted into the illustration.

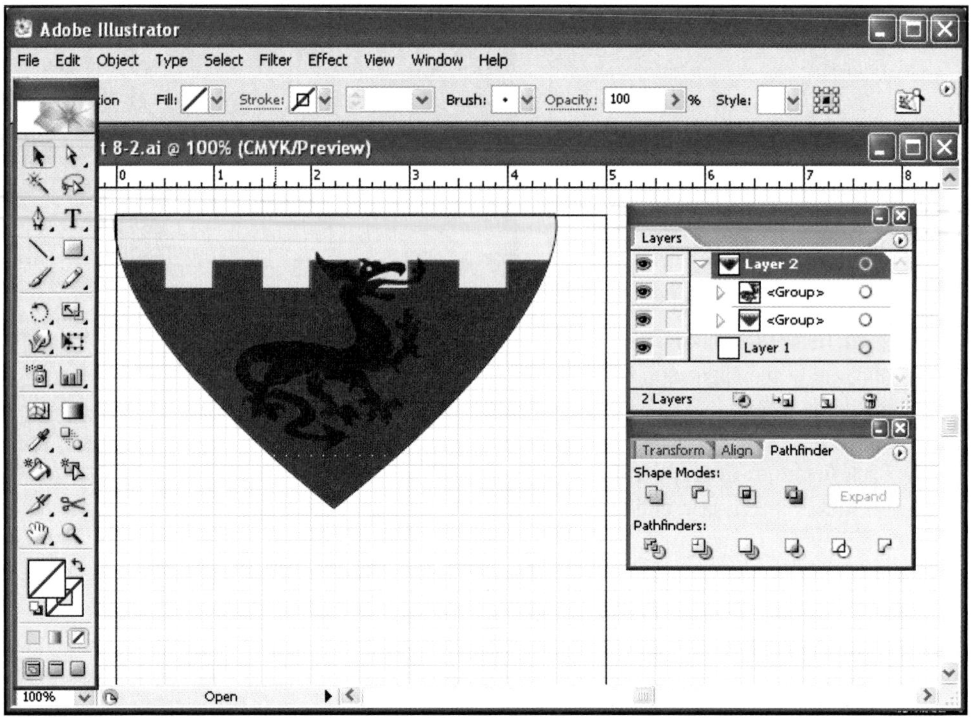

▼ Figure 8.11 Use a series of rectangles to create the scroll.

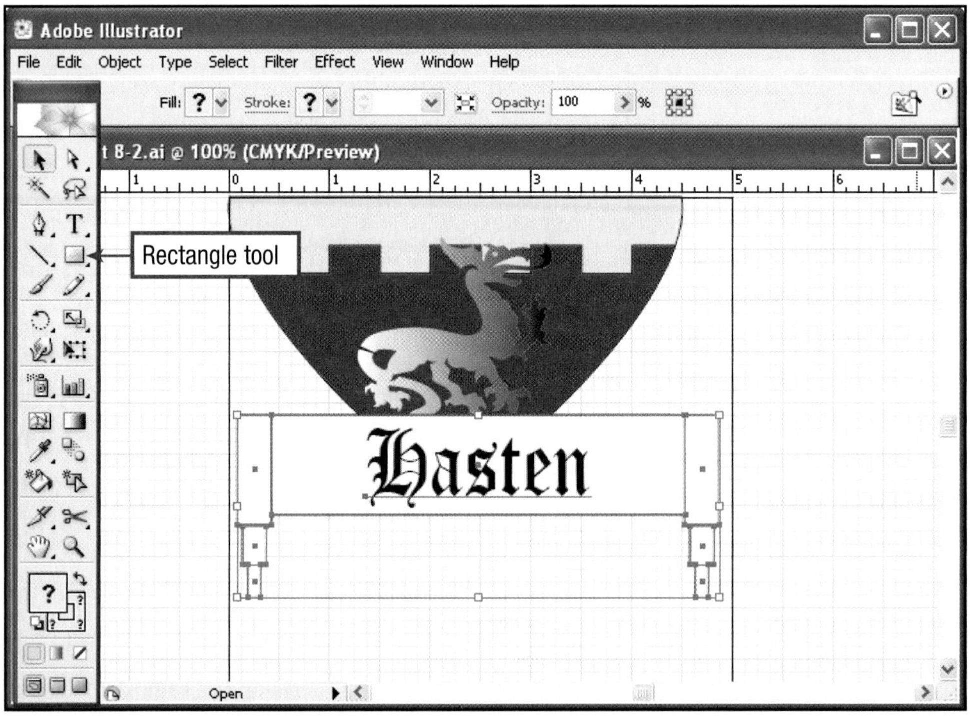

Project 4-5

Revise a Tri-fold Brochure

Spotlight on Skills

- Import a style sheet
- Apply CMYK custom colors
- Align objects

Key Terms

- export
- import

Academic Focus

Science
Evaluate computer hardware

Style sheets keep formatting organized within a document, but they can also be exported and imported between files. When you **export**, you send out a product or file to be used in another location. When you **import**, you bring in a file or product. In this manner, style sheets can keep a design consistent from page to page or from design project to design project.

Many companies have specific font schemes and colors to represent their brand. So style sheets can be used to create all official documents for a company. Also, if many designers are working on different parts of one project, style sheets can be exported from one designer to another to make sure the design is consistent overall.

Evaluate a Tri-fold Brochure's Design

The brochure shown on page 173 is very difficult to read. Word groups and text boxes collide with each other and make it almost impossible to read. Text boxes are powerful design elements and should be used sparingly. When overused, eyes are being constantly trapped by one box or another, making it difficult to read the entire message.

Use the table below to evaluate the effectiveness of the brochure on the next page.

Design Blunders

PARC Principle	Design Problems
Proximity	• Groups do not always appear to have related content. • Over-reliance on boxes reduces readability. • Clip art and graphs do not appear to be related to any information on the page. • The graphics look like an afterthought.
Alignment	• Many alignments are used, rather than using only one or two. • Some boxes are not aligned with anything. • Uses both center and left alignment. • White space is unequal in many places. • Corners are used for clip art with no obvious design reasons.
Repetition	• Repetition of boxes is overdone. • Too many fonts are used. • The inside and outside of the brochure do not look like they belong in the same document.
Contrast	• There is no clear entry point for the reader. • Different fonts are confusing, rather than providing contrast. • All caps and a complex script font are used for contact information and instructions, making it difficult to read important content.

Student Data File

Step-by-Step

1. Open the coat of arms you started in Project 8-1, and save it according to your teacher's instructions.

2. Open the **Layers** palette. Expand all the groups and layers. Unlock the group that you had locked in Project 8-1.

3. Your **Layers** palette should look like Figure 8.8. If you have extra layers, click the trash can icon on the bottom to delete them.

4. Use **Selection**, and then draw a marquee around all the objects on the page.

Apply the Pathfinder Palette

5. In the **Pathfinder** palette, click the **Crop** button to cut away the top shape from the bottom layer.

6. Select each part of the shield and add a **black stroke** color.

7. Select each of the shield pieces, then click **Object>Group**.

▼ Figure 8.8 Click the triangle to expand each layer in the illustration.

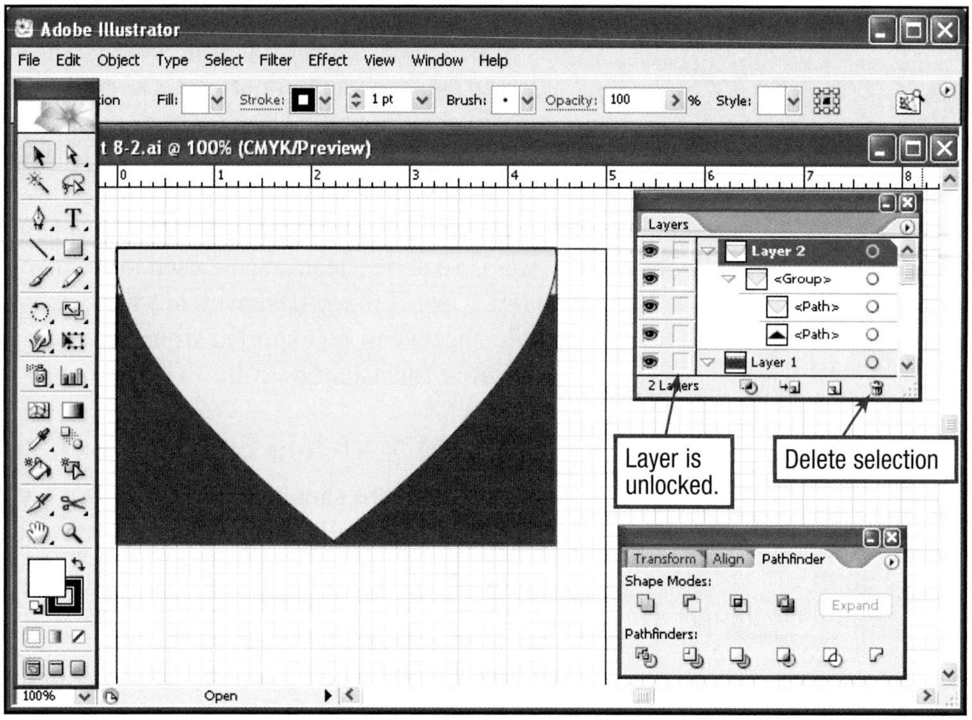

▼ Figure 8.9 The Crop tool will use the top shape as a "cookie cutter" to remove the bottom shape.

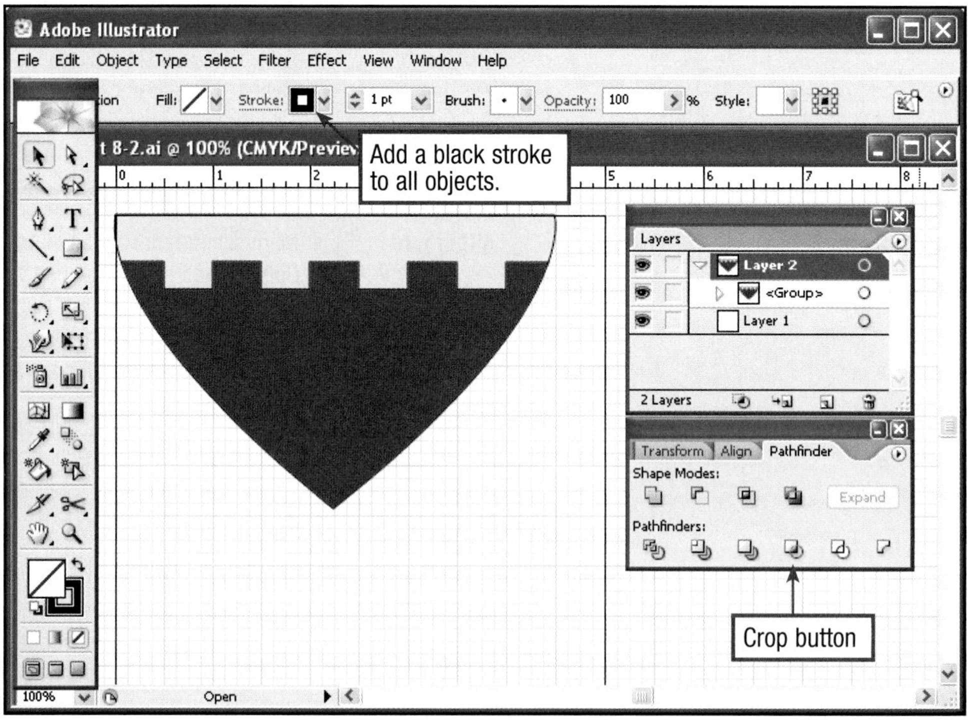

The designer needs to help readers find an entry point to a document by creating visual clues that present the information in a certain order. In this design, the reader skips around on the page and might miss important information.

► Brochure exterior

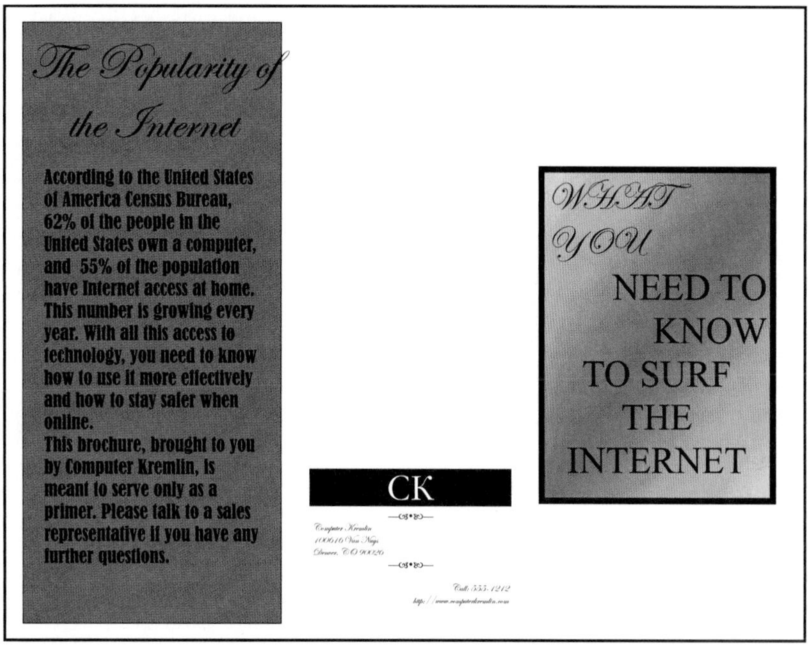
The Popularity of the Internet
According to the United States of America Census Bureau, 62% of the people in the United States own a computer, and 55% of the population have Internet access at home. This number is growing every year. With all this access to technology, you need to know how to use it more effectively and how to stay safer when online.
This brochure, brought to you by Computer Kremlin, is meant to serve only as a primer. Please talk to a sales representative if you have any further questions.
CK
WHAT YOU NEED TO KNOW TO SURF THE INTERNET

Sidebar

Align Objects The Arrange menu contains many of the tools you need to lay out a page effectively. The Align and Distribute tool gives you two ways to align objects. Objects can be aligned in relation to:

- **Margin Guides** If you aligned to margins in this brochure, the objects would be centered on the page, not within a panel.
- **Another object** You must first select ALL the objects that will share an alignment.

Identify What tool helps align objects in your designs?

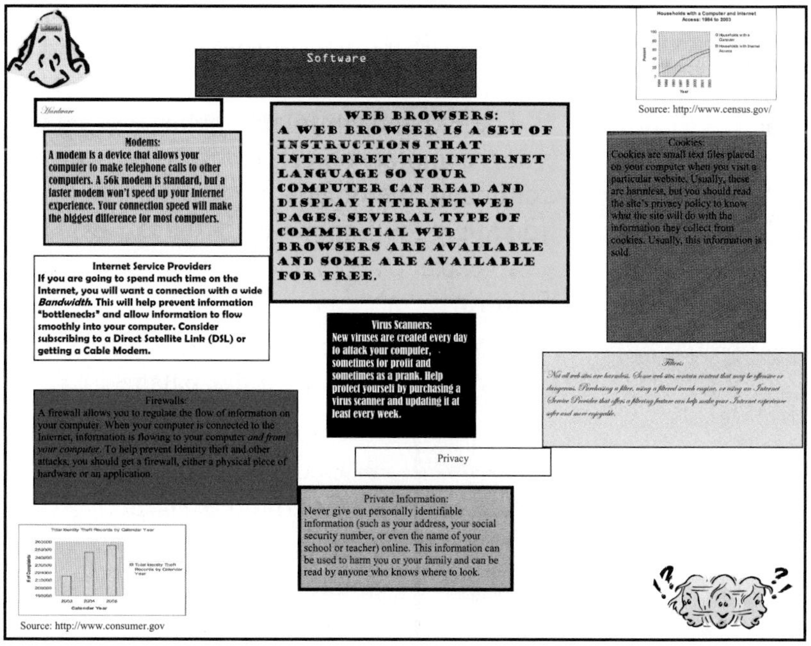
Software
Hardware
Modems:
A modem is a device that allows your computer to make telephone calls to other computers. A 56k modem is standard, but a faster modem won't speed up your Internet experience. Your connection speed will make the biggest difference for most computers.
Internet Service Providers
If you are going to spend much time on the Internet, you will want a connection with a wide Bandwidth. This will help prevent information "bottlenecks" and allow information to flow smoothly into your computer. Consider subscribing to a Direct Satellite Link (DSL) or getting a Cable Modem.
WEB BROWSERS: A WEB BROWSER IS A SET OF INSTRUCTIONS THAT INTERPRET THE INTERNET LANGUAGE SO YOUR COMPUTER CAN READ AND DISPLAY INTERNET WEB PAGES. SEVERAL TYPE OF COMMERCIAL WEB BROWSERS ARE AVAILABLE AND SOME ARE AVAILABLE FOR FREE.
Source: http://www.census.gov/
Cookies:
Cookies are small text files placed on your computer when you visit a particular website. Usually, these are harmless, but you should read the site's privacy policy to know what the site will do with the information they collect from cookies. Usually, this information is sold.
Virus Scanners:
New viruses are created every day to attack your computer, sometimes for profit and sometimes as a prank. Help protect yourself by purchasing a virus scanner and updating it at least every week.
Firewalls:
A firewall allows you to regulate the flow of information on your computer. When your computer is connected to the Internet, information is flowing to your computer and from your computer. To help prevent identity theft and other attacks, you should get a firewall, either a physical piece of hardware or an application.
Privacy
Private Information:
Never give out personally identifiable information (such as your address, your social security number, or even the name of your school or teacher) online. This information can be used to harm you or your family and can be read by anyone who knows where to look.
Source: http://www.consumer.gov

► Brochure interior

► **In this project,** you will revise the exterior of a brochure. You will re-design the interior of the brochure in Project 4-6.

Project 8-2 Design Vector Images

Spotlight on Skills

- Apply the Pathfinder palette
- Add Word clip art
- Apply text outlines
- Apply Expand Appearance
- Customize print output

Key Term

- mask

Academic Focus

Social Studies
Create a coat of arms

In Project 8-1, you used the Pathfinder palette to subtract rectangle shapes in order to create a castle. In that example, the tool worked like a cookie cutter, removing the excess parts and leaving the final shape. The Pathfinder palette also lets you add simple shapes to create more complex ones.

▲ The multiple objects in this illustration can be expanded as one piece of artwork that can then be used in multiple projects.

Apply the Expand Command

A **mask** is a feature that hides specific areas so that you can work on the part of the image that is not hidden. Invisible masks can cause problems as you work on your illustration. To avoid this, you should use the Expand command.

The Expand command makes the changes permanent, so that you have a new complete object, not individual objects. Until you apply the Expand command, the objects in the shape can still be moved and altered. After you apply the Expand command, the objects cannot be changed.

To expand a combined shape, you can select the object and do one of the following:

- Press ALT and click the command you want on the **Pathfinder** palette.
- Click the **Expand** button on the **Pathfinder** palette.
- Open the **Pathfinder** palette menu, and choose **Expand Compound Shape**.

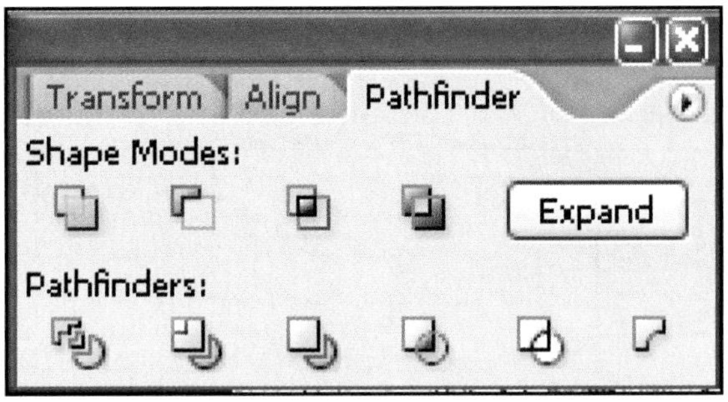

▲ Use Expand to save a file permanently as one piece of artwork.

If you change your mind and want to divide the compound shape back into the individual objects, you can use the **Release Compound Shape** command. You can also click **Edit>Undo Subtract** or press CTRL + Z.

► **In this project,** you will continue working on the coat of arms you started in Project 8-1, adding an image and the family name.

Student Data File

Step-by-Step

1. In Publisher, open **Data File 4-5a**. Save it according to your teacher's instructions.

2. Change the **margin guides** to **0.25 inch**.

3. Set the **grid guides** to **3 columns**, with a **0.2 inch gutter**.

Import a Style Sheet

4. In the task pane, open the **Styles and Formatting** pane. Click the **Import Styles** button.

5. Browse to **Data File 4-5b**. Click **OK** to bring all the styles in that file into your current document (Figure 4.24).

6. On **Page 1** of the brochure, select the text in the gold box.

7. In the **Styles and Formatting** task pane, click the **Title** style. If some text does not change, select it and apply the style again.

8. Change the fill color of the text box to **No Fill**. Change the line color to **No Line** (Figure 4.25).

Figure 4.24 Use the Styles and Formatting task pane to import styles from one document to another.

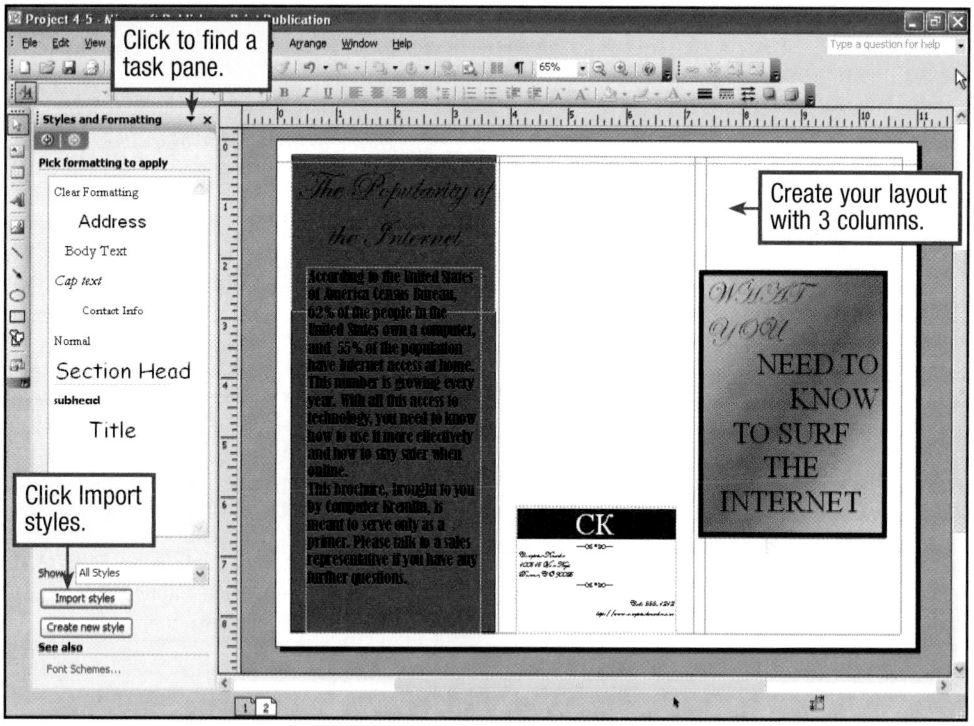

Figure 4.25 You may have to select individual sections of text to apply the style.

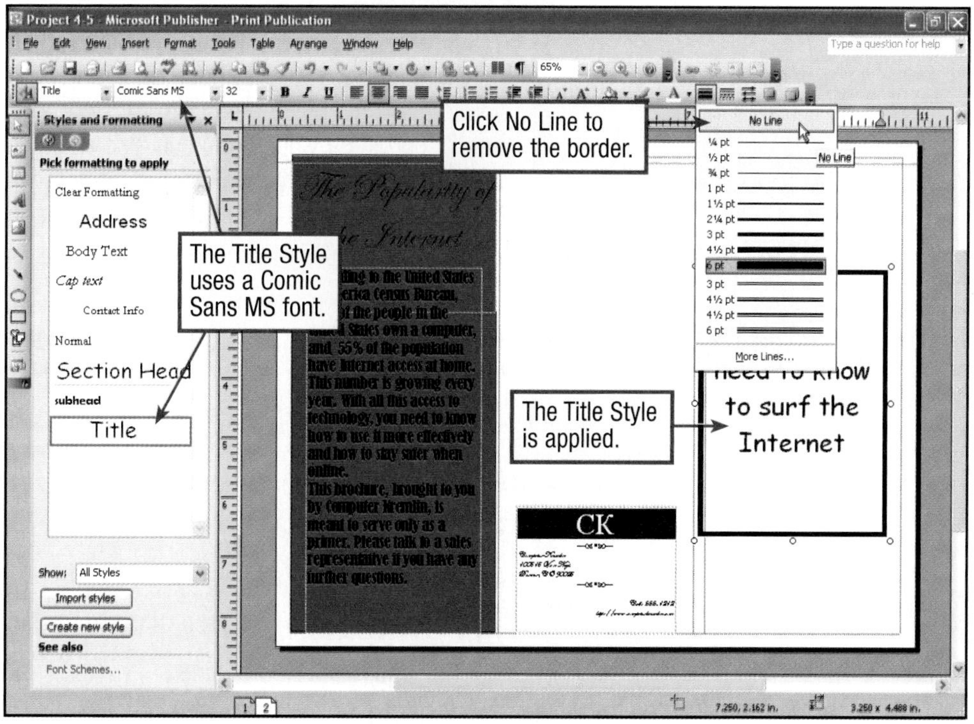

23 Use **Direct Selection** [icon] to drag a selection around the top end points of the shield.

24 Press CTRL + J to join the two halves together so they become part of the same shape, like the Pathfinder palette did previously (Figure 8.7).

25 If there is a gap, repeat steps 23–24 to join the bottom two points of the shield shape.

26 Follow your teacher's instructions for saving your work. You will continue working on your coat of arms in Project 8-2.

▼ **Figure 8.7** Unlike grouping, which joins objects on separate layers, the Join command joins objects on the same layer to create a new shape.

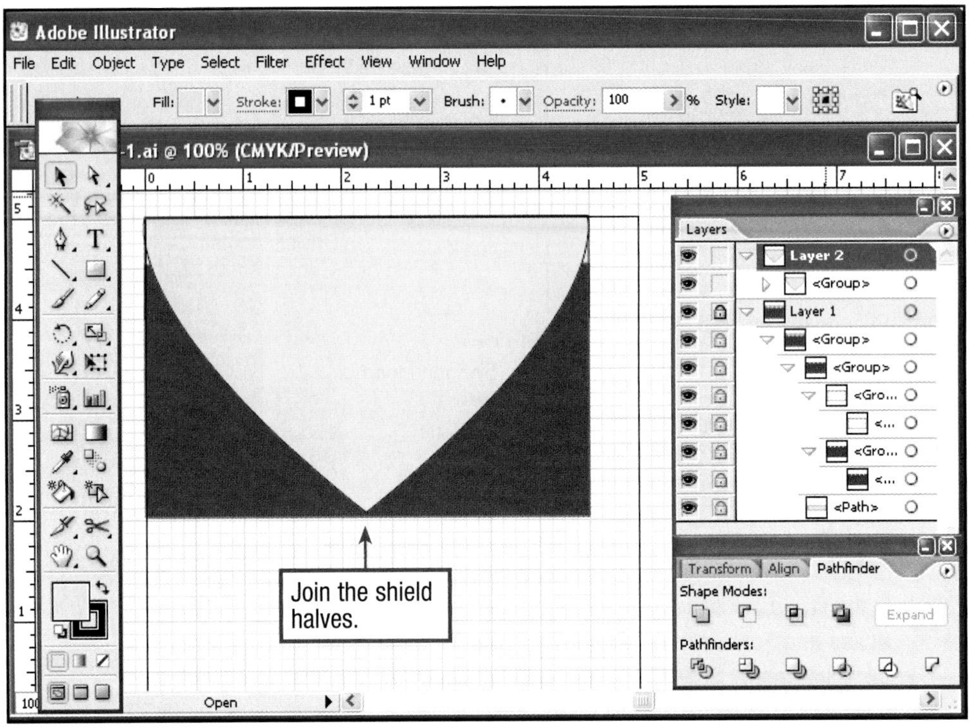

Instant Message

Transform Palette In Step 21, you chose the **Object>Transform>Reflect** option to create a mirror image of an object. The **Transform** palette allows you to make simple and precise transformations to objects by using the X and Y coordinate values. You can also change the size of objects by using the W(idth) and H(eight) values. Experiment with this palette and other transformation tools such as rotate, scale, shear, and blend.

REVIEW AND REVISE

Check your work Use Figure 8.7 as a guide and check that:

- ☑ The coat of arms is aligned to gridlines.
- ☑ The color sanguine has been applied.
- ☑ The castle group rectangles are yellow.
- ☑ The castle group has been grouped and sent to back.
- ☑ The shield halves are joined.

9. In the middle panel, select the contact information (but not the top black text box). Apply the **Contact Info** style.

10. Select the title text in the purple text box. Apply the **Section Head** style.

11. Select the rest of the text in the purple box and apply the **Body Text** style (Figure 4.26).

Apply CMYK Custom Colors

12. Select the purple text box and click **Fill** [icon]. Click **More Fill Colors**. Choose the **Custom** tab and change the **Color Model** to **CMYK**.

13. Change the CMYK settings to **1**, **40**, **0**, **0** with a **77% Transparency** (Figure 4.26).

14. On **Page 2**, **cut** the graph in the top right corner. **Paste** the graph on **Page 1** between the two paragraphs in the left panel.

15. **Wrap** the text **Top and Bottom**. Then resize and reposition the text and graphics so that the left panel looks like Figure 4.27.

16. Apply the **Cap text** style to the caption under the graph.

▼ **Figure 4.26** CMYK stands for Cyan, Magenta, Yellow, and Black, and the fill color is a blend of those four colors.

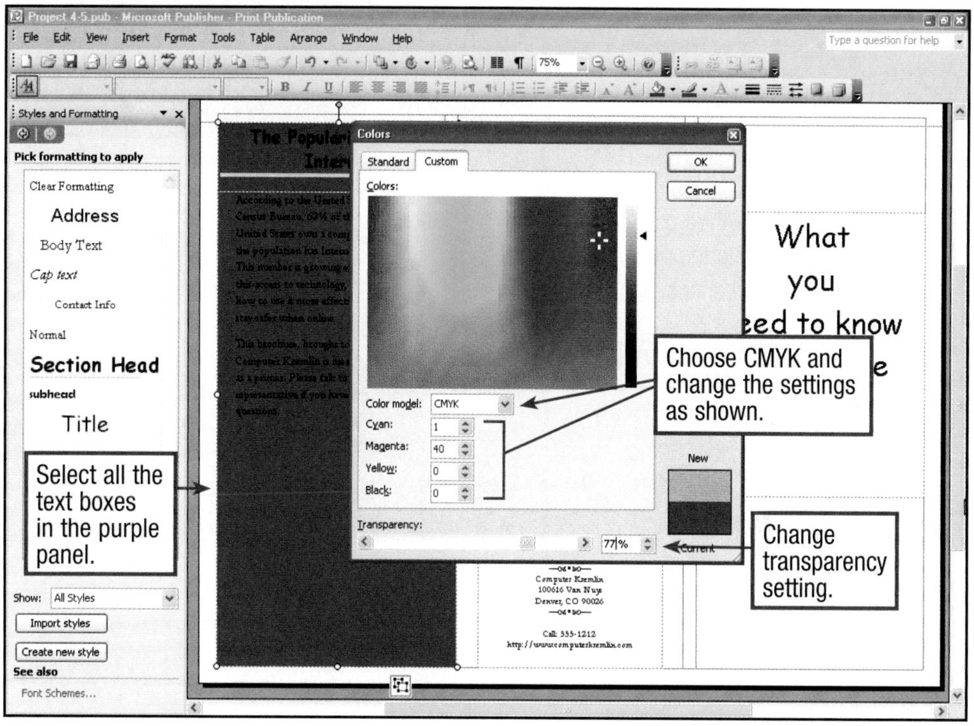

▼ **Figure 4.27** An eye-catching graph provides a visual break.

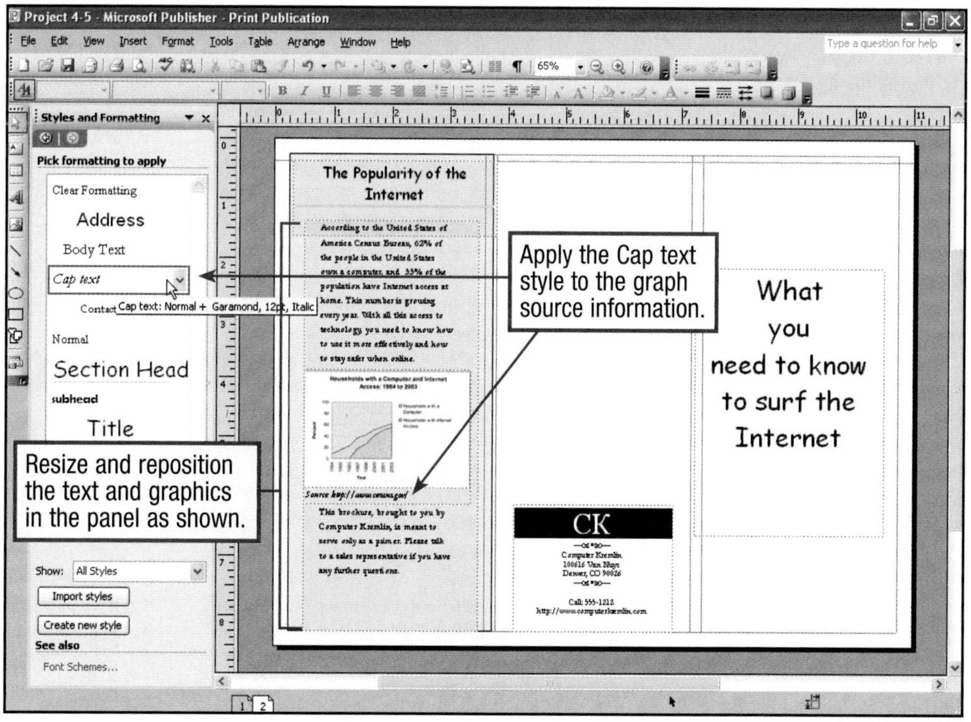

17 On the **Layers** palette, click the **Create New Layer** button.

Draw with the Pen Tool

18 In the toolbox, click **Pen**. Then click the three points shown in Figure 8.5.

19 As you click the third point, drag down and to the right to get the shield shape, as shown in Figure 8.5.

20 Use the **Selection** tool to select the shield half. Click **Edit>Copy**, then **Edit>Paste in Front** to create a second half.

21 Select one of the shield halves, then click **Object>Transform>Reflect**. Set at **Vertica**l and **90°**. Click **OK** (Figure 8.6).

22 Move the second shield half so it lines up with the first (Figure 8.6).

▼ **Figure 8.5** Click and drag with the Pen tool to create smooth, curved lines.

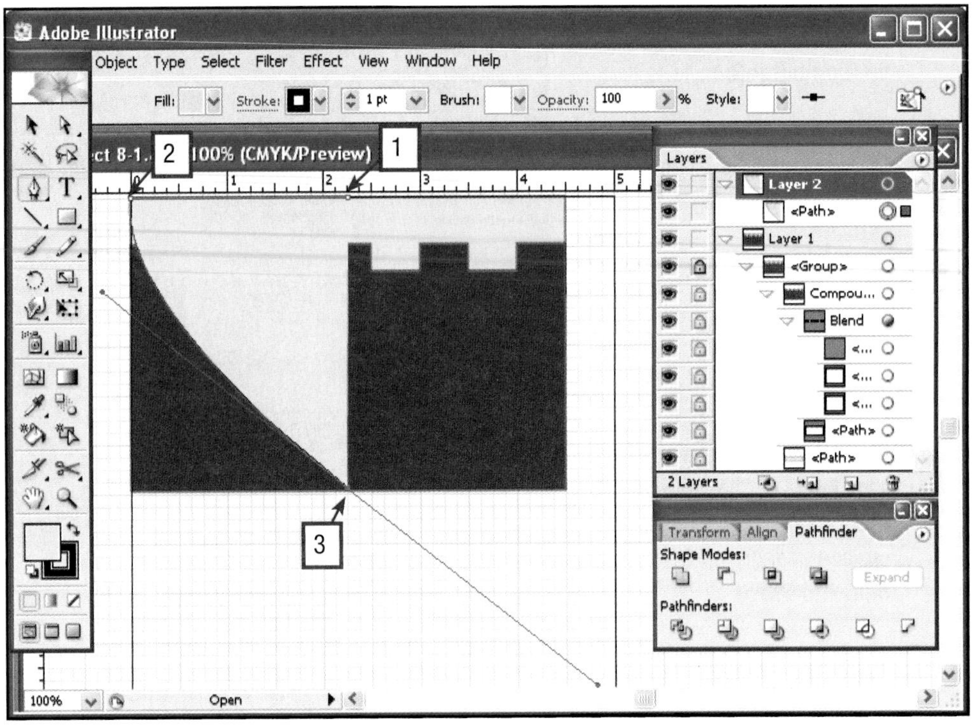

▼ **Figure 8.6** The two halves of the shield are mirror images, which is why you use the Reflect command.

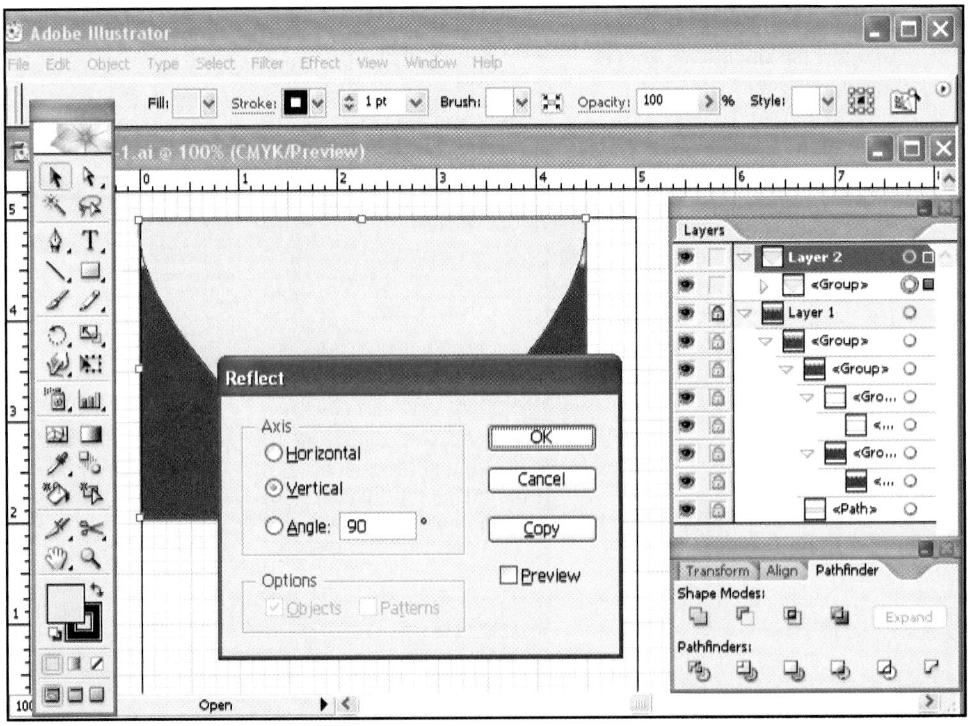

17 Insert **Data File 4-5c**, the picture of a "thought bubble."

18 Select the image, and click **Arrange>Send to Back**. Then move it behind the text in the right panel (Figure 4.28).

Align Objects

19 Select both the image and the text box in the right panel. Click **Arrange>Align or Distribute**, and choose **Align Center** and **Align Middle**.

20 **Group** the two objects.

21 On **Page 2**, **cut** the face clip art in the upper left corner. **Paste** it in the lower part of the right panel on **Page 1** (Figure 4.29).

22 Resize and reposition the objects until the page looks similar to Figure 4.29.

23 Click both the thought-bubble group and the face graphic. Choose **Arrange>Align or Distribute**, and choose **Align Center**.

24 Follow your teacher's instructions for saving and printing your work. You will continue revising this brochure in Project 4-6.

▼ **Figure 4.28** You can align objects relative to margin guides and to each other.

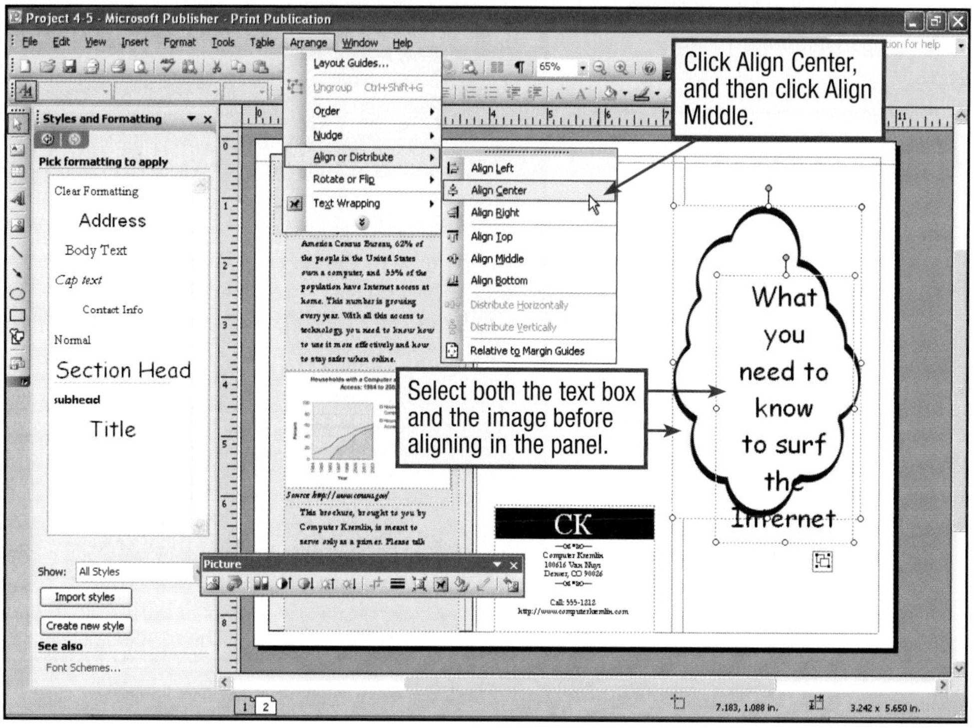

▼ **Figure 4.29** The revised exterior of the brochure.

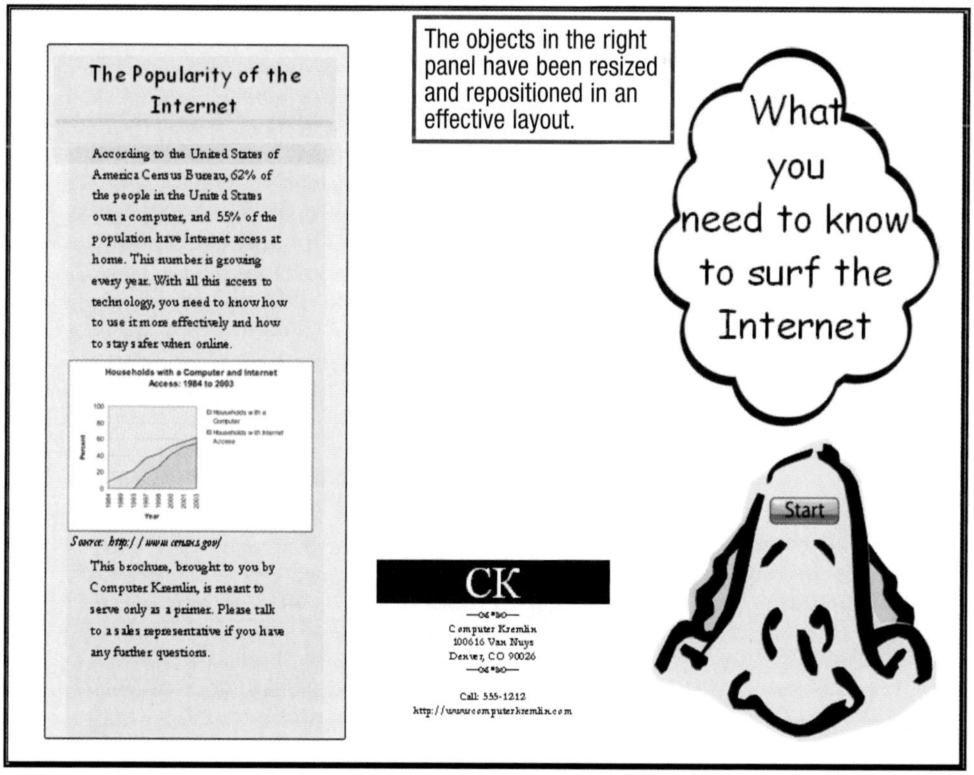

10 Select the castle shape, and double-click the **Fill** tool to open the **Color Picker**.

Create Custom Colors

11 Next to the # **symbol**, key the hexadecimal number AB343A to create the red color **sanguine.** Click **OK.** (Figure 8.3).

12 Create a new rectangle that is **4.5 inches wide** by **1 inch high**. Move the new rectangle so that it extends above the castle 0.5 inch (Figure 8.4).

13 Open the **Color Picker** and key the **RGB settings** 255, 255, 51. Click **OK**. Your rectangle should be yellow.

14 Select the new rectangle, and click **Object>Arrange>Send to Back**. Then select both objects and group them.

Work with the Layers palette

15 Open the **Layers** palette. Click on the **triangle** icons to expand the Layer list to see all the parts of the group (Figure 8.4).

16 On the **Layers** palette, click the empty box to the left of the **Group** item. A lock icon is displayed (Figure 8.4).

▼ **Figure 8.3** The color *sanguine* was used in the coats of arms of medieval knights.

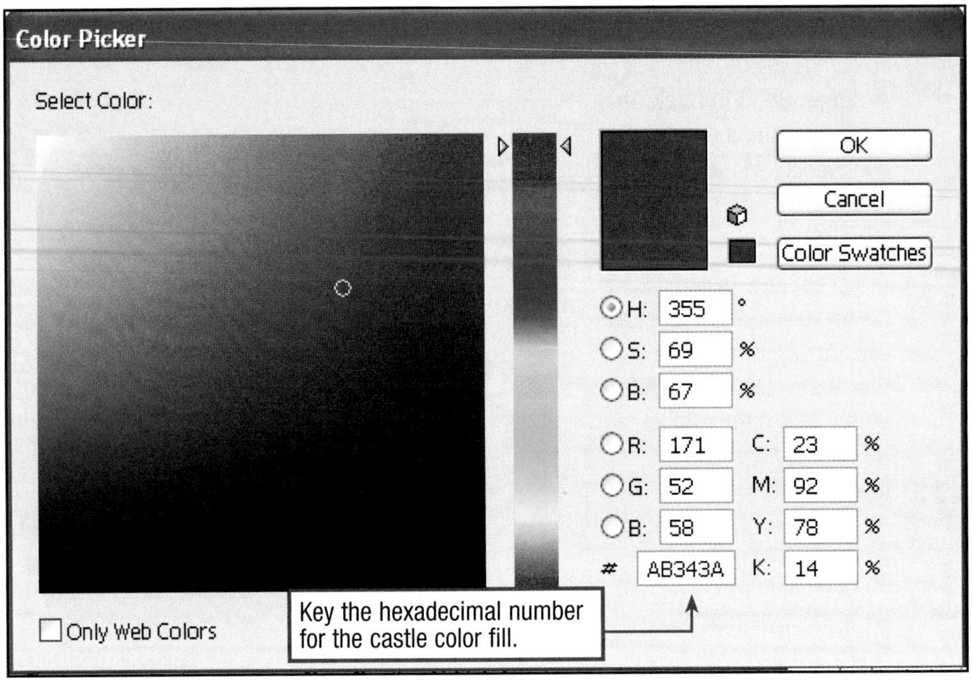

▼ **Figure 8.4** The Lock tool will keep the castle group from accidentally being selected during the next step.

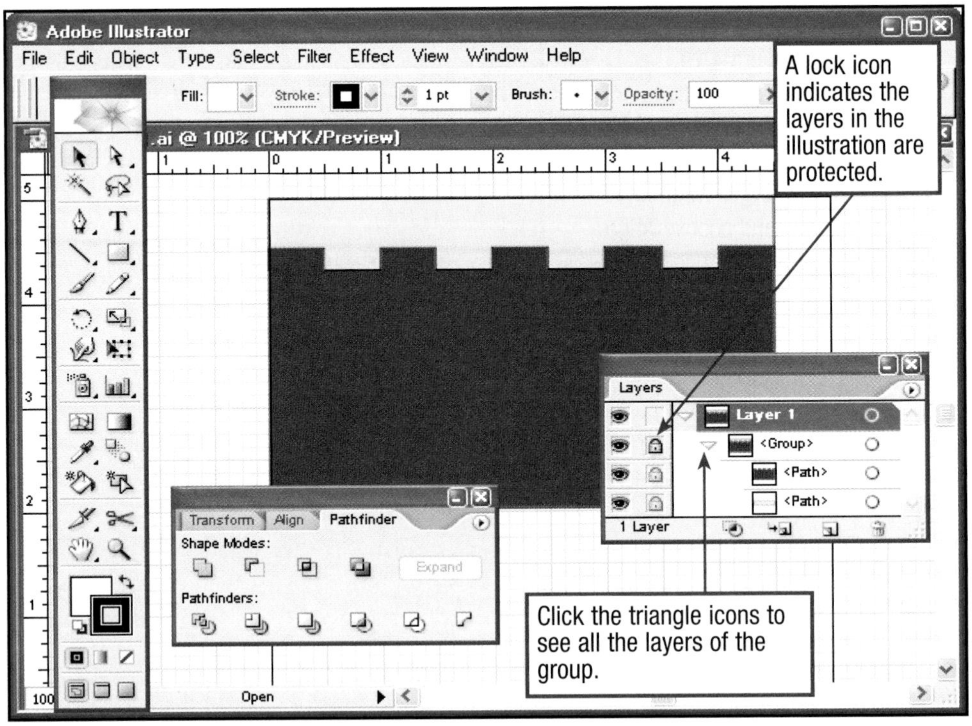

Project 4-6

Apply PARC to the Brochure Interior

Spotlight on Skills

- Link text boxes
- Re-align orphan text

Key Terms

- link
- orphan
- widow

Academic Focus

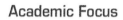

Science
Identify safe Internet usage

Student Data File

Step-by-Step

1. Open the file you created in Project 4-5, and save it according to your teacher's instructions.

2. On **Page 2** of the brochure, drag the graph and the clip art into the scratch area (Figure 4.30).

3. Delete all of the text boxes and remaining text on the page so you can start with a clean slate. (**Hint**: Hold **Shift** to select multiple boxes.)

The interior of the brochure is very confusing. There is no entry point for the reader, or clear direction to follow the message. The white space is poorly managed, and the colors are random. The poor design reflects poorly on the company. Readers might think the company's products, methods, and practices are as disorganized as its brochure.

The text boxes are confusing and make it difficult to read. One or two text boxes on a page can be an effective way to group information, but with so many boxes, the reader is not given a focal point. Also, the graphics in the corner do not seem to relate to anything on the page.

To make it easier to read the text, you will **link**, or connect, text boxes to flow new content across all three panels. When a linked text box is resized, text moves to and from the adjoining text boxes. You may have to resize the text boxes in each panel to avoid orphans and widows. An **orphan** is a line from the beginning of a paragraph that is left at the bottom of a page or column. A **widow** is a line from the end of a paragraph carried forward to the top of the next page or column.

► **In this project,** you will revise the interior panels of the tri-fold brochure you began in Project 4-5.

▼ **Figure 4.30** This design has so many problems that it is easier to start the makeover from scratch.

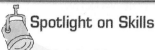

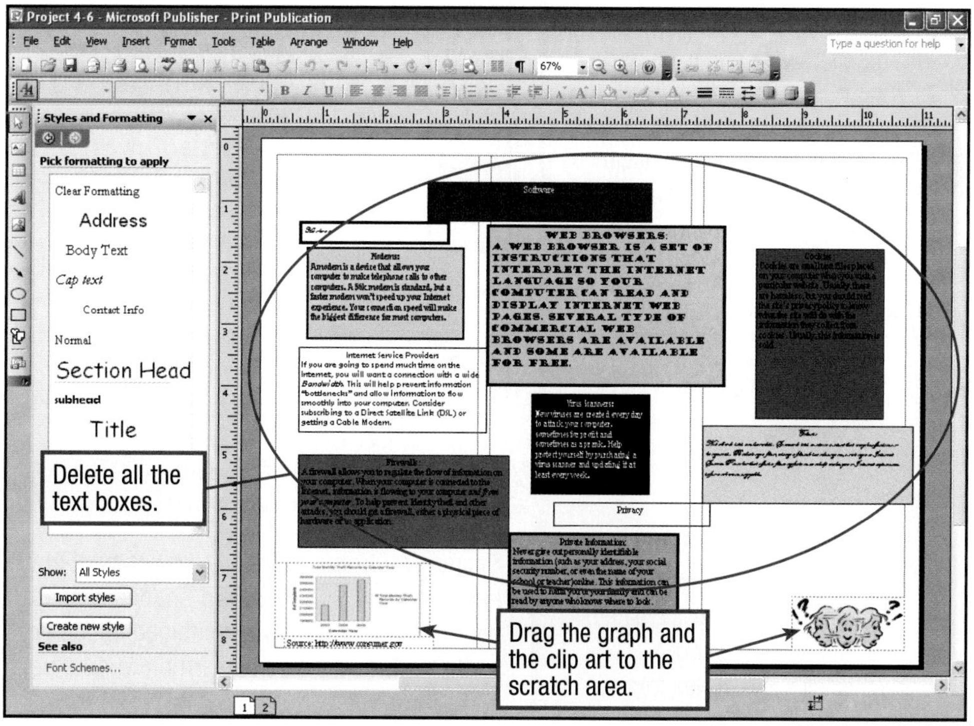

Step-by-Step

1. Open a new document in Illustrator, and set the size at **5 inches square**.
2. Open the **View** menu, and check **Show Grid** and **Snap to Grid**.
3. Click **Edit>Preferences> Guides & Grid**. For more precision, change the settings for **Gridline every** to **0.5 inch**. Click **OK**.
4. Click **Rectangle** [icon], and click in the workspace. In the **Rectangle** box, change the settings to **4.5 inches wide** and **2.5 inches high**.
5. Select the rectangle, and align it on the top and left as shown in Figure 8.1.
6. Create a new rectangle that is **0.5 inch wide** and **0.4 inch high**.
7. Position the second rectangle at the top of the first. Make three copies and distribute it as shown in Figure 8.1.

Apply Pathfinder Palette Tools

8. Use **Selection** [icon] to select all the shapes made so far, and then open the **Pathfinder** palette.
9. On the palette, press ALT and click **Subtract from shape** [icon]. A castle is created when the new layer of rectangles is removed from the back layer (Figure 8.2).

▼ **Figure 8.1** The smaller rectangles form a new layer over the large rectangle.

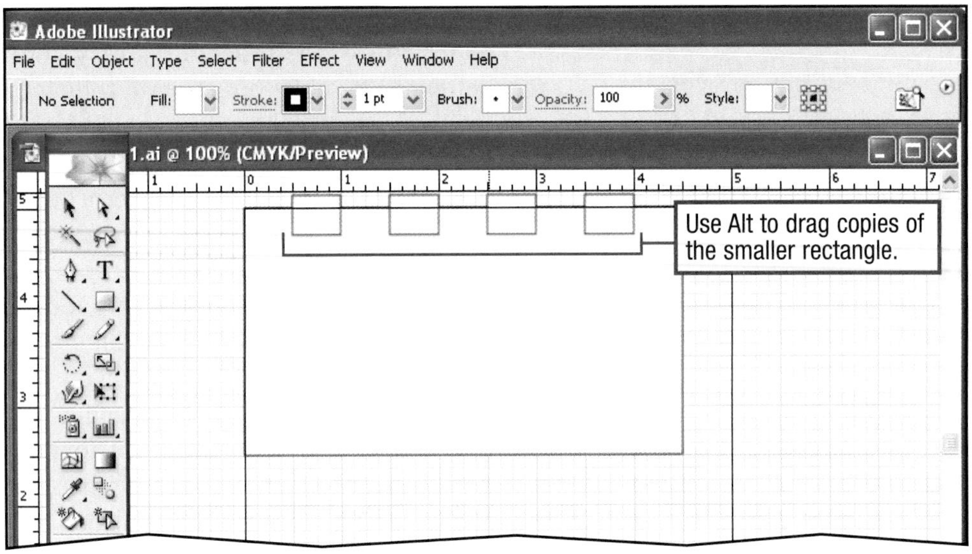

▼ **Figure 8.2** The Pathfinder palette combines or removes shapes to form complex ones.

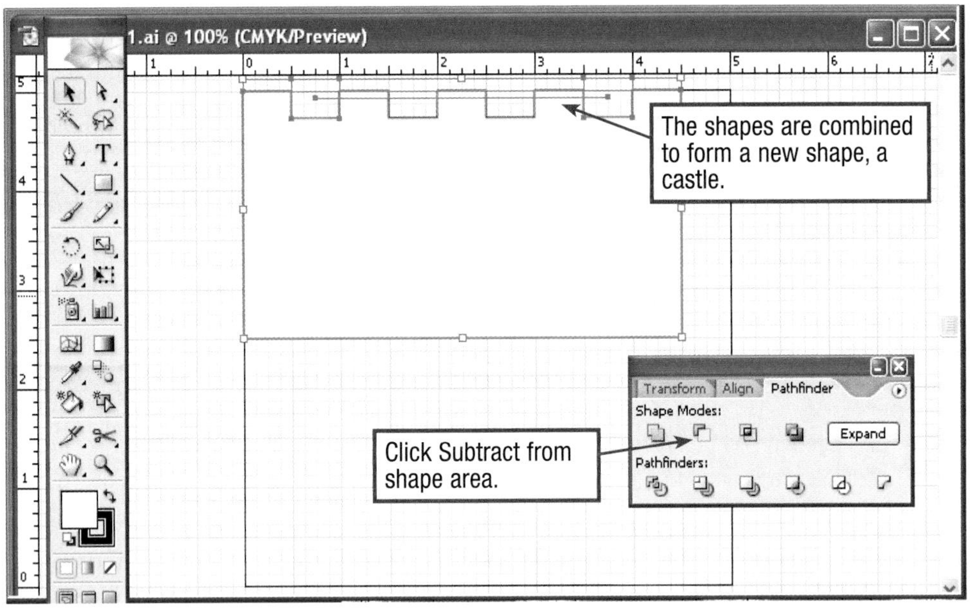

Instant Message

Expand a Shape In Step 9, you combined two shapes. By pressing the ALT key when you Subtract from Shapes, you **Expand**, which makes the change permanent. Expanding a combined shape creates a new single object of multiple objects. You will learn more about expanding in Project 8-2.

4. Create a text box in each of the three panels.

Link Text Boxes

5. Select the first text box. Click **Create Text Box Link** , and then click in the second text box.

6. With the second text box selected, click the **Create Text Box Link** button, and then click in the third text box.

7. Click the first text box. Insert the text file **Data File 4-6**. Under **Text encoding**, choose the **Windows Default**, and click **OK** (Figure 4.31).

8. Select all the text in the text boxes, and apply the **Body Text** style.

9. Select the words *Hardware*, *Software*, and *Privacy*. Change the style to **Section Header** (Figure 4.32).

10. Select the subheads highlighted in Figure 4.32. Change the style to **subhead**.

Re-align Orphan Text

11. See if you have any widows or orphans, like the *Software* header in the first column shown in Figure 4.32. Drag the bottom handle of the text box to decrease the size of the box and force the words to the next column.

▼ Figure 4.31 Flow text easily between panels by using the Link Text Box tool.

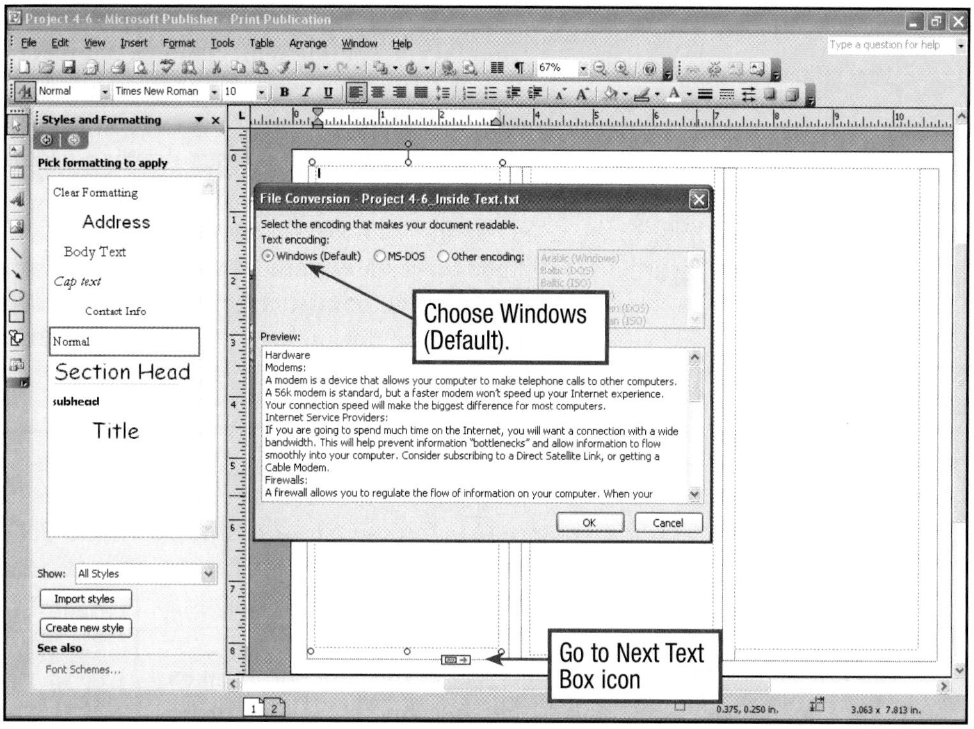

▼ Figure 4.32 When text flows automatically, be careful to avoid orphans and widows.

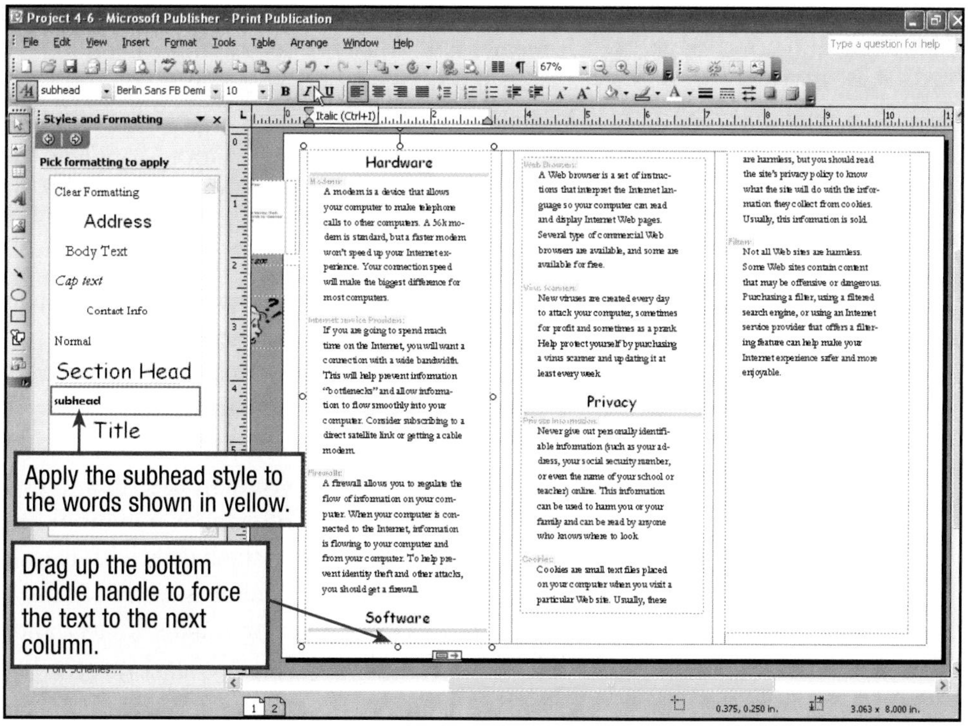

Project 8-1 Create Shapes with Tools

Spotlight on Skills

- Apply Pathfinder palette tools
- Create custom colors
- Work with the Layers palette
- Draw with the Pen tool

Key Terms

- Bézier curve
- anchor points
- control points

Academic Focus

Social Studies
Create a coat of arms

Go Online PREVIEW
www.glencoe.com

Before You Begin Go to **Chapter 8**, and choose **PowerPoint Presentations** to preview the documents you will be creating. Also, use the individual project **Rubrics** to help create and evaluate your work.

In the 1960's, French mechanical engineer Pierre Bézier (pronounced Bay zee yeah) devised a way of describing a curve to a computer by using very few points along a line. His equation, known as a **Bézier curve**, has been included in many vector-based drawing programs because of the precise way they can be used to create curved images.

Drawing with Bézier curves takes practice. Unlike drawing with a pencil, Bézier curves are more like working with push pins and wire. The pins are called **anchor points**, which hold the path on the workspace, while **control points** define the angle of the path to its next anchor point. The figure below shows the types of drawings that can be created using Bézier curves.

The Pen Tool

When drawing Bézier curves in Illustrator, you will be using the **Pen** tool. To draw straight lines with the Pen tool, simply click to establish anchor points. To draw curves, click and drag. Practice drawing a few simple shapes to help you understand the concept. It takes a few tries, but it will soon make sense. As you practice, notice how the symbols next to the Pen tool change.

▲ Bézier curves are a precise method of drawing curves that use anchor points on a path and control points that describe the direction of the path.

An "x" next to the Pen tool means that you will be placing a new anchor point when you click.

A "–" next to the pen tool means that you will be removing an anchor point when you click.

An "o" next to the pen tool means that you will be completing an enclosed figure when you click.

A ">" next to the pen tool means that you will change the anchor point's character from a curve to an angle.

▶ **In this project,** you will use Illustrator's Layers palette to create a coat of arms. A coat of arms is a symbol originally displayed on shields to identify knights on the battlefield. Families had their own coats of arms, where the colors, pictures, and even the shapes of the shields had meaning. Skill in layering makes it easy and fun to manage multiple layers for designing artistically and imaginatively.

12 Drag the clip art from the scratch area and place it above the **Privacy** header.

13 Right-click the clip art, and then choose **Order>Bring Forward**.

14 Change the text **wrapping** to **Square**. Resize the art so the column looks similar to Figure 4.33. (Be careful not to create a widow in the next column.)

15 Select the clip art and the text box in the center panel. Click **Arrange>Align or Distribute>Align Center**.

16 Move the graph from the scratch area to the top of the third panel. Repeat Steps 13–15 to align the graph and text in the panel.

17 Resize the graph so the interior of the brochure looks similar to Figure 4.33.

18 Apply the **Cap text** style to the graph caption.

19 Follow your teacher's instructions for saving and printing your work.

▼ **Figure 4.33** The content is now clearly laid out.

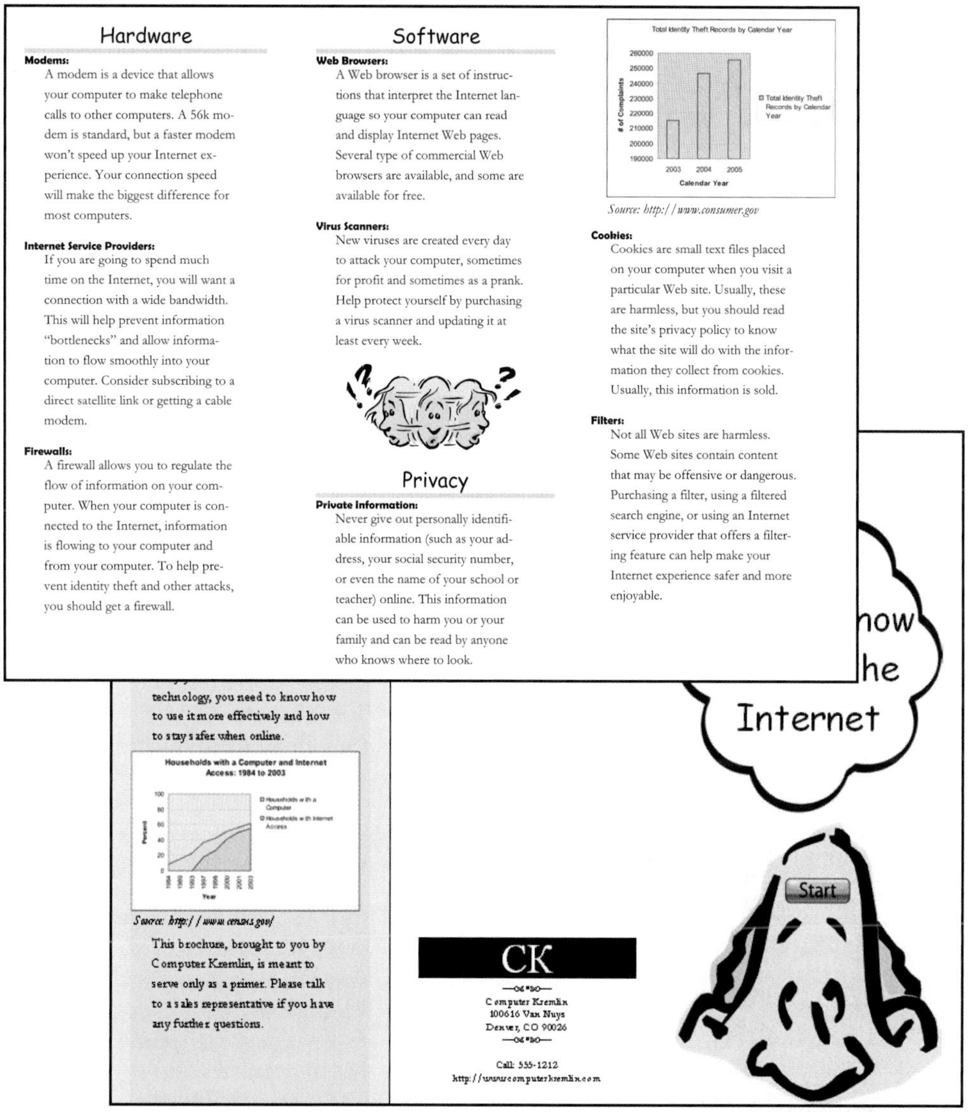

Hardware
Modems:
A modem is a device that allows your computer to make telephone calls to other computers. A 56k modem is standard, but a faster modem won't speed up your Internet experience. Your connection speed will make the biggest difference for most computers.
Internet Service Providers:
If you are going to spend much time on the Internet, you will want a connection with a wide bandwidth. This will help prevent information "bottlenecks" and allow information to flow smoothly into your computer. Consider subscribing to a direct satellite link or getting a cable modem.
Firewalls:
A firewall allows you to regulate the flow of information on your computer. When your computer is connected to the Internet, information is flowing to your computer and from your computer. To help prevent identity theft and other attacks, you should get a firewall.
Software
Web Browsers:
A Web browser is a set of instructions that interpret the Internet language so your computer can read and display Internet Web pages. Several type of commercial Web browsers are available, and some are available for free.
Virus Scanners:
New viruses are created every day to attack your computer, sometimes for profit and sometimes as a prank. Help protect yourself by purchasing a virus scanner and updating it at least every week.
Privacy
Private Information:
Never give out personally identifiable information (such as your address, your social security number, or even the name of your school or teacher) online. This information can be used to harm you or your family and can be read by anyone who knows where to look.
Total Identity Theft Records by Calendar Year
Calendar Year
Source: http://www.consumer.gov
Cookies:
Cookies are small text files placed on your computer when you visit a particular Web site. Usually, these are harmless, but you should read the site's privacy policy to know what the site will do with the information they collect from cookies. Usually, this information is sold.
Filters:
Not all Web sites are harmless. Some Web sites contain content that may be offensive or dangerous. Purchasing a filter, using a filtered search engine, or using an Internet service provider that offers a filtering feature can help make your Internet experience safer and more enjoyable.
technology, you need to know how to use it more effectively and how to stay safer when online.
Households with a Computer and Internet Access: 1984 to 2003
Source: http://www.census.gov/
This brochure, brought to you by Computer Kremlin, is meant to serve only as a primer. Please talk to a sales representative if you have any further questions.
CK
Computer Kremlin
100616 Van Nuys
Denver, CO 90026
Call: 555-1212
http://www.computerkremlin.com
Internet
Start

REVIEW AND REVISE

Check your work Use Figures 4.29 and 4.33 as a guides and check that:

- ☑ The exterior has the front panel on the right and the back panel on the left.
- ☑ Alignment and font styles are consistent.
- ☑ Contrast is used effectively to call out important information.
- ☑ Text flows between text boxes in the brochure interior, with no widows or orphans.

WORK SHOP

Toolbox

Layers Palette in Illustrator

You Will Learn To

- Identify palettes used to create complex shapes
- Apply the Layers palette

Key Term

layering

In this chapter, you will be working with a number of new tools and palettes. The Layers palette lets you view, create, delete, and manipulate layers. **Layering**, or stacking, is the process used to precisely position and align graphic objects in a design. You will apply the Pathfinder palette to combine simple shapes, like big and small rectangles, and to create more complex shapes, like the castle in the first project. You will also use the Pen tool for drawing precise shapes, lines, and curves.

How Do I Use Layers?

The Layers palette in Illustrator is more complex than the Layers palette in Photoshop. From Illustrator's Layers palette, you can:

- Rename a layer by double-clicking it in the palette.
- Expand or contract the Layers list to view sublayers by clicking the triangle icon.
- Drag layers above or below other layers to change the layer order.
- Show or hide a layer in the workspace image by clicking the Hide icon. Hidden layers will be saved with the rest of the document, but they cannot be selected and will not print.
- Lock layers so they will not be accidentally changed. Locked layers are visible, but they cannot be selected or altered.
- Add or remove layers and sublayers by clicking the buttons at the bottom.

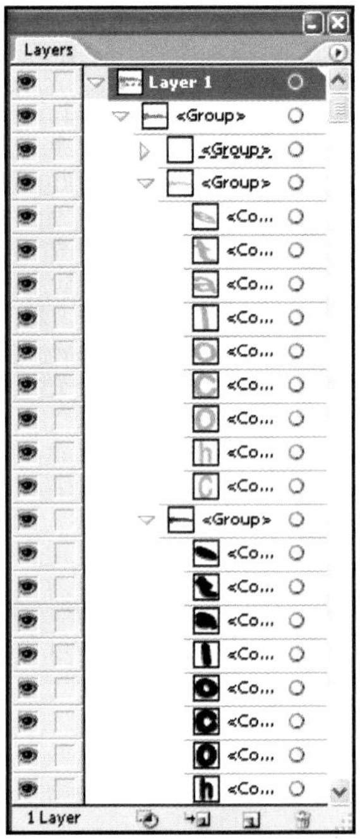

▲ The Layers palette lists groups, compound paths, and envelope distortions.

Sidebar

Keyboard Shortcuts Listed below are some tools that are used so often that they are not only included in Illustrator's toolbox, but they also have their own keyboard shortcut.

Selection	V
Direct Selection	A
Type	T
Rectangle	M
Scale	S
Gradient	G
Blend	W
Scissors	C
Zoom	Z

Identify What is the keyboard shortcut for gradient?

Reading Check

1. **Explain** Why is layering an important process in graphic design?
2. **Identify** What should you do to avoid accidentally changing a layer?

Project 4-7

Apply PARC to a Web Page

Spotlight on Skills

- Resize a Web page
- Resize a Design Gallery object

Key Terms

- dithering
- resolution

Academic Focus

Language Arts
Create a Web site about Shakespeare

> **Sidebar**
>
> **Add Music to a Web Page** Want to add music to your Web site? Use the *Help* feature to learn how! You can add MIDI files, which are small files that instruct the computer how to play a song. Since they are not actually recordings, the file sizes are small even though they can last up to a minute or two.
>
> **Identify** What type files are used to add music to Web pages?

Although Microsoft Publisher lacks some tools found in Web page software, it can still be used to create good Web pages. However, you must remember that an on-screen design is different from that on a printed page.

Design for On-Screen Publication

Computer monitors have different requirements from a printed page.

- **Screen layout is different.** Screens are wider and shorter than printed pages, so Web pages should be designed in landscape orientation.

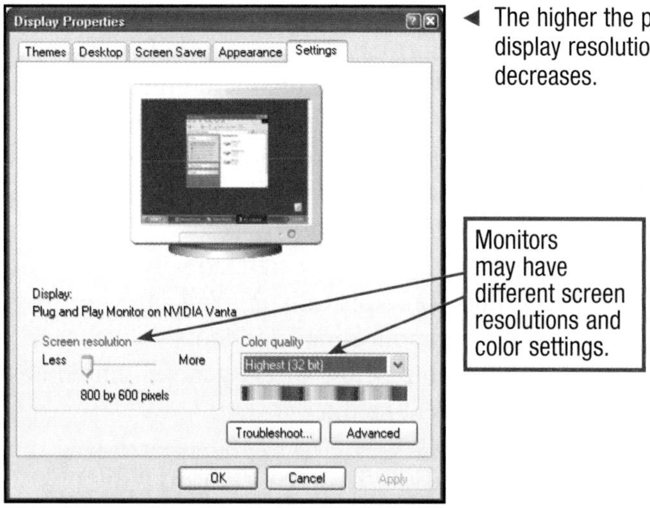

◄ The higher the pixel-count, the higher the display resolution. The size of the image decreases.

- **Screen resolution may vary. Resolution** refers to image clarity. On a computer monitor, resolution is measured in terms of **pixels per inch (ppi)**. When referring to printer output, resolution is measured in terms of **dots per inch (dpi)**. In both cases, the higher the number, the clearer the image. Most computer monitors can only display a maximum of 72 pixels per inch (ppi).
- A resolution higher than 72 ppi is not necessary for designs displayed on the monitor. This limitation can make text more difficult to read. Sans serif fonts are ideal for body text on Web pages or in PowerPoint presentations.
- **Not all computers use the same fonts.** Web pages should use the most common fonts. If unusual fonts are used, the visiting computer will substitute a different font—possibly a font that is unreadable.
- **Web browsers share a common 216 colors.** If a Web page is designed with colors other than these 216, the visiting computer will substitute the colors, which is called **dithering**. The computer uses this process because it is unable to display all the colors in an image. Although the colors are usually close to the original, in some cases they can be significantly different.

What Type of File Format Should I Use?

An important consideration in assessing project needs is how the final product will be delivered or published. Files must be saved in the proper format so that your message is deliverable both in print and online. Using the proper file type ensures that your message will reach your audience.

If your files are to be delivered on the Internet, you must consider your file size, image resolution, page size, page orientation, fonts, and even colors. Use file formats that work best for the medium. A **medium** is the delivery method of information, including print publications, CDs, DVDs, television and radio broadcasts, or Internet publishing.

If your project requires services such as scanning and high-resolution output, you might need to use a **service bureau**, a professional printer. The equipment used by a service bureau may require you to create your publications with specialized software applications, using specific tools and settings (see Appendix B). You and your service bureau need to use the same software applications and tools.

The table below offers general guidelines on formatting and resolutions for different media.

Media Formatting Guidelines

Medium	Picture File Type	Resolution	Types of Publications
Screen	JPG, GIF, PNG	72 dpi	Internet, PowerPoint, monitor, projection screen
Local printing (your personal computer)	Any	150 dpi	Printing from a local or networked printer
Professional printing	TIFF, PNG	300 dpi	Printing using an imagesetter

Some desktop publishing applications will work better with one type of file format than another. As you continue to develop your desktop publishing skills, you will be able to make decisions on the tools and file formats needed to meet project needs.

Reading Check

1. **Summarize** Why is it important to assess the client's project needs before you create a design?
2. **Explain** How does the final delivery method affect what file format to use?

Eye On Ethics

Cite Online Sources When you use information from the Internet, such as content, photographs, or art, you must cite the source of this information. To use an individual's work without giving that person credit is known as *plagiarism*, which is illegal. Use the Modern Language Association (MLA) guidelines for the information that you must include when citing online sources.

Analyze What types of online resources need citations when they are used in designs?

Evaluate a Web Page

The table describes some of the design problems on the Web page shown below.

Design Blunders

PARC Principle	Problems
Proximity	• Related items are not grouped together. • The page size is too small for an 800 x 600 screen resolution.
Alignment	• Objects on the page are not aligned horizontally or vertically. • Text is cut off in the bottom right text box.
Repetition	• Font choices seem to be somewhat random and are hard to read. • The clip art is almost all animated elements. The animation distracts from the message, rather than enhance it.
Contrast	• Background is distracting. • Items on-screen are in a random layout. There is no focal point for the reader. • There is no distinct entry point from which the user may navigate through the site.

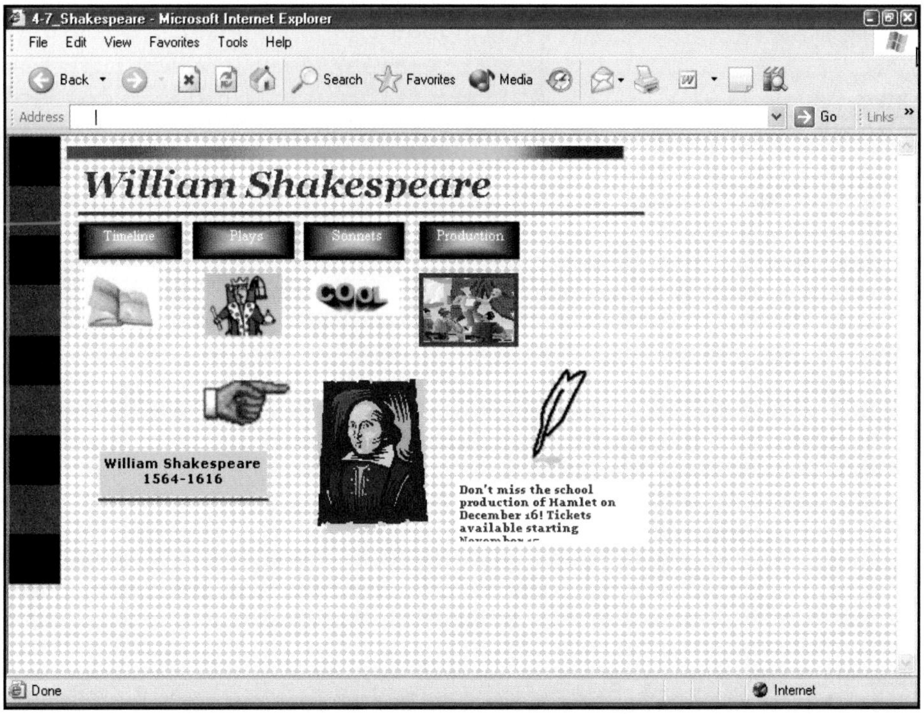

▶ **In this project,** you will redesign a Web site that discusses William Shakespeare, his life, and his works so that it effectively conveys the information included on the site.

WORKSHOP Foundations

Assess Project Needs

You Will Learn To

- Compare desktop publishing applications and tools
- Evaluate client needs
- Compare file formats

Key Terms

client
medium
service bureau

Before You Read

Check Your Understanding Stop often and think about what you are reading. Are you following along with the ideas? Have you immediately forgotten what you just read? Reread parts when necessary. On a note pad, draw pictures or diagrams to summarize the information. As you complete a section, see if you can connect the ideas. Write down the main idea on your note pad. Then write down supporting information or examples around the main idea. Draw lines or arrows to show the connections.

You have learned and applied design principles in the projects you have created and used tools in various desktop publishing applications to apply design principles. You should now have a basic understanding of the tools that are available in each application and how you can best apply them.

In this chapter, you will use the skills you have learned in both Illustrator and Publisher. Each application has tools to meet specific needs, so it is important to match a program's strengths to the designs you create. Graphic designers use many desktop publishing software applications to create their designs. For example, complex art illustrations should be created in software that is specifically designed for that purpose, and then layout software is used to insert the illustration in a brochure.

Choose the Appropriate Desktop Publishing Software

Tasks	Vector Drawing Software	Raster Editing Software	Word Processing Software	Layout Software
Design a Logo	X			
Create Scalable Graphics	X			
Edit a Picture	X	X		
Key and Edit Text			X	X
Professional Printing	X	X		X

Determine the needs for a project as soon as possible so that you can choose the best tools. Many desktop publishing projects are for a **client**, the individual or organization who pays for the work. To fully meet the client's needs, ask many questions, including:

- What are the specific goals for the publication?
- Who is the target audience?
- What is the budget and timeline?
- What text and graphics are required?

Student Data File

Step-by-Step

1. In Publisher, open **Data File 4-7a**. Save it according to your teacher's instructions.

2. Click **File>Web Page Preview** to view the document as a Web page.

3. Press the ESC key to stop the movement on the page. Click **Close** to close the window and return to Publisher (Figure 4.34).

Resize a Web Page

4. Click **File>Page Setup**. Change the Custom settings to **7 inches width**, **4.5 inches height**.

5. Drag the design into the scratch area.

6. Open the **Background** task pane. Choose the **Texture fill (Parchment)** background (Figure 4.35).

7. Set all **Margin Guides** to **0 inches**. Add **Grid Guides**: **5 columns, 8 rows, 0 inches spacing**.

8. **Ungroup** the old design. Drag the red and black **Design Gallery** object to the left side of the workspace.

Figure 4.34 You can access Web publication commands in the Web Tools toolbar.

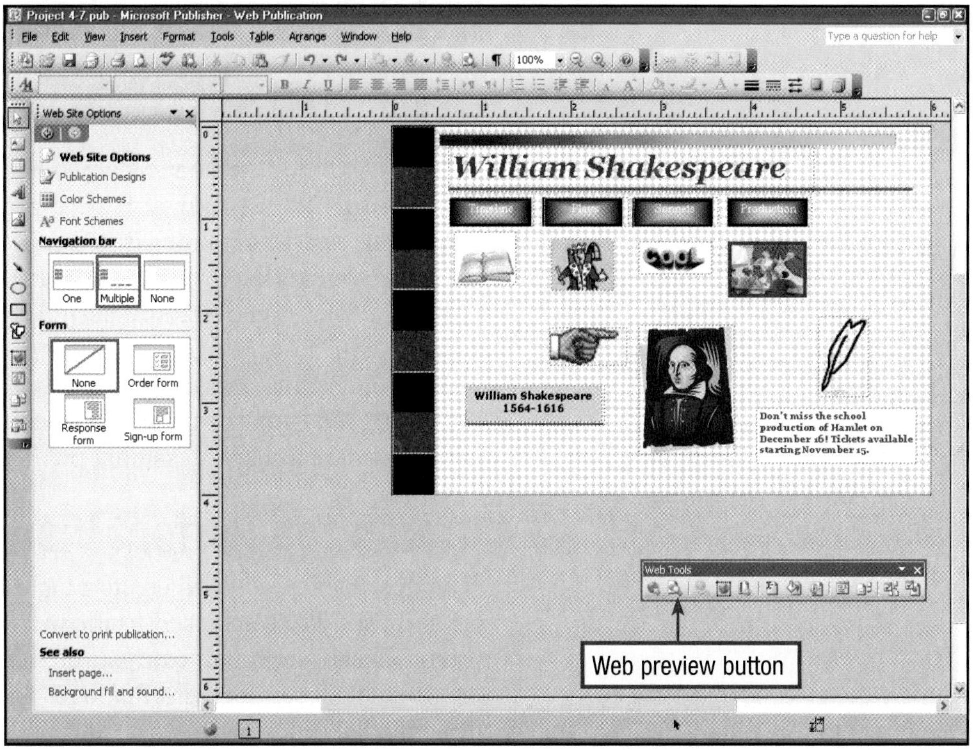

Figure 4.35 Zoom out to see the workspace and the design in the scratch area.

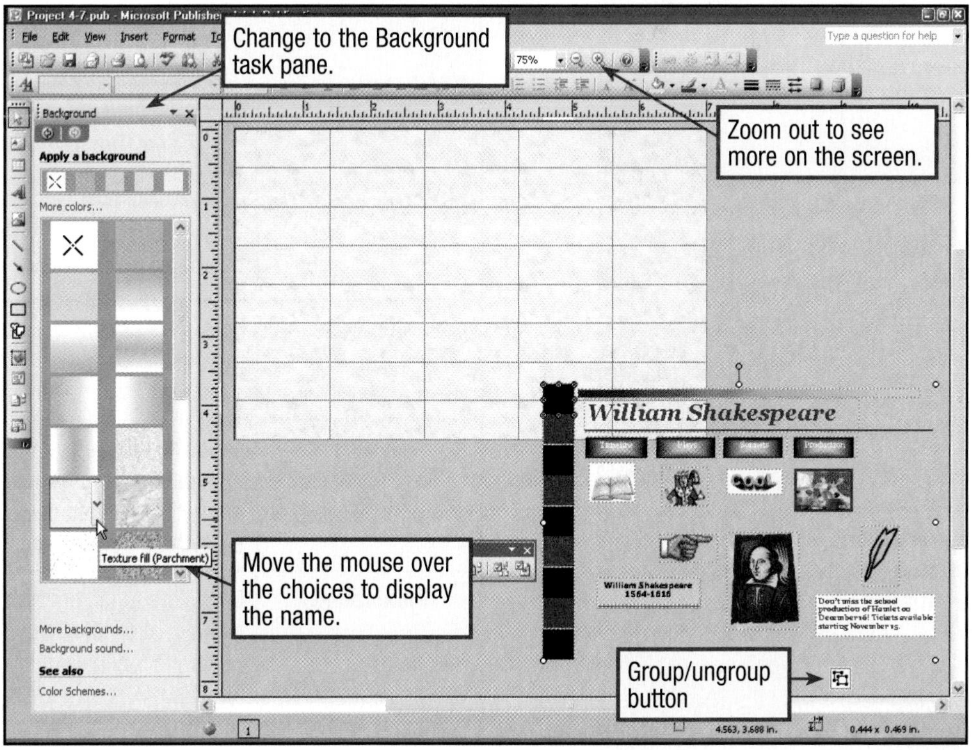

Chapter 8 Integrating Publisher and Illustrator

Skills You Will Learn

Workshop Foundations
Assess Project Needs

Workshop Toolbox
Layers Palette in Illustrator

Project 8-1
Create Shapes with Tools

Project 8-2
Design Vector Images

Project 8-3
Create a Tent Card

Project 8-4
Apply Live Trace

Project 8-5
Create Shattered Text

Project 8-6
Lay Out a Poster

Skills Studio

Design a 3D Product

Project 8-7
Create a 3D Cylinder

Project 8-8
Design a Product Logo

Project 8-9
Design a Product Label

Project 8-10
Add Symbols to a Label

In this textbook, you have learned how to create many well-designed publications using four software applications: Word, Publisher, Illustrator, and Photoshop. It is important to have skills in different software applications so that you can create artistic and imaginative designs. Professional graphic designers use different applications for editing text, modifying photographs, creating vector graphics, and laying out designs. Each of these software applications offers specific solutions for design issues, and using them together provides even more options for creating professional publications.

Create the Perfect Visual Message

In this chapter, you will create a logo. Logos are images that combine art and text. They are used to identify a product or business. A logo should visually communicate so well that people will instantly associate the product or service with the logo. Apply your knowledge of design principles, the design process, and desktop publishing software skills to create logos that stand out in the market.

DESIGN PROCESS: Logos

Elements	Issues
Purpose	Logos provide the first impression of a business, organization, or product. They should provide a unique identity that is quickly recognized.
Audience	Varies. Logos are used for many kinds of audiences. They can be businesslike or playful.
Content	Logos are unique and contain essential information identifying the organization or product. Simplicity will help the audience remember the logo. Readable fonts are essential.
Layout	Logos should be eye-catching and simple, visually communicating a professional image. Scalable vector graphics are recommended because the image must work well on everything from business cards to billboards.
Publication	Logos are found on business stationery, product labels, clothing, Web sites, advertisements, magazines, newspapers, and technical journals. They may be published on anything from an envelope to clothing, such as t-shirts.

Resize a Design Gallery Object

9 Click and drag a handle on the object to fill the left border, as shown in Figure 4.36.

10 Drag the *William Shakespeare* text box to the top row. Remove the italics.

11 Select the text box. Click **Format>Text Box>Text Box** tab, then change the **Vertical Alignment** to **Bottom**.

12 Add a **black**, **2¼ pt** line below the text box.

13 Insert a new text box in the second row and in **bold**, **16 pt Georgia** key 1564–1616. (Use an en-dash between dates.)

14 From the old design, drag the four buttons and the text boxes overlaying them. Position them in **Rows 2–5** in the last column, as shown in Figure 4.37.

15 Change the text on the buttons to **bold**, **Arial**, **10 pt**. Change the vertical alignment of the text to **Center**. (**Hint**: See Step 11.)

▼ **Figure 4.36** Design objects will automatically adjust their design when resized.

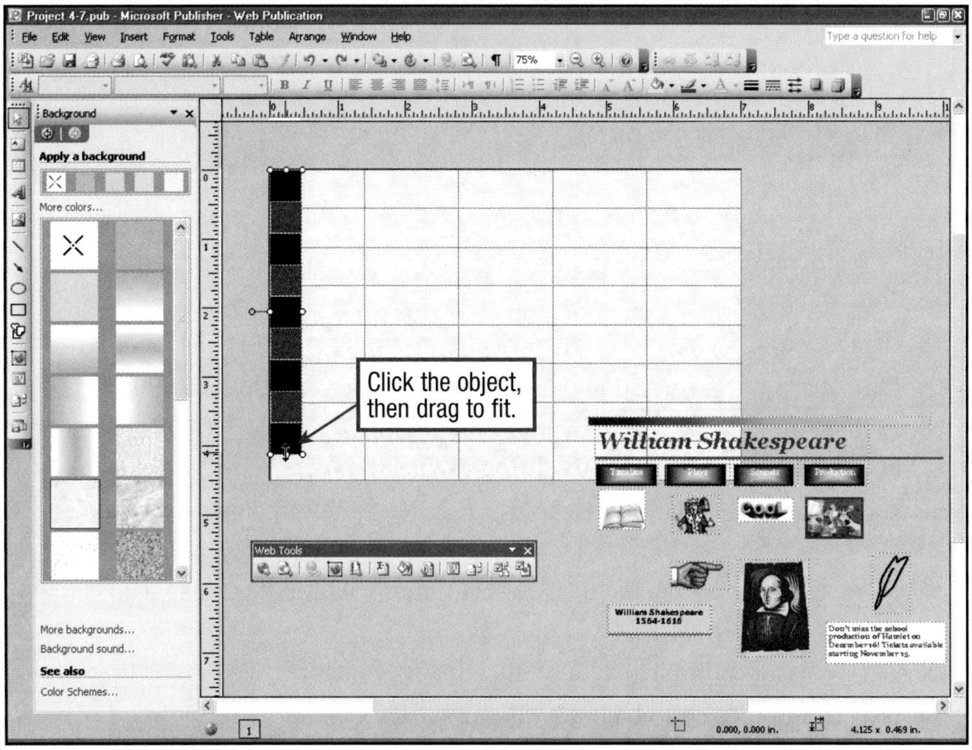

▼ **Figure 4.37** When pages are added, these buttons can be changed to hyperlinks.

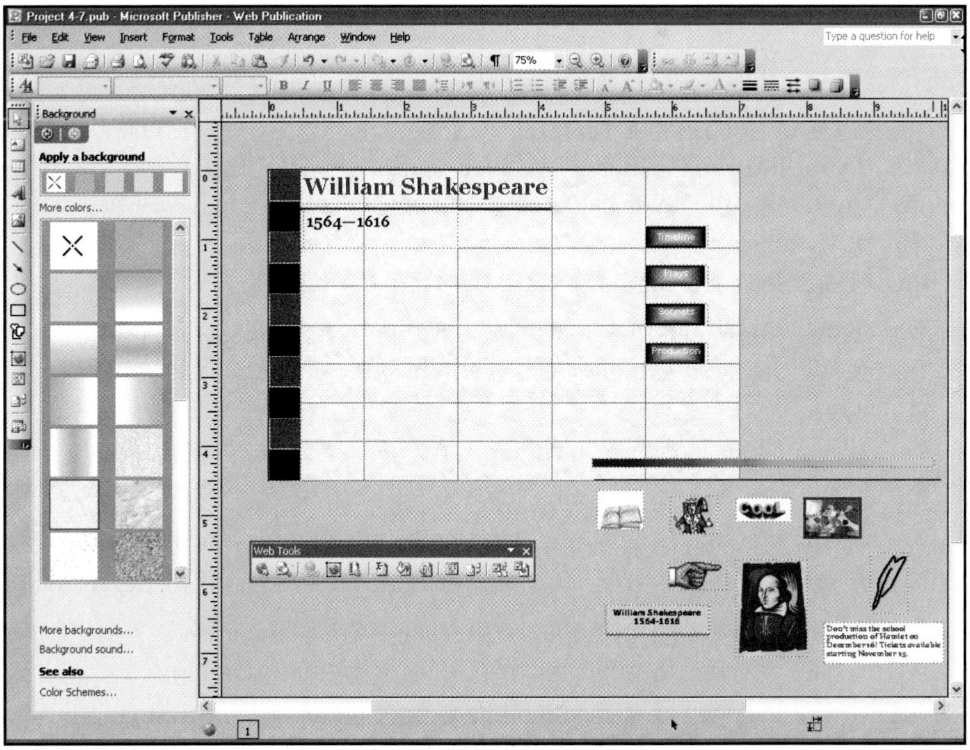

2 Independent Practice ★★

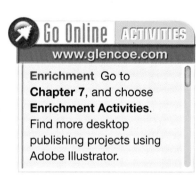

TEAM Create Food Illustrations Team up with a partner to create a breakfast banquet illustration that will make your classmates hungry.

a. Plan Decide what you want breakfast items you want to create.

- You and your partner should each create at least three food items.
- Include a range of food—such as orange juice, fried eggs, toast, and bacon—that will require different visual effects.

b. Create The following are examples of some of the effects you might use.

- Make the eggs and juice glass reflect light by using the transparency palette.
- Create wrinkles in the bacon with a distort envelope.
- Use gradient color to have lightly browned toast.
- Use the blend tool to create a very large stack of pancakes or patterns on a cup.

3 Independent Practice ★★★

SCIENCE Create a Technology Illustration Design your own version of your favorite technology: a cell phone, a car, a DVD player, a computer, or any item that you feel you can create with the skills that you have learned in Illustrator.

a. Plan Decide what technology you would like to illustrate.

- Research on the Internet the latest trends in the technology you have chosen.

b. Design Create the illustration as if it will be part of a publication, such as a brochure.

- Determine the size you will need.
- Draw at least three thumbnail sketches.
- Ask your classmates and your teacher which technology design they prefer.

c. Create Use Illustrator to create your illustration. Use a variety of tools including:

- Gradient and transparency effects to create texture and light.
- Text on a pathway to create a dynamic logo for the technology.
- Distort Envelope to create some interesting shapes or curves in your design.

Go Online ACTIVITIES
www.glencoe.com

Enrichment Go to **Chapter 7**, and choose **Enrichment Activities**. Find more desktop publishing projects using Adobe Illustrator.

16 Drag the text box with the Hamlet information below the bottom button (Figure 4.38). Change the fill to **No Fill**.

17 **Center** the text and change the fonts to **black Arial 12 pt** and **red 10 pt**, as shown in Figure 4.38.

18 Insert the clip art from **Data File 4-7b**. Position and resize it as shown in Figure 4.38.

19 Insert the clip art from **Data File 4-7c**. Position and resize it as shown in Figure 4.38.

20 Create a text box in the scroll image and in **bold**, **italic Georgia, 12 pt** key This above all, to thine own self be true.

21 **Preview** your document as a Web page. Close the preview to make any revisions in the Publisher document.

22 Follow your teacher's instructions for saving your work.

▼ **Figure 4.38** The final document as it would appear as a Web page.

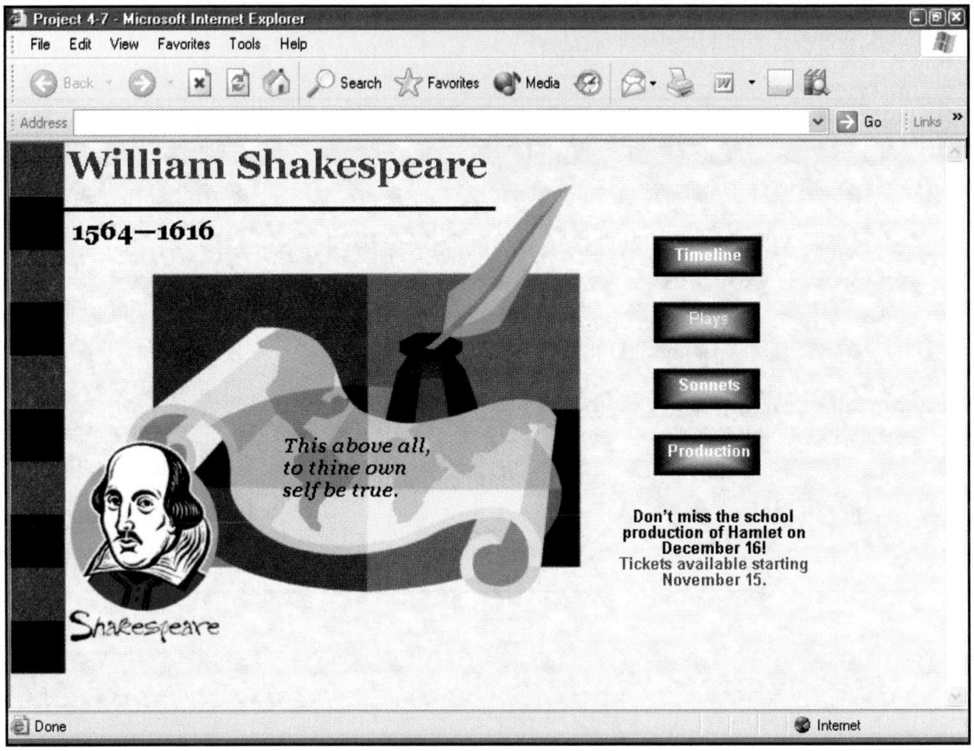

Instant Message

Web Page Display If your monitor's display is not set at a resolution of 800 × 600 pixels, your Web Page preview might not look exactly like the figure in this project. Do not change your monitor's display unless your teacher gives you permission, with appropriate instructions on how to do so.

REVIEW AND REVISE

Check your work Use Figure 4.38 as a guide and check that:

- ☑ The Web page is the correct size for the monitor display.
- ☑ Information is placed so it is easy to find.
- ☑ Objects are aligned in a consistent manner.
- ☑ Contrast is used effectively to call out important information.
- ☑ Font styles are readable and applied consistently for effective repetition.
- ☑ The images are sized and positioned so white space can flow.

Chapter 7 Assessment

Reading Check

1. **Define** What are vector graphics?
2. **Identify** What are common file formats that are used for saving vector graphics?
3. **Describe** Explain when you should use the Selection tool and when you should use the Direct Selection tool.
4. **Evaluate** Why is it useful to be able to use different palettes in Illustrator?
5. **Analyze** Why is scalability an important capability of vector graphics?

Critical Thinking

6. **Identify** Name four palettes that would be used for most illustrations.
7. **Describe** How can basic shapes be used to create more complex shapes?
8. **Summarize** What issues should you consider when deciding whether to use a vector or a graphic image?
9. **Compare** How is a drawing program such as Illustrator different from a program such as Publisher?
10. **Analyze** How is designing with text illustrations similar to creating logos?

1 Independent Practice

LANGUAGE ARTS **Prepare an Illustration for a Publication** Start with the crayon box from Projects 7-2 and 7-3, and create an illustration that will be used in an advertisement for an arts and crafts magazine. Think about how to enhance the crayon illustration that you created to get customers to buy a box. Be sure to include all the necessary information that the readers of your advertisement need to know, including the price for the box of crayons. Small items are often advertised in small spaces, so design your illustration accordingly.

a. Plan Look at some magazine advertisements and determine both the audience and the audience needs.

b. Design Create at least three sketches of potential advertisements.
- Get feedback from classmates. Consult with your teacher about your plan for the advertisement.

c. Create Continue with your crayon design, adding your own ideas to make it more interesting.
- Be sure the workspace is sized so that the advertisement is not too big.
- Add 2 more crayons to the front row and add a back row, all in different colors. Add effects such as reflections and shadows.
- Make the box larger, and place a couple of crayons outside the box.
- Add a new label with warped text reading "Now More Colors."

d. Publish Follow your teacher's instructions for printing your design. Evaluate it according to PARC principles, and revise if necessary.

Go Online RUBRICS
www.glencoe.com

Independent Practice
Go to **Chapter 7**, and choose **Rubrics**. Use the rubrics to help create and evaluate your projects.

Skills Studio

Reinforce Your Skills

Project 4-8

- Lay out a booklet
- Insert graphics
- Apply style sheets
- Link text boxes

Project 4-9

- Insert a calendar template
- Modify the calendar
- Align using tabs and bullets

Go Online ACTIVITIES

www.glencoe.com

Challenge Yourself Go to **Chapter 4**, and choose **Enrichment Activities** for more practice with the skills you have learned.

Create a Children's Newsletter

The following two projects will take you through the steps you need to create a bi-fold newsletter:

- **Project 4-8** Design for a young audience
- **Project 4-9** Complete your newsletter

Readable Newsletters

Creating a good newsletter can be very challenging. Like a brochure, it must provide a lot of information in a small amount of space, yet still be visually interesting and not too text-heavy. Also, newsletters can be many pages long. The information on the first page must invite the reader to open the publication and read what is inside.

Newsletters are usually published at regular intervals. The publications can be distributed weekly, biweekly, monthly, bimonthly, quarterly, or even yearly. Brochures, on the other hand, are generally designed once and simply reprinted when stockpiles are low. Newsletters with updated text and graphics must be designed so they can be laid out and republished quickly.

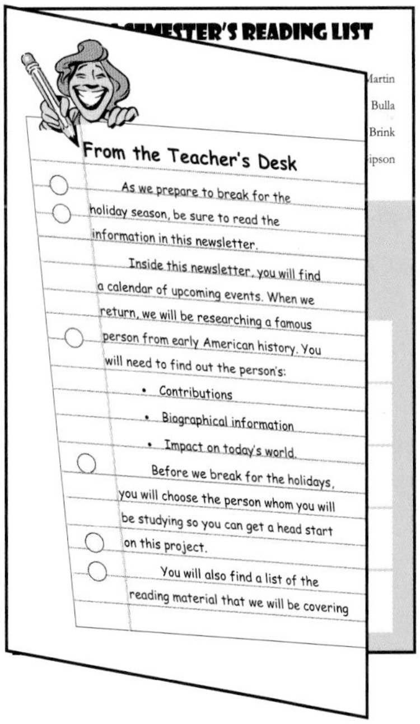

It is also important to create a unique design that makes your newsletter look different from the others in a mailbox. If your design does not appeal to your specific audience, they will ignore the information for which your newsletter was created in the first place.

In The Workplace

Illustrators

Illustrators work with clients to clarify and create the visual message that the client wants to express. They create two- and three-dimensional images for Web sites and printed material such as books, magazines, product packaging, greeting cards, and many other applications. Illustrators also create digital pictures for animation, computer games, films, and commercials.

On the Job

Illustrators have a solid understanding of drawing, perspective, color, layout, and other skills. And, while some illustrators work with traditional media such as pencil and paper, many illustrators create their work digitally using drawing programs like Adobe Illustrator, ACD Canvas™, and Corel® Draw®.

Illustrators may work with graphic design programs like Adobe Photoshop or desktop publishing applications such as Adobe InDesign, which can integrate Photoshop, Illustrator, and Acrobat files in a document. Illustrators working in both two and three dimensions may work with CAD (computer-aided design) programs like Autodesk® Maya® to create artwork for film, games, multimedia, broadcast, print, and Web pages.

Illustrators may develop specialized skills in specific fields. Advertising agencies, graphic design firms, game developers, publishing houses, manufacturers, the motion picture and television industries, and other businesses use their services. Highly specialized illustrators use their knowledge of technology and sciences to create technical, medical, and scientific drawings. Freelance illustrators work for various companies on a contract basis and may work in a number of industries.

Future Outlook

Demand for skilled illustrators is high and very competitive.

- **Society of Illustrators (societyillustrators.org)** promotes the art of illustration and features career tips for prospective illustrators.
- **American Institute of Graphic Arts (AIGA) (aiga.org)** provides design professionals with ideas and information.

Training

Although it is not absolutely essential for illustrators to have formal training, it is highly recommended. Illustrators gain skills at community colleges, art schools, universities, and specialized multimedia and design programs.

Salary Range

Salaries for illustrators range from $29,000 to $94,000 per year depending upon experience, skill, industry, and location.

Skills and Talents

Illustrators need to have:

- Good computer skills
- Knowledge of drawing and design
- Knowledge of digital illustration and design software
- Good communication skills
- The ability to work independently and meet deadlines

Career Activity

Why is it important for illustrators to develop their drawing and design skills in addition to learning digital illustration techniques? Why do you think salaries vary so much?

Project 4-8 Design for a Young Audience

Skills You Will Apply

- Lay out a booklet
- Position and resize graphics
- Apply style sheets
- Link text boxes

Academic Focus

Language Arts
Present children's material visually

When creating a design for a younger audience, you must remember that children's reading ability and interests are different from those of adults. Keep the following design guidelines in mind when designing for children:

- The design needs to be very visual.
- Fonts should be simple and larger than for adult readers.
- More white space can be created by using shorter line lengths and larger leading.
- The tone should be fun and friendly, with an appropriate reading level.

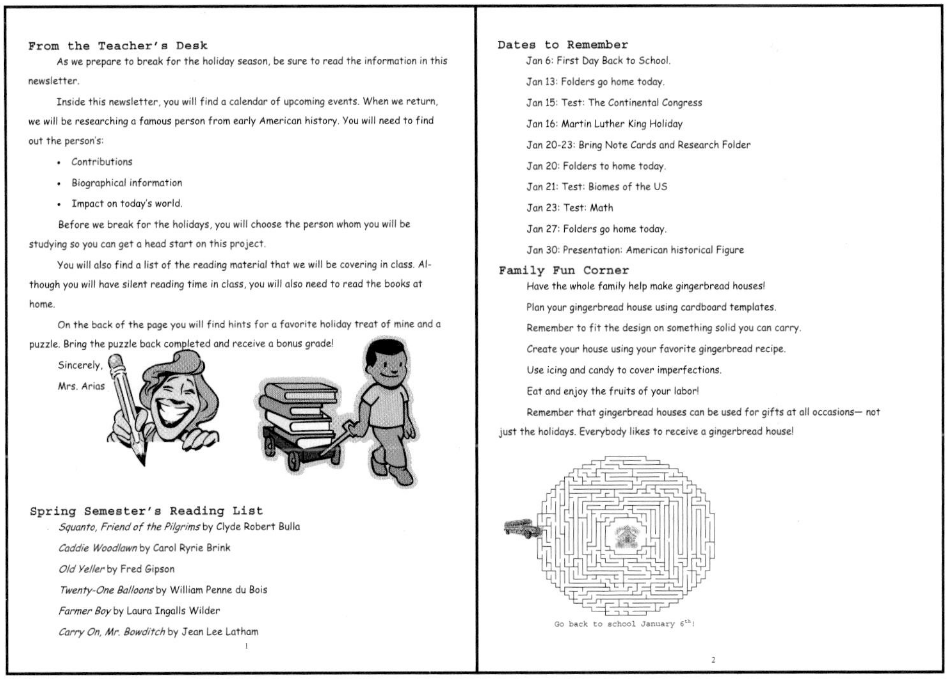

From the Teacher's Desk

As we prepare to break for the holiday season, be sure to read the information in this newsletter.

Inside this newsletter, you will find a calendar of upcoming events. When we return, we will be researching a famous person from early American history. You will need to find out the person's:

- Contributions
- Biographical information
- Impact on today's world.

Before we break for the holidays, you will choose the person whom you will be studying so you can get a head start on this project.

You will also find a list of the reading material that we will be covering in class. Although you will have silent reading time in class, you will also need to read the books at home.

On the back of the page you will find hints for a favorite holiday treat of mine and a puzzle. Bring the puzzle back completed and receive a bonus grade!

Sincerely,
Mrs. Arias

Spring Semester's Reading List

Squanto, Friend of the Pilgrims by Clyde Robert Bulla
Caddie Woodlawn by Carol Ryrie Brink
Old Yeller by Fred Gipson
Twenty-One Balloons by William Penne du Bois
Farmer Boy by Laura Ingalls Wilder
Carry On, Mr. Bowditch by Jean Lee Latham

1

Dates to Remember

Jan 6: First Day Back to School.
Jan 13: Folders go home today.
Jan 15: Test: The Continental Congress
Jan 16: Martin Luther King Holiday
Jan 20-23: Bring Note Cards and Research Folder
Jan 20: Folders to home today.
Jan 21: Test: Biomes of the US
Jan 23: Test: Math
Jan 27: Folders go home today.
Jan 30: Presentation: American historical Figure

Family Fun Corner

Have the whole family help make gingerbread houses!
Plan your gingerbread house using cardboard templates.
Remember to fit the design on something solid you can carry.
Create your house using your favorite gingerbread recipe.
Use icing and candy to cover imperfections.
Eat and enjoy the fruits of your labor!
Remember that gingerbread houses can be used for gifts at all occasions— not just the holidays. Everybody likes to receive a gingerbread house!

Go back to school January 6th!

2

▲ Your former teacher needs help redesigning her fourth-grade newsletter. It is difficult to find information in this design.

▶ **In this project,** you will help your former fourth-grade teacher, Mrs. Arias, redesign the monthly newsletter she creates for her students. She has found that very few students read the newsletters, and she needs your advice.

Mrs. Arias has a small budget, so you must use 8½ inches × 11 inches paper, and the newsletter cannot be longer than two pages. However, she can print 30 copies in color using a duplex printer.

6. Drag a selection box around the text and light bulb shape. Resize to fit the page, and **Group** all objects.

Add Gradient

7. Create a rectangle over the entire design, and choose **Object>Arrange>Send to Back**.

8. Choose a **Radial** type gradient to emphasize the radiating theme. See Figure 7.44.

9. Use the **Type** tool [T] to key Desktop Publishing in one text box and Powered by Imagination in another text box. Choose an appropriate typeface and size.

10. Create a yellow square "sticky note." Use the **Type** tool [T] to create a text box above the sticky note, and key Sign up Today! in a **script** font.

Apply Envelope Distort

11. Choose **Object>Envelope Distort>Make with Warp**, and select **Arch** (Figure 7.44).

12. Add a **Drop Shadow** to the sticky note, and then position and rotate slightly.

13. Your final flyer should look similar to Figure 7.44. Follow your teacher's instructions for saving and printing your work.

▼ **Figure 7.44** Your final text illustration flyer is an eye-catching design.

REVIEW AND REVISE

Check your work Use Figure 7.44 as a guide and check that:

- ☑ The flyer is in landscape orientation sized to be printed on an 8½ x 11 inch sheet of paper.
- ☑ The text illustration effectively conveys a persuasive message.
- ☑ The focus of the image is clear.
- ☑ The images add visual interest while displaying the content clearly.
- ☑ Text following the spiral pathway is readable.
- ☑ A gradient has been added to the background.
- ☑ The sticky note object looks realistic and has readable text and a drop shadow.

Student Data File

Step-by-Step

1. In Publisher, open **Data File 4-8a**, and save it according to your teacher's instructions.

2. On **Page 1**, select the old design and move it into the scratch area.

Lay Out a Booklet

3. Click **File>Page Setup>Layout** tab. Change the **Publication Type** to **Booklet**. Page size should be **5.5 inches wide**, **8.5 inches high**.

4. **Insert two pages**, and change the **View** to **Two-Page Spread** (Figure 4.39).

5. Under **Arrange>Layout Guides**, change **Page Margins** to **0.25 inch**. Set **Grid Guides** to **8 columns**, with a **0 inch gutter**.

Position and Resize Graphics

6. Insert the picture **Data File 4-8b** on Page 1. Resize and reposition it so it looks similar to Figure 4.40. Select the image, and choose **Send to Back**.

7. **Ungroup** the Page 1 design content in the scratch area.

Figure 4.39 In booklet format, each page is the width of a half page.

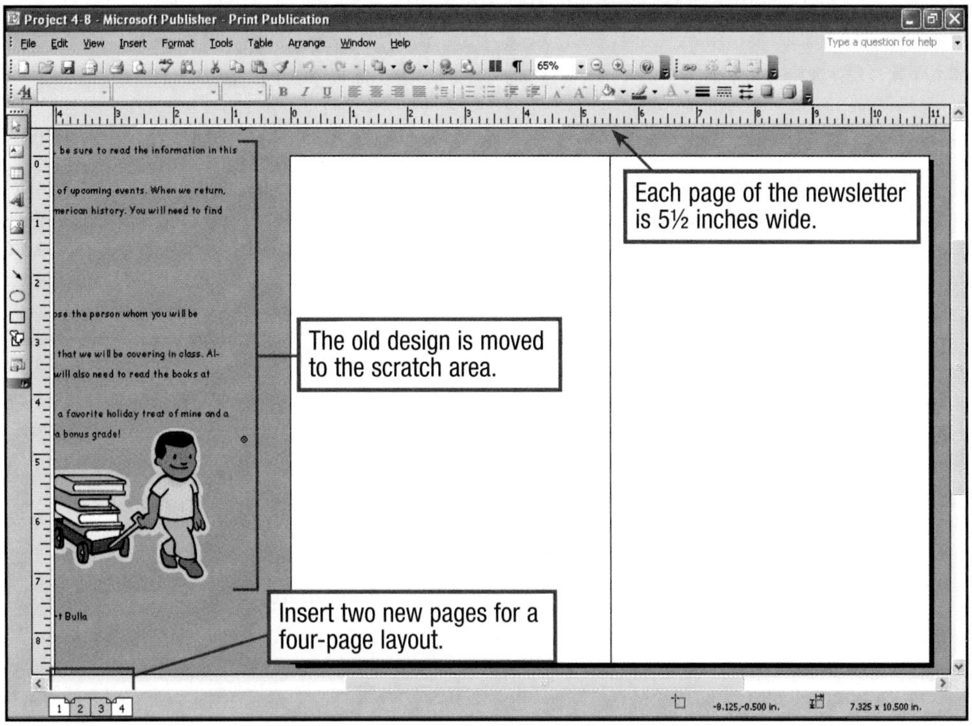

Project 4-8 - Microsoft Publisher - Print Publication

Insert two new pages for a four-page layout.

Figure 4.40 Any objects that stick out beyond the workspace will not print.

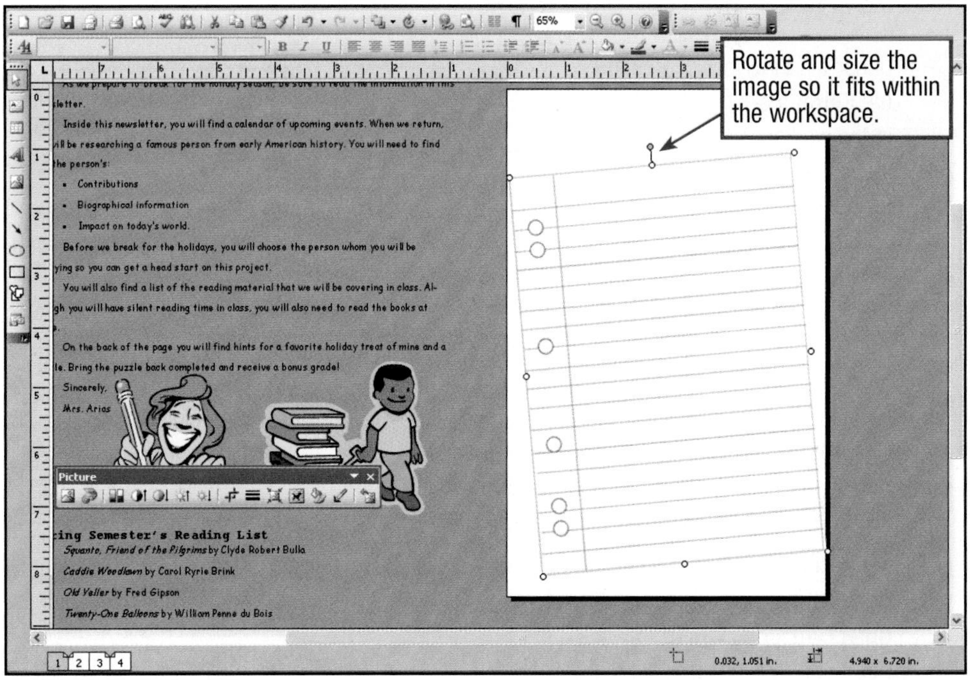

Rotate and size the image so it fits within the workspace.

Skills Studio

Project 7-9

Enhance Your Text Illustration

Skills You Will Apply

- Create a text path
- Add a gradient
- Apply Envelope distort

Academic Focus

Language Arts
Relate words to images

The Spiral tool creates spirals going clockwise or counterclockwise. Like the other drawing tools in Illustrator, you can drag out a shape or click the workspace to enter specific settings. You will be using the Spiral tool to illustrate radiating light from the bulb and add text following the spiral object's path.

▶ **In this project,** you will continue the text illustration flyer that you started to design in Project 7-8. Be creative, imaginative, and have fun. Think about what type of flyer would attract your attention because it is likely that it will then appeal to other students also. This project allows you to showcase your designer skills.

Step-by-Step

1. Open the flyer you started in Project 7-8. Save it according to your teacher's instructions.

Create a Text Path

2. Under the **Line** tool, open the **Spiral** tool. Left-click in the workspace. In the Spiral tool dialog box, key: 2.36 in for Radius, 95 for Decay, and 20 for Segments.
3. Under the **Type** tool, open the **Type on a Path** tool.
4. Select the spiral to key Radiated Outward. Press TAB, and key the text again. Repeat until the shape is filled. See Figure 7.43.
5. 5. Use the **Selection** tool to select the spiral. Choose **Object>Arrange>Send to Back** to move the spiral text behind the light bulb.

▼ Figure 7.43 Reinforce the light bulb theme by using the Spiral tool for a radiating effect.

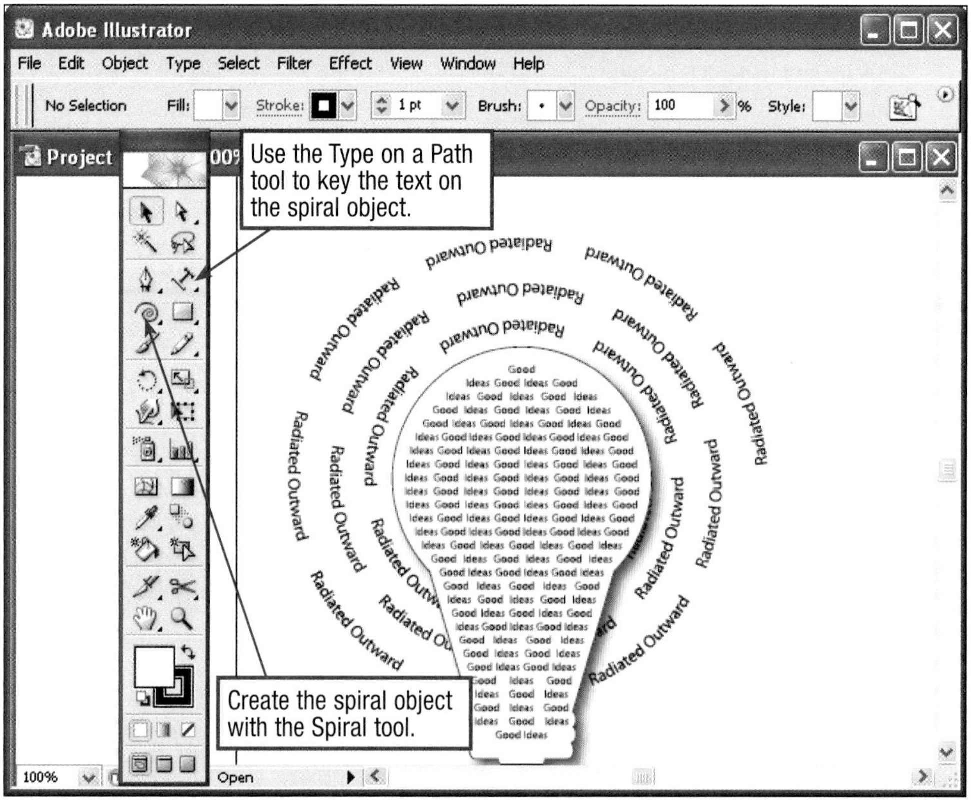

8. Drag the teacher clip art to the workspace. Resize and reposition it as shown in Figure 4.41.

9. Copy and paste the teacher letter in the scratch area to the lined memo paper. Click **No** to the question about the overflow.

10. Rotate the text box so that it aligns with the edges of the image. Resize as needed. (Figure 4.41). (**Note**: Ignore the Text in Overflow icon for now.)

Apply Style Sheets

11. Select *From the Teacher's Desk* in the text box. Redefine the style named *Copy*. Change the font to **18 pt**.

12. Reposition the text box so that the words align on the ruled paper image.

Link Text Boxes

13. Click **Create a Text Box Link**. The overflow text flows to page 2. Resize and reposition the text box (Figure 4.42).

14. Follow your teacher's instructions for saving your work. You will use this file in Project 4-9.

▼ **Figure 4.41** Rotate the text box so it aligns with the image.

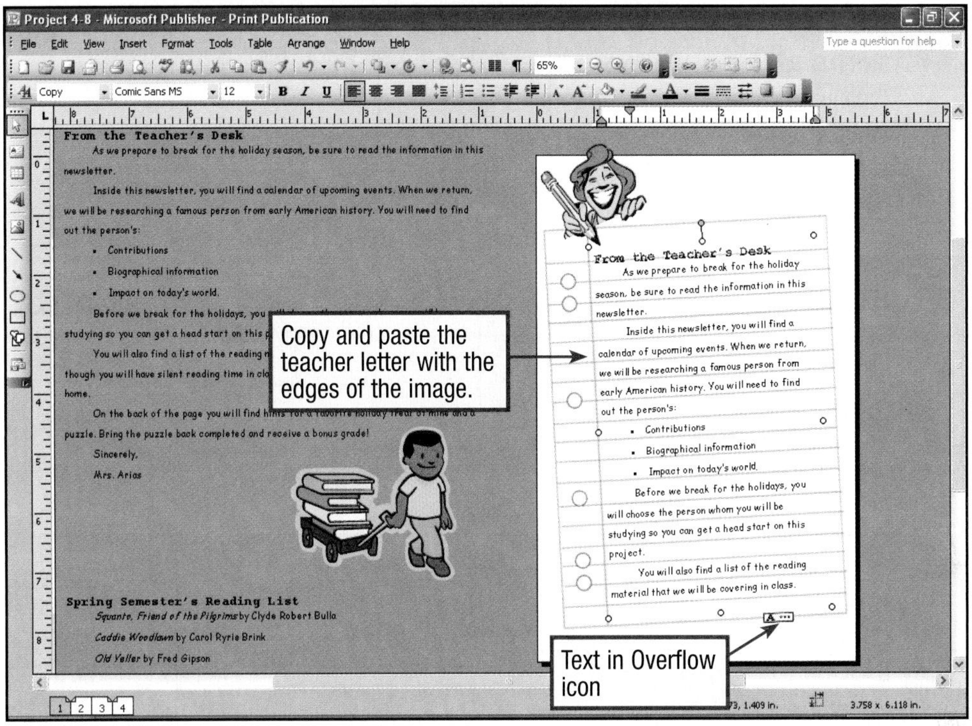

▼ **Figure 4.42** The text should be positioned on the ruled lines of the image.

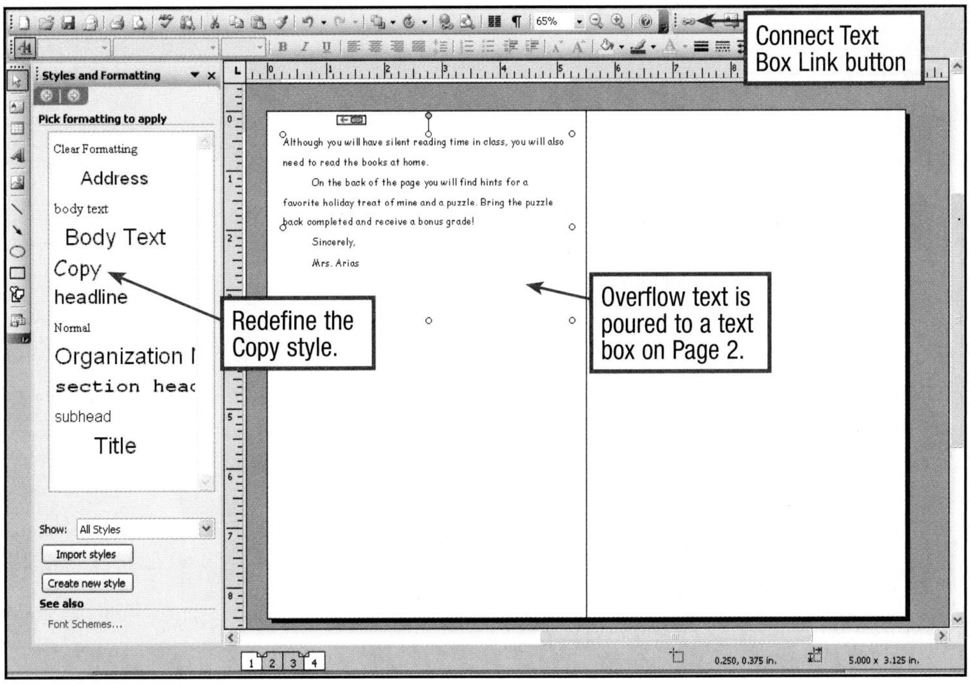

Add Shape to Area

10 Drag a selection box over the light bulb figure. Click **Window> Pathfinder** to open the **Pathfinder** palette. Hold ALT, and click **Add to shape area** to combine all the shapes.

11 Hold ALT to drag another copy of the shape to the side. See Figure 7.41.

12 Under the **Type** tool, open the **Area Type** tool. Select the light bulb. Key Good Ideas in the text box shape until the light bulb is filled. (**Hint**: Use copy and paste.) See Figure 7.41.

13 Click **Window>Type> Paragraph** to view the **Paragraph** palette. Choose **Justify with last line aligned center**.

Apply Text Outlines

14 On the **Menu** bar, click **Type>Create Outlines**.

15 Select the **duplicate** light bulb, and change the **Fill Color** to **No Fill**. Move the duplicate light bulb onto your design (Figure 7.42).

16 Click **Effect>Stylize>Drop Shadow**. Use the **Selection** tool to group all objects.

17 Follow your teacher's instructions for saving your work. You will use this file in Project 7-9.

▼ **Figure 7.41** Use the Pathfinder palette to combine or remove simple shapes.

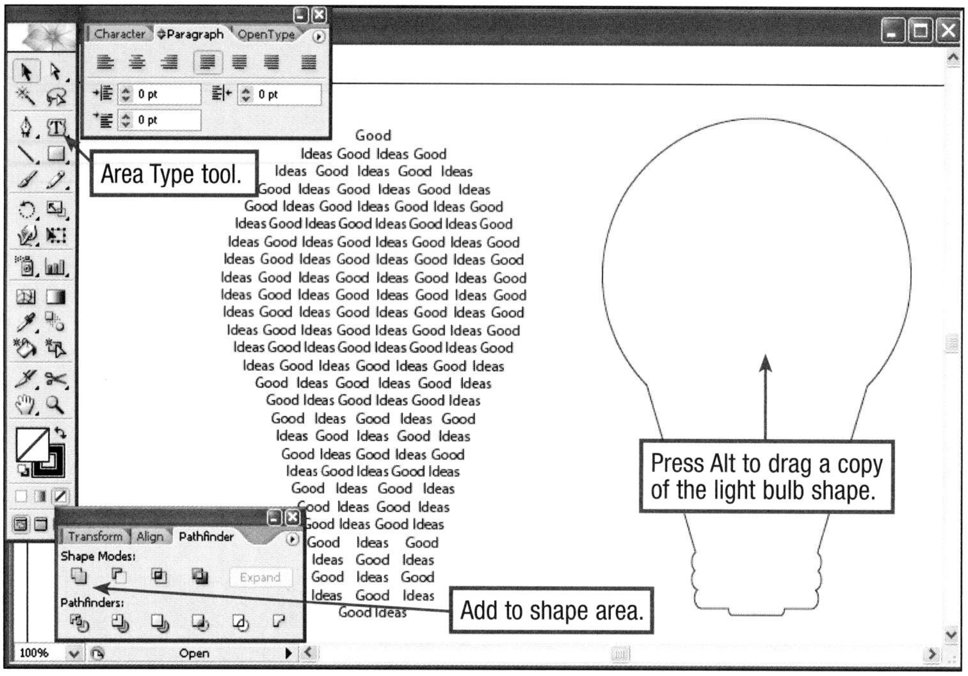

Area Type tool.
Press Alt to drag a copy of the light bulb shape.
Add to shape area.

▼ **Figure 7.42** Your design should look similar to this figure.

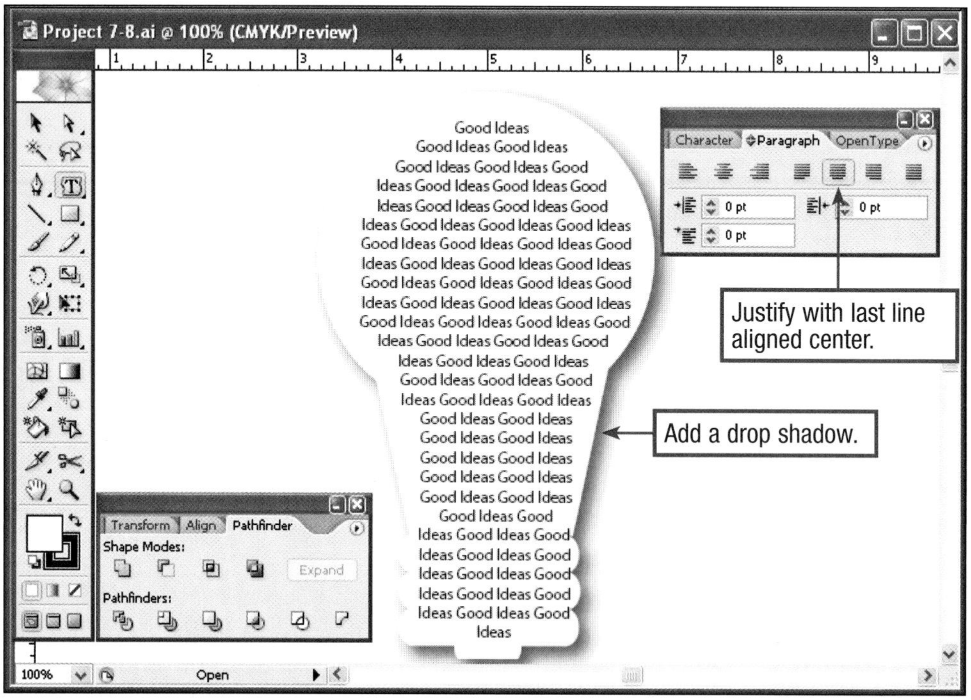

Skills Studio

Project 4-9 Complete Your Newsletter

Skills You Will Apply

- Insert a calendar template

Academic Focus

Social Studies
Arrange events sequentially

Step-by-Step

1. Open the newsletter file you started in Project 4-8. Save it according to your teacher's instructions.

2. Create a text box at the top of **Page 3**, the same size as the text box on Page 2.

3. On **Page 3** of your layout, copy and paste the *Spring Semester Reading List* from the old design. Apply the **Section Head** style to the title (Figure 4.43).

4. Change the font in the list to **Garamond** and the **spacing after paragraphs** to **3 pt**.

5. Create a right tab stop at the right margin of the text box.

6. Click **Format>Tabs**, and choose **Dot leaders**. Before each author's name in the list, **delete** *by*, and then press TAB (Figure 4.43).

▶ **In this project,** You will continue the newsletter that you started to re-design in Project 4-8. You will be using a template to create a calendar. Remember, though, that even though Publisher has many fine templates, you can make changes to a template to give it a new look.

▼ **Figure 4.43** The text on the interior pages has the same formatting as Page 1.

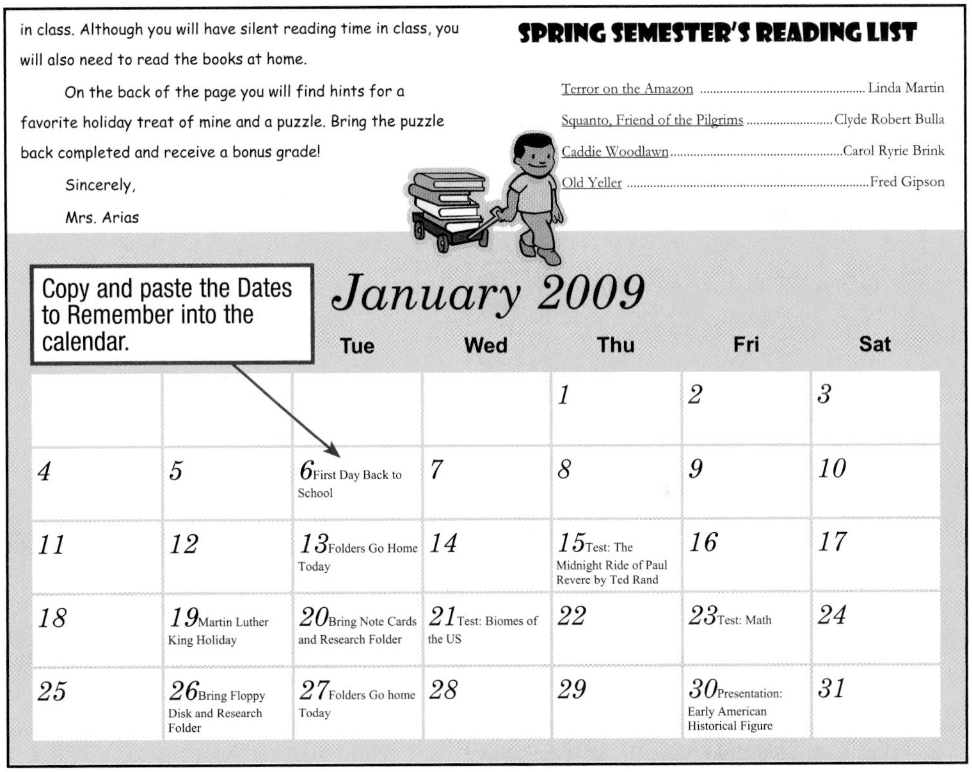

		Tue	Wed	Thu	Fri	Sat
				1	2	3
4	5	6 First Day Back to School	7	8	9	10
11	12	13 Folders Go Home Today	14	15 Test: The Midnight Ride of Paul Revere by Ted Rand	16	17
18	19 Martin Luther King Holiday	20 Bring Note Cards and Research Folder	21 Test: Biomes of the US	22	23 Test: Math	24
25	26 Bring Floppy Disk and Research Folder	27 Folders Go home Today	28	29	30 Presentation: Early American Historical Figure	31

Instant Message

Troubleshooting Tips Remember the following tricks to make your layout more attractive:

- Press CTRL SHIFT H to turn off **Automatic Hyphenation.**
- Use the **Arrange>Snap** menu and ruler guides to align objects.
- Press the ALT key to have more control when you move objects.
- Use the **Show/Hide** tool ¶ to help select text.

Step-by-Step

1. Open a new, 8½" x 11" file in **landscape orientation**. Save it according to your teacher's instructions.
2. Use the **Ellipse** tool and SHIFT to create the top part of your light bulb.
3. Use the **Rectangle** tool to create a narrow rectangle below the circle (Figure 7.39).
4. Use the **Direct Selection** tool to select the *top two* corners of the rectangle. Drag the anchor points to create a trapezoid shape (Figure 7.39).
5. Resize the trapezoid shape, if necessary. Use the **Selection** tool to move the trapezoid shape up to the circle (Figure 7.40).
6. Use the **Rounded Rectangle** tool to draw a small rectangle below the trapezoid.
7. Click the **Selection** tool, and hold ALT to drag three copies of the rounded rectangle.
8. Select the fourth rounded rectangle, and resize it similar to Figure 7.40.
9. Resize and reposition the shapes so that they overlap each other slightly (Figure 7.40).

▼ **Figure 7.39** Use the Direct Selection tool to change a rectangle into a trapezoid.

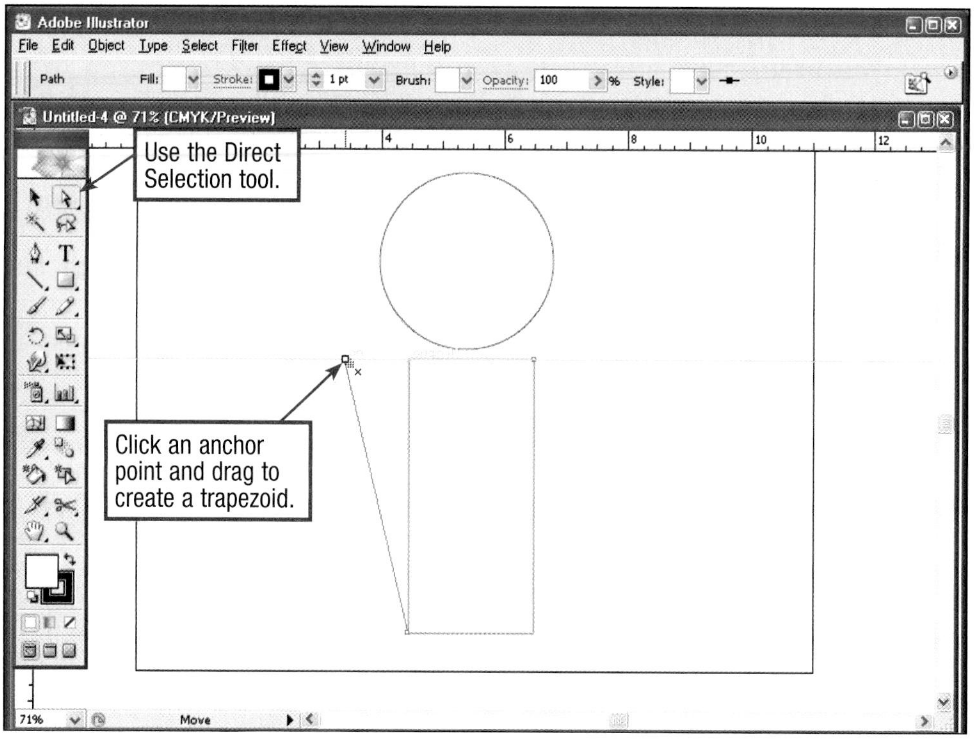

▼ **Figure 7.40** You can create a light bulb illustration using basic shapes in toolbox.

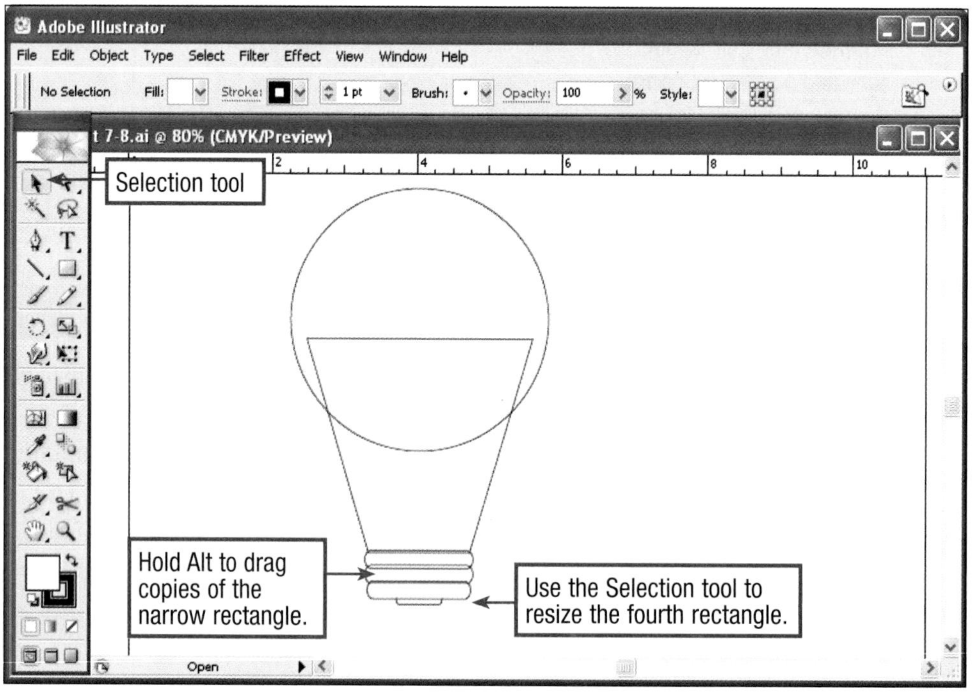

Insert a Calendar Template

7. From the **Design Gallery Objects**, insert a calendar template that spans the bottom of **Pages 2 and 3**. See Figure 4.43 on page 189.

8. **Center align** the calendar relative to the margin guides, and change the calendar month to January 2009.

9. Copy and paste *Dates to Remember* from the scratch area into the correct day on the calendar (Figure 4.43).

10. From the old design, drag the clip art above the calendar and **Bring to Front**. Size and position it so it looks similar to Figure 4.43.

11. **Ungroup** the objects from **Page 2** of the original design. Move them into position on **Page 4** of the new design (Figure 4.44).

12. Apply the **Style Sheet** to make the fonts consistent with the rest of the design.

13. In the *Family Fun Page*, add bullets to the list. (Figure 4.44).

14. Follow your teacher's instructions for saving and printing your work.

▼ **Figure 4.44** Exterior of newsletter.

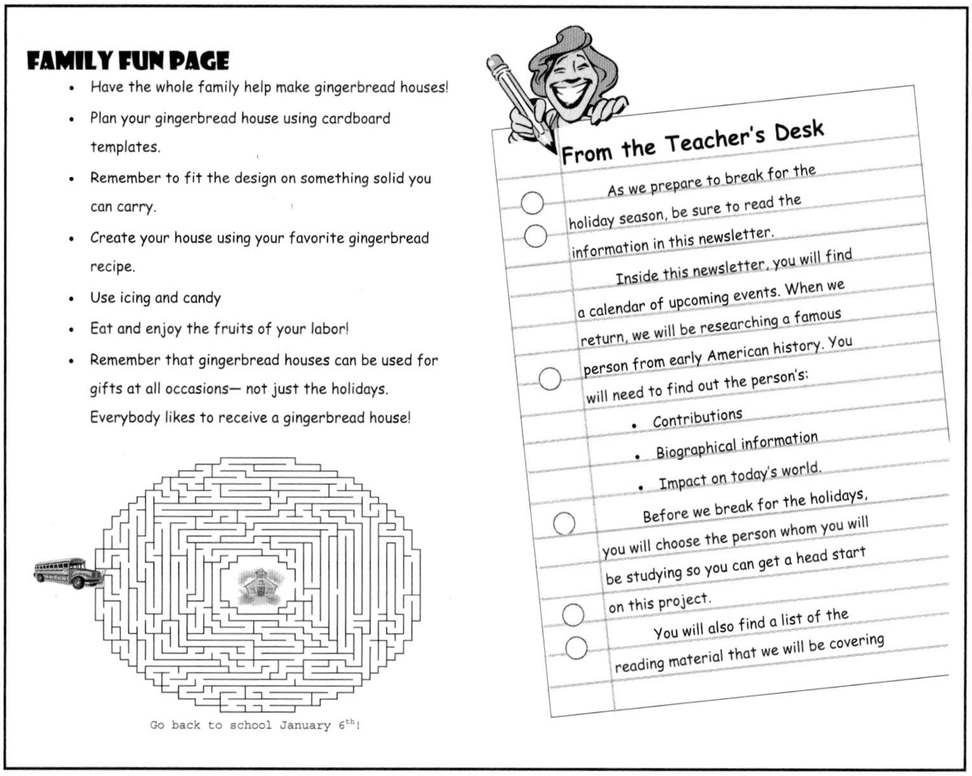

FAMILY FUN PAGE

- Have the whole family help make gingerbread houses!
- Plan your gingerbread house using cardboard templates.
- Remember to fit the design on something solid you can carry.
- Create your house using your favorite gingerbread recipe.
- Use icing and candy
- Eat and enjoy the fruits of your labor!
- Remember that gingerbread houses can be used for gifts at all occasions— not just the holidays. Everybody likes to receive a gingerbread house!

Go back to school January 6th!

From the Teacher's Desk

As we prepare to break for the holiday season, be sure to read the information in this newsletter.

Inside this newsletter, you will find a calendar of upcoming events. When we return, we will be researching a famous person from early American history. You will need to find out the person's:

- Contributions
- Biographical information
- Impact on today's world.

Before we break for the holidays, you will choose the person whom you will be studying so you can get a head start on this project.

You will also find a list of the reading material that we will be covering

REVIEW AND REVISE

Check your work Use Figures 4.43 and 4.44 as guides and check that:

- ☑ The newsletter is in booklet form, sized to be printed on an 8½ by 11 inch sheet of paper.
- ☑ Text flows between the first and second page.
- ☑ Images and text are effective for a young audience.
- ☑ Content is grouped in a way that makes it easy to read information.
- ☑ Alignment and contrast add visual interest, while displaying content clearly.
- ☑ Font styles are applied consistently for effective repetition.

Skills Studio

Project 7-8

Create a Text Illustration

Skills You Will Apply

- Add shape to area
- Apply text outlines

Academic Focus

Language Arts
Communicate a specific message

Well-designed text illustrations are effective eye-catching graphics that help your audience focus on the message of the publication. Like logos, the combination of text and graphics should communicate an instantly recognizable message. Keep the message simple, yet interesting. The design must attract the reader's attention, but it should not overpower the message.

Illustrator palettes help make it easy for you to follow PARC guidelines when you design publications using text illustrations. For example, the Character palette provides options to set the kerning, leading, and tracking in addition to the drop-down menus for font style and font size. Alignment and paragraph indentions are selected from the Paragraph palette.

To switch between the individual menus within the palette windows, click the tabs. Use the palettes below to quickly and easily manage text in your illustrations.

Palettes for Text Graphics

Palette	Usage
Character	Kerning and tracking are found under this palette. The Options button for this palette contains Small Caps, Superscript, and Subscript options.
Glyphs	Here you will find extended characters in a font (this is similar to the Insert>Symbol feature in Microsoft Word). Letters with accents, some ligatures, and special symbols are found here.
Paragraph	This palette contains the alignment options. The Options button in this palette also contains hyphenation settings.
Tabs	Use this palette to set tab stops and leaders. The leaders function is exciting to use: any symbol you can type can be a leader. The palette also includes a ruler and a magnet button to align the palette with text boxes. This feature enables you to use the ruler to set tab stops the same way you do in Microsoft Word and Publisher.

▲ The palettes described above help you control text in Illustrator. Use **Window>Type** to access any of these palettes.

► **In this project,** you will create a flyer using text graphics. Imagine that your desktop publishing teacher has asked you to create a flyer encouraging students to sign up for next semester's design class. Your teacher would like you to use a text illustration as part of the design. You decide to create a light bulb illustration with a text message to show how the class encourages creativity.

In The Workplace

Layout Artist

Layout artists are responsible for combining text and graphics in a document so that it is ready to be published. They are usually part of a team that puts together materials such as books, magazines, newspapers, catalogs, advertisements, or brochures. Even items such as greeting cards, directories, and business forms can require the skills of a layout artist.

On the Job

Layout artists might also be graphic designers, though often their job comes after the design stage. They make sure that the text and images are placed accurately and clearly on a page and that no elements are lost or run too long. Often layout artists need to work with editors or designers to make sure that the content fits a template or does not exceed the number of pages allowed for a particular publication.

Since publishing today is done electronically, layout artists must know how to use professional layout software such as Adobe® InDesign® or QuarkXPress®. It is also helpful for them to have broader desktop publishing skills that might include knowing about design, typography, graphics, and software such as Adobe Photoshop and Adobe Illustrator.

Publishing companies, print shops, and advertising agencies need layout artists to help create the many print products they produce. A wide variety of industries use layout artists for their own in-house publications. For example, large corporations, government offices, universities, and non-profit organizations often publish their own materials.

Future Outlook

There is a strong demand for layout artists as more in-house jobs become available. For more information about this field, go to the following Web sites:

- **U.S. Department of Labor Bureau of Labor Statistics (www.bls.gov)** has an online Occupational Outlook Handbook that provides information about careers related to desktop publishing.
- **A Digital Dreamer (www.adigitaldreamer.com)** is a Web site that provides information about a variety of careers involving digital graphics.

Training

Layout artists usually require graphic arts training in order to learn design and software skills. Certification programs and degrees are offered in vocational schools, technical colleges, online programs, and universities.

Salary Range

Depending on the employer, experience, or location, a layout artist earns between $20,000 and $53,000 a year.

Skills and Talents

Layout Artists need to have:

- Knowledge of various software programs
- Good design skills and visual perception
- Attention to details
- Understanding of print and publishing operations
- Problem-solving skills
- Communication skills
- The ability to work independently to meet deadlines

Career Activity

What is the difference between a layout artist and a graphic designer?

Skills Studio

Reinforce Your Skills

- **Project 7-8**
  Create an illustration with shapes
  Apply text outlines
- **Project 7-9**
  Design with Type on a Path tool
  Apply fills and effects

Go Online ACTIVITIES
www.glencoe.com

Challenge Yourself Go to **Chapter 7**, and choose **Enrichment Activities** for more practice with the skills you have learned.

Design with Text Illustrations

The following two projects will take you through the steps you need to create a text illustration:

- **Project 7-8** Create a text illustration
- **Project 7-9** Enhance your text illustration

Text Illustrations

The single most important element in a design is the message. The graphics, the layout, and all other aspects of the design help deliver the message more effectively. It is tempting to add more graphics than may be needed in a design simply because they are colorful and easy to use. The message may be lost, however, if the graphics are overdone.

Sometimes the text itself can be designed as a graphic. Illustrator's text tool options allow you to create text in a number of ways. You can enter text inside any path shape such as a rectangle, a circle, or even imaginative shapes that you create. Text can also be added to any path. The path can be circular, spiral, horizontal, or vertical. Even the alignment, orientation, and other type attributes of individual characters can be changed on the text's path.

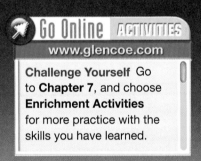

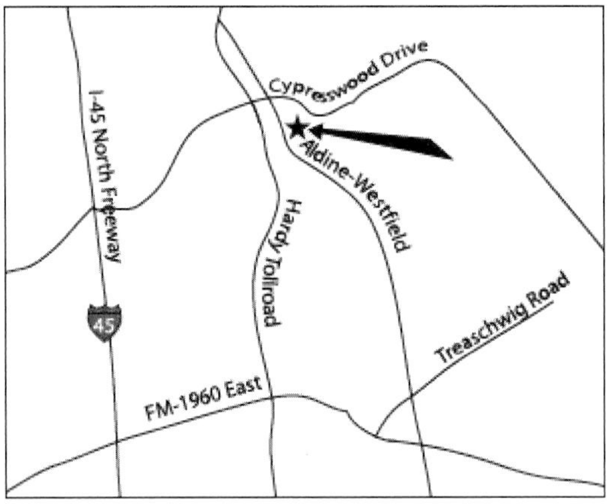

▲ Illustrator's tool for typing on text paths is especially useful for creating maps.

For maximum effect, consider factors such as the shapes to use, the alignment of text, and the use of horizontal and vertical space surrounding the text illustration.

Try to make these designs visually interesting and not too text-heavy. Challenge your imagination, and have fun creating designs with text. Though remember, the design must invite the reader to focus on the message of the text.

Chapter 4 Assessment

Reading Check

1. **Define** What are the four design principles known as PARC?
2. **Identify** What is the difference between an *orphan* and a *widow* in text layout?
3. **Describe** Explain the design process and why it is a spiral rather than a list.
4. **Analyze** Why did the ancient Greeks believe the Golden Ratio could be used to design buildings and artworks?
5. **Evaluate** Why is it useful to be able to export or import style sheets?

Critical Thinking

6. **Identify** Describe five ways to create proximity in a document.
7. **Describe** Discuss one way you can create an *entry point* in a publication.
8. **Summarize** Describe the planning stage of a project and why it is so important.
9. **Compare** Give four reasons how designing for a Web page is different from designing for print.
10. **Compare** Describe three differences and three similarities between a high school newsletter and a newsletter sent to bank customers.

1 Independent Practice

LANGUAGE ARTS **Evaluate and Design an Advertisement** Look in a local newspaper or Yellow Pages and find an ad that you think could have a better design according to PARC principles.

a. Plan Write an analysis of what works and does not work in the ad.

- Determine from the original ad what the client might have wanted, who the audience is, and any publishing restrictions you might have like size and color.
- Evaluate the design for proximity, alignment, repetition, and contrast.
- Identify specific problems, and explain how you would correct each one.

b. Design Create at least three sketches of new designs.

- Include at least one graphic and at least two alignments.
- Get feedback from classmates or your teacher to choose the best one.

c. Create Use Publisher to create a new advertisement.

- The advertisement should be the same size as the original.
- Use at least two colors. If you can only use black and white, include shades of gray.

d. Publish Follow your teacher's instructions for printing your design. Evaluate it according to PARC principles and revise if necessary.

Go Online RUBRICS
www.glencoe.com

Independent Practice
Go to **Chapter 4**, and choose **Rubrics**. Use the rubrics to help create and evaluate your projects.

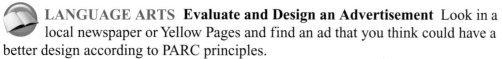

9 In the toolbox, click the **Type** tool [T]. Click below the flag, and key Old Glory.

10 Select the text. On the **Control** palette, change the font to **Poor Richard**. Resize as needed.

Warp Text

11 Use the **Selection** tool to select the text again. Click **Object>Envelope Distort>Make with Warp**.

12 In the Warp Options box, choose the *Style* **Flag** (Figure 7.37).

13 Check the **Preview** box, and adjust the settings until you have distorted the text in an attractive way. Click **OK**.

14 Select both the text and the flag. On the **Align** palette, choose **Horizontal Align Center**.

15 Your flag should look similar to Figure 7.38. Follow your teacher's instructions for saving and printing your work.

▼ Figure 7.37 Distortion effects can be applied to text as well as graphics.

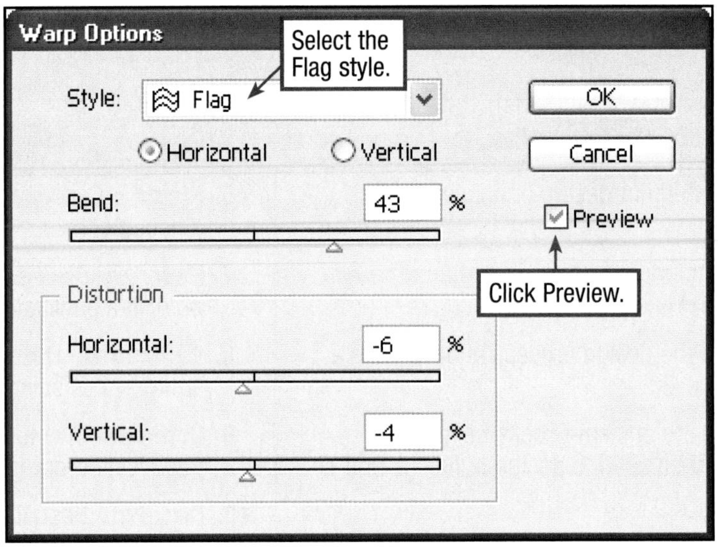

▼ Figure 7.38 Make sure your flag and text are in the printable workspace area.

REVIEW AND REVISE

Check your work Use Figure 7.38 as a guide and check that:

- ☑ There are 13 stripes and 50 stars on the flag. The colors are correct.
- ☑ Stripes and stars are all identical in shape and size.
- ☑ Envelope distortion effects have been applied in a realistic way.
- ☑ The text is accurate and readable, even with the warped effects.

2 Independent Practice ★★

SOCIAL STUDIES **Create a *Tips for Teens* Brochure** Your town's Chamber of Commerce wants you to create a brochure aimed at high school students. It will be a guide to places where students can find inexpensive and satisfying food, recreation, and culture.

a. Plan Choose at least three examples for each of the three categories above. Prepare short descriptions of each, including prices, locations, and hours.

b. Design Your brochure will be tri-fold.

- Decide what graphics and fonts you want to use for this audience. Use at least two graphics and two different fonts.
- By hand, sketch at least two designs for your brochure, following PARC principles.

c. Create Combine your text and graphics into a tri-fold brochure.

d. Publish Follow your teacher's instructions for printing the brochure. Evaluate it according to PARC principles and revise, if necessary.

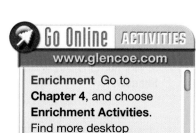

3 Independent Practice ★★★

TEAMWORK **Practice for an FBLA Event** Future Business Leaders of America (FBLA) is an organization that holds competitive events to prepare students who want to go into business. Desktop publishing is one of the competencies that is tested, and design is an important part of the score.

a. Plan With a teammate, choose a topic that you would like to develop.

- Go to the FBLA–High School Web site at www.fbla.org, and find the topics that will be discussed in the competitive events.
- Decide what type of publication you should create to present the topic. It must be either a newsletter or brochure.
- Research and gather content for your publication.

b. Create Design and create your newsletter or brochure using FBLA Competitive Event Guidelines for desktop publishing or Web site development. (You can find this information on the FBLA Web site.)

Go Online ACTIVITIES
www.glencoe.com

Enrichment Go to **Chapter 4**, and choose **Enrichment Activities.** Find more desktop publishing projects using Microsoft Publisher.

Step-by-Step

1. Open the flag file that you create in Project 7-6. Save it according to your teacher's instructions.

2. Use the Selection tool to select the flag shape.

Distort an Image

3. Click **Object>Envelope Distort> Make with Mesh**.

4. In the **Envelope Mesh** box, set **4 rows** and **4 columns**. Click **OK**. Then click off the flag to deselect it (Figure 7.35).

5. Click the **Direct Selection** tool to drag a selection around a single anchor point on the grid. This will activate the entire grid.

6. Select and drag individual points in the grid to distort the flag into an attractive shape. If you do not like a shape, press CTRL + Z to undo the move.

Add a Drop Shadow

7. When the shape is satisfactory, select the flag. Click **Effect>Stylize>Drop Shadow**.

8. In the **Drop Shadow** box, click **Preview**. See what happens to the shadow when you change the settings. (Figure 7.36).

▼ Figure 7.35 Setting more rows gives you greater control, but it can also make the process more confusing.

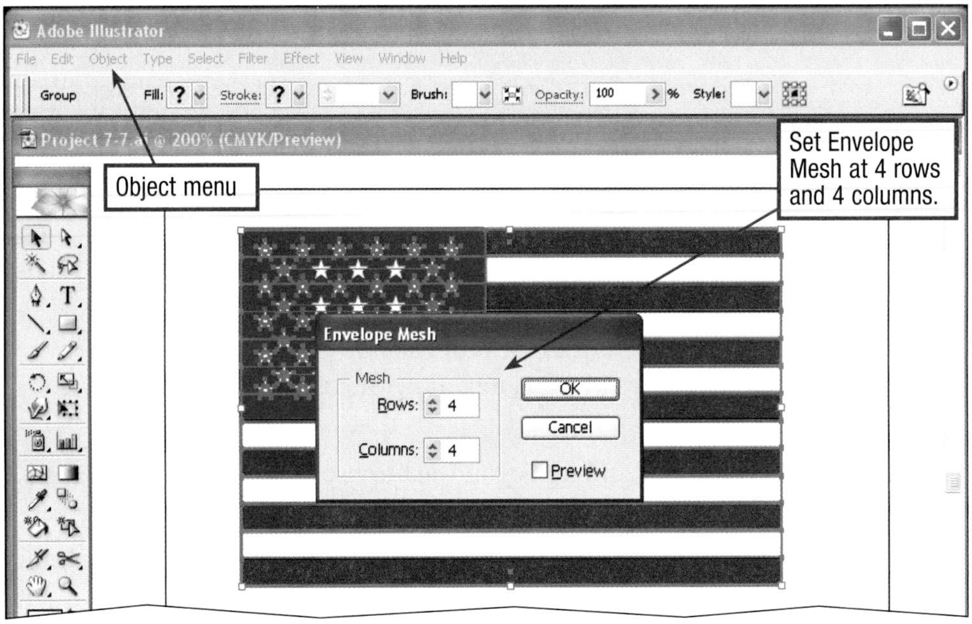

▼ Figure 7.36 Be bold with your mesh distortion. You can always make changes.

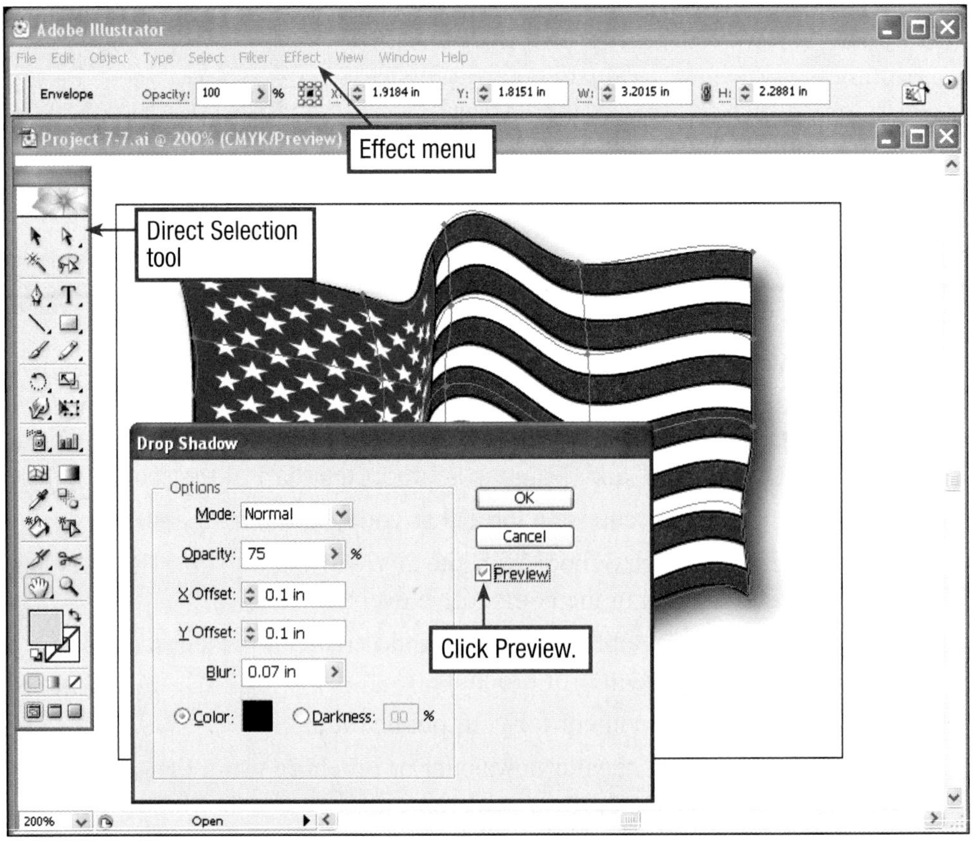

UNIT 2 Projects Across the Curriculum

The skills you learned in this unit will help you in your other classes, too. Use your desktop publishing skills to complete the following projects. Follow your teacher's instructions for saving or printing your work.

Project 1 Create a Flyer with Tear-offs ★

SCIENCE Your science class is sponsoring a Night of the Stars event, where you will set up telescopes to see astronomical sites. Create a flyer advertising the event.

Plan

1. Go to an astronomy Web site, like **StarDate.org**. Find an interesting event for people to view in your night sky.
2. Write up a description of the event.

Create

3. Design your flyer according to PARC principles. Include:
   a. At least one image (make sure you cite any source).
   b. At least two fonts and a spot color (use gray for printing in black and white).
   c. Tear-offs with the name, date, and time of the Night of the Stars.

Go Online RUBRICS
www.glencoe.com
Unit: Projects Go to **Unit 2**, and choose **Rubrics**. Use the projects to help create and evaluate your work.

Project 2 Create a Personal Budget Planner ★★

MATH Although often overlooked, business forms do require effective design and layout. Use your newly acquired design skills to create a budget planner.

Plan

1. Look over Publisher's Business Form templates to get an idea of how you might lay out your budget planner.
2. Draw a sketch showing the headers for columns and rows such as Date, Payment, Description, Total, Expense, and Balance. Insert enough rows to record your expenses for a week.

Create

3. Insert a table and format it so that it is visually appealing and easy to read. Use Publisher's Help if you need instructions about using a table.
4. Add Design Gallery objects, clip art, or borders to personalize your form.

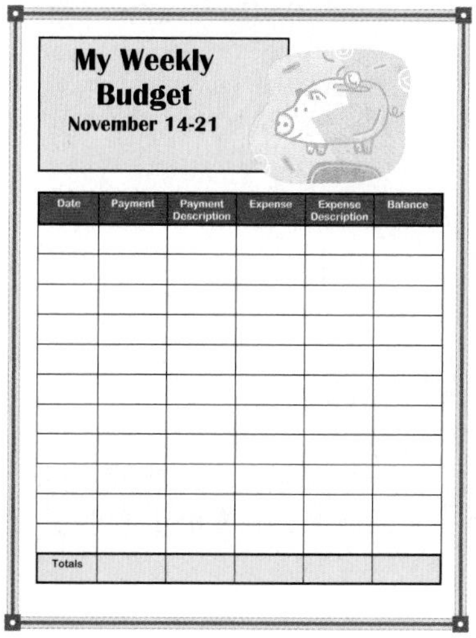
My Weekly Budget
November 14-21

Date	Payment	Payment Description	Expense	Expense Description	Balance
Totals					

Project 7-7

Add Distort Effects

Spotlight on Skills

- Distort an image
- Add a drop shadow
- Warp text

Key Term

- warp

Academic Focus

Social Studies
Create an American flag

Have you ever looked at yourself in a fun house mirror? Do you remember how the distorted images grabbed your attention? Illustrator has a tool called Envelope Distort, which places an invisible "envelope" over an object, allowing you to **warp**, or bend, the image to make it unusual and visually exciting.

There are three kinds of Envelope Distortion effects:

- **Make with Warp** has preset warp shapes.
- **Make with Mesh** gives you control over the distortion effect applied to your object. You can click and drag elements to stretch them like taffy.
- **Make with Top Object** adds effects to text so that it matches the shape of open books, or angled walls and signs, as in the figure below.

▲ A wide variety of warp options, each with customizable effects, is available to distort a drawing, photograph, or text.

The Envelope Distort tool is accessed through the Object menu. The mesh is activated by clicking and dragging a point or group of points with the Direct Selection tool. Once an envelope is applied, it is not easy to make changes to the object. Think of the envelope as a fun house mirror in front of the object, distorting your view of the object. You cannot recolor or delete part of a mirror, so you must switch to the object itself.

▶ **In this project,** you will use the Distort Envelope on the American flag you created in Project 7-6. The effect will make the flag look like it is waving in the breeze.

Sidebar

Distort Commands
Access these tools in Object>Envelope Distort:

- **Edit Contents** allows you to see the envelope to make changes without changing the shape.
- **Release** deletes an effect and reverts back to the original object.
- **Expand** makes the effects permanent and simplifies your document.

Evaluate Why do you want to see the envelope when editing?

UNIT 2

Projects Across the Curriculum

Project 3 Create a Brochure with a Coupon ★★

SOCIAL STUDIES Create a tri-fold brochure for a travel agency that specializes in time-travel tours. They want to include a coupon for booking a trip with them.

Plan

1. Choose a time and place in history that you think would be interesting to visit and write an itinerary for a tour. An itinerary includes the sites that will be visited, the dates of the trip, the modes of transportation, and the lodging details.

Create

2. Your brochure should follow PARC guidelines and include:
- Information about the tour and appropriate graphics to illustrate it.
- Contact information for the tourist agency.
- A coupon offering a 10 percent discount to the first ten customers.

Project 4 Add Hyperlinks to a Web Site ★★★

LANGUAGE ARTS Complete the Shakespeare Web site you started in Project 4-7. Add a page and hyperlinks for each button on the home page.

Plan

1. Research Shakespeare's life and work. Make a list of his plays and important dates in his life and times. Find at least two Shakespeare sonnets, and write an explanation of the sonnet form.

2. Create an information page for the Hamlet production.

Create

3. Create a master page for your Web site design.

4. Add four pages to your original page, one for each of the buttons.
- Add content from your research to the appropriate pages.
- Add hyperlink buttons to all the pages.

Publish

5. Proofread your work and, if possible, publish it as a Web page.

20 Drag a third copy, and place it below the first one.

21 Double-click the **Blend** tool. Change the **Specified Steps** to **4**. Click **OK**.

22 Click each star in the top row, making sure to click in the middle, not on an anchor point (Figure 7.33).

23 Use the stars in the second row to create a row of **5** stars with the **Blend** tool (Figure 7.33).

24 Group each row. Then select and drag copies of the two rows, alternating them as shown in Figure 7.34. Create **5 rows of 6 stars** and **4 rows of 5 stars**.

25 Select all the rows. On the Control palette, click **Horizontal Align Center** and **Vertical Distribute Center**.

26 Use the **Selection** tool to select the entire flag shape and press CTRL + G to group all the objects.

27 Follow your teacher's instructions for saving your work. You will continue working on your flag in Project 7-7.

▼ **Figure 7.33** The Blend tool makes it easy to quickly add the 50 stars to the flag.

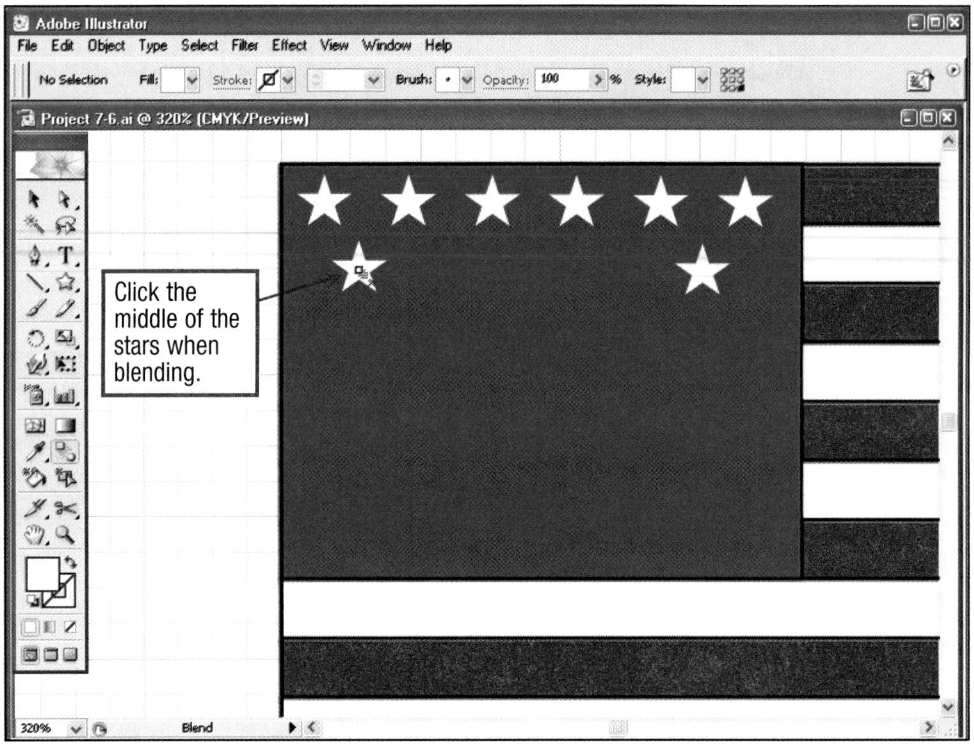

▼ **Figure 7.34** Group all the objects in your flag.

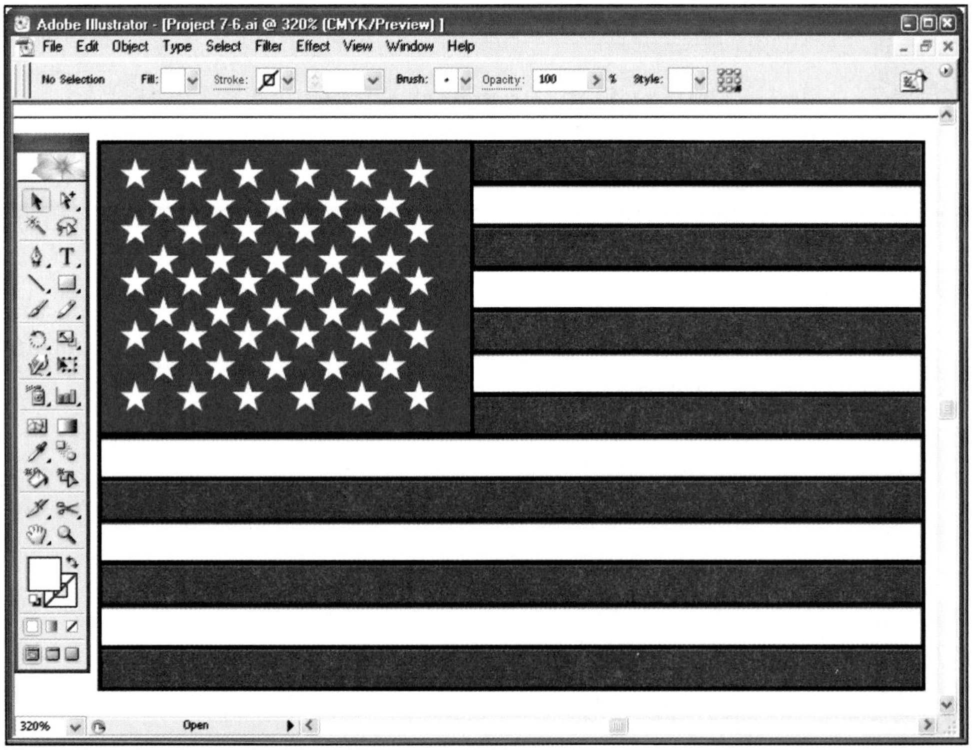

UNIT 3

Design with Adobe Photoshop

Contents

9 With the stripes still selected, click **Object>Ungroup**.

10 Press SHIFT and select the first stripe, and then every other odd stripe below it.

11 On the **Control** palette, click the **Fill** arrow to open the Swatches drop-down menu. Choose **Red** (Figure 7.31).

12 Select all the stripes, and press CTRL + G to group them together.

13 Click the **Rectangle** tool to drag out a rectangle over seven stripes (Figure 7.32).

14 Select the rectangle. Repeat Step 11 to change the square color to **Starry Night Blue**.

15 Click the **Rectangle** tool to open the **Star** tool ☆.

16 Click **Select>Deselect** to deselect the rectangle. Press D to restore default colors.

17 Change the **Stroke** color to **None**.

18 Select the **Star tool**. Then click to drag a star into the workspace. While dragging, use the Up or Down arrows on your keyboard to add or remove star points until you have a five-pointed star. Hold SHIFT to draw it straight ALT to force the points to be sharp (Figure 7.32).

19 Hold ALT and use the **Selection** tool to drag a second copy of the star to the top right corner of the rectangle.

▼ **Figure 7.31** The Control palette provides quick color options.

▼ **Figure 7.32** Magnify the flag to add stars.

Chapter 7 Project 7-6 Create a Drawing with the Blend Tool

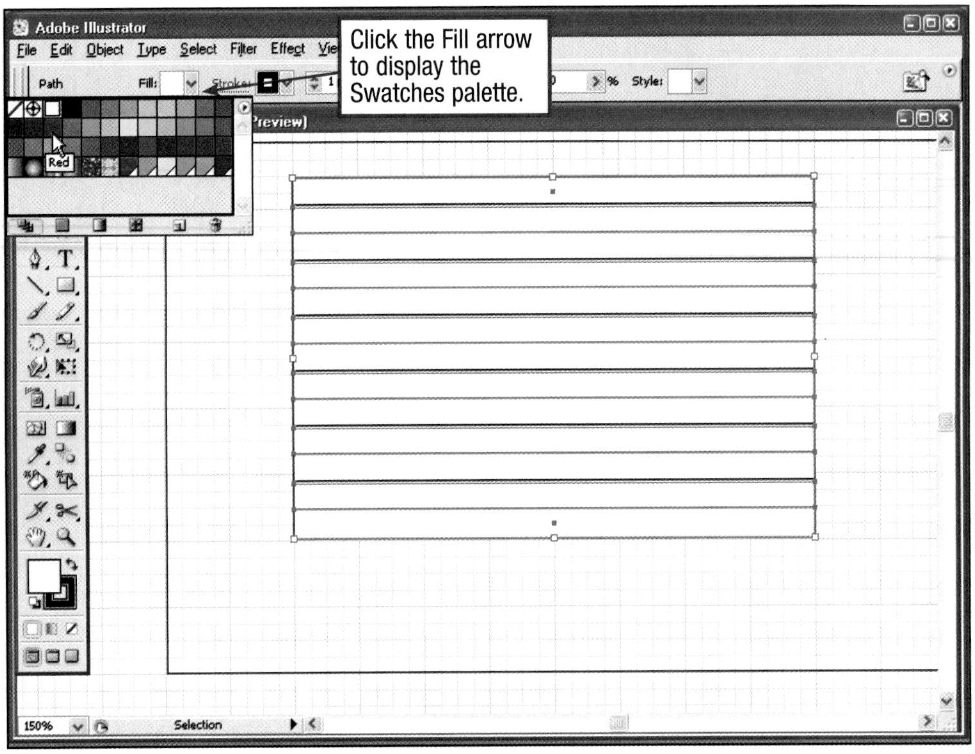

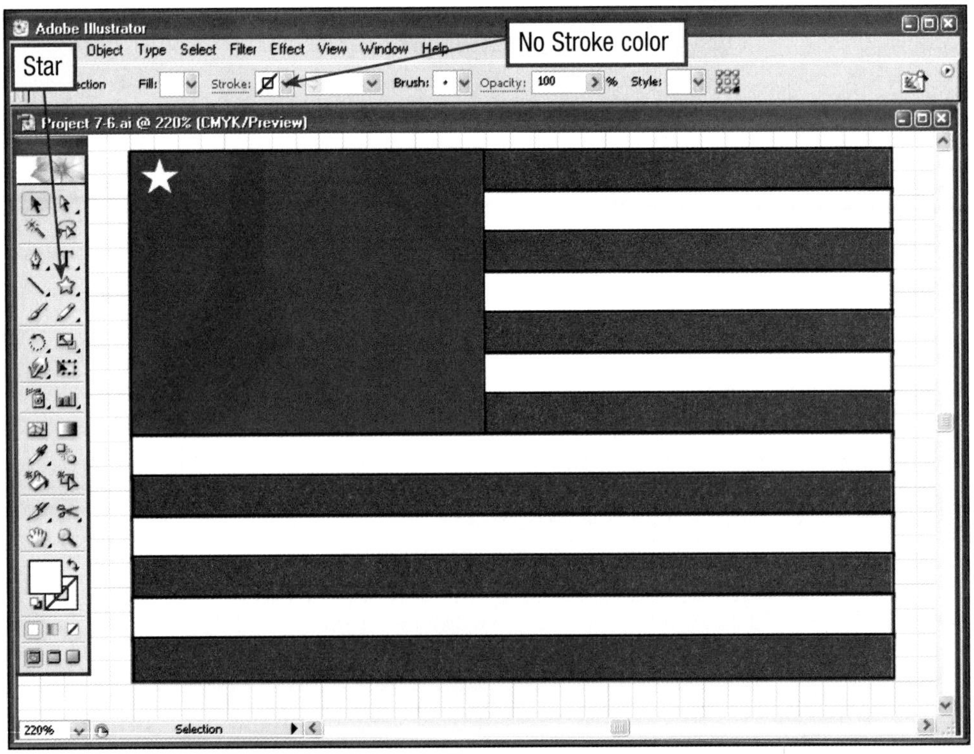

Chapter 5 Introducing Adobe Photoshop

Skills You Will Learn

Adobe® Photoshop® is a popular software application used to create and edit digital images. It is a very powerful program that is used by professionals like graphic artists, photographers, and Web designers. Many of the images you see on commercial products and in publications have been either created or refined with Photoshop.

Add Photographs to Publications

Photographs are an important part of everyday life. From food packaging to magazine covers to billboards, photographs create interest. They provide visual information in newspapers. In catalogs, they let you judge whether you want to buy a product. A photo on a cereal box might get you thinking about how those crunchy-looking flakes will taste for tomorrow's breakfast.

Although photographs themselves are not desktop publications, using them can make a publication more interesting and attractive. Photographs placed in documents should follow the PARC design principles. They should be in close proximity to the text that they illustrate, and they should align with other objects. Too many photographs can distract from the message and make it difficult to understand the purpose of the material. Photographs should be sized appropriately so they do not overwhelm other important elements on the page.

DESIGN PROCESS: PHOTOGRAPHS

Elements	Issues
Purpose	To provide visual information, add visual excitement, express an artistic vision, attract attention, or create mental associations.
Audience	Varies. Photos in a children's book, a training manual for adults, or a jeans ad for teenagers will each look very different.
Content	Photos providing visual information must show content clearly. Photos meant to attract attention might rely more on style.
Layout	Depends on whether the photograph is the main focus of the publication, or whether it is illustrating other content.
Publication	Photos appear in a variety of print publications, as well as Web publications and commercial products like CD covers, posters, product packaging, etc.

Step-by-Step

1. In Illustrator, open a new document. Set a **custom** size, **6 inches wide** by **4 inches high**. Save according to your teacher's instructions.

2. Click **View>Smart Guides**.

3. Press D to restore color defaults to white fill and black stroke.

4. Use the **Rectangle** tool to create a rectangle **4 inches wide**, **0.225 inches high**. (Click in the workspace to open the dialog box to see the object dimensions.) Place the rectangle at the top of the workspace (Figure 7.29).

5. Click the **Selection** tool. Press ALT to drag out a copy of the rectangle to the bottom of the workspace.

Apply Blending Options

6. In the toolbox, double-click the **Blend** tool. In the **Blend Options** box, change *Spacing* to **Specified Steps**, and set **11** steps (Figure 7.30).

7. In the workspace, click the top and bottom rectangles. Eleven copies of the rectangle are created between the first two (Figure 7.30).

8. Click the **Selection** tool to select the blended stripes. Click **Object>Expand** to make the effect permanent. **Click OK**.

▼ Figure 7.29 Press the Alt key to drag a copy of the rectangle.

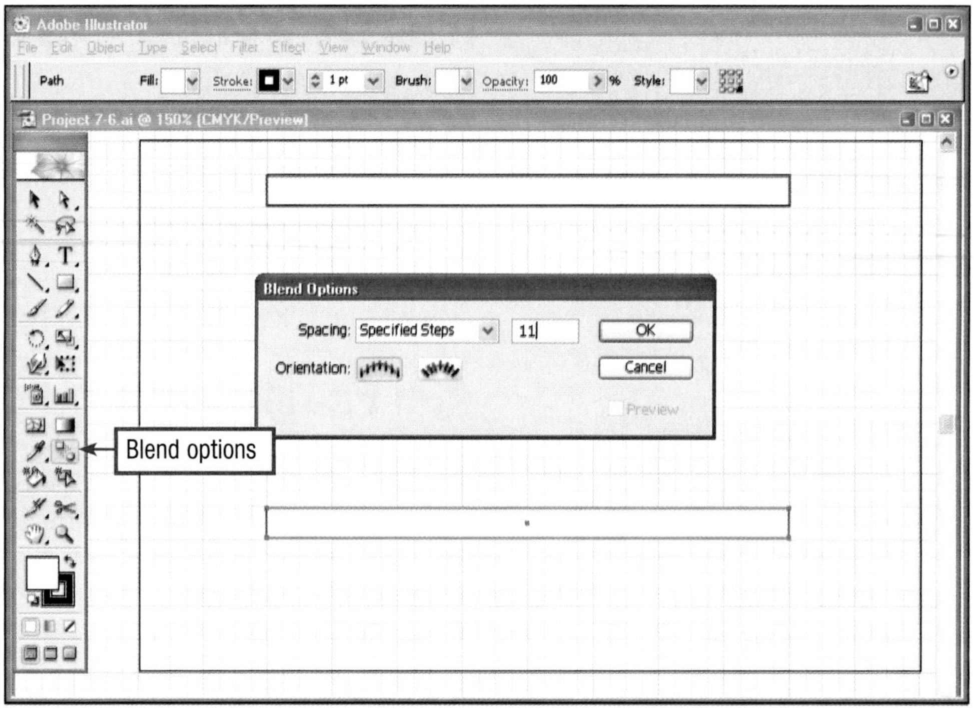

▼ Figure 7.30 Use the Expand command to make the blend permanent.

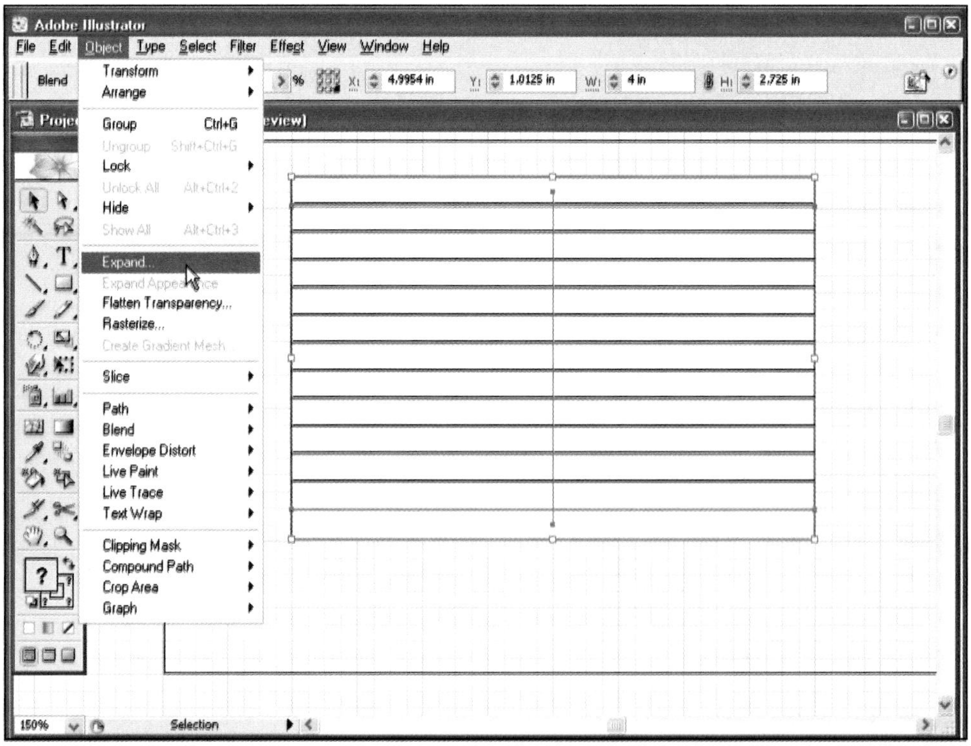

WORK SHOP

Foundations

You Will Learn To

- Identify raster images
- Determine resolution
- Identify raster image file formats

Key Terms

raster graphics
pixel
scalable
resolution
pixelated
file name extension

Before You Read

Reading for a Purpose
Just as an author's purpose helps determine what content will be put into a chapter, your purpose for reading helps you decide what is important to remember. Quickly read the "You Will Learn To" points and key terms. Look over the headings and assessment questions. Then complete this sentence before you begin to read: My purpose for reading this section is to ________.

Explore Raster Graphics

In Photoshop, you will create and edit different raster images. **Raster graphics** are digital images made up of thousands of tiny colored squares that blend together to form a picture. The squares are called pixels. A **pixel** is a picture element, the smallest square of color in an image.

▲ When you look at a close-up of a raster image, you can see the individual pixels.

For every square of color in an image, the computer stores the RGB (red, green, blue) settings. Information for thousands of pixels in the image must be stored. That is why files containing raster images can be very large. (For more information on color and how to use it effectively, see Appendix A, Color Theory, in the back of this book.)

What Is Resolution?

In Unit 1, you worked with vector images. The computer stores vector images as math formulas. When these images are moved or resized, the computer redraws the image by recalculating its dimensions. Vector images, therefore, are **scalable**. This means they can be resized without any loss of image clarity, or **resolution**. The higher the resolution, the greater the image detail.

Project 7-6 Create a Drawing with the Blend Tool

Spotlight on Skills

- Apply blending options

Key Term

- morph

Academic Focus

Social Studies
Create the American flag

The Blend tool can be accessed on the toolbox or by clicking **Object>Blend>Blend Options**. The Blend command is different from the blend modes you accessed from the Transparency palette. Blend modes change the transparency or opacity of an object. The Blend tool evenly distributes shapes or colors between selected objects.

If the tool is used to create shapes between two identical objects, it can create any number of copies of the object as shown in the figure below.

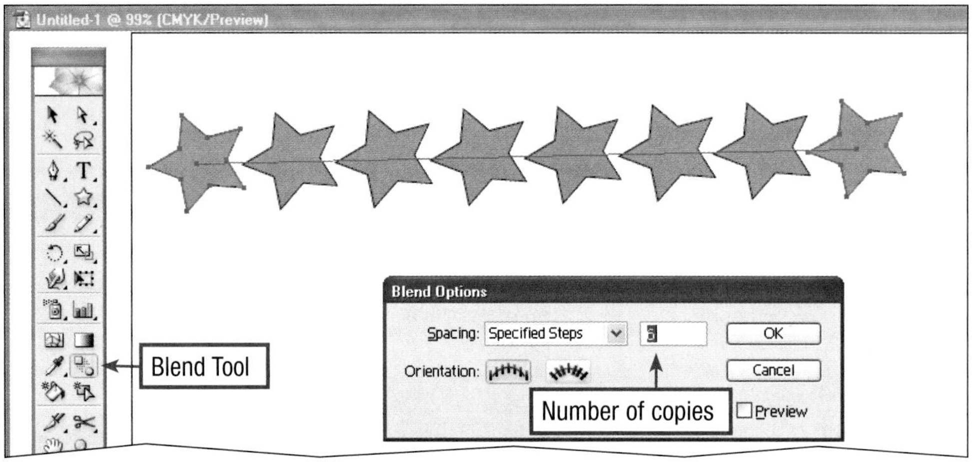

► The Blend tool easily creates as many identical shapes as needed for your design illustrations.

When the Blend tool is used to blend two different objects, it creates shapes and colors between the two that **morph**, or change from the first shape into the second. The tool can also be used to blend colors and shapes within an image. Smooth shading, complex contours, and animations can be created by using the features of the Blend tool.

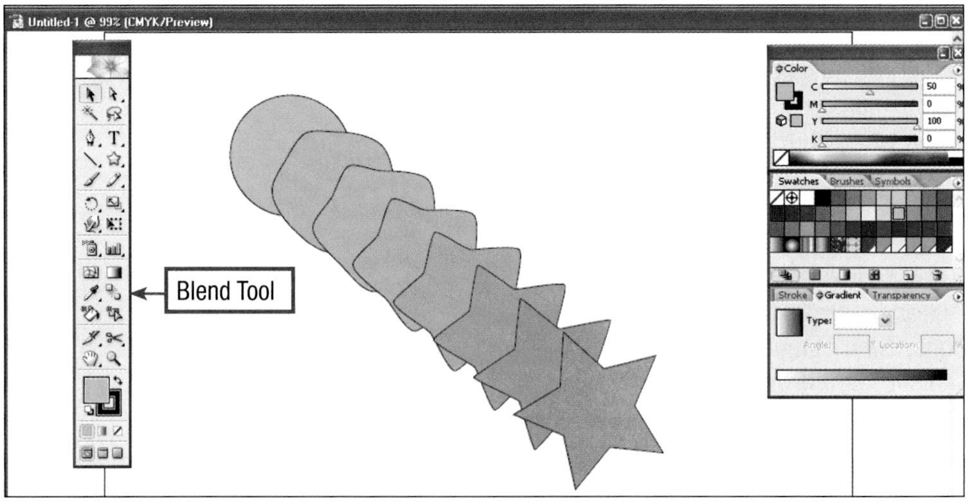

► Use the Blend tool to create shapes and colors morphing from one shape into a second shape.

► **In this project,** you will create an American flag using the Blend tool to duplicate the thirteen stripes and fifty stars.

Resizing Raster Images

Raster images are not scalable. When they are enlarged, the images look either blurry or **pixelated**, which means that the individual pixels are visible. When raster images are resized, it is actually the pixels in the image that are resized. If the picture is made larger, the pixels become bigger and more noticeable. If the picture is made smaller, the pixels are smaller, giving the image a better resolution.

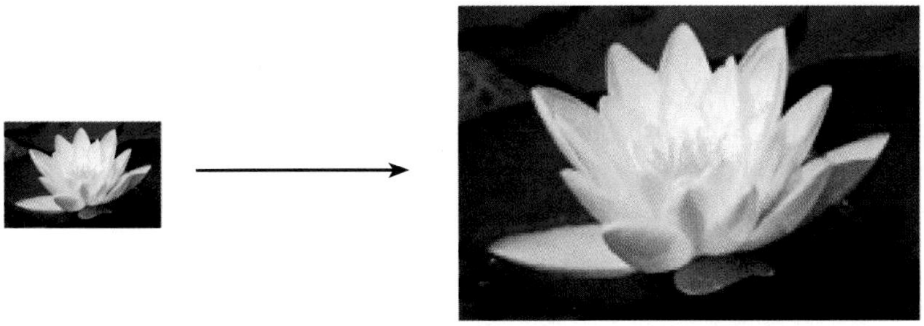

▲ When you enlarge a raster image, it loses resolution and detail because the pixels get larger.

Print and Monitor Resolutions

The resolution of a raster image is shown in dots per inch (dpi) or pixels per inch (ppi).

- Printer resolution is measured in dots per inch (dpi). Publications usually use images with a resolution of 300 or more dpi, depending on the printer.
- The resolution of a monitor is usually described in pixels per inch. Images displayed on monitors do not need as high a resolution as printed photos because a monitor cannot display as high a resolution as a printer.

When you print an image, the size and clarity of the image is based on the number of pixels in the image and its resolution. Two images with the same number of pixels, but different resolutions, will print out at different sizes. The image with higher resolution, such as 300 dots per inch, will be smaller. An image of 72 dpi, however, will be much larger because the same number of pixels are spread out over a wider area. If you plan to make an image a certain size, you must make sure that the resolution will be clear at that size. The more dots per inch in an image, the higher the resolution. The higher the resolution, the larger the file size. Only use the resolution you need. If you do not need high resolution, you should save your image at a lower dpi to save storage space and to make it faster to open or send files.

Sidebar

Storing Pixels With raster graphics, the computer remembers the Red, Green and Blue (RGB) value of each and every pixel. At a screen resolution of 800 x 600, the computer stores RGB information for 480,000 pixels. Even if the pixel is not actively used, the computer stores the code for white. Since the computer must store three color values for each pixel, it takes 1,440,000 pieces of data to recreate one screen!

Calculate In the example above, how is the figure 1,440,000 determined?

5 In the toolbox, open the **Ellipse** tool. Draw a small ellipse in the workspace (Figure 7.27).

6 Fill the ellipse with **white**, **no stroke**.

7 Select the ellipse, then rotate and reposition the ellipse on the eye (Figure 7.27).

Compare Opacity Levels

8 Select the ellipse. In the **Transparency** palette, change the blending mode to **Hard Light** and the **Opacity** to **40%**.

▼ **Figure 7.27** Play with the opacity levels to see how the effects change.

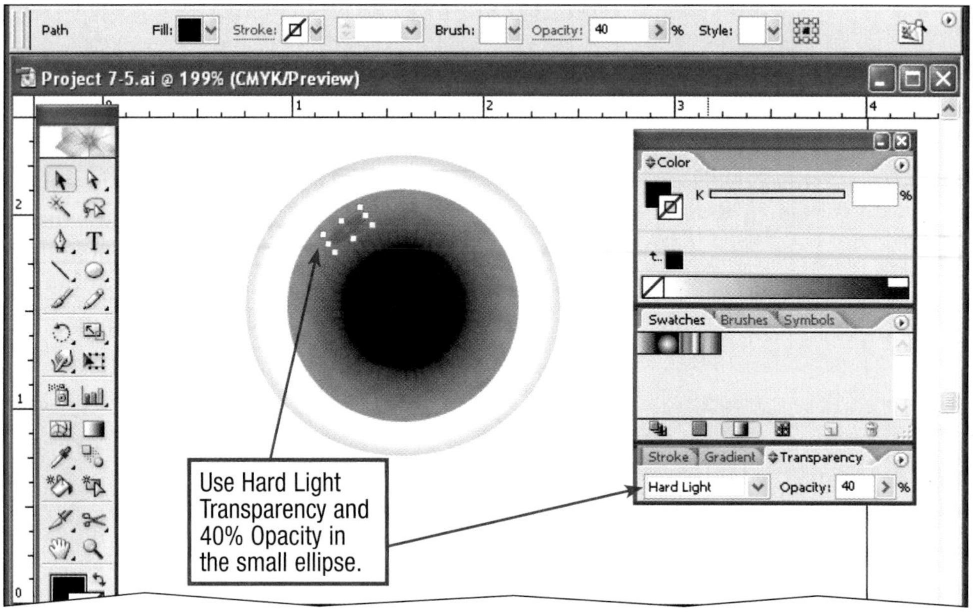

9 Create two smaller ellipses, one with **40 percent opacity** and one with **60 percent**. Position them as shown in Figure 7.28.

10 Use the **Selection** tool to select all the objects in the eye, and click **Object>Group**.

11 Your eye should look similar to Figure 7.28. Follow your teacher's instructions for saving and printing your work.

▼ **Figure 7.28** The blending makes it look like light is being reflected in the eye.

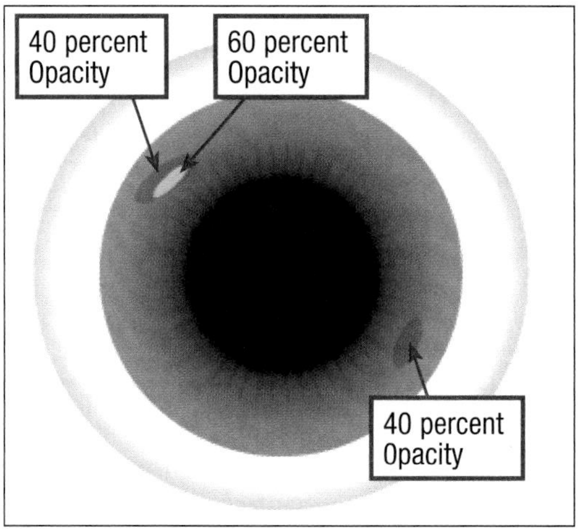

REVIEW AND REVISE

Check your work Use Figure 7.28 as a guide and check that:

- ☑ The pupil, colored iris, and white of the eye all use gradient colors.
- ☑ The pupil and iris are centered horizontally and vertically in relation to each other and the white of the eye.
- ☑ There is a 48 pt semi-transparent black star around the pupil.
- ☑ There are three ellipses of different sizes and opacities.

What Are Raster File Formats?

Raster images are often saved in the following file formats. You can usually tell a file's format by looking at the **file name extension**, the letters displayed after a file name.

Sidebar

Compressing Files Some formats allow you to compress a file size to make it smaller. These are called **lossy** formats, and they compress the file by removing or simplifying data. GIF is a lossy format that reduces the number of colors in an image. **Lossless** formats do not compress file size, but preserve image detail. PNG and TIFF are lossless formats.

Compare Which format would you use if you wanted to e-mail a photo to a friend to view on her computer? Why?

Raster Graphic File Formats

Format Name	File Name Extension	Description
Bitmap	BMP	Pronounced *bit-map*. Not considered appropriate for professional printing.
Graphical Interchange Format	GIF	Pronounced *gif* (hard g). Uses only 256 colors, so is common on the Internet, but not used for professional publishing.
Joint Photographics Expert Group	JPG, JPEG	Pronounced *jay-peg*. A general purpose format that uses smaller file size but reduces the picture quality based on user settings.
Tagged Integrated File Format	TIF, TIFF	Pronounced *tif*. Large file sizes, but good for professional publishing.
Apple Picture	PICT	Pronounced *picked*. File format created by Apple. Generally not considered professional quality.
PNG (Portable Network Graphics)	PNG	Pronounced *ping*. New Web browsers can read this file type, and it is appropriate for professional publishing.
Photoshop format	PSD	A "native file format," used mostly by Adobe products and not readable by other companies' software.

The files you create in Photoshop will have a PSD (Photoshop document) format. You will also see in Chapter 6 that you can save Photoshop files in various graphic file formats such as JPEG and TIFF. These file formats can then be used in other programs such as Publisher.

Reading Check

1. **Explain** How does a computer store raster images?
2. **Compare** Which has a higher resolution, an image that is 72 dpi, or one that is 300 dpi?

Project 7-5

Apply Blending Modes

Spotlight on Skills

- Use the Transparency palette
- Compare opacity levels

Key Terms

- transparent
- opaque

Academic Focus

Science
Compare transparent and opaque states

As you know, images are often composed of layers. A blending mode lets you change the effect that one layer has upon the colors above or beneath it. Illustrator's Transparency palette has a number of blending modes that change the transparency or opacity (opaqueness) of a layer color. The more **transparent** an object is, the clearer it is, so the layer beneath shows through it more. The more **opaque** an object, the darker it is so that nothing can be seen through it.

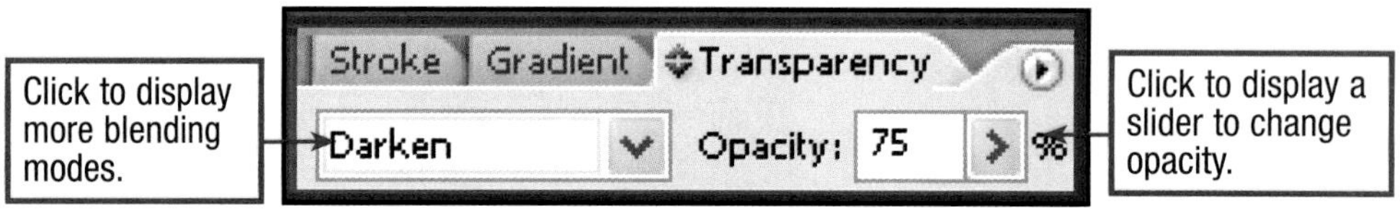

▲ Change blending modes in Transparency palette.

▶ **In this project,** you will use blending modes to add effects to the eye illustration you started in Project 7-4.

Step-by-Step

1. In Illustrator, open the eye illustration you created in Project 7-4. Save it according to your teacher's instructions.

2. Use the **Direct Selection** tool to select the star on top of the eye shape.

Use the Transparency Palette

3. Click **Window>Transparency** to open the **Transparency** palette.

4. On the **Transparency** palette, change the blending mode from **Normal** to **Darken**. Adjust the **Opacity** to **18 percent** (Figure 7.26).

▼ **Figure 7.26** Many of the blending modes are named after photography darkroom techniques.

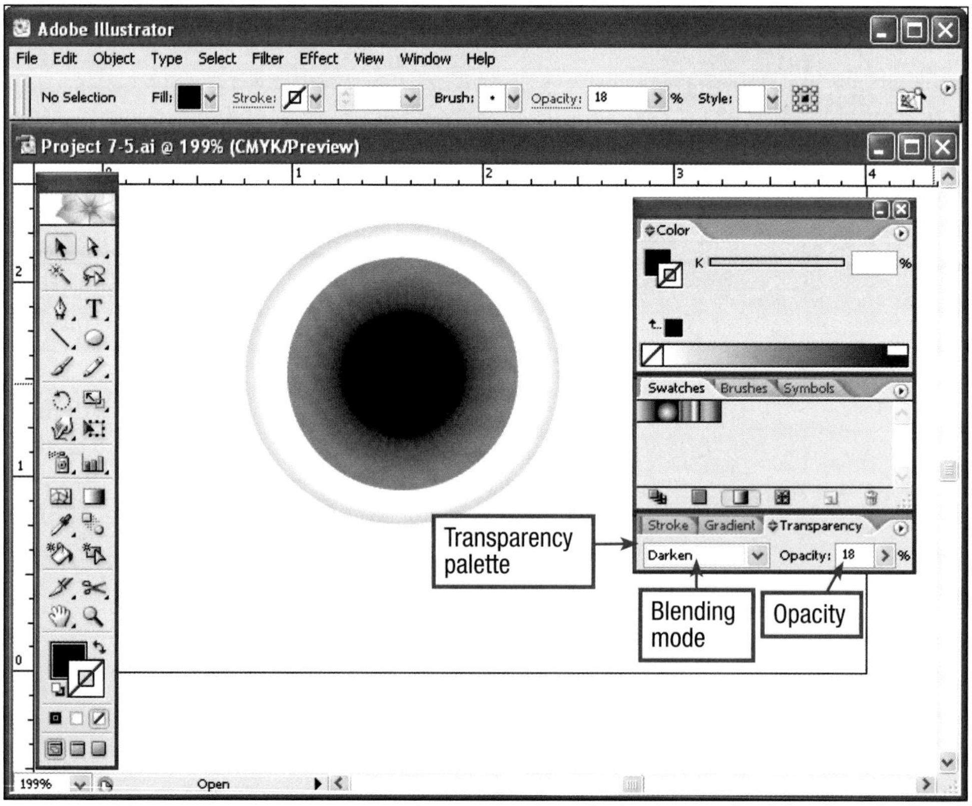

WORKSHOP Toolbox

You Will Learn To

- Identify parts of the Photoshop interface
- Indentify toolbox tools

Key Term

palette

The Photoshop Interface

The Adobe Photoshop user interface is quite different from Microsoft's interface. While Adobe and Microsoft share similar tools, these tools are in different locations on the screen. Adobe also offers new tools and toolbars, which are described below.

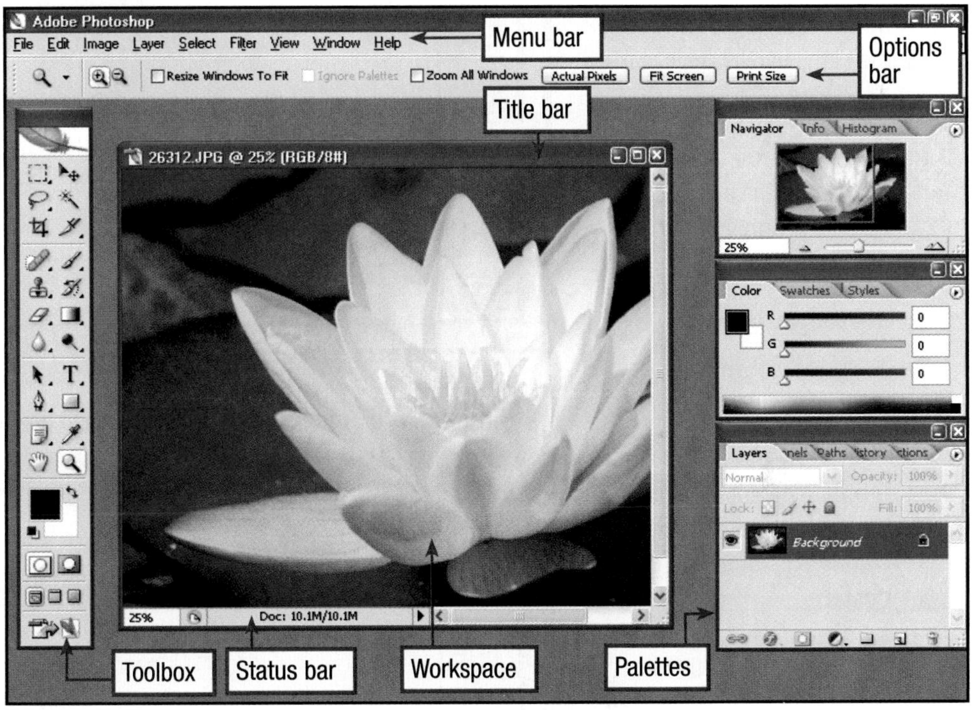

Workspace The image is placed on the workspace. It is the area that will be printed when the work is published. The size and shape of this area can be changed, and it can be moved by clicking and dragging the title bar.

Palettes A **palette** displays a variety of tools related to a particular action, such as adding color or working with layers. Palettes let you apply settings or monitor the work you have already done. Photoshop has many different palettes. They can be opened or closed through the Window menu.

Options bar The options on this toolbar change depending upon the tool that is being used. Like the palettes, the Options bar makes it easier to apply commands that relate to a particular action you are taking.

17 Use the **Ellipse** tool and SHIFT to create a circle larger than the eye on the workspace.

18 Select the new circle, and then click the gradient spectrum to display the gradient stops.

19 Click the right stop, and use the **Color Picker** to select a **light gray**.

20 Click the left stop, and set it at **white**. Slide the left stop to the right until the circle looks like Figure 7.24.

21 Select the circle, and drag it over the eye. Click **Object>Arrange>Send to back**.

22 Use the **Selection** tool to select the entire eye illustration. Click **Stroke>None**.

23 Open the **Align** palette and choose **Horizontal Align Center** and **Vertical Align Center**.

24 With the entire eye group selected, click **Object>Group**.

25 Follow your teacher's instructions for saving your work. You will continue working on the eye in Project 7-5.

▼ **Figure 7.24** Gradients add depth to your designs.

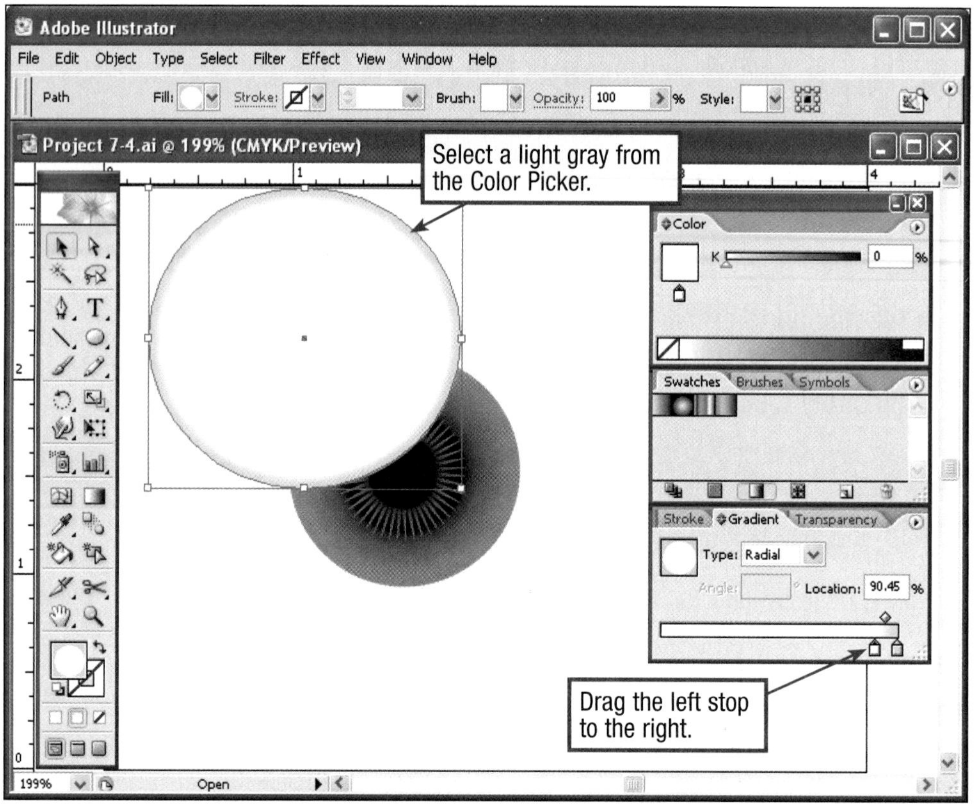

▼ **Figure 7.25** The object layers are aligned horizontally and vertically.

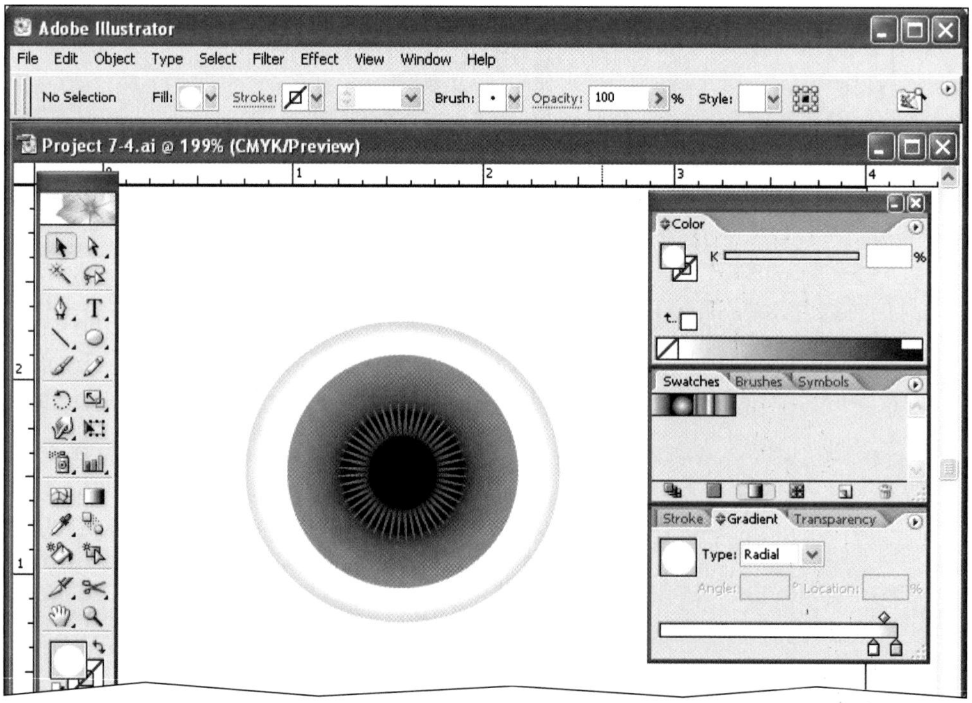

WORKSHOP Toolbox

What Tools Are in the Toolbox?

The toolbox contains tools for creating and editing your graphics. Many of the tools are duplicated in the palettes. When you choose a tool, the Options bar displays the options for that particular tool. When you move your mouse pointer over a button, the name is displayed, sometimes with a keyboard shortcut.

Tools with a small triangle in the corner have hidden toolbars that can be opened by right-clicking or by clicking and dragging to the right. Once you click a tool in the hidden toolbar, it replaces the one that was on the toolbar. Double-clicking most tools will set preferences.

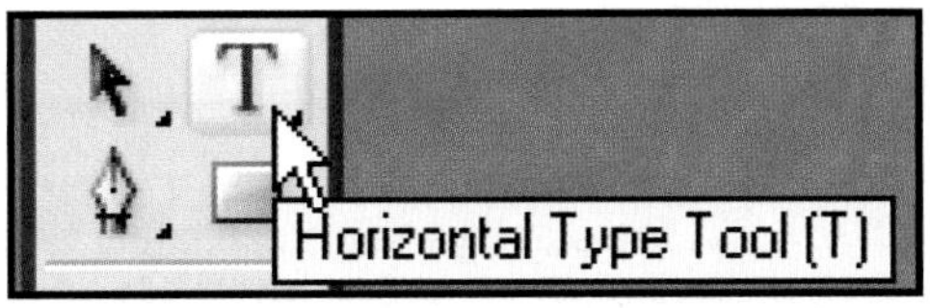

▲ Move the mouse over a button to see the name.

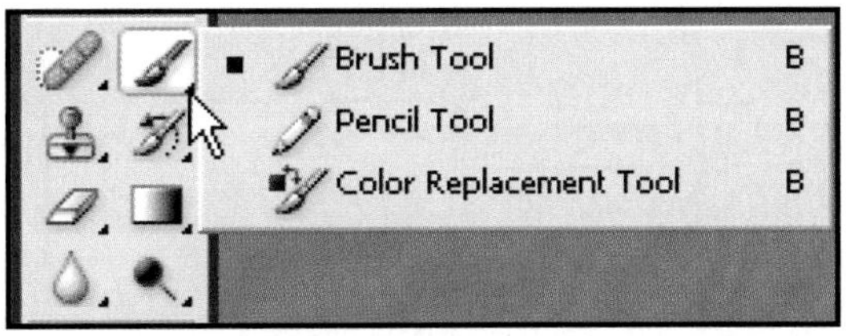

▲ Click and drag the corner triangle to display hidden tools.

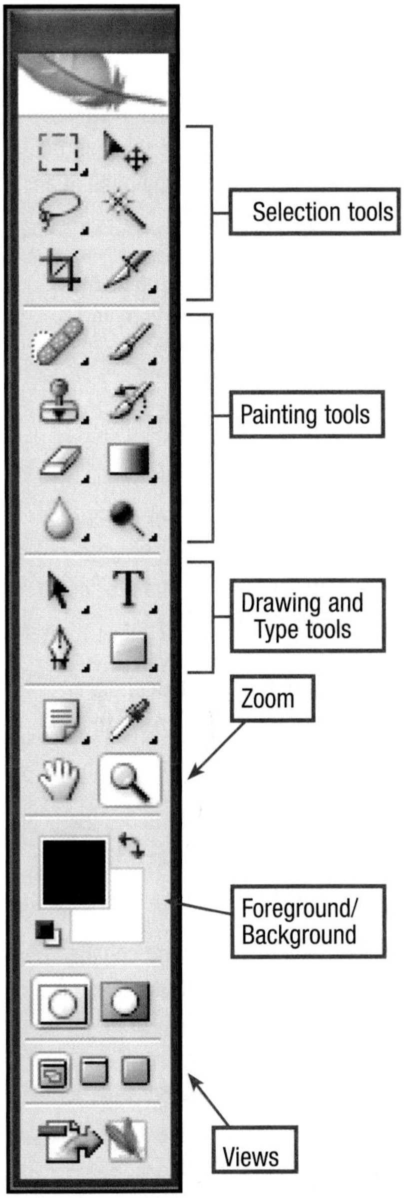

Eye On Ethics

Copyrights and Photos Just like text publications, photos have copyrights. Even if there is no copyright symbol, you should not assume that you can use a photo from the Web without permission or a royalty payment. There are many sites that offer royalty-free photos. These photos may still have a copyright, but you may not have to pay a fee for certain uses. If you are not sure whether you can use a photo legally, you can check the Web site or contact the creators to check the terms of use.

Connect Who might own the copyright of a photograph on a Web site?

Reading Check

1. **Identify** How can you tell which tools have hidden tools underneath?
2. **Explain** How can you change the commands on the Options bar?

8 On the **Gradient** palette, change the **Type** to **Radial**.

9 Single-click the left gradient stop.

10 On the **Color** palette, click the **black** rectangle on the right side of the spectrum.

11 Move the left gradient stop to the right until the shape in the circle looks like the pupil of an eye (Figure 7.22).

12 Click away from the image to make sure that nothing is selected, and then press D. (The **Fill** tool should become white, and the **Stroke** tool black.)

13 In the toolbox, click the **Swap between Fill and Stroke** arrow. The two buttons should switch colors.

14 From the **Ellipse** tool, open the **Star** tool. Click on the workspace.

15 In the **Star options** box, set **Points** to **48**. Click **OK** to display the star.

16 Select the star, and change the **Stroke** to **None**. Use the **Selection** tool to drag the star over the eye, and resize it to look like Figure 7.23.

▼ **Figure 7.22** Your gradient ranges from your chosen color to black.

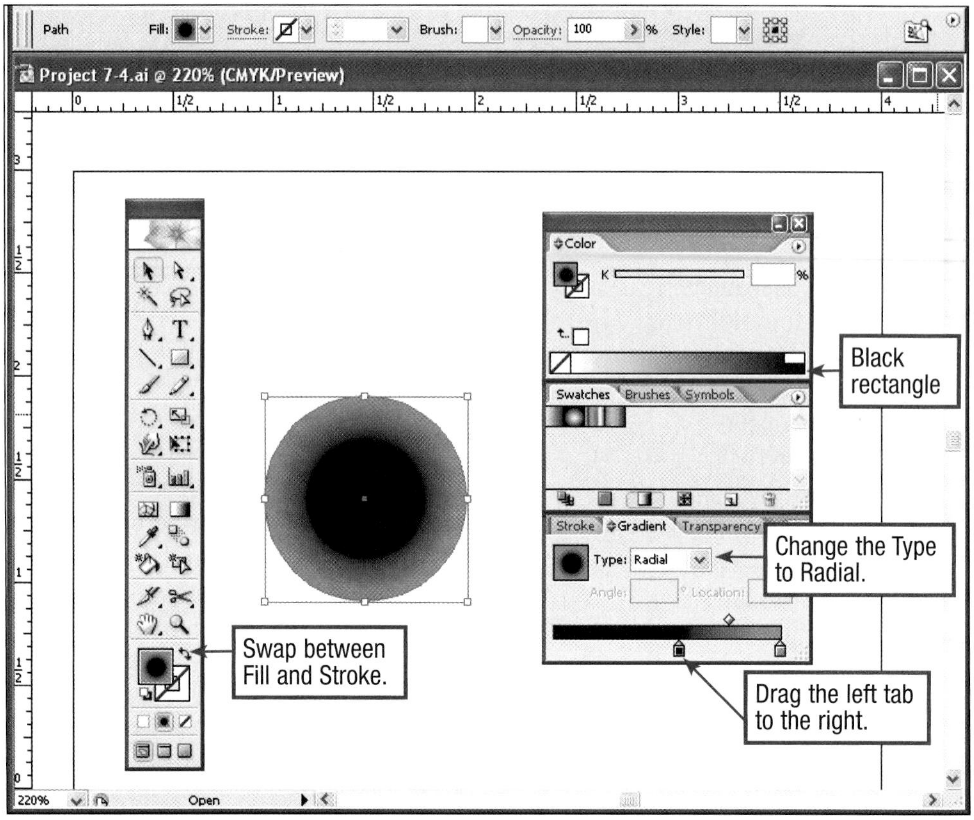

▼ **Figure 7.23** The star layer adds depth and visual interest to your design.

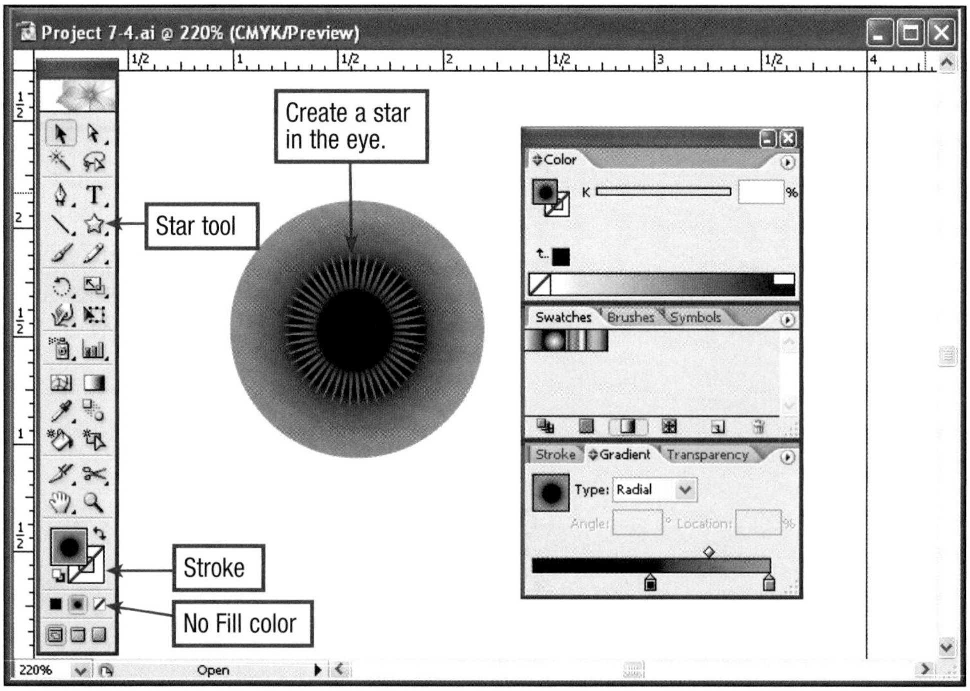

Project 5-1

Spotlight on Skills

- Apply the zoom
- Select with the Polygonal Lasso
- Copy and move an object
- Select with the Magic Wand
- Flip an object
- Select with Marquee tools
- Scale an object

Key Terms

- marquee
- polygon
- anchor point

Academic Focus

Math
Identify geometric shapes

Go Online PREVIEW
www.glencoe.com

Before You Begin Go to **Chapter 5**, and choose **PowerPoint Presentations** to preview the documents you will be creating. Also, use the individual project **Rubrics** to help create and evaluate your work.

Select Objects

In Word and Publisher, it is pretty easy to move an object. You simply click the object and drag it wherever it needs to go. This is not possible to do with raster images in Photoshop.

With raster graphics, the computer remembers the characteristics of each and every pixel. It sees each pixel as part of a grid on the monitor, not as a part of any particular shape. Therefore, in order to move or format an object, you have to select the specific pixels on which you want to work.

Selection Tools

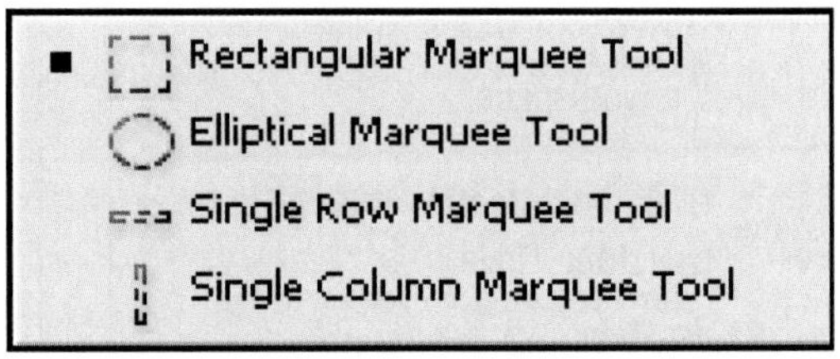

Photoshop's selection tools are listed in the top part of the toolbox. The marquee and lasso tools both have hidden toolbars with a number of options. **Marquee** tools allow you to select elliptical, rectangular, and other standard shapes in an object. A **marquee** is a dotted line that shows the area that is selected.

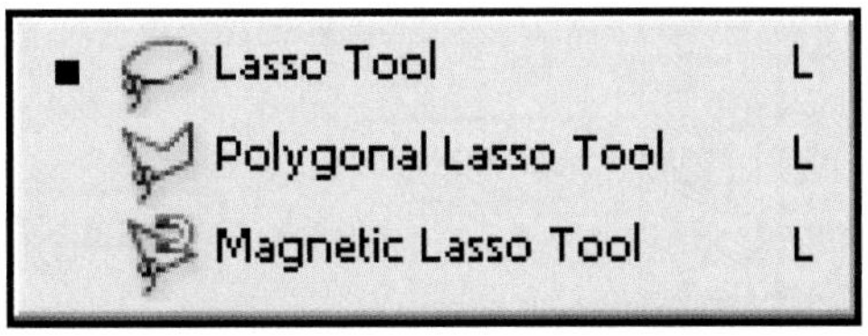

Lasso tools are used to select irregular shapes or unusual shapes such as **polygons** (multisided geometric figures). Each time you click, you create an **anchor point,** which is the beginning of a new line segment.

The **Magic Wand** tool selects objects based on the similarity of pixel color. This can be especially useful when you use a solid block of color, like a contrasting background.

When you click a tool, the **Options** bar at the top of the screen displays controls that are specific to that tool. For example, when you choose the Magic Wand, its options include a **Tolerance** setting, which determines how similar the selected colors must be. The **Contiguous** option selects colored pixels that are next to each other.

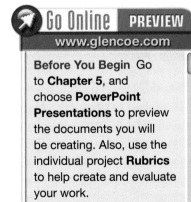

▲ When you click the Magic Wand on the toolbar, you open the Magic Wand options. Each tool opens a different Options toolbar.

► **In this project,** you will learn to use Photoshop's selection tools to move, format, and manipulate objects to create an image of a gingerbread house. Before you begin this or any other Photoshop project, it is recommended that you delete the settings set by other students to restore default settings. You will learn how to do this in Step 1.

Step-by-Step

1. In Illustrator, open a new document. Set a **custom** size, **3 inches high** by **4 inches wide**. Save according to your teacher's instructions.

2. In the toolbox, click the **Ellipse** tool. Then hold SHIFT, and drag a circle on the workspace.

3. Click the **Selection** tool select the circle.

Work with the Gradient Palette

4. If the **Gradient** palette is not open, click **Window>Gradient**. Click on the Gradient Slider to display the stops (Figure 7.20).

5. Single-click the **right** gradient stop.

6. In the toolbox, double-click the **Fill** tool to open the **Color Picker**. (Make sure the circle next to **H** is selected) (Figure 7.21).

Create Colors with the Color Picker

7. In the **Color Picker**, use the color slider and the color spectrum selector in the **Select Color** box to create a blue, green, or brown color (Figure 7.21). Click **OK**.

Figure 7.20 The default gradient is linear, ranging from white to black.

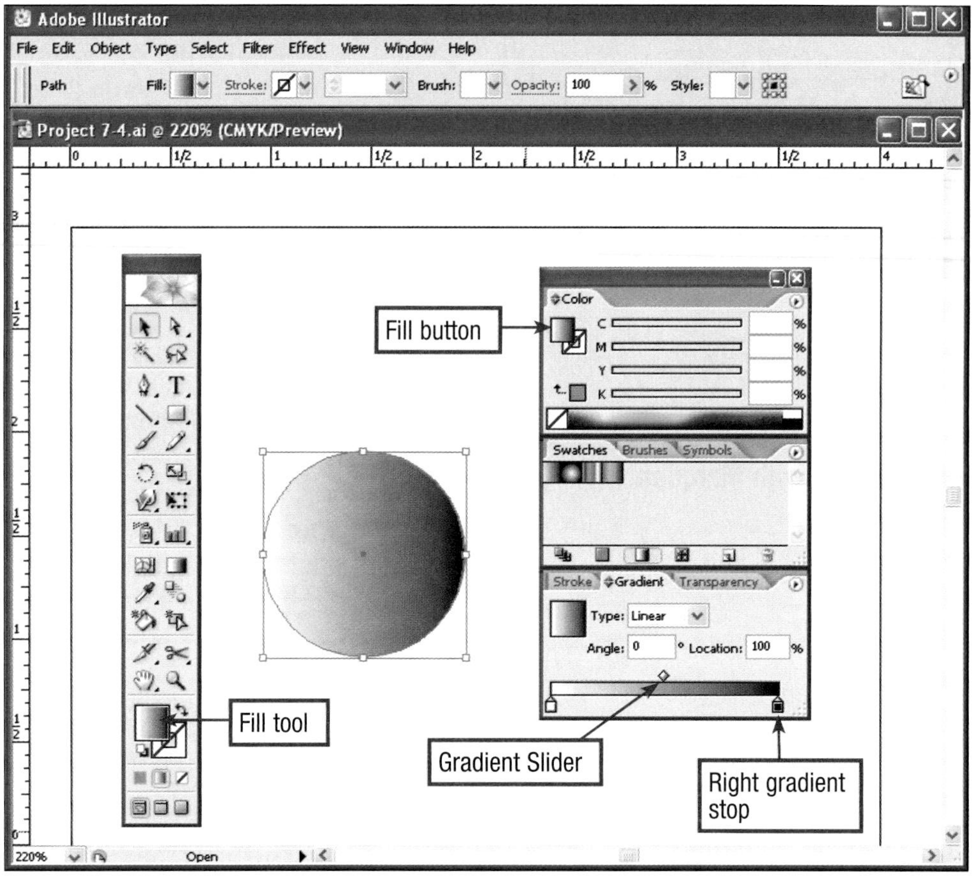

Figure 7.21 Use the Preview box to see what the color looks like.

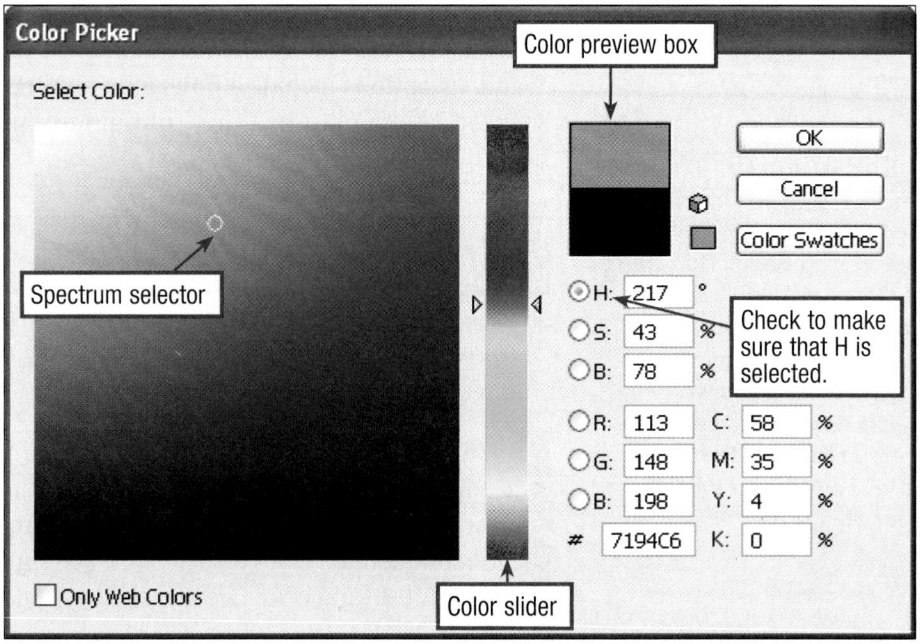

Student Data File

Step-by-Step

1. To restore default settings, hold ALT + CTRL + SHIFT when opening Photoshop. Answer **Yes** when asked if you want to delete settings. **Mac** users press OPTION + ⌘ + SHIFT.

2. Open **Data File 5-1** (Figure 5.1). Save it according to your teacher's instructions.

Apply the Zoom

3. In the toolbox, click **Zoom**. Then click the graham cracker until the magnification level in the title bar is 50% (Figure 5.1).

Select with the Polygonal Lasso

4. Right-click **Lasso**, and choose **Polygonal Lasso**.

5. Click each corner of the graham cracker to create anchor points.

6. Double-click **Hand** to zoom back out.

Copy and Move an Object

7. In the toolbox, click **Move**. Press ALT, then click and drag a copy of the cracker to the landscape image (Figure 5.2).

▼ **Figure 5.1** The zoom options are displayed on the Options bar.

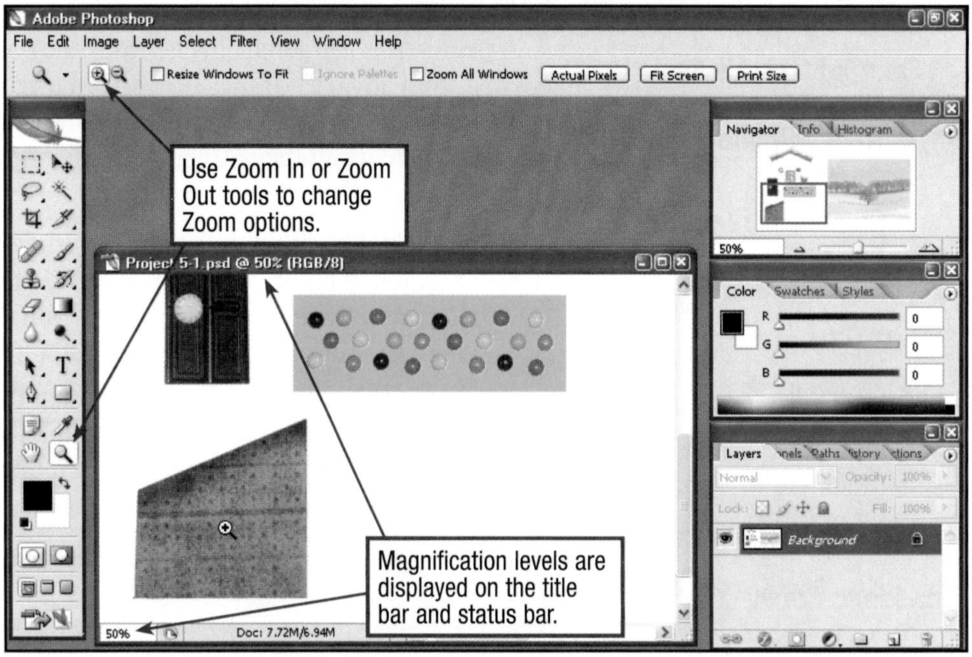

▼ **Figure 5.2** A moving line shows that you enclosed a selected area.

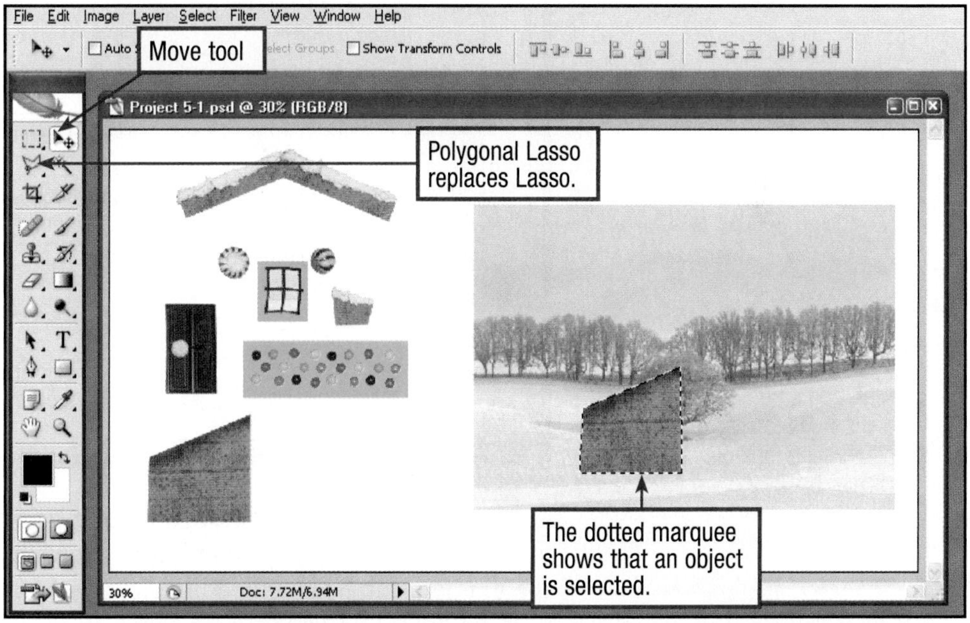

Instant Message

Screen Layout The screen layout in the figures may not always show the same palettes or screen elements on your monitor. It is not necessary to change the tools and palettes on your screen to match the figures.

Project 7-4

Apply Gradient Fills

Spotlight on Skills

- Work with the Gradient palette
- Create colors with the Color Picker

Key Terms

- gradient
- spectrum
- radial
- gradient stop

Academic Focus

Science
Create color gradients

► You can add a number of gradient stops to create gradients with multiple colors.

A **gradient** is a gradual change from one color to another. Gradients can be created from any part of the color **spectrum**, the entire range of colors from white to black. Adobe Illustrator has many kinds of gradient fills, which you can customize using the software's gradient palette.

From the gradient palette, you can:

- Change the gradient type to linear or **radial**, which is a circular effect.
- Set gradient color stops. A **gradient stop** marks the beginning or end colors used in a gradient. It allows you to set a specific color on the color spectrum for the starting or stopping point of your gradient.
- Change the gradient effect by moving the diamond-shaped slider or changing the color. You can also click the Gradient tool, then click and drag inside the filled object in the toolbox to adjust the direction and intensity of the gradient.

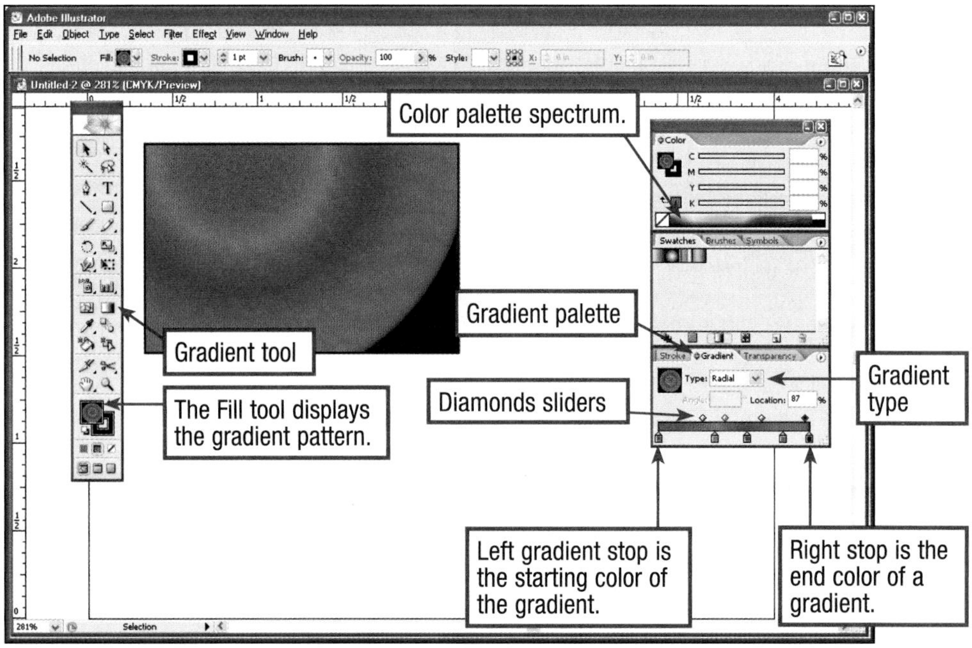
Adobe Illustrator
Color palette spectrum.
Gradient palette
Gradient tool
The Fill tool displays the gradient pattern.
Diamonds sliders
Gradient type
Left gradient stop is the starting color of the gradient.
Right stop is the end color of a gradient.

Gradient stops are added by clicking below the gradient spectrum. They are removed by dragging them away from the spectrum. The colors used in the gradient can be changed by clicking a gradient stop and then either

- Choosing a color from the Color palette spectrum, or
- Double-clicking the Fill tool to open the Color Picker.

► **In this project,** you will use the Gradient tool to create an illustration of an eye. The Gradient tool and the Gradient palette provide the options to create a realistic illustration.

Select with the Magic Wand

8. In the toolbox, select **Magic Wand** [icon].

9. On the **Options** bar, make sure the **Tolerance** is set to **100** and that **Contiguous** is checked (Figure 5.3).

Flip an Object

10. Click the graham cracker. The entire shape should be selected. Click **Edit>Transform>Flip Horizontal**.

11. Click and drag the selected object next to the first graham cracker. In this case, you do not need to click the **Move** button. (Figure 5.3).

12. Press CTRL + D to deselect.

Select with Marquee Tools

13. Use the **Zoom** tool to magnify the chocolate door.

14. In the toolbox, click **Rectangular Marquee** [icon].

15. Drag a marquee around the door image (Figure 5.4). (Hold the **Space bar** and use the **arrow keys** to reposition the marquee if necessary.)

▼ **Figure 5.3** Higher Tolerance values select a greater range of color.

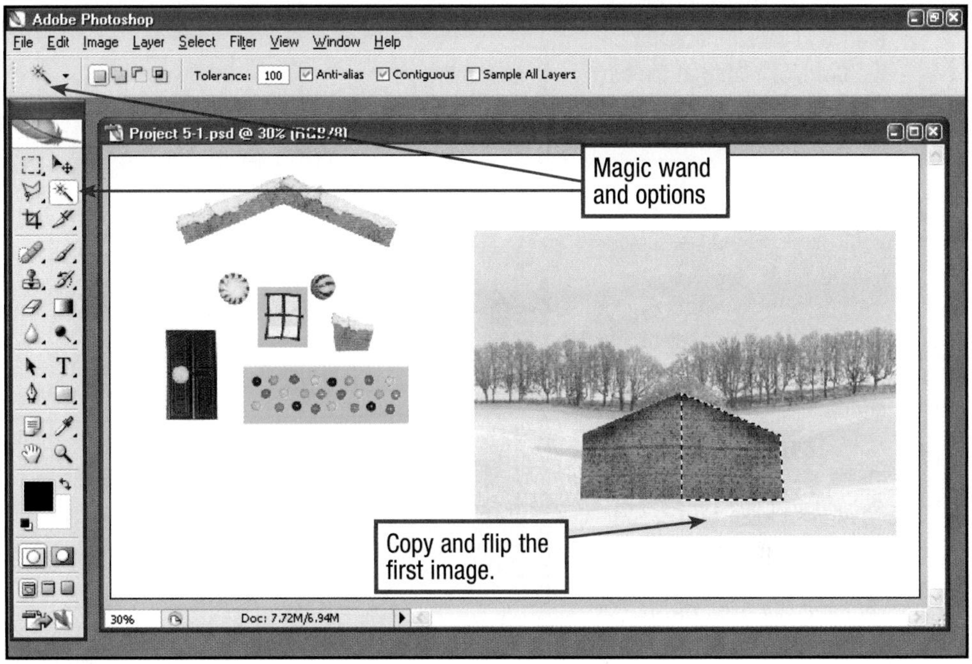

▼ **Figure 5.4** Use Marquee tools to select regular shapes.

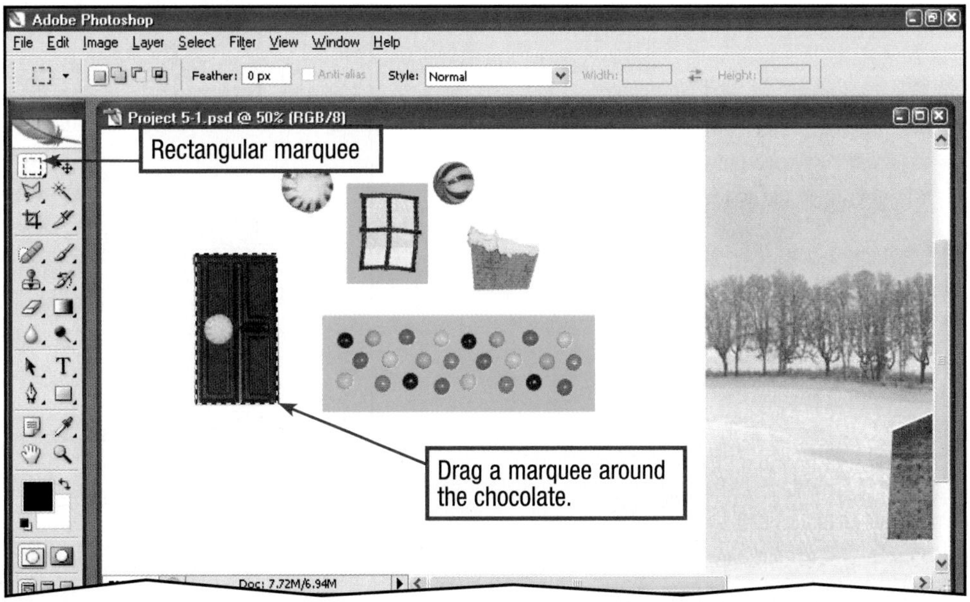

Instant Message

Deselecting an Object To clear a selection so you can select again, press CTRL + D or click **Select>Deselect**. To undo your last operation, click **Edit>Undo** or press CTRL + Z (**Mac** users press ⌘ + Z).

21 Click the **Type** tool [T], and drag a text box anywhere on the workspace. Notice that the **Control** palette at the top of your screen shows options for Characters.

22 In the text box, key Desktop Publishing 16.7 Million Colors (Figure 7.18).

23 With the **Type** tool, select the text. Click the **Align Center** button on the **Control** palette.

24 Select the text *Desktop Publishing*. Click **Type>Font**, and choose a slab font like **Wide Latin**. Choose a sans serif font like **Arial Narrow** for the text *16.7 Million Colors.*

25 Click the **Selection** tool, and then drag the text to the rounded rectangle.

26 Click the **Type** tool, and select the text. Press CTRL + SHIFT and < or > to resize the text to fit in the rectangle.

27 With the **Selection** tool, select the text box and the rounded rectangle. **Center align** the text, both horizontally and vertically.

28 For an optional effect, you can select two crayons, and drag them up from the box slightly.

29 Your crayon box should look similar to Figure 7.19. Follow your teacher's instructions for saving and printing your work.

Figure 7.18 Use the Type tool to create and select text.

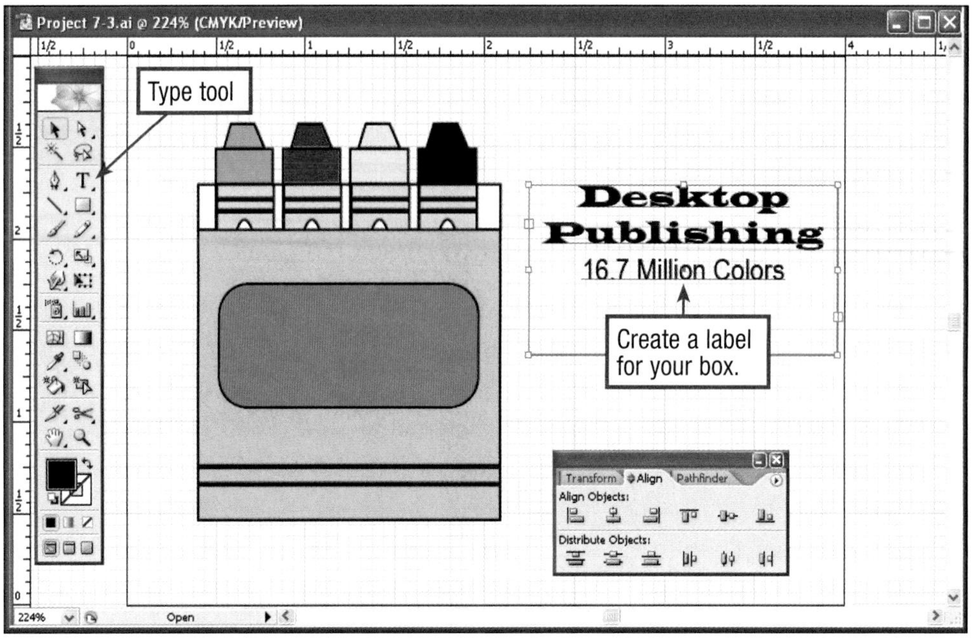

Figure 7.19 Resize the text box for the label, as needed.

REVIEW AND REVISE

Check your work Use Figure 7.19 as a guide and check that:

- ☑ The crayons are top aligned in the box.
- ☑ There is a white fill crayon box cover.
- ☑ The crayon box label uses two different fonts, and the text is centered.

16 Double-click the **Hand** tool to zoom back out to the whole screen.

17 Use the **Move** tool to move the door to the middle of the house.

Scale an Object

18 Click **Edit>Transform>Scale**. Drag a handle on the chocolate to resize it so it looks similar to Figure 5.5.

19 On the **Options** bar, click the **Commit Transform** check mark. Drag the door back to the middle of the house and deselect it.

▼ Figure 5.5 Use the Transform options to scale, rotate, or distort images.

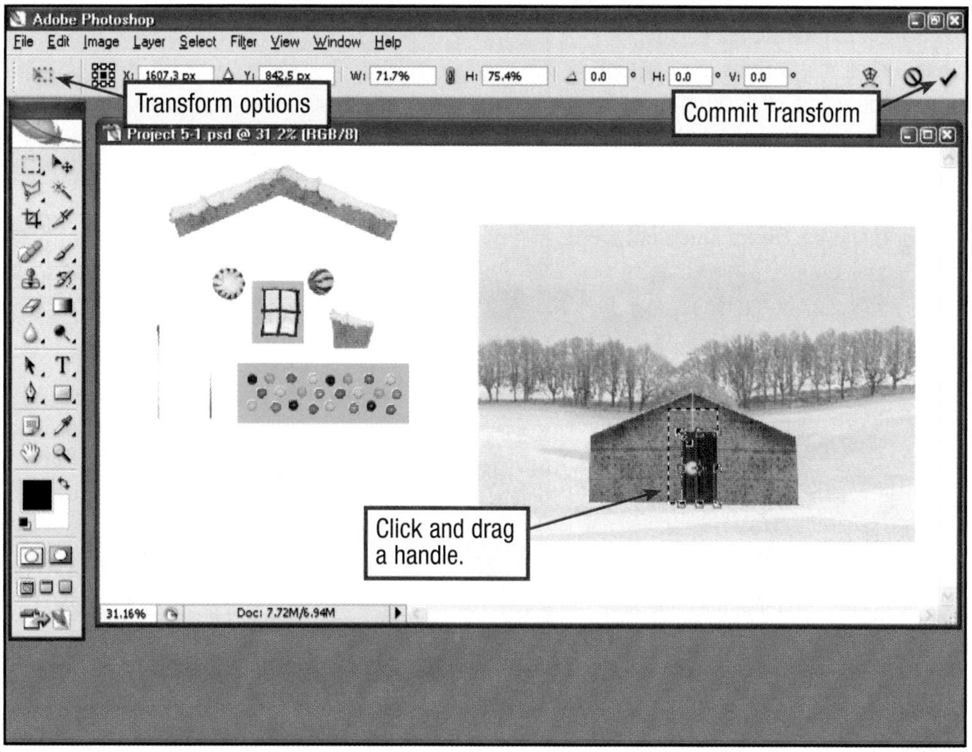

20 **Zoom** in on the peppermint disk. Then right-click the **Rectangular Marquee** tool to choose **Elliptical Marquee**.

21 Click just outside the peppermint disk, and drag across to select it. If you do not get it right, click off the disk and try again.

22 **Zoom out**, and use the **Move** tool to drag the disk above the chocolate doorway (Figure 5.6).

23 Your house should look similar to Figure 5.6. Follow your teacher's instructions for saving your work. You will continue your house in Project 5-2.

▼ Figure 5.6 Your gingerbread house is halfway built.

Work with the Swatches Palette

12. On the **Swatches** palette, click the **Options** arrow. From the menu, click **Open Swatch Library>Tints and Shades**. Choose a color.

13. Using the **Direct Selection** tool, press the SHIFT key to select all of the labels, and add the new fill color.

14. Click the **Rectangle** tool. Drag a box over the bottoms of the crayons. Make it wider and longer than the crayons (Figure 7.16).

15. Select the rectangle, and add a fill color and a black stroke around the border.

16. Click the **Rectangle** tool and drag right to choose the **Rounded Rectangle**.

17. Draw a rounded rectangle as a box label, and add a fill and stroke color.

18. Select both rectangles. On the **Align** palette, choose **Horizonal Align Center**.

19. Use the **Line Segment** tool to add two decorative lines to the bottom of the box (Figure 7.17).

20. Create a **white** rectangle at the top of the box. Click **Object>Arrange>Send to Back** to move the rectangle behind the crayons (Figure 7.17).

▼ Figure 7.16 Create a crayon box with the Rectangle tool.

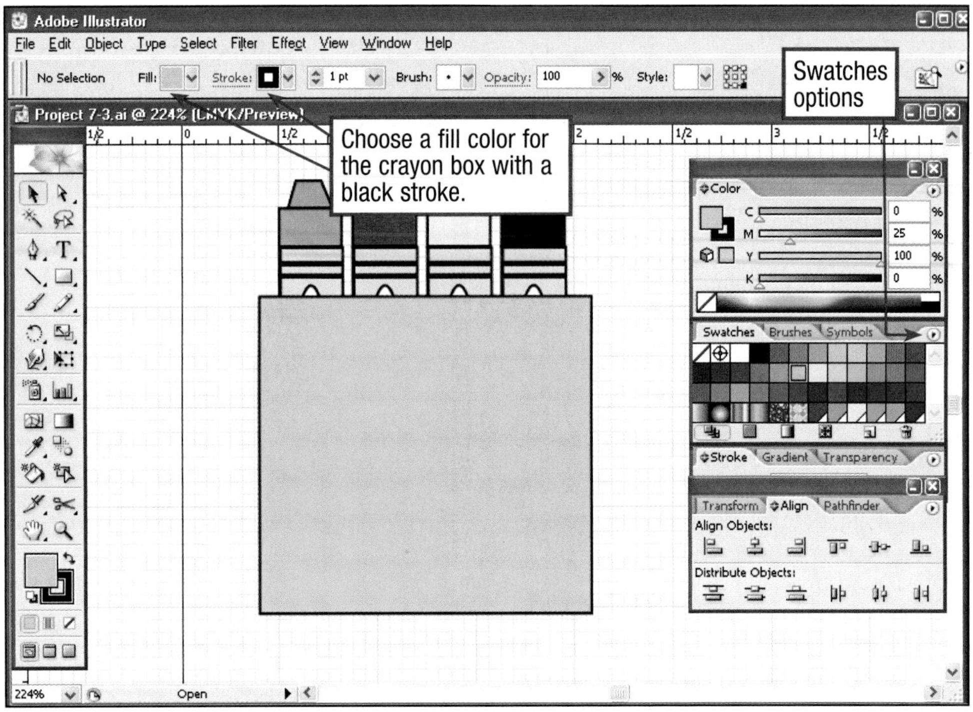

▼ Figure 7.17 Add a label to the crayon's box and an open cover.

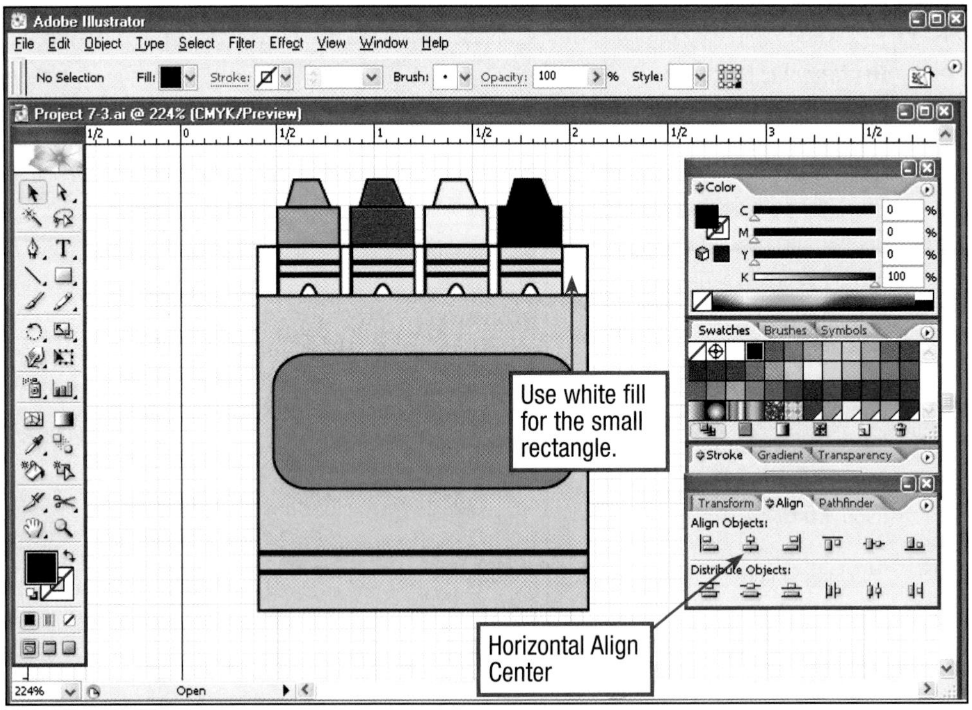

Project 5-2

Spotlight on Skills

- Select with the Magnetic Lasso
- Separate background images
- Resize and rotate objects
- Crop an image

Key Term

- fastening points

Academic Focus

Math
Work with geometric shapes

Complete a Collage

The Magnetic Lasso works well on objects that have irregular shapes, particularly when there is a high contrast with the background. As you select the shape, the border snaps into place along the edge, creating its own **fastening points**, which anchor the line and start a new segment. You can also click to create fastening points manually.

▼ You can adjust the sensitivity of the Magnetic Lasso by changing the settings in the Options bar.

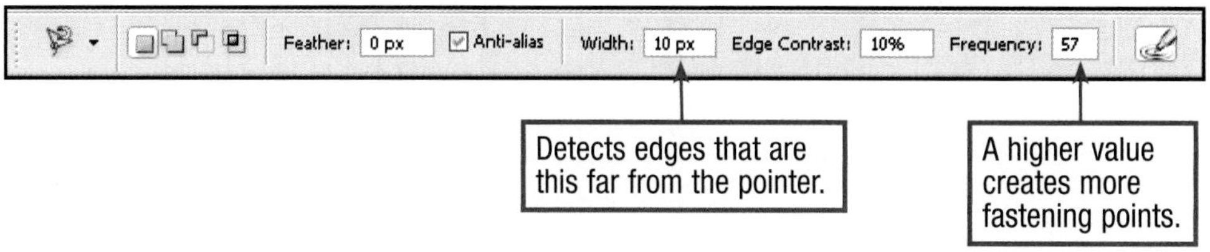

If you are having difficulty using the Magnetic Lasso to trace around the edge of an object, try reducing the Width and the Edge Contrast settings. You can also press CTRL + Z to remove the last segment of the line.

► **In this project,** you will continue to learn more about Photoshop's selection tools as you complete the gingerbread house you started in Project 5-1.

Step-by-Step

1. Open Project 5-1, and save it according to your teacher's instructions.

2. Click **Zoom**, and drag a marquee around the chimney.

3. Right-click **Polygonal Lasso**, and choose **Magnetic Lasso**. Change the **Option** settings so they are the same as Figure 5.8 on page 208.

▼ **Figure 5.7** Draw a marquee with the Zoom tool to magnify objects.

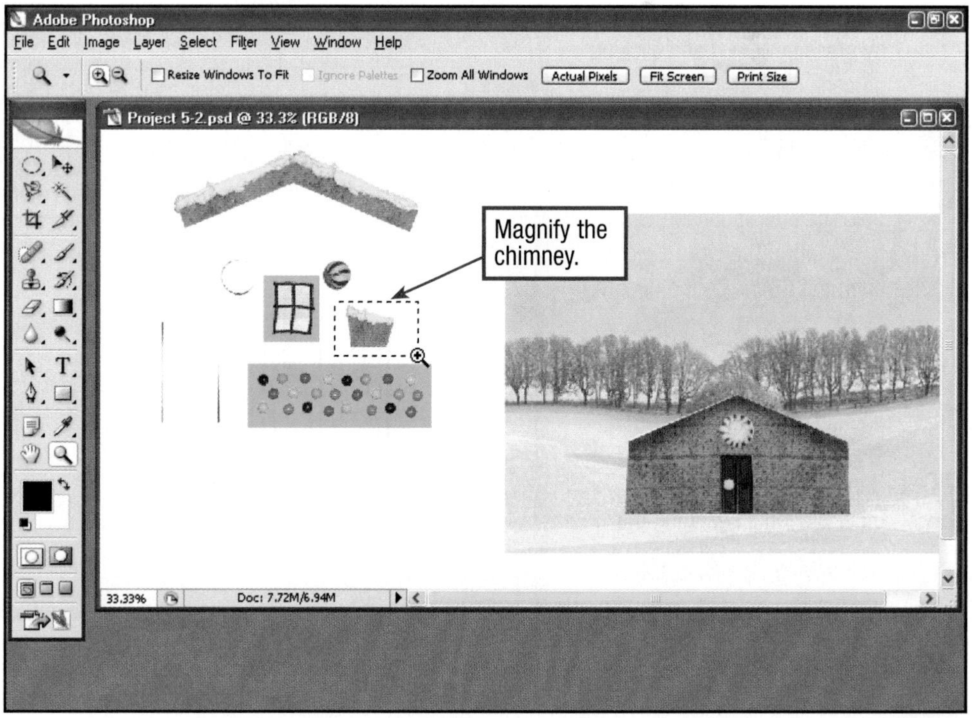

5. Deselect the crayons. Click the **Type** tool [T].

6. Double-click the word *Color* on the first crayon. Change it to Cyan.

7. Change the labels of the other three crayons to Magenta, Yellow, Black (Figure 7.14).

▼ **Figure 7.14** The Type tool changes the pointer to an I-beam.

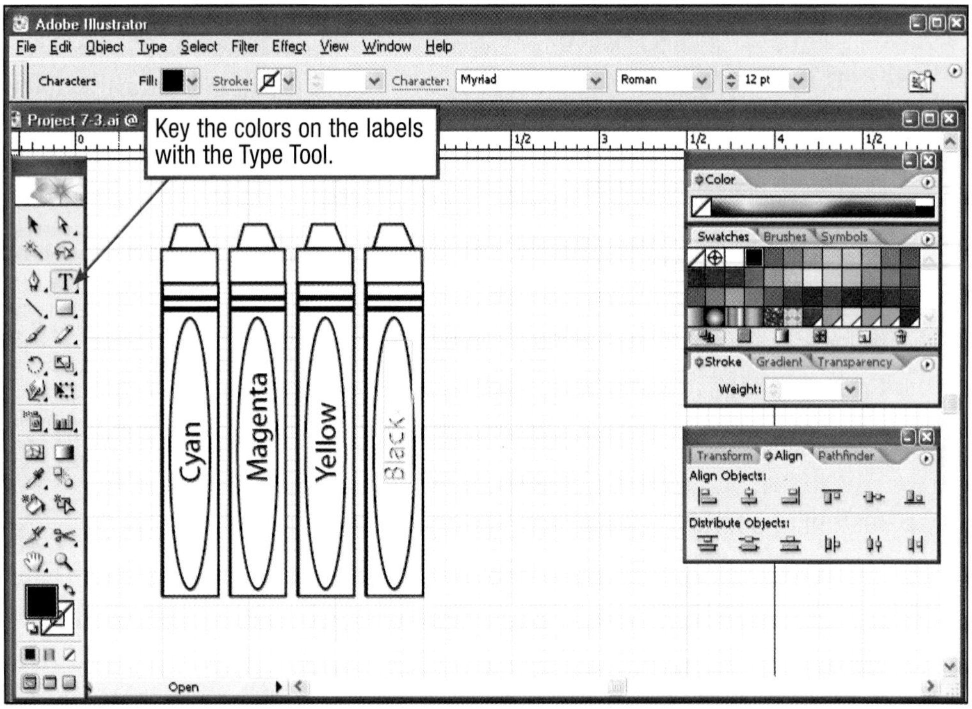

Work with the Color Palette

8. Click the **Direct Selection** tool [ ]. Select all parts of the **cyan** crayon except the label by pressing [SHIFT] and clicking on each section (Figure 7.15).

9. Click the **Fill** tool. Then, in the **Color** palette, click on the Color palette options button to the left of the word *Color* to open the **CMYK** option (Figure 7.15).

10. Under **C** (for cyan), key 100 and set the other values at **0**.

11. Repeat Steps 8–10 for the other crayons, changing the

▼ **Figure 7.15** Use the Direct Selection tool to select objects within a group.

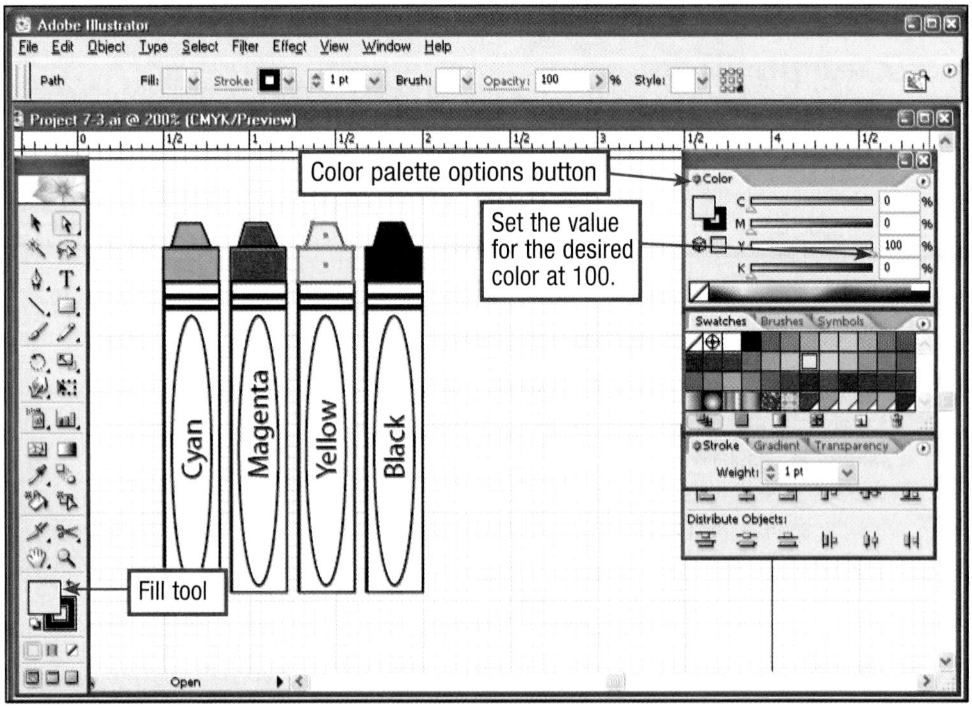

Select with the Magnetic Lasso

4. Left-click on an edge of the chimney. Then carefully move the mouse pointer around the outside edge of the chimney until the selection border is complete (Figure 5.8).

5. If the line does not go where you want, click to add fastening points. Press DELETE to remove the last line segment or CTRL + D to start over.

Mac users press ⌘ + D.

6. **Zoom out** and use **Move** to move the chimney above the house. There should be space between the house and the chimney.

7. **Deselect** the chimney. Then use the **Magnetic Lasso** to select the roof.

8. Move the roof into place, and deselect it (Figure 5.9).

Figure 5.8 Click the mouse to insert fastening points by hand.

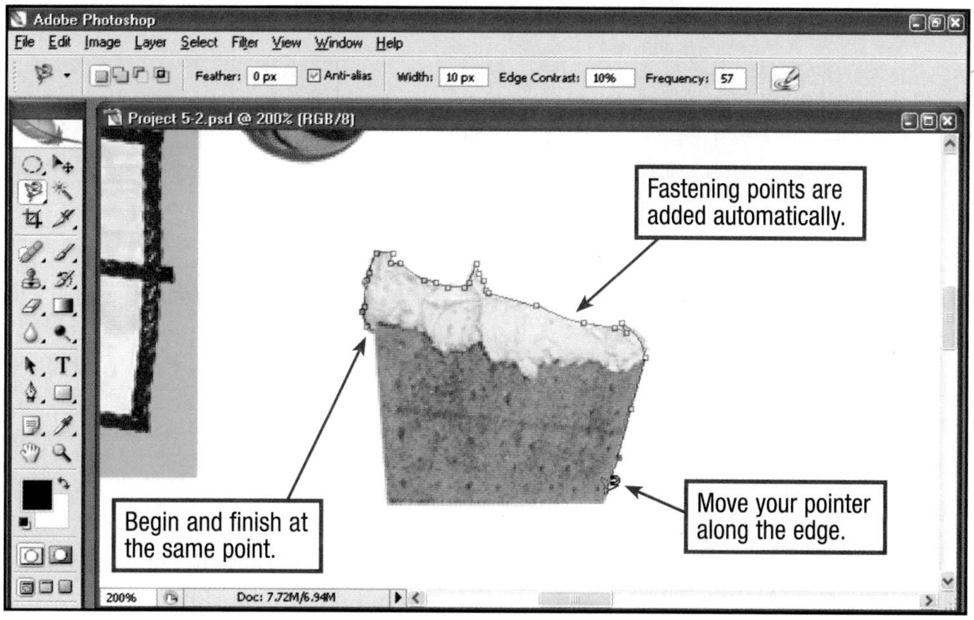

Figure 5.9 Place the chimney before you place the roof.

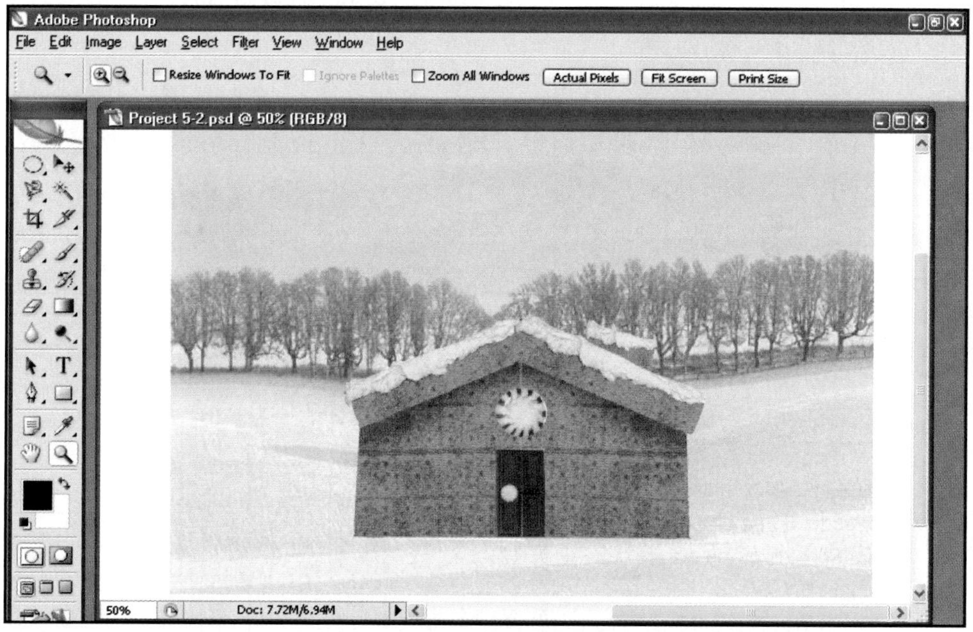

Instant Message

Undo Early Actions If you are unhappy with changes you made to an image and want to return it to an earlier state, open the **History** palette by clicking **Window>History**. The History palette displays previous states of the image. By clicking an earlier state, you can undo changes you did not like.

Sidebar

Tips and Shortcuts Remember these time-saving tips:

- Create perfect squares or circles by pressing the SHIFT key while dragging the rectangle or Ellipse tools.
- Use shortcuts to open tools or palettes. For example, Ellipse is L and Color palette is F6.
- If a shape is an odd color, press D to set default colors of white fill and black stroke.

Identify What are the shortcuts for the Rectangle tool and Gradient palette?

Color Palette The Color palette lets you change between the color modes and adjust colors by using a slider or by entering values.

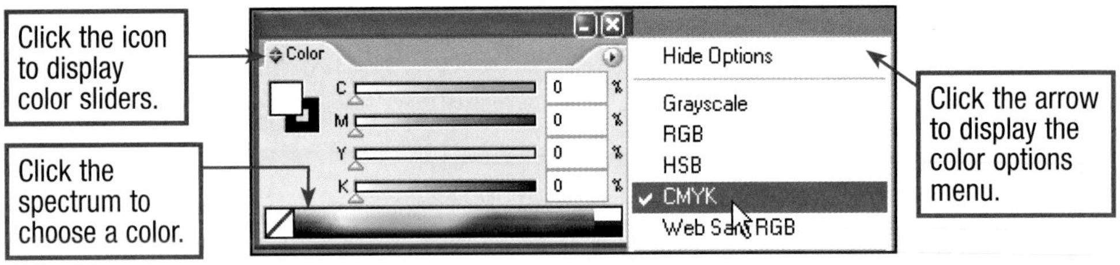

▲ Use the color options menu to choose a color mode.

- **Grayscale** ranges from white to black with shades of gray in between.
- **RGB** stands for Red, Green, Blue. These three colors, mixed in various proportions, create most colors in the visible spectrum. Web Safe RGB includes only colors that are suitable for Web sites.
- **CMYK** stands for Cyan, Magenta, Yellow, blacK. This mode is used for printed documents and is not meant for graphics on a monitor.
- **HSB** stands for Hue, Saturation, Brightness. Hue is the color. Saturation is the strength or intensity of the color. Brightness is how light or dark a color is.

▶ **In this project,** you will add color to the crayon you created in Project 7-2 and add it to a box of crayons.

Step-by-Step

1. Open the crayon file you created in Project 7-2.

Duplicate an Image

2. Click the **Selection** tool. Press ALT and drag out three more copies of the crayon (Figure 7.13).
3. If the **Align** palette is not open, click **Window>Align**.
4. Select all four crayons, and choose **Vertical Align Top**, then **Horizontal Distribute Center**.

▼ **Figure 7.13** Your crayons should be top aligned and spaced evenly apart.

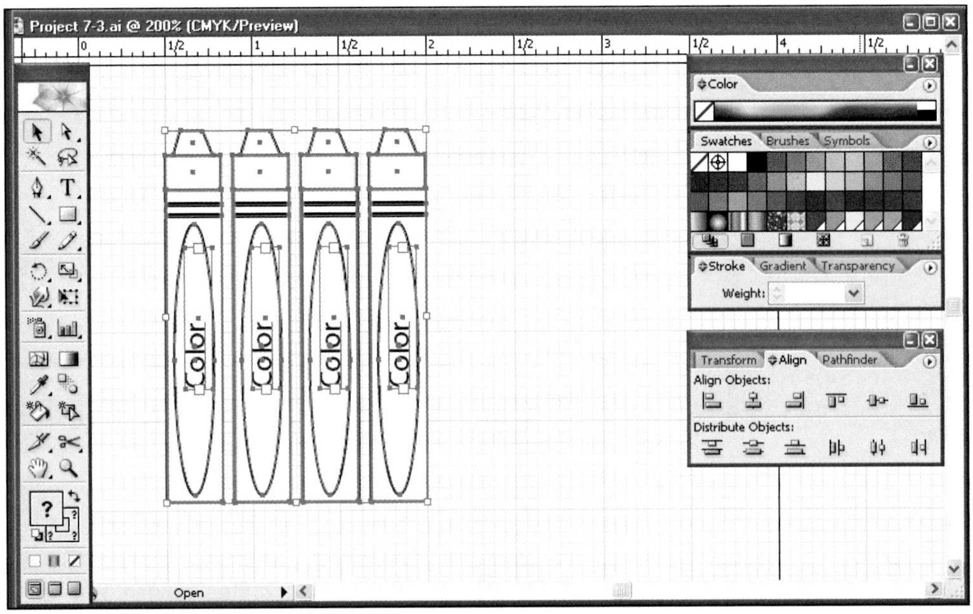

Separate Background Images

9 Zoom in on the green background with the candies and use **Rectangular marquee** to select it.

10 Click **Magic Wand**. On the **Options** bar, click **Subtract from Selection**.

11 Click the green background. The candies are now the only objects selected, and they can be more easily moved (Figure 5.10).

▼ Figure 5.10 The candies are difficult to move unless they are separated from their background.

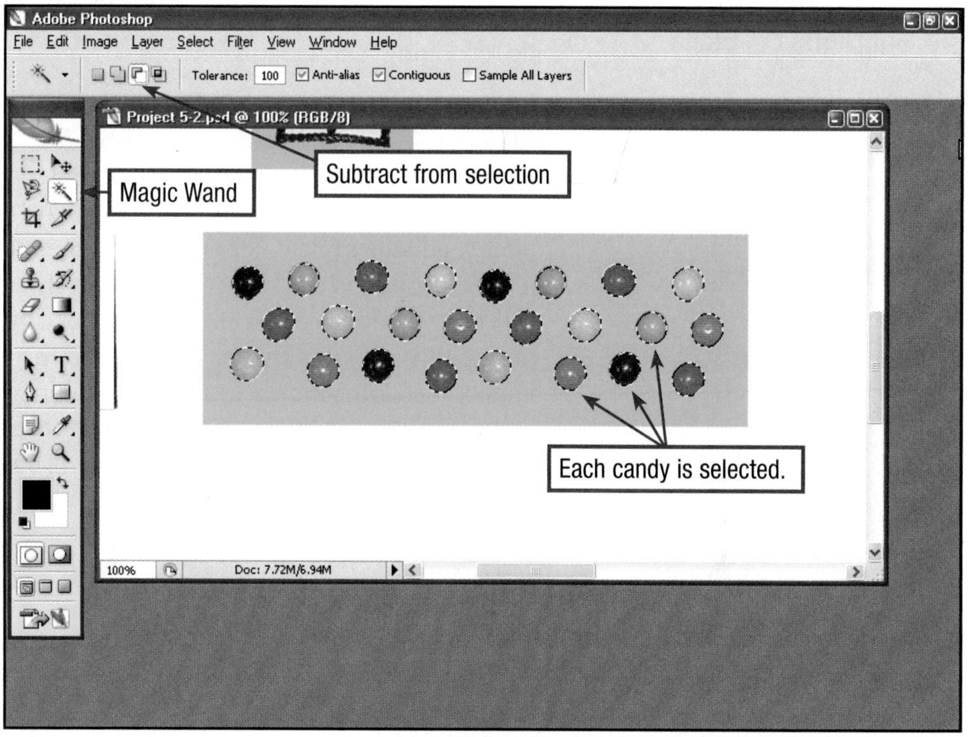

Resize and Rotate Objects

12 Click the **Move** tool. On the **Option** bar, click **Show Transform Controls** to display handles.

13 Move the candies to the roof of the house and resize them. **Note:** The **Move** options bar becomes the **Transform** options bar (Figure 5.11).

14 Position your mouse pointer outside the handles until you see a curved arrow. Click and drag the arrow to rotate the candies to align with the roof.

▼ Figure 5.11 Use Transform Controls to size and rotate an object.

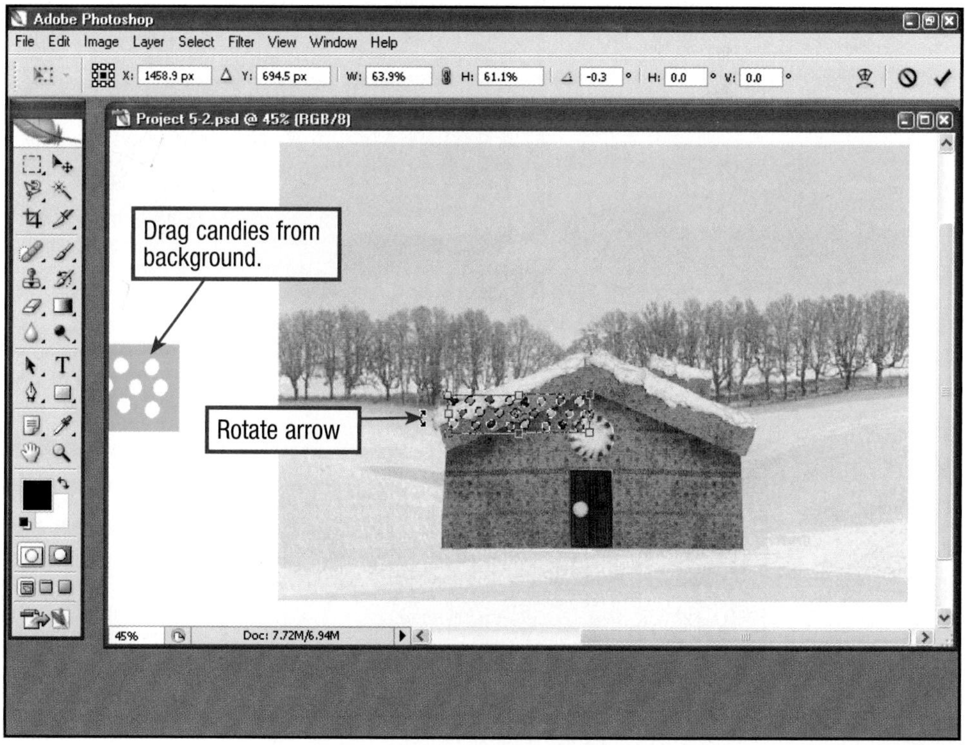

Project 7-3

Set Colors

Spotlight on Skills

- Duplicate an image
- Work with the Color palette
- Work with the Swatches palette

Key Terms

- grayscale
- RGB
- CMYK
- HSB

Academic Focus

Science
Identify color values

Adobe Illustrator gives you many tools for applying, changing, and creating colors.

Toolbox As you saw in Project 7-1, you can use the Fill tool to easily add color to an object. The Stroke button applies color to a border line or line segment. Below these buttons are other tools that let you quickly add the same color choices to other objects, or choose options such as gradient or no fill.

When you double-click the Fill or Stroke buttons, you open the Color Picker. Much like the Color palette, the Color Picker lets you set colors to precise specifications by keying in number codes. You can find out more about colors and their codes in Appendix A.

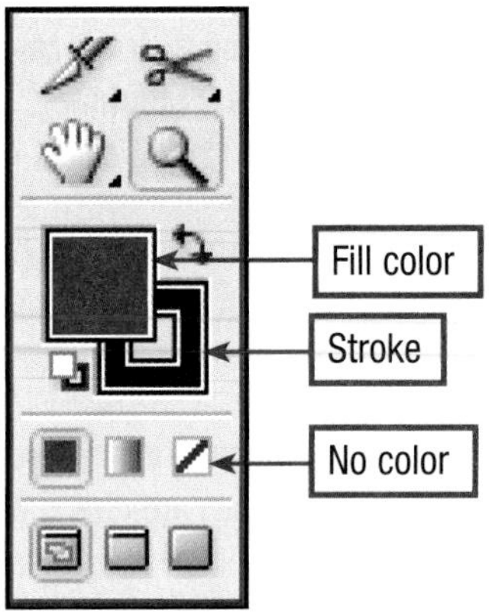

▲ Double-click a color tool on the toolbox to open the Color Picker.

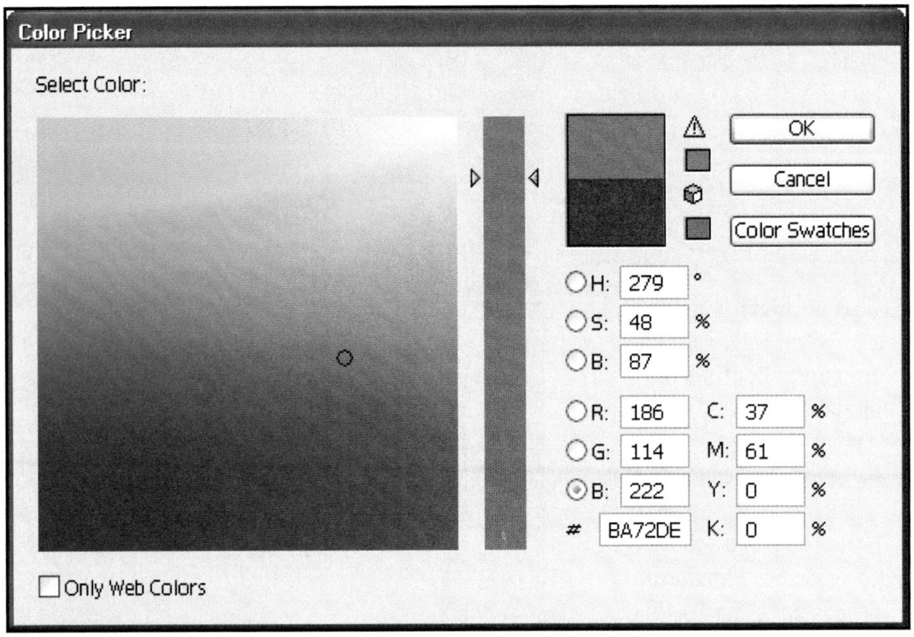

▲ The Color Picker lets you set colors with the color spectrum or by keying specific values.

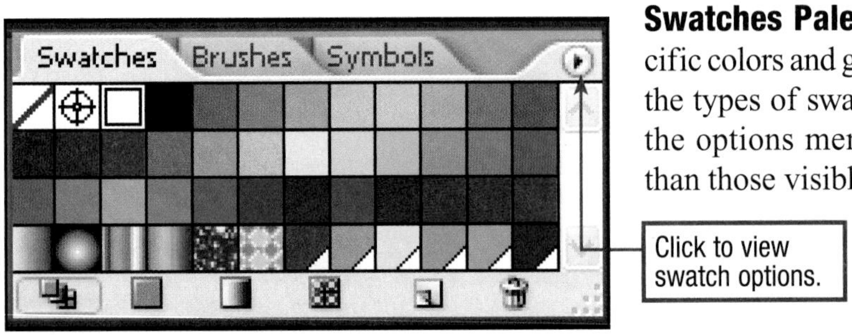

Swatches Palette This palette provides specific colors and gradient options. You can choose the types of swatches that are displayed. Click the options menu arrow to see more choices than those visible in the palette.

15 Click the **Move** button. When asked, **Apply the transformation**.

16 Press ALT and drag out a copy of the candies. Click **Edit>Transform>Flip Horizonal**.

17 Align the candies with the other half of the roof (Figure 5.12). Press CTRL + D to deselect. **Mac** users press ⌘ + D.

18 Repeat Steps 9–16 to **select**, **move**, **resize**, and **copy** the windows of the gingerbread house. Place them to look like Figure 5.13.

19 Use any selection tool to move the round peppermint balls into place.

Crop an Image

20 Use the **Rectangular marquee** tool to create a selection around the parts of the image you want to keep.

21 Click **Image>Crop** to delete the unwanted areas of the image.

22 Follow your teacher's instructions for saving and printing your work.

▼ **Figure 5.12** Align the candies with the roof.

▼ **Figure 5.13** Crop the excess parts of your image.

REVIEW AND REVISE

Check your work Use Figure 5.13 as a guide and check that:

- ☑ The house has a door, two windows, a chimney, and decorations.
- ☑ The elements are sized and placed correctly.
- ☑ The image has been cropped.

Add Text

19 In the toolbox, click the **Type** tool [T]. Click anywhere in the workspace and key Color.

Rotate an Object

20 With the **Selection** tool, select the word, then click **Object>Transform>Rotate**.

21 Key 90 as the **Angle** in the Rotate window, then click **OK** (Figure 7.11).

▼ **Figure 7.11** You can rotate text to any angle for visual accuracy and appeal.

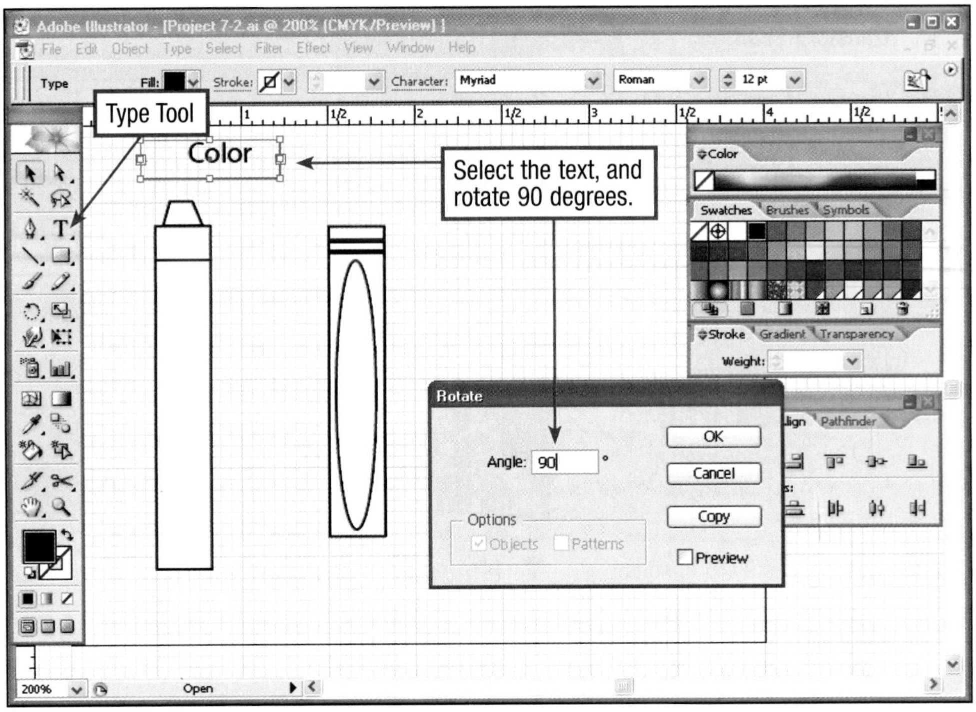

22 Drag the text into the oval. Position and resize as necessary.

23 Use the **Selection** tool to drag a marquee over the rectangle, and click **Object>Group**.

24 Move the label onto the crayon shape. Resize as needed and group (Figure 7.12).

25 Save your work. You will continue working on the crayon in Project 7-3.

▼ **Figure 7.12** Position and resize the crayon's label on the crayon to complete your design.

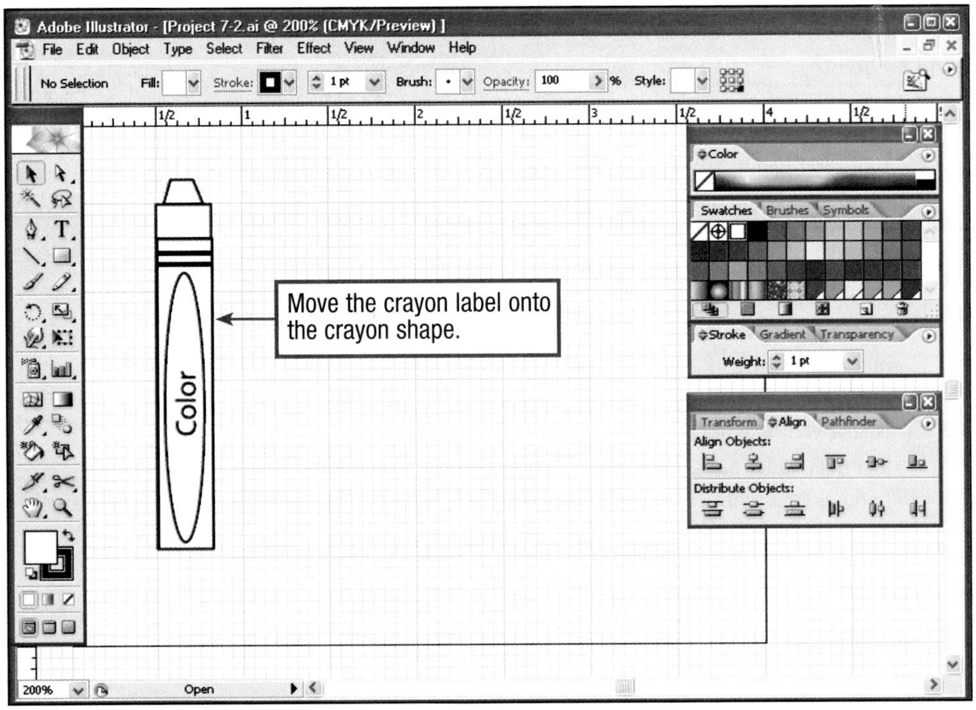

Project 5-3

Spotlight on Skills

- Use the Navigator palette
- Add to selection
- Subtract from selection
- Add a layer

Key Term

- collage

Academic Focus

Math
Work with geometric shapes

Create a Photo Collage

In Units 1 and 2, you saw how images were created on different layers. Photoshop allows you to manipulate layers so that you can change backgrounds and add or subtract images. You can use layers to create a **collage**, a collection of assembled images.

Introducing Palettes

Photoshop has many different palettes besides the ones that open as the default options. Display the palettes you need and hide the ones you are not using. The tabs in a palette can be brought to the front by clicking on them. They can also be dragged so that they become separate palettes.

To hide or display all the onscreen palettes, click SHIFT + TAB. Display or hide individual palettes by opening the Window menu and clicking the palette options. You can also close palettes by clicking the Close button in the top right corner.

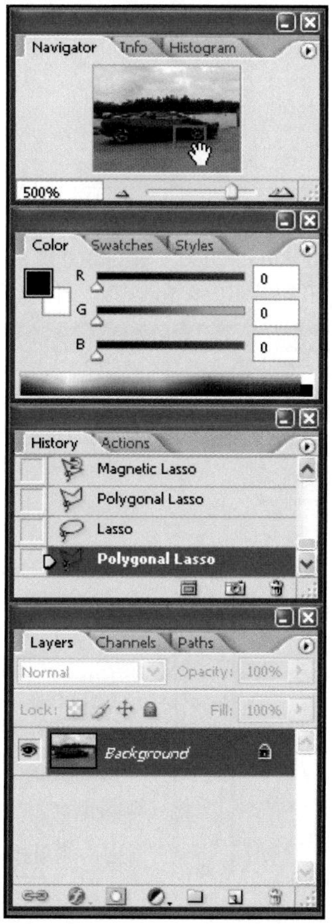

Navigator Palette The red rectangle shows the part of the image displayed in the workspace. You can move the rectangle to display a new area. You can zoom with the bottom slider.

Color Palette You can choose fill colors from the color palette using RGB, CMYK, or other settings.

History Palette If you made a mistake, click the last correct action that you want to return to. That will restore the image to that stage.

Layers Palette As you add layers, you will be able to view them, reorder them, and edit them using this palette.

▶ **In this project,** you will begin to create a collage. You will also continue to practice using the selection tools and the **Add to Selection** and **Subtract from Selection** options. These options allow you to remove or add selected parts of an object.

9. In the toolbox, click the **Hand** tool. Drag it over the image to reposition your view.

10. Click outside the crayon to deselect the rectangles. Click the **Direct Selection** tool.

11. Click the anchor points at the top of the top rectangle. Move them inward to create a trapezoid (Figure 7.9).

Align Objects

12. Click **View>Zoom Out**. Click the **Selection** tool, and drag a marquee around the three parts of the crayon.

13. Click **Window>Align** to open the **Align** palette. Choose **Horizontal Align Center**.

14. With the crayon still selected, click **Object>Group**.

15. Click **Rectangle**, and drag right to open the **Ellipse** tool. Draw an oval on the second rectangle (Figure 7.10).

16. In the toolbox, click the **Line Segment** tool. Draw a horizontal line at the top of the second rectangle (Figure 7.10).

Format a Line

17. Click **Window>Stroke**. Choose a **2 pt** weight.

18. Click the **Selection** tool. Press ALT. Then click the line, and drag downward to create another line (Figure 7.10).

▼ Figure 7.9 Use the Direct Selection tool to work on separate design elements in your illustrations.

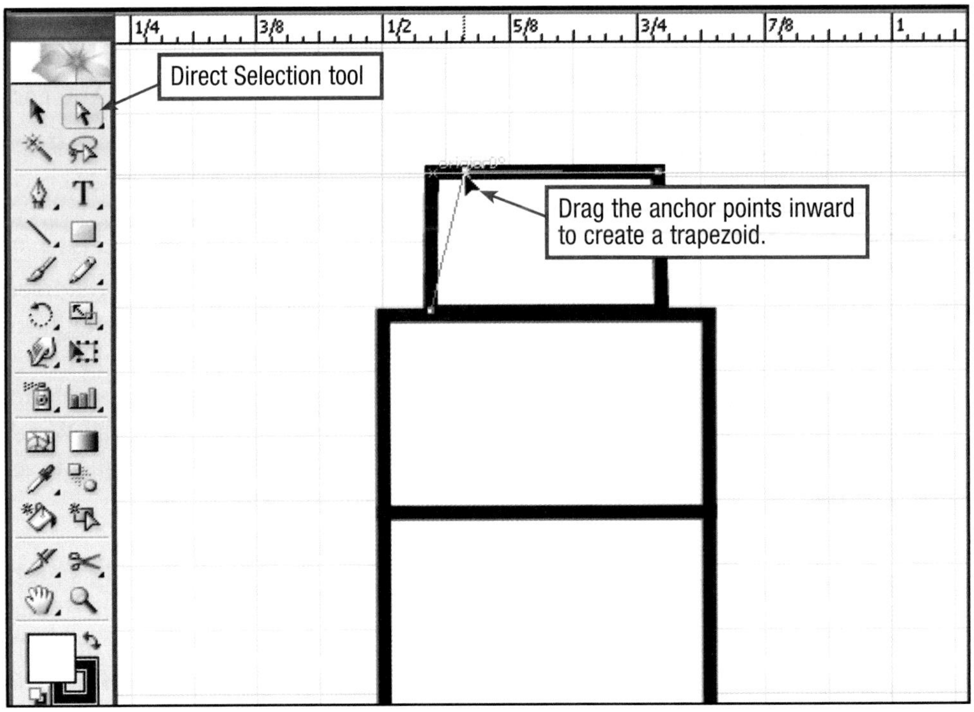

▼ Figure 7.10 When you choose a stroke, it is shown on the Control palette and toolbox as well as on the Stroke palette.

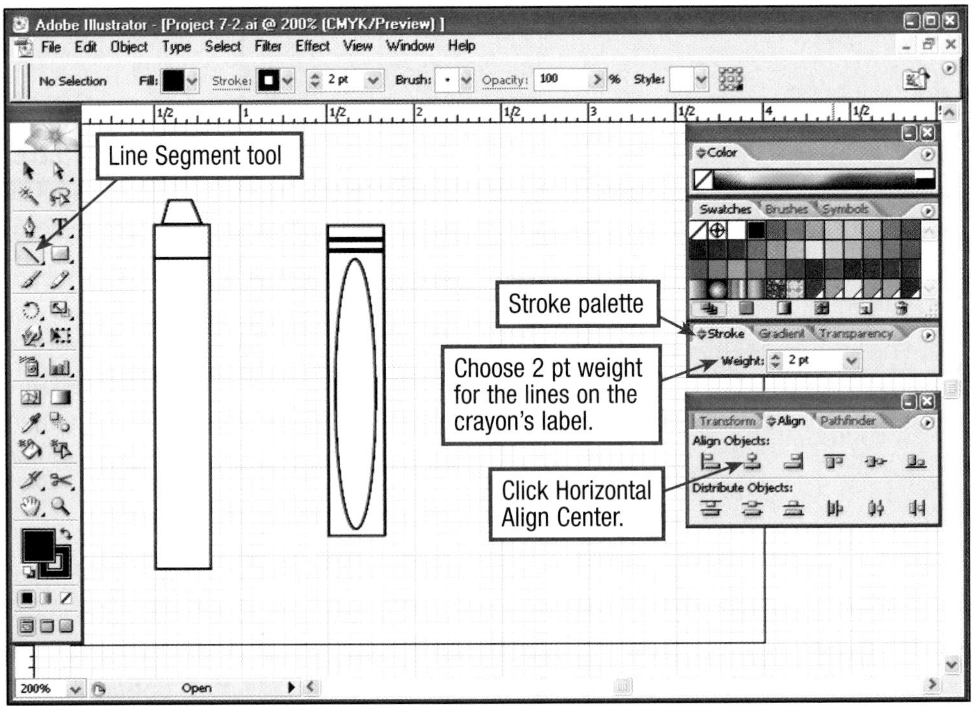

Student Data File

Step-by-Step

1. Press SHIFT + ALT + CTRL when starting Photoshop. **Mac** users press SHIFT + OPTION + ⌘.

2. Open **Data File 5-3**. Save it according to your teacher's instructions.

Use the Navigator Palette

3. Use the zoom slider in the **Navigator** palette to resize the workspace until it is as large as you can make it (Figure 5.14).

4. Right-click the **Rectangular Marquee**, and choose **Elliptical Marquee** .

Add to Selection

5. On the **Options** bar, click **Add to Selection** .

6. On the car image, select each tire by pressing SHIFT, then dragging a circle around it (Figure 5.15). Do not worry if you do not select the tires perfectly. You will correct it later.

7. Right-click the **Lasso** tool, and choose the **Magnetic Lasso** .

▼ **Figure 5.14** The Navigator palette helps you change the view in the workspace.

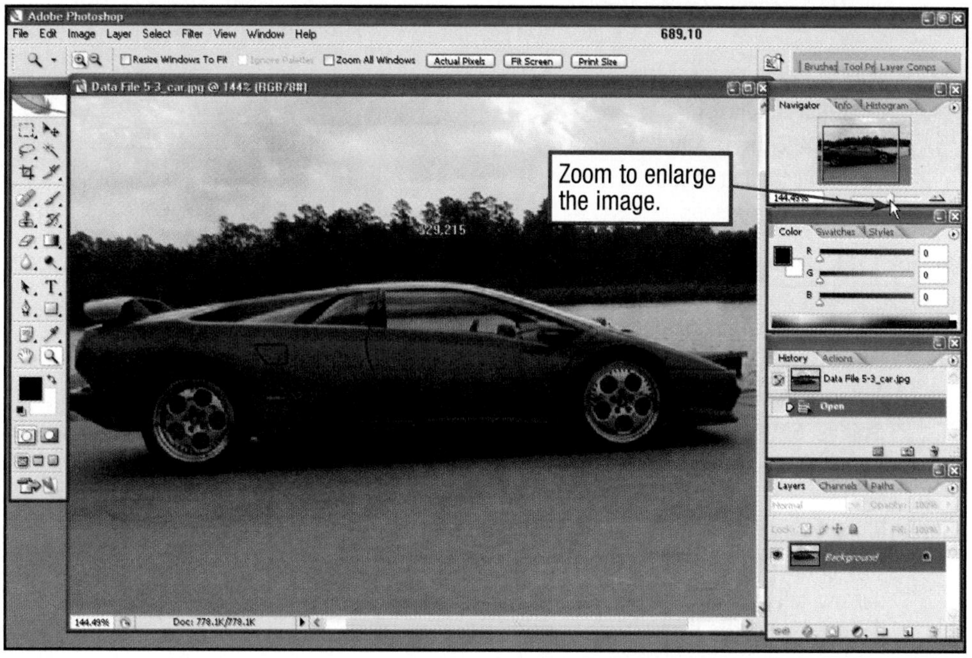

▼ **Figure 5.15** Use Add to Selection to select more than one part of an object.

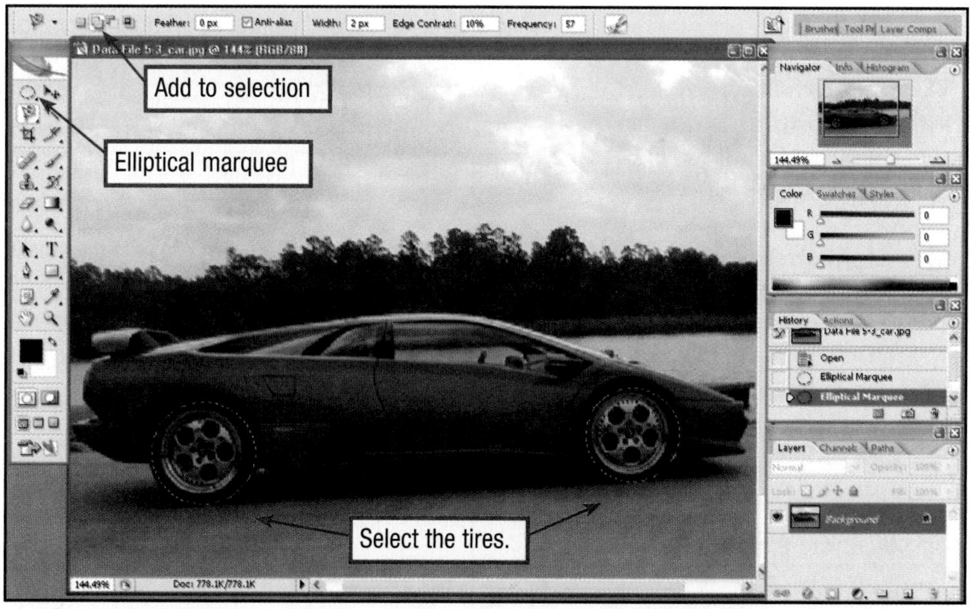

Instant Message

Keyboard Shortcuts Once you have clicked a selection tool, you can choose the **Add to Selection** option by pressing SHIFT. You can **Subtract from Selection**, by pressing ALT (or OPTION for **Mac** users).

Step-by-Step

1. Open a new document in Illustrator that is **4 inches wide** and **3 inches high**. Save it according to your teacher's instructions.

Display Grids and Guides

2. Click the **View** menu and make sure the following options are chosen: **Smart Guides**, **Show Grid**, **Show Rulers**.

3. In the toolbox, click **Rectangle** ▢. Drag a narrow, tall rectangle in the workspace (Figure 7.7).

4. In the toolbox, click the **Selection** tool ➤ and select the rectangle.

5. Click **Edit>Copy**, then **Edit>Paste** to copy the first rectangle. You will use this rectangle later.

6. Click **Rectangle**, and create a smaller rectangle at the top of the first rectangle (Figure 7.8).

7. Create another smaller rectangle, and position it at the top of the last rectangle (Figure 7.8).

Apply the Zoom Tool

8. In the toolbox, click the **Zoom** tool, and drag a marquee around the top two rectangles to magnify the section (Figure 7.8).

▼ **Figure 7.7** Use copy and paste commands to duplicate the objects you create.

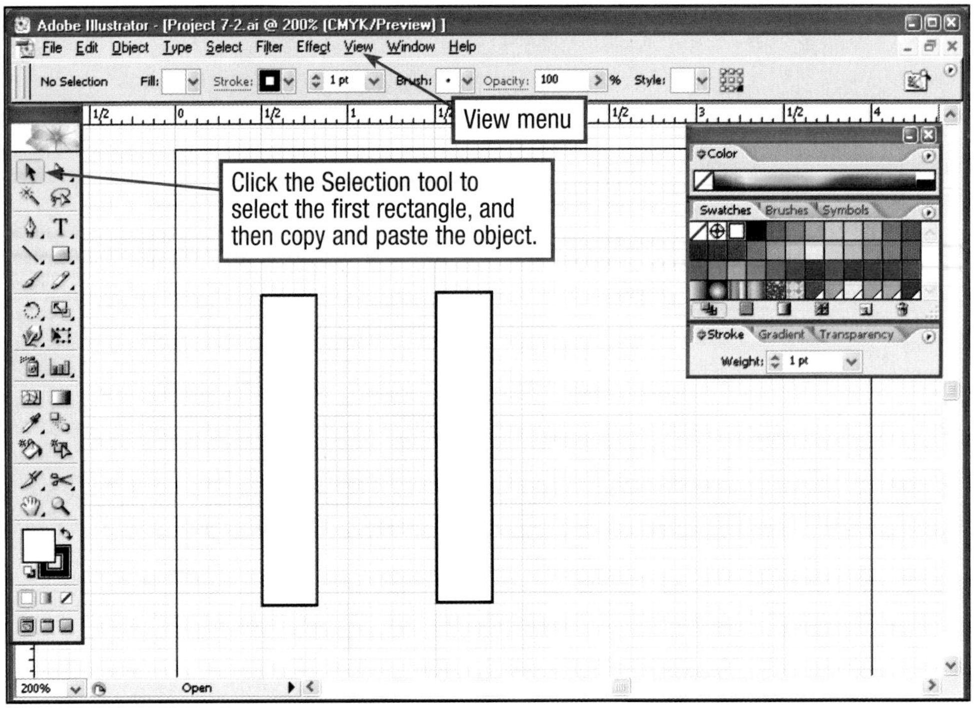

▼ **Figure 7.8** Draw a marquee with the Zoom tool to magnify a specific part.

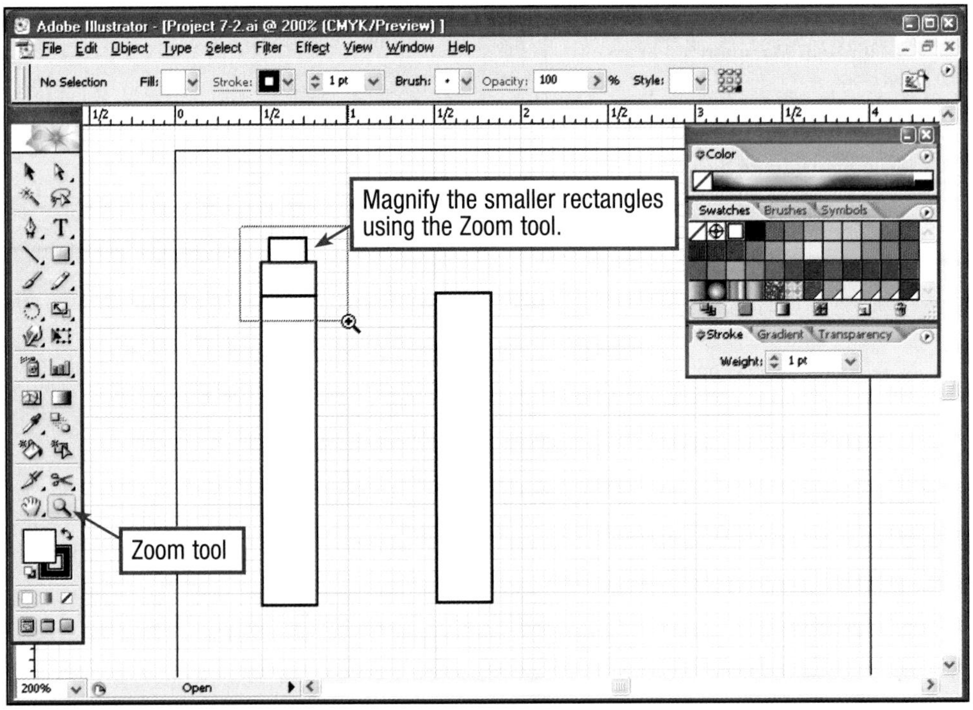

8 On the **Options** bar, choose **Add to Selection**. Change the **Width** to **2 px**.

9 Click the edge of the car, and move the selection tool around the perimeter. Do not worry about making the selection perfect at this point. See Figure 5.16.

10 Use the **Zoom** to magnify a curved area where the selection line is too far in from the edge of the car (Figure 5.17).

11 Click **Lasso**, and choose the **Add to Selection** option.

12 Draw a loop to select the area that was missed the first time (Figure 5.17).

13 Use **Hand**, or drag the rectangle in the **Navigation** palette to move around the car perimeter. Find a missed area at the bottom of the car.

14 Since the bottom of the car is a straight line, use the **Polygonal Lasso** to select it, and choose **Add to Selection**.

▼ **Figure 5.16** Use a smaller width, and click to add fastening points in areas without much background contrast.

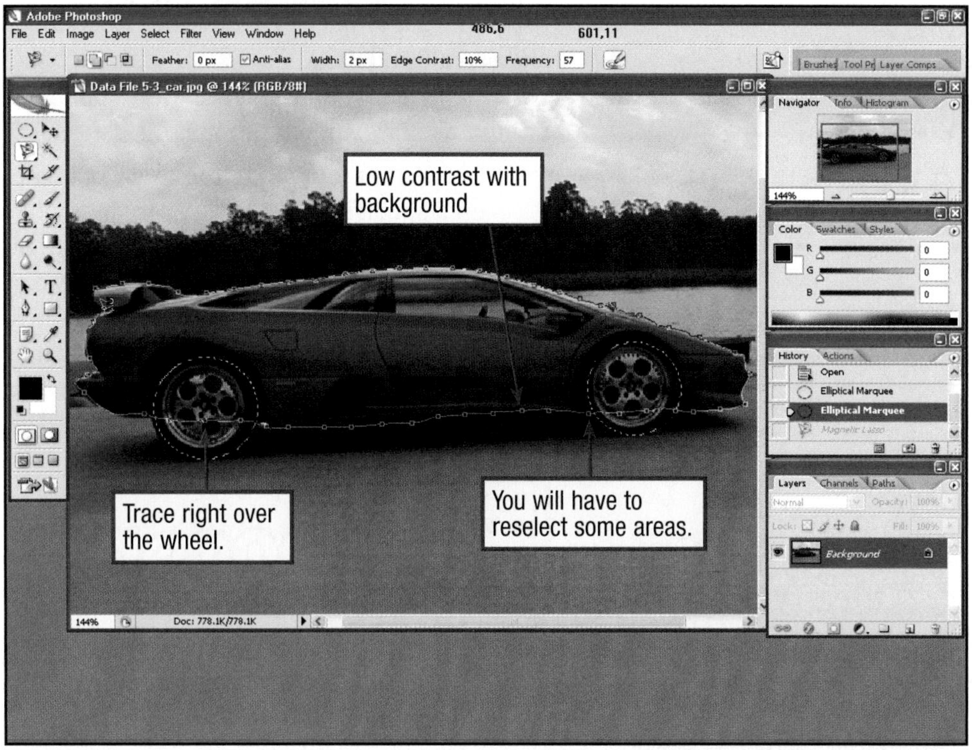

▼ **Figure 5.17** Zoom in close enough to see missed areas. When you choose Add to Selection, the new selection becomes part of the original selection.

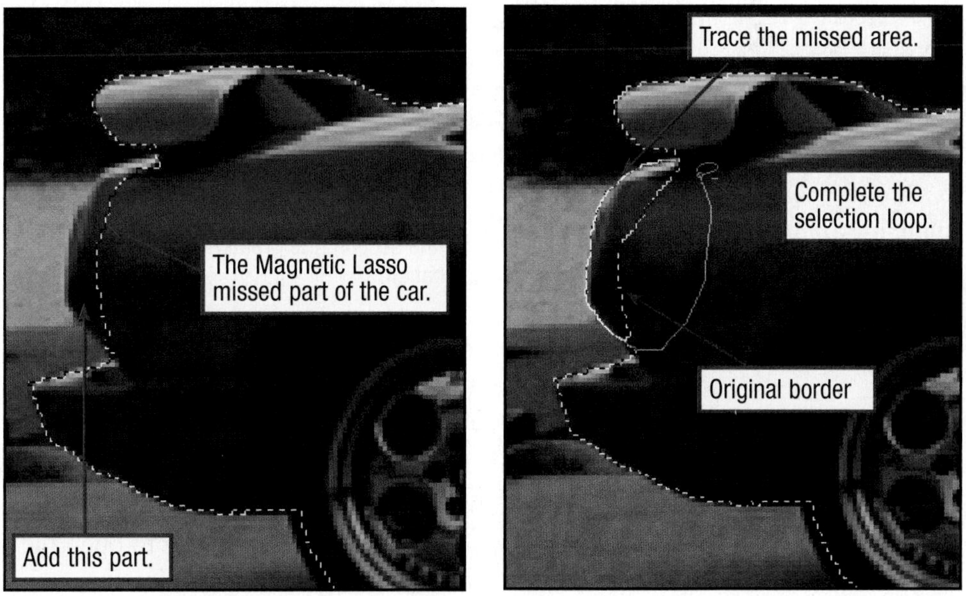

Zoom in Closer

Illustrator allows you view any part of an image or its layers in detail by providing a number of Zoom tools. *Zoom in* to **magnify**, or enlarge, an image and see close details. *Zoom out* to reduce the size of the picture to display a wider area. Depending on the tool, you can use preset magnification levels, or create your own percent magnification.

- The **Zoom** tool in the toolbox is often the quickest way to zoom in on a specific area. To enlarge the image, click the tool, then click the area you want to magnify. To reduce the image, press ALT and click the area. You can also drag a marquee around the area you want to view, and the selected area will magnify to fill the screen.

  Mac Tip Use the Option key rather than the ALT key to zoom out.

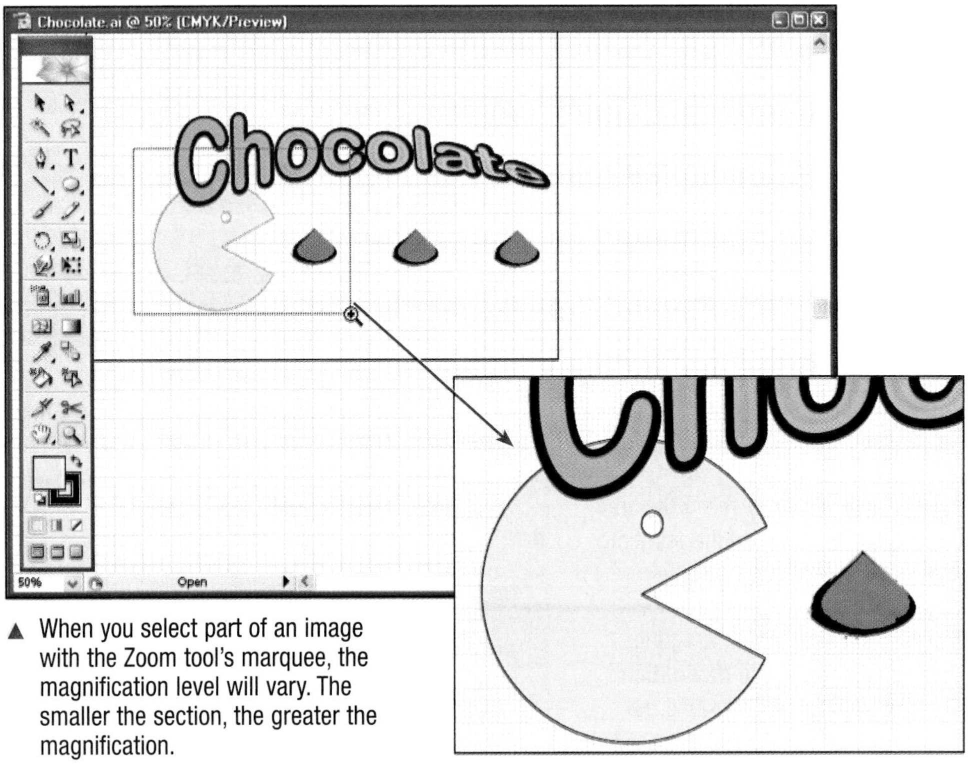

▲ When you select part of an image with the Zoom tool's marquee, the magnification level will vary. The smaller the section, the greater the magnification.

- In the lower left corner of the screen, change the zoom level by clicking the arrow and choosing from the drop-down menu, or setting your own percentage.
- Click **View>Zoom In** or **View>Zoom Out** to change the magnification to the next preset level.
- Click **Window>Navigator** to open the Navigator palette. Use the slide to change the magnification.

▶ **In this project,** you will use Illustrator's tools to draw a crayon.

Sidebar

Remember Undo If you make a mistake in Illustrator, you can undo it by using the same command you have used in previous programs. Click **Edit>Undo** or press CTRL + Z to go back to the previous command that you entered. You can also go back to the last-saved version of your file by clicking **Edit>Revert**.

Compare What is the difference between the Undo and Revert commands?

Subtract from Selection

15 Find an area where the selection marquee is drawn too far outside the edge of the car (Figure 5.18).

16 Use a suitable selection tool, and choose **Subtract from Selection** to fix the marquee (Figure 5.18).

17 Double-click the **Hand** tool to see the whole car.

▼ Figure 5.18 Use Subtract from Selection to redraw selection lines that are outside the image.

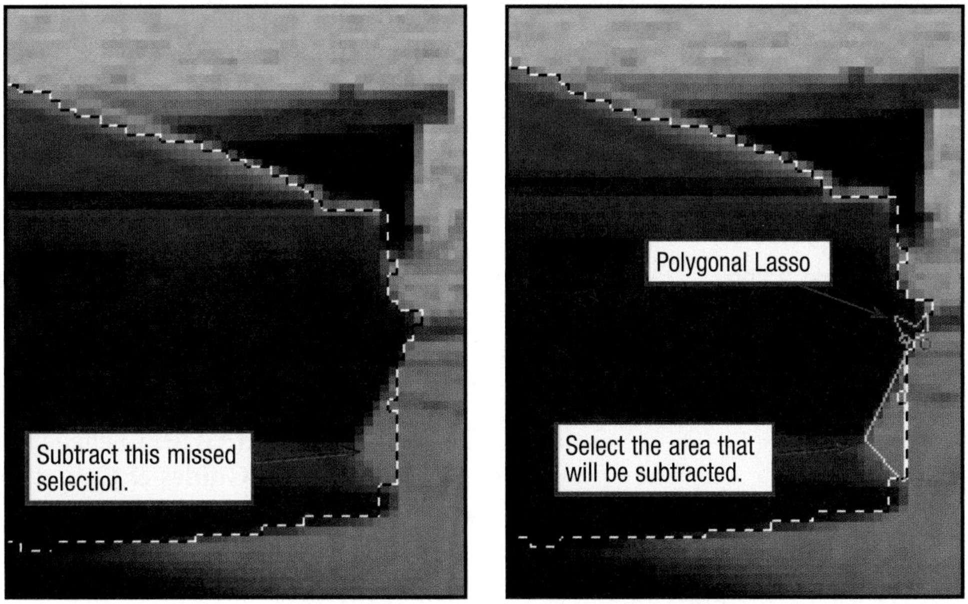

Subtract this missed selection.
Polygonal Lasso
Select the area that will be subtracted.

Add a Layer

18 Click **Layer>New> Layer Via Copy** to create a layer out of the selected area.

19 In the **Layers** palette, click the eye icon next to the **Background** layer to hide it. You will see a checkered background around the car (Figure 5.19).

20 Double-click the new Layer 1 layer, and rename it Original Car (Figure 5.19).

21 Follow your teacher's instructions for saving your work. You will continue your car in Project 5-4.

▼ Figure 5.19 A checkered background shows that transparent information is present.

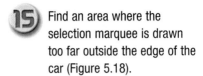

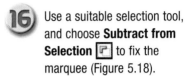

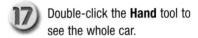

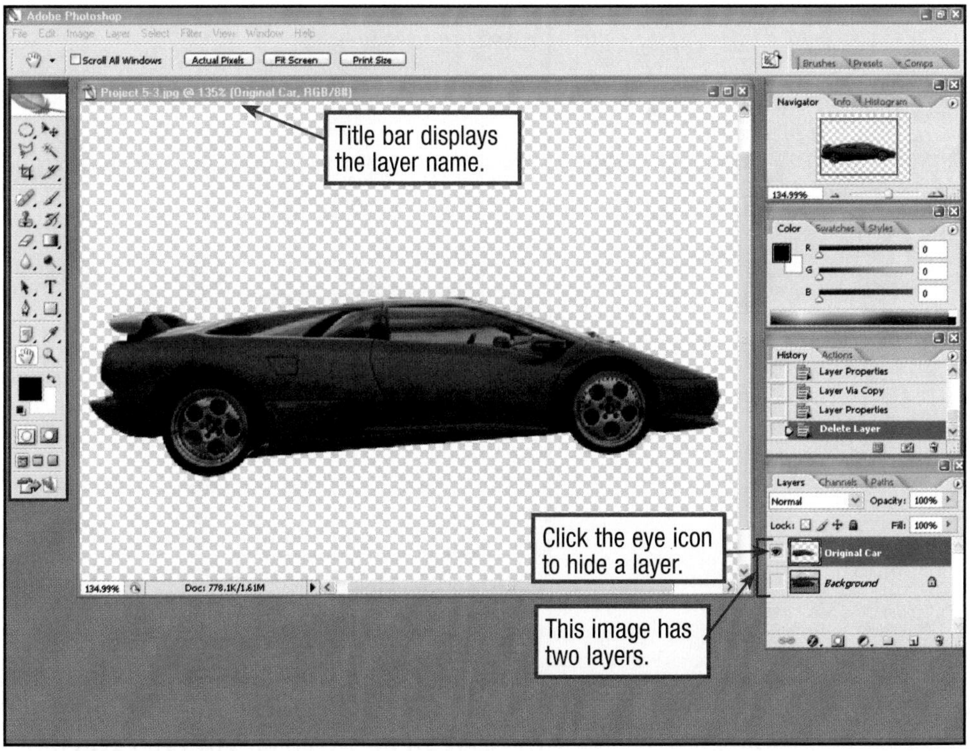

Project 7-2

Create an Illustration

Spotlight on Skills

- Display grids and guides
- Apply the Zoom tool
- Align objects
- Format a line
- Add text
- Rotate an object

Key Terms

- grids
- magnify

Academic Focus

Math
Work with grids

Illustrator provides a variety of tools that allow you to precisely create, format, and manipulate your drawings.

Align Objects

Illustrator offers new methods for aligning objects, as well as options that are similar to those you used in other software such as Microsoft Publisher.

- Guides and grids help you align objects in the workspace. **Guides** can be created by dragging a line from a ruler, or by right-clicking a border or path and choosing **Make Guides**.
- **Grids**, or the framework upon which you place objects, can be displayed behind your illustration and do not print. Display grids by clicking **View>Show Grid**. To change the size of the grid, click **Edit>Preferences>Guides & Grid**, then set the new spacing between gridlines.
- **Smart Guides** create temporary path lines that help you align objects in relation to each other.

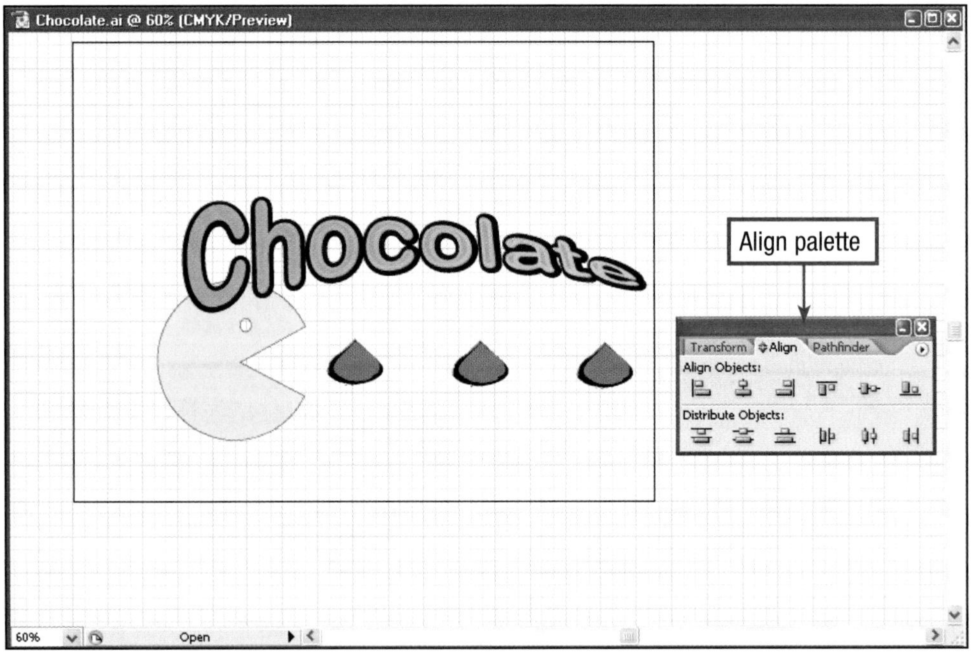

▲ Grids allow you to align objects in relation to the workspace. The Align palette helps you align objects in relation to each other.

- The **Align palette** lets you precisely align objects in relation to each other. Objects can be vertically aligned or horizontally aligned left, right, or center. They can also be distributed so that they are spaced evenly from each other. Open the Align palette by clicking **Window>Align**.

Project 5-4

Add Layers

Spotlight on Skills

- Change color
- Create new layers
- Reorder layers
- Add a new background
- Adjust contrast
- Insert a new image
- Erase parts of an image

Key Terms

- opaque
- opacity
- transparency
- blending modes
- hue
- saturation

Academic Focus

Science
Work with colors

The images you create in Photoshop will almost always be created from a combination of layers. For example, in an image of a haunted house, you might use one layer for the house in the background, one for a scary shadow in the window, and still another for the dark clouds you add.

In the Layers palette, you can rearrange layers in any order. Usually the background layer is at the bottom. The top layer in the palette is the top layer of your image. Some layers are **opaque**. That means you cannot see through them. Often, though, you do want to see through a top layer to a layer below, so you must change how opaque it is, or the **opacity**. The more you can see through a layer, the greater its **transparency**.

Apply Blending Modes

Blending modes control the way the pixels on one layer blend with the pixels in underlying layers. You might want the top layer to be semi-transparent so that colors from an underlying layer show through. Or, you might want colors from a top and bottom layer to blend into a new color.

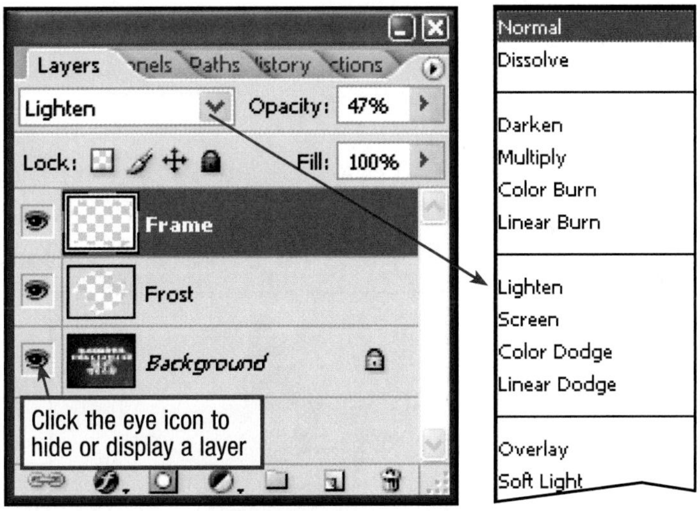

▲ View blending mode options on the Layers palette. The names of blending modes are based on photography darkroom techniques.

Use the **Help** feature in Photoshop to tell you more about each mode. You can also see their effect by clicking in the Blending Mode window in the Layers palette, then pressing the up or down arrows on the keyboard. The mode will change, and you can see the effect immediately on your image.

▶ **In this project,** you will finish modifying the car image that you started in Project 5-3. One change you will make is to the color of the car, using the Hue and Saturation command. **Hue** is basically the same thing as color. **Saturation** is the intensity of the color.

19 Click **Ellipse**, and drag to the right to choose the **Star**. Create a star on the workspace.

20 Click the **Selection** tool, select the star, and change the fill to **yellow**.

21 Move your mouse pointer near the bounding box handles until you display the curved, two-headed rotation arrow. **Rotate** the star (Figure 7.5).

Figure 7.5 The new object has the same fill as the previously selected objects.

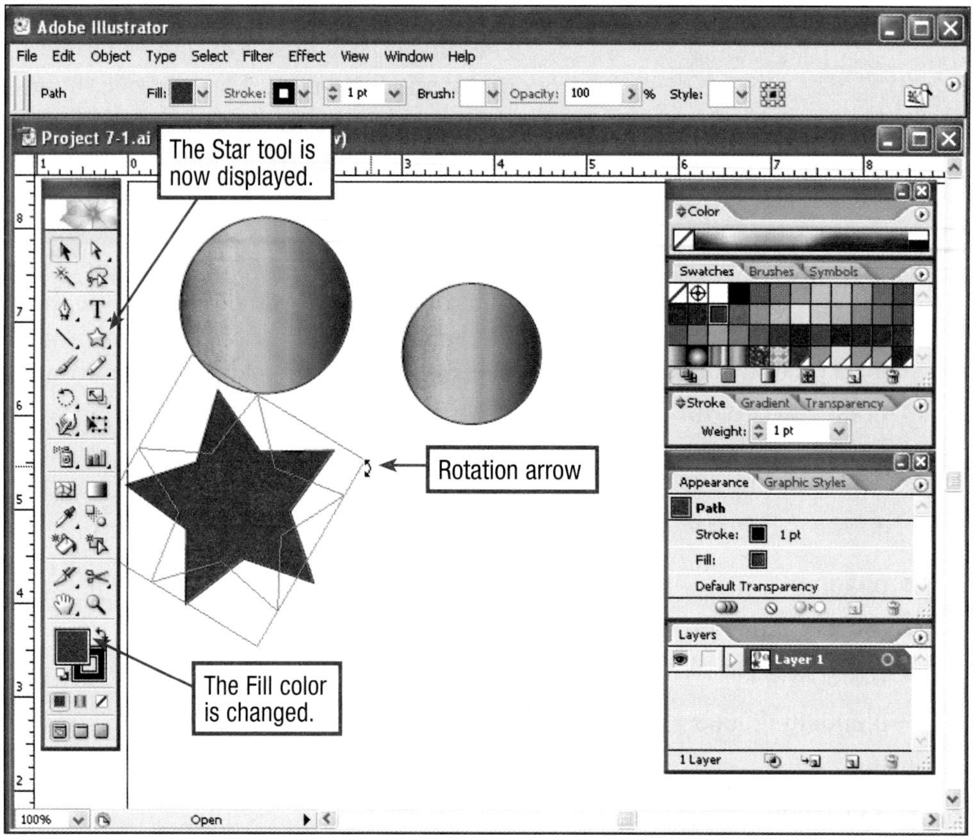

Apply the Direct Selection Tool

22 Deselect the star. Then click **Direct Selection**.

23 Move the pointer over an anchor point. When a white square appears next to the pointer, click that anchor point (Figure 7.6).

24 Drag the point to change the shape of the star.

25 Use the **Direct Selection** tool to drag a selection around one of the star's points. Click the point, and drag the shape further (Figure 7.6).

26 Follow your teacher's instructions for saving your file.

Figure 7.6 Use the Direct Selection tool to select a point or a section of an object.

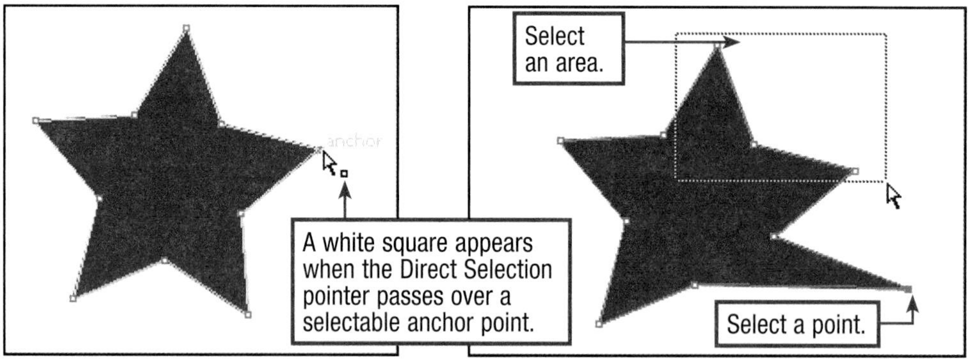

Instant Message

Restore Default Workspace Preferences When you exit Adobe Illustrator, the palettes and some of the commands you have used are stored as preferences. Since many people may use your computer, you may want to restore your settings to Illustrator's default settings whenever you start a new project. Follow your teacher's instructions for restoring the default preferences.

Step-by-Step

1. In Photoshop, open the car image you created in Project 5-3. Save it according to your teacher's instructions.

2. Make sure you are displaying the **Original Car** layer and the **Background** layer is hidden (Figure 5.20).

Change Color

3. Click **Image>Adjustments> Hue/Saturation**. Drag the three sliders to change the car's color. Click **OK** (Figure 5.20).

Create New Layers

4. Click **Layer>New> Layer Via Copy**. Name the new layer New Car. Hide the **Original Car** layer.

5. With the **New Car** layer still selected in the **Layers** palette, click **Layer>New> Layer Via Copy** to create another copy.

6. Click **Edit>Transform>Flip Vertical**.

7. Click **Move** [Move tool icon]. Drag the inverted car below the original car, so that the image looks similar to Figure 5.21.

▼ **Figure 5.20** Use the sliders to adjust the color of the car until you are satisfied.

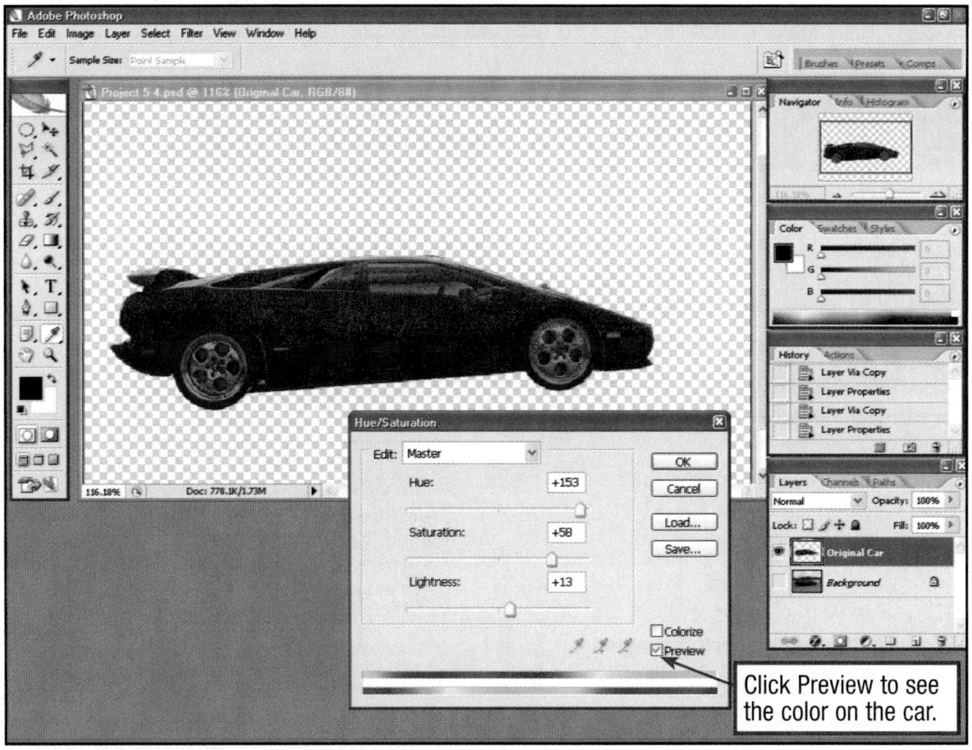

▼ **Figure 5.21** The two New Car layers are visible, and the original car is hidden.

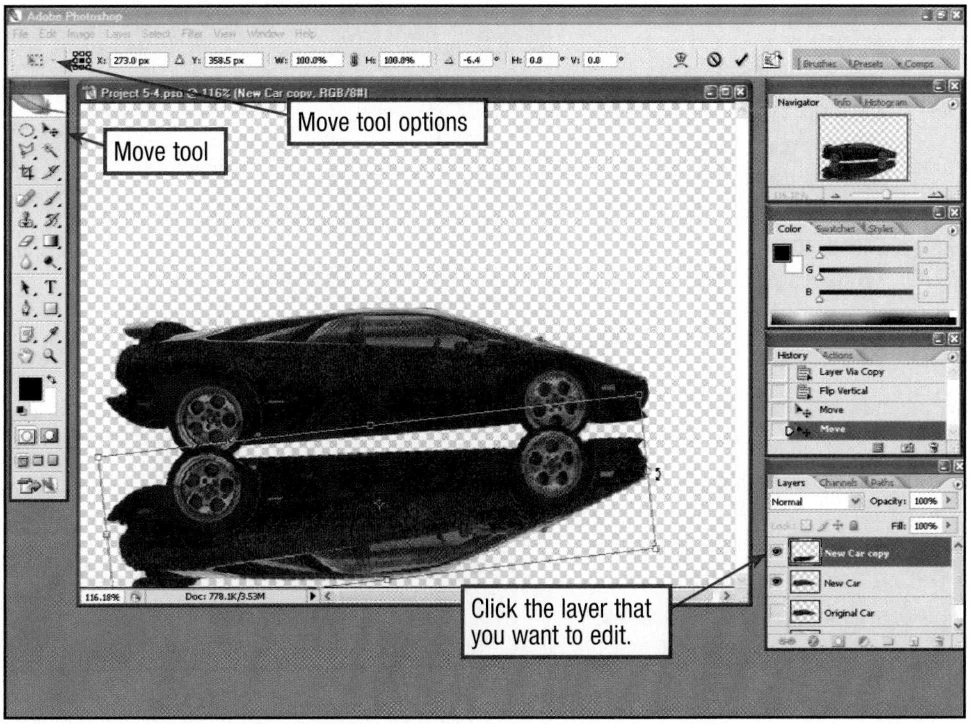

Add Fill Color

9 On the toolbox, click the Fill tool.

10 In the palettes, click the **Swatches** tab. Choose a color to fill your circle (Figure 7.4).

Drag Objects

11 Click inside the filled circle and drag it. Notice that you can click anywhere in the circle for it to be selected.

12 Select the white circle. On the color palette, click **None** ⧄ for the fill.

13 Run your pointer over the unfilled circle. You will see the black square as you pass it over the border (Figure 7.3).

14 Click on the border to select the unfilled circle, and drag it next to the first circle.

15 Click above the first circle, and drag a marquee over part of both circles. Both circles will be selected (Figure 7.4).

16 Click a new fill color on the **Swatches** palette. Both circles will be filled with the new color.

17 Deselect the circles by clicking in any part of the workspace with no objects.

18 Click the first circle to select it. Press SHIFT and click the second circle. Both should be selected. Change the fill to a new color.

▼ **Figure 7.3** Objects with fills can be selected by clicking in the center. Objects without fills are selected by clicking the border.

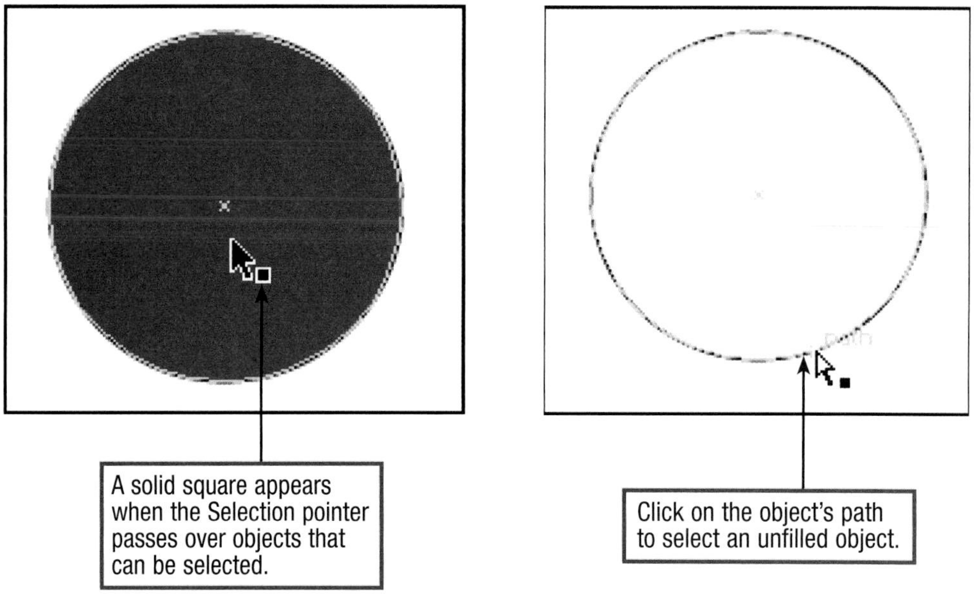

A solid square appears when the Selection pointer passes over objects that can be selected.
Click on the object's path to select an unfilled object.

▼ **Figure 7.4** Select multiple objects by drawing a marquee around them or holding the Shift key as you click on each.

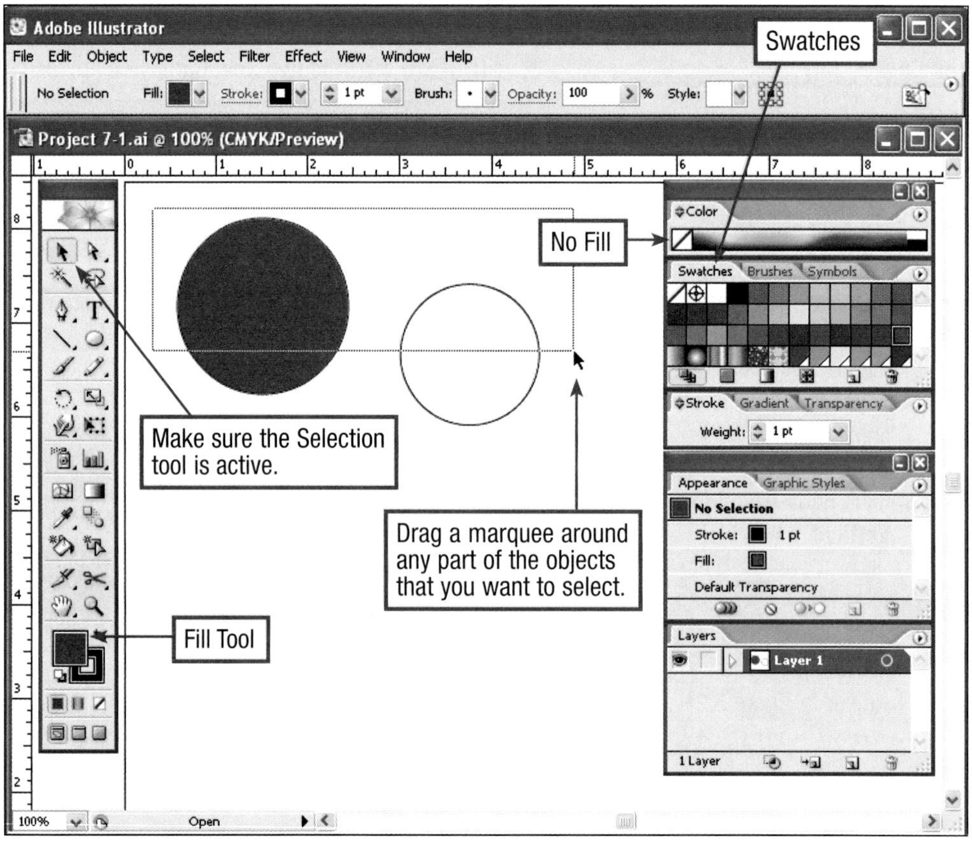

8. In the **Layers** palette, double-click the name of the **New Car Copy** layer, and rename it Reflection.

9. On the **Move Options** bar, click **Show Transform Controls**. Move your pointer outside the inverted car's marquee to display a curved arrow.

10. Drag the arrow to rotate the car until the tires line up (Figure 5.22).

11. Click the **Move** tool, and choose **Apply the transformation** when finished.

▼ Figure 5.22 Use the Move tool's Option bar to display handles.

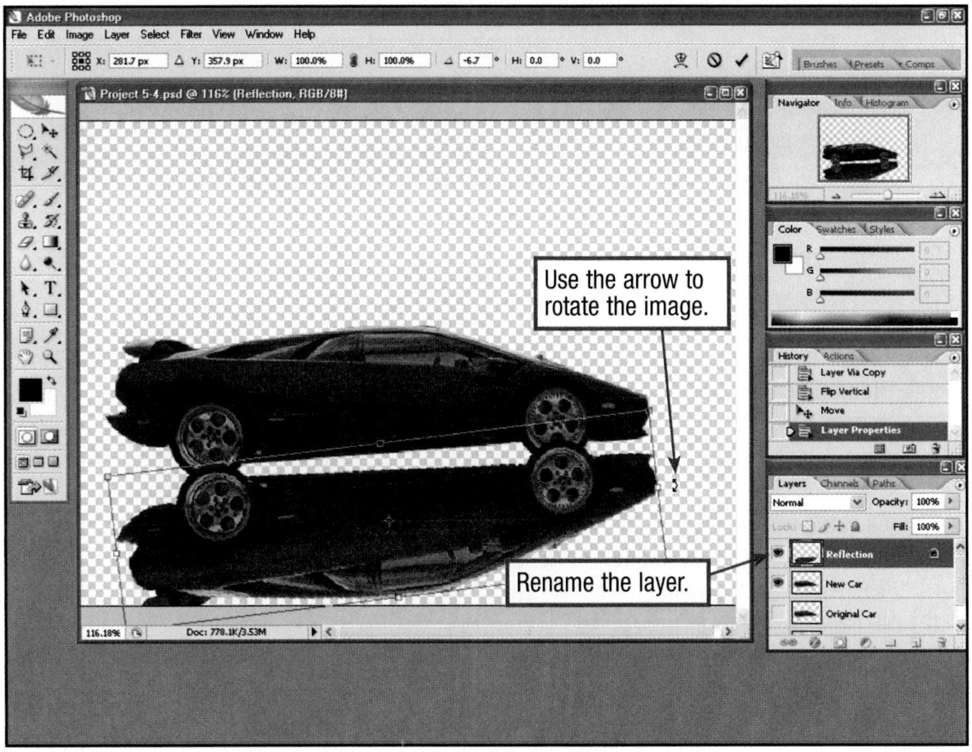

Reorder Layers

12. On the **Layers** palette, click and drag the **Reflection** layer below the **New Car** layer.

Add a New Background

13. Click **Layer>New>Layer**. In the dialog box, name the new layer Black Background (Figure 5.23).

14. In the toolbox, drag out **Gradient** , to open **Paint Bucket** .

15. Press D to reset the default colors, then click in the workspace. The entire background should be black.

▼ Figure 5.23 The layers have been rearranged in the Layers palette.

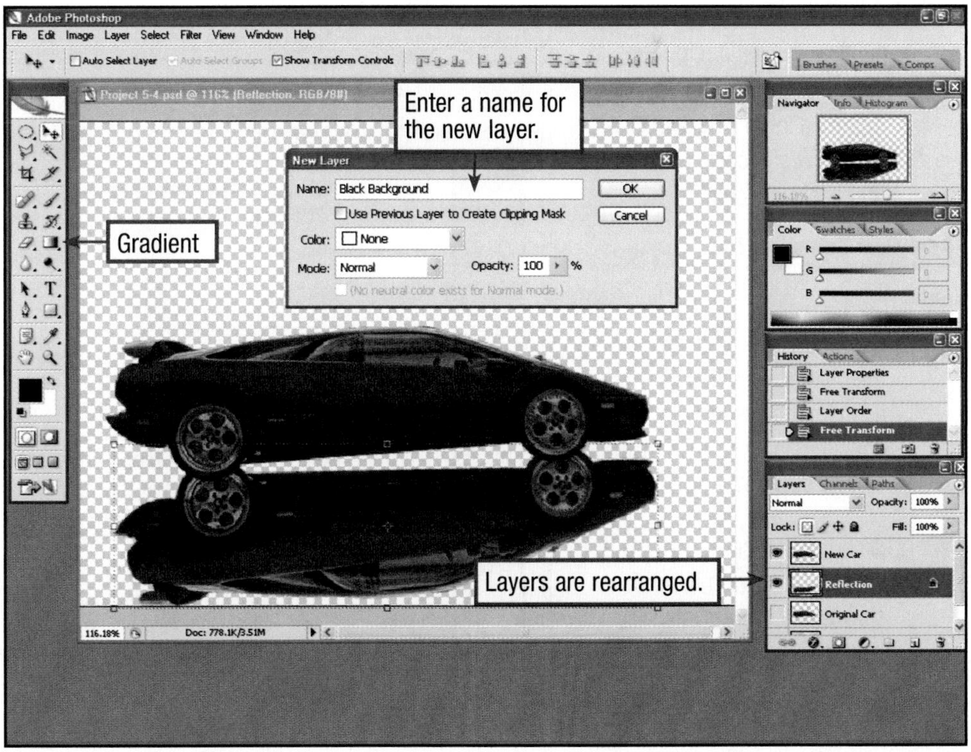

Step-by-Step

1. In Illustrator, open a new file and save it according to your teacher's instructions.

Create Geometric Shapes

2. Click **View>Show Rulers**.

3. On the toolbox, click the **Rectangle** tool. Then drag to the right to open the toolbar. Choose **Ellipse**.

4. Click the workspace and hold down the SHIFT, as you drag a circle about **1.5 inches** in diameter. (Holding SHIFT creates a perfect circle.)

5. Click the circle to display the **Ellipse** box. Under **Options**, see how close you were to drawing a **1.5 inch** circle.

6. Change the settings for both **Width** and **Height** to **1.5 inches** (Figure 7.1), and click **OK**. A second circle appears that is sized exactly.

Apply the Selection Tool

7. On the toolbox, click the **Selection** tool. When the pointer is moved over a circle, a black square appears, showing the circle can be selected.

8. Click the first circle. A bounding box with handles shows that it is selected (Figure 7.2).

▼ **Figure 7.1** The Ellipse tool will stay open until you choose another tool in the toolbox.

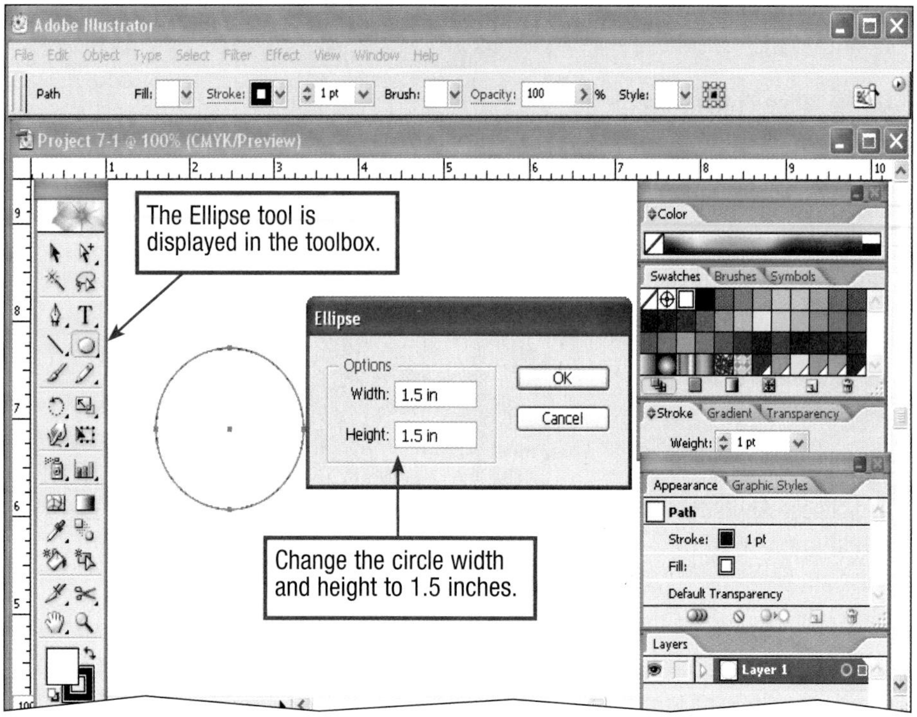

Adobe Illustrator
Project 7-1 @ 100% (CMYK/Preview)
The Ellipse tool is displayed in the toolbox.
Ellipse
Options
Width: 1.5 in
Height: 1.5 in
OK
Cancel
Change the circle width and height to 1.5 inches.

▼ **Figure 7.2** When a bounding box is displayed, you can reposition, rotate, or format the object.

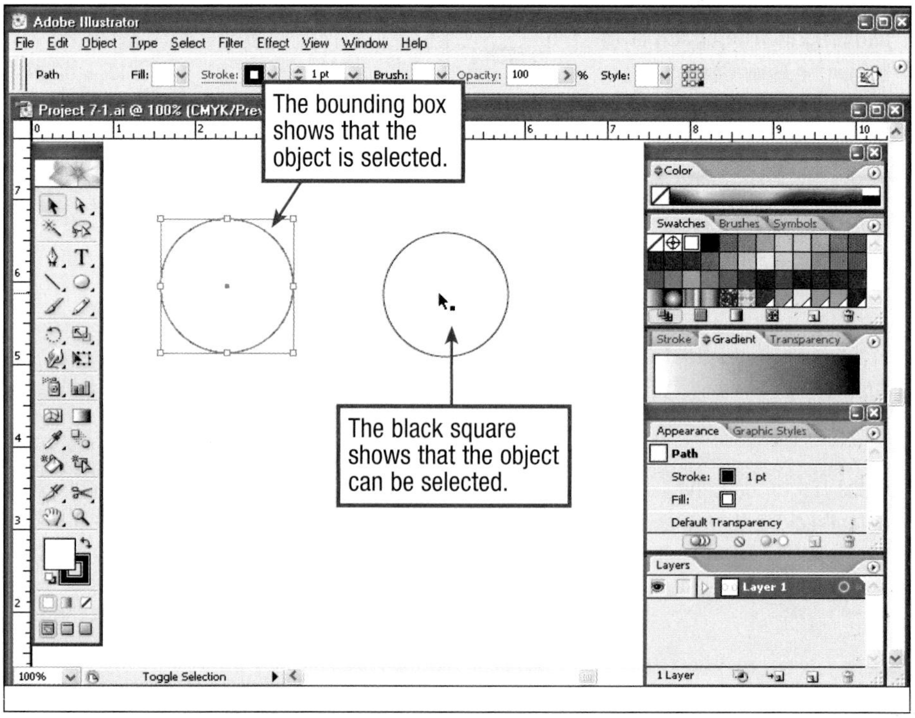

Adobe Illustrator
The bounding box shows that the object is selected.
The black square shows that the object can be selected.
Toggle Selection

16 On the **Layers** palette, drag the **Black Background** layer below the **Reflection** layer (Figure 5.24).

Adjust Contrast

17 Select the **New Car** layer, and click **Image>Adjustments> Brightness/Contrast**. Drag the **Contrast** slider until the tires are black.

18 Repeat Step 17 for the **Reflection** layer, until you are satisfied with the image.

19 Select the **Reflection** layer and click **Filter> Stylize>Wind**.

20 On the **Layers** palette, change the **Blending Mode** for the reflection to **Lighten** and the **Opacity** to **35%**.

Insert a New Image

21 In Photoshop, open **Data File 5-4**, a speedometer image.

22 Click the **Move** tool, then drag the speedometer into the car document. (Make sure you hold down your mouse button until the pointer changes shape in the car document.) See Figure 5.25.

Figure 5.24 The background is the lowest layer visible in the image.

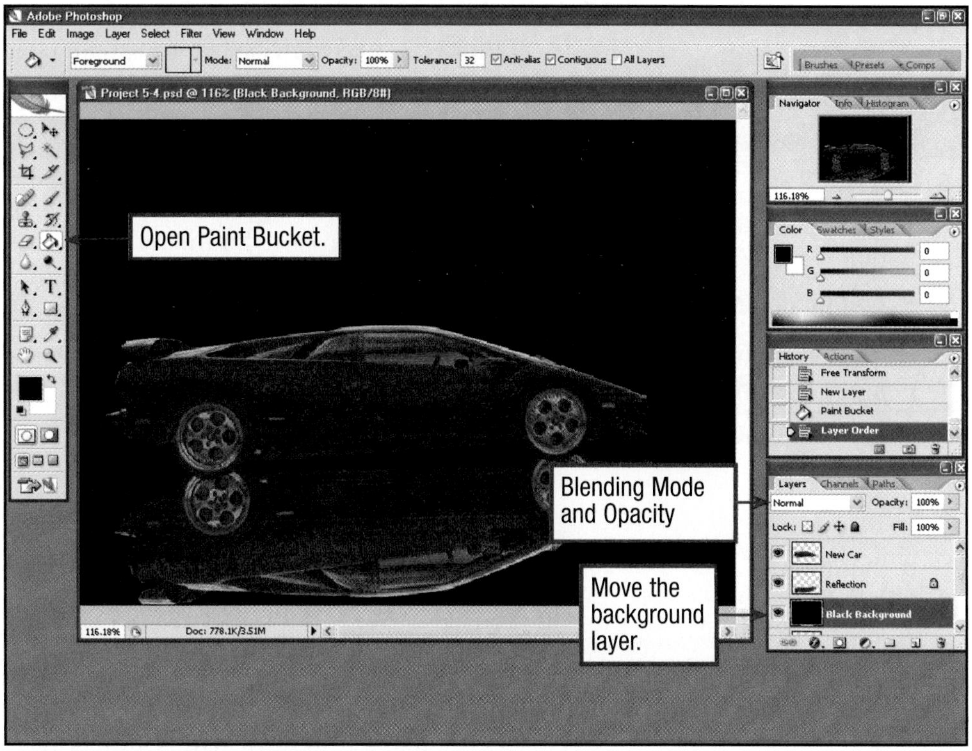

Figure 5.25 Even though the actual image does not move onto the new document, the pointer indicates that it is ready to be inserted.

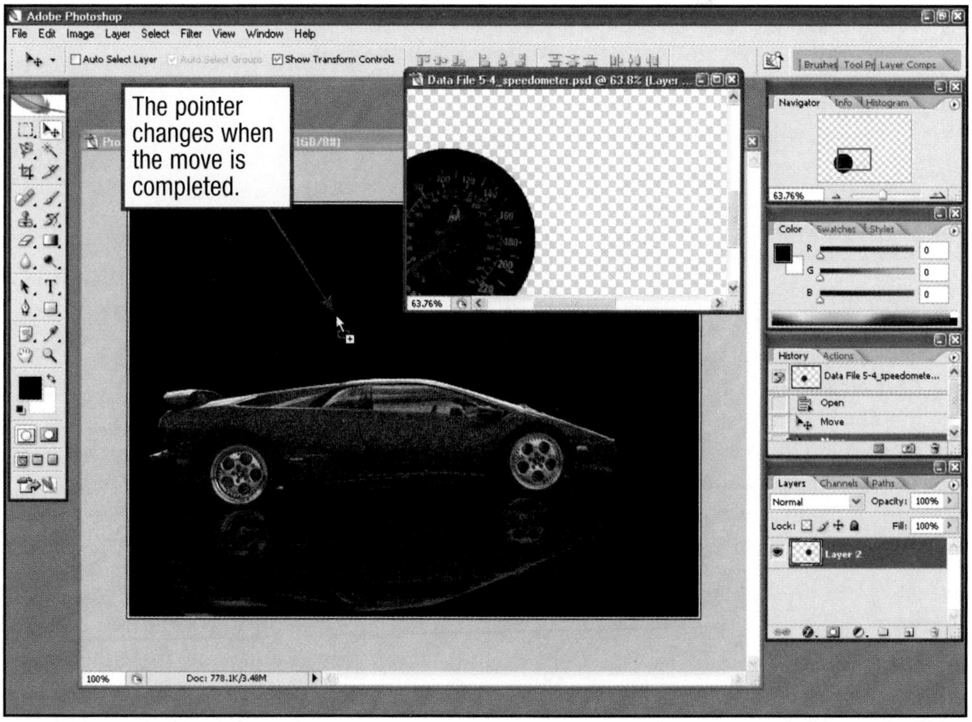

Project 7-1 Use Illustrator Tools

Spotlight on Skills

- Create geometric shapes
- Apply the Selection tool
- Add fill color
- Drag objects
- Apply the Direct Selection tool

Key Terms

- marquee
- object
- path
- anchor point

Academic Focus

Math
Create geometric shapes

Before you make any changes to an image, you need to know how to select parts of an image. Illustrator provides a number of selection options.

Selection Tools

The **Selection** tool is used in a similar way to the Selection tool you have used in Microsoft Publisher and Adobe Photoshop. You can drag a **marquee**, a dotted rectangle, over objects to select them. An **object** is any individual shape, image, or text that can be moved, edited, or manipulated. You can also select objects by clicking them individually or holding SHIFT down to select more than one object for grouping.

The **Direct Selection** tool is used to select anchor points or path segments that make up the border of an object. A **path** is the line that you create when you draw an object. An **anchor point** is the spot where you begin or end a segment. Each time you change the direction or shape of a line, you create a new anchor point.

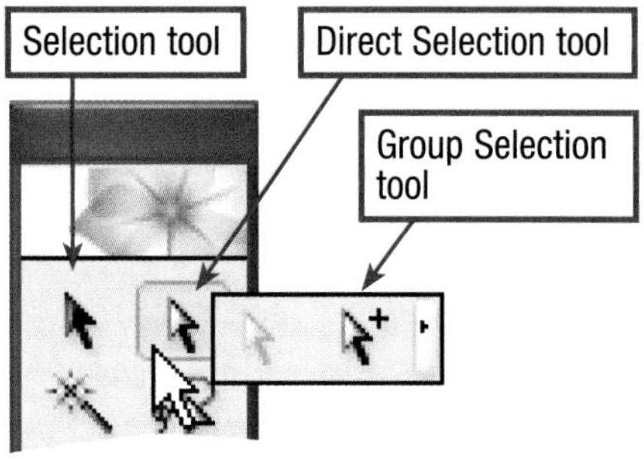

▲ Illustrator offers a variety of selection tools.

You can click the Direct Selection tool on a specific anchor point or path segment or use it to select an entire path. You can also drag a marquee around sections to change an object's shape or direction.

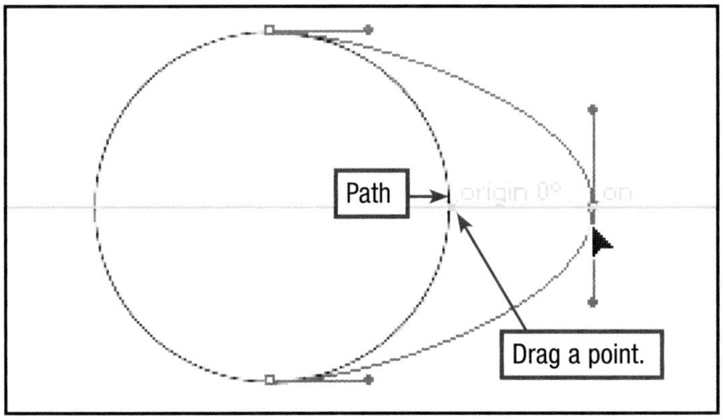

▲ Click and drag a point on a path to change an object's shape.

The **Group Selection** tool selects a single object within a set of objects that you have defined as a group.

▶ **In this project,** you will practice using Illustrator's selection tools. It is important to know how to use selection tools in order to use Illustrator effectively.

Go Online PREVIEW
www.glencoe.com

Before You Begin Go to **Chapter 7**, and choose **PowerPoint Presentations** to preview the documents you will be creating. Also, use the individual project **Rubrics** to help create and evaluate your work.

23 On the **Layers** palette, you will see a new layer with the speedometer thumbnail. Name it Speedometer.

24 On the **Layers** palette, drag the Speedometer layer below the New Car layer, if it is not there already.

25 Select the **Speedometer** layer. Use the **Move** tool to resize and rotate the image, as shown in Figure 5.27. Apply the Transformation.

Erase Parts of an Image

26 Click **Eraser**. On the **Options** bar, choose a **20 px** brush and **100 percent opacity**. (Figure 5.26).

27 Move your mouse (the eraser is now the pointer) over the parts of the speedometer below the car. Erase these parts.

28 On the **Layers** palette, change the **Blending Mode** to **Difference**, and adjust the **Opacity** as needed.

29 Follow your teacher's instructions for saving and printing your work.

▼ **Figure 5.26** Zoom in to see the parts you want to erase.

▼ **Figure 5.27** This finished image can now be placed in a brochure or ad.

REVIEW AND REVISE

Check your work Use Figure 5.27 as a guide and check that:

- ☑ The car's color, new background, and speedometer have been changed.
- ☑ A mirror reflection on a separate layer has been created.
- ☑ The speedometer has been resized and unwanted parts erased.
- ☑ Blending modes are applied to the reflection and speedometer.

WORKSHOP Toolbox

How Do I Use the Toolbox?

The toolbox has icons that you will need for creating illustrations and manipulating or editing the images. You can hide or display the toolbox by clicking **Windows>Tools**. You can also press the TAB key to hide or show the toolbox, along with all the palettes and the Control palette.

As with Microsoft Word and Publisher, you can choose a drawing tool, and then click and drag it into the workspace to create an object of any size. You can also click where you want the object to be placed in the workspace. A dialog box is displayed where you can set exact measurements for the object.

Some of the tools in the toolbox have small black rectangles. When you click one of these tools, the button expands to reveal additional tools. For example, when you click the Rectangle tool, it expands to show the Ellipse tool.

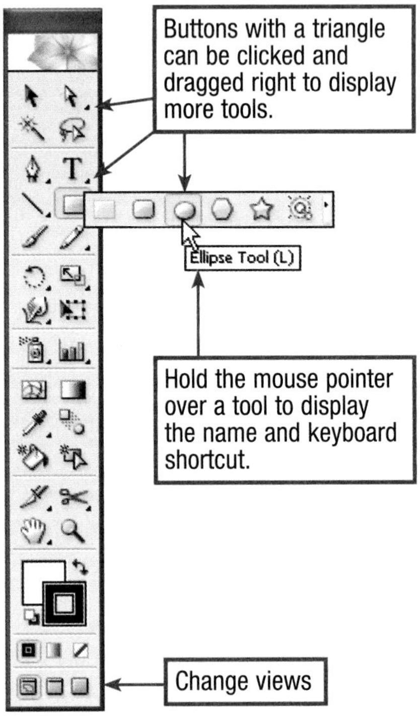

Buttons with a triangle can be clicked and dragged right to display more tools.
Ellipse Tool (L)
Hold the mouse pointer over a tool to display the name and keyboard shortcut.
Change views

▲ You can move Illustrator's toolbox to make more room for your workspace.

How Do I Use the Palettes?

Palettes make it easy for you to format or modify your image. They also let you see at a glance the settings you have chosen. There are 25 different palettes, but they do not all have to be displayed at once. You can press SHIFT + TAB to display or hide all the palettes, or click **Windows** in the Menu bar and select a palette name from the menu. You can move and resize the palette windows to allow more room for your workspace.

Sidebar

Use Help This unit only covers a few of Illustrator's many resources. For information about tools, palettes, keyboard shortcuts, and much, much more, go to Adobe's Online Help. Click on Help on Illustrator's menu bar. Scroll through the topics to see what you can learn.

Summarize Use Help to write a brief summary of three of Illustrator's selection tools.

Reading Check

1. **Compare** Describe five Illustrator icons that are similar to ones you have used in other software.
2. **Explain** How would you change the options displayed in the Control palette?

Project 5-5

Apply a Mask

Spotlight on Skills

- Resize a document
- Add a layer mask
- Set an RGB color
- Add text
- Align objects

Key Term

- mask

Academic Focus

Social Studies
Create an image of Stonehenge

As in Microsoft Word and Publisher, Photoshop documents can be made up of multiple layers. Unlike drawing programs, however, layers are not created automatically. You have to create the layers yourself.

Work with Layers

Working with multiple objects in only one layer can be challenging. Erasing or moving an object can affect all the other objects in the layer. While layers might seem confusing at first—and greatly increase the file size—they actually make it easier to create and modify images.

Layers can be edited independently of each other. Elements on one layer do not interact with another layer unless you want them to. If you decide you like one part of an image, but not the background, layers make it easy to delete that one element.

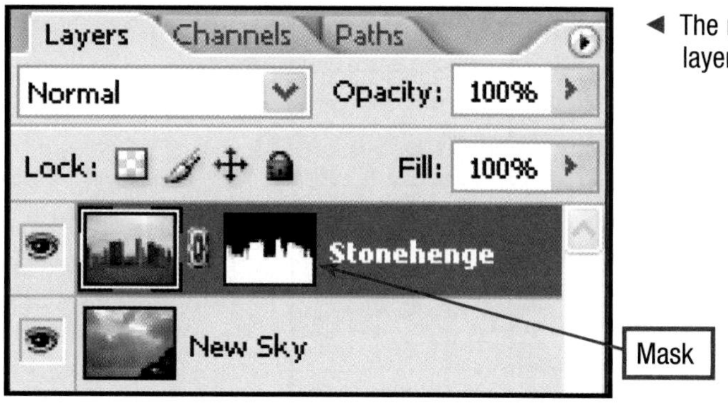

◀ The mask is displayed in the layer where it is applied.

You can also mask part of a layer. A **mask** is a feature that hides specific areas so that you can work on the part of the image that is not masked. It is only a temporary effect that does not change or delete pixels so that you can see how a modified picture would look.

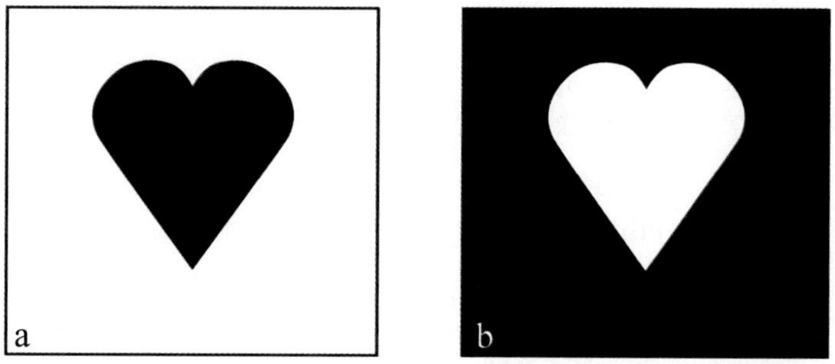

◀ a)The heart is masked so the background can be edited.
b) The background is masked so the heart can be edited.

▶ **In this project,** you will make the sky look more dramatic in a photograph of Stonehenge. Stonehenge is an ancient structure in England, erected by prehistoric people. Its purpose is still a mystery, though it was most likely used as a calendar marking the position of the sun.

WORKSHOP Toolbox

You Will Learn To

- Identify Illustrator's interface
- Identify toolbox drawing tools
- Identify Illustrator palettes

Key Term

palette

The Illustrator Interface

Adobe Illustrator has a similar look to most other Adobe products, and you should notice many features that are the same as Adobe Photoshop.

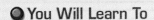

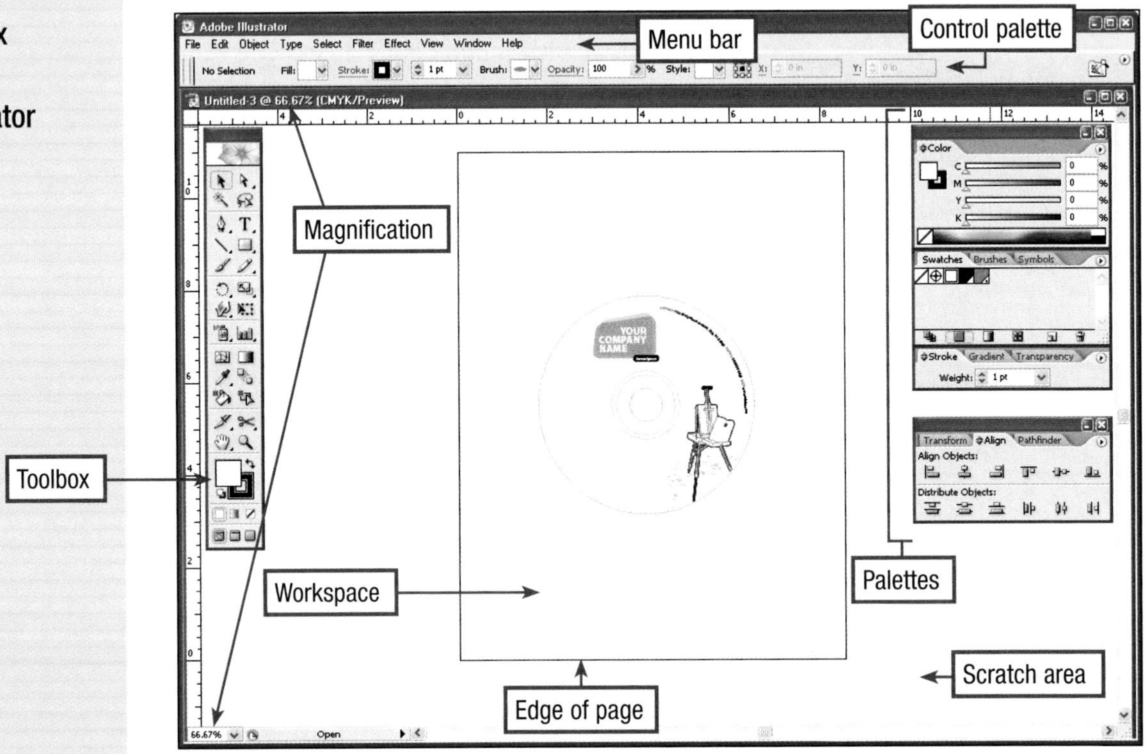

Workspace This area shows the page and where the image appears when printed. You can change the size and shape of the workspace.

Scratch Area The area outside the workspace can be used to assemble or edit your creations before placing them into the workspace.

Menu Bar The menu bar contains most of the commands you will need, though many of these are on the toolbox or palettes.

Control Palette A **palette** displays a variety of tools related to a specific action. The Control palette is displayed below the Menu bar at the top of your screen. This palette displays options related to the objects you select and changes depending on the object.

Magnification Levels The percent of magnification is displayed next to the file name and in the lower left corner.

Step-by-Step

1 Open Photoshop with default setting. Then open **Data File 5-5**, and save it according to your teacher's instructions.

Resize a Document

2 Click **Image>Image Size**. Under **Document Size**, change the **Width** to **5** inches, and the **height** to **3.75** inches.

3 Click the **Magic Wand**. On the **Options** bar, click **Add to Selection**, change the **Tolerance** to **50**, and be sure that **Contiguous** is checked.

4 Click on the sky, including the parts in and around the stones, until the whole sky is selected (Figure 5.28).

5 If parts of the sky are still not selected, click them again to add them. If the rocks are getting selected, make the Tolerance value lower and click the sky again.

Add a Layer Mask

6 Click **Layer>Layer Mask> Hide Selection**. The selected area will look like a checkerboard to show that it is hidden.

7 On the **Layers** palette, click the box to the left of the **New Sky** layer to display it (Figure 5.29).

Figure 5.28 A lower tolerance lets you select only the colors within a narrow range. A higher tolerance selects a broader range of colors.

Figure 5.29 The masked area is hidden, not deleted, so it can be changed later if necessary.

How Do I Identify a Vector Graphic?

Vector drawings are usually simple line drawings. However, in more complex images, it can be difficult to tell a vector graphic from a raster graphic.

You can identify a vector graphic by checking the image's file format or **file name extension**, the letters displayed after a file name that describe the file format. To view format information, open a folder with your graphic files, then click **View>Details**. Under **Type** you can see the format.

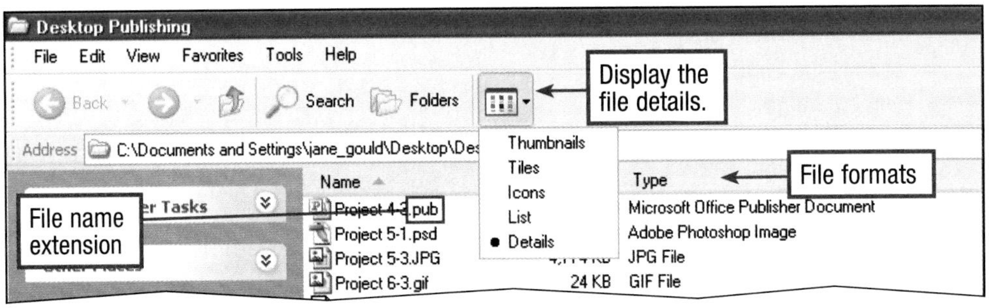

▲ Check the file format type to make sure an image is a vector graphic.

The chart below describes the different formats that can be used for saving vector graphics. Some formats can only be opened in a specific program.

Vector Graphic File Formats

Format Name	File Name Extension	Format used in
Windows MetaFile	WMF	Older Windows applications
Enhanced MetaFile	EMF	Newer Windows applications
Adobe Illustrator	AI	Adobe Illustrator
Apple's Picture format	PICT	Macintosh computers (and PCs)
Encapsulated PostScript	EPS	High quality PostScript printers
Scalable Vector Graphics	SVG	Web animations

Reading Check

1. **Explain** Why is it desirable to create scalable graphics?
2. **Summarize** How can you tell if an image is a vector or a raster graphic?

Eye On Ethics

Find Reliable Sources Make sure the information you find on a Web site is reliable. Check other sources to see if their information is similar. Find an update or copyright date on the site to see how up to date it is. Determine if the site is biased, or covers only one side of an issue. Find out who created the site. It may be owned by a company or person that is trying to sell products or services described on the site.

Draw Conclusions Why might you be cautious about health information that you find on a site created by a company that manufactures health products?

8. Choose **Layer>New>Layer** to create a new, blank layer. In the **Layer** dialog box, name the layer Gradient.

Set an RGB color

9. In the toolbox, click the **Set Foreground Color** button to open the Color Picker.

10. In the **Color Picker** box, change the **RGB** settings to **249**, **247**, **182** (Figure 5.30).

Figure 5.30 The Color Picker lets you set specific colors or create one using the color spectrum.

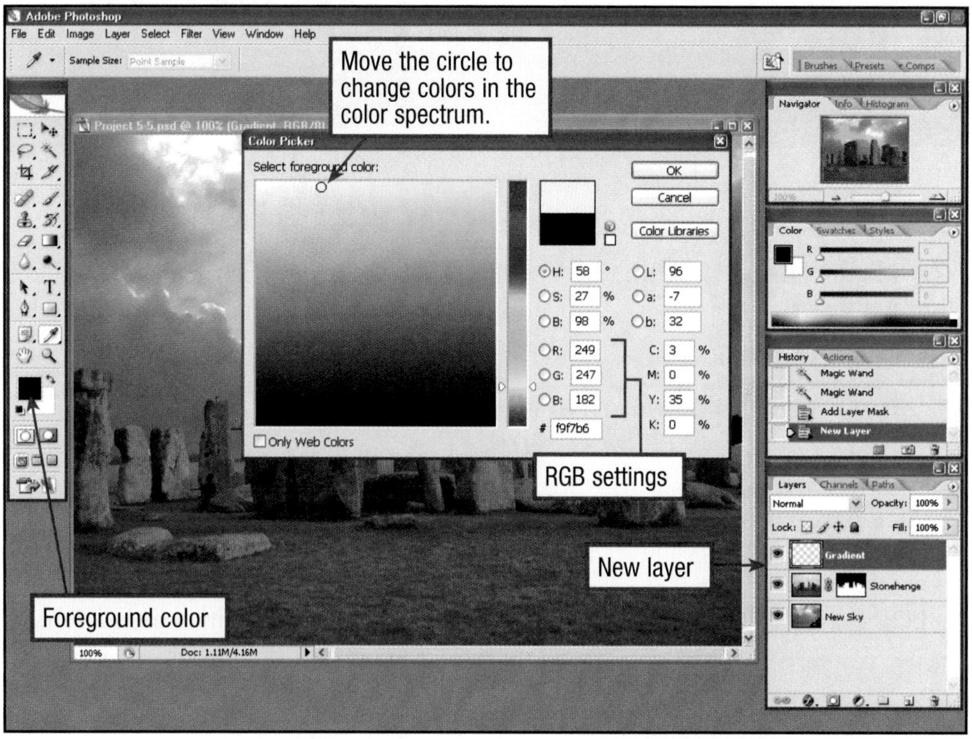

11. Click **Gradient** [button]. In the **Options** bar, click the drop-down menu. Choose **Foreground to Transparent**.

12. With the **Gradient** tool, click in the upper left corner of the image and drag a line down to the bottom right. The gradient color will cover the screen.

13. In the **Layers** palette, change the blending mode to **Color**. This should blend the top layer color with the layers below (Figure 5.31).

Figure 5.31 The gradient blended sky makes a more dramatic color.

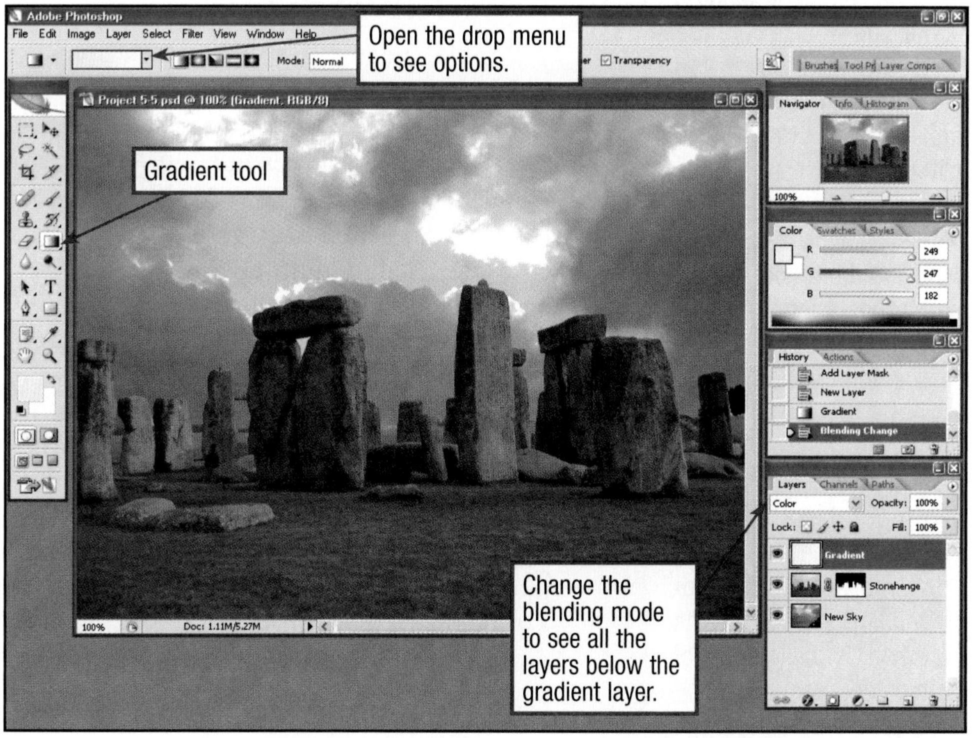

WORK SHOP

Foundations

You Will Learn To

- Identify vector graphic software
- Compare vector graphic file formats

Key Terms

vector graphics
scalable
file name extension

Before You Read

Prior Knowledge If your friends were talking about a movie you knew nothing about, you would soon lose interest. However, if you had seen a preview of the movie, you might be interested in what your friends had to say. The same is true of reading about a new subject. The more you already know, the easier it is to understand and be interested. Before you read a chapter, look over the *You Will Learn To* section, as well as illustrations and headers. Write down what you already know about the subject and what you want to find out by reading the chapter. As you read, find examples of both categories.

Work with Vector Graphics

In Unit 1, you used Microsoft Word to create some simple drawings and clip art. Drawing tools in Microsoft Word are easy to use and convenient for quick illustrations, but they are not intended to be used as a professional illustration package.

What Are Vector Graphics?

In Chapter 2, you had a brief introduction to vector graphics. **Vector graphics** are line drawings that are stored as math formulas in your computer. This makes them **scalable**, which means they can be resized without losing image quality. Vector graphics are different from the raster, or bitmapped graphics, you created in Unit 3 with Photoshop. Raster images will become pixelated when they are enlarged too much.

What Software Is Used by Professional Illustrators?

Popular vector graphics applications include Adobe Illustrator, Corel Draw!, and Macromedia Freehand. Animation software and CAD (Computer Aided Design) software, used for drafting in engineering and architecture, also use vector graphics.

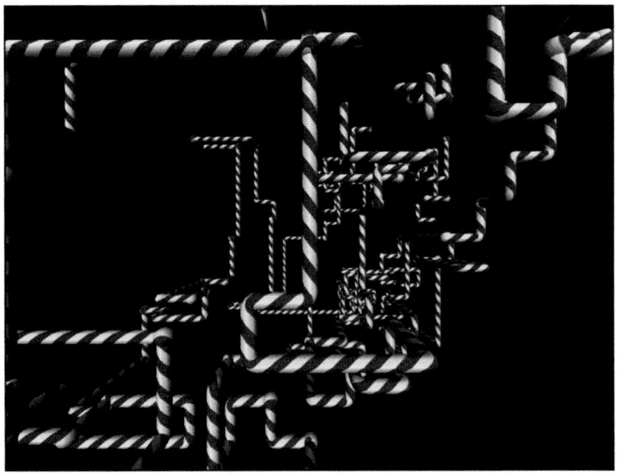

▲ Screensavers may use vector graphics.

Illustrator has many powerful tools. This book will give you an overview of some of its features. However, the images that you create will give you an exciting introduction to the many ways that Illustrator can help you create imaginative and powerful designs and illustrations. Specialized books also provide ideas for creating illustrations in Illustrator. Knowing how to use Illustrator can be challenging, fun, and an excellent skill to list on a job résumé.

Add Text

14 In the toolbox, click the **Horizontal Type** tool [T]. On the **Options** bar, choose **Papyrus** font, and change the **font size** to **36 pt**.

15 Key Stonehenge.

16 Click **Move** [Move]. On the **Options** bar, check the **Show Transform Controls**.

17 Resize and reposition the text to look similar to Figure 5.32. Click the **Move** tool and **Apply the Transformation**.

Align Objects

18 Press CTRL, and then select the Text and the Stonehenge layers (not the sky).

19 On the **Options** bar, click **Align Horizontal Centers** [Align] to center the text on the picture (Figure 5.33).

20 Follow your teacher's instructions for saving and printing your work.

▼ **Figure 5.32** Notice that a new layer is created automatically when you add text.

▼ **Figure 5.33** The final document.

REVIEW AND REVISE

Check your work Use Figure 5.33 as a guide and check that:

- ☑ The original sky has been masked and the new sky is visible.
- ☑ A gradient has been added to change the image color.
- ☑ The gradient layer has been changed to the color blending mode.
- ☑ Text has been added and centered on the workspace.

Chapter 7

Introducing Adobe Illustrator

Skills You Will Learn

Workshop Foundations
Work with Vector Graphics

Workshop Toolbox
The Illustrator Interface

Project 7-1
Use Illustrator Tools

Project 7-2
Create an Illustration

Project 7-3
Set Colors

Project 7-4
Apply Gradient Fills

Project 7-5
Apply Blending Modes

Project 7-6
Create a Drawing with the Blend Tool

Project 7-7
Add Distort Effects

Skills Studio

Design with Text Illustrations

Project 7-8
Create a Text Illustration

Project 7-9
Enhance Your Text Illustration

Many of the images you see every day are vector graphics: the pictures on your cereal box, the graphics in your cell phone, an advertisement on a billboard, and much of the clip art in these projects.

In this chapter, you will learn how to create simple vector images using Adobe Illustrator. Illustrator is professional software that is used to create drawings and artwork. You will see how much more powerful it can be than using the drawing tools in Microsoft Word.

Create an Illustration

An illustration can be as simple as the title design on this page, or it can be as complex as a full-color illustration on a movie poster. Before you design an illustration, you need to know how it will be used, how big it will be, and whether it is going to be published in color or black and white. Images may be simple design elements, but they can be used to tell a story. A picture in a children's book conveys a lot of information without using much text. An advertisement may use one strong, simple image to identify a brand or product. Stylish and sophisticated illustrations in a fashion magazine tell readers what to expect when they flip through its pages.

DESIGN PROCESS Illustrations

Elements	Issues
Purpose	To provide visual interest, to convey a message visually, or to create a particular graphic style in a publication.
Audience	Varies. Illustrations are used for many kinds of audiences. They are in advertisements, magazines, newspapers, technical journals, children's books, business publications, etc.
Content	Illustrations can be original or they can be copied from models or modified from other media. Their complexity depends on the message that is to be conveyed.
Layout	Because illustrations are used to enhance other content on a page, it is important to know the size and placement of the image. Consider whether elements of the illustration will be repeated in other parts of the publication.
Publication	Illustrations may be black and white or color. They can be printed or displayed online. The type of image and resolution will be affected by the publication method.

Project 5-6 Retouch a Photo

Spotlight on Skills

- Straighten a photo
- Remove red eye
- Apply the Clone Stamp
- Adjust color levels

Key Terms

- retouch
- clone
- histogram

Academic Focus

Math
Interpret a histogram

When you see an advertisement where the people, scenery, or products look perfect, chances are the images have been digitally improved. The ocean is bluer, the grass is greener, and human models have no freckles or wrinkles because they have been "Photoshopped."

Apply the Clone Stamp Tool

Photoshop has many ways to fix, or **retouch**, an image. One of the most powerful tools for retouching photographs is the **Clone Stamp** tool. When you **clone**, you copy a range of pixels and paste the pixels into another location.

▼ The Clone Stamp's Options bar

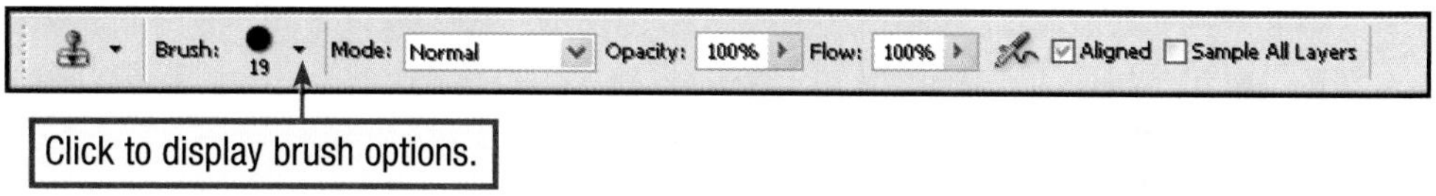

Take a Sample Before you can start applying the pixels, you must take a sample from an area that you want to copy. To clone effectively, you must make sure that the area you are sampling is a good match. The lighting, visual distance, and/or coloring should be similar to the part you are retouching.

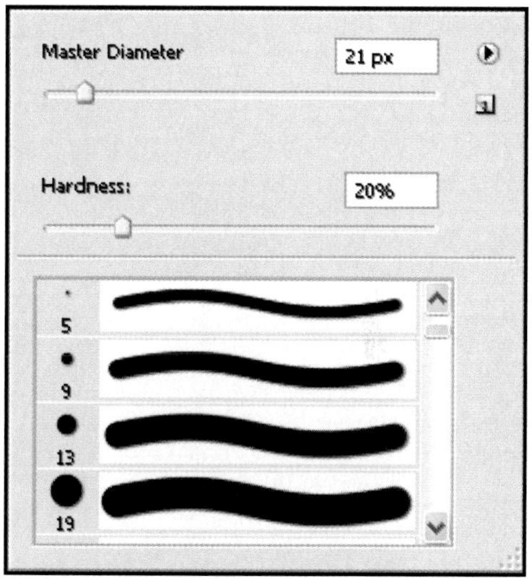

▲ Brush options

Choose a Brush When cloning, you have a variety of brushes to choose from.

- A hard-edged round brush makes brush marks less obvious. When in doubt, use a round brush.
- Avoid brushes with soft, feathered edges. These brushes leave an obvious blurred look in the area.
- Use a square brush when cloning small, square objects, or when the object is square itself.

Set Opacity It is much faster to clone an area using a high opacity (such as 100%), but your brush's edges will be obvious. Instead, choose a low opacity (such as 30%–45%). It takes a little longer, but the results are better.

UNIT 4

Design with Adobe Illustrator

Contents

Adjust Color

As often as possible, try to leave the original picture intact and make adjustments on separate layers. Even color adjustments should be done on a separate layer. Adjustment layers and layer masks allow you to make color changes without directly affecting the original picture.

Photoshop has many tools for correcting color. A **histogram** is a graph that shows the number of pixels for each color and tone in an image. When you change the histogram settings, a new layer is created on the Layers palette with a histogram thumbnail. You can double-click the thumbnail to make more adjustments.

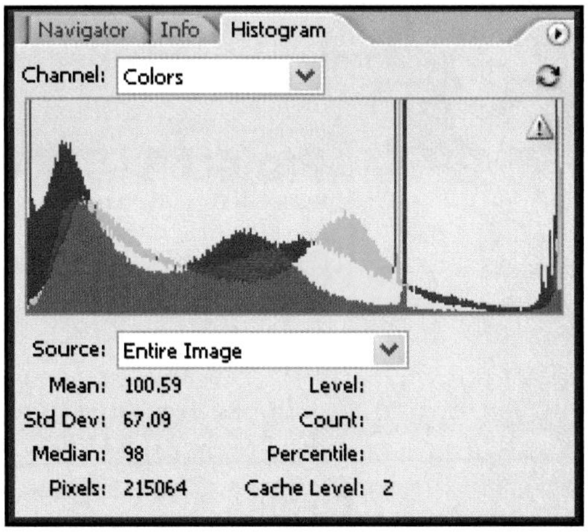

▲ A histogram lets you see a figure's range of colors at a glance.

Student Data File

▶ In this project, you will retouch a photograph that has many common image problems, including red eye, a blemish, and poor lighting.

▼ **Figure 5.34** This photo has a number of common problems.

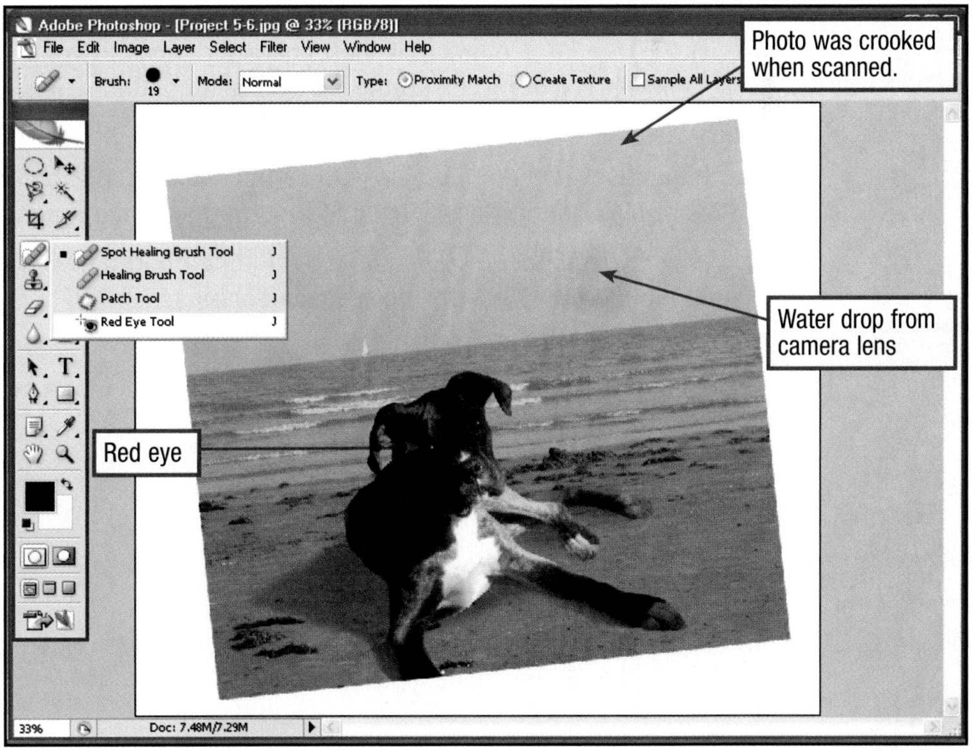

Step-by-Step

1. In Photoshop, open **Data File 5-6**.

Straighten a Photo

2. Click **File>Automate>Crop and Straighten** to straighten the photo. Save the straightened photo according to your teacher's instructions.

UNIT 3

Projects Across the Curriculum

Project 3 Create Geometric Shapes ★★

MATH Make a deck of 3 × 5 inch cards showing three-dimensional geometric shapes in everyday objects.

Plan

1. Choose at least six pictures of objects with different shapes for your cards, such as a ball (sphere), block (cube), can (cylinder), etc.

Create

2. Use Photoshop to edit the pictures and add effects such as gradients, shadows, and reflections so that they look three-dimensional.
3. Use Publisher to create the back of the cards. Write the name of the shape, a brief description, and the mathematical formulas for calculating area and volume.
4. Follow your teacher's instructions for printing your cards. If possible, print the cards on stiff paper, with the picture on one side and the text on the other.

Project 4 Create a Hybrid Animal ★★★

SCIENCE Combine the best characteristics of two or more animals to create a new breed of insect, reptile, bird, fish, amphibian, or mammal.

Plan

1. Research a variety of animals with distinct characteristics, such as wings, antennas, lots of legs, strange eyes, etc. Find images that contain the traits you want.
2. Write descriptions of your animal, including important facts like its animal kingdom and family, eating habits, life span, and habitats.

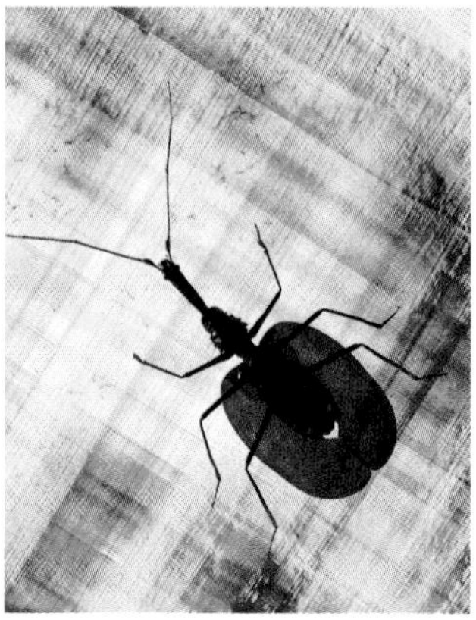

Create

3. Use Photoshop to combine the different body parts into a new creature.
4. Insert the creature image into a document of your choice, such as a brochure, flyer, poster, or booklet. Lay out the text you wrote, and add headers.
5. Use Photoshop text tools to write your new species' name.
6. Follow your teacher's instructions for printing your project. Use tile printing if you create a poster.

Remove Red Eye

3 In the toolbox, click **Zoom**. Drag a marquee around the dog's eyes to enlarge them.

4 In the toolbox, open the hidden tools for **Spot Healing Brush** and choose **Red Eye**.

5 With the **Red Eye** tool, click one eye, then click the other. The eye color will be fixed! (Figure 5.35)

▼ **Figure 5.35** Place the Red Eye tool in the center of the eye.

Apply the Clone Stamp

6 Use the **Navigator** palette to move to the water droplet.

7 In the toolbox, click **Clone Stamp**.

8 On the **Options** bar, choose the **Hard Round 19 px** brush. In the Brush drop-down menu adjust the **Master Diameter** slider to **95 pixels** (Figure 5.36).

9 In the **Options** bar, click on the **Opacity** arrow. Drag the slider to the left until the **Opacity** is **35 percent**.

▼ **Figure 5.36** The water droplet is in the square.

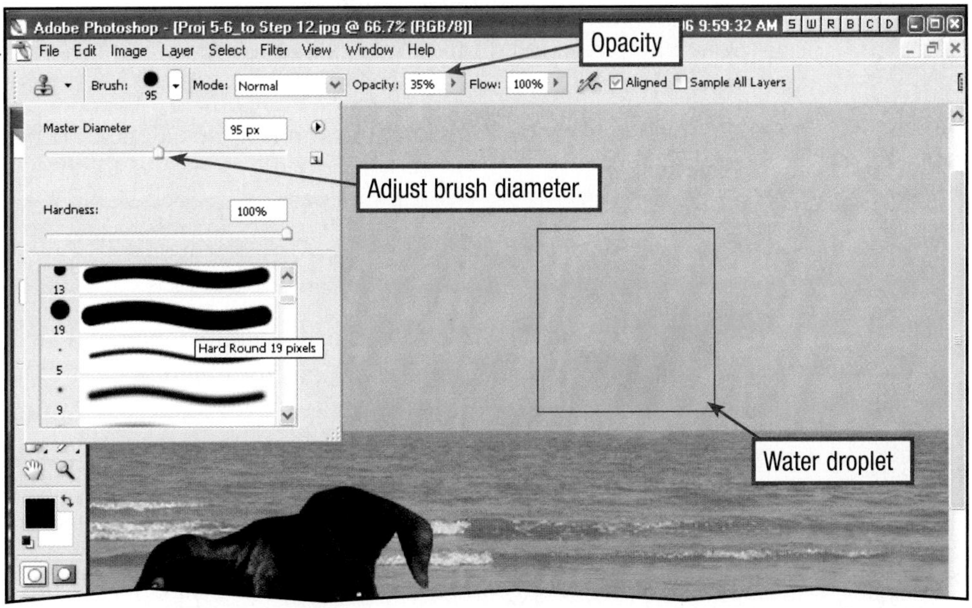

Instant Message

Red Eye Tips If you miss while using the Red Eye tool, press CTRL + Z to Undo before trying again on the same eye. If you do not cancel the first try, you might not get the results you want.

UNIT 3

Projects Across the Curriculum

The skills you learned in this unit will help you in your other classes, too. Use your desktop publishing skills to complete the following projects. Follow your teacher's instructions for saving or printing your work.

Project 1 Create a Personal Calendar ★

SOCIAL STUDIES Use Publisher and Photoshop to create your own personal calendar.

Plan

1. Brainstorm picture ideas to illustrate each month of the year.
2. Find out the dates of personal and federal holidays this year.

Create

3. Use Publisher's Calendar template and a digital camera or scanner to create a personal calendar.
4. Use Photoshop to edit the pictures and to create collages, montages, and special effects.
5. Follow your teacher's instructions to print the calendar. If possible, bind the pages together.

Project 2 Create a Book Cover ★★

LANGUAGE ARTS Read or research a book and create a cover for that book that would appeal to a specific audience.

Plan

1. Research the type of audience that reads the book and determine the design elements used for that audience.

Create

2. Create the correctly sized book cover. Use Publisher for the layout and Photoshop to create the title and the graphics.
3. Add a brief summary of the book on the back cover, and include a picture of the author (cite your source).
4. Follow your teacher's instructions for printing the cover.

Go Online RUBRICS
www.glencoe.com

Unit Projects Go to **Unit 3,** and choose **Rubrics**. Use the projects to help create and evaluate your work.

10 Position your pointer in a solid blue sky next to the water droplet. Press ALT and click to sample an area.

11 Hold down your mouse button and move the **Clone Stamp** brush over the water droplet. This paints the sampled pixels on top of the old pixels (Figure 5.37).

12 Continue painting until the water droplet is completely gone. You may need to resample various areas until the droplet completely vanishes.

13 Double-click **Hand** to zoom back out to the full view of your image.

Adjust Color Levels

14 Click **Layer>New Adjustment Layer>Levels** to open the histogram dialog box. Name the new level Color Adjustment. (Notice the new layer on the **Layers** palette.)

15 In the histogram dialog box, move the sliders until the settings are similar to those in Figure 5.38.

16 Double-click the **Hand** tool to zoom back out to the full view of your image.

▼ **Figure 5.37** The Clone Stamp copies pixels from one area and inserts them onto another area.

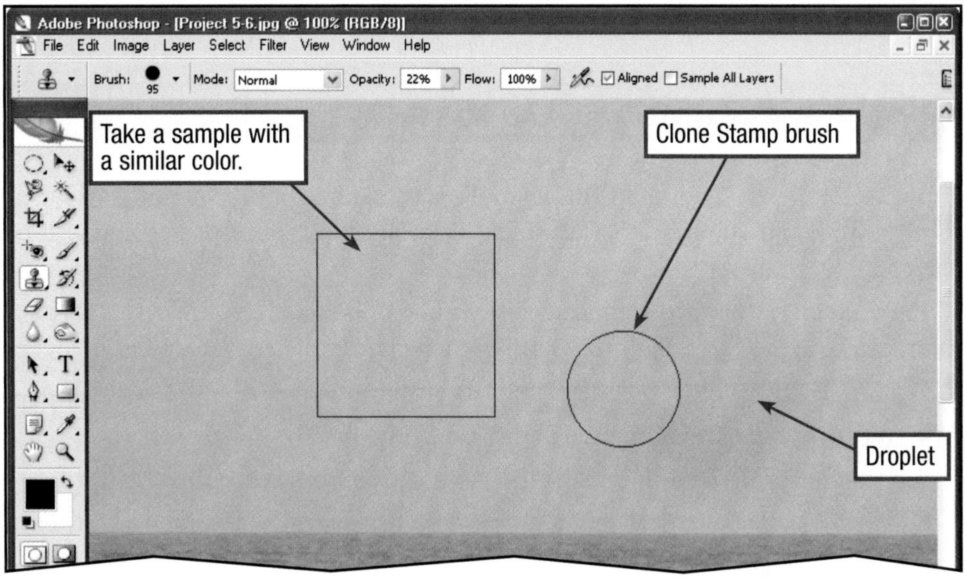

▼ **Figure 5.38** Notice the changes to your image as you move the histogram's sliders.

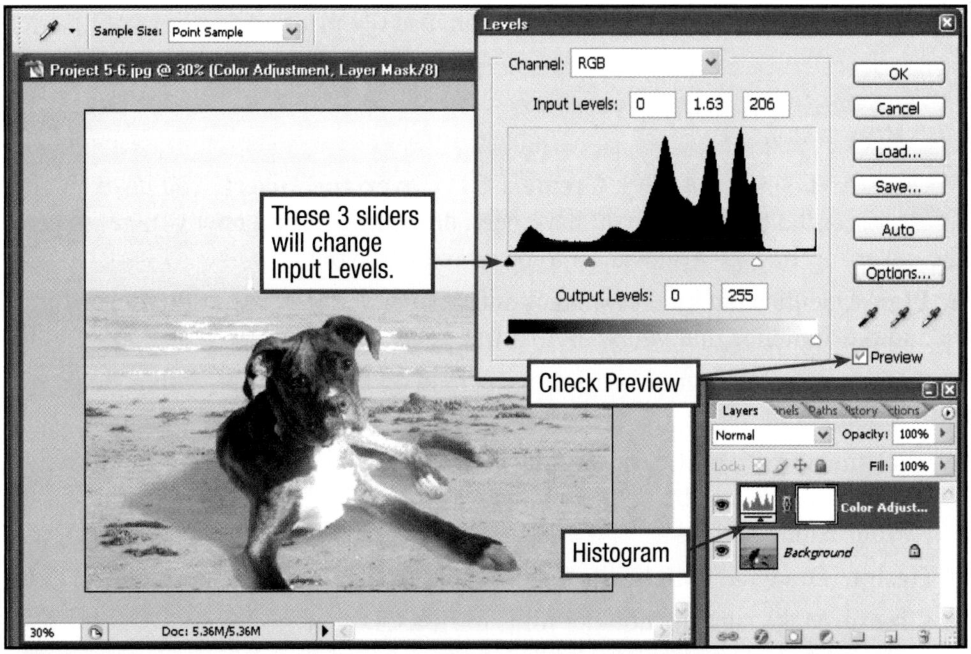

Instant Message

Interpret a Histogram The shape of a histogram depends on the colors, contrast, and brightness of an image. Darker images tend to have higher levels on the left side of the graph. Lighter images may have more peaks to the right.

Chapter 6 Assessment

2 Independent Practice ★★

SCIENCE Create a Banner or Poster Your school is hosting an Earth Day event, and you need to advertise it on a large banner or poster that will be displayed all around town.

a, Plan Decide what project the school will host. Is it a clean-up? A recycling program? An educational workshop on the environment? Decide on the event title.

b. Design Decide how large the banner or poster must be.

- Write the text, including the name, time, and date of the event.
- Design or find a strong image to attract people to the event.

c. Create Use layout software and Photoshop to create your banner or poster.

- Add an interesting background that does not distract from the image or text.
- Apply a filter or another effect to enhance the image you use.
- Apply layer styles to the type so that it stands out clearly.

d. Publish With your teacher's permission, use tile printing to print your poster.

3 Independent Practice ★★★

LANGUAGE ARTS Create a CD Cover and Insert You have finally recorded that album you have been dreaming of, and now you get to create the cover for the CD! You want it to be a booklet layout.

a. Plan Decide what kind of images and design would best suit the type of music and the audience that you want to attract.

- Take a photograph of yourself to include on the cover. Or, find a stock photograph.
- Come up with a title for the CD. Write titles and descriptions for all the songs that would be on the CD, as well as a brief biography for yourself or your band.

b. Design Draw the thumbnails for the back, front, and inside of the booklet.

c. Create Make sure the booklet folds to fit a CD case.

- Add a background and other design elements that repeat on all panels of the booklet.
- Modify the images and use effects to enhance the message that you want to convey to an audience.
- Make sure the text is accurate, readable, and well designed.

d. Publish With your teacher's permission, print the booklet on both sides of a sheet.

Go Online ACTIVITIES
www.glencoe.com

Enrichment Go to **Chapter 6**, and choose **Enrichment Activities**. Find more desktop publishing projects using Adobe Photoshop.

17 The sky now looks too washed out. On the **Layers** palette, click the **Layer Mask** for the **Color Adjustment Layer**.

18 In the toolbox, make sure that the **Foreground** color is **black** and click **Brush**. (Black removes the pixels in the mask.)

19 On the **Options** bar, change the **brush** to a **150 px soft round** brush (Figure 5.39).

20 Paint the sky and sea to restore the original color. If you mistakenly paint over a part of the picture, switch to a white brush to restore the pixels in the mask.

21 With the mask still selected, click **Filter>Blur>Gaussian Blur**.

22 Experiment with the slider at the bottom of the **Gaussian Blur** box to apply a softening effect to the sky.

23 Follow your teacher's instructions for saving and printing your work.

▼ **Figure 5.39** When you "paint" in the Adjustment layer, you are removing or adding the original pixel colors.

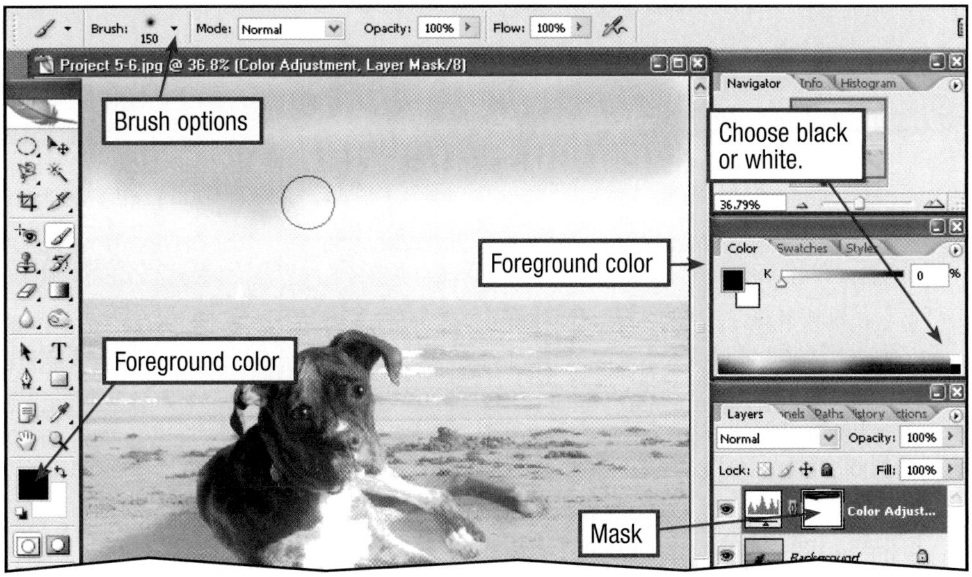

▼ **Figure 5.40** The foreground of the photo is now lighter.

REVIEW AND REVISE

Check your work Use Figure 5.40 as a guide and check that:

- ☑ The picture has been straightened, and the red eye has been removed.
- ☑ The water droplet has been cloned out.
- ☑ An Adjustment layer has been added to fix the strong backlighting.
- ☑ A mask has been used to restore the original sky color.

Chapter 6 Assessment

Reading Check

1. **Compare** How are native file formats and interchangeable file formats different?
2. **Identify** What kind of resolution is good for on-screen presentations?
3. **Explain** How can you use a paint brush to hide or reveal parts of an image?
4. **Evaluate** In your opinion, which of the following tools is better: Microsoft Publisher's WordArt, or Adobe Photoshop's text warping features? Explain your answer.
5. **Describe** What is tile printing?

Critical Thinking

6. **Analyze** What kind of information do you need before you print a document that contains images and text?
7. **Compare** Which software applications are best for text? Explain why.
8. **Analyze** Why might you question whether a photo you see online or in print is real?
9. **Evaluate** What kinds of questions would you ask a client to help you choose the best software to use to finish a project?
10. **Make Predictions** In terms of printing costs at a local printer, which of the following would be the most economical: 72 ppi, 150 ppi, or 300 ppi? Why?

1 Independent Practice

SOCIAL STUDIES **Create a Postcard** Create your own "Wish You Were Here" postcard for any location that interests you. It can be a state, city, popular resort, another country, or another planet.

a. Plan Research the location that you would like the postcard to be from.
- Find out what images would best illustrate the place. For example, in the Texas postcard you created, the state flag was the background, and the text was created from a picture of the state flower.
- Write a brief description that you can include on the address side of the postcard.

b. Design Decide which images you will use.
- Draw thumbnails showing different ways to use the images in the background and foreground.
- Decide what the text will say and where it will be placed.

c. Create Use Publisher and Photoshop to create the postcard.
- Use at least one filter to create interesting effects in the images.
- Use layer styles, such as drop shadows and glows, to make the text stand out.
- Create the address side of the postcard with a description of the location.

d. Publish With your teacher's permission, print the postcards, four to a sheet. If possible, use one sheet of paper to print both sides of the postcard.

Go Online RUBRICS
www.glencoe.com

Independent Practice
Go to **Chapter 6**, and choose **Rubrics**. Use the rubrics to help create and evaluate your projects.

Project 5-7

Create a Photo Montage

Spotlight on Skills

- Add a layer for a selection
- Add a shadow
- Apply a filter
- Flatten an image
- Create a vignette effect

Key Terms

- highlight
- montage
- vignette
- flatten

Academic Focus

Science
Apply light properties

When light comes in from a window or a bright lamp, the objects near it will reflect the light and cast shadows. The parts closest to the light might show highlights. A **highlight** is where the light is reflected off a surface. The parts furthest from the light, or hidden from it, will be in shadow.

When you create an illustration, details such as highlights and shadows make the picture more realistic. The play of light on an object gives the object weight and depth and shape. These effects often require adding many layers because each effect must blend with the object on the layer below it. For example, in the figure, the shadow on the background would be on a different layer from the shadow on the ball.

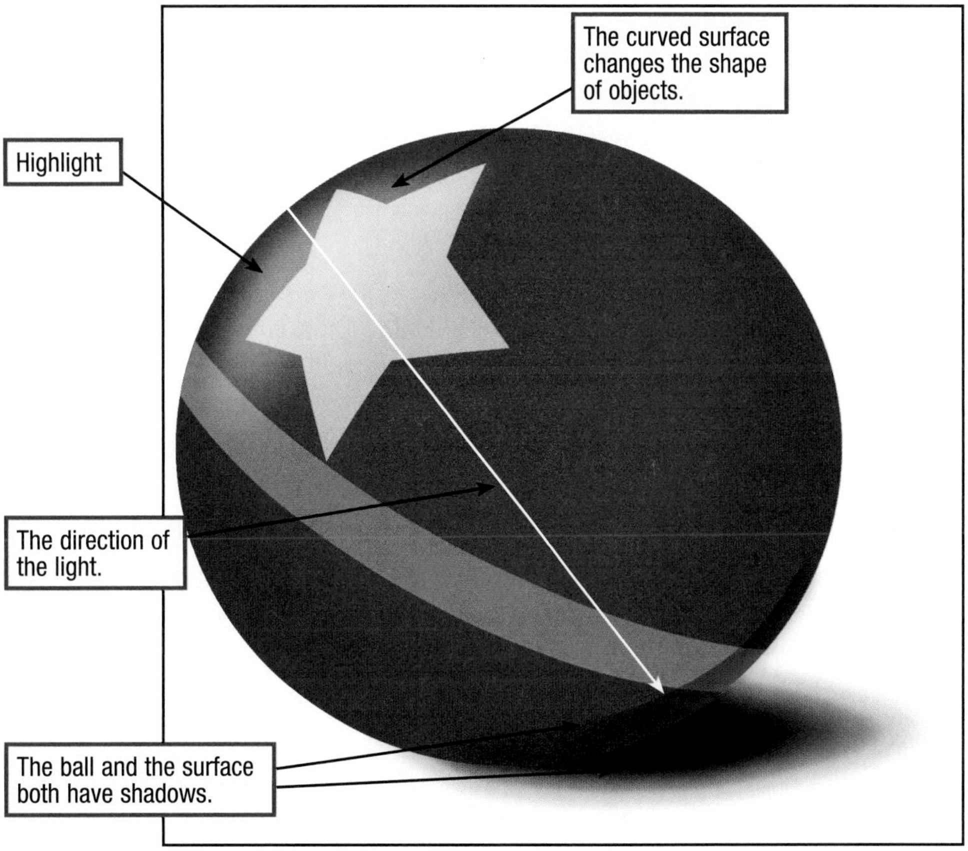

The curved surface changes the shape of objects.
Highlight
The direction of the light.
The ball and the surface both have shadows.

▲ The direction of the light affects where the highlights and shadows are placed.

▶ **In this project,** you will create a realistic photo montage. A **montage** is similar to a collage, except that the separate images combine to create a new image. The image will have a border that fades into the background, called a **vignette**. You will also **flatten** the image to merge all layers into one layer. This reduces the file size and makes the image more difficult to change if you send it to a client.

In The Workplace

Digital Imaging Technicians

Digital imaging technicians manipulate digital images to improve or alter the images' appearance. They are also known as digital finishing, retouching, and color correction specialists. The images they create are displayed on the Web, billboards, CD/DVD covers, packaging, magazines, books, displays, and countless other applications.

On the Job

Digital finishers, retouchers, and color correction specialists improve portraits by adjusting skin tones, blemishes, wrinkles, and facial hair; removing "red eye"; and erasing flaws from portraits. They restore or change colors and backgrounds, correct lighting, alter exposures, and improve composition. Digital imaging technicians may repair old or damaged photographs. Erasing scratches, fixing tears, and restoring faded colors help the technician prepare the photos for publication and display or preserve them for museums, archives, and families.

Digital imaging technicians work with custom and commercial photography labs, graphic design firms, professional photographers, publishers, printing companies, and advertising agencies, in a variety of corporate, commercial, and government settings. They work with digital images or with pictures that are scanned into a computer.

Desktop publishing applications such as Photoshop are used for finishing, retouching, and color correction. Digital imaging technicians may also use applications such as Quark, Illustrator, and InDesign. They are knowledgeable about color theory, understand photographic techniques like contrast and composition, and have a good artistic eye.

Future Outlook

Demand for digital imaging technicians is high. For more information about this career, consult the following Web sites:

- **American Institute of Graphic Arts (aiga.org)**, professional association for graphic design
- **National Association of Photoshop Professionals (photoshopuser.com)**, features training and tutorials for Photoshop users

Training

Digital imaging technicians can study graphic design, digital imaging, and photography at community colleges, art schools, universities, and specialized multimedia, computer, imaging, and design programs.

Salary Range

Salaries for digital imaging technicians vary greatly depending upon experience, skill, industry, and location.

Skills and Talents

Digital imaging technicians need to have:

- Knowledge of digital photography, illustration and design software.
- Knowledge of color theory.
- Knowledge of photography and composition.
- Good communication skills.
- The ability to meet deadlines and organize workflow.

Career Activity

Why is it helpful for digital imaging technicians to have a solid understanding of photography and photographic concepts?

Student Data File

Step-by-Step

1. In Photoshop, open **Data File 5-7**.

2. On the **Layers** palette, make sure all layers display the eye icon so they are all visible.

3. Click **Move** . The **Show Transform Controls** option should be checked.

4. Click the **Baby** layer to select the baby image. Press ALT + SHIFT to resize the baby to **71 percent** of its original size (without changing proportion or position).

5. Click the **Move** tool, and apply the transformation (Figure 5.41).

Add a Layer for a Selection

6. In the **Layers** palette, click the eye icon to hide the Baby layer. Then click the **Flower** layer.

7. Use **Lasso** to select the bottom part of the flower that would be in front of the baby (Figure 5.42).

Figure 5.41 The Transform options show the scale of a resized object.

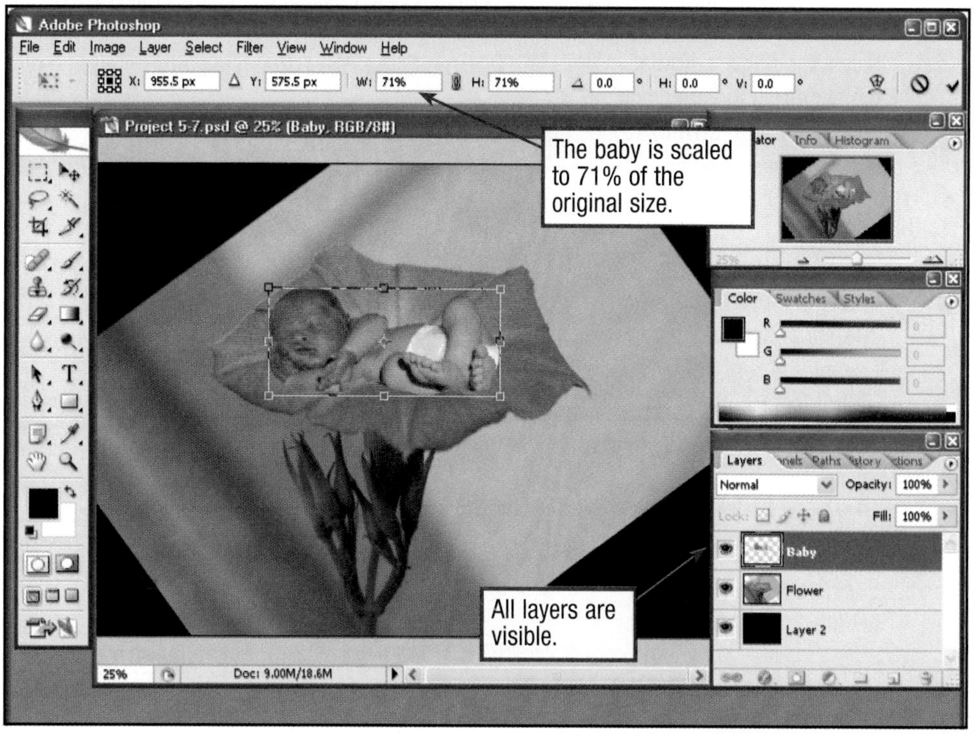

Figure 5.42 Select the parts of the flower that would logically be in front of the baby.

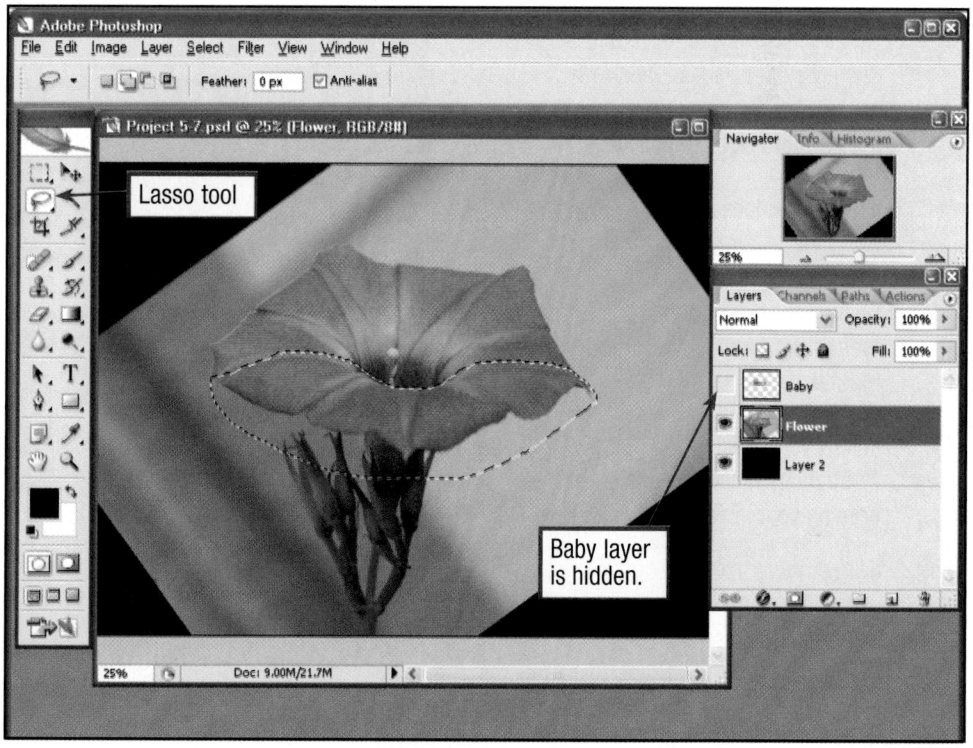

14. Select the **page # sign** at the bottom of the page and change the **font size** to **12**. In front of the sign, key The Classroom Counter in **Ravie**, **12 pt**.

15. Select the footer, and move it to the bottom of the page. Change the **font color** to **white**. See Figure 6.39 on page 284.

Insert a Textured Background

16. Click **Insert>Picture>From File**, and insert the Wood texture frame you created.

17. Position the frame over the **Master Page**. Click **Arrange>Order>Send to Back** to move it behind the footer.

18. Click CTRL + M to move to the newsletter pages. Check each page to make sure that the **Master Page** is applied.

19. If any page does not have the wood texture, open the **Master Page** task pane. Change the drop-down menu from **Ignore Master** to **Master A**.

20. Follow your teacher's instructions for saving and printing your newsletter.

▼ **Figure 6.40** Your final newsletter should have a texture and page numbers.

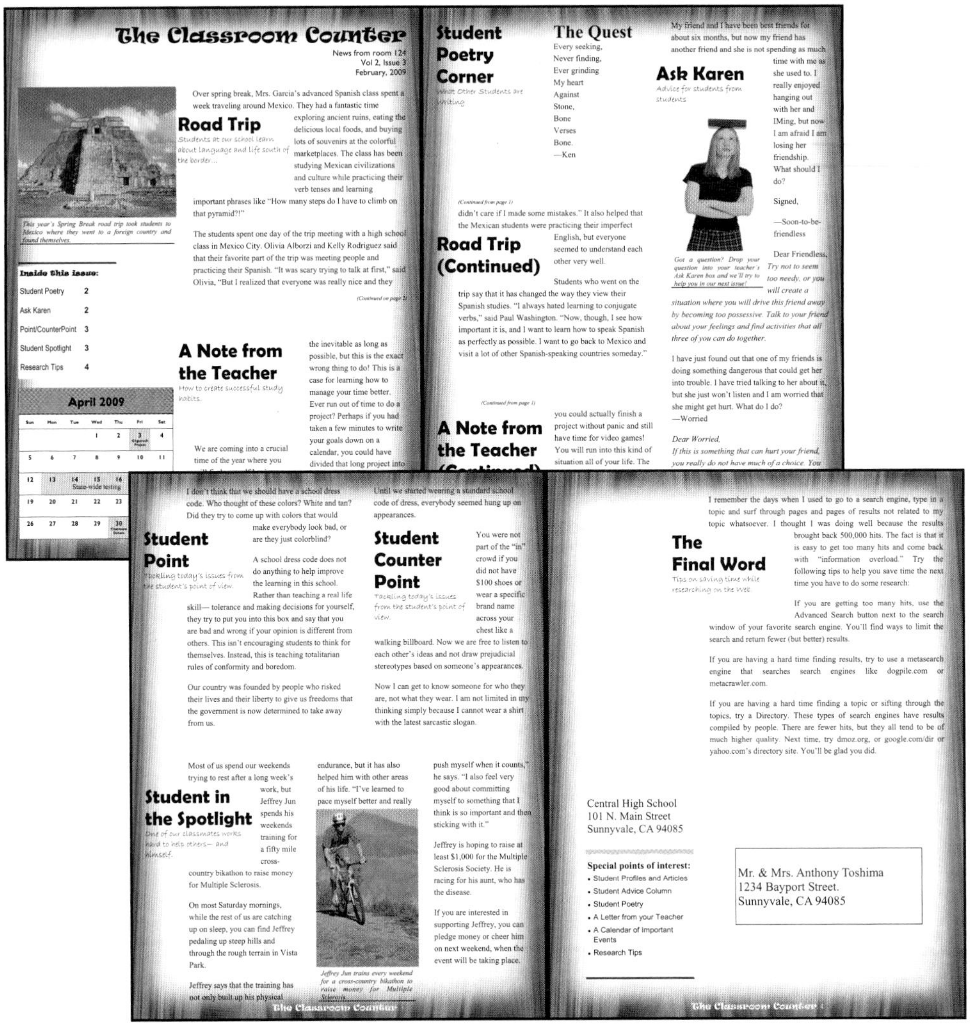

REVIEW AND REVISE

Check your work Use Figure 6.40 as a guide and check that:

- ☑ The text and graphics in the newsletter follow PARC principles.
- ☑ The wooden frame is present on the master slide and on every page.
- ☑ Page numbers and the newsletter name are visible on every page.
- ☑ Text is accurate, easy to read, with consistent fonts.
- ☑ There is a masthead, table of contents, calendar, pull quote, and sidebar.

8. With the flower half still selected, click **Layer>New>Layer via Copy**. Name the layer Flower Petal.

9. On the **Layers** palette, move the **Flower Petal** layer above the **Baby** layer.

10. Display the eye icon in the Baby layer and reveal the baby again.

11. Click the **Flower Petal** layer. Use **Eraser**, and **Zoom in** to erase parts of the petal that cover the baby's face (Figure 5.43).

Figure 5.43 The petal is covering part of the baby.

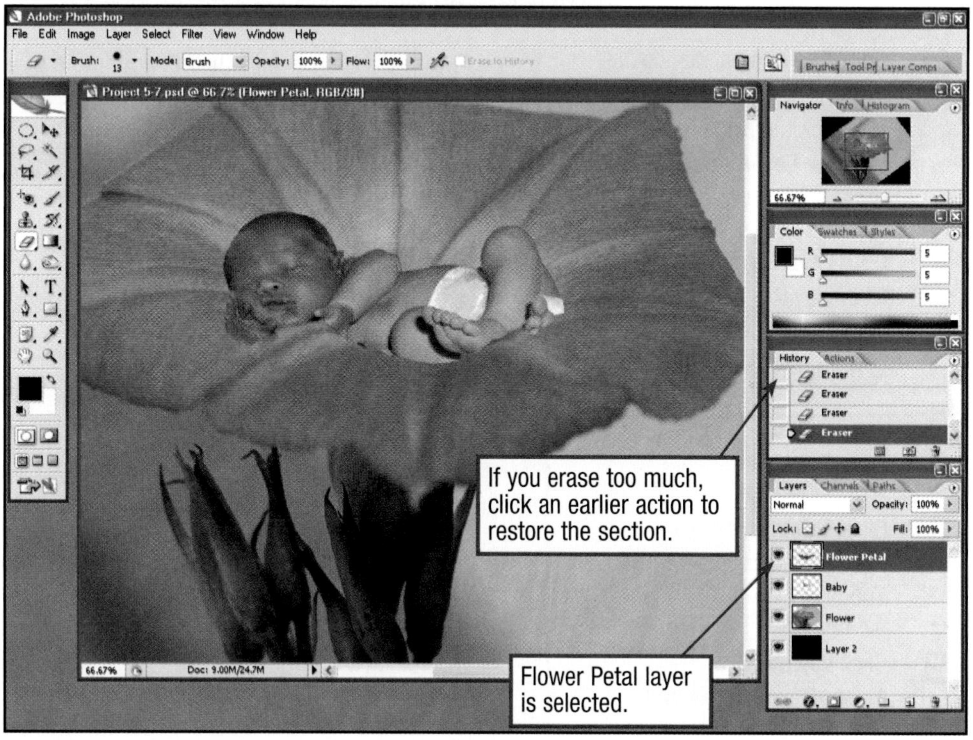

If you erase too much, click an earlier action to restore the section.
Flower Petal layer is selected.

12. On the **Layers** palette, select the **Baby** layer. Hide all the other layers.

13. Use **Magnetic Lasso** to carefully select the arm of the baby. (**Hint**: Set the **Width** to **2 px**.) (See Figure 5.44).

14. With the arm selected, click **Layer>New>Layer via Copy**. Name this layer Arm.

Figure 5.44 The high-contrast background makes it easier to select parts of the baby.

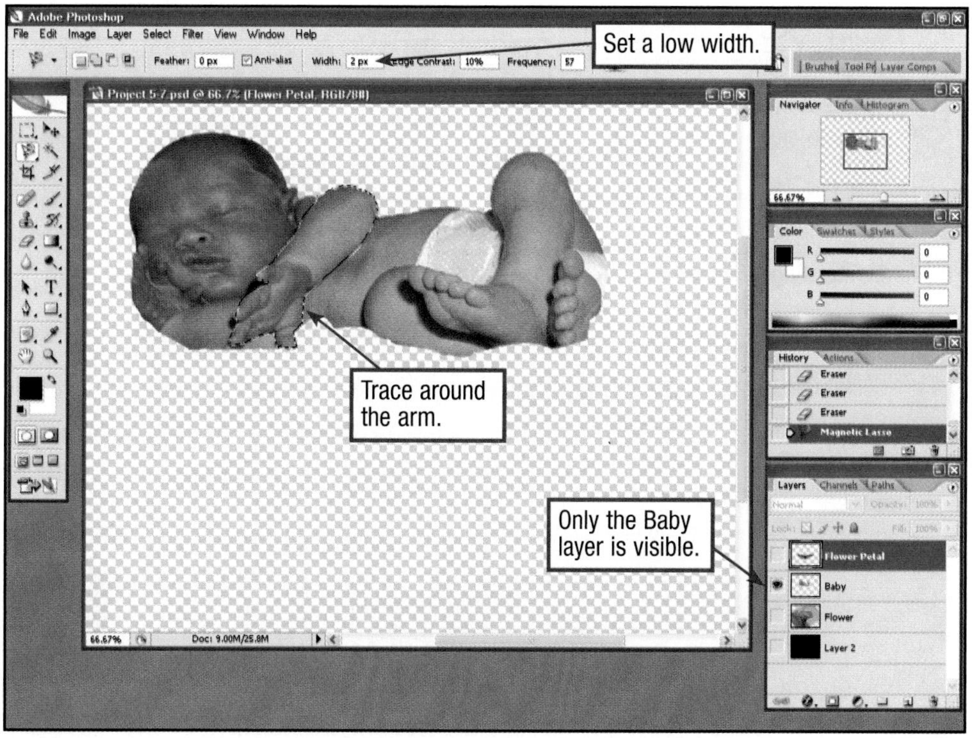

Set a low width.
Trace around the arm.
Only the Baby layer is visible.

5. On the **Layers** palette, double-click the **Background** layer to unlock the background. In the **New Layer** box, name the layer Wood and click **OK**.

6. Click **Layer>New>Layer**, and fill the layer with **white**. Name the new layer White, and move it below the Wood layer.

7. Select the **Wood** layer, then click **Select>All**.

8. Click **Select>Modify>Border**, and set the **width** to **100** pixels.

9. Click **Layer>Layer Mask>Reveal Selection** so only the border has the texture (Figure 6.38).

10. Save your work as a **JPG** or a **TIFF** file. Follow your teacher's instructions.

11. In Microsoft Publisher, open the newsletter you started in Project 6-7.

12. Click CTRL + M to open the **Master Page** (Figure 6.39).

Insert Page Numbers

13. Click **Insert>Page Numbers**. Choose a number position at the **Bottom of the Page** with a **Center** alignment. Do not check "Show number on first page."

▼ **Figure 6.38** Select only the outside frame of your texture.

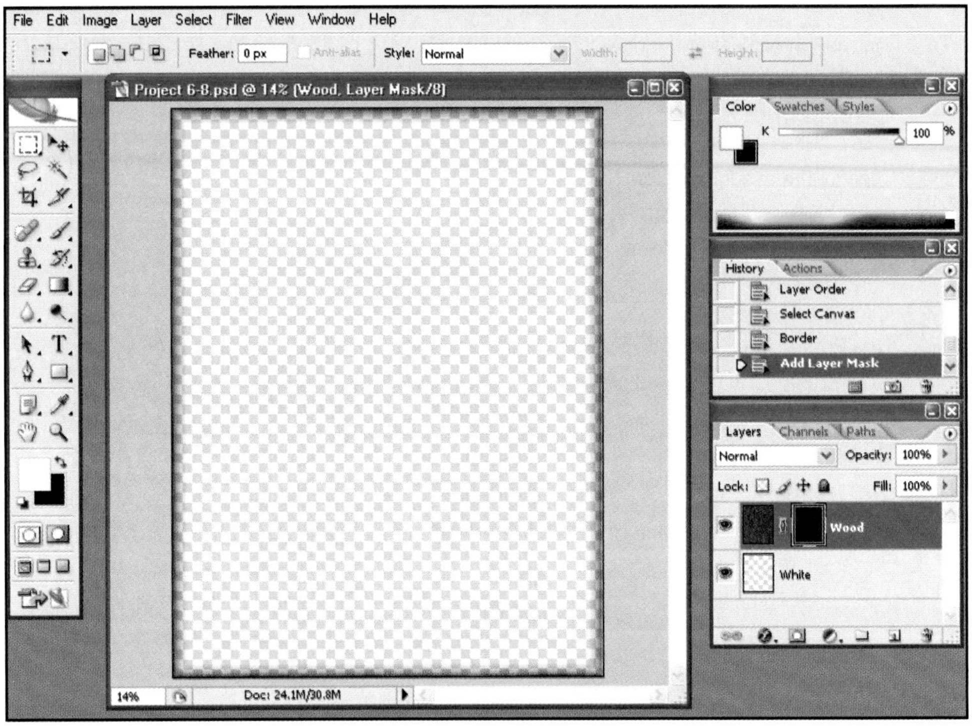

▼ **Figure 6.39** Your final master page should look similar to this.

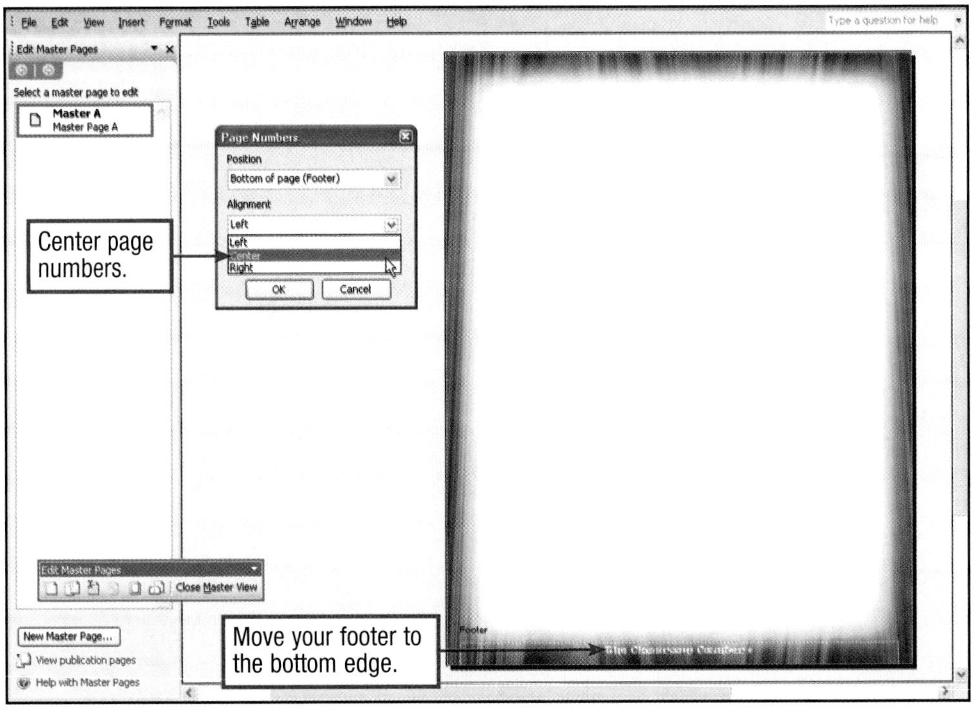

15 Make all layers visible. Then move the **Arm** layer above the **Flower Petal** layer (Figure 5.45).

Add a Shadow

16 Click **Layer>New> Layer**. Name this layer Arm Shadow. Move it between the **Arm** and **Flower Petal** layers.

17 In the toolbox, click **Brush** [brush icon]. In the **Options** bar, choose a **soft round** brush. On the **Color** palette, click the **Black** color square (Figure 5.45).

18 Use the brush to paint a small shadow beneath the hand on the **Arm Shadow** layer. Do not worry if it looks very dark.

Figure 5.45 The baby's arm is moved above the petal layer.

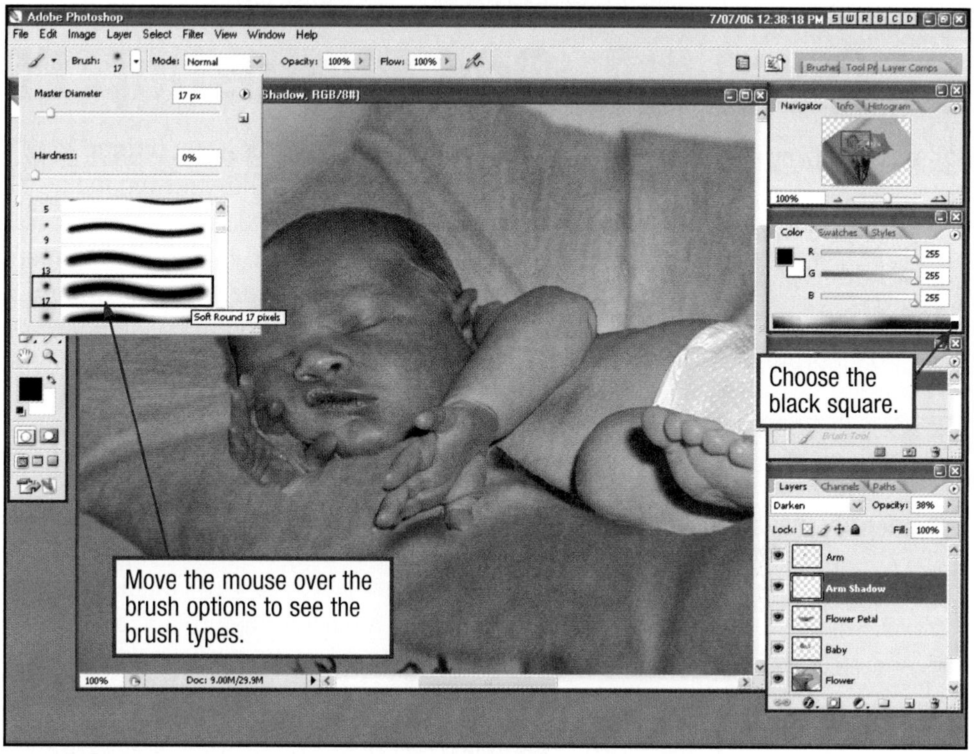
Adobe Photoshop
Choose the black square.
Move the mouse over the brush options to see the brush types.
Soft Round 17 pixels
Arm
Arm Shadow
Flower Petal
Baby
Flower

19 On the **Layers** palette, set the **Shadow** layer's **blending mode** to **Darken**. Adjust the **Opacity** so that the petal layer blends with the shadow above.

Apply a Filter

20 Click **Filter>Blur>Gaussian Blur** (which produces a hazy effect). Adjust the **Radius** pixels to create the effect you like (Figure 5.46).

21 Follow Steps 16–20 to create a new layer above the **Flower** layer. Add a shadow to the left of the baby's head. (The head rests on the **Flower** layer, not the **Petal** layer.)

Figure 5.46 The shadows should all follow the same light direction.

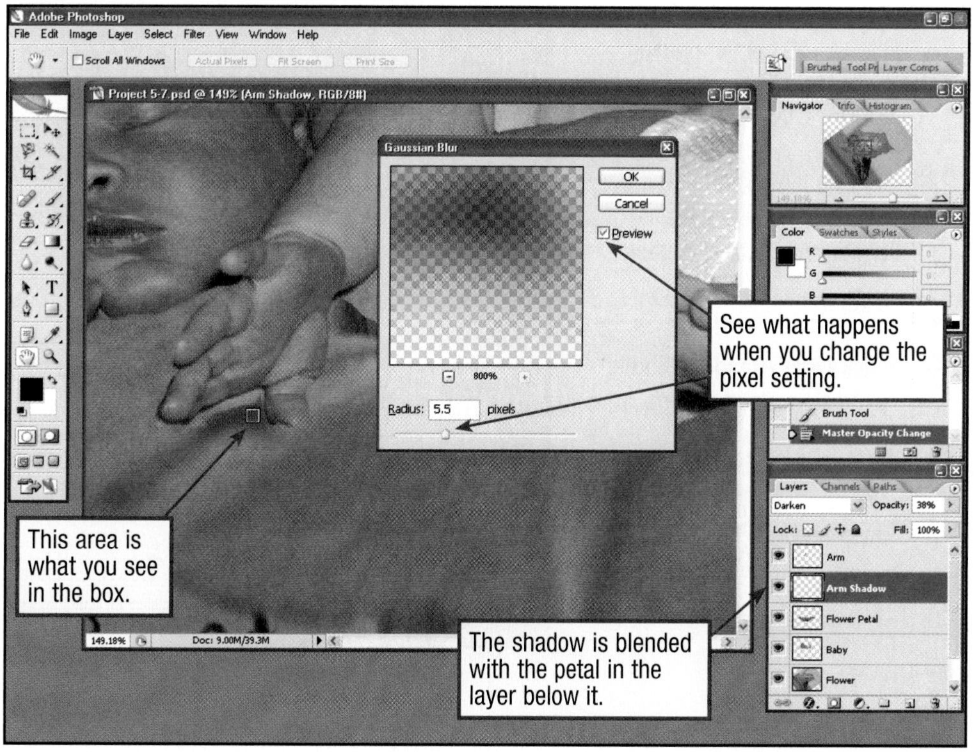
Adobe Photoshop
Gaussian Blur
OK
Cancel
Preview
Radius: 5.5 pixels
See what happens when you change the pixel setting.
This area is what you see in the box.
The shadow is blended with the petal in the layer below it.
Arm
Arm Shadow
Flower Petal
Baby
Flower

Skills Studio

Project 6-8 Add Photoshop Effects

Skills You Will Apply

- Create a texture
- Add page numbers
- Insert a textured background

Academic Focus

Science
Identify wave properties

An effective newsletter has a unique look that makes it stand out from its competitors. An eye-catching design makes an organization's newsletter easy to recognize for regular readers and more likely to be read by new readers.

Photoshop's filters let you create interesting background effects in your newsletter, like clouds, ice, fire, metal, and wood. Background textures are an interesting visual option to the standard stock photos and clip art that are often used in presentations, Web sites, brochures, and newsletters.

When you create your own background texture, you can customize the effect to your exact needs. Changing textures from other sources may be more difficult. They might be harder to modify. They also might be copyrighted, which means you may need to pay a royalty fee.

▶ **In this project,** you will finish the newsletter you started in Project 6-7 by using a master page to add a background texture.

Step-by-Step

1. In Photoshop, create a new **8½ by 11 inch** document, that is **150 ppi** (for printing purposes). Save according to your teacher's instructions.

2. Change the **foreground** color to **brown** and the **background** color to **black**.

Create a Texture

3. Click **Filter>Render>Clouds** to create a cloud pattern.

4. Click **Filter>Distort>Wave**. Change the settings to the ones shown in Figure 6.37.

▼ **Figure 6.37** The Wave filter can be used to create wood-like effects.

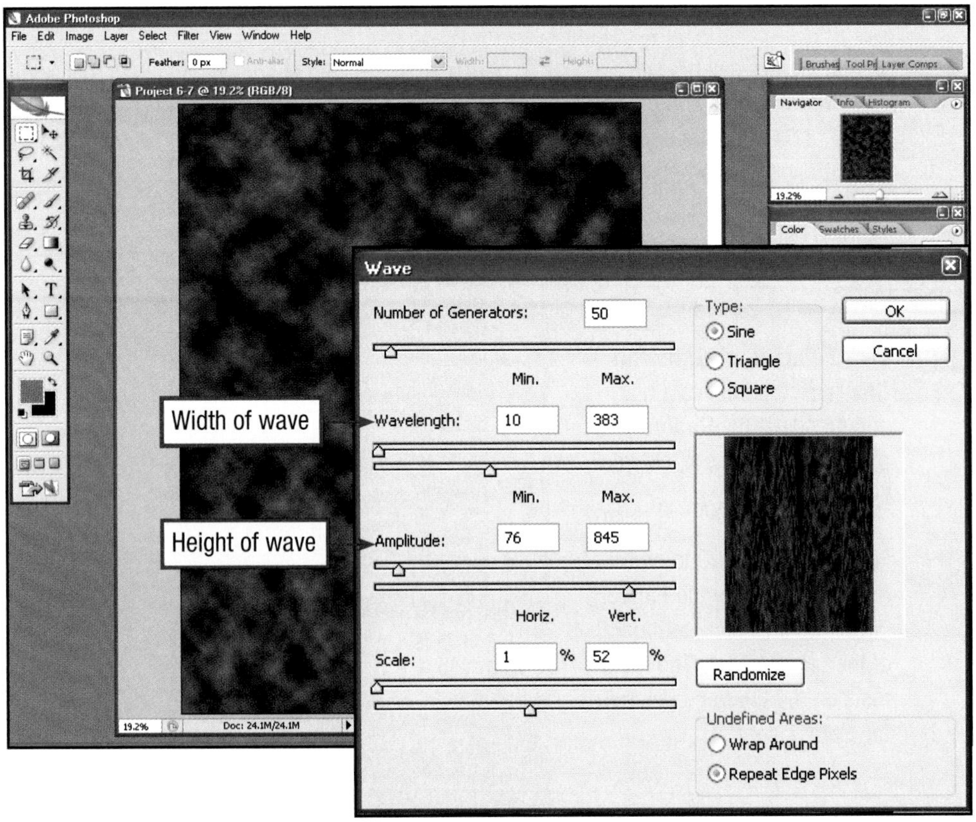

22. Open the hidden tools behind **Dodge**. Choose **Burn**.

23. Move the **Burn** tool over the **Flower Petal** layer. Create a light shadow near the baby to suggest a curve (Figure 5.47).

24. Change the **Burn** tool options until you are satisfied with the results. Use the **History** palette to undo any effects you do not like.

Flatten an Image

25. Follow your teacher's instructions for saving your work. Click **Layer>Flatten Image**. The **Layers** palette should only show one layer.

Create a Vignette Effect

26. Use **Elliptical Marquee** to create a large oval around the flower (Figure 5.47).

27. Click **Select>Feather**, and set the amount to **60 px**.

28. Click **Select>Inverse**, then press DELETE to remove the unselected background (Figure 5.48).

29. Follow your teacher's instructions for saving this flattened version of the document.

▼ **Figure 5.47** The Burn tool creates a curved look where the baby sinks into the flower.

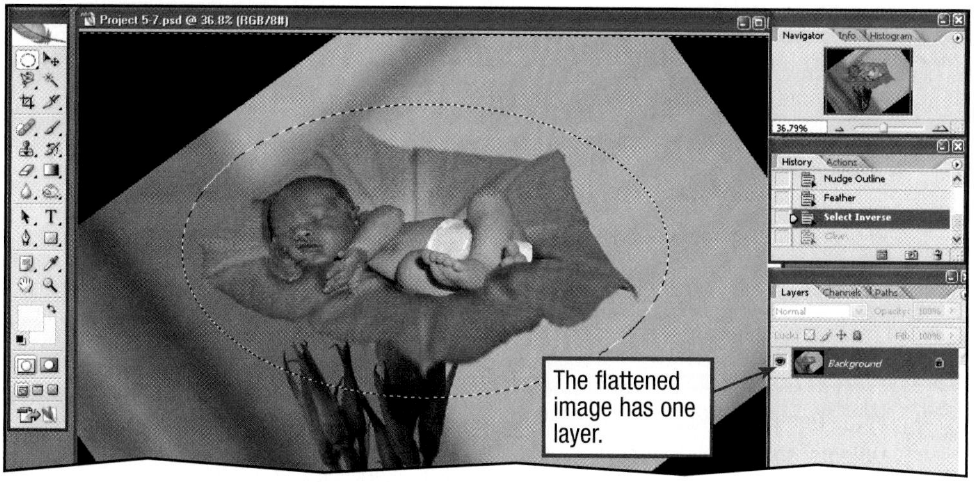

▼ **Figure 5.48** Save the flattened image in a different file from the layered image.

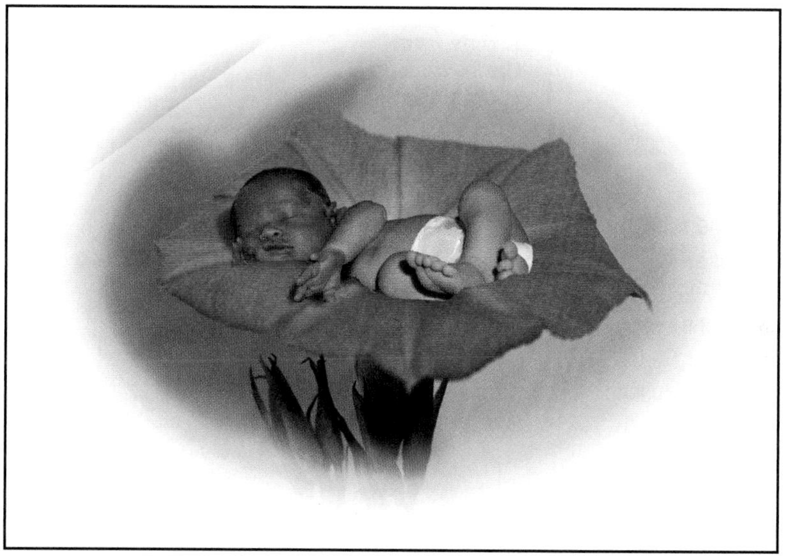

REVIEW AND REVISE

Check your work Use Figure 5.48 as a guide and check that:

- ☑ The baby has been resized and looks cushioned within the flower.
- ☑ The baby's arm is above the flower petal.
- ☑ The baby casts shadows onto the flower near his hand and head.
- ☑ A vignette effect has been created.
- ☑ Two versions have been saved: a flat and a layered version.

22. In the calendar, key the following information in the appropriate dates. Fill them with **gray**.
   - April 3 The Gilgamesh Project
   - April 30 Classroom Debate
   - Third Week of April State-wide Testing

Design the Final Page

23. In the **Design Gallery Objects**, choose the **Sidebars** section and choose a **Scallops** design.

24. Add brief descriptions of the newsletter contents as shown in the bottom page in Figure 6.36.

25. Place a text box above the sidebar and key the school's name and address.

26. Follow your teacher's instructions for saving your work. You will add Photoshop effects to your newsletter in Project 6-8.

▼ **Figure 6.36** Pages 2 to 4 of your newsletter should look similar to this figure.

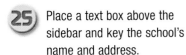

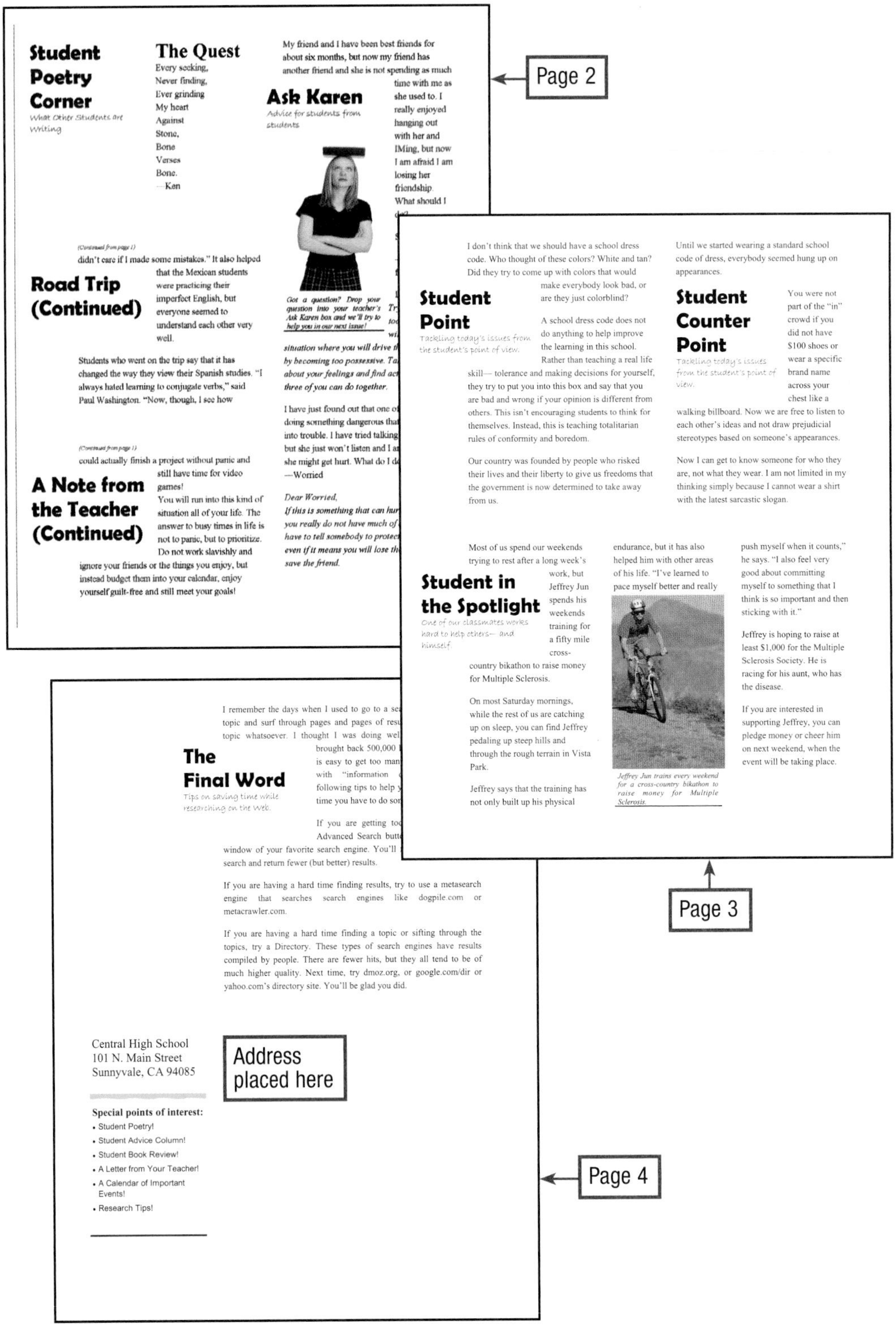

Project 5-8

Create Effects and Images with Filters

Spotlight on Skills

- Change the workspace color
- Apply filters
- Apply the Magic Eraser
- Add a gradient fill

Key Term

- filter

Academic Focus

Science
Create astronomy images

You have seen how Photoshop can be used to alter existing raster images, but it also can be used to create new ones. Many interesting images can be created by using filters. A **filter** is a tool that can create effects like distortions, textures, blurs, and more. As you learn more about the different filters in Photoshop, you will be able to combine them to create your own effects.

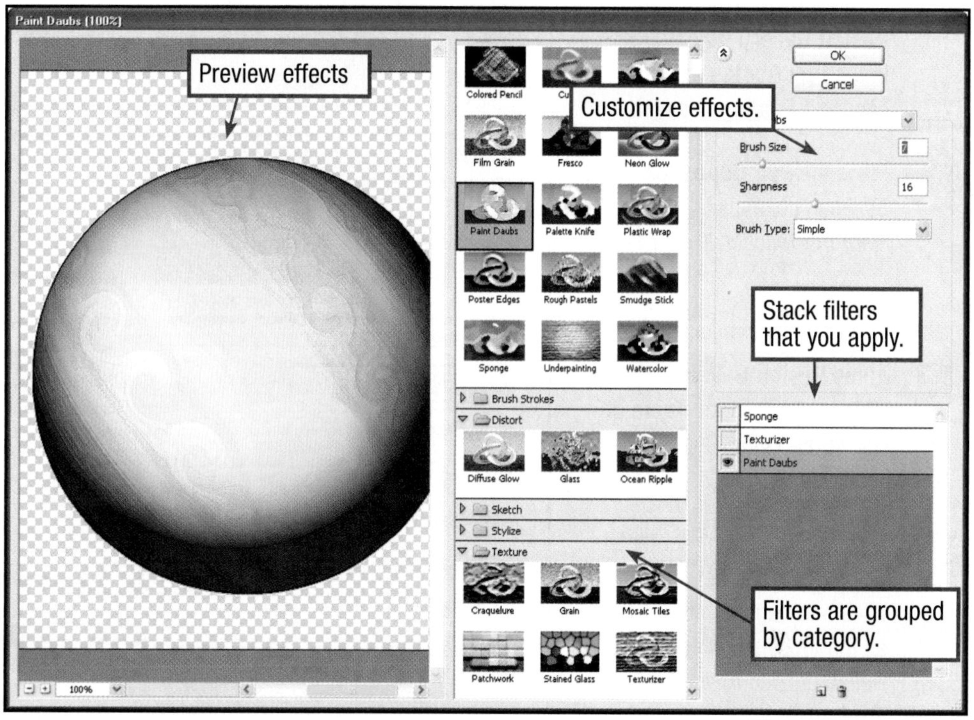

▲ Use the Filter gallery to preview filter effects.

Photoshop provides over 100 filters. Many of them can be previewed in the Filter Gallery. When you click a thumbnail in the gallery, you can preview how your object will look with the filter effect. You can then customize the effect by changing the settings. The effects that you applied to the image are stacked together and can be rearranged.

Like most effects in Photoshop, filters should be created and applied on their own layers. This makes it easier to change them without affecting other objects in the image.

► **In this project,** you will use filters to create images of a planet, stars, and a nebula (a gas or dust cloud in space). Included in the project are instructions on how to use many of the Photoshop filters.

Design the First Page

15. Create a text box for the newsletter title. Key the masthead information as shown in Figure 6.35.

16. On the **Object** toolbar, click **Design Gallery Objects** . In the **Pull Quotes** options, choose a **Scallops** design.

17. Place the **Pull Quote** box between columns in the *Note from the Teacher*. Key "The answer to busy times in life is not to panic, but to prioritize."

18. In the **Design Gallery Objects**, choose the **Table of Contents** option. Choose a **Scallops** design.

19. Format the Table of Contents' title with **Ravie**. Key the titles and page numbers of all the articles on Pages 2–4. Delete unused rows. (See Figure 6.35.)

20. In the **Design Gallery Objects**, choose Calendars. Choose the **Accent Box** design.

21. Select the calendar, and click **Wizard** at the bottom. Choose **Change Date Range**, and set the date to **April**.

Figure 6.35 Your first page should look similar to this figure.

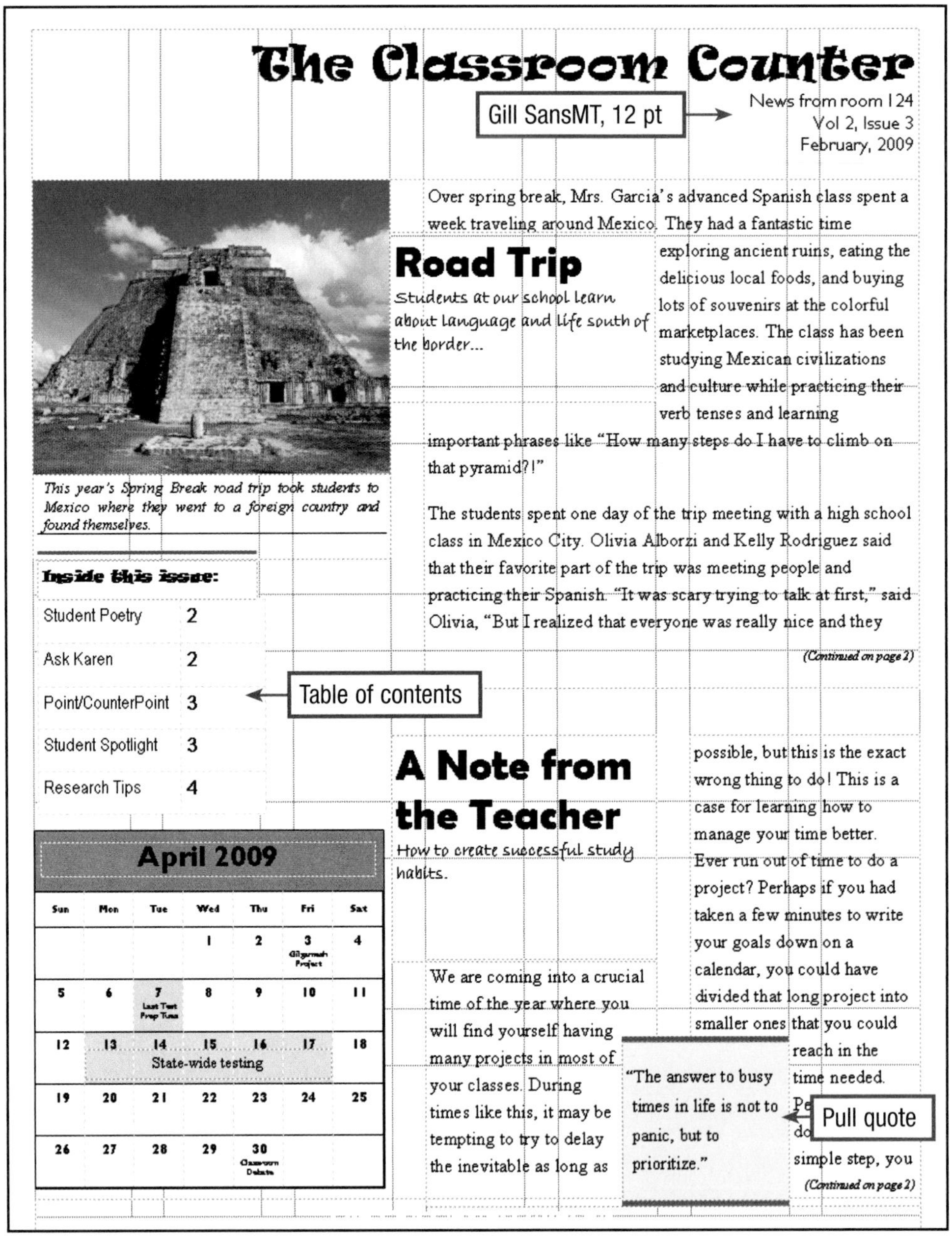

The Classroom Counter

News from room 124
Vol 2, Issue 3
February, 2009

Road Trip

Students at our school learn about language and life south of the border...

Over spring break, Mrs. Garcia's advanced Spanish class spent a week traveling around Mexico. They had a fantastic time exploring ancient ruins, eating the delicious local foods, and buying lots of souvenirs at the colorful marketplaces. The class has been studying Mexican civilizations and culture while practicing their verb tenses and learning important phrases like "How many steps do I have to climb on that pyramid?!"

The students spent one day of the trip meeting with a high school class in Mexico City. Olivia Alborzi and Kelly Rodriguez said that their favorite part of the trip was meeting people and practicing their Spanish. "It was scary trying to talk at first," said Olivia, "But I realized that everyone was really nice and they

(Continued on page 2)

This year's Spring Break road trip took students to Mexico where they went to a foreign country and found themselves.

Inside this issue:

April 2009						
Sun	Mon	Tue	Wed	Thu	Fri	Sat
			1	2	3 Gilgamesh Project	4
5	6	7 Last Test Prep Time	8	9	10	11
12	13 State-wide testing	14	15	16	17	18
19	20	21	22	23	24	25
26	27	28	29	30 Classroom Debate		

A Note from the Teacher

How to create successful study habits.

We are coming into a crucial time of the year where you will find yourself having many projects in most of your classes. During times like this, it may be tempting to try to delay the inevitable as long as possible, but this is the exact wrong thing to do! This is a case for learning how to manage your time better. Ever run out of time to do a project? Perhaps if you had taken a few minutes to write your goals down on a calendar, you could have divided that long project into smaller ones that you could reach in the time needed. Pe... do... simple step, you

"The answer to busy times in life is not to panic, but to prioritize."

(Continued on page 2)

Step-by-Step

1. In Photoshop, click **File>New**. Set the image to **6 inch width, 4 inch height** and **150 ppi resolution**. Name the file according to your teacher's instructions (Figure 5.49).

Change the Workspace Color

2. On the **Color** palette, change the **Foreground** color to **black**.

3. In the toolbox, open **Paint Bucket** behind the **Gradient** tool. Use it to fill the workspace with black.

Apply Filters

4. Click **Filter>Noise>Add noise** and adjust the amount to **25%**. Check the **Gaussian** and **Monochromatic** boxes.

5. Click **Filter>Render>Lens Flare** to set a bright star in the workspace.

6. Click **Filter>Render>Lighting Effects**. Set the **Light Type** to **Omni** and position it over the star.

7. Adjust settings such as **Exposure** and **Intensity** and the size of the light so that the star appears to be casting light.

8. Use the **Lens Flare** filter to create two more smaller stars (Figure 5.50).

▼ **Figure 5.49** Set resolutions and sizes to meet print requirements.

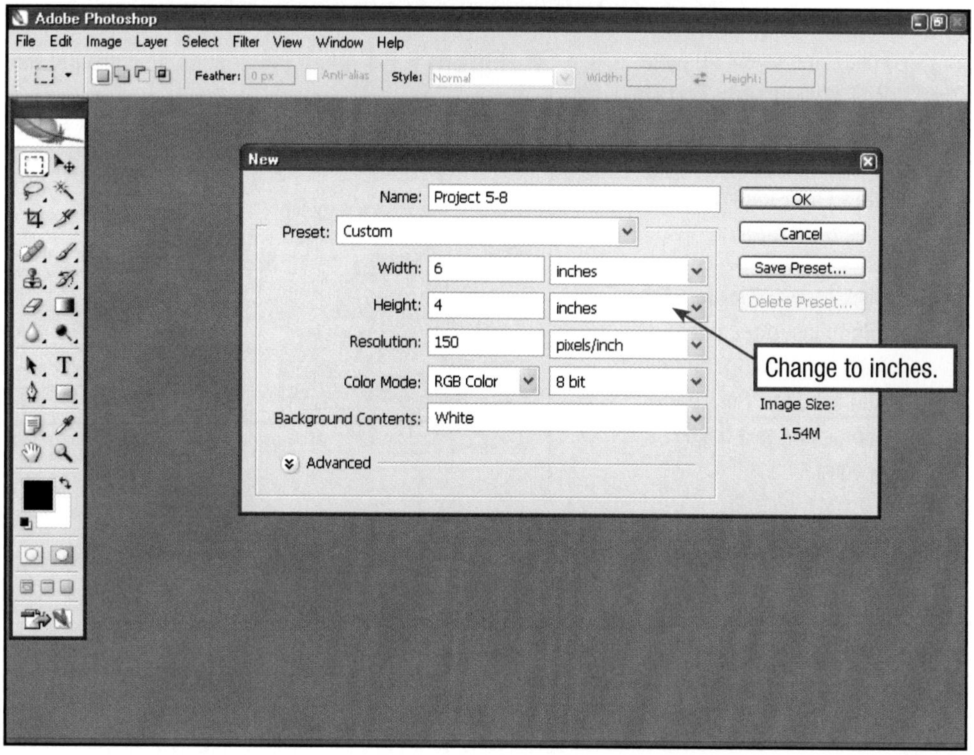

▼ **Figure 5.50** Change the lens flare setting to create different stars.

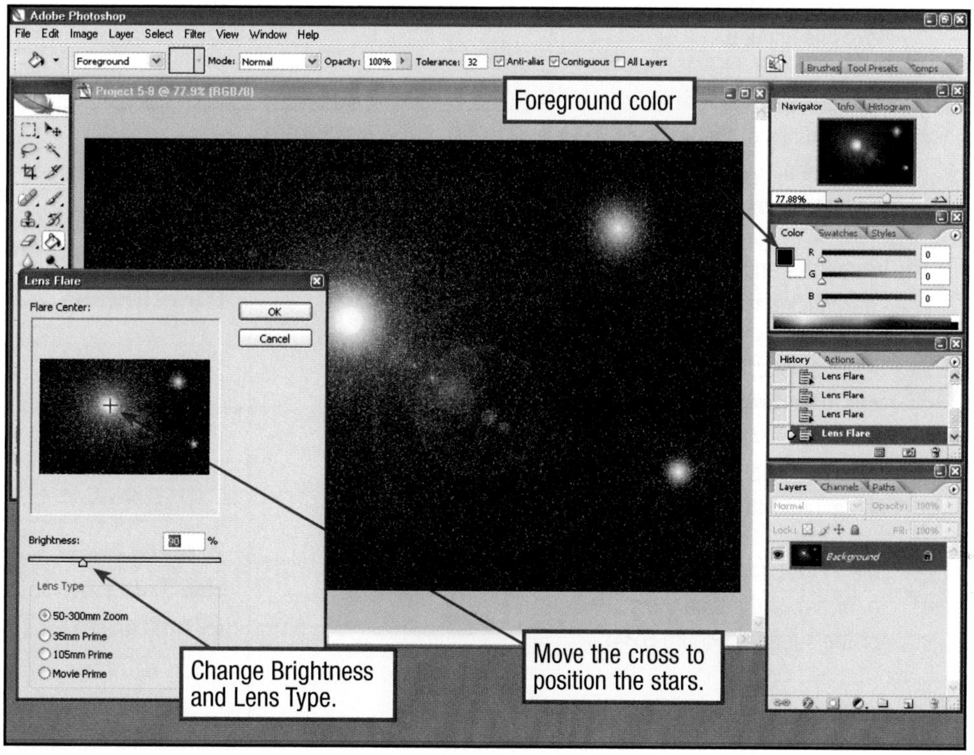

7. Follow the layout on page 279. Click **Insert>Text File** to insert the correct data file in each text box. (**DF** means **Data File**.) You will use Data Files 6-7a to 6-7k.

8. Click **Insert>Picture>From File** to insert the photo data files as shown in the figures. Add captions. Resize the photos and text boxes as needed.

9. Select the first article. Click **Format>Paragraph** to change the **leading** to **1.25 space**, with **12 pt after** each paragraph.

10. Define the style as **Article**, and assign the same style to each article in the newsletter. Resize the text boxes as needed.

11. Create text boxes for the titles and subtitles of the articles. Wrap the article text around the title boxes (Figure 6.34).

12. Write titles and subtitles (also called kickers) for each article.

13. Select a headline. Change the **font** to **Berlin Sans Demi** at **28 pt**. Define the style as **Headline**. Apply the style to all the headlines.

14. Use **12 pt Bradley Hand ITC** to format, and define the style for the subtitles (Figure 6.34).

▼ **Figure 6.34** Wrap the articles' text around the titles and photographs.

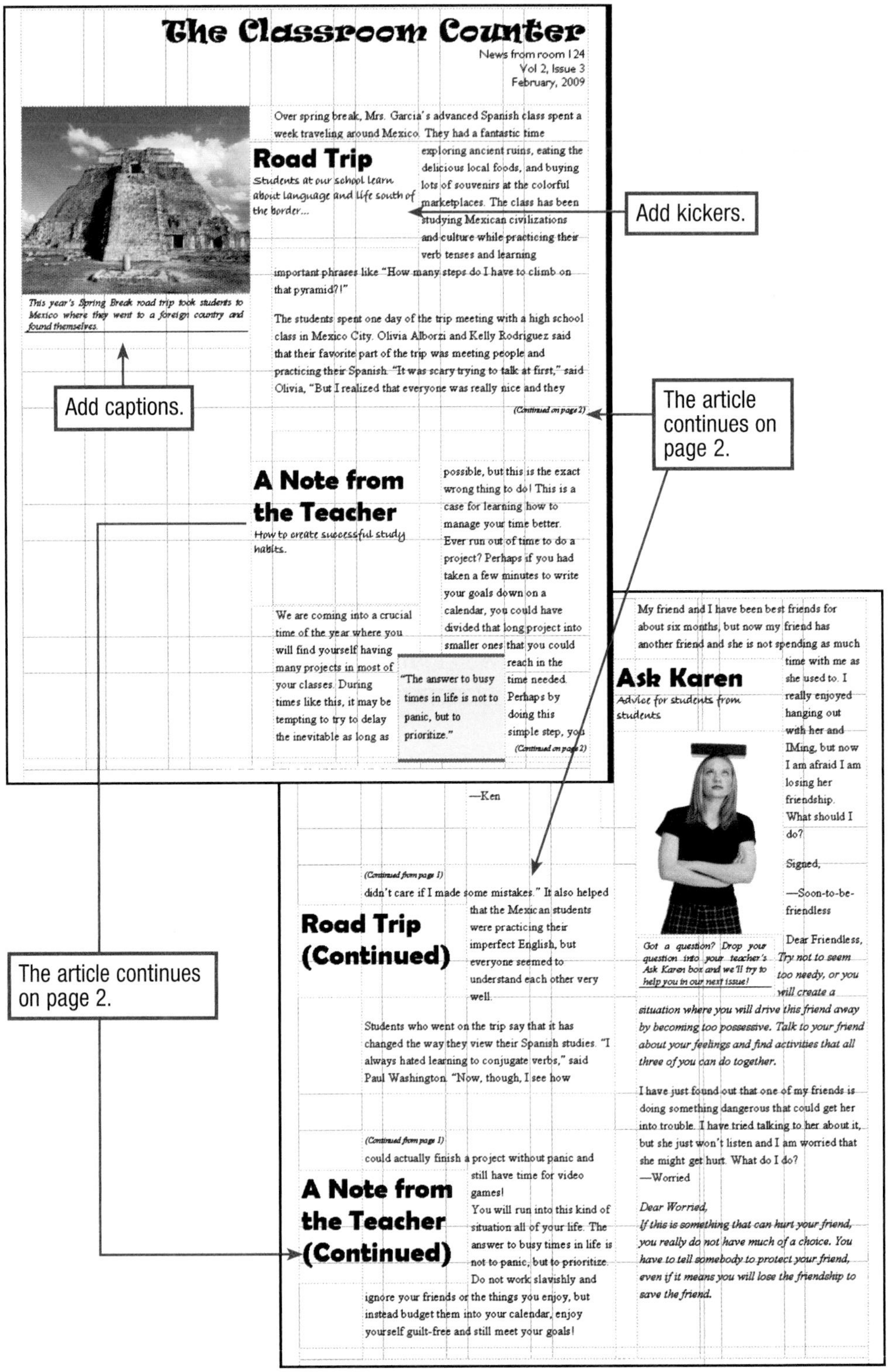

The Classroom Counter

News from room 124
Vol 2, Issue 3
February, 2009

This year's Spring Break road trip took students to Mexico where they went to a foreign country and found themselves.

Road Trip

Students at our school learn about language and life south of the border...

Over spring break, Mrs. Garcia's advanced Spanish class spent a week traveling around Mexico. They had a fantastic time exploring ancient ruins, eating the delicious local foods, and buying lots of souvenirs at the colorful marketplaces. The class has been studying Mexican civilizations and culture while practicing their verb tenses and learning important phrases like "How many steps do I have to climb on that pyramid?!"

The students spent one day of the trip meeting with a high school class in Mexico City. Olivia Alborzi and Kelly Rodriguez said that their favorite part of the trip was meeting people and practicing their Spanish. "It was scary trying to talk at first," said Olivia, "But I realized that everyone was really nice and they

(Continued on page 2)

A Note from the Teacher

How to create successful study habits.

We are coming into a crucial time of the year where you will find yourself having many projects in most of your classes. During times like this, it may be tempting to try to delay the inevitable as long as possible, but this is the exact wrong thing to do! This is a case for learning how to manage your time better. Ever run out of time to do a project? Perhaps if you had taken a few minutes to write your goals down on a calendar, you could have divided that long project into smaller ones that you could reach in the time needed. Perhaps by doing this simple step, you

(Continued on page 2)

"The answer to busy times in life is not to panic, but to prioritize."

—Ken

(Continued from page 1)

didn't care if I made some mistakes." It also helped that the Mexican students were practicing their imperfect English, but everyone seemed to understand each other very well.

Road Trip (Continued)

Students who went on the trip say that it has changed the way they view their Spanish studies. "I always hated learning to conjugate verbs," said Paul Washington. "Now, though, I see how

(Continued from page 1)

could actually finish a project without panic and still have time for video games!

You will run into this kind of situation all of your life. The answer to busy times in life is not to panic, but to prioritize. Do not work slavishly and ignore your friends or the things you enjoy, but instead budget them into your calendar, enjoy yourself guilt-free and still meet your goals!

A Note from the Teacher (Continued)

Ask Karen

Advice for students from students

My friend and I have been best friends for about six months, but now my friend has another friend and she is not spending as much time with me as she used to. I really enjoyed hanging out with her and IMing, but now I am afraid I am losing her friendship. What should I do?

Signed,

—Soon-to-be-friendless

Dear Friendless,

Try not to seem too needy, or you will create a situation where you will drive this friend away by becoming too possessive. Talk to your friend about your feelings and find activities that all three of you can do together.

Got a question? Drop your question into your teacher's Ask Karen box and we'll try to help you in our next issue!

I have just found out that one of my friends is doing something dangerous that could get her into trouble. I have tried talking to her about it, but she just won't listen and I am worried that she might get hurt. What do I do?

—Worried

Dear Worried,

If this is something that can hurt your friend, you really do not have much of a choice. You have to tell somebody to protect your friend, even if it means you will lose the friendship to save the friend.

9. Click **Layer>New> Layer** and name the layer Pink Nebula.

10. On the **Color** palette, click the **Foreground** color, then click the color spectrum to change the color to **bright pink**. Change the **Background** color to **black**.

11. Click **Filter>Render>Clouds** (Figure 5.51).

Apply the Magic Eraser

12. In the toolbox, open **Magic Eraser** [icon] behind the Eraser.

13. Click in the workspace until some of the nebula has been removed. (Press CTRL + Z to undo if too much has been removed and try again.)

14. On the **Layers** palette, change the **Nebula** layer's blending mode to **Lighten**. Adjust the **Opacity** to produce the best effect.

15. Click **Filter>Blur>Gaussian Blur**, and choose a **Radius** of approximately **20 px**, or whatever blends the cloud effect best.

16. Repeat Steps 9–15 to create nebulae in one or two other colors. (Figure 5.52)

▼ **Figure 5.51** The new layer covers the original layer.

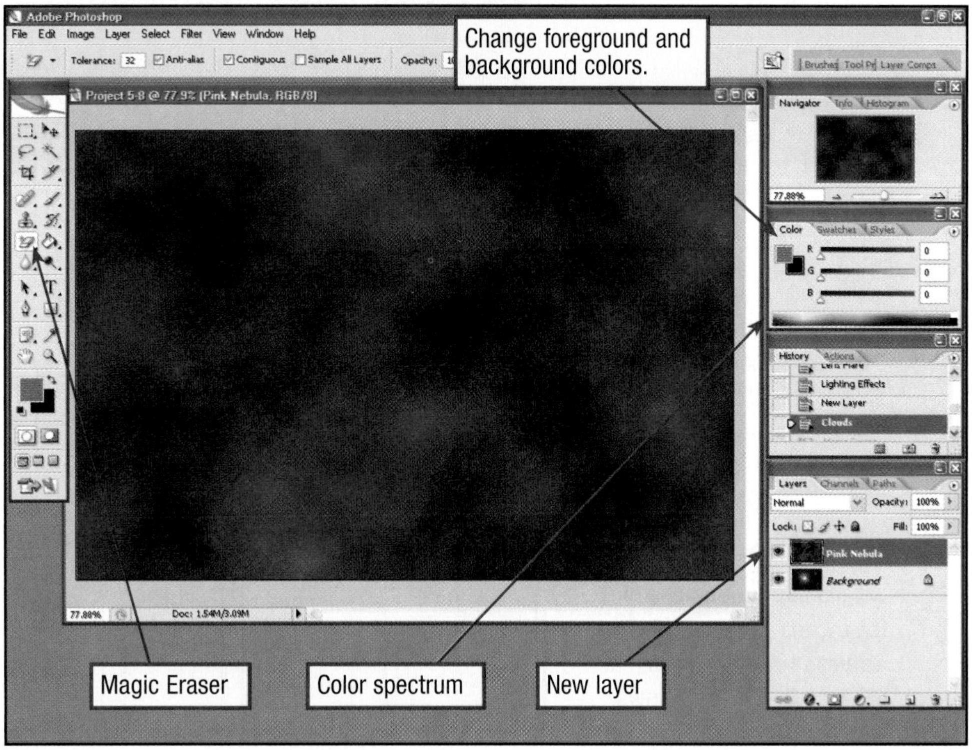

▼ **Figure 5.52** The nebulae should look like semi-transparent clouds.

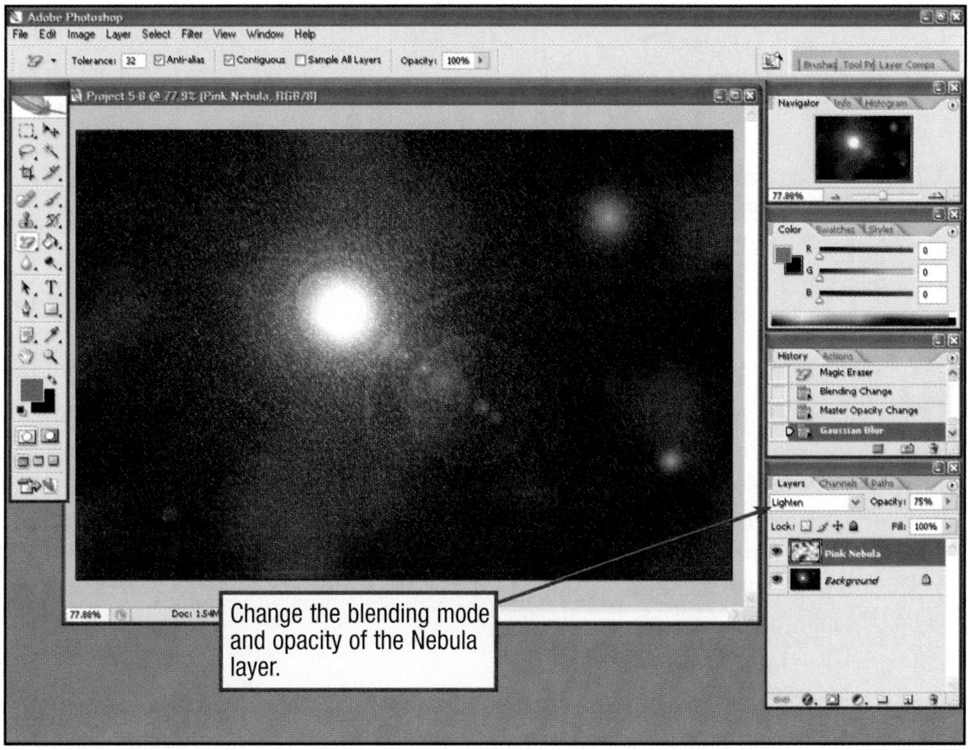

Student Data File

Step-by-Step

1. In Publisher, create a new blank print publication. Save it according to your teacher's instructions.
2. Insert three more pages for a total of four.
3. Set the **Margin Guides** at **0.5 inches**. Set the **Grid Guides** to **7 columns** with a **0.3 inch gutter** and **6 rows** with a **0.5 inch** gutter.

Lay Out Text Elements

4. Create text boxes following the diagram in Figure 6.33. Some articles flow into more than one text box.
5. To link text boxes, click the first text box, then click **Link** on the toolbar. Then click the second text box where the article will flow.
6. The two articles on Page 1 continue on Page 2. After linking the text boxes, do the following for each text box:
   - Click the text box.
   - Click **Format>Text Box**, and open the **Text Box** tab.
   - Choose either *Continued on…* or *Continued from….*

▼ **Figure 6.33** This layout is not exact. You will adjust the size of the text boxes after you add the text files.

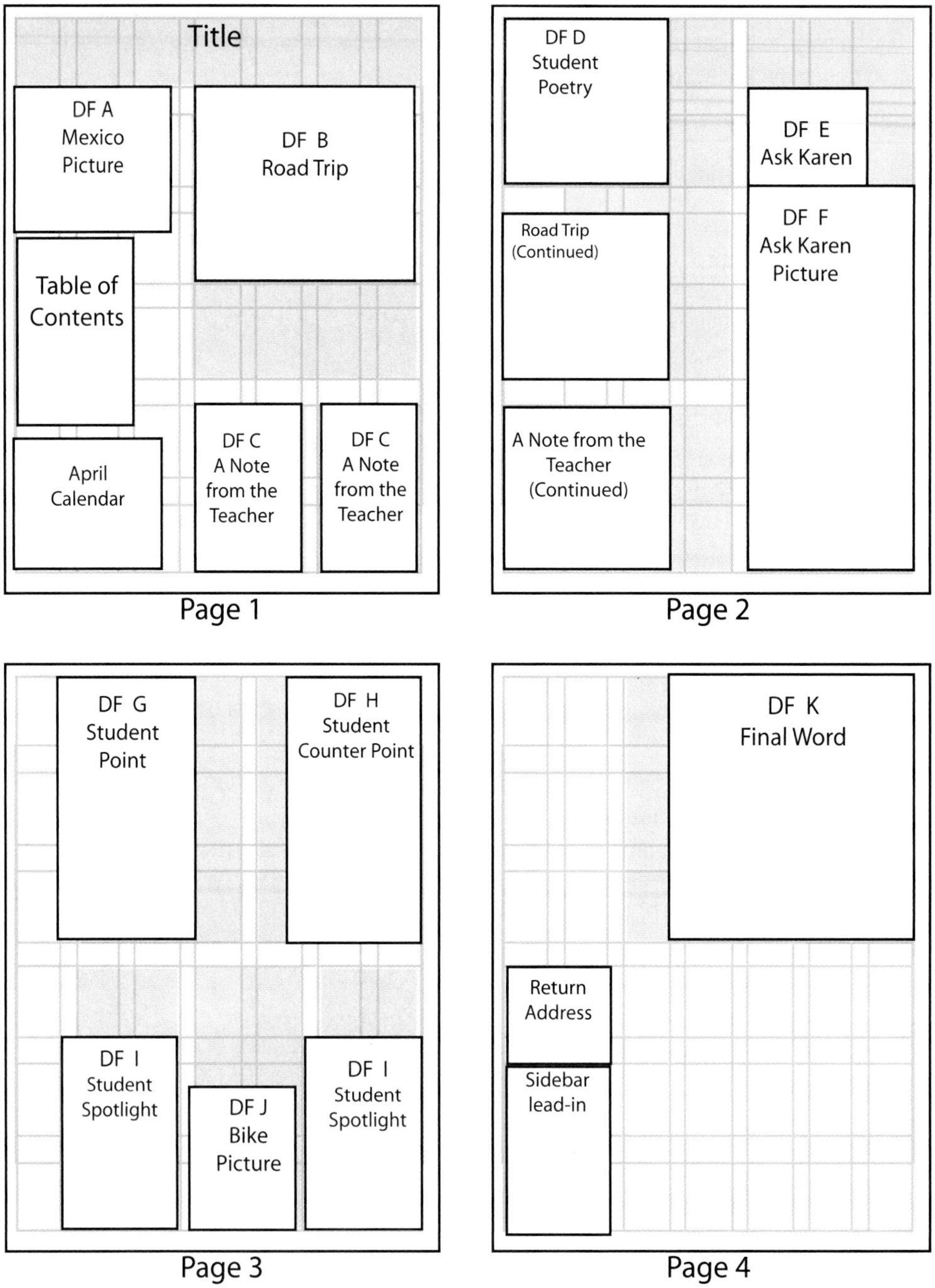

17 Create a new layer and name it **Planet**.

18 Click **Elliptical Marquee** [icon], then hold SHIFT to drag a circle in the workspace.

Add a Gradient Fill

19 Click **Gradient** [icon]. On the **Options** bar, open the gradient drop-down menu. Click the options button in the menu, and choose **Noise Samples**.

20 Click **OK** when asked to replace gradients. In the new menu, choose **Sunrise** (Figure 5.53). Click in the planet, and drag a line diagonally to add the gradient fill.

21 Click **Filter>Liquify**. Use the **Twirl**, **Bloat**, and **Pucker** tools to create your planet (Figure 5.54).

22 Click **Filter>Distort> Spherize**, and set the **Amount** to **100%**.

23 Click **Filter>Render>Lighting Effects**, and set a **Spotlight** on the planet. Adjust the sliders and **Preview** marquee so the planet fades into blackness (Figure 5.54).

▼ **Figure 5.53** You can change the type of gradients displayed in the drop-down menu.

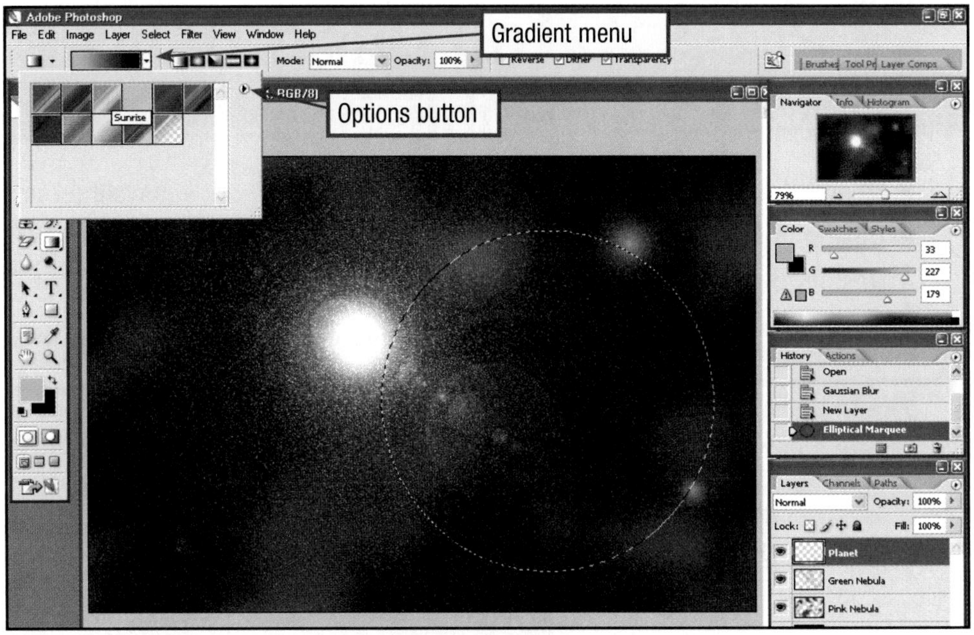

▼ **Figure 5.54** Create your own planetary effects with the Liquify and Lighting Effects filters.

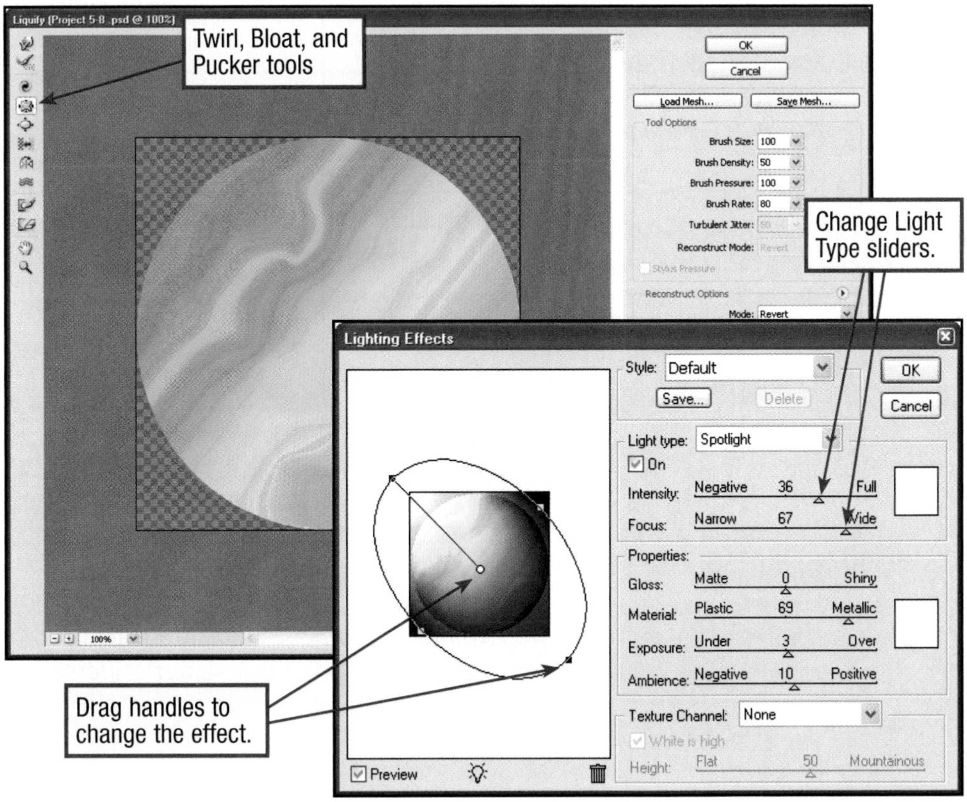

Skills Studio

Project 6-7

Lay Out a Newsletter in Publisher

Skills You Will Apply

- Lay out text elements
- Design the first page
- Design the final page

Academic Focus

Language Arts
Create a newsletter

The first step in laying out a newsletter is to decide where all the text will go. It must balance the twin goals of presenting important content and making it readable. If the newsletter has too much text on a page, it is difficult to read, and readers may throw it away. If there is too little text, the intended audience might not get the information they need, or the newsletter might need a lot of pages, which is costly.

Next, set the specifications for the printed page. The specifications include margin and column settings as well as your choice of page orientation (portrait or landscape). Keep in mind the PARC principles when designing your newsletter.

Apply PARC to Newsletters

PARC Principle	Application
Proximity	Titles should clearly identify articles. Headers, subheads, etc. should be grouped with the information that they describe. White space should break up text to give the viewer's eyes a chance to rest and focus.
Alignment	Use layout grids for consistent spacing and placing information so that it lines up with other items on the page. The tops of columns must align, even if the bottoms do not.
Repetition	Create a strong design element and use it throughout. Use a Master Page to add elements like borders, page numbers, or backgrounds to all pages. Experiment with different kinds of spot colors or paper.
Contrast	Make special information stand out with fonts or design elements that contrast with the surrounding design. However, keep the font scheme simple. Do not try to make every article different by using different fonts. Instead, vary the column widths and add boxes, clip art, sidebars, and pull-quotes.

▶ **In this project,** you will lay out a newsletter in Publisher. You will complete the newsletter in Project 6-8 using Photoshop tools. Take the time to set up the newsletter effectively so that it will be easy to add or change content.

24. Use the **Move** tool to move the planet as shown.

25. Create a new layer, and name it **Moon**. Create a smaller circle that overlaps the planet (Figure 5.56).

26. Press D to restore the default colors of black and white. Click **Filter>Render>Clouds** to fill the ellipse.

27. Click **Filter>Sketch>Bas Relief**. Set the **Detail** setting all the way up and the **Smoothness** setting all the way down. Change the **Light** to match the direction in your image.

28. Click **Filter>Noise>Add Noise**. Check the **Gaussian** and **Monochromatic** boxes, and change the setting to **18%** to give the moon some texture.

29. Repeat Steps 21–22 to spherize and add darkness to your moon.

30. Resize and reposition the moon as needed. Follow your teacher's instructions for saving and printing your work.

Figure 5.55 The Bas Relief sketch filter creates a three-dimensional texture.

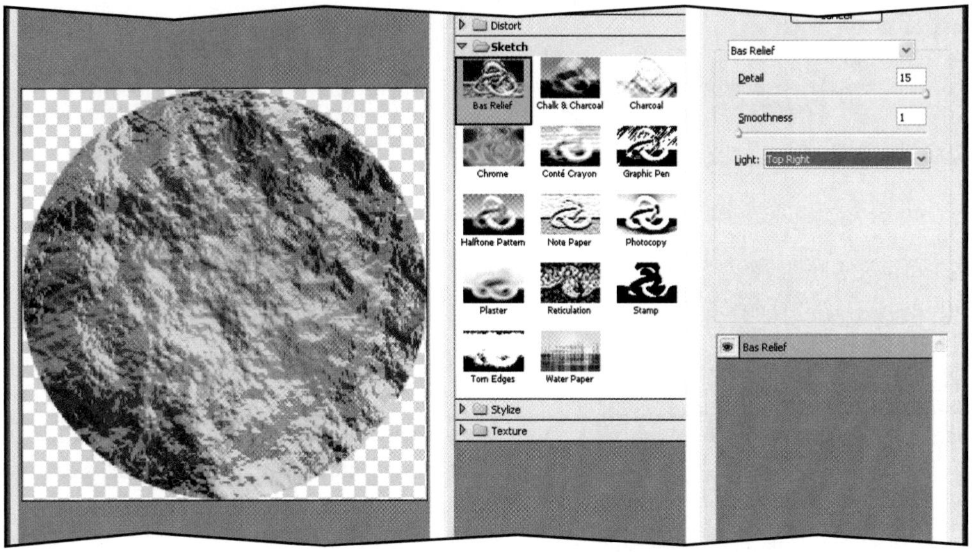

Figure 5.56 The finished image looks very realistic.

REVIEW AND REVISE

Check your work Use Figure 5.56 as a guide and check that:

- ☑ The background has stars and multicolored nebulae.
- ☑ The moon and the planet are spherical with textured surfaces.
- ☑ The moon and the planet appear to be lit from the same source.

Skills Studio

Reinforce Your Skills

Project 6-7

- Lay out text elements in a multi-page newsletter
- Link text boxes
- Add a masthead
- Add Design Gallery objects

Project 6-8

- Add a textured background
- Apply a master page
- Insert page numbers

Go Online ACTIVITIES
www.glencoe.com

Challenge Yourself Go to **Chapter 6**, and choose **Enrichment Activities** for more practice with the skills you have learned.

Create a Newsletter

The following two projects will take you through the steps you need to create a newsletter:

- **Project 6-7** Lay out a newsletter in Publisher
- **Project 6-8** Add Photoshop effects

Inviting Newsletters

Newsletters are perhaps some of the most challenging designs to create because they are so text-heavy. To interest readers, include lead-ins throughout your newsletter. Lead-ins literally lead readers to open the newsletter and read further. Examples of lead-ins include a table of contents, articles that continue on inside pages, interesting teasers below article titles, and captions for pictures. You have created a successful newsletter if you succeed in getting the reader to open it.

Newsletters are often distributed by mail, and they often have less than a second to convince the reader to open them. Mailed newsletters are often folded in half and stapled, and it is usually the last page that readers see first. This means that the last page, not the first, is often the most important page to design. If your newsletter is cleverly designed, readers will want to look inside.

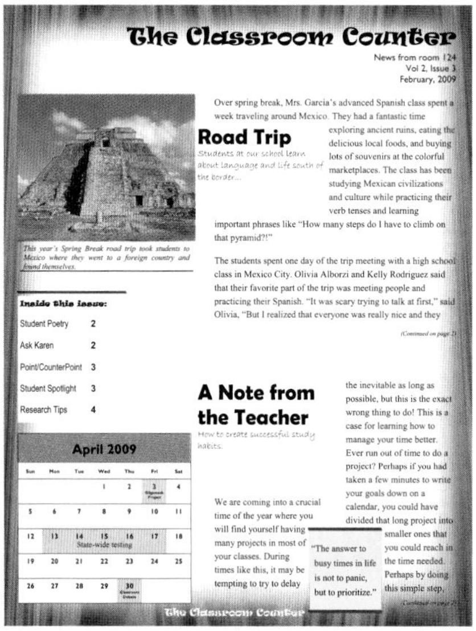

The Classroom Counter

News from room 124
Vol 2, Issue 3
February, 2009

Road Trip

Students at our school learn about language and life south of the border...

Over spring break, Mrs. Garcia's advanced Spanish class spent a week traveling around Mexico. They had a fantastic time exploring ancient ruins, eating the delicious local foods, and buying lots of souvenirs at the colorful marketplaces. The class has been studying Mexican civilizations and culture while practicing their verb tenses and learning important phrases like "How many steps do I have to climb on that pyramid?!"

The students spent one day of the trip meeting with a high school class in Mexico City. Olivia Alborzi and Kelly Rodriguez said that their favorite part of the trip was meeting people and practicing their Spanish. "It was scary trying to talk at first," said Olivia, "But I realized that everyone was really nice and they

(Continued on page 2)

This year's Spring Break road trip took students to Mexico where they went to a foreign country and found themselves.

Inside this issue:

Student Poetry	2
Ask Karen	2
Point/CounterPoint	3
Student Spotlight	3
Research Tips	4

April 2009

Sun	Mon	Tue	Wed	Thu	Fri	Sat
			1	2	3	4
5	6	7	8	9	10	11
12	13 State-wide testing	14	15	16	17	18
19	20	21	22	23	24	25
26	27	28	29	30		

A Note from the Teacher

How to create successful study habits.

We are coming into a crucial time of the year where you will find yourself having many projects in most of your classes. During times like this, it may be tempting to try to delay the inevitable as long as possible, but this is the exact wrong thing to do! This is a case for learning how to manage your time better. Ever run out of time to do a project? Perhaps if you had taken a few minutes to write your goals down on a calendar, you could have divided that long project into smaller ones that you could reach in the time needed. Perhaps by doing this simple step,

"The answer to busy times in life is not to panic, but to prioritize."

(Continued on page 2)

The Classroom Counter

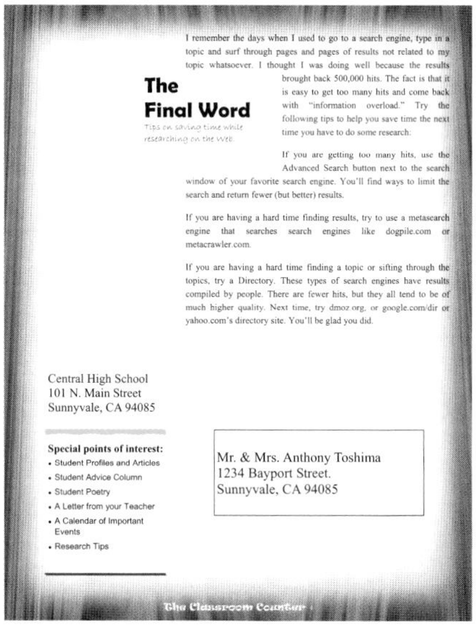

The Final Word

Tips on saving time while researching on the Web.

I remember the days when I used to go to a search engine, type in a topic and surf through pages and pages of results not related to my topic whatsoever. I thought I was doing well because the results brought back 500,000 hits. The fact is that it is easy to get too many hits and come back with "information overload." Try the following tips to help you save time the next time you have to do some research:

If you are getting too many hits, use the Advanced Search button next to the search window of your favorite search engine. You'll find ways to limit the search and return fewer (but better) results.

If you are having a hard time finding results, try to use a metasearch engine that searches search engines like dogpile.com or metacrawler.com.

If you are having a hard time finding a topic or sifting through the topics, try a Directory. These types of search engines have results compiled by people. There are fewer hits, but they all tend to be of much higher quality. Next time, try dmoz.org, or google.com/dir or yahoo.com's directory site. You'll be glad you did.

Central High School
101 N. Main Street
Sunnyvale, CA 94085

Special points of interest:
- Student Profiles and Articles
- Student Advice Column
- Student Poetry
- A Letter from your Teacher
- A Calendar of Important Events
- Research Tips

Mr. & Mrs. Anthony Toshima
1234 Bayport Street.
Sunnyvale, CA 94085

The Classroom Counter

Since newsletters are often created and distributed several times a year, your design should signal to the reader that this newsletter is from a particular source. Photoshop can help you add interesting and unique visual elements. If you can get someone to open or read your newsletter, you have created a successful design.

Skills Studio

Reinforce Your Skills

- **Project 5-9**
  - Take a digital photograph
  - Upload a photo from a camera
  - Remove a background
  - Insert a picture into an image
  - Edit the pictures
- **Project 5-10**
  - Group layers
  - Insert magazine cover objects
  - Add text

Go Online ACTIVITIES
www.glencoe.com

Challenge Yourself Go to **Chapter 5**, and choose **Enrichment Activities** for more practice with the skills you have learned.

Create a Magazine Cover

The following two projects will take you through the steps you need to create a magazine cover:

- ◆ **Project 5-9** Take a digital photograph
- ◆ **Project 5-10** Create a magazine cover

Digital Cameras

At one time, cameras required film, which meant that you could not see what a photo looked like until the whole roll was shot. You had to wait for a professional to develop and print the pictures. If you wanted to edit or retouch your photos, you again had to rely on a professional.

Digital photography has changed the way pictures are taken. Photographers can judge each photo seconds after it has been taken, and then they can print and edit them however and whenever they like. Most basic digital cameras today have many useful features and take clear pictures. Professional photographers, however, need cameras with features that allow them to take high-quality images for publications.

Commercial products require photographs that are clear, attractive, and often retouched. Although you may not have the equipment that a professional photographer has, the cover that you create in this project will surely catch the eyes of your friends and family.

17 On **Page 4**, create the layout as shown in Figure 6.32, repeating the design elements on the previous pages.

18 Insert **Data File 6-6e**. Format the text in **Times New Roman**, **12 pt**. **Single space** between lines, with **18 pt space** after each paragraph.

19 Select the first citation. Use the sliders on the ruler to create a hanging indent. Repeat for all the citations.

20 Create a text box at the bottom with your name and any other information that your teacher requires.

21 Select the first line of your information. Click **Format>Horizontal Rule>Before**. Add a **1 pt line** above and below the contact information.

22 Open the **Background** task pane. Choose the **Newsprint** background for all pages (Figure 6.32).

23 Follow your teacher's instructions for saving and printing your booklet.

▼ **Figure 6.32** Your printed booklet should follow the PARC principles.

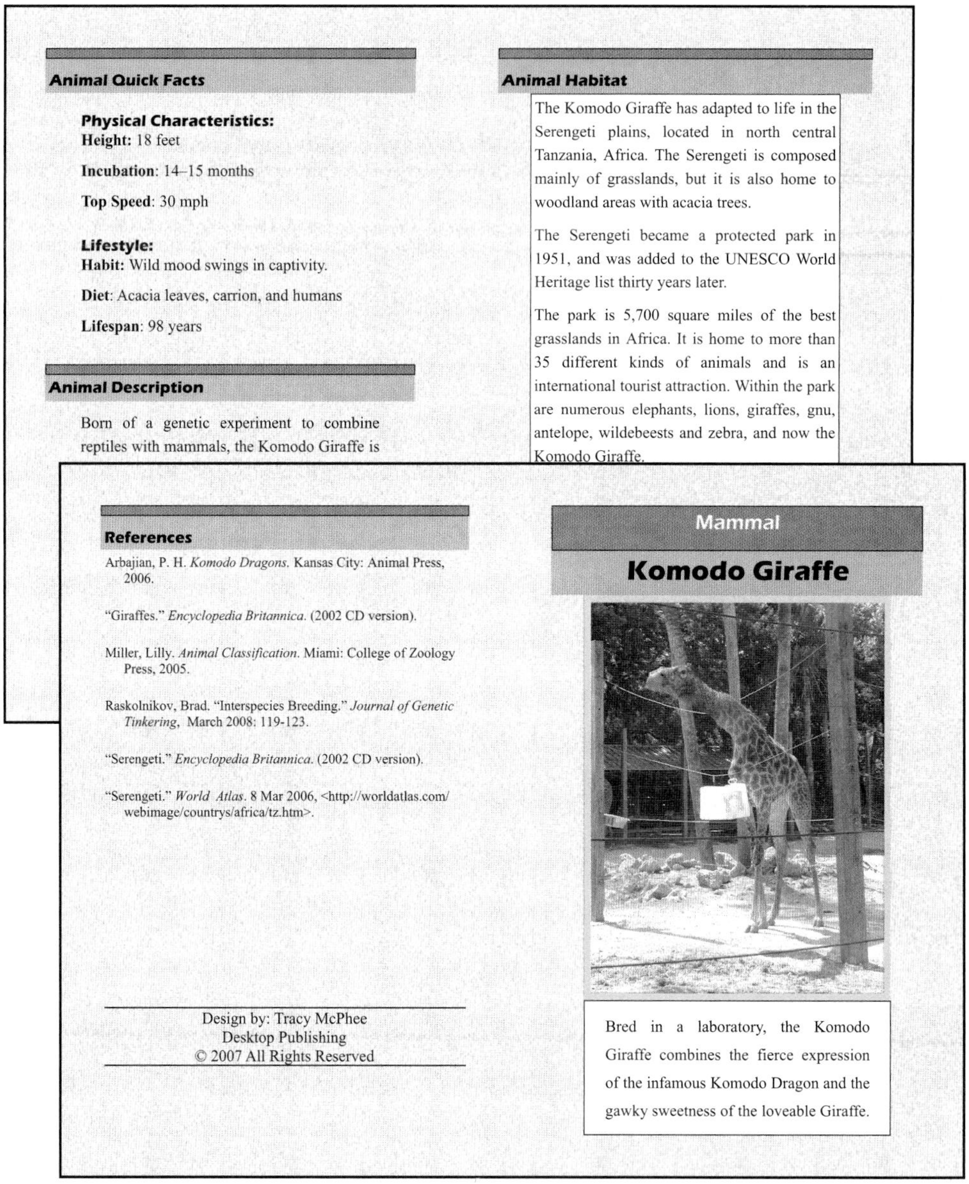

Animal Quick Facts

Physical Characteristics:
Height: 18 feet

Incubation: 14–15 months

Top Speed: 30 mph

Lifestyle:
Habit: Wild mood swings in captivity.

Diet: Acacia leaves, carrion, and humans

Lifespan: 98 years

Animal Description

Born of a genetic experiment to combine reptiles with mammals, the Komodo Giraffe is

Animal Habitat

The Komodo Giraffe has adapted to life in the Serengeti plains, located in north central Tanzania, Africa. The Serengeti is composed mainly of grasslands, but it is also home to woodland areas with acacia trees.

The Serengeti became a protected park in 1951, and was added to the UNESCO World Heritage list thirty years later.

The park is 5,700 square miles of the best grasslands in Africa. It is home to more than 35 different kinds of animals and is an international tourist attraction. Within the park are numerous elephants, lions, giraffes, gnu, antelope, wildebeests and zebra, and now the Komodo Giraffe.

References

Arbajian, P. H. *Komodo Dragons*. Kansas City: Animal Press, 2006.

"Giraffes." *Encyclopedia Britannica*. (2002 CD version).

Miller, Lilly. *Animal Classification*. Miami: College of Zoology Press, 2005.

Raskolnikov, Brad. "Interspecies Breeding." *Journal of Genetic Tinkering*, March 2008: 119-123.

"Serengeti." *Encyclopedia Britannica*. (2002 CD version).

"Serengeti." *World Atlas*. 8 Mar 2006, <http://worldatlas.com/webimage/countrys/africa/tz.htm>.

Design by: Tracy McPhee
Desktop Publishing
© 2007 All Rights Reserved

Mammal

Komodo Giraffe

Bred in a laboratory, the Komodo Giraffe combines the fierce expression of the infamous Komodo Dragon and the gawky sweetness of the loveable Giraffe.

REVIEW AND REVISE

Check your work Use Figure 6.32 as a guide and check that:

- ☑ The colors and fonts are consistent throughout the design.
- ☑ All objects line up with other objects on the page.
- ☑ Clear contrast exists between the headers and the body text.
- ☑ Paragraphs and sections of information are separated by space, creating visual groupings.

Skills Studio

Project 5-9 Take a Digital Photograph

Skills You Will Apply

- Take a digital photograph
- Upload a photo from a camera
- Remove a background
- Insert a picture into an image
- Apply blending modes

Key Terms

- megapixel
- optical zoom
- single lens reflex (SLR)

Academic Focus

Science
Evaluate camera optics

Besides price, the most important things to look for in a digital camera are the number of megapixels, whether it has an optical zoom, and whether the camera is a single lens reflex (SLR) model.

A **megapixel** is a unit that contains over one million pixels. The number of megapixels in a camera determines the quality of the picture and the types of pictures that can be captured. The higher the number of megapixels, the sharper the photograph and the more ways it can be used.

▲ An optical zoom uses lenses to magnify the image.

Many cameras use a digital zoom to magnify the subject being photographed. A digital zoom is similar to the zoom used in Photoshop. It increases the size by adding pixels, which can make the image blurry. Professional cameras use an **optical zoom**, which uses lenses inside the camera to magnify the subject without losing image quality.

◄ In an SLR camera, you are seeing an accurate view of the image through the lens.

In most cameras, there is a difference between what you see in the viewfinder and the image that the camera is actually capturing. **Single lens reflex** cameras allow the photographer to look through the camera's viewfinder and actually see the exact image that will be captured by the camera lens. This is especially important for close-up shots where a small movement can cause the picture to be out of the frame.

► **In this project,** you will begin to create a magazine cover. First, you will take a picture of the magazine's cover model using a digital camera. You will then save the photograph on your computer. In Project 5-10, you insert the photo in the magazine cover. You will need to photograph your subject in front of a blue or green screen so that the background can be easily removed from the picture. If a digital camera is not available in the classroom, use **Data File 5-9a** and begin this project at Step 10.

Apply PARC Principles

9. On **Page 2**, create a text box across the top row. Fill it with **CMYK 6**, **29**, **92**, **0**. Change the **Vertical Alignment** to **Middle**.

10. Key Animal Quick Facts in **Eras Bold ITC**, **18 pt**. On the Formatting toolbar, click the **Styles and Formatting** button [A]. Define the style as **Section Head**.

11. Draw a narrow, **¼ inch rectangle** across the top of the first text box. Fill with **CMYK 32**, **77**, **80**, **3** (Figure 6.31).

12. Under the heading, key and format the **top text** as shown in **Figure 6.30**, or insert **Data File 6-6a**.

13. Below the text you just keyed, follow **Steps 9–11** to create a new text box. Key Animal Description. Use the **Section Head** style.

14. Under the heading, key and format the **bottom text** as shown in **Figure 6.30**, or insert **Data File 6-6b**.

15. Create the layout for **Page 3** as shown in Figure 6.31. Insert **Data File 6-6c** into a **white** filled text box and format.

16. Insert the map from **Data File 6-6d**. Wrap the text and add the same border line as in **Step 6**. Use ruler guides to bottom align the figure with the text (Figure 6.31).

▼ **Figure 6.30** Key the following text on Page 2 of your booklet.

Physical Characteristics ← Use Section Head style, 8 pt space before the paragraph.

Height: 18 feet
Incubation: 14–15 months ← Use 14 pt, Times New Roman, 6 pt space after the paragraph.
Top Speed: 30 mph

Lifestyle

Habit: Wild mood swings in captivity.
Diet: Acacia leaves, carrion, and humans
Lifespan: 98 years

Use 14 pt, Times New Roman, with 1.25 space leading, 8 pt space after the paragraph. ↓

Born of a genetic experiment to combine reptiles with mammals, the Komodo Giraffe is the first scientific breakthrough in cross-species breeding.

The Komodo Giraffe combines both reptile and mammal characteristics. Despite its reptilian head, however, the Komodo Giraffe has fur and warm blood and, therefore, is classified as a mammal. It cannot produce offspring.

▼ **Figure 6.31** The Page 2–3 spread repeats design elements.

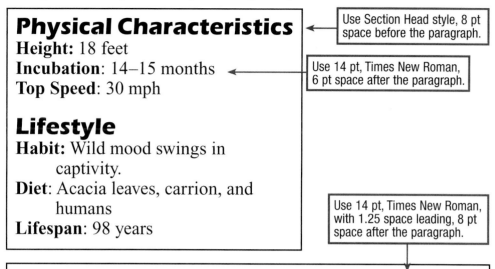

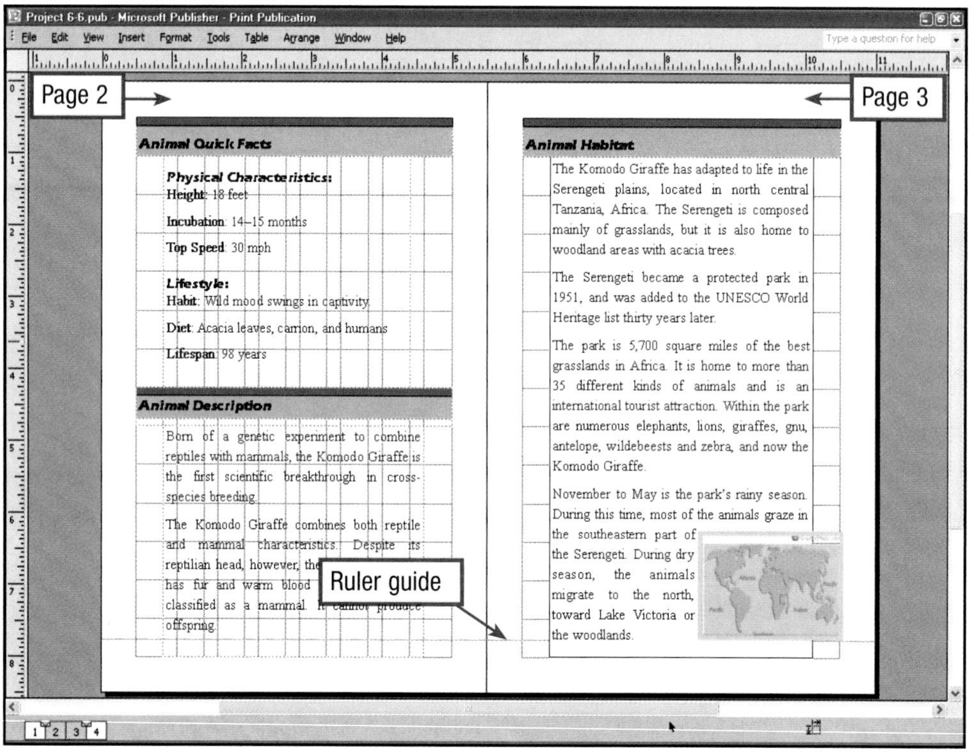

Student Data File

Step-by-Step

Take a Digital Photograph

1. Use Figure 5.57 to help set up the photo area. You will need about 8 feet of wide green or blue paper, a light source, and a digital camera.

2. Be sure that the colored paper is behind the subject.

3. Use two hands to hold the camera. One hand should hold the bottom to keep the camera steady and the other hand will take the picture.

4. Point the camera at the subject and look through the viewfinder. Use the camera's buttons to zoom in or out.

5. Compose the picture so that your subject is completely visible in the viewfinder (Figure 5.58).

6. To focus the camera, point the camera at the subject and press the camera shutter button halfway. The camera then determines the distance of the subject and the light condition.

7. Press the camera shutter button all the way and take the picture.

Figure 5.57 Set up your photo area.

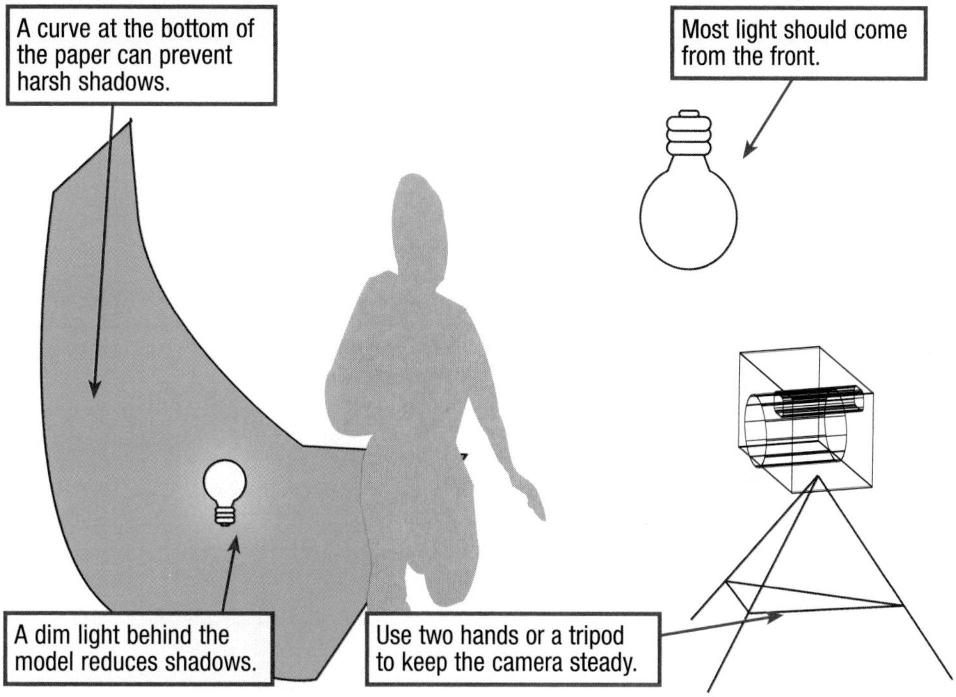

A curve at the bottom of the paper can prevent harsh shadows.
Most light should come from the front.
A dim light behind the model reduces shadows.
Use two hands or a tripod to keep the camera steady.

Figure 5.58 Frame your model and find a point on which to focus.

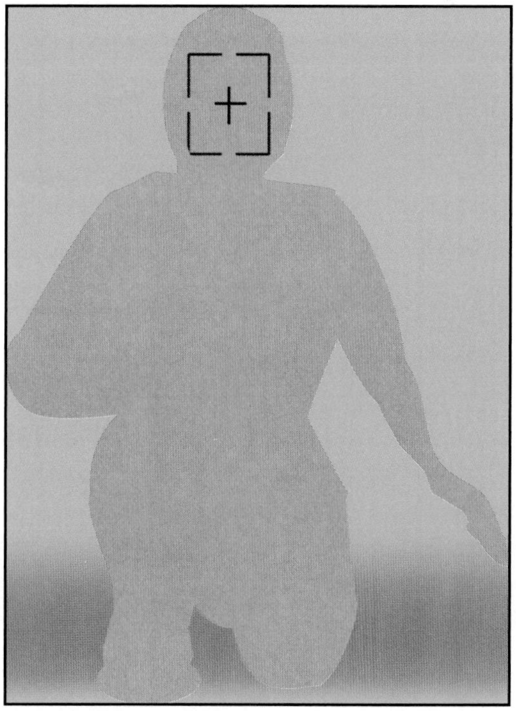

Student Data File

Step-by-Step

1. In Publisher, open a new document. Click **File>Page Setup**. Choose **Booklet** layout in **Landscape**, **5.5 inches wide**, **8.5 inches high**.

2. Click **Arrange>Layout Guides**. Set **margins** to **0.25 inches**. Create **grid guides** of **8 columns** with a **0.2 inch gutter** and **14 rows** with no gutter.

3. In the top row, create a text box. Fill it with **CMYK** values of **32, 77, 80, 3**. Key Mammal.

4. In the second row, create a text box filled with **CMYK** values **6, 29, 92, 0**. Key Komodo Giraffe.

5. Insert your picture from **Project 6-5**. Resize it to fit in **columns 2–7, rows 3–11**.

6. Select the picture, and add a **6 pt border** line with **CMYK** values **0**, **21**, **81**, **0**.

7. Below the picture, create a **white** text box with a **¾ pt black border** line. Key the text in Figure 6.29.

8. Select the white text box. Click **Format>Text Box>Text Box**, and change **Vertical Alignment** to **Middle**.

▼ **Figure 6.29** Follow the instructions below to create Page 1 of your booklet.

Mammal
Eras Demi ITC, 18 pt, centered
Komodo Giraffe
Eras Bold ITC, 24 pt, centered
Bred in a laboratory, the Komodo Giraffe combines the fierce expression of the infamous Komodo Dragon and the gawky sweetness of the loveable Giraffe.
Times New Roman, 16 pt, justified

8 Take several pictures from different angles and distances. It is much easier to take additional pictures now than it is to start over later.

Upload a Photo from a Camera

9 Connect the camera to the computer following your teacher's instructions. Transfer the picture from the camera to your save folder.

10 Open Adobe Photoshop. On the **Options** bar, click **Go to Bridge**, and navigate to the folder where you saved your camera's pictures.

11 Preview the pictures in the bridge. Double-click the picture you wish to open (Figure 5.59).

Remove a Background

12 Use the **Magic Wand** and the **Lasso** tools to create a good selection and isolate your picture from the background (Figure 5.60).

13 In the **Layers** palette, double-click the **Background** layer. In the **New Layer** dialog box, name the layer **Background** and click **OK**. That unlocks the layer.

14 Click **Layer>Layer Mask>Hide Selection**.

▼ **Figure 5.59** The Adobe Picture Bridge helps you organize your photos.

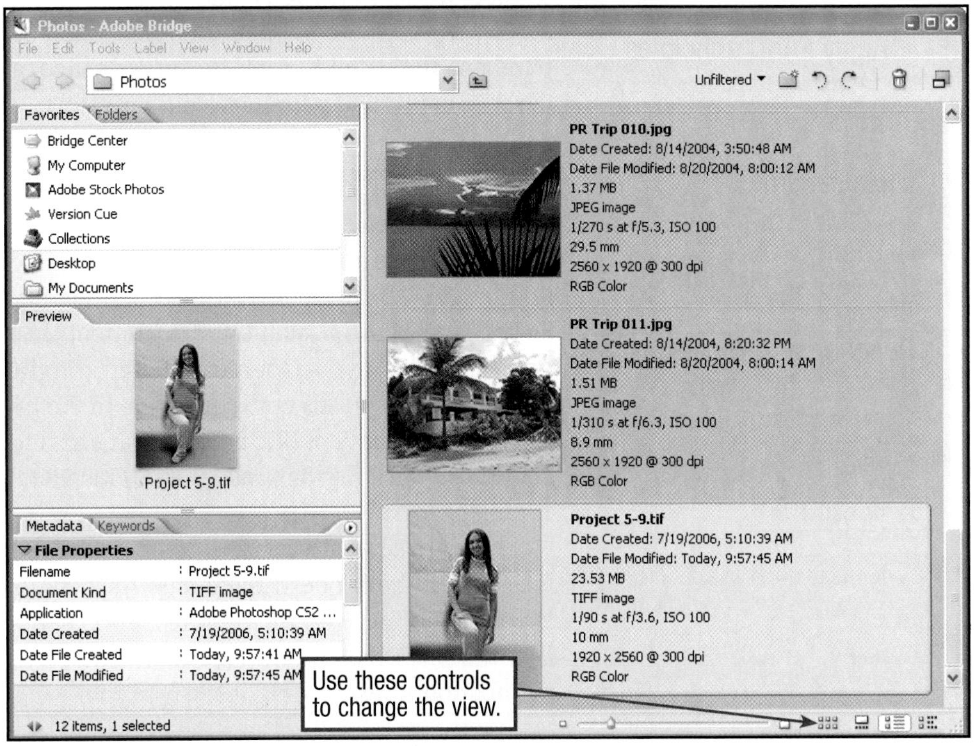

▼ **Figure 5.60** You may have to click different spots to select the whole background.

Project 6-6 Create a Booklet

Spotlight on Skills

- Apply PARC principles

Key Term

- plagiarism

Academic Focus

Science
Describe a new species

The material you find on the Internet, in textbooks, or magazines is copyrighted work. Somebody had to take the pictures, host the Web sites, create the music, and write and publish the books. Those people have paid to purchase the camera, rent the server space, and print the material, and they deserve credit and payment for their efforts.

Citing Sources

When you use material in a project—text, graphics, sound, and even layout—you should assume the material is copyrighted unless you created it yourself. Whenever you use somebody else's resources, even if you have permission to use it, you must document the source of the information.

To not credit your source is called **plagiarism**. It is like stealing, and it can have very serious consequences. In the business world, it could mean big fines, loss of a job, public embarrassment, and lawsuits. In school, plagiarism could result in a failing grade, loss of respect from teachers or friends, or even expulsion.

There are several ways to document sources, but one of the most common is based on the Modern Language Association (MLA) format shown below. If you do not have all the required information, include as much as possible. List the resources in alphabetical order, by the authors' last names or the publication titles.

Print Book
Author's Last Name, First Name. *Publication Title*. Place of Publication: Publisher, copyright date.

Print Magazine or Journal
Author's Last Name, First Name. "Title of Article." *Publication Title*. Volume or date of publication: page numbers.

Online
Author's Last Name, First Name. "Title of Article." Web site name. Date information was posted. Date accessed. <Web site address>.

▲ You can look online to find many excellent sites with citation guidelines for different types of sources.

► **In this project,** you will use Publisher to make a booklet that describes the Komodo giraffe you created in Project 6-5. The booklet will include a reference page to cite the information sources.

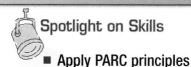

15 In Photoshop, open **Data File 5-9b**.

16 Use the **Elliptical Marquee** to select the soccer ball. Click **Layer>New>Layer via Copy** to create a new soccer ball layer.

Insert a Picture into an Image

17 Use the **Move** tool to drag your digital photograph onto the soccer picture and adjust the size.

18 In the **Layers** palette, arrange the order so your photograph is behind the soccer picture. (This creates a sense of depth.)

19 If the shadows and lighting on the model and the new background are not consistent, click **Layer>New Adjustment Layer>Levels**.

20 Create a new layer, and use a feathered soft, black brush to create some shadows on the ground below the model.

Apply Blending Modes

21 Change the layer's blending mode to **Darken**, and adjust the **Opacity** until the shadow is relatively convincing.

22 Follow your teacher's instructions for saving and printing your work.

▼ **Figure 5.61** The model and the background should look like they are one photograph.

REVIEW AND REVISE

Check your work Use Figure 5.61 as a guide and check that:

- ☑ The background behind the model has been removed.
- ☑ The model appears behind the soccer ball.
- ☑ The lighting for the model and the soccer ball appears consistent.
- ☑ The model is casting a shadow on the ground.

Apply the Smudge Tool

17 In the toolbox, right-click **Blur** and choose **Smudge**.

18 In the **Options** bar, adjust the **strength** to **100**, and choose a **9 px**, **hard edged brush**.

19 Click and drag on the rope where the giraffe's head used to be to create the missing rope.

20 Follow your teacher's instructions for saving the image.

21 Click **Layer>Flatten Image**.

22 Click **Layer>New Adjustment Layer>Levels**. Adjust the sliders until the image and creature look brighter (Figure 6.28).

23 Save the file as a **Copy** in **TIFF format** so that it may be used in Publisher in Project 6-6.

▼ Figure 6.28 Brighten the image to make it look more realistic.

REVIEW AND REVISE

Check your work Use Figure 6.28 as a guide and check that:

- ☑ The size, direction, and angles of the two animals' body parts are aligned so they join in a natural look.
- ☑ The animal hides appear to blend smoothly from scales to fur.
- ☑ No part of the giraffe's head is visible under the Komodo dragon's.
- ☑ Cloned areas look natural, without obvious repetition or blurry smudges.
- ☑ The image is clear and looks realistic.

Skills Studio

Project 5-10

Lay Out a Cover

Skills You Will Apply

- Group layers
- Add magazine cover objects
- Add text

Academic Focus

Language Arts
Create a magazine cover page

Student Data File

Magazines and other publications usually combine images and text on the cover. An interesting image will draw attention to the magazine. The reader's eye will then be drawn to the text to see how the image relates to the articles inside.

Obviously, a photograph or illustration is created separately from the other design elements on the cover, such as the nameplate (or masthead) and article titles. Often the text elements are created with layout software. However, when there is a limited amount of text, as on a cover or in an advertisement, Photoshop's Type tools are a very effective way of adding visually interesting text. Just as with images, Photoshop lets you add effects and filters to words and characters. You will learn more about Photoshop's Type tools in Chapter 6.

▶ **In this project,** you will use Photoshop to create a magazine cover that combines text with the photograph you created in Project 5-9.

Step-by-Step

1. In Photoshop, open the photograph you created in Project 5-9.
2. Click **Image>Canvas Size**. Change the size of the canvas to **8.25 inches wide** and **10.75 inches high**. If you are told the photo must be clipped, click **Proceed**.
3. Move elements on the page so there is room on the left and your image looks similar to Figure 5.62.

▼ **Figure 5.62** Leave room for text on the left.

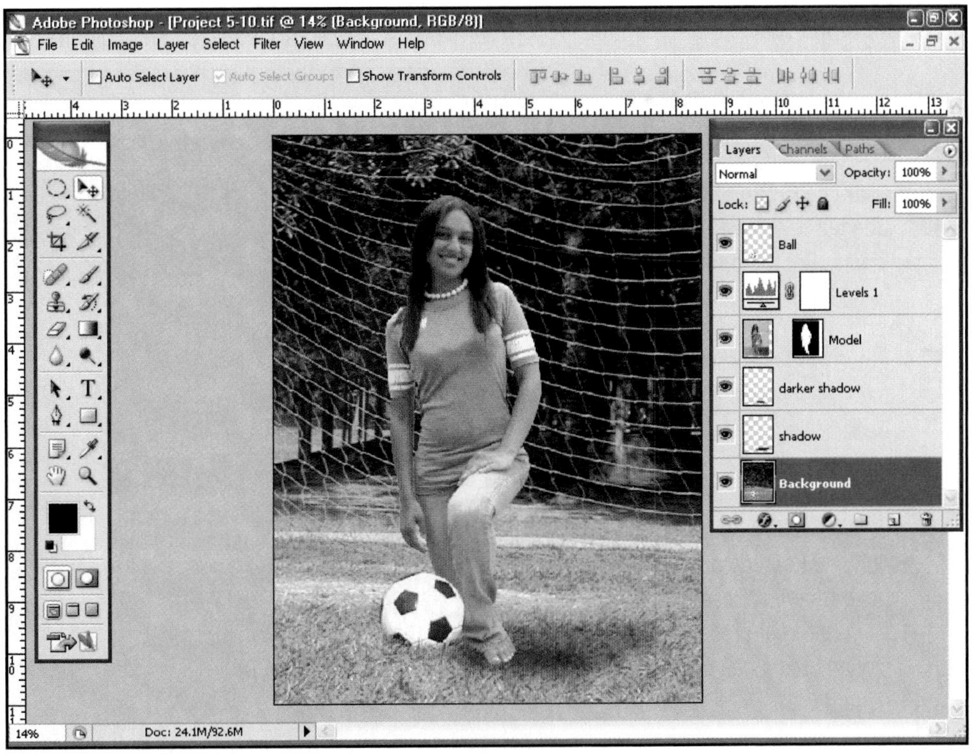

10 Use a soft, round brush to hide more of the layer until the giraffe and Komodo dragon start to look like one creature (Figure 6.26).

11 Change to a **black Spatter brush** and reduce **opacity** to **30%**.

12 Click the **Dragon layer mask**, and delicately paint the bottom half of the Komodo dragon to blend its hide with the giraffe's.

▼ **Figure 6.26** Use a black brush to hide the parts of the dragon that do not blend.

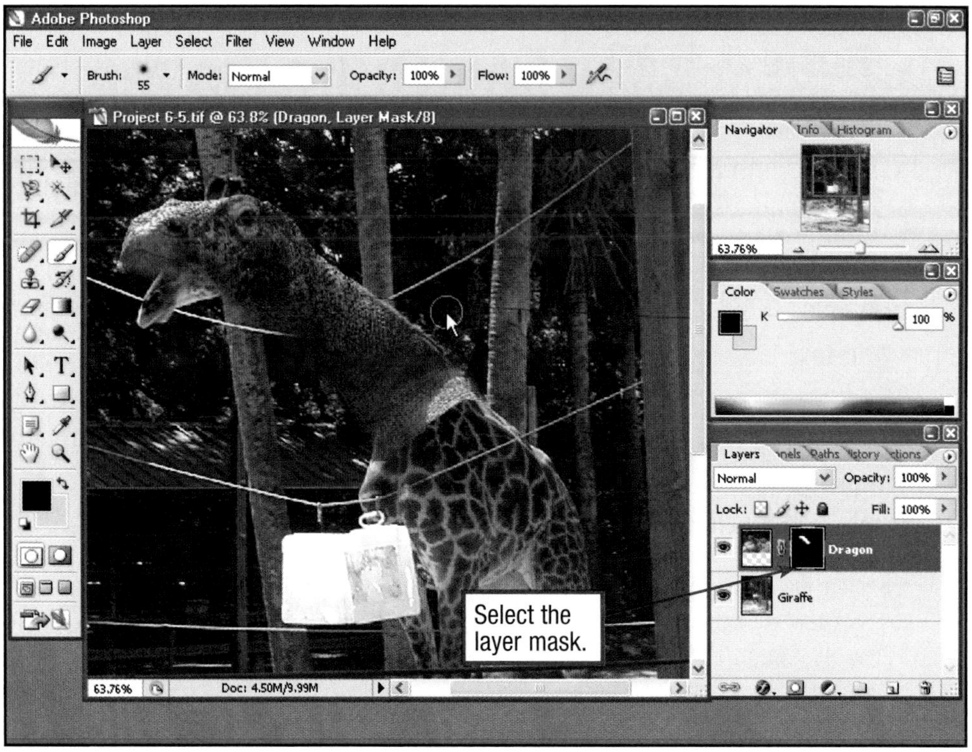

Apply the Clone Tool

13 In the **Layers** palette, select the **Giraffe** layer.

14 Click the **Clone Stamp**. Change to a **hard round brush**. Set the **opacity** to **33%**.

15 Press ALT and click on the background near the giraffe's head to sample an area.

16 Paint over the visible parts of the giraffe's head so only the Komodo dragon's head remains. Resample from different areas so the cloned area looks natural (Figure 6.27).

▼ **Figure 6.27** Use various sizes and opacities for the Clone Stamp.

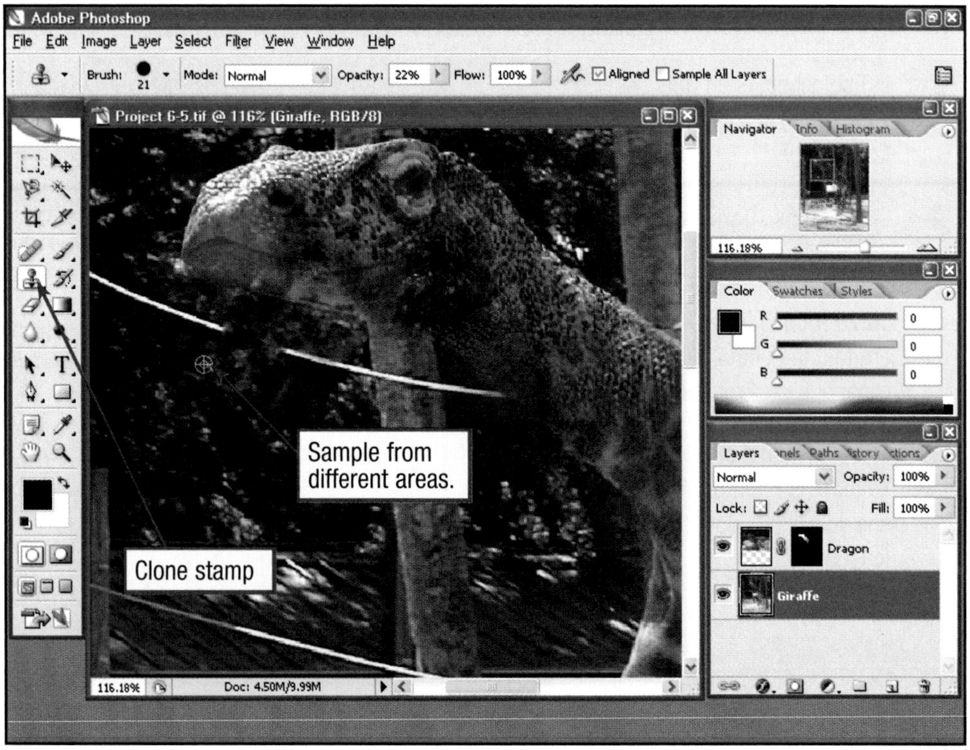

4. To unlock the **Background** layer, double-click the layer. In the dialog box, rename the layer **Background**, and click **OK**.

Group Layers

5. At the bottom of the **Layers** palette, click **Create a New Group** [icon]. Double-click the folder group that appears at the top of the palette and rename it Soccer Pic.

6. Click the layer below the **Soccer Pic** group layer. Hold SHIFT, and click the bottom layer. All layers should be selected.

7. Drag the selected layers into the **Soccer Pic** group. Click the triangle on the **Soccer Pic** layer to close the group (Figure 5.63).

Insert Magazine Cover Objects

8. Open **Data File 5-10a**, a nameplate. Use the **Move** tool to drag the Nameplate onto your picture document.

9. Zoom out and resize the nameplate as needed. Allow a small part of the nameplate to overlap the head of the model (Figure 5.63).

10. Open **Data File 5-10b**, and drag the bar code onto the image. Size and position the bar code as shown in Figure 5.64.

▼ **Figure 5.63** Organize layers by creating groups. Close groups to simplify the Layers palette.

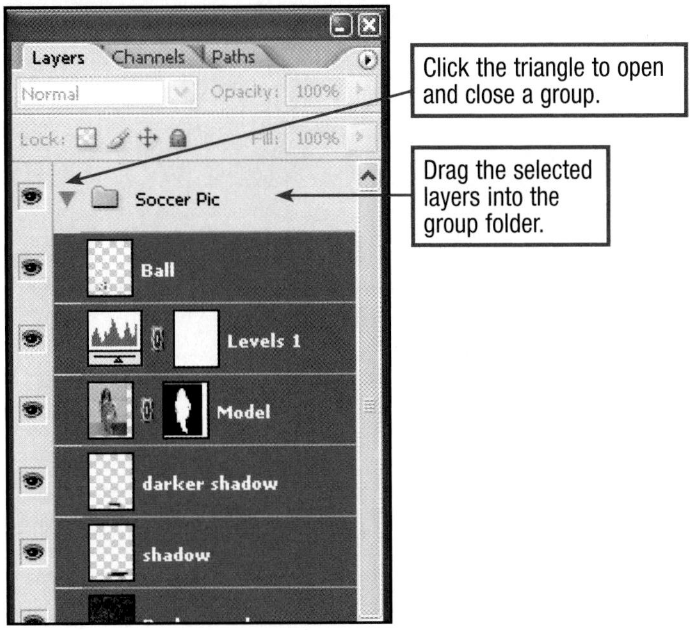

▼ **Figure 5.64** Add a nameplate and bar code on separate layers.

Blend Layers

4. On the **Layers** palette, adjust the **opacity** of the **Dragon** layer to **65%** so you can see through the layer (Figure 6.24).

5. Move the Komodo dragon's head over the giraffe's head. Resize the dragon so that it is proportional to the giraffe (Figure 6.24).

6. Restore the Dragon layer's opacity to 100%. Click the **Move** tool to **Apply the Transformation**.

7. Use **Magnetic Lasso** to select the top half of the Komodo dragon (Figure 6.25).

8. Click **Layer>Layer Mask>Reveal Selection**.

9. Zoom in closer to the head of the creature. Change the **foreground** color to **black**, and click the **Dragon layer mask** icon.

▼ **Figure 6.24** Reduce the opacity so that you can see through the layer.

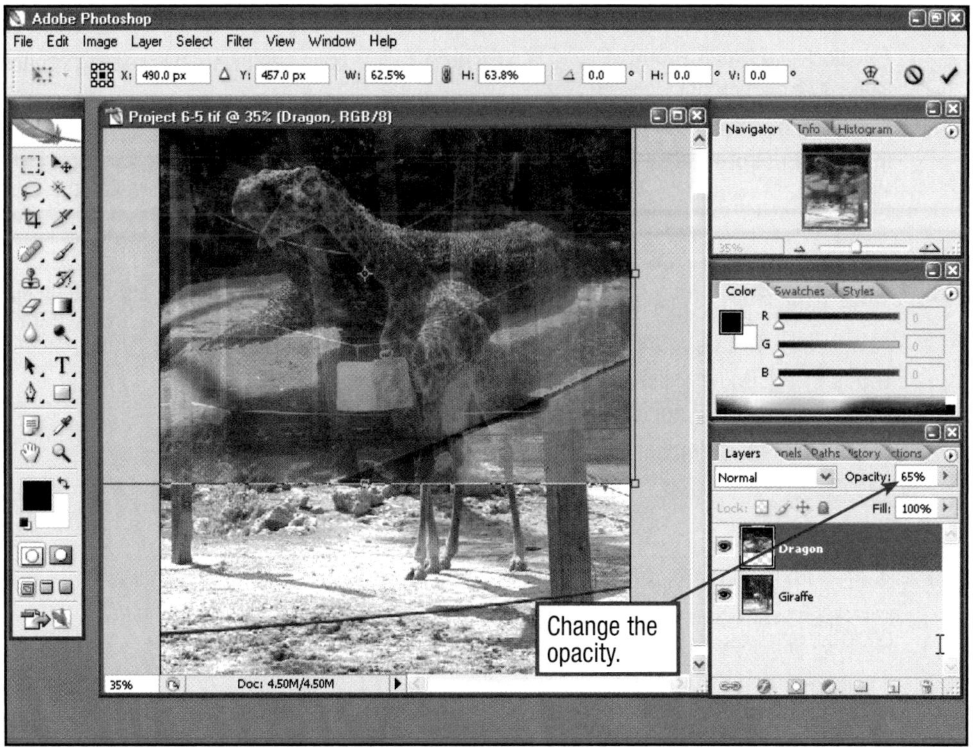

▼ **Figure 6.25** Only the selected part of the dragon will be displayed.

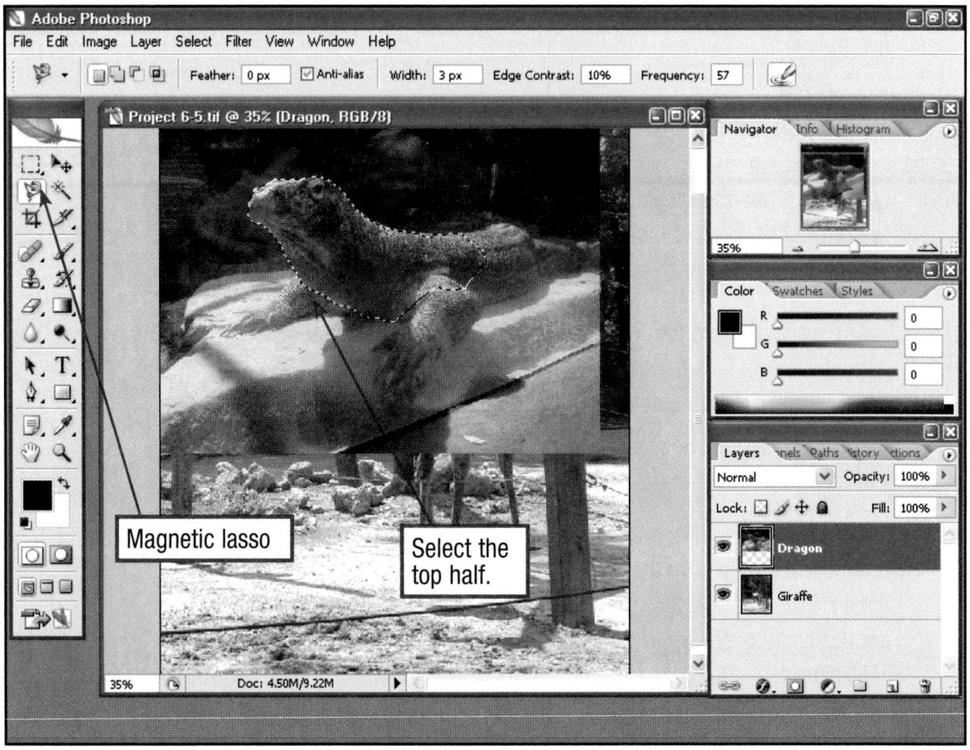

11 Press CTRL and click the nameplate thumbnail to select the entire nameplate.

12 Open the **Soccer Pic** group, and click on the Model layer. Click **Layer>New>Layer** via Copy.

13 Name the new layer **Model Head**, and move it above the **Nameplate** layer.

14 Change your **Foreground** color to **white**.

Add Text

15 Click the **Horizontal Type** tool. Drag a text box on the left side of the picture.

16 In the text box, use a font like **Haettenschweiler** to add the text in Figure 5.64. Format the text to look similar to the text in the figure.

17 Open **Data File 5-10c**, and drag the corner callout onto your magazine cover. Size and position it as shown in Figure 5.65.

18 Follow your teacher's instructions for saving and printing your work.

▼ **Figure 5.65** Your magazine cover should follow PARC principles.

REVIEW AND REVISE

Check your work Use Figure 5.65 as a guide and check that:

☑ The nameplate, bar code, and corner callout are sized and placed effectively.

☑ The model's head partially overlaps the nameplate.

☑ The text is accurate, readable, and has clear headers.

☑ The cover design follows PARC principles.

Project 6-5

Blend Images

Spotlight on Skills

- Blend layers
- Apply the Clone tool
- Apply the Smudge tool

Key Term

- clone

Academic Focus

Science
Create a new species

Student Data File

Step-by-Step

1. In Photoshop, open **Data File 6-5a**, a giraffe. Save it according to your teacher's instructions.

2. Open **Data File 6-5b**, a Komodo dragon. **Move** it into the giraffe picture (Figure 6.23). **Name** the new layer Dragon.

3. Select the **Dragon** layer. Click **Edit>Transform>Flip Horizontal**.

In Project 5-7, you used Photoshop to create a realistic picture of a baby sleeping in a flower. In that project and others, you have seen how Photoshop's tools can be used to enhance images by removing blemishes, changing colors, and even adding or removing objects. Often it is difficult to tell what is real and what is a creation.

▶ **In this project,** you will use Photoshop to blend two different animals together to create a whole new species. You will use cloning to fill in the background in the image. When you **clone**, you copy data to use elsewhere. You will then use your new creature as the subject of a booklet in Project 6-6.

▼ **Figure 6.23** It is a good practice to name the layers in your picture.

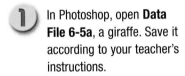

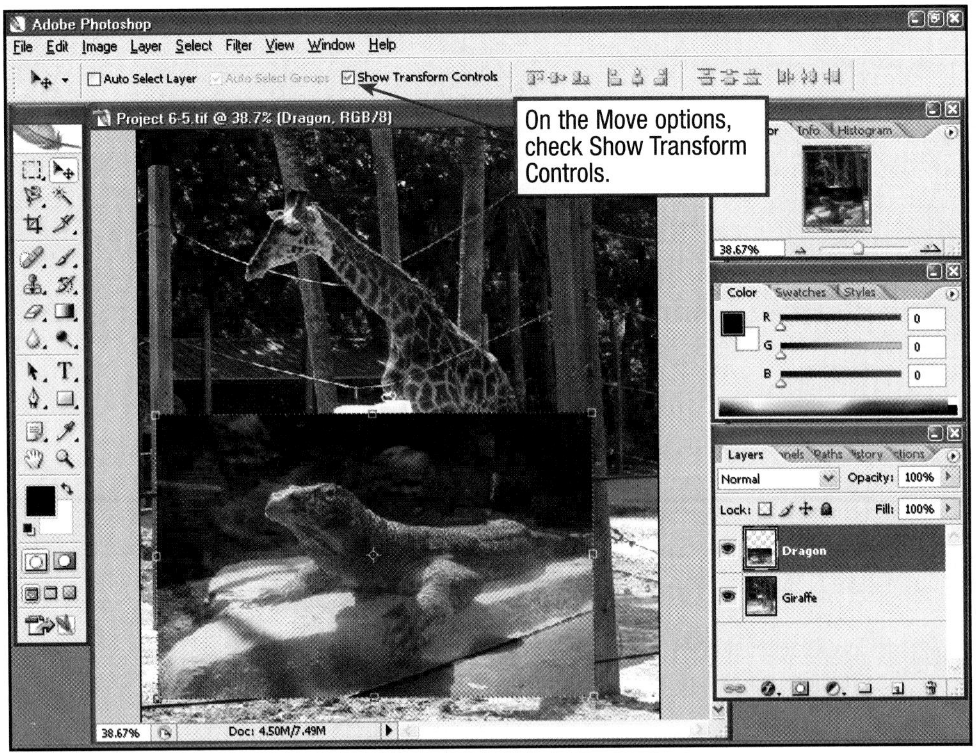

Instant Message

Troubleshooting Tips You may not get the visual effects you want on the first try. Remember to press CTRL + K to undo the previous action. Use the **History** palette to undo multiple actions. If you accidentally cover too many pixels when painting over an area in a layer mask, use a white brush to restore the hidden parts.

In The Workplace

Photographers

Photographers capture and produce an image using either film or a digital camera. Photographers must understand the technical aspects of photography, have a good sense of composition, and possess a creative vision. Many photographers today choose digital photography so their work can be easily incorporated into the digital workflow.

On the Job

Though some photographers have staff jobs, many are self-employed or freelancers. They may specialize in portrait, industrial, fashion, journalism, scientific, commercial, and fine arts photography. Some photographers work for advertising agencies, magazine publishers, or companies that sell and license photographs called stock-photo agencies.

All professional photographers must have a good grasp of lighting, lenses, filters, and other equipment in order to deliver the highest quality images. Photographers who work with traditional film cameras master darkroom processing and printing techniques, although some photographers rely on film laboratories for processing and printing.

Adobe Photoshop is an important tool for photographers, who must be able to create, alter, and edit their images. Desktop publishing and Web software help photographers market their skills, communicate with clients, and create electronic portfolios.

To succeed as a freelance photographer, business and communication skills can be as important as technical knowledge and talent. Photographers must know how to submit bids for future work, negotiate with clients, write contracts, reserve locations for shooting, hire models, market their work, and keep accurate financial records.

Future Outlook

Photography is an intensely competitive field and the number of applicants frequently exceeds the number of available positions. Successful freelancers must possess strong business skills and develop a visual style that distinguishes them from competing photographers.

For more information about this career, consult the Web sites of **The Professional Photographers of America (ppa.com)** and **The Society of Media Photographers (asmp.org)**.

Training

Technical proficiency can be gained through degree programs at universities, vocational and technical institutes, private trade schools, or experience. Degrees are often required for entry-level positions as photographic assistants.

Salary Range

Depending on experience and required duties, salaried photographers earn from less than $15,000 up to $50,000 or more. Full-time salaried workers tend to earn more than freelancers who do not always have steady earnings and who must buy and maintain their own equipment.

Skills and Talents

Photographers need to have:

- Technical knowledge of cameras
- Good visual skills
- Knowledge of various software programs
- Good communication skills
- Good problem-solving skills
- The ability to work independently and meet deadlines

Career Activity

Why is it important for photographers to master new technologies as they emerge?

Set Print Specifications

7. Click **File>Print**. Click the **Change Overlap** button. Make sure that the Overlap is set to **0.25 inches**. Click **OK** to return to the **Print** box.

8. In the **Print** box, click the **Advanced Print Settings** button. In the **Page Setting** tab, make sure that **Crop marks** are checked.

9. Follow your teacher's instructions for printing the banner.

▼ Figure 6.21 An overlap makes it easier to assemble your banner.

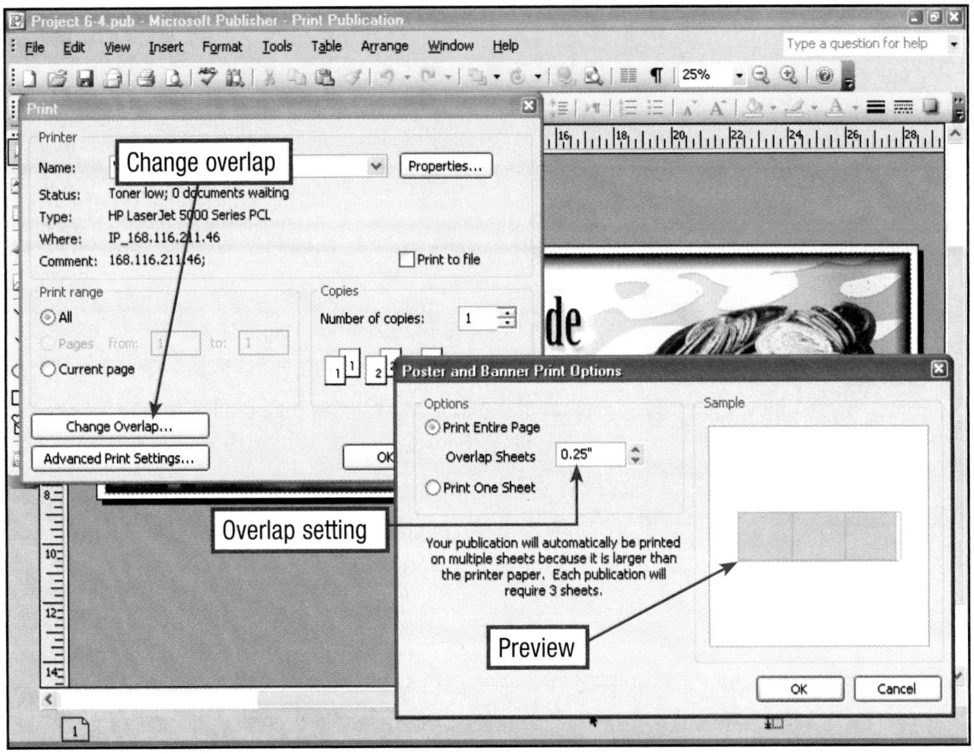

Assemble Printed Pages

10. Lay out the pages that you printed. Notice where the design is duplicated on the second and third pages.

11. Use a paper trimmer or scissors to cut off part of the duplicated area. Leave some duplication for overlap (Figure 6.22).

12. Overlap the pages, aligning the text and images. Tape the backs of the pages together.

▼ Figure 6.22 The banner is divided onto three separate sheets of paper. Trim and overlap edges that duplicate the design.

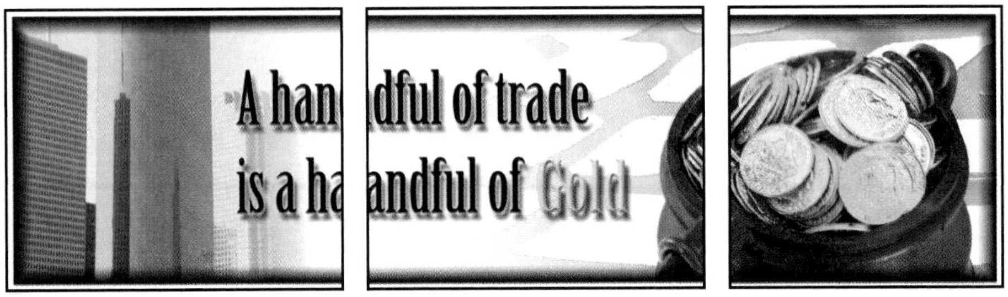

REVIEW AND REVISE

Check your work Use Figure 6.22 as a guide and check that:

- ☑ The design is printed across three pages.
- ☑ The entire banner design is visible, including your name.
- ☑ No leftover lines of overlapped white border are visible when the project has been assembled.
- ☑ The pages are aligned correctly.

Chapter 5 Assessment

Reading Check

1. **Analyze** What makes a raster image different from a vector image?
2. **Define** What is resolution?
3. **Explain** What is the difference between linking all layers and flattening the layers?
4. **Evaluate** When would it be better to use the Magic Wand tool and when would it be better to use the Lasso tool?
5. **Draw Conclusions** Which type of file would be better for the Internet, a TIFF or a JPG? Why?

Critical Thinking

6. **Analyze** How does the publishing method affect a publication's design?
7. **Compare** When would you need to use a raster image rather than a vector image?
8. **Explain** What are three advantages of using multiple layers in an image?
9. **Evaluate** What method can you use to separate a figure like a car or a person from a complex background of trees and a lake?
10. **Make Predictions** What would probably happen if you took a 72 ppi picture from the Internet and resized it to the size of a billboard using Photoshop? Explain your answer.

1 Independent Practice

TEAM PROJECT **Go on a Photo Tour** Use Photoshop to create an ID badge and tour the school on a photographic scavenger hunt.

a. Plan With the help of your teammates:

- Brainstorm ten positive aspects of your personality (friendly, funny, intelligent, artistic, athletic, etc.). List objects in the school that symbolize those positive aspects of your personality.
- Have a classmate take your picture. Then use Photoshop to create an ID badge that identifies who you are and what class you are with.
- Tour the school and (in 15 minutes or less) take pictures of 8 objects that represent positive aspects of your personality. For example, you might take photographs of awards, projects that are displayed, a basketball hoop, etc.

b. Create Choose at least five of the photos that you took.

- Use Photoshop to create a collage of yourself with those objects and your ID photo.
- Add brief text to explain what the objects symbolize.
- Create a title with your name, using text that is visually interesting but that does not overwhelm the images.

c. Present Print your collage and explain why you chose those photos to represent yourself.

Go Online RUBRICS
www.glencoe.com

Independent Practice
Go to **Chapter 5**, and choose **Rubrics**. Use the rubrics to help create and evaluate your projects.

Step-by-Step

1. Open **Publisher** and create a **New Blank Print Publication**. Save it according to your teacher's instructions.

2. Click **File>Page Setup** and choose **Custom**. Change the settings to **28.5 inches wide**, and **8.5 inches high**, in **landscape** orientation (Figure 6.19).

▼ **Figure 6.19** Publisher will automatically tile print publications larger than a single sheet of paper.

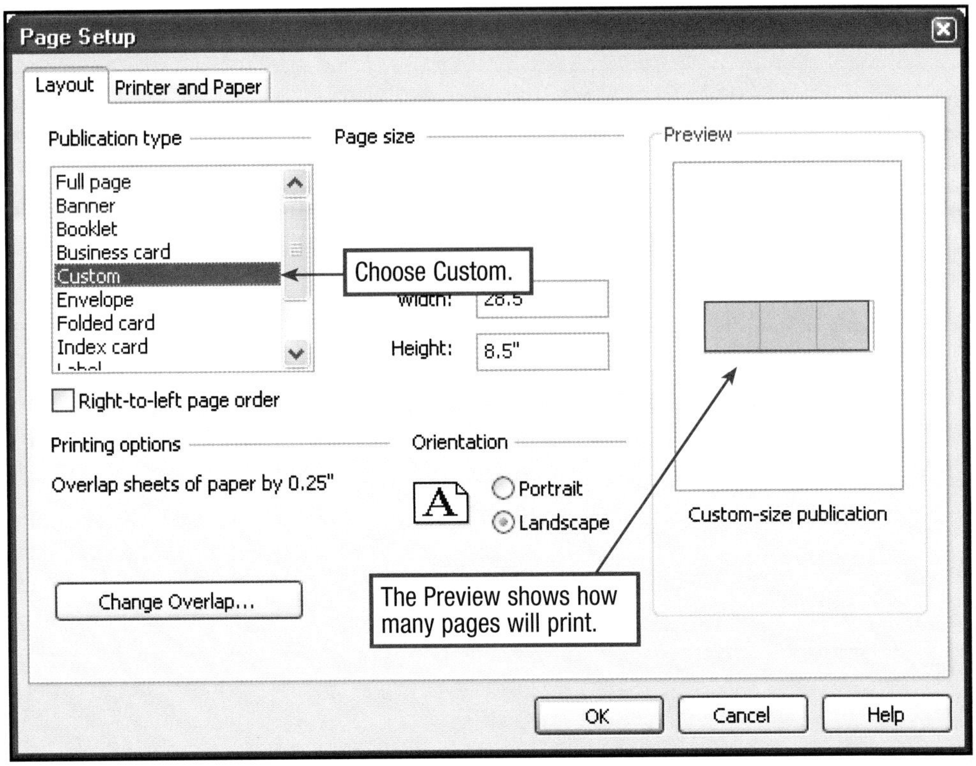

3. Click **Arrange>Layout Guides>Margin Guides**. Set **0.25 inch** margins for all four sides of the document.

4. Click **Insert>Picture>From File**, and open the banner from **Project 6-3**.

5. Move the image onto the workspace, and resize it so that it looks like Figure 6.20.

6. Click **Text Box**, and drag a text box to the bottom right corner. In a readable font, key Design by Your Name.

▼ **Figure 6.20** Leave the white margin around the banner.

Chapter 5 Assessment

2 Independent Practice ★★

SCIENCE **Create a Space Creature** Use Photoshop to create a space alien.

a. Plan Do research to determine what kind of planet the alien would be from. What characteristics are needed to survive in this environment?

b. Design By hand, sketch an alien. Note the effects that may be needed to create the look you imagine.

c. Create Use a photo of yourself or another person to:

- Remove yourself from the background and create a new background showing your alien's natural habitat.
- Use **Enhance>Hue and Saturation** to change your skin/hair color.
- Use **Filter>Liquify** to change the size of your facial characteristics.
- Use the **Clone** tool to add or remove features.

d. Present Give a presentation to show your alien and explain why you chose specific features for your creation.

Go Online ACTIVITIES
www.glencoe.com

Enrichment Go to **Chapter 5**, and choose **Enrichment Activities.** Find more desktop publishing projects using Adobe Photoshop.

3 Independent Practice ★★★

SOCIAL STUDIES **Create an American Montage** Use Photoshop to create a map showing pictures of famous American sites and famous people who were born or lived in a particular city or town.

a. Plan Do research to create a list of at least thirty well-known American places and people, and determine their locations.

b. Design Use the Internet to:

- Locate at least 15 pictures of the people and places on your list.
- Find an image of a map of the United States.

c. Create Use Adobe Photoshop to:

- Place the pictures on the map.
- Add text to create a title and identify each item on the map.
- Add effects and filters to make the map visually exciting.

d. Publish Print and display your map.

Project 6-4 Print an Oversized Document

Spotlight on Skills

- Set print specifications
- Assemble printed pages

Key Term

- tile print

Academic Focus

Math
Divide objects into parts

The banner you created in Project 6-3 was 28½ inches long. Since a normal sheet of paper is only 11 inches long, printing the banner could be difficult. There are three possible solutions shown in the table below. The option you choose depends upon your purpose, time, and budget.

Print a Banner

Options	Pros	Cons
Go to a professional printer.	Most professional, highest quality results. Could add a glossy coating and use custom-sized single sheet of paper.	Expensive. Must schedule it and go to a different location.
Purchase banner paper and print the design on your regular printer.	Relatively inexpensive and suitable for non-professional display.	Depends upon the quality of your printer. Could be difficult to find the custom-sized paper.
Print the design on standard-size paper.	Most convenient and least expensive option.	Have to print on and assemble multiple pages. Only suitable for non-commercial purposes.

Sidebar

Finding Graphic Files
Publisher lets you insert pictures with many different file formats. When you insert a picture from a file, check the **Files of type** window in the **Insert Picture** dialog box. It should be set to the particular format of the picture you are looking for. If you are not sure of the format, set the format type to All Files or All Pictures.

Explain What steps would you use to insert a JPEG image into a Publisher document?

Tile Printing

If you chose the third option in the table—printing on standard-size paper—you would not be able to print from Photoshop because it would only print one page showing part of the document. Instead, it would be best to print the document using layout software, which allows you to tile print.

When you **tile print**, the software determines how much of an image goes onto one page and how much goes on the next, until the entire image has been printed. The design would then need to be assembled (and laminated for best results) to create the full document.

In theory, this method of printing could print a design large enough to wallpaper the Empire State Building. The results depend upon the quality of your printer. The printer may slip out of register so that not all pages are printed to the exact same specifications. This could make it more difficult to align the pages when they are assembled.

▶ **In this project,** you will use Publisher to tile print the banner you created in Project 6-3. You will then assemble the individual pages.

Chapter 6

Integrating Publisher and Photoshop

Skills You Will Learn

Professional publishers will usually use separate software applications to create or edit graphics, and they will then combine the graphics with text using layout software. Photoshop generally does not handle text very well. Photoshop is a graphics program and includes some basic text tools, but it can be difficult to lay out and edit a lot of text with Photoshop. Unless the text is a special effect for a title, you should use layout software (such as Microsoft Publisher, Adobe InDesign, or QuarkXPress) for most text.

In this chapter, you will use Photoshop and Publisher together to create documents that combine text and graphics.

Design Posters and Banners

Commercial products such as movie posters and event banners often are created by combining the strengths of Photoshop with a layout program. Posters and banners combine large images and text to grab people's attention from any distance. The graphics that are used must be printable at a large scale without losing clarity. Text must be easy to read and kept to a minimum so that people passing by can quickly understand the message.

DESIGN PROCESS: Posters and Banners

Elements	Issues
Purpose	To advertise products, places, or events. Often used for educational purposes. Usually displayed in public places so that they can be easily seen by many people on the move.
Audience	Varies. Posters used as advertisements must be designed to appeal to the target audience. Instructional posters should meet the educational needs of the audience.
Content	In commercial posters, the message is usually conveyed through one clear image and minimal text. In educational posters, there is often more text.
Layout	Photos and text are usually large, so resolution is very important. Layout varies depending on whether the image is the main focus.
Publication	Posters and banners are typically printed, which may require special treatment because of the size. Banners can be printed on cloth, plastic, or other materials.

24 To display rulers, click **View>Show Rulers.** Drag a ruler guide to the bottom line of text. Use the line to align *Gold* with the other text.

▼ **Figure 6.17** Use ruler guides to align text from different layers.

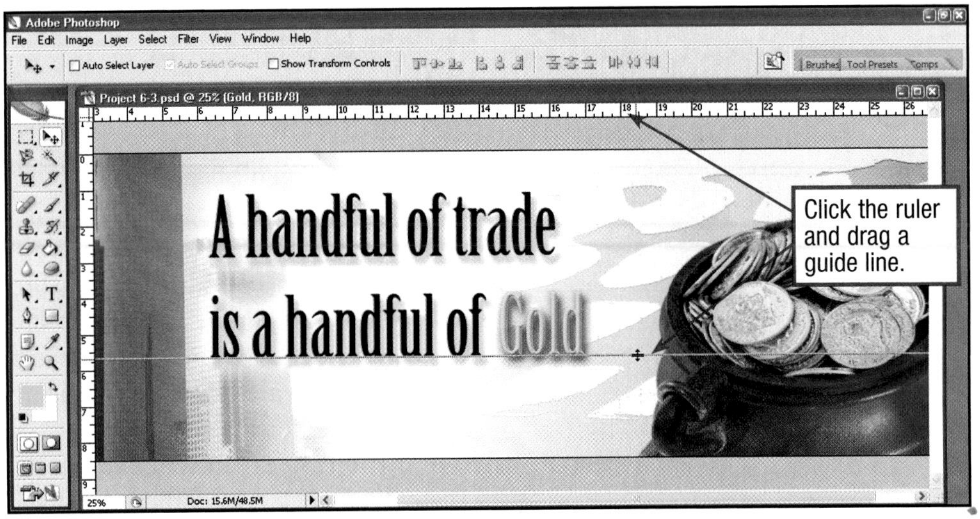

25 Create a new layer named Border.

26 Click **Select>All**. Then click **Select>Modify>Border**. Set the border to 100 pixels.

27 Change your **foreground color** to **black.** Fill the border with the color.

28 Click **File>Save As**. Follow your teacher's instructions for naming your file, and save it in **TIFF** format.

29 Choose to keep your layers. The file size is larger, but it can be edited like a Photoshop file. It also can be used with Publisher in Project 6-4.

▼ **Figure 6.18** Your final banner should be saved in TIFF format.

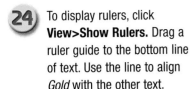

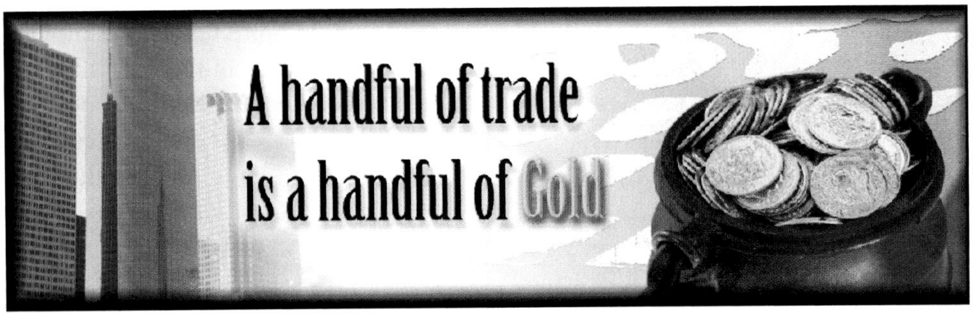

REVIEW AND REVISE

Check your work Use Figure 6.18 as a guide and check that:

- ☑ The City layer has a saturated color and the right side is partially hidden by a layer mask and gradient.
- ☑ The Keyboard layer has been modified with a filter and the left side is partially hidden by a layer mask and gradient.
- ☑ A rainbow effect has been added on top of the Pot of Gold layer.
- ☑ Black text has a drop shadow and an outer glow.
- ☑ The Gold text has a drop shadow and bevel and is aligned with the other text.
- ☑ The banner has a properly sized black border.
- ☑ The text is complete and accurate.

WORKSHOP Foundations

Find Photo Resources

You Will Learn To

- Find resources for photographs
- Determine legal use of a photograph

Key Terms

fair use
public domain
royalty

How do you begin to find digital photographs for a project? First, start with a general idea of what you would like the photograph to do in your publication. You have several available options to find appropriate photos for your publication.

Where Can I Find Photos to Use Legally?

Digital Photography The simplest way to obtain photographs is to take your own pictures using a digital camera. However, this might not be an option if you do not have a digital camera that can produce photos with the quality you need.

It also might be too difficult to photograph the subject you want. For example, you may need to take a photograph of a rainy scene, but there is not a cloud in sight. Fortunately, with programs like Photoshop, you can add effects to a sunny photo to make it seem like it is raining.

Scanning You can locate many good pictures in magazines and other print materials, but these products are all copyrighted. Copyrighted material may be used if it falls under **fair use** guidelines, which allow them to be copied for educational purposes. You can also find out if a publication falls under **public domain**, which allows you to use materials that are so old they no longer have a copyright, or materials that are published by the government or free to the public.

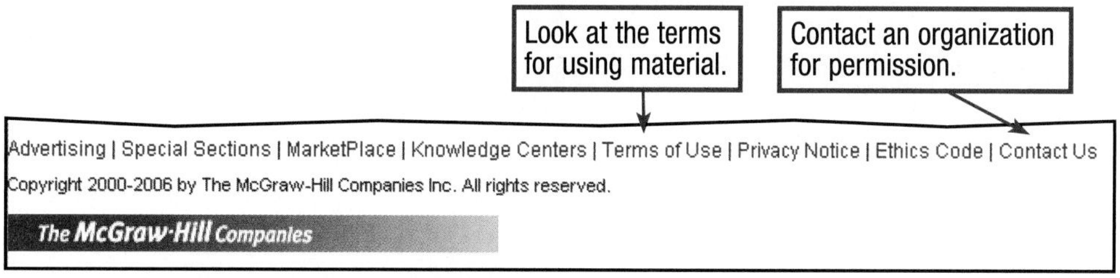
Look at the terms for using material.
Contact an organization for permission.
Advertising | Special Sections | MarketPlace | Knowledge Centers | Terms of Use | Privacy Notice | Ethics Code | Contact Us
Copyright 2000-2006 by The McGraw-Hill Companies Inc. All rights reserved.
The McGraw-Hill Companies

▲ Look for the Terms of Use and contact information at the bottom of a Web page to find out the legal way to use an image or other information.

If you are using material for profit and it does not fall under fair use or public domain, then you must get permission to use it. Sometimes, in order to get such permission, you may have to pay a fee, or **royalty**. Whether it is copyrighted or not, you should always cite a photograph's source.

Before You Read

Study with a Buddy Before you read a chapter, find a partner and ask each other questions about the topics that will be discussed. Use section headers or "You Will Learn" objectives as question starters. As you read, keep these questions in mind and see if you can learn the answers.

17 Use **Type** [T], and use a black, modern font (like **Birch Std**, **168 pt** or a similar font) to key A handful of trade is a handful of (Figure 6.15).

Add a Layer Style

18 With the **Text** layer selected, click **Add a Layer Style** at the bottom of the **Layers** palette. Click **Blending Options**.

19 When the **Layer Style** dialog box is displayed, select the **Drop Shadow** option. Adjust the sliders until you are satisfied with the effect.

20 Select the **Outer Glow** style. Adjust the settings until you are satisfied with the effect. Center the text so it looks similar to Figure 6.15.

21 Click the **Set foreground color** button to open the **Color Picker**. At the bottom of the Color Picker, key the color hexadecimal value dbd927.

22 Click the **Type** tool, then click the workspace to create a new text layer. Key Gold.

23 Click the **Add a Layer Style** button. Add a **Chisel Hard Inner Bevel** (or similar style) and a **Drop Shadow** to the Gold text (Figure 6.16).

▼ **Figure 6.15** Each blending option displays different setting controls.

▼ **Figure 6.16** The drop shadow on Gold should be similar to the shadow on the other text.

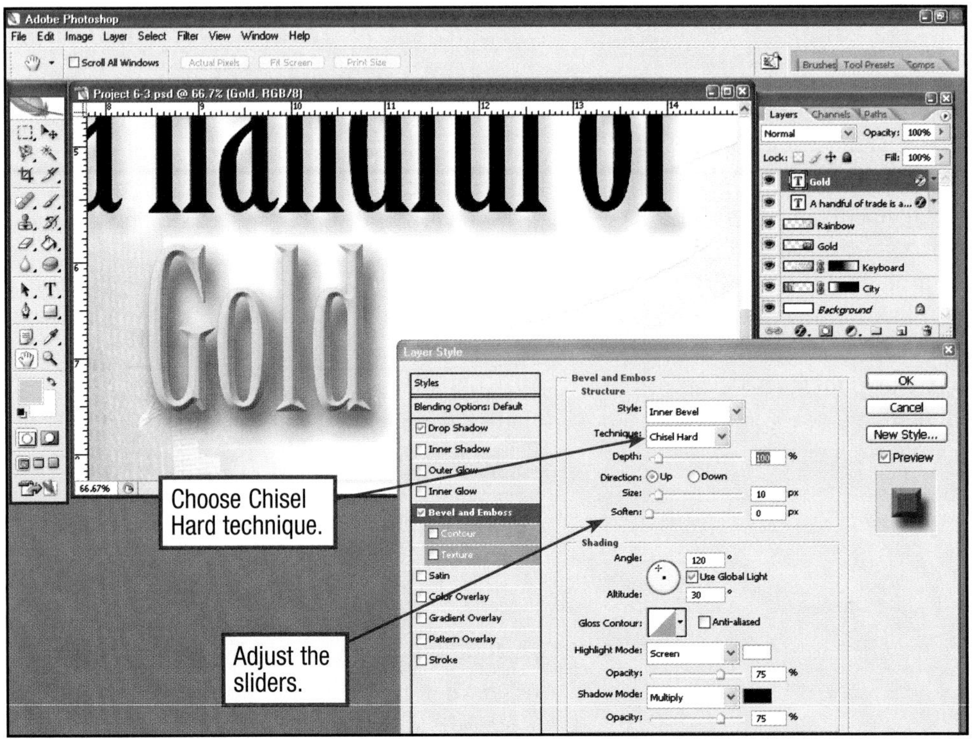

The Internet People often believe that any material they find on the Internet is free. This is not true. Most Internet sites contain copyrighted material, which cannot be used legally without permission. If you are not sure whether you can copy material legally, contact the site or read the Terms of Use. You can also do a search to find sites that offer images free of charge.

Stock Photography Stock photographs are generic photographs of models, places, and other subjects taken by a photographer to be sold and used in publications. A number of the photographs in magazines may be stock photographs.

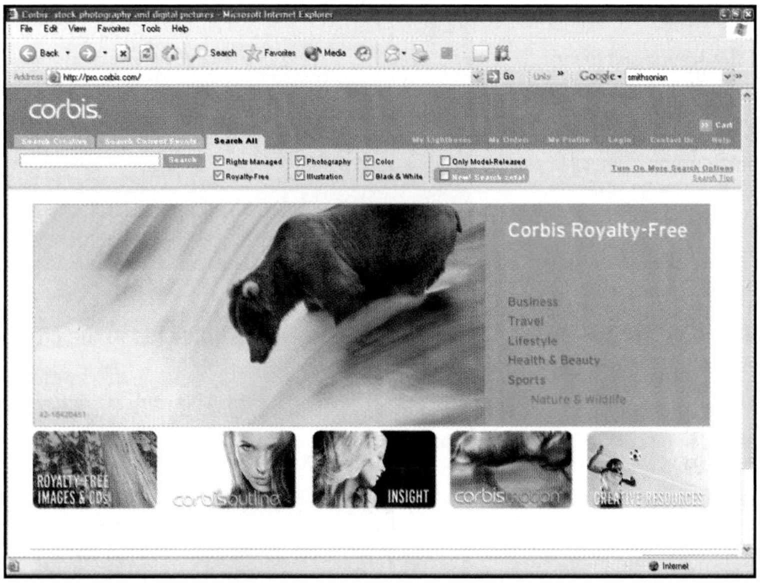

► Some stock photography suppliers offer royalty-free photographs, but you still may be charged a fee to use photos from their collections.

Stock photograph suppliers can be found on the Internet, usually charging a fee ranging from a few dollars to hundreds of dollars. Sometimes a fee is charged each time an image is used. Or, you might be able to purchase an image once and then use it for free as often as you like. You are sometimes able to pay an extra fee to guarantee that a particular photograph will not be used by anyone but you.

Reading Check

1. **Summarize** What are three ways you can obtain digital photographs?
2. **Draw Conclusions** Why is it important to consider sources for graphics and to do extensive research on photos you would like to use?

Apply Gradients

9 Set your **foreground** color to **black**. In the **Layers** palette, click the **layer mask** on the **City** layer.

10 Click the **Gradient** tool. In the drop-down menu on the **Options** bar, choose the **Foreground to Transparent** gradient.

11 Click and drag the gradient tool across the city image so it fades as in Figure 6.13.

12 Select the **Keyboard** layer, and click **Filter>Sketch>Note Paper**. (Click **OK** if the Note Paper dialog box opens.)

13 Repeat **Steps 8–11** to add a **layer mask** with a **gradient** to the **Keyboard** layer. Drag the gradient to create a fade effect that looks like Figure 6.14.

14 Select the **Gold** layer, and click **Layer>New>Layer** to create a new layer above the Gold layer. Name this new layer Rainbow.

15 Click the **Gradient** tool. On the **Options** bar, choose **Transparent Rainbow**. Set the **Opacity** to **40 percent**.

16 Select the **Rainbow** layer. Drag the gradient from left to right across the pot of gold. Change the **Blending Mode** to **Color** (Figure 6.14).

▼ **Figure 6.13** Layer masks let you hide parts of an image without destroying the image data.

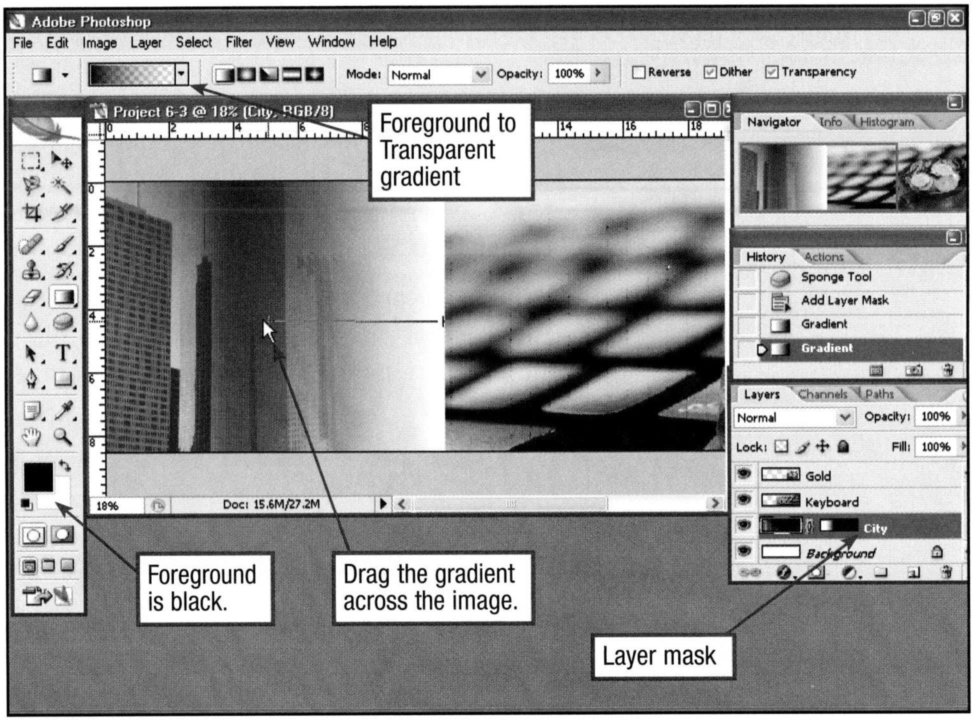

▼ **Figure 6.14** The gradients in the city and keyboard images should blend into each other.

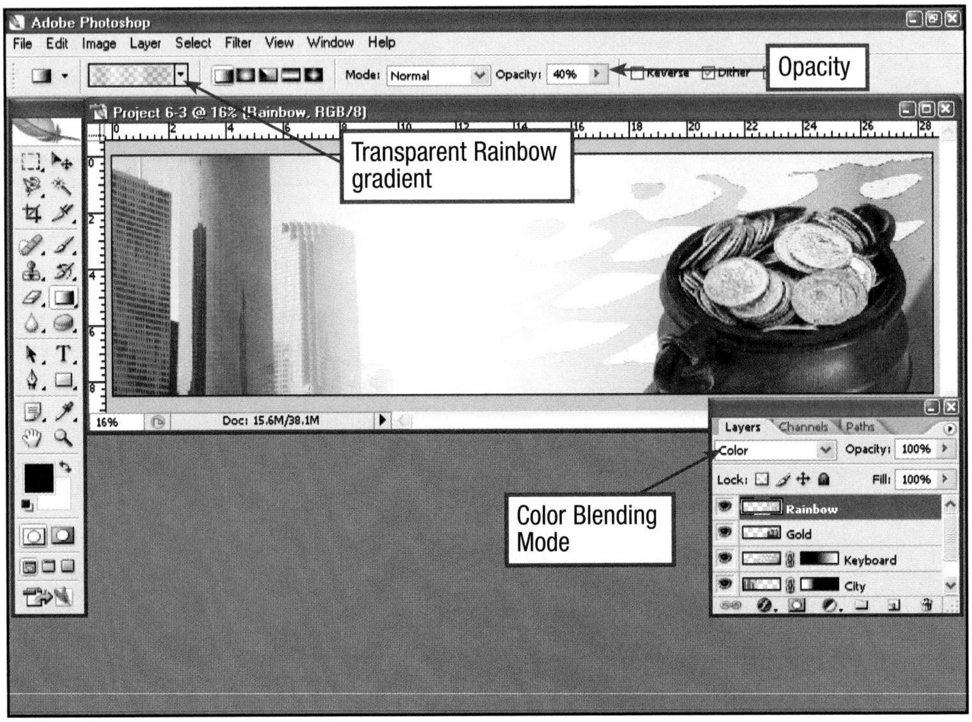

WORK SHOP

Toolbox

Image Resolution

You Will Learn To

- Evaluate resolution needs
- Identify printer resolutions

Key Term

pixels per inch (ppi)

Because images in Photoshop are made out of pixels and tend to be rather large files, it is especially important to keep track of their resolution, otherwise known as **pixels per inch (ppi)**.

With lower resolutions (72 and 96 ppi), the computer stores less detail for an image. This makes it easier to send files through the Internet or present them on-screen. Remember, the smaller the file size, the faster the computer can send or open information.

With higher resolutions (300 ppi and higher), the image is broken into smaller squares of color, and the computer must keep track of much more detail and more data. Considering all the color codes, layers, masks, filters, brushes, and distortion associated with high-resolution images, you can understand why your computer may start to slow down!

You do not need to use high resolution if you create a graphic for an on-screen PowerPoint presentation or if you are using a lower-quality printer. The following chart shows approximate ppi values for different printers.

Sidebar

Determine PPI Check the printer for *linescreen* (or Frequency) settings. Double the lines to find the ppi that achieves the printer's best quality print. A printer that prints a 65 linescreen will be able to print a 130 ppi image. More pixels per inch will simply slow the printer and the computer, and you will not print a better quality image.

Calculate What ppi should you use with a 150 linescreen?

Printer Resolutions

Type of Printer	Recommended PPI
None—publish on screen only	72 ppi or 93 ppi to adapt for new widescreen monitors
Inkjet Printer	Check your printer settings (see the Sidebar)
Laser Printer	150 ppi
Imagesetter	300+ ppi (ask for the print shop's recommendations)

Save yourself time, frustration, and disk space by creating files that match an image's resolution to the method of publication.

Reading Check

1. **Evaluate** What ppi would you use to create an image for a Web site?
2. **Explain** Why would a higher-resolution image slow down your computer?

3. Repeat Step 2 for each of the layers until all images are in your new document. Order the layers so that the **Gold** layer is on top.

4. With the **Move** tool selected (and **Show Transform Controls** checked), resize and reposition the pictures as shown in Figure 6.11.

▼ **Figure 6.11** Click the Move tool to apply your transformations.

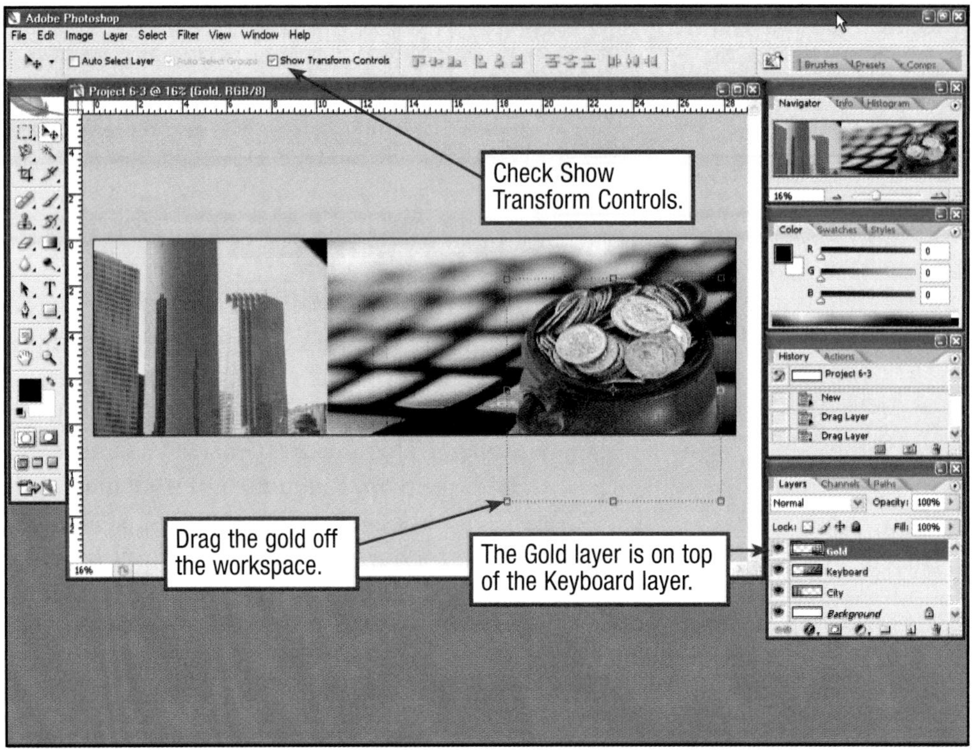

Saturate Colors

5. Click the **Dodge** tool to open the **Sponge** tool underneath.

6. In the **Options** bar, change the **Flow** to **78%** and the **Mode** to **Saturate**. Change the brush to **626 pixels**.

7. Select the **City** layer and **zoom in**. Then brush the city picture with the **Sponge** tool to make the colors more vivid.

Add Layer Masks

8. With the **City** layer still selected, click **Add Layer Mask** at the bottom of the **Layer** palette.

▼ **Figure 6.12** The sponge tool can saturate (intensify) colors to make them vivid.

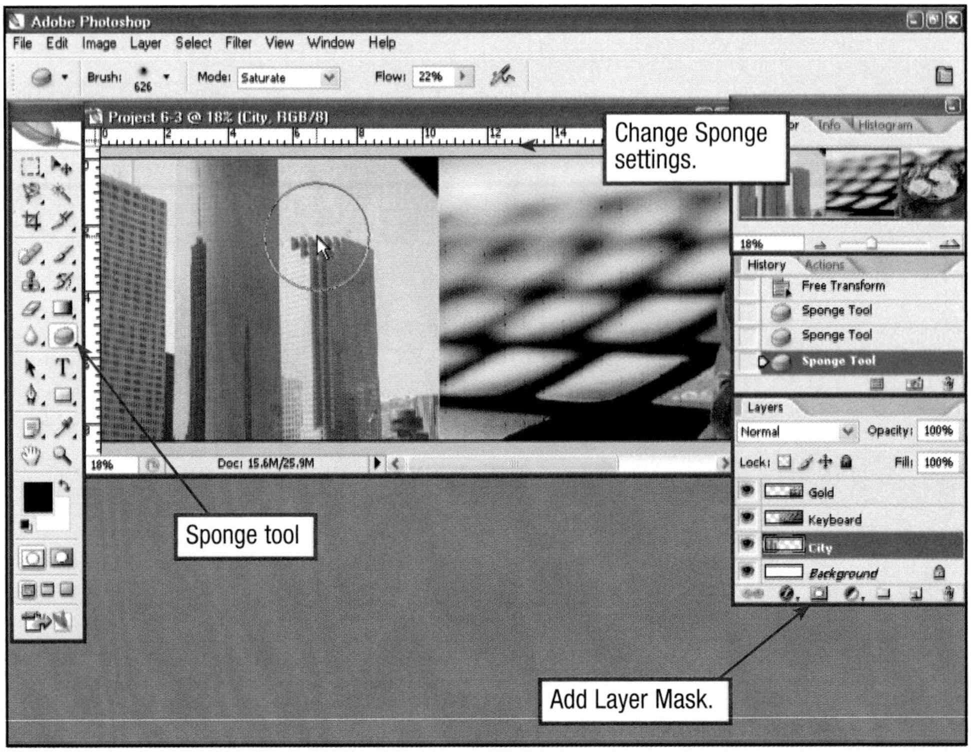

Project 6-1

Create a Postcard

Spotlight on Skills

- Insert a custom shape
- Add filters
- Apply a type mask
- Add styles
- Save in a new format

Key Term

- JPEG (JPG)

Academic Focus

Social Studies
Create a state postcard

In Photoshop, you can create text from images using the Type Mask tool, which works like a marquee or lasso selection tool. Instead of creating lasso or marquee shapes, however, the selected areas take the shape of letters. The Type Mask tools let you insert a picture within a letter, word, or a set of words.

One popular way that Photoshop is used is in the creation of correspondence forms, such as postcards. Postcards can be fun and educational at the same time. Postcards usually include quick facts relating to the eye-catching images and photos on the front of the postcard.

With Photoshop's digital imaging and text tools, you can design any type of postcard you can imagine. Showcase the photographs with appropriate text and shapes. Whether you decide to create a basic postcard or a very colorful one, you will discover that it is fun and easy to use Photoshop.

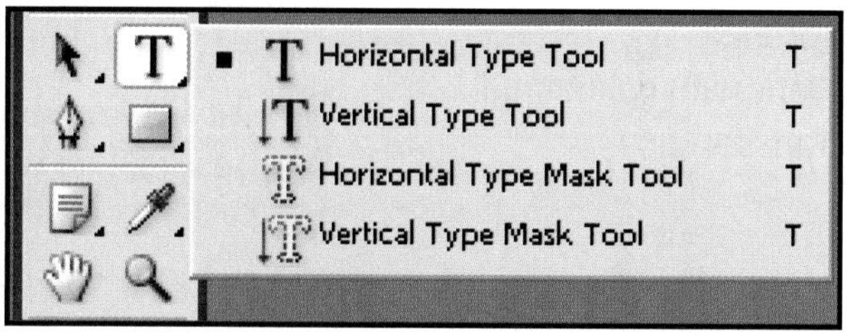

▲ You can turn your text into a picture with the Horizontal and Vertical Type Mask tools.

Go Online PREVIEW
www.glencoe.com

Before You Begin Go to **Chapter 6**, and choose **PowerPoint Presentations** to preview the documents you will be creating. Also, use the individual project **Rubrics** to help create and evaluate your work.

Saving Your File

One of the most important issues when working on a Photoshop file is how to save the file. All software programs have a default format, but most programs also allow for documents to be saved in multiple formats. It is important to know what formats are available in the program you are using. If you create a document in a format that cannot be used or is not compatible with another program, then you will not be able to work with or even open that original document!

Photoshop can save files in many different graphic formats, though its default format is PSD (Photoshop Document). Some applications cannot read the PSD format. Since you will be integrating Photoshop with Publisher to finish your postcard, you will need to save the postcard as a JPEG (pronounced jay-peg) file. **JPEG**, or **JPG**, (Joint Photographic Experts Group) format is commonly used for images that do not require transparency.

▶ **In this project,** you will begin to create a postcard from the state of Texas, using filters, layer styles, and an image embedded in text. You will complete the postcard in Project 6-2. Remember, when you start Photoshop, restore its default settings by holding SHIFT + ALT + CTRL (or SHIFT + OPTION + ⌘ for **Mac** users).

Project 6-3 Create a Banner

Spotlight on Skills

- Saturate colors
- Add layer masks
- Apply gradients
- Add a layer style

Key Term

- grayscale

Academic Focus

Science
Work with colors and transparency

Student Data File

Step-by-Step

1. In Photoshop, open a new document **28.5 inches wide** by **8.5 inches tall** at **150 ppi**. Save it according to your teacher's instructions.

2. Open **Data File 6-3** and select it. Use the **Move** tool to select a layer on the **Layers** palette, and drag it to your new document.

As you have seen, masks are used to hide or reveal parts of an image in a layer. They can create various effects in an image without changing any data in the image. The image is not changed, and the pixels are not altered. Only the mask is changed.

There are two kinds of masks: layer masks and vector masks. Vector masks are created with pen or shape tools. Layer masks are created with painting or selection tools. Only one mask can be applied to each layer. However, one image can have multiple masks. Both types of masks create thumbnails on the same layer where they are being used. The mask thumbnails are displayed in the Layers palette.

Masks use **grayscale**, the black to white color range, to create their effects. Whenever you paint a mask with black (Hide All), you cover the image. When you use white (Reveal All), you reveal the image. Grays will create a transparent effect.

▶ **In this project,** you will create a banner, adding effects with layer masks. You will complete the banner, using Publisher, in Project 6-4.

▼ Figure 6.10 **Note the document size on the ruler.**

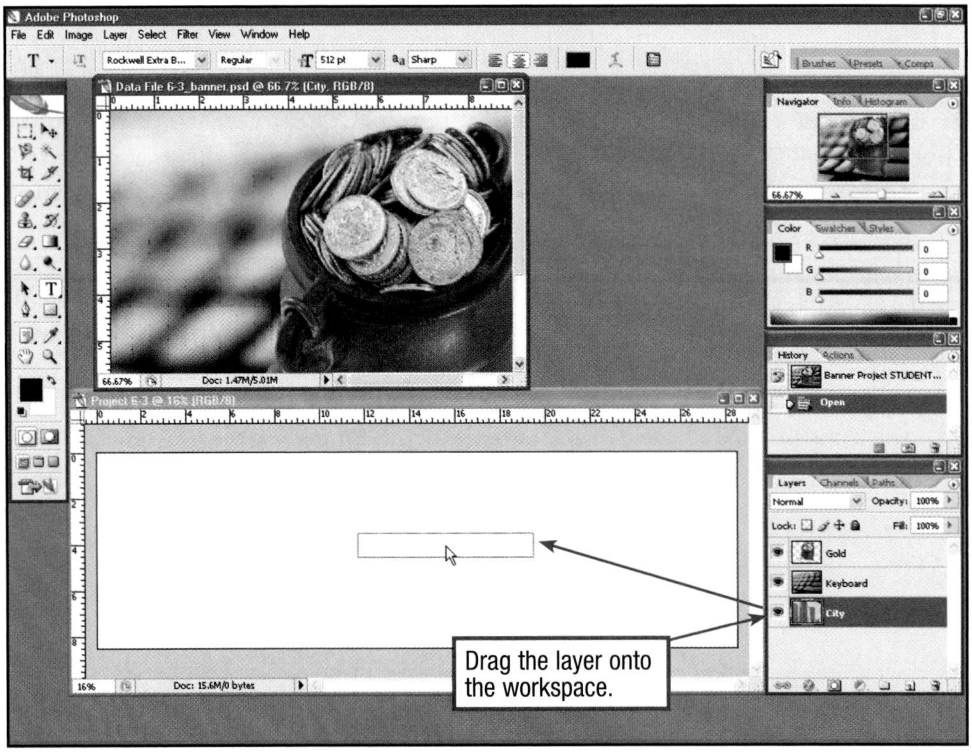

Student Data File

Step-by-Step

1. In Adobe Photoshop, set up a new document that is **5.0 inches wide × 4.0 inches high** at **150 ppi**.

2. Click **View>Show>Grid** and **View>Rulers** to help guide you in the next few steps.

3. Use the **Rectangular Marquee** to select the left third of the workspace. Change the **foreground** color to **blue**. Use the **Paint Bucket** to fill (Figure 6.1).

4. Use the **Rectangular Marquee** to select the bottom half of the white area. Change the **foreground** color to **red**, and fill the new selection. Press CTRL + D to deselect.

5. Press D to restore the default colors. Click the **Switch Foreground and Background Colors** arrow to make the foreground white.

Insert a Custom Shape

6. Press U to open a **Drawing shapes** tool. In the **Options** bar, click **Custom Shape**.

7. Open the **Shape** menu to select a star. If there is no star, click the arrow to open the options menu. Choose **Shapes**, then click **OK** (Figure 6.2).

▼ **Figure 6.1** Use grids and rulers to divide your workspace accurately.

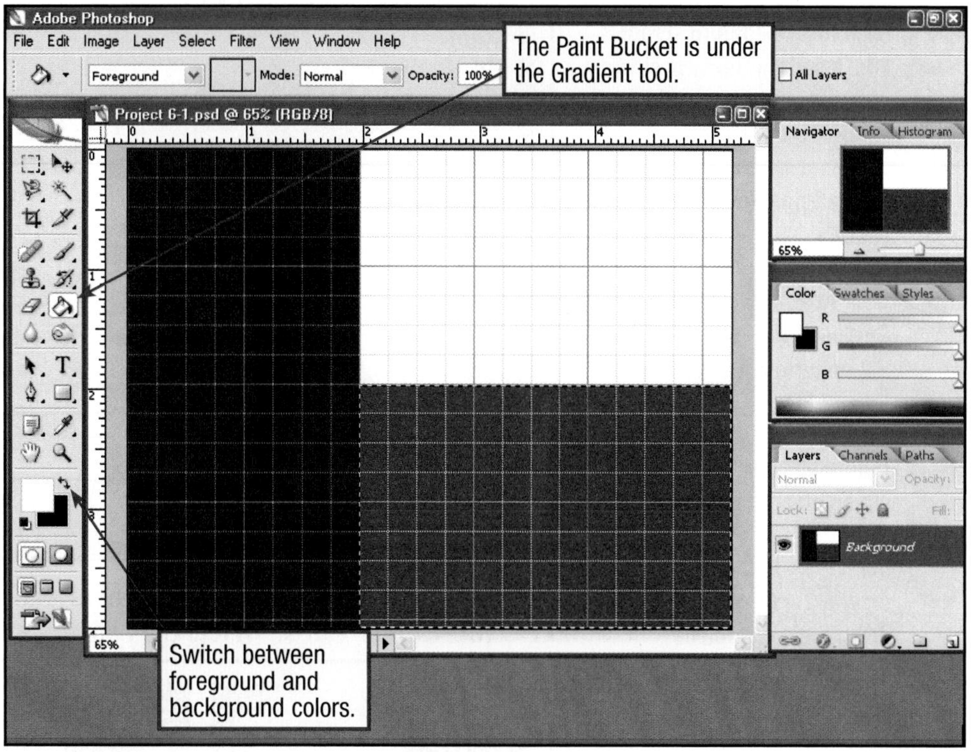

▼ **Figure 6.2.** Photoshop has many preset custom shapes.

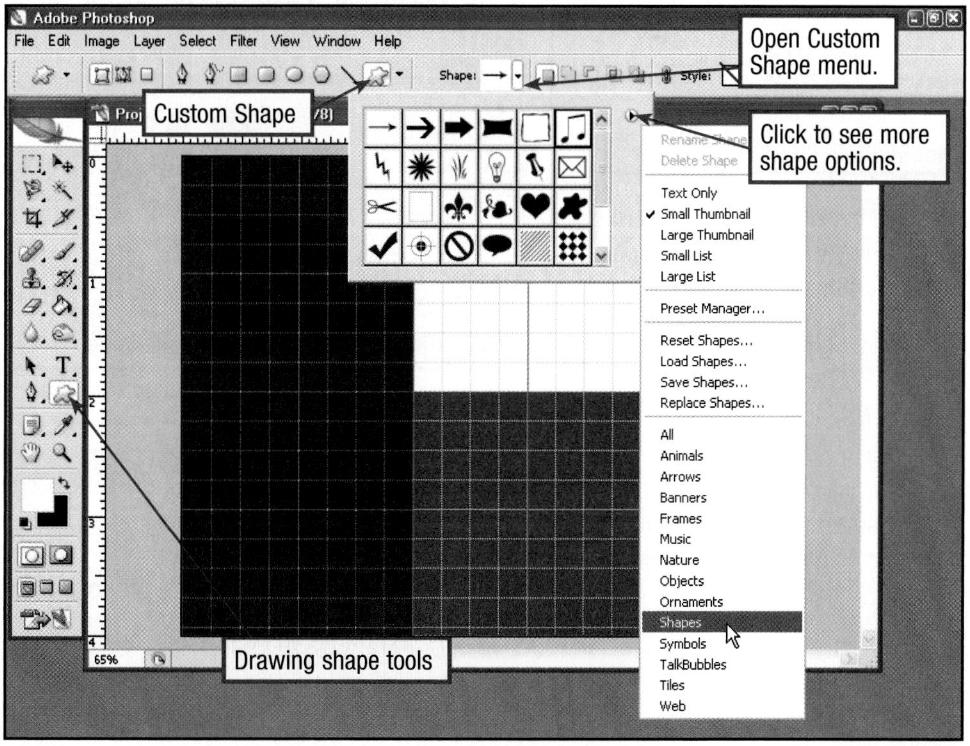

Lay Out a Postcard

3. Click **Insert>Picture>From File**. Insert the Texas postcard picture from Project 6-1 on Page 1.

4. On the **Page Sorter**, click Page 2.

5. Click **Arrange>Layout Guides>Grid Guides**, and set a **2 column** grid with a **center line**.

6. **Delete** all objects except the stamp area from Page 2.

7. Use the **Drawing** tools to draw a **2¼ pt vertical line** down the center guide.

8. Create a text box at the bottom of the postcard and key The Texas flag is red, white, and blue with a single star. This is why Texas is known as the Lone Star State. The Bluebonnet is Texas' state flower. (Figure 6.8)

Print Multiple Copies on a Sheet

9. In the **Postcard Options** task pane, choose **Multiple Copies per Sheet**. Use **Print Preview** to see how the postcards will print.

10. Follow your teacher's instructions for printing and saving your work. If possible, use a duplex printer to print on both sides of the sheet.

▼ **Figure 6.8** Publisher makes it easy to add text.

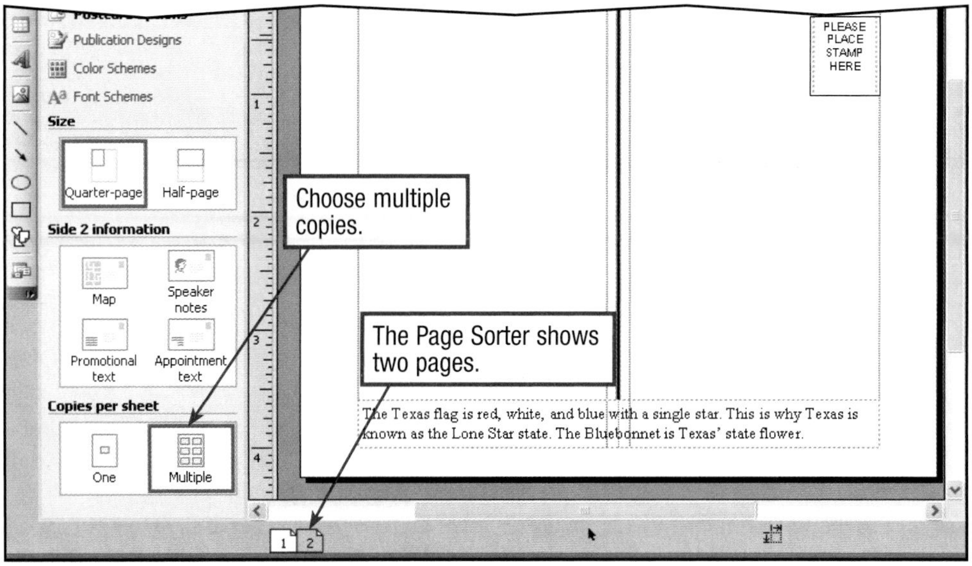

▼ **Figure 6.9** Print four copies to a sheet.

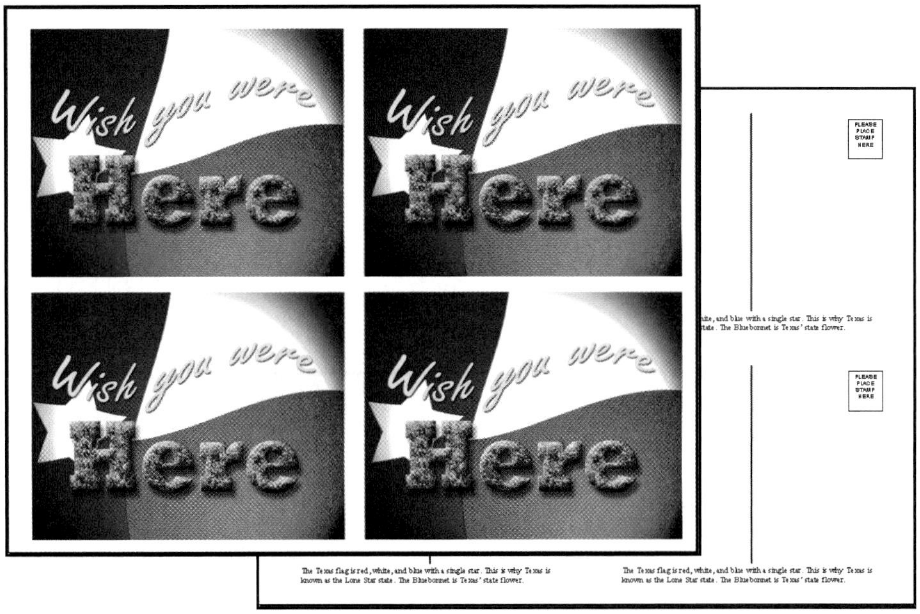

REVIEW AND REVISE

Check your work Use Figure 6.9 as a guide and check that:

- ☑ The Texas flag is on one side of the postcard.
- ☑ The text frame on Page 2 has been proofread for spelling and grammar.
- ☑ The postcard has been printed front/back with four cards on one sheet.

8 In the workspace, click and drag a star while holding the SHIFT key.

9 Use the **Move** tool (with **Show Transform Controls** checked) to reposition and resize the star as needed.

10 Click **Layer>Flatten Image** to move everything onto the same layer (Figure 6.3).

Add Filters

11 Click **Filter>Distort>Wave**. Adjust the settings to give the flag a wave effect that is not too distorted (Figure 6.3).

12 Click **Filter>Render> Lighting Effects**. Adjust the settings to set a dramatic lighting effect.

Figure 6.3 Experiment with the settings until you get the look that you want.

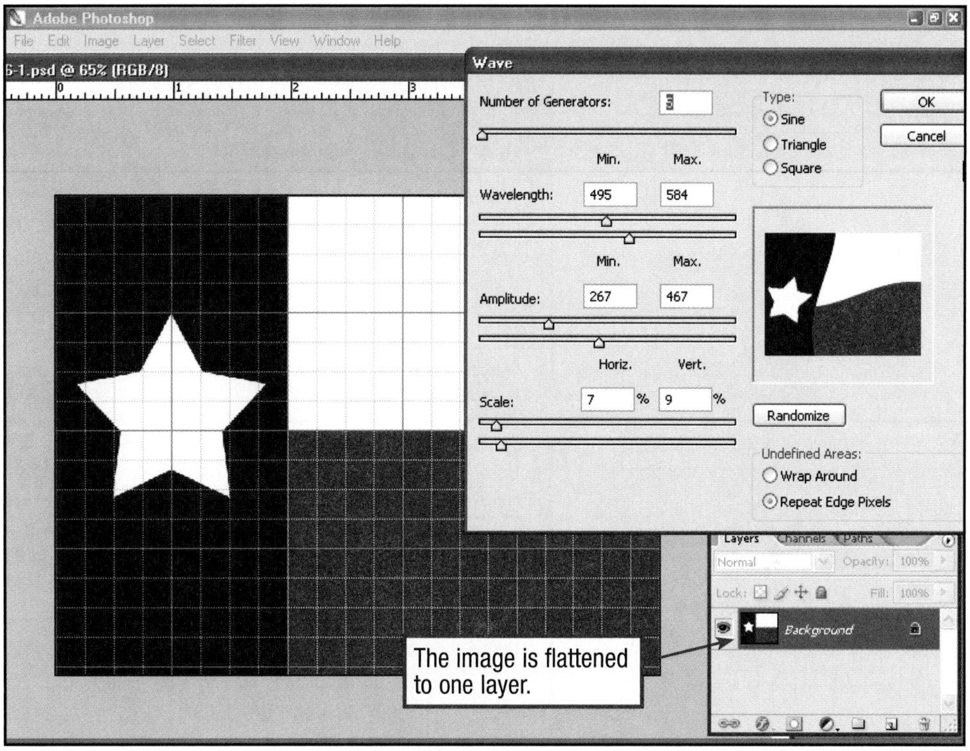

13 Open **Data File 6-1**, the bluebonnet flowers.

Apply a Type Mask

14 Under the **Type** tool, open **Horizontal Type Mask** . Click in the Bluebonnet photo.

15 Change the font to **Rockwell, Extra Bold**, **512 pt**. Key Here (Figure 6.4).

Figure 6.4 The screen turns pink when you apply the Type Mask.

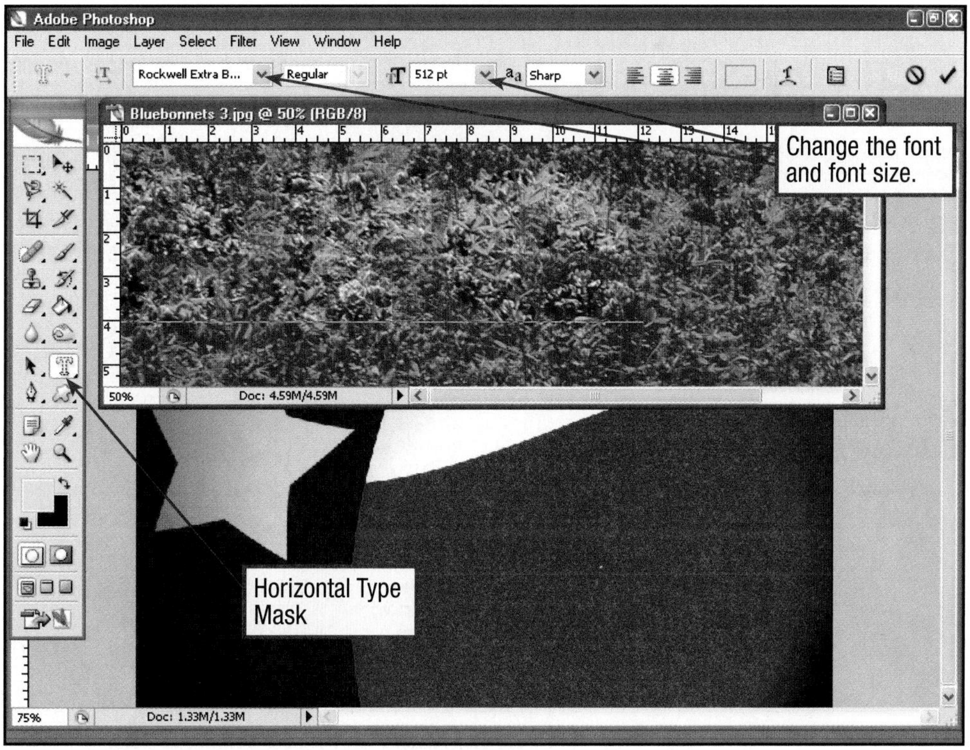

Choose a Format As you will see below, your choice depends mostly upon how you intend to use the graphic.

Compatible File Formats

File Format	Description	Transparency
GIF	Best for the Internet because it reduces the number of colors. Can be used for animations. Not recommended for pictures with drop shadows and outer glows.	Saves transparent information.
JPEG (or JPG)	Good general-purpose format. Good for the Internet because of excellent compression. Save pictures uncompressed for printing. May not be appropriate for high-quality print jobs.	Does not save transparent information. (A white box may appear behind your picture.)
TIFF (or TIF)	Most widely accepted file format for printing. Generally large file sizes. In Photoshop CS2, TIFFs can have layers.	Most software programs used today save transparent information in TIFF format.
PNG	Good general-purpose format. Can be saved for high, medium, and low resolution purposes. Relatively new format (1996).	Saves transparent information.

▶ **In this project,** you will create the back of your Texas postcard, using Publisher.

Step-by-Step

Insert a Photoshop File

1. Open Microsoft Publisher. In the **New Publication** task pane, open **Publications for Print>Postcards**. Choose any postcard design (Figure 6.7).

2. Press CTRL+A to select all the objects on Page 1 of the postcard. Then press DELETE.

▼ **Figure 6.7** The postcard has two pages, which are the front and back.

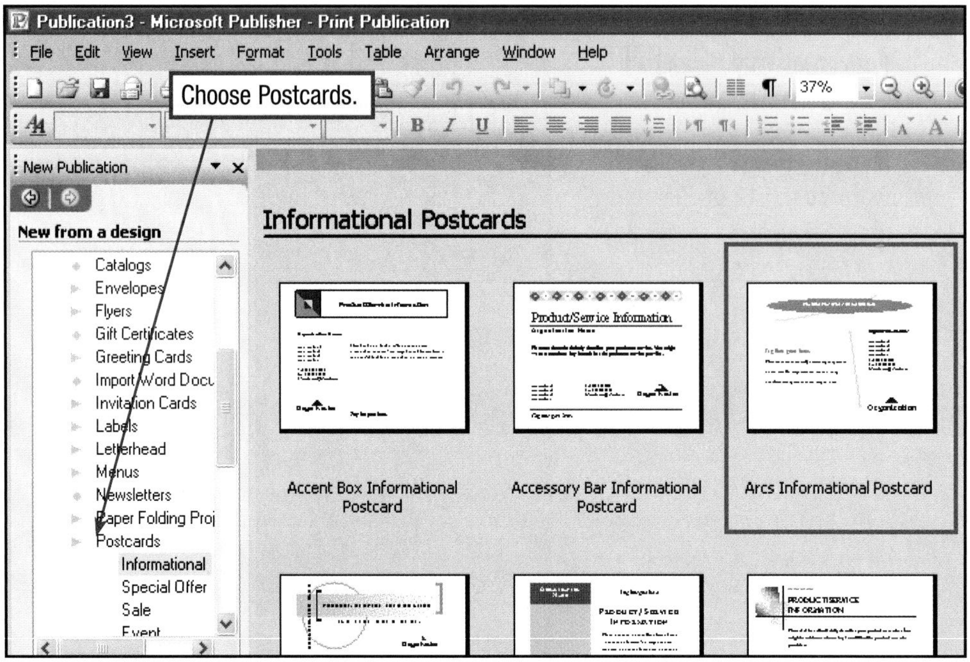

16 Click the **Rectangular Marquee** button. On the **Options** bar, click **New Selection** [icon]. Drag the text to the best part of the Bluebonnet picture.

17 Use the **Move** tool to drag the text onto the flag picture. Resize and reposition the word as needed.

Add Styles

18 On the bottom of the **Layers** palette, click the **Add a Layer Style** button [icon]. Apply a **Bevel** and **Drop Shadow** to the **Here** layer (Figure 6.5).

19 On the bottom of the **Layers** palette, click **Create a layer** [icon]. Change the **foreground** color to **yellow**.

20 Click **Horizontal Type** [T]. Change the font to **Freestyle Script**, **72 pt**. Key Wish you were.

21 On the **Options** bar, click **Create Warped Text** and choose **Flag**. Adjust the settings until your image looks similar to Figure 6.6.

22 Use the **Move** tool to reposition the text as needed. Use the **Styles** palette to add a **Drop Shadow**.

Save in a New Format

23 Click **File>Save As**. Save the postcard in **JPEG** format. You will continue working on it in Project 6-2.

Figure 6.5 Experiment with the Bevel and Shadow style settings.

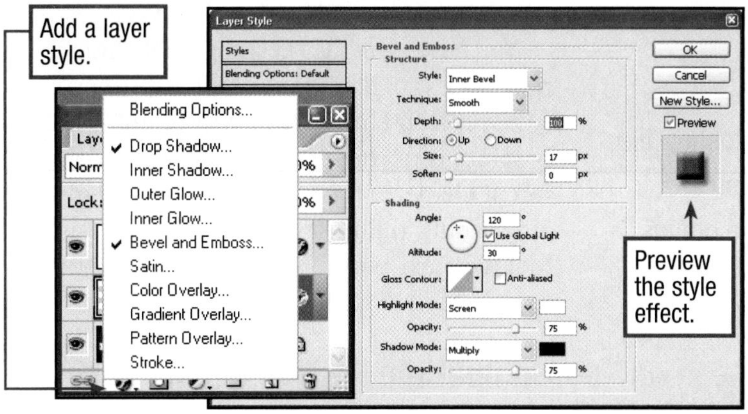

Figure 6.6 Add shadows and styles to make the edges stand out clearly.

REVIEW AND REVISE

Check your work Use Figure 6.6 as a guide and check that:

- ☑ The Texas flag is accurate and wave distortion has been applied.
- ☑ A dramatic lighting effect has been applied to the flag.
- ☑ The word "here" has an embedded picture of bluebonnets.
- ☑ All text has a layer style applied to it.

Project 6-2

Add Text with Publisher

Spotlight on Skills

- Insert a Photoshop file
- Lay out a postcard
- Print multiple copies on a sheet

Key Term

- native format

Academic Focus

Language Arts
Add descriptive text

You have seen that desktop publishing uses software for editing text (word processors) and software that is primarily for raster images (photo editing software). In Unit 4, you will be introduced to software that creates vector graphics (drawing programs). It is the role of layout software to put these different elements together to create a single, consistent product. The page you are reading right now was produced using page layout software. This page includes text boxes, a TIFF file, and graphic icons. Style sheets were used for repeated design elements such as headings, bullets, and captions.

Compatible File Formats

When programs have to work together, they need to use file formats that they can all recognize. Photoshop and Publisher are often used together to create documents using both text and graphics. However, these applications are produced by different companies: Adobe Systems and Microsoft. Each also has its own **native format**, which is a format created specifically for a single software program.

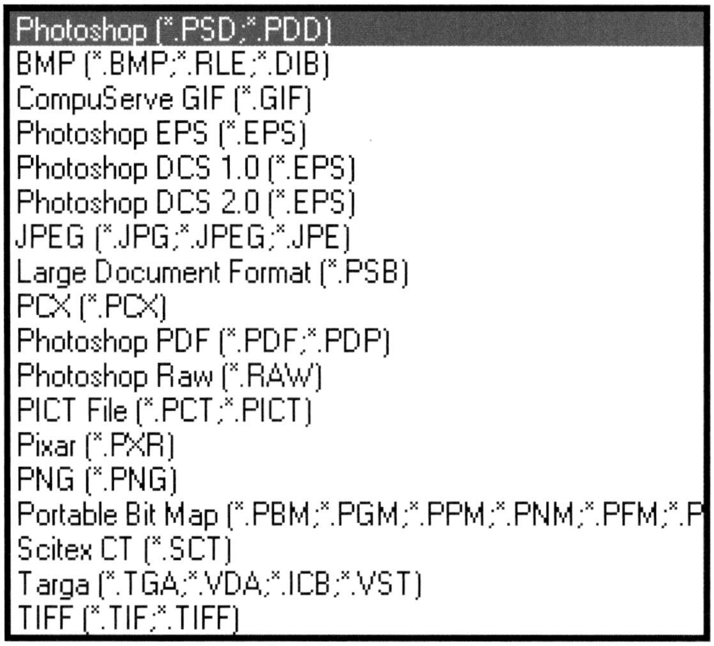

▲ Photoshop lets you save files in many formats recognized by other programs.

Fortunately, most software applications can work together through the use of compatible file formats. For example, even though Photoshop creates graphics with its native PSD format, it can save the graphics in a format that other programs will recognize. The interchangeable formats most commonly used are JPEG, GIF, PNG, and TIFF.